EYE OF THE FIRESTORM

THE NAMIBIAN-ANGOLAN-SOUTH AFRICAN BORDER WAR MEMOIRS OF A MILITARY COMMANDER

Roland de Vries

Major General (Retired)

Helion & Company Ltd

Helion & Company Limited
26 Willow Road
Solihull
West Midlands
B91 1UE
England
Telephone 0121 705 3393
Fax 0121 711 4075
Email: publishing@helion.co.uk
Website: www.helion.co.uk
Twitter: @helionbooks
Visit our blog http://blog.helion.co.uk/

Published by Helion & Company 2016
Designed and typeset by Farr out Publications, Wokingham, Berkshire
Cover designed by Johan Koortzen
Printed by Lightning Source, Milton Keynes, Buckinghamshire

Originally published as *Eye of the Firestorm: Strength Lies in Mobility* by Naledi, Tyger Valley, South Africa 2013

Edited by Willem Steenkamp, Friedel Hansen & Gustav Venter

Cover photo: Brigade night attack, Exercise Thunder Chariot, Lohathla, 1984

ISBN 978-1-909982-69-7

British Library Cataloguing-in-Publication Data.
A catalogue record for this book is available from the British Library.

Contents

List of Battle Maps

List of Figures

Glossary

61 Mech	61 Mechanised Battalion Group.
2IC	Second-in-Command.
AFU	Area Force Unit (citizen force units in South West Africa, similar to South African 'commando' units).
ANC	African National Congress.
Anhara	A grass-covered area in a woodlands landscape usually depicting a floodplain of a river. Not to be confused with a Shona or Omuramba.
APLA	Azanian People's Liberation Army.
ASO	Air Support Officer.
Ben-Ben	Another name used for Arlindo Salupeto Pena, one of the senior military chiefs of UNITA.
Buffel	South African four-wheeled mine protected troop carrier.
Casspir	South African four-wheeled mine protected troop carrier.
Civvie Street	Term used to refer to non-military life, home, friends and family.
C3I	An integrated military management system (comprising trained personnel, hardware and software) referring to command, control, communications and intelligence.
Combat Group (Battle Group)	An all arms fighting unit based on the headquarters of an infantry battalion or armour regiment.
Combat Team	An all arms fighting sub-unit based on the headquarters of an infantry company or armour squadron.
DET	Digital electronic transmission (text message) system used by the SADF to send classified radio messages.
EW	Electronic Warfare.
FAA	Forward Assembly Area (also referred to as an attacking position in close proximity to the enemy).
FAPLA (Angolan Army)	The *Forças Armadas Populares de Libertação de Angola* was originally the armed wing of the Angolan MPLA movement but later became the country's official armed forces when the MPLA took control of the government in 1975.
FNLA	National Liberation Front of Angola (*Frente Nacional de Libertação de Angola*). One of the original political parties and liberation movements of Angola, which participated in the civil war.
G-5	South African 155 mm artillery gun (gun-howitzer) which was capable of firing a 47 kg bomb up to 42 km.
GOC	General Officer Commanding.
HAA	Helicopter Administrative Area.
HEAT	High explosive anti-tank (type of high explosive munitions used to destroy armour).
HF	High Frequency.
HQ	Headquarter.

IFV (ICV)	Infantry Fighting Vehicle (Infantry Combat Vehicle).
Int	Intelligence.
ISSUP	Institute for Strategic Studies, University of Pretoria.
Jamba ("Umbundu" for Elephant)	UNITA's military base in south–east Angola.
Jati or Jati-strip	A strip of land, 1 km wide measured from the SWA/Angola border in the north and the Timo-cutline in the south treated as no-man's land by South African forces. The Jati-strip, sometimes wrongfully named as the 'Yati' stretched over a distance of 450 km from Beacon 1 in the west up to Beacon 45 in the east.
Koevoet (SAP)	Koevoet (Afrikaans for crowbar), also known as Operation K ("Koverte Operasies" Covert Operations) and officially denoted as a Counter–Insurgency Unit of the South African Police, was a paramilitary-trained police unit employed during the South African Border War.
Kraal	A kraal is the typical rural settlement form of northern SWA and Angola. Characteristically it consists of a roughly circular fenced space within which a smaller secondary enclosure containing a collection of huts is found. The primary space is used for the propagation of crops and the keeping of livestock when not taken out by herdsmen for daily grazing. Fencing is done to protect crops and stock from unwanted elements and is normally done by the stacking of thorny branches. Fencing of smaller enclosures is mostly done by implanted poles harvested from surrounding woodlands.
Leaguer	A temporary position involving the deployment of vehicles normally in a square or circle usually at night with the HQ in the centre as a defensive measure against surprise attack.
LWT	Light Workshop Troop.
MAOT	Mobile Air Operations Team.
MiG	Refers to Russian fighter aircraft used by the Cuban and Angolan air forces during the war in Angola, such as the MiG-21 and MiG-23. Both were armed with 23 mm cannon, a variety of modern air-to-air missiles and an assortment of air-to-ground attack weapons, such as rockets and 500 kg airburst bombs.
MK	Umkhonto we Sizwe (meaning "Spear of the Nation"), the military wing of the ANC.
MPLA	The People's Movement for the Liberation of Angola (*Movimento Popular de Libertação de Angola*) was a political party that has ruled Angola since the country's independence from Portugal in 1975. The MPLA fought against the Portuguese Army in the Angolan War of Independence of 1961–74 and defeated UNITA and the FNLA in the decolonization conflict of 1974–75 and the Angolan Civil War of 1975–2002.
MRL	Multiple Rocket Launcher.
OC	Officer Commanding.
Olifant	Main battle tank used by the South African Defence force. Essentially a modernised version of the Centurion Mk V with a 105 mm gun and an assortment of 7,62 mm Browning Machine Guns.
Omuramba	Channel-shaped shallow depressions typical of the braided drainage

	network of the Cuvelai drainage system found in the central region of southern Angola and reaching south to the Etosha Pan.
OP	Observation post.
Operational Area	See Red Line.
Ops	Operation.
OPSO	Operations Order.
Oshana	(also named Chana or Shona) Open pan inundated with water in the rainy season surrounded by bush, characteristic of northern Southwest Africa and southern Angola where natural draining systems are underdeveloped.
PAC	Pan Africanist Congress.
PLAN	People's Liberation Army of Namibia belonging to the South West Africa People's Organisation.
POQO	The armed wing of the PAC.
Ratel	Six-wheeled South African armoured infantry fighting vehicle.
Ratpacks	Daily food packages used during operations consisting of dry rations such as: Cereal, coffee, tea, high-protein biscuits ("Dog Biscuits,") condensed milk, and flavoured powder for cold drinks, tins of canned vegetables and meat and energy bars ("Tarzan Bars").
Recce	A member of the SADF's Reconnaissance Regiment s (formerly Reconnaissance Commando) from Special Forces.
Red Line	Also known as the Bravo line (cutline.) The Red Line was an east–west line based on the southern boundary of Ovamboland. All along the line vegetation had been removed to allow for daily patrols and tracing of tracks of movements across. The area to the north of the Red Line was known as the Red Area and was regarded as the Operational Area where terrorist activities could be expected at any time. This was also the demarcation for Foot and Mouth Disease between the extreme northern part of South West Africa and the farming area to the south.
RSA	Republic of South Africa.
RSM	Regimental Sergeant-Major.
SA	South Africa or South African.
SAAF	South African Air Force.
SACC	South African Coloured Corps
SADF	South African Defence Force.
SADC	Southern African Development Community.
SF	Special Forces.
SAI	South African Infantry.
SAM	Surface-to-air missile.
SAMIL	Range of South African heavy duty military trucks.
SAMS	South African Medical Services.
SANDF	South African National Defence Force (so named after the political changes in April 1994.)
SAP	South African Police.
SWA	South West Africa, now Namibia.
SWAPO	The South West Africa People's Organization was the main liberation

	movement of SWA.
SWAPOL	South West Africa Police.
SWATF	South West Africa Territorial Force (counterinsurgency-oriented) created by the SADF in 1980.
T34-85, T-54/55 and T-62	Various models of Russian tanks used in Angola.
Tac HQ	Tactical headquarters deployed in the field (either mobile or static).
Telstar	An aeroplane flying near deployed formations with the purpose of relaying radio signals otherwise obstructed by the terrain, hence improving communication over longer distances.
Tiffy	Nickname used for a member of the technical (mechanics and maintenance crews) services personnel of the SADF.
Timo cutline	A deforested line 1 km south of the Angola/SWA border named after Timo Bezuidenhout, a SWA politician of the time who, with fellow politician Jannie de Wet, conceived the idea of creating this lengthy 1 km wide strip of no–man's land.
UHF	Ultra High Frequency.
UK	United Kingdom of Britain.
UN	United Nations.
UNITA	The National Union for the Total Independence of Angola (*União Nacional para a Independência Total de Angola*) was the second-largest political party in Angola, founded in 1966. UNITA fought with the Popular Movement for the Liberation of Angola (MPLA) in the Angolan War for Independence (1961–1975) and then against the MPLA in the ensuing civil war (1975–2002).
US/USA	United States of America.
USSR	The Union of Soviet Socialist Republics or the Soviet Union.
VHF	Very High Frequency.
War Zone	A generic term used in this publication and which refers to the territory where the Border War was enacted.
WO	Warrant Officer (Class I or II).
Yati or Yati-strip	See Jati-strip.
ZANU	The Zimbabwe African National Union, a militant organisation that fought against the white minority government of Rhodesia. It formed as a split group from the ZAPU party and won the national elections of 1980 after which it merged with ZAPU to form ZANU-PF.
ZAPU	The Zimbabwe African People's Union, a militant organisation and political party that fought for the liberation of Zimbabwe.
ZIPRA	The Zimbabwe People's Revolutionary Army, the military wing of ZAPU.

If

by Rudyard Kipling

If you can keep your head when all about you
Are losing theirs and blaming it on you,
If you can trust yourself when all men doubt you,
But make allowance for their doubting too;
If you can wait and not be tired by waiting,
Or being lied about, don't deal in lies,
Or being hated, don't give way to hating,
And yet don't look too good, nor talk too wise:

If you can dream – and not make dreams your master;
If you can think – and not make thoughts your aim;
If you can meet with Triumph and Disaster
And treat those two impostors just the same;
If you can bear to hear the truth you've spoken
Twisted by knaves to make a trap for fools,
Or watch the things you gave your life to, broken,
And stoop and build 'em up with worn-out tools:

If you can make one heap of all your winnings
And risk it on one turn of pitch-and-toss,
And lose, and start again at your beginnings
And never breathe a word about your loss;
If you can force your heart and nerve and sinew
To serve your turn long after they are gone,
And so hold on when there is nothing in you
Except the Will which says to them: "Hold on!"

If you can talk with crowds and keep your virtue,
Or walk with Kings – nor lose the common touch,
If neither foes nor loving friends can hurt you,
If all men count with you, but none too much;
If you can fill the unforgiving minute
With sixty seconds' worth of distance run,
Yours is the Earth and everything that's in it,
And – which is more – you'll be a Man, my son!

Dedication

For The People I Served With,
My Family, My Friends
My New Found Friends;
Some Of Them Former Enemies

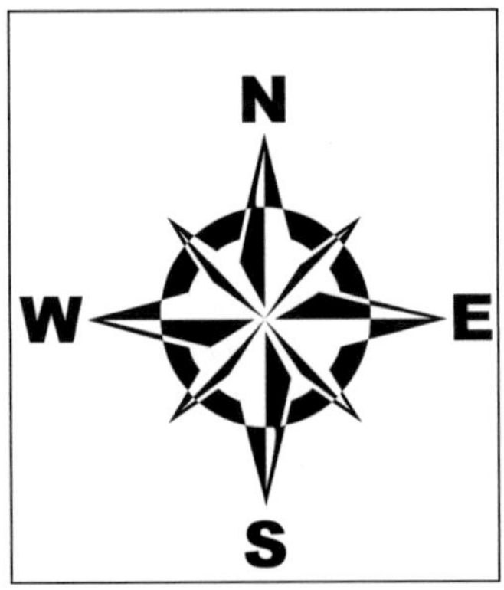

... That it may become as it ought to be, the career of Arms requires from those who seek it or are called on to pursue it, certain specific qualities which we call the military virtues: valour, fidelity, patriotism. The exercise of these virtues to a very high degree is so essential to the career of Arms that they constitute its characteristic feature, define its own peculiar spirit. They are the necessary conditions of the existence of the career, and if they disappeared it would disappear also.

– Oliveira Salazar

Acknowledgements

My appreciation reaches out to precious Henriette, my wife, who has manoeuvred enthusiastically with me for thirty years and finally managed to get me to sit down, when she convinced me that I should write this book.

My gratitude also envelops my adorable children, Roland Junior, Elmarie (and Ferdi), Melanie (and Jason) and Pieter, who all said, "do it, Dad" – which, I suppose, was something like being given a mission command.

To my father and mother, who are not with us anymore, but set my life on course by enticing me to both enjoy and internalise Rudyard Kipling's immortal poem *If.* They inspired me in many ways, yet never compelled me to their way of thinking. For this I have always loved and respected them. They did not force me to go to university, and therefore allowed me more time with my troops on the ground; those warriors with whom I had shared the inflictions of life and the rhythms of manoeuvre, and from whom I learned so much.

Thanks in so many ways are also due to our extended families and close friends in civilian life, whom I wish I could all mention name by name. However, for fear of leaving someone out or filling another chapter, I simply say: "Thank you all from the bottom of my heart for having knowingly or unknowingly inspired me during this writing campaign."

My colleagues and military friends, with whom I led operations, presented training and shared life's changing moments: Your names are embedded on a roll-call list not marked SECRET, which is kept in my active memory, never to be forgotten. You are all older now, as I am, but I am sure your memories remain bright, as mine do. Many of you are from the magnificent 61 Mechanised Battalion Group and its close circle of friendship. Many of you are still doing your duty in the ranks of its veterans' association. We shall always share the memory of our fallen comrades and the impact they had made on our lives and our writings and sayings.

As far as the technical details of this book are concerned, I am specifically grateful to the following individuals for their support and assistance, for whom I have a special word of thanks:

- My good friends, Camille and Charmaine Burger and their close-knit family for living with me through an exciting journey of discovery. The graphics in my book belong to Camille.
- My close friend, Loutjie Bouwer, who contacted me and said: "Roland, you have a story to tell – speak to Johan Coetzee of Naledi".
- Johan Coetzee, who spontaneously replied "let's go for it".
- My friend from the part-time forces and our enjoyable army days, renowned military writer Willem Steenkamp, with his unique sense of humour, who said: "I will be your editor. Let's fight through the objective".
- My friend and military writer, Leopold Scholtz, residing in the coolness of The Hague, Holland. Hey, man, did and do we still have exciting moments of sharing knowledge and ideas on the history of warfare?
- My friends and the new found friends of Naledi, as well as Friedel Hansen and Gustav Venter, who helped us with the final editing of the manuscript.

Another word of thanks is extended to erstwhile enemies, who could share some of their life stories with me; who became my friends. One man especially, from the former Umkhonto We Sizwe I wish to mention, Solly Mollo, who became a companion in 1994 and remains one today; the friendship flourished during those trying days of defence transformation... Ours was not to wonder why... but to manoeuvre through it.

I trust that this book will also serve as an inspiration to my comrades, for them to do research and put their own thoughts and results in writing – we owe it to all future generations... our children and their offspring. The latter (my little ones), seven of them, are close to becoming a full-blown mechanised infantry section, whilst young Pieter, currently in Saudi Arabia, is still out on reconnaissance.

Thank you, Dear Lord, for making the writing possible and for directing my path!

Roland de Vries
Middle East, April 2013

Foreword

The Wife of a Soldier and a Mother

by Henriette de Vries

On a crisp autumn morning in 1979 Roland de Vries crossed my radar screen for the first time. There was no way I could NOT notice this tall dark and handsome leader of men, as I entered the 1 South African Infantry Battalion (1 SAI) headquarters in Bloemfontein. I was part of an educational technology team from Military HQ and he the acting officer in command of 1 SAI. Little did I realise that the awareness was mutual.

I was engaged to be married later the same year and Roland was already married. Both being people who are loyal to our commitments, the awareness passed without any words or actions... like ships passing in the night.

Two years later, in the autumn of 1981, my daughter Melanie was born from my marriage to Captain Louis Harmse. Only three months later, during that very cold winter of 1981, I became a war widow and Melanie a war orphan when Louis was killed during the Border War. It was during this time that I really got to know Mrs. Ristie Viljoen, the wife of the then Chief of the Defence Force, General Constand Viljoen. She was and certainly is one of the most caring people I have ever met.

In the early summer of 1982 Mrs. Viljoen one afternoon knocked on the door of my mother's Pretoria residence, where Melanie and I were living. It was more than a courtesy call: she had a vacancy on one of the many high-profile ladies' group tours she escorted to the Operational Area at the time. These "Border tours" were undertaken to give the women of the country more insight in the life of operational soldiers. She wanted me to visit the last base where my deceased husband had served before dying in Angola during Operation Protea in August 1981.

At the time I was employed as a psychologist at the University of Pretoria's Child and Parental Guidance Institute. I initially hesitated to accept for various reasons. The trip was scheduled for mid-November and my leave was only due in December. My daughter, Melanie was only 18 months old and we had never been apart since her birth. But, most of all: did I really want to see places such as Oshivello and Omuthiya from where soldiers left to go into the war zone, some never to return?

Somehow, my mentor at the University, Professor Louis Jacobs, along with my mother and Mrs. Viljoen made the decision for me. It was only much later that I saw the hand of our dear Lord in the finely orchestrated process that lead me to visit Omuthiya on 22 November 1982.

We were flown in Puma helicopters from Oshakati to Omuthiya as part of our Border tour. As I disembarked at Omuthiya I was casually welcomed by Commandant Roland de Vries. The recognition was instantaneous. Not knowing about his imminent divorce, I took a deep breath and just walked on to greet some of the other officers I happened to know.

The day at Omuthiya however became a red-letter day in my life... our lives. Everywhere I went Roland subtly guided me to stay close to him. In the canteen he was just there next to me, assisting me as I looked for a small enough T-shirt to take home for Melanie; when we travelled in the Ratels to witness a very real fire and movement exercise by the troops, he made sure I got on top of his Ratel and we sat together at the back on top of the spare wheel. During lunch he sat opposite me at the table... By accident? I had my doubts.

As we left Omuthiya that evening Roland made certain that the three of us were the last people to leave the base: Tannie Ristie Viljoen, Roland and I. Being a romantic at heart and very much aware all day long of the electricity between Roland and myself, Tannie Ristie claimed she was cold and would not get out of the Ratel hatches with us to sit atop for the 20 kilometre journey to the airport at Operet. The three of us just smiled at each other for a moment. She realized that we did not really buy her excuse of being that cold during a 36 degree Celsius summer day in Namibia and Roland and I appreciated her discretion.

During that brief journey Roland made sure that a next meeting between us was discussed and confirmed. It was then that he told me about his divorce being in process.

Was it by chance that my mother owned a place in Plettenberg Bay where we went for our annual holidays? Was it destiny that Roland loved to sail his Hobie Cat on the same coast and had planned a holiday with his two children, staying over in the military base at George that December? Who cares? Hours in the scorching sun on his boat, not caring that we burnt to cinders, talking away as if we had never done so before, cemented a bond we both realised was rare. We were soulmates and a long-term relationship was assured.

Roland was transferred to Lohatlha in January 1983. No cell phones and computers were around at the time and we lived more than 800 kilometres apart. Since both of us were committed to our respective careers, we did not see much of each other. The telephone however proved patient and the old manual rural telephone exchange operator in Postmasburg, where Roland lived, even more so. (He probably enjoyed our lengthy loving conversations late at night as much as we did!) Fortunately, he accommodated the entertainment we afforded him by not billing us more than a single local call each night.

Around lunchtime on 21 May 1983 Roland phoned me from the office with a lilt in his voice. "I am a free man!" he said. "Let the sun set quietly on this day never to see it again. On my way to the field now, talk to you tomorrow! Let it be a new day when we talk about a new life."

As promised, he did phone the next day. He asked if Melanie and I as well as my mother could come and visit him at Lohatlha. Two days later he phoned again and suggested I bring something nice to wear. By this time I knew enough about Roland to realize he liked being surprisingly different, following the strategy of the indirect approach. I planned my outfit, my nice little dress to be suitable for ANY occasion.

Knowing the battlefield to be fluid I was not surprised when Hilda Potgieter, wife of Gunner Johan Potgieter, as he was known to me, met us at the Kimberley airport on Friday 27 May. No sign of Roland.

As we reached Postmasburg, I was more than pleasantly surprised by the quaint little cream coloured house with the red tiled roof. It was surrounded by a farm of Namaqualand daisies which welcomed me in all the colours of the sun. The small lawn was neatly manicured and the house spotlessly clean and extremely well kept. A trademark of Roland and it would become part of my life.

Stella, the Griqua woman who worked for Roland, received us with a lovely Devonshire tea and then showed us to our rooms. Still no sign of Roland.

Just as I prepared Melanie for her afternoon nap, I heard the now well-known rhythmic beat of an approaching Puma helicopter. Something urged me to walk outside and as I turned the corner of the house, I was enveloped in a gust of red Kalahari sand whirling up from the dirt road by the rotors of the Puma, as it settled down in an open plot close to the house. Roland jumped from the already open door and darted across the road with a broad but clearly tired smile.

It was wonderful to see him again after being apart for weeks. After a big hug, brief orders to all around us followed. Within a few minutes I was sitting next to him in his white Audi as we sped into the heart of Postmasburg. We stopped in front of an old house restored as a lawyer's office.

I did not know it then but the particular moment was but the first of a lifetime of pleasant surprises. It was typically Roland's style: mysterious and surprisingly different, he explained. Indeed, after thirty years I still appreciate that truth, the essence and the wonder of those claims.

Inside the office we read and signed a prepared prenuptial agreement which was perfectly drawn up. Some used to say he was not a good listener but he certainly listened very carefully to the conversations we had had about marriage and contracts. Everything was just the way it should have been.

While we drove home he apologized for being in a hurry as the manoeuvres in the field were still continuing and he had to get back as soon as possible. (Another refrain I had to get used to over the years to come.) As the Puma shrouded me in dust once more while taking off, I shook my head smiling. Who would have guessed that my nice little dress was going to be a wedding dress…? And he did not even ask me if I would marry him!

When he returned from the "battlefield" round about 14:00 the following afternoon, he warned me to be dressed and ready by 16:30 and then took himself off for a two-hour nap. This was another thing about him I had to get used to, the fact that he could rejuvenate himself from being bone tired to a point of being super-refreshed and alert within a mere two hours.

At 16:30 a red-eyed clearly exhausted chaplain, Ds. Attie Bezuidenhout, walked up the garden path. A freshly showered Roland went out to meet him. He introduced us as they stepped on the veranda. He came somewhat early for some pre-marriage counselling, Attie explained. As we sat down to talk to Attie, Roland instructed his 13-year old son, young Rolie to shower and dress for church. Rolie was surprised claiming that it was Saturday, but soon became enthusiastic as he heard there was going to be a wedding. My mother confirmed that she and Melanie had all they needed and would be marching ready within exactly 15 minutes. Roland's precision and time consciousness became an integral part of my life from that day forward.

I have to admit: I was impressed. Nothing was left to chance. Everything had been taken care of, even bouquets for the bride and her mother. We were married in the NG Kerk, Postmasburg at exactly 17:00 on 28 May 1983.

We lived in Postmasburg for three years as part of the Army Battle School family of Lohatlha. Our son, Pieter, was born on 17 April 1985 in 1 Military Hospital, Pretoria. At the beginning of 1986 we moved to Kathu for two years, when Roland became second-in-command of the Army Battle School.

Although life was a lot of fun for all of us out there in those days, the war remained part of our everyday lives. For wives to be without their husbands and the small children without their fathers for months on end was not easy for any of the army families. Many Sundays found groups of women together somewhere at someone's house sharing food and commiserating with each other. It was tough to accept that no news was good news when the weeks became months. The silence for the sake of security was our greatest frustration. Sometimes we would gather the week's newspapers, stick some of Roland's battle maps on the wall of our dining room and then try to figure out where in Angola our husbands might be. It was quite a triumph when one of the men came home and we learnt that we were not far off in our speculations.

Once the news came that our darlings were on their way home, nothing could hold us back. The fun we had in preparing together and also individually with our children was better than preparing for Christmas. The woman shared their little intimate efforts and the relaxed atmosphere and bouts of pealing laughter erased the hardships of the past lonely months. It is hard to describe the elation we felt at the approaching reunions. As the D-Day of arrival drew nearer we helped each other with new hair colour and styles, pedicures and manicures, new dresses... we just wanted the reunion to be perfect. Yet, once the husbands and fathers had arrived back every little family remained behind closed doors for a couple of days.

Roland had always been a true soldier in every sense of the word. Even the fun he had with the kids was part of the show. During weekends and holidays he playfully inspected their rooms where they stood to attention next to their little beds, which they had made themselves, no matter how haphazard. As they grew up, this improved without much effort from my side. Once they knew how to do it, they worked at it for the sake of the inspection. As Pieter was the baby, Melanie and Rolie always helped him with his chores for the sake of the group. (Rolie's younger sister, Elmarie, preferred alternate stays with Roland and her mother.)

Rolie did it right because he was the eldest and liked being praised for his leadership of the little ones. Melanie was a natural and never got caught out in the process. Pieter, as the youngest, soon learnt how to talk his way in and out of an inspection. Once something was not perfect he used to get Roland to show him, up to a point of actually fixing the problem in its entirety. Rolie shook his head, Melanie rolled her eyes and Roland thought the little guy's initiative highly commendable, so he carried on and eventually did the complete chore for him. I only looked on and wondered how these playful times together would impact on their lives.

The greatest fun for the children was the occasional opportunity when they did so well that Roland reversed the roles and the kids came to inspect us. Roland turned this into a big occasion and he made deliberate errors to teach and help the children to be always aware and observant. The same opportunity was used to teach the children that they could reprimand us as parents, but they had to do it in a respectful way.

Roland furthermore believed in self-confidence training and all our children playfully learnt to abseil from a roughly 80 foot cliff, without a safety harness before they went to school. Few things were considered more fun than a weekend out on the Lohatlha exercise terrain in tents with Ratels and ratpacks and two-way radios. The children played their own version of making war or in the summer swam in makeshift swimming pools (huge bladders used by the engineers for water purification and provisioning in the Operational Area.) The men made potjiekos or braaivleis[1] and the women competed silently with new salads and interesting dishes cooked on open fires. Each couple also had their own variety

1 Braaivleis and potjiekos are traditional South African ways to prepare food during social gatherings.

of "fire water" to assist the fun and laughter.

Sometimes the men put their families into their Ratels and we went bundu-bashing to a next venue for the next night. The women got their chance to take the driver's seat and the kids navigated loudly sitting on top of the hatches.

Roland arranged holiday camps for the army children on the base, to support families in which both parents worked and therefore had childcare issues during the school holidays. These became so popular that the civilians in town offered hundreds of Rand per child to have their children included in these camps.

At the end of 1987, during Operation Modular, Roland was the second-in-command of the operational brigade in Angola. Before he left he was informed that he would be transferred to Messina in the New Year as commander of the Soutpansberg Military Area Force Unit. We went there in the school holidays to reconnoitre, to look for a house and to mentally prepare. However, in his absence and without warning he was transferred to become the officer commanding of the Army College in Pretoria. What now? The only message I received from Roland somewhere out of Angola was: "Consider my authority hereby delegated to you, I trust you to make the best decisions for the family. You have all my love, trust and support. Go for it Mac Dough. In time I will head you off at medicine bend! Mission command!"

Packing up our house in Lohatlha (Kathu) with three children, and moving on my own to Pretoria was no mean feat. The 800 kilometres with a Hobie Cat and a trailer in tow was certainly the toughest driving I ever undertook in one day. Why I did it? Because Roland believed I could and expected it of me. Needless to say it was but one of the self-confidence exercises he threw my way during our years together. I think I felt just as good as the kids did receiving his praise and gratitude after successfully completing an odious task.

Little did I know that this would be the first of many solo home moves for me during the years to come. Somehow Roland always managed to be away when it happened. The excuses were so good and so well-timed that I could only shake my head at the perfect timing of military emergencies during the following twenty years.

The next twenty years of Roland's military career kept us based in the Johannesburg-Pretoria area. After an initial six months in Voortrekkerhoogte we moved into our first own home together in Wierda Park where we lived for thirteen years. I was very happy that things worked out this way because our kids, Melanie and Pieter could then complete their full school careers in the same primary and secondary schools without disruption. This was something that Rolie and Elmarie did not have.

While Roland was officer commanding of the Army College we were obliged to attend all official functions at the college. In those days young Rolie had already left for his own post-school military service and we were alone with Melanie (then six) and Pieter (only two). With a record of 354 functions in one of the years we were there, we were obviously not at home much of the time. In an effort to not overburden Lenkie, our wonderful Tswana housekeeper, we decided to take the children with us to many of the functions. This happened mainly over weekends. The children were bathed and fed before we left and a bed made for them in the back of our Volkswagen Kombi on a queen-size mattress which we bought for the purpose. They had their toys and bicycles with which they could go about freely within the Paratus square behind the Paratus mess.

One evening, during a very highbrow cocktail party, I was talking to some guests facing the back entrance of the mess hall. I suddenly noticed that something was out of place. I excused myself from the guests and moved quietly to the point of impact. There, sitting on his little black plastic motorbike, in his bright blue and red nightgown, was three-year old Pieter stuffing his pockets with crackers, caviar, exotic cheeses, anchovies, olives and other very expensive cocktail goodies. Patrick, the head waiter of the college mess, who adored our babies, very quietly pushed the plates with the best pieces to the edge of the low table and made sure that Pieter could reach them. Once Pieter cleared the one side of the plates, Patrick quietly and unobtrusively turned the plates for him to access the other side. When his pockets could take no more, he silently took off on his little scooter. I followed him quietly just to find him approaching Melanie. She was just coming out of the bar storage area with arms full of a variety of cold drinks used for cocktail mixers. It soon became clear that my "innocent" little children were quite adept at arranging their own parties behind the scenes with the help of the mess and bar staff. As I quietly sought out Roland to inform him of the irregularities, I only got a conspiratorial smile, a quick kiss on the cheek and an "I know...!" I should not have been surprised.

In the years to follow the kids grew up and became their own people. Roland was a quality-time dad as his work kept him busy all hours of the day, night and weekends. Whenever he had a moment with them it was always memorable. They had their own little tents and ratpacks which every so often appeared on a Friday evening and that was the sign for the kids to be ready for a fun-filled weekend. The children loved the little stories he told which always ended up in some problem-solving exercise for them. There were also many ladies' club or unit day meetings which the children could not wait to attend, as it was always outside somewhere with a lot of fun and games for the kids. Roland never failed to arrange a big Christmas party for the families which is something our children still talk about.

We managed to get away most December months to go to my mother's holiday home in Plettenberg Bay. These holidays found Roland and the kids either on his sailboat or somewhere along the beach up to something: gathering rare pansy shells, kite surfing or rowing. Roland was never a person to let a day go by without movement. Either we drove somewhere or walked around Robberg, or went fishing or engaged in whatever excitement he could find to entertain the family. I noticed but a year ago that all our children still uphold the family tradition of pizza and champagne on the beach at dusk when they are together.

All however was not fun and games or moonshine and roses all the time. In the 1990s Roland's career path became suddenly steeper and the road more treacherous. As he moved from the college to the Northern Transvaal command, to Officer Commanding of 7 Division and then to become Director Transformation at Defence Headquarters the political situation changed rapidly and Roland's career became part of it. The stronger Roland presented himself and his views, the more resistance he experienced from the older more conservative groups in the Defence Force.

Once, when the resistance became palpable, I asked him how he knew he was pursuing the right things and that the resistance he experienced was just because his ideas were too revolutionary and new for the powers that be. He then explained that change at that particular point was critical and inevitable to keep the country from entering a full-blown civil war. I believed and trusted him. He was a natural change agent. There was more than just practical evidence of this. The experts agreed:

Roland was invited to an extensive interview with the leaders of the Harvard Business

School. At his enquiry six months later about the extended publishing date of the book on change management in which Roland featured, John Kotter, dean of the school let him know, "You sent us back to the drawing boards; we had to re-think and re-do everything after you had left".

There was also his transformational leadership profile which was done by Productivity Development, leadership and management consultants which held an American franchise for psychometric tests, to test business and organizational leaders worldwide. He had an unusually high score on the transformational leadership profile, which was visible all along in his ways of doing things.

While doing an International Strategic Management Programme at the University of Stellenbosch Business School, Roland one evening approached the dean of the business school at the time, Professor Archer, to discuss some change management matter. As Roland explained the matter and shared his views, Professor Archer took a slow sip of his drink and then in my presence said to Roland, "You actually inhibit me when it comes to my own subject. You are just such a natural."

Once we realised that the waves of change had not only changed the country irrevocably but also the army, Roland decided that he could for the moment do no more. In April 1999 Roland retired from the Army as Deputy Chief.

The two of us then went on the extensive tour of Europe which we so long had promised ourselves. In typical Roland style we just bought the air tickets at short notice. He then grabbed a good map of Europe, made a rough figure "S" across the map to mark places we would like to see and off we went. No hotel reservations, no fixed itinerary, just cuffing it as we went along, grabbing a meal in a market place here and a sleeping place off the beaten track when it started getting dark.

This was wonderful, real fun and an unknown freedom. Needless to say, we managed to get to see many European battlefields from different wars over the centuries. It was only really on this trip that I came to realise what an outstanding scholar Roland actually was in spite of his claims to the contrary over the years. He recited European and especially military history and battle details as if he were reading it from an encyclopaedia. I was amazed at what he knew and could recite by heart. I knew he had an exceptional understanding of the Southern African battlefields, of the strategies and tactics employed, because we had often visited them with the children or with battlefield tours he arranged for special interest groups along the way. Mystification was his motto but I was still shocked that he had been able to hide such a wealth of knowledge from me for 17 years. When I said as much, he just replied, "You never asked."

Over the years I came to understand and share his knowledge and fascination with battlefields and wars all over the world. We never miss an opportunity to see another one. His excitement about one of my next missions early in 2013 brought a smile to my face. He was at 68 like a child who was promised a bicycle for Christmas when he heard that it might be possible for him to go to one of his favourite historical battlefields, namely Dien Bien Phu in Vietnam, since I was scheduled to do work in Cambodia. When I also indicated that I wanted to go to Russia on a Volga boat cruise in August of 2013, I should have expected his questions about which battlefields would be included in the trip... Kursk? Stalingrad?

Living with Roland has been living in the true sense of the word. There has been no time for sitting around. You have to be on the move all the time, manoeuvring and making sure that your rhythm is in harmony. For the past thirty years he has been the perfect gentleman, opening and closing doors for me and all ladies we incidentally travel with, carrying my stacks of parcels in and from the malls without complaining. He even on occasion protected me physically when I managed to aggravate some Arab patriarch with my western liberated ways. That has always been one thing with Roland. You do not touch what belongs to him. If you would dare, this controlled man becomes an aggressive and very dangerous opponent.

Amongst family and friends Roland is regarded as an enigma, always casually dressed yet impeccably neat at all times. Sometimes he will be the soul of the party having everyone in stitches and at other times quiet and remote somewhere in the background pondering his own thoughts. He was accepted as the military guy in the family all along. When he however began to really make his way in the business world over the last ten years or more, even close family members just shook their heads and agreed that he was indeed someone special.

He is a favourite uncle amongst the younger generations and a grandfather to die for. His 17-year-old grandson (Roland de Vries Jnr-Jnr) and all of the six granddaughters (Robyn de Vries 15, Sasha-Marie Grobler 8, Elysia Boschin 32 months, Briana Grobler 29 months, Danica Boschin 13 months and Wanya Grobler 11 months) will bear witness to this fact. When they see their grandfather approaching, they start laughing and dancing around.

It has been a joy and a privilege to walk next to Roland for the past thirty years There was literally never ever a dull moment. While I am quite happy slowing down at this stage, I fear Roland has no such inclination. Even the time spent in the elevator going to the ground floor from our 23rd floor apartment in Dubai, he uses for doing stretch exercises. As we walk down the marina to the grocery store to pick up our daily fare in the evenings, Roland still plans and dreams on about new horizons and new projects to launch and new ways to teach his grandchildren about the wonders of life and being alive. I guess that is Roland and that is the way he will always be.

Prologue: The Challenge

The decision to sit down and write this book was not an easy one. I primarily commenced writing, because my wife, Henriette and my four children and many of my friends who served with me in the South African Defence Force and others who crossed my path in remarkable ways, requested me to do so. I do not consider my life so significant in the greater scheme of things that I would have done it otherwise.

Once I decided to do so I realised that in a sense it was a way of finding closure on many things and perhaps unwittingly expressing words of explanation and encouragement to others. As I went along I began to realise that just perhaps in the writing thereof, I could share some experiences with my reader and relate valuable lessons I had learned through life. Knowledge shared, is knowledge gained. Therefore, thank you, Dear Lord for directing my path!

This book is about my life story and about living through the South African Border War … forcing heart and nerve and sinew … finding that strength lay in mobility, in the intimacy of motion and as such I was always searching for forward ground.

During the course of my existence two manuscripts played a significant role in my approach to life:

The first being the poem *If* by Rudyard Kipling which I received from my parents at a preschool age. The fundamental philosophy of trusting yourself, that all men counted, the importance of filling every unforgiving minute with sixty seconds' worth of distance running and the lesson of holding on in life I took to heart – to stand on your own two feet and to do your thing. The poem *If* therefore had a major influence on how I approached and witnessed life, viewed people and developed my own philosophy thereof. This was one of the main reasons I never belonged to organisations such as the "Afrikaner Broederbond"; in actual fact, disregarding it.

The second being the eight life stages by Erik Erikson as contained in the last page of this book.[1] Erik Homburger Erikson (15 June 1902–12 May 1994) was a German-born American developmental psychologist and psychoanalyst known for his theory on psychosocial development of human beings. He became famous for coining the phrase "identity crisis". Erikson believed that the ego exists from birth and that behaviour is not totally defensive as were described in his eight life stages.

How did the contents of these two manuscripts impact on the writing of my book? For starters, I tell my story exactly how I perceived it to be and where I challenged the system. I know damn well that I did so all along. Throughout my life I somehow always found myself in the "eye of a firestorm" from whence I had to manoeuvre, came hell or high water! Being somewhat free-spirited, I always found myself either confronting or questioning the conformists on the beaten track. I also thought deeply about work and life-related issues, studied on my own, experimented and wrote my own integrated leadership, command

1 The information used in my book concerning Erik Erikson came from an article by Arlene F Harder, MA, MFT (Revised 2012). It was compiled from *Childhood and Society* by Erik Erikson. With my friend Loutjie Bouwer I had studied the work of Erikson from the time I commanded the South African Army College in 1987.

and warfare philosophies with fervour. I can in all honesty say: I did it my way. In the process I did my darndest to take the people entrusted to me along in the process. With a natural transformational inclination I found that involvement, intellectual stimulation, inspirational motivation and individualised consideration were priceless (throwing fun in to boot). Just sometimes I fell into disfavour with a few of my seniors because of the latter; so be it, at times this was fun, as well. Refusing to be a member of the typical power play, brotherhood type of organizations, I was sometimes out on a limb. In an advanced stage of my career, I learnt that the latter fact was more irksome to some of the members of such organizations than I could ever imagine. However, I decided as early as my late teens that this kind of external control was something which I was not prepared to sell my birthright or individualistic beliefs for.

I furthermore decided to map out my life as a "military campaign" in terms of the eight life stages of Erikson – lines of operation, in my terms and of progressing from one firm base to the next.

Part 1 reviews the portion of my life from when I was born in Pretoria on 19 May 1944, bred in my family home in Vanderbijlpark and going to school there (my mom called me cheeky), until I turned eighteen. Thereafter I intentionally ventured back to Pretoria to join the South African Army in January 1963. It ends with a military and family career of 37 years, having experienced exhilarating times and eventually retiring on 30 April 1999 as the deputy chief of the army, a major general in rank, husband to one, father to four, friend to some, enemy of a few – later on grandfather to seven.

Part 2 appraises my experience in the Rhodesian Bush War and the South African Border War, intermittently from October 1979 until December 1988 and the influence it had on my life and the lives of some of my soldiers. This era gave me the opportunity to evaluate what was going on in the war for southern Africa and to question the sense and senselessness of stratagem, hopefully seeing both the wood and the trees.

Part 3 reveals my story experienced during the political changes in our country when the South African Defence Force embarked on transformation from January 1994 onwards – where all was not always what it seemed. I suddenly found out that "there is nothing more difficult to carry out, nor more doubtful of success, nor more dangerous to handle than to initiate a new order of things. For the reformer has enemies in all who profit by the old order and only lukewarm defenders in all those who would profit by the new order" (Machiavelli). So be it, as well! This section also reflects briefly on my second career until the moment I decided to write this book. All of this was utterly stimulating and helluva fun, careering all over Africa and the Middle East as well – same as manoeuvre warfare.

A final presumption if you would consider it. I also thought the writing of this book as being important to me, my family, friends and others in the sense that I am but one of a relatively small number of White South Africans left in this magnificent country of ours. The current members of the small White Tribe of South Africa are now no more than a mere three and a half million in a sea of others we co-exist in. I had lived in this country all my life and still am content, although we do not live on cloud nine ... few in other parts of the world do, I have experienced. I have fought for this country as others have done and experienced its transformation to what it is today. I sincerely believe that there is hope for this country of ours, endearingly called South Africa! I am proud of it and part of it. So, thank you, dear reader, for sharing in my adventure ... No, I don't have a business card.

Part 1

From Birth to Career: Achieving Identity and Meaningful Relationships

The era when I received "If" as a gift from my parents to the days I shaped my philosophy on leadership, command and management; the latter to be recognised by the Harvard Business School in a book that was written by John Kotter and Dan Cohen, "The Heart of Change".

Erik Erikson explains our personality traits in opposites. We think of ourselves as optimistic or pessimistic, independent or dependent, emotional or unemotional, adventurous or cautious, leader or follower, aggressive or passive. Many of these are innate temperament traits, but other characteristics, such as feeling either competent or inferior, appear to be learned based on the challenges and support we receive in growing up.

During infancy (from birth to eighteen months) there is major emphasis on the mother's positive and loving care for the child, with primary focus on visual contact and touch. If we pass successfully through this period of life we will learn to trust that life is basically okay and have confidence in the future. Failure in this may end with a deep-seated feeling of worthlessness and mistrust... Not surprisingly, the most significant relationship is with the maternal parent.

All through early childhood (from eighteen months to three years) we learn to master skills for ourselves. We learn to walk, talk and feed ourselves, master finer motor skills and are initiated into understanding basic emotions. We have the opportunity to build self-esteem and autonomy as we gain more control... of learning right from wrong; and in developing the important skills of the "WILL". During this stage, however, we can become extremely vulnerable if we're named, shamed, blamed and rejected by those closest to us. The most significant relationship is with parents.

In the course of our play-age period (from three to five) we experiment with the blueprint of becoming an adult and we start using the world "WHY" to explore our world. The most significant relationship is with the basic family.

All the way through school (from 6 to 12) we learn, create and accomplish numerous new skills and knowledge, in this way developing a sense of industry. This is also a very social stage of development we experience in terms of competence and self-esteem. Our most significant relationship is with the school and neighbourhood; however, parents are still important.

All through adolescence (from 12 to 18) development mostly depends upon what is done to us and what we do; we are neither child nor adult, as life gets more complex, as we attempt to find our own identity, struggle with social interactions and grapple with moral issues. Our task is to discover who we are as individuals separate from our family of origin and as members of a wider society. It is a time we can also develop strong devotion to friends and reason for existence. It is not surprising that our most significant relationships are with peer groups.

As young adults (from 18 to 35) we seek companionship and love, as we try to find mutually satisfying relationships primarily through marriage and friends. We generally also begin to start a family, if negotiating this stage successfully we can experience intimacy on a deeper level. If not, isolation and distance from others may occur, shrinking as if into defence... Our significant relationships are with marital partners and friends.

Through middle-adulthood (from 35 until 55–65) family, community and work-life is most crucial. We tend to be occupied with creative and meaningful aspects surrounding the latter; when we can expect to "be in charge". The significant undertaking is to perpetuate culture and transmit its values through those environments (guiding kids and folks and soldiers). Strength comes through caring for others and production of something that contributes to the betterment of society – "generativity". As our children leave home, or our relationships or goals change, we may be faced with major life changes – the mid-life crisis – and struggle with finding new meaning and purpose in life. If we don't get through this stage successfully, we can become self-absorbed and stagnate. Significant relationships are within the workplace, the community and the family – Eight Life Stages of Erikson.

1

My Early Years

You'll be a Man, my Son

If you can trust yourself when all men doubt you, but
make allowance for their doubting too ...
"If" – Rudyard Kipling

A Personal Glimpse: Trust versus Mistrust

From the time I was born I knew that I wanted to join the army. I can't explain why I wanted to do this, but what I did know was that nobody was going to stop me! My parents Divvy and Ellen, and my younger brother Herbert and sister Dorothea gradually came to accept my chosen destiny. Those who later became my next of kin, friends and the few enemies (from the ranks of own as well as enemy forces) had no choice in the matter – it was a done deal.

Although at first juggling a military career and then later a civilian one required some manoeuvring and at times the capturing of high ground to perform turning movements of sorts, it was a challenge I chose and enjoyed. Even today I use the joint operational planning cycle and principles of warfare to sort out my few nightmares and the other important things in life – and they still work for me, as they always have.

I was born at the Moedersbond maternity hospital in Pretoria on 19 May 1944. The Moedersbond was the most affordable venue for their firstborn that my father Divvy (full name Herman de Vries) and mother Ellen (née Riekert) could find. Let me say at this stage that by the powers vested in me by myself, my father and mother will hereafter be called Divvy and Ellen. My dear mother was eight years younger than my father, as Henriette, my beloved wife, is to me. The eight years' difference in seniority perturbed neither of these ladies; to the contrary ... I liked and still like it that these two women in my life were – and one still is – strong and caring ... Amazing!

The Moedersbond hospital was also close to my first home, about the same distance as the 2,4 km running test with full pack that we did later on in the Army. It was a modest wooden house north of Meintjieskop in Riviera, Pretoria which smelt of creosote, a smell I still love.

Divvy and Ellen brought me up to be forthright and honest at all times. Speak and live from the heart, they said, and because I was part of a wonderful loving family I received the priceless gift of natural pride. We were considered middle-class by ordinary material standards, but in fact we were much richer, because our real wealth was of a much higher order! Through my parents' positive and loving care and embraces I knew that I was OK, and I felt good about things from infanthood. Today I embrace and hold my own children and grandchildren as often as possible in the same way as my parents had held me, and when I became an officer and commander my soldiers became as dear to my heart as my own children.

I am a proud South African (okay, a white one), not an Englishman, an American, a Hollander, a Zulu or a German, nor from any other country or the United Nations. Perhaps there is a bit of Frisian in me. I like the part in heraldry which states that the Frisian people dwelt in the northern Dutch provinces of Friesland and Groningen. My system is north-seeking, and so I visited those places.

The Frisians were Germanic people who had occupied the North Sea coastal region since the times of the early Roman emperors. The Romans called them "Frisil", or plain hardegat or hardkoppig as we say in Afrikaans – hard-arsed or stubborn – and expressed a grudging admiration for this tribe which refused to be subdued. I had inherited a good share of this genetic code, as some of my seniors at Army and Defence Headquarters were doomed to experience in my not-too-distant military future, but that was just the way it was; so no names, no pack-drill. How could I have known in those early years after World War II that I would be having all these exciting encounters with them?

My parents instilled a crucial bit of personal philosophy in me at a very young age when they gave me Rudyard Kipling's famous poem, "If". It made an indelible impression on me which remains as sharp now as it was then, so it is hardly surprising that bits of it will pop up throughout this book. It is not the sort of high-flown poem that you have to struggle to understand, and it does not contain ambiguities that help the poet through rough patches that he can't or doesn't feel like explaining. It is as simple as the old .577/.450 Martini-Henry rifle that was the British soldier's personal weapon in Kipling's young days, and it hits just as hard as the Martini's fat lead bullet. "If you can trust yourself when all men doubt you, but make allowance for their doubting too ... "

Pure wisdom does not need fancy words or grave philosophical pronouncements to bring its message home. And so I still have my yellowed copy; all my children have copies of that old copy, and I often send other copies to my close friends as well. There is even one for you in this book. This poem became my guiding light as I set off on my journey to where I am today.

Fortunately, my parents spotted my invariable tendency to look at things from a different angle than most people, and accepted it. It is a tendency that frequently lands you in hot water because it goes against the accepted conventional wisdom, which is often not true wisdom but simply a restatement of long-held but not necessarily accurate perceptions, and naturally it often brought me in serious conflict with my teachers. But it served me well in life. I realised it was something positive; and as I progressed through the military I grasped its true value as the strategy of the indirect approach.

My life and person required that I be mobile at all times, and a small bicycle and lots of movement suited me well in my early life. I attended Sunday school regularly, but each Sunday at a different one. As a result I did not receive a year-end diploma like the other kids and was severely reprimanded by my parents. But I made many friends this way and even learned a bit of English and German along the way, more than I did at school.

I was certainly different from my brother, who became an engineer, and my sister, who qualified as a doctor of medicine. I felt extremely sorry for them because they would be trapped in such ordinary careers ... I'm just joking, of course; in fact I was very proud of them, even when they started earning much higher salaries while I had to get by on Army pay. This did not err on the side of generosity, even when augmented from time to time by the equally modest "bush pay" I received when I was deployed with my soldiers in the operational areas (when I got a parachute allowance after qualifying as a paratrooper, I reckoned I had it made).

In part the difference between us lay in the way our minds worked. My brother and sister were meticulous in their approach and extremely detail-orientated, and so did well at school. I spent a lot of time thinking, I remember, mostly with my right brain and in pictures. That was why I later preferred overlay-type operational orders during operational planning and execution – what the World War II German commanders called "graphic orders". There is much truth in the Chinese saying that a picture is worth a thousand words, as anyone who has suffered through a long planning session in a hot, stuffy tent or bungalow will agree.

One might say I started getting practice at an early stage – I was about four – by taking to saluting just about anyone who passed me. I expect it was something of an ordeal for my family to be saluted whenever I was in their vicinity. A while later I manufactured a parachute out of a dress belonging to the mother of my close friend, Jannie Swart. Fortunately Jannie jumped first off our garage roof at 46 Curie Boulevard, Vanderbijlpark, seeing that it was his mother's dress.

It was a large parachute, since Jannie's mother was a large lady, but obviously it was not large enough, because he made a hard landing and broke his arm. In technical language it was a "priority three casualty" and both our mothers were hopping mad, so I didn't attempt another parachute jump until August 1967 when I trotted out with the rest of Parachute Course 43V at Bloemfontein.

A bit of that early spirit must have clung on to me, though, because much later, having become a father in the interim, I decided intuitively one day that the time had come for my children to abseil down an 80-foot cliff without a safety line in order to teach them self-confidence. I trained Roland Junior, Elmarie, Melanie and Pieter-Riekert in the right procedures and down they went, while I prayed hard for them, since they averaged about four years of age. The details were not divulged to my dear wife, Henriette (who refused point-bank to undertake this stunt herself) for obvious reasons – the praying part is OK to divulge, though.

Anyway, they not only survived but thought it was a hell of a fun thing to do. My children still talk fondly about those days, and the eldest three tell their small children about our exploits amid much laughter (the fourth, 27-year-old Pieter, has at the time of writing not yet become a father, but no doubt he will do the same, if and when he gets around to producing an audience. Life is all about building great memories, is it not?

I did not know in 1944 that I was going to intermittently participate in a gruelling 22-year-long bush war, which would start in August 1966 and end in December 1988 on South Africa and South West Africa/Namibia's northern borders. I did not know either that I was going to spend umpteen hours in my beloved six-wheeled Ratel infantry fighting vehicle with a bunch of exceedingly great military compatriots... I always maintained later on that the smell of diesel mixed with dust and the aroma of broken foliage is much more exotic than Estée Lauder Private Collection (do not tell this to Henriette either – one must maintain operational security at all costs). Nor did I know that I was going to play a modest role in the political and military transformation processes which happened quite suddenly upon beleaguered South Africa in 1994. I loved those sudden surprises, revelled in the excitement of change and thrived on mobile matters.

South Africa then was about sharing exciting times – frequently exacting times – with others ... If I had known this I probably would have tried to get out of school sooner. The laws of the ruling National party apparently forbade that at the time, and many other stupid things I later came to know about, too. So I was going to remain non-partisan and only vote in referendums, and was definitely not going to join the groups like the Freemasons, the "Rapportryers" or the "Broederbond", which were all on offer at some or other stage of my life.

I was just not one who could swear to abide by the rules of a closed fraternity with secrets and to act towards others in accordance with their traditions and laws. There were quite a few Masons in the defence force of the day, I came to realise. To me such a system smacked of putting the interests of their own members first to the detriment of many perhaps more deserving others. This was definitely not for me. And I was certainly not a super-duper Afrikaner of the Rapportryer or Broederbond type, of whom there were many in the senior cadre. I saw myself rather as an ordinary man among super troopers. It was their individuality I enjoyed and appreciated. As our 'enemy' later on up north referred to us all as "Boere", I found that our "Boere" included English-speakers, Indians, coloureds, Jews and Blacks.

I have hated bullies with a passion from as far back as I could remember; one of the earliest was a massive overbearing character who used to grab and eat the peanut butter sandwiches I regularly gave to one of my exceedingly poor schoolmates during play-break when I was in Grade 2. Later on I found quite a few such bullies in the Army as well, people who abused their positions of power and did not understand the value of the personal part of such power – bloody authoritarian sticklers for the rules, control-crazy maniacs who smothered the people they were supposed to help like a bundle of wet army blankets. Leaders should be like thirst-quenching fountains, I became convinced, and I have never changed my mind.

I remember coming home from school one day, boiling with rage, and telling my mother that I felt like f ... ing up the aforementioned sandwich-grabber. "Now, Roland," she said, "do not use the "F" word again!". She explained to me in no uncertain terms what it meant. I was stupid enough to promise her that I would never use it again, and I kept myself to my promise – although at various times in the future I trembled on the very brink. Instead I took to using "bliksem", a very mild Afrikaans word which is acceptable even in polite company.

I have even told a number of people that I would give them R1 million if they ever catch me out. Admittedly this was and is a pretty rash thing to do, since I am no plaster angel and swearing is a time-hallowed Army custom, but so far I have got away without breaking that long-ago promise to Ellen.

Anyway, I had to deal with school because of that heartless insistence by the government that I needed to matriculate before I could join the Army (and, although I did not know it yet, meet Henriette, co-operate in producing my children and make both friends and enemies). It was as simple as that: Cross that hurdle labelled "Matric", or else. I did not want to become a politician, a businessman, a teacher, a preacher, a doctor, an engineer, a butcher, a baker or a candlestick-maker. I wanted to be a soldier and end up commanding a remarkable military unit of fighting men with a life and culture of its own. I wanted to have a wonderful family, too – which I got, and for which I thank the Dear Lord – and much, much more, including a small, battered backpack.

The said backpack, let it be understood, is a mental one. I am sorry to digress like this, since one has to keep moving, eternally seeking forward ground, but it goes like this: You will be a man, my son, Divvy and Ellen had said to me, sally forth into the wild green yonder (I understood this to mean Africa's bushveld). So there was my first mission command. Sally forth, travelling light with no more luggage than a small suitcase or backpack, preferably a battered one that no-one in Africa will be tempted to steal from you. Keep the people close to you un-battered and your enemies slightly battered until they change their minds and start talking peace.

Early Years – Inspiration, Trust, Drive, Hope and Energy

To me life was challenging and exciting, and if I had the choice I would do it the same way again (only better, of course, with the benefit of hindsight). The greatest joys in my life and sources of inspiration, trust, drive, hope and energy were my family, friends, a few enemies who are now new-found friends, my soldiers, Psalm 23, a few military books, six-wheeled Ratels, a tin cup, a fork, a beer, a campfire, my sleeping-roll, trees, the smell of the veld, movement and change – simple things really.

Soon, however, I learnt that life was not the way I had supposed it to be. I guess it is the way of things; what makes the difference is how you cope with the reality, the way you live your life, and the choices you make. The time for me had come to meet other people in a strange world, and to share with them and grow and learn and commit and do. It is a pattern that recycles itself to infinity. Caring for others who mattered and the possession of a passion for what you do, changed everything my soldiers taught me later on.

Before I reached school-going age we moved to Vanderbijlpark, south of Johannesburg. For some now-forgotten reason I disliked the place intensely, and when I became older I used to refer to it as "the Black Hole of Calcutta", which did not amuse either Divvy or Ellen. But this did not affect my plans, laid at an early age, to shake its dust off my feet. No doubt this was a bit unfair to Vanderbijlpark, a normal suburburban town where the quality of life was certainly better than Calcutta's – but that's how it was.

But back to 1949 ... My mother and I would often walk the four kilometres from our home to Barclays Bank. Each time we went out like this she would ask me to walk slightly behind her for a while to check whether the seams of her Berkshire stockings were exactly straight – no margin of error was acceptable. In so doing I learnt a lesson – not that I should wear nylon stockings with straight seams, I hasten to add, but to be neatly dressed at all times. She would have made a damned good sergeant-major.

By the way, the old German Army used to refer to their sergeant-majors as "the mothers of the company". In this sense, too, my mother acted like a sergeant-major. She would defend her three children to the death against any outsider, but this did not mean that they could misuse her protective instinct. I found this out one day when I was throwing stones at passing cars, as boys sometimes will. One driver stopped, scrambled out of his car and charged. I did not, to use a military phrase I learnt later, throw smoke and withdraw. As a result he caught me, gave me a good hiding on the spot (things were simpler in those days) and then dragged me home to 46 Curie Boulevard.

When my mother opened the door I was standing on my hands, with my torturer holding me by my feet. Ellen blew her top right there and sorted him out, six-love. "Who the hell are you to spank my child and hold him like this, you bloody bully?" she cried, so fiercely that the sorry soul dropped me without further ado, fled into the street and screeched away in his dented chocolate-brown Chevrolet Fleetmaster.

Then it was my turn for another subtle reprimand, Ellen-style: "Why the hell did you throw stones at passing cars?" Fine. Now I knew where I stood and how far I could manoeuvre. I proceeded to duck and dive, but without noticeable success, and eventually admitted under severe interrogation: that I was practicing my baseball and ambushing techniques, and all was fair in love and war (my justification for this was that an ambush is an attack on a moving enemy from a hidden position, but you must not get caught in the act).

With a slight smile, which I did not fail to notice, Ellen commented that she was pleased that I had not lied too directly to her, then added: "Sit down, Smiley (at that time my parents used to call me "Smiley" or "Cheeky"), I want to tell you a story about lies." And she did – a simple but remarkable story that I will never forget and over time told it to my own children as well. I think that in addition to being a good sergeant-major she could also have done well as an anti-corruption consultant in present-day Africa.

It was about honesty and not stealing from others. There was once a young man, she recounted, who used to steal things for his impoverished mother. One day he pocketed a safety pin and was caught in the act. His mother's response was: "Thanks for caring, my son, just don't let them catch you the next time around, OK?" Eventually he was arrested for murder and found guilty. His mother was at his side when he went to the gallows, and her last words to him were: "My dear son, I should never have allowed you to take that safety pin that first time, I should have taught you what is right and what is wrong from the beginning."

My father was a remarkable baseball player. He pitched for Northern Transvaal and played with Danie Craven[1] when both of them still worked at Iscor in the early forties. My father later played for Vanderbijlpark and he used to take me along to games at weekends. And at one game at nearby Boksburg he hit an amazing home run, far into the outfield. It was a truly remarkable feat, but in Divvy's opinion it was a "foul strike" (outside the boundaries of the field) and he indicated it as such with his arm. The umpire shouted at him. "It's a home run; you must run, if you don't run I'm going to give you out!" My father just looked at the umpire, then threw down his bat and walked back to the bench to sit down with his fellow players. They looked at him, astounded, but I was extremely proud of him.

Ellen's anecdote about the theft of the safety pin and Divvy's call on the baseball foul strike are stories that would definitely have been of benefit to many people around the world; including those inhabiting its various parliaments. The examples my parents set had an amazing effect on me. I decided in life that I would rather be honest in life instead give things away instead of holding on to them – one cannot slide into Heaven with a large rucksack firmly fixed to your backside, or even wearing a watch.

Perhaps I could get permission from higher authority, so to speak, to take a few pictures with me as well – a few nice ones of my family, friends, soldiers, Ratels and enemies; and perhaps my R-5 rifle and my sleeping-roll as well, just in case. Heaven was an objective I firmly set my sights on for some time in the future. In the meantime, however, I was and still am determined to stay around and remain fit for a little while longer – 68, and counting.

1 Daniël Hartman Craven (11 October 1910 – 4 January 1993), known as the famous Danie Craven or simply Doc Craven, was a former Western Province, Eastern Province, Northern Transvaal and Springbok rugby union player as well as arguably South Africa's best and best-known rugby administrator. He also coached the Springboks between 1949 and 1956 to become one of the most successful Springbok coaches of all time.

Working on Achieving Identity and Making Friends at School

School, yes, any other questions ... ? As far as I was concerned school was for left-brain, detail-orientated geniuses, while for me it was a war of attrition. If it were not for the cadets I would have had it, and I do not give in easily; that is the Frisian part of me. So I stuck it out, with a few provisos ... I need to confess something so that I can get it off my chest and out of my mind forever – I hated school with a passion most of the time.

But fortunately the Dear Lord saw to it that I had a bicycle, a few good friends, storybooks, comics, school cadets and the Boy Scouts. Yes, the Scouts, because they taught fieldcraft and a few other juicy military subjects at the time – and I liked and respected our "Skipper". I had tried the Voortrekkers (the Afrikaner youth organisation equivalent to the Boy Scouts), but they only held "grape festivals", sang "Sarie Marais" and did other boring things.

My bicycle was soon taken illegally and unlawfully from me by one of our local guys. I knew he was a local because at that time our beloved South Africa was not plagued by literally millions of illegal aliens from Nigeria, Zimbabwe, Mozambique and Somalia, as it is today. I have also registered with myself what the Army calls an "essential requirement of intelligence", namely to find out who the hell the guy was who had invented our school system. The words "yuck" and "uninspiring" come to mind. Please don't share this little secret with my four children and seven grandchildren, but I would have loved to get hold of that fellow during basic training!

I enjoyed the sport and social life at school, which was fun and made life bearable, attended all the cadet camps at Lenz that I possibly could, and before long became the one and only cadet student officer of our school. I spent wonderful times working with Mr. S.J.N. Swanepoel (nicknamed Swannie, the teacher who headed our cadet detachment) to develop our senior cadets into a formidable drill platoon – we were regularly asked to give drill demonstrations at many of our town's social and official events. We were so good that in 1962, after existing for only a few months, our platoon won the Southern Rand Open Drill Competition and came second in the Witwatersrand (now Gauteng Province). Did I feel great about this, or what?

Apart from school cadets I was soon dragged on to the "Debate and Social Committee" by Mr. J.J.N. Lauwrens (nicknamed "Kalimbo"). He said: "Roland, you enjoy arguing and always have an answer to everything; this is the place for you." I tried to decline politely by saying that I was quite happy running the cadets. He gave me that look and said: "Don't argue, next week you're going to entertain the school by doing the 'Journal' event at our next cultural evening."

I didn't know what he was talking about and politely asked him what the hell the "Journal" was. He replied: "You must tell stories, perform and make all the people attending laugh for two hours." I said: "Yes, sir," like a good soldier (cadet version), did it and then did it again, and it was great fun. But I definitely did not consider public speaking as a career, as Casper de Vries[2] had. Casper and I are not related in any discernible way, I might add, although obviously there is a common Frisian strain somewhere. But I must confess that my youngest son, Pieter, somehow received a social and comedian-like chromosome, so much so that as a student he made good pocket money as a disc jockey, and he still regularly receives invitations to act as the master of ceremonies at various functions, not to mention

2 Casper de Vries is a South African actor, comedian, entertainer, composer, director, producer and author, who had become famous for his one-man shows in Afrikaans.

friends' weddings – in fact, just a little while before I wrote this he flew to Pretoria from Saudi Arabia for four days to do just that. He is extremely fond of and loyal to his friends – my amazing youngster of 27 (who did not go to the Army, which proves that my way wasn't the only way).

The Debate and Social Committee was one thing, not that I had much of a choice about joining it, but I was able to strongly decline the appointment of prefect when I was in Standard Nine (Grade 11 these days). In my opinion the school was now pushing things a little too far – being a prefect would have hindered the personal mobility I strived so desperately to sustain.

If it had been up to me, Standard Nine would have been "hail and farewell" time in any case. My desire to join the Army had got even stronger as my teen years marched on. I was always somewhat of a rebel, and if I had been born in Angola, I might well have joined one of the liberation armies. But Rhodesia was closer to hand, in addition to having a fine army, so by Standard Nine I was ready to leave school and head over Beit Bridge to join up. As a matter of fact, by the time my parents found out about my devious intention I had already filled in my application papers.

Alas, Divvy and Ellen were having none of this, and they made their (and my) position quite clear: "Roland, our eldest, we love you dearly, but you will remain in school until you finish Matric. If it's up to us, you will remain there so long that your children will bring your lunch to school, but you will make your Matric ... " Put that way, I had to admit that they had made a pretty solid case and that I was not going anywhere soon. Fortunately, the cadets were there to make life bearable.

When I had accepted my fate and suspended my attempt to enlist in the Rhodesian Army, my final years in school in the early 1960s were spent reasonably productively at Transvalia High School in Vanderbijlpark – the old one with temporary classrooms made of asbestos, which luckily made them difficult to burn down. It also helped that when I passed Standard Nine my parents gave me a new racing Raleigh bicycle. This helped a lot to keep me sane, given that mobility was everything to me. They were so productive, in fact, that to the surprise of my parents, brother and sister I gained a reasonably good second-class Matric pass.

Transvalia truly was a great school, and in spite of my impatience with all that left-brain orientation I had many enjoyable moments. A particularly memorable one for me was also my parting shot, so to speak – I was the parade commander at a flag-hoisting parade when the new school building was opened in November 1962. My sister Dorothea had the honour of writing Matric in that same school five years later and came first in her class. My brother Herbert, however, attended the technical college in Vereeniging, because he was infatuated with my father's career and also wanted to become a mechanical engineer and working with all things metal.

For me greater things loomed, or so I believed, and I knew exactly where I would go looking for them. I had a university exemption – in those days a solid second-class Matric could get you in, since the era of 30 percent pass rates still lay well into the future – but there was no way I was headed for academia. In January I would be on the road to Voortrekkerhoogte (now Thaba Tshwane), the Defence Force's huge garrison and training complex outside Pretoria, where I would enlist at the Army Gymnasium.

I was fortunate to be applying at just the right time, when the South African Defence Force was on the cusp of an as yet unforeseen transformation process. In 1962 white male youths of 18 were liable to be called up for short-term training, followed by several years of part-time refresher training, or they could opt to apply for a long-term engagement in the Permanent Force; but things were about to start changing quite drastically. People of colour were not called up, but for the first time they could enlist in the peace-time Army (as opposed to serving in hostilities-only units in time of war).

In the Cape Province the Army was already re-raising what was to become the South African Cape Corps, a unit recruited from the coloured community which was the latest manifestation of a long line of such units dating back to the 1790s, several of which had made great names for themselves as fighting troops (in the 1850s Governor Sir Harry Smith, himself a veteran of the savage fighting during the Napoleonic War, remarked that "it is scarcely to be credited how rapidly these men trained as soldiers ... No nation in the world with the exception of the inhabitants of the South of France have such a natural turn to become soldiers"). There was also a black guard force in the SADF which within a decade would become a full-fledged military unit, and in the mid-1970s the first men of colour were commissioned as officers – and they were not token appointments, either; they were all survivors of a stiff training course.

I wonder where I would have ended up in 1962, however, if I had been a black 18-year-old. In an insurgent training camp somewhere abroad, perhaps? But I wasn't, and thanks to my mother and father I had the qualifications to join the South African Army, which for my money was the best army in Africa and probably one of the best small armies in the world (it wasn't in the latter case, but it would come pretty close some years down the line).

My belief was subjective, of course, since my main source of information was my large collection of recruiting pamphlets. I remember that the one which impressed me most was a colour depiction of khaki-clad infantrymen in battle order with their .303 Lee-Enfield rifles, piling out of a 1954-vintage six-wheeled Saracen armoured personnel carrier, shrouded in a cloud of pure honest-to-goodness dust. But that was good enough for me, being the right-brain thinker that I was.

At that stage the Army Gymnasium had only been in existence for about 12 years, but had already carved out a great reputation for its efficiency and smartness on parade. Its aim was to cultivate high-quality junior leaders for both the full-time Permanent Force and part-time Citizen Force. Entrants did a year's rigorous service consisting of a particularly strenuous version of the standard basic training, followed by special-to-arm training; great emphasis was also placed on ceremonial duties, of which there was a great deal.

When their year was up, those who had survived the full year's course could choose to return to civilian life or go on to more advanced leader training which would qualify them as instructors or officers in the Permanent Force. Just what I wanted! In its original conception the Army Gym was a win-win proposition. It helped to cultivate top-notch commissioned and non-commissioned leader groups for the Permanent and Citizen Forces, and fed the civilian commercial world with young men who had gained maturity and direction.

My mother took me to the Vereeniging railway station in our cream-coloured Opel Kapitan, accompanied by my saucer-eyed brother and sister. I had a small suitcase containing a red track-suit, PT kit, tennis shoes, jockey-type underpants, a towel and two tins of "The Real Makoya Zam-Buk ointment", which was then regarded as a sort of universal cure-all for any number of cuts, bruises, aches and similar ailments. I also had in my possession a precious miniature Sony transistor radio my parents had given me for Christmas (and which, sad to say, was stolen within my first month in the Army while I stood guard). In one hand I clutched an old Dunlop Maxply squash racket my dad had given me, and in the other the rail-warrant I had received from the local magistrate's office.

On my person I had my small Bible and six documents to see me into and through the Army Gym: a learner-driver's licence; my Matric certificate; my Army Gym admission form; my copy of Kipling's "If"; a letter of reference from Dr. S.I.W. Roos my former headmaster; and another from my Presbyterian padre (during my last year at school I had attended the Presbyterian Church because my Boy Scout friends did).

I quote Dr. Roos's letter because it might give an indication of whom and what I was at that crucial moment in my life's journey:

> To Whom It May Concern.
>
> It is a pleasure to provide the following information in the interest of Roland de Vries. This year (1962) he is a matric scholar at the High School of Transvalia, Vanderbijlpark. He is a boy who is extremely principle-centred and therefore handles his teachers and fellow scholars with utmost respect and dignity.
>
> Roland's great interest is with the military. Reasonably early in his school career he had shown remarkable aptitude for this. For the last two years he had been the Student Officer of our School Cadet Detachment. Also on the rugby field, Debate Committee and other such activities he had performed remarkably. It is an honour for me to recommend him for his future career.

Wow! To be honest, such praise came as a surprise to me, considering that I had never seen myself as an ideal pupil, but it did great things for my self-esteem, so I was ready to march into the great khaki-coloured embrace of the Defence Force with the utmost self-confidence and willingness to tackle anything, especially the Army.

At the station my mother, brother and sister kissed me goodbye, and Ellen said, "Roland, be good, look after yourself. We're proud of you." I was sad to hug them goodbye, because I would not see them again for three months, when I would receive my first weekend pass after completing the first phase of basic training. But I was also highly excited as I steamed north, compliments of the South African Railways, which in those days functioned like clockwork, with all the doors and windows in place and functioning. Finally – finally! – I was on my way to join the Army, just as I had dreamt of doing since the days when I surprised strangers by solemnly saluting them. How would I turn out – a Taurus in the making or a bull in a china shop? Only time would tell, and the clock was ticking.

2

You're in the Army Now!

If you can trust yourself

If you can force your heart and nerve and sinew to serve your turn ... And to hold on when there is nothing in you ... Except for the will which says ... Hold on!
"If" – Rudyard Kipling

In the Army, Now and Forever More – Learning about Soldiering and Minor Tactics

There was a formidable-looking sergeant waiting for me in the parking lot with a World War II-vintage Ford three-tonner when I disembarked from the train at Pretoria station on 2 January 1963. The station was designed and built by Sir Herbert Baker in 1908 – a majestic building, like all of his works, although it looks somewhat forlorn today because rioters burnt down its roof in 2001 during the reign of the African National Congress. But as I say, in 1963 it was in fine shape when I arrived to do my bit.

Not that I had much time to admire the station building or think fine thoughts. I was bundled unceremoniously into the three-tonner, along with a few other starry-eyed recruits, and we were rushed off to Voortrekkerhoogte. On arrival at the Army Gym we were told to report at a store, where we signed for an extremely heavy steel trunk filled with bedding. Then we were chased at the double to what was to be our home for the rest of the year, a typical red-brick Army bungalow with 12 beds in it. We were gasping for breath by the time we got to the bungalow, but for me it was an exhilarating experience. I was now a full-fledged member of Number 1 Platoon, Charlie Company! All that lay ahead was 12 weeks' basic training and then a nine-month instructor's course. OK!

My first encounter with the command structure occurred sooner than I anticipated, when our instructor, Corporal Cammie Botha, ordered me to report immediately to the Charlie Company HQ. There I was ceremoniously marched into the company commander's office by Company Sergeant-Major "Spoegie" (Spitter) Verster, a lisping, limping veteran whom we suspected of having been wounded in the famously bloody action at Delville Wood during the Battle of the Somme in 1916. He looked old enough to me at the time.

Waiting for me were the company commander, Lieutenant Hans Möller, and one of his platoon commanders, Second-Lieutenant Archie Moore. Möller ran his eyes up my six foot two inches and with a knowing smile said: "Ons gaan jou breek, mannetjie" (we're going to break you, little man). It is moments like this that fill the average recruit's soul with dismay, but I was so full of myself that I replied: "Dit sal die dag wees" (that will be the day). Möller's smile widened and we had an amicable chat about life and the army in general. I was impressed by his charisma (as it happened, in August 1967 we would both be learning the art of parachute-jumping at 1 Parachute Battalion in Bloemfontein – the Permanent Force was so small in those days that you tended to keep bumping into old acquaintances wherever you were posted).

And so commenced my Army career, a year-long adventure which I thoroughly enjoyed. My parents and siblings saw little of me during that time. There were no weekend passes for the first three months, and after that we got one a month, which started when you marched out through the gate at 12:00 noon on a Saturday and ended absolutely no later than midnight on the Sunday – and you had to be signed in at the guardroom no later than 11:59 p.m. I won't dwell on what followed; suffice it to say that we duly passed out as qualified infantry instructors at the end of that strenuous year, and to me it was a wonderful moment as the doors of the army opened up for us.

Unlike some of my colleagues, I was not interested in going on to the South African Military Academy at Saldanha Bay: I wanted a platoon of infantry under my command as soon as possible, and to my joy I was one of just 30 men who were selected to attend a three-month junior officers' course, which was also held at the Army Gym. I got through that all right, and on 19 March 1964 received my Deed of Commission, an impressive and much-cherished document bearing the seal of the Republic of South Africa and signed by then State President C.R. Swart.

It was actually handed to me on 16 April, and so at the age of 19 I was officially an assistant field-cornet (this unpopular re-designation for second-lieutenants was introduced in 1960 and abolished again in 1968). I was not yet firmly entrenched in the Army – my official status was that of a short-service Permanent Force subaltern on two years' probation. But there were no bounds to my anticipations.

I left Vereeniging by train for Bloemfontein with my bicycle clutched under my arm, my brown leather Army Gymnasium suitcase and the blazer for which I had paid in monthly instalments, the new R-1 rifle for which I had signed, a black duffel bag filled with army kit, an old suit passed on by my father and a new Dunlop Maxply Squash Racket.

My destination was 1 Special Service Battalion at its base at Tempe in Bloemfontein, where I spent the next four years immersed in learning and teaching basic infantry skills and mastering fieldcraft and minor tactics. In 1966 I got a step up to field-cornet (lieutenant). By 1967 I was becoming exceedingly bored with the day-to-day routine, but fortunately I had been made responsible for the facilitation of in-house junior leadership development. I was also playing good squash for the first league in the Orange Free State Province, and was selected for the South African Army team as well as for the SADF team, which was on provincial level.

But my inborn instinct for mobility made me realise that I had to make a plan to move on and do something elsewhere in the Army. I had completed a number of qualifying courses at the Infantry School and had done exceptionally well, and my personal reports had been excellent (I know this sounds boastful, but that is how it was), and naturally I felt good about it. And so in June 1967 I put in for the next basic parachute jumping course at 1 Parachute Battalion.

Actually getting on the course was not simple. 1 SSB's adjutant, Captain Jerry Coetzee, called me in and softly told me that the Commanding Officer, Commandant Jack Dutton, had said that I could not be spared and therefore he would not endorse my application. I thought to myself, Wow, a field-cornet who can't be spared! I didn't believe it and decided on an indirect approach, which is often a very good battle tactic, of course.

Now, this sort of sideways approach along the chain of command is not a career-enhancing idea in any army, but I got away with it because Jack Dutton was an outstanding commander and a gentleman throughout a long career which extended from the Korean

War, in which he commanded a troop of Centurion tanks, to his retirement as a lieutenant-general and the SADF's Chief of Staff Operations (and after that he went on to serve as South Africa's Ambassador to Chile). But his immediate problem was to sort out the bumptious Field-Cornet Roland de Vries.

In those days I played squash regularly with Commandant Jan Fourie the OC 1 Parachute Battalion, and I told him my sad story about how my application had been rejected rather than signed and forwarded to Army HQ in Potgieter Street, Pretoria. Like a true paratrooper, Fourie was not daunted by this obstacle. "No problem," he told me, "fill it in again and hand me a copy" – which I did the next day.

Two weeks went by without anything eventful happening. Then one day, while I was in the unit lines supervising some training, I saw our Regimental Sergeant-Major heading my way at speed.

"Sir," he said, "you better run to the commandant's office – you're on orders – and make it snappy." Somewhat apprehensively I did just that. Captain Coetzee marched me in, and within a minute I had accumulated no less than seven extra duties as orderly officer. It was like a blitzkrieg.

"What was that for, Captain?" I asked

"You violated the chain of command, Field-Cornet," he replied. And then he added: "By the way, you've been selected for Basic Parachute Jumping Course 43V in August – sign here!" I did so, jubilantly, even though it meant moving into the duty room for the next few days while I worked off my sentence. But my stint there was cut short on the third day when the Adjutant came over to me and said, "The Commandant said you only need to do three of your extra duties – he suspended the rest for taking initiative."

I remember thinking, what a man Jack Dutton was to serve under! But that was how he was. He had the last word, though. Next day at tea-time he looked me over and told the other officers, "Young De Vries is going on parachute course next month. Before he leaves, ask him to give you a lecture on the chain of command." Yes, what a man!

In August I went on course as scheduled, and managed to be among the 60 or so men out of a class of 150 who had managed to stick it out to the end. It was an amazing thrill to sew the wings on to my uniform. So far, so good! Now the question was where I would go next. Rumour had it that I was destined for 1 Parachute Battalion. But rumour lied. In November 1967 Commandant Jan Fourie was promoted to full colonel and tasked to establish a combat school for training members of the part-time Commando Force, the country's large network of area-protection units, and he wanted me there.

As a matter of interest, in the South African military lexicon "commando" had a unique meaning. The rest of the world had followed Winston Churchill's World War II example and used "commando" to designate special forces raiding units, but in South Africa, where the term originated, commandos remained what they had been since the 17th Century – units of citizen-soldiers.

Building Self-Esteem at the Danie Theron Combat School and Learning the Tricks of the Trade

Needless to say, this meant goodbye transfer to 1 Parachute Battalion, but I enjoyed tremendously giving training at section, platoon and company level to class after class of commando soldiers during the next two years. For at least one year I undertook a great number of courses for section commanders, and I can still recite the six battle drills which were supposed to pop into your mind if you happened to be woken up at dead of night to deal with some mango-encrusted fan.

During my time at Danie Theron I was honoured to be among 15 officers selected to attend the first-ever Specialist Infantry Course, which was presented by the legendary Major J.D. (Jan) Breytenbach and the almost equally legendary Staff-Sergeant M.J. (Yogi) Potgieter. The course lasted only from 20 May to 28 June 1968, but it was an extremely strenuous endeavour, highly invigorating and superbly presented.

Potgieter could have fought knife-in-teeth alongside Davy Crockett at the Alamo and he and Breytenbach spurned such pantywaist safety precautions as using blanks: during the tracking, patrolling, raiding and abseiling exercises they habitually shot into the ground around our feet with ball ammunition, which was disconcerting at first but soon became "ops normal" for us.

This excursion was not simply another training course, but a test trial to establish a programme for the selection of operators in the Special Forces which Breytenbach and Potgieter were soon to establish at the Infantry School at Oudtshoorn in the Western Cape.

The course ended with a gruelling two-week escape-and-evasion phase in the freezing dead of winter in the mountainous areas of the arid Little Karoo near Calitzdorp, Oudtshoorn and De Rust, and then across the Outeniqua Mountains to Swartvlei and Knysna – 240 plus kilometres. By the end of it, only six of us remained to pass out as qualified – the other nine had dropped out, particularly during that terrible final exercise, and some actually ended up in hospital.

I was quite proud of the fact that although I was caught and interrogated for 24 hours without interruption, I managed not to break – I still have a scratch-pad given to me by my interrogators which contains nothing but a few doodled drawings, a mirror of their frustration at being unable to get anything out of me except my rank, name and date of birth, the only information to be given by a prisoner of war according to the Geneva Convention.

Colonel Fourie congratulated me when I returned to Danie Theron – now a highly trained, supercharged infantryman with the papers to prove it. What a boost for my self-esteem! I promptly started taking my section leaders on weekend mini escape-and-evasion courses from Kimberley to Boshoff, to teach them to use their initiative, and they enjoyed it tremendously. In those days we did not have proper uniforms for field work, so I sought and received Colonel Fourie's permission to manufacture my own.

I dyed sets of khaki fatigues green for each of my students, then smudged the uniforms with dabs of Jik household bleach to give them a mottled camouflage appearance and bought them slouch hats to wear on the exercises. My course now stuck out like a sore thumb among the others in their authorised battledress. For good measure I also took them to see the movie "The Green Berets" when it was screened in Kimberley. Life was good!

Well, not all of it. Civilians do not always realise that by the nature of things there is inevitably an ever-present element of danger in military training, because soldiers are taught to handle lethal weapons and munitions under extreme conditions, and that past a certain point this can't be done by simulations or firing blanks. And so early in 1969 I lost my first soldier, a rifleman named Van der Zandt, from the small Orange Free State town of Winburg, while Staff-Sergeant Daan de Klerk and I were busy with field training at the De Brug firing range outside Bloemfontein.

De Klerk was guiding our soldiers through a "jungle lane" exercise at the time, which consisted of throwing a live Number 36 hand-grenade into an earth dam, then charging down the jungle lane, firing double taps (two shots in rapid succession) at targets hidden in the bushes. I was sitting to one side on the spare wheel of my Land Rover, directing the live field firing of our other students in another direction, when I heard the unmistakeable crunch of a hand grenade from De Klerk's direction and knew instinctively that something was wrong.

I jumped up with such speed that I tore the seat of my pants when it hooked on to some part of the spare wheel, and ran towards the jungle lane. There I found a shocked, dust-covered De Klerk standing amid the acrid stench of high explosive and Van der Zandt on the ground, bleeding from shrapnel wounds. He was dead: one fragment hit his heart and had killed him instantly.

There was, of course, a board of inquiry, but it found that De Klerk and I had adhered meticulously to the safety instructions; the board determined that Van der Zandt had frozen at the critical moment, dropping the grenade in front of him instead of lobbing it over the wall of the dam. The tragic incident was a shock to all of us, and I realised once again that the work we were doing was dangerous and that it required the utmost care by all. It was a lesson I never forgot.

I attended Van der Zandt's funeral at Winburg and afterwards visited his bereaved parents in their modest home, trying to console them by telling them what a fine soldier their son had been. I don't know how much this helped them, but the whole affair left a scar on my soul, the first of many to come in later years.

In 1969 I completed the 81 mm Battalion Mortar Course at the Infantry School (I came first, which did my self-esteem no harm whatsoever), and later that year came second on the Lieutenants' Qualifying to Captains Course Tactics and Training (Combat Team Commanders) at the Army College. Our instructors were three captains named George Kruys, Deon Mortimer and Daan Hamman (all later generals), and it was my good luck, because they were simply the best in the business.

In the 1960s the Army was still obsessed with the conventional-warfare methods of World War II, methodically and rigidly adhering to conventional wisdom – as we used to say, it was all about "what 'Major Brown' of the British Army said and did, what-what, old chap!" At the Army College, however, the whisper was going around that some people higher up had become convinced that South Africa faced not only a protracted insurgency threat but possibly a conventional one as well. There were clear indications that the Army wanted to shake off its old-brain thinking about how to fight a conventional war, if it ever came to that; this refreshing set of ideas, I was told, were based largely on the thinking of the forward-looking Colonel Constand Viljoen, who had taken command of the Army College in 1966 (and, of course eventually became Chief of the SADF).

I discovered that a few young officer instructors such as George Kruys, Deon Mortimer, Carel van Rooyen and Bill Sass were much taken with the idea of mobile warfare in the African battle space, for which the requirements differed considerably from the way Rommel had been fought in the Western Desert. George Kruys in particular fascinated me with his stories about the fighting methods of Vo Nguyen Giap and how his Vietminh had decisively beaten the French at Dien Bien Phu in 1954 by applying the manoeuvrist versus the attritionist approach to warfare

The in-depth study of warfare that they had made was an inspiration to me and I became one of their disciples. For the first time I embarked on some serious reading on military subjects, a habit I never lost. My first two favourite books were *Defeat in the East* by

Michael Elliot-Bateman (London Oxford University Press, 1967) and *Men against Fire* by S.L.A. Marshall (William Morrow, New York, 1966). I also started writing my own articles for military publications, which was not only fun but proved intellectually stimulating.

Two of my mentors at the college were to have a strong long-term effect on my thinking about the warfare of the future as our paths crossed in the years to come – Deon Mortimer as a colonel, when he was my commanding officer at the Infantry School in 1974, and George Kruys, by then a brigadier, who was in charge when I attended the Joint Staff Course at the Defence Staff College in 1985.

I went back to Danie Theron rejuvenated, with some radical new thoughts buzzing around in my head, but my time there was coming to an end. Towards the end of the year Colonel Fourie called me in and said: "Roland, you're doing extremely well in your work here and on your courses; I don't want to lose you, but I've been notified by Army HQ that you are to be transferred to the Infantry School with effect from 1 January 1970. This is good for your career. You're also being promoted to captain. Well done. I'll miss playing squash with you."

Revelling in Teaching and Tactics – and Realising that the Infantry Could Fight Mounted

I was sorry to leave Danie Theron, of course, but this new transfer sounded exciting, so I packed my bags and my squash racket, and off I went. It indeed proved exciting. I spent a satisfying six years at the Infantry School first as a captain and then from October 1973 as a major. In my time there I served under a succession of the most outstanding commanders any young officer could have wished for: Deon Mortimer, as I have mentioned, Pik van Noorden and Raymond Holtzhausen, all of whom later became generals and served with distinction.

The instructor clan I worked with at the school were highly dedicated individuals, professional to the core. I learnt much from them and soon I could share with others the huge amount of knowledge they had passed on to me. We had the most wonderful field range to the north towards the Swartberg mountain range, where we could train with live fire to our hearts' content in the most natural setting of bush and mountains (the terrain was one of the main reasons why the Infantry School had been established at somewhat out-of-the-way Oudtshoorn in 1962).

For me this was an astonishing finishing school to prepare me for my future career in a joint training and warfare environment. Just to get something of my own training said and done I attended a few interesting qualifying and promotion courses in between my working days. It was a busy time for me, as you will appreciate when I explain about the courses I had to attend, while at the same time I was deeply involved on an Army project on the new Ratel six-wheeled infantry fighting vehicle which was launched in 1973. To put it bluntly, I was not at home very much.

My first course was on the battle handling of the infantry battalion, which was conducted in 1971 at the school itself by Captain (later Brigadier) Bill Sass; the prime expert on this subject. Next was a three-week tracking course by Major Jan Breytenbach and Staff Sergeant Yogi Potgieter near Derdepoort, on the Botswana border – a course I truly enjoyed. In 1972 there followed a course on advanced military law at the Army College.

Then in 1973 I struck the mother lode when I was selected with five other paratrooper officers to attend a highly secret three-month special warfare course in Taiwan at the Special

Warfare School near Taipei and its Parachute Training Centre near Kaohsiung, which had been arranged by Brigadier Pik van Noorden, then the Army's Director Infantry, during one of his official visits to Taiwan.

The six officers selected were Major Louis Holtzhausen (Infantry School), Major John More (Special Forces), Major S.F. Mulder (School of Engineers), Captain Erich Lambrecht (1 Parachute Battalion), Captain Joe Verster (1 Parachute Battalion) and myself. This was my first trip overseas. These days young officers can attend courses in many places, but at that time Israel and Taiwan were about the only foreign friends South Africa had left (OK, Malawi as well). It was very hush-hush – the course was referred to as "Project Yuan", and we travelled very discreetly. In my case I had to pose as a Jordanian teacher, probably because of my black hair and brown eyes. What made this "cover" particularly intriguing was that in those days I didn't know just where the hell Jordan was!

The aim of the course was to teach the six of us about the ways of the communist's guerrillas of mainland China, Taiwan's arch-enemy, since the Red Army was the one training the liberation forces to the north of our borders. The course was an incredible experience. We referred to our training as "Chicom Tactics", and the subjects included guerrilla warfare, counter-guerrilla warfare, propaganda warfare, political warfare, ambushing, sabotage, expedient river crossing, abseiling, survival, raids, clandestine intelligence methods, special demolitions and even strange subjects such as "peeping, stealing and surprise killings". The latter three subjects were most relevant to our African friends up north. A subject of particular interest to me was the component on knowing your enemy.

Near the end of the course we travelled to the south and completed advanced parachute training at Kaohsiung. This included eight ordinary static-line jumps and four rough terrain jumps. When we had completed our training we were qualified for rough terrain jumping as well as Rangers[1], and subsequently received our emblems and certificates to prove it. Incidentally, we jumped with steerable static-line parachutes (the American PT-10 type), and a conversion by the Taiwanese Defence Force (referred to as a "Double-L") was copied for the SADF. There were even thoughts about establishing a guerrilla training centre for the SADF, but this was later shelved when Jan Breytenbach established the Special Forces.

In 1974 it was back to the Army College for the five-month-long combat group commander's course. Our course leader was Major (later Major general) Wessel Kritzinger, a tough, smart professional who did not suffer fools or humourists gladly, and on our very first day he set about making sure none of the former was among us. His method was to set us an entry examination which also happened to be the end-of-course exam our immediate predecessors had written. This was strictly a selection test, of course, and Kritzinger was so confident that we would fail it (which was to be expected) that he somewhat rashly promised that if anyone passed, that person would be exempted from the course and given full recognition for his achievement.

Well, as it happened, two out of the 35 students actually did pass, and to my glee I was one them, with the highest score of 72%. I could not help asking Kritzinger whether I could go home now, as he had promised. Strangely enough, he was not amused, and so I had to buckle down along with everyone else, 72% or no 72%. So I got to work, and to my further glee proved my early success had not been just a flash in the pan by emerging top of what turned out to be a most informative and enjoyable course.

1 The Taiwanese Special Forces had copied the term from the United States Army Rangers, which were elite members who had graduated from the U.S. Army's Ranger School.

There was more study awaiting me, however: near the end of the year my colleague Major Tony Savides and I attended the "Field Repair and Weapons Systems" course on the new Ratel Infantry Fighting Vehicle at the Technical Training Centre in Voortrekkerhoogte, because both of us were now deeply involved in developing the system and writing doctrine for it, as I shall explain below.

Early in my career I had decided to do my modest part in the development of mobile warfare concepts for the South African Army. So from the 1970s onwards I started studying and thinking seriously about the subject, writing articles and lecturing about it as often as I could. I was especially fascinated by the concept of the lightning war, as personified by the German Army's "Blitzkrieg" of World War II and the Israeli tactics in the Six-Day War in 1967.[2] I knew that the Israelis had been taught about mobile warfare and the strategy of the indirect approach by the famed Captain Sir Basil Liddell Hart, a seminal writer on mechanised warfare since the 1930s – "the captain who taught the generals", as they put it – so I started delving into his books.

I also made an in-depth study of the West Germans' Marder, a tracked infantry fighting vehicle operated by their army for the "Panzergrenadiere", or mechanised infantry, of which around 2,100 had been taken into service in the early 1970s. I was especially interested in its user-requirement specification, which had produced a successful and solid infantry fighting vehicle design. I was also enthralled by the myriad tactical possibilities presented – one of the unique features of the Marder was the side gun ports through which the occupants could fire on the move.

Looking back now on those days and specifically on the views I held on mobile warfare and a few trials and tribulations surrounding those views, I have just realised once again how much fun we had. Allow me to share some of it with you.

It all started seriously when I presented a highly successful platoon commanders' course at the Infantry School in May 1972, using our old six-wheeled Saracen APCs[3] and open Land Rovers to practice mobile warfare concepts. These experiments were encouraged by the enlightened and sharp-witted Colonel Raymond Holtzhausen, the new OC Infantry School. Soon afterwards a German UR-416 four-wheeled armoured personnel carrier, which had a chassis based on that of a Unimog, was sent to the Infantry School for trials. I was instructed to evaluate the UR-416, which we nicknamed "Boggelbees" (roughly "Hunchback Brute") – which it was – and in my subsequent report made it clear that I was not impressed.

During the evaluation process, though, I had learned more about the possibilities of fighting while mounted. Little did I realise that I was soon going to be converted into an ardent mechanised infantryman. By now Colonel Holtzhausen knew about my interests

2 Also known as the June War, 1967 Arab-Israeli War, or Third Arab-Israeli War, fought between 5–10 June by Israel and the neighbouring states of Egypt, Jordan, and Syria (known at the time as the United Arab Republic). The war began on 5 June with Israel launching a surprise pre-emptive air attack against Egyptian air-fields after a period of high tension that included an Israeli raid into the Jordanian-controlled West Bank as well.

3 The British Fighting Vehicle F.V. 603 Saracen Armoured Personnel Carrier (APC) saw service after the end of the Second World War. The first Mk 1s were powered by a Rolls-Royce B80 Mk 3A petrol engine. Throughout the 1950s and early 1960s the Saracen was the standard APC of the British Army and was replaced from 1963 by the FV432 tracked APC. The SADF acquired a number of Saracens during the late fifties for its Infantry, but was rarely used. A few of these vehicles saw service during the Sharpeville riots in 1960.

in mobile warfare and in early 1973 nominated me to serve as the Infantry School's representative on a newly launched project to design and develop a fighting vehicle for the infantry.

The project team was a high-powered one, not so much in rank as in talent. The project leader was Brigadier Tom van Dyk, the Director Technical Services. The senior Infantry Corps representative was Colonel Jannie Geldenhuys (later to become the Chief of the South African Army as well as of the SADF). Another important member was Colonel J.T. (Serge) Nell, a part-time Citizen Force officer who was not only a former infantry battalion commander (1 Regiment Noord-Transvaal) but also happened to work for the Council for Scientific and Industrial Research, where he was involved in the development of defence technology. It was a good background for the project and Serge, with whom I became lifelong friends, did outstanding work; the Ratel IFV and the later logistics and command variants were his pet subjects.

In 1974 our project team was joined by the astute and quick-witted Major Tony Savides, also from the Infantry School, of whom more later. The team also worked intimately with Armscor (Armaments Corporation of South Africa)[4] and its senior engineer at the time of the IFV trials, Mr. Willem Botha, became a close friend of Serge's and myself.

The team put a variety of prototypes through strenuous trials in South Africa and South West Africa during 1973 to find the best choice for the projected new infantry fighting vehicle (this type of vehicle is sometimes also called an ICV, or infantry combat vehicle). Some of the candidates came from abroad, from countries such as France and Germany. What made this even more enjoyable for me personally was that my membership elevated me into a new level among my rank-contemporaries. No more tedious train rides for me like my fellow captains – I commuted between Oudtshoorn and Pretoria on South African Airways and Air Cape flights which were paid for by Armscor, like some big shot carrying lots of rank on my shoulders.

It needs hardly be said that that the IFV project team was extremely dedicated and close-knit, and for me it was a great experience not only to learn about the Army's future combat systems and the evolving doctrine for them but to participate in both fields. I soon got a taste of what lay ahead when I spent the early hours of the morning on which I was to join the rest of the team in Pretoria scribbling down, in pencil, the initial set of user requirement specifications for our future IFV. On my arrival there I was plunged into an exhilarating experience which was actually more like an adventure, and I started reading and studying more and more about armoured fighting vehicles and mechanised warfare, anything I could lay my hands on.

The Ratel design – the only six-wheeled contender – won the competition hands down; it not only out-performed the others but also suited the Army's budget, which could not stand the strain of more than R45,000 each at the time, a price which now sounds laughably small. When Major Tony Savides came on board in 1974, he and I worked together at the direction of the Director Infantry, Colonel André ("Kat") Liebenberg to develop the combat system for mechanised infantry for the Infantry Corps, which included the creation and documentation for mechanised infantry employment in combat for section and platoon level doctrine. Colonel Mortimer was now OC Infantry School, and he gave us tremendous support in writing the doctrine. In the evenings we would go to his home to

4 Armscor served as the officially appointed acquisition organisation for the SA Department of Defence.

read and discuss the chapters we had written during the day.

In October 1975 Tony Savides and I presented the first mechanised-infantry leader course at the Infantry School. By this time South Africa had become embroiled in the civil war in Angola – Operation Savannah,[5] as we called it – and I volunteered to go, the natural reaction for a fire-breathing young officer, but Colonel Mortimer brought me back to earth immediately, telling me to get on with my mechanised infantry work; operational exposure would come later. I didn't like it much, but he was right. For the time being I was needed at home, not in the field. For six years I had been involved in presenting infantry battle-handling and tactics for officers and other ranks of both the full-time and part-time forces. Since teaching a subject is the best way to learn it, I had mastered tactics at platoon, company and battalion level for both counterinsurgency and conventional warfare.

Although still relatively junior in rank I was now being referred to by many of my colleagues as one of the "reformers" in our army, but I was still learning and thinking, and would do so for years – it would not be until 1987 that I put the fruits of it all into my book, "Mobiele Oorlogvoering – 'n Perspektief vir Suider-Afrika". It was to prove a long-lived work – many years later, while working in Jordan in 2009, I was surprised to receive a telephone-call from Captain Sollie Henning of the Infantry School, as well as a letter[6] from Colonel X. Mankayi, his commanding officer, requesting permission to translate my book into English (which for one or other reason had never been done) to be used there for in-house training and doctrinal development purposes. I was honoured by this gesture and naturally agreed to their request.

But back to 1975: In November that year I was informed that I was being transferred to 1 South African Infantry Battalion as the commander of Alpha Company, to render support with the establishment of the mechanised infantry system. I was also informed that for this reason I would only be nominated to attend the Senior Army Command and Staff course at the Army College at a later stage. Since the Army was very set on promotion being preceded by the appropriate course, this is an indication of the priority being given to full mechanisation in the infantry.

Originally 1 SAI had been based next door to the Infantry School, but had been relocated to Tempe in November 1973 to be converted into the Army's first mechanised infantry battalion and training centre. This meant it would be close to the School of Armour and 1 Special Service Battalion in the long-time heartland of the Armoured Corps, and within easy reach of the General De Wet Training Ground west of Tempe (generally called "De Brug"), which was suitable for mechanised training.

My Training Heydays at 1 SAI – Ongoing Mechanisation

I could feel excitement stirring in the frisky air of the Free State early in the morning of 5 January 1976 when I passed through the gates at Tempe, where I was to spend a fruitful three years at 1 SAI, revelling in my work as a mechanised infantryman (which kept me so busy that I would only go on the Senior Command and Staff Course in 1980).

My first commanding officer at 1 SAI was Commandant Len Meyer, an outstanding leader who had taken the newly established mechanised infantry capability to heart and

5 Operation Savannah was the name given to the South African Defence Force's 1975–1976 covert involvement in the Angolan Civil War following on Portugal's "Carnation Revolution" of 25 April 1974, which ended their colonial rule in Angola and Mozambique.

6 Letter from the Infantry School, Inf School/R/515/7, dated 16 April 2009.

was to provide immense support to its development. Our second-in-command was Major Frank Bestbier, who had gained valuable hands-on experience during Operation Savannah. I was destined to spend my first year at 1 SAI as the Alpha Company commander and then succeeded Frank Bestbier as second-in-command for another two years. It was a fine time to be at 1 SAI. Allow me to briefly explain what materialised during the three years I spent there.

While commanding my company and waiting for our Ratels to come off the production line at Sandock-Austral in Boksburg, I was twice detached to the Infantry School, where by now Colonel Rudolph ("Witkop") Badenhorst was in command, to help Tony Savides with presenting mechanised infantry orientation courses. Colonel Kat Liebenberg, the Director Infantry, also gave me an instruction to write an integrated manual for mechanised infantry operations at section and platoon level, which was to include an aide mémoire for section and platoon commanders, using the material Savides and I had originally written at the Infantry School. I was assisted by Major Lee le Crerar,

I finished the manual during a three-week tour at the school, and both the manual and aide-mémoire later became official army doctrine. I even appeared on a national television programme to explain what the Ratel IFV and the mechanised infantry were all about. Colonel Serge Nell also visited 1 SAI on several occasions with the results of his ongoing work on evaluating and upgrading of the Ratel system.

One innovative project he instigated was the development of an eight-wheeled platoon logistics vehicle to ensure that the replenishment component was as mobile as the Ratels themselves. Since I had long been a believer in the old Chinese proverb that a picture is worth a thousand words, I laid out all the equipment and supplies a mechanised platoon required in battle in Alpha Company's lecture room. It was an eye-opener. Prototypes of the amazing "Ratel-Log", as it was soon dubbed, with its pallet load system were later built and tested, but unfortunately the project was then shelved due to funding issues.

Halfway through my first year my company and I were deployed at very short notice to the Eastern Cape for two months to participate in counterinsurgency operations when riots broke out there, but when I returned near the last quarter I presented 1 SAI's first course for mechanised infantry. We were now ready to commence with full-scale mechanised training the following year, when I would become the second-in-command to replace a newly promoted Commandant Frank Bestbier on his transfer to Orange Free State Command as an operations staff officer.

In January 1977, with me installed as second-in-command and Major André Kruger in my chair at Alpha Company, Commandant Meyer was promoted colonel and took over as Director Infantry, from which position he continued to give his enthusiastic support in furthering the interests of the mechanised infantry. In his place appeared Commandant A.J.M. ("Joep") Joubert, like Frank Bestbier an Operation Savannah veteran from whom I would learn some valuable lessons on how to command an infantry battalion; it was a most rewarding experience to work with him.

We were truly fortunate in the high quality of our leader group, company commanders such as Majors André Kruger, Jos Rabie, Epp van Lill and "Doerie" van Deventer; in the more junior ranks we had professional officers who were acknowledged tacticians and instructors, such as Captain Koos Liebenberg and Captain Cassie Schoeman; and many other mechanised infantry officers, warrant-officers and non-commissioned officers who were also involved in training and development. Later, during and after the war in Angola, many of them were decorated or mentioned in dispatches and otherwise acknowledged in the annals of modern South African military history. They included men like Paul Fouché, Kobus Smit, H.G. Smit, Leon Marais, Hannes van der Merwe, Kowie Steyn, Laurence Maree and too many others to mention by name.

We set about delving thoroughly into the development of the training systems, training programmes, training doctrine and material required by the mechanised infantry, and trying out our new ideas on battle-simulation ranges we developed at De Brug; I look back on it as one of the highlights of my career. Eventually our exercises involved the sub-units of 1 Special Service Battalion, with whose second-in-command, Major Fred Rindel, I had established a firm relationship.

Over weekends we practised to our hearts' content with live ammunition attacking Bruintjieshoogte (a tactical feature at De Brug), as this was the only time the Air Force could fly close air support missions for us with their Impalas. Major Rudi Kritzinger was my South African Air Force colleague at Bloemspruit Air Force Training Base east of Bloemfontein – we played squash together – and these missions were therefore easy to arrange without too much formality. The Rhodesian Air Force pilots being trained at Bloemspruit also joined in these weekend close air support missions.

The practical training was not only great fun but also immensely beneficial for experimentation in evolving tactical and operational mobile warfare concepts – one of these being the comfortable utilisation of air support with the close co-ordination of indirect fire support and ground manoeuvre. Colonel H.B. ("Fido") Smit, an operations staff officer with 81 Armour Brigade, helped out by "unofficially" providing welcome transfusions of ammunition which had been left over from past Citizen Force brigade training exercises.

We taught our combat leaders about situational awareness, how to think one step ahead, about fast-moving action and leading from the front, quick orders and attacking smoothly while on the move. Sometimes we had to move further afield to have enough space – In September 1977 we held a battalion-size exercise nicknamed "Blits Een" (Lightning One) with live ammunition at Schmidtsdrif, about 70 km west of Kimberley because the sprawling Army Battle School had not yet been established at Lohatlha in the Northern Cape Province. Major Epp van Lill attended a mechanised infantry course in Israel and brought back valuable operational techniques. One which served us well in Angola later on was the method of breaking into, fighting through and clearing of extensive well-developed enemy trench systems. Subsequently we developed such a range at De Brug, which was similar to what was encountered in Angola.

Commandant Joep Joubert and I arranged with Army HQ for 1 SAI to be deployed operationally to northern SWA from mid-October 1976 until mid-January 1977 to gain practical operational experience. We converted 1 SAI to counterinsurgency mode on completion of Exercise Lightning One within two weeks and then deployed to Oshivello in Ovamboland for advanced training and acclimatisation.

During this phase our unit was evaluated by a team from the office of the Inspector-General, and we came out tops in comparison with the other counterinsurgency units. For me this was an indication that conventional training should remain the basis for counterinsurgency duties as well. 1 SAI was then deployed to Etale and did exceptionally well during operations, scoring the highest "kills" of any of the units deployed over the same period.

One such an operation was the successful ambush of a SWAPO unit by 35 men of 1

SAI under Major Jos Rabie in the Jati[7] in mid-November, where 11 insurgents were killed for a loss of two killed and four wounded. Part of the way through the deployment I took over as acting CO when Commandant Joubert left on a visit to Israel to benchmark the concept of a joint combat training centre.

On Boxing Day 1977, within a fortnight of our return home, I was well and truly "blooded" in every sense of the word. I was accompanying an infantry section which was deploying near the old Oshikango border post in a rather dilapidated "Bosvark" mine-protected vehicle when it went over an anti-tank mine. The Bosvark was a transitional MPV which was distinctly primitive compared to the superb Ratel IFVs which came into service about 15 months later, but its mine-resistant "dish" under the troop compartment did what it was supposed to do, although not very comfortably in my case.

I can't remember actually hearing the massive explosion that wrecked the Bosvark. What I do remember is being tossed about 30 metres through the air and coming down with a thump; fortunately I landed in a patch of soft sand, and as I hit the ground my training clicked in and I eased the shock of landing with a perfect paratrooper roll. Thanks to all this, I was not seriously the worse for wear, barring a little bleeding here and there and some bad bruises – although I have to admit that my self-esteem was somewhat dented. True, I still have trouble doing push-ups and suffer from a back problem, but it could have been much worse. The fact is that by 1977 we had virtually conquered the landmine with our ever more effective MPVs, and in later years most such casualties came from civilian vehicles which detonated the mines which SWAPO planted without much regard for what would set them off.

But at times I grow cold when I think back on what might have been. At the time that particular road was classified "yellow", and except for a change in plans André Kruger and I would have gone down it a little earlier in a Land Rover. If we had, we would have been goners. Subsequently I suggested, tongue in cheek, to Brigadier Kat Liebenberg, now OC Sector 10 at Oshakati, that he should change the road's classification to "Red"! At the end of January Frank Bestbier was promoted commandant and took over as OC 1 SAI to replace Joep Joubert, who had been made commander of the infantry branch at the newly established Army Battle School at Lohatlha – a milestone as regards training and development, because it provided far more space for heavy weapons than any of the other training areas and was located in such thinly peopled semi-desert bushveld that problems with accommodating the needs of local inhabitants were minimal.

But Joep Joubert was about to acquire another hat. In 1978 Chief of the Army, Lieutenant-General Constand Viljoen, formulated a plan to establish a mechanised battle group at Oshivello to conduct operations against SWAPO[8] at regular intervals, and Joep Joubert became the first commanding officer of what was called Battle Group Juliet.

As originally envisaged, Juliet had a structure which was tailored to fit the circumstances. In essence it was a temporary formation with the core of its fighting force being the Ratel IFV. The idea was to store all its equipment at the logistics base at Grootfontein; when the circumstances required, it would be manned with drafts of personnel from training units such as 1 SAI and 1 SSB.

In January-February Major Epp van Lill's company was deployed to Oshivello to test and evaluate the employment possibilities of such a unit in a typical Ovamboland bushveld

7 A strip of no-man's land on the northern border of SWA with Angola.
8 South West Africa People's Organisation and its armed wing the People's Liberation Army of Namibia.

milieu, but while he was thus engaged Battle Group Juliet was hastily activated and launched into southern Angola near the border base of Eenhana on Sunday, 19 February. This was an attempt to rescue a sapper named Johan van der Mescht, who had been captured at a waterhole the previous night, close to the base.[9] Van der Mescht was long gone, however, and Joubert returned with empty hands, but on the plus side, some valuable lessons were learnt regarding upgrades for the Ratels and improvements in the training at I SAI and 1 SSB.

In early May 1978 Battle Group Juliet saw its first action in its primary role when Commandant Frank Bestbier – who had now taken over from Joubert, with André Kruger as his second-in-command – provided the main muscle for the ground component of Operation Reindeer, a successful attack on SWAPO's "Western Front" headquarters and logistics base at Chetequera, 27 km north of the South-West African border.

The ground attack is less well-remembered than the simultaneous parachute attack on Cassinga, 240 km inside Angola, which caused an international uproar whose echoes have yet to die away, but the Juliet concept had proved its worth, and in January 1979 it was placed under Commandant Johann Dippenaar, renamed 61 Mechanised Battalion Group and given its own base at Omuthiya, separate from but handily located near the Oshivello training area.

My time at 1 SAI was enjoyable, to say the least. The training concepts we had developed were transmuted into an immensely satisfying and rewarding experience: we were building a very strong leadership core and a foundation of knowledge about mobile warfare in Southern Africa. Our young Permanent Force and national service leaders and their troops took to the new mechanised principles and procedures like fish to water – to my mind they were naturals in this evolving world in which warfare consisted not of holding static positions but swimming, as it were, in a fluid mechanised medium.

Most of these officers were to see operational service with 61 Mech, and some of the relationships we established in those days are as intact and strong today as they were then (it is a bond which became even more firmly embodied when the newly established 61 Mech Veterans' Association was established at Caledon, Western Cape, in 2007).

Some Excitement in the Creation of Matters of New Significance – Across the Limpopo and Back Again

In January 1979 I was promoted to the rank of commandant and transferred to the Directorate Infantry under my old mentor, Colonel Len Meyer, to make further contributions to the development of the mechanised infantry system, with André Kruger taking over from me at 1 SAI.

This was my first staff appointment ever, and frankly I did not overly favour it. Luckily for me, though, I was to be appointed in October as OC Task Force X-Ray, which was formed to participate in Operation Bowler in Rhodesia. Across the Limpopo I learned some more about counterinsurgency within a southern African context, the exploits of which are recounted in Chapter 10.

I returned from Rhodesia on 27 January 1980 to attend the Senior Command and Staff Course between February and December 1980. It was well-designed and an experience I thoroughly enjoyed, but I was perturbed by the fact that the outdated "Conventional Land Battle" was still being used as the basic conventional war-fighting doctrine.

9 In later years it was established that the abduction of Sapper van der Mescht was a deliberate act planned and executed by a SWAPO unit under command of the legendary Danger Ashipala.

This was the year in which Johann Dippenaar and 61 Mech burst into Angola on 10 June during Operation Sceptic (best-known, although incorrectly, by the name of its main objective, which was code-named "Smokeshell"). The Army College was subsequently tasked to compile a provisional doctrine, under the superb leadership of Major Johan Vorster, on the planning and conduct of jointly undertaken pre-emptive attacks. To me this was a good sign, indicating that the new thinking had taken root.

In November, towards the end of the course, I was suddenly detached to 61 Mech as Commandant Dippenaar's second-in-command for the planning of another cross-border "external operation", but it was called off, and I returned to the Army College to complete my course. For the usual end-of-course exercise I was made the commander of a notional division which was to attack an equally notional brigade manned by unspecified enemy troops which was notionally defending Mapai in Mozambique. Colonel Joep Joubert, now commanding 82 Mechanised Brigade, joined us for the exercise to sharpen his skills at conducting the joint operational planning cycle at formation level.

The division and the enemy might have been strictly notional, but the attack that never was did not degenerate into a mere token struggle. I managed to survive it with my reputation intact, however, and was subsequently informed by Commandant Louis Coetzee, the chief course instructor, that I had done extremely well and in fact had come first.

That brought its own reward, the one I had dreamt about for so long – a battalion of my own – when the Director Infantry, then Colonel Vos Benade, notified me in December 1980 that I had been appointed OC 61 Mechanised Battalion Group. A thrill ran through me when I received the news. I was in motion again, and I had no doubt that amazingly exciting times lay ahead. Thank you, Army, and thank you, dear Lord. It was a blissful moment!

Commanding 61 Mechanised Battalion Group Extraordinaire in 1981–82

I commanded 61 Mechanised Battalion Group in the northern operational area of SWA from 9 January 1981 to 10 January 1983. The story of my time in 61 Mech is related in Chapters 3 to 16; suffice it to say at this stage that it was a fighting unit which appealed to me and exerted a great influence on my life, especially the extraordinary people I served with. The motto of our unit was "Mobilitate Vincere" – victory through mobility!

My years in 61 Mech afforded me an opportunity to develop this first-line fighting unit's standing operating procedures for mobile conventional warfare. I participated in several internal and external military operations, and could therefore experience firsthand what it was like to apply mobile warfare concepts at battle group level within a formation context.

Operation Protea in 1981 was probably the most successful South African cross-border operation of all time.[10] On 9 and 10 September I attended the official debriefing at Grootfontein, along with all the other Protea commanders down to combat group level, plus the relevant senior staff officers. I still have my copy of the minutes.[11] In his message to us, the Chief of the Army, Lieutenant-General Jannie Geldenhuys informed us emphatically that he envisioned more operations like Protea in future. He added with equal emphasis that there was no substitute for winning battles; losing was not an option and the outcome of any battle was not going to be left to chance or luck in any way.

There was serious deliberation about the South African Army's future conduct of

10 Refer to Chapter 12.

11 C Army/Inspector General/305/3 1, Secret; Copy No 117 of 133 Copies.

conventional warfare. General Geldenhuys viewed Protea as a manifestation of the Army's operational readiness, and expressed his satisfaction with its overall conduct. He thanked the respective task force and combat group commanders for their support, and told them that they had done well. He also had a specific feather in the cap for 61 Mech: there was a need, he said, to study the operational conduct of Battle Group 10 (61 Mech) as it was carried out during Protea (Debriefing Minutes, page 15, paragraph 13). The case study he envisaged was to be used by the army to enhance mobile conventional warfare practices in the future.

Following on to this, the army historian, Commandant Casparus Bakkes, was requested to support the army with the writing of such a philosophy on the future conduct of conventional warfare in Africa. The Chief of Army Staff Operations (GS3), Major general Dirk Marais, was explicitly tasked to undertake the study and to develop a philosophy for conventional warfare. As far as I know, however, this philosophy never saw the light – perhaps because our army of the 1970s and 1980s was extremely counterinsurgency-oriented. This was a cause of some frustration to me. Years later, during a debriefing of the 1988 fighting during Operations Modular, Hooper and Packer, Lieutenant-General Jan van Loggerenberg, the Chief of Defence Staff Operations, would reflect that it was a limitation that the philosophy for conventional warfare had never been written!

In January 1983 I was promoted to colonel and transferred to the Army Battle School. One of my new tasks, Army HQ directed, was to go and teach exactly what I had learnt at 61 Mech and that which had been implied during the Grootfontein debrief on Operation Protea.

Manoeuvring at the Army Battle School at Lohatlha: "Si Vis Pacem Para Bellum"

The motto of the Army Battle School was the old Roman one – "Si Vis Pacem Para Bellum" (if you wish for peace, prepare for war). The school was founded on 15 January 1978 through the initiative of Lieutenant-General Constand Viljoen, the then Chief of the Army[12], and it became the leading landward warfare training institution in South Africa and the largest military base in the southern hemisphere at the time. Glorious red dust, Vaal bush and space to manoeuvre with anything imaginable in large numbers on the ground and from the sky, firing live day and night. Pure ecstasy for any fighting soldier!

For the first three years from January 1983 I was the Training Wing commander as a brand-new colonel fresh from 61 Mech. My 61 Mech comrades, Commandant Paul Fouché and Major Thys Rall, were transferred there with me, and the mere fact that I could work at Lohatlha with some of my trusted friends and colleagues gave me tremendous comfort. Initially I served under Brigadier Carel van Rooyen as my commander and Colonel Felix Hurter as his second-in-command, but for my last two years there I was the second-in-command under Brigadier Eddie Webb.

Webb had just returned from a three-year tour as our military attaché in Israel, he understood conventional warfare, and we were both wedded to the concept of the "indirect approach", as expounded in the many books written by Sir Basil Liddell Hart.[13] Webb fully supported me in establishing this way of thinking and doing as part of the mobile

12 Today it is known as the Combat Training Centre.

13 Liddell Hart, B.H.: *History of the Second World War* (G.P. Putnam, New York, 1971); *Strategy* (Faber and Faber Ltd, London, 1967); *The Rommel Papers* (Library of Congress Catalog Card No 53-5656, 1953).

conventional tactics we taught at the school.

The Battle School was responsible for presenting tactical courses to students at combat team (sub-unit) and combat group (unit) level by a Course Wing, while the Training Wing was responsible for the training and exercising of units and formations, both Permanent Force and Citizen Force, at the tactical and high tactical levels of conventional war. I came to appreciate the comment of Josephus (37–100 AD) that "The Romans are sure of victory... for their exercises are battles without bloodshed, and their battles bloody exercises."

The Training Wing consisted of a headquarters with a range safety office and branches representing the respective corps found within the army such as the infantry, armour, artillery, air defence, engineers, intelligence, maintenance (logistics), technical services and signals. I worked with outstanding officers and other ranks who were highly experienced in training and operations, men such as Paul Fouché, Les Rudman, Johan Potgieter, Daan Lotter, Francois Cilliers, Thys Rall, Gert Venter, George Ogilvie, Piet Lamprecht, Dick Els, Attie Bezuidenhout, Tokkie Strumpher, Bobby Keller, Frik van Zyl, Jan Malan, Chris Koch, Chris Human and Theo Wilken, to mention but a few.

Facilities at the school provided for all the requirements of forces under training, including a sick bay, air traffic control centre and air force node, mess facilities, ablutions, accommodation, store areas, technical, railway and refuelling services. Units and formations under training were accommodated in 13 fenced-in unit areas, each sufficient to accommodate a unit with its first and second line equipment. Ablution facilities with warm and cold water and a kitchen/store facility formed part of each unit area, while troops could be accommodated in tents for limited periods for mobilisation and demobilisation purposes.

The field training area, christened the P.W. Botha Training Area, was huge and covered 158,000 hectares, 60 km from north to south and 35 km from east to west. Modern infrastructure provided reasonably easy access to the school by means of national roads, rail and air. National airports were located within 200 km at Upington in the west and Kimberly in the east respectively.

I stopped counting how many training exercises we conducted at brigade and combat group level. In addition the SA Army called up Citizen Force sub-units on a three-month basis to form a combat group-sized "Force in Being", which was considered one of the SADF's landward mobile reserve capabilities; after one month's intensive training at the Battle School, these temporary groupings were either placed on high readiness or deployed to SWA for border duty.

My way of doing things seemed to stick a little in some people's throats; soon after I had commenced with my training work I heard that there were some senior officers in the halls of power at Army HQ proclaiming that "Roland de Vries is teaching his own doctrine at the Army Battle School." I wasn't worried, because they were exactly right. There were even some die-hard officers who alleged that they did not understand these "new operational concepts" that we were now propagating. I saw this as a compliment, considering where it came from.

There probably was a measure of professional jealousy to be read between the lines of all this sort of thing, but I sincerely believed that there were many officers in our army who did not understand mobile conventional warfare and neither knew how to operate at the operational level of war nor had studied past campaigns. To my mind they were hurting the progress and modernisation of our army without realising it.

Meanwhile we carried on regardless. Paul Fouché, Major Les Rudman and I had constructed a battle orientation range ("gevegsoriëntasiebaan") in the training area which was based on personal observation rather than mere book knowledge, and expert observation to boot, since both these officers were operational commanders of note, then and later (in 1988 Fouché commanded the forces in southeast Angola during Operation Hooper and Packer after taking over from Colonel Deon Ferreira and myself in mid-December 1987, while Les Rudman – today a major general and Deputy Chief of the Army – was decorated with the Army Cross for valour for his actions in southeast Angola in 1987–88).

In layout and construction the battle orientation range closely resembled the Russian-style defences the three of us had found at Xangongo during August 1981's Operation Protea[14] – we tactically deployed some of the Russian equipment we had captured at the time, so that suddenly we felt at home at Lohatlha. It was fun having mock fights through the Russian cum FAPLA[15] range, and some of the forces training there experienced the real thing later on in southern Angola; because the fighting work was not finished by a long shot – Operation Modular did not ring in its last phase till August 1987.[16]

August-September 1984 saw furious activity when 7 South African Division under Brigadier George Kruys held Exercise Thunder Chariot, the largest conventional warfare exercise in South Africa since World War II, which was intended not only as a show of force but by its very nature also to enhance the combat power and capability of the conventional forces. More importantly, it took place three years before the SADF would be engaged in an epic conventional battle fought in southern Angola.

Brigadier Kruys, his divisional headquarters, 71 and 72 Brigades and the plethora of support units spent three weeks literally eating the Northern Cape's plentiful dust, while the Training Wing commander (myself) and Colonel Johann Dippenaar, 7 Division's chief of staff, worked hand in hand at high pitch to plan and execute this amazing venture, the largest in our (or anyone else's) career. More than 11,000 Citizen Force troops were called up for the exercise, and about 4,000 vehicles were used. We tried to make the exercise as realistic as possible. Live ammunition was used throughout, and weeks of preparatory work had been undertaken to construct more than 35 km of Russian/Angolan-style trench systems to attack.

For the first time a large media contingent was allowed to cover a military exercise of this nature. They were present when the biggest peace time church parade in South African history with 10,000 troops on parade on that Sunday morning. Lieutenant-General Jannie Geldenhuys arrived by helicopter and he was available for TV, radio and press interviews. In a radio interview with Friedel Hansen of the SABC for "Monitor", the long-running current affairs programme broadcast on the Afrikaans radio service of the national broadcaster of the time he stated emphatically: "It is the responsibility of the military to create an environment for the politicians to be able to sit down and come to an agreement regarding the country's future."

Members of the media attended various stages of the exercise: some even had the opportunity to closely observe the exercise by night while live ammunition was used. Even the famed "rat pack" used by the SADF at the time came under scrutiny and the well-known independant defence analyst and correspondent for the Jane's Information Group,

14 Refer to Chapter 12.

15 *Forças Armadas Populares de Libertação de Angola*

16 Refer to Chapter 15.

Helmoed-Römer Heitman, described it as the best used by any defence force anywhere in the world. This serves to illustrate that nothing in our preparation was left to chance.

From our viewpoint, Thunder Chariot's main aim was to practice lightning warfare in a typical southern African milieu, jointly with the Air Force (which held its own full-blown exercise in the Northern Cape prior to its full participation in Thunder Chariot) and medical services, at division, brigade and battle group level.

The exercise was divided into five active phases: Phase One was the mobilisation and movement of the leader group to Lohatlha; Phase Two entailed training of the leader group and sharpening their combat skills over a seven-day period before the main force arrived; Phase Three consisted of the mobilisation, arming, equipping and movement of the main body to the training area, where the units joined up with their leader group. Phase Four comprised six days of training the main body, from sub-unit right up to brigade level;

Phase Five was the highlight, a spectacular and downright awe-inspiring divisional attack and defence between 17 and 20 September. The exercise included a night parachute jump on to one of the objectives and the building of two mobile bridges in pitch darkness. Among those who attended the divisional attack and defence phase were the State President, Mr. P.W. Botha, the Minister of Defence, General Magnus Malan, General Constand Viljoen and Lieutenant-General Jannie Geldenhuys.

The media praised the troops and described the exercise as a demonstration of the devastating power of the SADF. Paratus[17] of October 1984 stated that: "The South African Defence Force's military might, which was displayed during the recent Exercise Thunder Chariot, was not intended as a show of force – but it proved to the world that South Africa has the iron fist and the ability to use it with devastating effect if ever the need arises".

In spite of all the thunder and lightning there was not one fatal accident during Thunder Chariot and not many significant injuries either, in spite of the fact that prodigal amounts of ordnance, large and small, had been hurled about for several weeks. So we emerged with our safety record intact, because during my term at the Battle School we incurred no serious training accidents, notwithstanding the fact that almost every one of the countless day and night exercises we held featured the use of live ammunition. And speaking personally, one thing was sure: I now knew how to run both a brigade and a division.

With my rewarding and enjoyable time at Lohatlha almost over, I was nominated to attend the five-month-long Joint Staff Course at the Defence College (now commanded by Brigadier Kruys) from July to December 1985. For a career soldier in the SADF, this was not merely a ticket to be punched on the way to the next promotion: it was restricted to selected officers who were considered suitable for promotion to the most senior appointments in the SANDF in the future and we were therefore taught every aspect of military strategy. On successful completion of the course candidates were entitled to write "jsc"' after their names. I sincerely enjoyed the staff course, and although no positions were allocated, Brigadier Kruys indicated to me that I had done exceptionally well and had placed among the top six.

The course had one important effect for me, apart from any advantage my placing might confer: it inspired me to write my own book on mobile warfare. While doing so I became friends with Major general (retired) Friedrich Wilhelm von Mellenthin, who had been Field-Marshal Erwin Rommel's operations staff officer in the Western Desert, as well as chief of staff of the 4th German Panzer Army.

17 Official monthly journal of the SADF, which incidentally served as an intelligence source for both SWAPO and FAPLA.

Von Mellenthin gave me a valued token of our friendship, which I still possess: a signed photograph showing him standing under a camouflage net in the desert with Rommel and General Walther Nehring, the much-decorated commander of the Deutsches Afrikakorps during Rommel's absence from Africa during May 1942. He also gave me a signed copy of his well-known book "Panzer Battles", which related to his first-hand experiences about armoured warfare in North Africa and Russia – this was now the second copy I owned, and I still have them both.

He was then living in Johannesburg after having retired as head of the Lufthansa airline, and I knew very well that the American armed forces were tapping him for information to use in writing of their own "Air-Land Battle" doctrine; it was a most thrilling experience for me and my wife, Henriette to enjoy visits in the pleasant company of this old warrior and discuss the German concepts of "Blitzkrieg", "Auftragstaktik" and "Schwerpunkt" over glasses of dry sparkling wine.

My book was finally published in August 1987, with a foreword kindly written by Von Mellenthin, signed 15 March 1987.[18] In the book I expressed the view that our Defence Force would need the tactical prowess to fight against overwhelming numbers under an unfavourable air situation, and win... not knowing that very soon I would experience these very conditions during Operation Modular.*19*

On 17 September that year the book was launched at a function at the Army Battle School which coincided with a practical battle group exercise under my friend Commandant Jan Malan, with Von Mellenthin as one of the guests at both the exercise and the launch. What none of us knew was that within a month I would be in southeast Angola, knee-deep in Operation Modular.

The October 1987 issue of Armed Forces, a monthly non-government journal devoted to defence matters, had the following to say about our recent field manoeuvre: "This exercise was held to illustrate the doctrine in the recently released publication Mobile Warfare Concepts... the scenario for the attacking battle group comprised a tank squadron (eleven Olifant main battle tanks), three mechanised infantry companies with Ratels and Eland armoured cars... in support would be 155 mm artillery and multiple rocket-launchers... the planning for the armoured/infantry attack followed the doctrine of point of main effort tactics, while the theory of command from the front principle was strongly stressed."

An absolute prerequisite for these operations was to understand that mobility was coupled to devastating firepower, and that vast covered space was a factor for successful manoeuvre in Africa. By now I had written quite a number of articles on mobile warfare and command as well, which were published in the Infantry School journal "Infantry Forum". I had hoped that my simple written contributions would stimulate the South African Army to develop a required-to-read treatise on conventional warfare in the context of the African battle space, and soon after my book was published I asked my adjutant, Lieutenant G.I. McCaig, to write an article with me which we subsequently entered for a writing competition run by the University of Pretoria.[20]

We won the competition, and subsequently received R200 in prize money, which we

18 De Vries, R, Kolonel: *Mobiele Oorlogvoering – 'n Perspektief vir Suider-Afrika*. FJM Harman Publishers, Pretoria, 1987.

19 Refer to Chapter 15.

20 Colonel R. de Vries and Lt. G.I. McCaig: "Mobile Warfare in Southern Africa". ISSUP: Strategic Review for Southern Africa, a Publication of the University of Pretoria, August 1987 (ISSN 0250-1961).

shared with our other colleagues and used to pay for a few beers at Lohatlha. Incidentally, this article was translated into Spanish and published in the Spanish armed forces' military information bulletin (Number 232).

But in mid-October I had more pressing matters to occupy my mind than basking in the good reception of my book. When Kuruman conferred freedom of entry on the Army Battle School, the main guest at the occasion – the Chief of the Army, Lieutenant-General Kat Liebenberg – told me: "Pack your rucksack and be on your way to participate in Operation Modular in southeast Angola." When the "Mouse Catcher" said jump, you jumped, and without wasting any time I was off on yet another warfare adventure, which I describe in more detail in Chapter 15.

The Army College and One More Fling at the Cubans

I was still deployed near the Chambinga River in southeast Angola when a new appointment came through, as OC Army College, and when I came back to South Africa in mid-December 1987 with some additional grey hairs on my head, Henriette and the children had moved to Pretoria from our home in Kathu, near the Army Battle School, and had settled into an Army house at Voortrekkerhoogte.

The Army College was one of the superb postings of my career, with the best staff any commander could wish for. I had three outstanding colonels under command, André Kruger as chief instructor of the Senior Command and Staff raining Branch, André Hendriks as chief instructor of the Junior Command and Staff Training Branch, and Johan Potgieter, who served as one of Kruger's senior instructors. Colonel Alwyn van Niekerk took charge of the War Game Centre we established in 1990 and our instructors were all outstanding officers such as Commandant Kobus ("Bok") Smit, a veteran of Operation Modular.

The role of the Army College is not always clear to those outside military circles. Briefly put, it is a senior military academic establishment whose purpose is to provide training and education to experienced Army officers to assist their professional development as well as their tactical training from every level from combat team to formation.

I had always recognised it as a shortcoming that we did not have a Joint Services Command and Staff College to train selected officers of all the services jointly at one institution, especially with regard to campaign planning at the operational level of war. To bridge this gap, therefore, we established a joint college forum among the respective colleges of the Army, Air Force, Navy and Medical Service (the latter is a separate service division in South Africa) to enhance collective training. Each year we held a joint planning exercise among the respective senior command and staff courses so as to complete their training on an appropriate level, and I used my position as commanding officer to lecture as much as possible on the subject of mobile warfare and mission command.

In between all this I found myself being serving elsewhere as well. Double-hatting and stints of detached duty had become second nature to me by this time, and it happened again in May 1988, when I was rushed to the northern operational area as chief of staff of the newly established 10 Division under Brigadier Chris Serfontein, who was facing the sudden appearance of the elite 50th Cuban Division to his immediate northern front. This was all part of Operation Prone.[21] I took advantage of the situation by arranging for André Kruger's entire current Command and Staff course to join us at 10 Division, not only to

21 Refer to Chapter 16.

assist in the high-level planning but also to gain valuable operational exposure (see Chapter 16). I also "bagged" a new chaplain, the astonishingly creative Padre Loutjie Bouwer, who was then serving at Sector 10.

My Post-War Military Career – the Fortunes Outweighed the Ordeals by Far

Operation Prone marked the end of my fighting days. The long conflict popularly known as the "border war" ended quite abruptly after more than a quarter-century, and by 1989 all our forces were back in South Africa. It meant a considerable re-adjustment for many service people. Traditionally, wars tend to last for five or six years at most, whereas in our case the border war had gone on for so long that most of our people – both full-time and part-time – had never known what peace-time soldiering was like. It was quite clear that we had to prepare for drastic changes, both structural and political, and step back to digest all the lessons learnt in order to discern future military scenarios and prepare for them.

To this end the Chief of the Army ordered that a thorough debriefing session be held at the Army College early in 1989 to document, as it was put, "Lessons Learnt during Conventional Operations in the Western Sub-Theatre of War'. I participated in this exercise and still have my original copy of the document.

At the college I started working closely with Brigadier Chris Serfontein, who was now the Director of Army Staff Operations. We considered the possibility of writing the operational concepts for conventional warfare that we had tried and tested in practice, as this had never been achieved in theory. So we launched "Project Readhead" and held meetings, workshops and seminars on the subject.

But now that it was peace-time our effort somehow lacked lustre – and in any case the country started boiling over again as the African National Congress maintained its political pressure and its rolling mass actions – which consisted inter alia of a fierce and deadly struggle in the townships for supremacy over its main rival, the Inkatha Freedom Party – and brought such unrest that the military focus was switched to maintaining internal stability and security while the politicians argued about the future shape of things.

During all this time the Army College continued to go about its normal cycle of work, as it had been doing since 1912, through two world wars, the Great Depression and a number of smaller alarums and excursions. In between the normal courses I started conducting seminars and exercises to research the make-up of our future army as part of our command and staff training.

We referred to this as Army Vision 2010 and worked closely with "Milistan" (Armscor's defence research and technology centre) and recognised experts in this field such as Dr. André Buys and Mr. Peet du Preez, who supported us with studies of future force-design options and concepts of what the African warrior should look like within 10 or 20 years. It was all intellectually invigorating, but it remained just that.

On 1 January 1991 my time as OC Army College was up, and I made my farewells after three engrossing and fruitful years at its helm. Incidentally, I came within a hair of being made a brigadier into the bargain. For some time before my departure there had been rumours that the commanding officer's post was to be upgraded, and for once the rumour was true... but it only came into effect on the day I left, and my successor, Brigadier Anton van Graan, benefitted from his new appointment

My new posting took me to Northern Transvaal Command Headquarters at

Voortrekkerhoogte as the chief of staff. For those who do not know, the SADF had nine of these territorial commands, each responsible for internal security and the control and management of a number of units of all arms within their boundaries, although not the conventional warfare units. This was not really my kettle of fish, but nevertheless it was a great privilege to work with the OC Command, Brigadier Gert Opperman, an outstanding officer who would soon become a major general.

As a result I made good use of my time there; among other things, I was instrumental in establishing a leadership development programme nicknamed Project Spartacus, which all our commanders and senior staff members thoroughly enjoyed and which helped to forge them into a high-performance team. My former chaplain, Loutjie Bouwer, who had left the ministry and was now a budding management consultant with the Pacific Institute ("Investment in Excellence"), wholeheartedly supported us in running this programme. There were a few of the old school at Army HQ who frowned on our new-fangled ideas, but I used the time to hone my management skills and think about the future; much of my cogitation was based on the teachings of Peter Senge about the "learning organisation" described in his book "The Fifth Discipline"..

Then In November 1992 the Deputy Chief of the Army, Major General Jan Klopper, telephoned me to say that I had been made a brigadier, and I soon found myself on the way to the 7 South African Division Headquarters in Johannesburg to take over on 1 January 1993 from my friend of long standing, Brigadier Fido Smit, an armour man of note. I was destined to serve as divisional commander for almost three years, up to 1 October 1995, and I relished my work with the part-time forces. One of the highlights of my career was to work with those amazing volunteer commanders, sergeant-majors and non-commissioned officers who were leading and managing our part-time force units. Their dedication and zest for work after civilian working hours and over weekends were something to experience – they really were "twice the citizen".

At the time 7 South African Division was an active formation comprising part-time units of the army's conventional forces, and numbered about 50,000 fully trained officers and men. It was one of three such formations – 7 Division was headquartered in Johannesburg, 8 Division in Durban under Colonel Louis Rheeder and 9 Division in Cape Town under Colonel Flip Genis. Each was made up of 20 part-time combat, combat support and support units that could be organised into two or three brigade-sized fighting formations, as required. Each division was managed by a core of Permanent Force members and a reasonably large contingent of well-qualified part-time officers and other ranks that could be called up from time to time to serve in the HQ.

In May 1994 the Chief of the Army decided to place 8 and 9 Divisions under my overall command as well, which required directing and guiding the future functioning, training and operations of the conventional part time forces. So be it! Things were not as simple as they had been while the war was on. In those days a division could easily mobilise its substantial HQ and two brigades of up to 13,000 to 26,000 personnel for three-month periods at a time if need be. In 1994, however, this had become more difficult because of the political changes in our country, and in addition the Citizen Force members' long-suffering employers had begun to dig in their heels about call-ups.

For this reason the army instituted a study whose aim was to discern the future of our part-time forces. I was one of the participants, but first I had to get another job out of the way – I had been double-hatted once more, this time as the leader of an Army work group concerned with the transformation of the Defence Force, which lasted from 17 January to 21 April 1994 (I shall discuss this in more detail in Chapter 17 – A New Order of Things).

Our serene military world, which was accustomed to going its pre-ordained way, was about to be drastically shaken up. In fact, the shaking-up started before the year was very old, when almost overnight the South African Defence Force in which we had all grown up was transformed into a new South African National Defence Force soon after the first universal-franchise general election on 27 April that year.

The now-vanished SADF's last big conventional exercise had been a successful brigade-sized one with at the Army Battle School in 1993; now, in 1994, it was decided that a change of scenery was necessary for the new SANDF, and in view of the new developments regarding the future role of the restructured Defence Force22 Major general Chris Serfontein, the Chief of Army Staff Operations, directed me to test the concept of peace support operations.

The result was a large-scale all-encompassing joint map and planning exercise at the SAAF facility at Ananda, Rustenburg, called Exercise Southern Cross, whose purpose was to commence with the development of SANDF doctrine for future peace operations. Commanders and staffs from the Army, Air Force, Navy and Medical Services were involved, with me as "commander" of the notional force.

True to our remit, it took the form of a notional "peace enforcement" operation in Angola's Huambo region, and what materialised was an insightful exercise, engendering excitement and enjoyment among all the participants. It served to make us acutely aware of the fact that peace operations were a different kettle of fish to what we had been trained for. They were governed by strict protocols and rules of engagement which were laid down in terms of the International Law of Armed Conflict and were carefully overseen by the United Nations. I had a glorious time war-gaming (so to speak), at this level, and even managed to get my squash game up to scratch again in between sessions.

I was now operating in a very different scenario from the life in which I had grown to maturity. From January 1994 onwards I became ever more engrossed with and involved in the political change taking place in the country and the inevitable transformation of our defence force – including its internal politics.

More of that later – in Part 2 of this book, in Chapters 5 to 16, I shall explain how we arrived at peace, and tell about the few bloody exercises we had when the war on our borders seriously started escalating between 1978 and 1987. I will also tell about the final bout of high-intensity battles fought in southern Angola in 1987–88; when a few victories were lost and then won by all the fighting sides as the walls of old methods and mindsets from all sides suddenly began to crumble in 1988 after the much-chronicled (often inaccurately) Cuito Cuanavale incident.

To bring this outline of my military career to a halt pro tem (I shall explain more about it in Chapter 17): I was appointed Director of Transformation Management of the SADF from 1 October 1995, served in that post up to 1 April 1997; and then became Chief of Joint Training of the SANDF and member of the Defence Staff Council in 1 July 1997. I stayed there for exactly a year, was made Deputy Chief of the Army and a member of the Army General Staff, and on 30 April 1998 retired at the age of 55.

At this point I would like to share a few titbits of related information about my life

22 Refer to Chapter 17. By 1994 the old SADF had transformed into a new SANDF in the advent of our country's first democratic elections held on 27 April 1994.

before moving on to the fighting and peace-making. One can only hope to learn things one didn't know, make a few differences and leave a few legacies, and however much some observers and commentators would like to deny it, an offensive/defensive capability is part of all that. As Mao Tse-tung said, quite rightly, "politics grow out of the barrel of a gun".

Psychometric and Psychological Testing in the Army – to Be or Not to Be, That Was the Question

I need to get the following off my mind and out of my system. Starting in 1974, while I was still a captain at the Infantry School, psychometric and psychological testing in the army and performance appraisals and assessment boards, etcetera etcetera, were suddenly dropped on us and never went away again. I did not care too much for this sort of thing, but naturally the Army did not leave me with a choice in the matter.

It was not as if they would ask you in a friendly sort of manner: "Roland, would you like to participate in a process were we analyse your mind to bits and pieces?" Who the hell knows how your mind works anyway? I don't even completely know myself. So that famous and oft-quoted bit of advice from Sun Tzu, one of the oldest military writers (500 B.C.), to "know yourself, know your enemy, or succumb in every battle" is actually not that easy to put into practice. In consequence I was called in often to reveal to me secret things about myself by them (so what was new? – my mother, Ellen had told me exactly the same things, but more or less in words and ways I could understand, while sometimes employing a wooden spoon to drive her message home).

Some long-hair-and-thick-glasses type would say: "Roland, you are somewhat dominant in your approach and like to follow your own head... You are low on conformity and a bit challenging in this area, take cognisance that you are going to bump heads with the more traditional military men, of whom we have many". Yes, OK. And then:"Strangely enough, you enjoy applying the participative premise and to involve others in exciting ventures." Right, noted. "You are not too security-minded, mind you, when it comes to yourself; you tend not to lock up behind you, or close up things around you – probably a tendency to be somewhat claustrophobic..." Really! Interesting. What's next on the list, sir? "Well, you are quite sensitive to other people, but, man, you are very low on empathy when they screw up". Thank you for the feedback, sir, I'm aware of that. "Lastly, we would like to inform you that we see that you know your work and it seems to us that you enjoy it tremendously and you are exceptionally creative in many ways, which is commendable. All in all you are an ENTJ on the Briggs and Meyers – extrovert, intuitive, thinking and judging type – good commander's potential. Wowee... Noted. Thank you, thank you for not recommending that the conformists fire me; I truly love the Army and the people I work with. Note to myself: File these valuable insights immediately, Roland, then go ye forth and sin no more.

A little later on, in 1983, I acquired my own personal headshrinker in the form of my dear wife Henriette, who proved perfectly capable of sorting me out and keeping me out of trouble most of the time. And she didn't charge me one red cent for her services, either.

Truth and Reconciliation Commission

Only once was I called upon to answer to the Truth and Reconciliation Commission, a sincere effort to lance some of the festering sores of the past which kept veering over into an old-fashioned witch hunt, complete with anonymous and unproven denunciations (one can hardly call them anything else).

I was accused of allowing captured prisoners under my authority to be tortured during tactical interrogations in the field. To this day, I do not know the origin or source of this accusation, which was summarily dropped when the allegation could not be substantiated. The claim came as a complete surprise to me because it was such utter nonsense. The rule was that the SADF had to adhere to the Geneva Convention's provisions on the handling of prisoners, regardless of the fact that SWAPO was not a signatory and did not feel bound in any way to do the same, and 61 Mech went strictly "by the book" in this regard.

Obviously, captured enemy soldiers could be, and were, questioned on the spot for information of immediate tactical importance, but this had to be done within clear parameters, which included giving our troops the appropriate training. Our own unit order and various operational orders clearly stated how prisoners and civilians had to be treated. It was also seriously applied and overseen under strict guidance by our senior commanders. For example, during Operation Protea all churches and civilian concentrations were clearly marked on our maps as zones not to be engaged with fire.

I was extremely proud of the high discipline and exemplary conduct by units such as 61 Mech during operations in the field. However, as always, there were a few usual minor mishaps and contraventions, warfare being the untidy and high-stress business that it is, and these unsavoury little surprises had a habit of brewing away and then causing trouble, usually at inconvenient moments. The only remedy for this sort of things was to immediately and sometimes painfully nip each eruption in the bud. But to my knowledge nothing ever happened that was really outside acceptable norms.

In the meantime, however, I am hanging on to copies of those statements I made to the TRC – just in case. "Si Vis Pacem Para Bellum", after all.

Meeting Henriette, and Something about My Family

Many of my newfound and lasting friends, none of whom are getting any younger, knew that my first marriage was, to express it mildly, not a happy one, and ended abruptly at Tsumeb in 1982. I mention this, too, because throughout the long, arduous attritionist divorce ordeal I enjoyed the staunch support of my 61 Mech friends, including the combined personal touch of my two chaplain friends, 61 Mech's Padre Koos Rossouw and the Reverend Landman Vogel of Tsumeb. Landman was also a part-time force member of the Etosha Area Force Unit, and at times he deployed with us during external operations into Angola (which might have caused a few cases of cardiac arrest among the senior brass hats, had they only known).

I sincerely believed then, and still do, that this fraught personal situation of mine never adversely influenced my work at 61 Mech. In fact, I believe that it gave me a better-developed understanding of the lives and family values of the people serving under me, and on my part evoked a deeper feeling of loyalty and caring.

So far I have said little about my wonderful Henriette, but that's because I was saving it up for this moment. Henriette has told her side of the story in her foreword to this book, but now it is my turn.

She was delivered to me on my doorstep at Omuthiya in 1982 (after I had been divorced from my first wife), when I was OC 61 Mech, and I had a high-level VIP visit to thank for this revered opportunity. The VIPs in question were members of the parliamentary wives' working group, chaired by Mrs. Barbara Raw, wife of the much-respected senior opposition MP (and World War II veteran) Mr. Vause Raw. Accompanying them were General

Constand Viljoen's wife, Ristie, and Mrs. Helen Gleeson, the wife of General Ian Gleeson.

Also in the party was none other than Henriette, and when she stepped out of the Puma helicopter it was like a HEAT round chewing through my Ratel, and with the same inevitable result. We were married in May 1983 in Postmasburg in the Northern Cape, after I had taken over as commanding officer of the Training Wing at the nearby Army Battle School. Henriette was then, and still is, a wonderful, charismatic and imposing companion. She has stood at my side through all my long years of service in the military and she is still there. Our precious, dearly loved, outgoing, energetic, choleric, temperamental son, Pieter-Riekert, was born out of this marriage. He has some of my traits – enough said. He is now 27 and lives in Saudi Arabia, where he holds a senior management position with a soft drinks company (Aujan).

Henriette became my close companion from the start. She had to listen ad infinitum to stories of 61 Mech, and became more than just my wife – she turned into my partner in tactical thinking and could recite the six section battle drills and explain how to look through cover and not just at it, which terrain suited armoured warfare and which terrain was more congenial for the infantry.

She was also my sharpest critic during the writing of my modest book on mobile warfare in 1987, and we were both requested to lecture on mobile warfare concepts at the Army College, way before I became its commander in December 1987, handling the "know your enemy and know yourself, otherwise you will succumb in every battle" side of warfare. This was all fun, and we were friends. And then Pieter was there, and he was taught to abseil before he was four and to jump in the parachute position from a very old fridge.

Henriette was and still is a practicing psychologist, something dearly required by a former commanding officer who had served with 61 Mech. Today we live in the Middle East, and Henriette is the United Nations World Food Programme's staff counsellor for the Middle East and Asia. There is more to this story than it might seem. Our paths had crossed, in a manner of speaking, years before that crash-and-burn moment at Omuthiya. During Operation Protea in 1981 we of 61 Mech were very busy on the western side of the Cunene River, making sure that the Angolan-Cuban garrison at Cahama and points north did not send any reinforcements eastwards, where my predecessor, Commandant Johann Dippenaar, was heavily engaged in subduing a number of heavily defended strong points around Xangongo on the eastern bank. During the mopping-up operation on 25 August one of his officers, the veteran Captain Louis Harmse of 1 SAI, was shot and killed, leaving his three-month-old daughter Melanie... and his widow, Henriette (née de Lange). So little Melanie never had a fighting chance of getting to know her biological father, but I adopted her immediately after Henriette and I were married and have done my best to stand in for Louis.

Melanie is now happily married to Jason Boschin, also a war orphan – when he was a small child his father was killed in action while serving in the Selous Scouts during the Rhodesian bush war. They now live in Australia and have two cute little daughters, Elysia and Danica. But when they see me they immediately start moving and manoeuvring. Given time, they will become my mechanised girls! I sincerely hope that there are more children like Melanie and Jason who lost their parents in a war but still managed to find true happiness as they did. And that also applies to children like mine, from military families who went through the stresses and strains of the challenging times which are still fresh in our memories.

There was a happy ending to this as well, I am glad to say. My two precious children from my first marriage are good friends with Henriette, Melanie and Pieter (they also enjoyed the military, by the way, especially our regular visits to Omuthiya. My Signals Officer, Sean McSweeney, used to issue them with radios so that I could maintain some measure of control over them).

Elmarie is a very busy all-rounder today, homeschooling her children, running an aerobics class for the ladies of Albertinia, organising and training the local high school annual concerts and doing karate to boot. She is happily married to Ferdi Grobler, and they have three beautiful daughters (Sasha-Mari, Briana and Vanja). Roland Jr. is the wild one, physically gifted and adventurous. He joined the army and became a paratrooper and a mechanised infantryman, just like I did, and I had the honour of pinning his bronze paratrooper wings on to his chest at 1 Parachute Battalion in Bloemfontein in 1991.

He resigned from the Permanent Force as a captain and now runs his own paragliding school at Sedgefield. He and his wife Liza (later divorced) have one son, Roland Junior-Junior, and a daughter, Robyn. The skies are the natural habitat of Junior and Junior-Junior, and I have had opportunity to enjoy an exhilarating paragliding tandem with my eldest at Brenton-on-Sea. Together, Henriette and I thus have a combined arms team of seven amazing grandchildren. I am almost there in the making of a combat-ready mechanised infantry section.

With 61 Mech on My Retirement from the Army

I had had a full and satisfying 37 years of service – some of it lows but most of it highs, such as commanding 61 Mech – when I retired, but I did not quite realise then that at 55 I was still young enough to do many more satisfying things if I put my mind to it. But leaving was a wrench, and I asked the then Chief of the Army, Lieutenant-General Gilbert Remano, if we could forego the customary farewell parade for me; I was just not up to it.

General Remano reluctantly granted permission for a quiet exit, but some people had other ideas of which I was totally unaware. Specifically, Major general André Kruger and WO1 Koos Moorcroft dreamt up a little surprise for me, confiding only in my family. The three of us were, of course, old friends and at the time both of the conspirators were also serving on the general staff, André as the Chief of Army Structures and Koos as the Sergeant-Major of the Army. No doubt this helped to provide the "pull" for my surprise – a farewell parade laid on by 61 Mech, which was then based at Lohatlha under another old friend, Lieutenant-Colonel Jaap Steyn.

We flew to Lohatlha from Air Force Base Waterkloof, outside Pretoria – appropriately enough in a Hercules C130B, a type in which I had spent many hours in the course of my ultra-mobile career – accompanied by a few close friends, colleagues and relatives, among them Henriette, Roland Junior, Pieter and Melanie, all joining hands with me for a last momentous occasion with the unit I cherished.

The mechanised parade and taking the final salute as 61 Mech marched past in review were tear-blinking and highly appreciated – nothing more to be said about that – and was followed by an unforgettable farewell function given by Jaap Steyn and his staff. As a parting gift I presented Jaap with some framed historical photos of the 61 Mech of my time (which became part of carefully preserved memorabilia of 61 Mech after it was disbanded).

One of my final tasks, at the regiment's request, was to lead a discussion on dynamic military leadership and command concepts. Then that evening we made a fire and swopped memorable stories and anecdotes from our interconnected military pasts, and afterwards we spent the night as we had spent so many others, in tents, in the field.

This gesture by the commander and staff of 61 Mech, my family and my other friends will always remain etched in my memory. As we sat around the fire with its current young commander, some of his officers and my older friends of many years past, I did some deep digging into my memories. Next morning it was home to Pretoria with my mental rucksack crammed with beautiful things that were invisible to everyone but me.

On 1 May 1999 I woke up just before first light and realised I was out of uniform and out of my beloved Army, and before the end of the month I would turn 56. Now for civilian life.

Before doing anything else, Henriette and I decided, we would treat ourselves to an overseas trip, and so off we went to Europe for four weeks. Being who I am, I chose to take her northwards up the Rhine River to the Ludendorff Bridge at Remagen, near Bonn, the last one intact on the Rhine when the US 9th Armoured Division captured it on 7 March 1945.[23] From there we went through the Ardennes Forest, where Güderian and Rommel had fought their Blitzkrieg in May 1940, and across the Meuse River, right up to the Atlantic coast.

After that, it was on to the Netherlands to visit the town of de Vries and Fries-Haven, and I shared with Henriette the landing sites and the trials and tribulations of the Allied airborne forces which had jumped by parachute or landed by glider at Oosterbeek and Arnhem to fight an epic battle, Operation Market Garden in September 1944.

Market Garden's aim was to bring the Allies from the Belgian border to the Rhine and across it at Arnhem in one rapid thrust. Airborne troops were to capture the bridges over the Waal and the Rhine in surprise attacks, after which ground troops of the British Second Army were to drive a decisive wedge in the German defences. Optimists expected that this operation would bring the war in Europe to a close in 1944. But the attack failed because of bad flying weather and an overwhelming German counter-offensive. Only one out of every four of the Allied airborne soldiers survived. Cornelius Ryan got it right with the title of his book about Market Garden, "A Bridge Too Far". Just like the one at Cuito Cuanavale, but that is a story for a little later.

Then it was back to Pretoria to get going on my second career, whatever that might turn out to be. I didn't know yet that ultimately I would end up in Jordan and renew my acquaintance with the wonderful six-wheeled Ratels which had played such an important role in making 61 Mech what it was.

The Veterans' Association of 61 Mech

Many of the national servicemen who did their two years' compulsory service in units such as 61 Mech went on to serve equally well as part-time soldiers in the Citizen Force; during Operation Packer in 1988 the Citizen Force units of Colonel Paul Fouché's 82 Brigade participated in the battle of Tumpo, and in a few vicious skirmishes with FAPLA and the Cuban forces close to Cuito Cuanavale they gave an outstanding account of themselves.

When I was privileged to command 7 South African Division between 1993 and 1995 I met up with many of my erstwhile compatriots and we were now serving in various part-time units – we had become one mobile family. Today that kinship lives on in veterans'

23 It was known as Operation Lumberjack.

organisations such as those of 61 Mechanised Battalion Group and 32 Battalion.

Two national service officers who had served with me in 61 Mech in 1981, Gert Minnaar and Ariel Hugo, became the founding members of the 61 Mech Veterans' Association at a meeting at Caledon, Western Cape, in 2007. Former 61 Mech men and their families came from far and wide to attend the meeting; Chris Walls flew in from Bahrain; Hubrecht van Dalsen from Australia and Ferdie de Vos from Pretoria. All three had served with me as national service lieutenants, and they asked the regiment's retired Permanent Force members such as myself, Epp van Lill, Gert van Zyl, Kowie Steyn, H.G. Smit, Servaas Lotter and Duppie du Plessis to support them with their new 61 Mech venture – although this time it was a peaceful one which included extending the hand of friendship towards former foes.

Our now-vanished mechanised clan had come together again – we were somewhat older now, of course, but the shine remained bright on the enduring friendship which had been forged during our operations such as Carrot, Protea and Daisy in 1981; Makro, Yahoo and Meebos in 1982; and Modular, Hooper, Packer and Prone. At the end of the day, comradeship is what soldiering is about, a link born in the face of hardship and extreme danger. In a sense we were privileged to have served the SADF during some of the many military operations which took place in South-West Africa/Namibia and Angola over more than 20 years.

Every so often we have the pleasure of either enduring encounters formally arranged or unexpected ones. I have met with 61 Mech veterans all over the world – Africa, the Middle East, Europe and Australia. We meet, as always, with a knowing smile in friendship and pleasant remembrance of 61 Mech and our fallen comrades.

Epilogue – the Career of Arms as it Ought to Be

When I joined the Amy I was content with the long-established military virtues such as honour, courage and loyalty that were used as guiding principles to enhance military effectiveness and the moral behaviour of soldiers. However, I soon came to learn that military missions called for virtues that were more inclusive than these traditional ones, that there were other qualities that were just as important, such as respect for others' dignity, how you treated your subordinates, your enemy and the local population. I started thinking that a convincing case could be made by interpreting these traditional virtues in different ways. There was much, much more to military philosophy and war and conflict in general, I soon came to realise. One thing I knew for sure was that I would stand up for those entrusted in my care, even at a price.

This chapter then is an abridgment of my 37-year career in the military. It also serves as a backdrop to the anecdotes I share in Part 2 about the concepts of warfare and military operations I had participated in; and Part 3, which reflects on my last five fruitful years in the military and a civilian career of 13 years.

A career of arms is what I chose to pursue, and I succeeded. I made a satisfying amount of progress, took many decisions, some for better and some for worse, held some fascinating posts and earned a few gongs to hang on my chest. But one great truth remains to be mentioned: I could not have achieved this without a family and friends such as you; and a few enemies that made life extremely interesting and at times somewhat risky. The poet was right. No man is an island, entire unto himself.

But enough of this. Let us start on our march to battlefields now distant in terms of kilometres and elapsed time, but not in memory.

3

The Tenacious Ratel

And Other Lights of My Life

... Swiftness is an elemental factor ... making up for numbers on the battlefield by the quickness of marches ... aptitude for warfare is aptitude for movement.

The Lights of My Life

The Ratel features prominently in my life story because no one else I know has had such a long and intimate association with a specific combat vehicle, or derived so much pleasure and intellectual stimulation from that relationship. Fighting vehicles and aircraft come and go as progress catches up with them, but very occasionally one will appear which is so fundamentally sound that it serves on and on. A prime example is the Dakota aircraft which is still in service close on 70 years after it first took to the sky. The Ratel is another. Consider the facts: I was closely involved in the Ratel's early life-cycle, from its conception in 1973 through to its subsequent development into a versatile and constantly improving fighting vehicle which was operationally deployed with great success in 1978. In addition I was deeply involved in formulating early doctrine for the sort of mechanised warfare that its appearance made possible. A few years later I became OC 61 Mechanised Battalion Group, and I spent many exciting hours in it, either during training or on operations with my troops in the field, and made use of the opportunity to put my theories on mechanised warfare to the test. Later I watched our original IFV of the late 1970s develop into an entire family of fighting vehicles whose capabilities went far beyond the initial aims of the project.

It was a rare and highly enjoyable experience that lasted until 61 Mechanised Battalion Group and its Ratels (even better now after many battle-tested modifications and additions) said its final farewell to me at the Army Battle School in April 1999, when I retired from the military as the Deputy Chief of the Army – 26 eventful years since that early morning at the Infantry School when I had hastily scribbled down the user requirements for the unnamed and half-visualised new fighting vehicle before setting off to join the project team in Pretoria..

The Ratel is even part of my family memories. It will be remembered that I met my future wife, Henriette, at Omuthiya in November 1982 while commanding 61 Mech and I still cherish a photograph of her on the Ratel of my battery commander, Major Chris Roux, which just happened to be called "Henriette" in honour of his wife, another Henriette. So there you have it. The superb six-wheeled Ratels, my troops, my own Henriette and my children – all of them were to become the lights of my life.

In Mobility Lay Our Strength – the Role of the Ratel

I was there on the historic day in 1975 when the first Ratel prototypes rolled off the production line at Sandock-Austral in Boksburg. Forty years later – half the life-time of the average man or woman – it is still in service of the South African Army as the trusted steed of the country's armed forces. This is no co-incidence. What we conceived and developed was, and to my mind still is, the best vehicle for ultra-mobile African bush warfare ever to be made. Thanks to its swiftness, massive wheels, bush-breaking ability and variety of weapon systems, it ruled supreme on African soil through the 1980s, as tough and tenacious as the honey-badger, the "Ratel" in Afrikaans, after which it was so aptly named.

The Ratel was produced and employed at a time when South Africa was being subjected to virtually total economic, political and military embargoes because of the world's disapproval of the then government's views and policies, with the Cold War's surrogate struggles as a constant background to muddy all the issues. The South Africans, however, were then and still are extremely proud of the quality of their indigenous military equipment and high-spirited fighting men and women of our war-fighting days. In the end 1 800 Ratels were built; some went into the war reserve – in actual fact, only a fairly small number were operationally employed in southern Africa with units such as 61 Mechanised Battalion Group, 32 Battalion and 4 South African Infantry Battalion – some were issued to Citizen Force mechanised infantry units and many were used by other arms for a variety of purposes.

The Ratel combat system was commissioned in good time for the more conventionally orientated fighting which was waged from 1978 onwards as the border war escalated and external operations into Angola became larger and more frequent. It soon became the mainstay of all the conventional operations fought in Angola, and was a force to be reckoned with. Operating by themselves or in combination with a variety of other lethally effective locally manufactured weapon systems, the Ratels made it possible for the South Africans to influence the war and hold the line, even though usually outnumbered by a huge margin, and this remained so until peace arrived at the end of December 1988.

The Ratel was extremely versatile and suitable for a variety of military applications. Thanks to its exceptional cross-country capability, it ended up being widely used by other corps in the South African Army, such as the armour, artillery, engineers and signals. As a result the basic Ratel-20 IFV spawned a number of variants, including the Ratel-Command; the Ratel-60, which was armed with a 60 mm breech-loading mortar; the Ratel-90 with a 90 mm low-pressure gun, which was utilised as a fire-support platform and also became an effective tank-buster; the Ratel-81, configured as a "shoot and scoot" mobile platform for the 81 mm mortar; the Ratel ZT-3 anti-tank missile system; the Ratel-Ambulance; and the Ratel-Recovery.

The brilliantly designed Ratel-Log never went beyond the prototype stage because of financial considerations, but would have been a worthy addition to the family. In my time at 61 Mech the Ratel-90 even equipped the armoured car squadron because it equalled the Eland-90 in firepower and armour protection, was mechanically more reliable and was infinitely more mobile off-road.

The African battle space, especially southern Angola, served as the centre stage for the employment of the Ratel during high-mobility operations, and this particular theatre of war also provided the means with which to develop and refine concepts and doctrine for African-style mobile warfare.

The Ratel's primary role in fighting of this kind was to carry troops swiftly in and out of battle, and it was admirably suited for this purpose, because it provided all the required mobility, fire-power and armoured protection we required for combat conditions. It was remarkably robust and reliable and, most of all, it was proven in battle. The Ratel increased

South Africa's level of flexibility on the battlefield. High mobility combined with flexibility was the essence of the mobile war-fighting game.

The Ratel was not designed with full armour protection against all types of hostile fire – that would have made the hull too heavy and cumbersome. It provided adequate protection from 7,62 mm armour-piercing rounds hitting it from the front, side and rear, and the slanted armour plating in the front could stop a 12,7 mm armour-piercing round. But it was vulnerable to the formidable Russian 20 mm and 23 mm anti-aircraft rounds, which could slice through it from any side.

The infantry version's 20 mm quick-firing gun and 7,62 mm co-axially mounted Browning machine-gun provided the capability to lay down sustained fire; to suppress and neutralise or destroy hostile troops, even allowing the destruction of the enemy's light-armoured fighting vehicles during the close-in battle, and produce high rates of fire to support own forces during fire-fights. Sustained covering fire was also required to protect and support dismounted infantry and other friendly armoured fighting vehicles, to allow South African troops to move rapidly and more safely during battles – the ultimate aim in offensive operations is always to close with and destroy the enemy. The Ratel's high mobility and long range – 1,000 km at high speed on roads and approximately 600 km across country – made it easier to achieve surprise. Initiative could be fostered and freedom of action could be maintained under the most difficult combat conditions.

All of this formed part and parcel of manoeuvre and fire-and-movement tactics under all weather conditions. Decisive actions as well as sound command and control were enabled by the reliable tactical radio communications installed in the Ratel as a force-multiplying effect. The fighting whole was therefore greater than the sum of its parts.

The following anecdote illustrates, I think, our extreme enthusiasm and the frankly somewhat excessive eagerness that the development process inspired. Sometime in 1974 my brother got married, and naturally I was invited to the nuptials. I had to decline, however, because he was getting hitched at a rather inopportune time from my point of view, since I was knee-deep in an extremely engrossing experiment at the Elandsfontein vehicle testing range outside Pretoria with a small team which included my close friends Colonel Serge Nell and Major Tony Savides.

We were putting four prototype Ratels through their paces, and at the same time were training a few Citizen Force officers from Serge's regiment, 1 Regiment Noord-Transvaal, in the art of what we then believed mechanised warfare should consist of. I remember it well; a glorious Saturday morning was smiling down at us while we experimented with mobile formations and tactics. Some of the trainees were practising on the move with the four prototypes; others were going through minor tactics and formations on the side, using 20 mm ammunition cases whose drab metal sides were emblazoned with radio call signs.

Bear in mind that this miniature and rather makeshift field exercise took place well before Operation Savannah, the very first incursion into Angola, which only started late in 1975 and dragged on into early 1976. Savannah caught the South Africans on the wrong foot because it was hastily put together as a result of extraneous events in the Angolan civil war, and on top of that the operation – at least in the early stages – was shrouded in the utmost secrecy which prevented the use of much of our existing equipment (most of which dated from World War II in any case). So the SADF went into it without any of the means needed for fighting a modern conventional campaign; about the only really modern items were its four-wheeled Eland-90 armoured cars.

The SADF reaped a number of benefits from Operation Savannah, its first operational deployment in 37 years. A lot of rust was knocked off techniques and procedures, officers and men gained valuable operational experience, and it had a tremendous effect on technological innovations and enhancements for the mobile warfare of the near future. The result was that by the late 1970s and early 1980s the SADF was reaping the benefit of the experimental work done earlier.

There are many inconsequential but amusing anecdotes about the development of the Ratel which remain untold. I remember, for example, that the first driver's seat and turret only reached South Africa after being smuggled through no less than five other countries. To avoid embarrassment, I will not mention the country of origin... but our counterpart colleagues on the Ratel project, Herr Sieber and Herr Kamerad, will recall which it was, I am sure.

Fighting Against the Enemy's Tanks with Ratels

Halting a numerically superior conventional enemy force on the Lomba River in August-September 1987 during Operation Modular was an amazing and, frankly, seems an unlikely feat. But it was pulled off by the aggressive employment of a platoon of Ratel-90s and Ratel ZT-3s, commanded by Major Hannes Nortmann and crews of national servicemen, which proved to be a formidable tank-hunting pack in spite of its lack of teeth.

The fact was that Nortmann's tank-killers actually were not very well-armed for the purpose. The Ratel-90's gun had proved quite adequate against the old T-34s deployed in earlier operations at the beginning of the 1980s, but the heavier Soviet T-54/55 main battle tank that began to appear a few years later was a tougher nut to crack. The Ratels' 90 mm shell struggled to penetrate the T54/55s' thicker armour, and at times it required several successive HEAT (high explosive anti-tank) hits to bring about an opponent's demise – an encounter requiring not only remarkable adroitness (which the Ratels had) but also sheer guts (which, fortunately, the crews also had).

The Ratel ZT-3, on the other hand, was more than a match for the T-54/55s, not to mention thinner-skinned combat vehicles such as the PT-76 amphibious tanks, the BRDM armoured reconnaissance vehicle (the nearest thing the Soviets had to an armoured car), the BMP tracked armoured troop carriers and the old BTR-wheeled armoured troop carriers.

This was in spite of the fact (which is still not generally known) that Nortmann's ZT-3s were actually prototypes which were still in the test and evaluation phase. They did not work perfectly – some of the missiles proved rather erratic, for example – but thanks to Nortmann's use of surprise, rapid action and precision tactics the ZT-3s and Ratel-90s destroyed most of the tanks of 47 (FAPLA) Brigade in arduous close-in fighting. Paul Bester, an engineer at South Africa's arms manufacturer Denel and programme manager for the ZT-3 at the time, later told me the following story:

The ZT-3 was launched at the Pretoria show on 22 August in 1990; in 1987 and 1988 it was still being tested and evaluated in the battle at the Lomba... Some of the missiles flew wildly and plunged into the ground in front of the enemy's tanks. I read what Helmoed-Römer Heitman wrote in his book "War in Angola" about Hannes Nortmann and his anti-tank platoon's fight against the tanks of 47 Brigade at the Lomba:

"... the fourth missile hit the target. The detonation threw the turret 25 metres to one side. The next tank turned around and withdrew towards the river. The third continued to advance. Nortmann fired at it with his fifth missile, but it dived into the ground just ahead of its target. The sixth hit and destroyed the tank.

"Nortmann again pulled back to reload, and then manoeuvred into a new firing position. From there he fired at the furthest tank and hit it with two missiles. The third missile of this pack was fired at a tank that they could hardly see in the bushes on the north bank. The remaining tanks and their infantry now withdrew."

The satisfaction of knowing that your product has been used – and so successfully – is impossible to describe... this missile fills a gap that existed in our arsenal... the ZT-3, firing at a range of more than five kilometres, is comparable with the best available systems in the world."

The Ratels and the people who operated them formed the fighting core during the South African Border War right through the 1980s.

Other Tools of the Fighting Trade – Wheels, Tracks and Guns

Other exceptional military hardware developed and produced in South Africa became essential tools of our military's fighting trade on faraway battlefields in Africa. They included an assortment of wheeled and tracked vehicles and guns, most of which were designed, tested and produced in South Africa.

A crucially important addition to the South African order of battle through the 1970s and 1980s was the Samil range of robust transporters/troop carriers. There were three types in the series, the Samil-20, Samil-50 and Samil-100, each suffix indicating the payload (for example, the Samil-50 could carry five tons), and many of them had mine-protected drivers' cabs. The Samil was designed to be strong enough to deal with the most unfavourable terrain (remember, much of our movement was off-road in case of mines or the lack of anything resembling a direct route to wherever we were going), and its reliability was a critical factor in operations and logistical planning.

Supply is always a key factor when the winning of a difficult battle is balanced on a knife-edge, and a sustained logistical flow is essential in ensuring continual manoeuvre and maintenance of both the momentum and the tempo during a battle. This is particularly the case in Africa, where long distances, thick bush and generally bad road infrastructure (where any exists) are usually features of any mobile operation.

Mine protection was one of the South Africans' main preoccupations during the border war, and rightly so, because apart from the intrinsic damage they caused, they cut down on the mobility that became the SADF's stock-in-trade. They had been used with deadly effect against the Portuguese in Angola and Mozambique prior to the Portuguese regime's collapse in 1974, but few except makeshift measures had been used to combat them. The South Africans, in contrast, took the more aggressive attitude of attempting to tame the mine, and to a large extent succeeded.

High-mobility mine-protected vehicles of many kinds were used extensively for operations, and scientists like Dr. Vernon Joint became legendary for the role they constantly played in optimising the capability of South Africa's fleet of mine-protected vehicles (an amusing description of how they allegedly did it was given in a publication of the 7th International Seminar for Life Protection in Geneva in 2008, which said that the Department of Defence "filled a room with money, gave their scientists shovels and said; 'Replace what we can't buy, improve what we can buy and generally make it difficult for our enemies'").

They did, and not only for South Africa's enemies of yesteryear. South African vehicles from that era ended up protecting the lives of foreign peacekeepers in battles fought in Iraq and Afghanistan, and I refer specifically to the well-known Buffel and Casspir four-wheeled mine-protected vehicles, which were used in a combat role as infantry fighting vehicles in very similar fashion to the ways in which we used the Ratel.

Young industrial engineers like Wessie van der Westhuizen, Willem Botha and William Haddad deserve to be mentioned in this regard, but there were many others from Armscor and Denel as well. These dedicated specialists worked very hard behind the scenes, day and night, to produce near-perfect combat systems. Armscor served as South Africa's armaments procurement agency and Denel was the main state-owned defence industry in those fighting days, and to date still is.

The Olifant Main Battle Tank's Debut – Shock Action Unveiled

The main battle tank is the predator supreme of any landward defence capability. En masse it provides dearly sought-after physical and psychological shock action in battle. The tank is a renowned tank-killer in its own right, but its primary role is aggressive mobile action in the enemy's rear areas; the deeper it penetrates, the greater its leverage. The tank is not designed for static defence; when it is dug in and stationary, its users have hobbled it and reduced it to being simply an expensive pill-box. There is nothing revolutionary about these statements, of course, but I mention them because FAPLA and the Cubans generally used their armour in just such a way.

We did not when we deployed the Olifant main battle tank in the final battles in Angola. The Olifant is a prime example of what ingenuity and technical expertise can accomplish. Unlike the Ratel it was not born in South Africa, but it certainly grew to full maturity in our hands. Our Olifants started life as the British Centurion Mark V more than half a century ago. It was a good tank for European battles of the 1950s, but it didn't acclimatise well to Africa; among other things its range was totally inadequate, its petrol engine under-powered and unbelievably thirsty, it was prone to overheating, and by the 1970s its gun was distinctly under-powered.

We had some Centurions that we had bought in the 1950s and later acquired a number of under-the-counter gutted versions from Jordan and India (so much for sanctions). Then we set about turning them into modern battle tanks. It took a long time and much effort, but by the time we had finished, almost nothing of the old Centurions remained except the characteristic hulls, turret shells and track skirts.

The Olifant had been up-gunned to a powerful 105 mm rifled gun, for which it carried 72 rounds in its hull, and had two 7,62 mm machine-gun, one a co-axial in the turret and the other mounted on the commander's cupola. It had been up-engined with a diesel power-pack which gave it a road range of 250 km and a top road speed of up to 45 km/h. It had improved tracks and suspension which dramatically lessened its dependence on transporters to a remarkable degree. Its armour had been improved. And so on and so on.

By the late 1980s the Army had about 172 operational Olifants, and when the serious final battles in southern Angola broke out on 9 November 1987 they were ready for action. And they proved themselves.

On 3 October 1987 a South African battle group, of which Nortmann's platoon was part, destroyed 47 FAPLA Brigade at the Lomba River, a decisive encounter which routed the overwhelming offensive against Mavinga, UNITA's window to the outside world. Soon after this historic encounter, 12 South African Olifants arrived, with another in reserve, commanded by the tactically astute Major André Retief. This small but hard-hitting hunting pack crossed the Okavango River near Rundu and headed into Angola on 20 October; it was the first time South African tanks were seeing action since 1945.

The South African tank men distinguished themselves in the fighting that followed. FAPLA and the Cubans fielded more than 150 main battle tanks, while at no stage were there more than two Olifant squadrons deployed. The Olifants joined forces with the G-5 artillery pieces, SAAF Mirage ground attack fighters and Hannes Nortmann's hunting group, and by the time the fighting ended no less than 94 T54/55s had been knocked out between them, while large quantities of other enemy hardware had also been destroyed or salvaged and carried off. From personal experience I can attest to the fact that that handful of battle tanks made a vast difference to the morale of the few South African soldiers at the fighting front.

Our only significant tank losses were three Olifants, which were not knocked out in combat but fell foul of a minefield east of Cuito Cuanavale and were left there when the main combat force of South Africa were withdrawn to SWA/Namibia at the end of April 1988. Considering what had been accomplished, it was a small price to pay.

Guns, Rockets and Mortars Combined – the Ride of the Valkyries

The G-5 155 mm gun-howitzer, the 127 mm multiple rocket launcher and the 120 mm mortar were the South Africans' artillery backbone during the last battles in Angola. The amazing G-5 gun, one of the best in the world both then and now, fires a 155 mm base-bleed shell out to more than 48 km and was the scourge of the Angolan and Cuban forces. It accounted for the destruction of most of the Angolan and Cuban arsenal on the ground and even made long-distance attacks on the enemy's aircraft where they were parked on their airfields – the South Africans' long-range artillery, in fact, was a manoeuvre force in its own right. The G-5 was crewed by eight men, who travelled in the Samil gun tractor... but artillery commanders and forward observation officers usually rode in the ubiquitous Ratel-Command vehicles.

The Valkiri, the 127 mm multiple rocket launcher, made a name for itself in the later fighting of the border war. The Angolans and Cubans had long used the old Soviet BM-21 MRL against the South Africans, albeit somewhat ineffectively. Then the Valkiri, which had been in development since the late 1970s, appeared on the scene and effectively outmatched the old "Stalin Organs". It was hated and feared by the Cubans and the Angolans; the latter called it the "Shindingu", or "the red pepper that burns".

It was a typical South African design, efficient but cost-effective. It used the ordinary Unimog lorry chassis, on which was mounted a 24-tube pack which could fire rockets out to 22,000 metres; each rocket was tipped with a 60 kg fragmentation warhead that sprayed out 8 500 steel balls, giving a lethal spread of 1 500 square metres. Unlike the Ratel ZT-3, the Valkiri was a battle-proven weapon by the time the final battles started in 1987: the previous year, during Operation Alpha Centauri, it literally brought to its knees an Angolan force's advance from Cuito Cuanavale. To this day the skulls and bones of the unburied FAPLA dead still litter the battlefield.

The powerful 120 mm M-5 heavy mortar also did great execution. An Israeli import, the M-5s saw considerable action as an extremely useful support weapon during the late 1980s after they had been extensively modified by the South Africans to make them fit for deployment in African bush conditions. The M-5 could fire a standard bomb out to 6 250 metres, but also had rocket-assisted ammunition which had a "reach" of 10,000 metres.

FAPLA/Cuban propaganda to the contrary, only small numbers of artillery assets were deployed for the final battles, but in combination with the Ratels, tanks and ground-attack aircraft constituted a fighting force whose effectiveness was completely out of proportion to its size. It was, in fact, a force multiplier in its own right.

Vulnerable When Attacked from the Skies

South African combat technology had one yawning gap: its anti-aircraft capability. The South Africans were extremely vulnerable against a succession of overwhelming air attacks in Angola in 1987–88. Angry phalanxes of modern Soviet MiG fighters came out of the sky at us every day, and were almost uncontested. The SAAF Mirages were fine and very well-flown aircraft, but they were frankly outdated and outclassed for air-superiority fighting, and the ground forces had only a few not so classy anti-aircraft systems.

A handful of self-propelled Cactus surface-to-air systems – the product of a joint French-South African project dating back to the 1950s – ineffectively roamed the fields of Angola at that time. There were also a few Ystervark (Porcupine) self-propelled anti-aircraft guns, strictly stopgap systems consisting of the old manually aimed 20 mm light anti-aircraft gun bolted to a mine-protected Samil-20 chassis. Some twin Swiss Oerlikon 35 mm anti-aircraft guns with sophisticated fire-control and surveillance radars were also deployed, but they were meant for static defence and did not fare well in the rugged bush terrain.

More effective were the Soviet ZSU-23-2 twin-barrelled 23 mm anti-aircraft guns which the South Africans had captured in large numbers during previous operations such as Protea and taken into operational service, and many similarly captured and "turned" Soviet SA-7 Strela man-portable surface-to-air-missiles were used against their former owners. The best SAMs were owned not by the South Africans but by their UNITA allies, who had received shipments of Stingers[1] from the United States, and used them to some good effect against low-flying fighters during Operation Modular.

But at the end of the day none of these weapons were a real deterrent against the Angolan and Cuban air forces, and both the South Africans and UNITA had to rely heavily on passive air-defence measures such as camouflage and concealment.

Legacy of the Ratel Fighting Doctrine

The addition of the Ratel to South Africa's arsenal not only stimulated technological enhancement but also inspired fresh military thinking regarding the employment of this unique platform in mobile warfare. The fresh thinking included the design and application of newly crafted fighting doctrine, as the South Africans were out-and-out exponents of mobile warfare, and these concepts were successfully applied during the successive conventional battles fought in southern Angola in 1987 and 1988.

The dishes thus cooked up were served to the enemy with a dash of audacity, sometimes a considerable dash when dire circumstances required taking calculated risks (see Chapter 5, Warfare the African Way, for more about South Africa's emergent fighting concepts and battle doctrine).

The military incursions into Angola were normally referred to as pre-emptive strikes. Such pre-emptive operations were deliberate acts involving elaborate mission-orientated

1 Man-portable surface-to-air-missile systems, which were also used effectively by the Afghan forces against Russian aircraft during the Afghan war.

planning and customarily employing moderate force levels for forays of short duration, examples being Operation Protea in August 1981 and Operation Askari in 1984. Each cross-border operation varied in intensity, style and duration, according to operational circumstances, but two principles applied to all: ground must be seized but not occupied, and a force must not become bogged down in grinding battles – the rule was to go in fast and then get out fast again upon completion of the mission.

Force levels, too, ranged from purposefully grouped battalions to brigade-sized formations. Naturally, each operation differed from the last in some respects because of differing aims and circumstances. For example, Operations Modular, Hooper and Packer in 1987 and 1988 lasted about eight months, the longest of all the incursions.

In addition to taking part in conventional-type operations in the 1980s, Ratels were involved in a number of high-mobility counterinsurgency operations, mainly of short duration, inside SWA/Namibia. Operational units normally operated from temporary army bases in the northern border region, such as Omuthiya, Eenhana and Okongo. Although successful in this endeavour, Ratels were not viewed as being economically viable for such deployments, but the counterinsurgency operation served to exercise and sharpen the mechanised forces for conventional action. Thus 61 Mech was used extremely successfully in a succession of operations to counter SWAPO's incursions into the 'Death Triangle', the farming territory bounded by Tsumeb, Grootfontein and Otavi.[2]

The South Africans became quite adept at mobile warfare which required nimbleness in bush-manoeuvring. The essence of this concept was summarised as follows by renowned military writer Willem Steenkamp in *Challenge: Politics of Power – the Border War*:

> It cannot be mere coincidence that 1987 saw a marked interest in conventional armoured warfare emerging in senior South African military circles. Since the early 1970s the SADF had maintained a conventional force of two divisions, but for obvious reasons much of the practical stress had been laid on the counterinsurgency warfare. Then suddenly conventional warfare was in again.
>
> Why? Probably because with most of the fighting in Namibia now being handled by the South West Africa's Territory Force, the SADF has had time to stand back and re-assess its real function, and a clique of bright young SADF colonels has begun preaching a doctrine in which Güderian and Rommel rub shoulders with Patton, Mao Tse-tung and the Israelis. It is a curious mixture, but one well adapted to local circumstances.
>
> As elucidated by Colonel Roland de Vries, commanding officer of the South African Army College, the doctrine calls for high mobility by night as well as by day, maximum violence in execution, flexible thinking and the greatest possible use of deception. It is based on three premises: that there will probably be a hostile air environment; that the enemy will probably be numerically superior; and that the fighting will have to be concluded in only a few weeks, because South Africa, unlike Israel and other countries, has no generous allies to re-supply it at short notice.
>
> Who is this new doctrine to be used against? In principle, any enemy that attacks South Africa. In practice, the only immediate contenders would be the Angolans and their allies.

2 See Chapter 11.

Willem Steenkamp's words became a reality on the battlefields of southern Angola from 1987 until 1988.

After more than 40 years in service, some of South Africa's Ratels are currently serving in foreign countries such as Morocco, Jordan, Yemen and Ghana. Many Ratels are found in crisis areas, painted the trademark white of the United Nations peace-keeping forces. The mere fact that Ratels are still in service all over the world as well as in the current day South African National Defence Force is an amazing tribute to this remarkable vehicle; a tribute both to the people who designed and produced it, and those who operated it under fire.

On 21 July 2011, while living in Amman, Jordan, I received a telephone call from South Africa. It was from Frans du Randt of Denel Land Systems, who said: "Come and pay me a visit at Denel, we're building the new infantry combat vehicle, the Badger, the replacement of the Ratel." Nostalgia washed over me, and for a moment I was seized by sentimental recollections of the past. I thought fondly about 61 Mech and the people who had served it so faithfully during the stretched-out Border War. I thought about our trusty Ratels careering through the bush.

61 Mechanised Battalion Group was one of the South African fighting units commended by the Cubans for courage with which they fought in southern Angola in 1987–88. It is an ancient military custom for a commanding officer who is congratulated on some exploit of his unit to reply: "Thank you, sir, I'll tell the men." So once again I thank the fighting men of my one-time unit. They were very young, most of them, and they were performing their compulsory military service. But they gave the lie to the old adage that one volunteer is worth 10 pressed men. That is so in some cases, but every rule has its exceptions, and 61 Mech was one of them.

Our sons were warriors. They still are in heart, mind, body and soul.

4

With 61 Mech in the Field

Every Man Counted

If all men count with you ... If you can walk with
Kings, nor lose the common touch ...
"If" – Rudyard Kipling

Preamble – If You Could Walk with Kings

For an enthralling moment during the writing of this chapter about life with 61 Mechanised Battalion Group, I was a youthful 37 again. 61 Mech was a first-line fighting unit second to none, a regiment that touched your soul – one in which every person counted. My two years as its commander in the operational area in 1981 and 1982 had taught me that how important it was, as Kipling said, to be able to walk with kings – actually meaning any VIP – and yet retain virtue and never allow yourself to become distanced from the unsung heroes who actually got their hands dirty.

And Kipling was right about something else: it is possible to live a life in which you fill every forgiving or even unforgiving minute with sixty seconds' worth of distance run, if at all possible! What Kipling meant by "unforgiving minute" is that each one that passes is gone forever, and if you have not made good use of it you have thrown away 60 seconds of your life which can never be recovered. It was a personal philosophy that made for an existence which was invigorating and absorbing; one of learning, committing and doing and sharing danger with others.

This part of my life story took place more than 30 years ago, but to me it was and still is an era to be remembered, a vividly coloured collection of memories to be shared with family, friends and foes – and with myself.

61 Mech formed an essential combat element of South Africa's mobile conventional forces. At that time there were two military forces operating in SWA/Namibia. One was, of course, the SADF, while the other was the recently established South West Africa Territory Force, which was so designed that the two worked hand in glove. The SWATF was basically a lightly armed, locally recruited counterinsurgency force to which almost all internal security duties were being devolved by the SADF, which would remain responsible for deployment of conventional air and ground assets as required.

My new regiment straddled both stools. It was an SADF unit, but was the SWATF's conventional reaction force, and so came under command of HQ SWATF in Windhoek. It was also a regiment with a unique structure, since it consisted of organic mechanised infantry, armoured cars and field or medium artillery sub-units, rather than an infantry battalion to which armour and artillery could be temporarily attached when the need arose. The Germans and Russians had had multi-arm units since at least World War II, but not the SADF, barring the temporary grouping of Battle Group Juliet which was put together for Operation Reindeer in 1978 and was the inspiration for 61 Mech.

From my point of view, the most important military leaders at that time were General Constand Viljoen, the Chief of the SADF and the founding father, so to speak, of 61 Mech; Lieutenant General Jannie Geldenhuys, Chief of the Army; and Major General Charles Lloyd, General Officer Commanding SWATF. It was my good fortune that all three were inspirational commanders who had a marked influence on shaping and building the best army in Africa.

As I mentioned earlier, it was a joy to command 61 Mech from 9 January 1981, when I took over from Commandant Johann Dippenaar, who had done great work in creating it from almost nothing, to January 1983, when I handed over to Commandant Gert van Zyl. To command 61 Mech was stimulating, to say the least. To have been able to participate actively in the creation of its spirit, its leadership and skill at arms was one of the greatest and most satisfying experiences of my military career, both emotionally and intellectually. For this I have to thank the officers, soldiers and civilian staff with whom I served, my higher commanders, who afforded me the opportunity – and most assuredly the Dear Lord.

Into SWA and Taking Command of 61 Mech – a Quiet Resolution Taken

Early in January 1981, having just completed the year-long senior command and staff course at the Army College in Pretoria, I flew from Air Force Base Waterkloof to Grootfontein to take over 61 Mech. Sitting next to me in the cavernous, noisy interior of a droning C-130B transport plane were my two small children, Roland Junior and Elmarie, whose spirits were as high as mine as they stared around at the Herc's Spartan interior. It felt as if we could almost reach out and touch the excitement and anticipation in the tepid air.

Sitting next to my children in the row of uncomfortable red webbing seats were the youthful Captain Giel Reinecke and his family. Giel Reinecke was going to be my logistics officer and would become a superlative "Log O", one of the best in the Army (it was the beginning of a long association; years later he would serve with me again as my senior logistics officer-instructor when I commanded the SA Army College between 1988 and 1991 – and still later, we were destined to work together in "Civvy Street" after we had retired from the Army[1]). Giel's wife, Maureen, incidentally, was a staff-sergeant in the Army's Personnel Services Corps and was also going to serve at 61 Mech. Strapped down in the C-130s hold was yet another "passenger": a classically elegant beige Mercedes-Benz sedan belonging to the SAAF's Brigadier Bossie Huyser, who was on his way to SWA/Namibia to take over Western Air Command.

This was an important and extremely pleasant chance encounter for me. Later on, during both the April 1981 and April–May 1982 incursions of SWAPO's[2] "Special Unit" into the "Death Triangle", he would not beat about the bush when I asked for air support but would simply confront me at the Tsumeb airfield and ask: "Roland, how many aircraft do you need, and where and when?" That was typical of Bossie's spontaneous and supportive nature, enthusiasm and energy, which I enjoyed and utilised to the fullest extent during the extremely active and eventful two years I would spend in my new position.

Sprawling in the C-130's notoriously uncomfortable webbing seating, I spent the next two hours thinking about what awaited me as we droned northwestwards. What would life on the border hold for our young, for example? What would it be like, running my own

1 See Chapter 17.

2 South West Africa People's Organisation. Special Unit belonged to its military wing; namely the People's Liberation Army of Namibia (PLAN).

unit in action, which I had looked forward to for so many years?

I soon found out how it would begin when we got down to the business of taking over from Johann Dippenaar and his staff, first at Tsumeb and later on at Omuthiya[3]. It was an unbelievable experience. Dippenaar was a detail-orientated commander, and he put my party through a painstaking and procedurally perfect handing-over process. Everything had to be checked, inspected and signed for. There were scheduled visits and briefings; all the important stakeholders and key role players in 61 Mech's life had to be met, so that important issues could be discussed (my readers will make the acquaintance of many of these people in the ensuing chapters as they make their appearance in the story of our operation).

The formal handing over of command took place on 9 January 1981 at Omuthiya, the base near the Oshivello training area that Dippenaar created out of the virgin bush land. It was an impressive parade – as mechanised parades usually are – and as the sub-units passed by and gave us an "eyes right" Dippenaar quietly drew my attention to the fact that some of the vehicles were scarred by bullets and shrapnel. It was a sobering sight, and I started thinking again about my future responsibilities, not least of them the precious lives that I would hold in my hands. And right there I made a silent resolution: I was going to work extremely hard at building and maintaining a cohesive combat-ready unit and earning the respect of my people. But there was no gloom or apprehension about that resolution. I was looking forward to the challenge.

Something about the History of 61 Mech Extraordinaire

61 Mech was one of the finest combat forces in the military history of South Africa, and between 1979 and 1988 played a decisive role in the border war – and this is not a partisan statement: even our opponents acknowledged this. This combat unit extraordinaire was actually praised by the Cubans for its superb fighting in southern Angola under the direst of operational circumstances; a tribute which was the result of the regiment's widely recognised military professionalism and highly regarded operational standing.

61 Mech existed for only 27 years – not a long time in comparison to some of South Africa's "traditional" units with their continuity which sometimes goes back a century and a half. In that short lifetime it participated in more than 37 large-scale operations and a number of smaller ones, all in that one vast and almost trackless area which straddled both sides of the border between SWA/Namibia and Angola, a place of great distances, unforgiving terrain and frequently dreadful weather conditions which was populated by enemies ranging from artful, tenacious insurgents to conventional soldiers with tanks, artillery and fighter aircraft. Its official SADF designation was the Western Sub-Theatre of War,[4] although everybody, soldiers and civilians alike, called it by a simpler name, but one that said it all: "the border".[5]

The Operational Role of 61 Mech and its Ordered Commitments

61 Mech's purpose was to provide a mobile reserve and conventional strike force for the SWATF and to support the military objectives of the SADF for its counterinsurgency campaign. To carry out these tasks the unit had to be prepared to conduct pre-emptive

3 Operational base of 61 Mech, 120 km north of Tsumeb.
4 See Maps 1-5.
5 See Maps 1-5.

lightning strikes against threatening SWAPO concentrations inside southern Angola, the insurgents' jumping-off point for operations inside SWA/Namibia, hitting strategic and operational base areas which at first had been regarded as safe by the mere fact of being located behind the shelter of the international borderline.

The unit was also responsible for conducting offensive military operations, when so ordered, against any conventional force that might threaten SWA/Namibia's territorial integrity, or, for that matter, any force which interfered with the external operations conducted against SWAPO outside the borders of SWA/Namibia. Other responsibilities included waging counter-offensives against the deep infiltrations by the SWAPO Special Unit into the farmlands of the "Death Triangle", harrowing and traumatic – although unsuccessful overall – raids directed at thriving farming communities and the populace of major towns in the northern border region such as Tsumeb, Otavi, Grootfontein, Outjo, Kamanjab and Otjiwarongo.

Omuthiya – the Home of 61 Mech

Omuthiya was a combination of home base, training facility and operational staging area, ideally located and structured for all three purposes. It lay hidden from view in the bushy fringes of southern Ovamboland, approximately 20 km north of Oshivello near the northeastern edge of the Etosha Game Reserve. About 120 km to the southeast nestled the copper-mining town of Tsumeb. Comfortable, extremely neat and well laid out, it consisted of rows of tented accommodation and some prefabricated buildings, a parade ground, messing facility, a sick bay and the usual logistical infrastructure, plus the amenities typically found in semi-permanent bases in the operational area, such as a swimming pool and some other recreational facilities.

Its location could not have been better. To its north was a vast training area which extended right into Ovamboland, which was also, of course, the internal operational zone itself. Omuthiya was also a handy staging area for external operations, because the SWA/Namibia-Angola border was a mere 120 km away as the crow flies, which was no problem for a unit as used to bundu-bashing as 61 Mech.

This made it ideal as the launching-pad for stealthy incursions into Angola such as Operation Protea in August 1981, when 61 Mech penetrated into the so-called "shallow area" north of the border and seized control of the vital Cahama-Xangongo road without the Angolan forces even knowing it had arrived. So 61 Mech was ready at all times to strike swiftly in any direction, whether the threat was internal or external.

Operations Conducted by 61 Mech During 1981–82 and 1987–88

Under my command 61 Mech participated in the following military operations, which will be described in Part 2 of this book:

- Chapter 11: Triangle of Death – Carrot in April 1981 and Yahoo in April–May 1982 were fast-paced, action-packed counterinsurgency operations, conducted against the SWAPO Special Unit in the Death Triangle.
- Chapter 12: Battles of Encirclement – Protea in August 1981 was a classic large-scale conventional-type offensive operation launched against the conventional army of Angola in that country's southern Cunene Province.
- Chapter 13: A Flower Blooms – Daisy in November 1981 was one of the deepest mechanised border strikes ever undertaken against SWAPO in the central part of

southern Angola.

- Chapter 14: High Readiness – Makro (December 1981/January 1982), Meebos I (March 1982) and Meebos II (July–August 1982) were typical external operations in which 61 Mech's rapid deployment capability was fully utilised and in which its versatility and usefulness in switching from counterinsurgency to semi-conventional modes of warfare were aptly demonstrated.

Then in 1987–88 I had the privilege of serving once again with 61 Mech through the high-intensity conventional battles fought against FAPLA (*Forças Armadas Populares de Libertação de Angola*) and the Cubans in southern Angola; firstly as the second-in-command of the fighting brigade during the second phase of Operation Modular from October until December 1987; secondly as the Chief of Staff of 10 Division for the duration of Operation Prone in May-December 1988.

Once more I could observe this magnificent unit fighting with distinction and experience the immense pride I felt for my brothers in arms.[6] What was interesting about the operations I participated in with 61 Mech was their rich variety, from high-intensity counterinsurgency actions to high-tempo mobile operations of the conventional type.

Organisational Disposition of 61 Mech

When I took over command in January 1981 the main HQ of 61 Mech was located in Tsumeb, in a large house provided by the Tsumeb Mining Corporation on a more or less permanent basis. As the main force of 61 Mech was based at Omuthiya, however, I decided very early during my command term to relocate the main HQ to Omuthiya as well. When this had been done we maintained only a small administrative rear office and satellite operations and communications node at Tsumeb, where many of our civilian staff worked.

Adequate communication systems such as telex, telephone and radio linked 61 Mech with SWATF HQ at Bastion in Windhoek, Sector 10 in Oshakati, Sector 20 in Rundu, Sector 30 in Otjiwarongo and the respective Area Force Units in the region. Communication forums were established with municipalities to facilitate close co-operation with the local community and ensure operational expediency in case of a crisis. In addition, 61 Mech had the means to field a tactical headquarters for any operation quite rapidly, if and when required by operational practicalities.

For mobile operations 61 Mech was run from its Ratel-Command vehicles. These command vehicles were equipped with superb communication systems, including frequency-hopping radios, which were extremely helpful in maintaining secure communications against enemy interception (the frequency-hopping system, invented and manufactured by Grintek South Africa, was a world first).

61 Mech was organised to perform its primary role as a conventional first-line fighting unit. As I mentioned earlier, it was unique in the sense that there was no similar combined-arms team in all of the SADF, and as such it provided a well-balanced array of infantry, armour and artillery sub-units and combat-support elements. Chapter 4 explains more about the main equipment used by 61 Mech, the core of which was the six-wheeled Ratel in its various configurations.

The unit was led and managed by a professional core of Permanent Force officers, warrant-officers and non-commissioned officers, with a number of civilian staff members at

6 See Chapters 15 and 16.

the rear HQ. The leadership component included an essential team of well-trained young national servicemen – officers and NCOs of note, of whom the permanent members were extremely proud. The fighting element's other ranks were well-trained and daring young national servicemen, who to my mind had exceptional self-confidence and superb soldierly self-esteem.

During my term as commanding officer 61 Mech's generic composition (which is also given in graphic form in Figure 1) was made up of the following sub-structures: Battalion Headquarters; two mechanised infantry companies; an armoured car squadron; an artillery battery; a mortar platoon; an anti-tank platoon; and a headquarters company (combat-support services). An additional motorised infantry company, an engineer troop and an anti-aircraft troop were normally attached for external operations. Personnel strength varied from approximately 800 to 1 200 fighting men, depending on the scope and extent of a specific operation; for example, during Operation Yahoo in April-May 1982 more than 3,000 combatants and 500 vehicles were grouped under the command of 61 Mech as the designated task force headquarters.

For both training and battle our sub-units were usually organised into three combat teams based on the two mechanised infantry companies and the armoured squadron. Thus Alpha Company would become Combat Team 10, Bravo Company would be Combat Team 20 and Charlie Squadron would be Combat Team 30. This dispensation was not cast in concrete, however, and thanks to intensive training in both day and night operations 61 Mech was adept at rapid grouping and re-grouping in the field to fit any particular requirement. The combat teams themselves were organised into smaller combat elements to provide a balanced array of Ratel-20s and Ratel-90s; this allowed for integrated all-arms training and operational employment of mixed infantry and armoured assets.

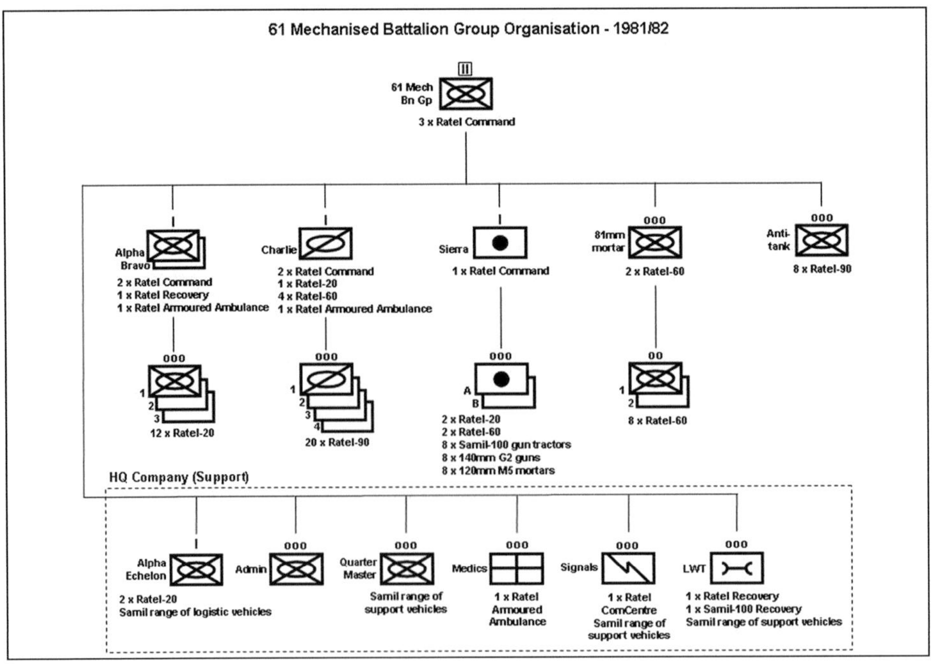

Figure 1: Organisation of 61 Mechanised Battalion Group in 1981-82

The following weapon types could generally be found in the combat groupings: The personal weapon was the 5,56 mm R-4 assault rifle, a locally modified and manufactured version of the Israeli Galil; platoon weapons such as light machine guns, light mortars and hand-held anti-tank weapons; and indirect-fire support weapons such as 60 mm and 81 mm mortars. These weapon systems were organised into appropriate groupings, such as the mortar platoon and the anti-tank platoon (which, like the armoured car squadron, was equipped with the formidable Ratel-90).

61 Mech was organised to operate independently in Angola for periods of up to 10 days, after which we became reliant on second-line supply. This meant that sufficient equipment, general supplies, spares and commodities – including a large number of Ratel spare wheels, engines and axles, packed on Samil load-carriers – went forward with us for extended operations.

Logistical (administrative) support bases were normally deployed further forward than usual, but still in relatively safe locations, to support the front line. The determinants for positioning were the prerogative of the respective sectors or higher field headquarters. Second and third line transport and aircraft supported these administrative areas, which were usually located close to airfields in relation to operational expedience.

In 1981 and 1982 our forces still enjoyed the advantage of operational, logistical and aircraft movement during day-time, thanks to our near-complete air superiority in southern Angola at the time. This situation changed dramatically from late 1984 onwards and seriously deteriorated nearer to Operations Modular and Hooper in southeastern Angola in 1987–88, due to almost complete air dominance by the enemy's MiGs. During the Angolan fighting in 1981 and 1982, priority casualties could be air-evacuated by both day and at night, but by 1987 and 1988 the air threat had escalated to the point where casevacs could only be carried out at night. Instead casualties were kept under well-organised medical care in the forward areas and then evacuated to rear-area medical facilities in record time.

Badges and Insignia of 61 Mech

61 Mech's officers and men proudly wore some distinctive badges and flashes which set them apart from their fellows in other units (Figure 2) and still engender the same sense of excitement and heightened pride as they did when we first put them up. The shoulder flash was approved by the Chief of the Army in 1981, during my command term and it stayed until 61 Mech was disbanded in 2005.

It consisted of a vertical fighting dagger and yellow lightning-flashes, which symbolised the elements of skill at arms and valour on the battlefield, and embodied the principle of the lightning war, which has been defined as "a conflict conducted with lightning speed and force... a violent surprise offensive by concentrated air and ground force...in close co-ordination and designed to achieve victory in a minimum of time" Our motto was "Mobilitate Vincere", meaning "the destruction of the enemy through mobility" or, in simple soldierly language, "Mobility Wins".

The much coveted operational participation bar – which could be earned only by taking an active part in 61 Mech's operations – was a horizontal dagger with red lightning-slashes springing from its blade. I adapted this one myself from a proficiency badge I earned when I graduated from the Taiwanese special warfare course in 1973.

61 Mech also adopted a range of sub-unit shoulder flashes and emblems with the idea of promoting ownership, cohesion and esprit de corps at that level. The soldiers were

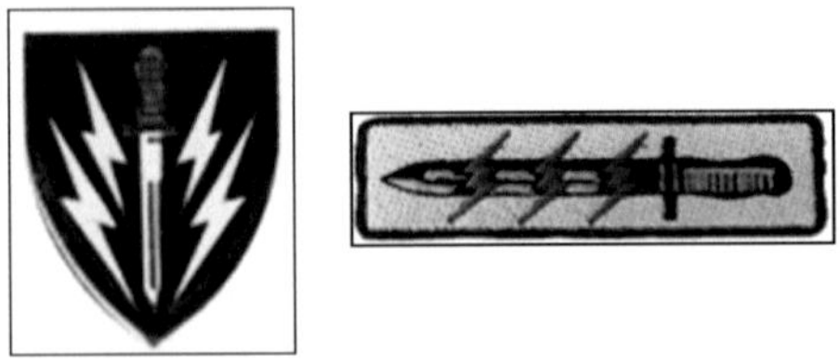

Figure 2: Badges and Insignia of 61 Mech and its Motto

extremely proud of their respective emblems and they were also displayed on their vehicles. Sub-unit commanders such as Captain Jan Malan, Captain Koos Liebenberg, Major Joe Weyers, Captain Bernie Pols, Major Giel Reinecke, Captain Hannes van der Merwe, Captain Cassie Schoeman, Captain C P du Toit, Major Jakes Jacobs and many others played an important role in designing these emblems from 1981 onwards.

Tricks of the Warfighting Trade – Keeping the Combat Edge Sharp

Simple battle procedures and deployment drills were instituted to enhance 61 Mech's overall operational efficiency and deployment. These included specific states of combat readiness – "March Ready" ("Marsgereed" in Afrikaans); "Combat Ready" ("Gevegsgereed"); and "Fire Ready" (Vuurgereed) – which could be communicated whether you were stationary or on the move, and by whatever appropriate means: verbally, by radio or by hand signals.

"March Ready" meant readiness to move from a designated position, either at a moment's notice or at a specified time, or denoted a specific operational grouping's readiness to move. "Combat Ready" meant that the unit or a sub-unit was fully prepared – weapons, equipment, communications and everything else – for a designated operation or action. "Fire Ready" meant that all weapon systems were locked, loaded and ready to fire.

As the SWATF's designated mobile reserve, 61 Mech customarily operated in rapid deployment mode and was on either 24-hour or three-hour stand-by, depending on what SWATF HQ deemed necessary. This meant that the unit had to be able to generate combat-ready mechanised forces for specified roles, tasks and operationally viable periods within the designated warning times and standby arrangements. Each sub-unit had its own staging area where the combat vehicles and other main armaments were permanently bombed up and ready to move at moment's notice.

I instituted stable parades ("stalparades") to push combat readiness to an almost extreme level. That involved continual inspection to ensure high levels of equipment care and the serviceability of weapons, vehicles and all other equipment required for maximum combat readiness and mobility. The participative premise of leadership was applied to stable parades, with every commander being physically involved with the cleaning and maintenance process. That included me – I normally placed myself under command of my driver for these tasks. I know that this made inroads on the military tradition that except in dire emergency the officer's role was to lead and supervise rather than become involved in the machinery, but that right brain of mine was at work again.

Everything would be unpacked, re-cleaned and inspected, with absolutely no detail neglected. Logbooks of all controlled items were filled in, checked and signed off. Where necessary, the tiffies of the Light Workshop Troop plucked engines out of the Ratels with "Yster" ("Iron"), their beloved recovery vehicle, and became so expert at it that they would have the massive lump of iron out in 20 minutes, and checked and back in place in another

25 (they were so good that when we went on operations we found they could do it in the bush as well). Integrated teams of troops and subordinate members carried out inspections, to make the point that everyone counted.

Then at the end of the day the inspection teams would provide feedback to the whole of 61 Mech – a grand affair in the bush, with boring maintenance and inspection chores made pleasant and culminating in a "bush braai", that beloved South African recreational ritual.

I placed a high premium on spiritual preparedness as well, and here our unit chaplain, Padre Koos Rossouw, and our sub-unit commanders played an exceedingly important role. What a man that Koos Rossouw was! He was not only a good preacher but had a slightly mischievous sense of humour and was a keen sportsman as well. All of this counted with our youngsters and contributed to his amazing rapport with them. Regular prayer parades were held, and every Sunday there was an 11am church parade in the mess hall at Omuthiya if we were not away in the operational area.

Sport and recreational outings added to the high morale of 61 Mech as well, because we firmly believed that all work and no play made soldiers dull fighters. Major Thys Rall, my second-in-command, organised regular bundu-rallies which were not only competitive but lots of fun as well, and took place amid much laughter, jostling and jesting. We also had our regular run, the 20 km "Ovambo Marathon", in which everyone participated – the commander not excluded!

Time permitting during those hectic days; we laid on some leisure outings for the troops. Our sub-units chose close-by venues such as the Etosha Game Reserve and the Olifantsfontein Dam, or visits to Tsumeb for a quick hour of essential shopping. Darts and volleyball were very popular and there was a good supply of soccer and rugby balls. We even organised an ice-cream machine, but unfortunately it was never operational, because it drew so much power that our generator was reduced to an ominous silence. Each man was entitled to two cold beers a day if he wanted them, and the Army's tightly-guarded coffers opened a crack to hand out special bush pay which was ample for our simple needs.

At times there would be individual "braais" in the unit lines, and the pleasant aroma of roasting meat and the chatter and laughter of the soldiers would waft through Omuthiya's trees on the evening breeze – all these little things contributed to the high morale of our unit; out there on our own in the night, behind the thick screen of the surrounding bush. We really were a band of brothers in our brown nutria battledress, entirely unto ourselves ... Marvellous!

Force Provision – Feeder Units

61 Mech's personnel feeder system was an interesting one. Its intakes came from sub-units provided by full-time training units located all over South Africa: 1 South African Infantry Battalion at Bloemfontein for mechanised infantry; 1 and 2 Special Service Battalions at Bloemfontein and Zeerust for the armour; and 14 Field Regiment at Potchefstroom for the artillery. Other corps training units provided the combat-support assets, such as the logistical, medical and signals components.

It was not, however, a composite unit in the accepted sense. A composite unit is usually assembled for a specific operation or exercise from whatever is available, with all that that implies in terms of teamwork and corporate identity. 61 Mech, on the other hand, was a permanent entity which took all its intakes and welded them into its own image before committing them to operations, starting on arrival at Omuthiya, where each new sub-unit was made mission and combat-ready for its anticipated operational tasks. That is vastly different to a hastily cobbled-together composite unit.

I made sure to maintain an excellent relationship with the commanders and staffs of the respective feeder units (not that difficult, since many of them were friends and colleagues who had worked side by side with me in the past). As a result, most of them viewed 61 Mech as the operational extension of their own units. This not only cemented our relationship but ensured that operational lessons learnt could be continuously evaluated and fed back to the training environments.

Operational Concepts and Leadership and Command Precepts Applied at 61 Mech

61 Mech played a significant role in my life, because it was an experience which allowed me to shape my future views about operational concepts, military leadership, command and management, which I finally put together in 1987 in my book on mobile warfare in Southern Africa, and thereby provided me with the privilege of contributing meaningfully to the development of operational concepts and doctrine for our army, the best in Africa (these concepts are explained in Chapters 5 to 8 of this book).

In a nutshell, we at 61 Mech firmly believed in the "train hard, fight easy" principle. I remember Captain Koos Liebenberg saying to me once at Omuthiya in 1981: "It seems to me that when we're not operationally deployed, or working on doing base development, or carrying out maintenance on our equipment, we're busy with SOP training and exercises with live ammunition."

That was a pretty good description of life at 61 Mech in my time. I enjoyed training; it allowed space for innovation, it was invigorating, it built spirit, rapport and self-confidence, and it provided valuable minutes in which I could interact meaningfully with my people. Moments I especially enjoyed were waiting for the men to finish practising clearing trenches with hand-grenades and small arms (the real thing – no dummies or blanks were used). You could smell and feel these moments. They were my dirty troops, satisfied troops, comfortable and relaxed in their adventurous achievements and skill at arms. These exercises afforded me the privilege of talking to, discussing, questioning and simply enjoying moments with 10 of them at a time. That was how training should be – fun, rewarding and uplifting, all rolled into one.

Our policy framework for training was based on conventional warfare, although we trained for counterinsurgency duties as well. This regularly included some focussed research and development on battle doctrine and force-employment concepts. We were therefore not only a "do-er" unit, but a thinking one as well. Our Standing Operating Procedure was a direct derivative of the evolving battle doctrine of the unit, contained in a yellow pocket book bearing the emblem of 61 Mech and signed by me. The motto on the SOP expressed an age-old truth: *Thorough planning and superb training saves lives.*

Official SA Army Pre-Emptive Attack Courses ("Voorsprongaanvalkursusse")

In addition to our normal role as a fighting unit the Chief of the Army also tasked 61 Mech to present a prestigious annual "Pre-emptive Attack Course" to selected Army officers and non-commissioned officers in 1981 and 1982. The purpose of the course was further preparation of the selected personnel for possible future deployment in similar operational circumstances.

The one-week course was strictly practical from start to finish, and was based on the operational experiences and doctrine of 61 Mech. Every course ended with a full-blown practical operational planning cycle and a strenuous mobile live-firing field exercise that was carried out over long distances. Both the courses were presented under the watchful eye of Colonel Willem Koekemoer of the Army's Training Directorate.

Sad to say, the first course was marred by a tragedy which touched us deeply, when 19-year old Rifleman Lionel van Rooyen was killed and 15 troops were wounded in a 120 mm mortar accident; all of them from Bravo Company. Both the Board of Inquiry that was held by the SADF and an official inquest by the Magistrate of Ondangwa found that nobody was to blame.

The 61 Mech Families

The families of 61 Mech's Permanent Force members were housed at Tsumeb, thanks to the town council and TLC, the mining corporation. Twelve families stayed in Langeberg mobile homes in a special area demarcated by the Town Council for 61 Mech and the mining corporation made available its beautiful recreation club, swimming pool and other sports facilities. Of course, there was also the excellent Minen Hotel, with a great pub and traditional German fare such as Eisbein, Kartoffelen and Sauerkraut – in fact, the Minen was adopted as the messing facility of the Air Force pilots who were brought in for the duration of the "Winter Games", the deep infiltration raids SWAPO mounted every April.

And let us not forget our 61 Mech babies. Here is a good story from my wizard "Log O", Major Giel Reinecke:

> My second child, Riekus, was born in the hospital at Grootfontein on 15 July 1982 at the time I served as the Logistics Officer at 61 Mech. Until today the name of my son reminds me of the two most fulfilling years of my military career, as well as Operation Meebos.
>
> More importantly, I can recall precisely how he was named. Towards the end of 1981 my wife became pregnant and the expected date of birth was somewhere in the middle of July 1982. There was no modern sonar scanning equipment available during those years to determine the sex of the baby. However, we were convinced that the second child would be a girl and never considered a name for a boy.
>
> 61 Mech deployed for Operation Meebos II on Sunday, 18 July 1982, and I was somewhat perturbed by the fact that my baby was not named yet and that Operation Meebos II was looming. My wife Maureen, who was a sergeant in the Army and the chief clerk of our unit, was as proud and dedicated as I was, and therefore understood my sentiments and the fact that I needed to go with my unit.
>
> In the early morning hours of the 15 July Maureen woke me up with the words 'it's time'. We left immediately for Grootfontein, and, lo and behold, to our surprise a boy was born ... but with no name. Four weeks after the birth the baby was still not registered and we still had not decided on a name.
>
> On Sundays the wives would gather at the Tsumeb rear headquarters for a quick chat over the radio with their husbands who were deployed in Angola. During this particular radio tête-à-tête our child was simply referred to as 'the Reinecke baby'. Our paymaster, Lieutenant Andy Weyand, soon visited us in Angola and brought some

parcels and mail from Tsumeb. Our command group was comfortably lounging on our camp chairs deep inside Angola, busy with our daily order group, when Weyand handed me a letter from my wife.

I immediately opened the letter, in which Maureen suggested two names for our now almost six-week-old boy. I simply had to make a choice so as to get our son's birth registered. Our commander, Commandant Roland de Vries, singled me out when he saw that my thoughts were not focussed. He said: 'Giel, why are you looking so worried – is something wrong?' I told him that the baby was not yet registered and it was necessary to inform my wife urgently about the name.

"Do you have any options for names?" he asked. "Yes." I replied, "Maureen suggested Riekus or Wynand." Immediately, in his typical style of participative management and the involvement of all Commandant de Vries called the attention of the leader group with the words: "Hey, you guys, Giel has a problem – his laaitie (son) doesn't have a name yet; he has two options – Riekus or Wynand – what do you say?" and pointed to the first member of the leader group.

Each member then responded with his choice. It was clear that the majority thought Riekus should be the preferred name. Roland de Vries promptly responded and said: "Signaller – inform Giel Reinecke's wife that the name of the baby is Riekus." That was it, problem solved.

On 25 August 2012 I addressed an assembly of 61 Mech veterans at the SA National War Museum in Johannesburg and told them the story about the naming of Riekus. My family was attending as well, and there was a spontaneous call from the gathering. It was my son Riekus: "Wowee, I'm a war baby from Southwest Africa!"

Riekus is extremely proud of his name today and specifically of how the naming came about. Today, when I think back to my two years at 61 Mech, together with my wife Maureen, my eldest son Michiel, who was only five years old then, and later Riekus, I realised what a magnificent unit we were. We were one family, working together, fighting together but also sharing in the joys of our families and children – even choosing their names."

The mere fact that our families were close-by was a valuable morale booster and force multiplier. Their support was cherished and dear to us. Among them we lived, worked and played as friends. We had our social events, formal and informal, and sometimes there was leave as well. We had our ups and downs, but nothing we could not handle. Places that the families occasionally visited were Windhoek, Swakopmund, Otjikoto Lake and the Etosha Game Reserve.

Some children went to boarding school, but most of them attended school in Tsumeb. My two children, Roland Junior and Elmarie, were among those schooled at Tsumeb. There were fine shops, an excellent hospital and good bretsjen (from the German Brötchen, traditional Namibian rolls, often served with various fillings or plain; like vetkoek to South Africans and doughnuts to the Americans. Many wonderful evenings were spent together relaxing at the "Buighuis" (our small unit pub) in Tsumeb. So life was good for our families as well – and every fighting soldier who has seen the amount of stress that even a small war can generate in a family will appreciate what I have just said.

Relationship with the Community

Our relationship with the community was exceptional. It was much more than just being friendly or mutually accommodating; it was more up front and personal than that. Mutual friendships were probably nurtured through the intimate relationships we shared with the area force units. These part-time force units, namely Etosha, Otavi and Grootfontein, were part and parcel of the community and they became part and parcel of 61 Mech as well. As such we celebrated successes and attended funerals together. There were always the prayers of the community and their tangible support for us when out on operations.

It did not matter whether our unit was inside or outside Angola, their friendship and caring remained, to the benefit of the few people of our unit who were sometimes left behind at Tsumeb and Omuthiya, and found themselves in the capable and generous hands of the community. At times we could reciprocate by holding the occasional magnificent parade through Tsumeb, or with social functions held at 61 Mech, which we did quite frequently. People such as Mr. Heinzie Hellwig, then mayor of Tsumeb, would officiate at these splendid parades, and at other times, we would invite the old German, South African or British World War II veterans to Omuthiya to share in our unit's splendour. Their combined esprit de corps and spontaneous singing were always tremendously appreciated; to us they were a prime example of the insight and wisdom of the elderly.

I had the privilege of having one German veteran, Feldwebel (sergeant-major) Robert Kaspar present his 1939 Iron Cross to me when my term at 61 Mech ended in January 1983. It was a gesture I appreciated tremendously, and of course I still treasure it, although "Uncle Robert" has long since marched off to join his comrades who died on the battlefield.

In 1983 Tsumeb bestowed the highest of all civic honours on 61 Mech, the freedom to march through its streets, as tradition has it, with swords drawn, drums beating, bayonets fixed and colours uncased – an accolade which dates all the way back to the walled cities of mediaeval Europe, whose rulers were very particular about which armed bodies were allowed to enter through their gates. By that stage I was a brand new colonel commanding the Training Wing at the Army Battle School after handing over to Commandant Gert van Zyl, but I had the honour of attending that proud and memorable day with my dear wife Henriette. The local newspapers wrote: "The death-blow of SWAPO shows its pride in Tsumeb".

Roll of Honour – We Will Remember Them

Chapter 9 of this book is dedicated to the memory of our comrades who fell or were wounded while serving in 61 Mech in 1981 and 1982, but this is a fitting place to note that three of our officers were decorated with the Honoris Crux for gallantry during that period: Major L.A. Anderson on 5 November 1981, during Operation Daisy; Lieutenant D.R. van der Westhuizen (posthumous) on 15 April 1982, during Operation Yahoo; and Second-Lieutenant S.S. Steyn on 30 July 1982, during Operation Meebos II – their individual stories are told in the relevant chapters.

Closure – Our Sons Were Warriors

I would like to make use of this chapter to acknowledge and pay tribute to the people I served with at 61 Mech. This includes the organisations and people who supported our unit in South West Africa, now Namibia. Their collective contributions made 61 Mech successful and kept our country safer such a long time. All of them played extremely important roles in holding the fort while the politicians were working towards a peaceful settlement in South Africa and Southern Africa.

This process, it should be noted, took place under severe external pressure which was exerted on South Africa by the United Nations and the international community. The process was advanced by the war in southeastern Angola in 1987 and 1988, the operational zone of which covered the whole operational area from Rundu to Ruacana on the northern border, which included well-known places such as Oshakati, Ondangwa, Calueque, Cahama, Jamba, Mavinga and Cuito Cuanavale.

It was a long, long war which was never officially declared, a war without winners or losers, because in the end the entire region scored and Southwest Africa achieved independence as a democratic republic without having first been turned into a charred, refugee-clogged wasteland. It remained intact throughout, so that the new nation got off to a good start, with a better infrastructure – made roads, dams, bridges, power stations, hospitals and everything else – than any other country in Africa except South Africa. All this happened because the armed forces carried out their laid-down function, which was to provide an atmosphere of relative peace and order in which the political process could run its course.

61 Mech played a significant and even decisive role in applying that function, and special credit, honour and recognition are due to the national servicemen in its ranks who served South Africa in the bundu, so far away from home. They, like their somewhat older colleagues of the Citizen Force and Commando Force, who were repeatedly called up for border service (especially in the early days, when we were thin on the ground), were the latest manifestation of a very old type of South African fighting man, the citizen-soldier, working hand in hand with his professional colleagues of the regular force.

They did sterling fighting work and soldiered like professionals in challenging and ferociously harsh operational environments which presented not only physical and psychological hardships, but also major challenges relating to overly adverse weather and difficult terrain conditions by both night and day. Many of the national servicemen I talked to in those days and later on in their lives found their work at 61 Mech rewarding, challenging and exciting. They were extremely proud of their regiment. My good friend Epp van Lill, who commanded 61 Mech in 1983, once said: "If you were with 61 Mech, you were there".

When I was a boy, one always looked up to men who had served in the Special Service Battalion, which had gained great renown in the 1930s and then during World War II, or those who wore an "8" on their Africa Service ribbon to show they had fought with the Eighth Army in the Western Desert. They are all gone now, but 61 Mech's men have stepped into their shoes.

So I look back now with pride on 1981 and 1982, when I commanded the regiment and its ranks of our young South African warrior sons, and 1987 and 1988, when I fought with them once again. And I think: What a great privilege, honour and joy God has afforded me!

I wish I could name all the good people who were taken up in the structures of 61 Mech over the many years. They were much more than cogs in a hierarchical organisation; they were a natural balance of ordinary people armed with rifles and thoughts and joy; who could become sullen at times because of lost ones, and at other times could cry without shame, because a real man need never be ashamed of honest tears. In my heart and mind all of them counted, and they still count today.

PART 2

War Stories – Forcing Heart and Nerve and Sinew

This was the period I developed my concept of mobile warfare for southern Africa and wrote my first book on the topic; one described by a renowned South African military historian as being significant for the time

I need to go back in history somewhat so as to get to my few war stories appraised in the following chapters. At the age of sixteen I saw the war clouds rising over South Africa during the Sharpeville tragedy in 1960 when the Sabre fighter jets flew provocatively over our school in Vanderbijlpark; when the worn shoes of those who had protested were left lying forlornly in the streets after the shots were fired and they had run off in disarray. In my adolescence throughout the sixties I saw a war caused through curfews and pass-laws, political turmoil, rioting and the sheer obstinacy of a government who dared not or did not want to listen ...

As a soldier I lived through the various stages of a drawn-out South African Border War which lasted close on twenty two years: From low-intensity counterinsurgency warfare in Rhodesia, South West Africa and southern Angola from 1966; through to escalation of the war through the eighties and eventually high-intensity conventional warfare in southern Angola in 1978-88; then finally the peacemaking following in southern Africa from 1988 onwards!

Part 2 is my story specifically of the time when the war started escalating and exploding into high-intensity warfare from 1979 until 1988. The epic conventional battle fought in southern Angola in 1987-88 became the turning point in politics and war which affected peacemaking in southern Africa from then on.

The Dialectics of War as I Saw It

Thesis, Anti-Thesis, Synthesis: Causes of War, Imperatives for Peace, Peace and Hope

Thesis: Immense provocations, angers and egos accompanied by the quest for power; for adversaries to have and to own regardless. The latter followed by a political and finally a military clash of wills. Then fighting with the heads and bodies of others for ideology and existence and so-called independence...

Anti-thesis: The will to have peace, to make peace, to find a way to get to a better form of peace by convincing and coercing friend and foe of the merits of a win-win situation. Encouragement processes of all kinds to achieve the goal of peace, to come to senses, to see the value of it to all and perhaps to learn from it...

Synthesis: Forced and unforced political and if necessary processes and peace talks leading to better forms of peace... perhaps... Shifted positions, endings and beginnings and hopes...

Will history repeat itself, filled with disillusionments instead of hopes ... ? Why don't we learn from history; instead of losing victories!

Overture to Chapter 5

On Terrain – An Amazing Phenomenon

Terrain, the landscape over which a battle is fought, forms the background of any military action. In any consideration of such actions, the sum total of the physical attributes of the theatre of war is of the greatest importance in helping to determine the planning and outcome of a battle – it often poses more formidable challenges than the enemy.

In a military action, terrain supports engagement at two basic levels, namely the strategic and the tactical. Strategic considerations ultimately determine decisions to engage in warfare, and are fundamental to the aims of a war. At the tactical level, however, terrain is analysed in terms of the execution of an operation or battle to determine how to employ it to defeat the enemy.

Physical terrain refers to the lie of the land and is used as a general term. Terrain includes key military factors such as spatial relationships; topography and drainage; geology and soils; vegetation; oceans and seashores; weather and climate; daylight and darkness; and gravity and magnetism.

However, human terrain factors – the aspects of geography resulting from human interaction with a given piece of terrain – also have an immense influence on warfare. Key military factors included in this aspect are racial and ethnic roots; population patterns; social structures; languages and religions; transportation networks; telecommunications and military installations. In its broadest sense thus, terrain is multi-disciplinary in nature.

Many military men have ignored the importance of terrain in planning and execution, and the result is that the history of arms is heavily populated with those who did so and were then condemned to pay a severe price for their neglect.[1]

1 Doyle, P. and Bennett, M.R.: *Fields of Battle: Terrain in Military History*; Wikipedia; and General (retired) John W. Vessey in the preface of *Military Geography for Professionals and the Public* by Collins, John M.

5

Terrain As We Knew It

The Neutral Factor

The African battle space allowed room for manoeuvre and protection from the enemy's searching eyes on high.

Preamble – Terrain and Warfare

Read the Ground and Understand

There is a pattern in everything. The wise commander identifies the pattern, finds the cracks in it, seeks out the chinks in the enemy's armour, and uses this accumulated knowledge to achieve victory in this regard. Analyzing terrain and using it cleverly is an engaging pursuit; combining it with manoeuvre is rapture. It was not for nothing that Sun Tzu stated in 500 BC that the secret lies in "attacking the enemy's plan". Or, in the words of the ballad singer Leonard Cohen, "there's a crack in everything, that's how the light gets in".[1] A thorough appreciation of terrain will illuminate those cracks to the perceptive soldier. It will allow him to see the light that seeps through; to discern what is, what is not and what has to be done to accomplish his vital mission. In short, the soldier must know the ground in every sense of the word.

To be able to read terrain and the enemy, and thus to understand varying operational situations, are the all-important factors for the field commander, and by this I mean mastering not only the physical terrain, as a neutral factor which can be used to his advantage, but also the psychological and sensory environments – "situational awareness", as the military describes it today.

There is no substitute for appreciating the battlefield beforehand and gaining a feel for the ground and for continuous observation and orientation of the terrain, even while on the move to determine what lies beyond the next tactical bound. Planning is elementary to action and the realisation of the excitement for manoeuvre – but prevention is better than a cure.

Situational awareness implies knowing, understanding and exploiting the relationships which exist between higher intentions, pre-ordained missions, the disposition of own forces, the enemy and friction de guerre. All these factors should be evaluated in the context of time and space within the ambit of unfolding events – all the time, night and day, through the disruptive and the undisruptive, unwholesome as well as wholesome surprises, the inglorious and glorious unforeseen occurrences.

You, rather than the enemy, should dictate unfolding events. Make the battlefield so fluid that the enemy can neither handle it nor build a coherent operating picture. Deception is an art of war; therefore exploit terrain well and in combination with ever-changing adaptations to the benefits of shifting positions and the rhythms of manoeuvre. Keeping

1 From the song "Anthem".

the enemy on his hind foot by being surprisingly different is the norm: seeking out and maintaining initiative and freedom of action; movement, fine-tuned timing, controlled dispersion and concentration in many ways provide the means.

The Western Sub-Theatre of War – Where the Killing Fields Were

The description of the terrain in this chapter relates to what the SADF[2] used to refer to as the "Western Sub-Theatre of War". The Caprivi Strip, situated to the east of this, will not be attended to.[3] The Angolans demarcated their areas of operation into "'Military Regions" while the South Africans called theirs "Sectors". Five areas of operation as military target areas will be further examined. They are:

- The Death Triangle south of the "Red Line" (the old quarantine control line against cattle diseases) in the Tsumeb, Otavi and Grootfontein region.
- The Cunene River Basin as a particularly important fighting arena situated in southern Angola, which included Cahama, Xangongo, Môngua and Ondjiva.
- The Area-In-Dispute within the Cunene Province, which the Angolans denoted the 5th Military Region.
- Mystical Southeastern Angola, labelled the 6th Military Region by the Angolans.
- The Western Front, covering Sector 10 in northwestern SWA/Namibia as well as the southwestern quarter of Angola's 5th Military Region.

Terrain and Warfare the African Way

The type of war that was fought in northern SWA/Namibia and southern Angola from 1966 until 1989 was of a revolutionary and counter-revolutionary nature for which the African battle space provided an excellent milieu. It was a war with clear communistic and political-military undertones – "peoples of all countries unite" as Mao Tse-tung would have propounded it. As such, it was a battle space with a myriad almost insurmountable problems for the environmentally inept – and as many challenges for the man who was not.

Ostensibly the aim of insurgencies in Africa has been the overthrow of colonial rule – although in fact the main colonial powers were happy from the 1960s onwards to rid themselves of what had become a financial burden. In the case of SWA/Namibia and South Africa, the *raison d'être* is even more obscure. In "liberation speak" the insurgency commonly known as the "Border War" went about the overthrow of a white minority government. In fact this was not so. On the contrary, South Africa strove from 1978 onwards and right through the 1980s to create conditions, in which a full-scale peaceful democratic transition could take place with the participation of all the population groups in SWA/Namibia, rather than step back and allow a full-scale armed communist take-over.

That these were the only choices cannot be denied. SWAPO was not overtly a communist organisation, but masses of Soviet propaganda material in its possession were captured in various cross-border raids, and as early as February 1978 SWAPO leader Sam Nujoma stated publicly in a television interview that when SWAPO came to power "the people will do away" with a variety of "traitors", including SWA/Namibians in the armed forces and "puppets" of the internal government.

Asked what would happen if a non-SWAPO popular independence government came to power, he replied: "The question of black majority rule is out. We are not fighting even for

2 South African Defence Force.

3 See Maps 1 and 2.

majority rule. We are fighting to seize power in Namibia, for the benefit of the Namibian people. We are revolutionaries. We are not counter-revolutionaries."

This being the situation, the opposing sides saw protracted war as the only way to accomplish political ends. The role of the SADF remained unchanged from beginning to end: to buy the time and ensure political stability while all the inhabitants of SWA/Namibia forged a democratic constitution which suited their needs. And in the end this aim was achieved in spite of extremely difficult internal and external conditions – political, economic, social and military.

The revolutionary form of warfare had been remarkably successful in the world, even when the insurgent movements had been defeated in Greece, the Philippines, Kenya, Malaya and elsewhere. The operational concepts applied by the respective belligerents in southern Africa during the Border War embraced mixtures of conventional, semi-conventional, unconventional, insurgency, counterinsurgency and guerrilla warfare, as well as downright dirty tactics.

In assessing the utilisation of terrain by belligerents during the South West African/Namibian Border War and Angolan civil war, the following should be borne in mind:

- South Africa's Border War was an arduous counter-revolutionary one which was fought internally and externally from 1966 until 1989. During a 22-year period the SADF had to dominate the northern border region of SWA and southern Angola. The SADF's approach was to follow the principles for conventional warfare and their reverse, the principles of revolutionary warfare.[4]
- SWAPO[5] was South Africa's main enemy during the Border War. Their combatants viewed southern Angola and SWA/Namibia as their operational domain. Heavily influenced and inspired by the proponents of protracted revolutionary warfare such as Mao Tse-tung, Vo Nguyen Giap and Che Guevara, SWAPO adopted a revolutionary armed struggle as its strategy and embraced the wily ways of the insurgent with immense reliance on the combination of suitable terrain conditions, nonconformity and guerrilla tactics.
- Then there were rather more than a few irksome enemies on one or other side of the list: The bedraggled conventional army of Angola, FAPLA,[6] the Cubans and their many Russian military advisors, which ardently supported SWAPO's revolutionary war, and in the process struggled and suffered endlessly to deny southern Angola to UNITA[7] and the SADF. Then there was UNITA, the potent guerrilla army of Dr. Jonas Savimbi, which was fighting its own liberation war against the Soviet-backed MPLA.[8] The UNITA fighters dominated large parts of northern, central and southeastern Angola and kept large numbers of the enemy widely dispersed and extremely busy, a great advantage to the South African counterinsurgency operations south of the border.

The vastness, the heavily bushed nature of the terrain and the general difficulty of using it suited the proponents of insurgency and guerrilla warfare as well as the exponents of manoeuvre, as the huge extended spaces of northern SWA/Namibia and Angola was

---

4 See Chapter 7.

5 The South West Africa People's Organisation.

6 *Forças Armadas Populares de Libertação de Angola.*

7 *União Nacional para a Independência Total de Angola* or National Union for Angola's Total Independence.

8 *Movimento Popular de Libertação de Angola* or People's Movement for the Liberation of Angola.

definitely not the place for positional warfare. Fortunately FAPLA and the Cuban forces favoured positional warfare; while the South Africans embraced the opposite. This gave the South Africans the winning edge in the field of battle.

The SADF's operations were conducted at any latitude, terrain and climatic region of northern SWA/Namibia and southern Angola, whether in the form of small-scale tasks (often contingency-driven) or large-scale deliberate armed actions. It was therefore essential that each and every soldier, his arms, equipment and fighting unit, as well as the command and control level, be ready and readily adaptable to meet any unforeseen event. Consequently it was crucially important for the SADF to develop dynamic leadership as well as vigorous methods, and acquire the means to master the harsh environmental and terrain conditions of the war zone – the enemy, heat, cold, humidity, mud, dust, rain, sweat, tears, joy, infections, and tropical diseases and their carriers, the ever-present flies or mosquitoes.

From beginning to end the African battle space provided all the belligerents with serious terrain and environmental challenges: poor road infrastructure and few access routes; long distances; difficult terrain to negotiate and fight through; difficult circumstances for logistical undertakings; minimal resources for sustainment; and major obstacles to cross. Add to these the fact that there were almost always numerous approaches to choose from; wide-open gaps and spaces through which to infiltrate; and endless cover from ground and air detection.

All these conditions and their effects could be either bothersome or beneficial. It could become challenging in the denseness and the darkness of Africa when a noisy fighting machine such as a large mechanised formation was used. This was especially true when fighting against a guerrilla enemy whose fighters could easily hide and was adept at running away in order to fight again another day.

The Lie of the Land – The Combat Zone in General

The Dominant Feature Was Fighting Space and the Bush

Northern SWA/Namibia and southern Angola possessed a harsh splendour, but it was not linked to either peace or freedom. Throughout the 1980s it was a place into whose thirsty sands much precious blood had seeped, willingly or unwillingly. The contested ground covered an enormous tract of territory, from east to west and on both sides of the border, from the Atlantic coast in the west, way past the magnificent Cuito Cuanavale River in the east.

The battle arena as we knew it was characterised by dense entangled African bush and enormous areas for manoeuvre. It was a sand-surfaced vastness which could swallow up large conventional formations as well as guerrilla armies. It could also stretch battle formations and logistical lines to unimaginable extents of vulnerability. Both danger and deliverance lurked in the shadows, waiting to pay a sudden visit to either friend or foe. Surprise could surge into exhilaration or alarm, regardless of the sweltering African heat and humidity or whether it was day or night.

The nature of the terrain in the fighting space that straddled the SWA/Namibian-Angolan border favoured deep operations, controlled dispersion and timeous concentration of forces. In the natural fighting medium of the African bush, smaller forces could successfully engage numerically superior mechanised forces and win through manoeuvre. The dense bush and overhead foliage had an added advantage. It provided a means for shrouded manoeuvres and adequate cover against hostile aircraft. The battle theatre, therefore, suited both mobile conventional and African-style guerrilla warfare.

Infrastructure was sparse. The few towns and roads in the area were susceptible to attack by any means and from any direction. Tarred roads in southern Angola were a rarity. One of these extended from Lobito on the Atlantic coast westwards to Menongue and Cuito Cuanavale, another from the port of Namibe through Lubango, across the bridge at Xangongo to Ondjiva and then to the border post at Santa Clara-Oshikango. South of Oshikango it became a fair gravel surface as far as Ondangwa. A main tarred highway reached out northwards from Windhoek as far as Ruacana in the west and Rundu in the east.

Tarred roads were fairly safe, but the few gravel roads in the operational area were easily mined, and passing vehicles sometimes ran into ambushes whose perpetrators lurked in the abundant vegetation along the verges. The safest way to get somewhere was to follow bush trails (where they existed) or open up new ones by "bundu-bashing", with men and machines thrashing their way through the thickest bush imaginable at a rate of 12-15 km an hour, night or day, a process that used up valuable time and energy, especially when the bundu-bashers consisted of a battle group moving in a single column approximately 45 to 55 km long.

Navigation in the flat Angolan bushveld was difficult, especially up to the mid-1980s: the main navigational instrument was still the traditional hand-held prismatic compass, which required frequent halts while the navigator walked ahead of the lead vehicle for about 30 metres and took a bearing, a maddening, endlessly repeated ritual. Night bundu-bashing was actually easier, because one could navigate by the stars, and in addition, it was cooler, there were fewer flies tormenting one, it was less dangerous and there were less hostile enemy aircraft to worry about.

Such was the backward state of bush manoeuvring in the earlier days – yet the South Africans became quite good at it during both day and night movement (they also developed superlatively tough transport vehicles, some of which are still in service today). As the 1980s ground on, the SADF acquired early satellite-navigation systems, but they were cumbersome and slow, and the prismatic compass did not disappear from the inventory.

Bush travel had some positive aspects – on the Angolan side there were many large and small rivers from which to pump clean, crystal-clear water for men and vehicles, and the sandy soil was easy to dig into for protection against hostile ground and air attack.

This was the terrain that made positive control of moving mechanised formations and the tight co-ordination and control of indirect-fire weapons such as artillery and mortars so difficult. Achieving the desired result required firmly established and continuously practised standing operating procedures. There was an SOP – carefully tailored to the requirement and intensively practised – for almost every contingency. Carefully worked out radio procedures allowed the sharing of information and the issuing of quick orders, precision engagement and rapid action; observation-orientation-decision-action was the drill and the norm.

At one time during Operation Modular in 1987 the South Africans' G-5[9] guns brought down accurate shelling on FAPLA forces crossing the Chambinga River with fire being adjusted by means of several relay stations, which at times used different languages

9 A 155 mm calibre howitzer/gun developed by South Africa and employed with great success later phases of the war.

(the South African and SWA/Namibian forces were a polyglot bunch speaking at least a dozen home languages) to make things that little bit more difficult for whomever might be listening in.

Occasionally the South African commanders in the fighting line used short pauses in the battle to come together, quickly re-assess an operational situation, discuss a change of mission or situation and issue new orders; then the forward movement would start again. Now and again fire-and-movement took place in such close proximity to the enemy that fighting vehicles and foot-soldiers got mixed up with one another, so periodically the South African commanders would withdraw their forces under fire to regroup, re-organise and attack again.

Another challenge was the difficulty in indicating the forward line of own troops, or FLOT, so that the Air Force could provide close support. The normal way of doing this is to throw smoke grenades of a specific colour, but frequently the battlefield would be shrouded in dust, wood-smoke from burning undergrowth or smoke thrown to indicate targets or extraction points. As a result it was all too easy for aircraft to bomb or rocket the wrong target. This happened quite a few times with the Angolan Air Force, with the South Africans helping the confusion by deliberately dropping smoke on to the FAPLA positions as target indicators for the MiGs[10] (this practice was possible because the South Africans had devised an efficient interception system that they could monitor the enemy's radio traffic around the clock in real time).

Variations in the terrain provided the opportunity to set up positions for a number of purposes, for example to delay, protect or defend. In the mountainous west, the passes, frequent high ground, undulating terrain and natural obstacles such as rivers could be put to good use: Operations were normally undertaken where the terrain forced channelling of enemy forces; high ground provided tactical bounds and firm bases for attack, or positions from where the enemy could be observed and supporting fire could be delivered by direct-fire weapons.

The huge fighting space on either side of the border was divided naturally into sprawling manoeuvre sectors which extended from SWA/Namibia across into Angola.[11] These manoeuvre spaces allowed for the exploitation of a full carte du jour of fighting schemes which included the offensive and defensive mobile battle; positional defence; counterinsurgency and special operations; unconventional tactics; deception ploys and guerrilla warfare. Within its protective folds and cover the potential existed to hide away or engage the enemy from unexpected directions by following carefully selected shrouded approaches.

The types of manoeuvre sectors in southern Angola were well-defined by a number of magnificent African rivers. Taking the general features of terrain into consideration, the manoeuvre areas discussed below could be identified. These sectors could be traversed from either side of the border, or forces could cross over from one to the other to evade danger or strike at viable targets.

The Western Manoeuvring Sector was situated to the west of the Cunene River and stretched all the way to the Atlantic Ocean. It was hemmed in by the Cunene to its east and south, and an inhospitable mountain range to its west. The Angolan forces used the

10 A fighter aircraft of Soviet origin. During the Border War the South African forces had to contend with various models of this efficient aircraft, namely the MiG-19, the MiG-21 and the MiG-23.

11 See Map 3.

harbour at Namibe for logistics and the embarkation of reinforcements for their Southern Front, but both Namibe and the port of Lobito to its north were more susceptible to attack by air or sea than by land; their isolation made them ideal for raids and sabotage by the South African special forces.

Inland the mighty Cunene River flowed from Matala in the north via Xangongo towards Calueque, presenting a significant natural obstacle to mechanised forces. It also contained crocodiles, to be noted by those daring to swim it. The Cunene was a formidable natural obstacle, problematic to cross and therefore easy to defend or to cut off opposing forces. Downstream from Calueque, near Rundu, the mighty river plunges over a waterfall and surges westwards till it eventually breaches the Atlantic coastline as the border between Angola and SWA/Namibia; mechanised forces moving southwards or eastwards from either Lubango or Cahama were funnelled towards the only permanent crossing sites at Calueque or Xangongo.

Attack or evasion lines, either into or out of the Western Manoeuvring Sector, or SWA/Namibia for that matter, came via these choke-points. For any force which needed to attack the defences at Xangongo straddling the Cunene River and guarding the bridge, it made sense to attack simultaneously from the west and the east – which is exactly what happened during Operation Protea in 1981, but more about that later...

The Central Manoeuvring Sector was located between the Cunene and Cubango Rivers, and constituted a potential manoeuvre area that extended almost into unbounded space. It included the Death Triangle inside SWA/Namibia and stretched all the way northwards across the border to beyond Techamutete, Cassinga and Indungo, way past the strategically important railway line leading from the Atlantic coast to Menongue near the border. One could either walk or travel by South African six-wheeled Ratel or Russian Ural[12] truck from Tsumeb in the south to Techamutete in the north, 475 km away, passing by urban centres such as Ondangwa, Ondjiva and Cuvelai (for an Angolan this was strictly theoretical, but not for South Africans during the time they actually controlled south-central Angola). The few smaller rivers in this sector, such as the Cuvelai, could easily be crossed at a variety of places. In this way enemy defensive positions could be skirted effortlessly and at will.

The Central Manoeuvring Sector was extremely important to the SADF because it provided almost limitless space for insurgency and guerrilla warfare, and also housed SWAPO's highest density of strategic and operational bases. After Operation Protea in September 1981[13] the SADF did not withdraw as it usually did after an external operation, but stayed on and dominated what came to be known as the "Area-In-Dispute" with its counterinsurgency forces until mid-1984; the South Africans' ceaseless patrolling effectively denied free movement by both the Angolans and the insurgents, and greatly hampered the activities of both.

What was the influence of terrain if a conventional enemy should threaten the territorial integrity of northern SWA? Certainly the following:

- A conventional foe could strike from Cahama via the river-crossing at Calueque or even thrust directly southwards from Xangongo and Ondjiva without encountering any natural hindrances. For that matter, a determined enemy force could attack southwards on many fronts, considering the available manoeuvre

12 A six-wheeled medium truck of Soviet origin regularly employed for the transportation of materiel and troops but also used as gun tractor and carriage of the BM-21 multiple rocket launcher.

13 See Map 5.

space and few natural obstacles.

- On the other hand, there was ample space for mobile defence and a subsequent counter-offensive from SWA/Namibia. The first truly defendable terrain hinged on an intimidating mountain range covered with near-impenetrable bush in the Tsumeb-Otavi-Grootfontein district, some 350 km to the south of the SWA-Angola border.
- By this time the enemy's MiGs already reigned supreme in the skies over the northern border region. The enemy therefore had free rein in choosing to attack any of the military forces and installations inside SWA/Namibia, including Calueque, Ruacana, Oshivello, Grootfontein, Oshakati, Ondangwa and Rundu.

In May 1988 the comfort of having defendable terrain in depth became essential for the SADF's mobile defensive scheme. This was when the South Africans were confronted with an uncomfortable surprise[14] in the form of the Cuban 50th Division of Havana. All of a sudden, manoeuvring space to the rear and flanks and the high grounds to the south became viable options to fall back on if it became necessary to entice the enemy into mobile defence on home ground.

The Eastern Manoeuvring Sector lay between the Cubango River in the west and the Cuito Cuanavale River in the east. The strategic hamlet of Cuito Cuanavale and its bridge, which are situated far north in this sector, could be attacked from the west through this particular manoeuvre sector or from the east via the Far Eastern Manoeuvring Sector across the Cuito River. Alternatively it could be attacked from both sides. Furthermore, this manoeuvring sector could be partitioned by controlling the crossing over the Longa River on the main road leading from Menongue to Cuito Cuanavale – and the SADF and UNITA forces had freedom to move in from the south to do just that.

The Eastern Manoeuvring Sector was the ideal manoeuvre area to be exploited by deep raiding forces tasked to threaten the enemy's critical 198 km-long logistical route from Menongue in the west to Cuito Cuanavale in the east. No wonder the Russian writer of a book[15] about the FAPLA-Soviet-Cuban coalition forces in this area gave it the appropriate title of "Bush War – The Road to Cuito Cuanavale".

The Far Eastern Manoeuvring Sector was located within Angola's 6th Military Region and to the north of the SADF's Sector 20 and the SWA-Angola border. Its eastern and western boundaries were respectively defined by the Cuito Cuanavale River and the Cuando River. This sector was UNITA's "liberated area" and contained its sought-after strongholds at Mavinga and Jamba. In the final phases of the war (1987 to 1988) the Far Eastern Manoeuvring Sector became the combat zone for an epic conventional battle fought between FAPLA and UNITA, the latter strongly supported by the SADF. To the South Africans it became known as Operations Modular, Hooper and Packer.[16]

The Far Eastern Manoeuvring Sector was nearly uninhabited, although some civilians could be found in the inconsiderable settlement of Cuito Cuanavale[17] in the northwestern

14 Explained in Chapter 16.

15 'Bush War – The Road to Cuito Cuanavale': was edited by Gennady Shubin and Andrei Tokarev and first published in Moscow in 2007.

16 Refer to Chapter 15.

17 Although Cuito Cuanavale is situated on the western bank of the Cuito Cuanavale River and thus falling within the Eastern Manoeuvring Sector, this hamlet together with the Tumpo area on the opposite side of the river formed a strategic defence complex located in and of significance for two manoeuvring sectors.

quarter of this contested area, where the Cuanavale River flowed into the Cuito. From here the Cuito River surged south to meet the Cubango River close to Rundu and form the Okavango River. The town of Cuito Cuanavale with its unsteady rickety bridge and strategically important airfield lay at the eye of a warring "'firestorm", because it became the ideal bridgehead and jumping-off point for the FAPLA and Cuban southward offensive into Savimbi's liberated zone in August 1987. Its handful of civilian inhabitants, let it be said, suffered greatly because of their village's unfortunate location.

The FAPLA-Cuban coalition force was logistically supported from Menongue and other important military bases in the west. This included the construction of fighter aircraft bases from where the Cuban MiGs could operate under adequate radar coverage. Rundu was located just south of the SWA-Angola border on the banks of the Okavango River. It was home to the military headquarters of the SADF's Sector 20. Rundu also housed the forward combined headquarters of the combined brigade-sized SWA/Namibian and South African task force operating inside southeast Angola, and was one of the forward strategic bases from where the South Africans developed their counter-offensive against FAPLA and the Cubans into southeast Angola.

The SAAF's transport aircraft and Mirage jet fighters could operate from its forward airfields, and lethal attacks on Angolan and Cuban ground forces were carried out almost on a daily basis, although the SAAF pilots had to fly outside their own radar coverage and rely on their usual flair and tactical efficiency to carry out their missions and come back to tell the tale. From Rundu a succession of ground convoys and transport aircraft supplied UNITA's guerrilla forces and the South Africans at Mavinga and Jamba, both of which had gravel airstrips of immense tactical value; transport flights were carried out mostly at night, due to the-ever present Angolan and Cuban air threat.

A few statistics might help readers to understand what this air-bridge operation implied. Mavinga was located about 150 km southeast of Cuito Cuanavale and 250 km from Rundu as the crow flies. Jamba was 310 km southeast of Mavinga, hidden away in the furthest southeastern corner of Angola. The South African brigade's administrative area, which was well-camouflaged against enemy air and ground observation, was located close to Mavinga and its important airstrip.

To the east of Cuito Cuanavale, along the banks of many of the rivers, countless bones and skulls of Angolan government soldiers were literally scattered around in the bush, an eerie, macabre sight. The skeletal remains were the unburied relics of violent clashes between the South Africans and UNITA against FAPLA and the Cubans in the not- too-distant past, and which were due to be repeated in these same killing-fields in 1987 and 1988.

But for a few derelict Portuguese houses at Mavinga and the gravelled "Old Portuguese Road" which linked Cuito Cuanavale with Mavinga, the Far Eastern Manoeuvring Sector was relatively devoid of infrastructure, and the Old Portuguese Road was deserted and desolate, although it was the only road of any significance in the vicinity – no-one used it any more because it was rotten with mines. It inspired the same eerie feeling as the boneyard nearby, as if it still retained the echoes of all the fighting it had seen.

Another strangely disquieting thing was the absence of any bird or animal life. This was probably due to the legacy of the many Portuguese hunting expeditions in the distant past which had plundered the country's wild-life, followed by years of rampant poaching, probably to help to pay for UNITA's war effort, or perhaps simply as self-indulgence.

During 1987 and 1988 the skies above southeast Angola were constantly filled by the howl of Russian MiGs flown by Angolan and Cuban pilots, scanning the ground rushing by below them for signs of the South Africans and UNITA; a nerve-wracking, ever-present sound. The MiGs searched for us in comfortable awareness of the fact that they had adequate radar coverage and that their more modern aircraft out-gunned and out-performed our Mirages.

This, then, was what FAPLA's and UNITA's contested area was like. The Cubans and South Africans were engaged in a clash of wile, muscle and will in one and the same battle, fighting on the same terms, in the same area and on the same stage. Southeast Angola was a most perilous and dangerous killing-field. What happened here, however, provided hope for peace in the future – if only the belligerents were prepared to learn from the past ...

Within these manoeuvring sectors, as I have said, major rivers and a mountain range formed natural obstacles, especially for mechanised forces. These choke-points – the bridges, the drifts or fords, the defiles and passes – which had to be used dramatically increased levels of vulnerability. A mechanised-cum-motorised column, 220 vehicles in single file could take more than three hours to pass any given point on the ground at an approximate speed of 12-15 km/h, which was time enough for deliberate or surprise attacks by ground troops, close-support aircraft or indirect fire at the time of maximum vulnerability.

Negotiating a defile or drift, therefore, had to be planned and executed meticulously, or the death and destruction would be catastrophic. This happened many a time when the enemy was crossing the Cuito, Cuanavale, Lomba and Chambinga Rivers in October-November 1987; and the SADF had a close call itself on 26-27 July 1988: while disengaging its combat force from southwest Angola it was nearly cut off by the enemy's advancing tanks at the crossing site over the Cunene River, close to Calueque.18

To compound the problem, few crossing-places in southern Angola remained in a sound or even just usable state. They were clogged with wrecked vehicles from the earlier fighting, crisscrossed by trenches and riddled with unmarked mines. Mechanised forces were channelled carefully over such precarious crossings, with the logistical line stretched to gossamer thinness. Alternative crossings required extreme efforts by military engineers on all sides – the Angolans had a number of mobile bridges, minelayers and mine-breaching equipment as well as amphibious armoured fighting vehicles for eventualities, but the SADF was very short of such equipment.

Crossing sites of high strategic and tactical value were vital for defence and vulnerable to attack, and naturally assumed immense strategic and tactical importance. They were clearly marked on all military maps and became the subject of regular ground and aerial reconnaissance.19 Many of them were permanently guarded, protected or defended by either the enemy or the South Africans.

The following vital choke-points influenced the methods and means of warfare in southern Angola and the northern border region of SWA/Namibia.

- The furthest to the west was the Leba mountain pass, on the road between the port of Namibe and the regional capital, Lubango.
- Five vital choke-points allowed entry into either the Western or Central Manoeuvring Sectors across the Cunene River. From south to north they were the two bridges close to Calueque; the 800-metre span at Xangongo, approximately 72 km to the north of the SWA-Angola border (which was demolished by the

18 Refer to Chapter 16.
19 See Map 3.

SADF during Operation Protea in September 1981[20]); the crossing at Quiteve, 95 km upstream from Xangongo; and the crossing at Matala, 200km upstream from Quiteve.

- The Central Manoeuvring Sector could also be entered from the east by crossing the Cubango River bridge at Caiundo.
- Then there was the strategic bridge located at Cuito Cuanavale, which linked the Eastern and Far Eastern Manoeuvring Sectors (In 1987 and 1988 it was this bridge that the fighting was all about and that drastically depleted opposing soldiers and their military hardware by the numbers; in this sense the bridge served its purpose well.)
- Other choke-points of tactical importance which did not, however, form links between neighbouring manoeuvring sectors were at the Chambinga River, on the way to Mavinga from Cuito Cuanavale; at the Lomba River in the south, close to Mavinga, where the Old Portuguese Road crossed over; and at the Longa River, on FAPLA's strategic logistical route, almost half-way between Menongue and Cuito Cuanavale.
- For the SADF to serve the battle arena it had to negotiate the Cubango River at Rundu, travel north-northeast for 60 km through the southern tip of the Eastern Manoeuvring Sector and then cross the Cuito River over the Bailey bridge the field engineers had built at the M'Pupa Falls. From this crossing site a make-shift bush road, harrowing for man and machine, extended north-northeastwards to Mavinga.

Extended Logistic Lines by Air, Land and Sea

Southern Angola's difficult terrain, vast distances and harsh environmental conditions seriously taxed the day-by-day sustainment of military forces in the field. This is, needless to say, a matter of cardinal importance; if a military force cannot be adequately and appropriately sustained, it loses combat power, momentum and eventually the will to fight. This happened many a time to the enemy, and sometimes to the SADF as well, for example, during the conventional operations in southeast Angola in 1978-88 the logistical support of the South African brigade was so gravely affected[21] that its momentum waned.

The Enemy Situation: At the strategic level it was important to note that the enemy did not lack supplies of modern land or air combat systems. From 1984 onwards there was an unstoppable flow of men and materiel right up to Cuito Cuanavale in the east and Cahama in the west. The actual logistics of the flow of supplies and heavy armaments were very difficult, but the recipients at the front had the comfort of knowing that they were being backed by serious heavies such as the USSR, East Germany, Scandinavia and Cuba.

In addition to pouring in masses of men and materiel through the evenly spaced chain of harbours at Luanda, Lobito and Namibe[22], the coalition's supporters built well-developed forward airfields at places such as Lubango, Cahama, Menongue and Cuito Cuanavale for the use of their efficient Soviet Antonov and Ilyushin cargo aircraft. Sometimes their external supply lines were adjusted to terminate at Dar es Salaam in Tanzania, for pragmatic reasons and also because of a potential threat environment, especially the chance of South

20 Refer to Chapter 12.

21 Refer to Chapter 15 and 16.

22 Previously known as Moçâmedes.

African special forces operations. From Tanzania the supplies were then taken overland to Angola by rail and road. Once in Angola, the supplies were distributed to the enemy's Southern Front by air, rail and road.

Namibe, the southernmost Angolan harbour, was a strategic point in the logistical lifeline which sustained the Southern Front – particularly as regards fuel and spares, the lifeblood of the large Cuban-FAPLA mechanised force deployed in southern Angola, but it had certain drawbacks. For one thing, it was isolated, quite near the SWA/Namibian-Angolan border, which meant there was always a danger of air and seaborne SADF assaults. Then again, the route to the Southern Front's Lubango-Cahama-Ondjiva area was a difficult one. The landed supplies had to be transported by road through the most difficult mountain passes imaginable, and were vulnerable to attacks by both the South African special forces and UNITA's guerrilla.

The other main enemy supply route to Ondjiva in south-central Angola ran from Luanda in the far north. It was long and arduous, and the South Africans and UNITA knew very well that FAPLA's supply-line troops were far less able to protect themselves adequately than the regular combat forces (who never really impressed us either, incidentally).

The enemy's way of providing logistical support to their front-line troops was arduous, time-consuming and often downright hazardous to themselves. Convoys crawled at a snail's pace along beaten tracks, usually with screening forces deployed on foot in open formation for protection. During Operation Modular in 1987-88 for example, the rear areas at Cuito Cuanavale were protected by a full brigade, while another brigade was used to ferry supplies over 189 km from Menongue to Cuito Cuanavale.

This was what the terrain and the nature of the threat forced the enemy to do, in the process making them utterly vulnerable to any form of land or air attack. To the South Africans, deep operations meant the disruption, dislocation and binding of enemy forces where the juicy strategic targets lay.

The South African Situation: For the SADF it was a gigantic challenge to support its massive combined counterinsurgency force in SWA/Namibia and southern Angola. The SADF and SWATF[23] deployments, such as those in Sector 10 and 20, were supported by air and ground assets from Pretoria and Windhoek via Grootfontein, Ondangwa and Rundu.

Grootfontein was the main general support base in SWA/Namibia. It was established in 1975, when Operation Savannah, South Africa's first incursion into Angola, made it clear that a conveniently situated base to support operations in northern SWA/Namibia was needed. The muddy sprawl of tents of 1975 – "Camp Swampy", as its temporary inhabitants soon dubbed it – swiftly grew into a large, well-planned and neatly laid out multi-functional installation.

Strategically located in the communication zone between Pretoria and Windhoek and the northern border region, it was also home to the Northern Logistic Command and a large SAAF base. Grootfontein was the nodal point for supply, technical repair, maintenance, transportation and medical care to both the front and rear; it contained a number of impressive logistical, technical and medical installations, and had its own busy railhead which effectively linked it to the national South African system. Supplies and war material received from Pretoria and Windhoek, were organised, managed and distributed northwards to the operational areas such as Sector 10 (Oshakati), Sector 20 (Rundu) and

23 South West Africa Territorial Force.

Sector 70 (Katima Mulilo) – munitions, fuels, lubricants, spares, dry rations and other consumables, equipment and clothing.

Grootfontein also became a mobilisation centre and transit camp, from where drafts of troops or entire units for major operations such as Protea in 1981, Modular in 1987 and Prone in 1988 were received, administered and dispatched to the "sharp end". Reinforcements mustered for major operations would arrive at Grootfontein by air in phalanxes of SAAF Hercules C-130 and Transall C-160 aircraft[24], mainly from Waterkloof Air Force Base in Pretoria, without any fear of enemy interference.

Carting tons of materiel over vast distances to support the combined SADF combat forces during external operations into southern Angola was a difficult undertaking. For example, during Operation Modular in October-December 1987[25] it was necessary to set up a large, well-dispersed Formation Administrative Area or FAA to supply the South African front-line brigade close to Mavinga and its vitally strategically important gravel airfield, which was also home to UNITA's Eastern Front headquarters. At night the FAA was a veritable beehive of activity, with a stream of C-130s and C-160s landing and taking off.

In addition to air supply there was also an extremely busy road traffic link. From Rundu the earth-bound logistical umbilical cord extended through Mavinga to the forward edge of the battle area by way of a harrowing network of roads pummelled out of the bush by a combination of bundu-bashing and sheer tenacity. To get from Rundu to Mavinga meant a horrendous 356 km by bush track, then another 120 km to 150 km to reach the front-line troops, wherever they might be – sometimes it was possible to arrange a rendezvous while they were temporarily halted, but mostly they had to be caught up with on the move.

Ammunition, fuel, lubricants, wheels, engines, axles, spare parts, batteries, rations ... There seemed to be no end to the struggle to feed the sharp end's ever-hungry maw (a major challenge was posed by the G-5 guns and the Valkiri MRLs[26], which were expending ammunition as if there were no tomorrow). Officers and men subsisted on their 24-hour ration packs, with fresh food no more than a distant dream, although they could console themselves with the knowledge that an exquisitely organised and managed medical support system would take care of them if they were wounded or fell ill.

Casualties were treated in and just behind the fighting line, and high-priority cases were flown out at night by helicopters from anywhere in the field and taken to the nearest forward airfield, then loaded on fixed-wing aircraft for transport to the appropriate base hospital. In one celebrated case a critically wounded sergeant was flown direct to 1 Military Hospital in Pretoria as the sole passenger in a big C-130.

Strangely enough, the belligerents more or less left each other's strategic logistical arrangements well alone, with no real inclination to undertake large-scale air and naval operations or interdictions at the strategic level. Perhaps the reason for this was to make sure that the fighting did not arouse too much anger in the breasts of the major world powers which were sponsoring either the Angolans or (very discreetly) South Africans, not to mention the fact that there was never any sort of formal declaration of war.

And so the Angolan/Cuban conventional land or air forces never tried to attack into SWA/Namibia to interfere with or disrupt the SADF's internal communications

24 South African Air Force.

25 See Chapter 12.

26 The Valkiri was a South African-developed self-propelled multiple rocket launcher system using 127 mm rockets. An improved version called the Bateleur is now in service.

or logistics. Even during operations inside Angola the SADF's external lines of logistics, communications and rear areas were rarely harassed. To any impartial observer this obvious neglect by the enemy was astounding. The South African Navy, interestingly enough, operated freely along the South African, Mozambican and Angolan coasts without noteworthy enemy encounters – a gap which was exploited many a time to insert special forces raiding groups for strategic operations far to the rear of the enemy's Angolan fronts.

Air Bases and Radar Coverage

In respect to the front line, the enemy's air force operated from airfields located at places such as Luanda, Namibe, Lubango, Cahama, Xangongo, Ondjiva, Menongue and Cuito Cuanavale. The SADF's main operational air bases were at Waterkloof at Pretoria, Rooikop at Walvis Bay, Windhoek, Grootfontein, Ondangwa and Rundu, with smaller airfields and helicopter landing zones at Oshakati, Oshivello, Tsumeb, Ruacana, and Katima Mulilo, and at most of the forward operational bases, such as Nkongo.

The enemy's radar installations at Cahama, Menongue and Cuito Cuanavale caused major distress for the SAAF[27] and the ground forces operating inside southern Angola: The enemy had much better radar coverage over the combat zone across the border than the SADF, although the SAAF had adequate coverage in the border region from their radars deployed at Ondangwa and Rundu, as well as mobile radar systems which could be deployed elsewhere as required.

Geology and Soils

Africa being Africa, the nature of the soil in the combat zone was of great and even obsessive interest, at least to the South Africans. The greater portion of northern SWA/Namibia and southern Angola is overlaid by sandy soils, varying in depth from thin layers above layers of silt or clay to deep layers of up to 150 metres in many areas. The areas close to the Angola/SWA border and within southern Angola are notorious for their highly penetrable sands, which are several metres deep. Towards the Kaokoveld and the coast in the west the terrain contains rocky outcrops as well as the usual sand. Directly north of the border, where most of the post-1975 battles were fought, the terrain was characterised by deep layers of sandy soil and some rocky outcrops and clayey depressions.

The sandy terrain had several significant implications – some favourable and others not, depending on one's point of view. Landmines were quick and easy to plant, and camouflaging afterwards did not pose problems for the skilled mine-layer; foot-soldiers became exhausted much more rapidly when traversing sandy terrain; effective tracking could be done if proper anti-tracking measures were not taken; vehicles were put under tremendous strain in deep loose sand, especially in wet conditions; ordinary artillery shells penetrated the sand deeply enough to reduce the shrapnel coverage; and digging trenches with ordinary light entrenching tools was relatively easy. South of the Red Line again, towards Tsumeb, Otavi and Grootfontein, soil conditions were remarkably different, firmer and with much less sand.

27 South African Air Force.

Dominant Geographical Positions

The soldier evaluates terrain in terms of its strategic and tactical value, classifying it as usable terrain, key terrain or vital terrain. Ground features can also be used to observe and fire from, mask forces or mask one's surreptitious movement. During the Border War strategic, operationally and tactically dominant positions took many forms and served many purposes. At the strategic level, one example was the occupation of SWA/Namibia by South Africa to keep communist forces at bay in southern Africa. Another was the dominant role Soviet Russia and Cuba played in Africa, especially Angola, as part of their Cold War aims. At the operational level of war the SADF controlled the central part of southern Angola (the Area-In-Dispute) to counter the external revolutionary onslaught by SWAPO more effectively.

At the tactical level, for example, and even operationally and strategically for that matter, controlling the bridges at Xangongo and Cuito Cuanavale was of immense importance for both sides. Many a time the fighting hinged on dominant geographical positions for the sheer benefit of manoeuvre, rather than merely for the sake of holding ground. Which it was depended on what the forces concerned wanted to achieve.

Ground can be held simply for the sake of holding it, the result being tactically inflexible positional warfare. On the other hand, manoeuvre warfare relies on making use of vital ground or key terrain in any one of many ways – exerting influence on the battlefield through observation or fire; threatening it and thereby forcing the enemy to divert resources in case of an attack; or actually attacking and capturing it, then denying it to the enemy. Alternatively, a manoeuvre force can make nonsense of a positional defence by simply bypassing key or vital terrain.

Time-Distance Factors

Battle space, together with terrain conditions and the requirements for manoeuvre and support, can take a heavy toll on time, which is one of the scarcest commodities in warfare. Furthermore, the performance of available transport and the disposition of fighting forces determine efficiency when moving from one sphere of influence on the battlefield to the next. Distance and levels of mobility ultimately determine how much time will be consumed before critical missions can be performed at the next venue. Greater distances obviously consume more time, reduce opportunities and increase risk, while simultaneously giving the enemy more time for his own movement.

During battle, the general rule is that the greater the distance, the higher the tendency to travel in groups or convoys. In this sense time and distance increases the overall vulnerability of a force. As a consequence, compromised safety then needs to be remedied by the addition of protective elements, thereby weakening forces needed elsewhere. Pre-positioning forces can improve response times, but if unforeseen problems arise, the question of time and distance will rear its ugly head again.

There is no formula for avoiding this type of problem. There will always be a play-off between time and distance on the battlefield, the result of which is balances of consequences, the advantages vis-à-vis disadvantages of the courses of action which commanders devise and undertake. In Angola the eternal quest for the adroit exponent of manoeuvre was to be at the right place at the right moment, and just in time.[28]

28 See Appendix B: Chart with Distances Relevant to the Border War

Topography and Climatic Conditions

Soldiers operating in the northern border region experienced distinct seasons every year – the cool, dry winter from May to September, and the rainy summer from October to April, with the heaviest rainfall occurring from December to March.[29] The distinct dry and wet seasons had a pronounced effect on warfare: Insurgents preferred the rainy seasons, because it provided them with easy access to drinking water and cover while inhibiting vehicular movement by the security forces. The SADF, on the other hand, preferred the drier months for mobile operations.

Maximum temperatures north and south of the SWA-Angola border exceeded 37° Celsius on a regular basis, but discomfort was caused not so much by the high temperatures as by other aggravating climatic conditions, such as the lack of wind and high relative humidity which limited perspiring.[30] The human body cools itself principally by exuding perspiration, which then evaporates, but this process becomes less efficient as the relative humidity increases. Physical exertion and too little water intake on hot, humid days can result in hyperthermia (when the body absorbs more heat than it can dissipate), and if preventative measures are not taken, the result can be heat stress, heat fatigue, heat syncope, heat cramps, heat exhaustion or heatstroke, which in severe cases can lead to death.

The levels of discomfort experienced by forces in the field in a near-tropical environment placed a high premium on the physical and psychological preparation of forces for battle and included acclimatisation of personnel for operations beforehand. As a rule, incoming troops spent approximately 14 days of preparation at the Oshivello training base before being deployed, if time allowed.

Humidity also influenced tactics, because the flow of air between depressions and high ground produced heat-waves which had a distinct influence on distance estimation and target acquisition and indication. Furthermore, knowing that SWAPO was an enemy adept in field-craft, the South African soldier needed to be trained to observe wind directions, to make sure he remained concealed and possibly also to spot an inadvertently exposed enemy. Smell, smoke, dust and noise travel with the wind, and were all vital indicators in the military games of hide-and-seek played during operations. The direction of the wind was an important factor to consider when determining the ideal direction of attack, and during the conventional battles in southeast Angola this became all-important because of the threat of possible attack or retaliation with chemical weapons from the Angolan side.

Topography and Radio Communications

The topography had a major impact on radio communications during the Border War. Higher-frequency signals tend to be obstructed by high ground; at low frequencies (below 2MHz) radio waves travel as ground waves and thus follow the curvature of the earth, while radio signals in the 1 to 30MHz range (shortwave radio) potentially have a global reach.

At higher frequencies the signal-transmission qualities of reflection and diffraction by atmospheric layers in Angola sometimes caused physical interference between sending and

29 Statistics were obtained from the *Atlas of Namibia: A Portrait of the Land and its People* by John Mendelsohn et al, Sunbird Publishers (Pty) Ltd, Cape Town, 2009. As statistics are not readily available for southern Angola, the northern Namibian weather patterns were assumed to be a close representation of conditions in southern Angola.

30 From the *Atlas of Namibia: A Portrait of the Land and its People.*

receiving antennas, which naturally resulted in snarl-ups. VHF[31] radio communication was less effective in terrain with prominent features because signals tended to be masked by high grounds, and UHF[32] signals were even more badly affected. During operations the SADF had to contend with what it referred to as the bedevilling skip-distances which influenced the quality of communications. To avoid the negative effects of the terrain, the SADF regularly deployed "Telstars" – aircraft flying near deployed formations to relay radio signals. Ground-based radio relay stations were also used.

Africa's Health Hazards – Diseases, Flies and Mosquitoes by the Million

Through all the ages of warfare, disease and pestilence have always been more destructive in exterminating human life than firearms. The border region was no exception. Dysentery (commonly referred to as "gyppo guts", a term left over from World War II), heat exhaustion, hepatitis and malaria were some of the more common diseases encountered, and during Operation Modular in 1987, diseases such as cerebral malaria and hepatitis took their toll on South Africa's small fighting contingent. From 5 August 1987 to 11 December 1987 a total number of 8,563 sick reports were recorded (an average of 67 per day); the total number of non-battle casualties extracted by air to the military hospital at Rundu were 187, of which seven were dead.

Quality medical and health care and scientific field sanitation succeeded to a large extent in controlling most of these endemic plagues, but the threat was ever-present, in the form of Angola's over-abundance of flies and mosquitoes. People do not often grasp the extent of such a threat. During the fighting in the Philippines in 1943, General Douglas MacArthur stated at one point that "this will be a long war, if for every division I have facing the enemy, I must count on a second division in the hospital with malaria, and a third division convalescing from this debilitating disease."[33] Diseases such as malaria are mosquito-borne, of course, and there was no shortage of them in Angola. Nor of flies, the carriers of various other maladies. This is not to mention the exasperation of many a commander who found himself inadvertently swallowing at least a dozen flies a day while giving orders. One often felt that one would rather face SWAPO and/or FAPLA than those damned flies and mosquitoes!

Cultures and Concepts of Warfare Influence How Terrain is Utilised

A soldier's society and culture influence the way he makes war and uses the terrain. This being the case, it was fortunate for the SADF that the Angolan and Cuban conventional forces were addicted to holding ground, favoured roads and river-lines as approaches for advance and withdrawal, and were enamoured of towns and sources of rivers as suitable places for building defences. This was probably due to their never-ending need for drinking water and its employment as natural obstacles for defence. The rivers also helped them with the control and co-ordination of indirect fire and air support, which, to the benefit of the SADF and UNITA, they were never good at. Conversely, the South Africans favoured the bush for manoeuvre and preferred not to hold ground.

It is interesting to speculate about how did the terrain conditions in the combat zone influence the choice between limited and protracted war. To judge by the dogmatic tactics

31 Very high frequency.

32 Ultra high frequency.

33 http://www.malariasite.com/malaria/history-wars.htm

they favoured so slavishly, it would appear that the Cubans, born and bred on a small and quite heavily populated island, were used to occupying and operating in a restricted space – during the peace talks at Calueque in August 1988, I remember, one Cuban officer told me": "The SWA-Angola battlefield was much larger than Cuba. In Cuba a G-5 gun could shoot from one side (of the island) to the other."

It was a revealing remark. My impression was that they were uneasy in Angola; that they felt that Africa – so far away from their homeland, so large, so dangerous, so undeveloped, and so climatically harsh – could devour them. SWA/Namibia and Angola could become anybody's Vietnam or Afghanistan (the SADF's rank and file, by contrast, were not culturally alienated – they were Africans, fighting in Africa). A protracted war suited the revolutionaries of SWAPO and UNITA because a long conflict could be used extremely well to trade the progressive attrition of numbers and materiel for time and space. But the Cubans in Angola were not revolutionaries any more, except in their rhetoric.

Fidel Castro's guerrillas of 1956 were mostly retired or dead of old age. These Cubans were trained and equipped – both physically and psychologically – for conventional warfare against other conventional soldiers, not a long-drawn-out war in the bush, with its immense attrition of man and machine, its soaring costs, the burden of disquieting internal and external political disapproval and all other entirely ghastly consequences.

These factors affected the South Africans as well, but within this battle arena the SADF's tactical prowess was much more than a match for the dogmatic, slow-moving Angolans and their FAPLA and its Cuban allies. Conversely, finding, fixing and striking nomadic guerrilla or insurgent units were another ball game altogether. In most instances accurate and timeous strategic and tactical intelligence were the decisive factors, rather than how well or how badly the enemy performed.

The Killing Fields – Where Blood Seeped into Thirsty Sands

The Death Triangle South of the Red Line: Haunted Ground

The Death Triangle was situated in the Central Manoeuvring Sector south of the Red Line in Sector 30's area of operations.[34] It derived its name from the fact that the three towns in the area – Tsumeb, Otavi and Grootfontein, with their surrounding freehold farming areas – formed a rough triangle, and because when SWAPO's Special Unit mounted its annual deep incursions its primary purpose was not to attack the military but, first and foremost, to commit acts of random terrorism.

The primary aim of the deep incursions was to terrorise the farming communities and towns in the triangle by killing as many civilians as possible, intimidating the local black population and generally disrupting farming and commercial activities. Among other things this involved murdering isolated farmers; striking at passing targets of opportunity along the many roads; sabotaging infrastructure such as railway lines, telephone poles and windmills, and harassing the security forces with mine-laying and ambushes.

At the same time the infiltrators would try to carry out political activation when possible. Then after about two months they would head northwards again and exfiltrate to the safety of Angola, all going well. But all did not go well with any of these deep infiltrations, none of which achieved anything significant apart from murdering a few innocents, and the terrain had much to do with it.

34 Read with Chapter 11 and refer to Map 4 and 7 to 9.

The timing of the Special Unit's annual raids was determined by climatic factors. The triangle is a summer rainfall region, with the rains normally coming down from November to April, so that at the start of winter the insurgents would be able to find ample surface water, a vital requirement for men travelling on foot through an arid semi-desert landscape. At that time of the year it was also more difficult for the security forces to mount hot pursuits to the north of the patrolled "cut-lines" (see below), especially when vehicles had to deal with inundated shonas (flood plains) and marshland.

And so at the beginning of every winter the security forces would brace themselves for what came to be called the "Winter Games", a high-tempo counterinsurgency operation (as it happened, two Winter Games of note took place while I commanded 61 Mechanised Infantry Battalion Group, a main player in both Operation Carrot in April 1981 and Operation Yahoo in April-May 1982.[35])

Conducting counterinsurgency operations in the Death Triangle was an awesome business. Sector 30 was responsible for an extremely large and often difficult swathe of territory. The front stretched over 450 km from Kamanjab in the west, across the Etosha Game Reserve and to the Rundu tarmac road in the east. From the Red Line in the north to Otjiwarongo in the south was close on 200 km. This vast tract of land included rugged mountains and varieties of unpleasant vegetation such as the "Haak-en-Steek" a dense, vicious type of thornbush with prickly barbs that claw at everything – "haak-en-steek" translates as "catch and stab", while its English name, the "wait-a-bit", is even more descriptive in describing its effects on the unfortunate traveller.

The Red Line, as has been mentioned, was a fence erected long before the Border War as a barrier to prevent the southward movement of cattle infected with the deadly mouth and foot disease, but after the war broke out it was also used to demarcate the boundary between Sector 30 in the south and Sector 10 (Ovamboland) and Sector 20 (Okavango) to the north and stretched from west to east across the northern part of the Etosha Game Reserve; to the military it was known as the Bravo cut-line.

The Red Line ran from west to east across the northern part of the Etosha Game Reserve and then went another 220 km eastwards from Oshivello to the Grootfontein-Rundu road. It sounds, perhaps, more impressive than it was (and still is) in the flesh, so to speak. In fact it consisted only of a straight, narrow sandy road, hemmed in by a cattle-fence on either side.

But it was patrolled daily by infantrymen mounted in Buffel[36] mine-protected vehicles which were controlled from an infantry company headquarters deployed at Tsintsabis. The road's surface was swept with improvised brooms pulled behind the vehicles to detect the track of insurgents heading in and out of the farming district, and when such tracks were spotted the Bravo cut-line was instantly converted into a killing zone.

The SADF developed three additional cut-lines across the enemy's infiltration approaches to facilitate counterinsurgency operations in Sector 30, which it code-named Alpha, Charlie and Delta. Alpha was located parallel to Bravo, but 10 kilometres further to the north; Charlie lay approximately 30 km north of Alpha, inside Ovamboland. On conclusion of Operation Carrot in 1981 it was decided to develop the Delta cut-line, 20 km to the south of Bravo, which cut across the farms and fences from the Tsumeb-Oshivello road in the west to the Grootfontein-Rundu road in the east (Delta was, in fact, still under

35 Refer to Chapter 11.

36 The Buffel is a South African developed armoured personnel carrier with proven landmine resistance.

construction when Operation Yahoo commenced in 1982).

Enemy tracks crossing these cut-lines provided not only early warning of crossings but also valuable tactical intelligence regarding infiltrations and exfiltrations – how many were in-country, how many were out, where were they and when would they do something? The raiders had guts and endurance, give them that. Their soldiers infiltrated far distances by foot to reach their designated target areas in the Death Triangle.

To achieve the purpose, the foe launched simultaneous infiltrations from Lubango via Cahama and Techamutete-Cassinga. From these jumping-off points all the way south, the insurgent groups had to cross extremely dangerous ground to reach their targets, carry out their tasks and then exfiltrate. This required thorough planning, crafty utilisation of terrain, and large amounts of time and effort. To track down and kill or capture the infiltrators the security forces needed even better planning and craftier exploitation of terrain, combined with an optimal utilisation of time and effort.

All enemy infiltrating routes led south and exfiltrating routes led north, and here the influence of terrain can clearly be seen. The vast, arid Etosha Game Reserve was and is a game-watcher's paradise, but for heavily laden men on foot it was effectively a no-go area unless each could carry 16 jerry cans of water, a manifest impossibility. As a result there were basically two viable routes south of the Red Line, one for each of the infiltrators' targets. They could skirt the western side of Etosha and strike at Kamanjab and Outjo, or they could creep through the bushveld east of Etosha and hit the Tsumeb-Grootfontein-Otavi-Otjiwarongo area.

- The western approach through the Kamanjab-Etosha corridor was the most perilous. It was difficult to survive and evade in this harsh, unforgiving terrain, in which it was relatively easy for the security forces with their vehicle and air assets to hunt the infiltrators down. The starting point for the western approach was the enemy's Volcano Base near Lubango in Angola. From Volcano they travelled by road to Cahama and then took to their feet, passing to the east of Ruacana, after which they struck southwards to the northwestern fringes of the Etosha Game Reserve – a gruelling 360 km and counting. Then it was action stations as they took on another equalling gruelling 124 km to Kamanjab and Outjo, which is where the fighting and dying began.
- The eastern approach was the preferred option. In Ovamboland and Kavango the veldt provided good cover and abundant food and water, all of which were literally life-giving resources that were needed to sustain a deep infiltration. A significant problem with this route, though, was the soft, sandy soil that started north of the Bravo cut-line and extended deep into southern Angola, which was ideal for picking up the infiltrators' tracks. To set off on this route, the infiltrators travelled in relative luxury by the prevailing standards (namely Soviet-built Ural trucks) from Volcano Base past Matala to Techamutete-Cassinga. From there, however, it was à la foot all the way southwards: first to the border itself, then about 120 km through thick bush to the Bravo cut-line, and then another 120 km or so of fighting the wait-a-bit thorn bush to Tsumeb. In all, infiltrating along this route meant a stiff 475 km on foot before the winking lights of Tsumeb could be seen.
- South of the Red Line, however, it was another winter ball-game altogether, and one in which the odds favoured the infiltrators. The ground was very firm and rocky, which made tracking difficult, and although the thorn bush made movement

difficult, it provided plenty of cover. On the other hand, the security forces also enjoyed certain advantages. One was that they knew the terrain better than the infiltrators, since the latter were mainly born and bred in the north, whereas many of the hunters were local inhabitants. Another was, of course, the excellent infrastructure, which allowed the rapid deployment of forces by ground and air.

One problem the security forces encountered had nothing to do with the terrain: the multitude of fences in the farming area, where most of the search and destroy missions took place. Quick reaction and maintenance of a high tempo were the order of the day, and the follow-up groups had neither the time nor the inclination to do anything except drive right over these inconvenient hindrances. Needless to say, the farmers hated to have their fences broken and became extremely agitated when this happened; but every problem has its solution, and in April 1982 we had fence-repair teams standing by around the clock.

The cut-lines, together with the excellent road network in the region, facilitated rapid movement by own forces for follow-up and cut-off deployments. There was an abundance of airfields and airstrips, and at selected farms there were fuel dumps so that the gunships could fly in to farms near where the action was, refuel and wait to be scrambled at the right moment.

One of the major problems own forces faced was the formidable mountainous area between Tsumeb, Grootfontein, Kombat and Otavi, which by the nature of things did not favour guerrilla-hunting, and it required extreme and innovative measures by the SADF to keep the foe out. Sometimes these measures worked well – in April 1981 not one Special Unit infiltrator reached the mountains, but the following year a few did, although they were so small in number and so harried by the security forces that they did not inflict any damage to lives or property.

What counted in the security forces' favour was their access to real-time and near-real-time intelligence, courtesy of the local population. Another benefit, as mentioned earlier, was the local knowledge provided by the resolute soldiers of the part-time area force units which were based on the towns and their communities – truly "twice the citizen". The intelligence system for the area was linked to a comprehensive network of contacts and agents, which in turn was inter-connected with the MARNET[37] and the landline telephone systems.

All the command centres, farms and crisis-points in the region were connected by the MARNET system, and almost all the farms and families were organised into ever-vigilant miniature strongholds for hearth-and-home protection. Radio and telephone communications were superb in the region, and could be described as one of the SADF's main force multipliers in Sector 30, principally for command and control of military operations, home safeguarding and intelligence gathering.

Such was the influence of terrain as the neutral factor on counterinsurgency operations in the Death Triangle. Whatever else might vary from day to day, the terrain remained a constant, and it was assessed day by day, minute by minute, hour by hour by the soldiers who implemented Operations Daisy and Yahoo.

37 Military Area Radio Network.

Cunene River Basin, Including Xangongo, Môngua and Ondjiva: Ground of the Vanquished

The Cunene River basin was the combat zone where the conventional part of Operation Protea took place in August-September 1981.[38] The contested area straddled the western and central manoeuvring sectors of southern Angola in close proximity to Cahama, Xangongo, Môngua and Ondjiva, and consequently became extremely important during the Border War.

For both sides the bridge at Xangongo was vital for the prosecution of the war effort in any direction and for any purpose – offensive manoeuvre, defence, delay and especially for logistics. The terrain and the military objectives selected could therefore be neatly partitioned for use as a plausible killing ground, which came to be to the advantage of the SADF. Once again, terrain as the neutral factor was exploited to offset the enemy's numerical strength and clumsy tactics.

Somewhat further to the southwest of the Cunene River basin, southern Angola was a moonscape. The terrain was extremely arid, with inhospitable mountains stretching northwards from the SWA-Angola border as well as towards the Atlantic Ocean. The only significant utilisation of this terrain was for the enemy's transportation of logistics from the seaport of Namibe to the logistical hub at Lubango, which happened to traverse the vulnerable choke-point of the Leba pass.

In 1982 SWAPO tried to set up an infiltration route in this unpromising natural buffer zone, but it was knocked out in the Cambêno Valley during Operation Super, and no further attempts to activate it were made.

Traditionally, fighting on terrain of one's own choosing is rightly regarded as a battle-winning factor, but it is just that – a factor, not a success formula in its own right. This was conclusively proved during the conventional part of 1981's Operation Protea, when more than two FAPLA brigades were destroyed in spite of the fact that they were, in fact, fighting on terrain where they wanted to fight. In spite of that traditional advantage they went under because their tactics did not allow them to make maximum use of the terrain benefit.

Around Xangongo, Môngua and Ondjiva, FAPLA and its Soviet advisors set up a comprehensive and heavily armed series of defensive positions which were, however, so static that even their tanks – of which the South Africans had none – were dug in. They were defeated by a conventionally orientated brigade-sized SADF task force which used unexpected attack routes to emerge through the darkness from the vast bush-covered manoeuvring areas on either side of the Cunene River; this meant that the Cunene itself became a north-south obstacle that divided the west from the east, cutting off many enemy escape-routes and preventing the arrival of reinforcements.

In this way the Cunene River basin allowed the manoeuvre exponents a prime opportunity – which was fully utilised – to destroy the enemy in his useless fixed defences on the eastern bank by the clever utilisation of terrain and tactics. West of the Cunene a brigade-sized FAPLA reserve was fixed in place at Cahama by a daring night-time dash to the western bank, and to the east the main defences at Xangongo and Ondjiva, unable to swing their focus and bereft of any help from Cahama, were overrun in quick succession.

38 See Chapter 12 and refer to Map 4, 10 and 11.

The Area-in-Dispute: Illusion and Elusiveness

Through the 1970s and 1980s SWAPO methodically established strategic bases in southern Angola to support their insurgent war south of the border, since their political-military struggle's centre of gravity was their main popular support base in Ovamboland (it is not realised that throughout the Border War SWAPO was almost exclusively recruited from Ovamboland, where the allegedly "apartheid" security forces were manned by people of a dozen or so different ethno-cultural groups – one of the most efficient security-force battalions, incidentally, was recruited in Ovamboland itself).

The central part of southern Angola was their proverbial guerrilla strategic base area and "free zone" as a Mao Tse-tung might have called it (the insurgents never succeeded in setting up a "liberated zone" on SWA/Namibian soil itself). The "free zone" formed part of an extensive strategic enemy base complex SWAPO had developed over time in the general vicinity of the Cassinga-Techamutete-Indungo-Chitequeta-Bambi-Cuvelai-Mupa region.

Until August 1981 SWAPO had been adequately protected by FAPLA, Angola's conventional army, but after Operation Protea in September 1981 the SADF created a no-man's land, the so-called Area-In-Dispute,[39] surrounding the territory they had captured from FAPLA. Thereafter FAPLA maintained a chain of defensive positions on its periphery. Fighting units of the SADF found first-hand evidence of this during Operation Daisy in November 1981 and Operation Meebos in July-August 1982: the overall area was littered with signs and symptoms of the enemy, with the intruders literally crossing abandoned trench systems, caches, bunkers and minefields wherever they went.

From its positions in the Area-In-Dispute the SADF regularly launched large-scale counterinsurgency operations against insurgent groups heading southwards to cross the border into the northern border region and the Death Triangle – usually during the drier winter months, when the going was better for vehicles and the natural cover somewhat sparser. These operations were directed from a tactical headquarters located at the Ondjiva airfield.

FAPLA naturally became extremely perturbed by the unnerving operational situation on their home turf, and this resulted in a steady build-up of their conventional fighting strength in the region, not only their ground forces but – to the dismay of the SAAF – their air power and air defences as well. Until the end of 1984 the FAPLA brigades closest to Xangongo and Ondjiva were based at Cahama and Quiteve in the west, Cuvelai and Techamutete to the north, Menongue to the northwest; and Caiundo to the east. The enemy's conventional brigades were liberally interspersed with Cuban units. Airfields at Namibe, Lubango and Menongue posed a threat to the South African occupiers, and at Cahama and Menongue the irksome enemy radars carefully watched the horizon in all directions.

All the while the Angolan conventional soldiers stared longingly from their trenches at the goings-on of the brown-clad hostiles gallivanting just beyond their weapons' range, operating more or less with impunity against SWAPO outside Luanda's immediate area of influence. The Area-In-Dispute became encircled by a ring of fire and steel but the Angolans and their allies did not intervene; even the menacing Russian MiG-21s remained on the fringes for the time being. For FAPLA the loss of its strongholds in central-southern Angola was a bitter pill to swallow – for the moment. For SWAPO it was exasperating – for

39 See Map 4.

the moment. For the SADF and SWATF it was fun – for the moment. But only for the moment. FAPLA was determined to recapture Ondjiva and Xangongo from the SADF, although it was content to bide its time till the right opportunity presented itself.

This is not to say that pouncing on SWAPO in the Area-In-Dispute was a simple task. Potential targets were dispersed throughout southern-central Angola. SWAPO's command structures were constantly on the move, and so were its operational and logistical field bases ... Hidden away in the ominous green of the bushveld, shaded in mystification, the insurgents kept dropping out of sight, hiding away or simply holing up in the dense cover so liberally available in southern Angola. When stationary, the insurgents were entrenched and well-camouflaged from enemy eyes, both on the ground and in the air. The hidden positions enjoyed all-round protection from defensive fire lay-outs and minefields.

But their best weapon was still their elusiveness: escaping and evading is the guerrilla's most effective stock in trade, and long practice had made experts of the insurgents. You seek him here, you seek him there, but all too often, finding him is a bonus. Nevertheless, northern SWA/Namibia and southern Angola became neatly insulated, to the benefit of the SADF's counterinsurgency campaign. But it remained a stupendous task. The Area-In-Dispute was enormous. It stretched in illusive serenity from the Cunene River in the west to the Cubango in the east – a distance of about 240 km as the crow flies. The operational zone extended from the SWA-Angola border in the south to the Namibe-Menongue railway line beyond Indungo in the north – about 370 km.

Much of it was sparsely populated, although there were a number of towns of varying sized dotted around it, such as Cahama, Humbe, Peu Peu, Xangongo and Môngua in the west; Ondjiva, Namacunde and Omupanda to the south; Anhanca, Evale, Mupa, Cuvelai, Techamutete, Cassinga and Indungo to the north; and Nehone, Dova, Ionde and Caiundo to the east.

No serious road infrastructure existed in this area, apart from some tarmac on the route northeastwards that led eventually to Luanda. Such "made" roads as existed were gravel-surfaced and, like their tarmac equivalents poorly maintained, if at all. Otherwise the norm was bush tracks of various stages of impassability. All gravel roads, bush tracks, river-crossings, defiles and occupied or abandoned enemy bases were heavily sown with explosive devices – ranging from anti-vehicle mines and anti-personnel mines to booby-traps. This knowledge always remained a hair-raising preoccupation for the security forces when they went to hunt for or attack SWAPO.

This vast, bush-clad salient also featured a number of picturesque catchment areas for rivers such as the Cuvelai, Mui, Bambi, Calonga, Dengo, Caiundo and Mulola; very often the rainy season transformed all these smaller waterways into formidable natural obstacles; since the region's sandy soil was quick to turn into quagmires which made movement by vehicle – the only way to cover the sprawling captured territory – extremely difficult.

The terrain was mainly flat, although near Cuvelai and Techamutete it undulated and there were some higher ground and rocky outcrops of note. The thick, sandy soil made daylight movement very difficult, because any large convoy would throw up huge clouds of dust, a dead give-away to anyone with eyes, and after the FAPLA/Cuban MiGs finally became active we made a habit of night movement – which brought its own problems, since off-road navigation by prismatic compass and protractor (all we had at the time) was no easy task.

This was the milieu in which Operation Daisy took place in November 1981 and

Makro and Meebos intermittently from December 1981 until the end of August 1982.[40] These operations were all of a counterinsurgency and force projection nature, but during Meebos there was a significant skirmish north of Cuvelai on 4 August 1982 in which a large mobile FAPLA column was completely destroyed.

For Operation Daisy[41] the target zone centred on Chitequeta and Bambi – the point of main effort. This piece of prime real estate nestled in glorious shadowy denseness; Chitequeta was situated about 35 km east-southeast of Techamutete and Cassinga, and 50 km south of Indungo, 120 km north-northwest of Ionde and 350 km directly north of the SWA-Angola border. For Operation Meebos[42] the northern quarter of the Area-In-Dispute was selected as the target zone. The general target area could be roughly demarcated by following the line of the Cuvelai River northeastward towards Indungo; then by encapsulating the densely covered terrain northwestwards towards the Calonga River and Techamutete.

Mystical Southeast Angola: Bloodied Land

The Angolan civil war, in which South African became such a reluctant participant, extended far into southeast Angola, officially FAPLA's 6th Military Region but popularly known in the Portuguese time as "the land at the end of the earth". Utterly remote, almost inaccessible and nearly devoid of a normal human population, it became an extremely lethal military playground in 1987 and 1988.[43]

This was UNITA's liberated zone, and FAPLA and its Cuban and Soviet allies were determined to gain control of it. The result was an epic conventional battle, Operations Modular, Hooper and Packer, between the FAPLA coalition and UNITA with its South African allies, who had a vested interest in keeping southeast Angola clear of FAPLA, so that SWAPO would not gain a foothold across the western border.

This drawn-out struggle was waged between the Lomba and Chambinga rivers, east of the magnificent Cuito River, a distance of about 120 km as the crow flies, plus another 25 km from the Chambinga crossing to Cuito River bridge. The width of the battlefield was about 180 km, from the Cuito and Cuanavale Rivers eastwards to a general south-north line through Mavinga.

It all started in August 1987, when an overwhelmingly large combined Angolan-Cuban force crossed the Cuito to capture Mavinga and Jamba from UNITA. The SADF entered this war to support UNITA and halted the enemy's advance on the Lomba River in September-October 1987. The enemy was routed and the SADF and UNITA followed up with a fierce counter-attack, and then kept up the pressure. By December 1987 FAPLA and the Cubans had been driven back into their defensive trenches at Cuito Cuanavale.

The Chambinga River, a tributary of the Cuito, and its marshy floodplains stretched obliquely to the east to define the northern periphery of the battlefield, and was vital ground for both sides. 16 FAPLA Brigade was entrenched at its source when the SADF's counter-attack commenced on 9 November 1987 (16 Brigade becomes important in the telling of this story.[44]).

40 Refer to Chapters 13 and 14.

41 See Chapter 13 and Maps 13 and 14.

42 See Chapter 14 and Maps 15 and 16.

43 See Chapter 15 and Maps 17 and 19.

44 See Chapter 15.

The crossing at the source – actually more of a drift or ford – was the strategic portal to Cuito Cuanavale town, so it is understandable that FAPLA wanted to capture southeast Angola from UNITA; this also explains why they passionately defended the crossing sites at Chambinga and Cuito later on, when it had become abundantly clear that their thrust at UNITA's home bases had failed.

By the same token, it is equally clear why the SADF and UNITA needed to drive the enemy westwards across the Cuito River whence they had come. In addition, the fighting process was a means of destroying so many of the enemy that it would be too ghastly for them to consider coming back for another round.

The Western Front: Final Clash of Wills

The Western Front encapsulated the Western and Central Manoeuvring Sectors and therefore included Angola's 5th Military Region as well as Sectors 10 and 30 inside SWA/ Namibia.[45] This was where the final clash of wills between the governments of South Africa, Angola and Cuba would occur during the last conventional battle of 26–27 July 1988. The final armoured clash between a mechanised South African combat group and an armoured advance guard of Cuba's elite mechanised 50th Division took place only a few kilometres north of Calueque, on the northwestern side of the Cunene River.

This episode derived from the arrival in May 1988 of the 50th Division, to a great welcome from everyone except, of course, the South Africans and UNITA. It completely upset what passed for a balance of power in southeast Angola with its overwhelming numbers and attached MiG jet fighters; Fidel Castro, desperate for a glorious victory for Cuban arms after 15 years of mostly undistinguished involvement, openly boasted that he was going to give the South Africans a "bloody nose" and a military beating second to none. The arrival of the 50th Division was an unpleasant surprise for the South African politicians and military grandmasters – strategic intelligence, or the lack thereof and all that?

Operation Prone, as this encounter is called, is therefore an interesting battle account which is worth studying, since it was the final momentous clash of wills and arms in the conventional war for southern Angola, a battle fought strictly between the South African, Angolan and Cuban military forces. After Operation Prone, Calueque became the point of main effort for the final throes of the conventional war.

The terrain presented significant obstacles which dictated the strategies and deployments for the enemy's southward thrust. Firstly there was the arid mountainous region at the western edge of the Western Manoeuvring Sector which eliminated a massive space from their list of options for conventional and insurgent movements; and then there was the Cunene River with its crossings at Xangongo and Calueque.

A popular comment by uninformed observers is that if the Cubans had invaded SWA/ Namibia they would have marched into Windhoek in about six weeks. This sounds very dramatic, but it does not take the terrain into account, or the Cuban island-dwellers' oft-demonstrated lack of both expertise at and inclination for manoeuvre warfare.

Theoretically the 50th Division could have launched a two-pronged attack to the south by making use of both these crossings while under cover of their superior air power based at Lubango, Cahama and Menongue. South African forces would then have had the flat expanses of Ovamboland, the emptiness of the Etosha Pans and the concealment of the

45 See Chapter 14 and Maps 4, 18 and 19.

tactical mountainous terrain in the Death Triangle at their disposal to defend or use as a launching-pad for a counter-attack.

This terrain was not only intimately familiar to the South Africans but also presented infinite possibilities for unconventional warfare and mobile manoeuvres, a game in which the SADF had already proven its superiority. Furthermore, the southward movement of the enemy into SWA/Namibia would have left their seaport at Namibe wide open for vertical envelopment by South Africa's 44 Parachute Brigade, which would have seriously disrupted their logistical lines in the blink of an eye.

Epilogue – Rhythms In Manoeuvre

To reap benefits from changing positions there should be rhythm to manoeuvre. The one who best utilises terrain as a neutral factor for artful manoeuvre has the advantage ... as the answer to numerical superiority is greater mobility.

The accomplished military commander exploits the terrain with confidence, making intelligent use of his forces, the terrain itself, movement, deception and appropriate tactics to compel the opposing force, either directly or indirectly, to act and to move according to his battle design. In doing so, own forces are able to maintain their initiative and freedom of action, and damned well keep the enemy in one precarious situation after another, endlessly impaled on the horns of a dilemma. Using terrain and manoeuvre the way they should be used was one reason for the SADF's fighting feats during the many operations which were fought in southern Angola and are described in this book.

Land warfare is not fought either in a vacuum or on a parade ground. If one can master the challenging conditions of the African battle space, keeping the whole greater than the sum of the parts, hell, man ... then mobile warfare can become fun!

So – know the ground and use it to the best advantage. Know your enemy and know yourself, or succumb in battle (more juicy bits about the latter will follow in the chapters to come).

Comment by the Publisher: This chapter was compiled by Roland de Vries and Camille Burger. The authors have been on several extensive tours of northern Namibia and southern Angola and its erstwhile battlefields since October 2010. The first trip was undertaken with the particular aim of reassessing the terrain conditions for the compilation of this introduction. In the process enthralling discussions were held with former enemies and local people on the ground that had experienced the torment of the protracted bush war. Seeing the terrain through the eyes of former enemies, the locals and others who had experienced it was an exhilarating and illuminating experience, and it has been captured in the pages of this introduction.

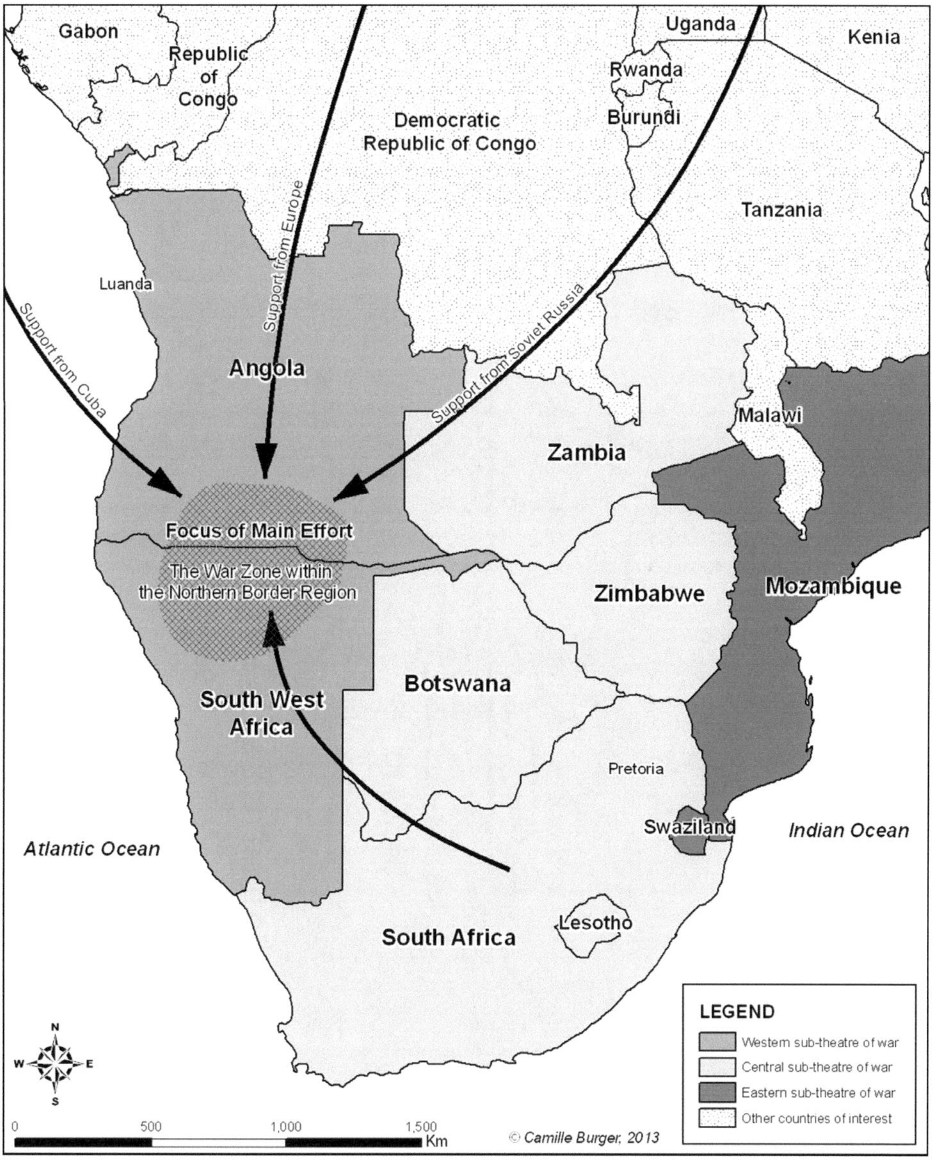

Map 1: The relative position of the Western Sub-Theatre of War

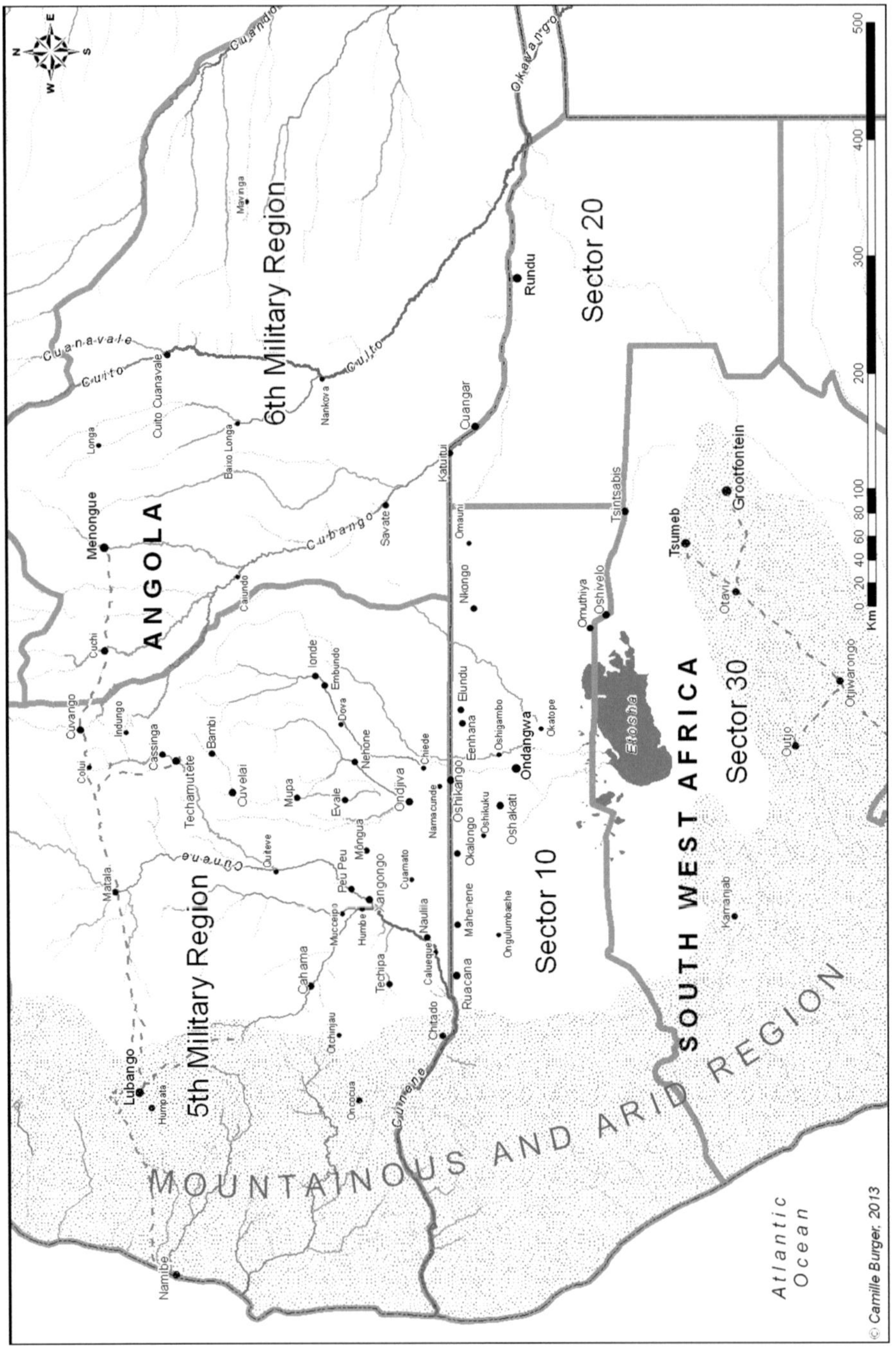

Map 2: The Western Sub-Theatre of War

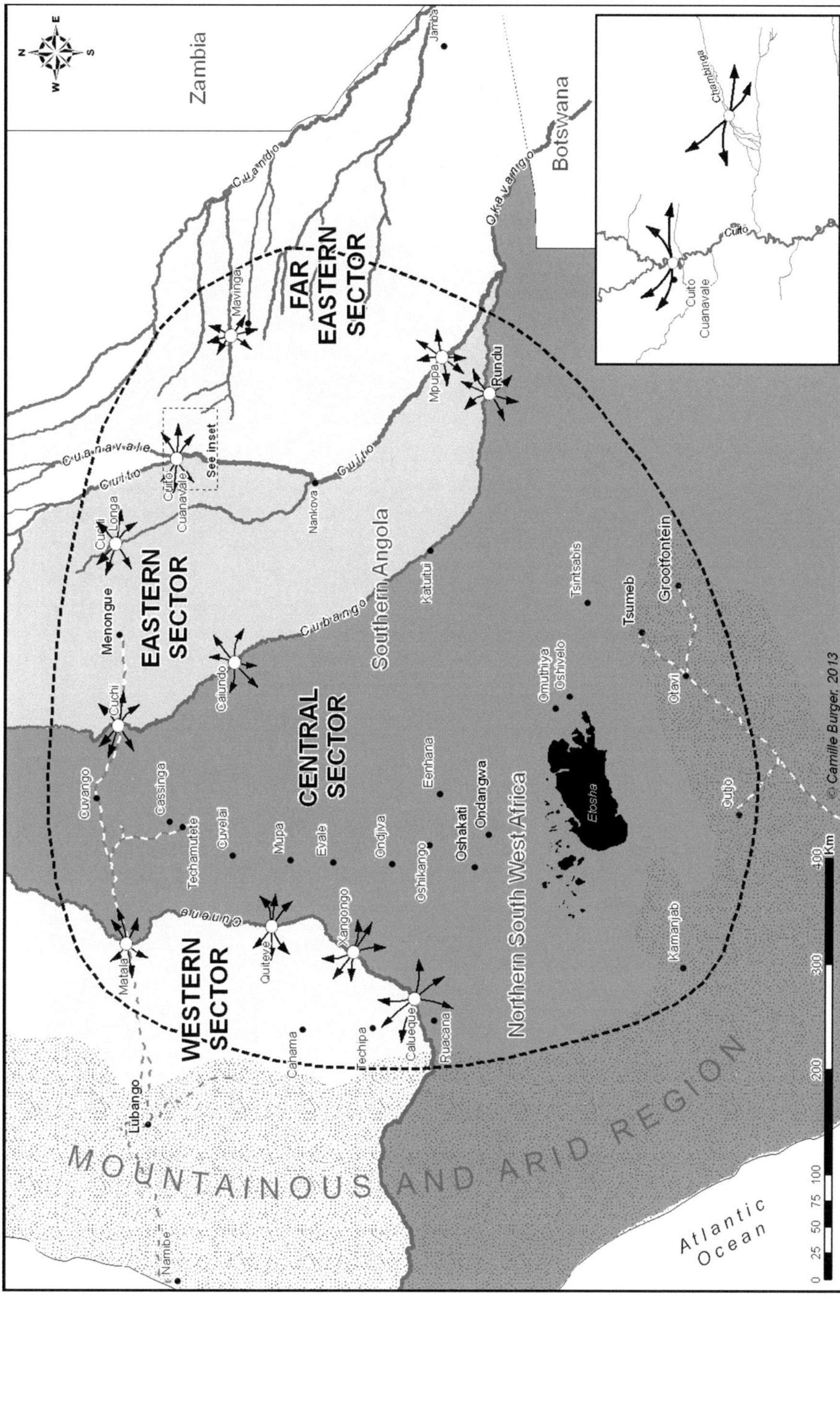

Map 3: Manoeuvring Sectors and Choke-Points within the Western Sub-Theatre of War

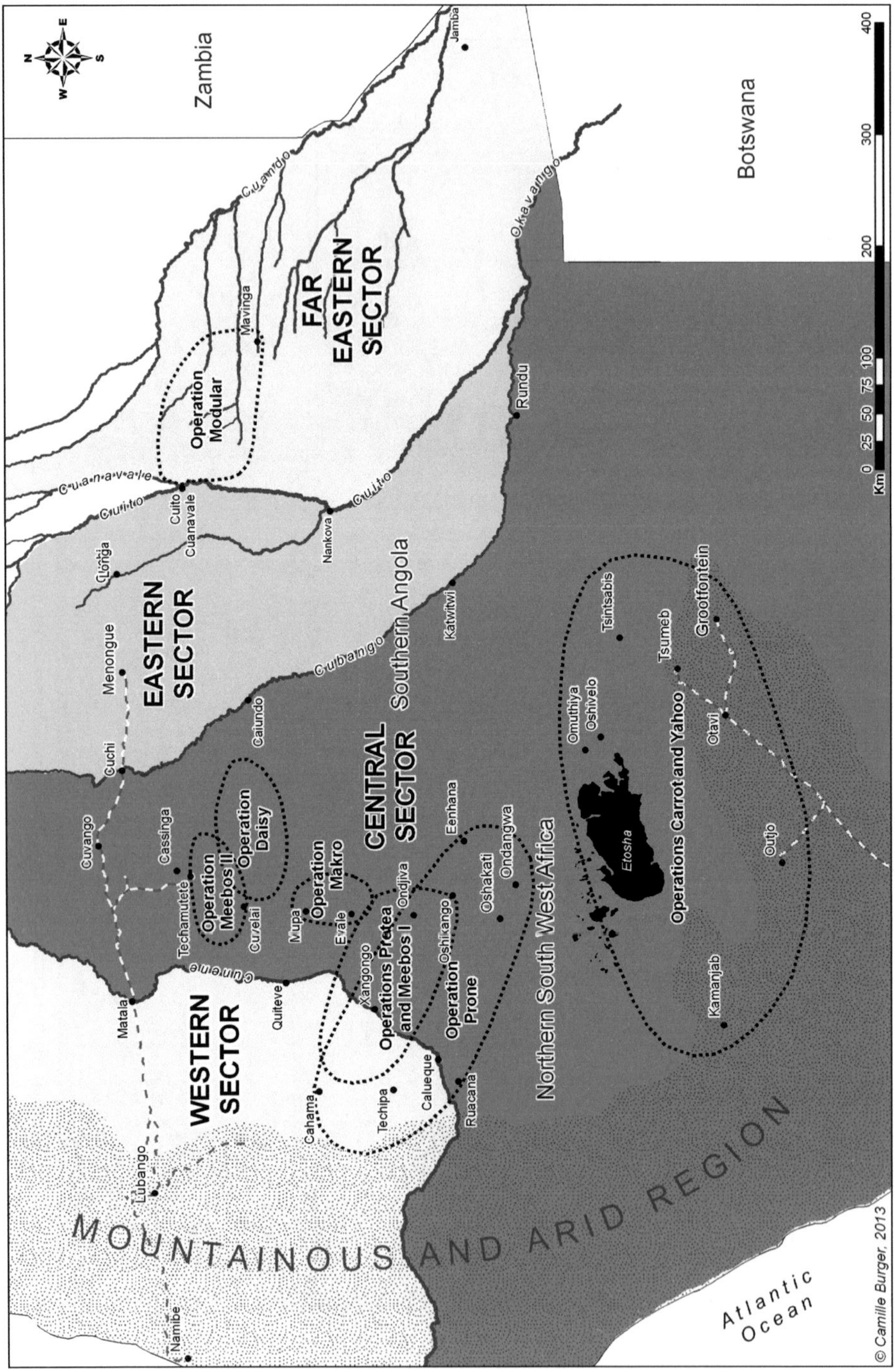

Map 4: Appraised target areas

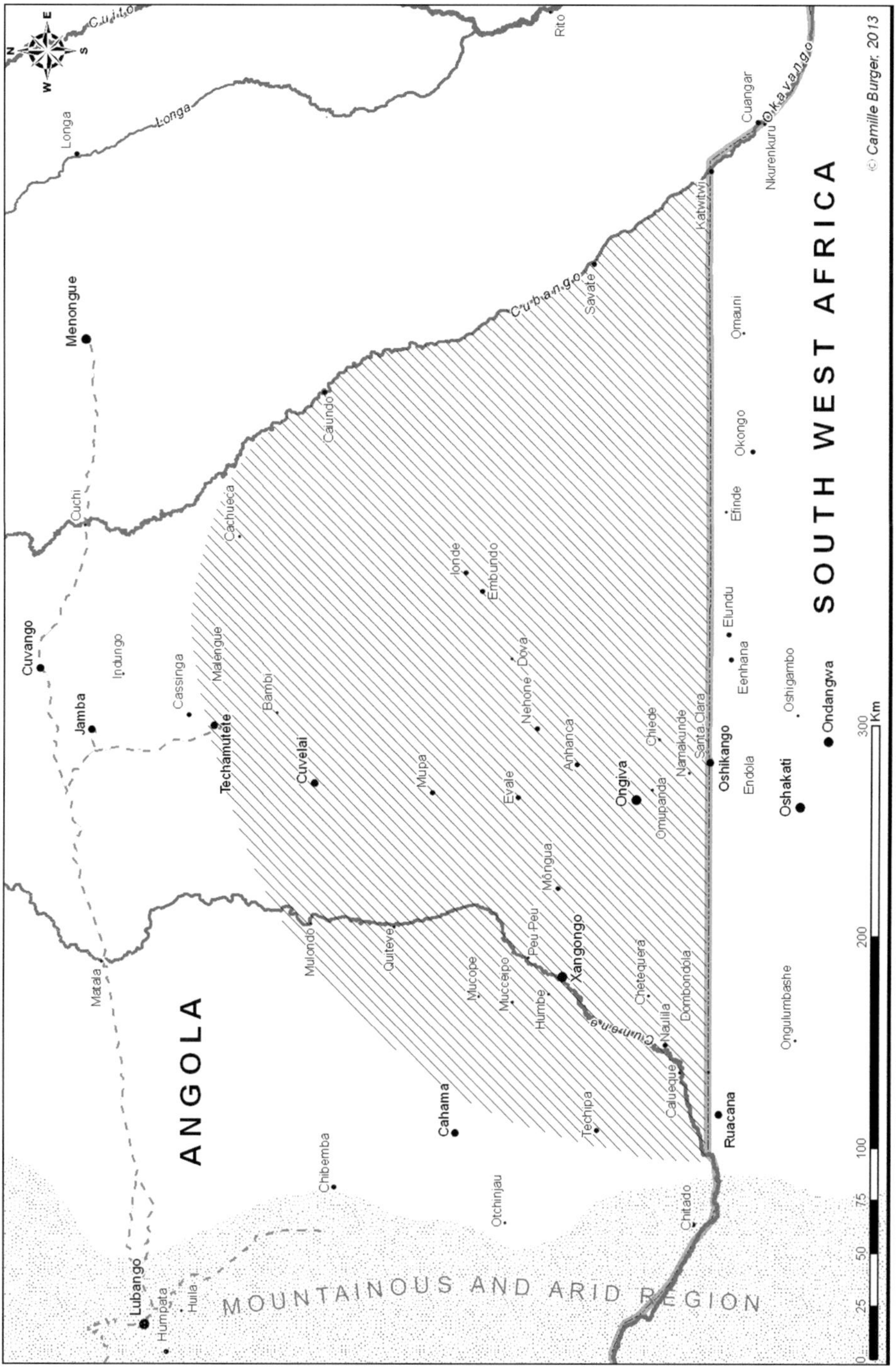

Map 5: Area in dispute activated in September 1981 on completion of Operation Protea

6

Warfare The African Way

Emerging Concepts of Mobile Warfare

There is one law of nature, one iron law that the Boer never forgets, the answer to superior forces is greater mobility.
Thomas Pakenham - The Boer War

Fluid Conditions are Necessary for Mobile Warfare to Flourish

Starting in 1970, I began what was to prove a neverending process of conceptualising my ideas on mobile warfare in southern Africa.[1] To me it was logical that any viable operational concept adopted by the South African Army from the 1970s onwards should embrace mobile warfare – especially as our potential conventional enemies up north were obsessed by positional warfare. In mobile warfare it is necessary to ensure maximum fluidity of movement on the battlefield, as so much depends on being able to destroy the stability so dearly loved by the exponents of positional warfare, and then to bring about tactical victory by seizing fleeting opportunities that follow any ensuing confusion. After all, Africa has the space for manoeuvring in great strides.

The only things that could restrict our degree of mobility were the problem of logistics and the burdens brought about by distances and difficult terrain, when mobility was reduced by heavy equipment such as towed artillery and vehicles. In truth, the latter was one of the reasons, I believed, why conventional enemies in Africa favoured positional warfare. Fortunately, our equipment such as the 155 mm G-5 gun had the range (42 km) and our progression of military vehicles that were being developed and brought into service were designed and built specifically for African bush warfare. The armoured Ratel, with its amazing cross-country and bush-breaking ability, operational range and fire power, was the prime example of this tough breed.[2]

This chapter focuses more on the mobile elements of conventional and semi-conventional warfare in southern Africa. The emphasis is on the fighting between the Angolan army (FAPLA[3]), supported by the Cuban forces on the one hand; and UNITA.[4] supported by the SADF[5] on the other. The tricks of the trade relevant to insurgency and counterinsurgency tactics will be reviewed by an analysis of operations against SWAPO[6] as

1 De Vries, R. Colonel. *Mobiele Oorlogvoering – 'n Perspektief vir Suider-Afrika*: FJM Harman Publishers, Pretoria, 1987. This book was published two months before I departed from the Army Battle School to participate in Operation Modular in October–December 1978 (Chapter 12–15) and Operation Prone in June–December 1988 (Chapter 16).

2 See Chapter 3.

3 *Forças Armadas Populares de Libertação de Angola* (People's Armed Forces for the Liberation of Angola).

4 *Uniao para a Independencia Total de Angola* (Union for the Total Independence of Angola).

5 South African Defence Force.

6 South West Africa People's Organisation, a liberation movement founded in 1960. After 1975 SWAPO fought an insurgency war for Namibian independence from Angolan territory. The military wing of

revealed in Chapters 11, 13 and 14. Similarly, supplementary information is considered in Chapter 7 regarding the fundamentals of warfare as a base-line for appraisals.

Conditioning of Man and Basic Cultures of Warfare – a Way of Life

There was one other vital facet I felt to be considered, namely the conditioning of the South African soldier and his training for mobile African warfare. Positional warfare does not present much of a problem in this regard, but mobile warfare is far more exacting. Constant movement, accompanied by uncertainty, endless attacks, rapidly changing situations and lack of full protection against harsh environmental conditions are all inherent to mobile warfare.

In a way this is similar to the conditions for guerrilla fighting.[7] Guerrilla warfare was and still is in the DNA and way of life of the black African, as was mobile warfare in the genetic material and mores of the white South African soldier, which was so clearly seen during Operation Modular in August–December 1987. In the same way, I felt, the guerrilla fighting talents of UNITA, 32 Battalion and 101 Battalion could be put to excellent use by the South Africans in defeating the more positional-orientated FAPLA and Cuban forces.[8]

The South Africans were extremely well versed in and adapted to mobile warfare. They were imbued with a will to win, regardless of the odds. One of their secrets lay in the operational concepts and doctrine they applied, a unique concept which embodied mixed mobile, conventional and guerrilla warfare.[9] 61 Mechanised Battalion Group, 32 Battalion, 201 Battalion and 101 Battalion, which at times fought in combination with the formidable guerrilla units of UNITA, were foremost examples.

These South African units were commanded by young men who understood the bush-warfare game and excelled at it. I always thought of our small mobile brigade, out on a limb and fighting against overwhelming odds in southeast Angola in 1987 and 1988, as a modern equivalent of General Christiaan de Wet's commando of the Anglo-Boer War days, which was so beautifully described by Thomas Pakenham: "De Wet's commando moved like a hunting cat on the veldt... It was not a majestic fighting machine, like a British column. It was a fighting animal, all muscle and bone; in one sense, the most professional combatant of the War."[10]

Let's be honest, during the Border War it seemed to us as if our conventional enemy would never master the dynamics of conventional warfare. This was fortunate for the South Africans and UNITA, given the fact that they were fighting against such an overwhelming enemy presence that in most wars their effort would have been described as a forlorn-hope mission.

Was this fighting deficiency rooted in FAPLA's African culture and its obvious incompatibility with the dogmatic Russian doctrine for conventional warfare, or was there a built-in lethargy which was due to a lack of intention or understanding, or was there something else to it? We did not complain or spend too much time analyzing these human dynamics, or rather the lack of them. What mattered was that it gave us the winning edge

---

SWAPO was known as the People's Liberation Army of Namibia (PLAN).

7 Refer to the Chambinga battles described in Chapter 15.

8 See Chapters 15 and 16.

9 De Vries, R. Colonel. *Mobiele Oorlogvoering – 'n Perspektief vir Suider-Afrika*: FJM Harman Publishers, Pretoria, 1987, p.117.

10 Ibid, p.119.

on the battlefield.

Looking back, however, it can be said that due to cultural trends and influences there were three starkly different forms of warfare being practised in southeast Angola at the time, and with some variations they can be found in other field armies as well:

- Firstly, there were the fortress and defensive-line holders, as FAPLA proved at Cuito Cuanavale. Here, in December 1987, the Angolans were pressured into blindly obeying the insistence of their Russian and Cuban henchmen that they must defend; hold the line and nothing else, world without end! One might ask whether this compliance stemmed from the traits bred into natural agriculturalists who had been tilling the same land for generations
- Secondly, there were the field fighters, as personified by the South African, SWAPO and UNITA forces, each in their own way, throughout the Border War. Was this the behaviour of traditional hunters rather than tillers of the soil? Interestingly enough, the African National Congress's Umkhonto we Sizwe, or MK, never fitted into this fighting mould. Its members were more likely to be stone-throwers and bomb-planters, due to their political frustrations and the fact that their leaders were bogged down in outdated notions of a Castro-style "people's war" which was totally inapplicable to South Africa because of the country's heavy urbanisation, unsuitable terrain and economic domination of its neighbours.
- Thirdly there were the besiegers, a local example being the Boers' decision to coop up the British garrisons at Mafeking (now Mafikeng), Kimberley and Ladysmith during late 1899. It was a fatal mistake, because, as at Cuito Cuanavale a lifetime later, the Boer generals surrendered their main asset – their mobility – and gave the British time to gather reinforcements from around the Empire. When the Boers realised their mistake and fell back on highly mobile guerrilla warfare they scored many successes under the exceptional leadership of the younger generals like Christiaan de Wet, Koos de la Rey, Louis Botha and Jan Smuts, backed by a core of more junior officers to whom this type of fighting was meat and drink. They proved so difficult to defeat that the British, as is known, eventually resorted to the drastic "scorched earth" policy and wiped out thousands of farms and all their crops and livestock in order to starve out the commandos.

Armies have always made use of one or other of the aforementioned methods of warfare, not only in Africa but all over the world, and not only in the past but in the present as well. Occasionally, however, it happens that an army can forge the different elements into one unified method of warfare which is precisely tailored to the conditions of a certain time and place. In a way the South African Army succeeded in achieving this during the Border War by harmonising its counterinsurgency, mobile conventional and guerrilla warfare methods and means into a unified operational concept.

Our field army was extremely small and relied mainly on white male conscript soldiers to make up its full-time units such as 61 Mech, whose rank and file consisted of national servicemen and the leader group of a core of Permanent Force officers, warrant-officers and non-commissioned officers, plus some rigorously trained national service officers and junior NCOs.[11] Then there were a number of locally recruited indigenous volunteer regular units,

11 See Chapter 4.

the best-known being 32 Battalion,[12] 201 Battalion[13] and 101 Battalion[14]. These first-line fighting units bore the brunt of the Border War and fought with distinction alongside units such as 61 Mech.[15]

In addition the SADF maintained a far larger, fully trained and organised part-time component, the Citizen Force and Commando Force, some units of which had territorial defence duties and others a conventional role; these units could be, and frequently were, called up in whole or in part for one or other role as the situation demanded.

The basic problem in land warfare is to find the proper balance between the positional elements (the attritionist approach) and mobile-warfare practitioners (the manoeuvrist approach), and throughout the history of warfare armies have see-sawed between these two extremes. Even the South African Army fell into this trap late in the Border War, when – completely out of character – it besieged Cuito Cuanavale from January until August 1988.[16] In one blurring moment the South Africans fell into an attrition trap by turning their backs on their highly successful manoeuvrist mode and allowing themselves to be bogged down (see Figure 5). It cost them dearly in terms of political and military prestige, although fortunately not in lives!

At the end of the day, an effective army must be designed to attack and defend well, and to deliver the ultimate attack far to the enemy's rear. An excellent example in our context is the deep thrust and then the successful attack by the South Africans and UNITA against FAPLA's 16 Brigade at the source of the Chambinga River on 9 November 1987 – the ultimate turning manoeuvre.

The Enemy – Operational Concepts as Applied by FAPLA for Conventional Warfare

To my mind FAPLA's military concept throughout the 1980s were based on rigid Soviet military doctrine, which demanded an attritionist (or positional) approach. This concept can best be seen in the static defence tactics used by FAPLA and the Cuban forces at Cuito Cuanavale from December 1987 until August 1988. Here they were remarkably successful, mainly because of their overwhelming numbers, massive international political support and an enormous amount of Soviet and Cuban aid, rather than fighting ability.[17] In the end the SADF could not take them on and exercised its choice of withdrawing to SWA/Namibia[18] by August 1988.

Such static strongpoint defensive concepts were no guarantee of success, it should be added. They were also applied by FAPLA and its Russian advisors at Xangongo and Ondjiva during Operation Protea in 1981 and at Cuvelai during Operation Askari in 1984; but with zero success. Although they enjoyed the advantage of fighting on ground of their own choosing, the Angolan conventional brigades were decisively destroyed by much smaller SADF forces at a very low cost to the South Africans in terms of personnel and vehicles.

12 Former guerrilla fighters recruited from Angolan liberation movements during Operation Savannah in 1975–76 and formed into 32 Battalion by Colonel Jan Breytenbach.

13 Bushmen Battalion made up of wily soldiers who were superb at field craft and tracking.

14 Ovambo Battalion stationed at Ondangwa in Sector 10. These soldiers excelled in counterinsurgency warfare, especially hot-pursuits from Casspirs.

15 See Chapter 4.

16 See Chapter 15.

17 See Chapter 15.

18 South West Africa.

To those of us who witnessed Operation Protea at first hand, this was a doctrine preset in the teachings of the Soviets. True to form, it was firmly rooted in the mindset of the Soviet society of that time, which rested on stability, rigid order and firm authority: One of the Soviets' sacred shibboleths was that "thou shall not use thy mobile reserve until given the explicit permission to do so" – which often did not arrive till it was too late, or even did not arrive at all!

This was one of the most surprising aspects of Operation Protea. At Cahama FAPLA had a large and well-equipped mobile reserve which included tanks – which we did not have – and there was nothing between them and Xangongo, a mere 46 km away except one under-strength battle group based on 61 Mech. But the Cahama force never once even probed or reconnoitred in force in the direction of Xangongo, where another SADF battle group was systematically destroying one strongpoint after another.

This was exactly in line with the SADF planning, which was to keep the Cahama force confused and therefore fixed in useless defensive positions by mounting a few feint attacks but keeping well out of harm's way for the most part.[19] And it worked brilliantly – they remained glued to the ground until our attack force withdrew at the end of August 1981, and thereafter as well.

The mental make-up, character and personality of FAPLA's Russian advisors and their Cuban surrogates were clearly influenced by the Soviet culture, which demanded blind obedience and little freedom for manoeuvre or the use of initiative by the field commanders. Such a system demanded the existence of a powerful controlling minority, a large executive organisation and strong conventional military forces that could be employed en masse. The result in Angola was a style of warfare which was rigid and deliberate, with slow-moving formations, cumbersome command-and-control systems and decision-making processes which were slow at best, with its practitioners most comfortable when burrowed into the ground, secure in the deceptive feeling of comfort and power conferred by their blind faith in their great amounts of military hardware.

As it transpired, our conventional foe was never able to slough off this mindset. So until the very end they remained predisposed to a war of position and preferred to defend their widely dispersed towns with heavily armed forces, where they feasted off the poor locals. Inevitably this meant that large gaps existed between defended localities, which weakened the mutual support so dearly required in defence and made them extremely vulnerable to surprise attacks. South Africa's mobile forces could therefore quite easily sneak through the gaps and strike at the enemy from unexpected directions, which was exactly what they did during many external operations.

The above being the case, any idea of the South Africans taking on the formidable integrated FAPLA-Cuban defences at Cuito Cuanavale from the east would have been extremely ill-advised. So why the hell did the SADF try to fight there in attritionist mode? It was the exact opposite of what might have been done. As early as mid-October 1987 the tactical commanders on the ground were suggesting that the enemy be attacked from west of the Cuito Cuanavale River; this way, fluidity would have been restored to the battlefield, with the opportunity to conduct mobile attacks from behind the enemy lines. It didn't happen. Enough said!

19 See Chapter 12.

About African Fighting Space and Other Soldierly Stuff

Please read this section in conjunction with Chapter 5 on "Terrain as we knew it – the Neutral Factor". Terrain had everything to do with warfare in Africa: Terrain in general; terrain and enemy; terrain and own forces; terrain and weather conditions; terrain and distance; terrain and people. Terrain was the playfield; terrain was everything – the neutral factor. Better use it well!

The wide, densely covered open spaces of SWA/Namibia and Angola suited the exponents of insurgency, guerrilla and conventional-type mobile warfare: For the insurgent and the guerrilla fighter to evade and to strike at many places; for the exponent of mobile warfare to manoeuvre through the gaps, to concentrate superior forces at points of decision and to strike quickly when least expected. I could clearly understand why Mao Tse-tung had said that "guerrilla warfare steps out of the bounds of tactics and knocks at the door of strategy, demanding that problems of guerrilla warfare be considered from a strategic viewpoint".[20]

We field soldiers, the 20th Century version of Shakespeare's "happy few", gallivanted around in the bush, doing what we knew and doing it well, while the politicians and the military high command sorted out the politics and strategies, or so we trusted. Oh, yes, there was one slight hitch on the ground: Most of the local population sided with the enemy and not with us. There were a number of civilian neutrals out there who did not really care which way the wind blew. Yes, strategic and tactical intelligence was another bedevilling factor. Otherwise we were quite good at the fighting game – if you don't believe us, ask our enemies.

Without accurate and timely intelligence, and the means to react quickly to such intelligence, mobility has little effect. In the denseness of Africa, human intelligence was much more valuable than aerial reconnaissance. Hence good intelligence and rapid deployment are two further conditions that must be present for a force to be able to engage successfully in mobile warfare. Quick reaction results from good communication and commanders who can take the initiative and make quick decisions.[21]

There was one more condition to be considered, which needed to be brought within the prescripts of a fighting recipe for the South Africans to win; and that was to understand the African way of warfare and to make it a way of life.

Warfare the African Way – Trials by Fire

Warfare in Africa as we experienced it was not neat and clean, easily comprehended or linear, with peace and war at the opposite ends of the spectrum. At the blink of a commander's eye you could switch from conventional warfare mode to counterinsurgency and back again, or apply a combination of the two. Therefore, embedded in our operational concepts within the African context was the habit of making the battlefield fluid, which was achieved through high mobility operations and deep penetrations behind the enemy's static positions. Many deep operations were launched from temporarily established helicopter bases. Those fighting methods were well attuned to the African battle space, and such trials by fire resulted in doctrinal innovations founded on the lessons of the battlefield.

20 De Vries, R. Colonel. *Mobiele Oorlogvoering – 'n Perspektief vir Suider-Afrika*: FJM Harman Publishers, Pretoria, 1987, p. 121.

21 These important elements of command, leadership and morale for mobile warfare are dealt with in Chapter 8.

The South Africans purposely planned their operations to out-think and outsmart the foe, among other things by means of interesting out-of-the-box innovations which we called "jackal operations". This tactical approach was taught to young and older officers alike by General Jannie Geldenhuys; basically, it amounted to the application of whatever type of battle craft and ingenuity would leave the enemy guessing or confused. It was a concept cleverly linked to what the renowned military author B.H. Liddell Hart referred to as "the strategy of the indirect approach".[22] I defined it for my own satisfaction as follows: Attack with strength against weakness; hit the enemy in his centres of gravity; take the enemy from least expected directions; strike deep and ferociously; threaten his lines of communication, rear areas and command centres.

Another obvious winning factor was that the South Africans and UNITA made much better use of the neutral factors – space, dense vegetation and darkness – than FAPLA and the Cubans. The dense bush and the night served as mediums for manoeuvring and were carefully utilised to offset a major deficiency in our mechanised land warfare capability: the lack of appropriate and adequate anti-aircraft weapon systems, including air fighter assets.

The shroud of the night was used for protection, controlled movement, dispersion and concentration of forces – to mask, to hide and to strike. Offensive mobile operations were the means by which to achieve this aim. It was also the main method of preserving one's own force and avoiding getting caught in any position where you were vulnerable to set piece attack or destruction in detail by enemy fire. This was very important to the South Africans, as we were not prepared to sacrifice unnecessary lives in futile exercises; blood was definitely not the price of victory. Tactics that suited the requirements of the South Africans within this particular operational sphere were applied as far as possible. These practices had to be stretched at times, and at Cuito Cuanavale in 1987 to 1988, they were forfeited to some extent. Some of these characteristics were:

- Ground was held only while it afforded a tactical advantage. When stationary for short durations, combat groupings leaguered in hides where all-round defence was possible. The artillery operated from well-camouflaged battery firing positions. Units such as 61 Mech and 32 Battalion were never stationary for very long and operated from well-concealed hides. When stationary for short periods, troops dug shallow slit trenches for protection against possible enemy air attack and ground and artillery fire. Combat was offensive by nature.
- Manoeuvring was characterised by constant movement, controlled concentration and dispersion of forces – hiding, camouflaging and planning; then purposefully moving once again. It was a process of continuous operational assessment, intelligence gathering and quick decision taking; of being constantly aware of the situation. It was crucially important to know yourself, know your enemy and know where he was all the time. Excellent timing was another essential requirement.
- The battle sequence constantly applied was to see (or sense), decide and then act; but quickly, so as not to allow the foe the latitude and privilege of quality thinking, timely response and sensible engagement.

Some of the SADF's manoeuvre warfare concepts were rooted in what General Jannie Geldenhuys taught us, values which were embedded in our subconscious minds and became second nature to us: "Make the battlefield fluid; strike deep; exploit your night-combat

22 Liddell Hart, B.H.: *Strategy*. Faber and Faber Ltd, London, 1967.

capability; use mobility and firepower to the fullest." He taught us to win, notwithstanding the odds, because there was no alternative. He taught us to apply the principles of warfare to the fullest. This was known as his "winning recipe".

To discuss this, it is necessary to put the concepts of attritionist versus manoeuvrist warfare into the correct perspective.

Attrition versus Manoeuvrist Warfare – Race to the Swift

Attrition warfare is similar to trench warfare – opposing lines of dug-in men with vast stretches of no man's land in-between, a classic example being the British and German network on the Somme River in France during World War I – which could be reduced to a formula of mass over time (see Figure 3). Conversely, classic manoeuvrist warfare is exemplified by the "Blitzkrieg" which its early exponents like Generals Heinz Güderian and Erwin Rommel unleashed on the French and British in May 1940, when World War II really got started. Their winning recipe was rooted in the application of momentum by utilising mass and speed to its best advantage, taking calculated risks, accepting open flanks and striking deep into the enemy's rear areas (see Figure 4).

On a continuum of war-fighting traits (see Figure 5); the attritionist approach (positional warfare) is viewed as the direct opposite to the manoeuvrist mode (mobile warfare). Mobile and revolutionary warfare are appreciated as sharing the same position on the continuum of warfare because of their dynamic nature. In a true sense, any exponent of

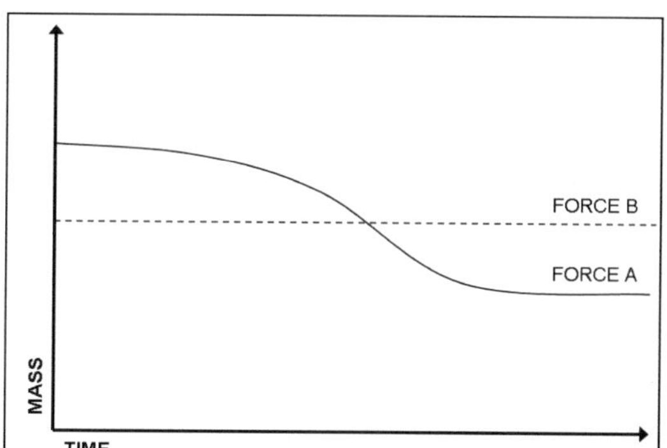

Figure 3: Attrition Theory – Two-Dimensional Figure

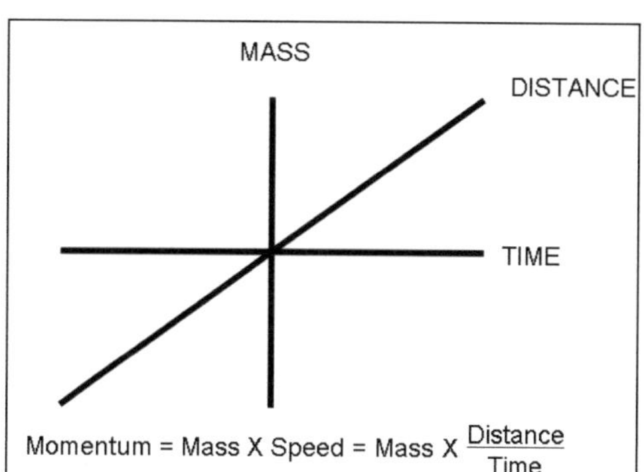

Figure 4: Manoeuvre Theory – Three-Dimensional Figure

warfare has a choice of adopting either an attritionist or a manoeuvrist approach.

It is often the case that a proponent of warfare leans more to the one than to the other. At the outbreak of World War Two, for example, the British and French armies favoured the positional concept, or to be more precise, linear warfare. In contrast, the German favoured their vision of mobile warfare, as manifested in the Blitzkrieg. In most battles, however, these two forms flow together (see Figures 6 and 7). In the deliberate attack, after break-in has been established, the grinding breakthrough battle necessarily needs to follow on in attritionist mode until breakout has been established.

The exponent of manoeuvre places his own force in an advantageous position from the outset, so that initiative and freedom of action can prevail. Surprise, disruption and dislocation of the enemy beforehand form part of the preamble to the main action, and are therefore deliberate acts which rarely derive from a commander's whim or sudden inspiration.

When adopting either an attritionist or a manoeuvrist approach, a choice needs to be made, but there is much more to it! Furthermore, regarding the theory, remember that the deeper the strike, the more the leverage, as is explained in Figure 6. As a general rule it can be said that "the nearer to the force that the cut is made, the more immediate the effect; the nearer to the base, the greater the effect. In either case, the effect becomes much greater and more quickly felt if made against a force that is in motion, and in the course of carrying out an operation, than against a force that is stationary." [23]

- The attritionist theory is more about head-on fighting and primarily about casualties, and material losses and massing forces over time, as the enemy did at Cuito Cuanavale.[24] The criterion for success lies in holding and denying ground to your enemy. That is why FAPLA and the Cubans said that they had beaten us at Cuito Cuanavale. Of course there was the political propaganda angle to it; the one thing the enemy was good at. For them it did not matter that the South African brigade and UNITA guerrilla units in situ were never encircled, cut off or threatened with destruction. Our own force was even allowed to withdraw from the Cuito front by the end of August without any enemy interference. In the same vein, did the enemy ever counter-attack? The answer is, "No". True to form, they remained rooted in their positions, as we had suspected they would be. Perhaps now is the right time and place to mention the reality (so often misconstrued) that it is quite possible to win a few battles and yet lose... something else.
- The manoeuvrist theory favoured by the South African conventional forces, on the other hand, was all about motion, appropriately defined as an approach to operations in which shattering the enemy's overall cohesion and will to fight is paramount. It calls for an attitude of mind in which doing the unexpected, using initiative and seeking originality is combined with a ruthless determination to succeed. The validity for manoeuvre warfare therefore lies in mobility.

Mobile warfare as such appears on any battlefield in the form of élan, audacity and the willingness to take calculated risks. This theory underscores dynamic determinants of warfare such as surprise; swift movement; momentum; manoeuvre; deep penetration; maintenance of the initiative and freedom of action; quick decision-taking; and command from the front. Mobile warfare by the South Africans emphasised point-of-main-effort

23 Liddell Hart, B.H.: *Strategy*. Faber and Faber Ltd, London, 1967, p. 331.

24 See Chapter 15.

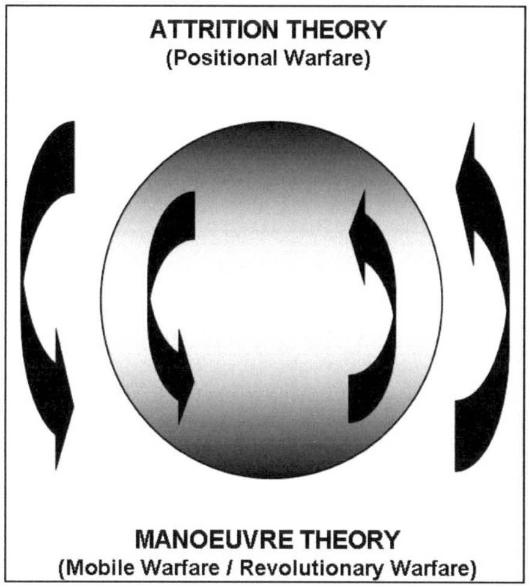

Figure 5: The Attritionist versus Manoeuvrist Theory of Warfare

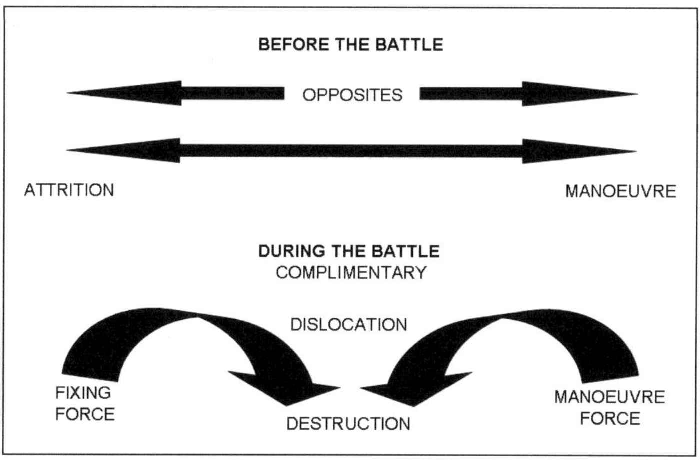

Figure 6: Attrition and Manoeuvre – Three-Dimensional Figure

Figure 7: Manoeuvre Theory –Three-Dimensional Figure

tactics and the principle of commanding from the front.

This was a way of warfare which many a time left our numerically superior foe aghast and floundering on the battlefield. This concept as we experienced it in southern Angola highlighted the validity of operations in depth, the quick thrust and the pre-emptive strike. Such emergent doctrine for the SA Army, moreover, initiated the professional development of officers and soldiers, who became attuned to mobile battles requiring quick decisions.

During the initial conventional battles fought in southern Angola the South Africans quickly learned that their smaller conventional forces could overcome a numerically superior foe through manoeuvre and then carry the day, but during the major battles fought at Cuito Cuanavale early in 1988, the tables were turned by our enemy's stubborn defence. The South Africans had allowed their combat force to be drawn into a heavily defended position which could not be overcome, and they were compelled to withdraw. In this example mobility was forfeited by the SADF and the initiative was subsequently lost to the enemy. The lesson to be learned from this is that the yardstick by which success on the battlefield is measured is the degree of freedom of action and retention of the initiative that one enjoys at the end of the fighting.

The characteristics of attritionist versus manoeuvrist warfare are summarised as follows:

- Attritionist or Positional Warfare (mainly followed by FAPLA):
  - Is more physically inclined, as men and material outweigh the psychological aspects of warfare, such as sound morale and the will to fight.
  - Is manifested in the dispersal of forces over a wide front and depth.
  - Places too much reliance on mobile reserves.
  - Can limit the choice of suitable terrain and obstacles to defend it.
  - Results in forces becoming fixed to static positions.
  - Is manpower and firepower intensive..
  - Requires deliberate defensive works and obstacles.
  - Could result in a protracted war of attrition.
  - Results in high casualty rates.
  - Is reliant on static command which is usually deployed to the rear.
- Manoeuvrist or Mobile Warfare (mainly followed by the South Africans):
  - Is proactive and offensive by nature.
  - Applies dynamic determinants of warfare, such as manoeuvre, rapid deployment, surprise, flexibility and secrecy.
  - Is intended to destroy the opposing force rather than to hold ground.
  - Uses ground as a tactical determinant for manoeuvring and fire and movement.
  - Creates fluidity on the battlefield, which keeps an enemy off balance.
  - Is characterised by battles of quick decision.
  - Pursues both the physical and the psychological elements of dynamic warfare, i.e. the destruction of the foe as well as the breaking of his will to fight.
  - Have low casualty rates as a main attribute.
  - Features dynamic command from the front.

In Conclusion – Hopefully Leaving a Legacy

A number of extremely important lessons were learned by the South Africans during the conventional and semi-conventional warfare in southern Angola. Those trying but invigorating years most definitely paid dividends. The ideas and innovations which emerged suited the African terrain and its vegetation, and useful practical knowledge resulted from direct operational exposure and experiences. The most important of these lessons were:

- High mobility based on wheels as the mainstay of a force, with a critical core of tanks and armed helicopters for the main punch and psychological effect, but without compromising maintenance and supply support too much.
- The ability to deploy rapidly over hundreds of kilometres with little or no road infrastructure.
- Airdrop and air-landed capability for purposes of both strategic and tactical mobility, and also to overcome the lack of any road infrastructure.
- Mine-protected vehicles throughout, as African conflicts are characterised by the heavy mining of routes, river-crossings and defiles.
- Reliable and secure communications to cover the great deployment distances involved and for sound command and control purposes.
- The ability to function in small deployments independent of larger defence formations and authority.
- Survivability in harsh environments characterised by heat, dust and a mixture of intense dryness and high humidity, and as well as great numbers of flies and mosquitoes.
- Serviceability in an operating environment in which users and support personnel may not possess the same degree of technological sophistication enjoyed by first world armies.
- Technical support decentralised to battery, company or squadron – and even troop or platoon – level to ensure serviceability in a dispersed small unit deployment scenario.
- Equipment, ordnance and personnel capable of maximising the use of local protection and passive air defence measures.
- Simple and reliable command and control systems allowing for deployment in a complex and fluid battlefield environment.
- Logistical support for small units deployed independently for sustained periods.
- Reduced dependence on a constant supply of consumables such as batteries, cabling and similar commodities.
- Robust equipment capable of withstanding rough treatment in a rough environment.
- Long shelf life of munitions with little maintenance, as the intensity of operational requirements will be sporadic.
- Simple optical target acquisition as a backup to sophisticated technology.
- Ability to read the mind of the enemy and infiltrate his command and control system.
- High reliance on human intelligence.

To my mind over-reliance on high technology warfare in Africa was not the norm during our fighting days – practical command and control systems utilising appropriate technologies with the person-in-the-loop, yes. Military operations in Africa are soldier-intensive, boots-on-the-ground and human-centric in nature. The idea should be to equip soldiers appropriately without overburdening them, and to refrain from overindulging in high technology.

The need for the following will remain extremely relevant for the African battle space:

Appropriate, affordable and sustainable technology; the important role of dismounted soldiers as well as semi-modern mechanised forces; and the requirements for higher levels of interoperability within a joint and combined fighting environment.

To survive under arduous African battle conditions always necessitated thorough tactical planning and decisive action, a trait the South Africans were well versed in. Tactical prowess as applied by them enabled fast movement and precision engagement, so as to close in on and surprise the enemy at the right moment and place.

It was amazing that under these arduous African battle conditions a diminutive South African fighting brigade and a few UNITA guerrilla battalions could halt an overwhelming FAPLA-Cuban coalition force of eight angry mechanised brigades and two tactical groups at the Lomba River in September–December 1987, then chase them all the way back to Cuito Cuanavale; and that the enemy, with all his mechanised might, superior air power and enthusiastic Soviet and Cuban support, never had the guts to counter-attack from Cuito Cuanavale afterwards. Never had the guts, for that matter, to cross the border into SWA/Namibia, right up to the moment a ceasefire agreement was signed at Calueque on 22 August 1988.

The international perception during the 1980s was that South Africa had one of the toughest armies in the world, honed and sharpened by 22 years of bush war on the Angolan/Namibian border. This military force had proved its steel as a formidable fighting force. It was something to be proud of.

7

Ways of the Warrior

Fundamental Truths

Generally in war, use the normal force to engage; use the extraordinary to win.
Sun Tzu

Introduction – Operational Concepts and Norms of Warfare

This chapter addresses the fundamentals of warfare which can be used as a baseline to appraise the operations reviewed in the chapters which follow.[1] As a point of departure it is accepted that armies such as those of South Africa, Angola and Cuba as well as SWAPO[2] and UNITA[3] fought according to distinct concepts and norms of warfare they had chosen.[4] and that these concepts and norms determined the way in which they did battle.

An operational concept forms the core of an army's doctrine, while the principles of warfare provide the basis for how to fight battles and campaigns. Doctrine ensures a particular force's unity of opinion on the battlefield, and is intended to secure or retain the initiative and exercise it aggressively to defeat the enemy.

Ideally the destruction of the opposing force is achieved by throwing it off balance with powerful initial blows from unexpected directions and then following up rapidly to prevent its recovery; the best results are obtained when the initial blows are struck against critically important units or formations and vital areas whose loss will degrade the cohesion of enemy operations.

I sincerely advise that this tactic be followed rather than merely attacking the enemy's leading formations frontally, as the SADF[5] did at Cuito Cuanavale. The "unbalancing approach" should develop opportunities which enable your force to shift its main effort swiftly and take continuous advantage of the enemy's weaknesses. Military operations consequently require proper planning, preparation, execution and successful completion, with adherence to the principles of warfare.

This chapter is pertinent to the final campaign fought in southern Angola, where the blood of many soldiers had seeped into the ever-thirsty sands on the banks of the Lomba, Chambinga, Cuito and Cunene Rivers[6] in the 12 months of turmoil, blood, sweat and tears that separated August 1987 and August 1988. The final epic clash of arms occurred between 61 Mechanised Battalion Group and the advance guard of the 50th Cuban Division a few kilometres northwest of Calueque during Operation Hilti/Prone on 26–27 June 1988. This last battle led to the signing of a peace treaty between South Africa, Angola

1 Chapters 10 to 16.
2 South West Africa People's Organisation.
3 *Uniao para a Independencia Total de Angola* (Union for the Total Independence of Angola).
4 Refer to Chapter 6.
5 South African Defence Force.
6 See Chapters 15 and 16.

and Cuba in New York on 22 December 1988.

In that long, bloody year of battle for control of southern Angola almost 5,000 enemy soldiers died, as well as about 3,000 UNITA fighters and 43 South Africans. Inevitably the question arises: Who won? To this day a controversy still exists about who can claim victory, with the hard facts so obscured by ignorant comment, wishful thinking and (particularly from the Angolan/Cuban side) outright propaganda that it is likely to last for many years to come. Strangely enough, it is not the soldiers who were there who do the arguing (after all, they know very well what happened, whether they talk about it or not), but the politicians, the political commissars and the commentators – and, let it be said, a few die-hard senior soldiers.

It is not surprising that the topic remains hot even after all the time that has passed. The intensity of the fighting and the scale of the casualties surpassed anything in Southern Africa's military annals, and so people continue to seek reassurance that the precious lives of those fighting soldiers were not wasted, and that every 60 seconds' worth of distance run was worth the effort. But the problem with too much argument (as opposed to civilised discourse) is that there is a danger that the essence of what truly happened in southern Angola will be lost. And that would serve no purpose whatever.

Given the enormous international implications of what happened there, a tireless squabble about who won and who lost is not the point, is it? So I am going to share my simple viewpoints and try to bring enlightenment about what is meant by military campaigning, so that my readers can follow the facts and decide for themselves.

About Military Strategy and Tactics – Battles Fought Courageously for Victories that were Lost

There is no question about the fact that artful campaigning and crafty tactics should be linked to sensible military strategy for the successful conduct of a war. Strategy is the planning, coordination and general direction of military operations to meet overall political-military objectives. Military campaigns and tactics, on the other hand, are concerned with engagements in the field of battle which implement strategy over the short to medium term.

That renowned military theorist, Carl von Clausewitz, has a very succinct definition in this regard: "tactics is the art of using troops in battle". A campaign therefore is a series of tactical engagements fought within space over time. Theoretically, it would therefore be reasonable to assume that winning engagements in a campaign should lead to winning that campaign as well and ultimately to winning the war of which that campaign is a part. But is it ever that simple?

Informed military thinkers postulate that there should be a clear correlation between political goals and military strategy formulated by the grandmasters on the one hand, and on the other the campaigning of those mere mortals doing the dirty work on the ground. But do the politicians know this? I wondered about this many a time as I ate dust out there in the front line.

If there is such a clear correlation, why was the SADF[7] surprised by the massive FAPLA[8] and Cuban advance into southeastern Angola on 13 August 1987, and again by the 50th Cuban Division's arrival in southwestern Angola in May 1988? Why, why, why was our small force committed piecemeal into battle in southeast Angola in August 1987

7 South African Defence Force.

8 *Forças Armadas Populares de Libertação de Angola* (People's Armed for the Liberation of Angola).

against overwhelming odds, with one brigade fighting at the end of a teetering logistical limb against more than eight enemy brigades and two tactical groups? It was fun in a sense, was it not? At least we learned a helluva lot about fighting while outnumbered, and then winning all the same.

At times one can win all the battles and yet lose the war, as the Americans did in Vietnam, and are currently doing in Afghanistan and Iraq (the technospeak which makes this sound a little less embarrassing is "tactical victory, strategic defeat"). This phenomenon was aptly described by Harry G. Summers in his insightful analysis of the Vietnam War, "On Strategy". He makes a trenchant comment on the Vietnam affair by quoting an exchange between two colonels at the peace talks in Hanoi in 1973:

"You know we were never defeated on the battlefield," said the American Colonel ... His counterpart, a colonel from the North Vietnamese army, pondered his remark for a moment and then replied: "However, it is irrelevant ... "

Let us return then to one of those erstwhile battles of Vietnam for a meaningful moment from the pre-American era, described by Michael Elliott-Bateman in "Defeat in the East":

The place was Indo-China, the year 1954; the victors came in sand-shoes, trudging through the mud with ammunition slung on bamboo poles, signals wire in tricycles, the despatch riders on pushbikes. The vanquished went in tanks and armoured cars and half-tracks and lorries, trailing their howitzers and other weapons of conventional war. And all the while the rains the French had prayed for to save Dien Bien Phu splashed down cheerlessly on their retreat from Hanoi, a melancholy ending to an inglorious war.

The French Commander-in-Chief, General Henri Navarre, believed that he could draw the communist Vietnam Liberation Movement into a set-piece battle at Dien Bien Phu which would then lead to its ultimate defeat. Navarre had hoped to force the hand of the elusive Võ Nguyên Giáp, commander-in-chief of the Vietminh forces, and win a decisive conventional-type positional battle in open combat. Giáp was, however, far too wily a guerrilla fighter to let himself be lured into such an obvious trap.

He had been a most successful communist guerrilla leader against the Japanese in Indo-China from 1943 until the end of World War II, after which he set about fighting the French (and later, of course, the Americans). The result was almost inevitable. Cut off and under continuous artillery fire from high ground, Dien Bien Phu fell on 7 May 1954, and the commander, General Christian Marie Ferdinand de la Croix de Castries, and all his surviving men were led away into captivity.

It was a humiliating defeat for a major military power to suffer at the hands of a backward little Third World territory which most Westerners would have struggled to find on a map. Worse still, the French had been defeated in open combat on ground of their choosing. What makes Dien Bien Phu particularly interesting, however, was that it was not only a tactical victory for the Vietminh but a strategic one as well, because the French then decided to withdraw all their forces from Southeast Asia.

There is a certain similarity with what happened here almost 40 years later by the time peace finally took hold in Southwest Africa/Namibia. In 1990 the South African Defence Force had already left its soil and the hordes of Cubans north of the border had departed not only from Angola but from Africa itself. Long before that, however – almost from the beginning of my military career, in fact – Dien Bien Phu had been one of my favourite case studies and I had long known that Giáp was a leader of standing, although not always recognised as such. And the lesson I had drawn from the battle was that within the folds of strategy lies the essence of something else, that in reality winning and losing are not always what they seem. Think about it – this is exhilarating stuff.

In the same vein we could contemplate the relevancies vis-à-vis irrelevancies of either losing or winning in southern Angola. Let us face it, the South Africans and UNITA did not dislodge FAPLA and the Cubans who were defending Cuito Cuanavale for dear life in 1988; but neither was the South African-UNITA coalition force beaten there. During the convulsions of the war, Fidel Castro's sabre-rattling rose to a well-nigh deafening crescendo, but the fact is that the Cubans never had the guts to cross the border and stage an aggressive advance into SWA/Namibia.

Please note that this is fact, not fiction. Castro turned the alleged "Battle of Cuito Cuanavale" into an amazing propaganda victory to soothe his own ego and provide the Cubans with some hollow "glory" as a parting gift to themselves before they gave up on Angola. Similarly, the die-hards of the "old SADF" beat a victorious tattoo on their wheezing chests. However, as far as I am concerned the mythological elements of those victories/defeats were then, and still are, irrelevant today. So, like that proverbial anonymous voice from the rear ranks, I ask the following questions:

Were fabled victories not lost while a war was won by all belligerents through the creation of a better form of peace, watered by the spilt blood of so many soldiers in southern Angola and northern SWA/Namibia? Was Cuito Cuanavale not then a turning-point for the creation of democracy in Namibia in 1990, South Africa in 1994 and Angola in 2002? Why quarrel about the fairy-tale elements of such an important facet of history? Should we not rather focus on the plus points of the factual story? I fought for that; so did many of my friends, and our enemies as well.

It is absolutely true that the momentous clash of arms in southern Angola in 1978–88 was the final act of a war that had never been declared and was never fought through to its final conclusion, with one or other belligerent party being forced into unconditional surrender. So bloody what, then?

During the Yom Kippur War in 1973 the Israelis and the Arab coalition learned that a limited war could lead to political negotiations and a better form of peace which benefitted all parties. Every October those sworn enemies of the fairly recent past still celebrate victory for the same battle. Is this not similar to what happened in southern Angola, Namibia and South Africa? It is ironical, though, that present-day Egypt seems to be doing its damnedest to destroy itself.

Of one fact I remain certain: The tactical prowess of the South African soldier on the ground and his combat leadership and sheer tenacity saved the day for our politicians. It made FAPLA and Cubans think seriously about whether they dared cross the border and launch an offensive into SWA/Namibia.

I leave these few thoughts for your contemplation. Questions and answers concerning wars are never that obvious! Histories of long-gone wars are still being written, even rewritten, such as the narrative of the Second Anglo-Boer War. No doubt time will tell and it will all come out in the wash ... Probably when all of us who were there are long gone.

About Politics and Military Campaigns

In northern SWA and southern Angola in 1987–88 the politicians on both sides of the fence – shaken by the enormity of the extremely dangerous and precarious political and military events they had set in motion – realised that time was finally running out. There was none left for grand strategizing and political waffling, and only a little in which to work out how to get out with their hides semi-intact.

What went on then in the proverbial smoke-filled rooms at higher level is beyond the scope of this book, so I shall rest my case and let the jury decide. What I can say from personal experience is that we who were being shot at on the ground had some interesting hold-your-breath moments and some extremely exciting times. Things were simpler at grass-roots level – however much the political process might falter and the grand military strategies waver, down on the ground it was merely a case of us or them!

Consider the following observations about campaigning in general and fighting in the front line in particular; they might prove useful indicators with which to gauge what the hell actually happened in the war and help in understanding the descriptions in the pages that follow:

- A campaign is fought in a particular theatre of war, a sub-theatre or an operational area, such as the "Western Sub-Theatre" of the Border War.[9] A military campaign, furthermore, is phased into smaller campaigns or operations, such as Operations Modular, Hooper, Packer and Prone, which form (or should form) an integrated whole.
- A campaign should result in the realisation of political-military objectives or campaign goals, which need to be attained to either, terminate or resolve a conflict on favourable terms. At the next level, clear operational objectives are set which need to be achieved in the campaign to accomplish the desired strategic end-state.
- Fundamental rules (the principles of warfare) which govern the conduct of warfare apply at the strategic, operational and tactical levels. Specific principles are also devised for the conduct of different types of tactical actions, for example offensive, defensive and retrograde (withdrawal) operations.
- Battle doctrine is devised and used according to the way a force fights. Doctrine can be compared to the civilian concept of "best practice methodology". It describes the nature and characteristics of current and future military operations and ensures uniformity of execution. The purpose of doctrine is to teach people how to think, not what to think. It is authoritative, but requires judgment in its application.

Campaigns can include many forms of offensive manoeuvring schemes, such as penetration, envelopment or encirclement. Within the defensive domain, a campaign can include both positional or mobile defence as well as any of the many forms of retrograde operations. It is interesting to study Napoleon's methods of fighting because he was a master at manoeuvring; he usually applied its many forms in combination, utilising surprise and deception throughout as a means of grasping the initiative before going for the kill. Essentials regarding the planning and conduct of military campaigns and its operations include the following:

- Manoeuvre. Manoeuvre is applied to obtain a favourable position in respect of the enemy. Manoeuvre warfare is aimed at breaking the cohesion of enemy operations and/or undermining your opponent's morale. This type of operation is aimed at the enemy's weak points.

9 See Maps 1 to 3.

- Sequencing. Sequencing implies the successive or parallel arrangement and subsequent application of actions in a campaign in order to reach the enemy's centre of gravity via the lines of operation. Operations are broken up into stages and phases to facilitate timing, and the concentration and dispersion of forces.
- Centre of Gravity. The centre of gravity is that element of the enemy's capability which, if attacked, destroyed or neutralised, will lead either to his inevitable defeat or to a desire on his part to pursue peace through negotiations.
- Combat Operations. Successive tactical combat operations are used to achieve either the intermediate or the final objective.
- Close Operations. Close operations are used to attack the enemy force directly on its front line so as to neutralise its combat power.
- Deep Operations. Deep operations are conducted far behind the enemy's front line and create preconditions for own forces' close operations, thus depriving him of his freedom of action and his ability to take the initiative. Furthermore, deep operations support the disruption of the enemy and thus the creation of confusion, which is vital for breaking the cohesion of his combat power.
- Psychological Operations. Psychological operations and actions can be applied to influence or destabilise the enemy's spiritual or intellectual component, making it hard for him to take considered decisions – or even any decisions at all.
- Lines of Operation. Lines of operation describe how military force is applied in time and space in order to reach the enemy's centre of gravity via decisive events or points. The commander normally endeavours to concentrate his forces in both space and time, while
- at the same time seeking to split the opposing forces and destroy them at different times.
- Decisive Points. Decisive points are those events whose successful outcome is a precondition for the successful elimination of the enemy's centre of gravity. A major operation can be launched as part of the process to achieve partial or predetermined operational objectives within a certain area or period of time. It is the coordinated design of a series of successive or simultaneous actions which are aimed at achieving a particular objective.
- Operational Pause. Because military operations cannot be conducted continuously, there may be a need for periodic pauses in a campaign or operation. The initiative must nevertheless be retained somehow during these pauses.
- Planning Factors. Planning factors are instruments which help the commander to estimate the situation. Some of these factors are derived from the higher level and some are derived from the planning process, or from other sources which are relevant for operational consideration. Examples of such factors are terrain, enemy, own forces, weather conditions, deception and so forth.
- Situational Awareness. Situational awareness implies informational superiority which enables quality decision-making. It requires early warning of a situation, optimised by means of surveillance and reconnaissance, and is based on quality intelligence, which in turn requires real-time and near real-time intelligence.
- Culminating Point. An operation reaches its culminating point when the momentum of the current operation can no longer be maintained.

"Operational" has taken on a new meaning in both general military comprehension and in its association with manoeuvre theory – that is, if you want to achieve success at the operational level so as to make a strategic impact. For a concept, plan or warlike act to be considered "operational" it must meet at least five criteria:

- It must have a mission – and one mission only – which is derived from an aim which can be stated in politico-economic terms (in other words from a strategic viewpoint);
- It must contain a dynamic closed-loop system which is characterised by speed and appropriateness of response;
- It must consist of at least three components, one of which reflects the opponent's will – others could be own forces and terrain;
- It must support the means of achieving synergy – that is, its whole must have an effect greater than that of the sum of its parts; and
- It must be self-contained within the scope of its mission.

The manoeuvre theory concept stemmed from thinking of this kind, and I am going to emphasise the next vital issue once more because it is such a core value – the strategy of the "indirect approach" as propounded by Sir Basil Liddell Hart: "Throughout the ages, decisive results in war have only been reached when the approach has been indirect ... It brings out the point that in almost all decisive campaigns the dislocation of the enemy's psychological and physical balance has been the vital prelude to a successful attempt at his overthrow ... "

Pre-emption, disruption and dislocation are therefore the norms applied by both the gifted strategist and the wily tactician. To this end make damn sure, to use the words of Sun Tzu, to "know yourself and the enemy, so as not to succumb in battle."

Reviewing the Last Conventional Battle Fought in Southern Angola in 1987–88

In reviewing the question of who was winning or losing the last conventional battle in southern Angola in 1987–88 when the fighting stopped, one can apply some quite simple criteria; just ask yourself which side held the initiative and was enjoying freedom of action and room for manoeuvre during and at the end of each battle sequence.[10]

- In July–August 1987, when the enemy started with his massive advance from Cuito Cuanavale towards Mavinga, the SADF and UNITA were caught by surprise, one might even say "wrong-footed". So FAPLA and the Cubans undoubtedly had the initiative and dictated the moves, moving up to the banks of the Lomba to a great fanfare in the government-controlled media.
- On 3 October 1987 a small SADF and UNITA force launched a decisively executed turning manoeuvre (the first of several) which destroyed 47 FAPLA Brigade at the Lomba; the enemy advance was halted in its tracks and disintegrated, with the entire FAPLA force fleeing hastily back to take up intermediary defensive positions hesitantly between the Lomba and Chambinga Rivers. They had lost the initiative, and the SADF and UNITA had regained their freedom of action and room for manoeuvre.
- The next turning manoeuvre followed when the SADF and UNITA destroyed 16 FAPLA Brigade at the source of the Chambinga River on 9 November 1987.

10 See Chapters 15 and 16 and Maps 16 to 18.

Once again the enemy forces fled precipitately and did not stop until they reached Cuito Cuanavale, which they prepared to defend at all costs. From October until December, therefore, the SADF and UNITA enjoyed total freedom of action, with the initiative firmly in their grasp. Then, to the SADF's astonishment, FAPLA stood its ground at Cuito.

- Unfortunately, the moment of operational autonomy was then lost when the SADF high command opted for a frontal attack by the lone South African brigade and its handful of attached UNITA battalions on the formidable defences on the eastern bank of the river. Those grinding battles lasted from January until March 1988, and as a result of this regrettable decision the South African forces and UNITA temporarily forfeited their room for manoeuvre and eventually had to withdraw from southeast Angola at the end of August. The initiative was handed to FAPLA and the Cubans on a platter.
- In the meantime, on the western front near Cahama and Calueque, the Cubans had come up with another uncomfortable surprise, their ultimate turning manoeuvre when their 50th Division suddenly appeared over the horizon from Havana. The SADF was compelled into a feverish skittering with small scampering steps. Was this battle the culminating point? Who had the initiative now?

At this point, one could delve into the deep recesses of the mind for a moment and pose the following questions: Were the political aims and directions set by the South African government for the winning of the war in the whole of southern Africa sensible? Did the SADF flounder in the domain of military strategy by biting off more than it could chew; or fall short in devising a viable campaign strategy for the western sub-theatre of war? Was the entire latter aspect disjointed, yes or no?

I am not speaking about the guile of tactical commanders in the field at places such as Cuito Cuanavale and of the attritionist predicament in which Colonels Paul Fouché and Pat McLoughlin landed when their troops were forced to hold that line; nor of astute combat group commanders such as Commandants Jan Malan, Cassie Schoeman, Robbie Hartslief, Jan Hougaardt, Gerhardt Louw, Mike Müller and Koos Liebenberg, who had to save the show! I pose the questions to people far higher up the political and military command chain. What are your answers?

In spite of what has been claimed – whether in ignorance or with malicious afterthought – it is as well to realise that the Cubans never made use of this moment of weakness and indecision to roll over the border and proceed with the conquest of SWA/Namibia during the ensuing months between 50 Division's deployment and the ceasefire on 22 August at Calueque, which preceded the peace settlement in New York on 22 December.

By then the last battle had been fought with a Cuban advance guard near Calueque. This uncomfortable situation was saved by the SADF in July when the newly formed 10 Division was hastily deployed in Sector 10, ready for either offensive or defensive action, or both. This move allowed for a breathing space and a deadlock, and all role players subsequently opted for peace. In the words of Antoine-Henri Jomini: "The art lies in turning to your advantage any chance that you can possibly foresee". The SADF had used delay and deception to restore the situation. So who had won the bloody war in the west and applied the principles of warfare the best, including the principles of revolutionary and counter-revolutionary warfare?

Principles of Conventional Warfare – Fundamental Truths

The principles of warfare were originally proposed by the renowned Prussian general and writer Carl von Clausewitz in his celebrated book "On War". This ageless military treatise reveals war stripped to the bone, an exercise of force for the attainment of a political object, unrestrained for a moment by any law save that of the military. In addition the logic of those principles of warfare is the foundation of the pioneering work that was done by Napoleon Bonaparte, the great military thinker and commander of his time.

The principles of warfare have become guiding precepts for many military organisations to focus the thinking of political and military leaders in order to successfully plan and conduct wars and smaller military operations. As such the principles are viewed as fundamental truths which have stood the test of time and are used to this day in many countries and their armies at the political, strategic, operational and tactical levels of war. That included the SADF where it was taught to military leaders at all training institutions.

During conventional warfare as experienced in southern Angola, opposing forces used conventional military weapons and tactics in open combat and were organised and equipped along classic military lines. Military structures were therefore organised into subunits (companies or squadrons), units (battalions or regiments) and formations (brigades or divisions). The purpose of such conventional structures and the operations in which they were employed was to destroy or weaken the enemy force.

Operations at this level are normally conducted without the employment of nuclear, biological or chemical weapons, but at least one of the opponents usually resorts to unconventional warfare tactics (and sometimes the other as well). The South Africans certainly did, using 32 Battalion, the Special Forces, UNITA and even the Air Force and South African Navy. In many cases, the latter operations were conducted behind the enemy's lines with the purpose of destabilising him.

Underlying the way the SADF fought, though, were the principles of conventional warfare as described below. These principles can be applied to my accounts of the battles in later chapters of this book to allow my readers to form an opinion as to where the planning and execution of the various operations and sub-operations went well, and where they did not, and likewise for our opponents, of course. Simply stated: To thine own self reveal the truth.

- Selection and maintenance of the aim – The first principle: Carefully considered so as to determine the true aim, well-formulated, clear, concise, unambiguous, decisive and binding. The execution should lie within the grasp of those entrusted with the achievement of the end-result. Once the vision is clear, the "how to" will be invented along the way.
- Concentration of effort – The critical principle: Concentration of forces at the decisive point and time; it is the concentration of strength against weakness, all in one, conceptually, physically and psychologically – to be there first with the most.
- Economical use of force – The regulating principle: The sensible application of military capability, including cost, space and time, in relation to the intermediate objectives and the results stated as achieved in the end. Implied is sustained resilience, the ability to bounce back, where the whole is bigger than the sum of the parts.
- Unity of command – The force-multiplying principle: The cohesive and binding power of dynamic command and leadership in attaining unity of effort at each

organisational level, tempered by sound judgement, responsibility, teamwork and mentorship – an unbroken chain of mutual trust, respect and understanding.

- Manoeuvre – The victory principle: The baseline here is to seek and maintain the initiative and thus your freedom of action by any means possible. Place the enemy on the horns of a dilemma. Use agility, mobility, flexibility of mind and the clever utilisation of combat power to achieve the mission.
- Offensive action – The élan/audacity principle: Aggressiveness tempered with initiative creates opportunities to be grasped with the aim of winning engagements and battles so as to win the war. Set the terms of the battle by your actions.
- Cooperation – The integration of effort principle: The unvarying quest to achieve interdependence, teamwork, mutual support, spontaneous cooperation and shared responsibility. At the lower level it implies combined arms integration and the decentralisation of control.
- Flexibility – The setting the pace principle: Acting faster than the enemy. The ability to meet changing situations rapidly, tempered by mental agility and the ability to improvise.
- Surprise – The physical and psychological shock principle: Mystify, mislead and surprise by means of agility and creative conception. Hit the enemy in his centre of gravity. Simultaneously attack the enemy's sensory, physical and psychological assets – pre-emption, disruption and dislocation are the name of the war-fighting game.
- Security – The "keep our secrets secret" principle: Deny information to the enemy and create conditions on the battlefield that will induce own initiative and freedom of action; so that the mission can be achieved more freely.
- Intelligence – The finger on the pulse principle: Maintain information superiority and situational awareness at every level within the sensory, physical and psychological spheres of warfare. Avoid being surprised by the enemy at all costs.
- Maintenance of reserves – The aces-high principle: Adequate reserves should be planned for and maintained at each appropriate level of warfare. Reserves allow commanders to influence the battle at the most opportune moments. This also makes it possible for soldiers to be reinforced when so required, provides comfort and positively influences morale. At times reserves allow the weary and stressed-out to be relieved and to rest. Reserves provide the substance to maintain momentum and exploit opportunity.
- Logistical support – The enabling principle: This principle implies that a sound balance exists between the teeth and the tail. It embraces both the physical and moral components of warfare within the spheres of logistics and administration. If support is adequate and appropriate, mission accomplishment is made possible.
- Maintenance of morale – The final principle: This principle is based on Napoleon's famous maxim: Morale is to the physical as three is to one. The principle of morale implies engendering esprit de corps by caring for your people and by being successful on the field of battle. The principle embraces tenacity, resilience and confidence in yourself and the others you are fighting with. Its strengths manifest themselves through high discipline, sound leadership, excellent training, skill at arms and comradeship.

To clinch the best possible usage of those principles according to the teachings of the renowned Liddell Hart, "one must, on the one hand, strive by all means to prevent the enemy from acting on sound principles; on the other hand, a supreme planning effort must be made to exploit those principles in order to facilitate the achievement of our aims and objectives. For this purpose, every principle which the enemy is likely to apply must serve as a target for the ingenuity of those who plan the operations of our forces..."

Soviet Principles of Warfare – The Style of the Steppe

Normally the national variations in war-fighting principles such as that of the SADF vis-à-vis the Soviets (or FAPLA, for that matter) are found in minor semantics and emphasis. The great differences come through cultural urges which are reflected in war priorities, operational concepts and the fighting methods of units and formations on the ground. By themselves the principles of the Soviets are grand and quite comprehensive. They are considered to be encompassing for the planning and conduct of military operations on land, sea and in the air, and include the following:

- High combat readiness.
- Surprise.
- Aggressiveness and decisiveness.
- Persistence and initiative.
- Combined arms coordination and joint operations.
- Decisive concentration of forces.
- Deep battle or deep operations.
- Information warfare.
- Exploitation of moral-political factors.
- Firm and continuous command and control.
- Comprehensive combat support.
- Timely restoration of reserves and combat potential.

Soviet and Western systems are similar, but the emphasis is different. Western systems allow more control and decision-making at lower levels of command, which comes with a consistent empowerment of people lower down in organisational structures. Offensive, mass and manoeuvre principles for the Western-type commander engender a sense of personal responsibility and authority to ensure that those principles are followed through by appropriate action.

In contrast the Soviet system stresses preparedness and obedience. This places more responsibility at the better prepared and informed higher level centres of command, and provides more overall control of the battle. FAPLA never seemed to master the principles of conventional warfare or the fighting tactics derived from them which were taught by the Russians, with the possible exception of their air defence, which in my view operated at a slightly higher level of competence.

The Angolans experienced extreme difficulty in conducting smooth-flowing operations and effecting tight control of indirect fire weapons during manoeuvres, and this applied to their air force as well. They were much more comfortable in static defence, preferably close to the home comforts of towns or other settlements. In addition, the maintenance of their fighting equipment was appalling (not that the SADF complained about that). FAPLA competence levels were better when it came to the maintenance of static reserves, their latent combat potential, which was provided by the Soviets and the Cubans, and the exploitation of political and propaganda factors.

To my mind our enemy's problem did not stem from the intrinsic value or otherwise of the Soviet principles but from their incompatibility with the hapless FAPLA soldiers' actual needs and the lack of suitable understanding and adaptation to make them fit into their new milieu. Specifically, I believe that the problem resulted from wrong interpretation of the Russian and Portuguese languages they were subjected to, a misunderstanding of the Soviet war-fighting dogma of fighting with forces en masse and with the rigidity of their command and war-faring theory which was originally devised for countering the German thrust over the steppes during World War II.

As far as I am aware, modern conventional African armies have generally been ineffective; they fare much better at insurgency and guerrilla warfare which has a less formal nature (which does not imply, I hasten to add, less personal courage or endurance) than the conventional environment. It is my sincere belief that this is why both UNITA and SWAPO were so effective in their guerrilla role.

I am afraid I could never say the same about the African National Congress's armed wing, Umkhonto we Sizwe, or "MK"[11], which operated so haphazardly inside South Africa or externally in some cases – to my knowledge the only semi-conventional service MK ever saw was when a battalion which was training in Angola was used for internal security duties in the hinterland during one of the Angolan/Cuban "pushes" against Mavinga and Jamba. To be honest, I did not see them even once until we started with defence transformation in January 1994.

But back to the original question: Why do conventional African armies generally have such an unimpressive record? In my opinion there are many factors which contribute to this less than acceptable level of competence, among them the economic, ideological and technical aspects, but the most important one has to do with culture and certain societal attributes which hinder the development of effective conventional forces.

The formal nature of conventional warfare and its highly disciplined environment, its dependence on stringent and almost obsessive attention to the control, coordination and timings of swift-flowing manoeuvres, just does not suit their temperament – let us be honest and admit, for example, that "African time" is not just a racist joke but a real phenomenon which is frequently encountered. Prove me wrong, if you can, but so far I have not seen evidence to the contrary.

There is no racist undertone to these remarks. I have dealt with too many black people of stature – as equals, as subordinates and as superiors – to have any prejudices of this kind. More than anything else, it is a matter of deeply rooted culture which is especially strong among the less Westernised, and it is my experience that a soldier's culture exerts a tremendous influence on his favoured methods of fighting.

So African armies tend to not to fare well when it comes to hands-on Western-style conventional fighting; they excel at waiting, delaying, evading and indirection, and therefore perform more successfully as insurgent, guerrilla or unconventional type forces. They also excel at political and propaganda warfare within the African context – or, as some commentators would have it, intimidation and twisting the truth.

As a result, when firmly entrenched cultural attributes are simply transplanted on to a Eurocentric conventional war fighting milieu in Africa it usually leads to over-centralisation, loss of flexibility, lack of initiative, the discouragement of leadership at the more junior levels and the manipulation of information. It needs hardly be said that the SADF did not complain about this when we were fighting FAPLA, since it suited us down to the ground, both figuratively and literally.

I am not alone in making statements as provocative as the above, and by way of proof I would like to quote some remarks by a Soviet officer named Vladimir Vasilievich Kostrachenkov in the book "Bush War – The Road to Cuito Cuanavale":

The only things that held together well were Kalashnikov assault rifles and Kalashnikov machine-guns. FAPLA used only those weapons. Once I went and asked a fighter, show me your weapon. When did you last clean it? We never clean them, he answered. They shoot fine as they are! The guy just laughed. They never cleaned their guns; never greased them with oil ... [11]

The Angolans hear gunfire and run. They aren't really brave soldiers. The Angolans were terrified of the South Africans. When we in the 16th, 21st and 47th Brigades went on a three-month offensive from Cuito Cuanavale to Jamba, many Angolans just ran away as soon as the South Africans advanced.[12]

I should add that Kostrachenkov and other Russian advisors who were attached to FAPLA do not come across as prejudiced in their writings. They were well-trained professional military officers who were doing a job of work in Angola and were fish out of water who frequently found themselves frustrated by the African way of doing things.

Once again I rest my case. In a sense I felt sorry for our Russian and Cuban equivalents, who, as military advisers and surrogate force members, had to contend with the "otherness" of Africa and, unlike us, did not understand it. Oh, well, that's the way they had to earn their campaign medals and bush pay. But it is interesting to read the accounts of the Soviets who served on the Cuito Cuanavale front. I respect their trials and tribulations, many of which were similar to what we as ordinary soldiers also experienced during the bush war.

Principles of Revolutionary Warfare – For the Guerrilla Warrior

Such acknowledged experts on revolutionary fighting as Mao Tse-tung and John J. McCuen present two sides of the same coin in their examination of the principles of warfare – one focuses on the art and science of revolutionary combat and the other on counter-revolutionary conflict.[13]

Revolutionary war is one of the most difficult types of war to deal with, because its proponents are willing to keep it going for many years. If it is not dealt with effectively, a long-term war will slowly weaken the nation's resolve while simultaneously strengthening the enemy's, and such conflicts are expensive, and sometimes bring a staggering cost in dead and wounded, as we saw during the SWA/Namibian Border War (although the bulk of the losses were SWAPOs and FAPLAs) and in many others elsewhere in Africa.

Liberation movements such as SWAPO knew that they could not defeat the SADF in a stand-up fight, but realised that it might be possible to weaken the government's resolve by what Mao Tse-tung refers to as "protracted war". The African National Congress applied the same stratagem in South Africa from the 1960s to 1994 to bring about political change in South Africa. In the process, counter-revolutionaries (a handy catchall term, normally used by revolutionaries to describe anyone who does not actively support them) customarily suffer at the hands of the insurgents, as happened in SWA/Namibia and is happening right now in Afghanistan and Iraq.

11 Chapter 2, p.24.
12 Chapter 2, p.27.
13 McCuen, John J.: *The Art of Counter Revolutionary War*. Faber and Faber Ltd., London, 1969.

It is extremely difficult to halt a determined revolutionary onslaught! In effect, revolutionaries use guerrilla warfare to turn the locals against the government. Mao Tse-tung, for example, based his revolutionary war in China in the 1930s and 1940s on a well-integrated political-military philosophy which he used to defeat first the Japanese invaders and eventually the nationalist forces (Kuomintang) of Chiang Kai-shek with the support of the local population.

Revolutionary war is about intangibles, about emotions and ideology rather than the killing of enemy forces. The fighting and the killing of the enemy is a means to an end, not an end to itself. Mao Tse-tung refers to this as the "People's War, a war of the masses which can be waged only by mobilising the masses and relying on them. What is the true bastion of iron? It is the masses, the millions upon millions of people who genuinely and sincerely support the revolution".14

How do you beat such a revolutionary surge, which has been making its appearance on the battlefield since the earliest times? "Guerrilla" is a Spanish word meaning "little war", and it became a permanent part of the international military lexicon during Napoleon's invasion of the Iberian Peninsula, when the French forces were harried by small groups of Spanish fighters driven by a political ideal, namely the desire to drive the invaders out of their homeland, even if this meant supporting other conventional forces (in this case the British).

Originally the actions of guerrilla warfare were purely military in nature, but by combining those with political and psychological aspects there emerged the concept of modern revolutionary warfare –that is, the practical application of Mao's military-political philosophy and doctrines. The nature of guerrilla and unconventional warfare is indirect and extremely fluid by nature, and could therefore be fully adapted to war-fighting conditions in Africa, since the natural geographical milieu and the people living in it are well-suited to this type of warfare.

The maintenance of momentum and the creation of fluidity in operations are core requirements for the successful waging of guerrilla operations; in the infected areas, guerrillas are present everywhere and virtually unassailable. Success is rooted in the effect of numerous small-scale attacks, actions, harassments and threats, which continually destabilise the security forces. Hit-and-run tactics, or to put it differently, disrupt-and-run tactics, are the order of the day. This emphasises the disruptive and psychological effect of such tactics on the enemy.

Therefore, it is possible to formulate a good definition:15 Guerrilla warfare consists of military or paramilitary operations, carried out by unconventional, mainly indigenous forces in areas occupied by the enemy, or in enemy areas; unconventional warfare, on the other hand, consists of operations that include everything from guerrilla, special, pseudo and paramilitary actions to psychological warfare and the spreading of rumours and disinformation.

The phases of revolutionary warfare are briefly discussed in Chapter 10, where I relate my Rhodesian experience. Briefly, though, they are: Phase 1 – organisation and subversion; Phase 2 – terrorism and low-scale guerrilla warfare; Phase 3 – guerrilla warfare; and Phase 4 – mobile warfare. These phases need to be considered when contemplating the principles

14 Mao Tse-tung: *Quotations from Chairman Mao Tse-tung*. Foreign Language Press, Peking, 1972, p. 88.

15 De Vries, R., Kolonel: *Mobiele Oorlogvoering – 'n Perspektief vir Suider-Afrika*. FJM Harman Publishers, Pretoria, 1987, p. 118.

of revolutionary and counter-revolutionary warfare.

SWAPO and UNITA conducted their wars the revolutionary way, and the SADF's strategy should have been to apply the exact opposite – if it had been playing with a full deck of political-military cards, that is. The SADF definitely knocked SWAPO for a six on the military side, no question about that. But this was not the case on the political side. Similarly, FAPLA and the Cubans should have countered UNITA by applying this concept, whose underlying principle is quite simple – in a nutshell, what the revolutionaries do, the counter-revolutionaries must undo, and proactively. This takes much more than mere one-upmanship, and until today it remains one helluva tall order. As we speak it is happening all over again in Somalia, Libya, Syria, Afghanistan and Iraq; and we can see how it happened all over Africa and is still happening.

The principles of revolutionary warfare can be summed up as follows:

Strategic Principles

- Self-preservation and annihilation of the enemy – this is the essence of revolutionary war and the basis of all war activities.
- Establish strategic bases – it is impossible to sustain a war effort without bases.
- Mobilise the masses – the war can be carried out only by mobilising the masses, by respecting the people, helping them, defending them and relying on them.
- Secure external support – international support is necessary for the struggle in any country or any nation.
- Unity of effort – the whole point of what is to be done is the basic principle behind unifying the war effort, the strategy, tactics, planning and organisation.

Tactical Principles

- Initiative – to dictate unfolding events.
- Intelligence – to know beforehand and at all times what is happening.
- Mobility – to be there first with the most.
- Surprise – to surprise and to take advantage of that surprise.

In Chapter 5 the notion of our war being 80% political and 20% military has also been dealt with in a way. The problem lies with the political side of counter-revolutionary war and not so much with the military. If the politicians and the military grandmasters do not get that part right, any way the wind blows could result in finding yourself dying for the enemy's cause. I have never, but never, seen politicians operating at the tactical level as military section leaders and platoon commanders do. I have rarely seen ruling politicians of a beleaguered state putting an acceptable alternative vision and national policy to the madding (and maddening) crowds.

In a sense, this part of my treatise follows the mode with which Mao Tse-tung made his mark on war. That was the way my revolutionary enemies were taught in those days. My fellow counter-revolutionaries (as it were) and I were trained and educated to go it the John J. McCuen way. At the military level we did damn well, I believe. During all those years in the bush the enemy threat was contained in the extreme northern sector of SWA and they never succeeded in prospering beyond the terrorism phase. However, SWAPO kept us involved for close on 22 years while they merrily continued to win the hearts and minds in Ovamboland and the sympathies of the whole world. Think about it – they sit quite contentedly in Namibia's parliament today.

How does one reap the political rewards of one's magnificent tactical successes in counterinsurgency warfare? I believe that this particular question from our fighting days in northern SWA/Namibia, southern Angola, Rhodesia, and Mozambique still needs to be answered ... A failure to reconcile the political, strategic and tactical situations can only result in the inevitable defeat of any counterinsurgency effort, no matter how large it is or how many slaughtered enemy heads are counted. From my instructors in Taiwan I learned from the teachings of Mao Tse-tung that "to be bound rigidly in the tactical field by the tactical advantages and disadvantages of the moment, without applying these to the strategic and the political plan, is the way to disaster."

It needs hardly be said that politicians and senior military men who are embroiled in such wars should take account of those conflicts' strategic portion. Does anyone teach this to politicians at their schools as the military thinkers have done at theirs? Michael Elliot-Bateman seeks to answer this in his book "Defeat in the East". Pondering this particular common dilemma, he writes:

"The fundamental purpose of this book is to find a sound military basis for victory in Eastern Asia, if military means are to be used at all for Western political ends in that region. Indeed, this book is the product of an attempt to discover the secrets of war; an attempt that originated from a desire to find the root causes of British defeat at the early stages of the Second World War and which led to the realisation that present British military thought (is) on a similar course with defeat."

On home ground in northern SWA/Namibia, counter-revolutionary action came to be known as counterinsurgency by the military. In this regard, consider the concentration of forces in the countering of insurgency. Mao Tse-tung provides much food for thought: "Troop concentration seems to be easy, but is very difficult in practice. Everybody knows that the best method is to defeat the few with the many, but many people are incapable of doing that, and on the contrary divide up their forces because they become perplexed and enslaved by complicated circumstances, and lose the initiative."

The enemy then succeeds in fixing you, instead of the other way around ... Hello, northern SWA/Namibia, Rhodesia, Afghanistan, Iraq! It is easy to start a conventional war in such places; it takes but one command and a generous dose of shock and awe. It is not so easy to stop the political consequences once it explodes into a multi-faceted revolutionary onslaught.

I can remember well how, as a young paratrooper captain at the Special Warfare School in Taiwan in 1973, I was told: To effectively stop a guerrilla movement, the target country needs at least a 50 to 1 troop to guerrilla ratio. If its forces are highly mobile, a 10 to 1 ratio might suffice. Operation Yahoo of April–May 1982 proved the point: A brigade-sized counterinsurgency force of 3,000 men, 500 vehicles and many helicopters took 14 days to destroy a company-sized insurgent force just 156 strong.

Next, let us examine mobility as a tactical principle of counter-revolutionary warfare. Even here it is possible for tactical methods and means to become ensnared in an attritionist mindset. As the counterinsurgency war dragged on there was a proliferation of SADF military infrastructure and temporary bases across the depth and breadth of northern SWA/Namibia; and even in South Africa, for that matter. Every base became a comfort zone with which the enemy became intimately acquainted, including its inter-force boundaries. Every base required a staff, "IN" and "OUT" trays, a guard force, a reserve force, a mess tent, a canteen, logistics and so forth. All of this decreased the number of feet on the ground.

On the other hand, the South African Police, which fielded the highly mobile and effective Koevoet counterinsurgency force in the operational region from 1980 onwards, had a completely different strategy. The Koevoet men went wherever the action was, with their careering Casspirs in hot pursuit of the enemy. They operated from Oshakati in highly versatile teams, extremely base-independent, with flat organisational structures and maximum feet on the ground and on the move.

According to Mao Tse-tung a guerrilla depends on three main components: a big country; the support of the people; and a secure base area. SWAPO, however, did not become dependent on bases as we did. For them the term "base" had another meaning. Their prime concern was not war material and infrastructure but the people who had been through all the processes of indoctrination and mobilisation, and also the suitability of the countryside for their insurgent activities and political work.

The concept of "protected villages" that the Rhodesians used never ceased to amaze me when I served there. It was another one of those attritionist defensive line-ups. Instead of separating the people of the community from the guerrillas, it alienated them and drove them into the arms of the revolutionaries. In this way the security forces worked energetically for the opposition. It was crazy, if you think about it now. By the same token, the many miles of electrified fences along South Africa's northern and eastern borders, which were designed to keep the enemy out, only succeeded in fixing its own forces. In the meantime the enemy merrily taught their insurgents where the safe places were through which the border could be crossed in no time flat.

So what should the tactical solutions to this conundrum have been? Most probably the answer should have been to invest more heavily in intelligence, as the key driver, and in sound command and control and high mobility as the force multipliers; and of course in obtaining the loyalty of the people you are supposed to protect and serve in the first place. What was the aim of this whole thing in the first place, then – unity of effort?

By the way, there was a time in South Africa when it was illegal to possess or read Mao's "Military Writings" because "they" were afraid that you could become a communist. Ridiculous! Such debilitating factors by the former ruling party gave new meaning to the simple dictum of "know your enemy". I mean, what the hell, it was exactly what our enemy was doing. When I returned from the training course in Taiwan I brought with me – illegally, of course – quite a few of Mao's books. In actual fact, our small group of six officers who were there was taught "Chicom" – Chinese Communist tactics. It makes you think, doesn't it? You are tempted to misquote Shakespeare and say: "To be a counter-revolutionary or not to be, that is the question."

8

On Leadership and Command

Physical and Psychological Effects

The psychological is to the physical as three is to one.
Napoleon Bonaparte

Prologue – Command Brings Great Responsibility

Command – a Very Personal Matter

During my 37 years of service in the military I came to realise that command was a very personal thing. It brought great responsibility – for fulfilling your mission, for looking after the people you served and who in turn served you, and for dealing with and using the environment you functioned in which you found yourself.

This included your nearest and dearest, who supported you throughout all your life's endeavours – and in fact it seemed to me that command was very much like being the father of a family. It required a good deal of caring for and understanding of others as well as providing guidance and mentorship. In the military, especially when performing dangerous missions, people under one's command could flourish, shrivel, live or die. The success achieved by a fighting unit on the battlefield depended to a great extent on the decisions and actions of the commander, but sometimes matters were taken out of your hands by circumstances beyond your control.

When that happened, the pain of failure and the grief of loss proved slightly more bearable if you knew you had acted to the best of your knowledge and experience and according to your moral values; it was only the knowledge that you had acted in the most responsible and appropriate way possible which allowed you to move on to the next challenge awaiting you.

To me it seemed logical to merge leadership, management and command into one, with leadership being the most important element, the binding factor. Command was the positional power component in the equation, and leadership emphasised its personal element. It also allowed and encouraged the empowerment of people under your command. As I saw it, leadership was about unleashing potential, management was about executing plans, programmes and projects, and command about successfully achieving missions and preserving innocent lives.

The Levels of Command

At second hand, so to speak, I learned a valuable lesson about military leadership and command from "Defeat into Victory" by Field-Marshal William Slim, First Viscount Slim.[1] This detailed his successful campaign against the Japanese in Burma in 1945, for which "Bill" Slim justly achieved great fame.

1 Slim, Viscount, Field-Marshal: *Defeat into Victory*. British Library Cataloguing in Publication Data, London, 1986, p. 3.

Slim was an immensely experienced veteran of both world wars and in his opening passages had the following to say about military leadership in relation to the chain of command within an army:

> It was good fun commanding a division in the Iraq desert. It is good fun commanding a division anywhere. It is one of the four best commands in the Service – a platoon, a battalion, a division, and an army. A platoon, because it is your first command, and because, if you are any good, you know the men in it better than their mothers do and love them as much. A battalion, because it is a unit with a life of its own; whether it is good or bad depends on you alone; you have at last a real command. A division, because it is the smallest formation that is a complete orchestra of war and the largest in which every man can know you. An army because the creation of its spirit and its leadership in battle gives you the greatest unity of emotional and intellectual experience that can befall any man.

I had the good fortune of experiencing life and leadership to the fullest at the respective levels of command portrayed by Field-Marshal Slim in various positions in our army, as either a commander or a second-in-command: First as a young platoon commander at 1 Special Service Battalion; officer instructor at the School of Infantry; as company commander and battalion second-in-command at 1 South African Infantry Battalion; as the commander of a battalion-sized task force in Rhodesia; as the commander of 61 Mechanised Battalion Group during the border war; as a training wing commander and later on second-in-command at the Army Battle School; as commander of the South African Army College; as Chief of Staff of Northern Transvaal Command; as OC 7 South African Division; as commander of the Joint Training Division of the SADF and member of the Defence Staff Council; and finally as Deputy Chief of the South African Army and member of the Army General Staff.

Of all these, as my readers will be aware by now, my tenure as OC 61 Mech was my favourite time and the most rewarding of all my appointments. On the whole it was the most emotionally and intellectually stimulating experience a soldier could wish for. As my friend and colleague Epp van Lill, also a former OC 61 Mech, used to say: "If you were with 61 Mech, you were there."

61 Mech was where I learned a good deal about leadership and command within an operational milieu, and where I was able to shape my philosophy about these things.2 The primacy of output at 61 Mech was always the mission. It went hand and hand with initiative and empowerment. It entailed the limiting of all aspects which impeded creativity, intertwined with efficient and effective delivery. Our primary focus was placed on professionalism and cultivating self-discipline. People, their safety and their wellbeing were our first and foremost concern, above all other things.

My Philosophy on Leadership and Command

Leadership and Command – An Essential Ingredient to Combat and Life

During military operations in southern Africa, commanders and soldiers of the South African Army proved the crucial significance of leadership. I learned that the leadership

2 See Chapter 4.

qualities – inspirational motivation and continuous intellectual stimulation – served as essential ingredients in both combat and ordinary life. Sometimes I was amazed by how our young leaders and soldiers improvised when in dire straits and then simply got things done. It was particularly heartening to see our junior leaders and their national service soldiers in action, whether in close encounters with the enemy, playing games or just going about their ordinary daily tasks. They thrived on initiative, decentralised control and freedom of action.

Pure military leadership played a crucial role in the livelihood of units such as 61 Mech and its preparation for operations and battle. It was something our senior permanent staff members carefully and diligently nurtured in our national servicemen; I dearly appreciated our young soldiers' obvious natural aptitude for leadership.

First Principles – Cultivating Self-Discipline and Building Teams

I believed in mission command, both tight and loose control being the median.3 It worked for us at 61 Mech and in all my commands later on. I have always been extremely proud of and confident in my subordinates. To me, cultivating self-discipline was much more important than merely enforcing it. My basic rule was: If you push people and organisations, they push back. The moral was quite simple: So don't be stupid, don't do that – all you will achieve is the destruction of your own command.

South Africans don't respond well to that sort of treatment; to get the best out of them they need to be led, not driven. Some over-enthusiastic and overbearing military bullies I encountered never learned that all-important lesson. They should have read Kipling's "If" instead of strutting about like latter-day Genghis Khans. My attitude was that every person counted, that our sons in uniform clearly were men to be entrusted with the dangerous military work on hand!

Underlying these leadership and command precepts was the unremitting process of building interlocking sets of high-performance teams at the various levels in our organisations. To do this we had excellent combat leaders and supporting staffs. For example, at 61 Mech our basic fighting organisation was the company level subunit, which would normally be formed into an integrated all-arms combat team for operations. Our policy frameworks, military doctrine and standing operating procedures provided for integrated planning methods and the seamless execution of that planning. It was due to the combination of the planning and the unfettered enthusiasm of the people concerned that the whole became so much greater than merely the sum of its parts.

In my mind's eye I viewed leadership as being similar to a spider's web – if you touched one iota of it, it was energised throughout. In this way 61 Mech was probably one of the best conventionally trained and most completely cohesive operations-ready units in Africa, and as far as learning and experiencing about command and leadership are concerned, I was privileged, as were many others, to have served with this regiment. It was disbanded in 2005, but its memory lives on in the pages of this book and will continue to live on in our military annals.

3 See Figure 9.

The Participative Premise and Basic Precepts

Life's endeavours have convinced me that sustainable results can only be achieved through the active involvement of others, and that by and large people want to be productive and successful in life. I therefore fully believed in the premise of participative leadership, albeit without driving it (or us) around the bend. This philosophy was in harmony with modern military command principles such as "mission command", which I had studied thoroughly – the emphasis is on the mission and not a myriad tasks and lists of do's and don'ts.

During World War II the Germans applied the concept of what we now call "mission command", and they called "Auftragstaktik", with great success. From the 1980s onwards both the British and American forces began teaching the mission command concept as part of their newly adopted battle doctrines based on the manoeuvre theory of warfare. At 61 Mech Captain Jan Malan referred to this command style as "command initiative" ("bevelsinisiatief"). This concept is most aptly described by the following passage about the German military of the past, by Colonel T.N. Dupuy in "A Genius for War":[4]

> A favourable situation will never be exploited if commanders wait for orders. The highest commander and youngest soldier must always be conscious of the fact that omission and inactivity are worse than resorting to the wrong expedient. (Moltke).

A major (from a yesteryear Prussian Army), receiving a tongue-lashing from the prince for a tactical blunder, offered the excuse that he had been obeying orders, and reminded the prince that a Prussian officer was taught that an order from a superior was tantamount to an order from the king.

"Frederick Charles promptly responded: 'His Majesty made you a major because he believed you would know when not to obey his orders.'" This simple story became an inspiration for all following generations of German officers.

Some members of the old South African Army of the 1960s–1990s who were more set in their ways frowned on the new-fangled leadership and command approaches we were practising at 61 Mech; at the time, their approach was often inclined to be more authoritarian, with "rules-are-rules" management – checklists by clipboard, heart-breaking inspections and control measures to the extreme (no disrespect intended). Their methods were not for progressive 61 Mech, or for me.

The participative premise did not imply that you could not fire someone if it was truly warranted; or even that a serious or a subtle reprimand could not be handed out now and then. I have reprimanded, transferred and fired my fair share in the military; although I believed that I always did so in a responsible way and with consideration for the dignity of the individual.

Learning from mistakes was justified in my book (I made a few spectacular blunders in my time) and my dictum was therefore that one could make a few responsible mistakes, but not too many. If this was not the case, how the hell could mission command call for the taking of a calculated risk on the fluid battlefield? For this reason the framework for any decision taken required prior knowledge, the need for thorough planning beforehand and the maintenance of situational awareness at all times.

Decision-taking was not a luxury. Many a time it needed to be done without the luxury

4 Dupuy, T.N., Colonel: *A Genius for War – The German Army and General Staff 1807-1945*. A.T.N. Dupuy Associates Books, Macdonald and Janes, London, 1977, p. 116.

of having all the facts and information at hand, otherwise an opportunity might pass you by and leave you with your thumb in your bum and your eyes swivelling back and forth as if you were watching a tennis game. If you found you had taken a wrong or skewed decision, take another one and move on swiftly. Decisions triggered action and generated fresh information, allowing insight to flourish. A plan was merely a basis for change, a framework to enable you to move from one firm base to the next so as to remain one step ahead of any situation.

The norm was: See, decide and act; if an objective is achieved, follow through to the next, otherwise you flatten out – in other words, maintain perpetual motion between any advantageous shifting positions. Equitable and sensible delegation of work, with the concomitant responsibility to people under one's command remained an essential requisite; however, accountability was the prerogative of the commander, and he should never have shied away from it. It went hand in hand with the consideration for each individual, and the responsibility of the leader to encourage the people entrusted to him through intellectual stimulation and inspirational motivation. To achieve the latter was extremely rewarding.

Furthermore, as a leader I believed in setting the example and therefore worked very hard throughout my career, as all my people knew. Many a time at 61 Mech I would return from Omuthiya to my alternative office at the Tsumeb rear HQ in the company of my adjutant, a national service lieutenant named Henri Boshoff. We would then work together on administrative tasks, sometimes until 3 o'clock in the morning, before going briefly to bed, and at 6am we would be off to Omuthiya again, taking cat-naps during the two-hour drive.

Similarly, the office lights of other officers often burned through the night, especially those of my logistics expert, Major Giel Reinecke. Reinecke's office was situated in a temporary building at the rear of our office at Tsumeb which was screened off with mesh to keep the ever-attentive mosquitoes away. A steaming hot tin mug of agreeable coffee close at hand kept him company as he worked through the night on stacks of logistics files, estimates, plans, indents, stock sheets and ledgers. Now and then, when the work allowed, we would meet at night for an stimulating chat. In 1982 his dedication and hard work at 61 Mech were recognised by the well-deserved award of the Military Merit Medal which was presented for "service of a high order" in both peace and war, and which certainly applied to his efforts.

Giel's office was not the only theatre in which the "paper war" was waged. Public administration had to be applied meticulously as well: the books and the ledgers had to balance, fair audit reports had to be achieved and logistics competitions won; ask my 2IC, Major Thys Rall, about this, and Giel Reinecke as well. Ask Lieutenant Andy Weyand and Sergeant Bets de Klerk about paying more than 1,000 people – basic pay, danger pay, allowances, deductions and all the rest, not to mention sorting out pay problems (which infuriate a soldier more than anything else). Ask my tiffy Sergeant-Major, Duppie du Plessis, about his technical journals, maintenance schedules and his tireless personal quest for 100% serviceability.

A magic phrase any officer needs to learn at the very start of his career is "carry on". This does not imply walking away from work but of picking the right people for a job (about which they might well know more than you do) and then letting them get on with it. Micro-managing commanders sometimes come close to being "enemy" saboteurs.

On Mission Command – Exploiting Favourable Situations

Command and Control – the Mission Came First

Command and control was designed through all the ages of warfare to achieve unity of effort throughout all the various organisational levels. It clearly underscored the requirement of commanders to exercise authority, discretion and direction over assigned and attached resources in the accomplishment of their missions. In the military this is denoted C3I, which refers to an integrated system embracing the functions and supporting elements of command, control, communications and intelligence.

Sophisticated computer systems were not available to the SADF during the Border War – the days of Desert Storm still lay far into the future. But at 61 Mech we more than made do by personalising our own highly integrated command and control methods and support systems for mobile operations down to a fine art. These procedures were repeatedly practised and war-gamed at Omuthiya[5] and included the effective integration of direct and indirect fire support, air support and air defence in total harmony with the manoeuvring of ground forces.

This included the rapid grouping and regrouping of combat units according to the mission, combat situation and terrain. Similar methods were used by the South African forces in combat, for example during Operations Protea and Modular (Refer to Figure 8).[6] We went further than merely mastering these concepts and successfully completing military missions; this particular competency became a lifesaver on the battlefield.

How did fast-paced action influence the choice of the leadership and command styles we adopted – especially in an operational environment where there was always an acute need for timely, accurate and relevant information to enable quality decision-making and therefore precision engagement? The answer is simple and unassailable: Successful manoeuvring had to be based on mission command.

The Parameters of Mission Command

Mission command has three enduring principles: Timely decision-taking; the importance of understanding the superior commander's intention; and, by applying one's own actions, a clear responsibility to fulfil that intention. The underlying requirement is to act (or, in certain circumstances, not to act) within the framework of a mission. This required a style of command which promoted decentralised control, freedom and swiftness of action and initiative at all levels. But for this method of command to flourish it was necessary to develop teamwork, and trust and mutual understanding between leaders and their men.

While the principles of initiative and freedom of action formed the backbone of the concept, they needed to be tempered by good judgment and responsibility. Their application, however, could not be stereotyped.

A commander's style of leadership needs to reflect a grasp of the situation and the capacity to understand his subordinate commanders and troops. As such it provides a common baseline which applied not only to operations but also much of the regulation of military affairs in peacetime and even in everyday walks of life. Command and control should form the dynamic component of military doctrine. As new technology becomes available its principles and application should be reviewed and revised when necessary.

The parameters of command are illustrated in Figure 9. The lower left quadrant of

5 Operational base of 61 Mech in the northern border region of SWA.

6 See Chapters 12 and 15.

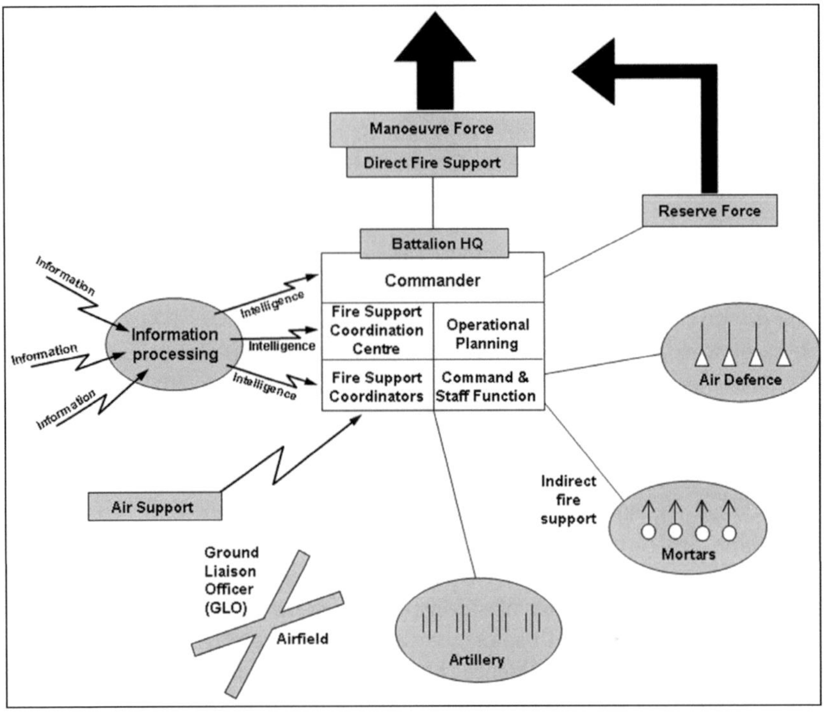

Figure 8: Manoeuvring and Fire Support Coordination

the diagram represents the attritional or positional theory, as opposed to the manoeuvre or mobile theory illustrated at the top right[7]. My experience was that at any given time the physical aspect of war, the technological state of the art and the prevailing political-economic constraints could all influence command application, especially within the domains of "loose rein – tight rein" (I shall address this aspect when we appraise the influence of politics on the course of Operations Makro and Meebos in Chapter 14).

- Loose Rein – Tight Rein. This dimension represented the ability to decentralise control, but at the same time also to know when to tighten the reins. To use a metaphor, the experienced horseman rides loose-rein at high speed, allowing the horse to select its own route within the parameters he sets. However, on a busy highway he will rein in tightly and carefully control the horse's movements.
- Physical-Psychological Sphere. The physical dimension focuses on human and material attrition, while the psychological parameter embraces the clash of wills and morale. The ability to read the mind of an opponent and then to negatively influence his will (namely, to your own advantage) impacts on his morale while at the same time it reinforces your own will, resolve and morale.
- Positional versus Dynamic. The positional dimension relates to the concept of "chateau leadership" seen, for example, in the French Army during World War I and the start of World War II, in which headquarters were deployed far to the rear. These practices resulted in rigid control since commanders were remote from

7 Simpkin, Richard: *Race to the Swift*. Brassey's, London, 1984.

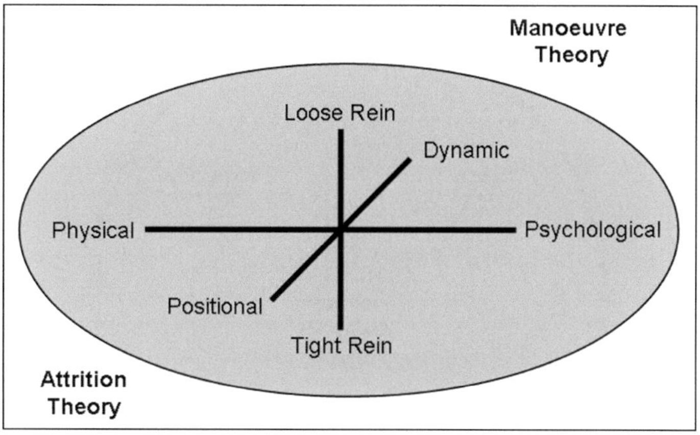

Figure 9: The Parameters of Command

the action and were reliant on reports coming in from front to rear. Dynamic command, on the other hand, supports the command-from-the-front principle by allowing mobile, lean command structures and systems to be where the action is, ready to make quick decisions by being in personal contact with own forces; to direct and to support – but not to micro-manage. Headquarters are rarely stationary and are practised in moving swiftly from one command location to the next.[8]

Observation; Orientation; Decision; Action – Commanding from the Front

The concept of mission command alluded to above supports the "command from the front" principle, which requires commanders to be close to the action and in feeling with any unfolding situation. It was a concept I always drummed into my subordinates, commanders and junior leaders.

Achieving situational awareness provides a commander with the ability to collect, process and disseminate an uninterrupted flow of information, while exploiting or denying an adversary's ability to do the same. This makes it possible to take swift action or resolve situations which arise suddenly, while at the same time ensuring inter-operability between the different combat units and their headquarters.

For this reason mobile operations necessitate the application of the decision-action cycle, commonly referred to (see Figure 10) as the OODA Loop: Observation; Orientation; Decision; Action. Its purpose is to get inside the enemy's observation-decision-action cycle and take decisions so swiftly that you leave him breathless and astounded. Communication systems are susceptible to disruption and dislocation by electronic means or measures or otherwise by either side. The conditions of the fluid battlefield therefore call for extremely robust and reliable tactical command and control systems and tested procedures to allow the men in the loop to take successful action at ground level.

8 Refer to Chapters 11, 12 and 15.

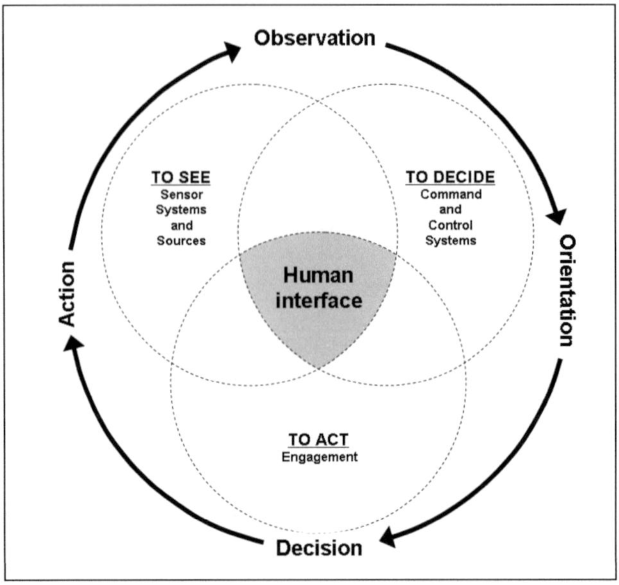

Figure 10: Decision-Action Cycle

The Inverse Face of Command – The Clash of Wills

The Secret of War Lies in Mastering Command and Control – Force Multiplication

"The whole secret of the art of war lies in the ability to become master of communications," as Napoleon once stated so accurately, obviously referring to the merits of mastering command and control on the battlefield as a force-multiplying factor. Similarly Sun Tzu had already affirmed 500 years before the birth of Christ that "you must know the enemy and yourself, or succumb in every battle".

The annals of warfare provide abundant proof that the command and control arrangements of a military force, along with its communication systems and lines of communication, can be either its strong point or its Achilles heel. For example, they were the focal point of the successful strategy and tactics Allenby and Lawrence used during the Arab rebellion in Palestine against the Turks in 1918. During the Second Anglo-Boer War (or the Second Freedom War, as many South Africans prefer to call it) this concept was the main reason for the numerous successes General Christiaan de Wet enjoyed as a famous guerrilla leader when he fought the British on his home soil.

His opinion was that the way to combat the enormously larger British forces was by using smaller mobile columns to plague the enemy's long lines of communication and the huge columns of ox-carts and mule wagons moving along them. In his most spectacularly successful attack, De Wet proved his point (as he had already done earlier) and humiliated one of Britain's most famous soldiers, Field-Marshal Lord Roberts of Kandahar, by capturing nearly 200 supply-wagons at Watervaldrif in spite of the presence of a battle-hardened, combat-ready brigade.

What is particularly interesting in the context of this discussion is the fact that Lord Roberts reacted by ordering his fighting troops to withdraw to the railway whence they had come, abandoning the convoy to its fate. Why he did this depends on which source one consults. In what amounted to a semi-official history of the war, "The Great Boer War",

Arthur Conan Doyle gives what could be described as the authorised version of Roberts's astounding decision:

If Lord Roberts needed justification for this decision, the future course of events will furnish it. One of Napoleon's maxims in war was to concentrate all one's energies upon one thing at one time. Roberts's aim was to outflank and possibly to capture (General Piet) Cronje's army. If he allowed a brigade to be involved in a rearguard action, his whole swift-moving plan of campaign might be dislocated.

It was very annoying to lose a hundred and eighty wagons, but it only meant a temporary inconvenience. The plan of campaign was the essential thing. Therefore he sacrificed his convoy and hurried his troops upon their original mission. It was with heavy hearts and bitter words that those who had fought so long abandoned their charge, but now at least there are probably few of them who do not agree in the wisdom of the sacrifice.

Our loss in this affair was between fifty and sixty killed and wounded. The Boers were unable to get rid of the stores, and they were eventually distributed among the local farmers and recovered again as the British forces flowed over the country.

There are certain weaknesses in this explanation. One is that losing 180 wagons crammed with supplies for an advancing field force was surely not merely a "temporary inconvenience" but a crippling blow to its mobility. Another is that by hastily withdrawing his brigade, an awesomely powerful force in those circumstances, he surrendered the initiative to the lightly-armed and numerically inferior Boers.

In his book "The Boer War", however, Thomas Pakenham provides evidence of a different kind which indicates the tremendous psychological blow inflicted by De Wet's attack, one that affected even as doughty a veteran as Lord Roberts.

According to evidence before the later Royal Commission of Inquiry into the war (evidence that has not been refuted), Roberts temporarily lost his mind when he learnt of the convoy's setback. His first reaction was to abandon the advance, give up his chances to catch Cronje and to quickly retreat to the railway."[9]

Getting the enemy commanders to lose their minds is fine with me. The De Wet case study makes one think about how FAPLA's overwhelming mechanised force abandoned all hope of capturing Mavinga and Jamba from UNITA when a tiny but lethal South African contingent intervened in southeast Angola in August 1987.

The lesson here is that the effect that certain forces, their actions and subsequent events may have on the other side's commanders must never be taken lightly. The destruction by 61 Mech of FAPLA's 47 Brigade and a tactical group on the Lomba River on 3 October 1987 led to the disorganised flight of three other enemy brigades and a tactical group.[10] This surprising feat was repeated a few days later when the enemy was once again routed by a strategic attack. This was when 4 South African Infantry Battalion, supported by one squadron of Olifant main battle tanks and a UNITA guerrilla battalion, destroyed FAPLA's 16 Brigade at the source of the Chambinga River on 9 November 1987 – a consequence which had been deliberately planned for by the South Africans.

It is exactly those potentially catastrophic consequences for an opponent which must be identified and exploited during the fighting – or, better still, before any significant clashes take place, if this is at all possible. The outcome of many a battle has hinged on a clash of wills. Which of the forces locked in combat will break first, as in the Lomba

9 Pakenham, Thomas: *The Boer War*. Jonathan Ball Publishers, Johannesburg, 1981, p. 338.

10 See Chapter 15.

and Chambinga actions? Conversely, of course, such effects should be guarded against and defused as soon as possible if they show signs of appearing in the physical and/or psychological edifice of one's own forces.

That inspirational retired Prussian veteran of World War II, Major general Friedrich Wilhelm von Mellenthin, taught me in the early 1980s that sound command and control was the bulwark against military collapse.[11] The essence of what Von Mellenthin passed on to me is best expressed in his own words on one of the many occasions when Henriette and I visited him:

> The modern battle of combined forces is fought in mobile fashion. The technique, especially the computer technique, requires a high level of intellectual flexibility, untainted discretion and independent action of the officers of the modern army. Leading by means of commands is the prerequisite for carrying out the numerous tasks of combat forces.
>
> The size of the battle terrain, the quickly changing condition, the amount of intelligence, but also the uncertainty, are all elements of the modern battle that require the free action of the military leader within the framework of the mission. Only training, with the fundamental principles of mission command and centre of gravity tactics at the core, makes the officer fit for these requirements.

As the founder of the German Armoured Corps (General Heinz Güderian) said, "*Nicht kleckern, sondern klotzen*" (do not kick your heels when in dire straits, rather form cores of strength). Command and control in a battle is an art, a free creative activity that is based on character, ability and spiritual power.

Great military successes are reached by boldness and daring – although thorough consideration is necessary before one can dare, and careful appreciation of the situation must always lead to a crystal clear decision. "Intellect without will is useless", said General Marshal Von Moltke, and Major general Von Seekt says: "A will without intellect is dangerous."

History is rich in striking examples of battle situations where the principle of good command and control played a decisive role in bringing success for leaders ranging from Ramses I of Egypt, Frederick the Great and Napoleon to Erwin Rommel, the Israelis during the Six-day War in 1967 and the South Africans at the tactical level in southern Angola in 1987–88. Let me repeat Napoleon's sage advice that salvation lies with those who successfully master "communications" (or what we would call "command and control").

Similarly, command and control structures and lines of communication are attractive targets – I think here, for example, of how FAPLA's lines between Menongue and Cuito Cuanavale were harassed by the marauding raiding parties from 32 Battalion, Special Forces and UNITA during Operation Modular in 1987-88.[12] This cuts both ways, of course, and so while the destruction of the enemy's command and communications is being pursued, care must be taken to guard one's own structures against a similar attempt by the enemy.

---

11 I had befriended Major General F.W von Mellenthin in 1985 when he lived in Johannesburg. He was the operations staff officer for Field-Marshall Rommel in the Western Desert as well as the Chief of Staff of the 4th German Panzer Army during World War II. He also wrote the foreword for my book on mobile warfare.

12 Appraised in Chapter 15.

Liddell Hart describes this concept in a particularly convincing and rather moving manner:

> To exploit the principles of war for our purpose and base ourselves upon strategic indirect approach, so as to determine the issue of the fighting even before fighting has begun, it is necessary to achieve the three following aims: To cut the enemy's lines of communication, thus paralysing his physical build-up; to seal him off from his line of retreat, thus undermining the enemy's will and destroying his morale; to hit his centres of administration and disrupt his communications, thus severing the link between his brain and his limbs.

Reflection on these three aims proves the truth of Napoleon's saying that "the whole secret of the art of war lies in the ability to become master of communications."[13] Note that Liddell Hart's approach in fact embraces the following three dimensions of command and control: The physical, the psychological and the sensory which includes electronic communications. Actions are not necessarily aimed only at breaking the enemy, but also at affecting his good judgment and similarly disrupting his decision-making processes.

A thorough study of the enemy's command, communications and lines of communication is therefore required when determining your own courses of action. This was carefully built into our overall planning during Operation Protea in August 1981, to make sure that the enemy's mobile reserve at Cahama was kept at bay;[14] with the surprise attack in depth on FAPLA's 16 Brigade during Operation Modular in November 1987 to overthrow the remainder of their forces;[15] and also when 50 Cuban Division was kept in confusion in July–August 1988 by means of deception measures, which made it difficult for them to decide about whether they wanted to cross the SWA-Angolan border offensively or not.[16] Such tactics were intended to dislocate and disrupt the enemy beforehand and keep him confused throughout.

Personalising the Battle – Knowing the Enemy and Yourself

Then there is the personalisation of the battle. The psychological approach played an extremely important role in southern Angola, the emphasis being on the opposing force which needed to be identified, analysed, neutralised, undermined or destroyed. In this sense man is extremely vulnerable. If a leader is demoralised, confused or eliminated, the chain reaction strikes his subordinates and consequently his organisation with a vengeance. The result in Angola was the destruction of the will to fight, followed by the collapse of the enemy's cohesion.

The opposite is also true. Actions aimed against the mass or key elements of an enemy force can likewise have a negative influence on the enemy's command. A classic case is the ambush and almost complete destruction by a small element of 61 Mech under Captain Jan Malan of a large FAPLA convoy sent out by the utterly confused enemy commander of 11 Brigade at Cuvelai during Operation Meebos in August 1982[17] – the command and control of the brigade had collapsed due to psychological pressure, which created the ideal situation

13 Liddell Hart, B.H.: *Strategy*. Faber and Faber Ltd, London, 1967, p. 387.
14 See Chapter 12.
15 See Chapter 15.
16 See Chapter 16.
17 See Chapter 14.

for further exploitation.

Commanders need to make the destruction of the command and control of their enemies a personal goal – this is super critical. We can learn a great deal from the Far East in this regard; that renowned military sage, Sun Tzu, says: "If your opponent is of choleric temper, seek to irritate him ... the good tactician plays with his adversary as a cat plays with a mouse ... a whole army may be robbed of its spirit ... a commander-in-chief may be robbed of his presence of mind ... "

This succinct statement of intention needs no elaboration, and it is a meaningful one that every military commander should embrace and apply with great enthusiasm. To analyse this important concept, let us consider the command disposition of the Cuban General Arnaldo Ochoa Sanchez, which is fully described in Chapter 16. Sanchez – nicknamed "El Moro" – was a charismatic military leader who was highly respected by the Russian military advisors as well as the Angolan and Cuban forces. But, like all of us, he was fallible.

From November 1987 onwards the Angolan and Cuban governments were set on re-establishing a formidable military presence in the 5th Military Region, the "Area-In-Dispute",[18] as the SADF called it. During Operation Prone's critical period of June–November 1988 I was serving as the Chief of Staff of 10 Division, and in June I asked our senior Staff Officer Intelligence, Colonel Deon Steyn, to undertake a study of the command and operational disposition of the 50th Division.

It became known to us that Sanchez was falling out of favour with Castro. We perused a case study Commandant R. Gibson (Army Intelligence) had written on the Ogaden Campaign of 1977–1978, when the then Ethiopian regime had driven Somali forces out of the disputed Ogaden region with the help of the Russians and Cubans,[19] and intelligence officers and psychologists at 10 SA Division did a profile analysis on Sanchez, using a document which had been released by Army intelligence on 18 August 1988.[20]

In addition I obtained permission to have Henriette flown to Oshakati for a few days in August to assist us in the Sanchez study – this was not mere indulgence on my part: Henriette was not only a psychologist by profession but a reserve major in the SADF, and when I was OC Army College we had both lectured on the "personalisation of warfare", a fascinating subject. She was accompanied by our son Pieter, who was then four years old, which gives a good indication of how little we expected the Cubans to actually cross the border or even send their MiGs to bomb Oshakati.

It became apparent from Henriette's study that Sanchez's arrogance was becoming immensely irksome to Fidel Castro, and she predicted that he would not last long as the commander of the Cuban forces in southern Angola, a conclusion that was based to a great extent on rumours that Sanchez was concentrating more on self-enrichment than on his military responsibilities, specifically by involvement in a cross-continental drug trade.

Sanchez's record was also carefully examined. It appeared that he had been involved in the planning of Operation Badr – the Egyptians' surprise offensive across the Suez Canal in October 1973 which marked the start of the Yom Kippur War – and commanded Cuban troops in Syria in 1975 during the war of attrition against Israel. Henriette and the divisional planning staff concluded that Sanchez would most probably carry on

18 See Chapter 5 on terrain. Also refer to Map 5.

19 C Army/GS2/205/1 dated 23 August 1988.

20 Departamento de Intelligencia Para: Buro Politico Regarding Arnaldo T. Ochoa – Divisional General, dated 16 August 1988.

using deception measures like the one employed in the successful crossing of the Suez Canal in 1973.

There was thus a particular focus on the intelligence indicators of a surprise offensive like Operation Badr's, and these indicators were compared with the intelligence and deception signatures which emanated from 50 Cuban Division and were then monitored by the intelligence staff on a daily basis, and it soon became apparent to us that the Cuban division did not have either the will or the heart to launch a major offensive into SWA/Namibia; it seemed that their offensive moves and statements were more sabre rattling than anything else.

10 SA Division, however, remained on high alert, on the assumption that the Cuban division could attack at moment's notice – there was no question but that the combined Cuban and FAPLA presence in the 5th Military Region had the ground and air capability to invade if it had been inclined to. I might add that if the positions had been reversed, the South Africans would have taken the gap and invaded SWA/Namibia. It all comes down to temperament and daring.

As a footnote: Sanchez did not live to see the official end of the border war.[21] In 1989 he and a number of other Cuban officers were arraigned before a military "honour court" in Havana, charged with everything from drug-trafficking to smuggling diamonds and ivory. At the trial – broadcast on Cuban television – a mass of evidence was produced which specified the crimes committed, complete with dates, places and the amounts of money and drugs involved. None of the accused pleaded innocent, only that there were mitigating circumstances. The court did not agree and found Sanchez guilty on all charges, including the capital offence of treason. On 13 July that year, at age 59, he was executed by firing squad.

Training Commanders to Act Decisively during Fluid Battle Conditions – *Friction de Guerre* and the Fog of War

Interestingly enough, during October and November 1986 I had held an exercise at the Army Battle School to practice the concepts I have discussed above. Among other things, the exercise was aimed at training commanders and staffs to act quickly, efficiently and decisively during fluid battle situations. At its conclusion I was left deeply convinced of the importance of a formidable command and control setup, implying capable military leadership and staffs.

Once again it was remarkable to see how the success of a battle – even a mock one like this – revolved around command cohesion. It was obvious to me that any force which enjoyed initiative and freedom of action must win the battle, irrespective of the relative strengths involved. From this it followed that the planning and conduct of any battle needed effective and flexible command. It was also clear beyond a shadow of a doubt that virtually all actions – the foreseen and unforeseen; the successes and failures; behaviour; incidents and events, whether planned or unplanned, natural or artificial – had a dynamic influence on command.

It was then, and is now, universally accepted that in conducting military operations, the commanders and planners have to factor in and take account of two concepts. One is friction de guerre (a term thought to have been coined by Von Clausewitz), meaning all the small unforeseen or coincidental events which can pop up to interfere with your

21 Wikipedia, the free encyclopaedia - Arnaldo Tomas Ochoa Sanchez.

performance. The second is another Von Clausewitzian phrase, "the fog of war", which could be summed up as a lack of full situational awareness, leading to uncertainty about your own capability, and the capability and intent of your adversary.

All such events can influence commanders' decisions and the timings of the action or operation, and a high incidence of such events and crises can result in catastrophe. This phenomenon is usually characterised by a loss of initiative, freedom of action and an all-out effort to maintain control.

A succession of unforeseen events can require commanders to take numerous critical decisions within a very short period of time. Inevitably this will require continuous coordination and liaison, and it often happens that fatigue or complete exhaustion overtakes the decision makers at critical moments, so that it begins to feel as if everything and everyone is working together to break down the cohesion of command.

At such moments especially commanders need to guard against an inner feeling of "I'm tired ... things have to stop now". This critical stage is exactly when the leader's firmness and inner strength must be the determining factor. He must avoid subjective anxiety about his forces' position, and a slackening of self-discipline due to panic or a feeling of helplessness; both in the battle and in the broad organisation, when his seniors and comrades will evaluate the operation retrospectively as a whole (once again, compare the concept of command tactics that has been designed to overcome this problem).

Commanders should realise and accept these moments of semi-chaos and friction as an unavoidable feature of war and learn to deal with them. During training my commanders were repeatedly subjected to both. The bottom line here is that the successful bridging of a catastrophic phase – the key test of a true commander – is the most satisfactory moment of command. It cannot be emphasised enough that the successful military leader must already have his inner self under control. Only the leader with a positive self-image can forget about his formal position and approach and control the situation tactically, objectively and scientifically.

Consider the sequence of events experienced by 61 Mech and me when a large group of SWAPO infiltrators surged into the Death Triangle during the night of 14–15 April 1981. We lost 10 men due to enemy action within 12 hours,[22] and during this period there was a clearly detectable feeling that the enemy had seized the initiative and was enjoying freedom of action. Heavy demands were made on qualities of personal command and leadership, but these proved more than adequate, and total control of the situation was soon regained. The scale tipped clearly and noticeably in the favour of own forces,and the infiltrator groups were hunted down and neutralised.

A commander's aim must be to overcome catastrophe as quickly and effectively as possible. During this phase he must not think about mistakes that might be made; instead, his entire being must be directed at taking the pre-emptive and positive actions the situation requires. His thoughts must revolve around decisions and action plans that are true to principle and designed to achieve success by being decisive. Negative factors must be vigorously turned into positive ones – initiative, freedom of action and control must be reclaimed and maintained at all cost.

At the same time everything possible must be done to turn his enemy counterpart's command into a fatal tragedy. This was exactly how the Israelis trained and exercised

---

22 See Chapter 11.

their combat commanders for their mobile battles in 1973 and 1976. They referred to this technique as "change of mission tactics": Commanders under training would be subjected to a gruelling planning process for a specific mission; then, as they entered the exercise area, the original mission would abruptly be changed by their instructors.

A word of warning here: commanders and their command and control structures must stand ready to deal with any and all types of enemy attacks. During operations this required us to maintain an efficient command and control structure which was armoured against the tests of the mission, circumstance, place and time; mission command and inspirational leadership was the answer to these challenging conditions.

The Amajuba Phenomenon – As if by Signal, All Cohesion was Lost

Let us reach far back in our history and consider a classic case of how a catastrophe can impact on command – the Battle of Amajuba, during the First Anglo-Boer War of 1880–1881. This battle, which took place on Sunday, 27 February 1881, was the decisive action of that war and a truly stunning victory for an outnumbered force of Boers which deeply humiliated the British (see Figure 11).

The ways of warfare have changed a great deal since then, but Amajuba remains an excellent example of the application of the indirect approach and the degrading of the enemy's command capability. Moreover, it is a clear and superb example of how to generate initiative and freedom of action through surprising, powerful offensive action and manoeuvring, the danger involved in subjective thinking and how a numerically inferior force can triumph over a larger one.

Major general Sir George Pomeroy Colley, with just over 300 infantrymen and a small naval contingent, climbed Amajuba at dead of night and occupied a position just below the summit, a most unpleasant surprise for the contingent of Boers encamped below to discover when day broke. General Piet Joubert directed that the British be dislodged, and the Boers did just that. A hundred and fifty men under two field-cornets named Roos and Malan started climbing the mountain under covering fire from below, and by midday between 70 and 80 of them had reached the summit.

There followed a short but fierce three-pronged shootout at close range. The British force's functional coherence was completely disrupted, and battle and command cohesion vanished like dew before the sun. Panic surged through their chaotic ranks and the well-nigh incredible happened: troops from two famous regiments fled in wild disorder. Colley and 92 of his officers and men lay dead, 134 officers and men were wounded, and 53 were taken prisoner. The Boer losses? One killed and five wounded.

The key to the Boers' success at Amajuba lay in their forceful and unexpected offensive action, which took Colley totally by surprise. In his book "The First Boer War", Joseph H. Lehmann writes:

Colley decided to occupy Majuba ... That the surprised enemy would try to dislodge his force seemed remote. After all, the Boers were committed to fighting on the defensive, and the Sekhukhune War demonstrated that they were incapable of taking a hill from even poorly armed natives ...

Much of the cohesion of the clannish regimental system was missing on top of Majuba. No instructions were given to dig in. When a (Gordon) Highlander officer asked the general if they might entrench themselves, Colley replied, "No, the men are tired, and there is no necessity for it." Sheltered behind the rim, Colley believed that his position was

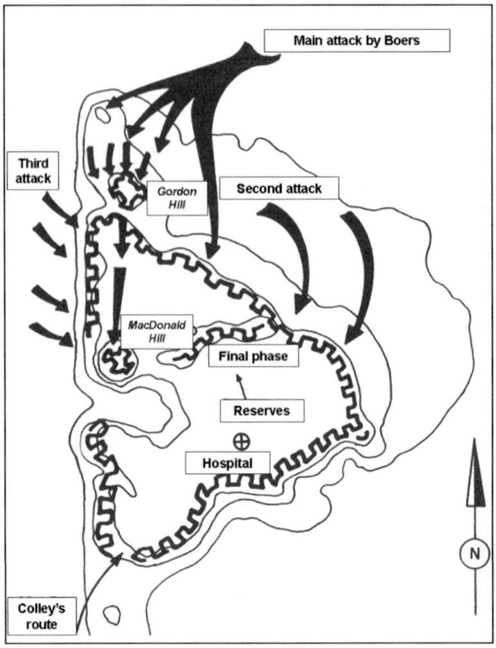

Figure 11: The Battle of Amajuba
(Figure from De Vries, R., Kolonel: *Mobiele Oorlogvoering – 'n Perspektief vir Suider-Afrika.* FJM Harman Publishers, Pretoria, 1987, p. 75 and p. 109)

impregnable ... "We could stay here forever," Colley confidently told Stewart. Since most of the crest was obviously inaccessible, his plan did not call for battle.[23]

... The sudden piercing cry of terror ... rose from the line ... all cohesion was lost as men, as if by signal, stampeded towards the drop behind them and leaped down the mountain.

The student of military history has much to learn from this testimony by Lehmann. An important facet is the danger involved in subjective thinking. A further lesson is that the success potential of an indirect action often lies in the approach over inaccessible, inhospitable, apparently non-negotiable approach, as the Germans similarly demonstrated with their unexpected Ardennes offensive in May 1940.

This is not to mention other defects. One was the lack of defensive precautions and a contingency plan. Another was the underestimation of the enemy, based not on facts but on a subjective assumption deriving from a totally different set of circumstances. Yet another was the lack of a unified team spirit, although this was not Colley's fault but is the latent weakness of any hastily assembled composite force.

Provoking a Battlefield Catastrophe – Throwing the Enemy off Balance

The reason for resurrecting the Amajuba disaster is to explain the "Catastrophe Theory".[24] The shrewd planner has the power to organise something like this on a battlefield whose nature virtually begs for it to be done. The aim is to significantly disrupt an opponent's

23 Lehmann, Joseph, H.: *The First Boer War.* Jonathan Cape, Thirty Bedford Square, 1972, London, pp.234, 235 and 239.

24 Zeeman, E.C.: *Catastrophe Theory.* Addison-Wesley Publishing Company, Massachusetts, 1976.

balance by forcing a catastrophe on him and by degrading his organisational cohesion. Actions following the turning point are not always predictable. Sun Tzu's words serve as warning in this regard: "Do not press a desperate foe too hard ... always let an outlet free." If he plays his cards right, however, the military planner can predict behaviour and actions with fair certainty. Knowledge about the enemy and knowledge of self are indispensable criteria. Thus:

- Anger and Fear Influence the type of Action. An increase in anger causes an increase in the probability of aggressive action. An increase in fear causes an increase in the probability of retreat or flight. A numbness which implies little or no driving force at the time results in a perceived neutral reaction or even no reaction at all, just a state of inertness. An increase in both of the first two evokes a conflicting "fight-and-flight" interaction. The result is bi-modal, frustration causing acute stress and a continuous, dynamic response which alternates between fight and flight.
- Stress and Alienation used to Unleash Chaos. In the broadest sense of the word, stress represents frustration and anxiety. Once again alienation can be regarded as a condition of isolation, the experiencing of a lack of communication, psychological affliction, instability and polarisation. Of course circumstances on the battlefield contribute naturally to alienation. Physical actions such as firepower, the use of smoke at night, the cutting of lines of communication and the destruction of command are options that can be used to create alienation and stress. Therefore, in the military sense, chaos implies the disintegration of command and control as well as combat and organisational cohesion. A drastic increase in stress and alienation may cause a sudden intense eruption of chaos.
- Fear and the Unknown may Evoke Uncontrolled Anxiety. The actual enemy on the battlefield is naked fear and not the bullet or the bayonet's cold steel. The battlefield is bleak and sinister. If one does not guard against fear, it may degenerate into uncontrolled anxiety. This condition is one that petrifies fingers on triggers, causes shivering and trembling, and persuades masses of people to take off in wild flight. Cold facts and cruel disillusionment allow the best theories and most formidable plans to crumble, break down complex command and control structures, let organised military battle formations scatter and make glorious leaders disappear. This manifestation can be described as a battlefield catastrophe – a condition that can be mercilessly stimulated by continuous pressure.

The catastrophe theory was successfully applied by us for the attack on FAPLA's reinforced 16 Brigade at the source of the Chambinga River on 9 November 1987, the guardian angel of the enemy forces' most vulnerable extreme eastern flank and final gateway and escape route to Cuito Cuanavale – in other words, the chink in their armour.[25] A telegram sent to Cuito Cuanavale on 11 November 1987 by a Russian military advisor said it all:

> Telegram 91 to Cuito, 11 November 1987, 09:00 – To the Advisor of the Military District Commander: The enemy hits each brigade separately and nothing is being undertaken to inflict a blow collectively. Thus all the brigades will be killed off one by

25 See Chapter 14.

> one. The there are few military personnel in the combat units. Commanding officers of all ranks are scared. They are scared to start counteractions against the enemy. Signed, Brigade Commander Advisor.

The writer then continued:

> Something quite unimaginable is happening now. The Angolan troops are almost completely demoralised; the brigades are on average at 45 percent strength. For every 10 to 15 shells launched by the enemy, the Angolans are able to send one, if even that much. Our reconnaissance operates poorly and the enemy knows everything about us.
>
> The Angolans fear the South Africans like fire and if they hear that their "Buffalo" (32 Battalion) is part of an attack; they throw away all their equipment in panic and flee ... Despite all this, orders and instructions continue to stream out from the district military command to occupy defensive positions, to create a strong reserve (but out of what?) for confronting the flanks and rear of the attacking enemy.[26]

As a point of departure it needs to be mentioned that the planning and application of the catastrophe theory in this case gave concrete shape to the principles of warfare and the concept of the indirect approach. The opponent needed to be struck with complete paralysis and indecisiveness for a moment before chaos and naked anxiety was provoked. Especially in this sphere creative thinking was particularly important, and people with a natural talent for battlefield shrewdness were used for planning in such instances.

Preventing a Battlefield Catastrophe – Maintaining Own Forces' Balance

These factors can be turned on their heads in order to prevent catastrophe among one's own forces:

Alienation. The combination of knowledge in a group, faith, harmony, good morale, trust in one another and self-confidence are powerful elements to confound alienation. Isolation on the battlefield can be counteracted by realistic training and practical battle drills. The improvement of a force's firepower provides further stimulation in this regard. Another critical aspect that is often ignored is the need to keep people informed. Knowledge about the current situation and the importance and necessity of the action affects morale in a positive sense and improves harmony. At the other extreme, tactical combat cohesion, good leaders and commanders, and an efficient command and control system, are obviously indispensable.

Fear, Anxiety and Stress. We know now that a powerful interaction exists between these respective poles, and as with the measures to be taken against alienation, counteractions will have a positive effect in fighting fear, anxiety and stress. The opposite of anxiety is the aggressive and unyielding will to resist. Similarly, the idea addresses aspects like cultural inheritance, education, human characteristics, and abilities and dispositions, as well as physical fitness. A single powerful mechanism for proactively countering potential chaos is "Battle Talk". This implies continuous repetitive communication of actions in a fighting group or unit during battle.

26 Shubin, Gennady and Tokarev, Andrei: *Bush War – The Road to Cuito Cuanavale.* Jacana Media (Pty) Ltd, South Africa, Sunnyside, 2011, pp.56 and 57.

Leadership As An Art – Physical And Psychological Effects

Simple Things Matter – Comradeship

During my career I learned that simple things matter and I should like to share a few stories on the topic. Weaving a fabric of such happenings can be used by a leader to create his leadership philosophy and, through example, to strengthen resolve and unit cohesion and instil esprit de corps.

Leadership must be felt, experienced and created, and so leaders do not inflict pain; they bear pain. The first responsibility of a leader is to define reality, then to inspire and support, and lastly to express appreciation. Good leaders understand that the needs of organisations are best satisfied when the needs of individual people are met. Above all, one needs to transcend the drive for delivery by nurturing the quality of relationships, the quality of communications, mutual trust and the quality of promises to each other.

Is leadership, then, not about liberating people to do what is required of them in the most effective, supportive and humane way possible? One of the tricks of the trade is to be hospitable to unusual people. Quite a few of those can be found and experimented with in the military. My commander extraordinaire of the Light Workshop Troop at 61 Mech, Sergeant-major Duppie du Plessis, was one such unusual specimen. Another was an enemy of military decorum known as "Captain" Payne (let me hasten to add that this rank was self-bestowed), the leader of a group of similar opponents of orthodox military order and discipline.

Sergeant-Major Duppie and His Tiffies Extraordinaire – Building Trust through Promises Kept

61 Mech's Light Workshop Troop provided first-line technical support[27] and their job description included on-the-spot repair and recovery of vehicles and weapon systems in the field. It was not strange to see the LWT's tiffies (in the SADF all mechanics bore the generic nickname "tiffy", apparently a corruption of the now-archaic "artificer") working at night under hostile fire to increase the serviceability ratio of the unit's battered equipment.

Sergeant-Major Duppie du Plessis used to tell me: ""In the morning, when the sun rises, all your vehicles will be mobile." That was good enough for me, because he and his extremely dirty, extremely hard-working clan always delivered on their promises, or as near as damn-it, because he was one of those rare and remarkable people whose words could be taken to the bank – even if it meant cutting up a wrecked vehicle during the night and loading its remnants onto another to make sure we maintained our mobility (SADF policy was leave nothing behind if this was at all possible).

What they accomplished was the stuff of legend. It was nothing strange to see a pair of booted feet sticking out of the engine compartment of a disabled Ratel which was under tow, belonging to a tiffy who was making sure that at the next halt the vehicle would be fit to move under its own steam again. At our Omuthiya home base the lights of the LWT shed always burned right through the night, accompanied by the clamour and commotion of constant activity. Our tiffies were truly among the shining lights of 61 Mech ... and they were not the only ones.

27 See Chapter 4.

"Captain" Payne and the Rough Hands – Cometh the Hour, Cometh the (Unlikely) Man

While OC 61 Mech I learned a generous portion of life's lessons from the plight of one "Captain" Payne and his crew of nonconformists, popularly known as the "Rough Hands" or "Skurwehande". They taught me something about destiny and providence; they surely taught me lessons in humility, humanity and dignity, and how to be thankful for small mercies and the little things in life. And they also taught me about simple leadership and what loyalty truly meant when experiencing dire straits. After I had had the privilege of meeting up with Payne and the Rough Hands I valued my own children and my young troops at 61 Mech all the more.

They were called "Rough Hands" because they were men who worked extremely hard with their bare hands, performing the major portion of the SADF's manual labour. The then national service system was fairly indiscriminate – it scooped up just about everybody except tertiary level students, the medically unfit, certifiable lunatics and conscientious objectors without regard for station in life, background, home language, religion (about 99 different varieties) or alternative gender preference (as long as it was kept quiet), and that included long-term permanently resident aliens of military age. Then it sorted them out and fitted them in somewhere or other.

Most of the Rough Hands came from distinctly questionable walks of life. Most were natural troublemakers, others had a history of drug use and some were outright criminals with dossiers as long as your arm. They were posted to the South African Engineer Corps training centre at Kroonstad, classified as "Code Sevens" (i.e. members who were not allowed to bear arms or render operational service) and taught the tricks of manual labour before being deployed where they could do the most good and the least harm. They enjoyed a well-earned notoriety for generating disciplinary nightmares ... and yet I found some jewels among them.

At Omuthiya in late July 1981 I had just received the warning order that Operation Protea would be going ahead the following month, as scheduled.[28] In utmost secrecy we embarked on our final planning and preparations, marking our maps with code words and nicknames which were to become as familiar as the ones we had been christened with. One of the targets allocated to 61 Mech was "Apple Pie", a little hamlet called Humbe which was located about 8 km west of Xangongo and the Cunene River. About 45 km further to the northwest lay the town of Cahama; home to FAPLA's local mechanised mobile reserve.

I knew that if the bulk of 61 Mech left Omuthiya for Operation Protea I would need extra hands to look after and maintain our base in our absence, carrying out a variety of humble and sometimes arduous but important tasks – kitchen and messing fatigues, cleaning the ablutions, maintaining the evaporation dams of our sewage system and removing refuse daily with the help of our trusted Russian Gaz truck which we had previously liberated from the communist yoke. So I sent a telex message to Army HQ to request extra bodies for base maintenance. I did not anticipate that they would be Code Sevens, or realise what influence they were going to exert on my life and the lives of a few other people at 61 Mech.

In due course 12 Skurwehande arrived at Grootfontein in a C-130 transport aircraft – a luxurious first for them – including "Captain" Payne, their unofficial but undisputed leader, who spent the trip (so I learned later) sitting calm and relaxed in one of the C-130's

---

28 See Chapter 12.

red jump seats, completely confident in his own personal strength, ability and authority. They did not know where the hell they were going or what the Army was letting them in for, and I suspect did much care either.

At the Grootfontein airfield my base maintenance manager, WO1 J.N. ("Valie") de Vaal, went to receive them (and a big surprise when he met his customers). They were then trucked to Omuthiya, where they were put up in a 16 x 32 tent which was pitched on the eastern side of the base at a discreet distance from their social superiors, the operational subunits. So the scene was set for something unforgettable to happen in the lives of the 12 unsuspecting Skurwehande and an equally unsuspecting 61 Mech ... Well, meeting with surprises was the spice of our life.

We soon got used to Payne and his minions in their sweaty, dirty nutria overalls, cleaning the base, carting away loads of rubbish in the Gaz or wandering down to maintain the evaporation dam with brooms, spades and rakes and so on, as per the laid-down (and strictly observed) base routine and maintenance instructions. Their tent was regularly inspected by the staunch Regimental Sergeant-Major, M.C. Barnard, and the amiable Sergeant-Major Valie de Vaal..

While Payne's private army slogged away at its unsavoury tasks, the rest of us were equally busy with the more serious stuff of preparing for battle – driving north out of Omuthiya in our Ratels, exercising repeatedly on the training range with live ammunition before coming back in the evenings, exhausted but totally content with ourselves and extremely satisfied with our progress, to relax by knocking back a cold beer at the canteen while enjoying a marvellous SWA/Namibian sunset (although sometimes this pleasure was denied us when we went out into the field again to exercise our night manoeuvring, navigation and movements). Meanwhile the Skurwehande were left in peace to carry out the inglorious tasks which were their preordained lot in military life.

But things were not as tranquil as they seemed. One day, not long after Payne and his merry men arrived, my subunit commanders informed me that we had an outbreak of some serious but mysterious trouble, the evidence consisting of sundry troops lying in the sick bay with various wounds inflicted during the night by the proverbial blunt instruments.

The next night more of them sustained the same type of wounds. But who had inflicted the wounds was a total mystery; nobody was shedding any light on the matter, not even the victims themselves. All we could discover was that they had been hit with iron bars which should have been in safe storage in the quartermaster's tent. That was it. To use the correct military terminology, no real-time evidence was forthcoming.

I deployed an expert intelligence-gathering team consisting of the chaplain, Padre Koos Rossouw, and the RSM, WO1 Barnard – to find out what the hell was going on. Even they could not penetrate the veil of secrecy; 61 Mech's entire strong informal internal intelligence system failed to yield any valuable information. My subunit commanders were astounded, as was I, and we wasted no time in sitting down to thoroughly assess the troubling situation: We were getting ever closer to Operation Protea and if it went on like this I risked running short of serviceable troops.

The only logical conclusion was that Payne and his merry men were behind the mayhem, since it had started after their arrival. That settled the "how". Now we needed to find out the "why", and the best way was to confront the notorious Payne, who by all accounts was gifted with a sixth sense and had a notable command presence, and was therefore the obvious ring-leader in whatever was going on, So at 10:30 next morning I had him called over to the white prefab office which I did not use very often. It would be a one-on-one meeting, I decided, without either the adjutant or RSM present.

Payne rolled up as scheduled, expecting Heaven knows what. To his surprise, I think, I invited him politely to sit down in a camp chair facing me and opened the discussion by asking why his followers called him "Captain" Payne. With so much as batting an eyelid he pulled down his dirty, sweaty, odoriferous nutria overall with hands bearing the blue inkspots which indicated that he was a user of some devious and harmful substance or substances. Tattooed on each shoulder were the three "pips" of a captain.

I thanked him for the information, and now, with the battle-lines drawn and my control of the proceedings clearly established, went straight to the heart of the matter: "Why are you knocking the shit out of my troops?"

Payne showed no signs of the anxiety which normally featured in such proceedings, and did not even bother to deny it. "Nobody respects us here," he said coolly. "I know you're preparing to go to Angola. We want to go along. If you don't take us, I'll destroy your base while you're gone."

It was an unbelievable situation. Here I was, the master of life and death over more than 1,000 men, armoured by a hierarchical organisation whose very pillars were instant obedience and respect for rank, being threatened by a manual labourer of dubious reputation swimming around at the very lowest level of our little society's food chain! I could just imagine what the RSM would have said if he had been present, not to mention my distant masters in Windhoek and Pretoria. At the very least Payne and his troops would have ended up as unwilling guests at "Durban-by-the-Sea", as the troops called the dreaded detention barracks at Grootfontein.

On the other hand, that maverick right brain of mine told me, Payne's was one helluva powerful argument. I had no doubt that he meant what he said, and I did not want Omuthiya to be turned into a war zone while most of 61 Mech was in the bush. There was also the question of maintaining secrecy about Protea, since I was tasked to venture deep into Angola in what might well turn out to be a sticky situation, in which case I would always be able to use a few extra bodies.

So I gave it some deep thought and came to a decision: Ah, hell, I thought, in for a penny, in for a pound. I could carry out an interesting experiment that might be a morale booster for 61 Mech into the bargain. So I made one of the more stupid decisions of my career and said:

"OK, but here are my conditions ... "

My conditions were that the Skurwehande tent would be uprooted and pitched close to my living quarters at Omuthiya – within spitting distance, to be more exact, which in this case was more than just a figure of speech. When I did my daily inspections of the base, Payne would accompany the RSM and me. There was to be no more knocking the shit out of my troops.

The Skurwehande, I went on to say, would be issued with a Buffel mine-protected vehicle and brand-new R-4 rifles (they would now be armed to the teeth and dangerous, but I tried not to think about that). Then, under command of one of my national service officers, Lieutenant Marche Mucho, they would undergo strenuous combat training and be deployed as a protective element for Sierra Battery, our organic 140 mm guns under Captains Bernie Pols and Frans van Eeden, and for the duration of the operation would be with the artillery as Ruth was with Naomi.

Payne was not to tell a single soul that we were going into Angola – sharing that knowledge with 61 Mech at a later date was my prerogative (incidentally, the troops were only told the day before we crossed into Angola, and they responded with a spontaneous cheer). Payne graciously assented to all these conditions, so I sent him off and gave Marche Mucho a thorough briefing on what awaited him, making it plain that if at all possible, no harm was to come to my special squad.

Mucho – one of those exquisite national service junior leaders, tall, knowledgeable, charismatic and commanding – rose to the challenge; the Skurwehande could not have wished for a better officer. Without wasting any time he had the tiffies paint "Phantom" diagonally on the side-plates of the Skurwehande Buffel, then plunged the former Rough Hands, now the "Phantom Squad", into intensive training so that they could protect Sierra Battery if the need arose.

The RSM was not very excited about my plans – he clearly thought that I had gone slightly whacky, which was understandable under the circumstances – but he threw himself into the new dispensation and became quite comfortable with it. Other reactions were mixed. My subunit commanders were amused, the gunners were perturbed by the excess baggage they had acquired, and Padre Koos Rossouw realised he would have some extra work to do.

But it turned out surprisingly well. It even had an unexpected benefit. As far as Payne was concerned he was now my partner in command, and the odd disciplinary problem among 61 Mech's wilder spirits disappeared – Payne took it on himself to sort out any issues in a strictly unofficial way, and my small group of problem children clearly knew it. Life returned to normal at 61 Mech, and it was business as usual. Nevertheless, I prayed a bit more fervently from then on, while the Phantoms trained hard at becoming combat soldiers. Nobody realised that a hair-raising adventure was brewing in which they and their new-found skills would be put to the test.

The Phantom Squad's time of testing came after we had captured Humbe on D-Day. I ordered Combat Team Charlie under command of Major Joe Weyers to deploy rapidly towards the west and establish a delaying position in case FAPLA's mobile reserve tore itself loose from the Cahama defences and advanced on Xangongo while we were still fighting there.

For this vital task I made Combat Team Charlie (which was based in the armoured car squadron) as potent as possible by attaching a troop of 140 mm guns under Captain Frans van Eeden, as well as a small but extremely deadly pathfinder group from 44 Parachute Brigade under the renowned Colonel Jan Breytenbach, which had found itself at a loose end after doing what was necessary at Xangongo, and whose men were mounted in Land Rovers bristling with heavy weapons.

Joe Weyers deployed 17 km west of Cahama, well within range of Frans van Eeden's guns, which were deployed to the rear of the fighting line with the Phantom Squad in close proximity, while I took most of my remaining men on a sweep in search of stragglers or refugees from the Xangongo fighting. That night, not too far away to the east, I was lying up near a place called Mucope after an unproductive day of scouring the bush. Then suddenly we heard the crump of mortars and other more intensive fire coming out of the darkness.

Without any of us knowing about it, a large FAPLA column – an assortment of Soviet armoured vehicles, military trucks and BM-21 multiple rocket launcher systems – had escaped our attack on Xangongo and had lain up in the dense bush somewhere to the north and slightly west of Peu Peu, then set off to exfiltrate stealthily to the safety of Cahama under cover of darkness. The column moved back on to the tarred road and then headed for Cahama in single file, keeping their engine revolutions low and navigating by their infrared lights.

All went well until the column arrived unheralded at the rear of Weyer's delaying position. They had got halfway between the guns and Charlie's forward line when they were detected and the shooting started; in an amazing demonstration of expert redeployment Weyers and Breytenbach swung around and between them destroyed or captured virtually the entire column in a short, fierce engagement. We were too far away to provide any support, and I waited anxiously till the news came that the enemy column was no more, and that we had suffered no casualties except for three soldiers who had been lightly wounded by enemy mortar fragments.

I describe this incident – which, incidentally, had such a demoralising effect on the Cahama force that it never once ventured out of its defences – because a few days later I personally debriefed Payne and his Phantoms, and got their version of what they had been up to.

Payne had told his troops that they could relax for the evening, because they had worked hard throughout the day. They neatly piled their R4s in classic military fashion and stretched out on the sun-warmed road, some of them naked, to enjoy a little downtime, although they kept their ears to the ground.

When Payne heard the low drone of the approaching enemy column he reached the logical conclusion that it was the squadron sergeant-major coming up to replenish the guns. Then all hell broke loose. Tracer bullets flew overhead and explosions made the night hideous.

Payne's troops were scattered on both sides of the road, and a natural first impulse would have been for them to take cover as best they could. But, Payne said, there was only one thing uppermost in his mind, based on the promise he had made me at Omuthiya: "Regroup, get my people safely back to the artillery and protect the guns." And that is exactly what he and they did, miraculously unharmed in spite of all the metal flying around.

That was his story; whether everything about it was the exact truth I did not know, but their telling matched the circumstantial evidence, and I believed them. I was happy. I had got away with a gross contravention of the regulations, and my instinct in judging Payne to be a man of his word had proved to be correct.

But the real point of this story is that the incident had a tremendous effect on their self-esteem, something about which I was extremely happy. They had arrived at Omuthiya as the Army's bottom feeders, adjudged fit for little more than to be hewers of wood and drawers of water (and much worse). They came back from Angola, I was convinced, as men whose lives had changed forever, real soldiers who had smelt powder and won the right to look any other fighting man straight in the eye. I could just imagine how their wonderful war story would be told and retold to their envious fellow Skurwehande when they got back to wherever they had come from.

Sometimes I wonder where they are today and what happened to them. Like so many stories about war, this is one about ordinary people and extraordinary outcomes. I suppose one could sum this whole thing up with another misquote: "Cometh the hour, cometh the man ... namely Captain Payne."

An Unexpected Visit to Omuthiya by Israeli Generals – Building Self-Esteem

Sometime in 1982 a small group of Israeli generals paid us a surprise visit at Omuthiya. They had been flying back to Grootfontein in a Puma helicopter after a visit to Oshakati, and on the way south they decided on impulse to drop in at Omuthiya without any advance warning. This sort of thing can be a commander's nightmare, but at that time, there were very few things that could still surprise 61 Mech, because we were always ready for anything.

We duly received these seasoned Israeli commanders and I asked them whether they wished to view a battle drill demonstration by one of the combat teams. The answer was: "Yes, of course!" I then asked them to select one of the three combat teams for a fire and movement demonstration, and the dice fell on Captain Jan Malan's Combat Team Alpha. I called Jan and said only: "Battle drill demonstration – march- and combat-ready within 30 minutes. Movement due north, axis of advance, North Road ... "

Jan mustered his force without any fuss and started moving north exactly on time, with his Ratels in their designated combat groupings and marching order. I followed behind them with the Israelis poised on top of my command Ratel, call sign Zero. I then invited the Israelis to select any target on the move for Malan's combat team. One general immediately responded with: "Anti-tank knot, right two o'clock, 350 metres, thick clump of bushes."

I got on the radio to Jan and repeated the target indication. The combat team swung into action, veered to the right and cut loose on the notional anti-tank position. Then one of the Israelis said: "Make the commander a casualty." I promptly radioed Jan: "You're dead!" Jan instantly slumped over in his turret, and without a single hitch or glitch one of his lieutenants took over and continued with the assault. It was a demonstration of superb leadership and good training, and before the visitors left, a senior general told me that rarely in all his operational experience had he encountered such swift and effective response and the laying down of fire in such intensity.

On this unexpected high note the memorable surprise visit ended and the Israeli departed, leaving me with a feeling of great satisfaction. Unscheduled though it was, it had served several purposes. It had impressed the battle-hardened Israelis, who were not easily impressed; it had been an excellent snap exercise for Combat Team Alpha, and it had proved once again that the South Africans were masters at mission command and the ability to attack smoothly on the move from the line of advance. I was very proud of Combat Team Alpha on that day, and Jan Malan and his followers felt the same. And so the all-important process of promoting self-esteem had been served. Napoleon would have understood my satisfaction.

High Drama and Low Comedy – All Build Team Spirit

While returning to SWA/Namibia after Operation Protea one memorable day in September 1981, I was viewing the long column of 61 Mech Ratels from my stationary command vehicle as they travelled south from Ondjiva on the road near Omupanda. We had taken an immense amount of booty of all sorts at Ondjiva, and most of the Ratels and Samil cargo trucks were towing "liberated" FAPLA weapons and enemy equipment, sometimes three in a row, while various 61 Mech troops were driving an assortment of captured enemy trucks and armoured vehicles.

Needless to say, this was a slow process, and every two hours we would halt for 10 minutes to allow a quick brew-up of coffee and attention to Nature's calls. But as I surveyed this particular halt I noticed a strange, somewhat spectacular event taking place before my bewildered eyes. One of Captain Koos Liebenberg's drivers of Bravo Company, who was at the wheel of an ex-Soviet Ural truck, ignored the halt, turned off the road and started bashing out a circular track in the dense bush on the verge.

Strange things frequently happened in Bravo Company, but this one stumped me, so I jumped up on the Ural's running-board to find out what the hell was going on. But the driver had a perfectly logical explanation: "I don't have a clutch, Commandant, so I can't stop, but nothing is going to stop me from bringing my Ural back home to Omuthiya!" That's what I call tenacity – how could I help loving those 61 Mech troops? Give Koos Liebenberg and his company a job and they would see it through, come hell or high water – and that applied to the rest of them as well. For me, the team spirit of 61 Mech and the guts of our troops were the zingy spices of life.

Frankie Fiser – Fighting Barman

A vibrant young national serviceman from Cape Town named Frankie Fiser served at 61 Mech in mid-1982. As he was a businessman at heart, Frankie occupied an extremely important position as our barman and tuck shop manager – after all, as Napoleon once remarked, an army marches on its stomach. Everybody liked Frankie for his lively disposition, fast mouth and quick answers.

Now, Frankie was not operationally trained and was destined to be left behind when we set off on that year's Operation Meebos.[29] But like "Captain" Payne he thirsted after stronger waters, and being adept at negotiation, confronted me directly with an urgent request – he wanted to go with us to Angola. I just couldn't turn my back on such a display of spirit, and after a while gave permission, albeit with a firm proviso: "You will not drive over a mine with your soft-skinned mobile tuck-shop or get killed or wounded in any ensuing skirmish, got it? I don't want Cadbury chocolates, Mars Bars, Windhoek Lager and tins of Coca-Cola spread all over Africa!"

Both of us knew, of course, that no such thing could be guaranteed in a shooting war, but I did what I could by positioning his mobile tuck-shop at the very end of the fighting column, which stretched back for about 50 km. Well, I am glad to say that Frankie returned to Omuthiya without a scratch, having done a sterling job of keeping the troops' stomachs in marching order.

There was a sequel to this. After returning from Meebos in August I received a call from Cape Town. It was his father, Dr. Frankie Fiser, and when he heard I would be down there in December he invited me to dinner at his home. I spent a wonderful evening with Dr. and Mrs. Fiser, and was humbled by their gratitude for "the boost in self-esteem and personal growth that Frank experienced at 61 Mech," as they put it.

I left their home that night feeling content and fulfilled. Frankie had had the spirit all along, of course, or he would not have begged to go along on Meebos. But I had fostered it, I think, and most important of all, I had given him the opportunity to prove himself which is so important to any young man. He was already enrolled at the University of Cape Town for 1983, and I knew his experiences under my command would assist him in his studies. Such was the calibre of the soldiers of 61 Mech. To me they were an amazing collection of unusual people!

29 See Chapter 14.

Exercising the Tactical Headquarters (Tac HQ) of 10 Division – Building Unity

On 1 August 1988, during Operation Prone,[30] a combined Cuban-FAPLA-SWAPO raiding force attacked the temporary military base at Okalongo – a typical installation of its kind, sand-walled with a watchtower – which was located 59 km north-northwest of Oshakati and 29 km north of Ogongo, and manned by an infantry company from 1 South African Cape Corps, which had recently deployed from Cape Town. The base lay approximately five kilometres south of the Jati Strip.[31]

Right in the middle of the witching hour (10 minutes past midnight, to be exact) Okalongo was bombarded with rockets and mortars. This was an indirect stand-off bombardment – a "wegstaanbestoking" in Afrikaans, not a prelude to a ground attack but a harassing attack fired from a distance, and it came as a complete surprise, something these newly-arrived soldiers had never before experienced in their lives – a terrifying blast of death materialising without warning out of the darkness from the northwest, north and south-southeast of the base.

One soldier had it particularly hard. His comrades could still take cover behind the ramparts, but he was marooned in the watchtower high above them, not only feeling very vulnerable but witness to the full horror of the bombardment. With each salvo he shouted frantically: "Hier kom hulle nou weer" (here they come again) as the incoming rockets' fiery trails arced across the night sky and explosions erupted all around him.

It was a soul-shocking initiation to border soldiering for the younger Cape Corps men as they crouched palefaced behind the ramparts, rifles at the ready, peering wide-eyed into the darkness to fight off a nonexistent enemy attack. At 01:20 the enemy indirect fire ceased abruptly. Now the cost could be counted – and it was negligible, More than 50 122 mm rockets and 82 mm mortar rounds had exploded inside the walls, but by a miracle not one man was killed or wounded, although there were naturally some cases of shock; but while they might have been shaken, their spirit was not broken.

Meanwhile at Oshakati I had scheduled a practical exercise for the 10 SA Division's mobile tactical HQ from 2 to 3 August, the idea being to establish team cohesion and exercise battle procedures, navigation, movement, formations and radio procedures (these last included supplying the enemy radio interception teams with some interesting items of speculation).

I chose Okalongo as the Tac HQ's first destination to bolster the occupiers' morale after their recent ordeal – so recent; in fact, that when we arrived there the mortar and rocket craters were still fresh and a slight whiff of high explosive lingered in the air. The arrival of our 13 Ratels and additional hardware did the trick. That night some interesting stories were told by the undaunted Cape Corps men, and it was clear that our arrival had been therapeutic, as had been intended.

The next day's plan was to move our Tac HQ through the dense bush along the southern edge of the border towards the Etale base, about 70 km further to the east, and before I left I appointed my Ratel's driver as the colonel in command, while I took his place at the wheel. This was just one of the tricks I had up my sleeve which was intended to make life interesting and exciting for the command team, build team spirit and heighten awareness.

30 See Chapter 16.

31 Jati or Jati-strip – A strip of land, one km wide measured from the SWA/Angola border in the north and the Timo-cutline in the south treated as no-man's land by the SADF. The Jati-strip stretched over a distance of 450 km from Beacon 1 in the west up to Beacon 45 in the east.

Here and there navigational issues and formation-changing hitches cropped up during our steady move eastwards, but all in all the young national service "colonel" did well, and no enemy interfered. Colonel Cassie Schoeman and his operational team were deployed at Etale; knowing me of old, he understood very well what I was up to, and fell in with the game. He accommodated the young "colonel" in the officers' quarters after that worthy had been briefed by the operational and intelligence staffs on the current state of affairs, while his new temporary rifleman (namely myself) played darts with the troops, had a few beers with them and spent the night in a sleeping bag in their quartered area. I don't know about my temporary replacement, but for me it was a brief but welcome and enjoyable respite from the thinking game.

The following day the Tac HQ returned to Oshakati and the young "colonel" handed his rank badges back to me as we arrived. Everyone had enjoyed the exploit and the Tac HQ had duly been exercised; and hopefully the enemy was appropriately confused by now. All this being the case, I had no hesitation in declaring the HQ combat and mission-ready.

An Extremely Young Commander at the Army College – Being Surprisingly Different

I had one leadership creed I shared with no one; that was to be surprisingly different! Every so often I would use this ace up my sleeve on the spur of the moment, as I did at Okalongo, just to shake things up a little and make life more interesting, but at other times I would do so for a very specific purpose.

When I was OC Army College I sometimes used the weekly parade to pull my little tricks out of the hat. I would call on one of my national service staff members and, much to the surprise of all present, hand over my colonel's rank badges and responsibilities to him for the day. Harrowing though it might have been for at least some such temporarily "promoted" officers, the purpose was not torture but to expose the recipient of my gift to the privileges of senior command and also to experiences the downside, the daily struggle through the tedious content of an in-and-out tray.

At first the more senior staff members of the college frowned on my little rank games, but later they came to accept them and even appreciate the fun (my seniors at Army HQ would most probably have fired me if they had known how I was playing fast-and-loose with rank, that most sacred of military things).

There was actually another benefit to this. Palming off the burden of rank on to an unsuspecting subaltern for a day was like a sort of holiday which gave me the time to wander around among my people, talk nonsense and simply enjoy a few amazing encounters at grass-roots. I still maintain that it is expected of leaders to walk the tight rope and to make the self vulnerable at times!

An Essential Ingredient Required for Combat – High Morale

Esprit de Corps – Morale is to the Physical as Three is to One

My soldiers had taught me the importance of high morale as we prepared for and executed Operation Protea.[32] The following section is all about building the high morale of this extraordinary unit of fighting men, which, as we have seen, included exercising leadership and command.

Esprit de corps was an essential ingredient for successful combat and healthy unit

32 See Chapter 9.

livelihood. We needed to establish this before we departed from Omuthiya for Humbe-Xangongo in southern Angola on 22 August 1981. In battle, death rides on the shoulder of every soldier. There is always the subtle fear of being wounded or even dying. However, the greatest fear of any true commander and his soldiers is not the bayonet or the bullet, but failing to carry out the mission.

Fear of failure is not necessarily a bad thing when it serves as a holding principle to ensure balance at critical moments of decision; for me as a commander it was therefore extremely important to keep building the esprit de corps of my unit. I saw this as one of my main responsibilities, with the full support of my cadre, of course. Napoleon Bonaparte had expressed a fundamental truth for soldiers and units such as ours almost two centuries before 61 Mech existed when he said "Morale (the psychological) is to the physical as three is to one".

It was all about building character, of the individuals as well as of the clan. In practice one finds a powerful interaction between the individual, the leadership and the unit. This all adds to self-confidence; mutual trust; physical and psychological preparedness; faith in oneself and the unit; and belief in appropriate battle doctrine. There was an immense feeling of pride in belonging to a unit such as ours – a spontaneous sense of identification.

I could almost tangibly feel the loyalty which existed between the members of the respective subordinate groupings and in 61 Mech as a whole, notwithstanding the different combat, combat support and combat service corps serving in it. It is an old thing for soldiers the various corps to give the others nicknames (usually unflattering ones) and tell equally unflattering jokes about them. But in a healthy army or unit the jokes and nicknames are all submerged in a common corporate loyalty, and this was certainly the case with 61 Mech. The reason was that we trained mainly as integrated combined arms teams, in which marrying-up drills played an essential part – full integration of arms, in other words, not make-believe stuff or lip service.

You could not get up at 05:00 one morning at Omuthiya and declare: By the powers vested in me as the commander, from today onwards there shall be high morale, mutual respect and trust. It needed to be earned through hard work. Needless to say, of course it brought tremendous personal satisfaction. These were emotions of a transitory nature, which could be created to remain steadfast.

As Michael Elliot-Bateman wrote in "Defeat in the East":

> Morale is the instinct that enables men to face the fear of death and injury undaunted and to endure hardship. It is the will of man and of a unit to fight and suffer heroically. The strongest natural instinct of man is self-preservation and his most basic motivation is self-interest. Both these are quite contrary to man's exposing himself to danger and to physical hardship. This is the nature of morale; it is an instinct that transcends the natural instinct of self-preservation and raises man above the pettiness of self-interest.[33]

This was how I knew 61 Mech.

33 Elliot-Bateman, Michael: *Defeat in the East.* London, Oxford University Press, 1967, p. 227.

Individualised Consideration and Inspirational Motivation

In the field where the danger was to be found, I found that intimacy lay at the heart of camaraderie and competence. Young national servicemen at 61 Mech had taught me this simple value. I could read it on their faces; discern it in their way of talking and walking, and judge it by their jesting and laughter. I made it a habit to wander amongst the tents in the evenings, many a time accompanied by Koos Rossouw our chaplain.

Sometimes we would find small groups of soldiers war-gaming on sand models they had made between the tents. Sitting down on my army camp chair in their midst, Koos would say a quick prayer and then we would chat, crack a few jokes and have some tactical jostling – great. I did the same when our troops fought with live ammunition and hand grenades through the mock trenches in the bush just north of Omuthiya – great fun.

No better place to have talks with troops appearing out of the dust and the gunsmoke – dirty troops, smiling troops, accomplished troops. These special moments made me feel happy, confident and relaxed. And I wished their fathers and mothers; brothers and sisters; teachers and girlfriends, could have seen them as I did – what a God-given privilege!

Building Morale Worked Both Ways – Something about a Soldier

I was working on my battle maps alongside my Ratel-Command vehicle the day before departing on Operation Protea. With a sideward glance I saw one of my troops passing by. He saluted, suddenly stopped, turned sideways, walked towards me and said with extreme confidence and visible self-esteem: "No matter the odds, Commandant, we'll fight a hole through any enemy." I felt emotionally uplifted and appreciative of this simple gesture by an enthusiastic, friendly, spontaneous young soldier. Such was the calibre of my national servicemen! Enthralled, I saluted him.

Afterthoughts on Leadership and Command

Effective leadership provides the winning edge, and leaders should therefore have the ability to act independently within the framework of given guidelines and accept their command responsibilities in a spirit of joyfulness, even under unpredictable circumstances. They should recognise that all means of union of power demand the union of knowledge and preparedness. In all of this, man is the most important element on the battlefield. As such I had the privilege and honour to could have served in the company of heroes!

9

Our Fallen and Those Maimed For Life

Sixty Seconds' Worth of Distance Run

If neither foes nor loving friends can hurt you ... If you can fill the unforgiving minute with sixty seconds' worth of distance run, yours is the Earth and everything that's in it, and ... Which is more ... you'll be a Man, my son!
Rudyard Kipling

Our Sons were Warriors – I Will Remember Them

I remember all those who fell while under my command; their losses resonate in my soul because they were my soldiers, and I cared deeply for them. And in my heart and mind I still feel the weight left by the sacrifices of the wounded. There are many soldiers of those times who were left with physical and psychological scars that mark their sacrifice for our country. You will not find their names on any memorials, but we who were there and came through unscathed will always carry their names and faces around with us.

On 25 August 2012 I had the honour of officiating at the memorial service of the 61 Mechanised Battalion Group Veterans' Association at the Ditsong National Museum for Military History (formerly the South African Museum of Military History) in Saxonwold, Johannesburg. On a glorious, sunny winter's day we basked in the companionship of old comrades, and let our thoughts range far away in time and distance to the battlefields where we had walked arm in arm with death and wounds – and lived to tell the tale. It was a truly moving moment for all of us as we gathered in front of the memorial needle, its names of fallen comrades evoking memories undimmed by time.

In its 27-year existence 61 Mech lost 105 officers and men. Some were killed in action and others died in service – although real soldiers make no distinction between the two; it is enough that they left us while we were all engaged in some life-or-death enterprise. Of those, 20 fell while I commanded this magnificent first-line fighting unit in 1981–82. I remembered them as they had been then, young, vigorous and ready for battle, and I shed a tear and part of my essence for each of them.

It had been almost exactly 30 years since our unit had returned from southern Angola after Operation Meebos.[1] During Meebos, on 30 July 1982, Second-Lieutenant Sarel Steyn earned an Honoris Crux for gallantry when he saved a number of his comrades from their burning Ratel after it had detonated a double landmine, and recovered the body of Rifleman Daryl Peter Croeser from the stricken vehicle while it was being ripped apart by explosion after explosion as its ammunition detonated from the heat.

Later that day Sarel Steyn spoke for all of us when he expressed his deeply felt grief for Croeser in a few simple words that resonated louder than the most flowery graveside eulogy: "He was my gunner and my orderly, he was a good soldier." I had great sympathy

---

1 See Chapter 14.

for this young officer, just 19 years old, who had run Kipling's 60 seconds out there in the anonymous Angolan bush without flinching, and had become a man overnight.

These and other memories, of our young leaders and their fallen brothers in arms, of those fighting days ran through my mind as I stood there, reading the names on the memorial. They are always with me, those blithe warriors who had had their lives snatched away from them. Sometimes I think that in a way they were the fortunate ones, because no one could hurt them anymore; they would never know betrayal or sadness or misfortune, and were now beyond the reach of any enemy who might wish to do them harm. Their lives, too, were worth every 60 seconds of the distance they ran before they were taken from us, and we mourned them then and mourn them still, because every soul in our defence force counted dearly. Our sons were warriors! I shed a tear for all those fallen men who proudly wore the coveted dagger and lightning-flashes of our regiment.

In Memoriam – 61 Mechanised Battalion Group from 1981 until 1982

Operation Daisy from September – November 1981 (3)
Lieutenant G. van Zyl – 4 November 1981.
Corporal J.L. Potgieter – 4 November 1981.
Candidate Officer S.F. Coetzee – 5 November 1981.

Operation Yahoo from April 1982 – May 1982 (9)
Second Lieutenant D. Van der Westhuizen – 15 April 1982.
Corporal M. J. van Jaarsveld – 15 April 1982.
Lance Corporal J.J. van der Berg – 15 April 1982.
Rifleman B.J. Wolfaardt – 15 April 1982.
Rifleman M. Peterson – 15 April 1982.
Rifleman J.H. Potgieter – 15 April 1982.
Rifleman L.P. Hough – 15 April 1982.
Rifleman J.D.G. Du Toit – 16 April 1982.
Rifleman G.P.C. Hattingh – 20 April 1982.

Operation Meebos from July – August 1982 (1)
Rifleman D.P. Croeser – 30 July 1982.

Other Fatalities (7)
Rifleman P. Hall – 1 March 1981
J.J. Kotze – 9 April 1981.
Rifleman L. Van Rooyen – 10 July 1981.
Bombardier D.J. Loubser – 17 August 1981.
Lance Bombardier H.V.L. Olver – 17 August 1981.
Rifleman G.J. Myburgh – 17 September 1981.
Cavalryman D. A. Steyn – 19 September 1981.

Blood was Not the Price for Victory – Perspective in Life

Before we go on to the war stories in the next chapters, I would like to give some perspective to certain issues concerning our soldiers who died or were wounded during the South African Border War

The purpose of any just war is to contribute to a better form of peace, is it not? Is that a worthwhile cause to die for? I leave the answer to my readers. But I want to make it clear that in the old SADF the price of victory was not to be measured in terms of the blood shed to achieve it! What counted was whether the mission had been fulfilled, because every South African field commander bore two permanent pressing responsibilities wherever he went and whatever he did: One was the mission he had been given, and the need to win every time, because there was no alternative; the other was to avoid incurring undue casualties.

This latter principle was clearly enunciated by Napoleon Bonaparte: "He who allows 10 men to be killed where at most two need have died is answerable for the lives of eight men". And in the Boer commandos of former days, the loss of a burgher's life because of his commander's failings was regarded as little less serious than outright murder. One could be cynical and say that our responsibility was simply to avoid political fallout at home, but the student of history knows that this reluctance to waste lives has been a consistent theme in all of South Africa's wars.

What made the burden even heavier was the fact that the men we flung into many a high-intensity action, especially during the external operations into southern Angola in the 1980s, were not professional soldiers, to whom death was an occupational hazard. They were precious national servicemen, the citizens of the future (and, we hoped, a vastly better) South Africa and we owed it both to the country and to their families to bring them home safely if at all possible.

At the same time, however, this could not and did not mean that their commanders (or their men, for that matter) shrank from taking a calculated risk where it was necessary or advantageous, even though this might entail the loss of life. Weighing up these conflicting responsibilities and their possible or likely consequences usually took place under the most demanding battle conditions. The only solution lay, as with everything else, in thorough planning and preparation for any operation or contingency, coupled with reliance on sound leadership and sensible military doctrine.

At times plans went askew and unforeseeable contingencies arose, either because of dire emergencies or simply because a fluid battlefield often sets its own rules. Then casualties occurred, as could be expected; and so many of our operational commanders knew what it felt like to lose people in battle. Let me recall a few examples of lives lost during our darkest hours:

- On 21 May 1980, 15 soldiers of 32 Battalion died during Operation Savate near an insignificant hamlet on the western bank of the Cubango River, when their unit attacked in the face of withering FAPLA ground fire.
- In Operation Sceptic on 10 June 1980, 61 Mech lost 13 soldiers killed. This happened during a pre-emptive strike on a SWAPO base at Chififua in southern Angola nicknamed "Smokeshell", when a platoon of Ratels unexpectedly ran into a complex of anti-aircraft guns deployed in a ground role.
- During Operation Protea in August 1981 10 South African soldiers were killed in action in a number of small actions or incidents.
- During Operation Yahoo, a high-intensity internal search-and-destroy operation against infiltrators of SWAPO's Special Unit, 61 Mech lost nine soldiers killed and 41 wounded between 15 April and 25 May of 1982; in the same operation five civilians were killed and three wounded through contacts with the enemy or in landmine explosions, and two members of the community were murdered by

the infiltrators.

- On 9 August 1982, during Operation Meebos, SWAPO anti-aircraft gunners shot down a Puma helicopter over the Mui River in southern Angola. It burst into flames on crashing, killing 15 soldiers.
- Between 28 December 1983 and 27 January 1984 61 Mech lost 14 soldiers during Operation Askari.
- During the little-known Operation Firewood in October 1987, 5 Special Forces Regiment lost 19 killed and 64 wounded.
- 61 Mech lost 14 soldiers killed in action during the conventional fighting in southern Angola between 16 September 1987 and 27 June 1988.
- On 27 June 1988 the Cubans retaliated to a ground attack conducted by 61 Mech across the border near Techipa with an attack by six Russian MiG-23s on South African air-defence position at Calueque. One bomb missed its intended target but killed 12 soldiers of 8 South African Infantry Battalion.

The memory of those who were killed or were wounded in battle, and the speculation about what the dead could have achieved if they had lived, is forever buried in the deep recesses of every commander's mind and the minds of their comrades – I often think about them when I lie awake during a restless night. It is not an easy matter for a commander to lose people in battle. When your people are killed or wounded, whether in action or otherwise, it brings with it an immediate feeling of shock, tremendous loss and deep sorrow.

In the military such news usually reaches the field commander amid life-threatening operational circumstances. The loss of a precious life or an injury to one of those under your command has a momentary numbing effect that leaves a feeling of profound sadness; the feeling of loss is inevitably made even worse by the thought of those loved ones and friends who are left behind.

It is a feeling not to be dwelled on for too long, because the life-threatening circumstances have not necessarily changed, and there still remains your tremendous responsibility for those who have not been killed or wounded. The grief and mourning have to be pushed to the back of your mind for the time being, because the war must go on: The momentum must be maintained as aggressively as the situation demands, people must be inspired, morale must be restored and spirits brought back to a high pitch, emotional states must be uplifted. This happens during and after every battle ... the Cunene ... the Cuvelai ... the Caiundo ... the Lomba ... the Chambinga ... the Hube ... the Cuito.

It did not seem to us that our enemies cherished the lives of their soldiers as much as we cherished ours. At one stage during the battle for southeast Angola, South African soldiers watched from a distance as FAPLA soldiers executed their own wounded in the field – not exactly the ideal best practice to induce or foster high morale, I would say. Strange people, those enemies of ours.

About Troop-Carriers on Land and in the Sky – The Ratel and the Puma[2]

We learned a few hard lessons during operations in SWA/Namibia as well as in southern Angola. The Ratel was wonderful but not invincible and if the enemy took one out, eight or more people would normally die. On 15 April 1982 61 Mech recovered eight bodies from a Ratel destroyed in an ambush by SWAPO near Tsintsabis during Operation Yahoo.

2 Refer to Chapters 11 and 14.

The same thing applied to the Puma transport helicopters. On 9 August 1982 61 Mech recovered 15 bodies from the Puma which had been shot down by SWAPO gunners over the Mui River near Cuvelai.

When 61 Mech arrived at the scene the helicopter was still burning. Deaths in such horrendous ways were always heart-rending to witness. It scarred our souls, and while the scars might grow fainter in time, they will always be there.

A Few Consequences of Dying in Battle – Dying is No Accident

- Apprehension of War, Escalation and the Losing of Many Soldiers. On 31 October 1987 a South African raiding force of 5 Reconnaissance Regiment of the Special Forces, backed by soldiers from 1 Parachute Battalion and 101 (Ovambo) Battalion, struck deep into central Angola during Operation Firewood. Their objective was SWAPO's well-defended Northern Front headquarters near Indungo. The insurgents concealed in the shadows of the dense Indungo forest put up a tremendous fight; the powers-that-were had decided that the attackers would not have any artillery in support but would have to rely on their 81 mm mortars, and it was a literally fatal decision – for the attackers, that is, who lost 19 killed and 64 wounded – an extremely heavy price to pay for one operation.

  The deep Firewood raid did have some unintended but welcome consequences, however. At this time we were preparing further to the east to obliterate 16 FAPLA Brigade at the source of the Chambinga River during the second phase of Operation Modular.[3] The Firewood raid had been too close for comfort, and caused a ripple of unease in the ranks of FAPLA's commanders; they could feel the heat licking at their lifeline, close to Menongue. I suspect that they were worried that if the South Africans were willing to raid that deep to take out a SWAPO headquarters, what might be coming at them?

  However, a similar ripple of unease went through the South African senior ranks when their heavy costs were counted. The more prudent military strategic and operational decisions were then taken to approach Cuito by way of the eastern flank rather than the western one which the fiery younger South African field commanders strongly favoured. It was clear to us on the ground that the military and political powers brass-hats were extremely wary of further escalation and possibly taking more heavy casualties as a result. So the senior generals of the SADF4 decided to opt for a more cautious approach to the conventional fighting in southern Angola, and to limit the operational objectives.
- Deep-Felt Sorrow Came with Mourning and Measures of Closure. On successfully completing Operation Yahoo on 25 May 1982, the passing bells tolled from the churches of Tsumeb as the community and 61 Mech met to mourn their dead and wounded. A measure of closure was found in the close companionship and the sharing of memories by those left behind. Like the security forces, the small communities of Tsumeb, Grootfontein and Otavi had suffered dearly – too many had been killed and wounded for so few people to accept their passing with anything less than great sorrow and a sense of loss.

  A meditation by our 61 Mech chaplain, Padre Koos Rossouw, was published

3 See Chapter 15.
4 South African Defence Force.

in the Otjikoto Journal of the Tsumeb district in June of 1982. It started with a passage from the Book of Micah, Chapter 6, verse 8: "He has showed you, O man, what is good; and what does the Lord require of you; but to do justice, and to love kindness; and to walk humbly with your God...? Then Koos asked, "What is the meaning of this"?

Together with 61 Mech the Tsumeb community had suffered a heart-breaking loss of loved ones. Lieutenant Daantjie van der Westhuizen, his son-in-law Rifleman Hendrik Potgieter, and Bushman Tracker Jan Kouswab who had died in the ambush on 15 April; Mr. D.J.J. Erasmus, who lost both his legs due to a SWAPO mine laid on his farm near Tsintsabis and died on the operating table in Tsumeb Hospital; Mr. J.P. Steyn from the farm Masaus, who died instantly when his vehicle detonated a mine on his farm; Mr. L.P.J. Fourie from the farm Ruimte, who was killed together with a soldier, a Corporal Bester, when the infiltrating insurgents riddled his civilian vehicle with AK47 fire.

Then there were the commanding officers of the training and feeder units in South Africa, like my friend Colonel Tony Savides at 1 South African Infantry Battalion, and their chaplains, who had the heart-rending task of taking tidings of our losses to their parents, families and loved ones on behalf of the Chief of the Army. They did so with great dignity and genuine sorrow.

- Human and Worldly Outcries Lead to Peace-making. During the ill-fated air attack by six Russian MiG-23s at Calueque on 27 June 1988 seven of the 12 South African soldiers killed were 19 years old, and the eldest 23. Questions directed at the politicians and generals were sharp, damning and less than flattering. The following quote from "The War for Africa" by Fred Bridgland[5] provides a telling perspective of the prevailing moods:

  In South Africa it caused waves of wrath, anguish and fear as international newspapers blazoned such headlines as: Angola War: Pretoria's Plans Go Awry; (International Herald Tribune, 13 July 1988); Military Balance Shifts Against Pretoria, (The Times of London, 16 June 1988); 12 South Africans Die in Angola Border Clash, (Washington Post, 29 June 1988); and "the nightmares of Pretoria's generals are coming true ... South African whites for the first time are starting to feel the effect of casualties in a distant war of which they are told very little" (Africa Confidential, 15 July 1988). Heated questions were asked about why the SADF had allowed the enemy to make a deliberate attack on such a vital installation.

A kind of a stalemate was reached in the war. A weary calm settled over the battlefield. The magnitude of events and time had caught up with the politicians and the generals on opposing sides, and they opted for a ceasefire and subsequently sued for peace. What is worth dying for in battle? No wonder that the pressures exerted so strongly by the regional and international community contributed to peace-making in Southern Africa by December 1988. It was about time.

The Memorial Needle of 61 Mech and the Names of the Fallen

61 Mechanised Battalion Group's striking memorial needle bears the unit's original emblem, and on its base, a block of grey granite from Karabib in SWA/Namibia, are carved

5 Bridgland, Fred: *The War for Africa: Twelve Months That Transformed a Continent*. Ashanti Publishing Limited, Gibraltar, 1990, p. 363.

the names of the fallen. The names are recorded under the specific emblem 61 Mech worn at the time of their death, with the dates and names of the appropriate operations.

It is better-travelled than most memorials, because it went with the regiment wherever it moved in its 27 years of existence. Originally the needle was erected at Omuthiya; from there it went to Walvis Bay and eventually to Lohatlha, where 61 Mech was disbanded on 18 November 2005. Now it has reached its final resting-place at the Ditsong Museum of Military History in Johannesburg, where it was unveiled on 12 June 2010; as it happened, the date of the unveiling coincided almost exactly with the 30th anniversary of Operation Sceptic (Smokeshell), which began on 10 June 1980.

Those who cannot visit the Museum of Military History for one reason or another will also find the names of the honoured dead listed in the regimental veterans' association website at www.61mech.org.za. And if you do visit the memorial needle or call up the website, please do not forget those who were maimed for life in body, mind or soul. Their unsung war against pain and disability will continue for the rest of their lives.

Epilogue – How Far is Far Enough?

We have made peace now with our enemies of the war in Southwest Africa/Namibia and Angola, and so it is incumbent on us to respect their dead and wounded as we respect our own. Theirs is by far the greatest wounds that must heal, for their losses were much higher than ours. During the South African Border War, from its beginning in 1966 to its effective end in 1987 SWAPO[6] incurred 11,292 known dead, in comparison with 715 members of the security forces. How militarily effective was our foe? During Operation Modular in 1987, 31 of our soldiers were killed in action, while FAPLA[7] and the Cubans combined lost almost 5,000 and UNITA[8] about 3,000.

It is a strange irony that in each of the 20-plus years of war in SWA/Namibia and Angola the annual civilian death-toll on South Africa's roads was many times greater than the war losses on the border. It is even more ironical that in the years since the African National Congress took power in April 1994, there has been an undeclared (and officially ignored) war of a new type raging in South Africa – a series of savage attacks on isolated farms which the police appear unable to put an end to.

Between 1991 and 2007 there were 10,412 attacks on farms, in the course of which 1,650[9] people' (almost all white) were murdered, many of them with such brutality that it turns the stomach of the most hardened observer. And the killing goes on without signs of abating: During the merry month of August 2012, for example, 30 farmers were murdered in just 13 terrible days – this in a country which officially has been at peace for almost two decades.

More and more observers – both in South Africa and overseas – are asking if this is sheer uncontrolled criminality, or something even more sinister. The brutal killings on our farms and in our homesteads of old and young (including babies) are on the brink of amounting to genocide – it could be related to revolutionary warfare by violent criminal means,

6 South West Africa People's Organisation, our main enemy.

7 Forcas Armadas Popular de Angola.

8 National Union for Angola's Total Independence – *Uniao Nacional para and Independencia Total de Angola*.

9 Official Survey by the South African Institute of Race Relations (SAIRR), 2008/2009, data provided to SAIRR by the Agricultural Institute of South Africa (Agri SA) and the South African Police.

It has become so serious that the international Genocide Watch organisation's table of escalation places South Africa at level 6 – the preparatory phase for a campaign of genocide. As long ago as 2001 Genocide Watch stated that "2.2 percent of ethno-European (white) farmers had already been murdered and more than ... 12 percent of these farmers had been attacked on their farms." And that was 12 years ago!

In plain words it is a catastrophe, not just for the farmers but for our future food security, but the current government is effectively doing nothing about it, apart from washing its hands in a style worthy of Pontius Pilate; the official line is that no ulterior motive can be found, the attacks are just part of the general wave of violence and criminality sweeping the country. It shrugs off any suggestions from the farmers that there is evidence of a campaign to drive them off their land.

At the time of writing, the latest ghastly murders were recorded on a farm near Trompsburg in the Free State Province on 11 September 2012 – South Africa's own shameful 9/11.[10] This is far worse than the 31 young soldiers we lost during four intensive months of honourable war in southeast Angola during Operation Modular in 1987.

Meanwhile there are still energetic attempts to build the fighting at Cuito Cuanavale up to an earth-shaking defeat for the SADF which single-handedly changed the history of the subcontinent and led to the deaths of hundreds, if not thousands, of South African soldiers. To warrant their military ineptness during their revolutionary war, members of the African National Congress's Umkhonto we Sizwe recently went on record (without producing any evidence, of course) that mass burial sites of South African soldiers had been unearthed near Cuito Cuanavale.

To my mind blatant lying is embedded in the indirectness of a lying nature; what more is there to say? In the 1970s and 1980s the South African press was freer than any other in Africa (not to mention in such ANC sponsors such as Cuba, East Germany and the Soviet Union); many of the newspapers were fervently opposed both to the government and the war in SWA/Namibia. There was no way in which either the government or the SADF could have suppressed news of losses on the border, family death notices in the newspapers or media coverage of funerals without being enmeshed in a massive public uproar, even from its own supporters. Not one of the crusading journalists of the time ever found evidence of any such cover-up.

Yet the stories go on, and have been going on for years. In 2008 I was invited to a panel discussion on the battle of Cuito Cuanavale at the South African War College in Pretoria. There I heard one Colonel Rickerts, a former MK member, passionately retelling the old lies to gawking students of the senior army command and staff course of the new South African National Defence Force. The students just smiled knowingly (later Rickerts went further and through the media whipped new life into that threadbare old story about mass graves in Angola). Not even Google – that fount of truth, lies and misconceptions – has anything to say about this.

Our soldiers were precious to us, as I have said, but sometimes in those battle-torn days I wondered if our enemies' military and political masters held the lives of their soldiers in the same high regard as we did, because on occasion I had experienced the contrary![11] After the end of hostilities in SWA and Angola, fortunately, I met many of our former enemies' proud ex-combatants, and I know that for many the memory of their dead was as precious

10 *Beeld*, South African Newspaper, Johannesburg, 11 September 2012.

11 Refer to Chapter 9.

to them as ours was to us.

I remember a tall Angolan MiG-21 pilot I met at Calueque during the peace negotiations in August 1988; we told one another a few war stories, and he wept as he told me about one of his friends who had been shot down over the fields of southeast Angola during Operation Modular. There remains hope for a country when its people can shed tears of sadness and joy and even compassion, not just of suffering like the people in so much of Africa.

Unwarranted deaths, no matter their cause, hurt those who are left behind; they can destroy a magnificent country, and it makes one wonder about the future. We will remember all of our fallen, "at the going down of the sun, and in the morning", in the words of Laurence Binyon's famous prayer. For many of us, the South Africa we held and still hold in such dear regard – with all its many faults and equally many virtues – is our beginning ... and our end. How far is far enough? Was the war worth the all that it cost?

Or will history repeat itself?

10

Into A Foreign Country

Operation Bowler

The inevitable is only what a fool hasn't the wit to avoid.
Somerset Maugham

The Cycle of Knowledge – Why Don't We Learn from History?

In January 1979 I was transferred to Pretoria from 1 South African Infantry Battalion to the Directorate Infantry under Colonel Len Meyer. This was, of course, work of significant importance, but the fire in my belly kept me wondering about where my next adventure would come from. It arrived in mid-October, when – by the grace of the Dear Lord and Colonel Meyer – I was ripp'd untimely (as Shakespeare would have said) out of Army Headquarters by the seat of my nutria-coloured pants and appointed commander of Task Force X-Ray in Rhodesia.[1]

I was frankly ecstatic at being pulled out of Army Headquarters and given a field command which was remote enough from the headquarters machine to give me enough elbow room – Task Force X-Ray was operating in the Sengwe Tribal Trust Land as part of Operation Repulse, an area veiled in bush in the southeastern corner of Rhodesia. And so I became a very small part of the bush war to the north of the Limpopo River.

In the Sengwe I would realise that the excitement lay in the creation of new significances, in understanding and learning more about what was happening in Southern Africa, not only the shooting part, but the realisation that no man or country is an island, whether he or it did things one way, as was the case in Rhodesia, and we in another, as with SWA/Namibia and southern Angola (one should be wary of direct comparisons, though – the Rhodesian government was fighting a straightforward insurgency which was aimed at taking power, whereas the South African government had no intention of hanging on to SWA/Namibia, and had tasked the SADF to keep the peace while SWA/Namibians of all races worked out their constitutional future – no more, no less).

And so I found myself wearing Rhodesian camouflage and the rank insignia of a Rhodesian lieutenant-colonel, absorbing things I had never been exposed to before. Where, then, was the worth of the new experience I would pick up n Rhodesia? Well, I found value in the teachings of Mao Tse-tung:

> Knowledge starts with practice, reaches the theoretical phase via practice and then has to return to practice; practice, knowledge, more practice, more knowledge ... the cyclical repetition of this pattern to infinity, and with each cycle the elevation of the content of practice and knowledge to a higher level.

---

1 See Map 6. Rhodesia is better known to the world today as embattled Zimbabwe under the rein of the infamous President Robert Mugabe.

And so it was a good experience to command a battalion-sized task force in the Sengwe from 19 October 1979 until 27 January 1980; it is a good experience to command a battalion anywhere, but this was especially the case here, because I was fortunate enough to serve under Brigadier Peter Rich, who commanded 4 Rhodesian Brigade – a charismatic man who had served in the British Special Air Service during the Malayan campaign before emigrating to Rhodesia.

The headquarters of both 4 Brigade and Operation Repulse were located at Fort Victoria (now Masvingo), a small town near the famed Zimbabwe Ruins and Lake Kyle. The brigade flash was a golden lion on a blue shield – a most appropriate insigne because this beautiful countryside had been wracked by a ferocious counterinsurgency war which had started in 1962 and would not end till December 1979. The Sengwe taught me a lesson I had learned already, namely that life is not the way you feel it should be. In fact, it is the way it is, and what makes the difference is how you cope with that immutable reality.

What was the Point of the War in Rhodesia and with Strangers going to a Strange Land?

I am not going to discuss the origins or course of the Rhodesian Bush War, the Zimbabwe War of Liberation or the "Second Chimurenga", as it had also been known since 1962 (the choice depends on which side you were backing), since the subject has been documented extensively in other publications – let me say only that it was a typical revolutionary war fought in an African country, with all that that implies. What I intend to talk about is the situation that arose when three small South African task forces were hastily put together and dumped into the interior of that embattled country in October 1979 by the joint decision of the South African and Rhodesian governments.

Our intervention came very near the tail-end of 18 years of turmoil against the backdrop of Black Nationalism which was bent on taking power by force of arms. One might even regard it being a type of civil war rather than an independence struggle, since the Rhodesian government of Ian Smith was already independent in fact, even though nobody recognised it. But it was basically a government run by a white minority, and its opponents were two armed Black Nationalist movements, the Zimbabwe African National Union (ZANU)[2] and the Zimbabwe African People's Union (ZAPU).[3] Broadly speaking, when one looks at the 1979 map of Rhodesia, ZANLA operated into the country from strategic bases located in Mozambique in the east, and ZIPRA (The Zimbabwe People's Revolutionary Army) mainly from Zambia to its west, north and northwest.[4]

The war had been going on for longer than, I suspect, anyone of its participants had expected, but by 1979 it was clear that Rhodesia was entering the final stages and was fighting a rearguard action. Tremendous political, military and economic sanctions were reaching their peak, the Rhodesian economy had been flatlining for some time, and large parts of the interior had been lost to the insurgents and become "liberated zones", especially the tribal trust lands like the Sengwe TTL; in fact, by the time I arrived there in October

2 ZANU and its military wing ZANLA (Zimbabwe African National Liberation Army) were initially headed by the Reverend Ndabaningi Sithole and later Robert Mugabe. This movement consisted mainly of the Shona speaking tribes.

3 ZAPU and its military wing ZIPRA (Zimbabwe People's Revolutionary Army) consisted mainly of Ndebele ethnic groups and were led by Joshua Nkomo.

4 See map 6.

1979, Rhodesia as we knew it was within a year of disappearing and re-emerging as the Zimbabwe of Robert Mugabe.

Rhodesia's only reliable external ally at this disastrous time was South Africa to the south of the Limpopo River, which had its own external and internal problems to deal with. In October 1979 South Africa decided to throw Rhodesia a lifeline in the form of Operation Bowler, in the form of a token force which was legally and lawfully attired in Rhodesian camouflage. One consequence of this was, as I have said, that a temporary lieutenant-colonel named Roland de Vries found himself in the Sengwe, a situation about which he was definitely not going to complain.

I use the word "token" because in all conscience the South African force – Operation Bowler – was far too small for the task it had been given. X-Ray was battalion-sized, but the other two "task forces", Zulu and Yankee, each consisted mainly of a company-sized contingent from 1 Parachute Battalion; both would be hedge-hopping through the bush as fire forces.[5]

The Sengwe TTL's operational area spanned the southeastern corner of Rhodesia, across to Mozambique in the east and South Africa to the south. The primary enemies, therefore, were the ZANLA insurgents. We were soon to be involved in low-intensity counterinsurgency warfare with the senseless purpose of stemming the unstoppable tide of infiltrators from all directions.

I say "senseless" because it was the age-old story – too little, too late. The tide was turning as the dominoes tumbled before the forces of "liberation" in Southern Africa. In fact, Rhodesia was the last of the dominoes standing between South Africa and its African enemies. The Portuguese were long gone from the west, and now Rhodesia was clearly on its last legs; it was no brain strainer to guess that the next battle line would be along the Limpopo.

Was this the reason for South Africa's involvement in Rhodesia's war at such a late stage? In any case, there we were, strangers in a strange land, burning time into nothingness within its strangeness as we chased an elusive enemy who flitted through the dappled shadows of its ominous green vastness. As highly trained professional soldiers it was engrossing work, but it would end up making me think deeply about the validity of this kind of warfare within the greater scheme of things.[6] Inevitably it led me to ask another question: Were those in power in South Africa channelling political and military energy and stratagems in the right direction, or merely squandering resources?

So you might ask what the hell I actually learned from the Bowler episode. Well, I soon learned that in what Mao called a "protracted war" there was no substantial gain to be achieved by a country and its people over time without the accompanying pain, especially in Africa. In many instances it was self-induced pain, caused by politics with explosive military bangs, as a result of intermittent stupidity – it will be remembered that politics grow out of the barrel of a gun, as Mao Tse-tung famously said. One also recalls that pithy Afrikaans military phrase which was current in the SADF: "As jy dom wil wees, moet jy maar afkak" (roughly "If you choose to be stupid, you'll just have to be satisfied with seeing your arse").

This cut both ways, incidentally. Our enemies also needed to climb a steep learning-curve and struggle through bouts of immense suffering – to live and learn under fire, while many died; hopefully to leave enduring legacies of peace at the end of the whole vicious

5 The two fire forces were provided by 1 Parachute Battalion from Bloemfontein.

6 See Chapter 7 – Principles of Revolutionary Warfare appraised.

cycle. Notwithstanding "the Struggle", is Zimbabwe not a pure example of a lost victory today? Could Zimbabwe ever prove the contrary to us? The same question could be asked about South Africa, or is this far too difficult for the peoples of Africa to contemplate? The other conflicting parties in Southern Africa, us and them, were not ready for peace either by 1980. Angry energies still needed to be expanded and expended before they could be channelled into something more valuable and enduring for posterity in SWA, southern Angola and South Africa.

Shooting and killing, political strife and dialogue were still necessary, it seems, before the politicians and the military grandmasters could come to their senses. There was to be no ecstasy for some time, until the obstinate hard-arsed political paradigms shifted. Lesson learned: People (sorry, politicians and those others that the military shoe fits) don't act according to the real truth, but the truth as they have come to perceive it; one can only change the way one feels and acts by changing the way one thinks. Yes, we were definitely not there yet in those days! A question which is still pending is whether we have arrived at all.

Until 1980 the resolute Rhodesian minority government and its small but exquisitely efficient military machine fought a harsh bush war in which they were never beaten on the ground (politics was something else), and there were many excellent military lessons for us to learn from their tactics. But one wonders if the politicians and their military high commands ever learned the strategic lessons that emerged so painfully from the quagmires of African warfare and revolutionary conflicts, conflicts which ended with the imposition of imperfect political and security settlements which carried within them the seeds of their eventual failure? Rhodesia-Zimbabwe was one such.

The answers to these amazingly intricate conundrums of politics, war, peace and hope, I realised, would not come easy. But it is so that the South African Army used its first-hand experience of the Rhodesian war to customise its own bush tactics and then to successfully fight its own battles 1 700 km to the west. This frustrated the Soviet and Cuban military and political designs on Southern Africa till the Soviet Union collapsed, the Cold War fizzled out and the time was ripe for a peaceful, democratically principled process to be applied from December 1988 onwards. So South Africa and the SADF learned something from the Rhodesian conflict – if not necessarily about the political part!

Operation Bowler was not, of course, the first South African intervention in Rhodesia. For years South African police contingents, seconded South African Air Force pilots and various individuals had served with distinction in Rhodesia, learning the tricks of the bush war fighting trade.

The South African Alouette gunship and Puma transport helicopter pilots had participated in countless cross-border raids into neighbouring Zambia and Mozambique, as well as in the internal "fire force" operations. A number of our army officers attended the superb counterinsurgency and tracking courses presented at the Rhodesian Infantry School at Gwelo (today's Gweru). Military training programmes included escape and evasion courses presented by the famed C (Charlie) Squadron of the Rhodesian SAS. Such courses were attended by well known paratrooper officers of the South African Army in the late seventies, including Jan Breytenbach and Barrie Ferreira.

I wanted to attend one of those courses at Gwelo myself, but instead I and five other paratrooper officers were nominated to spend three very secret months on a special warfare course in Taiwan, where we were instructed in the tactics the Communist Chinese were teaching the enemies we were fighting in Southern Africa. The Rhodesians, on the other hand, had learnt much from the British military during the successful Malayan counterinsurgency campaign between 1948 and 1960, and the Rhodesian Bush War and studies of the Malayan campaign became the foundation for the counterinsurgency doctrine adopted by the South African Army from 1966 onwards.

Revolutionary Warfare According to Mao Tse-tung, John J. McCuen ... and Roland de Vries

Did the South African government perhaps miss something out there about the effects of bedevilling politics and the need for sound international relations? I saw many good things being done by the counterinsurgency forces in Rhodesia; mostly military. Those included practical grassroots military actions; well-planned and well-executed large scale offensive feats and pre-emptive cross-border strikes when it was necessary; and adequate mobility and small-unit actions to aggressively locate, pursue and annihilate insurgent units while keeping the remainder under control and on the run. What did I miss in the Rhodesian way of fighting insurgency and the way the South Africans did as well later on? Well, mainly that nothing much was done about the politics and the time factor.

Those drawn-out conflicts steadily wore away the phoney democracies, while foreign assistance dwindled into nothingness. Did we really care about cultural sensitivity; about being familiar with the local culture, mores and languages? Did we even understand that the ordinary people were the key base to be secured and defended, rather than territory won or enemy bodies counted? Did we have a clear political vision, with clearly articulated aspirations which could excite and even outmatch the designs of the revolutionaries?

Of course we talked about it in the classrooms at our military colleges. Counterinsurgency warfare was all about small-unit action, they said, the lieutenant's and corporal's war, the people with boots actually on the ground. Well and good, but you did not see the civilian politicians' well-polished shoes on the ground as well, fighting the political war while we handled the shooting. But the revolutionary forces did not make the same mistake. Their young cadres were the messengers of hope and freedom for their people. Where did we miss out? Who were the masters of intelligence on the ground and within the higher realms of political, economic and military power? Us or them?

In the Sengwe we were operating blind, as we did most of the time in the northern operational area of SWA/Namibia and southern Angola in this type of low-intensity warfare. What was low-intensity warfare anyway? I found it most frustrating. You worked your backside off and wore out the soles of your boots, yet seemed never to find the enemy. Positive yields were small. You could not really discern progress as the days dragged by. I knew of infantry units which were deployed for three months at a time in northern SWA/Namibia without once setting eyes on the enemy.

Somewhere out there on the periphery, useless political talks continued sporadically on how to resolve a semi-invisible protracted war. Where were we going with all of this? Although exciting, this dangerous, intangible game was both physically and psychologically demanding and exhausting. To top it all, it came at a terrible price to any country involved, in terms of both dollars and trauma.

As I saw it, the wars in Africa started small and then escalated, and gradually wore you down. Time, that vital commodity on the battlefield, is as important to the African soldier as it is to the Westerner, but the difference is how it is viewed and used. To the Westerner it is an enemy to be beaten; but Africa has a vast, resilient patience which makes a friend of time. The Western style of counterinsurgency warfare was demeaning and tainted with haughtiness; it was overeager in its application and over-confident in its ability to achieve, and one saw edginess and impatience with the mere "dumb" mortals in the villages and kraals.

Who were they anyway? How does this view coincide with the strategic phases of either revolutionary or counter-revolutionary warfare? In a sense it is easier for the exponents of revolutionary warfare, I believe. They go with the flow, while the followership builds up behind them. Time and space in Africa was on their side: to fight, evade, hide, and fight again another day – and in between to do the political and propaganda thing, because tomorrow was another day. What did they have to lose anyway, they who had nothing?

In "The Art of Counter-Revolutionary Warfare", John J. McCuen advocates that the principles of Mao Tse-tung's teachings which are adopted by the insurgents should be applied in reverse by the counterinsurgents.[7] I support this theory, but I would advise the counterinsurgent to think matters through before actually turning Mao's teachings on their heads, because this is easier said than done.

Setting up protected villages, constructing "cordons sanitaires"[8] and generally treating ordinary people in an undignified manner are not the solutions. Let us see how those revolutionary war-fighting measures more or less worked, according to a Rhodesian case study, as simplified by De Vries (definitely unofficially). We, with our Western outlook, just could not get that political thing right, could we? If one uses the simple landscape and stages of revolutionary warfare which are illustrated below as a yardstick for what had happened in Rhodesia, SWA/Namibia and South Africa, it becomes somewhat scary. So let launch a brief appraisal of theory and practice:

- Phase 1: Organisation and Subversion: The revolutionaries usually start from nothing and then organise in secrecy against the governing power. They subsequently develop extensive terror networks of conspiracy until the cracks in the social and administrative fabric appear.

  In Rhodesia this phase began in 1962–1965 with minor acts of subversion when ZANU and ZAPU were formed and their novice insurgents were sent to China for guerrilla training. On 4 July 1964 ZANU insurgents ambushed and murdered a white foreman from the Silverstreams Wattle Company, Pieter Johan Andries Oberholzer, the first major act of terrorism. The government first deployed the British South Africa Police, and later more and more military units to contain the ever-widening insurgency threat. It was to no avail: the lengthy bush war had started.
- Phase 2: Terrorism and Low-Scale Guerrilla Warfare: Before long governing authorities are faced with unprecedented acts of terrorism, a brief reign of terror follows during which the revolutionaries make their mark and establish political-military baselines.

  Between 1965 and 1972 the insurgents received more and more Soviet and Chinese military and political aid, and even assistance from some Western countries. This period was initiated by Prime Minister Ian Smith's Unilateral Declaration of Independence. This was the signal for both ZANU and ZAPU to

7 Refer to Chapter 7.

8 See Map 6. This was an extensive belt of land mines stretched out on the border with Mozambique from Chikwarakwara (Limpopo River) to Chicualacuala further to the northeast.

intensify their insurgency activities from neighbouring countries.

The armed struggle within Rhodesia then escalated all over. The interior was divided into military areas by the government and a sophisticated combined command structure was formed to direct concerted operations. Simultaneously large numbers of the black population were herded into protected villages. Meanwhile Rhodesia became more and more isolated from the outside world as the international shunning increased.

- Phase 3: Guerrilla Warfare: The raging conflict usually swirls out of control as the revolutionaries shift to full-blown guerrilla warfare – ambushing and attacking, collecting taxes, policing, administering justice, recruiting and so forth, in their own persuasive ways. Meanwhile they increase their effort to mobilise the people in support of the rebellion. The revolutionaries continue their efforts to build up their strength and gain the legitimacy needed to win broad popular and international support.

  From 1972 until 1975 the insurgency inside Rhodesia reached a level of impressive strategic dimensions. To the east, Mozambique became an independent and hostile neighbour in which ZANU insurgent force took up residence. In Zambia to the northwest, ZIPRA not only moved its insurgents in but started building up a conventional army as well. Levels of incursions from the two countries increased dramatically, and the Rhodesian government started losing control over large parts of its interior, which became the insurgents' "liberated areas".

  Political isolation and economic and military sanctions against Rhodesia increased significantly, and the Rhodesians became isolated (made easier by the fact that as a landlocked country it had no access to the sea). Operation Bowler of October 1979 was a response to a desperate cry for help, but it was too late, and peace talks between 1979 and 1980 led to the so-called Lancaster House constitution (which President Robert Mugabe later went on record as calling "a dirty piece of paper"), followed by the formation of a black majority government.
- Phase 4: Mobile Warfare: The final phase is mobile warfare, intended to destroy the government forces in open battle. For success, this phase requires regular troops, organised along conventional lines and outfitted with conventional heavy weapons and equipment. Normally the aforementioned steps require extensive outside aid in the form of military advisers and material.

  The authorities usually face the dilemma of inadequate forces in the field. They therefore start training auxiliary units to take over static and local defences. The revolutionaries find these organisations easy to infiltrate. Initially the government forces inflict some stunning defeats on the new rebel regulars, but rebel losses are quickly replaced from the ranks of the regional forces.

  The authorities soon find themselves surrounded by an unfriendly sea of people and start falling back phase by phase. Unfortunately most counter-revolutionaries fail because they do not adjust to fit into the changed strategy and tactics they now face. The authorities become engulfed by the revolutionary forces. They withdraw or surrender piecemeal as the untenable situation evolves into a checkmate or mere unconditional surrender.

Fortunately the war in Rhodesia never moved to this final stage, notwithstanding the protracted period of guerrilla warfare.

Benchmark this pattern of revolutionary warfare with what had happened in South Africa from the 1960s through to the middle of the 1980s as it, too, became a beleaguered pariah state. Our precarious situation evolved into a war without boundaries in SWA/Namibia and southern Angola through the 1960s and 1970s, progressed into low intensity war and wavering politics by the middle of 1980, escalated into high-intensity conventional warfare and political turmoil by 1987–88, and then between 1989 and 1994 settled down as belligerent countries and various political groupings came to their senses.

South Africa surprised the world when our country magically entered a new democratic era in April 1994 after Nelson Mandela was freed, and there was hope (unrealised, for the most part) for a carefree future Africa. I had to cross the Limpopo River to learn what I have written above. More practice, more knowledge, as Mao would have said. The three South African task forces, X-Ray, Yankee and Zulu, now had only to find their rightful places within the structure and operational framework of Rhodesia's security forces.

Security Framework of Rhodesia and Areas of Operation

Rhodesia's security forces consisted of its Army and Air Force, the British South Africa Police, or BSAP, the National Intelligence Organisation (CIO), and the Internal Governmental Affairs (INTAF) and its Guard Force of auxiliaries; one could even class the Prisons Service and the Rhodesia Railways Security Unit as constituents of the broader security apparatus.

The BSAP, as the first line of defence in Rhodesia (as the South African Police once was in South Africa), had the specific responsibility of maintaining law and order and also of providing intelligence for military operations. INTAF formed part of the security structure and included the administration of the Tribal Trust Lands and African Purchase Areas (land specifically set aside for black farmers to own and use for agricultural purposes). In addition INTAF managed the establishment and protection of all protected villages; the Guard Force was established under its auspices to secure the protected villages (although this role was soon expanded to include more traditional infantry tasks). INTAF also had an intelligence gathering role in support of and in close cooperation with the BSAP.

The Rhodesian security forces very sensibly established a combined operations headquarters in Salisbury to integrate the various counterinsurgency efforts so that they were all working towards a common security goal. The army was the senior service, and so Lieutenant General Peter Walls was appointed the overall commander, with Air Marshal M.J. McLaren as his deputy. Walls reported to the Minister of Combined Operations, Mr. Roger Hawkins, who in turn was directly responsible to Prime Minister Ian Smith. The last intelligence representative was Provincial Commissioner Lewis Walter, who was appointed on 1 July 1979.

A senior SADF officer was stationed at the combined operations HQ for the purposes of liaison and coordination between the two armed forces; another of his responsibilities was to oversee the interests of the SADF with regard to the insurgent threat to South Africa from the north. To my mind this security framework was a practical arrangement, and facilitated application of the principle of sound combined command and control and effective integrated operational conduct.

Rhodesia was promptly divided into seven operational areas, each with a joint operations centre (JOC for short); with HQ Combined Operations exercising direct overall command. For practical reasons – the nature of the country, the threat and the need to expedite command and control – the operational areas were organised as follows:[9] Operation Hurricane was responsible for the northeastern border, across Malawi and northern Mozambique; Operation Thrasher for the eastern border across the central part of Mozambique; Operation Repulse for the southeastern border across Mozambique and South Africa; Operation Tangent for Matabeleland and across Botswana; Operation Grapple for operations in the midlands of Rhodesia; Operation Splinter for the area of Lake Kariba and Zambia; and Salops for operations in and around Salisbury.

Task Force X-Ray's JOC was to be Fort Victoria, Repulse our operation; 4 Brigade our higher HQ; Brigadier Rich our commander and Mabalauta and the Sengwe our new domicile.

Operation Bowler – Faring across the Limpopo

The South African troops were soon nearing the moment on 19 October when they would sneak discreetly across the Limpopo River, wearing camouflage uniforms and personal kit issued by the Rhodesian Army. The world were not to know about this ... hello! All three task forces would be supplied and provided with medical evacuations from South Africa, and for this purpose a temporary base was established at the airfield at Madimbo – Madimbo was an established Army field training base, located about 55 km due east of Messina and 80 km from Pafuri, on the border between South Africa and Rhodesia. It was very close to the Limpopo, which made it a suitable jumping-off point, and it now also became a transit camp for personnel operating inside Rhodesia.

Each task force had its own first line support and maintenance system, as well as a medical post with a doctor, and a chaplain. Each of the task forces also maintained a sophisticated telecommunications rear link to the army operations centre in Potgieter Street, Pretoria, where the Director of Operations, Brigadier Hannes Botha, held sway – soldiers of that time will remember him as a keen paratrooper, a staunch militarist, a stickler for rules, the scourge of junior officers and incidentally a Springbok rugby player. The operations directorate was situated at the north entrance to Army HQ.[10] Situation reports, it was impressed on us, were to be telexed to Army HQ, Director Operations on a daily basis, marked "Exclusively for Brigadier Botha".

Task Force X-Ray's mission was to conduct area operations in the Sengwe under the operational command of Brigadier Rich, and as far as possible regain military control over the area. He suggested that we establish our base of operations and HQ at Mabalauta, 115 km map-distance from Madimbo, and about 45 minutes' flying time by Dakota; this was mainly because, although the road infrastructure was sparse, Mabalauta had an excellent gravel-surfaced airfield, and there was a wooden prefabricated building which would be a suitable operations centre.

Task Force X-Ray was a motorised infantry organisation, based on three infantry companies and a support company, and equipped with 30 Hippo mine-protected vehicles[11] – unwieldy things with limited armour protection, already made obsolete by better MPVs, which could only be used for road transportation of personnel (they dealt fairly well with

9 See Map 6.

10 Incidentally, in 1998 I would mount and brief countless army project teams in the hall adjacent to the former operations centre to kick-start the transformation process of the new SA Army. I was then the deputy chief of the newly established national army under a new democratic dispensation.

11 First generation South African manufactured mine-protected vehicles based on the chassis of a Bedford.

mines, however, and were much to be preferred over unprotected vehicles, of course). Our transport could move two full companies – about 300 men – in Buffels at any given time, and we had an Alouette helicopter allocated to us on a full-time basis.

By 19 October Task Force X-Ray consisted of 800 men and an attached field engineer section, with most of the combat troops drawn from 3 SA Infantry Battalion at Potchefstroom. My second-in-command was Major Willem Welgemoed, a sturdy infanteer who was well-versed in counterinsurgency operations and later on commanded a top border unit, 101 (Ovamboland) Battalion of Sector 10. The Regimental Sergeant-Major was WO1 P.J. Oosthuizen., and my three company commanders were Captains Mucho Delport, Jan Hougaardt and "Twakkies" du Toit.

Du Toit was killed in action during Operation Bowler, but Delport went on to command 32 Battalion during Operation Modular in the October 1987–88 fighting in southern Angola, while Hougaardt would later became famous as one the SADF's outstanding guerrilla fighters while serving with 32 Battalion.

Task Forces Yankee and Zulu were provided by 1 Parachute Battalion, each based on the typical structure of a paratrooper company. Using Puma helicopters provided by the SAAF, they were tasked to operate as fire forces throughout Rhodesia within the operational context of the Rhodesian Army, which included close cooperation with the Rhodesian Air Force, Special Air Service and Selous Scouts. Before crossing the Limpopo, both task forces received some extra training at Madimbo by the Rhodesian Army, which had developed fire force operations to a fine art (of which more later).

Area of Operations of Task Force X-Ray – More About the Sengwe

Was Task Force X-Ray thrown willy-nilly into the vast hinterland of the Sengwe as part of a last-ditch stand by the Rhodesian armed forces? We who were actually on the ground did not worry about such philosophical questions, because we had much else of more immediate concern with which to occupy our minds.

For all of us as – national service troops and a sprinkling of Permanent Force members – Operation Bowler was an amazing adventure, something extraordinary to experience. Our area of operations was a beautiful part of Rhodesia, very much like the Pafuri district we knew in the northeastern quarter of the Kruger National Park. In the northwestern quarter towered the majestic Mateke Hills. To the south the Limpopo River flowed through South Africa and then Mozambique, gracefully wending its way towards the Indian Ocean. In the central part, where the buffalo and elephant roamed in the Ghonarezou National Park, we had the wide, welling elegance of the Nuenetzi River to bless our zone of operations (African rivers are in a class of their own). Rumour had it that close by was a farm owned by the Four Jacks and a Jill, then a popular South African pop music band, but if so they seemed not to be at home during our deployment.

Its disadvantages were that the ground was hard and rocky, which made tracking difficult, and covered with dense, harsh, thorny bush. It was also cloaked in sweltering sub-tropical heat and the accompanying humidity. In addition our area of responsibility was so vast (7,225 square kilometres) that it swallowed up our 800 men as easily as if they had been a mere platoon. In one way this last was a good thing – the whole deployment was supposed to be a deathly secret, but it would take only a few words from any of our men for their accents to give away their nationality in spite of their brand-new Rhodesian camouflage uniforms.

We also discovered in short order we were going to have a major struggle to provide fresh drinking water to our troops, who were often deployed for days at a time on patrols and area operations. We came to use plastic 60 mm mortar ammunition containers filled with water that we could drop from an Alouette helicopter, and sometimes it was also possible to land our robust old go-anywhere Dakota in small clearances hastily hacked out of the bush. The Dakota and a few Puma helicopters were kept on constant standby at Madimbo.

Mabalauta was also home to some other new-found friends, the local Rhodesian game rangers. They were as heavily armed as soldiers, because the Sengwe was a dangerous place. Towards the east lurked the menacing border of neighbouring Mozambique, home of the ZANLA insurgents. The border was protected by a vast minefield, nicknamed the "Cordon Sanitaire"[12], which looked impressive on a map. Unfortunately it did not daunt the insurgents, who regularly picked their way through it at night with the aid of probing sticks, spades, electric torches and even candles – talk about a low-tech solution to a high-tech problem – and even laid out safe pathways.

To my mind the minefield served no purpose other than providing the Rhodesians with a false sense of security, and laid an immense burden on the Rhodesian sappers, who were expected to maintain it on a day-to-day basis. Mines are unpleasantly dangerous things to handle, even when the greatest care is taken, and during our stay of nearly four months we casevacked many Rhodesian "own goal" casualties ... but not one ZANLA insurgent, although numerous elephants fell foul of the mines and were left to rot where they fell. It was a heart-rending sight to witness these bitter fruits of the much-vaunted Cordon Sanitaire from the safety of our Alouette helicopter.

The cordon sanitaire and its false value made me think deeply about the attritionist approach to warfare. Later we tried similar tricks on our northern and eastern borders in South Africa, although not on this scale, but with the same futility. In my experience such alleged obstacles fix only your own forces, not the enemy's, and in any case an obstacle is essentially useless if you cannot effectively cover it by fire and observation.

I forgot to mention another doubtful benefit of visiting the Sengwe – mosquitoes, flies and ticks by the million. One could almost regard them as a ZANLA auxiliary force, because within the first three weeks of operations more than two-thirds of the Task Force X-Ray men contracted either tick fever or malaria.

In reality the Sengwe TTL was a ZANLA liberated zone which served as a transit route along which the insurgents could move in relative safety to the Rhodesian interior. The Rhodesian military simply did not have the numbers required to control it, and in practical terms the government had reduced its responsibilities by surrendering the Sengwe to ZANLA. Now Task Force X-Ray and its 800 men were thrown into this enormous area and expected to make a difference.

There were a number of protected villages ("PVs" for short) at dots on the map like Chipise (close to the Limpopo on the Rhodesian side), Malipati and Chicombedzi, which provided me with much food for thought. The idea behind the PVs was to separate the local population from the insurgents. One of Mao Tse-tung's much-quoted principles, of course, is that an insurgent is like a fish swimming in a sea of people. He who controls the masses obviously enjoys a tremendous advantage in fighting a protracted revolutionary war, in which, for obvious reasons, the elements of space and time are on the side of the insurgents.

---

12 See Map 6.

From this amazingly wise concept was born the amazingly obtuse idea of confining people to the PVs (which the insurgents, always quick on the propaganda trigger, labelled as concentration camps).

The whole idea was wrong for the time and place. The Sengwe was a vast no-man's-land inhabited by what might be called the national herd – thousands of wild cattle belonging to no one. Among the cattle roamed a few extremely poor and innocent "Povo". The Povo just could not settle down happily in the PVs; even when they were coerced to enter, they often simply trickled out again into the wild green yonder. My sympathies were with them: If I had been a Povo I would have done the same thing.

I visited the PVs many a time and had great conversations with their patient chiefs. Did they know where we came from? Yes, South Africa! Did they know where the war was going, the one in SWA/Namibia and South Africa as well? Yes! (adding that time and space favoured the insurgent forces). Were they friendly and tolerant towards us? Of course, they were!

This is where Westerners often run aground in their dealings with the locals. Africa is extremely patient and accommodating. The people agree with everything you say or suggest; after all, tomorrow is another day. Did we know and understand this? I don't think so, which is disgraceful, because Rhodesians and South Africans were, after all, Africans themselves. Did the PV concept work? Absolutely not! At the time many staunch bush fighters propagated the concept of the "strongman image" – absurd, think again (not that they or anyone else did)!

So the Sengwe was a difficult row to hoe, any way you looked at it. But we went in, boots and rifles and all, determined to do our customary utmost. As ever, the mission came first and had to be executed in the most professional manner possible. So there we went barrelling across the Limpopo.

Time Spent on Reconnaissance is Never Wasted – Into Rhodesia by Dakota

I geared up for Operation Bowler in the week of 15 to 19 October, the day Task Force X-Ray was scheduled to cross the Limpopo. First of all, on Monday, 15 October, Brigadier Hannes Botha briefed me at Army HQ in Pretoria, while at Potchefstroom, I knew, 3 SAI was putting my infantry together for the road and air trip to Madimbo – they were new troops who had not yet seen operational deployment, and I looked forward to building my new operational team.

But first I had other pressing business. After Brigadier Botha's briefing I left for Air Force Base Waterkloof to join the core element of my command group: my second in command, Major Willem Welgemoed, my company commanders, Captains Mucho Delport, Twakkies du Toit and Jan Hougaardt, and a few other stalwarts. From Waterkloof we flew 710 km north-northeast to the airfield at Fort Victoria and the combined 4 Brigade and Operation Repulse HQ.

We asked our pilot to fly low because we wanted to see what we could of the ground we were going to be operating over. He did so, and what met our eyes was an enormous expanse of bushveld which was densely covered by trees and undergrowth, a scattering of "gommas" (rocky outcrops) and here and there some magnificent baobab trees. Then we were over the dry river bed of the Bubi River and the Great Zimbabwe Ruins near Lake Kyle, and closing in on Fort Victoria.

The almost overpowering heat welcomed us as we stepped out of the Dakota at Fort

Vic, as the locals called it. Awaiting us were a few robust "Rhodies" in green army shorts, camouflaged T-shirts and velskoene worn without socks – I should have joined you when I left school, as I wanted to, I thought enviously as my orthodox uniform clung to me. An open Land Rover whisked us away to HQ 4 Brigade – a typical British military layout of prefabricated wooden buildings – which I found pleasantly exciting, given the circumstances.

The base complex was a hubbub of activity, but a relaxed, informal atmosphere prevailed, and everybody greeted us in an exuberantly friendly manner. Brigadier Rich and his staffs welcomed us and gave us a thorough briefing – I noticed that nothing much was said about the insurgents occupying the Sengwe, since nothing much was known about them. Then we spent some time with the brigade intelligence staff, squeezing them dry of everything we could get. I couldn't help thinking: Who were the masters of intelligence on the ground and within the higher realms of political, economical and military power? We ... or the enemy?

That evening we stayed over at the Fort Victoria Hotel, all part of the process of building my new command team. We watched the Rhodesians playing bingo in the hotel, drinking beer, chatting merrily, as if there were no war going on outside – robust, resilient people, I thought, not dissimilar to your typical, ordinary household Afrikaner. Outside in the parking lot was an assortment of improvised mine-protected and armoured vehicles which attested to the Rhodesians' talent for making the best use of whatever came to hand.

The next day we flew 217 km southeastwards to Mabalauta – definitely the place for the task force HQ, I decided. We spent some time with the local game ranger, adding to our situational awareness about the forthcoming operation. When we were done, I told him: "See you on Friday 19 October at about 10:00; I'll be arriving with a Dakota and my Tac HQ to set up communications and an operational base. That will only be the advance team. The rest of the battalion will be arriving soon after."

Our new-found friend seemed to be extremely relieved, and when we left his home I could see why. The fences around it carried row on row of improvised claymore and shrapnel mines, linked with detonating cord, and the area was dotted with slit-trenches; the "vibe" here was drastically different from that of the roomful of cheerful bingo players at the hotel.

We used some of our remaining time at Mabalauta to refine our appreciation for Task Force X-Ray's participation in Operation Bowler, We saw herds of elephant and buffalo wading through the Nuenetzi – it was an amazing setting – then flew back to Pretoria, where a mountain of work awaited us: including introducing ourselves to the incoming troops, welcoming, briefing and preparing them for their deployment at Madimbo. Time was so tight that there was none to be spared to acclimatise our troops for the sweltering heat and humidity they would encounter; it was a case of in for a Rhodesian cent, in for a Rhodesian dollar.

Somehow we managed it. Our logistics officer and the RSM got their acts together in double-quick time, and by the afternoon of 18 October the troops had been kitted out in Rhodesian camouflage uniform. This was a much more glamorous outfit than the SADF's efficient but frankly dull brown nutria, and had a hugely positive effect on their morale; it was quite clear to even a casual observer that they were ready for the adventure and raring to plunge into the exciting unknown. I felt immense pride by just looking at them and seeing young smiling faces – great troops, the South African kind, simply the best.

Operation Bowler Commences: Into the Sengwe

Next morning early I flew to Mabalauta in a Dakota with my small operations staff, established my Tac HQ and set up my communications. As soon as we were safely on the ground we were joined by the Alouette gunship with its Browning 7,62 mm machine-gun which had been put under my operational control for the duration of the operation, and Captain Allan Lindner from the Rhodesian Army Intelligence Corps made his appearance (he, too, became part and parcel of our HQ until Bowler ended). While we were organising ourselves, our troops set off from Madimbo, 800 of them in dappled green, faces camouflaged with "black is beautiful" (as the SADF called camouflage cream), final inspections completed, watches synchronised, radios humming.

The first phase of the plan was simple: let's see whether our diminutive force could give the enemy a little surprise right from the word "go". One infantry company crossed the Limpopo on foot and patrolled its way towards Mabalauta over a wide front – "cross-grain patrolling" we called it, covering all the potential infiltration routes of the enemy from the southeast to the northwest. When they finally reached Mabalauta, however, they reported that they had not picked up any fresh spoor, and that they had rarely encountered any local inhabitants. I was philosophical about this: they were new to this game and that might have missed some enemy sign, because they were not trained trackers.

The remainder of Task Force X-Ray travelled by road to Mabalauta in our Hippos, via Messina and Rutenga. One of the companies dismounted in the vicinity of the Mateke Hills, broke up into smaller groupings and started patrolling their way towards Mabalauta, while the remainder of the force carried on to Mabalauta itself.. The dismounted company had a fleeting engagement with a small insurgent group, and after an exchange of fire the insurgents broke contact and fled. Our troops followed up, but lost their tracks in the hard, rocky-strewn soil. Still, a contact was a contact, and at 18:00 on that first day on Rhodesian soil the first Sitrep went off to HQ 4 Brigade at Fort Victoria and Army HQ in Pretoria, the latter marked "Top Secret – Exclusive for Brigadier Hannes Botha, Director Army Operations", as ordered. It was the first of many.

The convoy and the remainder of the force carried on to Mabalauta. The troops began to feel the extremes of heat and thirst; and sub-unit commanders on the ground kept an eye open for possible cases of heat exhaustion. The Alouette soon started working overtime ferrying water to the troops in the bush, which achieved the purpose but did not bode well for security

The method of controlling the Sengwe was by means of area operations, which relied heavily on patrolling, one major problem being that we did not have any intelligence about the enemy with which to work. Regular mobile patrols were also undertaken to the respective protected villages, to liaise with the local population and see if we could glean some fresh intelligence about our elusive enemy (we couldn't, and so nothing of value resulted). Area ambushes were set up as well on possible enemy infiltration routes through the Cordon Sanitaire, but without any result.

The point here is that if you want to be successful at ambushing, you need near real-time tactical intelligence – fact, not fiction – and we soon realised that apart from the intelligence drought, a major problem was that we had no trackers or interpreters; there were so many high-priority requirements for them elsewhere that the Rhodesians simply did not have any to spare for the Sengwe. We learned that the insurgents used youngsters ("Madjibas") to scout ahead of their patrols and provide early warning of security force presences, and so our patrols were equipped with silenced .22 rifles to shoot and kill any they might come across ... which they did not.

Captain Lindner and I spent hours flying across the Sengwe in a Lynx light aircraft of the Police Reserve Air Wing (PRAW) which had been allocated to us, carefully marking all the possible infiltration routes and what seemed to be possible enemy base-camps; we used this information to deploy the companies for area operations. In the process I had a few pleasant visits to Buffalo Range (Chiredzi), were the Sub-JOC[13] was located. This gave me an opportunity to establish a firm relationship with my BSAP counterpart there, and we went through umpteen operational planning sessions, but nothing of value to Task Force X-Ray ever resulted.

So the days passed in the Sengwe – lots of arduous work and not much to show for it. Which is not to say that there were not certain distractions from time to time. During an operation along the Limpopo River, one of our patrols walked slap-bang into an enemy camp – unfortunately just as darkness was falling. Nevertheless there was a short but heavy firefight before our patrol broke contact and withdrew because of the lack of visibility. Next day the insurgent camp was thoroughly investigated, and it was found that the ZANLA men had withdrawn through the night, taking their dead and wounded with them (and got clean away since their tracks were lost); it was clear that the base had been occupied for some time.

During our second month Brigadier Rich asked me for a few days' accommodation at Mabalauta for a fire force which wanted to try its luck in the Sengwe. I said that they were most welcome, and in due course the fire force arrived in a flurry of rotor-blades. I asked the fire force commander how they intended to go about their work, and he replied that they were going to do a few blitz operations on suspected enemy camps. I said, Oh, interesting, and left it at that. The next morning the fire force set off after breakfast with another flurry of rotor blades, its light aircraft already airborne and searching for something viable to strike.

The force returned after a while with a few children and an aged Povo who were shot to pieces and handed over to our medical officer and ops medics. The fire force then went out again and brought back more wounded Povo, who were also taken to our sick bay. I could see that our troops were not at all happy about all this, and asked the fire force commander if his men had encountered any enemy. He said no.

I said: "Stand by", got Brigadier Rich on the radio and had an in-depth discussion with him, telling him: "We don't do things this way." Shocked, he asked me to call the fire force commander to the radio, and the upshot was that early next morning the fire force left us with a final flurry of rotor-blades. I watched them go and thought: Goodbye, good riddance ... No enemy kills!

On another occasion I returned from a patrol, went straight to the operations centre and found my adjutant staring apprehensively at me with saucer-sized eyes. It turned out that in a moment of distraction he had sent a Sitrep[14] to Army HQ without the caveat "Exclusive to Brigadier Botha" on it. The reaction was a signal to me, ordering me to charge him with a military offence.

I called for a telex pad and penned an "exclusive for signal", stating: "I am the commander here; I do not deem the minor error made by my adjutant as serious. If you want to charge somebody I am probably your man". We never heard anything further. That

13 Joint Operations Centre.

14 Situation Report sent daily normally at 18h00.

evening a relieved adjutant offered to buy me a beer at our field canteen. It was clear to me that at Army HQ there were certain people who were in dire need of Dale Carnegie's famous book about winning friends and influencing people.

During our second month, too, one of our mobile patrols was ambushed while deploying to Malipati by road. A white-hot slug from an enemy RPG-7 sliced through one of the Hippos above the head of our engineering officer as he bent down to tie a bootlace. The patrol executed a perfect counter-ambush drill and drove the enemy off. Fortunately, none of our own forces sustained any injuries, but during mopping up of the enemy position two dead insurgents were found, cut to pieces by our return fire, and there were blood trails indicating that others had been wounded and dragged away.

Eventually I became fed up with the slow pace of operations. What the hell to do? One Sunday I said to my helicopter pilot and his gunner: "Let's go." I bombed up with enough R-1 and hand grenades, and we flew off wildly into the Sengwe to look for enemy sign. Every so often the Alouette would drop me on the ground so that I could investigate a suspect area or position, while the chopper orbited overhead with the gunner's finger on the Browning's trigger to provide covering fire in case one of my rash forays got me into trouble. This went on till the Alouette's fuel started running low and we had to head for home.

On the way back I cooled down. It had been a rash and fruitless exercise. Stupid, I thought, stupid! What frustration won't make you do! I would have felt even more of an arse if I had been patrolling my way towards Mozambique right now with a jubilant ZANLA escort, thanks to my brainless antics. I made a mental note to tell the adjutant: Adj, omit this part of the operation from the Sitrep.

During early December we suffered a serious loss. Captain Twakkies du Toit's company deployed westwards towards the central part of the Sengwe by Hippo as part of the area operations, and reached the position selected for the night's temporary base just as it was getting dark. What they did not know was that the enemy had got there first, and as they started occupying the base they came under heavy fire.

Twakkies jumped on to one of the logistics vehicles to bring the 60 mm mortar in action, but he was killed in the first exchanges of fire. The company was not put off its stroke by either Twakkies's death or the surprise ZANLA had sprung on them, and the ambushers were soon driven off by a ferocious counter-attack that cost them a number of dead or wounded, to judge by the blood trails.

This was Task Force X-Ray's last notable action. On the morning of 12 December, the day the ceasefire was signed, our Alouette flew over a rivulet close to Mabalauta, and the pilot looked down and saw a large number of insurgents bathing in the stream. They looked up at him and waved ... it was infuriating, but the irony of it all struck me.

Fire Force Tactics – Offensive Heli-Borne Operations

Before we leave the story of Operation Bowler behind us I would like to say something about fire force operations, a concept which deeply impressed me, in spite of the bad example I quoted earlier. So here goes. This exquisite tactic was tailor-made by the Rhodesians for the African war-fighting milieu to find the enemy, fix him in place and then strike him from above; and during Operation Bowler the South African paratroopers and chopper boys learned this particular trick of the battle trade and became experts at it.

The fire force concept incorporated several distinct components:

- The commander's mind, to outthink, outmanoeuvre and generally bedevil the foe.

- Real-time tactical intelligence, to find the enemy on the ground.
- The Alouette gunship, to strike by surprise, to support and annihilate from above.
- The Puma transport helicopter, to take fresh sticks of fighting men directly into battle.
- The light aircraft, to reconnoitre, observe, fix, guide, mislead and report.
- The trusty Dakota, to drop the airborne soldiers so as to cut off the fleeing insurgents and stop up the gaps.

The fire force was a killing machine *par excellence*, but the exponent needed the right terrain conditions and full acceptance that it was a waiting game. Hilly areas from where you could secretly view the elusive enemy's movements along preferred infiltration routes helped; or a scout in the bush with eyes on the front. In Africa, many a time, those infiltration avenues were the slave and pioneering routes of yesteryear – lesson: learn from history and mark your battle maps accordingly. What did I personally learn by watching fire force operations?[15] In the bush it was Blitzkrieg by checker-board, a helluva effective and exciting game of hiding, seeking, fixing and striking with precision.

The Contingency Plan for the Attack on an Insurgent Assembly Point – Dirty Tricks

A week before 12 December when the armistice was to be proclaimed, I was flown to Madimbo by Dakota for a top secret operational planning session. It concerned the assembly areas which were to be established across Rhodesia where thousands of insurgents were supposed to gather to be processed and disarmed as part of the preparation for the country's first universal franchise election.

The idea was that the assembly processes were to be carefully monitored by international observers to make certain that no foul play was involved from any side. The insurgents were extremely jittery about the roll-out of the process – understandably, because for a short time they would be extremely vulnerable to an all-out concerted attack by the security forces.

My mission was simple, but highly hush-hush: I was to develop a contingency plan to attack one of the insurgent assembly areas to the northeast of Mabalauta, if the need for such a devious deed should arise. As our Dakota headed back to Mabalauta at the customary tree-top level, some unfriendly groundling or other took a pot-shot at us with an AK-47. The first we knew about it was when there was a ping inside the Dakota, and the appearance of sunbeams through the small entry and exit holes.

I felt a sudden great need for a steel helmet on which to sit, since I did not fancy getting a short 7.62 mm round up my fundamental orifice at this late stage. The professional part of my mind noted that it was interesting to discover that there were still a few hostiles in the Sengwe who did not realise that a truce was about to be signed.

In any case, the objective selected for Task Force X-Ray was located south of Chiredzi, near Chicombedzi. It was estimated that up to 1,000 insurgents would move into the collection area at some stage following the signing of the ceasefire agreement. The next day I duly went on my physical reconnaissance of the target area and within another day had completed my appreciation and plan, all still in the utmost secrecy, and sent it off for

15 Incidentally, what I had learned about those mini blitzkriegs in the Rhodesian bush 61 Mech applied with great success during Operations Carrot and Yahoo in 1981 and 1982 respectively. (Chapter 11). This was when we annihilated the insurgents of SWAPO's Special Unit in the Death Triangle (the Tsumeb, Otavi and Grootfontein district) in northern SWA.

approval by the higher headquarters.

The plan outlined an uncomplicated surprise air attack. Activation would be by the transmission of a codeword, on receipt of which a few SAAF Canberra light bombers which were standing by at Air Force Base Waterkloof would take off with their bomb bays loaded with Alpha bombs. The Alpha bomb, for those unfamiliar with it, was a Rhodesian invention. Dropped by bombers flying low in attack formation, the Alphas could carpet an extensive target area with a large number of miniature explosive devices.

Its one disadvantage was that the low-flying aircraft were, of course, extremely vulnerable to enemy fire from the ground. Nevertheless, the Alpha bombs were very effective when used correctly, and in fact improved versions were dropped by the SAAF during the airborne raid on Cassinga in May 1978.

Quite probably the attack would have done great damage if the code word had gone out, but, needless to say, it was never issued; the contingency plans were either destroyed or now lie buried somewhere under a layer of dust in one or other military archive.

British Observers Arrive – Captain Featherstonehaugh of the Royal Green Jackets, I Presume

Early in December 1979 we received two temporary British Army additions to our ranks when Captain Featherstonehaugh (Royal Green Jackets) and Staff-Sergeant Kendrick (Royal Artillery), who were posted to Mabalauta to observe, report and generally keep the playing fields level while the peace process progressed.

The two British soldiers were extremely professional and more or less became part of our group, sitting in on our planning and order groups and travelling with us on patrols – the only drawback was that to make sure they understood everything we had to desist from using the cheerful mixture of English and Afrikaans, various indigenous words and obscure local acronyms that constituted the normal SADF mode of discourse.

During one of the patrols they drove over one of the landmines ZANLA had kindly left behind to help us to stave off the boredom of peacetime. This brightened up the lives of our two "Pommes" and served them right for forcing us to give up our customary incomprehensible "Englikaans" when planning or giving orders! I can record that they immediately had kind thoughts about the Hippo MPV in which they were travelling at the time, and distinctly uncharitable ones about the minelayers.

As a footnote: Naturally I was interested in what Captain Featherstonehaugh and Staff Kendrick thought about the way we were running things, and I was gratified to find that they were impressed by the professional conduct and discipline displayed by our young conscript soldiers. Coming from the horse's mouth, as it were, it proved we were well up to international standard.

Leaving Rhodesia – with a Touch of Nostalgia

On 27 January 1980 I said goodbye to Task Force X-Ray. It was a nostalgic moment for me. By now I knew the leader group and the troops well, had learned to respect and trust them, and had grown fond of them. Before I left I attended a formal dinner in the bush with my leader group and the two observers, and said goodbye to my men. Then I handed over to Commandant Chris Prinsloo (South African Infantry Corps) and flew back to Madimbo in our Alouette helicopter, en route to the Army College to attend that year's command and staff course.

My Rhodesian experience had been extremely valuable, not only in terms of on-the-job training – for which there is no substitute – but also because it had given me a career direction: Roland, my son, I told myself as I passed through those hallowed doors at Voortrekkerhoogte, counterinsurgency operations are much too slow for you; stay with the mobile stuff!

I still treasure some mementos from that little excursion into the Sengwe. I have an old army dishcloth which bears the names of so many of my colleagues – some have faded now, but I can still make out the signatures of people like the RSM, WO1 P.J. Oosthuizen; M. Hill, our range warden; Captain J. van Wyk; Commandant M. de Beer from Messina; and WO II W.J. du Plooy. Then there are my Rhodesian lieutenant-colonel's insignia, and a 4 Brigade shield with its golden lion that Brigadier Rich had presented as a farewell gift.

Winning or Losing – Africa is Still Calling – Wozani Ma Africa

What is the winning or losing of a revolutionary or counter-revolutionary war? Invariably in Africa I saw the military commanders and their troops on the ground mopping up the mess made by politicians. If we claim that counter-revolutionary warfare is 80% politics and 20% military, wherever and whenever will we then see the politicians in front, leading on the ground? If we say that the military is an extension of politics, who teaches politicians about strategy and tactics and the principles of war?

With Operation Bowler we succeeded only in scraping the bottom of the barrel. The entire fighting and subsequent peace-making process was taken over by political events from late 1979 onwards. As far as adventures go, Bowler was an extremely interesting operation. It was a wonderful experience working with the robust Rhodesians – they knew their military work, that was for sure, and nothing could get them down. Then there was Task Force X-Ray. Once again I experienced the superb qualities of the South African infantry soldiers – they were simply the best. It was a privilege and honour for me to have served with them.

Collectively we had learned more about counterinsurgency, and realised we would have to do much better in SWA. The main swindler, as far as I was concerned, was tactical intelligence. The enemy had the intelligence advantage in the Sengwe, no doubt about that, and probably throughout Rhodesia as well. Without first-class intelligence you are fighting blindfolded, with your hands tied behind your back, and that includes disposing over essential assets such as trackers and interpreters – of whom we had none in the Sengwe, so that finding, fixing and striking at the elusive enemy depended mainly on luck.

And, looking back at the Cordon Sanitaire and the protected villages, I offer the following advice free of charge to any government or military force which might feel like following suit: Find another solution (not that those with an attritionist mindset and blockade mentality would listen to what I say).

One final lesson learned was that counter-revolutionary warfare in Africa was not easy or simple. To really grasp this, it is necessary to read and apply the military and political writings of Mao Tse-tung very carefully if you want to win at this game. The main thing is the population and by that I do not imply that killing them off is the solution. What one does out there in the field of combat had better be done with the utmost responsibility and caution in mind, not to feed the ego or self-interest of political and military powers.

Protracted warfare in Africa is not a tidy affair with accepted rules and clearly defined boundaries. It is even more important to understand that human intelligence, the people's culture and traditions, the interaction of individual personalities, trust, respect and leadership are highly relevant in African conflicts (I would relearn all this once more before very long).

Were we missing the point? To my mind, all of these humanistic elements of warfare and of the soul were more important than those modern high-technology-shock-and-awe wars fought in the Middle East, such as in Iraq and Afghanistan, at a political whim which derived from the American dream. It was easy to start and fight wars like that, but it is not so easy to stop them, especially when you are dealing with truly hard, merciless men like the Afghans!

It is important for the war fighter to realise that there are real people out there ... people who live and toil on the land, love their land, are not easy to get rid of and are the true factors to be reckoned with! Those simple people are often poor and have nowhere to go. Time and space is on their side, and they will sit out your most protracted best efforts and still be there when you are long gone.

Spending some time in the Middle East in 2011 and 2012, I was fascinated by the conflict world Lawrence of Arabia had once lived in, thinking about the ongoing wars in Africa and the Middle East and about the '27 Rules' he had written:

> Managing, understanding and working with Hejaz Arabs ... is an art, not a science, with exceptions and no obvious rules. At the same time we have a great chance there, as they trust us; and have given us the position towards their government, which the Germans wanted to win in Turkey. If we are tactful, we can at once retain their goodwill and carry out our job, but to succeed we have got to put into it all the interest and skill we possess.
>
> Learn all you can about the people ... Get to know their families, clans and tribes, friends and enemies, wells, hills and roads. Do all this by listening and by indirect inquiry. Do not ask questions. Get to speak their dialect, not yours. Until you can understand their allusions, avoid getting deep into conversation or you will drop bricks.[16]

How did "we" fare in Africa and were "we" trusted? One can dominate the earth for a while with the might of one's military machines, but not the soul of man. Look behind their eyes, read between the lines, listen to what is not being said ... ! It is simple, really, when you come to think about it, it's about listening and talking and caring! What is the winning and what is the losing of a war, then? Let us see if we can find the answers in the chapters following this one; in the way the South Africans applied counter-revolutionary stratagems and tactics in SWA/Namibia and Angola

Let the old master, Mao Tse-tung, have the last word:

> The development of things is full of twists and turns and does not run in a straight line. It is the same in war, and only a formalist cannot understand the truth.

16 From the *27 Articles* of T.E. Lawrence – 1917.

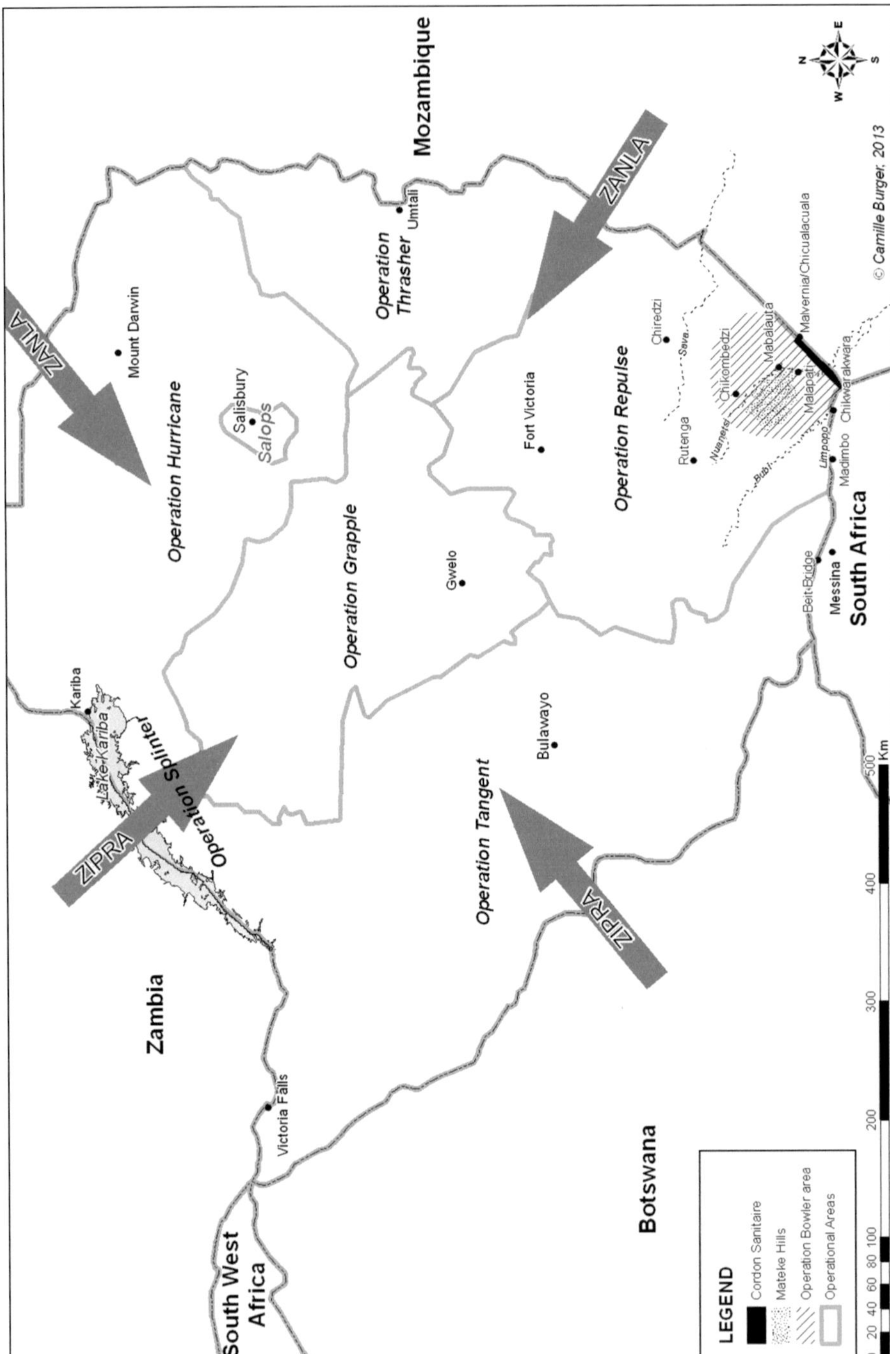

Map 6: Operation Bowler during the Rhodesian War, 1979/80

11

Triangle of Death

Let the Winter Games Begin

By deep knowledge of principle one can change disturbance into order, change danger into safety, change destruction into survival, change calamity into fortune, bring tasks to great fulfilment.
Sun Tzu

Overture for Living and Dying – In the Grip of Terror

For the civilian communities of Tsumeb, Otavi and Grootfontein, danger furtively approached from the north with the advent of the winter rains during April and May. This was the area known as the Death Triangle – one more place marked in blood on the battle map of Africa[1], where the threat of acts of terror by infiltrators of SWAPO's Special Unit[2] held innocent communities in its grip once a year.

It is a matter of record, however, that not one of the Special Unit infiltrations succeeded in achieving its operational goal; unless you considered propaganda engendered through human sacrifice as the primary outcome. There is another way of looking at it, though. One might ask whether their aim was not something entirely different. For example, could it be that the security force losses were seen as tactical successes from their point of view? might the massive mobilisations on our side as result of their presence and efforts not represent strategic milestones to them?

Whatever the case, it must be emphasised that the deep infiltrations were not stopped in their tracks as a result of incompetence on the part of the infiltrators, who were tough, handpicked men, most of courage and great tenacity of purpose. Nor were they stopped by happy chance or co-incidence on the part of the security forces, and especially not where 61 Mech was concerned.

But stopped they were when they ventured south of the Red Line into Sector 30s area of operations. To find out how, let us accompany 61 Mechanised Battalion Group down memory lane, and for a moment revisit Operations Carrot in April 1981 and Yahoo in April–May 1982.

The counterinsurgency operations conducted in the Death Triangle were of the high-intensity variety and therefore differed from Operation Bowler, which I described in Chapter 10. One constant was the terrain factor (see Chapter 5) – not because of any similarity, since the harsh, densely bushed countryside of the Death Triangle with its "haak-en-steek" thorns was vastly different from the Sengwe Tribal Trust Land, but because of the way it affected the infiltration routes and the security forces' counter-measures.

As an aside, the "haak-en-steek" thornbush's malign presence whose capacity for

---

1 See Maps 5, 7, 8 and 9.

2 South West Africa People's Organisation and its armed wing which was known as the People's Liberation Army of Namibia (PLAN)

making the ground fighter suffer is almost inconceivable to a European or American soldier. It not only entangles its victim but inflicts grievous damage to both his flesh and his clothing, and saps his energy by the sheer effort of getting through it. Its very descriptive Afrikaans name translates literally as "catch and stab"; its English nickname is equally descriptive: "wait-a-bit". Neither of the two is exaggerated. In one famous case in 1975, a field exercise came to a shuddering halt when an entire infantry battalion carrying out a bayonet charge was stopped as if by a brick wall when it ran into an unplotted belt of haak-en-steek.

A vitally important factor too was the difference in the Rhodesian and SWA/Namibian war situation. The Rhodesian economy and security forces were physically, although not spiritually, worn out after a classic protracted revolutionary 15-year war and oppressive international sanctions, so that they were desperately short of money, men and machines.

In contrast, the South African economy was basically sound, trade (mostly clandestine) with the rest of Africa was booming, almost the entire territory was at peace, the area in question was sparsely populated and we had ample manpower resources to call on, both conscript and volunteer. This meant that unlike the Rhodesians we had the means to apply the necessary countermeasures.

The Special Unit infiltrations have been and still are misunderstood in many circles. They were not kamikaze-like "suicide missions", as was popularly believed (by the SADF, as well) but propaganda stratagems which were building-blocks of SWAPO's liberation ideology – insofar as it had one, other than simply an armed seizure of power.

Viewed from that perspective, the sacrifice (one can hardly call it anything else) of the deep infiltrators was clearly outweighed by the greater considerations in the eyes of SWAPO's leaders; their definition of success and ours differed, since their best interests always led to the unnecessary deaths of others, even their own soldiers.

Like practitioners of protracted revolutionary warfare everywhere, SWAPO's leaders based its liberation strategy on three pillars: the internal insurgency itself, fed by infiltrations from southern Angola into northern SWA/Namibia; the on-going political mobilisation of the populace, especially the Ovambo tribes, from which it drew almost all its support; and the tireless quest for foreign political and military support.[3]

For these reasons SWAPO needed to prove its worth as a viable revolutionary movement, both to the outside world and to the populace of SWA/Namibia. It was therefore essential for its leaders to launch regular daring incursions into the so-called "white farming areas" to demonstrate their organisation's strike capability, on which depended its international funding, as well as external political propaganda and military support.

It is to be remembered that the outside world's perceptions about what was going on in SWA/Namibia differed from ours. We basked in our tactical military successes, measured by the head-count of those killed... but our enemy revelled in the opportunities for mass mobilisation and spin-doctoring by their own and allied propagandists. But at the end of the day, all these advantages were bought with the blood of the men doing the infiltrating.

I could not help but admire the immense effort our foe undertook to infiltrate so deeply on foot, even though each annual deep infiltration was most assuredly destined to end in little more than death and wounds. Was there honour for them in defeat? Clearly we did not fight according to the same norms as our enemy.

So, who was going to win this war in the end – politically and strategically, not only

3 See Chapter 7 appraising the revolutionary and counter-revolutionary principles of warfare.

militarily? The viewpoints will always remain a matter of perception and interpretation, depending on which side you look at it from, and how you perceive the fairness or otherwise of the conflict. The satirical game of politics and war at the higher levels was maddening to the man on the ground, although the fighting was fun! So let the "Winter Games" begin.

Operational Outline for Fighting in the Death Triangle

Plans to Safeguard the Community – the Call of the Guinea Fowl

Soon after I took over command of 61 Mech in January 1981 I was thoroughly briefed by Sector 30 about the possibility of a SWAPO incursion that April. Naturally I saw this as one of my immediate operational priorities, although 61 Mech was not a dedicated counterinsurgency unit. My staff and I immediately carried out an appreciation of the situation and steps were taken to prepare for such an emergency.

We drew up and war-gamed a comprehensive and finely detailed contingency plan. So when SWAPO came in April as predicted our forces were married up,[4] painstakingly prepared and ready to fight, and the part-time Area Force Units and their members' families had prepared their plans for hearth-and-home protection, with 61 Mech playing a crucial support role for the local communities. Needless to say, the all-encompassing security systems were never foolproof; at times the countermeasures faltered, and some innocent people and their families were killed in attacks, ambushes or landmine explosions. But on the whole they worked well, and mostly better than well.

The influence of terrain on operations has been discussed in some detail,[5] so I do not intend to return to the subject. At the same time, however, it is important to realise that 61 Mech's operational area of responsibility was extensive, since it included the districts of Grootfontein, Tsumeb and Otavi – even Otjiwarongo and Outjo at times.[6]

Operations to counter surprise incursions south of the Red Line were activated by the code word "Tarentaal" (Guinea Fowl), which could be issued by either the South West Africa Territory Force (simply "SWATF" to everyone) or Sector 30. Crisis plans were then immediately set in motion, which included activating standby forces earmarked by the South African Army, South African Air Force and the SWATF.

The emergency plan for the region, entitled "Operation Awake", was viewed as the bulwark against any major enemy incursions to the south. But I did not like it, because to my mind it was completely reactive in posture, a "wait-and-see" and then "come-awake" plan.

The result was that Sector 30 was more attuned to farm protection and continuous training of its part-time units and members than anything else, with one lone infantry company[7] expected to continually patrol and sweep the 200 km Bravo cutline from its base at Tsintsabis in spite of its meagre manpower resources, leaving the Alpha and Charlie cutlines further to the north completely exposed.

So the innocent communities to the south had to stand and take it on the chin – although the SWATF solemnly cautioned them that they must "neither develop a war psychosis; nor become over-relaxed". What choice advice for any sane man whose very life might hang in the balance! So the cutlines and the ever vigilant, super-efficient part-time area force units formed the main rampart against terrorism... and it was simply not enough.

4 Military term used for force integration and war preparation.
5 See Chapter 5.
6 Refer to Maps 7 to 9.
7 Designated the Northern Border Company (Noordgrenskompanie) based at Tsintsabis.

The tracks of SWAPO infiltrators were usually not detected till after they had crossed the Bravo cutline, and only then would the codeword "Tarentaal" be sent out.

After we had successfully completed Carrot by 18 April 1981 I pushed hard on a number of occasions for a reinvention of Operation Awake, but to no avail. 61 Mech always got stuck with the conundrum after the fact; and on 15 April 1982 we were going to lose eight good men because of that! What it amounted to was that Sector 30 more or less sat twiddling their thumbs, waiting for the enemy to strike first every blooming April, after which they would start defending their wickets.

It just did not make sense to me. The most sought-after military solution should have been to make sure that the Special Unit did not have the opportunity to undertake the annual Winter Games. It was fortunate for Sector 30 and the local communities that 61 Mech lurked in the bushy fringes of Ovamboland at Omuthiya, within striking distance of the Death Triangle – and unfortunate for the Special Unit, which would be consumed every time in the end.

Central to the demise of the insurgents was real-time and near-real-time tactical intelligence, superbly networked with the invaluable local knowledge supplied by the local community; the farmers in the network not only supplied information but could provide an invaluable local tracking capability as well.

Major keys to success and readiness were mobility and unremitting, carefully coordinated search-and-destroy missions. Superior command and control arrangements, extensive and reliable communications and unparalleled teamwork delivered the final dividend. The right spirit was, of course, crucial to the entire effort. Hunting down terrorists was a serious business, and all the combat participants involved on the ground were totally focussed, committed and in dead earnest. To appreciate these circumstances I intend to review Operations Carrot and Yahoo in succession. They were exciting times, exacting times... tragic times.

Own Forces and Command Arrangements – The Bulwark against Terrorism

The detailed composition of the task forces for both Carrot and Yahoo and their employment particulars are described in Appendix A. Sector 30 was commanded by Colonel J.T. Louw from his headquarters at Otjiwarongo. The sector, as well as 61 Mech, fell under General Charles Lloyd, who commanded the SWATF from HQ Bastion in Windhoek (as a matter of historical interest, the post-independence Namibian Army, which was naturally composed mainly of ex-SWAPO men, not only moved into Bastion on the disbandment of the SWATF but even kept its name!).

For both Carrot and Yahoo a task force tactical headquarters, equipped and maintained by 61 Mech, was activated at the Tsumeb airfield; during Yahoo, lower-level Tac HQs were established at Grootfontein, Otavi, Tsintsabis and Kamanjab. In addition, every part-time area force unit in Sector 30 had its own HQ, which featured a dedicated operations centre with guaranteed communications.

61 Mech usually provided the major share of the task force from Omuthiya, and in 1981 actually commanded Operation Carrot, as laid down in its commitment. This changed quite drastically when Yahoo started in 1982. By that time, command had reverted in its totality to Sector 30; but 61 Mech summarily took charge of Yahoo in the east when no decision about the status of command for the unfolding operation came from on high during the frenzied early stages, and the powers-that-were decided to leave it that way.

The subunits of 61 Mech were superbly commanded and the men were outstanding – well-trained, ardently committed to their operational work and anxious to gain operational experience. I dearly respected and appreciated them, and enjoyed having them under my command, and by the time the Special Unit crossed the Bravo cutline in April 1981 we had become a close-knit fighting team.

Other major role-players and key decision-makers in the war against terrorism in the Death Triangle were Colonel T.W. (Tommy) Thomasse of the SWA Police and the commanders of the part-time Area Force Units at Grootfontein, Etosha (Tsumeb), Otavi and Outjo. The AFUs formed the main fabric for the counterinsurgency war; their commandants (lieutenant-colonels in today's dispensation) were exceptional in character and seasoned by much experience.

These officers and their families all became close friends of 61 Mech through years of working together, during which time strong bonds were forged by shared responsibilities and danger. They were characterised by selfless service to their respective communities, men like C. H. (Stoffel) Rothman of Outjo; L.M.J. ("Uncle Lukas") Nel of Etosha; P.C. (Piet) Oosthuizen of Grootfontein; and H. (Henne) Volkmann of Otavi.

Other extraordinary local people were Rheinard Friedrich, Alex Britz, Frank Bosch, Ockert Britz; Dave Keyser, Horst Körner, Daan van der Westhuizen, Klaus Meich Riche and many others who played unparalleled roles in the security and livelihood of the region. Many AFU members were farmers who had maintained private tracker teams, recruited from their black and white farm workers, which became legendary for their skill in reading the ground.

The farmers and their trackers operated closely with the security forces' follow-up teams, not only tracking but providing invaluable services as guides and operational advisors. It is impossible to underestimate the importance of these men: they knew the habits of the enemy, and, even more importantly, they knew the terrain.

I think here particularly of AFU Lieutenant Daan van der Westhuizen of the farm Koedoesvlei, near Tsintsabis – he and his team, which included his son-in-law, Rifleman Hendrik Potgieter, were exceptionally skilled at tracking and general fieldcraft; it was a stunning blow, both personally and professionally, when he and Hendrik Potgieter, together with several others, were killed in a SWAPO ambush at the very start of Yahoo on 15 April 1982.

One of those who died with him was his master tracker and long-time employee, a 64-year-old Bushman named Jan Kouswab – respectfully referred to by both the troops and the community as "Jan Kaka" – who was particularly renowned for his ability to follow well-nigh invisible spoor. Kouswab was not officially a member of the armed forces, but he was held in such estimation that he was buried with full military honours.

It was my privilege to write the citation for Daantjie van der Westhuizen's posthumous Honoris Crux decoration for gallantry, and in 1983 Daantjie's HC was handed to his widow, during a ceremony at which the Minister of Defence, General Magnus Malan, officiated.

Mrs. Van der Westhuizen – affectionately known as "Tannie Pompie" to the officers and men serving in SWA/Namibia – was a celebrity in her own right. Herself a full member of the Etosha AFU operated a round-the-clock radio relay station from Koedoesvlei farm which was the rallying point around which the military area radio net (MARNET) functioned. But she was particularly renowned for making long-range radio contact with field units hundreds of kilometres away (including 61 Mech on several celebrated occasions) when this was theoretically impossible.

Major Alex Britz was another farmer who lived just outside Tsumeb alongside the main gravel road stretching towards Tsintsabis. He unsurprisingly became the operations officer for 61 Mech during every incursion. Alex Britz was granted the honour of accompanying 61 Mech during Operation Meebos deep into Angola in July 1982. He was an exceptionally fine man and a superb operations officer who became a true friend as well as an honorary member of our unit.

The SAAF commanders and their task teams were staunch supporters of these operations. I do not have the space to mention all their names, but they were men like Brigadier Bossie Huyser, Colonel Ollie Holmes, Commandants Hap Potgieter and Daantjie Beneke, Majors Jaap du Preez and Mossie Basson, and helicopter ace Captain Neall Ellis. The Northern Logistics Command (NLC) at Grootfontein, commanded by Colonel Willem Enslin, provided logistics and transport services for operations to the north. His second-in-command was the super-efficient Commandant Thys Snyman, who gave us excellent support when we needed it. Serving with them was the hyper-energetic Commandant Callie Kaltwasser of the Technical Service Corps, commanding 101 Medium Workshop. He guaranteed the second-line vehicle maintenance and repair services for the region.

Another stalwart was Commandant Buks Koen, OC 1 SWA Special Unit at Otavi. Closely allied to the community, his unit provided an excellent tracking capability and at very short notice could swiftly deploy motorcyclists, horsed infantry and dog handler teams for operations.

I mention all these men and their units for a reason. During the long years of peace after World War II the vital necessity for very close co-operation between the military and the police, and between the SADF's many arms and services, had faded somewhat. But the border war had brought the concept to the fore again in no uncertain terms, and by 1982 it was working at full steam.

An Account of Operation Carrot (6–18 April 1981)

The Next Suicide Mission of SWAPO Erupted with a Bang

Twenty-two insurgents of Special Unit left Lubango by the middle of March 1981 under command of a veteran insurgent named Engine.[8] They were transported by vehicle to rendezvous with a 30-strong escort party close to the SWA-Angola border, each of them was issued with R100 in cash, tinned food and ammunition before setting off further southwards on foot.

One day's march from the Charlie cutline the escort party turned back, its task done, and the 22 infiltrators set out on their lonely mission. About 07:00 on 6 April they crossed the Bravo cutline to the north of the farm Vaalwater. At this stage the security forces were oblivious of the approaching threat; at Omuthiya 61 Mech was ready for action, as always, but by midday we were still unaware that the infiltrators had arrived and were now inside the farming area.

The usual practice up to that time had been for a party of infiltrators to cross the Bravo cutline and then bombshell into smaller groups, which would then deploy in all wind directions and commit various acts of terrorism. This time, however, there was another

8 Combat name used by PLAN insurgents for security reasons.

group of about 15 infiltrators, who crossed the border more to the west and headed southwards through western Ovamboland to take the perilous Kamanjab corridor to the farming area.

This group, about which we knew very little, soon came to grief. Sector 10 patrols picked up their tracks at an early stage, followed up and twice made contact on 10 April, killing two insurgents before they had even got through western Ovamboland. The rest bombshelled and fled northwards, and no more was heard or seen of them.

Now the cat was out of the bag. In Windhoek, the GOC SWATF, Major General Charles Lloyd, made Operation Carrot public on 7 April when he briefed media representatives in Windhoek, saying that a ferocious group of 22 insurgents had struck south of the Red Line and that the security forces "were in hot pursuit".

It was no more than the truth. The high-intensity operation which followed was fast and furious, 13 days of intensive search-and-destroy actions before Operation Carrot ended quite abruptly (of which more later). General Lloyd later described it as an outstanding success and a benchmark for the future, likening it to a "miniature Blitzkrieg". This, too, was no more than the truth. Of the 22 infiltrators, 18 had been killed and another three taken prisoner, with one managing to evade his pursuers and get back to Angola.

The SWA/Namibian media were now referring to the deep incursion as a suicide mission, reporting that the infiltrators had found no place to hide and that they had been "tracked down and killed by the security forces with determined skill. The quick response by the security forces caught them off-guard." How did this happen?

Operation Carrot Commences – Search and Destroy Relentlessly

On 6 April I was minding my own business at Omuthiya, engrossed in the usual command duties, when I was called to our operations centre to take a radio call. It came from the Etosha AFU and informed me that an infiltrator group of unspecified size had crossed the Bravo cutline near Vaalwater; the local police special counterinsurgency platoon had been dispatched at breakneck speed to follow up on one of the insurgent sub groups.

I told my second-in-command, Major Thys Rall, to inform Colonel Louw at HQ Sector 30, and set our contingency plan in motion, starting by summoning my command Ratel and immediately heading for the spot where the insurgent tracks had been found; riding with me was my logistics officer, Captain Giel Reinecke, so that we could assess the situation on the ground before he threw his all-important planning and preparation process into top gear.

Near Vaalwater we hooked up with a waiting patrol from the Etosha AFU, which took us to the tracks. There was little doubt that they had been made by insurgents because the bootprints showed the chevron pattern soles that SWAPO wore; and it was clearly a reasonably large group, at least 20 strong. Just to make sure, though, we followed the tracks on foot for some distance.

It soon became clear that our initial identification had been correct when we tracked them into the ferocious "haak-en-steek", which in some places sported "trophies" of clumps of hair and pieces of the "rice pattern" camouflage clothing supplied by China.

I immediately got on the radio and instructed my artillery battery commander, Captain Bernie Pols, to deploy his farm protection details without delay (this was the gunners' secondary role in counterinsurgency operations, which did not require heavy ordnance). I also got hold of Thys Rall and told him to have the "Operation Awake" commanders available for orders at the Tsumeb airfield on my arrival there, which would be at 21:00. Then, as we high-tailed it to Tsumeb, I spoke to Colonel Louw by radio, told him what I knew and said that it was necessary to activate "Tarentaal" immediately.

When I entered the unadorned corrugated-iron operations centre at the airfield at 21:00, relief washed over me as I saw all the familiar faces waiting for me. The briefing, exchange of information and forward planning began without delay, and I was pleased to note the utter confidence and seriousness of those present.

By this stage the wheels were turning elsewhere as well. The area force units were mobilising and deploying. The police counterinsurgency platoon reported that it was steadily closing in on one of the subgroups just north of Tsumeb, and that contact was imminent (good news for me, as it implied the collection of fresh real-time intelligence). The standby paratrooper company under Captain Herbie Pos was flown in overnight by SAAF Puma helicopters and C-160 Transall transports, and our air support was due to arrive next day.

Within the next 13 days there were more than 15 contacts and near-close encounters. The upshot was the total failure of the deep operation: before being killed or captured they had managed only four mine incidents, three minor acts of sabotage and one break-in at a farm. Among the dead were one Sheendo, who had cold-bloodedly murdered two farmers named Dressel and Van der Bank during the 1980 infiltration, as well as three other 1980 participants, named Bybel, Nakule and Mukondo. Another casualty was the group's leader, the veteran Engine.

The three captured insurgents – Lucius Nangala Malambo; Theofilus Jason and Josef Sagarius – were interrogated at length by my intelligence officer, Captain Gerrie Hugo, and when they were later brought to trial in Windhoek some interesting stories emerged about their life in the SWAPO ranks, their training in Angola and their instructions for the infiltration (to terrorise the communities in the south).

At the end of the trial Mr. Justice Kenneth Bethune found the three young insurgents guilty of contravening the Terrorism Act. We became embroiled in this drawn-out and heavily publicised trial, which meant that at one stage I had to send Major Rall to Windhoek to give evidence. This was definitely a distasteful experience, and we decided that there would be no more of it during the next fighting round.

Next time, we decided, we would see if we could "turn" them instead, so that they voluntarily operated on the side of the security forces (and we succeeded; it is interesting to note that during Operation Yahoo the following year, all our captives opted to transfer their loyalty rather than become prisoners of war – more about this later on).

As a historical footnote, the three accused were defended pro deo by Windhoek advocate Anton Lubowski, a prominent SWAPO activist, and Mr. Pio Teek, then Windhoek's only practising black attorney. Lubowski was assassinated in 1989 by persons unknown.

There were repeated claims that his assassination was a contract hit put out by the notorious secret organisation, the Civil Co-Operation Bureau, in an unauthorised attempt to destabilise the impending Namibia's progress to independence, while the then Minister of Defence and a retired Namibian policeman claimed Lubowski had actually been a police informer (the implication being that SWAPO had liquidated him).

Neither the South African nor Namibian governments later displayed any real enthusiasm for putting named members of the CCB on trial, and eventually the 20-year statute of limitations expired. These chilling stories all became common knowledge during the Truth and Reconciliation Commission's (TRC) proceedings in South Africa after 1994.

My Deadly Encounter with SWAPO – One Unforgiving Minute in the War

On 18 April I decided to join a follow-up by Captain Herbie Pos and his paratroopers, which by then was north of the Alpha cutline and well on its way into Ovamboland, on the spoor of two of the remaining insurgents, who were hot-footing it northwards. To the west, Captain Cassie Schoeman's follow-up team was in pursuit of a lone insurgent way past Tsintsabis.

These were the two maddening final pursuits, with tracker teams from the Etosha AFU leading the chase while a few helicopter gunships were standing by at Tsumeb airfield and a Bosbok light spotter aircraft was twisting and turning overhead. Talk about overkill – but what the hell?

Being a bit bored at the way the operation was dragging on when in fact it was over for all practical purposes, I made the following deathless spur-of-the-moment suggestion to my staff: "Who wants to go out with me and shoot a few terrorists?" Reinecke and Hugo, who were immersed in some unfinished administrative work – time and the paper war waits for no man – looked up and said: "No, thank you, not today, perhaps later". Oh, well...

I soon found two more enthusiastic recruits, however – Major Thys Rall and Sergeant-Major Hennie Blaauw – and a few minutes later we were travelling north at high speed, trailing the customary long dust-trail. Thys Rall and Hennie Blaauw were riding shotgun (actually with their assault rifles), and I was standing on my seat in the turret – rank hath its privileges, after all – with my R-5 rifle to hand and two extra magazines within easy reach. My gunner, meanwhile, was in close conversation with his 20 mm quick-firer.

My situational awareness did not diminish as we tacked steadily northwards: to the east, Cassie Schoeman reported by radio that they were closing in on their quarry, while further north Herbie Pos reported that he was now following very fresh tracks and a contact was imminent. We joined hands with Pos around 16:35 and adopted a two-up formation – Pos in his Ratel-60 on the left, myself on the right, with relays of trackers in the centre, running at full speed with their skilled eyes glued to the insurgents' spoor. I couldn't help thinking that it reminded me of Shaka's famous "horns of the bull" tactic with which he destroyed almost everyone he came across. Behind us came the rest of Pos's force, ready for action.

I soon observed the two insurgents in their rice-pattern camouflage, running for all they were worth slightly in front of us. I confirmed my sighting with Pos, just to make sure they weren't own forces who had somehow got out of place, and said I was going to make a quick right sweeping movement to cut them off.

I did so, and we saw the two insurgents about 300 metres away, high-tailing it towards a dense thicket of bush. Tallyho! We rushed forward with the rest of the force hot on our heels. Pos's forward movement was momentarily delayed when he ran into a massive anthill, so that my Ratel was on its own, in front of the pursuit line.

I started firing at the insurgents, and I could see my tracers flying, the bullets kicking up dust all around the two fast-moving insurgents. Thys Rall now joined in from one of the rear hatches; his bullets came perilously close to my head and I glanced back to give him that well-known military stony glare, which persuaded him to stop firing. To my gunner's disgust, things were happening so fast that he did not get a chance to fire his 20 mm.

One of the insurgents now glanced over his shoulder, and, (understandably) seized by fear at all the thunder and lightning descending on him froze in place. I shouted to my driver to stop, which he did so close to the SWAPO man that when Hennie Blaauw leapt off the Ratel to take him prisoner he literally landed on top of him.

Then we were off again, while I kept firing. The remaining insurgent disappeared into the long grass. I halted the Ratel again, jumped off and started running towards him, spraying the area with bullets because I didn't know whether he had been hit or was lying low and preparing to take me out.

As it turned out, he had taken no less than seven hits and was dying. But he remained full of fight; when I came up to him he rolled over and aimed at me – a classic case of staring death in the face (or muzzle, if you prefer). But he did not fire, just collapsed and died. I had a look at his rifle and realised with great relief why he had not got his final shot off – a cartridge from the magazine had jammed his AK.

The dead man turned out to be a section commander. He had a map case and a Russian Tokarev pistol with him, and on the side of his camouflage forage cap a metal SWAPO badge was proudly displayed. I still have that forage cap which I keep in remembrance of a courageous soldier who was not willing to surrender in spite of being completely outnumbered and in enormous peril. Every so often I think about that man. He had a family somewhere, and if they ever read this they can do so with pride.

Now for the first time I realised what great hardship the infiltrators had endured; the soles of his feet were bleeding, worn away by walking hundreds of kilometres through harsh terrain and deadly danger. But he had not given up. He had stuck it out to the bitter end.

I tell this story not in a spirit of braggadocio but to illustrate an important point: that in mobile warfare the commander must lead from the front, for two sound reasons – to be able to make instant decisions, and also to show his troops that he does not expect them to face dangers that he is not willing to face himself.

This was a given in the days of the foot infantry and horse soldiers, but it became somewhat diluted with the growth of modern communications, which tended to turn senior commanders into what might be called battle managers; but in certain circumstances it still has its place. If at all possible, leaders must not only lead, they must be seen to lead.

Cassie Schoeman, who was deep into Ovamboland by now, then came through on the radio to inform me that his man's tracks had been lost. I told him to call it a day, at which he sounded somewhat disappointed. But there was really no point in prolonging the chase; Carrot was over, with all 22 infiltrators accounted for, one way or another. So he did a 180-degree turn and headed southwards again, and so did we. My friend Colonel Tommie Thomasse of SWAPOL could now balance the books and draw a line under Operation Carrot, 1981.

By the way, when I got back a regretful Giel Reinecke, who had obviously had second thoughts about abandoning the paper war in favour of the shooting variety, came to me and said: "Hell, I was stupid not to go with you." A little smugly, I admit, I consoled him with: "Sorry for you." I don't think it helped much...

61 Mech returned to Omuthiya to resume its endless training, and Herbie Pos's company of paratroopers to Sector 10 for further counterinsurgency deployment. They had performed excellently – of the 22 insurgents they had accounted for five killed, and had suffered only two paratroopers wounded. Captains Koos Liebenberg and Cassie Schoeman and their companies had also done extremely well during a few furious follow-ups and area ambushes which channelled the infiltrators to selected killing zones.

In his report on Operation Carrot, Pos highlighted the following observations and lessons learned:

- There was great value in mounting sufficient tracker teams and rotating them rapidly during mobile hot pursuits; and the local AFU tracker teams' tactical prowess and knowledge of terrain had paid huge dividends and invariably led to success.
- Thorough planning, rapid action and precision engagement were the factors which turned the tables on the enemy. The immense planning effort, together with the excellent management of the operations and the amount of intelligence invested, had led to a number of rapid successes.
- The commanders and their men were always well-informed and knew exactly what was happening in every busy bushy corner of the area of operations.

Initiative and decentralised control were allowed to flourish at lower levels of command and were found to be invaluable for operational success. In actual fact, all members were freely allowed to generate bright ideas. According to Pos, this contributed to shared responsibility, force cohesion and high spirits.

All I could add to this was to say: What an amazingly effective team those paratroopers and the other members of the task force were! It was an honour to could have served with them.

General Lloyd subsequently asked me to brief his command cadre and senior military staff on the conduct of the operation in Windhoek the following week. This was good for my self-esteem as the commander, of course, but I never forgot that I had my people to thank – they were superb, as ever.

Debriefing Operation Carrot at Otjiwarongo and Getting into Trouble

At 61 Mech we occasionally played, celebrated success and got into some trouble as well. The aftermath of Carrot saw a comprehensive debriefing exercise at Otjiwarongo. We were staying in the Hamburger Hof Hotel with its extremely pleasant bar, and on the final evening, with the debrief over, we settled down to celebrate.

The evening found Gerrie Hugo, my intelligence officer, walking around the bar (not in too straight a line) with a large square German beer advertisement under his brown combat jacket and generally looking like the Mad Hatter out of "Alice in Wonderland", but quite content with himself and his surroundings.

After this the celebration in the bar things allegedly (I admit nothing) got slightly out of hand. The celebrants bombshelled in good SWAPO fashion and somehow the action moved up to the hotel's first floor. There Cassie Schoeman ended up lying flat on the lower shelf of a stainless steel mobile serving tray – how he managed to get in there in the first place, and how we managed to get him out again later on, was nobody's business.

In his arms he cradled a purloined fire extinguisher in case he had to mow down any enemies (unspecified) who might appear. It is my understanding that this was the fault of our attached SAAF pilot, who was flying the serving tray (I mean that literally, since it was only touching the floor here and there) and had made Cassie his nose gunner.

The follow-up ended in the room of distinguished Commandant "Uncle Lukas" Nel. Somehow the novice nose gunner allegedly discharged the fire extinguisher's load of fine white powder (this is also still under investigation), leaving Uncle Lukas's abode – and most of the rest of the Hamburger Hof, for that matter – with a beautiful snowy coating. Talk about nights in white satin!

Our master tracker, Daan van der Westhuizen, then appeared on the scene, declared that the tracks in Uncle Lukas's room were approximately 20 seconds old, and warned that a contact was imminent. I consoled Lukas Nel by explaining that these were extraordinary operational circumstances, but to no avail – he was at the end of his tether after our taxing operation, being the oldest of us all (he was one of our very few remaining World War II veterans), and suffered a slight sense of humour failure.

At 03:00 I had to leave the fun so that I could reach Windhoek in time to catch a flight to Cape Town to give a presentation at the Artillery Symposium, which I was a little doubtful about because I was not feeling too operationally sharp. Before I left I held a snap order group with Major Thys Rall, who was in command during my absence, because I just knew that there was going to be hell to pay and that some of the proverbial matter would be hitting the fan.

I told Thys to make it up with the hotel proprietor and send me a Sitrep on the outcome as soon as possible; as evidence he was to keep the red fire extinguisher, which we had now got out of Cassie's clutches (we had also carefully dusted the mobile serving tray to ensure that no fingerprints were left behind).

These precautions proved inadequate. When Thys phoned me in Cape Town next day he told me that the fallout was more serious than we had anticipated, the situation had escalated out of proportion after Colonel Louw received a full report from an unknown source which had left him in a choleric frame of mind (to be absolutely truthful, Thys used the Afrikaans phrase "de moer in", a polite translation of which would be "bloody furious"). On the positive side, though, he had used our expertise at successfully "turning" captured SWAPO members on the proprietor, who was now co-operating fully with us.

I decided that, given the circumstances and the nature of the "enemy", the only approach was to tackle the matter like a good mobile soldier, so I carried out a pre-emptive strike by immediately phoning Colonel Louw to say: "Sorry, sir, I'll come and see you as soon as I get back."

He assented although he did not sound overly friendly, and I thought deeply about our predicament and the appropriate tactics to use. Bearing in mind that the colonel would be bound to have cooled down by the time I returned, I decided to adopt the indirect approach advocated so strongly by Liddell Hart and myself: I called Rall and asked him to take the fire extinguisher, the very symbol of our disgrace, and have it bronzed like a pair of baby shoes.

Then when I returned from Cape Town I sallied forth to Otjiwarongo with the bronzed fire extinguisher and presented it to Colonel Louw as a war trophy, saying earnestly: "Well, sir, we're sorry – but hell, it was great fun." Being a soldier at heart as well as by Act of Parliament, he understood, accepted the extinguisher and remained the true friend of 61 Mech that he had always been.

Thus Operation Carrot ended on a high note and with a good thrash to round it off. This might sound like a strange way for grown men to act, but any fighting soldier will understand. What we were really doing was joining hands with one another in a moment of true comradeship and sharing something of communal value that blew away the last remnants of almost two weeks of the crushing responsibility that only the commanders of fighting men in battle ever experience. And so, all these years later, we still remember that wild night at the Hamburger Hof with a smile of satisfaction.

We each took away a more respectable memento. Everyone who attended the debriefing session received a silver beer mug proudly emblazoned with the 61 Mech insignia and inscribed with the words "Operation Carrot 1981". I was also given another silver mug by Colonel Tommie Thomasse with the compliments of the SWA Police. In effect we were already cementing friendships and networks in preparation for 1982s Operation Yahoo, which started with another SWAPO infiltration on 14 April 1982. There was no doubt about it – life with 61 Mech was great fun and full of surprises!

Recollection of Small Gestures Highly Valued

I cherish some other highly valued personal mementoes of Operation Carrot. Just after we returned to base my dear friend Cassie Schoeman wrote me a letter in his typical clear and concise style and signed with his characteristic flourish: "19 April 1981. Congratulations with the April birthday celebrations of SWAPO! The mechanised infantry company of "Schoombie"' (the nickname I had fondly given him, and still use today when we meet after a long interval – Author) wishes to express sincere appreciation for the privilege of having been able to participate in Operation Carrot. Congratulations on the manner in which you led and conducted this operation. Be ensured of the loyalty and friendship of Alpha Company".

I also received a brief telex message from Colonel Louw after the final shots of Operation Carrot had been fired: "Secret: O/OPS/042/Apr 81/182 302B. From: Sector 30. To: 61 Mech Bn.1.309/OPS/Carrot/General. 2. With reference to today's contact. 3. Col Louw personally wishes to congratulate Cmdt De Vries on his outstanding performance. The conduct of the operation was truly exemplary, continue doing the good work."

I do not quote these responses in order to beat my own drum, because there were too many excellent groupings and individuals involved for anything of the sort – the whole thing was an example of teamwork to the utmost degree. I do so to record how tremendously inspirational it was to be at the receiving end of praise like this; especially since I had been the commander of such a demanding venture.

The praise was of particular significance to me because it came not from someone on high whose only knowledge had been gleaned from various reports, but from close friends and colleagues who had been there with me, and I advise all those in command, or those who will one day be in command, to remember to do the same for the people serving under them.

Little gestures of appreciation – a brief note, even simply a pat on the back – if made with sincerity, tend to make complex ventures successful and give meaning to a person's life. This was what I had learned from outstanding leaders such as Cassie Schoeman and the many others I shared my life with – my second family.

A final comment: Carrot was not a big operation, compared with some of the later ones. But in terms of rapidity it was one of a kind from beginning to end, and for me personally it ended on a high note in one unforgiving minute in the fields north of Tsintsabis.

The Enemy Went Back to Brew a Volcano Special

On our return to Omuthiya we plunged into some serious preparation for our next operational task – not that we knew what it would be. What we did not know was that when it came along later in the year it would be Operation Protea, 61 Mech's largest operation so far, and our first true excursion into the highly mobile mechanised warfare for which we had been raised in the first place.

But Protea was still a deathly secret, hidden in the bosoms of Pretoria and Windhoek.

What we did know was that next year would most likely see a new session of the "Winter Games", and we were not wrong. But we did not realise quite what we would be in for during the 1982 round.

The total defeat of the 1981 incursion had been tremendous shock for PLAN – the People's Liberation Army of Namibia, to give SWAPO's military wing its proper name. The insurgent planners went back to the drawing-board, and when they returned for the next round in 1982 it would be with a bang, and with a few new tricks up their camouflaged sleeves. The as-yet unplanned and unnamed Operation Yahoo was not going to be as sweet as Carrot, and we would suffer death and wounds. But all that still lay hidden in the unforeseeable future.

Chronologically, Operation Protea lies between Operation Carrot and Operation Yahoo; but I am going to leave Protea till Chapter 12, because Carrot and Yahoo are so closely related that they are almost two phases of one episode, since both were fought by the same people over the same terrain. They were not identical, however, because no military operation is a duplicate of either its predecessor or its successor, and in the case of Yahoo the extent of the fighting was considerably greater.

In addition, Operation Yahoo would be fought under the pitiless glare of the limelight cast by the media, so that political apprehensions were aroused and propagandistic onslaughts from all sides reverberated in the halls of the South African parliament. This claimed the focussed attention of the highest military commanders to bear; and out there in the bush, far from South Africa's and the world's council chambers, a few soldiers from opposing sides translated the whims of their political and military masters into bouts of fierce combat for a ragged moment in time.

So here is the story of Operation Yahoo as I saw it.

Operation Yahoo (14 April – 25 May 1982)

A Surge with Bitter Flavours – Setting the Scene for Yahoo

It is not an easy story to tell, and it is not a straightforward one either. While I was writing this part of my memoirs I kept thinking about something written by David Diop, a famous Senegalese poet of the 1960s: It is Africa, Africa that surges up again, patiently, persistently, and whose fruits, little by little, acquire the bitter flavours of freedom.

Operation Yahoo was such a bitter flavoured surge, in which many died and were wounded within the first few days of intense fighting! Yahoo would explode during the eventful night of 14 and the fateful morning of 15 April and 61 Mech was destined to play a vital role throughout. We had had a busy 12 months following the conclusion of Carrot in early 1981: Operation Protea; Operation Daisy; Operation Makro; and Operation Meebos I. By 7 March 1982, however, we had finally returned to Omuthiya from southern Angola and, as always, had got right down to preparing for the next call-out.

HQ SWATF had placed us on a 24-hour readiness status, which I had changed to three hours; this meant that all our subunits were bombed up and ready to go from wherever we were to wherever we were needed; at 61 Mech we lived permanently on the edge, a frequently tiring but always exciting existence.

While we trained, SWAPO's political masters and military commanders were engaged in preparing an enormous play for their international propaganda effort. This time they were going to mount their largest incursion yet, and squeeze every scrap of propaganda value out of it, regardless of the amount of their soldiers' blood that would have to be spilt in the process.

Once again it would be suicidally daring, with no quarter offered or expected. If it entailed dying at the hands of a persistent and overwhelmingly larger counterinsurgency task force, so be it. And the counterinsurgency task force would be just that. Under command of 61 Mech, it would comprise more than 3,000 military and paramilitary combatants, 500 vehicles and an impressive mini air force.

Operation Yahoo was not your ordinary low-intensity type of counterinsurgency fighting, but high-intensity fighting, with no holds barred. The numbers of killed or wounded tell the disturbing story of the intensity with which this miniature campaign was fought:

- Ten members of the security forces were killed during contacts and by mines, and another 41 wounded.
- Five civilians were killed and three wounded in contacts or mine explosions, and two innocent community members were deliberately murdered by SWAPO.
- Of the original surge of 200 Special Unit fighters, 156 succeeded in infiltrating the Death Triangle. Of this number, 56 were killed and 16 captured (all of the prisoners were subsequently "turned" by the security forces, so that the total loss for the infiltrators actually amounted to 72). Almost 69 managed to make their way back to Angola – most quite early in the incursion – while a few stayed behind and merged quietly with the local community.

It is possible that the SWAPO losses were even greater, because it will never be known how many of the walking wounded (and the indications were that there were many) succumbed to their injuries for lack of the appropriate medical attention.

What amazes me to this day is that the 16 who were taken prisoner were quite willing to turn their coats and serve enthusiastically with the security forces against their erstwhile comrades. The pay and the service conditions were probably much better, I thought cynically at the time... Africa my beginning, Africa my end. Yet there must have been something else. But what that "something" was, if it existed, I never discovered. But the fact remains, as I have mentioned, that Operation Yahoo was not your common or garden low-intensity type of counterinsurgency effort. It was high-intensity fighting, with no holds barred.

There Remained an Unending Quest for Situational Awareness and Early Warning

Forewarned, as it is rightly said, is forearmed. March 1982 crept towards its end, and we knew what would come next; the drenching rains, which started in October, would last well into April. Its intermittent downpours provided the insurgents with sufficient drinking water to stay alive, washed away their tracks and obscured the view of scouting aircraft. The foliage grew even denser, providing more cover for movement; the soggy ground hindered the security forces' vehicular movement, making cross-tracking and follow-ups more difficult.

The responsibility of countering the movement from the north was in the hands of Sectors 10 and 20, while prevention and containment south of the Red Line was Sector 30s commitment. As the SWATFs mobile reserve, 61 Mech watched, remained aware and made sure it was ready to respond swiftly from Omuthiya if and when a crisis erupted. But I worried: it was as if those responsible for the region were not heeding the approaching firestorm.

And, unbeknown to either the security forces or the community, it was definitely approaching. No less than seven large insurgent groups were already moving stealthily southwards to sow death and destruction. Yet the telltale red flags were there for all to see. One clear battle indicator was 32 Battalion's Operation Super in southwestern Angola's Cambêno Valley on 3 March. A 75-strong force, supported by Alouette gunships, attacked an unprecedentedly large insurgent group which was calmly preparing to infiltrate southwards through the mountainous wastes of Kaokoland, and killed 221 of them.

This should have provided a surfeit of food for thought. Such a large group? And via a route which had never been attempted before? Was this perhaps part of a greater operation which was meant to stretch the security forces as thinly as possible over an enormous area? A forewarning if ever there had been one, surely, and to my mind the signal for immediate pre-emptive and proactive countermeasures by Sector 30. If there were such intentions, however, I could see no sign of them.

So the looming threat loomed on, and there was practically nothing 61 Mech could do about it. Oh, we could and did guess, assess, plan, prepare, train and exercise as vigorously as always to keep sharpening our combat edge, while my intelligence staff carefully listed all battle indicators that we could use as yardsticks to monitor the situation and detect anything unhealthy that might emerge from the vast expanse of bush cover in the north. But till HQ SWATF pressed on our button we couldn't move.

This did not prevent me from worrying about three not-so-little issues which kept nagging at me. The first was that 61 Mech was not in control of threat containment – that mandate resided in Sector 30, and we were hearing very little about the operational requirement they would have of us. The next was what would happen to the local communities if the balloon went up. Would we be there to support them if the time came, given the fact that we were also on standby for other crises that might arise in southern Angola? The third – not Sector 30s fault, this one – was that we had just received a new intake of subunits from our feeder training units in South Africa. The newcomers still required extensive mission training and were not yet fully acclimatised or used to our operational ways.

The picture was not all bad as far as this last matter was concerned, however. The new intakes had been thoroughly trained before being deployed to Omuthiya, and we had outstanding soldiers, both Permanent Force and national servicemen, to show them the ropes. And we had a few tricks of our own up our dusty sleeves. Firstly, our combat element was ready for any undue emergency; secondly, we had dusted off and reviewed our contingency plan for just such an emergency; thirdly, we were cramming as much mission training into the newcomers as possible, just in case of sudden developments.

I believed that this third issue, therefore, was certainly a nail-biter but not actually a problem, and that if Sector 30 did press on our button the regiment would be able to respond instantly and would acquit itself well. The major concern was thus the perceived operational lethargy at HQ Sector 30.

Overview of the Special Unit – the Enemy Had Done Their Homework

The SWAPO deep infiltrations should be viewed as a holistic sequel to their decisive defeats during all previous such operations, which had a marked effect on the infiltrators' operational conduct during Yahoo. This time the SWAPO planners had done their homework thoroughly and had clearly studied our tactics; in 1982 they came back better prepared and more dedicated and ferocious than ever before, so much so that it would take the security forces close on two months to run them into the ground.

They planned to cross the Bravo cutline during the night of 14 March, supported by a well-designed deception plan, and as one soldier to another I would like to express my admiration; there would be no walkover this time. If things went well, the lights of the copper mining town of Tsumeb and the red lights on the communication masts near the Otjikoto Lake would soon be winking at them in the night. But as it transpired, the lights would guide them southwards into a killing field, as a moth is enticed into the candle's flame.

The Special Unit comprised well-trained insurgents, and by 1982 had an active strength of about 400 combatants who were, theoretically at least, devoted to the political ideals of SWAPO (I say "theoretically", bearing in mind the 16 prisoners who did not hesitate to change sides, and at least one subgroup which retreated to Angola very early on). Their command cadre had undergone rigorous training in Eastern Bloc countries and China, and new recruits were carefully selected for these deep raids.

Their legendary commander was the charismatic Danger Ashipalo, whose staff consisted of his second-in-command, Kapoko, a political commissar named High Court and an engineer commander, Kandove. Many battle names like these became legendary during the border war (I met a few of them subsequently over a beer or two... nice people, really).

Volcano, their operational base, was located about 35 km southwest of Lubango and was home to 10 platoons of between 35 and 45 men, each commanded by seasoned leaders like Kilimandjaro; Amin; Mandume; Nangobe; Castro; Ndowishi; Kayofa; Kalulu; Shikongo; and Kaunda.

Before the insurgents left Lubango for the Death Triangle they were briefed and motivated by the senior cadre of SWAPO, including Sam Nujoma in person, supported by Martin Shalli (the Senior Staff Officer PLAN, who, incidentally, I met in October 2010) and Danger. Secrecy was so strict that they did not receive their final instructions until just before their departure.

Their main mission was to infiltrate the designated target areas and fight until those areas were liberated, because 1982, they were told, was "the Year of SWAPO". Specifically they were to lay ambushes and mines; kill white farmers; sabotage infrastructure; shoot at vehicles; attack and raid shops on farms; attack the towns; conduct progressive political actions to boost the cause of SWAPO; reconnoitre enemy bases and plot targets of opportunity; and establish and develop underground networks to support future infiltrations to follow.

That was it. Close on 200 fired-up PLAN fighters headed southwards, bound for Kamanjab and Tsumeb. Utter dedication to the cause – or a conditioned reflex of the kind that made Pavlov's famous dog react to a command given in a certain way?

I remember asking myself about that when we eventually found out what we were facing. I could not make up my mind whether the infiltration was a reflection of sheer guts and tenacity of purpose or plain stupidity which had been harnessed to the propaganda wagon.

It is interesting to note that the Special Unit men were planning to infiltrate as far southwards on foot as we had raided northwards by vehicle and parachute during Operation Daisy in November 1981[9] (being a mechanised man, I would rather have bummed a lift somewhere in a Ratel or Ural).

They set off on their infiltration notwithstanding the fact that after Operation Protea the SADF/SWATF had turned all of south-central Angola into their personal

9 See Chapter 13.

hunting ground, or that Daisy had disrupted their operations, or that there were constant counterinsurgency operations on the go not just in Ovamboland but also in southern Angola, across their transit route to the border. I couldn't help wondering whether these deep raids – and particularly this one – were not some sort of warning about the future.

My speculation got me nowhere, of course. Remember, this was a politico-military war, not simply a military one, and the high-level political games being played elsewhere did not form part of our agenda. Yahoo was only part of the bigger picture, but it was the part we were concerned with.

The 52-strong Western Group under Kilimandjaro travelled by vehicle from Lubango to Cahama, from where they walked to the border and crossed over near Ruacana on 7 April, then bombshelled into three smaller groups. A few of the groups made contact with the security forces in Sector 10; some infiltrators became disheartened and decided to return to Angola. Those who were left unscathed (and unintimidated) continued their stealthy southward trek, and on 29 April the first group to be reported to the security forces was spotted on the farm Welkom, in the district of Kamanjab.

The seven Eastern Groups aimed at the Death Triangle and the Mangetti Block left Lubango in Ural trucks at the beginning of April, bound for the Techamutete-Cassinga area via Matala, their jumping-off point. They were commanded by Nangobe, Castro, Ndowishi, Kayofa, Kalulu, Shikongo and Kaunda. They marched southwards for about 370 km, crossed the border and set off for Tsumeb, about 240 km further on. In the process several of these groups were involved in contacts with security forces in Ovamboland, but in each case their tracks were lost.

On 10 April the tracks of an significant number of infiltrators – about 150 of them – were located near Nkongo. A hot pursuit followed, but somehow this group also managed to evade their pursuers. They soon made their presence felt, however: at 19:00 on 11 April a patrolling Sector 10 Buffel MPV detonated a mine along the Charlie cutline, 30 km due north of Tsintsabis. A 20-strong group were later detected to the east, but the follow-up failed when their tracks vanished. Let us pause for a while and consider the specific taskings five of the seven groups had received before leaving Volcano[10] (those of Nangobe and Castro were never ascertained by us). Kayofa and Kalulu had been tasked to activate the Mangetti Block and to lay an ambush for the security forces on the Bravo cutline for deception purposes; Ndowishi was ordered to commit acts of terrorism in the vicinity of Mount Aukas, near Grootfontein; Kaunda was instructed to infiltrate and subsequently activate the Tsumeb, Otavi and Kombat districts; Shikongo was tasked to infiltrate further south to Omaruru and Otjiwarongo.

It was exciting to watch the enemy picture evolving and coming alive as the operation proceeded. Intelligence management was in the capable hands of Captain Gerrie Hugo, supported by a joint intelligence team comprising Colonel "Foffie" Badenhorst from the SWAPOL special branch; Major Derek Botha of Koevoet, of the SWAPOL counterinsurgency unit; Major Henk Coetzee from Special Forces; and Captain Lukas Delport from military intelligence.

This team of talented operators worked day and night to out-think the infiltrators. They spent countless hours with our captives, so as to extract information from them (and found that most of the involuntary guests spilt the beans within 30 minutes of being captured...

10 See Maps 8 and 9.

an amazing sight). Another extremely valuable source of intelligence was the captured enemy documents yielded up by both the living and the dead. Proof of just how good our men were could be seen in the way the intelligence requirements they had formulated at the beginning of the operation – who, what, where, when, why and how – were satisfied, one after the other.

It was now time for Kayofa and Kalulu to implement their deception plan in the Mangetti Block and on the Bravo cutline, the plan we did not know or think about... Keep this in mind when I explain about the tragic events which unfolded on 15 April. Full marks for the enemy on Day 1! But the other three terrorist groups, led by Ndowishi, Kaunda and Shikongo, were about to be cut to pieces by our task force in being.

A Concert and a Crisis – Pulsating Energy, Swirling Action, Unending Motion

My disquiet remained as the days crawled remorselessly on, past the end of March and into the first half of April. So did the vagueness about what was expected and what, precisely, 61 Mech's role would be if something did happen. No practical pre-emptive plans were generated by Sector 30, none whatever; "wait and see" remained the watchword.

So in the meantime we at Omuthiya watched, waited... and kept preparing for any eventuality. Our only guideline was that if and when it happened, it would be a counterinsurgency effort rather than a conventional one, which was better than nothing, but not by much. We did not know it yet, but the crisis was only days away – 15 April, to be exact – and its deadly brunt would be borne by Alpha Company, under Captain Jan Malan.

I was confident that Alpha Company could handle anything the enemy might throw at it. Malan was a vibrant commander, one of the new breed of mechanised infantrymen, and had shown himself to be an astute tactician. His second-in-command, Lieutenant Hubrecht van Dalsen, had had his baptism of fire in a short but fierce action at Môngua during Operation Protea; the acting company sergeant-major, Staff-Sergeant E. Koen, was an experienced man – all in all, a young, enthusiastic and committed command team. Their national service rank and file were of equally quality, 150 lively, well-trained troops who would be going into action for the first time in their young lives and were looking forward to it.

As April approached its mid-point it became ever clearer to us that an infiltration was imminent, and so I decided to deploy Alpha Company to the north of Tsintsabis, between the Bravo and Alpha cutlines. This was a carefully calculated choice: it was an area we regularly used for training, so they knew it well, and, more importantly, Tsintsabis lay on the traditional infiltration route. The deployment served two immediate purposes – Malan could complete his troops' orientation training and at the same time provide a rapid-reaction force within easy reach of a crisis situation.

I informed Colonel Louw of my decision, and he was ecstatic at this boost to his meagre force numbers. So was Lieutenant Daan Liebenberg of the Northern Border Company at Tsintsabis – as well they might be, since Alpha Company with its HQ, three mechanised platoons mounted in 14 Ratel-20s and an anti-tank group with four Ratel-90s represented a formidable addition to the northern patrol force.

Alpha Company, geared up for any eventuality, left Omuthiya for Tsumeb on 14 April, the intention being to attend a concert at the Etosha High School that evening and then deploy directly to Tsintsabis; the rest of 61 Mech would come from Omuthiya in Samil-100 trucks and join them at Tsumeb for the concert. The concert was staged by the SADF's

Entertainment Group, and was one of the recreational outings we regularly organised for our soldiers. That was the idea, anyway, but SWAPO had plans for entertainment of rather a different sort.

It started off well enough. Alpha Company's Ratels and the three of my mobile tactical headquarters were parked at the rear HQ of 61 Mech on the eastern outskirts of Tsumeb, the big six-wheelers still sighing gently as they cooled down after a day's labour, while the national servicemen and the Permanent Force members with their families sat in the school hall, my RSM, WO1 H.G. Smit, and his wife Ansie making sure that decorum was observed (the PF members' next of kin lived at Tsumeb – my family home was actually adjacent to the rear HQ).The RSM, incidentally, was known among the rank and file as "Killer" – although not to his face, needless to say. This was not a tribute to any murderous qualities but rather a mark of respect; I have always liked the way the sergeant-major was referred to as "the mother of the company" in the old German army, because that pretty much described the role of Killer Smit and his subordinate sergeant-majors played in 61 Mech.

Traditionally, of course, a sergeant-major's primary role is to keep an eye on standards of drill, dress and discipline, but in practice his duties cover a wide spectrum. An officer's role is to lead, to set goals and see they are achieved, but warrant-officers and non-commissioned officers are the unit's primary man-managers, and if they do not do their jobs the unit will be no good.

In any case, all went well at first, and by 21:30pm the concert was in full swing, when I was called to the radio room at our rear HQ, and was informed by Daan Liebenberg that there had been a massive influx of insurgents over the Bravo cutline during the course of the evening; as yet he had no details, he said, but he had despatched a number of patrols to investigate and had informed Colonel Louw at HQ Sector 30.

With great regret I went back to the school and summarily stopped the concert. The civilian entertainers watched wide-eyed as their audience evaporated. Good-bye, thanks very much, see you somewhere in the future, don't call us, we'll call you. I had already instructed my second-in-command, Major Thys Rall, to activate our contingency plan. It swung into motion quite smoothly, since it was all SOP.

I ordered Jan Malan to deploy Alpha Company into a suitable stopper position to the north of the Bravo cutline and close to Tsintsabis until we knew more about what was happening, then told Giel Reinecke to join me in my command Ratel for the trip to Tsintsabis (part of this derived from the fact that next day happened to be his 27th birthday). As an afterthought I also told Padre Rossouw to get his kit together and join the Tac HQ. Soon we were on the road to Tsintsabis, 65 km to the north-northwest – a mere hop and skip by SWA/Namibian standards. Close behind me followed Gerrie Hugo in the intelligence Ratel.

Quick off the mark though we were, we were eating the dust of Alpha Company's 18 Ratels. The super-efficient Malan was wasting no time: he had crammed his entire leader group into his command Ratel, and under the dim cabin lights they were already assessing the scanty information at hand and working out tentative plans and orders as they bucketed through the night towards Tsintsabis.

Ninety minutes later we arrived at Tsintsabis. Our first task was to set up the Tac HQ; like RSMs, SADF chaplains were much more versatile than their mandate required them to be, and Koos Rossouw proved once again his expertise at assembling, mounting and marking the intelligence and operational maps. He did not know it yet, but he was going to be working overtime on 14/15 April to handle all his spiritual and temporal tasks.

I informed Colonel Louw that for the time being I was taking control of events and asked him to activate Operation Awake (Sector 30s emergency plan) and dispatch a few Puma helicopters and Alouette gunships to Tsintsabis as soon as possible while 61 Mech held the fort. The show was on!

By 01:00 on 15 April Jan Malan reported that he was deployed north of Tsintsabis and was ready for anything, be it vigil or action or both. I was pleased but not surprised. So now we had a foot on the ground, just in case (as it happened there was no activity that night, but if there had been he would have provided any interlopers with a hot reception – contingency plans are never a waste of time, since crises mostly do not provide advance warning).

In the meantime my command group was communicating with the farmers in the Tsintsabis-Tsumeb district via the Etosha AFU, using the military area radio network and the telephone, warning them of the impending threat and trying to find out what the hell they knew about the situation on the ground.

Although we snatched desperately at each scrap of relevant information, there wasn't much to be had; the only item of solid intelligence was the infiltrators' tracks, and we needed to know a great deal more than that. How many were there, where did they cross, when did they cross, where were they heading, what exactly were their intentions? Absolutely basic information, but we didn't even have that. All we could do was mark the known crossing sites on the map and assess the situation in terms of time and space to the best of our ability. It was both maddening and worrying.

While we battled to shed light on the darkness, Giel Reinecke was busying setting up his liaison with Northern Logistic Command at Grootfontein to activate the logistical support plan which would provide the sinews of this particular war – accommodation, vehicles, fuel and technical support, all to be deployed at the Tsumeb airfield as soon as possible.

The region's area force units were notified that the 1982 Winter Games had begun. All got the same message: Action stations – activate your crisis plans and warn the farmers and the communities forthwith. Fully man your respective operations centres now. Put your tracker teams on immediate standby. Start cross-tracking on the farms. Notify the respective mayors and town clerks to activate crisis plans and procedures now. Colonel Tommie Thomasse and Commandant Buks Koen of 1 SWA Specialist Unit got the same message.

Next I contacted Daan van der Westhuizen – veteran master tracker and fieldcraft expert par excellence – at his farm Koedoesvlei, 15 km west of Tsintsabis, explained what was happening and said we needed his renowned tracker team to report soonest to the Tac HQ. Without hesitation he said he was on his way.

In due course the team arrived at Tsintsabis in Daan's cut-down drab brown Land Rover – tall, imposing Daan himself; his son-in-law, farmer-rifleman Hendrik Potgieter, who was married to his daughter Olivia; his friend and long-time Bushman employee, Jan Kouswab (widely known as "Jan Kaka"); and two other Bushman trackers. Back at Koedoesvlei, Daan's wife, the legendary "Tannie Pompie", was on all-night duty at the radio relay station which had been installed in her kitchen, reaching out to everyone and knotting together the strands of the communication network.

Giel Reinecke caught my attention: "Alex Britz is on the phone, he wants to speak to you." I was not surprised that Alex had called – we had passed his farm, about 12 km from Tsumeb, on our way to Tsintsabis a few hours ago – or that the first thing he said was: "Where must I report, at Tsintsabis or Tsumeb airfield?" Sixty Kipling-style seconds' worth of comfort washed over me. The plan was coming together swiftly. Only one nagging problem remained: Where the hell were the insurgents – and what were they up to?

All this time the remainder of 61 Mech had been girding its loins, high-tailing it back to Omuthiya under Major Chris Roux of Sierra Battery and the RSM, and then getting ready to move out. There was nothing haphazard or ad hoc about all this – the 61 Mech SOP provided for simultaneous action by its components when required. When their vanguard arrived at Omuthiya I contacted Major Roux by radio and said that his first priority was farm protection. He replied that he had already given orders and that his gunners were making ready to deploy southwards without delay. I said "OK" and dismissed the matter from my mind; Sierra Battery knew precisely what to do.

Almost unnoticed, 14 April had passed into 15 April – except by me, because I had two reasons to accost Giel Reinecke, who was pulling an all-nighter, as usual, in his highly efficient way. Our hurried conversation went along the following lines: Congratulations, my friend, may you have a fruitful life and many more such exciting celebrations in the future – have a luke-warm beer on me. And by the way, what is Northern Logistics Command reporting about the umpteen activations of our logistics emergency procedures? Are they ready to equip the stand-by forces on early arrival this morning? When there is a war on, you mix business with pleasure.

So all the well-oiled wheels were turning – except one. As the hours passed we remained perplexed and ever more concerned about the enemy situation, about which we still knew next to nothing. Again I phoned Colonel Louw, who was now in his office at his HQ in Otjiwarongo, to pass on a brief Sitrep. The conversation went something like this:

> Me: Colonel, good morning, a bit busy here, who have you appointed as the commander for this operation?
>
> Colonel Louw: Thank you, Roland, for handling the crisis so far; I'll let you know soonest about the command thing.

Right! Well, at least someone was in charge pro tem. I could live with that. I filed this particular protocol question away in the back of my mind and concentrated on more pressing matters.

During the early morning hours a little more intelligence came in. Four separate insurgent crossing places had been found on the Bravo cutline, all of them heavily mined and booby-trapped. So far, so good, I reckoned as I stood amid all the frenzied but ordered activity at Tsintsabis, with the squelching of the radios as background music. I didn't know yet that 15 April was about to become the longest and most tragic day in my life.

The sun rose in its usual stately fashion over an amazingly beautiful bushveld landscape, out of the fiery haze of Botswana and Bushmanland to the east; soon first light would be along. Usually I enjoyed these spectacular sunrises, but not this morning: there were just too many life-and-death things to consider. But daylight was going to give us an advantage.

In my heart of hearts I knew that we were going to lose a few good men and some innocent civilians in the next few days. That was a given! How long will this infiltration last? I thought, if you can think, Roland, but not make thoughts your aim? On the one side was an unknown number of determined insurgents from the Special Unit; on the other side the counterinsurgency task force I was about to command – even if only temporarily – was still being formed.

Dawn brought our first casualty. Around 06:00 one of Sierra Battery's Ratels left the road and overturned while speeding over the Ovambo Omuramba low-water bridge, 4 km south of Oshivello, killing one of our gunners, although there were no significant injuries to anyone else on board. Chris Roux gave me the news from the scene of the accident. I was still dealing with grief at this needless death when I got the next shock at about 09:00.

One of Northern Border Company patrols on the Bravo cutline had found what looked like an insurgent crossing between 30 and 40 km west of Tsintsabis. While inspecting the site, one of the soldiers accidentally detonated a personnel mine which had been boosted with an 82 mm mortar bomb. In the massive explosion which followed he was killed and eight other members of the patrol were wounded. It was a grievous moment. Two good men dead and eight wounded with nothing to show for it, and the day had barely started! All we knew was that we had found four sets of enemy tracks receding into the distance, leading Heaven alone knew where. And worse – much worse – was to follow.

In the meantime I clung on to what good news there was. Thys Rall informed me that the main Tac HQ at the Tsumeb airfield had been established and that the ground and air forces earmarked under the standby arrangement were being marshalled at great speed and were converging on the airfield; I was happy to leave the task of receiving and briefing them as they arrived in his capable hands.

At the same time the RSM was busy establishing an operational and logistical base at the airfield. The two Puma helicopters and two Alouette gunships I had requested were airborne and on their way to Tsintsabis from Ondangwa, estimated time of arrival 09:00. I acknowledged and carried on: with my other tasks, as per the overriding rule: Within the ambit of the mission, the commander must remain focussed and maintain freedom of action. It was not easy. What a night and what an early morning it had been! Little did I realise that the next shock would hit me at high noon.

Tentacles of Terror Unfurl and Reaches Out of Mangetti – Disbelief and Shock

The surreal friendliness of full daylight at last reached Tsintsabis on the morning of 15 April, the first day of the battle for the Death Triangle, and once again, first blood went to the enemy. This day terror and trauma would reach out from the Mangetti Block and strike down eight of our young soldiers; four of them were national servicemen going into action for the first time in their lives.

I would like to pause here and tell a sad story about the brave and the young; about a captain and his soldiers who were doing their job under the harshest imaginable conditions... about a venture into the gaping, deadly jaws of an ambush. The word "ambush" is not always correctly used. Its simplest definition is the best one: A surprise attack on a moving enemy from a hidden position. No more, no less, and if that surprise attack is properly handled its effects can be devastating.

So stay with me for a moment while I reveal something about soldiering and missions, and about what happened on a fateful, never-to-be-forgotten morning so very many years ago.

I had recalled Alpha Company to Tsintsabis early on 15 April to explore the nearest enemy tracks reported, across the Bravo cutline 15 km to our west. We knew by now that all the enemy crossing places were heavily mined, and it was obvious to my small command group at Tsintsabis that things were not as they had been during previous infiltrations. Something fishy was going on: what was and what was not?

For this reason I instructed Jan Malan to go and investigate with one of his platoons and Daan van der Westhuizen's seasoned tracker team. Before they left I warned them to be extremely vigilant because somehow things seemed not right. By now the Pumas and the two Alouette gunships squatted at Tsintsabis, their drooping rotors ready to start turning, their pilots briefed and ready to take off at moment's notice to provide air support. But we all knew that a contact might be decided before the choppers had time to get there. For a soldier conceptualising the border war was simple in a sense. We did not dwell on the politics of the thing, but concentrated on a much more immediate issue: was it going to be us or them? The fighting on the ground could be both simple and complex. The difficult part, I believed, arrived when tactical plans needed to fit into the operational scheming, or vice versa. My belief at the time, speaking as a tactical commander, was that the challenges were usually to be found during the dogged pursuance of the mission and the execution of the plan – friction de guerre, the unexpected. This usually came into play when the first shots were exchanged. Then the plan usually changed as if it had a will of its own.

For Jan Malan and his platoon, fresh out of training at Bloemfontein, this happened quite suddenly at 11:00 on 15 April, when eight of his soldiers were mown down and then devoured by fire, all within the first furious minutes of the contact. Three of the enemy succumbed during the ensuing firefight, but that small handful of minutes would be the most traumatic to be experienced by the survivors.

I personally debriefed the platoon concerned soon after the ambush, and my story is one that I have reconstructed from what they told me. I also have Jan Malan's personal account, which I asked him to write for me when we were both serving at the Army Battle School at Lohatlha in 1983. I kept that report, which included an accurate sketch he made of the incident, and still have it (about two years ago I gave him back a copy, and he was deeply touched by the memory. As a leader he always remained close to his people, a man who led by example).

This was what Malan wrote[11]:

> On my arrival at Tsintsabis I met the tracker team of Lieutenant Daan van der Westhuizen for the first time. After a quick marrying-up and a motivational talk to my platoon, we left for the area where the enemy tracks had been found. Just before we left Tsintsabis, Hendrik Potgieter still remarked how joyful it was to work with such motivated and dedicated men.
>
> The trackers travelled with us, mounted on our Ratels. As we moved westwards along the cutline the Bushmen maintained a close watch for signs and tracks of the enemy. Arriving at the crossing site, we observed numerous sheets of white paper strewn about. I instructed my men to dismount and we approached the suspect area on foot in open formation. Closer inspection revealed typical SWAPO propaganda pamphlets.
>
> The next moment one of the Bushman trackers came to an abrupt halt and pointed to a suspect area in the sand. I halted our search and marked the suspect

11 Translated by me from Afrikaans.

area with a mine marker I had on me. I then tasked the trackers to do an allround search of the area. Three enemy tracks were leading in a southerly direction. We found shallow trenches of the enemy alongside the northern edge of the cutline. The signs on the ground clearly indicated that they had evacuated their positions hastily the previous night.

We found a clear path of approximately 20 tracks leading in a northwesterly direction. After a brief discussion with Van der Westhuizen and Potgieter, we decided to do a 360° search of the whole area. All of us were in agreement that the enemy tracks would most likely swing back and cross the cutline on a southerly tack. It was now about 10:45 and the trackers indicated that the tracks were approximately 12 hours old.

At this stage I gave feedback by radio to Commandant Roland de Vries at Tsintsabis. My suggestion was to carry on with the search, and he agreed with me. The plan was now for one infantry section to move to the south of the cutline and search for enemy tracks for 200 m in a westerly direction. At the same time Lieutenant Daan van der Westhuizen, with the remainder of the trackers and another infantry section, continued with the search to the north in a westerly direction for 200 m.

The terrain alongside the cutline in both directions was extremely dense. From the moment Ratel 12A with Van der Westhuizen on board left they were out of my sight. Daan van der Westhuizen, apparently occupying the Ratel turret, reported that the enemy tracks were leading west. The next moment there were maddening explosions and rippling small arms fire coming from their receding Ratel's direction.

I immediately recognised that the fire was not from the Ratel's 20 mm quick-firing gun. I tried to call the section on the radio, but there was no answer. I immediately deployed the remainder of the platoon and started moving in the direction where the fire was coming from. The bush was dense and our movement was slowed down considerably.

At one o'clock from our position in front of us we observed two 300 metre signal flares bursting in the sky. By now the fire had ceased. I instantly reported our dilemma to my battalion commander at Tsintsabis and requested the gunships. Without delay the Alouette gunships were airborne and flying towards us.

We then sighted our burning Ratel. My troops dismounted into an open formation as we moved forward. We did not fire for fear of hitting our own people in front of us. At that same moment two of our soldiers came running anxiously towards us from our left front. They were streaked with blood and totally shocked. The two soldiers reported to me that they had driven right into an ambush. They said to me that many of their section members had been killed.

Massive black clouds and flames erupted from the Ratel. I deployed two of our sections and moved to the other side of the inferno, and we took up a defensive position. There were no sign of enemy nearby. I quickly moved towards the burning Ratel, accompanied by the platoon commander. We peered inside; it was obvious that nobody was alive. At this stage the ammunition inside the Ratel started exploding and the roofhatches were blown sky-high.

All around the burning Ratel I found our remaining soldiers... They were all wounded and shocked. The medical orderly, company HQ and platoon HQ personnel removed the wounded to a safer area, and rendered first aid... At that moment the

Alouette gunships arrived. I indicated to them the assumed direction in which the enemy had retreated. Approximately one kilometre further west of our position we heard the gunships firing at the ground.

In the meantime I had requested the HQ at Tsintsabis to dispatch the two Puma helicopters for casualty evacuation. The Pumas were on their way immediately. By now we had adopted an allround defence. We started preparing a helicopter landing zone. The Ratel was still burning profusely. The tyres were sending up columns of black smoke and explosions ripped large pieces off the hull.

The Pumas landed and our dead and wounded were taken on board and flown south to Grootfontein. The gunships were still firing into the bushes to the west of us, where three terrorists had been killed. One of the gunships evaded a SAM-7 fired in retaliation from the ground. I then followed up with two sections in the direction of the contact. We found the three bodies as well as the SAM-7. One of the dead terrorists was later identified as a section leader.

I had lost a total of eight men killed in this one ambush (See Figure 12). Five mines were later lifted by our engineers in the area where the ambush had been sprung. The enemy had left a clear trail for us to follow. The ambush had been carefully planned and cleverly set up. It was in the form of a horseshoe. It was located in a thicker part of the forest, on the verge of a more open area. The enemy had prepared shallow trenches for their RPG-7s, SKS rifle grenades and machine guns. We found the position for the SAM-7 and a 60 mm mortar as well.

Our Ratel was allowed to approach to within 15–20 metres before the enemy opened fire. It was later found that the Ratel had been penetrated by seven RPG-7 rockets and rifle grenades. The enemy platoon returned to Angola after they had completed their mission.

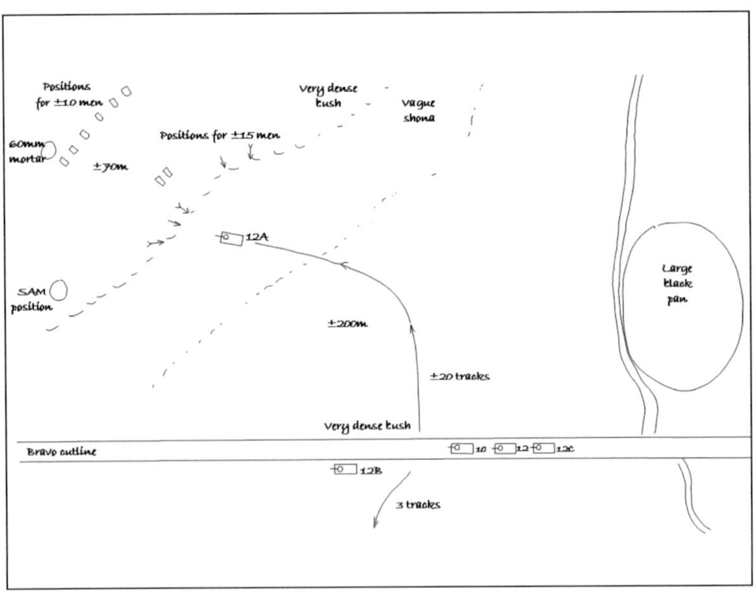

Figure 12: Ambush Sketch by Captain Jan Malan (Operation Yahoo)

I felt deeply for Jan Malan, his soldiers, their loved ones, even for myself. I can't describe to anyone what I felt that tragic morning in the war... If you can meet with triumph and disaster... If you could risk it on one turn of pitch-and-toss... with sixty seconds worth of distance run... Within five hours of one morning we had lost 10 of our young.

What made it even more heart-rending was that on the Van der Westhuizen farm just 15 km away, Tannie Pompie was monitoring the crisis unfolding over her radios, calmly relaying messages between Jan Malan and myself to help with dispatching the helicopters and evacuating the dead and the wounded. Then I could hear her iron resolve cracking, and knew that she was at the end of her tether, so I asked Padre Rossouw to console her over the radio as best he could – Koos had become a good friend of the Van der Westhuizens, like the rest of us at 61 Mech – and as soon as one of the Pumas returned from Grootfontein I had him flown out to Koedoesvlei.

That was how Operation Yahoo began for 61 Mech and the community it was sworn to protect. While the wrecked Ratel smouldered where it had been killed – it was to be three days before it could be recovered to the Tsumeb airfield and the remains of our men removed – we gritted our teeth and got on with the job. This was only the first day... the battle was not over yet, not by a long shot!

South Africans are not great breast-beaters. They tend to internalise their grief, and now the sorrow was overtaken by grim determination. Friction de guerre plagues all soldiers; the art of war consists in making it plague the other side more than yourself, and this means wresting the initiative from them and then keeping it. This was what Operation Yahoo was all about.

Incidentally: On 21 April 1982 we received a visit from the high brass in Tsumeb, one of them being General Constand Viljoen, the Chief of the SADF. We discussed the course of the operation, and he asked me: "How did Captain Malan allow his platoon to run into an ambush and get eight of his men killed?" I replied: "General, remember, I was in command, he only carried out my orders". I then described what had happened that morning, and why. When I had finished he said: "Tell the captain he did well, he did what he had to do, I feel sorry for our loss!" I passed this on to Jan when I saw him next day, and I could see that it meant a lot to him. As it did to me, because I shared his tremendous, painful burden.

When I found some night-time quiet the following week, I wrote the citation for Daan van der Westhuizen's Honoris Crux Decoration, recognition not of just one act of bravery but of many committed in extremely dangerous situations. It was a small thing, perhaps, in material terms, but that is how an army expresses its gratitude, and it is meaningful beyond the comprehension of civilians because (certainly in the SADF), a decoration for gallantry could only be won by an act or acts of courage. That simple orange-and-white ribbon sets its wearer apart from other men.

In a sense Daan's decoration not only commemorated his many acts of courage in the face of the enemy but also immortalised the seven men who died with him: Corporal M.J. van Jaarsveld; Lance-Corporal J.J. van den Berg; Rifleman M. Peterson; Rifleman J.H. Potgieter; Rifleman B.J. Wolfaardt; Bushman Tracker Jan Kouswab; and a second tracker whose name is unknown.

But I digress. There was an operation to be executed before we could allow ourselves the luxury of mourning our dead. First of all we had to move our small command team to the Tsumeb airfield. Giel Reinecke, Gerrie Hugo and I had to be at the nerve centre, taking control: briefing the incoming elements of our force, deploying the plan, setting the operation in motion. Seek forward ground...!

Turning the Tables on SWAPO – When in Charge, Take Charge

When the sun set over the Death Triangle on the evening of 15 April I had not yet heard anything from Sector 30 about who officially commanded Yahoo, so I decided simply to carry on and run activities in the eastern sector until I had orders to the contrary. We dared not slow down; the insurgents had kept moving southwards throughout the night.

The morning of 16 April dawned, and the enemy still held the initiative while we reacted to events, rather than initiating them ourselves. But before long that would change. The reinforcements were still converging on the Tsumeb airfield (See Figure 13), and soon the hunt would begin in all earnest.

The combined task force for the east comprised units from the South African Army, South African Air Force, Special Forces, SWATF, SWA Police and South African Police Koevoet (SAP-K).[12] The ground force fielded close on 16 infantry companies; one armoured car squadron; an additional artillery battery (personnel only); one field engineer troop; and no less than nine SAP Koevoet teams which totalled 340 men. The SAAF task team provided a Mobile Air Operations Team (MAOT) and commanded an impressive number of Puma transports, Alouette gunships and Bosbok light aircraft, plus the private light aircraft flown by the part-time air commando units. The South African Medical Service provided all the medical support we needed.

Task Force West for Kamanjab and Outjo was formed at the same time although their trouble would only arise on 30 April. In the meantime Commandant Stoffel Rothman, the OC Outjo AFU, took command and established his tactical headquarter at Kamanjab. Sector 30 was also keeping a watchful eye there with what they could spare of their meagre resources. To facilitate optimal command and control the area of operations was subdivided into Area East (Tsumeb) and Area West (Kamanjab). For the latter my main tactical headquarter (Tac HQ East) was established at the Tsumeb airfield.

Later I established smaller Tac HQs at Otavi, Grootfontein and Tsintsabis to support command and control as the operation progressed. Originally I had asked Daan Liebenberg to man the Tsintsabis Tac HQ and Commandant Buks Koen, OC 1 SWA Special Unit, the one at Otavi, supported by Major Henne Volkmann, another seasoned part-time warrior and commander of the Otavi AFU. The Grootfontein Tac HQ was sponsored and manned by the Grootfontein AFU under command of Commandant Piet Oosthuizen. During Operation Yahoo our newly established combined task force headquarters adhered to 61 Mech's proven integrated planning system. This provided for all operational planning and control assets to be integrated into joint specialist or functional teams which worked closely together. All maps were marked and updated minute by minute, and displayed corresponding time-dated situational awareness pictures. Layers of information reflected the enemy situation as well as on-going operations; all contacts with the enemy and wide-ranging relevant information were carefully marked and analysed.

Each contact or critical event was followed by a quick war-game between the intelligence and operations staff, with the supporting staffs standing by to provide inputs as required and design supporting actions. At 07:00 there would be a 10 minute planning session at which everyone stood rather than sat; then at 17:00 a more formal get-together to

12 Refer to Appendix A for the composition of the Task Force.

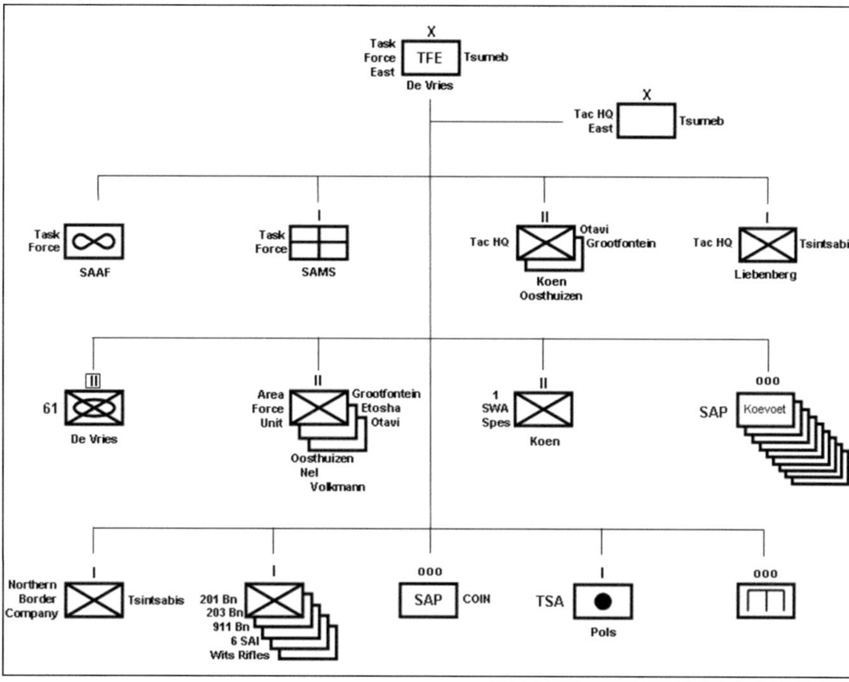

Figure 13: Task Organisation for Operation Yahoo, 1982

review the events of the day.

The hours of darkness were used for deliberate planning, and at first light the follow-up and supporting operations would kick off. From then onwards the focus was on the minute-to-minute controlling, orchestrating and supporting operations and unfolding events. Start at 06:00, shoot dead before 18:00: that was the pattern of a good 12-hour day's work. Then it was back to the devious stuff as darkness cloaked the land, another 12 hours of solid work: at all costs the relentless pressure on the enemy must be maintained, zero tolerance and zero empathy.

In between all this we slept and ate now and then. On occasion I would snatch a few minutes to go next door to my home for a bath – no leisurely soak, though; while the water ran into the tub I could be found sitting next to it on the toilet seat with my clip-board balanced on the plastic laundry bin, busy with the appreciation for the next phase of the operation.

On 17 April the security forces regained the initiative at last, and now the hunt was on; by 1 May there had been more than 23 contacts in our eastern sector, with over 36 infiltrators killed and 16 captured.[13] Another 19 insurgents were killed by follow-up forces from Sector 10, which were operating in the area north of the Charlie cutline and feasting on the remnants fleeing from the south.

The traffic in death and wounds cut both ways. On the 16 April the insurgents gunned down and killed an innocent black farm labourer in the Mangetti Block, north of Tsintsabis. On the same day Rifleman J.D.G. du Toit of 61 Mech was killed in action. On 18 April

13 See Maps 8 and 9.

67-year-old Mr. L.P.J. Fourie was shot and killed by one insurgent subgroup while driving near his home on his farm, Ruimte; with him died a Corporal Bester, a national service soldier from 6 South African Infantry Battalion.

That same day, 51-year-old Lieutenant Dave Keyser of the area forces had a close shave while following another subgroup's spoor with his tracker team; he ran straight into the insurgents on the farm Toevlug, and a fierce shootout ensued in which he was wounded when an RPG-7 grenade exploded in a tree next to him. Fortunately for him it was only a light wound, and he was back in the field on the 19th.

19 April turned out to be one helluva hectic day:

- Early in the morning, 18 insurgents were reported as far south as the farm Uithoek, and the tracks of another 15 insurgents were sighted at Grasvlakte farm... The tentacles of terror were reaching out to all the corners of the Death Triangle.
- Six insurgents, heavily laden with munitions, were killed less than 10 km north of Tsumeb. The booty captured included five AK-47s, 1 x RPG-7 launcher with 6 grenades, seven anti-personnel mines, 17 hand grenades, 15 blocks of explosives and a large quantity of ammunition (there were also a medical kit and six FAPLA uniforms).
- Mr. D.J.J. Erasmus (54), whose wife Ria was a civilian employee at the 61 Mech rear HQ, was mortally wounded when a mine exploded underneath his vehicle near his farm, Vaalwater. He was rushed to the Tsumeb hospital, but succumbed to his wounds on the operating table. What made it particularly sad was that earlier that morning he had told me that he wanted to visit his farm, and I had warned him explicitly not to do so. But for some reason he disregarded my warning... and paid with his life. I had the heart-rending task of trying to console Ria. The deaths of our civilian friends in the Tsumeb district were mounting steadily, and the situation was disconcerting.
- During a follow-up, tracker Reinhardt Friedrich of the Etosha AFU was wounded in the ankle by an exploding Soviet-made POM-Z anti-personnel mine while he was leading his tracker team (Bushmen were the acknowledged experts at reading the ground, but not the only ones with this ancient skill). The wound was serious enough for him to be evacuated to 1 Military Hospital in Pretoria, but this time there was a happy ending, although when I visited him at Tsumeb in October 2010 he still retained a limp to remind him of his narrow escape.
- Another farmer, 48-year-old J.P. Steyn, was blown up and killed by a mine on his farm Masaus, 25 km west of Tsumeb. A Bushman tracker and a national service soldier travelling with him were also blown up, but escaped with light wounds.
- A mine explosion in the Mangetti Block killed two black children, aged 7 and 11.

That was the high point of insurgent activity. By 20 April the infiltration began to unravel (as far as the shooting war was concerned, that is – the propaganda war was another story). From 21 April onwards the security forces suffered very few casualties, although we were initiating so many contacts that at times we did not know where to dispatch the Alouette gunships. The tables had been turned in no uncertain terms.

Allow me to digress again. Operation Yahoo was to last for 42 days and nights of almost continuous activity. What was this war all about? Let me indulge briefly in a discussion of theoretical relevancies before taking up the narrative again.

Conventional war-fighting wisdom holds that any offensive or counteroffensive should develop from one firm base to the next, and that each fighting step should be followed through to the end. The end comes when the winner destroys his opponent physically and breaks his will to fight.

But consider the wisdom of revolutionary warfare, which is choreographed for the unconventional ways and means propagated by Mao Tse-tung and others. SWAPO, the "masters" of revolutionary warfare, intentionally allowed martyrs to be sacrificed for their cause, ruthlessly estimating that the aims of political propaganda could be achieved through human losses, pamphlets left in the wake of receding tracks and the dissipating reek of cordite fumes. All's fair in love and war! So was SWAPO winning or losing... and what margins were used to measure success or failure?

I was extremely pleased not to be employed by SWAPO at the time. It was bizarre for a conventional soldier like me to think that my enemy could deliberately sacrifice his soldiers to achieve his war aims and higher political outcomes. The question was whether the ordinary combatants of SWAPO knew this when they crossed the Bravo cutline in darkness on 14 April – most of them as highly motivated to carry out their assigned tasks as we were to stop them.

Notwithstanding either conventional or unconventional wisdom: The task force marshalled for the counteroffensive needed to destroy the enemy ruthlessly and swiftly, and absolutely break his will. This we achieved to the letter after a few days of bitter fighting. By and large, operational successes are ensured by maintaining the initiative and this retaining freedom of action. This being the case, I firmly believe that the norms of war which apply to initiative and freedom of action apply equally strongly to politics. This I had observed in Africa on many an occasion.

So who was winning the shooting and political wars by the end of May (and in fact throughout the bush war), us or them? Please work out your own answer to this one. We who were on the ground had no time to think about such things: we had a serious battle to fight, regardless of the shaky politics and political pressures coming to bear on us.

But back to the war. By 22 April it was clear that 18 determined insurgents were still pushing towards the southwest of Tsumeb to find refuge in the rugged mountains formed by the Tsumeb, Otavi and Grootfontein triangle. For us, that was a serious no-no; we had to get them out of the area at all costs or we would lose them. How to do so required some creative thinking, because this was obviously the moment for what we called a "jackal operation", a psychological gambit which would take advantage of the insurgents' utter exhaustion and their cultural superstitions. So that night we concocted some interesting and downright unorthodox things:

- The first ace up our sleeve was our light artillery, Sierra Battery's 120 mm mortars. We did some time and distance calculations to determine more or less where the insurgents would be hiding out in the mountains and Major Chris Roux was directed to calculate and then deliver a spectacular indirect harassing fire mission on their presumed location. There are very few things as exciting (for the gunner) or as terrifying (for the recipient) as rocket-assisted 120 mm mortar bombs streaking into the air and then, many minutes later, exploding on the target with an imposing "crump", quite often setting off a veld fire into the bargain.
- The next move was up to Giel Reinecke and our German pilot, Tickly Kessler in

Tickly's Beechcraft Bonanza, which he had modified into a warplane of sorts.[14] They would float silently over the target area and then drop thunderflashes on to the presumably unsuspecting enemy below. Thunderflashes, for those who don't know, are essentially training devices which are used to simulate hand grenade explosions and go off with an almighty bang and flash without any fragmentation (they are not toys, however, and I couldn't help warning Giel to be very careful not to drop one inside the Beechcraft's cabin). Not that he needed the advice, being an experienced soldier, but sometimes a commander can be a bit of a nanny.

- Throughout the night a few Ratels would carry out fake maintenance runs on the roads surrounding the target zone; every so often each Ratel's crew would call a halt, build a large fire next to the road and then carry on again; the idea was to make it look as if we were deploying a massive cordon-and-search force.

A mind-bender action which did not take place was one dreamed up by our psychological warfare team, Colonel Basjan van Niekerk (quite a joker) and Commandant Jan Greyling, who spurned such mundane ideas as dropping pamphlets. What they suggested was that Tickly's Beechcraft fly over the target area, trailing a brightly illuminated artificial "snake". This was too much, even for as convinced a believer in the indirect approach as myself. I inquired as to how they proposed to illuminate the improvised serpent – with candles, perhaps? – and sent the unrepentant pair back to the drawing board, no doubt enjoying a good chuckle.

To cut a long story short, the plan worked excellently. In the next few days we found tracks indicating that the infiltrators were legging it northwards, away from the mountains. By 1 May the tables had been turned; that day saw the last contacts in our sector, with four insurgents killed and the rest in frenzied flight back to Angola as their mission dissolved around them. They had a long way to go – 400 km to Lubango, all of it on foot. How many were going to make it was an open question.

On 2 May I was lurking in my command Ratel in the bush on the northern side of the Tsintsabis-Oshivello gravel road, facing southwards, near where Rassie Erasmus had been mortally wounded on Vaalwater farm on 19 April. Yahoo was clearly running out of steam by now, but needless to say we were not relaxing – one of the truest battlefield maxims is always "be alert, be alive". So we sat there, rifles "locked and loaded", while a mere 3 km to our south the gunships were twisting and turning in the air, firing lethal 20 mm bursts into the bush below, while two Pumas circled close by, each with a stick of paratroopers on board. One of them, I knew, also carried Captain Gerrie Hugo, my intelligence officer.

Just then I then received a radio message from the operations centre in Tsumeb which informed me that two wounded insurgents had been sighted by farm labourers at one of Vaalwater's outposts. Right! Start up and go – driver, advance! We made haste towards the outpost, and within a few minutes we had them.

Now we could see at close range just how far gone the infiltrators were. They were lying in the open near the outpost, bone weary, their camouflaged uniforms in tatters. One was bleeding profusely from a mangled arm which was attached by a piece of skin and nothing more, obviously the work of a 20 mm round. The other insurgent threw his AK-47 to one side as he saw our Ratel appearing out of a haze of dust and diesel fumes.

As we took them prisoner the Pumas arrived. Gerrie Hugo's landed close by and

14 Renowned part-time force pilot from SWA with pipes for hand grenades fitted to his Beechcraft and twin AK-47 rifles fixed below his fuselage.

the paratroopers tumbled out to deploy for allround defence, while Gerrie came jogging over to me through the dust clouds thrown up by the rotors. After a quick exchange of information he took custody of the two prisoners and assured them: "Yes! You'll receive medical attention as soon as you've pointed out the stash of personnel mines and goodies hidden somewhere in the bushes." In the circumstances, I suppose this amounted to an offer they simply couldn't refuse.

By 3 May Operation Yahoo really began winding down. It seemed that the insurgents had lost all interest in their instruction to carry out attacks on 3/4 May in commemoration of "Cassinga Day" (the extremely successful airborne attack on the SWAPO forward base at Cassinga in Angola on 4 May 1978 during Operation Reindeer). There was not too much serious commanding to be done now, so I told my crew to mount up, and headed out to join one of our follow-up groups north of the Bravo cutline, which was following six sets of enemy tracks going into Ovamboland.

This was more or less what I had done on 18 April 1981 at the end of Operation Carrot, except that this time I was not involved in any shooting. The reason for this could, I suppose, be described as a matter of professional courtesy. Close to the Charlie cutline we ran into a follow-up group from an Ondangwa-based Sector 10 unit, 53 Battalion. The major in command pointed out that he and his men were hot on these tracks and added very politely: "Sir, these are our tracks now; if you take the enemy you'll spoil our kill ratio."

Kill ratio?! It turned out that in Sector 10 there was a stupid competition about which battalion could get the most kills. Ah, well... We were somewhat pissed off, but acknowledged 53 Battalion's prior claim. "Fine," I said, "this is your area, so carry on and have fun." I couldn't help adding: "By the way, radio Commandant Daan Nell and tell him that we have lots of bodies in the Tsumeb mortuary. If he wants to boost his kills he can come and fetch some."

On that rather sour note we headed south while the major and his men headed north. What happened subsequently I have no idea. All I know is that not very long after this incident an elephant was killed on the Charlie cutline. Perhaps it was also included in the kill ratio.

Our immediate preoccupation was with a thorough mopping-up operation, carrying out a methodical search for enemy stragglers and cleaning up the mess left in the wake of the firestorm. The Yahoo force started demobilising; SWAPOL's 340-strong Koevoet contingent returned to Ovamboland to go back to doing what it did best, and the other components similarly went their own way, some to their home bases and others to operational deployments elsewhere, like Koevoet.

On 25 May word came from HQ SWATF in Windhoek that Yahoo was officially over and we could stand down. I thanked my men for doing a magnificent job and being a great team. I meant every word. Once again 61 Mech had completed its mission successfully and contributed to the arsenal of operational experience and war-fighting knowledge which was our most valuable stock-in-trade.

Another important milestone had been passed by my soldiers. No matter how much you may believe in your own judgement, the fact is that you can never really get the measure of a man – and he can never really get a measure of himself – until he has been in harm's way. Now my young soldiers had been blooded, and they had turned out to be simply the best, as I had expected. It was something that would stay with them; they were now fully-fledged embers of the band of battlefield brothers.

I spared a moment to think about the Special Unit's suicidal foray. They had come south facing one of only two options: to fight and die, or to fight and be captured. What a choice! Mentally I flicked a casual salute at the enemy soldiers we had met and bested. In a way I had come to respect and even pity them. But only for a brief moment. We had things to do – to support the local communities in their mourning, and join them in rejoicing that it was all over – and places to go, namely Omuthiya, and the leisure to remember our fallen and celebrate our successes. It had been a hard and a triumphant time for us, one I will never forget!

It needs only to be said that Operation Yahoo lingered on for a while longer – as late as the middle of June there were reports that a small number of insurgents, seven to 10 of them, were still at large in the farming areas, but were lying extremely low. But the "Winter Games" were over in no uncertain terms... until the next year.

As a footnote: The last of the "Winter Games" took place the following year. By that time I had been transferred to the Army Battle School, and there was some talk of temporarily recalling me. However, it was then decided to assign the task to Colonel Tobie van Schalkwyk, who happened to be in-theatre with 82 Mechanised Brigade. But I was there in spirit, because 61 Mech was attached to 82 Brigade for the operation.

The War in the West, Where the Searching and Destroying Continued until 2 June

For the sake of completeness, I think I should end my personal account of Yahoo with a summary of what happened in the west, outside our sector.

The western group under Kilimandjaro gained access through the Kamanjab corridor and then went to ground in the northwestern fringes of the Etosha Game Reserve. There they waited patiently for a high-density operation by Sector 10 to subside before they continued to infiltrate southwards towards Kamanjab and Outjo. What happened then was a tale of misfortune and disaster. On 30 April five insurgents were reported on the farm Bakenkop. The security forces launched an immediate follow-up and killed four of them, including Kilimandjaro himself. The remaining insurgent fled northwards and eventually got away when his track was lost. Between 29 April and 2 June there were another eight contacts in the Kamanjab area.

Of the 18 infiltrators who had originally infiltrated through the western corridor, 12 were killed and one was captured, while the remaining five escaped back to Angola. That really was the end of the show in the west. The long-planned raid had achieved nothing; one improvised anti-personnel mine was detonated by a local inhabitant and another by a giraffe.

War Stories and Other Tales from Yahoo

On the Logistics, by Giel Reinecke

Major Giel Reinecke's voice deserves to be heard. In a fighting regiment, the sharp-end elements naturally garner most of the glory, but the fact is, of course, that without the "back-room boys" such as Reinecke they would achieve nothing. He was responsible for organising the gigantic logistical support effort for Yahoo between 14 April and 25 May, and not once did it falter – an outstanding achievement, given the diversified requirements of the various elements and the vast distances over which the sinews of war had to be supplied, day and night and invariably on time.

So I am going to let Giel have his say in his own words:

The demand on the operation for logistics, personnel and medical support was enormous. The RSM of 61 Mech, WO1 H.G. Smit, and my support personnel helped me in setting up an immense logistics support base at the Tsumeb airfield. It was done within 24 hours. As with Operation Carrot the previous year, military and police forces, equipment and commodities arrived en masse to support the gigantic counterinsurgency effort.

Yahoo lasted six weeks and deployed over a vast area of more than 30,000 square kilometres. The support base at Tsumeb Airfield was equipped with tented accommodation for the troops, with kitchens and canteens, and included facilities for technical support, tyre repairs and diesel and petrol provision. Two large 45,000-litre rubber cushion tanks for helicopter fuel and mobile bunkers for refuelling of light spotter aircraft were held in constant readiness.

16 Maintenance Unit from NLC at Grootfontein served as our second-line logistics installation and delivered diesel, petrol and helicopter fuel daily as requested. Our support company was responsible for the collection and distribution of normal general stores, canteen items, rations and vehicle spares.

The operation had its own specific logistics challenges. Those were mainly due to the long duration of the operation and the distant outskirts to be reached. This was to satisfy wide-ranging logistical and maintenance requirements coming from the front line, spread out in all wind directions.

Second-Lieutenant Koenraad Schultze established various logistic delivery points for the forces deployed in remote areas. This included supplying commodities such as diesel, ration packs, vehicle spares, spare wheels and canteen items far out in front. Another unique logistics task undertaken was to pre-position 200-litre fuel drums of helicopter fuel at preselected points and on farms. This saved time in refuelling our helicopters and allowed the Alouette gunships longer air time and gave them the ability to be close to the action.

The key to operational success was the integrated planning process followed by 61 Mech... All the staff members were involved in the process. The planning and control measures cascaded down to ground level. This allowed everyone to be fully informed and committed to the overall mission of Operation Yahoo. That mission was to track down and destroy the SWAPO insurgents.

We were involved countless times in ongoing operational planning as well as anticipating future events. We made support plans for each unfolding action and developed ranges of contingency plans for plausible courses of action. The level of dedication, cooperation, respect and loyalty experienced all-round was tremendous.

Everything considered, Operation Yahoo was an all-encompassing, all-systems-go operation of brigade size. The combat force of 3,000 men and 500 vehicles either gobbled up or guzzled the following: 3 150,000 litres of fuel (7 tankers per day); 126,000 sets of rations (ration packs as well as dry or wet rations); 15,000 litres of water per day (3 tankers); 1 160 spare wheels repaired (by a team of three utterly dedicated national servicemen); 36,000 rolls of toilet paper ("DD1000" in military terms) supplied.

Today, as I reflect 30 years later on those days of my life, I realise how focussed we were. I was only 27 years old at the time, with a huge responsibility. So was the responsibility of our commander and all the other officers and men deployed for operations in the northern border region. The quality of our training, dedication to the task and the level of leadership and teamwork displayed by all remains fixed in my mind as a treasured memory.

Even now my birthday is celebrated with a luke-warm beer and a cheer from close friends. I am proud and honoured to have served with 61 Mech and experienced Operation Yahoo.

The Christmas Tree Ambush at Kombat – Fighting in a Lighter Vein

Whatever my faults, no one could say of my stint at 61 Mech that I was a chairborne commander.

At the end of April we received a reliable intelligence tip-off that two SWAPO insurgents had evaded all our forces and were now comfortably entrenched with a collaborator in an informal settlement near Grootfontein itself, and Colonel Foffie Badenhorst (an intelligence operative of note in his own right), Colonel Tommie Thomasse, Captain Gerrie Hugo and I decided to capture them ourselves by laying an ambush halfway along the road between Otavi and Kombat.

Our chosen site for the ambush was one of those resting places for weary travellers that you find at intervals along the main roads of SWA/Namibia – a concrete table and four concrete stools underneath a massive maroela tree. We decided this was an eminently civilised place for an ambush, so we reconnoitred the lay of the land and deployed the ambush party, which consisted of a platoon of enthusiastic paratroopers under Major McGill Alexander. Foffie Badenhorst, in the meantime, had acquired an old brown Ford Grenada for one of his trusted informers, who had made contact with our two guests-to-be.

Like all great military plans, the one we worked up for the occasion was a simple one. The informer would entice them into the old Grenada on the understanding that he would drive them through to Windhoek to continue their work there – needless to say, a far preferable alternative to foot-slogging it – but before leaving Grootfontein they would stop at a café to buy fish and chips, and about 20:00 they would stop to eat by the roadside... at the resting place of our choice, of course.

The ambush was carefully prepared, although not in a way that conformed to any doctrinal handbook. My creative signals officer, Sean McSweeney, prepared the maroela tree as if he were TV's MacGyver setting up for a Christmas party. Pin-prick lighting was strung along its branches from carefully concealed heavy-duty electrical cable which was connected to a mobile generator chugging away far out of earshot. Badenhorst armed himself with a bright blue loudhailer and McSweeney with the light switch.

By last light the Christmas tree was ready and Mac Alexander's paratroopers were lying patiently in ambush. Nearby I was stretched out comfortably on the ground with Badenhorst, McSweeney, Alexander, and Tommie Thomasse; by now we had acquired an extra operator in the shape of Giel Reinecke, who had insisted on abandoning his logistical battles.

Eight o'clock came... and went without either the insurgents or anyone else heaving into sight – in that time and place the only people using the roads at night were the SADF and the odd SWAPO pilgrim. We sat tight. This was Africa, and we knew that African time was not necessarily the same as ours. Close to 21:00 Mac Alexander's listening post to the east of the ambush position reported hearing the droning engine of a vehicle which sounded not dissimilar to that of a Ford.

We braced up in anticipation. Sure enough, a few minutes later the Grenada appeared out of the dark and rolled to a gentle stop next to the concrete table. The informer and the two insurgents climbed out and strolled towards the table with their supper, completely relaxed.

Action time! McSweeney pressed his switch and the maroela blazed into light. The insurgents stared up at it, open-mouthed, their fish and chips forgotten. Now it was Foffie's turn. From the bush he roared an ear-splitting demand for them to surrender through his loudhailer, which was now brilliantly illuminated as well, and the paratroopers burst out of concealment, brandishing their weapons. It goes without saying that the flabbergasted insurgents offered no resistance, and when we searched the Grenada an interesting assortment of weapons, grenades, explosive devices and camouflage uniforms was found tucked into the boot.

All in all it was a most satisfactory outcome, and there was an equally satisfactory sequel. Foffie Badenhorst applied his great knowledge and turned both insurgents, who readily exchanged their rice-pattern camouflaged uniforms for SADF/SWATF "browns", and within two days were in the field, chasing their late colleagues with all signs of enthusiasm... Strange people, those SWAPO types.

I quote this tale as further proof (as any old fighting man will agree) that any war is a strange mixture of triumph, defeat, tragedy and sorrow, joy, high drama and sheer comedy. Operation Yahoo was no different from any other. When you think about it, interludes like this are as necessary as moments of sorrow; they create a balance that preserves a soldier's sanity while he is engaged in activities which cry out against the instinct of self-preservation genetically engineered into every human being.

Tsumeb and 61 Mech Mourns – We Shall Remember Them

The sorrow was very real as we counted the cost in dead and wounded of Operation Yahoo, not only ours but that of the entire local community. I have written about this in Chapter 7, but I would like to add one last recollection. Daan van der Westhuizen's death deprived his little 11-year-old daughter, Riana, of her father, but not of her memories – of Daan himself, and equally of her valiant mother, Tannie Pompie, sitting cigarette in hand in her kitchen at Koedoesvlei, manning the radios in spite of her great grief. Tannie Pompie is gone now, too, but as with Daan, her memory lives on.

On 16 June 2007, almost 25 years after that terrible morning when I learned of Daan's death, I made contact with Riana, who was now 36 and living in Swakopmund, to renew that old but cherished bond of friendship, born of both love and tragedy.

As a postscript: I have a friend named Deon Lamprecht, who was a soldier in 61 Mech in 1982 and 1983 and is now a reporter for Beeld, the well-known newspaper. A few days before writing this I received an e-mail from him which read as follows:

I went to visit Riana van der Westhuizen in Swakopmund a few days ago. It was for a story I am writing about the border war... She showed me the military medals of her father and mother. The Honoris Crux Decoration for bravery as well – the citation you had written for her father in April 1982. She was proud of all of this. She then showed me a gold lighter engraved with the words "Yahoo 1982", the gold lighter you had given her when Operation Yahoo ended in May 1982.

I was moved and grateful when I read that e-mail. I had completely forgotten about that lighter. But there it was still after all those years as a constant reminder of a defining moment in my life and hers.

Epilogue – A Perspective of Life

On 24 May 1982 Sector 30 issued a communiqué summarising the security situation to the communities of the Death Triangle. The communiqué emphasised that SWAPO was not finished yet, that a few dangerous stragglers might well be lurking in the region, disguised as ordinary civilians, that in a year's time the infiltrators might well return once more to deal with unfinished business.

The following day Operation Yahoo was officially closed down and we went back to Omuthiya – Operation Meebos was already showing the first signs of its appearance in July. That will be another one of my stories.[15] Yahoo's debriefing at HQ Sector 30 during late May 1982 was an interesting exercise. Among other things it laid down a "must" which made me want to cry "Eureka!" – the plan for Operation Awake needed to be urgently reviewed. The comprehensive debriefing document (Secret/Operation Yahoo/Sector 30/305/3/1 dated 11 June 1982) was signed, sealed and handed out; I still have mine, Copy Number 12. We ended with a minute of silence to remember our fallen; but my minute remains in place, even now. I think it is only fair that I credit SWAPO for the sheer guts, determination and tenacity its men showed in their annual raids into the Death Triangle. They kept us feverishly busy for a while in spite of our numerical and technological superiority. I might add that for us it was also a learning experience in which we picked up new tricks of the counterinsurgency trade.

I would summarise our seven most important keys to success as follows, considering that our fighting mix and creative leadership made all the difference:

- Maximising the operational employment of trackers fairly mixed with the optimisation of local knowledge of terrain, own forces and enemy – this is about sixth sense and hunting foxes with hounds.
- Outstanding communications as one of the main force-multiplying dimensions – this is not only about hi-tech communication systems, but about agreeable dialogue between us and our enemy captives.
- Accurate tactical intelligence, real-time and near-real-time, so that one could strike while the iron was hot. Go all out for information superiority, while denying it to the enemy. This mix led to quality decision-making and precision engagement.
- Optimal utilisation of the terrain and environmental conditions – exploiting the neutral factor, no more, no less.
- Fool-proof follow-up systems to find, fix and strike the foe at critical moments, again and again and again, with overwhelming air and ground assets – swift and sweet, one after the next, a mini-blitzkrieg by numbers.
- The need to be surprisingly different in finding creative solutions and having some fun in the fighting process – jackal operations to out-jackal the jackals, with allowances made for some exuberance to be liberally spread amongst own forces – the psychological is to the physical as three is to one.

In the end, who won the fight in the Death Triangle? And before you answer that question, remember that more than one dimension has to be considered. At one level the outcome must be judged by the respective numbers of dead and wounded; on another by the immense propaganda engendered by our enemies' deaths for a political effect.

At the end of the Border War our erstwhile enemy won the majority of seats in the new

15 See Chapter 14.

Namibian parliament, a not unexpected outcome, since this is Africa, and the Ovambos – virtually SWAPO's exclusive power base – form the largest ethnic group in the country.

Some of our people who fought there believe it means we lost the Border War. But it is not as simple as that. The SADF was not there to ensure that one or other party or movement got into power. From beginning to end it was an enabler, no more and no less, whose laid-down task was to ensure the public order so that all Namibians could work out their constitutional future for themselves. The military did just that, and then, its job done, marched back to its barracks.

As a result the first election was a free and fair one that propelled Namibia into the family of democratic nations. There was no forcible communist-backed takeover, marred by widespread death and destruction. The adjacent nations of Botswana, Zambia and South Africa did not face future problems with an unstable and belligerent neighbouring dictatorship. Because the Soviet Union had collapsed, partly through our efforts, there would be no exporting of revolution. The new Namibia started its existence with everything running in its favour, rather than as a ruined basket case.

SWAPO had to work damn hard for what it finally got. So did we. But hard work never harmed anyone in the long run.

So think twice before making any snap judgements about who won and who lost. The peace that descended on Southern Africa at the end of the Border War was a living one, not the peace of the dead. That makes our region a little different from some others in Africa.

In October 2010, three decades after Operation Yahoo, I visited Tsumeb again during a battlefield tour of Namibia and southern Angola by a few veterans of 61 Mech and 32 Battalion.

The mining town was at peace with itself, drenched in the scent of its jacarandas and bougainvilleas. Many black and white people in Namibia greeted us with friendliness in Afrikaans, which was first taken across the Orange River by "Oorlams" Hottentots at the beginning of the 19th Century and remains a lingua franca which is widely spoken by all races.

I introduced my two good friends, Louis Bothma, the renowned military writer, and Camille Burger to Alex Britz, my friend from those war years, who came to greet us when we arrived for our stay-over at Tsumeb. We shared a few Windhoek beers, shed a few tears and laughed a little as we talked about the old days. As we reminisced the Southern African sun went down, wearing its usual coat of many colours, over the rugged, densely bushed mountains west of Tsumeb at which we had fired our artillery in 1982 during that successful jackal operation. Now we sat here comfortably around a smouldering fire on old army camp chairs, cloaked in the never-forgotten companionship that had arisen between men at war.

Ockert Britz – once the town clerk of Tsumeb, once a part-time major of the Etosha Area Force Unit, a man who had lived through Operation Carrot and Yahoo with us – said thoughtfully: "61 Mech was good for us, our town thrived in those days... We learned a lot during the war... and afterwards we made peace and friends... black and white... Namibia is the best country in the world to live in!"

Memories came rushing back as I wrote the story of these two operations that I shall never forget! It was one of the most challenging and exciting parts of my life and military career. The military and civilian people who lived and died during that period touched my soul.

I reflected that the many years of bitterness and fighting had resulted in the creation of real peace in our part of the world. Seen from that perspective, it was clear to me that operations such as Carrot and Yahoo had done their bit in the long process of bringing peace to everybody. But the foundation of that peace was the ordinary people of the Death Triangle, who had left me with a lasting impression of hopefulness and filled me with infinite optimism for Africa.

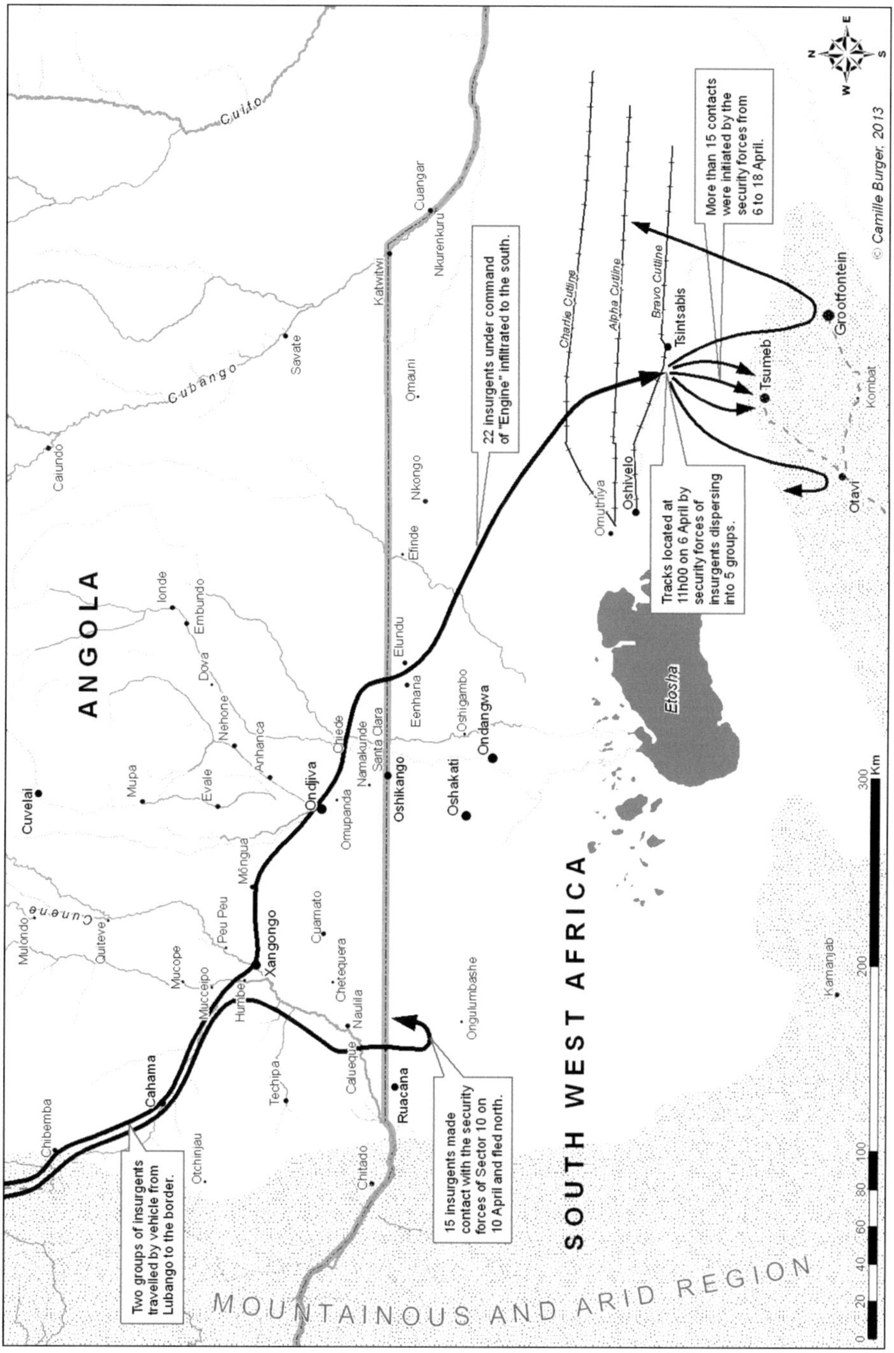

Map 7: Operation Carrot, April 1981

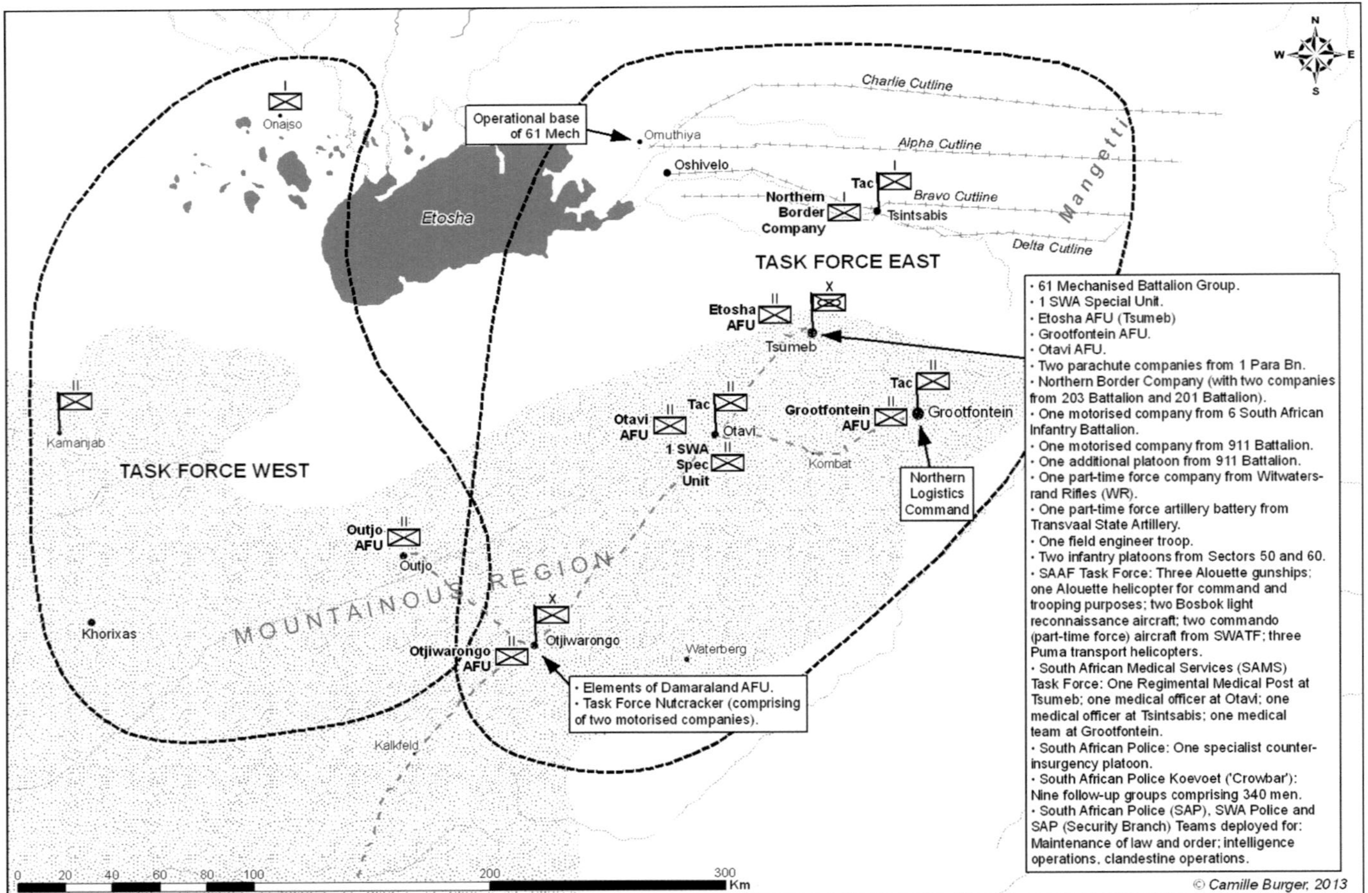

Map 8: Operation Yahoo, April to May 1982 – Deployment of Own Forces

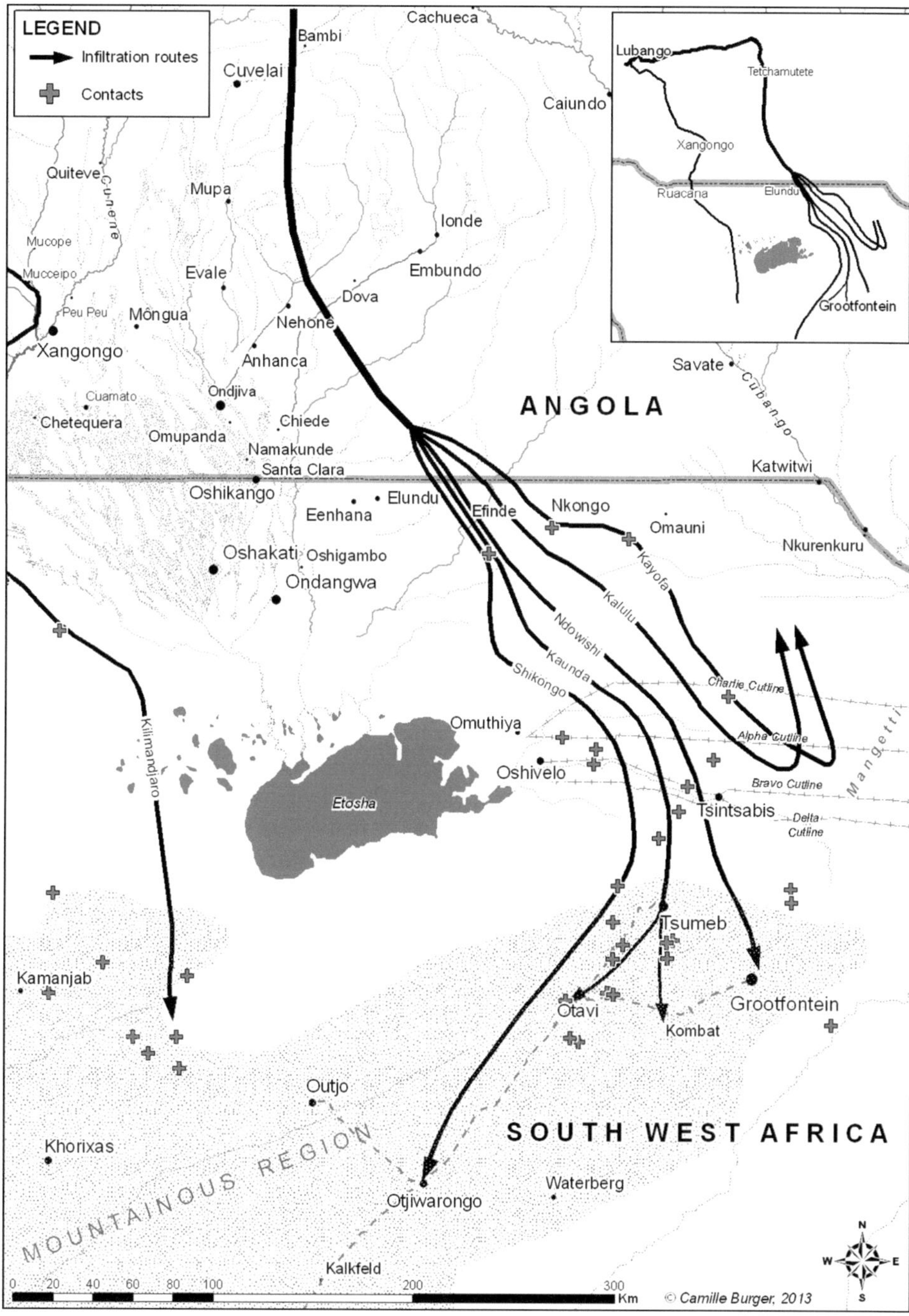

Map 9: Operation Yahoo, April to May 1982 – Enemy Infiltrations and Contacts

12

Battles Of Encirclement

Operation Protea

We should strike only when we are positively sure that the enemy's situation, the terrain, the people and other conditions are overall favourable to us and unfavourable to the enemy ... There will always be opportunities and we should not rashly seek battle.
Mao Tse-tung

Operation Protea In A Nutshell – The Enemy Had A Surprise Coming

Operation Protea took place in August 1981, but it is still as clear in my mind as it was 30 years ago. The SADF was about to launch its first significant conventional cross-border strike into southern Angola against FAPLA since Operation Savannah in 1975. 24 August was appointed D-Day for attacking the enemy's conventional fighting core in southern Angola, and it would be one of the largest mechanised operations undertaken by South Africa since World War II. The main question was this: did FAPLA have what it would take to defend itself and its installations?

Operation Protea was designed as a surprise offensive, executed with lightning speed and maximum violence, whose aim was to achieve victory in a minimum of time. A characteristic of mobile warfare throughout history has always been and always will be the integration of effort and violent execution by concentrated and closely coordinated ground (and latterly air) forces, normally conducted with a fair measure of mobility and what I call "élan audacity". This was done during Protea. No wonder that afterwards it was studied as a military classic by command and staff courses in other parts of the world.

It was my privilege to participate between 23 August and 2 September 1981 in this conventional operation as the commander of 61 Mechanised Battalion Group. Our fighting unit formed part of a brigade-sized conventional formation designated Task Force Alpha. Simultaneously, another task force, named Bravo and orientated more towards counterinsurgency duties, struck at selected SWAPO targets in the surrounding area.

With a tip of the hat to Sun Tzu's wisdom, let us start by reviewing what we would have to face.

Enemy and Terrain – Know the Enemy or Succumb in Battle

Overview of the General Enemy Situation – Steady Build-Up as the Plot Thickens

In 1981 there was no way that SWAPO was giving up the fight for SWA/Namibia in spite of the havoc wreaked by recent SADF operations such as Reindeer in May 1978 and Sceptic in June 1980. The centre of gravity for its political-military struggle remained Ovamboland, its main ethnic powerbase and the source of almost all its recruits (and a fair number of ours, incidentally).

The insurgents continued to strike relentlessly into northern SWA/Namibia from relatively safe lairs located inside southern Angola, where they could rely on the protection and support of FAPLA, some Russian advisors and a large number of Cubans. All these supporters now inadvertently became the enemies of the SADF; the South African position was that it had no quarrel with FAPLA or anyone else, except if they got in the way when it wanted to get to grips with SWAPO. This became more and more common as SWAPO was ever more firmly drawn into the FAPLA camp, to the point where some insurgent units training in Angola were used in Luanda's campaign against Dr. Jonas Savimbi's UNITA.

The result was that the South African and SWA/Namibian security forces began crossing swords regularly with FAPLA's conventional units during their pre-emptive external operations into Angola. Immense integrated enemy forces and logistic support were deployed at staging points such as Cahama, Xangongo and Ondjiva. The military situation had become untenable, according to the SADF's threat assessment, and was viewed as being strategically more serious than could be tolerated.

This posed a clear and present danger as far as a conventional military threat to the region was concerned; in addition, FAPLA's complex of air defence systems equally and consistently posed a real threat to ongoing air operations inside southern Angola by the South African Air Force. This being the case, a surgical incision by the SADF was therefore required to dismember FAPLA's military corpus.

And so an extensive military operation was conceived in intense secrecy in Pretoria and Windhoek. By August 1981 two brigade-sized defensive strongholds at Xangongo and Ondjiva were marked for destruction by Task Force Alpha; simultaneously, Task Force Bravo would take on a number of carefully selected SWAPO targets to the north of Ondjiva.

Conventional Foe for Operation Protea – FAPLA was Task Force Alpha's Enemy

FAPLA's defensive strongholds at Xangongo and Ondjiva lay approximately 60 km north of the SWA/Namibian-Angolan border – too close for comfort in the eyes of the SADF. FAPLA's regional headquarters for the Cunene Province, controlling the extensive defences in the region, was located at Lubango (previously known as Sá da Bandeira). It was protected by a network of air defence screens which were carefully linked with modern Soviet radar systems, and each defensive layout was set up in depth, which clearly indicated that Russian planning and doctrine had guided their design.

At Xangongo and Ondjiva there were layers of defensive echelons, interlocked with communication trenches and reinforced concrete bunkers, and protected by all-inclusive minefields. A large number of tanks, anti-tank guns and artillery pieces were deliberately positioned throughout the respective defensive localities. The defences generally faced southwards, the direction from which FAPLA naïvely believed any South African onslaught would come; in fact, they played into the hands of the South Africans' mobile warfare philosophy, since it made them extremely vulnerable to attacks from alternative directions.

The entire conventional enemy strength in the Cunene Province amounted to slightly more than a full Russian type division. A careful analysis was made of these deployments, both those designated as actual targets and those which might pose a danger of intervention, and intelligence sources indicated that the following main deployments were to be found in the designated target area:

- FAPLA's 19th Brigade defended Xangongo and the bridge over the Cunene River. The bridge became a key strategic target because it carried the main Cahama-

Ondjiva highway over the river and was therefore of critical importance to both the South Africans and FAPLA. It was appreciated that a component of the enemy force might be situated at Humbe, across the river west of Xangongo, and that a tactical group of the Cahama brigade might be deployed at the Peu Peu base near Xangongo as a local mobile reserve. Intelligence indicated that about 500 SWAPO insurgents were deployed in the vicinity of Xangongo, and that another 500 semi-regular fighters were integrated with the FAPLA regular forces.

19 Brigade was to be taken in a pincer manoeuvre by the full might of Task Force Alpha and the SAAF on D-Day. Battle Group 10 (basically 61 Mech with some add-ons) would execute a flanking movement west of the Cunene. The remainder of the task force was to storm the eastern approaches. Just how well the South African planners had read their opponents' minds can be seen from the fact that before the shooting broke out on the morning of D-Day FAPLA's Russian military advisors and their families at Xangongo were enjoying a pleasant breakfast, completely unaware of the attackers approaching from east and west (there was no such surprise at Ondjiva, however – in actual fact they were given prior warning by a SAAF leaflet drop).

- FAPLA's 21st Brigade lurked at Cahama. This force served as the mobile reserve for the region. It was also suspected that a reinforced SWAPO battalion could be found at Cahama, or alternatively might be hidden in the bushveld somewhere between Cahama and Xangongo. The intelligence picture on 21 Brigade was not entirely clear, and neither was the situation with regard to enemy movements or positions between Cahama and Xangongo. It was assumed, however, that FAPLA would push defensive outposts further southeastwards and southwards from Lubango to secure Cahama's integrity if the need arose.

  What happened to 21 Brigade would depend on what it was told to do while Xangongo was being assaulted from the west and east. Thus it was not a primary target, but had to be prevented from interfering with the attack on Xangongo. The task of making sure that it stayed put in Cahama – or beating it off if it did not – was assigned to 61 Mech, the only available fully conventional fighting unit in SWA/Namibia.

- FAPLA's 11th Brigade was deployed at Ondjiva, tasked with defending the town and its airfield, as well as the SWAPO district headquarters located there. Task Force Alpha's Battle Groups 20 and 30, and Combat Team Mamba were to tackle Ondjiva as soon as Xangongo had been taken (as it transpired, taking Ondjiva proved to be more difficult than anticipated, and had to be supported soon after the attack commenced on D+3 by Combat Team 2 of Battle Group 10, otherwise 61 Mech's Bravo Company under Captain Koos Liebenberg).

  There was also a strong FAPLA outpost at Môngua, midway between Xangongo and Ondjiva, which was not discovered till after the attack on Xangongo had started. Combat Team Mamba took out this juicy target of opportunity on D+1.

Revolutionary Foe for Operation Protea – SWAPO was Task Force Bravo's Enemy

Task Force Alpha's primary concern was FAPLA, but Task Force Bravo's was SWAPO, pure and simple. Potential enemy targets were dispersed throughout the central part of southern Angola to the north and northeast of Ondjiva. Military objectives were presented as command and control structures and a few carefully selected operational bases. The enormous designated target area stretched north of a notional line , called the "Tango Line", which linked Evale, Dova and Ionde, and therefore included Mupa, Cuvelai and Techamutete.

Terrain as the Neutral Factor – Encircle and Annihilate

The SADF made intelligent use of the terrain to encircle and annihilate the enemy in accordance with the precepts I described in Chapter 5, and in assessing how this was done it should not be forgotten that FAPLA favoured positional warfare, while the South Africans concentrated on manoeuvre tactics.

The plan the SADF devised worked supremely well, and the FAPLA brigades at Xangongo and Ondjiva were slaughtered, even though they had the advantage of fighting on terrain of their own choosing, as they made futile attempts to defend their outflanked positions. Their routes of escape were completely cut off as the South Africans and their war machines moved into place in the vast bush-covered manoeuvre areas on either side of the Cunene River and attacked out of the darkness in the east and west, the directions from which they had been least expected.

The river was used to isolate the target zone, effectively dividing the west from the east. This meant that the enemy's two main static defence zones, bereft of mutual support, could be taken in quick succession. At Cahama the enemy mobile reserve was shocked into immobility, and for more than 10 nights and days they remained inactive while the South Africans systematically reduced Xangongo, then Môngua and finally Ondjiva. In fact, they did not move even after Protea was over.

Stratification for Operation Protea – Ends, Ways and Means

Higher Stratagems and Force Structures

By July 1981 the campaign strategy for Operation Protea had been neatly packaged by Major General Charles Lloyd, General Officer Commanding South West Africa Territorial Force, at HQ Bastion in Windhoek. He was an outstanding commanding general, and I had immense regard for his ability in the fields of high command and strategic planning. Protea formed part of his stratification for the war in the Western Sub-Theatre – simply stated, the military plans which shaped the ends, ways and means of defeating the foe. His strategy was aligned with the SADF's higher intention, which was to incapacitate SWAPO's military forces in southern Angola.

Operation Protea was about going straight for the jugular. The strongly defended bridge at Xangongo over the Cunene River, which was both vital to the operation and vulnerable to surprise attack, was selected as the point of main effort. Ondjiva, 88 km to the southeast, was the secondary military objective and was to be attacked a few hours later.

As I have said, Cahama was not on Operation Protea's agenda as an objective, although attacks on other targets such as Cuvelai in the northeast might be undertaken, depending on the circumstances – a decision would be taken after the fall of Xangongo and Ondjiva, because the strategic outcome that the South Africans sought was the ability to influence and dominate the area in southern Angola, soon to be referred to as the "Area-In-Dispute", which SWAPO used for administration and the transit of infiltrators.

At the higher tactical level Protea was commanded by Brigadier Rudolph "Witkop"

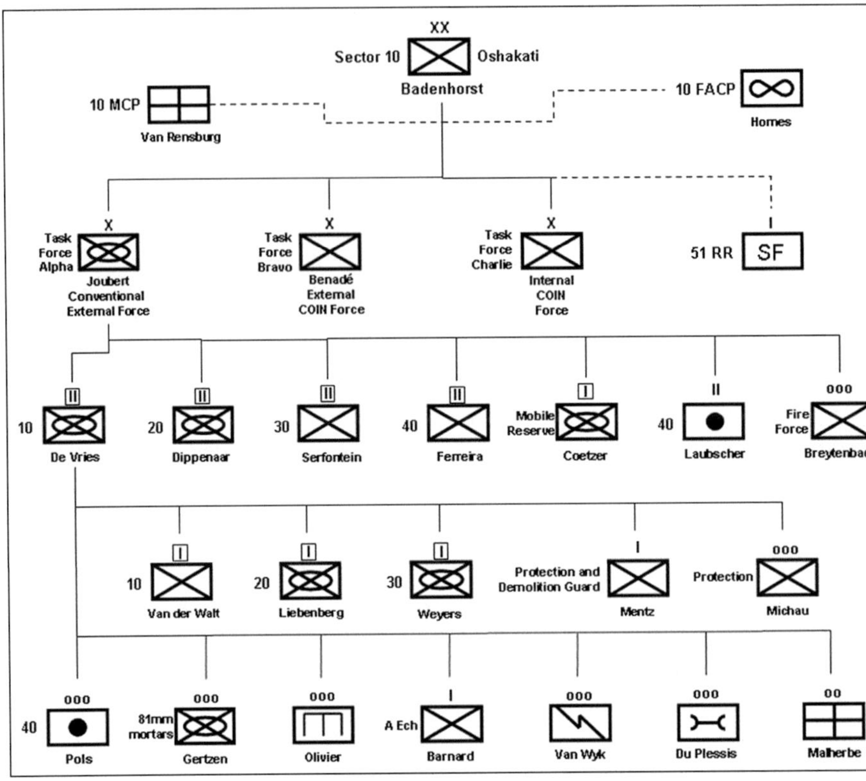

Figure 14: Task Organisation for Operation Protea, 1981

("Blondie") Badenhorst, OC Sector 10, from his HQ at Oshakati. He was well-suited in terms of both experience and place. A veteran of the border war, he was responsible for the ongoing internal counterinsurgency war in Ovamboland, the centre of gravity for both sides in this particular conflict. Thanks to Protea, the hinterland of Angola just north of the international border was destined to become a long sought-after killing zone, and thereby logically extended deliberate operations deeper into southern Angola.

To achieve this Badenhorst structured Operation Protea's combat force into three separate but operationally interdependent brigade-sized tactical groupings. The force arrangement readily facilitated unified command and control, the appropriate delineation of operational responsibility, operational interdependency and the sound management of intelligence (See Figure 14).

- Task Force Alpha was the main force marked for external mobile conventional operations against targets held by the combined forces of FAPLA and SWAPO at Xangongo and Ondjiva.
- Task Force Bravo, on the other hand, was appropriately structured to conduct an external search-and-destroy mission against SWAPO and its bases beyond Ondjiva.
- A third task force was designated Task Force Charlie and constituted the internal counterinsurgency units already operationally active inside Sector 10. The conduct of Task Force Charlie was of less significance for Protea and will therefore not be

further discussed.

51 Reconnaissance Regiment (and elements of 52) formed an integral component of the force. So did the task elements of the South African Air Force and South African Medical Services which had been provided to support Protea. Colonel Ollie Holmes commanded 10 Forward Air Force Command Post (10 FACP) and Major Rinus van Rensburg the medical contingent. For Protea the SAAF mustered an impressive array of ground support assets, operating either from Air Force Base Waterkloof at Pretoria or from forward airfields such as Ondangwa or Grootfontein: 12 Mirage F1AZs; eight Mirage F1CZs; seven Mirage IIICZs; six Mirage IIID2Zs; 16 Mk IIs; five Buccaneer strike bombers; and five Canberra light bombers.

At that time our combat aircraft were still fortunate enough to reign supreme and uncontested in the skies over southern Angola. On the other hand, southern Angola had become one of the most hostile air environments in the world at the time, able to mount substantial anti-aircraft fire from the ground, which made our air operations anything but a pushover.

In addition to the fighter jets a substantial number of transport and light reconnaissance aircraft were deployed, as well as Alouette and Puma helicopters, and a few unmanned aerial vehicles were quietly settling down in-theatre as well. The statistics tell the story of the SAAF's amazing work during Operation Protea, ranging from offensive air missions to transportation and evacuation duties. In just 11 days more than 1 112 individual sorties were flown from Grootfontein and Ondangwa; 333 tons of bombs were dropped and 1 774 rockets and 18 AS-30 missiles were fired.

In spite of the anti-aircraft fire, SAAF air losses were small: a Mirage 111 CZ was damaged by an SA-7 missile, but returned to base and landed safely; and near Môngua an Alouette was shot down on 25 August and the crew – Lieutenant Johannes Gysbertus Roos and Sergeant Clifton Stacey – killed.

Mission and Organisation of Task Force Alpha for Encirclement and Annihilation

As the conventional strike force, Task Force Alpha was made up of a mobile headquarters, four battle groups and a mobile reserve. The force commander was Colonel A.J.M. ("Joep") Joubert, an accomplished operational commander who understood mechanised warfare. His second-in-command was Commandant Tobie van Schalkwyk, while that astute gunner, Commandant J.H. ("Koos") Laubscher, commanded the artillery. The other senior commanders were:[1]

- Battle Group 10: Commandant Roland de Vries.
- Battle Group 20: Commandant Johann Dippenaar.
- Battle Group 30: Commandant Chris Serfontein.
- Battle Group 40: Commandant Deon Ferreira.
- Task Force Mobile Reserve (Combat Team Mamba): Commandant Johan Coetzer.

Battle Groups 10 and 20 were mechanised and 30 and 40 motorised infantry. 61 Mech (Battle Group 10) and 32 Battalion (Battle Group 40) were first-line combat units, permanently structured and deployed in northern SWA/Namibia at the time, and formed core components of the task force. Battle Groups 20 and 30, however, were temporary composite units which had been formed for the operation and were manned by subunits

1 Refer to Appendix A to appraise the detail of the force structures and its groupings.

drafted from training establishments located in South Africa, and were disbanded again after the operation.

Combat Team Mamba was also a composite unit, but of a slightly different kind – its infantry company and anti-tank platoon were both loaned from 61 Mech and were commanded by Captain Hannes van der Merwe and national service Lieutenant Chris Walls respectively, and were therefore thoroughly imbued with the mechanised mindset and used to working together.

The planning made provision for the task forces to change their composition at different stages of the operation. Thus, when Xangongo had fallen, Battle Group 40 would come under command of Task Force Bravo, as would Battle Group 30 after the capture of Ondjiva. After Ondjiva, too, Combat Team Mamba's mechanised company and anti-tank platoon would return to 61 Mech, which was still tasked with safeguarding Protea's western flank.

Mission and Organisation of Task Force Bravo – to Search and Destroy

The OC Task Force Bravo was Colonel Vos Benade, an accomplished infantry officer who had commanded a battalion on the border as long ago as 1977 and was well-versed in counterinsurgency warfare. The drastic depletion of SWAPO personnel strength and the destruction of its infrastructure in his target zone was high on Benade's agenda, and his task force was structured for counterinsurgency operations.

For the first part of the operation Bravo consisted of Battle Group 50 – basically 201 (Bushman) Battalion under the experienced Commandant Frans Botes – and Battle Group 60 under command of the even more experienced Commandant James Hills. Each unit comprised four motorised infantry companies and an 81 mm mortar platoon. The task force reserve was made up of two companies of paratroopers, a pathfinder platoon from 44 Parachute Brigade and Special Forces teams from 52 Reconnaissance Regiment.

Foremost Operational Phases, Guidelines and Operational Outcomes

The hunting season would open with the initial attack on Xangongo on D-Day (24 August); the assault force would withdraw to SWA/Namibia again when Xangongo and Ondjiva had been taken and the respective target zones to the north pacified. Each task force and its respective battle groups would determine its own designs for battle within the overall operational framework, and these plans would be implemented in eight logical operational phases:

- Phase 1: Deployment of cut-off forces inside southern Angola and preparatory operations by the SAAF and Special Forces.
- Phase 2 (D-1 – 23 August): SAAF strikes on FAPLA air defences and radar installations deployed at Cahama and Chibemba.
- Phase 3 (D-Day – 24 August): The main assault, the simultaneous capture of Xangongo, Peu Peu and Humbe by Task Force Alpha. This would include preparing the Cunene River bridge at Xangongo for demolition. At the same time measures would be taken to prevent any intervention from the FAPLA force at Cahama, then and later, so that Xangongo could be defended. Thus the western flank would be protected so that Task Force Alpha and Task Force Bravo could proceed with the operation without fear of interruption.
- Phase 4 (D+3–27 August): The capture of Ondjiva by Task Force Alpha, which

would then hold it until D+14, the date initially scheduled for the withdrawal of the strike force to SWA/Namibia.

- Phase 5: External counterinsurgency operations against SWAPO by Task Force Bravo during Phases 3 and 4 of the operation until the completion of the operation on D+14.
- Phase 6: Deep operations of a classified strategic nature, to be performed in the rear areas of the enemy. One of the selected targets included an important bridge far to the enemy's rear which was to be destroyed by Special Forces (this was later called off – probably as a result of changing imperatives at the political level).
- Phase 7: Withdrawal of the strike force to SWA/Namibia on D+14 (as it turned out, Protea was successfully completed by 1 September – D+8).

The guidelines received for our planning made it clear that Protea was limited to the bare military necessities, and we commanders adhered to these operational restrictions to the letter, right down to the level of our individual soldiers.

The guidelines laid down that striking at FAPLA was a go, as far as it was operationally warranted; that during the fighting the civilian population and its property was to be spared as far as possible (all churches and hospitals in Angola were specifically marked on our maps as places not to be harmed); victory would depend on capturing the maximum amount of enemy equipment, and as many enemy leaders and foreign military advisors as possible – getting hold of a few Russians in the process would be nice; careful planning and execution of security, surprise and deception as essential determinants for overall operational success; and as always, care was to be taken to incur a minimum of own casualties.

The immediate short-term operational outcome of Protea was a devastating defeat for the enemy. However, we did not know then that in due course the conflict would escalate to a massive conventional battle in southern Angola from August 1987 onwards.[2] It was a classic example of the proverbial law of unintended consequences, with an immediate tactical venture giving rise to unforeseeable medium to long-term strategic outcomes.

Just a short digression about Protea's operational outcomes before we delve into the preparation for the battle itself:

- Operation Protea left the enemy aghast. The Russian military advisors and their families abandoned Xangongo in such haste that we found their breakfasts lying untouched on dining room tables; clothes were still flapping in the wind on washing lines, while FAPLA and MPLA[3] flags had been left hanging limply on flagpoles. Numerous enemy soldiers lay dead among the trenches, and wrecked vehicles lay smouldering in the streets and fields of Xangongo and Ondjiva. Many defensive positions had simply been abandoned without any pretence at holding them. It was a total victory for the South Africans – and, needless to say, it was followed by an immense political hue and cry from the Angolans and much of the rest of the world.
- The civilian population we encountered stared wide-eyed and bewildered at the unknown belligerent forces rumbling by in their war machines through the strange emptiness left in Xangongo and Ondjiva; the desolation and destruction left behind were sad to see.
- Protea's resounding success drove FAPLA and the Cuban forces far away from

2 Refer to Chapters 15 and 16.

3 Popular Movement for the Liberation of Angola

this vital "shallow area", the operational zone immediately north of the Angolan-SWA/Namibian border, to Cahama in the west, Cuvelai, Techamutette and Cassinga in the north, Menongue in the northeast and Caiundo in the east. The "Area-In-Dispute", as it was soon to be nicknamed, became a hunting ground in which our counterinsurgency forces could operate freely against SWAPO without interference from FAPLA.[4]

- Only 10 South African soldiers were killed during Protea, and 58 wounded. These low (but deeply regretted all the same) personnel losses stood in stark contrast to those of the other side – more than 1,000 dead, and a large number wounded and captured (calculating or estimating the total number enemy wounded with any sort of accuracy was, of course, totally impossible).
- More than 4,000 tons of war material and equipment were captured, including a large number of enemy T-34 tanks, armoured cars, troop-carriers and logistic vehicles, multiple rocket launchers, artillery pieces and anti-aircraft guns, supplies of ammunition, food and fuel, and a trove of sensitive documents. The enemy's military hardware, I may add, was mainly of Russian origin.

Operation Protea was therefore limited warfare in the true sense – a bloody sequence of movement, surprise, encirclement, annihilation and withdrawal. The main operational guideline irrevocably stated "in and out within 14 days". In actual fact, as I noted earlier, the operation lasted only 11 days.

Task Force Alpha Mobilises at Oshivelo and Omuthiya

Concentration of Task Force Alpha at Oshivelo and Omuthiya

By 3 August Task Force Alpha started mobilising and its units began to move to their allotted staging areas between Oshivelo and Omuthiya, but when the countdown began on D-21, 61 Mech was already deployed at Omuthiya and had its various combat groupings planning, training and preparing in conditions of utmost secrecy.

The pace was intensive, and almost inevitably there were heartrending incidents of loss. Some of our artillerymen were involved in a serious accident with a Buffel MPV near Oshivelo, and precious lives were lost, and a serious accident during a fire-and-movement exercise resulted in a number of our soldiers being killed or wounded. People who have not served in the military do not always understand that for a soldier, death is a constant companion even in times of peace or preparation for war, because the tools of his trade are lethal ones, so that when accidents happen – as they sometimes do in spite of all precautions – the results can be much more devastating than would have been the case in the civilian world.

During the mobilisation phase, Northern Logistic Command played a vital but mostly unsung role. The NLC was located at Grootfontein, about 162 km south of Oshivelo, a huge integrated general support base with an extensive airfield of its own. The NLC was commanded by Colonel Willem Enslin, and the SAAF component by Colonel "Pottie" Potgieter of the SAAF. The base also served as a transit camp where incoming units and individual soldiers were received, in-processed and dispatched to the front in the SAAFs Hercules C-130 and Transall C-160 transports.

Protea rapidly gathered momentum as the tempo of preparation for battle increased –

4 See Map 5.

the force needed to be declared combat and mission ready by 22 August 1981 (D-2), and the clock was ticking.

Setting the Scene for the Coming Battle, and Organising the Force

This part of my story tells of certain features about the gathering of the fighting clans for Operation Protea (the organisation of the two task forces is explained in Appendix A, including the force composition of 61 Mech, otherwise known as Battle Group 10).

On 4 August the senior command and staff course of the army arrived from Pretoria, and about 30 of its students and instructors were appointed to various senior positions in the combat groupings; this was one of the methods the Army used to expose its future commanders and senior staff officers to combat to gain operational command experience of the kind that cannot be taught in classrooms.

The course's chief instructor, Commandant Johan Coetzer, was made commander of Combat Team Mamba, the mobile reserve, and several students ended up in key positions at 61 Mech. Commandant Epp van Lill became my senior operations officer, Commandant Joe Aveling my intelligence officer and Major Dawid Mentz the commander of the protection company which was to perform essential garrison duties at Xangongo, which would include guarding the bridge after it had been prepared for demolition. I also acquired a guest of sorts – the experienced Colonel P. P. Robberts from the Office of the Inspector General of the Army, who was to record the operational lessons learned.

On the same day a paratrooper company from 1 Parachute Battalion at Bloemfontein arrived at Omuthiya under command of the charismatic and tactically astute Captain Pale van der Walt. I found the paratroopers lounging casually under some trees after travelling from Grootfontein in three Magirus Deutz cargo trucks. They were a welcome sight. As excellent as my men were, we were going to play on what might be a very sticky wicket, and South African paratroopers were superb fighting soldiers, tops at their job and brimming with *esprit de corps* (OK, as an old paratrooper I might be considered prejudiced, but our "parabats" had already proved over and over that they were second to none, and would do so again later in the year, when the same company joined us for Operation Daisy).

At the call of a general one should not falter, and so at 14:00 on 5 August I and my subunit commanders presented ourselves at Operet, the Oshivelo airfield, to join the other senior leaders of the task force for a briefing by General Lloyd. In his characteristic blunt, uncompromising style he told us that the force build-up was due to the combined threat posed by FAPLA and SWAPO on the other side of the border. The pep talk also served as a morale booster and an aid to improve force cohesion. That same evening at Omuthiya my subunit commanders passed General Lloyd's message on to our troops. Now the scene was set, and the level of anticipation rose noticeably.

On Thursday, 6 August, Lieutenant H.P. ("Grobbies") Grobler of Charlie Squadron and three of our Ratel-90 armoured car troops (12 Ratels in all) and their support sections were detached to Battle Group 20 (incidentally, two of Grobler's troop commanders were the remarkable Second Lieutenant Johan Grové and Candidate Officer Andries ("Doibie") Helm from 2 Special Service Battalion, Zeerust, who were soon to be decorated with the Honoris Crux after knocking out several FAPLA tanks during the fighting at Xangongo and Ondjiva). In their place 61 Mech would receive fresh armoured car troops equipped with eight Eland-90s from 2 Special Service Battalion.

This decree from Windhoek was aimed at providing Battle Group 20 with a more balanced anti-armour component for its assault east of the Cunene. While I could appreciate the need, I was furious at this untimely decision to dismember my tightly knit and intensively trained armoured squadron virtually on the eve of D-Day, and so was Major Joe Weyers, Charlie Squadron's commander. But there was nothing to be done about it, and when the newcomers arrived from Zeerust we made sure that they were warmly welcomed and immediately imbued with the 61 Mech spirit before plunging them into Charlie Squadron's force preparation process.

What worried us was not the quality of the troops but the Eland-90s with which they were equipped. We ogled the "Noddies" with frank trepidation. The French-designed Elands, though heavily modified for African conditions, were notorious for leaving their users in the lurch at inopportune moments, and, being four-wheelers, were far less mobile off-road than the Ratel-90 – a serious problem, considering the amount of bundu-bashing that was part of our style. The fact was that the Ratel with its amazing combat potential and home comforts, so to speak, had thoroughly spoilt us.

On 10 August the Elands had their baptism of fire north of Omuthiya, and our fears were realised. The training had to be adjusted to accommodate the four-wheelers' limited mobility, and major technical problems soon surfaced, with more than half the Elands breaking down on the exercises at one time or another. Sergeant-major Duppie du Plessis and his tiffies of the light workshop troop ramped up their already frenetic work schedule, however, and by Monday, 17 August, our small herd of Elands had had their problems sorted out. Charlie Squadron was smiling again. We're almost back to combat-readiness again in spite of Windhoek's best efforts, I thought with grim satisfaction.

Then, to my horror, I received two more unasked-for additions, and distinctly unwelcome ones into the bargain – a pair of bright yellow road-graders driven by sappers from the Engineer Corps. I couldn't believe it. Here I was scheduled to embark on a swift, top secret dark-of-the-night dash into hostile territory, and Windhoek had decided in its wisdom to encumber me with these lumbering monsters, which were not only highly visible but arrived without any spares or enough spare wheels.

It turned out that some brainless staff officer further up the food chain had come up with the idea of attaching the graders for the purpose (so I was told from on high) of burying the as yet unkilled FAPLA dead in their own trenches, come D+1! I was staggered. But I was also stuck with the graders. I wasted no time in palming them off on the hapless Major Dawid Mentz, the designated Xangongo garrison commander, and fell to thinking unhappy thoughts about how the hell we were we going to bundu-bash through the dense bush from Ruacana and across the Caculuvar River to Humbe and Xangongo with these unwanted appendages dragging us down. Well, suffice to say that eventually we did it, flat wheels and all. But I would still like to meet that staff officer some day!

Disposition of 61 Mech as Battle Group 10 for Operation Protea

This telling is not a comprehensive account of Operation Protea, since it concentrates on the conventional side of the operation, conducted by Task Force Alpha, and the role 61 Mech played. Protea was a milestone for the unit as far as its real role was concerned. In April 1981 we had successfully carried out Operation Carrot in the Death Triangle, but Carrot had been a counterinsurgency action.[5] This time around 61 Mech would be involved

5 Refer to Chapter 11.

in a mobile conventional operation, the sort of hard-charging enterprise for which we were trained, structured, equipped and motivated.

The troops were not altogether surprised when my subunit commanders made the great revelation about Protea after General Lloyd's briefing; in spite of the deathly secrecy that had been maintained, the battle indicators had inevitably started to become glaringly obvious, and it was clear that something awesome lay in the offering; that FAPLA on the other side of the border did not sense the same thing was astounding – and from their units' reactions when we fell on them on D-Day they clearly had not.

For our part there was a general spirit of excitement and a heightened creative tension which boded well for the final moments of force preparation and training. The concentration area at Oshivelo-Omuthiya was a beehive of feverish activity. Everything was being done at a high tempo. Talk about living in the fast lane! It was positively exhilarating.

Planning is Preparing for Action – The Design for Battle Unfolds

I am going to lift the shroud of secrecy somewhat and provide a sneak preview of how 61 Mech, in its guise of Battle Group 10, planned for the coming operation, before getting into the training and field exercises. I received my warning order at the beginning of August, when 61 Mech had embarked on a final sharpening-up process lasting from 3 August to 21 August (D-3) ... and, for the record, I was furious!

The reason for my fury was that when I analysed our mission for the first time it became glaringly clear, according to my initial perception, that our unit had been handed the more mundane of the combat tasks, which was why certain of 61 Mech's organic elements had been irresponsibly taken away and attached to some of the other units which had been cobbled together for the operation.

What made it worse was that these moves by some staff officer in Windhoek – no names, no pack drill – materialised out of the blue just a few critical days before D-Day. Try as I might, I could not fathom the reason or reasoning behind the decision to rob 61 Mech of its assets just before the operation; it flew in the face of lucid military thinking, and at the very least might well affect the cohesiveness which was such an important part of any unit's effectiveness in action.

Were there selfish reasons for playing with the lives of others in such a reckless fashion? I don't know. What I do know is that I was not the only one to object – some of the strange groupings baffled the Inspectorate General of the Army, as emerged very clearly at the post-operation debriefing in September. I spoke my mind about this during a coordinating meeting a few days later at Oshakati, but to no avail: I was told that it was too late to change the situation, that the planning had gone too far. I did not protest any further: Orders were orders. As always, the mission came first and had to be achieved in the most professional manner. So I would do the best I could with what I had ... and in any case I had the utmost confidence in my subordinate commanders and my troops, even though I had been deprived of some of my most important assets.

Early in August Brigadier Witkop Badenhorst and Colonel Joep Joubert held an all-encompassing order group and coordinating conference at Oshakati which was indisputably Operation Protea's kickoff. I left my second-in-command, Major Thys Rall, to carry on with the force preparation and headed for Oshakati with Major Giel Reinecke so that he could see to the logistical side of things, a huge undertaking in its own right.

On Friday, 7 August, I was back at Omuthiya, and we started with the joint operational planning cycle to prepare for our part of the mission. The way we did it at 61 Mech was to have a top-down process which started with the subunit commanders and staffs and junior leaders, and percolated right down to grassroots level. The idea was to build a shared operational picture and engender mutual trust and understanding. We realised these outcomes and some others, and we had some fun during the process as well.

The venue was the cosy corrugated iron operations and communications centre at the centre of our base, with the battle maps on the walls displaying the code words and nicknames – as I have mentioned before, I believed strongly in visual aids for planning and giving orders.

In addition to the field training we also wargamed on a daily basis. Operational forecasting was built into our planning process – our capabilities and the enemy's, doctrine, time, terrain factors – all these were factored in. The contingency plans that resulted from each forecasting session would then be exercised the following day. "Know yourself, know your enemy ... " as Sun Tzu had said. Well, we did our damnedest to achieve just that.

Simultaneously with all this, my intelligence staff was assessing incoming intelligence on a daily basis. Sometimes we had special help. On one occasion that renowned pilot, Major "Mossie" Basson, took off in his Impala on a distinctly unauthorised mission to reconnoitre potential crossing sites over the Caculuvar River for us ... Somehow Mossie Basson was always getting into trouble with the SAAF brass for failing to ask permission to do some trifling thing or other. I knew what that felt like.

Our plan took the manoeuvrist approach, making provision for both a mobile attack and a mobile defence against a numerically much larger enemy force, namely the brigade lying up at Cahama. Surprise and deception were therefore essential factors to be considered, because we needed to deprive the enemy not only of any early warning of our intentions – of our very presence, in fact – but also the ability to make accurate assessments about what we were up to. To this end, our initial direction of attack and our subsequent actions were seen as key elements for achieving the initial surprise and thereafter continuously deceiving the enemy. To achieve this we would have to keep the battlefield fluid and the enemy at Cahama guessing – persuading them to think that they would be the next to be attacked and slaughtered.

Initial intelligence indicated that Humbe might not harbour an enemy presence. Needless to say, we were not happy about this. Empty trenches had been observed on a number of aerial photographs taken a few days before D-Day, and when we were doing the enemy appreciation this seemed strange – if there were no enemy force at Humbe, the FAPLA strong points at Xangongo would be completely exposed to an attack from the west, along with the bridge which was so vital for both sides.

It just did not seem to make military sense. Logically one would have expected a reinforced FAPLA battalion, or at the very least a company-sized combat team, to be in place at Humbe to defend towards the west and south. The fact that Humbe was undefended when the aerial photos were taken did not necessarily mean that this was still the case – if Cahama had a more flexible defensive scheme than we suspected, it could send a force down to occupy those trenches at Humbe whenever it chose.

We worked on the expectation (correct, as it turned out) that the potential enemy air threat would be completely dormant throughout, although the SAAF was ready to counter any such danger if it arose. Given air superiority, our SAAF ground attack aircraft would be able to fly close-support missions throughout the operation, with Lieutenant Jacques du

Randt at Charlie Squadron acting as our forward controller.

In addition we had been allocated a Bosbok light spotter for reconnaissance, and we also planned to fly some unmanned aerial vehicles, so we would be able to actively monitor the areas where we were vulnerable. The Bosbok would serve the purpose of airborne forward air controller for close air-support missions and artillery fire control. We knew we had some extremely valuable sources of real-time and near-real-time intelligence, specifically intercepted and decrypted enemy radio traffic and reports from judiciously deployed Special Forces teams; once the operation was in progress, active patrolling and reconnaissance in force would fill in the gaps, along with information gained from prisoners of war and friendly locals.

By mid-August our operational plan had been finalised, produced and approved. Now all we had to do was implement it – and quite likely improvise at some stages to cater for unforeseeable situations and developments, which usually happens in any operation. Basically, however, it went like this:

- The primary mission of Battle Group 10 on D-Day was to capture Humbe and secure the area further eastwards on the way towards the bridge at Xangongo, about 8 km away. This would include cutting off any remnants of the Xangongo defenders who were trying to escape westwards to Cahama.
- A possible secondary target on the first day of attack was Mucceipo (known as Techiulo today), about 8 km northwest of Humbe, where a hospital and Roman Catholic mission were located. This particular target, we were told, was allegedly a place where SWAPO was deployed. Whether Mucceipo actually harboured a SWAPO presence was something Intelligence was never clear on, and this vagueness – and the soft nature of the target – caused some raised eyebrows in our planning team (as it turned out, Mucceipo proved to be only a slight embuggerance factor).
- We were to cross the Xangongo bridge at 08:00 on D+1 (25 August) to link up with Battle Group 40 and then join hands with the remainder of Task Force Alpha.
- On D+1 we were to exploit towards Cahama and northwest of our target zone, conducting sweeps in areas of immediate responsibility. The aim was to seek out and destroy enemy remnants we might encounter, especially SWAPO; determine the lay of the land; provide early warning of possible enemy intervention from Cahama; and secure our area of operations. If FAPLA elements ventured out of Cahama, we were to prevent their intervention and defend Xangongo.

Battle Group 10 had been assigned a number of non-operational tasks as well. We were to:

- Prepare the Xangongo bridge as a "reserve demolition" task by noon on D+1and then guard it to make sure it was not actually blown until the right moment arrived, if it arrived at all.[6]
- Help to mop up the objective at Xangongo.
- Carry out some mundane garrison duties, inter alia making essential repairs to damaged infrastructure and establishing friendly relations with the local inhabitants (although we did not know it yet, we would be given an unscheduled additional task following consolidation, which was to provide a second mobile

6 Reserve Demolitions are vital demolition tasks which, on account of the critical role they play in the tactical or strategic circumstances, are specifically controlled.

reserve for Task Force Alpha in addition to Combat Team Mamba when Battle Group 30 was confronted by T34-85 tanks during the attack on Ondjiva).

- The day we withdrew from Xangongo at the end of Operation Protea we were to hand over the town, including the demolition-ready bridge, to our new UNITA allies.[7]

Our battle group's final task would be to cover the withdrawal of the remainder of Task Force Alpha, and assist with the removal of captured war material from Xangongo to Oshakati (as mentioned earlier, all this was completed by 1 September, or D+8 – well ahead of the projected withdrawal date).

As a formality the final operations orders were given by the four battle group commanders about five days before D-Day. In reality the operational plans were constantly evaluated and refined, right up to 21 August, as more information about the evolving enemy situation flowed in or the higher HQ altered the timings.

On Thursday, 20 August, Battle Group 10's battle plan was formally approved by General Constand Viljoen, the Chief of the SADF, who arrived in company with Lieutenant General Jannie Geldenhuys, the Chief of the Army; Lieutenant General Jan van Loggerenberg, the Chief of the Air Force; Major General Lloyd; Brigadier Badenhorst; and Colonel Joubert. In their wake followed a horde of staff officers from Pretoria, Windhoek and Oshakati.

During my presentation General Viljoen asked me only one question: "Tell me, Roland, what your plan is if you run into trouble along the axis of attack with the enemy's mobile reserve deployed behind your back at Cahama while you're on the way to Humbe?"

I briefly explained the rationale of our battle plan, which had been previously endorsed by Brigadier Badenhorst and Colonel Joubert. Immediately General Viljoen replied: "Fine", and signed off on our plan. I returned to Omuthiya, feeling uplifted, and gave due credit to my command cadre and support staff for their relentless toil over the hectic and eventful days of preparation. Now there was nothing to stop us from heading into Angola except the Angolans ... if they found out about us before it was too late, and if they felt like venturing out of Cahama if they did find out.

Preparing for Battle – Sharpening the Combat Edge

Mission and Force Training – Knowledge is Power

What remained for us to do from 3 August onwards was to prepare for the mission on hand in accordance with our order of battle.[8] Subsequent lower level force groupings were to be handled along the way as the course of the operation unfolded. Man and machine needed to be at the highest attainable state of combat readiness; among other things as regards sound leadership, command and morale (as I emphasised in Chapter 8).

Until Wednesday, 12 August, the various subunits were deeply immersed in advanced combat training – the sounds of firing and the manoeuvring could be heard all day from the training area north of Omuthiya – and after dark the subunits exercised their night movement and navigation. Simultaneously there was relentless day-and-night maintenance

7 *União Nacional para a Independência Total de Angola* is the second-largest political party in Angola. Founded in 1966, UNITA fought with the Popular Movement for the Liberation of Angola (MPLA) in the Angolan War for Independence (1961–1975) and then against the MPLA in the ensuing civil war (1975–2002).

8 Refer to Appendix A describing the composition of forces for Operation Protea.

of weaponry and equipment which included test-firing and calibration. A major portion of the 12th was spent on the repair and maintenance of vehicles and equipment, and I directed a comprehensive war game for the leader group in order to test the emerging operational plan.

At 12H00 on Saturday, 15 August, all the troops were given a ground attack demonstration by Mirage fighters just north of Omuthiya, followed by a showing of the artillery's lethal 127 mm Valkiri multiple rocket launchers, their debut in southern Angola (the rockets' fiery tails would soon give them their nickname of "Shindungu", the "red pepper that burns"). Such demonstrations were useful as a type of battle orientation, but they also combined with the vigorous training and the mounting general excitement to give a further boost to 61 Mech's existing high morale.

Exercising the Combat Force – Battles without Bloodshed

At Omuthiya we applied to the full Josephus's famous dictum which has survived through so many centuries of warfare because it is so true: Battles are exercises with bloodshed, and exercises battles without bloodshed. Fortunately there was no bloodshed during the training and exercising for Protea – although, to be honest, we came close to it at times. The subunits exercised independently at first, then as combat teams and eventually as part of an all-encompassing shooting and manoeuvring battle group. We had a rule: If a combat team fought well, the battle group fought well; if the battle group fought well, the brigade or task force fought well. This is what the schedule looked like for the final phase of training and preparation:

Between 13 and 17 August the respective combat teams went through the marrying-up drills of the different combat and support elements, then commenced their joint exercising, all of it carried out with live ammunition.

By 17 August the intelligence team and engineers had carefully prepared a mock enemy defensive locality a few kilometres north of Omuthiya. The layout was orientated and designed to resemble what we could expect at Humbe. In addition a mock enemy trench system of the typical Angolan pattern was prepared on the northern fringe of Omuthiya. Here the respective subunits and sub-subunits regularly practiced to put an extra edge to their high tempo trench-fighting techniques: breaking in, fighting through, clearing the trenches, replenishing ammunition, evacuating casualties, taking prisoners of war and breaking out. These were adrenalin-boosting exercises which the troops enjoyed tremendously.

On 18 August Battle Group 10 set off to launch its first simulated attack on the mock enemy defensive locality that lay awaiting its baptism of fire and brimstone north of Omuthiya.

On 19 August Battle Group 10 was already well on its way to the mock "objective" at 04:00 for a repeat of the previous day's attack. By 12:15 it had been done and the weary, sleepy troops were stood down to enjoy some rest.

On 20 August General Viljoen gave our ops plan the green light, and we had a final run-through on the "objective", all guns blazing and the artillery and mortars thundering away in support. A certain spice was added when we were reminded once again (not that we really needed it) that field exercises were an exciting but dangerous pastime.

A fin broke off a 60 mm mortar bomb while it passed overhead. I could clearly see it tumbling down, twisting and turning as it dropped out of the sky on to the fighting line, and I shouted, "Fall down! Lie still!" to the troops in the assault formation in front of me. It landed right among them, but to the relief of all concerned (particularly mine) it hit the ground sideways on and did not explode. We were fortunate: the new troops had learned an important lesson at no cost to themselves.

Our forward air controller, Lieutenant Jacques du Randt, spent the nights renewing his friendship with Freddie, our Bosbok pilot, who was an old schoolmate of his, and the two of them occupied the little aircraft's cockpit for hours at a time, experimenting with and sharpening up their air-to-ground-to-air techniques for aerial reconnaissance and artillery fire control. Our gallant Bosbok pilot didn't know it yet, but he was destined to be caught up in an astonishing enemy encounter one dark and eerie night a scant 18 km from Cahama – and this on the ground, where no airman likes to be when there is shooting in progress.

Then, quickly, it was Friday, 21 August, and Battle Group 10 was combat and mission ready, all set to sally forth into the bowels of Angola. There was a final inspection in the morning, and we got ready to move out in the small hours of 22 August, D-2.

Execution by Battle Group 10 – The Mission Comes First

On the Move Northwestwards to Our Forward Assembly Area at Ruacana – D-2

At 00:00 on D-2 the forward combat and support groupings started rolling out in the dark towards "Long Drop" (Ruacana). Shaking Omuthiya's dust from our heels took some time, given the length of our column and the loose sand: the time past point[9] exceeded 60 minutes. A heady aroma of diesel fuel hung in the cold predawn air, and the armour types were happy to huddle inside their green Nomex flame-retardant jackets. The battle group headed for Ruacana in two separate packets, each following its own route.[10]

Under Thys Rall's supervision the command group and the assault force's mechanised element set out on what the operations order had designated as "Route 1", across country north of the Etosha Game Reserve and then eventually turning towards Ruacana via the Kamanjab road, a distance of 470 km. While Rall's packet slogged through the veld, throwing up the heavy dust clouds that were an inevitable feature of any large scale vehicle movement in the dry season, the remainder of the battle group, including the light workshop troop and those bright yellow millstones around our neck, headed for Ruacana along "Route 2", a 336 km road journey via Ondangwa and Oshakati, under command of Major Giel Reinecke and the supervision of our RSM, WO1 M.C. Barnard.

Our two-part trek to Ruacana resulted from the great emphasis on maintaining operational security during the move. Route 1 took the combat component slightly to the north of Etosha's game fence, through an area so sparsely populated that there was barely a kraal to be seen, which meant there was nobody to send out word of our temporary presence. Halfway along the route the column halted briefly at a dot on the map called Onaiso, where Giel Reinecke had arranged for diesel bunkers from Grootfontein to top up the Ratels' tanks. Here and at every other halt, young Captain Kobus "Bok" Smit hauled out Second Lieutenant Etienne Gertzen's 81 mm mortar platoon to give it a bit of extra training. In the meantime, Major Giel Reinecke and the second component were eating up the tarmacked kilometres to Ruacana on Route 2.

About 22:50 the two components joined hands at Ruacana's airfield, replenished once more and then went into laager at a forward administrative area near by which

9 The time it takes the whole of the battle group to pass one stationary point on terra firma.

10 See Maps 10 and 11.

Commandant Eric Lambrecht, commander of the resident 51 Battalion, had secured at my request. When his coordinating officer had met us at a prearranged checkpoint and led us to our temporary domicile, we carried out some final-final preparation and then got our heads down. The border was very close now, although invisible in the total darkness.

I let the men sleep in till 07:00 – quite late for us. There was no reason to hurry, since we would not be moving again until after last light, and when we did it would be the start of days of frenzied activity, fatigue and little sleep. Generally there was a good relaxed feeling, although one could feel a stirring of excitement as we counted the hours to nightfall. There was a cool winter breeze and the Ratels' armour was cold to the touch, although that would change as soon as we got going.

Relaxing did not mean idleness, however, just a slowing of our tempo, and we kept ourselves busy with any number of tasks, so that little by little there were pools of activity everywhere. All-important were the final checking of personnel records by the combat teams and other subordinate groupings; here and there the combat team commanders sat surrounded by their men, completing administration and giving final briefings ... Everyone was cool, calm and collected, I noted with satisfaction.

The tiffies were fully occupied with final repairs and the other technical chores, large and small, that never seemed to end in a mechanised force, while Giel Reinecke and his fellow expert, Captain Phil Jaeckel, busied themselves with final staff checks on fuel, ammunition and spares, just to make sure that everything was in order. We could hear a few weapons being calibrated and test-fired near the airfield. I walked about, coffee mug in hand, feeling fine, enjoying the splendid morning and leaving my well-drilled subordinates to get on with whatever they were doing. It was one of those times when the best thing a commander can do is keep out of everyone's hair.

About 11:00 I held my final briefing and pep talk, with each and every one of my soldiers in the audience. My makeshift dais was the top of Ratel Zero Bravo (Commandant Joe Aveling's intelligence vehicle), with young Padre Koos Rossouw perched next to me on the spare wheel, Bible in hand. Joe had hung oversized battle maps from the side of the Ratel, a blaze of blue and red symbols and arrows depicting own and enemy forces, and he opened the proceedings with the standard the-enemy-is-there-and-we-are-here briefing. Then Koos held a quick church parade.

The troops lounged peacefully in front of me on the sandy soil while all this was going on. Their eyes were shining, the anticipation clearly to be read in their faces. I wished that everyone could see them as I did – their fathers, mothers, sisters, brothers and girlfriends, young and energetic. Awesome! Their lives would literally be in my hands. I tried not to think too much about it just then – that burden was going to descend on me the minute we crossed the border, and it was going to become heavier with each passing hour.

Then it was my turn. My message was simple: This is not an exercise – this is Operation Protea, the real McCoy! Then something happened that could not have been more dramatic if I had deliberately arranged it: Without warning a gaggle of Mirage fighters thundered over us, heading west to east after a strafing run on enemy radar installations north of Cahama, near Chibemba.*11* The troops were jubilant and a spontaneous cheer went up.

11 With regards to the Mirages which flew over us: Operation Protea was initiated by the South African Air Force (SAAF) attacking enemy targets inside Angola on 23 August 1981. The air force targets were the key enemy radar installations and few air defence positions which could interfere with the coming operation. The air attacks by the SAAF simultaneously served as psychological dislocation of our conventional foe

I was filled with a calm confidence as I outlined our forthcoming dash across the border that night, feeling extremely assured and relaxed. The only thing that jarred my general spirit of wellbeing was the sight of those two damned yellow graders, sticking out like sore thumbs among the lines of dun-coloured Ratels and other vehicles tucked away in the surrounding winter foliage. For a moment I could not help harbouring renewed aggressive thoughts about that unknown staff officer in Windhoek, then gave myself a mental shake. Ignore! The clutch of conspicuous albatrosses would be hanging around my neck whether I liked it or not.

At 15:00 we had a brief visit from the top brass when General Jannie Geldenhuys and General Charles Lloyd arrived in a Puma and wandered around, chatting briefly with some of the troops. I knew they were just satisfying themselves that everything was ready for whatever deeds of derring-do awaited us. I watched them with equanimity – of course we were ready; the operation was rolling out like clockwork. I knew that at my request Commandant Lambrecht would secure our entry into Angola across the Cunene River at Calueque under cover of darkness.[12] After that we would be on our own.

Soon afterwards Freddie arrived with our Bosbok. He was going to be a busy lad, helping us to navigate in total darkness through the virtually trackless bush, and then scouting ahead and, if necessary, spotting for the guns. He snugged down the Bosbok and then went into conclave with my two artillery commanders, Captains Bernie Pols and Frans van Eeden, to finalise the coordinating arrangements.

The pace picked up as the time for our departure came nearer and last minute affairs were tended to. By late afternoon the C-130s were still flying in a few spare Ratel engines, axles and other items, and Giel Reinecke, Phil Jaeckel, the RSM and Sergeant-major Duppie du Plessis of the LWT were running about coordinating and organising the final logistical loose ends: steel helmets still needed to be issued to a few of our troops, and various things had yet to be stowed away in the assortment of SAMIL load carriers that made up our "tail". "Yster" ("Iron"), the tiffies' large, much-loved recovery vehicle, was doing some heavy lifting, swinging the spare engines and axles on to the big 10-ton armoured SAMIL-100s.

To an outsider it might have looked like chaos, but it was an ordered chaos, and at last light Battle Group 10 started forming up near the airfield in marching order, testing communications and generally making ready for departure. By 18:00, dead on time, the messages came crackling down the line to me: "March and combat ready!" Our balloon had gone up in no uncertain terms.

The Move from Ruacana to the Forming-Up Place Northwest of Humbe

We left Ruacana behind us at 19:15 and set off northwards in orderly fashion. Our eventual destination was the forming-up place from which we would attack Humbe, about 12 km northwest of the little hamlet. At 22:50 we crossed the Cunene at Calueque. From now on, I knew, there was not going to be much sleep for any of us during the next three days. Oh, well, that was the way of warfare; we would just have to catnap whenever the opportunity presented itself. Fortunately soldiers had the knack of sleeping anywhere and at any time, sometimes even during a lull in the middle of a battle.

---

and disruption of their command and control.

12 Incidentally, Commandant Mike Müller crossed into Angola with 61 Mech across the same low-water bridge on 26 June 1988. They were on their way to attack the advance guard of the 50th Cuban Division near Techipa. This was to be the last epic battle of the war. See Chapter 16.

As we moved into Angola I spared a thought for the task force HQ, our three brother battle groups and the mobile reserve, which would move off from Okalongo, far to the east, at 03:00. Personally, I thought that was leaving it a bit on the late side, but I had no time to worry about it, because feeling our way to the forming-up place (FUP) in the dark – and getting there in time – was the primary priority.

Scouting and navigating at the head of the column as we smashed our way through the Angolan bush was a small grouping consisting of the Charlie Squadron commander, Major Joe Weyers, one of his Ratel-90 troops and a mechanised platoon in Ratel-20s from Captain Koos Liebenberg's combat team. Liebenberg himself was also with the vanguard, because as the lead assault force commander he had to be in a position to make a rapid assessment of our situation when we approached the forming-up place for our attack on Humbe. Another add-on was our engineer troop, in case assistance was needed when we crossed the Caculuvar River. Somewhere behind me, I remembered with regret, were the two growling yellow graders.

At first we followed a bush track running due north in the direction of Humbe. I had little confidence in it since it was marked on a vintage Portuguese topographical map we had which probably dated from the Dorsland Trek of the late 19th Century. Sure enough, the track soon disappeared without trace, and from there on it was bundu-bashing all the way.

Navigation in those pre-GPS days was a laborious business which entailed sliding off the sloping armoured nose of one's Ratel with a prismatic compass in hand; walking at least 35 paces ahead to ensure that there was no magnetic deflection from the steel hull and electronics, taking a bearing and then climbing back on again ... over and over and over.

I double-checked all the bearings to make sure I knew where we were every step of the way; how many times I went through the navigational ritual during that long, long night, I can't remember, but it was utterly exhausting. But I didn't mind: remaining orientated and maintaining situational awareness at all times are crucially important for every commander, especially when (as was the case with us) his information about the location and activities of enemy forces was a trifle patchy.

As we bucked and crashed northwards through the night, though, we got a little unexpected help in the form of a lone black man riding a typical African-style bicycle with a groaning chain and heavily sprung saddle. We could see the whites of his eyes gleaming in his sweaty face (cold or no cold) as he saw our large herd of Ratels appearing out of the gloom. But he proved to be an amiable type, and in the process of a quick friendly chat he gave us some valuable information.

He had come from Humbe, he said; everything there was quiet and peaceful, but there were some enemy elements deployed on the Cunene's floodplains, with the bulk of the heavies at Xangongo. The main Xangongo-Cahama road, too, was quiet. We rewarded our new-found friend with a ration pack – a great delicacy for the locals, we knew – and he resumed his southward journey. We rumbled the opposite way into the country of this friendly man who never was.

Tough though our Ratels and SAMILS were – and nobody knew more about building bush-proof vehicles than the South Africans – the bundu-bashing took its inevitable heavy toll. But we had Duppie du Plessis and the LWT to take care of that, and his grease-smeared tiffies toiled right through the night, repairing broken down vehicles on the move in spite of the jolting and lack of light. I was awed by their accomplishments – consider the difficulty of plucking a bulky six-cylinder Büssing diesel engine from an armoured hull like a rotten tooth and replacing it with a new one under these conditions.

This is not to say that the rest of us had it easy. The short Mopani stumps played havoc with our tyres, and the Ratel crews spent many hours wrestling with their vehicles' huge wheels when one of them suffered a puncture and had to be swopped for a new one. But there was no rest for the wicked – H-Hour would wait for no one, and when the bell rang we had to be in position at the forming-up place (FUP), come hell or high water.

Then we struck a problem for which even our wizards of the LWT had no immediate solution when Murphy's Law intervened and one of the graders ground to a halt with a flat tyre and technical problems. Blessed be the senior staff officer who decided that we needed these ogres in our arsenal, I thought, for I shall surely strangle him when we get back. But in the meantime I had to deal with the immediate problem of what to do with our highly visible cripple.

Change of mission! I told Dawid Mentz and Marche Mucho and his Phantom Squad to stay with the grader, see to its repair and then hit the road and follow us.[13] Goodbye, Phantoms, farewell, God speed, see you later. I sent up a hasty but heartfelt snap prayer as they disappeared into the night behind us: Dear Lord, if it pleases you, please don't let SWAPO come across our lonely yellow grader and the Phantoms and take them to Cahama to display to the world; thank you, dear Lord!

Oh, it was an interesting night, all right, short and endless, all at the same time. And the grader was not the last of our problems, not by a long shot. On one occasion the exhausted driver of a SAMIL decided to catnap during one of our short 10-minute halts. But instead of catnapping he fell into a deep sleep, probably dreaming of home comforts and some other things ... with the break over, the vehicles ahead of him moved on and the ones behind naturally stayed put, and as Battle Group 10 trundled steadily northwards, a large gap of about 10 km opened up in its ranks. I am still waiting for your driver's name, Major Reinecke!

There is no doubt about it: Troops have the uncanny habit of making life interesting for military commanders. However, I would go nowhere without them, especially the South African kind, and in this case we were able to scramble Freddie at Ruacana to lead our lost flock back to the straight and narrow. After midnight we were reunited in the pitch black African night. Our family was back together again ... and not a moment too soon, because the clock was ticking.

The plan called for Battle Group 10 to swing 45° to the northwest near a small kraal, (roughly kidney-shaped, according to a recent aerial photograph) which our ancient map named as "Rotunda". We found a kraal, but the problem was to make sure that we reached Rotunda rather than some other inconsequential huddle of bush dwellings. Thys Rall and I did it the hard – but only – way. We went forward with torches in hand and literally felt our way around the perimeter, a painful business, since bushveld kraals in that part of the world are surrounded by palisades with thorn bushes in the gaps.

Many bloody scratches later, Thys and I were satisfied that this was, in fact, the kidney-shaped destination we had been looking for. We set off into the pre-dawn mist, away from the crimson-tinged horizon, the remaining grader's yellow hide silently shouting about our presence in Luanda's backyard.

I got on the radio to Colonel Joep Joubert and informed him that all was well and that

13 Read about the amazing exploit of the 'Skurwe Hande' (Phantoms) in Chapter 8.

we were running according to plan. He, in turn, informed me that the eastern part of the task force had encountered movement and navigation problems, and so he was moving the hour of reckoning from 10:30 to 11:30. This could not have been an easy decision for him, because H-Hour was the all-important core of everything: The thorough coordination of all the respective movements; the timing for the air attack; the safety of our own aircraft; and the tight fire-support coordination and control of indirect firing weapons. But obviously he had no alternative.

On our side, too, things now started to go wrong. From Rotunda we had planned to follow an old Portuguese cutline running northwest, which showed up as a thin grey line on the aerial photograph we had studied at Omuthiya. Then we discovered that there wasn't one, so we settled down to another dose of relentless bundu-bashing through extremely thick vegetation.

I remember it very well, the growling of the vehicles, the rising chorus of birdsong as daybreak brought the cold morning light ... and our battle to move forward, relying on brute force and sheer navigational skill with prismatic compass and dead reckoning as we burrowed through a maze of giant trees, stunted shrubbery and tangled undergrowth.

In one sense it was a magnificent sensory experience. The smell of freshly broken foliage lay heavy in the morning air as we purposefully tunnelled our way through the intertwined bush with its dappled shadows; the foremost Ratels' sloping sides were smeared with the sap of shredded shrubbery. In another it was eerily threatening, because our watches told us that our movement time was being relentlessly consumed.

Daylight brought a new concern. In a number of open areas we found clusters of fresh enemy tracks leading westward towards Cahama, some made by FAPLA combat boots and others showing the chevron sole patterns indicating the wearers were SWAPO men. Who these men were and what they were doing was something for which we never found an answer; but at that precise moment in time the first question that came to my mind was this: Had we succeeded in retaining the total surprise factor?

The only assumption I could make was that some FAPLA and SWAPO soldiers had become aware of the impending attack and were hightailing it out of the danger zone, that the more far-seeing ones had had a sixth sense warning that something was not right, and that they crossed the crocodile infested Cunene River to get out of the way. We knew that occasionally our opponents would give way like this without bothering to request permission from higher authority (understandably so, since the said higher authority in question often fled without telling them).

Our battle group soon arrived at a chosen forward waiting point just to the south of the dry Caculuvar River, although the potential crossing site was still masked by the dense foliage. Here we planned to wait for 60 minutes, a best practice established during training exercises – past experience had shown that this was enough leeway to cater for timing hitches along the way, and we could afford the time, because in spite of our battles with the bundu we were still on schedule.

Radio contact was made with the task force HQ, which passed on some valuable titbits of information. The revised H-Hour timing was confirmed; no fresh intelligence regarding the enemy's disposition at Xangongo had been received; our electronic watchers reported that nothing new was coming out of Cahama; the air attack on Xangongo was going in on time; it was all systems "go".

Time now for a few quick prayers, friendly nods here and there, the final clearing of fallen leaves and debris from the open mechanisms of the 20 mm quick-firing guns of the Ratels (the guns were mounted upside down, and the open slots through which expended cartridges were ejected were vulnerable to falling leaves and other flotsam from above, of which there was plenty). Young Padre Koos Rossouw flitted among the vehicles, having quick chit-chats with those troops who were not sleeping.

Final confirmation of our orders followed, and the respective parties which could see one another exchanged quick thumbs-ups. Battle Group 10 was now combat and fire ready. Time to cross the Caculuvar for the final leg to the forming-up place for the attack on Humbe. Needless to say, it was not as simple as that, and an unpleasant though not major surprise was waiting for us when we neared the actual crossing place. Mossie Basson's aerial photos of the Caculuvar River had depicted a wide, hard, mud-caked floodplain, but he had missed one important feature, as we discovered when we ran slap-bang onto a deep, steep-sided donga.

I knew from experience that the agile Ratels would just be able to get through, albeit with some difficulty; but what about the four-wheeled vehicles in the rest of the column? In my mind's eye I could see the hands of my imaginary clock starting to sweep faster and faster around the dial. A moment of apprehension and conflicting emotions swept through me. H-Hour was approaching fast. At Ondangwa the Mirages were already screaming on the tarmac. East of the Cunene, the rest of Task Force Alpha was pushing hard towards Xangongo. Contact with the enemy was imminent and urgent work would soon need to be done ... and we weren't there yet to do it!

Then suddenly I was filled with a strange calm and a feeling of immense confidence, especially in the people around me. I called a brief halt, radioed my combat team commanders and explained our minor dilemma: "Small problem. Slight obstacle on our front encountered. Wait, out." Then I dispatched a single Ratel-20 to breach the donga. Going down into it was a breeze, but climbing out was another story. The Ratel managed it, however, rearing up precariously on to its hind wheels before reaching the lip of the donga and crashing forward on to all six axles on the other side.

That partly solved one problem – at a pinch we could get the Ratels across here, but the last thing we needed at this stage of the game was to lose one of them – but we still had to find a way to get our "tail" over the Caculuvar. Commandant Epp van Lill, my operations officer, took the matter personally in hand. He jumped down from my Ratel and ran westwards up the donga, scouting for a less strenuous fording point, and soon found one a little further on. But it was still only suitable for Ratels. Relief washed briefly over me before I bent my mind to the remaining problem. Decision time ... H-Hour was just 45 minutes away ... Maintain the momentum! Get there on time at all costs, and fight with what you have!

There was only one thing to do. I would cross with the Ratels and head hell bent for leather towards the Humbe-Cahama highway; the rest of the force would have to bundu-bash westwards along the Caculuvar till it found a viable place to cross, then try to catch up with us. Splitting the battle group at this late stage was not a comfortable undertaking, of course, but that was the way of it. What the hell, do it and carry on. We growled our way over the river and carried on. But once again fortune was with us. The "tail" soon found a good way across and before long joined up with us again. Alpha Echelon and the protection company now halted and laagered in a relatively safe position further to our rear and flank.

More good news: Freddie was on his way in his Bosbok and the Mirages and Buccaneers were lining up to take off for the attack on Xangongo and Peu Peu. Then even more comforting news came over the radio. The ailing grader had been repaired and was rolling along slowly but surely in our wake. Sighs of relief, particularly from me; we definitely did not need to have FAPLA taking ownership of it and my men.

It was a massive weight off my mind; at times during that desperate trek I had felt like leaving our uninvited burden behind for the enemy do to with as they pleased, and damn the consequences. But only briefly: when 61 Mech returned after an operation it brought all its possessions back with it, if at all possible – even if they were wrecks hoisted on to the back of a truck. If we couldn't do that, we blew them up or shot them to pieces. I had a fleeting thought about that staff officer, what was his name again?

It was a great moment when the battle group emerged from the bush on to "'Bloody Mary", the Humbe-Cahama highway, a sort of catharsis which momentarily washed all my inner tension away. Our first action, of course, was to look to left and right for signs of an enemy presence or activity – after all, we were now squarely inside hostile territory. To the east and just 18 km away lay Humbe; harbouring Heaven knew what enemy force. About 42 km away to the west lay Cahama, and we knew what they had there to unleash against us if they were so inclined.

First things first. Ignore Cahama for the time being and concentrate on taking Humbe. Swing southeastwards and focus on the front. We were now suitably deployed for a running fight coming from the direction of Humbe-Xangongo; in a sense we had already achieved the mission of dominating this crucial stretch of road, simply by planting our lethal presence squarely on it.

To wax philosophical for a moment: Our operational movement thus far, bundu-bashing our way through the night with a minimum of navigational aids and ending up ready for battle in the right place and at the right time, had been a feat in itself – so much so that after the operation was over the Inspector General of the Army asked me to write a case study about it.

In it I gave due credit for the planning and execution of this exceptional tactical move to Thys Rall, my subordinate commanders and their seconds-in-command. Swift and effective tactical movements by mechanised forces are essential ingredients for mobile warfare, and in a wider sense all of Protea's combat participants were steadily and surely building a solid knowledge base and the skills needed for mobile warfare in Africa, attributes which would be urgently required later on during Operation Modular in 1987–88.

To my mind mobile warfare was a combination of art and science. The South Africans mastered the tricks of this particular war fighting trade in the wide expanses of bush around us, but our conventional foe seemed unable to embrace the war of movement effectively. Russian war fighting doctrine as adopted by FAPLA was dreary and unimaginative. Their fighting style lacked dynamism – it inclined towards positional fighting, as would soon be clearly demonstrated (with grave consequences for its practitioners) at Xangongo and Ondjiva.[14]

West-Flanking towards Humbe-Xangongo – Advancing on Bloody Mary

The enemy's integrated defensive stronghold with its centre in Xangongo was now locked in a pincer-hold, ready to be taken by simultaneous attacks from both the east and west of

14 See Chapters 6 and 7.

the Cunene, whose two sectors interfaced at the vital Xangongo Bridge. Then the South Africans would be able to probe steadily and with determination towards the heart of the encircled enemy.

But first things first – in Battle Group 10's case, the capture of Humbe from the west, with Bloody Mary as the axis of attack.[15] We reached our forming-up place ("Sweet Sam") with limited time to spare. The forward mechanised combat team swiftly deployed into an extended fighting line, straddling the road. The plan for the two-phase attack was simple. Leading the attack would be Combat Team 2 under Captain Koos Liebenberg – Bravo Company 61 Mech in 14 Ratel-20s and two armoured car troops with eight Ratel-90s. Major Joe Weyers would be the second-in-command and also commander of the two Ratel-90 troops. In direct support was the 81 mm mortar group Bok Smit had been training so assiduously along the way.

For the duration of the attack Captain Pale van der Walt would be the mobile reserve with his one Ratel-60 command vehicle, Alpha Company in 14 Buffel MPVs and the eight Eland-90s of the other two armoured car troops, with Captain Chris Gildenhuys as acting second-in-command as well as commander of the Eland-90s. Combat Team 1, like Combat Team 2, would have an 81 mm mortar group in direct support.

The order of advance was straightforward. Koos Liebenberg would lead with Combat Team 2. In the centre of the assault formation was my command group, with my second-in-command, intelligence officer and air support officer in their own command vehicles in open formation. Close by was Captain Bernie Pols, my artillery commander, whose Ratel acted as the fire support coordination centre. Behind us came Pale van der Walt's Combat Team 1. With the four 140 mm guns to our rear was Captain Frans van Eeden, who could also act as a forward observation officer, or FOO; the guns would come into action 12 km from Humbe, guided by Freddie in his Bosbok, but the two mortar groups would start shooting when required by their respective combat team commanders.

Together our portion of the command team inter alia was responsible for operational safety and close coordination of direct fire and movement in relation to the indirect fire and air support. We had refined this act to a fine art during our training at Omuthiya, and we were very relaxed about it.[16] The RSM followed one tactical bound behind the fighting force with the fuel, water, ammunition and other bits of logistics. A Ratel armoured recovery vehicle and armoured ambulance moved with each of the combat teams.

Excitement gripped us as we advanced, the rays of the mid-morning sun penetrating the deep shadows of the thick bush around us. I remember seeing a few magnificent baobab trees along the road to our front. We passed an isolated kraal to our left front, but there was no living soul to be seen anywhere. We pressed on, ready for anything. The smell of diesel fuel mingled with dust hung over the relaxed hum of the powerful engines, which sounded strangely subdued, as a slight breeze stirred the cool air and pushed the dust gently away, improving the observation we required so desperately.

Now suddenly the energy level ratcheted up, as if in response to a signal – 11:30, H-Hour, was approaching fast. I could hear the squelch of the high frequency radios. Then it arrived. In the east, the South African attack aircraft pounded Xangongo's defence complex, and our own 140 mm guns started firing on Humbe, guided by Freddie in his Bosbok. Battle Group 10 rolled forward, ready to erupt into an orgy of controlled fire and movement at

15 See Map 10.

16 Refer to Chapter 8.

any moment. We knew exactly what we had to do: Capture Humbe, then move eastwards to the river, dealing with any enemy elements escaping from Xangongo; on standby all the time to take action if FAPLA decided to intervene from Cahama.

The Battle for Xangongo and Peu Peu to the East of the Cunene

Battle Group 10's flanking move allowed the remainder of Task Force Alpha to deal with the enemy on the eastern side of the river without any fear of an intervention from the west. HQ Task Force Alpha and Battle Groups 20 and 40 started forming up 7 km to the east of Xangongo at around noon, much later than expected because of the difficulties they had encountered with movement and navigation.

By now Battle Group 30 under Commandant Chris Serfontein had been released to assault Peu Peu, on the Cunene 10 km to the north of Xangongo, after it had been softened up by air attacks and artillery bombardments. To the south, a similar softening-up was applied to Xangongo before Battle Group 20 under Commandant Johann Dippenaar (my predecessor as OC 61 Mech) tackled the major part of the attack, the assault on its southern and eastern defences and the airfield. Dippenaar launched a ferocious attack on his objective which literally forced the enemy soldiers on to the layers of defensive minefields which were supposed to protect their southern flank.

While Dippenaar's mechanised battle group was flaying the southern defences, Commandant Deon Ferreira and his motorised troops of Battle Group 40 were fighting through the northernmost of the Xangongo defences and capturing the "old Portuguese Fort" (actually a cantonment rather than a fort) which stood on high ground on the outskirts of the town itself, as well as a tall water tower next to the river and just south of the road.

The fort and tower were important objectives, because the high ground was an important tactical feature which could be used for either defence or attack. The tower provided excellent observation over the town and to the west, and the high ground overlooked both the critically important bridge over the Cunene and the main road leading from it to Humbe and points north and west. That meant both the bridge and the road could be watched and effectively influenced with direct fire weapons, small arms and short-range mortars.

When we moved over the bridge into Xangongo on D+1 and on to the salient of high ground – the westernmost edge of the Xangongo defences – Dawid Mentz made good use of the tower to keep an eye on what was now his domain as garrison commander, and later our battle group would use the river and the high ground in combination for designing the defence of Xangongo.

A serious battle took place in and around Xangongo in the next two days. Out on his own in the north, Commandant Serfontein took Peu Peu, fighting a stiff action that led to the destruction of a locally stationed FAPLA mobile reserve force with a number of T34-85 tanks when it started heading south to intervene at Xangongo. The upshot was the destruction of the FAPLA force and the capture of Peu Peu and its large stocks of supplies and ammunition.

Meanwhile at Xangongo heavy fighting was taking place, and in the end it took Battle Groups 20 and 40 two days of stop-and-start combat to stamp out the last resistance from the complex of strongpoints guarding the town.

Capturing Humbe and Exploitation towards the Cunene

While this was happening we took Humbe without a shot being fired, barring a few shells from Frans van Eeden's guns; it was almost a formality. As Battle Group 10 advanced down the road, 140 mm shells wailing overhead and the Ratels ready to steamroller over anything in sight, our spotter aircraft informed us that the trenches in Humbe's vicinity seemed neglected and abandoned; no hostile movement was observed or enemy forces sighted trying to break out of Xangongo. We were grateful but frankly amazed at this tactical lapse on FAPLA's part.

In any case, Bernie Pols immediately told the gunners to cease firing but to stand by for an immediate resumption if necessary, and we carried on. While we were doing this, a now unemployed Freddie flew westwards and reported that the coast was absolutely clear in that direction as well. This was what we had predicted and hoped for back at Omuthiya, but we were relieved all the same, since expecting the unexpected is SOP for any battlefield soldier. Quite clearly our surprise had worked, almost miraculously so, when you think about it.

Now it was decision time for me again. It will be remembered that my original orders from Task Force Alpha included an alternative objective in the advent of Humbe being deserted, namely the settlement at Mucceipo – today's Techiulo – which might be harbouring a SWAPO presence of unspecified strength. Otherwise the nature of the target was undefined; our planners' suspicion resulted not from hard evidence but from a deduction based on the fact that Mucceipo – which consisted of a few outbuildings, a mission station and a hospital – would offer the insurgents some home comforts.

I had had some reservations at the time about Mucceipo's suitability as a target because of the mission hospital, but had not given it much attention, and so the alternative attack had been planned and our battle maps had been marked accordingly. Now, with Humbe having fallen into our lap, Mucceipo became a serious target.

And it had to be a quick decision, because we were closing in on Mucceipo, which would come up 1 700 metres to our northeast as soon as we reached a turnoff we were approaching. I decided to secure it, and halted my command group and Combat Team 2's attack line at the turn-off, from where I had a clear view of the outbuildings, the hospital and the mission. On my command Koos Liebenberg told off a subordinate grouping commanded by Joe Weyers to secure Mucceipo at all speed.

As I glanced up the road I saw numerous FAPLA soldiers frantically fleeing through the settlement in a northwesterly direction. They were clearly visible through the sparse trees and bush around the station. Some were carrying AK-47s, but many others were unarmed. Through my binoculars I could see fearful sweat-streaked faces glancing back at us. But not for long because moments later they had all disappeared into the sanctuary of the dense bush.

Liebenberg ordered Weyers's party away on its quick encircling movement, but for some reason or other there followed a short argument between the two of them. What the nature of the altercation was I did not know or care much. What I cared about was that it resulted in Weyers having difficulty swinging his group 90° to the north to carry out the encirclement.

I wanted things to move faster than that, and spoke to Weyers about this across the gap between our Ratels. Then something cold momentarily touched my soul. I leaned over my turret again, looked at Joe and said: "Move and encircle. Don't shoot unless we're fired on first." This was, of course, not good war fighting practice, but that cold feeling was telling me something. Weyers set off, accompanied by Pale van der Walt in his Ratel-60 so that he could summon his paratroopers if something happened.

Weyers's group surrounded the mission forthwith without encountering resistance, although Van der Walt got involved in a spur-of-the-moment scuffle and shot down one sorry soul who tried to break out. Now the perfection of that God-given instinct of mine was confirmed when seven white nuns and a collection of sick, lame and lazy came out of the mission to meet us.

Yes, the nuns said. There had been some SWAPO and FAPLA at Mucceipo, but they were not there anymore. I sent up a silent prayer of thanksgiving. Already there was a furious international outcry in progress about Operation Protea. I could only imagine the condemnation that would have befallen myself, my unit and South Africa as a whole if we had gone in there with guns blazing. Mucceipo taught me a personal lesson: Heed your inner voice – and make damn sure about the quality of the higher intelligence you receive.

By 12:30 Battle Group 10 had extricated itself from the Mucceipo intercession and was advancing towards Humbe again. We passed some milestones and then we were there, seeing the derelict trenches for ourselves. We felt some apprehension about running into minefields, so we probed forward carefully, keeping our eyes peeled for any tell-tale signs.

But there were none, and no signs of any escapees from Xangongo either, although Battle Group 20 and Battle Group 40 were going at it hammer and tongs in the east – we could hear the firing and explosions reverberating from across the river, and see the dark ominous smoke of battle spiralling up. It was clear that they had the defenders pinned down in their trenches. All the while our trusty Bosbok pilot roved around overhead, scouting the ground ahead, secure in the knowledge that we enjoyed air superiority (by 1987 things would be vastly different, so that the days of light spotter aircraft roving unhindered in the skies above Angola would be gone forever).

As we advanced through Humbe I stopped at the police station, a small building just off the road to my right. Like any good souvenir hunter I leaned out of my Ratel to cut its limp, tattered FAPLA flag from the flagpole, and then jumped down to pay a courtesy visit, so to speak, on the local police chief. Everything had been abandoned as is, however.

I would have given the police chief a talking-to about the disgraceful state of his facility, but strangely enough he was not there. I noticed that the in-tray in his disordered office was brim-full of bundles of paper, among them probably a few charge sheets against some of the miserable souls living in the vicinity. Having acquainted myself with the Angolan justice system, I mounted my Ratel again and moved on behind the advancing combat line ... In passing I couldn't help noticing a few graders, not at all as bright and pristine as our own two yellow ogres. So what! In any case, goodbye, Humbe.

About three kilometres from the bridge I halted the battle group and ordered it into an open laager at a reasonably defendable spot, making sure that we remained totally alert for anything hostile which might come our way from any direction. This done, I radioed a brief Sitrep to Colonel Joubert on the other side of the river. He said that we had done well, but I could sense that he was preoccupied with the grinding battle to our east.

Now our "tail" started arriving – the artillery, Alpha Echelon and the protection company – and we took the time for a quick coffee break. But our day was not yet over by a wide margin on either our side of the river or the other; it was time to exploit towards the Cunene, clear the area of possible enemy remnants and consolidate our position for the night. As planned, I released Combat Teams 10 and 20 to start exploiting.

Fighting on the Flood Plains

Koos Liebenberg and Pale van der Walt set off without delay to exploit swiftly eastwards towards the river and clear the area of any enemy remnants, but they did not encounter many escapees from Xangongo. A few FAPLA soldiers had managed to make their way across the bridge, and some – the braver among them, or perhaps the more desperate – had swum across in spite of the Cunene's resident crocodiles.

Some of them ran into Van der Walt's paratroopers, while Liebenberg's Ratels killed more than 14 in the floodplains. One of the dead was the quartermaster of a FAPLA unit, cut down in a burst of crossfire with his complete stock book and other papers (what the hell was he thinking?) – although this dedication to duty impressed my own loggie, Giel Reinecke. Combat Team 2's skirmishers reported that Battle Group 40's men could be seen scurrying around on the high ground at the old fort, obviously in control, so now our flanks were secured from both ends.

Lieutenant Gert Minnaar, of Combat Team 2's platoon commanders, later recalled his eventful firefight on the floodplains. It is an unembellished and somewhat clumsily written account, eloquent in its simplicity, which describes a young soldier's baptism of fire and his growth to full adulthood:

My platoon and the one commanded by Second Lieutenant Ariel Hugo proceeded from the bridge in a northerly direction in open combat formation. We did not travel far before we encountered at least a platoon of FAPLA soldiers on the run. The wind was blowing from their direction and the sounds of our Ratel engines were obviously muffled.

At first the enemy was oblivious of our ominous presence. I ordered a "skiethalte" drill (firebelt action). I spotted some more enemies, approximately 150 metres away towards the bushes at my 10 o' clock position. At first they were also unaware of our presence.

Then one of the enemy soldiers turned around, looked at us and proceeded to walk on as if we did not exist. I could not believe my eyes. My Ratel gunner, Rifleman Anthony Pike from Port Elizabeth, opened fire with the 7,62 mm Browning machine gun. Three hapless FAPLA infantrymen were caught in the open. The FAPLA soldiers spun around and started to return fire.

At that point in time I was still standing in the turret of my Ratel, but I very quickly decided not to expose my body as a target to the enemy any longer when I saw one of the FAPLA soldiers taking specific aim with his AK-47 at that part of my body which protruded from the turret. I needed no further encouragement to disappear into its relative safety and firmly shut the hatch. I can remember thinking that that enemy soldier was making it much too personal for my liking by aiming at me without knowing who and what I was!

The rest of the fighting I had to watch through the confined view of the turret's vision blocks, while the bullets filled the empty space between us. It was not that I was that much concerned about the bullet with my name on it, because there was nothing I could do about that, but I was more terrified of those bullets with the inscription "to whom it may concern" ...

I caught sight of Corporal Anton Viljoen of Bravo section, from Patensie in the Eastern Cape. He had moved forward in his turret with his R-4 rifle. By now he had been so taken up by the situation that he had decided to add firepower with the Ratel's 7,62 mm Browning machine gun as well; he did not seem to care about the return fire from the enemy.

Another picture that I can still recall vividly was when Rifleman Pike hit the target with the Browning ... This picture has been ingrained on my mind since that day. I was

Chapter 1

The De Vries family with mother Ellen, father Herman (Divvy) and younger brother Herbert.

On holiday at Margate – our mother Ellen with my sister Dorothea and younger brother Herbert catching on fast.

My drill platoon at Transvalia High School, 1962.

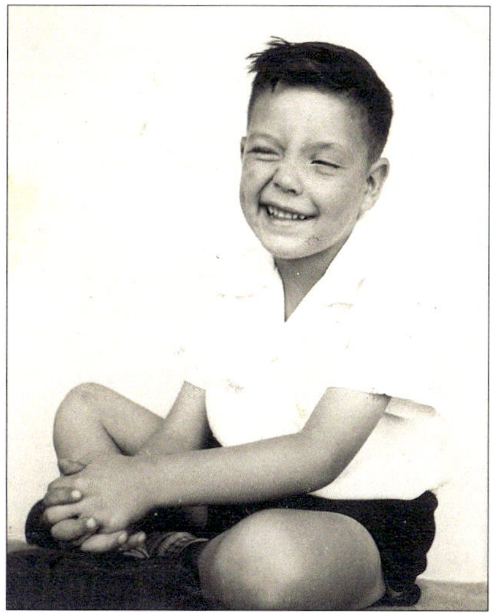

My mom called me Cheeky... She said: "You'll be a man, my son".

Inspecting my first platoon at Transvalia High School, 1962.

Press-ganged into the school debate committee. From left to right: Frans Beetge, Marietjie van der Walt, Mr J.J.N. Lauwrens, Sakkie van der Merwe, Yvonne Pringle, Ina Jamneck and Roland de Vries.

Chapter 2

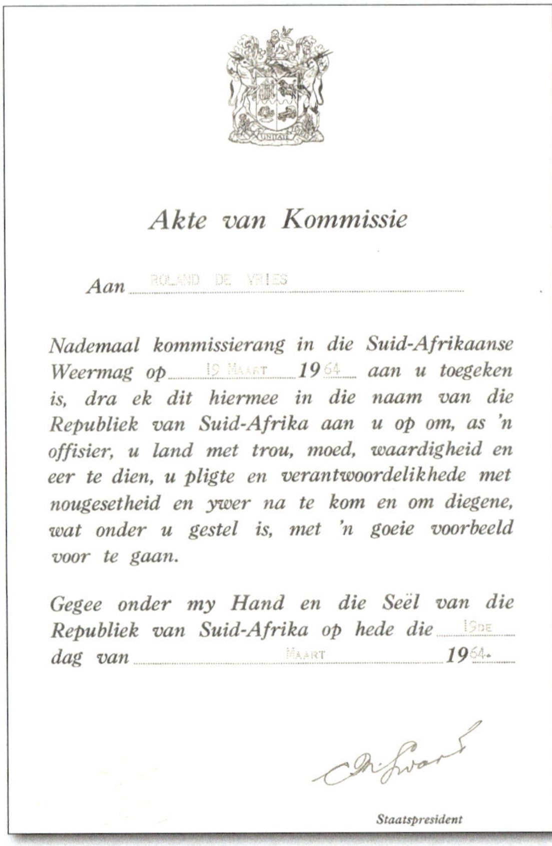

Akte van Kommissie

Aan ROLAND DE VRIES

Nademaal kommissierang in die Suid-Afrikaanse Weermag op 19 MAART *19*64 *aan u toegeken is, dra ek dit hiermee in die naam van die Republiek van Suid-Afrika aan u op om, as 'n offisier, u land met trou, moed, waardigheid en eer te dien, u pligte en verantwoordelikhede met nougesetheid en ywer na te kom en om diegene, wat onder u gestel is, met 'n goeie voorbeeld voor te gaan.*

Gegee onder my Hand en die Seël van die Republiek van Suid-Afrika op hede die 19DE *dag van* MAART *19*64.

Staatspresident

My Deed of Officer's Commission signed by State President C.R. Swart.

Army Gymnasium, Voortrekkerhoogte, 1963 – the work of Corporal Cammie Botha.

Specialist Infantry course with Colonel Jan Breytenbach in May to June 1968. Front from left: Mac Beets, Johnny Lottering, Size Zaayman, D.R. Toll, J.H.H. Smith, J. Pearce, James du Toit, S/Sgt M.J. Potgieter. Rear from left: Louw Trichardt, Johnny Coetzer, Dan Lamprecht, Louis Heap, Maj J.D. Breytenbach, Roland de Vries, André Bestbier, Ken Leviton, Lucas Moulder.

Those who completed the escape and evasion exercise. Front from left: Mac Beetge and D.R. Toll. Rear from left: Johnny Coetzer, Dan Lamprecht, Louw Trichardt and Roland de Vries.

With our Chinese instructors and crew of the Fairchild C-119 Flying Boxcar – parachute training at Kaohsiung, Taiwan, 1973.

Ranger training at the guerrilla warfare school in Taiwan, 1973.

Getting ready to become airborne – at Kaohsiung, Taiwan, 1973.

Chapter 2

The photo presented to me by the Special Warfare School of Taiwan, 1973.

Airborne exercise in Taiwan, 1973.

Qualifying for Rough Terrain Jumping in Taiwan, 1973.

With Colonel Raymond Holtzhausen at the Infantry School in 1972 – talking about mobile warfare.

Teaching mobile warfare at the Infantry School to one of my platoon commander's courses, 1972.

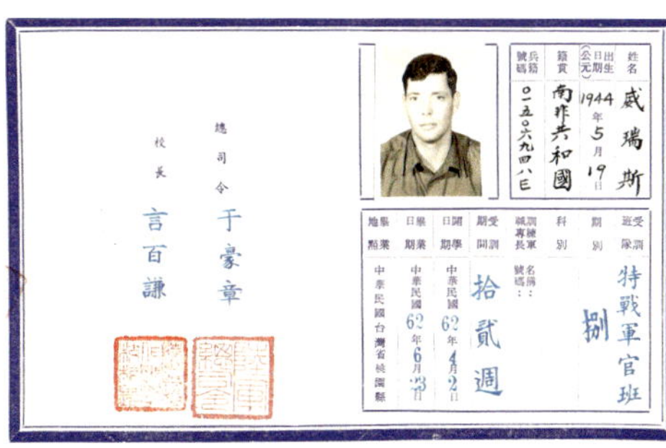

Taiwan, 1973 – My certificate for parachute training with their Special Forces.

Pages 34, 35, 36, 37, 39, 40, 42 and 43 sponsored by SADFI

EXERCISE THUNDER CHARIOT

• Journalists: Pte P.N. John
Pte J. de Smidt
• Photographers: Sgt L. Rourke
Pte P. Hollander

THE South African Defence Force's military might which was displayed during the recent Exercise Thunder Chariot was not intended as a show of force — but it proved to the world that South Africa has an iron fist and the ability to use it with devastating effect if ever the need arises.

◄ *Die Staatspresident, mnr P.W. Botha, die Minister van Verdediging, genl Magnus Malan (regs) en die Hoof van die Suid-Afrikaanse Weermag, genl C.L. Viljoen, het die oefening bygewoon.*

'n Olifant-tenk ploeg deur dik sand

34 PARATUS • OCTOBER 1984

Exercise Thunder Chariot – practicing lightning war at the Army Battle School – October 1984.

Devastating power of the SADF . . .

THIS simulated warfare exercise is the largest that has been carried out in South Africa since World War II. It was a conventional war exercise that involved over 4 000 vehicles and more than 11 000 Citizen Force soldiers from 7 Infantry Division of the South African Army.

The South African Air Force also participated in this exercise which was held at the Army Battle School's P.W. Botha Training Area, Lohatla.

"The aim of Exercise Thunder Chariot is to practise lightning warfare conditions in typical Southern African operations with the air component and medical service totally involved, on division, brigade and batallion/regimental group level," said Brig G.P.H. Kruys, Officer Commanding 7 Division.

THE exercise was divided into six phases. In phase one, the mobilisation and movement of the leader group took place. This included the arming and equipping of this group. After the arrival of the unit leader groups at the training area, phase two began. Here the leader groups were subjected to a seven day training programme to sharpen them up before the arrival of the main force.

Phase three consisted of the mobilisation, arming, equipping and movement of the main force to the training area where they joined the leader group.

Die skouspel van die nagaanval op ▶ Long Jump.

In phase four the main force underwent six days of training from the lowest to the brigade level. In phase five, the highlight — the division attack and defence — took place.

The last phase was the demobilisation from 17 to 20 September.

THE spectacular and awe inspiring aspect of the exercise, the divisional attack, occurred from 11 to 14 September.

At about 16h00 on the 11th, 71 Motorised Brigade attacked a target area on the western flank called **Grand Slam.** Later that evening on the eastern flank, 72 Mechanised Brigade unleashed its firing power at another 'enemy' target known as **Cobra 1.** The third objective, which was also taken during this night attack, involved a paratroop drop who then took the target **'Longjump'.** They were assisted in their offensive by a regiment of tanks.

Both of these 'enemy strongholds were bombarded with artillery before the various units of 71 and 72 Brigades moved in for the kill.

Included in the night's activities were the building of two bridges and repairing a third which gave further mobility to the bigades in their offensives.

• **Continued on p 36**

BELOW: The G5 gun smoking after wiping out yet another target.

PARATUS • OKTOBER 1984 35

Exercise Thunder Chariot – race to the swift, Army Battle School, October 1984.

Signed specially for me – WW2, El Alamein. From left to right: Lt Col F.W. von Mellenthin, Field Marshall E. Rommel and General W. Nehring.

Left: Those were the days – during a Battle Group exercise in October 1987 with General Friedrich Wilhelm von Mellenthin and Commandant Jan Malan at the Army Battle School.

With my favourite Prussian general – Launch of my book on Mobile Warfare at the Army Battle School, August 1987.

Renovation of the SA Army College, April 1990 – with Defence Minister, General Magnus Malan.

Chapter 2

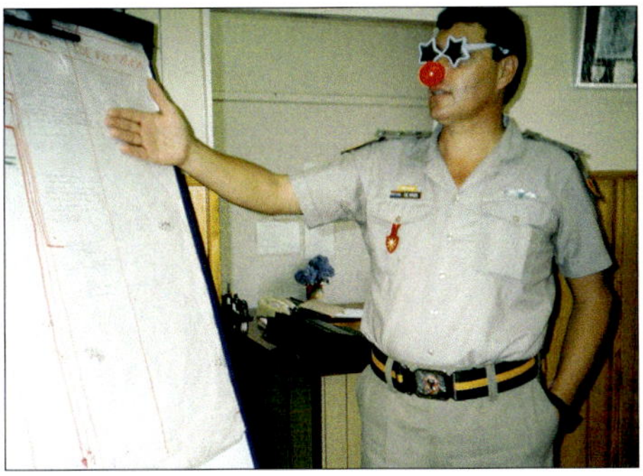

Presenting an Ops Plan at Northern Transvaal Command – my kit for creative thinking.

White water rafting on the mighty Tugela with Brigadier Gert Opperman in 1991.

The Chief of the Indian Army, General Ved Malik, visits Army HQ in 1989.

Departing from Waterkloof with friends and family for my going away parade at Lohatlha, April 1999.

Nostalgia – 61 Mech in review order at my parade, April 1999.

Addressing 61 Mech at Lohatlha during my going away parade in April 1999 as Deputy Chief of the Army.

Chapter 2

A common bond of friendship – establishing the 61 Mech Veterans' Association at Caledon in Aug 2007. Front from left: Gertjie van Zyl, Ariel Hugo, Hubrecht van Dalzen, Duppie du Plessis and Servaas Lotter. Middle from left: Ferdie de Vos, Kowie Steyn, Chris Walls, Gert Minnaar, Roland de Vries, Epp van Lill and Jan Malan. Rear: HG Smit.

That was it – meeting Henriette at Omuthiya, November 1982.

Married to Henriette in Postmasburg on 28 May 1983, with Padre Attie Bezuidenhout, Melanie, Roland (Jnr) and Henriette's mother Jo de Lange.

Teaching infant Pieter the ropes, Plettenberg Bay, December 1985 – "You'll Be a Man, My Son."

Pieter (3) standing to inspection.

Melanie (7): stable parade and kit inspection.

Chapter 2

My eldest son Roland (Jnr) and eldest daughter Elmarie.

My eldest daughter, married to Ferdi Grobler, with Sasha-Mari, Briana and Wanya.

Amazing Henriette obtained her PhD in Psychology in 1996 after years of exposure to me.

My Aussies – the Boschin family: Melanie, Jason, Elysia and Danica.

Chapter 2

Still enough of my grandchildren remaining in South Africa to make up a fighting platoon... Roland Jnr-Jnr, Briana, Sasha-Mari, Robyn and Wanya.

With my eldest grandchildren, Roland (Jnr-Jnr) and Robyn de Vries from the marriage of Roland Jnr and Lisa, Plettenberg Bay, 2012.

Writing my chapter on Ops Prone in Dubai, assisted by Elysia from Australia, December 2012.

Young Pieter remains close by – sailing in Bahrain, 2012.

Commandant Roland de Vries, Officer Commanding 61 Mech, 1981-1982.

Bevelvoerderserekode van 61 Meg. Gn. Gp.

Diep in Owamboland se uitgestrekte bos het die bevelsoorhandiging tussen die uittredende bevelvoerder, kmdt. J. M. Dippenaar van 61 Gemeganiseerde Bataljon Groep en kmdt. T. De Vries, nuwe bevelvoerder, om 09h00 op 9 January 1981, plaasgevind.

Gemeganiseerde vegspanne het aan 'n indrukwekkende gemeganiseerde kolonne deel gehad, wat 'n luisterryke geleentheid was. Staflede en hul gesinne is diep beïndruk deur die slaankrag van die Eenheid soos uitgebeeld deur die magsvertoon van hierdie besondere Eenheid.

Die uitgaande bevelvoerder, kmdt. Dippenaar, het ook 'n PMM (Pro Merito Medlaje) aan RSM AO1 M.C. Barnard (SAPK), oorhandig. Hierdie medalje word toegeken aan onderoffisiere wat voortreflike diens lewer.

In sy toespraak het kmdt. Dippenaar die staflede van die Eenheid geloof vir hulle diens en ondersteuning en gesê: "Elke soldaat kan 'n medalje verdien, mits hy bereid is om getroue, harde, eerlike en lojale diens te lewer." Hy het die Eenheid voorspoed en seën toegewens.

Nadat 'n oorhandigingsaluut geskiet is, het kmdt. Roland De Vries die 61 Meg. Bn. Gp.-bevelvoerderserekode voorgelees in Engels en Afrikaans: Dit lui soos volg:

"Ek verklaar dat ek bewus is van die belangrikheid van die voortbestaan van alle Christelike volke en aanvaar hiermee die verantwoordelikheid van die groot eer en geleentheid aan my gebied as Bevelvoerder van 61 Gemeganiseerde Bataljon Groep.

Ek onderneem om alles in my vermoë te gee tot die beskerming van Suidwes-Afrika teen aggressie van buite en tesame met my gade te help om 'n vreedsame en stabiele gemeenskap binne die landsgrense te skep.

Ek beloof om nooit my eie voordeel te soek nie, maar my altyd te beywer vir die hoogste heil van hierdie Eenheid en die S.A. Leër.

Ek sal alles in my vermoë gee om hierdie Eenheid tot die hoogste standaard van paraatheid en doeltreffendheid te lei.

Ek gee aan God die hoogste eer en aanvaar Hom as die hoogste gesag oor my lewe en Sy Woord is my finale lewenskode.

My leuse sal steeds wee:

"Vir my Makker
Vir my Eenheid
Vir my land en Volk
Vir my God!"

Kmdt. J.M. Dippenaar, SAPK
1 Januarie 79 - 9 Jan. 81
Kmdt. R. De Vries, SAIK
10 Januarie 81

All about the 61 Mech commander's code.

My Spartan office at Omuthiya where I met with "Captain Payne" in August 1981.

Being smart even in the bush – Inspection at Omuthiya, 1981.

Our bread and butter – Operational planning at Omuthiya was the regular thing.

Ops normal – Sergeant Piet Slow presenting the intelligence picture. From left to right: Major Leon Marais and Captain Koos Liebenberg.

Mark you, SWAPO and FAPLA – the sharp end of a Ratel-90 of Charlie Squadron.

Young Padre Koos Rossouw at Omuthiya, 1981.

From a long-gone era – Images in cement at Omuthiya in 2010.

The Iron Cross (dated 1939) given to me by Robert Kaspar in Tsumeb, 1982.

Handing over command of 61 Mech to Cmdt Gert van Zyl.

Chapter 4

What was left in 2010 of the guard house at the entrance to Omuthiya.

The troop mess-hall at Omuthiya today (thirty years later)

Sharing the podium of 61 Mech at Omuthiya with my friend John McMahon in October 2010.

The rear HQ of 61 Mech in Tsumeb, thirty years later – sharing a nostalgic moment with Andy Weyand in October 2010.

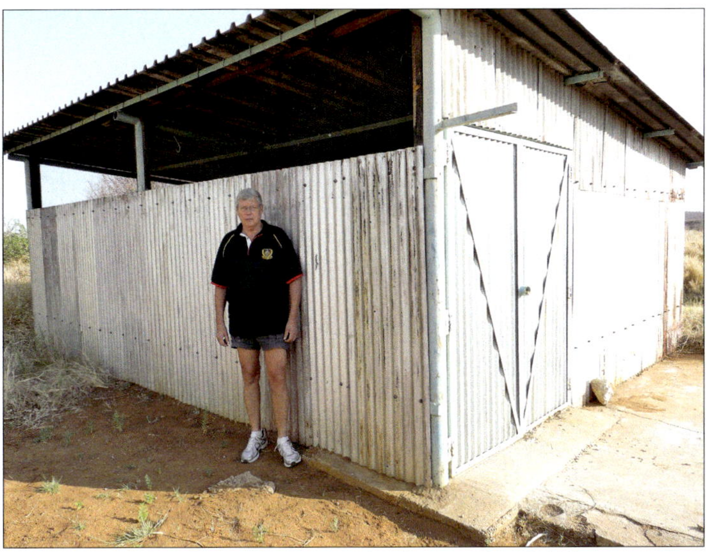

Where the tac HQ of 61 Mech was located at the Tsumeb airfield for operations Carrot and Yahoo, October 2010. (Photograph: Deon Lamprecht)

Chapter 5

Killing ground – the thorny bushveld and mountainous terrain surrounding Tsumeb. (Photograph: Krige van Heerden)

Illusive serenity – A typical kraal in southern Angola. (Photograph: Camille Burger)

The sandy conditions of southern Angola.

Vital ground – the water tower near the bridge at Xangongo on the west bank of the Cunene River.

Not for the faint-hearted when bundu-bashing – terrain in the vicinity of Evale. (Photograph: Camille Burger)

The road between Cuvelai and Techamutete – ideal for ambushing and mine laying. (Photograph: Camille Burger)

Chapter 5

An anhara near Indungo providing great fields of fire (Ops Firewood area) (Photograph: Camille Burger)

Ask the enemy all about it – on Death Road between Menongue and Cuito Cuanavale. (Photograph: Camille Burger)

The easy-to-defend-or-ambush crossing at the Longa River, viewed from the turret of a Russian T54/55 tank. (Photograph: Camille Burger)

Dense terrain near Cuito Cuanavale. (Photograph: Camille Burger)

No question about it – the Cuito River formed a formidable natural obstacle. (Photograph: Camille Burger)

Sharing memories from a bygone era – 61 Mech parade at the Ditsong National Military Museum, August 2012.

61 Mech veterans from the Border War on parade, 25 August 2012.

25 August 2012 – veterans Lukas Nel and Dave Keyser from operations Carrot and Yahoo seated to the left of Henriette. (Photograph: Deon Lamprecht)

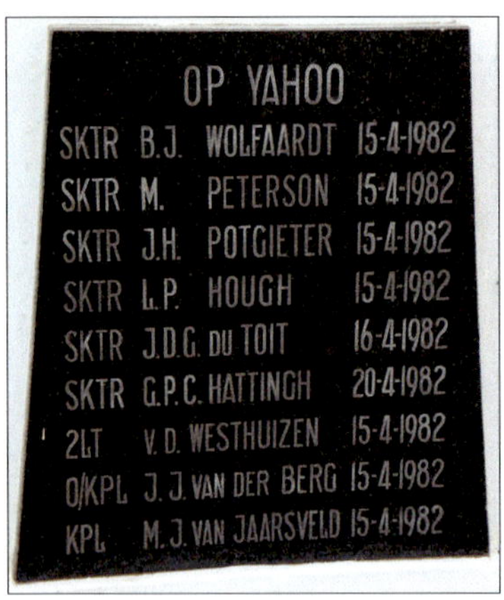

Ops Yahoo 1982 – Some of the names on the Memorial Needle of 61 Mech and in our thoughts.

Chapter 9

61 Mech Remembrance Day, 25 August 2012 – laying a wreath. (Photograph: Deon Lamprecht)

Cmdt Lukas Nel (Ret) remembering the fallen from Ops Yahoo.

Soulmates – With Ariel Hugo and the legendary Lukas Nel during the 61 Mech Parade in August 2012.

Jaap Steyn and Camille Burger share my moment at the Memorial Needle of 61 Mech, August 2011.

Chapter 11

WINDHOEK OBSERVER

SATURDAY APRIL 11, 1981 The Paper for the People Registered at the GPO as a Newspaper No. 157 Price 30c (Tax included)

SUICIDE MISSION

Armed clash with guerrillas at Otjikoto

Ops Carrot, April 1981 – “suicide mission” by SWAPO.

An armoured strike force gets ready on Wednesday of this week to search the northern perimeters of the Tsumeb district for two groups of Insurgents. The Observer was present for most of the day while the search was in progress.

LEAFLET WAR IN OTAVI VALLEY

STAFF REPORTER
WINDHOEK:

Swapo insurgents, believed to be saboteurs according to top staff officers of the Army High Command in Windhoek, have distributed a large number of propaganda leaflets and other literature such as the movement's constitution in areas south of Tsumeb where they are currently deployed, to strike at what is believed are “soft targets” and in that manner, the Army says, to catch the headlines.

There did occur though, at yesterday azfternoon is military briefing, an incident, which this newspaper feels was directly aimed in an effort to discredit us. Swapo guerrillas have a newspaper of their own called The Combatant.

This 'newspaper' was among the documents distributed in the early hours of the morning yesterday at settlements where black people live. On page 16 there is a heading: “SWA flotsam and jetsam (SWA press looks at the so-called internal leaders.” The combatant then takes 12 quotes from the Windhoek

Continued on Page 8

Ops Carrot – “leaflet war” in the Death Triangle.

Swapo finds no place to hide

A GROUP of Swapo terrorists who tried to penetrate into the farming areas of northern South West Africa were tracked down and killed by the Security Forces with determined skill.

The gang, heavily armed with Russian-supplied weapons, were on a futile mission — to wreak havoc and destruction among the innocent inhabitants in the area. themselves the hunters, they became in the hunted as the Security Forces swiftly turned the tables on them and relentlessly persued them to their deaths.

But instead of the hunters they found themselves the hunted, as the Security Forces turned the tables on them and persued them relentlessly to their deaths.

The quick response by the Security Forces caught the terrorists off guard.

Sector 30, which the terrorists tried to penetrate covers nearly a third of South West Africa/Namibia. Comprising 278 273 km², the security of the area is the responsibility of a single unit. Sector 30 is equivalent in size to Lesotho, the Orange Free State and the whole of Natal combined.

Otjiwarongo is known as the 'capital city' of the North, and here Sector 30's headquarters are to be found, its name emblazoned in Afrikaans, English, and German. The area around Otjiwarongo is particularly suited to grazing, at least according to its name. It is from here that 11 other bases are controlled.

There are some rather large towns in this area, such as Grootfontein, Outjo, Otavi, Tsumeb, Otjiwarongo, as well as the whole of Damaraland and Hereroland. Some 32 000 and 103 000 Whites and Blacks respectively, live in Sector 30. Apart from those who work in the towns, the overwhelming majority reside on cattle farms. There are sheep and goats

What happened in the Death Triangle is alluded to by the military periodical Paratus – Ops Carrot, April 1981.

WINDHOEK OBSERVER FEBRUARY 27, 1982

Bobos strike

COURT REPORTER

WINDHOEK: A surprise turn of events put a temporary end to the trial of three Swapo insurgents, charged under the Act on Terrorism. As the people started filing into the Courtroom with an air of expectancy, because the Court is entitled to impose the death penalty, it was learned that money had arrived, and that Senior Counsel could be briefed to appear for the three young blacks who throughout the trial so far, have shown no outward signs of their feelings.

The rail tracks at Bobos between Otavi and Tsumeb after saboteurs had set explosive charges to them. The saboteurs also carried considerable quantities in propaganda literature on them. These were distributed on the hills and on farms.

The three insurgents were members of a group of 22, of which 15 were killed and four managed to escape the steel clutches of a vast mechanised security force thrown over the north in April of last year. The order was 'exterminate them'.

On Wednesday Mr Justice ... convened Mr Bryan O'Linn SC walked in. He was followed by Mr Ruppel, of the law firm Lorentz and Bone, instructing attorneys in the new turn of affairs.

It soon transpired that money had been received to enable the three young men to obtain the services of a Senior Counsel.

Mr Justice Bethune appeared slightly irritated when he addressed the Court after he had learned that a advocates who were formerly in Court in pro deo capacities, would be his juniors, both having been instructed by Lorentz and Bone.

The Judge wanted to know why from the start there was pro deo representation, if now the accused were in a position to pay for their trial.

Mr O'Linn explained the three men were held in solitary confinement for a long period. They were not in received to appoint Senior Counsel. Those who were now assisting the three accused with money, were not aware of the trial said Mr O'Linn, and only through subsequent reports, did they learn about it. That at least, Mr O'Linn made clear, was his surmise.

He applied for a postponement of the trial which had reached the stage where the Judge had already make a submission without a proper investigation into the circumstances. He proposed, saying that this was entirely subject to the approval of the State, that the matter be postponed until Tuesday May 11 and be set down for three days until May 14. He would then possibly call witnesses to testify in mitigation. There was even the possibility, he said, that he could call expert witnesses to testify. Counsel did not elaborate on what he circumstances of the case. Under the circumstances, Mr Hiemstra said, the State could hardly oppose Mr O'Linn's application.

Thereupon Mr Justice Bethune issued an order, saying a date must be arranged with the Registrar of the Supreme Court, Mr Hank Peters, for a date for the matter.

Mr Peters subsequently confirmed that the trial would

Bobos Strike, Ops Carrot.

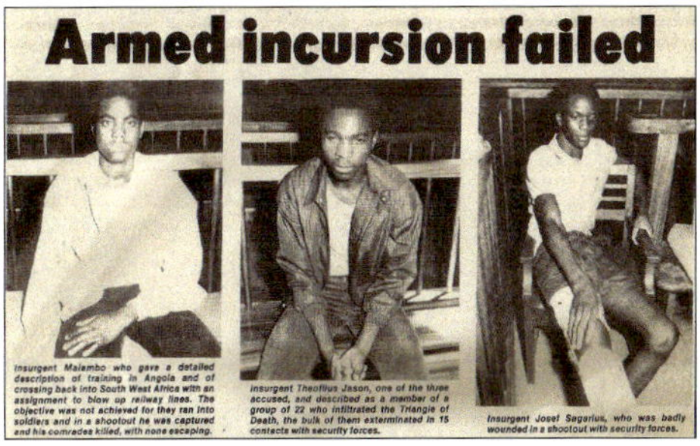

Armed incursion failed

Insurgent Malambo who gave a detailed description of training in Angola and of crossing back into South West Africa with an assignment to blow up railway lines. The objective was not achieved for they ran into soldiers and in a shootout he was captured and his comrades killed, with none escaping.

Insurgent Theofilus Jason, one of the three accused, and described as a member of a group of 22 who infiltrated the Triangle of Death, the bulk of them exterminated in 15 contacts with security forces.

Insurgent Josef Sagarius, who was badly wounded in a shootout with security forces.

Three captives during Ops Carrot, 1981.

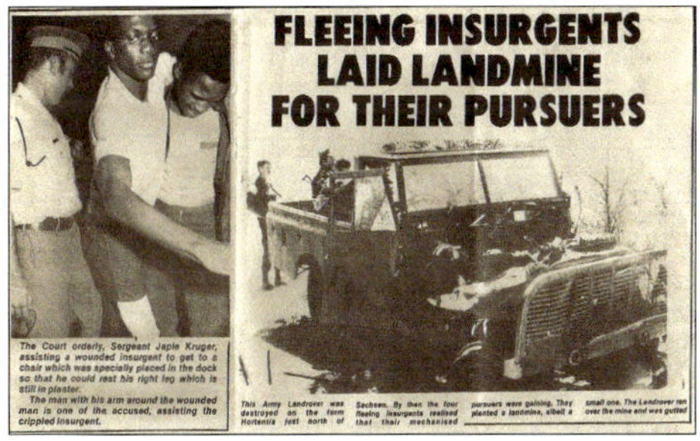

FLEEING INSURGENTS LAID LANDMINE FOR THEIR PURSUERS

The Court orderly, Sergeant Japie Kruger, assisting a wounded insurgent to get to a chair which was specially placed in the dock so that he could rest his right leg which is still in plaster.

The man with his arm around the wounded man is one of the accused, assisting the crippled insurgent.

This Army Landrover was destroyed on the farm Hortensia just north of Sachsen. By then the four fleeing insurgents realised that their mechanised pursuers were gaining. They planted a landmine, albeit a small one. The Landrover ran over the mine and was gutted

Ops Carrot – "Fleeing insurgents laid landmines for their pursuers".

The Court would have met on Thursday morning for the purpose of listening to an address by the State, represented by Mr Joe Hiemstra, and by addresses to be made by both Mr Pio Teek and Mr Anton Lubowski, who appeared pro deo for the three guerrillas.

Just before the Court circumstances had arisen. There was now an instructing attorney and no longer pro deo representation for the accused men.

Mr Teek extended his apologies to Mr Justice Bethune.

Mr Bryan O'Linn then rose. He said he was appearing for all three and that the two

Mr Anton Lubowski who is appearing pro deo for the insurgents.

JUDGE'S REASONS

COURT REPORTER

WINDHOEK: Mr Justice Kenneth Bethune stated his reasons on Thursday morning why he had convicted three young blacks under the Act on Terrorism and why he had found that they were guilty of contravening all the provisions contained in that Act.

The Judge said that the three men were charged under Article 2(1)(c) of the Act on Terrorism, Act 83 of 1967.

When they were brought before a Magistrate, Accused Number One, Josef Sagarias and Accused Number Two, Theofilus Jason, submitted a plea of guilty. Accused Number Three Lucius Malambo, did not make a plea.

Hereafter the Attorney General decided the three must appear in a Supreme Court, and when the Supreme Court met to hear them, all three submitted a plea of not guilty. Counsel for Josef Sagarias and Theofilus Jason, informed the Court that the two accused had not meant to submit a plea of guilty when they appeared in a lower court, and that there could possibly be some misunderstanding with the interpreter in Court.

Mr Justice Bethune said in the circumstances he had decided to exercise his discretion and note a plea of not guilty by all three men before court.

The State, the Judge said, had filed an application that the names of State witnesses must not be revealed, and such an order was made.

A statement by Colonel R. was served on the accused and none of the three men before court had indicated that they desired that Colonel R should personally testify in the Supreme Court. When Colonel R's statement was handed in at the Supreme Court, Counsel for Defence indicated that they would want an opportunity to cross examine Colonel R. The statement by the Colonel was not handed in, but on the second day of the trial, Defence Counsel withdrew its objection against the submission of this statement.

The statement was then handed in.

Mr Justice Bethune said that according to the evidence led by the State, a group of 22 members of Swapo's forces infiltrated the socalled white area of South West Africa early in April of last year. Military steps were immediately invoked to stop them and if necessary exterminate them.

Cont. on next page

Mr Pio Teek, Windhoek's practising black member of the Bar Council, who has also been instructed pro deo to appear on behalf of the insurgents. Mr Teek is a devoted barrister who also appeared for Markus Kateka and who fought his case in the Appelate Division in Bloemfontein which resulted in Kateka's death sentence being commuted.

Ops Carrot – the trial I wrote about.

MORE INTEREST THAN FEAR

An armoured car in the streets of Tsumeb

Ops Carrot – living on the edge in Tsumeb.

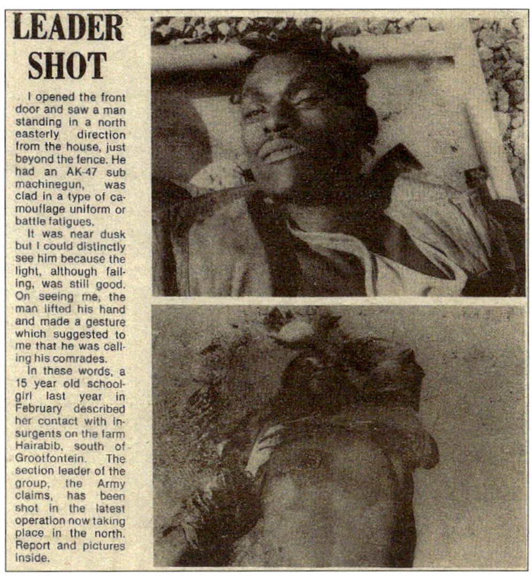

LEADER SHOT

I opened the front door and saw a man standing in a north easterly direction from the house, just beyond the fence. He had an AK-47 sub machinegun, was clad in a type of camouflage uniform or battle fatigues.

It was near dusk but I could distinctly see him because the light, although failing, was still good. On seeing me, the man lifted his hand and made a gesture which suggested to me that he was calling his comrades.

In these words, a 15 year old schoolgirl last year in February described her contact with insurgents on the farm Hairabib, south of Grootfontein. The section leader of the group, the Army claims, has been shot in the latest operation now taking place in the north. Report and pictures inside.

Ops Carrot – SWAPO "leader shot".

Ops Yahoo – the Ratel of Captain Jan Malan destroyed in the ambush, 15 April 1982.

Ops Carrot, 18 April 1981 with Sergeant Major Hennie Blaauw soon after our contact with SWAPO's Special Unit.

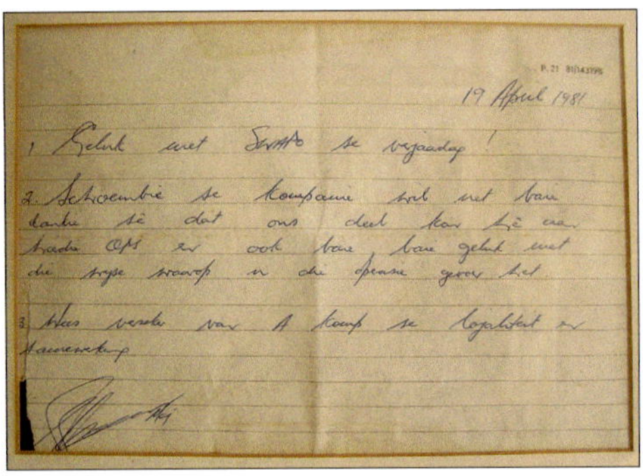

P.21 81/143795

19 April 1981

1. Geluk met SWAPO se verjaardag!

2. Schoembie se kompanie wil net baie dankie sê dat ons deel kon hê aan hierdie OPS en ook baie, baie geluk met die sukses waarop u die operasie gevoer het

3. Baie dankie vir A Komp se lojaliteit en samewerking

Ops Carrot – Letter to Roland de Vries from the legendary Captain Cassie Schoeman.

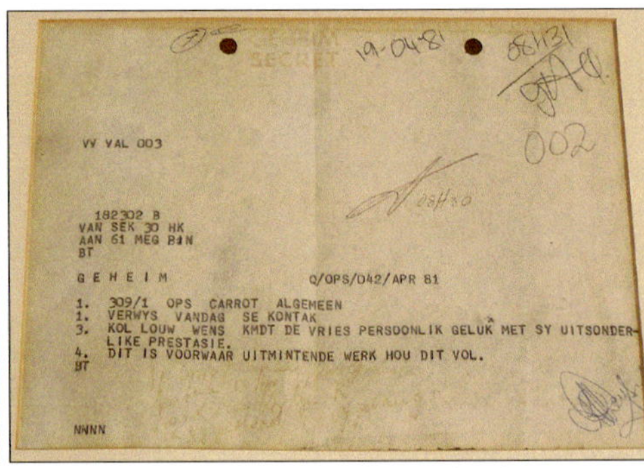

SECRET 19-04-81 081131

002

VY VAL 003

182302 B
VAN SEK 30 HK
AAN 61 MEG BN
BT

GEHEIM Q/OPS/042/APR 81

1. 309/1 OPS CARROT ALGEMEEN
1. VERWYS VANDAG SE KONTAK
3. KOL LOUW WENS KMDT DE VRIES PERSOONLIK GELUK MET SY UITSONDERLIKE PRESTASIE.
4. DIT IS VOORWAAR UITMINTENDE WERK HOU DIT VOL.
BT

NNNN

Ops Carrot – Telex message from Colonel J.T. Louw.

Addressing my troops at Omuthiya on the successful completion of Ops Carrot in April 1981. (Photograph: Giel Reinecke)

I Say Thank You. From left to right: Louwtjie and Bets de Klerk and Pompie and Daan van der Westhuizen. (Photograph from the 61 Mech archive)

April '82-Infiltrasie

Komdt. R. de Vries saam met Kol. J. Louw.

DIE vier bevelvoerders van die veiligheidsmagte gemoeid met Tsumeb, naamlik kol. J. Louw, bevelvoerder van Sektor 30, kol. Thomasse van die S.W.A.-polisie, komdt. De Vries van 61 Meg. Bn. Gp. en komdt Nel van Etosha A.M.E. het onlangs 'n aantal gaste van Tsumeb en omgewing genooi om die April '82 infiltrasie te bespreek.

Hoofde van verskeie instansies en departement van T.C.L., asook boere uit die omgewing was teenwoordig.

Komdt. De Vries en lede van sy personeel het 'n uiteensetting gegee van die groot area waar opereer is, die magte wat aangewend is en die koste daaraan verbonde.

Komdt. De Vries het die belangrikheid van wedersydse kommunikasie, veral om operasies op die kaplyn meer effektief te maak, benadruk.

Die veiligheidsmagte gaan 'n groot poging aanwend om die vyand daar meer effektief te monitor. Dit is 'n uitgestrekte gebied en daar word alles gedoen wat prakties moontlik is om infiltrasie te stuit.

Die belangrikheid van suksesvolle rapportering van inligting is beklemtoon.

Kol. Louw en komdt. De Vries het met groot lof gepraat van die wonderlike samewerking tussen die Weermag, die S.A. Polisie, die S.W.A. Polisie, S.A.P. Veiligheid, die Lugmag, die Leër en die A.M.E.'s Daarby kom nog die goeie samewerking van die publiek.

Kol. Louw het gesê hy is dankbaar vir die meerderheid van die publiek wat hulle waardering vir die werk van die veiligheidsmagte uitgespreek het. Hy het onder andere die telegram van dank van die Burgemeester van Tsumeb genoem.

Hy het hulde gebring aan al die verskillende veiligheidsmagte en hulle bevelvoerders wat meegehelp het om die operasie suksesvol te laat verloop, asook die dames wat tydens die operasie so mooi na die diensdoende lede omgesien het.

Read all about it – with Colonel J.T. Louw on completion of Ops Yahoo, April-May 1982.

MILITARY CORRESPONDENT

WINDHOEK: The latest situation in the incursion which occurred in the triangle of death is that a further six guerrillas were shot, Army Headquarters announced in Windhoek before the noon hour yesterday.

The Army statement says that three of these men were shot on the farm Kakuze (no district mentioned) and another three just north of the Mangetti area. The statement adds that in summarising the situation the following facts transpired in recent days:

Two groups of insurgents attempted to infiltrate the farming land south of the Mangetti area. One of the groups with a strength of between 25 to 30 men succeeded in the attempted incursion while a second group of 13 could not manage to infiltrate.

Until the noon hour yesterday, Wednesday April 15 ten of the group of 25 which succeeded to make an incursion, were shot and killed. The survivors have broken up into smaller groups and have taken refuge in the thick bush of the Tsumeb-Otavi-Kombat area.

The second group of insurgents which failed to penetrate the farming area, was currently fleeing through western Kavango in the direction of the Ovambo-speaking region, the statement said, adding that two of this group were shot and killed.

Six guerrillas shot – Ops Yahoo, 1982.

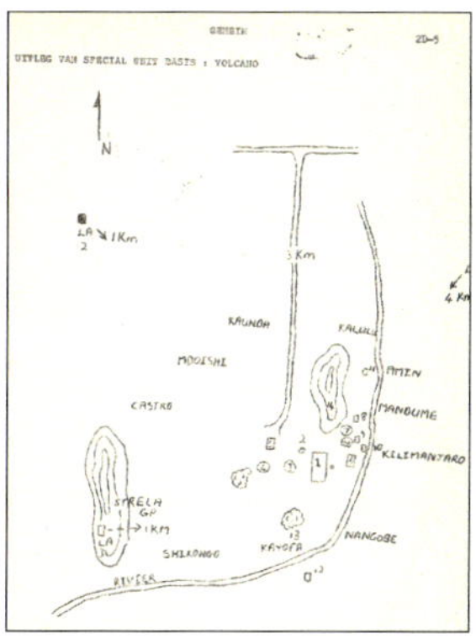

Layout of Special Unit's base (Volcano) in Angola – Ops Yahoo.

Mnr. D.J.J. (Rassie) Erasmus

Hendrik Potgieter

Ops Yahoo, April to May 1982 – about the fallen.

THE OTJIKOTO JOURNAL

BESOEK AAN BESEERDES

DAMES van Etosha AME, Noordgrens Kompanie en 61 Meg. Bn. Gp. het die gewondes in die Militêre Hospitaal in Pretoria gaan besoek.

Die twee bekwame vlieëniers wat ons veilig terug besorg het.

REINHARD VORDER NA WENSE

Reinhard Friederich, 'n plaasboer uit Tsumebdistrik wat in 'n landmynontploffing beseer is, vorder na wense.

Yvonne, sy vrou, het ook saam met die dames daar besoek afgelê.

DANK AAN FIRMAS EN PERSONE

Ons wil graag die volgende persone en firmas bedank wat bygedra het vir die geskenkpakkies vir die gewondes:

Alfa Ko-op
Inge Scholz
Model Supermark
Nictus
Gerdi Müller
Joey Nel

Ops Yahoo, 1982 – visiting the wounded.

Steeds vol Moed

"Dit staan soos 'n paal bo water: Ons gaan terug plaas toe," sê tannie Pompie. Sodra alles weer normaal is wil tannie Pompie, Olivia en die kinders weer teruggaan plaas toe. Sy hoop dat Mannetjies, wat nou besig is met diensplig, haar sal kan help.

Terug in Tuig

Net die dag na die begrafnis was tannie Pompie weer terug op haar pos voor die radio. Tydens ons besoek aan haar was sy weer volstoom aan die gang.

Olivia is ook betrek deur Etosha AME waar sy diens doen. Albei staan hulle plek vol, en dit help om die smart en gemis draagliker te maak.

Baie Dankie!

Die Van der Westhuizens en Potgieters wil die gemeenskap van Tsumeb hartlik bedank vir hulle wonderlike hulp en bystand na die dood van hul geliefdes. "Die mense in Tsumeb het hulle harte oopgemaak en ek sê dankie daarvoor," sê tannie Pompie.

Mev. Pompie van der Westhuizen, weduwee van lt. Van der Westhuizen, terug voor die radio's.

Ops Yahoo, 1982 – a grieving Tannie Pompie.

61 Mech Command Group, Ops Protea, August 1981. Front from left: Second-in-Command Major Thys Rall, Operations Officer Commandant Epp van Lill, Phantom Platoon (Protection) Commander Second Lieutenant Marche Michau, Medical Officer Dr Reitz Malherbe. Second row from left: Artillery Commander Captain Bernie Pols, Unit Chaplain Padre Koos Rossouw, Logistics Officer Major Giel Reinecke, Personnel Officer Lieutenant Willem van der Vyfer. Third row from left: Sergeant Major M.C. Barnard (Regimental Sergeant Major), Protection Company Commander Major Dawid Mentz, Bravo Company Commander Captain Koos Liebenberg, Officer Commanding Commandant Roland de Vries, Charlie Squadron Commander Major Joe Weyers, Unknown Officer, Engineer Officer Major Leon Terblanche. Back row from left: Intelligence Officer Commandant Joe Aveling, Signals Officer Captain Thinus van Wyk, Alpha Company Commander Captain Pale van der Walt, Technical Officer Captain Philipp 'Jakkals' Jaeckel, Mobile Reserve (Combat Team Mamba) Captain Hannes van der Merwe.

Ops Protea – A young soldier preparing for battle at Omuthiya.

Ops Protea – A short halt north of the Etosha on the way to Ruacana.

Chapter 12

Up close and personal – refuelling from a Lappies mobile fuel pump.

Left: The 61 Mech Command Group refuelling during Ops Protea.

Final briefing to 61 Mech (Battle Group 10) for Ops Protea at Ruacana on D minus 1.

Splendour and pride – to see the open young faces of my troops in this way at Ruacana, Ops Protea, 23 August 1981.

A young tiffy replacing a Ratel engine at night in the field during Ops Protea.

My Command Ratel (nicknamed Repulse) during Ops Protea, August 1981.

Chapter 12

Ops Protea – 61 Mech advancing on Humbe on D-Day, 24 August 1981.

Ops Protea – meeting our well-regarded teacher and his adopted son near Humbe.

Left: Ops Protea – Padre Koos Rossouw and a few of his followers – smoking could kill you.

Right: Catching up with my shaving on D plus 1 with explosives already affixed to the bridge, Ops Protea.

The bridge at Xangongo stacked with explosives during the night of 24-25 August 1981.

Ops Protea – my command group crossing the Cunene on D plus 1.

Chapter 12

Ops Protea – A young sapper killed in a booby-trapped house across me near the bridge at Xangongo on 25 August 1981.

A lone Eland armoured car guards the local inhabitants at Xangongo, Ops Protea.

Ops Protea – meeting up with the Pathfinders of Colonel Jan Breytenbach at the bridge.

61 Mech crossing at Xangongo with captured enemy 23 mm AA-guns.

For them the war was over – FAPLA prisoners of war at Xangongo, Ops Protea.

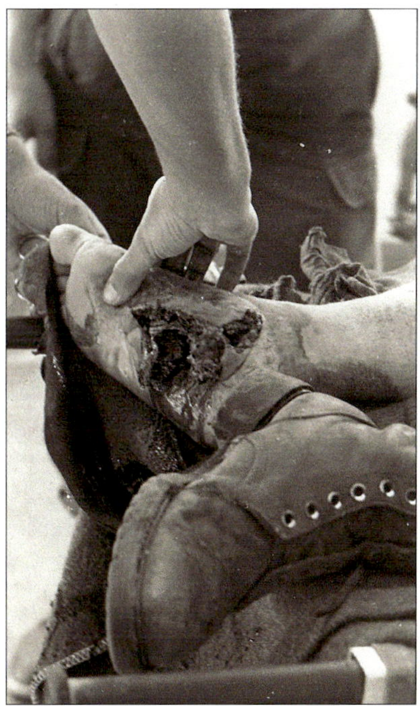

Ops Protea – medical treatment for a personnel mine victim of the Pathfinders.

Ops Protea – The Phantom Platoon commanded by Lieutenant Marche Mucho. (Photograph: 61 Mech Archive)

"Captain Payne" of the Phantoms – after action, satisfaction – looking extremely intimidating in his Buffel (where are you today, my friend?) (Photograph: 61 Mech Archive)

61 Mech exploiting through Mucope during Ops Protea on 25 August 1981.

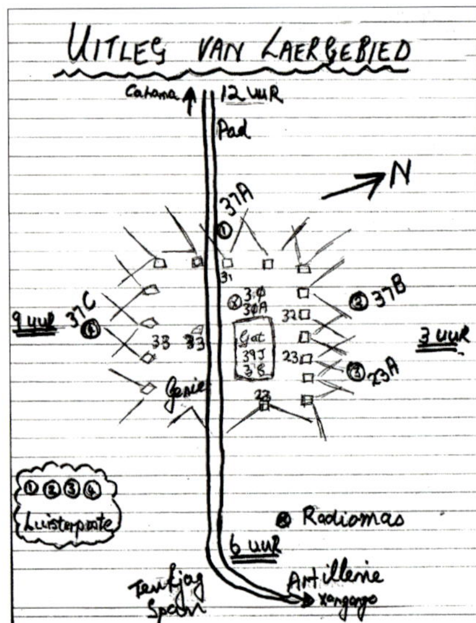

Deployment of Combat Team 3 at Chicusse.

Xangongo – One of the Russian BM-21's captured by 61 Mech's Combat Team 3 during Ops Protea.

Ops Protea – a contact site near Chicusse on the road between Xangongo and Cahama.

The former home of the Minister of Education of the Cunene Province which became our HQ at Xangongo during Ops Protea – with appreciation from 61 Mech.

What a man, always smiling! – Major Les Rudman arrives at Xangongo.

One of my order groups at Xangongo during Ops Protea.

Captured Russian SAM-7s at Xangongo, Ops Protea.

An intelligence briefing by Commandant Joe Aveling to the 61 Mech Command Group during Ops Protea.

FAPLA defences at Xangongo, Ops Protea.

Dawid Mentz and I meet with the locals and make friends.

Ops Protea – propaganda display by FAPLA at Xangongo – "Destroy the Racist South Africans..."

SOLDIERS AND SHIMBUNDUS PLAY SOCCER

The spectators at a soccer game between the South Africans and the local soccer team of Xangongo.

The well-known soccer game at Xangongo initiated by General Jannie Geldenhuys – Ops Protea, August 1981.

Ops Protea – appraising the FAPLA sand model of their defences at Xangongo on how they defended in the wrong direction.

Inspecting a FAPLA air defence position at Xangongo during Ops Protea.

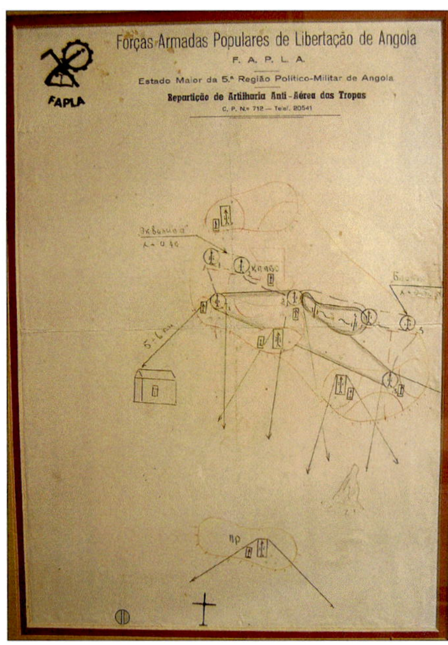

Exquisite staff work – A FAPLA sketch I found in the trenches at Xangongo left by the fleeing, Ops Protea.

A AJUDA MILITAR DOS PAISES CAPITALISTAS AOS RACISTAS

O RATEL

Existem duas palavras quase semelhantes, mas completamente diferentes pelo significado. Trata-se das palavras "Embargo e Embarque".

A primeira significa proibição de venda ou de fornecimento de mercadoria, e a segunda, ao contrário, significa pôr mercadorias sobre os barcos.

Os paises capitalistas fazem uma voluntária confusão destes dois termos em relação à ajuda militar que continuam a fornecer aos racistas da África do Sul.

Pode dizer-se que esta situação foi planificada cientificamente para sempre encontrar maneira de ajudar os racistas, principal fornecedor de produtos energeticos (ferro, ouro, urânio, diamantes, carvão etc etc. do capital internacional. Oficialmente ou não os racistas continuam a receber ajuda e assistência militar dos paises capitalistas que nas assembleias internacionais proclamam o Embargo e depois procuram acelerar o embarque das armas aos racistas.

No ano de 1978 as publicações militares francesas, inglesas, italianas, Norte-Americanas e da R.F.A. publicaram fotografias e deram pequenos dados sobre o novo blindado da África do Sul: O RATEL.

Distinguiram nesta acção de publicidade as seguintes revistas: Defence Interarmées (francêsa) Eserciti e Armi (Italiana).

O problema não é especificamente com estas Revistas que como todas as publicações militares da Europa capitalista são controlados pelos vários serviços secretos ocidentais e pelo "Bureau de Informação da O.T.A.N.; que se ocupa da dita "Guerra Psicológica ao Comunismo".

O problema está na mistificação que foi feita deste novo blindado, para apresentar a indústria-militar Sul-Africana como um fenómeno excepcional, incrivelmente competente e funcional.

Temos que dizer que a dita funcionalidade e perfeição da tecnologia militar Sul-Africana é artificial, quer dizer sem a ajuda directa das potências capitalistas, a Africa do Sul nunca teria fabricado tal blindado RATEL.

Considerando que todo o armamento da Africa do Sul sempre foi de importação Ocidental, a fabricação deste representa uma manobra psicológica que reforça a política de agresão que os racistas estão a levar a cabo na África Austral. Nenhum país Africano está em condições de construir por si próprio armamentos pesados, portanto o estado que desenvolve uma tal actividade claramente demonstra a sua agressividade politico-militar.

Elementary, my dear Watson. The enemy knew all along about the Ratel – found during Ops Protea at Xangongo.

Top: Ops Protea – 140 mm guns keeping the enemy's mobile reserve in place at Cahama.

Above: On the way home – blowing up FAPLA's underground fuel tanks at Ondjiva, Ops Protea, September 1981.

Aftermath of war – viewing the destroyed bridge at Xangongo during Ops Meebos, March 1982.

An aerial photograph of the bridge at Xangongo after its destruction in September 1981. (Photograph: 61 Mech Archive)

WINDHOEK OBSERVER

SATURDAY JULY 11, 1981 The paper for the People Registered at the GPO as a newspaper No. 171 Price 30c (Tax included)

ARMY THRUST POUNCES ANGOLA

"I can assure you that the information I have is that as yet my men have not bumped into FAPLA forces. Soldiers of FAPLA and civilians are targets with which contact is not to be sought.

"We are bent on the utter destruction of these bases. We are looking for a fight...but we do not get one. They are running," General Lloyd said.

HANNES SMITH

THE BORDER: South African shock troops converged on various targets in the south of Angola in a strike which for its murderous sting, has had few parallels in the long and bloody bushwar of South West Africa. At one stage a clash was held up and the ground troops could not

In Windhoek the supreme military commander, General Charles Lloyd admitted that his forces had struck at Swapo bases in Angola. But he denied contact with FAPLA, the regular army of Angola, or with

destruction of a village from the air near a place called Ombedja.

Climate creation – The *Windhoek Observer* reports on thrusts into Angola.

WINDHOEK OBSERVER JULY 11, 1981 PAGE 3

KUNENE BLITZ

Media report on the "Kunene Blitz", September 1981.

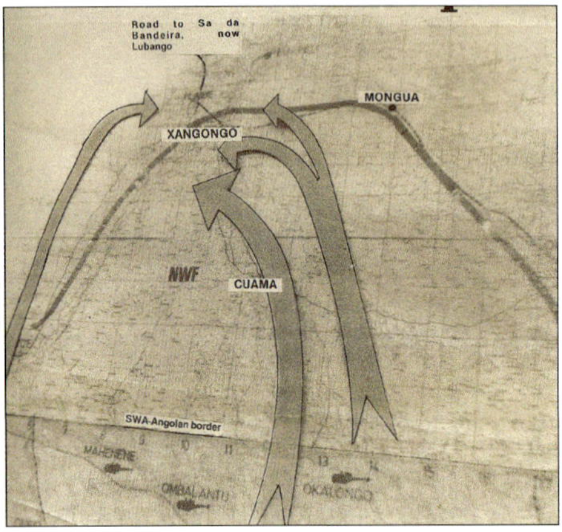

Another media report on Ops Protea, September 1981.

Angola 'loses radar screen'

5 Sept '81

Australian Associated Press-Reuter

JOHANNESBURG, Friday — All Angolan radar and anti-aircraft sites within a 150-kilometre strip north of the Namibian frontier have been destroyed, informed Western sources say.

They were knocked out in raids by South African aircraft.

The principal targets were Soviet-made Sam3 surface-to-air missile installations at Cahama and Chibemba, 130 kilometres and 200 kilometres north of the Cunene River, the sources said.

Neutralisation of Angola's protective "umbrella" was believed to have been one of the main objectives of Operation Protea, which was launched by South Africa when her troops crossed northward from Namibia.

The recent installation of radar and missile sites in southern Angola was a major problem for the South African forces, ruling out any element of surprise in future operations against the Angolan rear bases of the South West Africa Peoples Organisation, the nationalist movement fighting for an independent Namibia.

South Africa, long ostracised by the West because of her racial-segregation policies, is hoping that proof of Soviet involvement in Angola will win support for her white-minority Government.

A diplomatic source in Pretoria said South African security forces inside Angola had killed two unidentified Soviet lieutenant colonels and two Soviet women.

One of the women was the wife of Sergeant Major Nicolay Pestretsov, who was taken prisoner by the South Africans.

The Defence Department in Pretoria so far has acknowledged only that the two senior officers were among "some Soviets" killed.

So what is new? Angola loses Radar Screen.

WINDHOEK OBSERVER AUGUST 29, 1981 PAGE 3

MURDEROUS ASSAULT

Continued from Page 1

showing the vestiges of Portuguese architecture, with roomy, lovely homes.

The first objective was the Russian headquarters at Xangongo. Here worked about 20 officers and non-commissioned officers of the Russian army, aided by seven women.

The man in command of the place held the rank of Lieutenant and he vacated his headquarters and house 2 hours and 50 minutes before the arrival of the South African mechanised units.

Russian writing is difficult to read, but I made out his name as Boris Burin, but this may be erroneous. He is a handsome man in his thirties, married to a striking young woman, who was in a great hurry to put the proper shoes on, for fleeing in a hurried state. Her shoes were lying in a disorderly fashion in her bedroom.

In the Russian headquarters, there is an atmosphere which speaks of only one thing -- organised militarism. Maps in Russian on the walls showed how Xangongo must be defended in case of an artillery attack or air raid. A lovely, huge colour picture of President Brezhnev, looks on from the wall. Likewise one of Fidel Castro, who is pictured with Che Guevara, the famed guerrilla, who has become the number one name in the

Ops Protea viewed as a "murderous assault" by the media.

Sept 4

2 WORLD NEWS The Advertiser, Friday, Septe

Soviets training Angolan troops, envoy admits

Australian Associated Press-Reuter

PARIS, Thursday — The Angolan ambassador to France, Mr. Jose d'Almeida, acknowledged today that the Angolan Army was being trained by Soviet officers and some might have been killed in the South African attacks on Angola.

TROOPS CAPTURE ARMS

ABOVE: South African soldiers walk past equipment captured in Angola. It includes a Soviet-made 122mm multiple rocket launcher mounted on a Soviet-made ZIL truck and, at left in foreground, anti-aircraft guns of unknown origin.

RIGHT: Sergeant-Major Nikolai Pestretsov, the Soviet soldier captured by South African forces this week.

World News reports about Ops Protea and captured Russians.

PAGE 10 WINDHOEK OBSERVER AUGUST 29, 1981

Russian bomb-proof bunker

Russian bunker found during Ops Protea as reported in the *Windhoek Observer* on 29 August 1981.

MURDEROUS ASSAULT LEAVES 400 DEAD

The attack on Xangongo leaves 400 dead.

WINDHOEK OBSERVER SEPTEMBER 5, 1981 PAGE 47

INCURSION ENDS

WINDHOEK OBSERVER

FULL ACCOUNT OF THE STRIKE AT FAPLA-SWAPO HQ

THE INVASION

MURDEROUS ASSAULT LEAVES 400 DEAD

On 5 September 1981 the *Windhoek Observer* reported the end of Ops Protea.

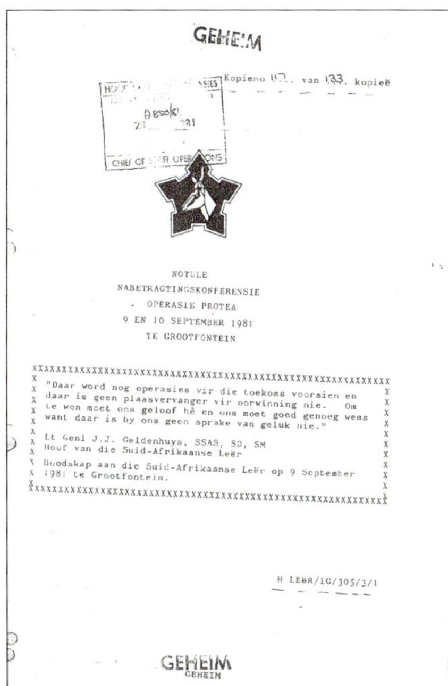
GEHEIM

Kopieno ... van 133. kopieë

CHIEF OF STAFF OPERATIONS

NOTULE
NABETRAGTINGSKONFERENSIE
OPERASIE PROTEA
9 EN 10 SEPTEMBER 1981
TE GROOTFONTEIN

"Daar word nog operasies vir die toekoms voorsien en daar is geen plaasvervanger vir oorwinning nie. Om te won moet ons geloof hê en ons moet goed genoeg wees want daar is by ons geen sprake van geluk nie."

Lt Genl J.J. Geldenhuys, SSAS, SD, SM
Hoof van die Suid-Afrikaanse Leër

Boodskap aan die Suid-Afrikaanse Leër op 9 September 1981 te Grootfontein.

H LEëR/IG/305/3/1

GEHEIM

The cover page of the Ops Protea debriefing conference held on 9–10 September 1981.

TROOPS RETURN

Ops Protea, September 1981 – our troops return (*Windhoek Observer*, 5 September 1981)

Chapter 13

In between the operations – 61 Mech parade at Tsumeb in July 1981.

Having a luke-warm beer broadens the mind... Captains Koos Liebenberg, Pale van der Walt and Frik Schade sharing a brief respite at Omuthiya before leaving for Ops Daisy.

A Ratel column on the move during Ops Daisy, November 1981.

Anhara Chitequeta: A helicopter landing site and water provisioning point during Ops Daisy, November 1981.

Our trusted 81 mm mortar platoon in action during Ops Daisy.

Chapter 13

Our sons were warriors... young conscript soldiers at Chitequeta.

Never go without them – our Air Support Team during Ops Daisy.

Ops Daisy – I share a pensive moment with my Command Group at Chitequeta – we had lost a few good men on 4 November.

The Sappers in action at Chitequeta – none but the brave.

A large bang and the smell of cordite – Ratel 72A of Lieutenant Chris Walls stranded at Bambi due to a SWAPO landmine, Ops Daisy.

A SWAPO soldier killed by Bravo Company during Ops Daisy.

The luxury of still having air superiority in 1981 – stable parade at Ondjiva airfield (note the bomb craters repaired by the Air Force)

Tactical interrogation of SWAPO soldiers by Captain Gerrie Hugo according to the book, Ops Daisy.

61 Mech at Anhanca during Ops Makro on the way to Evale, December 1981.

What we found at the hamlet of Evale.

61 Mech Command Group for Ops Meebos, August 1982. Front from left: Quintus Deacon, Padre Koos Rossouw (Unit Chaplain), WO 1 Duppie du Plessis (Light Workshop Troop Commander), Major Giel Reinecke (Logistics Officer), Captain Gerrie Hugo (Intelligence Officer), Padre Hennie Pretorius. Rear from left: Captain Jan Malan (Alpha Company Commander), Staff Sergeant Kokkie de Kok (Technical Staff), Captain Sean MacSweeny (Signals Officer), Major Alex Brits (Adjutant and Operations Officer), Commandant Roland de Vries (Commander 61 Mech), Captain Chris du Toit (Charlie Squadron Commander), Major Thys Rall (Second-in-Command 61 Mech), Major Jakes Jacobs (Ops Officer), Major Chris Roux (Artillery Commander), Sergeant Adriaan Louw (Military Police), Major Jaap du Preez (Air Support Officer SAAF) (Photograph: Giel Reinecke)

61 Mech's Alpha Company of Captain Jan Malan assembling to ambush a FAPLA convoy – Ops Meebos, 3 August 1982.

At the ambush site between Cuvelai and Techamutete on 4 August 1982. (Photograph: Giel Reinecke)

Chapter 14

Captain Jan Malan approaches me after their successful ambush with a Russian Ural spoil of war trailing behind him. (Photograph: Giel Reinecke)

Exhiliration during Ops Meebos – 61 Mech soldiers bathing in the Cuvelai. (Photograph: Giel Reinecke)

61 Mech recovering the wreck of the Puma – Ops Meebos, 10 August 1982.

Ops Meebos, 9 August 1982 – at the site of the downed Puma helicopter in the Mui River where we lost fifteen good men.

Homeward bound – a gift from Henriette for my 45th birthday (painting by Nick Meyer with an air-brush from a slightly out of focus photograph I took when returning to Omuthiya during Ops Meebos)

The captured FAPLA reconnaissance vehicle during the surprise encounter – Ops Meebos, July 1982.

Baptism of fire for the young – a national serviceman prepares for the attack on 16 Brigade alongside his Olifant tank during Ops Modular. (Photograph: André Retief)

A destroyed Russian T54/55 tank near the Lomba River – Ops Modular, October 1987. (Photograph: Hannes Nortmann)

Brothers in arms – an Olifant tank and a Ratel in cahoots north of the Lomba River – Ops Modular, November 1987. (Photograph: André Retief)

Shock action unveiled – Olifant tanks in Angola at long last... Ops Modular. (Photograph: André Retief)

I can still smell the cordite – hugging my modest foxhole in the Catato Woods after a close encounter with a Russian MiG-21.

Chapter 15

Lean and mean – the tac HQ of Task Force 10 in the Catato Woods, November 1987.

```
-- Msg #[0069] -- Time [B09h35] -- Descriptor -- [OPS          ]--
VAN:TM HK 10
AAN:BDE HK 20     INFO:TAK HK RUNDU
DEEL 1
VOORSTELLE WESTELIKE MISLEIDINGS- EN ONTWRIGTINGSPLAN TER ONDST
VAN OPS OOS VAN CUITO RIVIER
1.DOEL VAN BG PLAN.VY MAG TE SKEI,BEV EN BEH TE ONTWRIG,MAGTE WE
S VAN RIVIER TE BIND EN SELFS WES TE TREK.
2.D- DAG VIR OPS OOS VAN CUITORIVIER 25 OF 26 NOV 87.
3.HOOFUITVOERDER-VOORGESTEL DAT BDE HK KOORDEN BEH.VOORSTELLE SO
OS VOLG:
4.WEGSTAANBESTOKINGS OP CC VANAF NW DEUR UNITA.
5.ART AANSLAG CC HK OP D-DAG
6.INFILTRASIE -AANVAL UNITA NW OP CC OP NAG D-1/D-DAG.
7.GERUGTE OFFENSIEF DEUR UNITA WES VAN CC D-4 TOT D DAG TOV MOON
TLIKE HOOFAANVAL OP CC UIT WESTE.
BT
NNNN
-- Msg #[0070] -- Time [B09h48] -- Descriptor -- [OPS          ]--
VAN:TM
AAN:BDE  INFO:TAK HK RUNDU
DEEL 2
8.PAMFLETTE OP CC-PLAASLIKE BEVOLKING MOET UIT CC ONTTREK.
9.OORBELADING VY INSAMELINGSTELSEL
10.KWELAKSIES DEUR UNITA IN VY AGTERGEBIEDE EN IN CC ASOOK MYNLE
11.SKEP VAN RADIOSTASIE TE LONGAKRUISING WAT BERIGTE STUUR TOV M
OONTLIKE KRUISING ALDAAR.
12.LUGVERK AS GEVEGSAANDUIDINGS:
A.CC WES
B.LONGA
C.MASSECA
D.BAIXA-LONGA
E.NANCOVA
13.LUGAANVALLE AS GEVEGSAANDUIDINGS
BT
NNNN
-- Msg #[0071] -- Time [B09h56] -- Descriptor -- [OPS          ]--
VAN:TM
AAN:BDE     INFO:TAK HK RUNDU
DEEL 3
A.MENONGUE VLVT UITHAALVAN AANLOOPBAAN OP D-DAG EN HERHALING DAA
RVAN OP D PLUS 2/3
B.LONGA
C.MASECCA
D.NANCOVA
E.BAIXA-LONGA
14.UNITA KOMMANDO EN SPES MAGTE AKSIES TUSSENMENONGUE EN CC.
15.AANWENDING EO
16.ALG ART BEST CC
17.NAVRAE KOL R.DE VRIES
```

Ops Modular – a radio DET message sent by me to coordinate the next battle action.

MAJOR Armindo Moreira strode to the centre of a patched-together bridge and waved a hand towards a hillside of mud-and-thatch huts.

"We brought you here," the Angolan major said in Portuguese, "to show you that we still control Cuito Cuanavale."

Raising his voice above the roar of the river, he added: "The South Africans will take it over my dead body."

With that, a dozen South African G-5 artillery shells screamed out of the low, dark clouds and shattered the valley floor about a kilometre away. "A little gift from the racists," said Moreira as we scrambled off the bridge to a waiting Soviet-built personnel carrier.

THE CATWALK TO CUITO

MARGARET KNOX, an American journalist, reports from Cuito Cuanavale, where she spent several days with the Angolan forces . . .

IT'S A SMALL AND SHABBY TOWN — BUT CAPTURING IT HAS BECOME CRUCIAL TO ALL

Places preferably to avoid – the cat-walk at Cuito Cuanavale.

What was left by the Mirage strike of 8 December 1987 – on the Death Road between Menongue and Cuito Cuanavale.

Castro praises strength of SADF

WASHINGTON — Cuban President Fidel Castro has a high regard for the fighting qualities of the South African Defence Force, his enemy in the Angolan bush for more than 14 years.

The SADF is powerful, well-trained and well-equipped, he says.

The leader of the communist island gave his view on South Africa's military capability during a recent tripartite conference in Havana to set the record straight on the 1962 Cuban missile crisis which led the United States and the Soviet Union to the brink of atomic war.

Illustrating a point about moving a large force quickly, Castro referred to the clash between his own soldiers and South African troops at Cuito Cuanavale, Angola.

"A crisis arose in Cuito Cuanavale that forced us to send large numbers of troops, and we did so with decisiveness, because one must do things decisively. Otherwise one will be defeated. If 20 000 are needed and you send 10 000, the most likely thing is that you will be defeated," he said.

"We were facing the South Africans. They are very powerful. They manufacture weapons. They have good training, good equipment, and very good aircraft.

"We prepared for battle with the South Africans. To give you an idea, when our troops advanced, they had 1 000 anti-aircraft weapons so that they could have superiority . . . So we also have some experience in troop movements, and we know what it is like to carry out an operation."

Castro disclosed that the number of Cuban forces in Angola rose to 53 000 after the Cuito episode and insisted that all the transport operations were carried out by Cuba. He also insisted that Cuba was never paid for the presence of its troops.

"The only thing that came from the Soviet Union was worries," he said.

Castro gave the conference no further details of the Cuito operation, but it is routinely touted by the Cubans as a glorious military event.

But Cuba's glory days are over now and the regime is trying desperately to stave off economic catastrophe.

The collapse of the former Soviet Union has removed cash-starved Cuba's principal source of foreign aid, forced it to import essential goods at world prices it cannot afford, and dried up its supply of fuel.

Cubans are abandoning cars and buses for bicycles and replacing diesel-driven farm equipment with oxen. Electricity, like most other things, is rationed.

Analysts predict Cuba will be the next communist regime to tumble, but they admit there is no sign of a significant decline in Castro's personal popularity. — Sapa.

Castro praises the strength of the SADF.

Chapter 16

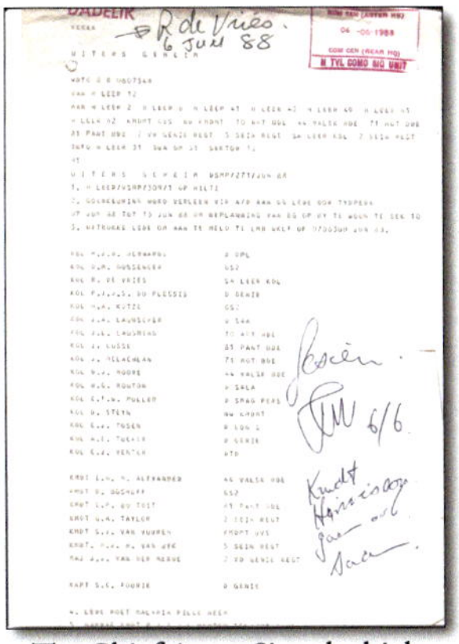

The Chief Army Signal which kick-started Ops Hilti (Prone) – mustering the planning group for 6 June 1988.

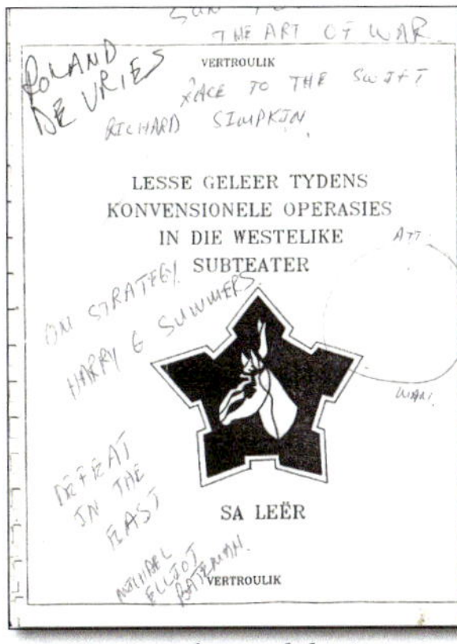

VERTROULIK

LESSE GELEER TYDENS
KONVENSIONELE OPERASIES
IN DIE WESTELIKE
SUBTEATER

SA LEËR

VERTROULIK

Lessons learned during conventional operations in the Western Sub-Theatre of War in 1987–88, a document kept by me all these years.

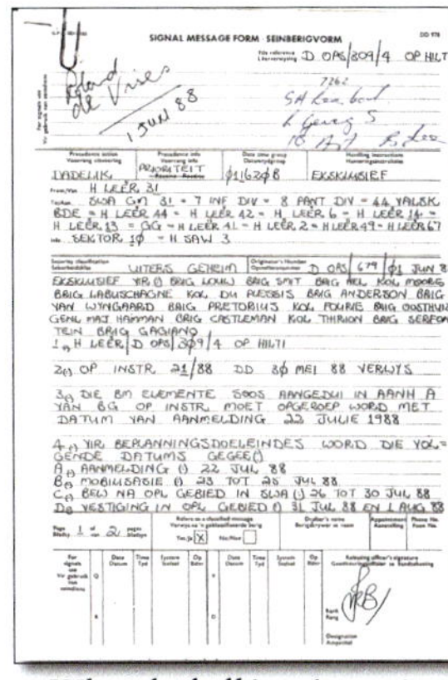

SIGNAL MESSAGE FORM SEINBERIGVORM

D OPS/809/4 OP HILTI

IXDADELIK EKSKLUSIEF

H LEËR 31

2(a) OP INSTR 21/88 DD 30 MEI 88 VERWYS

3(a) DIE BM ELEMENTE SOOS AANGEDUI IN AANH A VAN BG OP INSTR MOET OPGEROEP WORD MET DATUM VAN AANMELDING 22 JULIE 1988

4(a) VIR BEPLANNINGSDOELEINDES WORD DIE VOLGENDE DATUMS GEGEE

A(a) AANMELDING 22 JUL 88

B(a) MOBILISASIE 23 TOT 25 JUL 88

C(a) BEW NA OPS GEBIED IN SWA 26 TOT 30 JUL 88

D(a) VESTIGING IN OPS GEBIED 31 JUL 88 EN 1 AUG 88

What the hell is going on? Another Chief Army Signal – Mobilising head over heels for Ops Hilti (Prone), 1 June 1988.

With Cuban Colonel Richard Wilson at Ruacana in August 1988. Leonie, the wife of Commandant Leon Lamprecht (OC 51 Battalion Ruacana) is to our left (our families did not flee the 50th Cuban Division – no way; well, almost!)

Making peace with the Cubans at Calueque... and afterwards drinking their rum from Havana, whilst they relished biltong and red wine – Ops Prone, August 1988.

Taking young Pieter and some of the children of Ruacana to play with the jubilant Cuban MI-18 pilots at Calueque during the peace talks – their own families were far away, August 1988.

Taking chances ... and why not? Henriette and Pieter (3) crossing the border with me into Angola near Calueque (I only told her later about the mines and that SWAPO had not opted for peace yet) – Ops Prone, August 1988.

Chapter 17

What John Kotter of the Harvard Business School wrote about in the Heart of Change – sailing at Plettenberg Bay with my former enemies from MK, Solly Mollo (left) and Bongani.

Most serious things – briefing the Army General Staff and its task groups on transformation, 1989.

Just like war – Peacekeeping Exercise Southern Cross held at Rustenburg in 1993.

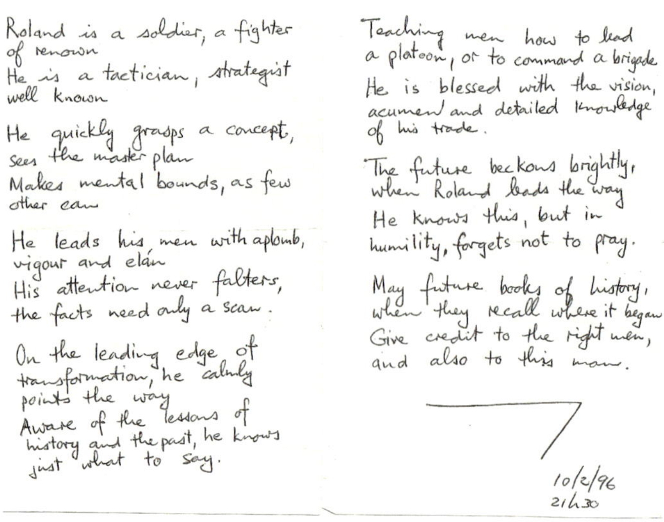

Roland is a soldier, a fighter of renown
He is a tactician, strategist well known

He quickly grasps a concept, sees the master plan
Makes mental bounds, as few other can

He leads his men with aplomb, vigour and elán
His attention never falters, the facts need only a scan.

On the leading edge of transformation, he calmly points the way
Aware of the lessons of history and the past, he knows just what to say.

Teaching men how to lead a platoon, or to command a brigade
He is blessed with the vision, acumen and detailed knowledge of his trade.

The future beckons brightly, when Roland leads the way
He knows this, but in humility, forgets not to pray.

May future books of history, when they recall where it began
Give credit to the right men, and also to this man.

10/2/96
21h30

With appreciation – A simple thank you from me for a poem written by Lt Col Willem van Rijn during the advent of Defence Transformation in 1996.

Chapter 18

On Kinmen Island on 12 June 1973, a day between the token firing at each other with artillery and loud-speaker callings from mainland China.

Workshop on defence transformation in the Democratic Republic of Congo – the one I wrote a paper about.

A few smart members of the Nigerian Army working out their "Terms of Reference" for transformation (don't visit one of their transport parks), Port Harcourt, 2007.

A new order of things – workshop on the transformation of the Nigerian Army at Port Harcourt with Major General O.A. Azazi to the right, 2007.

Great people, the South Sudanese – workshop with the Southern Sudan People's Liberation Army, Juba, 2009.

Extreme fun – my simple way of congratulating a Nigerian officer on a sharp remark, Port Harcourt, 2007.

Chapter 18

Let us put the plan together – with one of my favourites, the amazing down to earth Major General Peter Bol Koang, Commander Division 8 at Bor, South Sudan, 2009.

My new family looking after me at my humble dwelling in South Sudan, Juba, 2009.

With enemies of yesteryear at SWAPO's Heroes' Acre in Windhoek ... 61 Mech, 32 Bn and SWAPO Veterans together as friends.

Having a friendly discussion with Colonel Ben Khadila and General Martin Shalli (who briefed Special Unit for their deep incursion during Ops Yahoo in 1982) of SWAPO about the past, Windhoek, October 2010.

A friendly chance encounter – meeting a former SWAPO member at Okatope, October 2010.

Inside a bunker at Okatope, October 2010.

Chapter 18

Look-out post at Okatope, October 2010.

Touring the Angolan battlefields where the Dorsland Trekkers also passed through. With Louis Bothma, Deon Joubert and Blackie Swart in the Naulila area, October 2010. (Photograph: Camille Burger)

The bridge at Xangongo in October 2010. (Photograph: Deon Lamprecht)

My thoughts wander – the house that was booby-trapped near the bridge at Xangongo, October 2010. (Photograph: Krige van Heerden)

The FAPLA War Memorial at Môngua (where Combat Team Mamba of 61 Mech fought their battle in August 1981), October 2010.

I have a stake here, thanks Minister – 61 Mech's former HQ at Xangongo during Ops Protea in August 1981, as in October 2010.

Chapter 18

A briefing to our 61 Mech and 32 Bn veterans during our Battlefield Tour in October 2010 close to Evale.

The stately church at Mupa surrounded by derelict shell-cases. (Photograph: Camille Burger)

The church gong at Mupa, October 2010 (Photograph: Camille Burger)

What a woman – Sister Eria tells us her story at Mupa, October 2010.

Our new friend Antonio Vicente tells us what happened at Cassinga (the true account, one not marred by propaganda), October 2010. (Photograph: Camille Burger)

In the killing ground – the Ops Meebos ambush site revisited in October 2010.

What happened here? At one of the SWAPO mass graves of Cassinga, October 2010.

Playing "la-dee-da" with my new recruits at Menongue, October 2010. (Photograph: Krige van Heerden)

It is peaceful now at Cuito Cuanavale... except for the minefields, October 2010.

An amazing moment – sharing thoughts with two young FAPLA soldiers at the bridge across the Cuito Cuanavale in October 2010 – do they know about Mirage attack aircraft and G-5 guns?

Remembering our fallen from both sides at Cuito Cuanavale.

At the old British Fort overlooking Uniondale. "Out there are two choke-points and some vital ground..." (Photograph: Camille Burger)

Chapter 18

Bliss is all about "terrain" – in the beautiful, classical, period city of Assisi, Italy, and the historic Roman battlefields behind me.

Happiness is being close to the terracotta warriors of 210-209 BC near Xian, China. With Henriette, of course, in 2008.

Bridge on the River Kwai, Kanchanaburi, November 2012.

From the Crusades – Ajlun Castle overlooking the Jordan Valley where my son Pieter and I could wander.

The fort Lawrence of Arabia used during his desert campaign at Azrac – attacking deep from the flank.

The fort at Aqaba held by the Turks in Jordan which was attacked by Lawrence of Arabia and his Arab Army in 1918 – surprise, surprise.

Nothing like brewing tea with my friend Saleh Moosa where Lawrence of Arabia roamed in Wadi Rum, Jordan – living off the land.

shocked to see how a burst struck one of the enemy soldiers and caused him to perform a macabre dance of death in the air until he slumped to the sand. The realisation that war was a matter of life and death then really struck home to me. I was grateful that I was the one who survived that ferocious clash.

We took note of where the enemy soldiers fell, and fought through the target until a kilometre or so past the point where we had first engaged them. We then moved back to the area where we had the contact with the enemy the first time, to consolidate the target area and also to collect any survivors, enemy dead and their weapons and equipment – our Intelligence Officer also needed to be provided with any valuable information we could source from the skirmish.

We found one enemy soldier alive. He turned out to be the platoon commander of the group, and had dragged himself into the shade of a tree. He was badly wounded in the chest and his thumb was shot off, but he showed amazing tenacity. I could not help but admire the man. He was duly evacuated back to our battle group HQ on the Ratel of our company second-in-command, Lieutenant Kowie Steyn. Later on I learned that the FAPLA lieutenant had survived the ordeal.

While searching through the pockets of the dead enemy soldiers we found photos of their loved ones, letters from home and also a passbook in terms of leave taken, just like ours; the leaves were meticulously recorded, date by date. I realised that they were soldiers and human beings just like us, who longed to be with their loved ones and who also looked forward to passes to go home, as we did, that they also could not wait for a letter from a special person to arrive.

It became plain to me that we were fighting human beings with families and feelings just like us, and not necessarily evil indoctrinated communist-inspired socialists, who were hell-bent on destroying South Africa.

By late afternoon the two combat teams were back at the laager position, still feeling the adrenaline rush we felt during the fighting through the floodplains. It was good for the overall morale of our combat force. I was proud and also relieved. Our national service soldiers had been blooded, at no cost to themselves. They had been in harm's way, and now they were warriors.

Settling Down for the Night – Goal-Set Through

While Koos Liebenberg and Pale van der Walt were securing the floodplains, Giel Reinecke and the RSM set up a replenishing point at which each of our tail-end vehicles (and later those of the combat teams as well) stopped as it came into the laager from the west so that our contentedly humming multi-hosed Lappies pumps could top up its tanks while the occupants scavenged around for stories about what had been happening.

Around them the other specialists had set up their own little pools of activity. Outside the laager the tiffies had established a stragglers' collection area and repair point for ailing or broken down vehicles, and the signallers, whose generator was already droning monotonously away, were installing some subdued lighting beneath and behind the camouflage nets so that the LWT would be able to work through the night if necessary. A protection platoon was in place to guard all this, and would be on the alert until we left and only a few patches of oil in the sand remained to mark the spot.

Huddled on camp chairs, my little command group and I were wrapping up the comprehensive agenda of things to be done on D+1. When this was done there would be a quick order group, my subordinate commanders would give their own orders, and then, all going well, we would all settle down for some hard-earned rest. I knew all that would happen quickly because they were well-versed in their deployment drills.

Thys Rall and Giel Reinecke were finalising their own bits of orders, respectively for the defence of our laager and for what was to follow on. It was like all the pieces of a jigsaw puzzle falling neatly into place. When the last piece had found its home we would have everything we needed for a night routine, from an allround defence with interlocking arcs of defensive fire and passwords to radio watch schedules, a guards and sentries roster, early warning procedures in case of enemy action and calculations of our logistical needs for the next 24 hours.

Major Joe Weyers was also organising Combat Team 3 for a westward move towards Cahama the next morning as soon as I let him loose – exactly when this would happen would depend on the enemy assessments we made in the coming night – and Joe Aveling and his men were already deeply involved in re-evaluating the emerging intelligence picture. So far all the news was good. Battle Group 30 had taken Peu Peu, and most of the sprawling Xangongo complex – all but its outlying southern outposts, in fact – was in the hands of Battle Groups 20 and 40.

Occasionally we could hear individual shots, machine gun bursts and huge explosions as the battle groups continued to sweep, but the steam had gone out of Xangongo, and in the morning the last loose ends would be tied up as well. Then Task Force Alpha would be able to give its full attention to the next major objective, Ondjiva. With the Xangongo bridge secured at both ends, Major Leon Terblanche and his sappers from 25 Field Engineer Squadron were already placing the demolition charges on the pillars and surface area of the 800 metre long single span.

I was feeling cheerful, although extremely tired. It had been a very long and exhausting night and day for all of us, and the wear and tear on man and machine had been heavy. By now my fighters and support personnel knew that a number of our soldiers lay dead on the other side of the Cunene – how did they feel about it? Thus far our battle group had been fortunate. It had not lost a single man dead or wounded, and in fact would have preferred more action than it had got.

Battle Group 10 commenced settling down for the night as the late afternoon started fading into dusk. The allround defensive and mutually supporting posture had been set up. Local protection patrols were already deployed, and early warning and security arrangements were in place. Sentries had been posted and the first radio watch of the night was manning the sets. Other activities were up and running without any fuss or bother – it was all SOP.

During short moments of personal inactivity I enjoyed sitting on a camp chair next to my Ratel and experiencing the tangible aura of 61 Mech all around me. I drank an aromatic and refreshing cup of army coffee with my crew, a welcome touch of luxury after our recent furious activity. But at the same time I was eyeing the barracuda camouflage net where it lay bundled up next to my Ratel. It looked very soft, very comfortable and very inviting as it lay waiting with open arms to clasp my weary bones to its inviting bosom.

First, though, we experienced one of those odd and touching moments that one lives through in even the most brutal war. A distinguished-looking Angolan, bespectacled and smartly dressed, came riding sedately over to us on a dilapidated Moped motorised bicycle with a small tattered boy perched on the front. There was no anxiety or uneasiness about him, and nobody challenged him as he chugged over to the command group through the ranks of war machines as if it were a daily occurrence for him to encounter a battle group bristling with weapons of death and destruction.

We invited him to have a chat, and he was happy to do so. He explained that he was the local schoolteacher at that very Humbe at which we had been hurling 140 mm shells only a few hours earlier. He felt no apprehension about the South African forces and was quite willing to talk about the local situation. Humbe's inhabitants and the police had fled that morning, he said, just before the air strike on Xangongo. No, there had been no element of FAPLA deployed there for some time.

I was intrigued by the small boy, who was clearly of Portuguese origin, and he explained that he was the stepfather of the boy, whom he had found wandering around somewhere, a victim of the civil war that had been raging in Angola since the mid-1970s.

Our conversation over, our gracious black visitor and his adopted white son putted away into the setting sun towards Humbe. Before he left I took a photo of them with their Moped, victims of dreadful circumstances – but survivors of those circumstances as well. It was a cheering thought. I still have that the photograph and sometimes wonder what became of them. One day, perhaps, I shall be able to visit Humbe again and ask after them.

My command group assembled for our routine evening debriefing session and quick orders. There we shared our feelings – our satisfaction with our performance thus far, our disappointment at not having had a worthy fight that day. Things took their normal course – orders were reaffirmed and commitments assigned, maps were checked and marked, watches synchronised. Through it all I thought quietly about our move to Humbe, the consolidation of our objective, the state of our equipment and even the viciousness of the few successful fleeting skirmishes that had taken place. Had I done everything right? Could I have done it better? A good commander is his own severest critic.

All around 61 Mech was settling in. Our soldiers were digging shallow scrapes for themselves out of the soft sand and piling up low berms around their sleeping bags. Arcs of interlocking defensive fire were being arranged, set up carefully and coordinated by the seconds-in-command and junior leaders of the combat teams; left to right, front to rear. Last parades were being carried out on the vehicles and weapon systems by their crews.

The tiffies had no time for such frivolity – they were too busy at their never-ending task of repairing vehicles and other hardware, with the chugging of the generators as their background music. Koos Rossouw was doing his rounds among the crews, dispensing quick, quiet prayers and words of comfort for those in need of them.

Everywhere the troops were getting down to the treat of the day, preparing a hot meal from their 24-hour ration packs, so that there was a pleasant aroma of food wafting around, spiced with the smell of their little pocket cookers' solid fuel tablets. Luxury supreme! When my orders had filtered down to squad level the activities began to peter out. There were the usual pleasing settling down sounds and the sighing of cooling metal, a sure sign of the work we had put in. Now and again small bursts of subdued laughter drifted to my ears through the cold night air.

And so night settled over our battle group's defensive laager on 24 August. Now there was no more sporadic shooting from across the river. I had a vague sense of unease, a feeling that something more was going to happen before the night was out, but no more than that. There were still no signs or indications of an enemy advance from Cahama, and this blessed inactivity was confirmed by our interceptions of their radio traffic, some as recent as 21:00.

Now, at last ... With final orders given, I simply flipped back on to the camouflage net, clutching my R-5 rifle with the sights set at 200 metres. It was 22:00. My commanders and I had had 42 hours of tension, snap decisions, nerve-racking night navigation, endless jolting and bumping and repeated spurts of adrenalin to burn up our blood sugar. Some of the troops had managed occasional catnaps along the way, but this was a luxury denied us, the people who were responsible for them. Small wonder, then, that I fell asleep as soon as I closed my eyes.

I think many civilians through the ages have been puzzled by the soldier's obsession with sleep and his ability to drift off into dreamland anywhere and at any time without even having to lie down. But it is a luxury whose true value a man cannot appreciate till he has had to do without it. And the irony of it is that the soldiers who need sleep the most – the commanders, who are expected to keep a clear head at all times – are likely to get the least.

I wish I could say that I slept all the more soundly because I knew that we were safe and secure in the capable hands of our operations officers, our sentries and our signallers on radio watch. But to be honest, I was so far gone that I simply passed out like a light.

Not all of us slept. A few kilometres east of our laager, Major Leon Terblanche and his sappers were pulling an all-nighter to complete the preparation of the bridge for possible demolition. I knew that he would make a first-class job of it because he was a first-class soldier, extremely professional and totally mission-orientated.

As it turned out, I got my long anticipated sleep in batches. At midnight or just beyond I was rudely awakened by my radio operator calling me frantically to his set. Instantly awake, I threw myself into my jump seat in the rear of the Ratel, headset on, subdued red light glowing, battle map in front of me.

It was Colonel Joubert, clearly excited over whatever was in progress on his side of the river. Exactly what it was I did not know yet, although I could hear explosions, but Joubert did not leave me in the dark for long. It appeared, he said, that a rogue FAPLA column was hell bent on breaking out of Xangongo and crossing the bridge. Battle Groups 20 and 40 were hastily preparing to ambush the column. Battle Group 10 must waste no time in occupying an immediate ambush position on our side.

I started rousing my commanders from their well-deserved slumber as soon as I signed off, ready to issue quick orders as soon as they were capable of absorbing them. But then a few minutes later the battle noises to the east of us subsided and Joubert called back to say that we could stand down again – the column had been knocked out in the streets of Xangongo. Those of us not on night vigil went instantly back to sleep again. That took no effort; we were all still bone weary.

Link-Up by Battle Group 10 – Entering Xangongo from the West

25 August – D+1 – dawned over a very different Xangongo. Most of its laboriously constructed rings of defences were ruined and abandoned after full day and part of a night of fighting. Close on 500 of its defenders lay dead, and the killing was not over yet, because Commandant Dippenaar was still reducing the last few pockets of resistance; ten more of his soldiers would be dead before the final shots were fired.

But at Battle Group 10 we were preoccupied with our own lurking challenges. We moved towards the bridge in the very cool morning air and halted temporarily in open formation to wait for the right time to cross over and join hands with Battle Group 40 on the other side. While we waited we made ourselves a hasty rat-pack breakfast and brewed up some longed-for coffee, and with Colonel Robbie Robberts and Commandant Epp van Lill I dawdled over to the western end of the bridge with my shaving kit and "basin, canvas, for washing purposes only: drab veld: Mark I with stand: wooden: collapsible".

Colonel Robberts had been working hard on observing Battle Group 10, making copious notes and recording the lessons learned. It would all come out in the wash when we held a debriefing session in September. I put my thoughts about the debrief in my mental "pending" tray and concentrated on the most immediate task – namely, having a shave. The three of us looked over the railings to see what Leon Terblanche had been up to. Scores of explosive charges in canvas bags like oversize schoolbags hung suspended on the pillars as far as the eye could see along the 800 metre span: one press of a button and the bridge would be levitated in grand style.

There was shooting to be heard now as Dippenaar systematically dealt with the remaining strong points on the southern flank, Behind us, meanwhile, Joe Weyers was getting ready to take Combat Team 3 up the road and Dawid Mentz's company-sized garrison force was busy mopping up the floodplains in the vicinity, and the flared-out sweeping formations were turning up all sorts of abandoned booty, including a large number of brand new three-barrelled 23 mm anti-aircraft guns which had been deployed as part of the air defences.

The weapons were made safe, dragged out of their entrenchments and the bushes and towed behind the troop carriers towards the bridge and Xangongo. With them went a number of spanking new AKM-47s, the successor to the AK-47, which were still smothered in grease. Together with the guns, hordes of other abandoned equipment were scooped up to be taken back.

Close on 08:00 we rolled over the bridge, with my command Ratel leading our procession, and proceeded to the eastern end for the link-up. As I halted, we could see the Portuguese fort with its red-tiled roofs slightly to the left, the smoking wreck of a T34-85 tank squatting close by. Near the wheels of our Ratel lolled a slain FAPLA soldier, not far from one of the sandbagged pressure charges the sappers had positioned during the night. It struck me that if the man had survived he would probably have had an interesting tale to tell (at some stage the body disappeared; perhaps helped over the side by persons unknown, presumably to the delight of the crocodiles below).

I witnessed a terrible incident while I waited to establish our link-up with Battle Group 40. A Buffel MPV, filled with jubilant sappers sped towards a house near the fort. The Buffel halted at the house and stood swaying in its loose-jointed way while the troops dismounted in leisurely fashion, smiling and joking. Suddenly I was seized by an amazing feeling of dread, so strong that I called Juliet Nine, the medical officer's Ratel, and ordered him to move forward as fast as he could.

As I spoke, I saw one of the sappers saunter towards the house and enter it. Instantaneously there was a massive explosion that ripped the house apart and threw a great column of black smoke into the morning air. The house had been booby-trapped by the fleeing foe! Our medics tore across the bridge – they were, in fact, the first elements of Battle Group 10 to cross over – but there was nothing for them to do except retrieve the mangled remains of the sapper.

I still keep a photograph of the slain sapper, but I have blotted out his sorrowful face, sometimes in the still of the night I think back to that unnecessary tragedy. Who knows what that soldier might have become if he had lived? And I think of his loved ones. Did they know what had actually befallen him? Who was he? I never found out, since he was one of Battle Group 40's troops, but I remember him and the unnecessary manner of his death.

Link-up with Combat Group 40 was eventually established close to 09:00, and I led Battle Group 10 into Xangongo, which was to be our domicile until 31 August (D+7). As we trundled into town we encountered groups of refugees assembled along the main road near the fort and the river, guarded by a lonely Eland-90 armoured car poised on a high rise. The locals seemed calm and at peace with themselves – lethargic and brow-beaten, more likely.

Burning wrecks were scattered everywhere, and the sweet smell of burning flesh and decay clung to the particles of dust our wheels stirred up. We could see a number of slain FAPLA soldiers lying near some abandoned trenches further to the south where they had fallen the previous day. Elsewhere a group of wounded prisoners of war lounged gloomily about near a small church which had been converted into a medical post.

Xangongo was like an overturned anthill, with all sorts of things going on. Media representatives with their nuisance-making cameramen were there already – ignore them, Roland! Teams of intelligence personnel and other inquisitors were rummaging through houses and buildings, searching for maps, documents and other juicy titbits of enemy information. No doubt the more macabre-minded were also on to some interesting souvenirs. One house which had been abandoned in frantic haste by a Russian military adviser and his family was of particular interest to the rummagers.

We deployed into an open laager near the Portuguese era hospital, and I noticed that it still proudly bore Xangongo's old name, Vila Roçades, on its battered red tiles. Below them the remnants of glass in its shattered windows winked in the late morning rays of the sun.

Brief Respite in Xangongo – Quick Orders and Turning Around

When we were all in place we made good use of what we knew would be only a brief respite, because we still had plenty of things to do and places to go to. We gobbled down "doggies" – the ubiquitous ration biscuits – dunked in mugs of coffee. to a clangour of tools from the tiffies, who were at it again to one side, maintaining and repairing.

Our immediate task was to reorganise as soon as possible before moving off in different directions, with various parts of the battle group taking on specific tasks. The name of the game would be simultaneous action and flexibility, each warrior king running his own castle. To this end immediate orders were issued:

There would be some swift exploitation 45 km northwestwards to Mucope, by a part of our mechanised elements; Weyers and Combat Team 3 plus add-ons would set off in the direction of Cahama as a covering force and set up a stopper line near Chicusse nicknamed "Big Boy 1"; Alpha Company's paratroopers would deploy northwards to hunt for SWAPO, while the protection company and the engineers would make an immediate start on defence and administrative arrangements. The bridge's reserve demolition must be finalised and then it must be guarded; Alpha Echelon must set up the administrative and logistical baseline at Xangongo.

I left my commanders to attend to their preparations and hastened over to Colonel Joubert's command post on the eastern outskirts of the town. There I found him with his second-in-command, Commandant Tobie van Schalkwyk, who was sitting on a folding camp chair next to their command Ratel, map boards spread out on the ground in front of them. Over some more coffee I provided a concise feedback about what I had been up to, and we exchanged valuable items of information about the operational developments of the past 36 hours.

My orders for the next phase at Xangongo and beyond were reaffirmed, and Joubert informed me that he was putting a pathfinder group from 44 Parachute Brigade under the renowned Colonel Jan Breytenbach under my operational command. The pathfinders had been wandering around doing some interesting fighting work to the north of us near Peu Peu and were now seeking further interesting conversations with the enemy.

Apparently no other commanders wanted Breytenbach and his gang of handpicked veterans – many of them soldiers of fortune recruited from the recently defunct Rhodesian Army's special forces – because he was a difficult character who tended to use his initiative to an extreme degree and somehow always got away with it. But my response was: "Yes, Colonel, thank you!" I was happy to take the chance because, having trained under him and gone on many a practice jump with him, I had immense respect for the man and his operational aptitude as a combat soldier of note.

I also knew exactly what I was going to do with this newly acquired combat asset. I was going to put him and his men with their heavily armed Land Rovers and similar vehicles in Combat Team 3 for the venture towards Cahama. Weyers might well end up having a very tough job to do, and the pathfinders' added firepower, inherent aggression and solid operational experience were a bargain not to be passed up. Breytenbach and his warriors not only had what it took but liked their job, and I knew that wherever they went, shooting was apt to follow. It was a decision which would bring me both joy and grief, but definitely more of the former than the latter.

I returned to my battle group close to midday. The subunits were ready to move on, and so was I. Dawid Mentz's minute garrison force and the field engineer troop would stay behind so that they could get on with the various duties they had been assigned (don't laugh, but these included organising a soccer game between Battle Group 10 and the Xangongo town team).

Most of Alpha Echelon would remain behind as well to carry out its administrative and logistical duties in the relative safety of Xangongo while the rest of us crashed about in the bush, hunted for SWAPO and generally nibbled away at the Angolans' morale to keep them off the highway. I was very anxious now to get Combat Team 3 on the road so that the task force's open western flank could be positively secured as soon as possible, and I still had to marry up Weyers's men with Breytenbach's small but potent group of pathfinders.

I soon found the pathfinders close to the bridge with their handful of "sabre" (i.e. heavily armed) Land Rovers. My medics provided some urgently required medical aid, as one of his sabres had run over a landmine and a number of his soldiers had been seriously wounded. I passed Joubert's orders to Breytenbach and told him that I was attaching him to Joe Weyers, from whom he would receive further instructions.

Needless to say, this flew in the face of normal Army protocol, since Breytenbach outranked Weyers by a considerable margin, but the "Brown Man", as he was universally known, did not mind about such sacrilege and neither did Weyers. The pathfinders, I calculated, were there to smite the foe, wherever and whenever he was to be found. There was no doubt about the fact that they were fierce fighters, not pleasant opponents to be encountered on a dark and eerie road like the one leading to Cahama. And smite them they would.

The pathfinders' sabre Land Rovers were equipped with an assortment of machine guns and 106 mm recoilless guns, not to mention an assortment of other munitions, and would form a deadly alliance with Combat Team 3's Ratels, Eland-90s and 140 mm G2 guns.

Our troops were fascinated by the Brown Man's seasoned, strangely attired soldiers, and nicknamed them the "Tandeborsels" (Tooth brushes) because of their variety of foreign accents and their outlandish habit of speaking on the inside of their mouths, rather towards the outside as was normal. In short order, Weyers reported he was "march and combat ready"; I unleashed his combat team without further ado and he and his men set off up the Cahama highway at their best speed.

I was getting ready to leave for the sweep towards Mucope when we received some tragic news from Battle Group 20. Captain Louis Harmse (1 South African Infantry Battalion) had been killed while clearing trenches with his company. I could see that the news was a particular blow to Captain Koos Liebenberg and Lieutenant Kowie Steyn, both of whom had been close friends of his.

A comforting word was all I could offer. It was the Harmse family's second devastating blow in just five years; Louis's father, Colonel Des Harmse, had been killed by enemy action during Operation Savannah in 1976. Louis himself had had a harrowing experience during Operation Sceptic on 10 June 1980, just over a year earlier, when his platoon had suffered heavy losses during the main attack, and had volunteered for Protea to make up for it, although no one had blamed him in the least for what had happened.

But we had little time to mourn for dead friends just then; 25 August was destined to be another long, hard day which did not lack for incidents.

Exploitation towards Mucope – Reconnaissance in Force

Battle Group 10's exploitation mission to Mucope (41 km north-northwest of Xangongo and 63 km due east of Cahama) derived from our enemies' almost invariable habit of making themselves comfortable in and around existing settlements. Our reconnaissance in force was to concentrate on part of no-man's land west of the river where, we strongly suspected, some enemy remnants were still in hiding (there were, but not where we thought, as I shall soon explain). The other purpose of the mission was, of course, to destabilise 21 FAPLA Brigade at Cahama and to secure our area of operations.

We – that is to say my HQ, Koos Liebenberg's mechanised company, a troop of armoured cars and the 81 mm mortar platoon – looked forward to running into the enemy and enthusiastically scoured the endless kilometres of bushveld west of Xangongo, where we were convinced they were lying up. Unfortunately, our efforts came to naught, although here and there we found signs of recent enemy occupation. Someone photographed the water tower at Mucope from a moving Ratel, and that was it.

Somewhat disgruntled, we laagered for the night in dense bush to the west of Mucope, 35 km east of where Combat Team 3 was deployed at Chicusse. It was cold, the ground was extremely hard to dig in to, a lone enemy reconnaissance aircraft passed over our heads in the night sky and we had difficulty maintaining communications with Weyers because our communications were bedevilled by skip distances[17] – another quirk of African bush warfare that would baffle and frustrate the average European soldier.

Close on 22:24 there was a hurried radio message from Joe Weyers, relayed by our old friend Tannie Pompie van der Westhuizen, the only viable link we had with Chicusse just

17 See "skip distances" explained in Chapter 5 on terrain,

then, although she and her radios were about 430 km away on her farm, Koedoesvlei, at Tsintsabis!

The message was short and frustrating: "Contact ... Contact ... Wait, out". We waited, grinding our teeth while listening to what sounded like a tremendous fight coming clearly in the night air from somewhere near Cahama. All we could do was stand by for rapid deployment in the direction of the fighting. What the hell had Joe Weyers got himself involved in? Then the noise of battle subsided as quickly as it had begun, and Tannie Pompie managed to relay another message to us. Combat Team 3 had had a shootout following a surprise encounter with a FAPLA artillery column on the road near Cahama, and had thrashed it.

The full story came out next day, when I took my exploitation force back to Xangongo and in passing paid a fleeting visit to Chicusse, accompanied by Epp van Lill and Colonel Robberts. Wrecked weapons and vehicles were strewn over the road, and as a memento I took a picture of a ruined Russian BTR-152 armoured troop carrier.

The position to the west of the Cunene River was now reasonably secure and I decided to withdraw all of Battle Group 10 to the east of the Cunene for the night, to let the troops have some much needed rest. As we rolled back towards Xangongo I gave some thought about the next job at hand, reflecting on the planning we had done earlier at Omuthiya and how it related to our current situation and the fresh insights we had gained.

The battle indication about the future intentions of FAPLA's forces at Cahama was quite clear to me. The bloody encounter at Chicusse had demonstrated our conventional enemy's incompetence, passivity and extreme slowness at reacting offensively. When considered together, all of these factors were sure indications that the enemy was not going to launch a deliberate counter-attack against Xangongo from Cahama any time soon; the threat posed by the FAPLA mobile reserve at Cahama had been swiftly and efficiently turned around by force projection and manoeuvre.

I uttered a quick prayer as I sped along, throwing up dust and listening to the comfortable drone of the Ratel engines: Thank you, dear Lord, for saving our people from harm ... I felt extreme gratitude towards my soldiers. They had tackled the job passionately and willingly in spite of facing danger and hardship. These extremely young warriors were something extraordinary, as you will find out when you read the story of what happened at Chicusse.

Contact, Contact, Wait, Out – Unexpected Fighting near Cahama

A rogue enemy artillery column of FAPLA came to its bloody demise during the night of 25 August because the South Africans manning the stopper line at Big Boy 1 near Chicusse were alert and had been comprehensively trained to prepare for and react quickly and decisively to any unforeseen crisis.

As we later reconstructed the preamble to the shootout, the ill-fated FAPLA column had broken out of the encirclement of Xangongo on D-Day and then lain up somewhere west of the Cunene, waiting for the fighting to die down before making its escape back to Cahama and the presumably welcoming arms of 21 Brigade.

Initially the FAPLA men bundu-bashed through the dense bush – something they were famously reluctant to do – until they reached the Cahama highway, then headed westwards with understandable caution, crawling along at low engine revolutions to keep their noise down and relying on infrared lights instead of their headlights. But these precautions were not enough to save them from the painful shock they received when they reached Chicusse (in all fairness, they were not the only ones to be unpleasantly surprised, as you will see). There are several layers to this story:

Firstly: Combat Team 3's mission and something about their advance to the Chicusse position.

As the western covering force, Combat Team 3's purpose was to provide early warning of a possible counter-attack from the west by FAPLA's mobile reserve, and to fight if it did eventuate. For this purpose Combat Team 3 had been turned into a formidable fighting package. It now consisted of its combat team HQ (two Ratel-90s); armoured car troops 1, 2 and 3 (four cars per troop, Ratel-90s as well as Eland-90s); support sections 1, 2 and 3 (Ratel-60s, totalling platoon strength, operating as support infantry for the armour); one mechanised infantry platoon from Bravo Company (four Ratel-20s); one medium artillery troop (four 140 mm G-2 guns); the pathfinder group from 44 Parachute Brigade (referred to as a tank hunting team by Combat Team 3 in its diary); an engineer section; and the administrative and supply echelon.

In the event of a FAPLA advance the combat team was tasked to make contact with the enemy vanguard and to either stop it in its (tank) tracks or to fight a delaying action while withdrawing to Xangongo. This would give the remainder of Battle Group 10 and the SAAF time to counter-attack if need be.

An unmanned aerial vehicle and a Bosbok were used for reconnaissance as Combat Team 3 advanced westwards towards Big Boy 1 but there was no sign of any enemy presence. By late afternoon the combat team reached their deployment position, 18 km from Cahama, which was now just within range for Captain Frans van Eeden's old but trusty 140 mm G-2 artillery pieces.

There they found signs that the position had recently been evacuated by a reasonably large enemy force. Why? No one knew for sure. Had FAPLA withdrawn its force to cater for the eventuality of an attack on Cahama? We concluded that our recent manoeuvrings had probably reinforced a perception of impending peril and that this should keep them at bay for the time being.

There was a tall radio mast at Chicusse, near Combat Team 3's new positions. Colonel Breytenbach immediately suggested that it be blown up. Weyers said no, being perfectly aware of the fact that the higher headquarters had ordered that such infrastructure was to be left untouched. Weyers' second-in-command, Captain Chris Gildenhuys, personally confirmed the hands-off policy, as he noted in the war diary.

That should have been the end of the story, but no one could be certain of anything involving the Brown Man, and a few minutes later the mast collapsed into ruin amid the rending of steel. In his typical devil-may-care way Breytenbach had trampled all over a standing order and collapsed the mast by undoing one of its support cables in utter disregard of the danger of compromising the combat team's presence.

I was disappointed when I heard about this. I had expected the immensely seasoned Breytenbach to mentor and support Weyers, who had obviously seen less operational service, rather than defy a direct order from him; in the military one expects any command instruction to be respected, whether one agrees with it or not, except if changing circumstances dictate otherwise.

At the end of the day, however, the damage done was immaterial; much more important was the damage that might have been inflicted on the status of command and personal relationships in the field, particularly considering the imbalance of the respective ranks. But no rupture occurred, as was proved when the uneasy marriage between Combat Team 3 and the pathfinders was put to the test during the surprise encounter with the FAPLA column that night.

Back to the story. The combat team was deployed astride the Xangongo-Cahama highway, facing west, with the position laid out in such a way that it could both observe the Cahama-facing front and cover it with interlocking arcs of fire, and also simultaneously mount an allround defence if the need arose. The pathfinders deployed independently at a slight distance to the rear in a flanking position south of the road – a disposition which later proved to be a fortunate one. Van Eeden's guns were deployed still further to the rear, facing west.

While they dug in, the team intercepted an interesting news report by the South African Broadcasting Corporation which Chris Gildenhuys subsequently recorded in the war diary: South Africa had attacked Angola with tanks, the SABC said, without quoting any source. It was an intriguing item of news, since De Vries, Weyers, Gildenhuys and everybody else knew that our nearest tanks were the Olifants parked at Bloemfontein, thousands of kilometres away.

Apparently the Americans were keeping silent about South Africa's latest military intervention into Angola. All it really did was emphasise Combat Team 3's isolation in the face of an overwhelming enemy presence.

On the other hand, no one in Combat Team 3 really expected anything except a quiet night, given FAPLA's clear lack of enthusiasm for emerging from its cosy lair at Cahama – an inertness confirmed by our ever vigilant aerial scout, Freddie, who had ventured nearer to Cahama, staying in constant communication with his old schoolmate, Lieutenant Jacques du Randt.

Things seemed so calm that Freddie ignored a standing SAAF instruction and, instead of returning to base for the night, landed on the road and parked his Bosbok inside the covering position. With everything in place, Combat Team 3 settled in for the night, tired but as vigilant as ever.

Secondly: To give an explanation about the rogue enemy force.

Given FAPLA's reluctance to operate at night, it was a fair assumption that on the balance of probabilities there would be no unpleasant surprises during the hours of darkness on that silent highway that in times of peace carried streams of back-and-forth traffic but was now deserted.

But of course the unexpected is always to be expected in war, and at that very time the rogue enemy artillery battery was stealthily making its way towards the South African position – from the wrong side. Soon all hell would be brought down on the heads of the bewildered enemy by a somewhat less bewildered combat team after some quick thinking and equally rapid action by both Weyers and Breytenbach.

Thirdly: To clarify what actually happened:

At 22:20 the artillery troop deployed to the rear of the blocking position reported possible enemy movement from their southeast which appeared to be approaching on the road from the direction of Xangongo; eight suspect vehicles had passed the guns and were moving steadily towards the stopper line. The vehicles were identified as being of Russian origin, travelling without lights – FAPLA, lo and behold.

Weyers called the combat team to immediate readiness. The first enemy vehicle, a BRDM armoured scout car, passed through the laager's 12 o'clock position and was knocked out by a shell from a Ratel-90 of Armoured Car Troop 1. That was the signal for wholesale firing in all directions. Not one of the other seven reported vehicles reached the forward line, many being wiped out on the road, which became an instant killing ground for Breytenbach's veteran tank hunters.

The next day it was determined that the rogue enemy column had been a composite artillery battery, consisting of the artillery observer's BRDM, three BTR-152 armoured troop carriers full of FAPLA soldiers, two motorised 122 mm BM-21 multiple rocket launcher systems, four towed 23 mm anti-aircraft gun systems, four Gaz trucks fully loaded with ammunition, and a radio vehicle which served as a fire control post.

The rest, as they say, is history. The coolheaded Chris Gildenhuys did not get his water hot about it, however: In the war diary he noted laconically that there was a "contact with the enemy at Big Boy on 252224B August 1981," although he obviously could not resist a touch of dry humour when describing the immediate aftermath: "There was no further sleep that eventful and operationally active night. Any suspect enemy movement was immediately answered with Browning machine gun fire. At some stage even the rising moon was engaged".

On Wednesday, 26 August, the sun crept up from the east to reveal the full extent of the action, a mournful sight. At 07:30 the combat team commenced mopping up the killing zone with its sorry wilderness of smashed guns and burnt out vehicles like the slain BRDM with its charred FAPLA corpses. Still there was no reaction from Cahama, apart from some salvos from 122 mm multiple rocket launchers, which to everyone's relief all fell short. The only other enemy contact, if it could be called that, consisted of a lone FAPLA soldier, still armed with his AK-47 rifle, who came wandering in out of the bush and surrendered to Gildenhuys.

Freddie, our gallant Bosbok pilot, nonchalantly lifted off the tar road at Chicusse and disappeared into the wild blue yonder towards the east into the rising sun, leaving exploding 122 mm rockets behind him. Miraculously there were no holes in his aircraft.

I was, needless to say, extremely thankful that the combat team had suffered truly negligible injuries – three soldiers with minor head wounds from mortar fragments. We were all extremely proud of the achievements of our combat team and the pathfinders, and more of our young warriors had had their baptism of fire without suffering any losses.

I recalled Combat Team 3 to Xangongo for some rest and recuperation, and soon afterwards the pathfinders reverted to Task Force Alpha's command, not that they really bothered themselves all that much about whose command they were under, I suspect. To my mind the fighting at Chicusse had been successfully performed under difficult operational circumstances, and again I was particularly pleased about the battle experience my soldiers had picked up, especially the flock of national servicemen under my command.

All the war booty that was still intact – including the two Soviet-built BM-21 MRLs, the only ones netted during Protea – was recovered to Xangongo and driven back to Oshakati under their own steam at the end of the operation. And during all this FAPLA's mobile reserve at Cahama remained quietly at ease (or should I say "unease"?), not daring to venture further to the east or do anything except fire those haphazard 122 mm rockets which didn't even reach their targets.

What were they thinking? That the South Africans were coming for them next, or what? They had not seemed to care about the plight of their bleeding and dying companions and even less about the captured BM-21s and the assortment of armoured vehicles and trucks that were soon travelling calmly in the other direction.

Next day Joe Weyers and his troops presented me with a memento which I still treasure, a slab of flat shining metal which had melted off the burning BRDM armoured car and congealed on the road. I still hold it in remembrance of my soldiers of 61 Mech. I also brought back a pristine optical sight block from the BRDM which was probably blown off as the car exploded, and which in 2011 I handed to the Museum of Military History in Johannesburg in the safekeeping of the 61 Mech Veterans' Association.

And on the return of Charlie Squadron to Omuthiya on 2 September I asked Chris Gildenhuys to deliver a bouquet of flowers to Tannie Pompie at Tsintsabis as a token of appreciation for her invaluable relay service. The visit was, so he reported, a memorable one.

The designated exploitation area to the west had now been satisfactorily cleared of enemy remnants, and we had also acquired a much better grasp of the lay of the land – time spent on reconnaissance is never wasted, after all. We calculated that the FAPLA mobile reserve would be kept guessing, and therefore immobile, for some time to come. Just in case, however, I sent Combat Team 3 off westwards again on 27 August to establish another stopper line nearer to Xangongo at "Big Boy 2", in the vicinity of Catequero.

Cahama Remained a Thorn in the Flesh after Operation Protea

To give a quick preview into what was then the not-so-distant future: Cahama remained a thorn in the flesh of the SADF long after Operation Protea and was never subdued at any time during the Border War. This was especially true as regards the airfield and the formidable air defences protecting this important military stronghold, and in operations in 1983 and 1984 the SAAF was faced with its modern Soviet-built SA-8 and SA-9 surface-to-air systems, which resulted in a number of Impala Mark 2s being hit by missiles.

In December 1983, during Operation Askari, 61 Mech (by then under Commandant Epp van Lill) knocked at Cahama's gates. Brigadier Joep Joubert, who had replaced Brigadier Badenhorst as OC Sector 10, had instructed Van Lill to "cut the water and lights" at the base and disrupt its rearward line of communication to Chibemba and ultimately Lubango.

By means of feint attacks and artillery bombardments Van Lill succeeded in temporarily isolating Cahama from Chibemba, but avoided a toe-to-toe confrontation with FAPLA's newly acquired Soviet T54/55 tanks, for which the SADF had no effective countermeasure at that time. Essentially, Van Lill reprised 61 Mech's role in Operation Protea – albeit with more shooting involved – namely, to keep the Cahama-based forces in place to prevent interference with the rest of Operation Askari further to the east.

Having done all that could be accomplished at Cahama, Van Lill was sent off on a spur-of-the-moment quest on 13 January 1984 to capture 11 FAPLA Brigade's heavily defended position at Cuvelai in the east after an earlier South African attack had been beaten off. This he did, annihilating 11 Brigade after some intense fighting in which the Ratel-90s of Charlie Squadron (Major Chris du Toit) and those of the anti-tank platoon proved that the heavily armoured T54/55s might be formidable but were not invulnerable at close range.

The war was definitely escalating, and it was clear that things were getting worse rather than better. In the light of all of this I asked myself many a time whether Pretoria had a medium to long-term political-military strategy in place for this war. I did not get a clear answer. Oh, well, ours was not to reason why ...

In any case, during Operation Hilti-Prone in May 1988 the fiercely defended Cahama area became the stronghold of the supposedly élite 50th Cuban Division, which had provided the South Africans with a nasty surprise by arriving unexpectedly in the war zone. The airfield was extended and used as an operational base for modern Russian MiG fighters.

The Cuban ground and air forces were now capable of striking into SWA/Namibia if they wanted to (but they did not, as I have noted). In 1987/1988, however, their intentions were not that clear. What was perfectly clear was that the war in southern Angola had escalated out of all proportion.[18] What would happen next?

About Mobile Defence and the Relevance of a Bridge

To return to Protea. 61 Mech gained valuable operational experience across the spectrum of offensive as well as defensive operations during Protea. The offensive lessons had been learned. Now it was time for the defensive part. On 26 August, after returning from Mucope, I started setting up our mobile defence for the western flank. Any defence, but especially a mobile one, should be an active rather than a passive operation. Fortunately for us, the Russians did little to teach their FAPLA protégés about this important characteristic.

If cleverly conducted, a mobile defence can be used to maintain the initiative. This implies the skilful use of obstacles to impede the enemy's ability to manoeuvre, while at the same time preserving the mobility of one's own force. This was exactly what Battle Group 10 had in mind for the successful completion of Operation Protea.

Obstacle planning for mobile defence is closely linked to the enemy's most probable offensive manoeuvring courses of action. The latter need to be assessed with close attention to the utilisation of terrain, time and distance, and we meticulously identified and analysed the possible forming-up places and approaches the enemy could use for an attack.

Logic dictated that we use the Cunene as a natural obstacle for defending against a Cahama-based force, with Xangongo as the centre of gravity, or pivotal point, so to speak, for our defensive manoeuvring. We did not favour entrenchment or the holding of ground: Tactical ground is given to us by the Dear Lord to fight on, not to hide in.

Shallow trenches were used by our own forces for the purpose of local protection – that is, at times when we were stationary for limited periods. But we were never stationary for long. The tactical positions of our mobile command group and the combat teams were dispositional tactical features on the eastern bank of the Cunene.

The defence was covered by observation posts on the eastern bank, which were linked to mobile covering patrols operating westwards towards Cahama, since early warning of possible enemy intervention was crucial for counteractions from our side. The normal intelligence gathering process was supplemented by means of enemy radio intercepts and aerial reconnaissance.

The defensive plan called for counter-attacks by our combat teams from carefully selected staging positions; these positions were mostly occupied only at night; during the day the combat teams were kept busy with a multitude of chores in and around Xangongo. Captain Koos Liebenberg's Combat Team 2, as a pure mechanised force, was our mobile reserve.

---

18 See Chapters 15 and 16.

Our two artillery commanders, Captains Bernie Pols and Frans van Eeden, developed a deliberate defensive fire plan for all our indirect fire weapons, and in addition the gunners sallied forth now and again to taunt the enemy with some impressive harassing fire on Cahama with their 140 mm guns. Surprisingly (or perhaps not), however, Cahama continued to stew in its own juice and did not take any aggressive or offensive action.

The preparation of the bridge as a Reserve Demolition was, of course, integral to our defence and formed part of the counter-mobility operations we had planned, the aim of which was to impede the enemy's mobility in the west while at the same time enhancing the security (and therefore room for initiative) of Task Force Alpha's activities east of the river. It is fascinating now to recall the detail which went into the planning and execution of this aspect, and the carting of tons of explosives and special demolition equipment to the bridge site by Battle Group 40 under the supervision of its second-in-command, Major Eddie Viljoen.

A Reserve Demolition only takes place when the boss says so (in this case the GOC SWATF, General Charles Lloyd). It is therefore understandable that the actual execution of a Reserve Demolition is governed by strict battle handling procedures, and that a specific unit – in this instance Battle Group 10 – is selected to manage the operation.

The role of demolition guard commander I delegated to Major Dawid Mentz, at the time the uncrowned king of Xangongo. This meant that he was now responsible for the tactical command of all troops at the reserve obstacle site – the guard force as well as the firing party. A demolition guard force is responsible for protecting the reserve obstacle and preventing its capture by the enemy prior to execution of the demolition order. Mentz was expected to secure the site; prepare the bridge for demolition; transmit the demolition order to the firing party commander when so ordered; and ensure its successful execution.

25 Field Engineer Squadron was designated as the firing party; this meant that Major Leon Terblanche was responsible for commanding the demolition, which entailed technical control of the preparation for demolition, and then firing the charges when and if ordered. The entire process was regulated by code words for the activation of readiness states and the demolition itself. Transmission of "Bride" meant the demolition process must be activated; "Rubicon" would be the signal for the actual demolition. To make sure that the process worked smoothly, we set up special communications and alternative communication arrangements.

For Protea the arrangements for the bridge's demolition were stipulated in an official classified message to General Lloyd and an operations order to me as the commander of Battle Group 10. From 12:00 on 25 August the bridge and other means of crossing were ready for immediate demolition, and stayed that way until completion of Battle Group 10's defensive mission on 31 August. I then officially handed over responsibility both for the defence of Xangongo and the Reserve Demolition to a UNITA party which had just arrived. The specific responsibility for the Reserve Demolition I delegated to Captain Charl Naudé of the Special Forces, who remained behind with UNITA when the rest of us departed after the handover.

I can now make an interesting revelation about the bridge and the Reserve Demolition which only became known to me in recent times when the archives of the old defence force started spilling some of its formerly heavily guarded classified secrets.

On 26 August a telex message marked "secret" was dispatched from Cape Town by General Constand Viljoen to General Lloyd in Windhoek, the contents of which made it clear that the South African government had decided not to blow the bridge, due to political considerations stipulated in the telex I quote verbatim (translated from the Afrikaans):

> Secret – Immediate; 26 Aug 81 at 07h50; From CSADF[19] to GOC SWATF[20]; For Information To: Minister for Defence, Chief Army, Chief Air Force, Chief of Staff Intelligence and Chief of Staff Operations: For Attention Maj Gen Lloyd from Gen Viljoen regarding Reserve Demolition of bridge over Cunene at Yankee (C Army/003/Aug 81 refers).
>
> After political discussion, further consideration and for the sake of good sense, it was decided that the bridge should not be demolished. You are therefore not to demolish the bridge, unless it becomes absolutely necessary in the event of a possible enemy intervention and to prevent the enemy from capturing the current position at Yankee [the code for Xangongo – Author]. In such an instance you are the highest approval and controlling authority. Acknowledge.

The abovementioned is particularly interesting when one considers what eventually happened. Not to put too fine a point on it, the imposing structure was eventually blown at three o'clock in the morning by a one-man demolition squad in the shape of the ever creative and somewhat mischievous young Charl Naudé: "Ek het die brug geblaas, ek alleen," he later told me gleefully ("I blew the bridge, all by myself").

I am not sure of the date, but it was probably close to 9 September, a few days after we had withdrawn and were already safely back in SWA/Namibia. As Naudé recollects, there was one almighty bang and much of the bridge fell into the Cunene, no doubt to the surprise of the crocodiles, not to mention the war weary inhabitants of the battered little town. Naudé then made his own way back to SWA/Namibia (rumour has it that he did not walk back with his tremendously large backpack, and that his departure was not unconnected with a captured Scania truck which was seen heading southwards soon after the explosion).

As a historical footnote: This was the second time in six years that South African explosives had dropped the Xangongo bridge. During the withdrawal from Angola in March 1976 at the end of Operation Savannah the bridge was prepared for demolition by 3 Field Engineer Regiment for exactly the same reason. It is said that the actual deed was handled somewhat more diplomatically than in 1981, though: When the charges were in place the unsuspecting local UNITA commander was given the honour of pressing the button, so that the South Africans would not be blamed (they got blamed all the same, of course).

It is also interesting to note that just over two years later, during Operation Askari, Commandant Epp van Lill and 61 Mech were ordered to attack missile sites on the outskirts of Cahama, and to get them over the Cunene it was necessary to mount one of the first operational bridge crossings undertaken by the SADF since World War II. This entailed the construction of a Bailey bridge just north of Xangongo for 61 Mech to cross over on the same day of the attack.

Alas, the sappers' hard work was in vain. The hastily planned attack (according to Van Lill he was simply given the green light over the radio) was called off after a vigorous

19 General Constand Viljoen.

20 Major General Charles Lloyd.

counter-attack by the FAPLA tanks. This was 61 Mech's last involvement with Cahama during Askari – immediately afterwards it was summoned to Cuvelai for the successful attack there.

Later the sappers had to construct a crossing over the site of the original and now-demolished bridge to facilitate ongoing operations by the SADF against FAPLA on the other side of the Cunene River. I suppose the moral of this story is that one should not be too eager to burn (or blow) one's bridges.

The Fight for Môngua – a Spitting Mamba

On 25 August, with Xangongo taken, Commandant Johnny Coetzer's Combat Team Mamba was ordered to capture Môngua – which lay squarely in the way of the attack planned for Ondjiva for 26–27 August, and where a strong and previously unknown enemy outpost had been discovered.

I was not there, but of course had a close personal interest in the attack, seeing that Mamba's main components came from 61 Mech, Captain Hannes van der Merwe's Alpha Company and the anti-tank platoon under Lieutenants Chris Walls and Hubrecht van Dalsen. So I followed its progress and maintained close radio communications with my people there, out on a limb to the east.

Mamba overran Môngua and destroyed the mechanised force there after a fierce firefight, the enemy losses including some T34-85 tanks at the hands (and guns) of Chris Walls's eight wily anti-tank Ratel-90s. Our own losses were minor; barring the deaths of Lieutenant Bertus Roos and his gunner, Sergeant Clifton Stacey, when their Alouette was shot down by 14,5 mm FAPLA guns while providing fire support (what made this particularly harrowing for Chris Walls and Hubrecht van Dalsen was that they actually saw the stricken helicopter falling to its doom).

Now, with Môngua out of the way, Coetzer and Combat Team Mamba stood by to join hands with Task Force Alpha when it arrived to attack the last main objective, Ondjiva.

Combat Team 2 and the Battle for Ondjiva – Rapid Response Southeastwards

On 26 August (D+2), Task Force Alpha set off for the attack on Ondjiva, minus Commandant Ferreira's Battle Group 40, which had now come under command of Task Force Bravo and was well on its way to Mupa, and of course Battle Group 10, which was engaged in establishing the western flank's mobile defence. Task Force Alpha still disposed over a formidable main assault force – the mobile task force's mobile HQ; Battle Group 20 (Commandant Dippenaar); Battle Group 30 (Commandant Serfontein); and Coetzer's Combat Team Mamba as the mobile reserve. At a later stage, though, an element of Battle Group 10 would play a decisive role at Ondjiva, although no one knew this as yet, of course.

The task force's HQ and the two battle groups moved swiftly southeastwards from Xangongo along the tarmacked highway, picking up Combat Team Mamba along the way, and occupied forward assembly areas located slightly to the east of Môngua and north of Ondjiva.

Meanwhile the SAAF dropped leaflets on Ondjiva which warned civilians and the FAPLA soldiery to evacuate the town forthwith, because the SADF's fight was with SWAPO, not Angola's soldiers or population. Since FAPLA's commanders were not visionaries and believed they were able to beat off all-comers, the leaflets had precisely the opposite effect to the one intended. The regional headquarters at Lubango instructed 11

Brigade to stay put and to defend the town at all costs – which was what happened in the end, the costs being mainly theirs.

The only effect of the leaflet drop was that the element of surprise was forfeited and the defenders were ready when the SADF attacked from the northwest on 27 August. As a result it eventually took two days of heavy fighting before Ondjiva fell.

- During stage 1 of the assault, Battle Group 20 attacked the airfield and the military complex on the northwestern and western edges of Ondjiva. More resistance was encountered than expected, including retaliation by enemy tanks, so that the counteractions required intervention by the task force reserve, Combat Team Mamba. This delay had a negative impact on the predetermined overall timings for the attack.
- Stage 2 consisted of an attack by Battle Group 30 on Ondjiva itself, followed by the clearing of the town. Once again more resistance was encountered than had been expected, among other things aggressive action by tanks, and the battle group hit minefields on the way to its objective while the sand ran steadily out of the task force's hour glass.
- At Task Force HQ Brigadier Joubert grew so concerned about the delays that on the morning of D+3 he called on Battle Group 10 to provide an extra mobile reserve to reinforce Mamba. Captain Koos Liebenberg's Combat Team 2 deployed with such speed that he arrived without maps or the benefit of a briefing, and between Alpha and Mamba the last enemy resistance was eventually neutralised by last light (more about Combat Team 2 and how it came to participate will be told later).

On 28 August the town was finally secured and mopping up commenced. Only minor resistance was encountered during the final clearing-up phase, with many FAPLA members escaping under cover of night.

The story of Koos Liebenberg's helter-skelter dash into harm's way clearly illustrates 61 Mech's thoroughly rehearsed ability to respond rapidly to an unforeseen crisis.

It began soon after the attack went in on 27 August. Colonel Joubert realised that his task force was in for a heavy fight and that he urgently needed reinforcements – specifically a mechanised combat team with adequate anti-armour capability. Joubert contacted me by radio around 10:00, explained his dilemma and requested immediate support.

I swung into action without delay. I tasked Liebenberg about his new venture and recalled the two Ratel-90 armoured car troops (a total of eight vehicles) deployed with Combat Team 3's stopper line a few kilometres west of the Cunene. The two troops rushed to Xangongo, where Liebenberg was already finalising things and readying his force for immediate departure to Ondjiva.

There they were immediately attached to Combat Team 2. Marrying up the two mechanised infantry platoons (Ratel-20s) and two armoured car troops (Ratel-90s) took place with unceremonious haste in an open square in front of the battle group HQ, after which the combat team immediately moved southeastwards on the highway to Môngua and then Ondjiva.

Liebenberg later gave me a written account of his actions at Ondjiva which I translated from Afrikaans as follows. It is a bald, unvarnished narrative that sketches a good picture of what the last stage of the fight for Ondjiva was like:

... At about 10:00B, I received an instruction (from Commandant Roland de Vries, the commander of Battle Group 10) to move to Ondjiva to act as the task force reserve. I arrived at Ondjiva with my combat team at about 13:00B. I did not have the required maps or aerial photography.

The situation at Ondjiva was foreign to me. Everywhere one could hear shots fired and explosions erupting. It seemed as if I was the only person concerned about it.

At approximately 15:00B, I received an order from the task force commander (Colonel Joep Joubert) to clear an enemy mortar position south of Ondjiva. After acquiring the necessary aerial photograph I started moving. As soon as I started moving I received an instruction to hold fast. I paused for some time, observing the apparent chaos unfolding at the airfield.

I was monitoring the command net of the task force (and) about one hour before last light I heard that the assault troops of Commandant Serfontein (Battle Group 30) were under threat by enemy T-34 tanks from the east. I received an order to block the counter-attack of the enemy tanks. I immediately moved forward with the two Ratel-90 armoured car troops.

I located Commandant Serfontein at the eastern edge of the town. As our small force advanced I could observe the enemy tanks. We also came under fire. The enemy tanks were on the side of a shona and were making their way steadily towards Anhanca. Dusk was approaching fast.

I deployed the two armoured car troops to the left and right of the road at the edge of the town. The exact position was at the intersection where the road turns south in the direction of Namacunde. The Ratel-90s had excellent firing positions and commenced with the delivery of fire within their respective troop formations.

The main threats were from two enemy tanks approximately 900 metres further to the east. It was becoming dark very quickly now and we resorted to speculative fire. We could only deliver pinpoint fire when we observed the gun flashes of the enemy tanks momentarily lighting up the darkness.

By now it was completely dark. All our Ratel-90s fired simultaneously at the enemy tanks, when suddenly two huge balls of fire erupted. The incoming fire of the enemy tanks ceased immediately. We assumed that there had been two successful hits.

In the meantime own forces had received the order to withdraw and to regroup halfway between the town and the airfield – it was chaos. Everyone rushed back at the same time and the road became completely congested. The problem was only resolved at about 01:00B the next morning.

My combat team was the last to leave the fighting zone. We laagered adjacent to the town. My orders were now to prevent any enemy intervention which could come from Ondjiva. It was a restless night. I was speculating (about) what would happen the next day. I had not received any further orders from anyone.

At approximately 04:00B I received an instruction by radio to join up with Combat Team Mamba under command of Commandant Johnny Coetzer. An enemy target to be attacked northeast of the airfield was designated to our joint force. We rendezvoused at Ondjiva airfield and quickly determined our course of action. There were clear indications that neither orders nor snap orders were going to be given to us.

Our attack was launched at 08:00. Phase 1 of the attack was executed by Captain Hannes van der Merwe and his mechanised company. I bypassed the next (target)

> during Phase 2 and attacked my designated target. Another disappointment awaited our combat team, as the target was void of enemy.
>
> Our involvement with the task force was completed by 12:00B (28 August 1981 – D+4). I received an order (from the task force HQ) to return to Xangongo. We arrived at Xangongo at about 16:00B and were afforded the opportunity to rest for the night.

The armoured car troops of Charlie Squadron had their own story to tell when they reported back to Combat Team 3 HQ. Their call signs 31 and 32 – 2nd Lieutenant A.J. de Jager and Lieutenant J.H.B. Kleynhans – had accounted for two T34-85s by a judicious use of the fire and movement tactics we had drilled so thoroughly into them during training, and their mechanised support troop had killed a number of FAPLA soldiers. Charlie Squadron celebrated the two troops' exploits as a major success for their subunit, which it was.

Naturally I was very pleased. Both Bravo Company and Charlie Squadron's detached Ratel-90s had given a good account of themselves; it was good for my soldiers' morale, it was a great learning experience, and it had provided indelible memories for their later lives.

Their actions at Ondjiva had once again proved the value of mobile forces within the context of the African battle space – speed, mobility, firepower and flexibility are norms of paramount importance for the success of fast-flowing battles.

The battles for Ondjiva and Môngua also demonstrated the mettle and leadership of the South African soldier in rough conditions – fighting diligently by day or night amid dire situations, sleeping by catnapping wherever and whenever opportunities came up, in shell scrapes if they were lucky or on the move if they were not, with a full night's rest an almost unheard-of luxury. A few more of South Africa's sons had become warriors overnight.

Keeping the Western Front Quiet – Parrying and Sparring

To return to 25 August at Xangongo: From that date until the completion of Operation Protea the western front needed to be kept quiet and the continued offensive operation of Task Force Alpha to the east neatly partitioned off by the Cunene. The enemy had to be kept guessing about the stretch of no-man's land stretching out towards Cahama; an area which provided equal opportunity for manoeuvre by both friend and foe.

Our operation was of an offensive-defensive nature and entailed continuously blocking any possible enemy interference from the west. This made life extremely interesting for us during Protea's short lifespan because there was such a diverse range of offensive and defensive tasks – and some others which did not fall into any clear categories. So we went from taking on attacking and defending postures to playing soccer (of which more later). It amounted to sparring without any standing rules.

We believed, with considerable justification, that by its mere threatening presence Battle Group 10 was fulfilling its next mission of denying Xangongo to FAPLA's 21 Brigade. But we did not relax, even though we thought it highly unlikely that Luanda's men would get up to any nasty stuff in the short term, in spite of the fact that they possessed more than enough latent potential to make things very sticky for us, if only they could summon up the resolve to use it. But there was always that off-chance, so we kept our eyes wide open for signs of damage from *friction de guerre*, or of being caught on the hop.

In the meantime Battle Group 10 was sitting pretty, literally "occupying the high ground", guarding the explosive garlanded bridge and making sure that we were ready to exploit every possible advantage that the Cunene River offered as an obstacle. Colonel Jan Breytenbach and his pathfinders were doing their mysterious own thing in the north, somewhere in the vicinity of Peu Peu, like a force of Jedi knights armed with machine guns instead of light sabres. Combat Team 3 sat tight in its stopper line to the west, covering the enemy's most likely approach route; their vehicle inventory, incidentally, now included a camouflaged Soviet ambulance that FAPLA had abandoned.

Life in the stopper line was tranquil, war or no war. From time to time a few members of the local population passed by of whom some were questioned and others searched. Regular maintenance on vehicles and equipment helped to pass the time. From 19:50 onwards on 28 August they smelt (distant) powder when there was an intense artillery bombardment about 10 km to 15 km to their west, which they concluded was probably harassing fire 21 Brigade had laid down because it feared a deliberate SADF assault.

At 11:00 on Saturday, 29 August, Koos Liebenberg and Combat Team 2 arrived to relieve them, accompanied by the two Ratel-90 armoured car troops and their "supporties", which remained behind in the stopper line with Combat Team 2; before Combat Team 3 withdrew they proceeded to regale their Charlie Squadron colleagues with stories about knocking out the two enemy T34-85s at Ondjiva and sowing death and destruction among the FAPLA infantry.

Back at Xangongo, Combat Team 3's troops settled down to enjoy some well-earned rest and recuperation, including the luxury of bathing in the Cunene River and eating some "wet rations" in the form of three bartered goats which were slaughtered and immediately barbecued.

That same day I recalled Combat Team 2 to Xangongo as well. This came as somewhat of a disruption for Koos Liebenberg and his men, who had settled in on the stopper line, but I had just received orders that Battle Group 10 was to withdraw to SWA/Namibia on 1 September – well ahead of schedule – and I needed Combat Team 2 to start organising the recovery to SWA/Namibia of the bulk of the captured enemy weapons and equipment. The reason for this mundane tasking was that Xangongo had yielded a massive amount of booty, and each of their powerful Ratel-20s would be able to tow two to three pieces on the way home.

Fortunately Combat Team Mamba had been disbanded by now, so that Hannes van der Merwe's Bravo Company and the Ratel-90 anti-tank platoon had rejoined us on 29 August and could take over the stopper position until Monday, 31 August, the day before the great goodbye to Angola.

On Sunday, 30 August, I instructed elements of Combat Team 3 to escort the artillery troop on a harassing fire mission to the northwest of Mucope. The G-2s delivered a fire plan in the direction of Cahama, after which the group embarked on the retrograde move. Then at about noon a significantly sized enemy force was located near Mucope. Additional elements of the combat team were sent off immediately to support the artillery group with a snap attack, but by the time of the attack, about 15:00, the FAPLA force had beaten a fast retreat back to Cahama.

In their haste the FAPLA soldiers left behind a complete medical post on which Combat Team 3 promptly laid hands on; judging by the substantial pieces of equipment and medications, it was clear to us that the enemy had started to probe carefully outwards from Cahama to discern what was going on around them (Mucope was one of their traditional defensive outposts).

On Monday, 31 August, I instructed Combat Team 3 to move at once into the stopper position at Big Boy 2 and act as a rearguard to cover the eastward withdrawal of Battle Group 10 from Xangongo. At 12:00 Combat Team 3 handed over their responsibility to a UNITA contingent, then withdrew to Xangongo, where it deployed in allround defence near the airfield. Then at 14:50 Battle Group 10 withdrew from Xangongo in good order after handing over the defence of the town to UNITA.

Life to the Full at Xangongo – To Live is to Experience

Life with 61 Mech was Always Interesting

Back to a few anecdotes about life at Xangongo when we provided for its mobile defence from 26–31 August. If this was what mobile defence was like, I would probably volunteer for it again. There was some fun in it; especially with interesting souls such as those belonging to 61 Mech as they busied themselves with things that were not usually listed in the job profiles of soldiers.

A Town Called Xangongo and its Wonderful People

In the Portuguese era Xangongo (then still Vila Roçades) had been a pleasant enough little town, but that was before the civil war had engulfed Angola, and now our new domicile was a typical African slum, crowded and inhabited by desperately poor people living in (and sometimes outside) rickety shacks or tenements composed of all sorts of scrap material, and lean-to's that were made of anything from rusty sheets of corrugated iron to ordinary sacking. They looked as if they might collapse under the weight of the people crammed into them, and often did.

The nameless alleys were unpaved and in perpetual darkness. A morbid atmosphere clung to the place. The town stank, because the streets ran with raw sewage and were choked with mounds of uncollected garbage. At night the town was ruled by packs of skinny half-feral dogs. The children wore rags, drank water from cesspools and lived in fear of being eaten alive by rats. There was little running water, only brief interludes of electricity, and even less hope.

Spraypainted on to several propaganda billboards around town were derogatory remarks about the racist South Africans and how the MPLA and the Cubans were the saviours and how they were going to stuff us up. "*Viva Castro, Viva MPLA, Viva Cuba ...* " and so forth. Okay, noted. Also noted: If the average black township in good old apartheid South Africa had looked like this you would have instant riots all over the place, and the opposition would be screaming its head off in Parliament.

Xangongo's environs were hardly more aesthetically pleasing. It was surrounded by an interlocking trench system with sophisticated concrete bunkers, but the effect was somewhat spoiled by a myriad of wrecked vehicles of various types, shot to pieces in the recent fighting (and incidentally, when I drove through Ondjiva and Xangongo on a battlefield tour in 2010, it looked pretty much the same, after almost three decades of so-called freedom and the influx of billions of dollars from the off-shore oilfields).

That was the bad news. The good news was the people of Xangongo were great. We established a relationship of trust literally overnight and soon were helping them to restore order and repair critical installations – the tiffies working overtime to repair and maintain facilities that had not had a lick of attention for Heaven only knew how long – and providing medical aid, another thing that, we gathered, had been in short supply for a long time. Padre Koos Rossouw enthusiastically dished out spiritual comfort and even converted a few Angolan souls when he was not busy playing darts or volleyball with the troops.

Providing municipal services suddenly became part of our operational portfolio. I will not say that I was exceedingly overjoyed about this, but as always the mission came first and needed to be executed in the most professional manner. This is the trait of the South African soldier, and I wondered at times what the FAPLA soldiers, the Russians and the Cubans had done to these people. We heard horrific stories of ill-treatment which really stuck in our throats, because the SADF had strict guidelines about the appropriate handling of civilians and prisoners of war, and enforced them, too.

Major Dawid Mentz was not overjoyed about becoming mired in municipal matters either but he also buckled down and did a sterling job, not only improving the almost nonexistent services but handing out gifts of captured Cuban food supplies and cigars to the local traditional chiefs and their people. If we had stayed there for months rather than days he would probably have been a shoo-in for Mayor. I was extremely pleased that this creative and resolute paratrooper's path had crossed mine and that of 61 Mech – thank you, Dear Lord.

The Amazing Soccer Game at Xangongo

In addition to all his other duties, Dawid Mentz also turned into Xangongo's sports king. I had a hand in this, but the prime mover was none other than General Jannie Geldenhuys, who came visiting on D+3, when the locals were still somewhat shell-shocked and deeply apprehensive about the comings and goings of the Ratels, the Elands and the big, mean-looking 140 mm guns.

Amid the hustle and bustle as Battle Group 10 rapidly adjusted to its new role of setting up defences and restoring order, General Geldenhuys called me to one side and said: "Roland, organise a soccer game against the town." I was more than somewhat astounded, but like any good mechanised combat commander I responded with a "yes, sir!" He is a very intelligent man but not a mind reader, so he did not realise what I thought of this extraordinary idea, and I am still not prepared to state my thoughts in writing.

But I did not simply dismiss the idea. I had immense respect and affection for him and realised that he had something up his sleeve; he was one of our most unusual generals, with amazing insight and a flair for indirectness and creativity. So if "Jannie G" wanted a soccer game, he would have it. I promptly delegated the responsibility to an equally astounded Dawid Mentz, forestalling any comment by adding: "No backchat." This done, I went off to pursue my duties in overseeing the more military-orientated, and, to my mind, more important work at Xangongo.

Dawid appointed one of his national service lieutenants, Henri ("Bossie") Boshoff, as the official referee, and they got down to organising the soccer match in true military style – probably no bundu soccer match has ever been so carefully planned and expertly executed.

The town team turned out in their official jerseys and the 61 players in their regimental T-shirts, and Xangongo's fanatical soccer fans attended in droves, full of a high-spirited exuberance which drove out their grief and fear, if only for a little while. It was a grand success; we lost 3–1, but this was one struggle where I didn't mind being defeated, because 61 Mech became the instant and trusted friends of the locals.

On 19 November that year, long after Operation Protea, General Geldenhuys wrote me a letter of appreciation in which he stated that the soccer match had paid an immense dividend in the national and international community; this one little game had softened the United Nations' surge of anger against South Africa's aggression.

These were not just kind words: That very reaction had been reported by then Foreign Affairs Minister, Pik Botha to his other colleagues in government. South Africa's ambassador, Mr. Riaan Eksteen could also use the game at Xangongo as a means of swinging around the bursts of negativity that were repeatedly aimed at South Africa in the United States.

The reports by at least four journalists who accompanied the SADF during Operation Protea helped to create a more positive view about South Africa's exemplary military conduct in Angola with reports that clearly showed the positive relationship existing between our soldiers and the local Angolan citizens. To my knowledge there were more than two television broadcasts abroad that featured the soccer game. I suppose you could call this a non-military mission accomplished in a military manner to satisfy a strategic aim.

My heartfelt appreciation went out to Dawid Mentz, Henri Boshoff[21] and 61 Mech's soccer team ... and to the battered citizens of Xangongo, who were still able to muster some spirit in spite of their tribulations. I couldn't help thinking that 61 Mech would clearly have to add soccer and rugby tactics to its battle doctrine and SOP.

Mopping Up Xangongo ... with Mopeds

"Mopping up" is a traditional military term which pretty much describes what the process consists of, but sometimes it can lead to unexpected outcomes. For example, our days were filled with various routine mopping-up tasks, together with the repair and maintenance of equipment and even some training. But then we noticed an odd thing: More and more of our troops were putting around on brand new Mopeds, which were surely not part of the standard FAPLA vehicle inventory.

Finding out what this was all about fell in the province of the RSM, WO1 M.C. Barnard, and it did not take him long to get to the bottom of it. It turned out that Giel Reinecke's loggies had come across a warehouse full of the things; my troops being the creative characters that they were, the result was inevitable and so some of the Mopeds began filtering out of the warehouse.

I had a friendly one-on-one discussion with Giel about this matter, and the RSM took the sort of direct action for which RSMs are famous – suddenly and mysteriously the tyres vanished off the Mopeds' wheels. Oh, well ... it was good while it lasted.

My magnificent troops took it in good part; they had an uncanny ability to test the proverbial envelope and, if they found a weakness, to stretch it almost to breaking point. In this sort of game you win a few and lose a few, and most of the time they got away with it. It's when troops stop complaining or chancing their arm that you know something is drastically wrong.

From Counterintelligence, I Presume

There was no shortage of gentlemen from counterintelligence sloping around Xangongo. One of them was my very tall good friend Commandant Durrie van Deventer, who once approached me in the early days of our occupation of Xangongo and enquired very seriously: "Do you know anything about R10,000 which was allegedly stolen from the local bank?"

This took me by surprise. I stared at him in honest amazement and asked for details.

21 Both Dawid Mentz and Henri Boshoff have since died.

Durrie explained that a bank had been blown open by a shell from a 90 mm gun and an unsanctioned withdrawal made. I was baffled, because by the time we arrived in Xangongo the opportunities for carrying out this type of financial transaction were over. "Ask Battle Group 20 or Battle Group 40," I said. "They were in Xangongo before me, and they also have Ratel-90s or Eland-90s."

I considered this to be a perfectly logical response, but for some reason or other it never quite allayed Durrie's suspicions. Now and then I run into Durrie, and even now he asks me: "Roland, don't you know anything about that ten thousand?" And invariably I answer with my hand on my heart: "No, Durrie – look at the car I'm driving and the house I'm living in."

It is just one of those great unsolved military mysteries. But if it did happen, somebody scored, all right – in those days 10,000 bucks was a lot of money.

With Compliments from FAPLA, an Enquiry from the Top and Mentz's Goat Barbecue

The following inconsequential tale has several seemingly random ingredients, since it involves a house, a jeep, some kwanza (the local currency) and a goat which provided an unpleasant surprise.

Firstly, the house. It was quite a nice house with a little garden (the latter sadly neglected, I have to admit). It had been the domicile of the Minister of Education of the Cunene Province. The "mod cons" were not quite up to scratch – for example, whoever had occupied it just before the SADF arrived had obviously taken the lack of running water in his stride and just continued using the now non-flushing toilet until he had filled it up. Maybe he switched to the garden after that.

It was still a lot better than living rough, however, and we turned it into our static command post, with the lounge serving as our operations centre. I suppose the décor was quite tasteful if you are into the military look. The constantly hu-ing and crackling radios reposed on the sideboard and the maps were tastefully arranged on the walls; outside the window Zero Charlie, the signals Ratel, stood in the driveway with its cables trailing gracefully inside.

Parked in front of the house was a scoot-about vehicle I used to tool around in Xangongo, making a nuisance of myself – one of those little Russian Jeep-equivalents which the mopping up had produced, almost without direct human intervention. It was a cool-looking piece of equipment, to be sure, but it qualified for the "nice from afar" stakes, because it was bloody uncomfortable to get in and out of. Don't try and sell on Soviet engineering and design.

Then there was the case of the kwanza. Somehow a large cardboard box, filled to the brim with the useless local currency, appeared on the veranda and became part of the general scene. How it got there in the first place was a mystery I never could solve: one day there was nothing on the veranda, next day the box was squatting there with its worthless cargo.

The box nagged at me. Surely there was something we could do with all that Monopoly money stuffed into it? Then I had an idea. "Dawid," I told our garrison commander and sports king, "go and buy us a goat for this evening – the command group is going to have a braai in our garden."

By now, I think, Mentz was no longer capable of being surprised by any of the bizarre tasks I laid on him. He took up the money box, mounted his Buffel and vanished into the wild green yonder of the rural area outside Xangongo. In due course he returned with a suitable carcass, which was duly converted into edible form that evening.

It was a pleasant occasion. Having momentarily shrugged off our responsibilities, we grouped our camp chairs around a moderate fire and chit-chatted about nothing of world-shaking consequence. We talked a bit of shop, of course, being soldiers, shared stories about our families and had some good discussions about rugby and soccer. To oil the general bonhomie I shared out some of my private hoard of tinned smoked oysters.

Then I thoughtlessly spoiled it all. While my merry men were tucking into the meat, I asked Mentz where he had purchased our much-prized (and now well-barbecued) goat. Mentz told us in minute detail, as garrison commanders sometimes do, that he had made a careful appreciation of his mission. He had closed in tactically on a particular kraal just outside Xangongo. There he was involved in some serious negotiations before he could close the deal for the goat.

He had laid a bundle of kwanza in the beckoning hand of the local chief, who replied: "Not enough." Mentz produced another handful. Still not enough. Like a good paratrooper Mentz then applied maximum violence in execution, in the form of a double handful of kwanza. This worked. "Enough," the chief said and gave one handful back. Mentz was not quite sure about the greater financial implications of this act, but did not care since he had successfully transmuted useless paper money into a useful ration.

I should have stopped right there. Instead I had another question. I noticed that of all of us, he was the only one not eating: "Dawid," I asked, "why are you not enjoying some of this delicious goat with us?"

"Naw, no appetite," he replied. "When I bought the goat they were gnawing on some dead FAPLA lying around nearby."

Suddenly some of the diners around the fire lost their appetites. Mentz could really have spared us that explanation. But he was a sturdy paratrooper and the garrison commander, and if you asked him a question you got a straightforward answer. But, still ...

Incidentally, that bloody box of useless banknotes was to plague me later on, after the operation. It was rumoured that at senior level there was some concern because I had allegedly given an instruction to hand the remaining kwanza to the UNITA party which took Xangongo over from us. Apparently there was an official letter written about this as well (which proves my point about the useless work performed by some senior staff officers with nothing better to do – I would not be surprised if the letter writer was the same man who had hung those two graders around my neck).

In any case, the famous kwanza conundrum died away of its own accord. I still don't understand the reason for the minor fuss – we certainly could not have caused inflation or done any further harm to the corpse-like Angolan monetary system. At least the old chief scored a little when he sold Dawid Mentz the FAPLA-eating goat.

Gert Minnaar and the Irish Nuns He Encountered at Mucceipo (Techiulo)

Mission stations and expatriate nuns are comparatively rare phenomena in South Africa, a developed and largely urbanised country, so for Lieutenant Gert Minnaar, Platoon Number 1, Bravo Company (Combat Team 2), it was a new experience when we stopped briefly at Mucceipo during our exploitation mission and he made the acquaintance of the Roman Catholic sisters there. Later he wrote down his impressions:

My platoon visited the Irish nuns at the hospital at Mucceipo, north of Humbe, on the afternoon of 25 August 1981. I can remember that one of the nuns was quite young and pretty. I wondered what motivated her to be out here, spending her life in the outskirts of Africa. The other nuns were much older.

They were extremely friendly towards us. They told us that many of their patients had fled into the bushes the morning of 24 August 1981, when the battle planes of our air force passed over. It was somewhat strange for me to walk with the nuns on the veranda of the hospital and have a casual conversation in English, while they as women were so deeply embedded in a war zone.

We were able to do these dedicated women a good turn, by the way. The water pump at the hospital had broken down and required urgent repairs. Sergeant-major Duppie du Plessis and his tiffies were called in; compared to the things they normally had to do, this was child's play, and in no time they had the pump running again.

Our Enemy Never Ceased to Amaze – The Defences at Xangongo

At one stage during our stay at Xangongo I took my Ratel crew, Colonel Robbie Robberts and Commandant Epp van Lill with me to study the FAPLA defences. This was the first opportunity we had had for a good look-see at the defences, and we were amazed at their intricacy and sophistication. As I have mentioned, the town was locked into an allround defensive system with extensive minefields to the south, the direction from which they had naïvely expected our attack to come, if it ever came. Now, however, we could see for the first time just how extensive and expertly constructed the defences were.

The system was set up in depth, Russian style, with rows upon rows of carefully prepared earthworks – trench after trench, all linked by communication crawl-ditches and dugouts, some with metal bedsteads inside ... quite comfortable, if you enjoy living underground for months on end. Another interesting leftover from the Russians and FAPLA we found at Xangongo was a large, detailed relief map, neatly constructed out of concrete, showing the exact layout of the Xangongo defences. Near it was a wooden construction which was probably used as an observation tower for their artillery.

We noted with some amusement that they also used red and blue to mark the disposition of own and enemy forces, just like us – except that in their system the good guys (themselves) were marked in red and the bad guys (us) in blue. The result was that it was very easy for us to read the relief map! They were spot on, full marks to them. The model had obviously seen a lot of use for training purposes – not that it had helped FAPLA much. If things had been different we could have sent them better training staff than the Russians did, certainly ones with a finer understanding of African-style bush warfare.

Close by I picked up a beautiful single-page sketch made by some junior FAPLA commander. I still have it. The staff writing on the sketch was carefully and neatly done in Russian text and tactical symbols. Wow, I thought, if they could just have fought as well they did their staff work, we would have been in for a surprise.

The Final Phase – Withdrawal from Angola

On 28 August the Chief of the Defence Force, General Constand Viljoen, publicly declared that the SADF's mission in Angola had been successful and that the strike force would withdraw on 1 September (D+8). It had taken just 11 days of ceaseless activity. At 18:30 on 29 August I was hastily summoned to Ondjiva by Colonel Joep Joubert to receive my orders for the withdrawal.

Captain Chris Gildenhuys escorted me there and back the same night with a small armoured group. Along the way we encountered a few tiffies who were still repairing captured enemy tanks, and one lot gave us a helluva fright when we came unexpectedly on a repaired T34-85 straddling the road.

Well after midnight, while we were on our way back to Xangongo, I issued a warning order to my leader group about the impending withdrawal. It was all over; soon we would leave behind us the sorrowful sights of the battlefield. Our impending withdrawal would take us via Môngua to Ondjiva, where we would laager for the night near the airfield before departing to Omuthiya the next day.

My orders covered the handing over on 31 August of the defences and the Reserve Demolition to a UNITA force – "Silver", as the SADF codenamed them so that the outside world would not be aware that the SADF was in such close cahoots with Savimbi's forces. The "Silver" guerrilla unit arrived on 31 August (D+7); more to keep Xangongo safe from FAPLA and SWAPO intruders, we thought, than to keep Captain Charl Naudé company. We were wrong in both instances, as it turned out.

Our UNITA contingent was accompanied by Commandant Mo Oelschig, their SADF liaison officer (liaison teams provided by the Chief of Staff Intelligence were attached to all the UNITA forces – Oelschig was particularly effective because he spoke fluent Portuguese, the Angolan lingua franca).

The first batch of UNITA soldiers arrived by Russian Ural truck from who knows where. The trucks were in an appalling mess. All available space was stacked to the brim with anything you could think of – blankets, ammunition, RPG-7 rocket launchers, spare uniforms, you name it. I could see Major Giel Reinecke eyeballing all this, his meticulous loggie's eyebrows arched. The second batch of UNITA arrived by Puma helicopter; probably they had first flown to Air Force Base Ondangwa by SAAF C-130 from Savimbi's headquarters at Jamba, then embarked on the Pumas for the second leg to Xangongo.

This was my fastest relief operation in the line ever. It went more or less like this: Hello, UNITA, this is Xangongo; this is the current enemy situation, goodbye and good luck. The UNITA contingent did not seem very interested in their surroundings or perturbed by the tactical situation on the ground. Later on I understood why. They were not going to remain there for long; as experienced guerrillas they knew better than to fix themselves anywhere.

Battle Group 10 said goodbye to the courageous Captain Charl Naudé, who promptly settled down in the plumbing disadvantaged ministerial home, the bridge's detonating device having been carefully handed over to him by the engineers. Then at midday we were on our way, leaving behind our new-found friends, the amicable local people and their soccer stars; the inert FAPLA mobile reserve at Cahama; the UNITA contingent; the Xangongo Bridge; and Charl Naude and the detonating device that could bring instant ruin to the bridge.

We must have looked a little like a modern-day equivalent of the Israelites departing from Egypt. Nearly every vehicle in the battle group had an enemy vehicle in tow – and sometimes two or three. In a way it was a forlorn sight, but it delighted the troops (though not, be it said, either Giel Reinecke, the combat team commanders or the tiffies, whose responsibility it was to keep this raggle-taggle procession on the move in reasonably good order).

Troops found themselves converted into instant drivers of Soviet military hardware and sat proudly behind the steering wheels. I wished FAPLA and their mothers could see them as our battle group moved steadily down the highway towards Môngua and then Ondjiva, along with a few civilian refugees who had decided to shake the dust of the new workers' paradise from their heels, and Mo Oelschig, who had hitch-hiked a lift back to SWA/Namibia in my Ratel.

We passed some tiffies who were still struggling to get a T34-85 tank in running condition and stopped briefly at Môngua to load Lieutenant Roos's wrecked Alouette. Eventually we approached Ondjiva itself; overhead a Puma hovered while television teams dutifully recorded the withdrawal of the victorious South Africans. It was a reminder that there was a political and propaganda war going on at the same time as the shooting war down on the ground.

And Xangongo? Well, it soon became a semi-deserted ghost town, and it took a while before some of the local inhabitants started filtering back. We met them a few months later, in March 1982 (Operation Meebos 1), when 61 Mech was tasked to conduct a hasty force projection operation into southern Angola which was all about striking fear into FAPLA's hearts and minds. FAPLA had to be kept at bay and in animated suspension, away from our newly acquired hunting ground in their part of the world.

Incidentally, the UNITA guerrilla force only occupied Xangongo and Ondjiva for a short while: they were bush fighters, and holding towns was not their style – Mao Tse-tung had taught that what was necessary was annihilation of the foe and self-preservation. They were not ready for mobile warfare yet. That would come in 1987, when Jamba and its vitally important airfield at Mavinga were seriously threatened by FAPLA and the Cubans.

As we drove away it seemed that Battle Group 10 had handed Xangongo over to UNITA on a silver platter – plus a cardboard box filled with kwanza. But of course the bridge did not survive the handover for very long.

Incidentally, to the uninformed observer it might be thought that the destruction of the bridge was an act of wanton destruction. But it will be remembered that General Viljoen had authorised its demolition it if became "absolutely necessary in the event of a possible enemy intervention and to prevent the enemy from capturing the current position ... " It could be argued that this was surely now the case, since 61 Mech was no longer there to dominate the western approaches and UNITA had no intention of holding the town.

We laagered close to the Ondjiva airfield for the night, and before anything else replenished our vehicles. For the first time an abundance of cold beer and soft drinks were available for our troops. My command group settled in under a large wild fig tree near the entrance to the airfield, dug our shallow shell scrapes and set up local protection for the night – SWAPO was always present, and we were not particularly keen to invite an unwelcome standoff bombardment with mortars and rockets by some of the more stout-hearted insurgents who might still be left in the area. Somewhere in the near future we would stop over at our fig tree again, although we did not know it yet.

That same evening Captains Koos Liebenberg and Hannes van der Merwe sat with us under the tree and told us in minute detail about the fight for Ondjiva. It was a calm night, its tranquillity only disturbed now and again by the sporadic crumping of the artillery's allround harassing fire.

Battle Group 10 had one final task left. I received an instruction from the task force HQ early the next morning to demolish the underground fuel bunkers adjacent to the air field – a stupid move, as it turned out, because we were back by the end of September and could have made good use of them!

The engineers immediately warmed to me, and soon afterwards the three underground tanks erupted into impressive balls of fire and clouds of black smoke; from my vantage point on top of my Ratel I took a photograph of the spectacle. The smoke hung for quite a while over the airfield as testimony of the South Africans' successful clash of arms; one might say that as far as Battle Group 10 was concerned, Operation Protea ended on a fiery note.

The road home took us through Ondjiva, Omupande, Namacunde and Oshikango. Those Angolan place names were like mystical music in our ears as we went through them. It was now downhill all the way; figuratively speaking (the border region is as flat as a table top). Koos Liebenberg had to swing away to deliver his burden of captured clobber at Oshakati, and by the time he arrived at Omuthiya considerably later for a well-deserved cold Windhoek Lager he was, as he told me, highly fed up.

At Oshakati one of our favourite staff officers had told him to park all the enemy wrecks in neat little rows, as colonel-type staff officers are wont to do. This was too much; as any good mechanised commander should do when he receives a nonsensical instruction from a staff officers who is not in his chain of command, Liebenberg ignored him (he put it to me in somewhat stronger terms), simply unhooked the wrecks where they stood and made haste to Omuthiya, about 170 km away to the south. The staff officer was last seen standing caught up in a heavy cloud of dust and diesel fumes as the combat team hightailed it home.

It was a homecoming of note. My wonderful staff, creative as always, had organised a magnificent welcoming braai (I believe our old comrade, Tannie Pompie, had something to do with this). The cold beer was like mothers' milk as it went down our throats while the aroma of the braai fires drifted gently over us in the soft light of the setting sun. There was pleasant conversation and bursts of spontaneous laughter everywhere, and a spirit of comradeship so strong that it felt almost tangible.

Chaplain Koos Rossouw's thanksgiving was solemn and thought-provoking. We sat listening, on camp chairs for those who had them, or with backsides nestling in the warm sand for those who did not, in deep thought. What were my soldiers thinking? I stared at their faces, trying to read their minds. They had changed, even though they might not realise it. They had been blooded; they were warriors now. Tired warriors, let it be said, bone tired, and filled with the almost euphoric dream state that comes at the end of any operation. Tomorrow was another day, but tonight they would sleep the long hours away like babies.

As I write this now, the youngest of them are deep into their forties and some into their fifties, weighed down with the responsibilities of families and business or similar things. Their children should know what amazing warriors they were. That is why I write these words – not to praise myself but to praise my men.

Closure – Mission Accomplished

Self-criticism – as distinct from self-justification – is an important aspect of leadership. Our subunit commanders were highly satisfied with 61 Mech's general operational conduct, especially the unit's movement, grouping and regrouping abilities. As Koos Liebenberg commented, the SOP had been tried, tested and found to be valid for operational circumstances.

Mission accomplished ... Complete strategic and tactical surprise had been achieved. Protea was a classic military operation, effectively integrating the offensive and defensive dimensions of mobile conventional warfare with those of counterinsurgency duties. 61 Mech had established a benchmark for the effective conduct of mobile warfare at battle group level within the context of the African battle space. In a sense the operation heralded a turning point in the way the SADF would conduct mobile conventional warfare in future.

This, then, is my account of Operation Protea and its accompanying reflections and truths as I saw it. As I said a little earlier, I have told it to honour those who did their duty and played their part with the utmost loyalty and conviction.

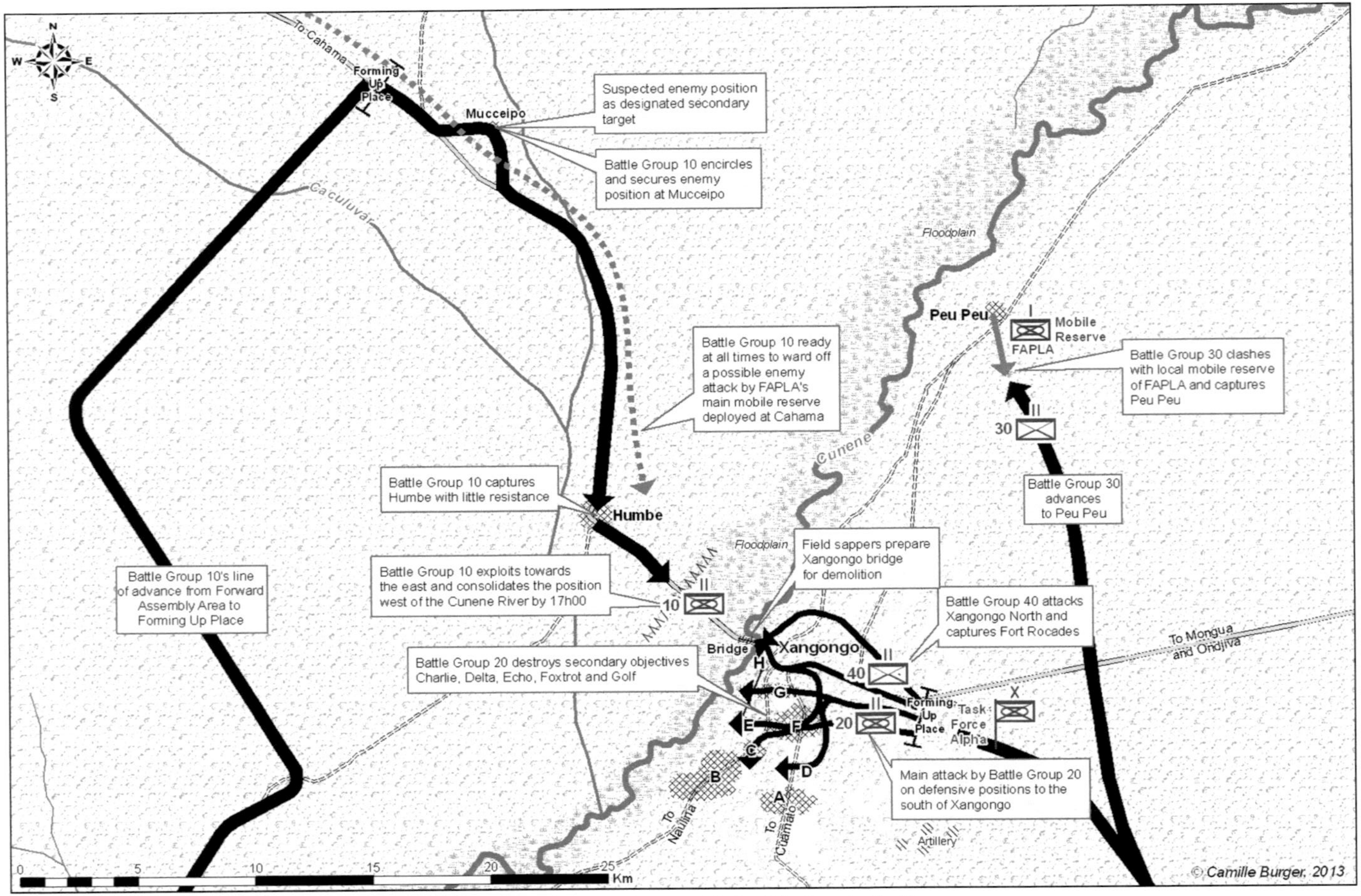

Map 10: Operation Protea, August 1981 – The Battle for Xangongo

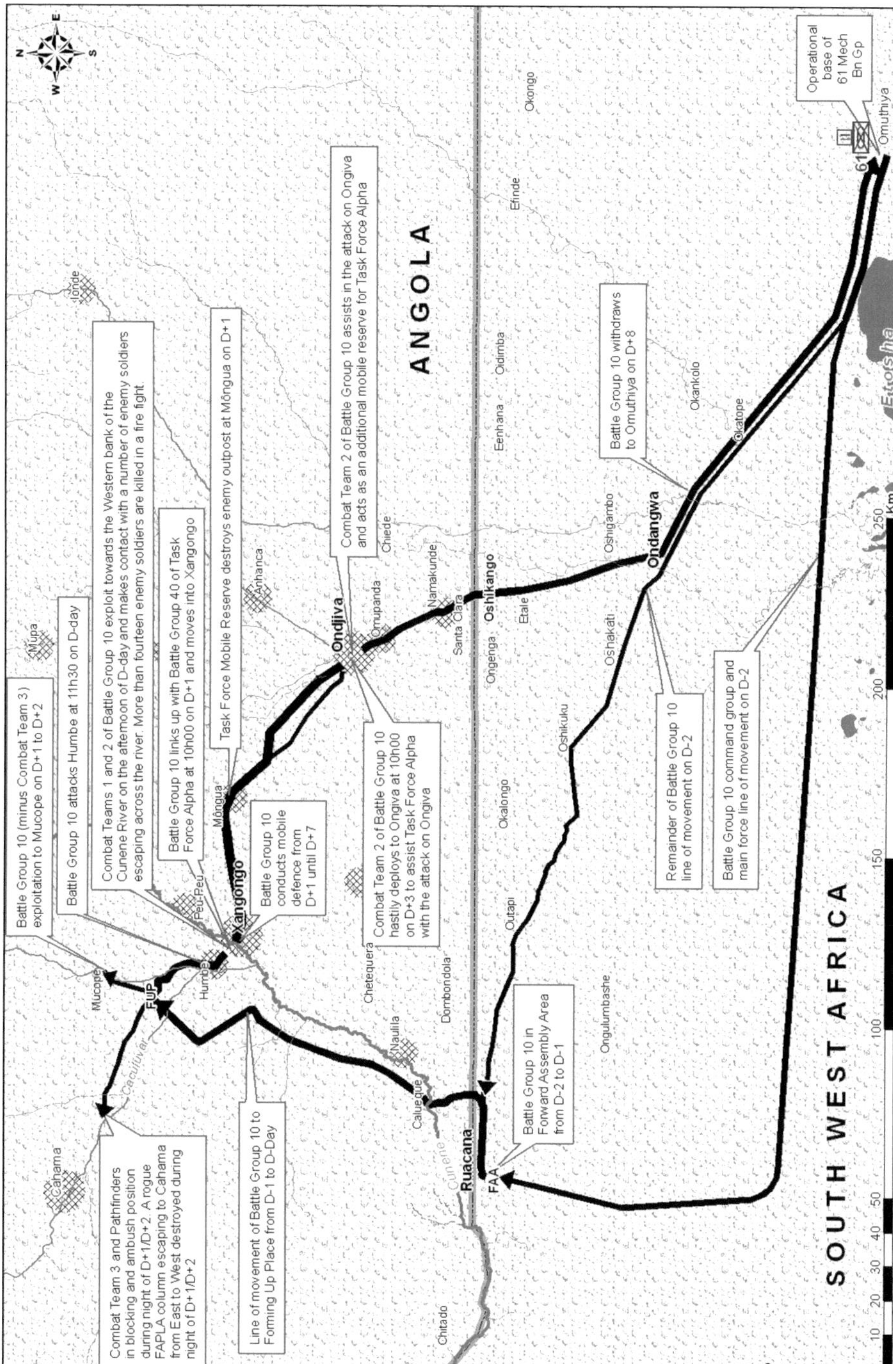

Map 11: Operation Protea, August 1981 – Actions by Battle Group 10

13

A Flower Blooms

Operation Daisy

Superficiality is evinced when a person... takes a glance at a distance and having noticed some factors would proceed to direct a military operation.
Mao Tse-tung

Just One of Those Externals – Ironically So

Operation Daisy took place from 29 October to 20 November 1981 and was conducted by a brigade-sized formation of fighting units from the SADF and SWATF, involved in the deepest mechanised strike launched into southern Angola since Operation Savannah in 1975–76. Once again, this account centres on 61 Mechanised Battalion Group, the main strike force.

By the standards of the South African Border War, Operation Daisy was a massive undertaking, with thousands of troops on the ground, backed up by an enormous air support and logistical organisation; it would be fair to say that the organisational breadth and operational depth made this cross-border strike truly unique.

Operation Daisy was a sequel to Operation Protea, less than two months earlier. Protea had yielded much valuable intelligence gained from interrogations of enemy prisoners and examination of captured documents. The indications were that an important SWAPO base was located in the vicinity of Chitequeta, 224 kilometres north of the SWA/Namibian-Angola border.

Buoyed by Protea's success, the SADF immediately became fixated on the possibility of having yet another juicy target in its sights. The Special Forces and 32 Battalion were commissioned forthwith to search the area for our most sought-after enemy – the wily fighters of PLAN. The fact that the enemy was exceedingly active in the potential target area was confirmed by aerial reconnaissance, and Chitequeta was duly selected as the most desirable spot in the dense Angolan bush at which to strike next.

The operational concept devised by the SADF and SWATF for Operation Daisy was basically sound, but a mite overambitious, perhaps (not that 61 Mech was going to complain about that: We were in it for the fight). The operation was well-planned and well-executed at all the levels under the command of Sector 10, and, as I have mentioned, there was no lack of resources.

There was, however, one small problem. In a nutshell, the targets that had been selected were not viable; a fact that, unfortunately, was only established after Chitequeta had been captured on 4 November 1981. As a result, the operation did not yield the enemy losses and equipment captured or destroyed that had been hoped for, notwithstanding the fact that the vast target area had become saturated with security forces in search of more than 1 500 insurgents.

By the end of it, 18 days of intensive effort had yielded only a marginal benefit: 71

insurgents killed, a few enemy vehicles seized or merely shot at, and a measureable but unremarkable amount of equipment, arms and ammunition captured, although there was no doubt that there had been further disruption of SWAPO's activities.

Daisy also proved once again that in Africa, time and space and shelter often seemed to benefit the elusive insurgent, allowing him to flee, hide and strike again another day. Nevertheless, the SADF concluded that the operation had been worth our while. Continuous disruption of the foe, winning the Bush War, learning lessons, etcetera, et cetera – all of this was trumpeted into the ears of those who wanted to hear. But Daisy's outcomes were a huge disappointment for the security force personnel who were actually involved on the ground.

Daisy served as a polite wake-up call to the high command of the SADF and SWATF. It was necessary to rethink future large-scale counterinsurgency warfare ventures. It also resulted in the intelligence community becoming subdued for a while as its leading lights quietly pondered their contribution to what was a genuine faux pas.

I certainly believed that in more ways than one Daisy provided an important lesson to be added to our ever-growing arsenal of knowledge. Apart from that, it was an amazing experience for all who participated, although not a cheap one. We need to remember that a few good men died out there and many were wounded ... not merely good men but our friends.

Learn, Commit and Do, the frequently used phrase has it. Correct – but learn what and do what? Take the war to the enemy, is it? Let us find out!

Overview of the Operational Situation – Fighting for Initiative

The loss of Xangongo and Ondjiva to the SADF in August 1981 had driven the FAPLA conventional forces back to the outer fringes of the Area-In-Dispute, as far back as Cahama-Quiteve in the west; Techamutete-Cassinga in the north; Menongue in the northwest; and Caiundo in the east. It was decided not to withdraw all forces at the end of the operation but to continue to dominate the Area-In-Dispute. HQ Sector 10 therefore established a tactical headquarters at Ondjiva in September and expanded its counterinsurgency operations to search for the scatterings of SWAPO within the wide expanse of contested bushveld. The first consideration, of course, was to find the enemy. The PLAN insurgents were in the area all right, but where, precisely? By October the intelligence pattern of their whereabouts and operational activities started crystallising again. The Chitequeta-Bambi area became suspect and Operation Daisy was launched, although Protea's dust had hardly settled.

To the east of the Cubango and Cuito rivers UNITA willingly helped to keep SWAPO at bay and FAPLA quite busy, allowing the SADF and SWATF more time and freedom to concentrate on hunting the insurgents in the Area-In-Dispute. This was the state of play when Operation Daisy was being conceptualised in October 1981.

The hostile area had a deceptive serenity. It nestled in shadowy dense vegetation between the Cunene River in the west and the Cubango in the east – a distance of approximately 242 km as the crow flies. The operational zone extended from the SWA/Namibia-Angola border in the south to the Namibe-Menongue railway line beyond Indungo in the north – a distance of about 370 km (it will be remembered that the type and nature of terrain and their influence on operations were discussed in some detail in Chapter 5, so little more needs to be said here on this topic).

Chitequeta, the point of main effort for Daisy, was situated about 65 km east-southeast of Techamutete, 71 km southeast of Indungo, 106 km north-northwest of Ionde, 224 km north of the SWA/Namibia-Angola border – and 350 km north-northwest of Omuthiya, from where 61 Mech deployed northwards on 30 October.

Enemy Forces in the Target Zone

Setting Up SWAPO as the Primary Enemy

SWAPO directed its nomadic operations in the central part of southern Angola from Lubango. Its leaders had divided their operational area into the Western, Central and Eastern Regions, each with its own roving regional headquarters. Their command-and-control in this particular area effectively directed insurgent activities against the northern parts of SWA, particularly Ovamboland – the centre of SWAPO's revolutionary struggle, where it rolled into one with South Africa's counterrevolutionary war.

Here both South Africa and SWAPO applied military and political methods and means to achieve their ends. Neither the Angolan Government nor the Soviets and Cubans cared to keep their dirty fingers out of the pie, which is why the Border War had become an all-in fighting arena, a war without frontiers which involved a variety of political, military and ideological agendas.

It was alleged that by September SWAPO's Military Command Post – the one the SADF was seeking so eagerly – had been relocated northeastwards to Chitequeta. In close proximity to this HQ, it was concluded, other juicy targets were likely to be found.

Scraps of information gathered from radio intercepts and captured insurgents started filling the gaps in the intelligence picture, and it became clear to the intelligence boffins that SWAPO was attempting to regroup its scattered combatants in the vicinity of Chitequeta and Bambi. If the insurgents settled in there, the result would be a doable target.

So scouts from 32 Battalion and Special Forces were sent out to tiptoe through the dense bush and plot the exact positions of the enemy at Chitequeta and Bambi. At the same time, aerial photo interpreters huddled over their stereoscopes at Oshakati, Windhoek and Pretoria, carefully annotating enemy locations with Indian ink to provide the stage setting for the projected attacks.

It was no easy task. By late October SWAPO's exact positions had yet to be determined. The SADF saw no reason to pause while this was being sorted out, however, and by the end of the month Operation Daisy was set to be launched regardless. An additional factor that helped to settle the matter was that the southern Angolan rainy season (December to April) was drawing closer with every passing minute.

The interpretations and conclusions of the SADF's Chief of Staff Operations regarding SWAPO in our target zone was summarised in Operations Instruction Number 21/81 – 309/4/Rekstok, dated 22 October 1981. The content of this operations instruction was echoed by a similar one which was issued by Chief of the Army in Operations Instruction Number 14/81/ – 309/1/Afval, dated 22 October 1981, a direct crib of the first.

The information reflected in the two instructions was provided to the Chief of the SADF and the Chief of the Army by HQ Sector 10 on 23 September 1981. Who did what planning, I wondered later, and how thoroughly was it done? "Afval" (Offal) was the code word originally selected for the operation, whose name was only changed to Daisy in October, but frankly, "Afval" would probably have been more fitting. Anyhow, Military Intelligence surmised that the SWAPO forces (PLAN) were deployed in the target zone designated for Daisy as follows:

- The Military Command Post. It was reported that the military command post was concealed about 20–30 km north of Chitequeta. It was suspected that the well-protected HQ comprised 400 men, equipped with about 70 vehicles.
- Bravo Battalion. Bravo Battalion was supposed to be deployed at Chitequeta and it consisted of 500 hundred combatants. According to Intelligence, the battalion's troops occupied one-man slit trenches; mortars were deployed to the south of the base, anti-aircraft guns to the east and the west, and B10s (82 mm recoilless guns) to the north. It was presumed that Bravo Battalion was deployed there to protect the eastern flank of the command post against UNITA guerrillas.
- The Protection Battalion. It was suspected that a 1,000-strong SWAPO protection battalion lurked to the southwest of Chitequeta, in the direction of Bambi. The battalion, supposedly, was there to protect the southwestern flank of the command post.
- Other forces of evil noted. In passing it was mentioned at times by Military Intelligence that a number of enemy bases could be found in the region of Chitequeta – up to seven, in fact, each holding between 400 to 1,000 combatants. There were also random mentions of numerous smaller, vehicle-mounted insurgent groups.

The combat participants of the SADF and SWATF were explicitly warned that the insurgents were maintaining an effective early warning system – the bush telegraph was formidable, we knew. The enemy did not want to be caught with their rice-patterned pants down again, as had happened during Operation Sceptic in 1980 and Operation Protea in 1981.

Intelligence warned that the protection battalion would fiercely resist any attack in an all-out effort to protect their command post. Serious counteractions by SWAPO, once they started fleeing after D-Day, were not truly contemplated. It was believed that the insurgents would flee northwards and northwestwards towards Indungo and Techamutete-Cassinga after the first shots were fired.

All of the aforementioned intelligence and the inferences drawn from them were neatly documented and packaged by 22 October. But we still did not know exactly where the enemy at Chitequeta or Bambi was! Our battle maps were marked with a certain degree of misplaced optimism ... Lord Tennyson's famous lines about "theirs not to reason why, theirs but to do and die" illustrates a great and ageless military truth, namely that an assumption is the great-grandmother of all balls-ups!

Toying with FAPLA – No Foreplay (or Any Other Play) Anticipated

Whether or not FAPLA's conventional forces would intervene in Daisy was one of the questions that the planners considered. FAPLA had not been extremely friendly towards the SADF since Protea (not that we, the men on the ground, were overly concerned about their emotions) but the SADF's high command had issued an unambiguous instruction that the Angolans were to be left strictly alone for the moment.

International sensitivities, regional politics and peace talks and all that it entailed, remained lucid realities in playing with FAPLA, so much so that the authorisation for Daisy remained in the balance till a late stage because high-level talks between South Africa and the Western Contact Group were in progress. It was rumoured that the operation might be rescheduled or even suspended sine die if necessary; it had happened before. For us it was a case of "Ours not to reason why, but to wait and sigh."

But to get back to the planning map and the areas on it marked red. The closest conventional FAPLA brigades and battalions, interspersed with Cuban mechanised forces, were deployed at Techamutete and Cassinga, within 60 km of Chitequeta, and this uncomfortable fact warranted serious scrutiny – way back in May 1978 during Operation Reindeer, our paratroopers had fought a serious engagement at Cassinga with Cuban-crewed tanks from Techamutete.

The gravel road leading from Cassinga via Techamutete and Cuvelai to Mupa and further southwards to Ondjiva was another important consideration. This particular road, which lay approximately 69 km to the west of Chitequeta, formed one of SWAPO's main logistical routes to the south and served as a command axis as well. In addition, FAPLA could use this road for a counter-attack from the west.

We did not truly expect any interference by the FAPLA forces deployed at oblique angles to our target area. Nevertheless, possible plans concerning intervention and counter-intervention were carefully considered, as was FAPLA's will to fight or the lack thereof. Our conclusion was that this was not something to be too worried about.

The known positions which posed marginal threats from ahead and the flanks were duly marked in red on our battle maps as follows: Caiundo, one brigade; Menongue, one brigade plus; Techiesso, two battalions; Cuchi, one battalion; Cuvango, one battalion; Dongo, one Cuban brigade; Techamutete, one brigade plus, reinforced with one additional battalion; Cassinga, two battalions.

We were somewhat wary about possible enemy air intervention this time around. The enemy's MiGs could strike from Lubango, 315 km from Chitequeta, and from Menongue, a mere 170 km away. This was not of the greatest concern; the SAAF was still man enough for the moment to take on the foe in the skies. But Cahama remained a thorn in our flesh, because some of the closest enemy radar systems were located in its proximity.

Enemy air reconnaissance posed the larger threat for our ground forces. Our dust in the clear skies remained a major risk and when observed by the enemy could forfeit surprise and give away our position. Worse still, it could indicate an attack. (Note that to a certain extent the SAAF ignored the rule of not playing with FAPLA, as a few MiG pilots and their mates at Cahama were soon to realise.)

Own Forces – Readying for a Firestorm into Southern Angola

Setting the Landscape for Operation Daisy

Major General Charles Lloyd, the GOC SWATF, was in overall command of Operation Daisy, with Brigadier Witkop Badenhorst at HQ Sector 10 in charge at the operational level. It was an effective combination, since both were operationally perceptive and well-attuned to the vibrations of the Bush War.

There was no shortage of first-line fighting troops to take part, since a number of good units were readily available in the northern operational area by October 1981. The choice fell on 61 Mech, 201 (Bushman) Battalion, a company of 32 Battalion and a number of Special Forces reconnaissance teams; later it was decided that five paratrooper companies from 1 and 3 Parachute Battalions, the latter a Citizen Force unit, would be added. All these units maintained a high level of combat readiness and were regularly employed in operations in the northern border region.

At that time 32 Battalion was commanded by Commandant Deon Ferreira and 201

Battalion by Commandant Frans Botes. They operated from the Buffalo and Omega bases respectively, both of which were located close to the border near Rundu. It was a good overall mix of skills. 61 Mech was a conventional mechanised unit, 32 and 201 Battalions were counterinsurgency experts and the paratroopers were versatile light infantry who could be deployed at short notice on anything from airborne assaults to counterinsurgency sweeps.

32 Battalion's veterans were already in the field with Operation Dahlia, probing, patrolling and striking at SWAPO in the area to the west and north of Ondjiva. East of them, the Bushmen of 201 Battalion were occupied with Operation Mispel, hunting insurgents towards Anhanca, Nehone and Dova (from where they would deploy towards their target zone to the southeast of Chitequeta once Daisy began).

In mid-October the preparations for Daisy were jointly taken in hand by the SADF, SWATF and Sector 10. At this late stage the aerial reconnaissance over Chitequeta and Bambi had been halted although Special Forces patrols continued to snoop around the suspect area to establish SWAPO's exact positions.

Now the scene was set, and D-Day was scheduled for 4 November. Beyond the border the terrain lay patiently in wait and ultimately was to prove a tougher adversary than SWAPO itself.

Operational Framework and Design for Battle

The force marshalled for the next firestorm into southern Angola was an interesting combination of skills, talents and capabilities. The main difference compared with Protea was that Daisy would include a sizable airborne operation. The order of battle (see Appendix A and Figure 15) provided for a large mechanised and motorised ground force and substantial air, medical and logistical support; a mere head count of the water tankers and fuel bowsers, and a quick look at the SAAFs statistics, would have been enough for even an uninformed observer to grasp Daisy's considerable scope.

From 1 to 17 November, the SAAF flew 272 sorties from Air Force Base Ondangwa and between 4 and 12 November a total of 207 Alouette, Puma and Bosbok missions were dispatched from Ionde. 61 Mech carted no less than 15 bowsers of helicopter fuel part of the way to Ionde.

The directives for Operation Daisy were issued by the Chief of the SADF and Chief of the Army to the GOC SWATF on 22 October and from here they went down to Brigadier Badenhorst at HQ Sector 10. Similar operations instructions from the HQs of the South African Air Force and South African Medical Services in Pretoria proceeded down the line to the SAAF command posts and the SAMS medical task teams at Windhoek and Oshakati.

The mission, as defined by the Chief of the Army for Sector 10 via HQ SWATF, was "to launch an operation against the military command post of SWAPO and other subsequent targets in the area of operations determined for Operation Daisy. Close cooperation with the air force and medical commands in SWA needs to be ensured."

The following was particularly stipulated: "Destroy the military command post of SWAPO; incur maximum casualties of enemy insurgents during the operation; capture members of surrogate forces if possible; disrupt FAPLA and SWAPO logistics from the north."

As I understood the mission, SWAPO's military command post was to be the focus of main effort – the problem being, of course, that even at this late stage Military

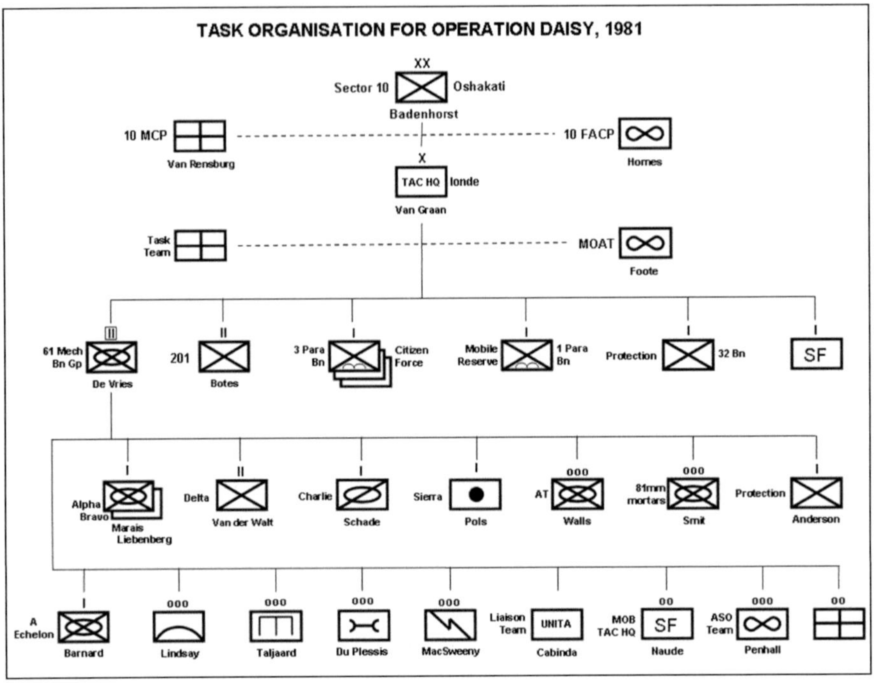

Figure 15: Task Organisation for Operation Daisy

Intelligence did not know exactly where the military command post was located. A few (some contradictory) operational guidelines stressed the importance of achieving surprise and taking measures to protect the strike force against interference by FAPLA elements, but at the same time avoiding contact with them.

As the operation was to unfold outside our radar coverage, adequate air defence measures needed to be taken, which included the employment of our own (ex-Angolan) SAM-7 missiles with our forward troops. 61 Mech needed to withdraw southwards under our radar coverage as soon as possible after D-Day. The safety of own forces and those of local inhabitants were stressed, but, it was underlined, not at the cost of jeopardising the success of our operation.

Allow me a moment to express my opinion about how our drawn-out counter-revolutionary war was brought to the fore by operations such as Daisy! The essence of the mission, as constantly stated by the higher command, was to inflict maximum casualties on SWAPO in a not too friendly manner. For military men the mission is all-important; it comes first and is the centre of one's being. You live or die for it. But, ...

But it takes strong leadership to do that, as well as the unequivocal commitment from the men. It should be the product of an accurate intelligence assessment, deeply rooted operational thinking, thorough planning, originality in conception and clear direction. It needs to be achieved in the most professional manner by you, not the enemy. You know whether you win or lose by simply measuring the degree of initiative and freedom of action you enjoy or do not enjoy, not only during the fighting but also at the end of each phase. Achieving the mission becomes a case of ensuring that the right domino falls at the right time, come hell or high water; and then the next one and the one after that – not elegantly, perhaps, but always commendably at all costs. To put it in another way: You must not only win but you must be seen to be winning, without any shadow of doubt about your victory. A campaign is meant to be a serious shakeup of the enemy. You win, he loses, or else ...

Normally the next item on the list is to dutifully tally the heads of the dearly departed and the stuff that belonged to them when the fighting is over. That's it – then you respectfully report back. The idea of killing as many insurgents as possible remained a central military theme throughout the counterinsurgency war in the border region, but thinking back about this, one has to ask whether the counting of heads is a true measure of operational success.

Looking at it from a different angle (and this is not meant as a snide remark), how many innocent civilian heads, from both sides of the border – such as those we drove past in our Ratels in the dead of night or during the sweltering heat of daytime – were converted to whomever's worthy cause? How many by the politicians higher up whose work this really was?

Not too many heads changed over to our side, I believe. That was really the point, is it not? One man, one vote, or what was it in the end? How many were dying while we fought for time to allow the constitutional process to run its course?

In the end someone wins a war. If it goes well, everybody wins in the end. It is said that the purpose of fighting is to create a better form of peace. Let us see. How well were our missions thought through? How did these fit into the larger scheme of things? Who said that counter-revolutionary war was 80% political and 20% military? It seemed that it was all about the body count, more or less, right or wrong, win or lose, hope or despair ...

Command-and-Control and Design for Battle

Operation Daisy was commanded from a tactical headquarters at Ionde, whose gravel airfield was protected by a company from 32 Battalion. Located approximately 120 km inside Angola, it was close enough to the action at Chitequeta to facilitate proper command-and-control.

Commandant Anton van Graan, whose normal appointment was Staff Officer 1 Operations ("SO 1 Ops" in Army jargon) at HQ Sector 10, was in command on the ground. Van Graan was a dedicated paratrooper who had earlier commanded 1 Parachute Battalion at Bloemfontein. He had also served in Rhodesia on counterinsurgency operations and therefore came to Daisy with the right operational experience to command it. A serious and conscientious military professional, he was trusted by the field commanders.

The Tac HQs functions included the planning, execution and support of ongoing joint operations and the evacuation of casualties and prisoners of war. The operation was adequately supported by the SAAF aircraft flying out of Grootfontein, Ondangwa and Ionde. A main helicopter administrative area ("HAA") and forward air force operational base were established at Ionde. The overall plan subsequently made provision for the establishment of secondary helicopter administrative areas as determined beforehand and as the operation unfolded.

The plan for D-Day itself made provision for a combined attack on Chitequeta by 61 Mech, three companies of 3 Parachute Battalion and 201 Battalion.

- 61 Mech was designated to execute the main attack, a surprise strike from the east after a cautious northward approach from the Omauni base near the SWA/Angola border.
- Frans Botes and 201 (Bushman) Battalion were to act as one of the cutoff and

flank protection forces. Their deployment position lay about 20 km southwest of the main enemy complex, and their selected approach northwards followed the course of the Mulola River.

- The three companies from 3 Parachute Battalion would be inserted by parachute from Grootfontein into the bush northwest of the main objective as a complementary cutoff force. On completion of their mission they were to sweep towards Chitequeta in search of any enemy presence.
- The 1 Parachute Battalion company would operate from Ionde for the duration of the operation as the mobile reserve.
- A number of Special Forces' teams would be deployed ahead of the operation to provide intelligence as well as early warning of potential enemy movements.
- The main attack would be followed up with area operations for 17 consecutive days.

The phases for the operation selected by Sector 10, as described below, will be used as a baseline for the telling of the story that follows.[1] This explains how a complex military undertaking was effectively planned and executed in logical order. It is significant to note how well the overall operation progressed according to plan, notwithstanding the intelligence dilemma.

- Phase 1: Force preparation from 23 September to 29 October (D-42 until D-6).
- Phase 2: Movement from the respective staging areas to preselected forward assembly areas (FAAs) between 30 and 31 October (D-5 to D-4).
- Phase 3: Movement from the FAAs to final deployment positions between 1 and 3 November (D-3 to D-1).
- Phase 4: Execution of the main attack on Chitequeta on 4 November (D-Day).
- Phase 5: Mopping-up and area operations from 5 to 8 November (D+1 to D+4).
- Phase 6: Movement southwards from 9 to 18 November (D+5 to D+15).
- Phase 7: Withdrawal of the combat force to SWA on 19 November (D+15).
- Phase 8: Demobilisation of forces as applicable, including a debriefing of the operation.

On completion of Daisy, the situation would be allowed to settle down until the next viable target for a deliberate pre-emptive strike in southern Angola presented itself. So the tidy counterinsurgency war would continue.

Aim and Scope of Air Operations

The SAAFs role was to provide maximum support to the ground forces. Air attacks against FAPLA positions were only to be launched in extreme situations – principally if and when interference with our ground or air operations became imminent. The air component's specific tasks were: Air strikes against preplanned targets; air defence missions to counter the enemy air threat; close air support for the ground forces; interdiction of enemy logistical supply routes; visual and photo reconnaissance; trooping, paratrooping and resupply; casualty evacuation; and search and rescue.

- 10 Forward Air Command Post at Oshakati was commanded by Colonel Ollie Holmes. Its role included operational planning and the tasking of aircraft from AFB Ondangwa.
- A Mobile Air Operations Team (MAOT) was deployed at Ionde under

1 See Maps 12 and 13.

Commandant D. Foote. The MAOT was responsible for controlling and coordinating air operations in the forward areas. This included the tasking and employment of Alouette and Puma helicopters and Bosbok light aircraft allotted to it.

- An Air Support Operations Team (ASO) was attached to each ground unit. These teams supported the ground forces with the planning, controlling and coordinating of air operations in their immediate areas. ASO Team Alpha, commanded by Major Rod Penhall, accompanied 61 Mech; Team Bravo (Captain H.P. Cook) went with 201 Battalion; and Team X-Ray under Major P.W.H. "Knoppies" Coetzer was held in reserve for the greater part of the operation.

Executing Operation Daisy – Into Southern Angola with a Vengeance

Bush, Dust, Distance and Darkness – Unending Movement and More

Although the matter of terrain has been thoroughly discussed in Chapter 5, it is nevertheless necessary to make a few comments about its influence on this particular operation in southern Angola before we proceed.[2]

Daisy often reminded me of that ancient but undimmed cavalry dictum which states simply that "strength lies in mobility." Battling with (and overcoming) the terrain was nothing new for 61 Mech, which had experienced many awesome movement challenges since its establishment (and would experience many more till the war ended in 1988). But the terrain we encountered during Daisy was the most difficult of all.

To achieve our full operational "reach" we had to fight constantly against what one might call the four Horsemen of the Bushveld Apocalypse – Bush, Dust, Distance and Darkness. But I am glad to say that we were past masters at cheating these rogues. We had learned time and again that a large mechanised force could be inserted deeply into enemy terrain without being detected at critical moments – most of the time, in fact.

This would stand the SADF in good stead during Operation Modular in 1987, when one lonely SADF brigade fought successfully against numerically overwhelming enemy odds – in fact, more than eight conventional enemy brigades and two tactical groups[3] – and won. They, incidentally, achieved this in spite of the fact that by 1987 the enemy's MiGs reigned supreme and uncontested in the skies over Angola, the wings of our Mirages having been effectively clipped due to their obsolescence and the lack of adequate radar coverage in southern Angola.

To counter the MiGs on the ground we had to rely on leadership, tactical prowess, superior manoeuvring and the clever utilisation of dense bush and darkness to survive and win. The enemy air threat remained uppermost in our minds during all movement, and with Daisy it became a serious factor for the first time – the dust in the clear Angolan daytime skies, patiently following our mechanised column, was a menace because airborne observers could spot its great swirls from far away.

During the advance to Chitequeta the watchful SAAF could not detect any enemy air activities or impending air threats. The danger from above only became a factor to be reckoned with at 08:15 on D-Day (4 November), when the enemy's radar screens came alive with the blips made by attacking Bosboks, Mirages, Buccaneers and Impalas.

The following figures provide an interesting perspective on the deployment and

2 Also refer to Chapter 5 appraising terrain.

3 See Chapter 15.

movement challenges experienced during Daisy: Our mechanised-cum-motorised column with its organised spacing boasted close on 250 vehicles and was more than 55 km long; time past a given point was a whopping three hours plus. The approximate rate of advance was 12–15 km/h.

During the operation we bashed through 1 600 km of the thickest bush imaginable in 22 gruelling days. To give a bit of perspective, this is further than the distance between Pretoria and Cape Town – and unlike a South African holiday maker, you are not travelling on a well-maintained, tarmacked national highway which is not only guaranteed to be free of mines (which is why we avoided such few roads that existed in southern Angola) but has great numbers of filling stations, truck stops, motels and other amenities along the way.

Given all that, it is amazing that so very few technical hitches were encountered during the operation, although, needless to say, our tiffies worked day and night to keep the force moving. Convert the abovementioned equation into requirements for diesel, helicopter fuel and water and the bowsers and bunkers needed to convey these essential fluids. Guess how many spare wheels, engines and axles were required? This operational perspective can be drawn through to interesting conclusions, particularly about the logistical requirements needed to sustain such a large force deep inside Angola.

Anyhow, it was magnificently managed by our logistics officer, Major Giel Reinecke, technical staff officer Captain Jakkals Jaeckel and their support personnel. In a sense the oil-smeared tiffies, the versatile mechanics of Sergeant-major Duppie du Plessis's light workshop troop, became true heroes of Operation Daisy.

The thorny, tangled bush tested the staying power of man, machine and pneumatic tyre to the utmost. Broken sticks and stunted Mopani trees had a field day with us, so that there were flat tyres by the dozen. Amazingly, this was only experienced for the first few days. Then the drivers caught on, and all of a sudden the back-breaking, time-consuming toil of replacing heavy Ratel, Buffel or Samil wheels lessened dramatically. This becomes of paramount importance to a force operating on its own: wheels and tyres, mobility, serviceability, fuel, shooting stuff, ration packs, the safety of the participants – the very mission itself – all depend on each one of these elements and many others.

As challenges go, there were a few which towered above the others: Navigation; maintaining movement control; bundu-bashing; just keeping sane. In the process of unending forward motion many vehicles had to be recovered from the thick sand with towbars, kinetic ropes and recovery vehicles. Many a time vehicles needed to race abreast across deep patches of thick sand encountered in some of the floodplains to prevent them from being bogged down to axle-depth – the sandier and marshier, the merrier.

The troops started cutting short stumps from trees with power saws and dumping them into the watery traps behind each Ratel; the next one along would trample them down and add its own contribution, to be trampled down in turn, and so on. No one told them to do this. The youngsters were simply "making a plan," that traditional South African response to a problem.

The eggheads would probably call this "lateral thinking." Most of our young soldiers would have scratched their heads if you asked them what lateral thinking was. All they knew was that there was a problem and it had to be overcome somehow, no matter how odd the solution might look. South African troops were awesome!

Closer to the objective it was to be all-night movement, something we had experimented with and practised over and over at Omuthiya. We knew that the enemy could hear our movement and discern the dusty reflection of our vehicle lights from approximately 12 to 15 kilometres away. In spite of this handicap, the ever-present requirement was to maintain operational security and to achieve surprise onwards to H-Hour.

How you actually managed this in spite of the general conditions and the unavoidable problem of moving forward with a large, noisy collection of machines like 61 Mech, especially when your opponents were bush-wise insurgents who were adept at concealing themselves or running away so as to fight again another day – well, you did what you could. Hell, it was fun being with 61 Mech!

Phase 1: Force Preparation from 23 September until 29 October (D Minus 42 until D Minus 6)

Excitement stirred in the sweltering heat and humid air of northern SWA/Namibia as the forces gathered and prepared for Operation Daisy. But there was concern as well: By late October, with the kickoff only a few days away, we still had not yet been provided with certain essential elements of intelligence, the most important being, of course, the exact positions of the enemy and the nature of their deployments in the Bambi-Chitequeta-Indungo area.

There was no time for sitting back and waiting, however, and while the intelligence gatherers toiled away, we continued resolutely planning and preparing for the operation. The tactical commanders duly received their operations orders from Sector 10; I frequented HQ Sector 10 at Oshakati to participate in the joint planning, accompanied at various times by my second-in-command, Major Thys Rall, my logistics officer, Major Giel Reinecke, and my intelligence officer, Captain Gerrie Hugo.

As always 61 Mech oozed confidence, but that did not prevent us from attending to every detail as if it were our first excursion into the field. Our medical officer kept feeding us malaria pills, with the routine warning that they were for swallowing, not chewing. Padre Koos Rossouw kept himself busy sorting out our souls. During one of the planning phases I told him jokingly, "Koos, remember to consider the devil as a planning factor." Long exposure to the military mind had made him immune to such incursions, however, and he replied casually: "No, I leave that to the anti-aircraft gunners." How do you reply to that?

Thys Rall, an armour man of note, was an exacting man for detail, and therefore became our movement and navigation patron saint, apart from supporting me with the combat training of our fighting troops.

Many a time I would find Thys Rall, Koos Liebenberg and Lieutenants Ariel Hugo and Chris Walls poring over the maps in the operations room, prismatic compasses and protractors in hand. Great stuff! There was no chance of getting lost in Angola's vast hinterland with those four experts on the job. I could trust them to get us where we wanted to be and at the right time. So it suited me fine – I had suffered a few embarrassments of my own in the past and the possibility of getting lost was simply too ghastly to contemplate.

In our corrugated-iron operations centre the constantly updated battle maps and aerial photographs were up against the wall, ready for each of our succession of planning sessions, with my operations officer-cum-adjutant Captain Cassie Schoeman keeping a watchful eye over everything.

I need to say something about this man, who had just gone through Operation Carrot with me.[4] Schoeman was a brilliant operations officer, but also a leader of men whose troops adored him. We had become close friends in the 1970s, during our training days at 1 South African Infantry Battalion at Bloemfontein. He had commanded my Alpha Company with distinction during Operation Carrot, and then returned to Bloemfontein, but my good friend Commandant Tony Savides, at the time OC 1 SAI, had acceded to my request that Schoeman be detached to 61 Mech as my operations officer for the duration of Daisy.

Cassie Schoeman travelled with me in my command Ratel. He was an amazing man, a pillar of strength. Did he ever sleep? If so, I didn't ever catch him at it. His voice, always crisp and clear, could be heard over the radios from front to rear, up to the Dear Lord as well, which superseded the 61 Mech chain of command. This is not a mere flippant remark because Cassie was then and still is a religious man. During the next demanding 25 days I would give him a sideways glance every now and then, and each time I would see him sitting in his jump seat in my Ratel, cool, calm, collected, forever positive and enthusiastic.

I did not know it yet but we would be operating together again during Operation Modular in 1987 and Operation Prone in 1988[5] – that time I personally asked Lieutenant General Kat Liebenberg, the then Chief of the Army for Cassie's presence at the front and like Tony Savides years earlier he also said "yes". During the fighting in the late 1980s Cassie commanded 4 South African Infantry Battalion in Operations Hooper and Prone ... also with distinction. It was an honour to have this man as a colleague and a friend.

As usual, the planning was serious business. Our studies told us that the densely bushed terrain would allow us to strike with equal ease (or perhaps I should say "difficulty") from the south, west, north or east. One thing was a certainty: No matter which direction we chose, getting there would place extreme demands on both man and machine. On the other hand, if any vehicle could handle it, it would be our very tough six-wheeled Ratels.

This being the case, we decided to strike Chitequeta with a two-pronged attack from the north and the east, the directions from which the enemy would be the least likely to expect us. In addition, we calculated that it would lessen the security risk and hasten the disruption of our foes. Artillery fire and an air attack close to H-Hour would have to suffice for dampening the noise of our painstaking approach to contact, which would take 45 to 60 minutes at least, given the vegetation.

So be it! H-Hour would have to be as close as possible to first light. However, the Bosbok light aircraft, the Mirages and the Buccaneers needed some light in order to secure their targets, and the sun had to be high enough so that the insurgents could not take to the dappled shade of the bush to hide from the circling Alouette gunships. After much discussion we settled on 08:30 as the best time. The approach we chose would take us northwards via Omauni, halfway between the Cubango River to our east and the Mulola River to our west, to an attacking position 60 km east of Chitequeta.

While we were beating our brains out in the ops centre, our troops were raising purposeful hell in the training area north of Omuthiya – furiously training and exercising, manoeuvring at will and tearing up the earth with live ammunition. WO1 "Killer" Smit, our incoming RSM, and the troops of Alpha Echelon even composed a little song called "Oopse Daisy", the gist of which was that we were heading for Chitequeta, where we were going to administer a serious lesson to all those present (this is the polite version). Well done, RSM, I thought. After all, the psychological is to the physical as three is to one, right?

4 See Chapter 11.

5 See Chapters 15 and 16.

Two staid and respectable businessmen of today who were then 19-year-old national service second lieutenants, Gert Minnaar and Ariel Hugo[6] (although they were already veterans of Operations Carrot and Protea), later wrote down their recollections of this time, which I think are worth quoting.

Firstly, Gert Minnaar:

At 61 Mech we believed in training hard which made the fighting part easier. During October 1981 we were at it again, preparing for Operation Daisy at Omuthiya.

> We knew that it was going to be an arduous undertaking. What we could discern from the planning and the maps was that the target lay more than 250 km inside southern Angola. I was excited about our new venture. I was a mechanised platoon commander under command of Captain Koos Liebenberg of Bravo Company. He was an excellent commander and looked well after us national service "loots" and his men. We had worked closely with him in the bush for many months now.
>
> Bravo Company was a close-knit team. Our icon was the Ratel-20. It was armed with a 20 mm quick-firing gun and a turret-mounted 7,62 mm Browning machine gun. We could fight either mounted or dismounted. As young national service officers we felt extremely confident due to the meticulous force preparation and training we continuously underwent at Omuthiya. This good feeling was amplified by us being veterans now from both Operation Carrot in April 1981 and Operation Protea in August 1981.
>
> What marked our training in preparing for operations which I would never forget? It was manoeuvring endlessly, day and night, in the dense bush surrounding Omuthiya; navigation exercises; fire and movement and contact drills with live ammunition; clearing enemy trenches and, above all, maintaining our vehicles and equipment at a high state of readiness. We worked hand in hand with the other subunits of the armour, artillery, engineers and support groups. Omuthiya was our home from home. We were proud of Bravo Company and of 61 Mech...

And then Ariel Hugo:

> I commanded Number 2 Platoon (mechanised) of Bravo Company. Our company commander was Captain Koos Liebenberg, in whom we had the utmost confidence. Our company comprised a company HQ with two Ratel-20s and three platoons equipped with four Ratel-20s each. In addition the company was supported by a Ratel armoured ambulance, Ratel-Recovery vehicle, 81 mm mortars and an assortment of logistics vehicles.
>
> Bravo Company was usually organised as a combat team, which normally included four Ratel-90s of the anti-tank platoon under Second Lieutenant Chris Walls. We were both trained at 1 South African Infantry Battalion in Bloemfontein before we came to 61 Mech at the beginning of 1981. Walls and I had become close friends and had participated in Operations Carrot and Protea. We were veterans and old hands now, and felt good about it.

6 I have remained friends with Gert Minnaar and Ariel Hugo until today. The same accounted to the other names mentioned in the script; all currently members of the 61 Mech Veteran's Association thirty years hence.

Commandant Roland de Vries, the commander of 61 Mech, had observed our "unholy" alliance. During some of our exercises he made an approving comment about our navigational abilities with map and prismatic compass, which was not easy in the dense bush and flat terrain of Ovamboland or, for that matter, southern Angola. As a 19-year-old national service officer, my chest swelled at the praise.

On or about 15 October Captain Koos Liebenberg told Walls and myself that we had been selected to navigate 61 Mech on to the objective for Daisy. The operation apparently was scheduled for early November. I experienced a surge of apprehension, but pride and anticipation as well.

After this Walls and I exercised endlessly to sharpen our navigational skills. This happened many a time on our own during the day and night in the bushes north of Omuthiya. There was no way that we were going to get lost. We were also privileged to plan the operation, especially the movement and navigation part, with the command group of 61 Mech. This was truly an amazing experience for us youngsters.

Our soldiers did not spend their time wondering about who, what, where, when, how or why – they all knew this well. But for now their entire attention was concentrated on doing.

Phase 2: Movement from the Respective Staging Areas to Preselected Forward Assembly Areas from 30 until 31 October (D-5 to D-4)

Thursday 29 October 1981 found the task force ready to move from its widely dispersed staging areas to the preselected forward assembly areas and eventually to the final deployment and attacking positions. At this stage 61 Mech was still deployed at Omuthiya, getting the last-minute things done, while 201 Battalion was closing down Operation Mispel in the Ondjiva-Dova area and was making ready to move northwards towards Chitequeta. The infantry company and reconnaissance team of 32 Battalion had moved from Buffalo base to Omauni and were still in final force preparation mode.

The 1 Parachute Battalion company was finalising its battle preparations at Ondangwa prior to the airlift to Ionde. The three companies of 3 Parachute Battalion were still training and preparing at Oshivello but were ready to move to Grootfontein airfield at a moment's notice to fit their parachutes.

By 30 October the field base at Omauni – 61 Mech's FAA, it will be remembered – was ready to receive us. Back at Omuthiya we were still waiting anxiously for intelligence on the precise location of the enemy positions, but we knew there would be no turning back now, and so we rose very early and were rolling out of the base by 04:00.

As with Protea, we travelled by two separate routes for security purposes. The combat element, commanded by Thys Rall, took "Route 1," which struck out due northwards through the Ovamboland bush until it reached the Chandelier road, then swung east towards Omauni, taking extreme care from here on to avoid falling victim to any SWAPO mines which might be there. After 14 hours and 195 km the combat element arrived safely at Omauni.

The remainder of our force, under the overall command of Major Giel Reinecke, with the RSM, WO1 M.C. Barnard, who was in charge of the administrative echelon, used the road system via Rundu to Omauni. This was far longer than Route 1 (575 km), but we calculated that a long convoy of load carrying vehicles was a fairly common sight in Ovamboland and would not cause any undue interest. Although "Route 2" was much longer than Rall's, it was far easier on the springs and allowed more speed, and Reinecke made it to Omauni in one gruelling 14-hour dash.

I remained rather forlornly behind as the two columns set off from Omuthiya because some members of my flock were still arriving from Grootfontein, mainly our new drivers from Army HQ and those of supplementary logistics vehicles from Northern Logistics Command. These drivers were not operationally experienced; their mission training would have to take place on the hoof in hostile country, and I wanted to make sure that they were as well-prepared as possible for what might lie ahead. I made a mental note about a memo I would like to send to Army HQ and the SWATF: Please take note of our slight predicament for future reference – this does not make life easy in the field.

All I could do right then was to apply what civvies called "total quality management," that is to say, "continuous improvement and management of risk." So I made sure that each newcomer was shown the way to Omauni on a route map, accompanied by a cheerful word and a prayer (now I knew what Padre Koos Rossouw felt like when praying for soldierly souls – well, drivers, anyway. But I was sure they had souls like everyone else). I then left for Operet airfield near Oshivello and flew directly to Omauni in a light aircraft.

As we flew northeast we could see the dust of the Ratels below us as they headed for Omauni. I could not help thinking about the air threat we might face once we had crossed the border, and silently I gabbled another prayer for my flock travelling below me. I knew that 176 km to my east Reinecke and his clan would be on the road as well. I couldn't help hoping that the Dear Lord had dedicated a special staff officer up there to process my snap prayers for drivers with trucks which needed fuel, could break down or might be shot at.

By late evening the component parts of 61 Mech reached Omauni, having suffered only a few breakdowns. Our flock was together again, dust-feathered veterans and a large number of starry-eyed fledglings. The latter were quickly welcomed into the 61 Mech fold and told: Keep your distances, drivers, when driving in Angola – take note, there are umpteen enemy MiGs up there.

While the fledglings were being pushed out of the nest at Omauni Frans Botes and his diminutive bush veterans of 201 Battalion were moving via Dova towards the Mulola River and then northwards to Chitequeta; a fiery little surprise and a few enemy mines awaited them along the way, although neither they nor anyone else knew that yet, of course.

It was pleasant to enjoy a cold beer with my command group at Omauni. My dust-covered troops were relaxing in the easy comfort of the base, enjoying some trouble-free chatter, hot food and two beers per man. Tomorrow would be the closing moment south of the border, the prelude to action, so there was checking, more checking and then a final inspection before 61 Mech declared itself combat ready.

At Omauni I acquired a passenger, no less a person than Lieutenant General Jannie Geldenhuys, the Chief of the Army, who had decided to travel with me in my command Ratel until we had attacked Chitequeta on 5 November. Somehow we found some space for the battered brown leather suitcase he lived out of and welcomed him on board. Fighting a battle under the direct gaze of the Army's top soldier is hard on the nerves of any young battalion commander, but Jannie Geldenhuys was never your common or garden type of general, and he fitted in very comfortably, acting as part of the Ratel's crew and never interfering with my command.

He was, in fact, a great asset, because his presence had a tremendously positive effect on the troops' morale. Our generals' habit of accompanying their soldiers into battle – right out in front where the shooting was taking place, which was very different from a quick in-and-out visit before the fighting started – was something one did not and does not see in many other armies. But it was the sort of thing a soldier of the old SADF expected and appreciated (incidentally, General Geldenhuys was known for washing his own underpants on such an occasion in spite of all the brass on his shoulders).

The renowned war correspondent and writer, Al J. Venter (sporting a very large pistol) and his media team also joined us at Omauni to record a complete video account of the operation. They were duly welcomed and Giel Reinecke assigned them a Buffel of their own ... which he made sure they signed for! Captain Cassie Schoeman assigned them a position in the marching order, which meant that pro tem they were now members of 61 Mech, cameras, tripods, slouch hats, impressive field gear and all. The troops (and some of the officers) spent much time eyeing these strange and exotic beings.

Phase 3: Movement from Forward Assembly Areas to Final Deployment Positions from 1 until 3 November (D-3 to D-1)

The Omauni base was still shrouded in darkness at 04:00 on 1 November when 61 Mech bade its comforts farewell and started moving out, the dust-dimmed red rear lights of the vanguard fading rapidly into the darkness as it bore away to the north. About 75 km away to our west, I knew, Frans Botes and 201 Battalion were also feeling their way northwards along the Mulola River, while at Grootfontein the 3 Parachute Battalion companies were in final preparation mode for their airborne deployment to Chitequeta on D-Day. Meanwhile the 1 Parachute Battalion company was standing by at Ondangwa at high readiness, waiting to be trooped to Ionde as the mobile reserve on D-1.

Over the next three days 61 Mech's long column moved systematically northwards for 295 km to our final attacking position, 60 km east of Chitequeta (also designated as Helicopter Administrative Area 2). At night we laagered to allow time for our soldiers to get some rest and to replenish and maintain our force.

The first day we were obviously still in UNITAs area; we came across groups of UNITA soldiers in tattered camouflage, armed with AK-47 rifles, who greeted us with smiles and thumbs-up signs, and our UNITA liaison team's members came erect with their chests swollen with pride. The troops reciprocated by treating our new-found comrades to some of our ration packs, which were greatly esteemed luxuries to the bare-bones UNITA men. But I knew we would not be in friendly territory for much longer, and I could not help worrying about continued security. Who would report on us, and what would they report? The African bush has eyes even when it appears deserted.

General Geldenhuys worried about this as well, and at one stage cautioned me about the air threat to which we might be exposed. He had observed (as had I) that every so often some of our vehicles would bunch up instead of maintaining the proper distance, and he was as concerned as I was about this serious potential threat to man and machine. Once again I cautioned my subunit commanders about the impending danger prowling the sky, but there was little more that I could do.

One reason for the bunching up was, of course, that many of our drivers and troops were still new at the war-fighting game, but on the other hand they were learning fast on the job, so to speak, experiencing firsthand what it was like to operate in difficult terrain and to maintain control as parts of large moving formations. It was somewhat different, as they were discovering, from what they had been used to in the serene (and un-bushy) surroundings of Bloemfontein and Kimberley.

In the meantime a helicopter-borne company of 32 Battalion and a party of Recces under the justly renowned Captain Willem Ratte had secured a position designated Helicopter Administrative Area 1 about 50 km east of Ionde, and two Pumas and two Alouettes under Major "Knoppies" Coetzer had landed there with his MAOT.

The runway was in good condition, suitable for use by light aircraft and even Dakotas, and in the course of the day eight Alouette gunships and six Pumas landed and were ready for deployment; the 32 Battalion men also swooped on a suspected enemy base at Embundo, about 6 km southwest of Ionde, found it unoccupied and secured it.

Throughout what was left of the day a succession of Dakotas landed at Ionde, ferrying in additional personnel for the Tac HQ and MAOT, as well as a suitably stocked medical field post. Twenty Buffel spare wheels that were urgently required by 61 Mech were flown in as well, preparatory to falling into Giel Reinecke's eager hands. The first of three pairs of Bosbok light aircraft which would support the operation arrived.

The last Dakotas landed at about 18:00 with the company of paratroopers from 1 Parachute Battalion, and by 19:20 the MAOT was in place and preparing for our arrival next day; this would allow my command group time for a final liaison meeting with Brigadier Badenhorst and the Tac HQs command cadre before D-Day.

At 22:38 the MAOT personnel marked the HAA position with strobe lights and flares for a Hercules C-130 flying towards Chitequeta with the eight Special Forces operators ("Recces", as they were called by everyone except, apparently, themselves) who were to be inserted to the northwest of the target zone. Their mission was to confirm the presence of the enemy at Chitequeta by 18:00 on D-1 (3 November), and also to mark out a suitable drop zone to the northwest of the main target area for the insertion of the three paratrooper companies the following night.

One of the operators in the C-130's noisy, cavernous hold was Captain Jeremy Wiley, an astute and creative character who had a special trick up his sleeve. Earlier he had befriended a SWAPO deserter, allegedly from Bravo Battalion, who claimed to have headed for the hills because of ill-treatment. Wiley's unlikely recruit had been hurriedly taught how to jump from an aircraft at night with a parachute – thrown out, more likely – and was now going to accompany him as a guide.

Radio communications with 61 Mech was maintained inter alia via the Special Forces mobile tactical HQ which was moving with us under command of Major Charl Naudé, the Xangongo bridge-killer. Communications were a problem, however, because of radio skip distances, and at times were sporadic and sketchy. The same problem hampered our UNITA liaison team (both, incidentally, used Morse code most of the time).

201 Battalion acquired an absolutely unforeseeable possible security problem while moving up the Mulola River when it had a surprise encounter with a strong SWAPO contingent at map reference XN 450 095. The insurgents were put to flight after a short but intense firefight, with the gunships providing support, and at 16:00 four wounded soldiers and one captured insurgent were evacuated to Ionde in a Puma.

When Botes laconically but proudly radioed the news to me, I replied, "What the hell about security, Frans?" I suppose I was being a bit of a wet blanket, but the uppermost thought in my mind was: Will the contact compromise the attack on Chitequeta? Events were to prove that it was a legitimate concern.

On a lighter note: Among the spoils of this contact was a brand new six-wheeled Volvo field vehicle, and Frans Botes dreamed fond dreams about using his new acquisition as his personal staff car after the operation. Alas, his grand plan was soon smashed by Brigadier Badenhorst, who was also much taken with it, and since "rank hath its privileges" this executive toy duly found its way to Oshakati at the end of the operation.

While Ionde was being put into functional shape the SAAF flew a reconnaissance mission to Cahama and found that the radar installations there, which had been destroyed by the Air Force during Operation Protea in August, were active again. This was a matter of considerable concern for the SAAF, which wished to ensure a favourable air situation for the duration of Operation Daisy, and so an air strike was planned for D+1.

In the meantime HAA 2 was established for 61 Mech by Major Coetzer and his ASO team. From here helicopter operations would be directed westwards during the next few days. Late afternoon on 3 November found 61 Mech arriving and completing its laagering procedure.

We made final preparations for the next day's assault. Meanwhile, 60 km to our west, the Recces roamed discreetly around, looking for the alleged enemy positions – I say "alleged" because so far nothing new had been forthcoming from Oshakati. We reassessed our position and confirmed that the orders remained unchanged; so far it was all systems go.

We knew that when we moved out in the morning there would not be a moment for rest or reflection about anything but the task at hand until it was finished. Forget about sleep. What might happen next? What must happen next? What unforeseen and unforeseeable thing might happen during the next tactical bound?

Perpetual motion had totally absorbed our very beings so far, as our minds and bodies were battered by the constant pitching and tossing of the Ratels' armoured hulls, moving ever forward, checking and checking again at every brief pause, concentrating one step ahead all the time, a huge volume of thought from a thousand people vanishing into the ether ... A thousand people whose lives were my responsibility.

The light was fading away as night advanced on us. Soon it would be dark, and then it would be D-Day. There was little or no sleep for the soldiers of 61 Mech that night; the adrenalin level was simply too high. Perhaps there would be some catnapping in the vehicles next morning, whether stationary or on the move, as we advanced.

In the Tac HQ at Ionde itself with its wall decorations of battle maps, even that small luxury was denied its occupants as the night hours wore by to the accompaniment of the radios' constant squawking. Nor would there be any sleep for the SAAF personnel preparing for the next morning's strike, the paratroopers strapping on their parachutes at Grootfontein, 201 Battalion moving stealthily nearer to Chitequeta in the darkness, Captain Jeremy Wiley creeping through the darkness around Chitequeta with his turncoat companion in tow.

The trap was about to snap shut on SWAPO. What were they thinking? What were they doing? And, most of all, precisely where the hell were they?

No time to worry about that now. We had room in our thoughts for only one thing, and that was to cover the remaining 60 km secretively and accurately, and to do it so that we would be on the right objective at the right time. The essential for any attack, and this is even more the case in darkness and densely bushed terrain, is to reach the forming-up place and starting line mere minutes before H-Hour.

This is the soldier's witching hour and minute; from this baseline all critical happenings would flow – in fact, would start flowing before he had even got there, because it was the point of coordination for everything that would happen: the fire-and-manoeuvre of the ground force; the air support and the safety of our aircraft and our forces from our own fire, indirect fire support and coordination.

We were now very close to this critical juncture, and the minutes were slipping away at a steady clip. From here on everything would depend on a sequence of properly coordinated actions and simultaneous moves. For the advance to the FUP my trust and that of 1,000 soldiers would reside in my small team of stalwart selected navigators: Koos Liebenberg and Ariel Hugo of Bravo Company and Chris Walls of the anti-tank platoon. We knew how good they were at this. Now they were going to have to do it again.

Phase 4: Execution of the Main Attack at Chitequeta on 4 November (D-Day)

The total time that the planning provided for moving the main force over the 60 km between the final attacking position (HAA 2) to the forming-up place was five hours and 30 minutes (03:00 to 08:30), but Koos Liebenberg, Ariel Hugo and Chris Walls left at midnight, escorted by a mechanised platoon.

The four Ratel-20s moved cautiously through the night at low speed and engine revolutions to reduce noise to a minimum, marking their path with their own wheel tracks and garlands of white toilet paper, that material of a thousand military uses.

For 45 km they ground westwards through the dark thickets of bush until they reached their preselected waiting area without encountering any hostile presence except a snake which had the audacity or misfortune to fall into Liebenberg's turret. The occupants took out their consternation on the unfortunate snake, but did not interrupt their forward progress for long – the timing was far too tight for that; the main body would be following in the vanguard's tracks by now. When they reached the waiting area they stopped to wait for the main body's arrival.

The main body departed HAA 2 at 03:00, as scheduled, leaving the Alpha Echelon behind to catch up with it at Chitequeta on D+1. The immensely long fighting column advanced as stealthily as possible, similarly reached the waiting area without incident and joined hands with Liebenberg's navigation team. Now they were just 15 km east of Chitequeta, an inconsiderable distance, to be sure, but thanks to the terrain it would take another two arduous hours of bundu-bashing to get there.

While 61 Mech battled with the bundu, Captain Jeremy Wiley's small Special Forces team was doing some sterling work. His team came into contact with an enemy lookout post in the early hours of the morning and shots were fired; Wiley hoped that he and his men had been mistaken for locals, or even UNITA scouts. Wiley's attempts to report on the contact and the general enemy situation were bedevilled by faltering radio contact and unnerving skip distances, but at about 04:00 he finally got word through to Major Charl Naudé in our command group.

The news was not good. Wiley reported there was no question that enemy elements were to be found in the target zone, but not where we had thought, and he believed our main objective was unoccupied. These tidings were disheartening, to say the least. Wiley added that he had heard the C-130s flying to his west as they dropped the paratroopers and had picked up the distant drone of our main body far to the east, although its direction could not be pinpointed. He had also heard the movements of several small enemy groups.

When I heard this, there was no doubt in my mind about what was happening: Our surprise was blown and our wily opponents were scattering to stay out of harm's way. Well, now we had been forewarned that we could expect a contact anywhere and at any moment!

I radioed all this to my subunit commanders and cautioned them to remain on high alert and be ready to fight at moment's notice. As for us, we would continue with the attack as planned, in spite of the uncertainty about the enemy and the newly discovered fluidity of the situation within our target zone – what it amounted to was that the target had now become infinite, without boundaries.

For a few dreadful moments ripples of disappointment washed over me when I thought about the painstaking preparations and immense effort all the combat participants had put into Operation Daisy, and the struggle we had put up to get where we were now. How would this affect the morale of my men?

I knew one thing, however: I could not allow the frustration of missing the enemy, combined with sheer fatigue, to wear away my people's combat vitality and sound morale. Danger could be lurking anywhere. So: Don't fret, remain composed. Focus on the job at hand, inspire and motivate, keep the goal in mind ... Faith, faith in self, faith in the people around you. These are the true pillars of strength ... Be ready to adapt at moment's notice. A plan is a basis for change ... Provide the purpose to carry you and them through.

By this time 3 Parachute Battalion's three paratrooper companies were on the way to the target area for a drop at P-Hour[7], and were girding their loins for what promised to be an interesting and eventful day. They had taken off from Grootfontein at 03:00, packed into six Hercules C-130s and Transall C-160s. They flew without incident to their drop zone, about 20 km northwest of Chitequeta ... and then ran into a snag.

A Recce party was supposed to have illuminated the DZ for them but had been unable to do so in time, so the aircraft had to circle the area, and as a result missed the DZ by several kilometres. The paratroopers jumped into the darkness nevertheless. As they floated down, the C-130s and C-160s banked away, having completed one of the SAAFs two main tasks for D-Day (the other was the air strike on Chitequeta a few minutes before H-Hour).

By a near miracle all the paratroopers landed without serious injury – although five of them got entangled in their harnesses on the way down – and started making their way to their cut-off position. But the question was: What had the enemy in the target zone heard, and what were they thinking?

The first of the four Bosboks we had been allocated was airborne and on its way from Ionde to the target area by 05:45, followed by the other three soon after 07:30. This handful of courageous young pilots was to render wonderful service in the course of D-Day, providing the ground forces with invaluable navigational assistance, scouting ahead, and acting as the forward air controllers for the attacking aircraft, carrying out aerial observation and spotting for the artillery.

At about 06:00 we picked up Jeremy Wiley and his SWAPO compatriot and stashed them in one of the HQ Ratels; understandably, they were bone tired after spending a long, dangerous night in close proximity to the enemy, continuously dodging and diving for cover. We resumed our journey to the objective with Major Peter Lemon and his crew of industrious signallers listening for enemy radio chatter in their special signals Ratel with its electronic surveillance equipment. But although they were well-versed in the tricks of electronic warfare, they intercepted nothing of any value.

At about the same time six Alouette gunships took off from Ionde and flew to HAA 2

7 Similar to H-Hour for a ground attack, P-Hour indicates the time that paratroopers are dropped.

where they landed around 06:30 and went on standby to provide fire support as required by 61 Mech, 201 Battalion or the 3 Parachute Battalion companies. They would remain on call for the rest of the day for such missions as cutting off any enemy fleeing southwards from the target zone. An hour later they were joined by four Pumas for trooping and casevac[8] duties.

61 Mech carried on forcing its way through to the objective, with the course of the Caiundo – little more than a rivulet at that time of year – serving as the axis of attack from the north. Here and there pools of fresh water could be sighted in the shonas and riverbeds we crossed, a warning that the rainy season would wait for no one, least of all the military. About 5 km east of the target Captain Bernie Pols peeled off and set up Sierra Battery's eight 120 mm mortars, then stood by for H-Hour.

At 08:15 flights of Buccaneers, Mirages and Impalas started attacking preselected targets with high explosive bombs. Bursts of 23 mm gunfire and the trails of at least two SA-7 missiles were noticed, but no aircraft were hit. One Mirage pilot reported that he had seen spectacular secondary explosions as he left the target area, presumably from enemy ammunition caches. Some of the bombs did not release due to electrical malfunctions and others were jettisoned off-target (during mopping-up operations two days later it was found that these bombs had killed six insurgents).

Minutes before H-Hour our four Bosbok aircraft carried out dummy runs over the target area from the south. This was to disrupt and deceive the enemy about the direction of the attack. This done, they got down to aerial reconnaissance, artillery target indication and forward air controlling for the attacking Mirages and Impalas.

At 08:30 Bernie Pols's 120 mm mortars went into action, not only to soften up the main objective but also to mask the noise of our vehicles and the direction from which we were coming (incidentally, the artillery fired more than 800 120 mm mortar rounds on suspected enemy targets during Operation Daisy).

61 Mech was organised into three combat teams for the attack, which was planned to take place in three uncomplicated phases:

- Phase 1 was the main attack, to be carried out, after the air strikes, from the north by Koos Liebenberg's Combat Team 2 (mechanised) with indirect covering fire from the 120 mm mortars, thickened up by Major Bok Smit's 81 mm mortar platoon. Combat Team 1 (mechanised) under Major Leon Marais, with Captain Frik Schade as his second-in-command, was the mobile reserve for this phase, and moved one bound (200–400 metres) behind the combat group HQ and Combat Team 2 on the same axis of attack. Combat Team 3 (motorised) under Captain Pale van der Walt would be deployed in a cut-off position 3 km to the east of the objective. This was also its attacking position for Phase 3 of the attack, which was set to develop from east to west.
- Phase 2 entailed the continuation of Combat Team 1's attack, through to the next objective further to the south. This attack would also be supported by 120 mm and 81 mm mortar fire. Combat Teams 1 and 2 would then follow through with the attack and exploit southwards to the general line of Mabilue, a recognisable point selected from the map on the southern perimeter of the main target.
- Phase 3 made provision for a final east-to-west attack by Combat Team 3 on a selected depth target, supported by the six gunships. For this purpose a helicopter

8 Term used in the SADF for medical or casualty evacuation.

administrative area had been prepared 6 km to the east of Chitequeta. Here the helicopters could refuel and rearm in relative safety. The plan was then for Combat Team 3 to exploit further westwards to the north-south line of the Caiundo rivulet, with Combat Teams 1 and 2 earmarked as mobile reserves.

As our fighting line entered the fringes of the objective from the north we were still hoping for a major contact with the enemy, but no fire was drawn. We continued moving southwards with the artillery and mortar fire being shifted further southwards in front of our skirmish line, amid clear signs that although the enemy had once occupied the base, they had been gone for at least two months, leaving behind nothing but cobwebs and booby traps.

Everywhere we saw derelict trench systems and bunkers which had decayed and collapsed over time. As we swept through the objective we found numerous tree stumps and stunted trees protruding all over. The trees had been cut off at the axle height of a Ratel and were clearly intended to serve as obstacles against attack. We also noticed that fields of fire had been carefully cleared – although not recently – for defence against a mechanised force.

We ceased firing with the 120 mm and 81 mm mortars, which remained on call for opportunity targets with the assistance of our spotter aircraft. For a while we kept more or less to the original plan of attack as we swept through the target zone, even though the circumstances had changed, to make certain that our target area was truly void of an enemy presence.

As we moved through the objective I could hear an enemy 23 mm anti-aircraft gun firing far to the south of our immediate target zone. One of our light aircraft, Bosbok 264C, which was flying Telstar (radio relay) in the area to our west, observed the same AA fire to the south. The Bosbok pilot later reported:[9]

> 08:15 to 12:50: Circled area 10 km west of target to provide Telstar for ground forces. During attack troops reported AA fire from ground photo CJ 089 420. Airbursts exploded 100 m from aircraft while at 1,000 feet. Could not determine origin of fire and ground forces reported AA fire at the same time.
>
> Impalas were brought on to AA positions. Did forward air controlling with Impalas on to another AA position at ground photo CJ 098 436; results unknown.

At 08:55 Major Rod Penhall, 61 Mech's air support officer, called in two Mirages for a re-strike in the area where the Bosbok had reported the anti-aircraft fire. The Mirages fired rockets and drew 23 mm anti-aircraft and SA-7 fire as they pulled out of their dive. At 09:30 Penhall called in another re-strike, and from 10:30 to 12:00 two pairs of Impalas attacked with 68 mm rockets. After that there was no further anti-aircraft fire.

Later on, as we swept through the objectives further to the south, we found some tattered enemy corpses in the bush not too far from our original target area. Apparently, a medical field post had been hit by a stray bomb from the attacking Impalas. By now it was obvious that any sane enemy would be hightailing it southwards out of the danger zone – especially considering the commotion caused through the night by the closing of the trap from the east, west and the north.

That impression was strengthened when a few Mirages and Impalas flew interdiction

9 I still have his top secret mission report – Misrep/Top Secret/003/ 4 Nov 81 – from AFCP10 at Oshakati in my possession.

and air reconnaissance missions over the bush tracks leading from Techamutete and Bambi to the target area between 12:00 and 14:00, but reported that they had not observed any suspected enemy movement, whether vehicular or otherwise.

The SAAF had done what it had been asked to do and was just as disappointed with the results as the ground forces were with the attack. Its later report pulled no punches: "Once again a great deal of firepower and effort had been expended with no visible result. Once again the intelligence regarding the SWAPO bases was found badly wanting. All the Air Force had to show for the tremendous tonnage dropped on the target during D-Day was six bodies found two days later."10 These words echoed the mood of the ground forces.

We carried on through the objective for a while longer, but still found nothing. Clearly we had ended up attacking a phantom enemy, so I called a tactical pause while we reassessed our situation. It was decided to exploit swiftly to the south and west of the target area, since there was still enough daylight left.

I released Koos Liebenberg's Combat Team 2 to look for enemy stragglers further to the south, with Leon Marais and Combat Team 1 standing fast on the high rise forming the most dominant part at Chitequeta as our mobile reserve. I tasked Pale van der Walt's Combat Team 3 to sweep eastwards towards the Caiundo River.

The original idea had been to use the gunships to search for escaping insurgents, but the SAAF had refused to employ them for this purpose, and in any case we did not want to expose the helicopters unnecessarily to either friendly or hostile ground fire, something which could erupt at any moment, or waste precious flying time unless or until a viable contact had been made.

So it was left to the ground forces, mounted or dismounted, to flush out any insurgents who were somewhere out there – an exhausting, seemingly endless struggle through the unrelenting, dense bush. At 16:30 Combat Team 2's three mounted platoons, who were pushing ever further southwards, finally made contact.

They were following up on enemy spoor they had found when they spotted seven insurgents running southwards. Some of the riflemen immediately dismounted and gave chase on foot, while the Ratels paced the skirmish line, ready to provide fire support. In due course Second Lieutenant Ariel Hugo's platoon made contact (at map reference XN 564 913, to be precise) and a short, sharp firefight took place in which one insurgent was captured and the rest shot dead.

It was a small but expensive victory: Major Cabinda of the UNITA liaison team and a UNITA orderly were killed, along with Lieutenant Gert van Zyl (one of the SADF's UNITA liaison officers) and Corporal Johan Louis Potgieter. Rifleman George Peter Boorsma and Lance Corporal Russell James wounded. Two Puma helicopters were immediately dispatched to the scene from Ionde, and at 17:58 evacuated the dead and wounded, the prisoner and the booty – AK-47 rifles, military rucksacks and an attaché case filled with documents.

Ariel Hugo later wrote a vivid account of the incident:

> We made contact with the enemy on the afternoon of 4 November 1981. When the first shots were fired the enemy instantly killed a UNITA major, his orderly and Lieutenant Gert van Zyl (who) were travelling on my Ratel (Call Sign Two-Two).

10 61 Mech archive – SAAF Report marked Top Secret: Summary of Air Force Participation in Operation Daisy.

> Gunner Peter Boorsma and Corporal J.L. ("Pottie") Potgieter immediately jumped off my Ratel.
>
> Peter Boorsma was seriously wounded in his legs in those critical first couple of seconds. This followed seconds after the three soldiers on my Ratel were killed. Boorsma was now pinned down 15 metres from his attackers. He came under intense AK-47 fire. Pottie dived forward to cover Boorsma, thereby saving Boorsma's life. With this heroic act Potgieter was killed – a single shot through the mouth.
>
> In those chaotic moments Rifleman C.P. Spangenberg (Rifleman Number 5 of Bravo Section) jumped up, ran forward and shot the insurgents where they lay hidden in their position. It happened at point-blank range under covering fire from my other platoon members. Corporal Potgieter was a brave man. He was our comrade, a friend and our cook of note in the platoon. We will remember him and all our other fallen.

For 61 Mech it was a moment of great sadness. In some armies and some wars casualties are taken in a commander's stride as a necessary cost of battle, but we were too close simply to shrug off our losses. There is a particular burden on a commander at such times. He is literally the master of life and death, and the loss of every man diminishes him. My only consolation was the courage shown by my soldiers. They were national servicemen, not long out of high school, and yet they had fought like seasoned professionals against a group of equally resolute enemies. So there was pride, too, to soothe my grief.

At about 17:00 Commandant Frans Botes reported from the southwest that 201 Battalion had come across an empty base and had seized a large quantity of abandoned enemy equipment. They had also taken a few casualties from mines, he added.

In the late afternoon we moved into an allround defensive position alongside the Caiundo rivulet. The battle we had prepared for had eluded us, but our work here was not done yet; next day we would have to mop up the target zone and do some exploitation – not at all a pleasant task, because we were sure that there were mines and booby traps everywhere, lying silently in wait to strike at the unwary and unfortunate.

I wondered what tomorrow held in store – for us, for 201 Battalion, for the paratroopers surrounding the target zone, even for the enemy. Obviously there was no answer to that question: What would happen would happen.

As I sat and pondered, our crews were getting on with the tasks at hand, carrying out last parades on their vehicles and equipment, while to one side the tiffies were busy as usual on some of the inevitable repairs that needed to be carried out, as cool and calm as if they were back in their shed at Omuthiya. We held a debriefing, shared our thoughts about the day's events and gave orders. Security measures were put in place and the mortars tasked to lay down harassing fire throughout the night.

We had settled in by the time the sun went down over 61 Mech and our comrades of 201 Battalion and 3 Parachute Battalion, invisible to us, 15–20 km to our west. With a few moments to spare at last, I allowed my thoughts to take over. What were my soldiers thinking about at the end of this day of frustration, gunshots and loss? Obviously it had been a severe rite of passage that would forever change their view of the world and probably of themselves as well. What had been the effect on the feelings and beliefs that are embedded in the deepest recesses of every man's mind?

Other thoughts flitted through my mind: For 61 Mech the operation had not resulted in a noteworthy operational gain – that is, if the enemy head count was really the prime criterion. We had attacked an old enemy base which clearly had been unoccupied for some time, thanks to the inaccurate intelligence about SWAPO's exact deployments that we had received during the planning phase and, in fact, right up to the moment we reached our forming-up place at Chitequeta.

I couldn't help wondering whether the operation had been compromised beforehand, and if so, to what extent. I knew that 61 Mech had not been detected by the enemy during our exhausting three-day easterly approach, a heartening thought. But had the enemy picked up 61 Mech's deployments prior to forming up?

What about the untimely contact by 201 Battalion and then their movement further northwards? Or Jeremy Wiley's unfortunate but unavoidable contact near Chitequeta on the morning of D-Day; or the problem-plagued airborne deployment, which must have been a dead giveaway? I was sure that all these indicators had been picked up and diligently reported to the PLAN HQ at Lubango.

I filed these dark thoughts away for future reference. These things had happened and could not be undone. We had done what we had been tasked to do, and had done so in the most professional way we could manage. Our young citizen-soldiers had performed extremely well. I had no regrets on that score.

So, back to business. We were not sitting fat and happy back at Omuthiya, slugging down a cold beer or two. We were on the ground deep inside Angola, in the middle of an operation, with large enemy forces on nearly all sides. Put the regrets aside for the time being, learn, absorb – and above all, stay focussed on the mission!

Phase 5: Mopping-Up and Area Operations from 5 until 8 November (D+1 until D+4)

5 November found 61 Mech mopping up the target area and planning our next move, a strike 35 km southwestwards towards Bambi as soon as possible. While thus occupied we received some cheering news. Further to the west the SAAF had hit Cahama very hard, flattening the radar installations, some fuel dumps and parts of the town. The SAAF had also flown some reconnaissance missions nearer to us, along the roads near Techamutete and Cassinga, and reported that nothing had been seen to get excited about.

By 09:00 Rod Penhall had established HAA 3 for us in a nearby shona at Chitequeta, close to our tactical HQ, and soon a huddle of gunships and Pumas was standing by to support our mopping-up operations and to assist with any casevacs and fire support, as required. Guarding these precious assets was Major Lourens Anderson ("Andy", inevitably, in the nickname-happy SADF), and his protection group. Neither Andy nor ourselves knew it, but he was about to feature in an act of derring-do which did not surprise anyone who was acquainted with this engaging character.

We experienced a few embarrassing moments after Major Leon Marais's combat team, which was operating to the southwest of Chitequeta, reported suspect vehicle movement to its southwest. This caused something of a stir: Would there be an opportunity to strike at either SWAPO or FAPLA?

On the other hand, we knew very well that elements of 201 Battalion were operating in that direction, and might be responsible for the movement Marais had reported. The problem was that we did not know exactly where they were, thanks to lapses in the accurate reporting of their positions and also the unreliable communications that had plagued us all along.

Rod Penhall requested the MAOT at Ionde to investigate, and some Mirages and

Impalas were duly scrambled. It turned out that the 61 Mech and 201 Battalion had been reporting each other's movements. Red faces at Chitequeta! But it was better to be safe than sorry, we consoled ourselves.

At one stage the SAAF sounded the alarm because it appeared that the FAPLA MiGs might be planning a strike on Chitequeta, something both General Geldenhuys and I had feared. It was an unpleasant prospect – our helicopters were particularly vulnerable to air attack, as were 61 Mech's 250-plus vehicles and their crews, even though they were widely dispersed as they roamed the target zone; and our anti-aircraft capability was poor.

But to our relief nothing came of it and no real air threat developed; the MiGs remained on the defensive to the west, north and the northeast of us. The FAPLA MiGs were scrambled on numerous occasions at Moçâmedes (Namibe), Lubango and Menongue, but apparently only for the defence of their airfields. However, the air activity would become more venturesome as the operation progressed ... We had, it seemed, kicked over a hornets' nest.

In the meantime Major "Tallies" Taljaard's sappers[11] were doing sterling (and extremely dangerous) work as part of the mopping up. There were bunkers and caches crammed with obsolete ammunition and mines all over the place, most of them protected by booby traps. Clearing all this away was hazardous, strenuous and time-consuming, since each bunker or cache had to be fine-combed with probing sticks and mine detectors, and the sappers were well aware that ammunition which had been improperly stored in hot conditions soon deteriorated and became extremely unstable. If ever there was a display of sheer cold guts – what Napoleon called "two o'clock in the morning courage" – this was it.

Another section of sappers had established a water point in a nearby shona and were purifying and collecting clean water for our 1,000-plus souls, and also for the three companies of paratroopers which were closing in on Chitequeta – almost 300 exhausted and extremely thirsty airborne soldiers.

At midday our activities were interrupted by another of those unforeseen and unforeseeable events that crop up so regularly during any operations, which also led to a display of awesome courage. Near the helicopters the sappers had parked a Buffel full of dangerously unstable old SWAPO ammunition that had been removed from the bunkers, and suddenly it caught fire, probably because of some or other chemical reaction. Rod Penhall immediately instructed the Puma and Alouette helicopters to move to safety. Meanwhile Major Andy Anderson casually walked over to the burning Buffel, climbed in, started it up and drove it away.

At a safe distance from the helicopters he stopped, climbed out and walked calmly away, not flinching or even looking back when the Buffel erupted in flames and black smoke behind him. The only casualties were three men who suffered slight injuries: Sergeant P.J. Slow, our intelligence clerk, and two paratroopers named J.J. Wood and A.L. Swart.

It was an almost unbelievable illustration of the cool courage shown by so many South African soldiers in all our country's wars, the personification of that line in our national anthem that "at thy call we shall not falter," and the memory of it remains vivid in my mind to this day.

It was my privilege to write the citation for Andy's Honoris Crux decoration for gallantry. To no one's surprise it was later approved and in due course he was decorated by

11 The field engineers from 25 Field Engineer Squadron.

the Chief of the Army in person. I might add that the burden of becoming a living legend lay lightly on Andy's shoulders; he remained the same unassuming and humorous character that he always had been.

I wish I could say that he went on to great things in the military, but in later years he was paralysed below the waist in a road accident and invalided out of the service. This did not totally cramp his style. Among other things he went on to fly microlight aircraft, and during the 1994 general election he played a crucially important role as a civilian monitoring coordinator at the main joint operations centre in Pretoria. Andy died prematurely a few months before this writing, but he left a simple legacy that I have never forgotten: Let nothing get you down.

Soon after this our ground forces reported an unidentified twin-engine aircraft flying high over the Daisy target area. Mirage F1s were scrambled to intercept it, but by the time they arrived the aircraft was long gone. The SAAF surmised that it could have been deployed either for electronic surveillance purposes or for the controlling other enemy aircraft in flight. It was just another little worry to add to all the others.

At approximately 13:00 a Puma brought General Lloyd, Brigadier Badenhorst and Commandant Anton van Graan from Ionde, the purpose of their visit being to plan the operation's future direction, which amounted to no more than the continuation of the area operation southwards and then the scheduled withdrawal to SWA/Namibia.

It was decided that at first light on 7 November 61 Mech would advance to Bambi – perhaps we would be in luck and find an occupied base there, although we were not really optimistic about our chances. Enemy remnants were expected to be on the move all over, fleeing the danger zone; in a nutshell, the battlefield had become completely fluid, and Military Intelligence still could not provide a coherent enemy picture.

Clearly, the enemy knew more about our whereabouts and moves than we did about theirs – we were relying purely on luck to bring us some fleeting opportunistic engagements. We all knew that using 61 Mech for area operations was like swiping at mosquitoes with a bludgeon. But that's how it was. So we would venture southwestwards, anyhow and hope for the best.

Mopping up continued late into the afternoon. At about 13:00 the enormously dangerous nature of the engineers' task was brought home again in tragic fashion when Candidate Officer S.F. Coetzee was killed by an exploding booby trap while clearing a bunker. Three others with him were wounded, one of them – Sapper N.M. Domoney – seriously. The dead and the wounded were immediately evacuated to Ionde in a Puma.

I spent a few precious minutes thinking about my brave sappers as the Puma scissored away to Ionde. One more life had been sacrificed in the struggle for South West Africa/Namibia's future. Coetzee had died clearing an abandoned base of derelict Soviet ammunition, but in practical terms he might as well have been killed during a contact; the Army is a machine with many components, each essential to the functioning of the others.

I knew that no matter how much ammunition we carried away with us, more would flow in from the Soviet Union to replace it. Were this day's death and wounds truly necessary? Who could share the thoughts of the one who stood in command ... those of their friends ... their loved ones, far away in South Africa, who would soon receive the heartbreaking, soul-wrenching news?

At 14:00 the three paratrooper companies who were sweeping towards us from the southeast reported that they had killed three insurgents. It was just one more indication that the enemy were scattered all around us.

At the close of the afternoon General Geldenhuys, General Lloyd, Brigadier Badenhorst and Commandant Van Graan lifted off for Ionde in their Puma, from where a Dakota took the two generals on to AFB Ondangwa. I felt good about having been privileged to share their pleasant and supportive company.

Captain Jeremy Wiley and his ex-SWAPO colleague also left us, rested now and clothed in the fresh combat dress we had given them. Before he left Wiley concluded that a number of the enemy, equipped with vehicles, out of immediate reach to the north, had escaped the net on D-Day. I could only sigh. Would we ever know what the true deployments of SWAPO were during those eventful days? One day I would ask them. Until then, best wishes until the next time, and meanwhile let's get on with the job at hand.

Now the sun set on 5 November, a long, eventful and tragic day. There was an evening debrief, and we settled down to another uncomfortably quiet night, camouflaged and dug in. Now, I knew, my soldiers were left to their own thoughts. We had now lost several good men, good friends. How do you describe to anyone what it is like to feel sporadic thrusts of sorrow and utter frustration at the same time? It stays buried to the hilt in your innermost being.

My thoughts were not all dark ones, though. I was very proud of my young men of 61 Mech as I lay there, listening to the sounds of approaching rest. I could hear the men's quiet sighs of relaxation and the subdued clatter as they settled down. I could hear the sighs of the Ratels, too, as their armour plate cooled down after their hot and arduous day, and they seemed almost human. I knew that in spite of everything, high confidence and self-esteem still prevailed among my soldiery as they lay in their shallow shell scrapes all around me.

You sleep differently in the bush, especially on operations: less deeply, your instincts alert, even if you don't realise it, ready to shake you awake and propel you into action in the blink of an eye. Countering alienation and anxiety is enhanced by creating safe spaces and assurance for your people inside the surrounding darkness. This is a physical as well as a mental phenomenon.

I had marvelled at its encouraging effects under similar experiences in the past. At the heart of it lay close camaraderie and sound morale from which stems confidence and cohesion. I knew that our evening debriefs, filtered down to grassroots level, made life easier and strengthened confidence. Focussing yourself and others on the positives broke through the hindrances and the negatives. You had always to search for forward ground, either physically or mentally.

A gentle day dawned on 6 November. The mopping up and area search continued, uneventfully this time, praises be. There was time for planning and issuing new operations orders all the way down the line, and some serious equipment maintenance. The tiffies and vehicle crews lurked camouflaged among the trees, preoccupied as usual with the necessary upkeep and repairs, and the Alpha Echelon was engaged in the administrative war, having joined us from HAA 2. I watched and listened to the soldiers' usual jostling and jesting with one another; it was good to see and hear, because it meant that their morale was as solid and unwavering as ever. "Keep on keeping on", that was the motto.

Only two events stirred our interest. The first was when some of our troops doing ground searches came across six decomposing SWAPO dead, the ghastly fruit of that D-Day air attack. The second occurred far out of sight but nevertheless aroused considerable excitement. Two Mirage F1CZs piloted by Major Johan Rankin and his wingman,

Lieutenant Johan du Plessis, had tangled with the enemy in the Cahama-Lubango area in the west, and Rankin had shot a MiG-21 down in flames. It was the first enemy aircraft to be shot down by the SAAF since the Korean War in the early 1950s.

What made Rankin's exploit even sweeter for us was that it did something to counter the ominous signs that the FAPLA Air Force was becoming more active in southern Angola, something which did not bode well for future external operations. We instantly became much more focussed on passive air defence measures. Captain Carl Lindsey, commander of our anti-aircraft troop,[12] kept himself and his men on perpetual high alert. Fortunately, we never encountered any hostile aircraft during Daisy, and Lindsay (probably to his frustration) had nothing to shoot at with his hand-laid 20 mm guns and SA-7 missiles.

Our artillerymen seemed to be on high alert as well, so much so that some of them reported that they had spotted a small number of MiG-21s roaming around, although it is possible that what they saw were our Mirages. I certainly never saw any MiGs, and frankly, it was only during Operation Modular[13] in October–December 1987 that I would come to fully appreciate the wrath of the MiG-21s – that was really high-intensity conventional warfare.[14]

During the day a company of 32 Battalion further to our south made contact with SWAPO insurgents 15 km northwest of Ionde. They swooped in by Puma helicopters supported by Alouette gunships. Pertinent question: Was our enemy fleeing southwards from Chitequeta?

The Mirages and Impalas flew more reconnaissance missions in the Techamutete-Bambi area, but failed to locate enemy vehicle movements, and at various times during the day Bosbok missions were flown to support the area operations being conducted by 201 Battalion, the paratroopers and ourselves in the target area.

Then our time at Chitequeta was up, and at first light on 7 November 61 Mech struck 35 km southwestwards towards Bambi. We did not really expect to run into serious, if any, enemy resistance, but our approach was always to prepare and act as if you were going to attack a first-class enemy.

So we moved as if we expected an imminent full-scale fight, with ground attack aircraft and helicopters standing by to support us if a contact eventuated. This package deal had been carefully put together by our air support officer, Major Rod Penhall, who was a good Air Force man but by now had become an integral part of 61 Mech as well.

The terrain we were moving through was exotic, lush undergrowth and gigantic trees of which some we estimated at more than 60 metres high. It was a beautiful landscape, spoiled by some not-so-beautiful reminders of the business at hand. Every so often we spotted deserted trenches and foxholes; we dodged tracks and defiles and kept our eyes peeled for enemy mines and ambushes.

The move went swiftly and smoothly. We were getting quite good at this, we started to feel. It was getting to be second nature, just about. But we were due to be shaken out of our nonchalance. We were conscious of a strange alien atmosphere at our vanguard as we came in from the northeast and entered the fringes of where we thought the enemy base at Bambi was located, Koos Liebenberg's Combat Team 2 scouting ahead.

What we found, though, was another deserted enemy base; the story of Chitequeta

12 20 mm Ystervark anti-aircraft system and shoulder-launched Russian SAM-7 (Strela).

13 See Chapter 15.

14 See Chapter 15.

all over again – semi-depleted bunkers, caches and foxholes everywhere. SWAPO had also been thoughtful enough to leave us a parting gift, although we did not know it till two of Liebenberg's Ratels were blown up within 15 minutes of our arrival. We were to discover that there were anti-vehicle and anti-personnel mines everywhere, as well as booby traps.

Soldiers are strange beings even under the most unpleasant of circumstances, and the sight of Combat Team 2 being waylaid by SWAPO's unwelcome presents evoked some heartless amusement among the other subunit commanders and Sergeant-major Du Plessis – possibly less exuberant in the case of Duppie, seeing that obviously there was going to be some heavy work for his tiffies. Fortunately, when the combat team emerged from the resultant cloud of dust, black smoke and cordite it became clear that the only wound suffered had been to Liebenberg's self-esteem. From personal experience I knew how it felt, and my heart was with Koos and his men.

Then soon afterwards one of the diesel bunkers ran over a third landmine. Once again there were no casualties, although the driver was painfully deaf for a while. Judging by his smile, however, I gathered that this was something he could live with, considering the alternative.

Bambi was a waste of time, with very little to be found except the damned mines, so the air support was stood down with the exception of two Alouette gunships, which remained on standby throughout the day while we commenced with area operations in its surroundings, as planned.

A number of 61 Mech patrols searched the area along the Bambi River, and at about 13:00 some cooking fires, still warm, were found nearby. A Gaz truck was also located in the area, and our two Alouettes machine-gunned it, but when the patrols closed in they found it had already been abandoned. Was this the remnant of a reconnaissance effort, or what? The ground forces found more abandoned SWAPO bases as they started searching the area.

The Gaz incident gave rise to an illuminating signal from Rod Penhall to the MAOT which describes the circumstances and terrain very well:

> From ASO Alpha to MAOT ZULU: Top Secret/Int 013 Nov 81. Mission 351 2 x Alo; Close Air Support; 0712h00 to 0713h30: Flew from HAA 3 (61 Mech's previous position at Chitequeta) to area south of Bloody Mary (Bambi River); saw big empty camp at XN 240 820. It is about 2–3 km in diameter and could house 400 to 500 people.
>
> Another empty base was swept by the army (61 Mech) at XN 30 88. There are lots of huts in the base, but no trenches or bunkers were seen by the Alo crews. Fresh vehicle tracks leading to the northwest, west and north from that base. At XP 190 280 the A/C shot at a Gaz vehicle. Ground forces did a follow-up and found the vehicle. No anti-aircraft positions were seen and no fire was drawn during the sortie. Small buildings were observed at Bambi XN 23 87.
>
> General ... There is lots of water (even in pools) around XN 30 88. The whole area 10–15 km and south of the Bambi River between XN 40 90 and XN 17 83 is full of small bases, vehicle tracks and mielie lands.

More air reconnaissance missions were flown by the SAAF in the vicinity of Bambi and Cuvelai at various times during the day; the enemy's MiGs were extremely active slightly to the north of Cassinga, only 45–60 km away. The SAAF believed there was a possibility that they would attack the ground forces at any moment, and Colonel Ollie Holmes placed Mirages on hold over Cuvelai to counter them if they made their appearance. Down on the ground, we kept a close vigil on the skies as well.

It became clear that however much we had disrupted their activities, the insurgents had not merely gone to ground: Military intelligence informed us that they had intercepted an enemy radio message in which SWAPO had been tasked to capture one of the SADF soldiers operating in the Bambi-Chitequeta area.

Then at about 15:00, Frans Botes and 201 Battalion started sweeping southwards from their previous cut-off position. Almost immediately they sent back an intelligence report about enemy activity close to them, saying that the insurgents were laying mines among their dispersed vehicle columns as they started moving. This was definitely too close for comfort, and two gunships were scrambled to investigate, but had nothing substantial to report.

We found that we were quite literally trapped at Bambi by the unmarked enemy landmines and booby traps. We sat stranded for the moment with the damaged tanker and two Ratels, eloquent reminders that death and destruction lurked wherever we walked, stepped or drove, which we did with extreme care; all in all it was an unnerving experience.

That afternoon we laid out our defences with the greatest care; interlocking arcs of fire all around and a meticulous fire plan for the 120 mm and 81 mm mortars, so that we would be ready for anything that might come our way – which it did, albeit more or less by accident.

Andy Anderson and I spent some time walking about as dusk set in, visiting some of the troops: Only one of our patrols was still outside the perimeter, protecting some sappers who were filling a few water bowsers at a waterhole about 500 metres to our west-northwest.

Everything was tranquil. "Tools, entrenching" clanged pleasantly as the troops dug in next to their vehicles, while others brewed coffee and prepared meals from their 24-hour ration packs, so that a pleasant smell of hot food and smouldering Esbit fuel tablets spiced the cooling air. I looked them over: Haggard, covered in dirt ... but smiling. That was what I saw. That was good; it meant their tails were still up.

We got back to the HQ vehicles as the dusk slid softly into darkness. Tonight, I thought, tonight we'll all catch up on some seriously deserved shuteye. We found Cassie Schoeman dispensing some lukewarm whisky he had hidden away for the right moment. A tot gurgled agreeably into my tin mug, and I leaned back comfortably with my elbow against the side of our Ratel while Cassie measured out much appreciated slugs for our crew as well. No doubt they wondered how a mere officer had managed to conceal a bottle of booze from his wide-awake troops.

Peace settled over Bambi. I relaxed on my "camp chair, canvas, nutria, with metal frame, folding, Mark 1." Then without any warning we were suddenly treated to a healthy display of fireworks coming out of the darkness to our north. Volleys of AK-47 tracer ripped over us ... crack, thump ... crack, thump ... crack, thump ... My immediate thought was for our lone patrol at the water bowsers a few hundred metres away, outside our defences. I forgot about my whisky and told Cassie to get them on the radio and report back ASAP.

We discovered later that a SWAPO group had accidentally walked into our northern flank and challenged the patrol with a password which (so we were told) sounded very much like "Vietnam." When they failed to get a satisfactory reply they opened fire, which any defence consultant in his right mind would have advised them not to do.

Koos Liebenberg made that clear right away with a single order: "On my command, fire-belt action." This was the signal to create a small hell on earth. A cocktail of small-arms fire and 20 mm and 90 mm rounds, with a few 81 mm mortar bombs added, chewed up the source of the AK-47 bullets. No doubt the enemy operators enjoyed a few moments of surprise at this swift, strong reaction before they departed for the hereafter and allowed me to return to drinking my whisky.

Overkill, I grant you, but what the hell, we had plenty of ammunition which would have been used for attacking Chitequeta – not to mention Bambi – and Combat Team 2 enjoyed the long-awaited opportunity to fire their weapons and exact some payback for their two mine-crippled Ratels. After this, we presumed, it would be a case of "all quiet on the northern front" more or less, and so it was.

Later we listened to my dialogue with Liebenberg, which had gone out over the radio and been taped by Tannie Pompie at her radio relay station at Tsintsabis, and I was surprised at how matter-of-factly we sounded – you would have thought we were on the telephone, organising a game of cards with some friends:

"Two Zero, this is Zero, Can you determine what is happening on your front ... ?" "This is Two Zero ... yes, but we're also somewhat concerned about the patrol at the water hole ... A fire-belt action should do the thing ... Two Zero: Do you need some mortar fire to the rear of the enemy position ... ? Roger, out ... "

If this had been a scene in a war movie, I think a lot of viewers would have regarded it as being a bit too much of the proverbial stiff upper lip to be accurate. The fact was, of course, that we had rehearsed this sort of contingency measure so thoroughly that it had become like second nature to us.

Since we could not see further than about 50 metres through the bush and the darkness, we did not investigate until the next morning. Then we found several dead insurgents, one of whom had apparently placed his AK-47s muzzle against his throat and killed himself. Whether this was so or not, it was enough to convince some of our troops that 61 Mech was able not only to drive the enemy insane, but to give them a death wish as well.

We spent two more days at Bambi, combing the area, while the tiffies worked industriously at maintenance and repairs, especially on the two mined Ratels and the damaged tanker. They worked around the clock and by morning after our arrival we were mobile again, with the exception of the Ratels, each of which needed a new axle.

We started to frame detailed plans for our extrication from Bambi's mine-infested precincts, determined to depart its unwelcome environs without suffering any more losses as soon as we were told to move. 8 November was a quiet day for 61 Mech (well, actually, for Operation Daisy as a whole).

At 04:00 the SAAF carried out a successful and particularly welcome supply drop in the area of HAA 3 at Chitequeta, 35 km away, where our Alpha Echelon and their protection group were waiting with open arms. Then at 05:00 another drop was made, this time further south to 201 Battalion, which detonated another mine as it patrolled steadily down the line of the Caiundo River.

Major Penhall had requested the SAAF to fly an interdiction and air reconnaissance mission from Ondangwa over Bambi and the roads linking Cassinga-Techamutete-Cuvelai, which it did, only to report that no enemy vehicle movement whatever could be detected. We stayed put, cocked and locked, but there were no incidents.

Phase 6: The Southwards Move from 9 to 18 November (D+5 until D+15)

9 November was a noteworthy day for Operation Daisy. An insurgent base had been located to the north of Ionde (the position XN 600 700 was recorded in a mission report from the Air Force), and a helicopter-borne assault operation got under way as rapidly as possible.

At approximately 10:20 a command Alouette and four gunships were airborne, flying a reconnaissance mission up-river in the direction of the suspected enemy position, and by 10:30 a Bosbok light aircraft from Ionde was also in the air to search the suspect area. Neither the helicopters nor the Bosbok spotted anything, and four Pumas full of paratroopers who arrived at 10:42 also drew a blank.

The Pumas returned to Ionde, and at 13:12 the four gunships landed at our HAA to refuel before heading for Ionde as well. On the way there, however, they spotted a group of about 20 insurgents at XN 600 700, near the original suspect target area at XN 600 700. When this was reported back to Rod Penhall, he called MAOT Zulu (the one at Ionde) and asked that the Pumas immediately bring the paratroopers back to the original position.

At 13:35 the Pumas were on their way again, with four Alouette gunships for fire support. This time there was a contact with what turned out to be a group of about 40 insurgents. A sharp action followed in which 24 insurgents were killed and five wounded and captured. It transpired that they were all from Bravo Battalion and had been fleeing southwards after the attack on Chitequeta on D-Day.

They were not the only ones. There were now clear signs that several enemy groups were fleeing southwards because of our activities and those of 201 Battalion, and this became the nature of the gallivanting game: Loose fighting all over the place with small enemy clusters.

The SAAF jets kept on flying interdiction and aerial reconnaissance missions as far north as Techamutete and even up to the railway line leading to Jamba and Donga. Each time they were warned that the enemy's MiGs were active to their north, although nothing ever came of it.

10 November found 61 Mech moving steadily southwards at last after the echelon had joined up with us from Chitequeta with the aid of two Bosboks to support the link-up. Around noon the terrain struck its own blow while we were bundu-bashing through (surprise, surprise) dense bush, when a large tree toppled over on to one of our Ratels and crashed down on the head of one of our soldiers which was protruding from the turret.

Our medical doctor immediately attended to the soldier's injuries and reported that his condition was extremely serious; we came to an abrupt halt and quickly prepared a helicopter landing zone in the thick bush, and he was soon bound for Ionde in an Alouette escorted by two gunships.

At 16:30 two Super Frelon helicopters arrived from AFB Ondangwa (via a stop at Ionde for refuelling) with the two axles we needed to get our mine victims moving under their own steam again; the axles were offloaded at great speed and the tiffies got to work with equal swiftness, so that within an hour the Ratels were combat ready once more.

At the same time the Ionde Pumas trooped 23 Special Forces operators into the Daisy target area to leave a few surprises of our own for the enemy by laying mines at Chitequeta and on all the roads and tracks leading towards the Daisy target area, the idea being to make it difficult for the insurgents to return to their old haunts. One bad turn deserves another, as one might say.

Then at 22:00, soon after we had laagered for the night, a C-130 made a successful low-level supply drop whose goodies included much-needed technical supplies that had been requested by our technical staff officer, Captain Jakkals Jaeckel, and our chief loggie, Giel Reinecke. Major Penhall expressed our appreciation to the SAAF.

As we continued southwards the next day we had a surprise encounter with the legendary 32 Battalion scout, Captain Willem Ratte. Unlike the rest of us, Ratte was moving northwards up the dry floodplain of the Mulola with his trusty platoon of ex-Angolan rebels in four Buffel MPVs, on a mission which we didn't waste time asking about. The consensus was that Ratte was probably on his way to take on the rest of SWAPO's army on his own.

61 Mech eventually swung eastwards and on the way to Mupa rendezvoused with a massive convoy of closely guarded diesel bunkers from 5 Maintenance Unit which replenished our almost depleted diesel reserves. Having delivered their most welcome load, they set off on their long journey back to Oshakati, while we moved on to Mupa itself.

We arrived there on 15 November and moved into a laager in one of the folds of the Cuvelai River. Our immediate necessities now were to allow the troops some hard-earned rest, to replenish and to carry out urgent repairs to our equipment. It was a short but extremely pleasant respite, with abundant fresh water pumped out of the Cuvelai by the sappers for drinking, washing clothes and scrubbing away layers of accumulated dirt.

Most of all, it was a break from the endless jolting through untamed bush that had been our lot since leaving Omuthiya. Our rule was never to be stationary for more than two or three days at a time if it could possibly be avoided, but there is a time and place for everything.

The first evening at Mupa brought a treat we had not enjoyed since setting out on Operation Daisy, when Rod Penhall, Thys Rall and Giel Reinecke arranged for the SAAF to drop some fresh rations, as well as some spares and consumables for the vehicles; the drop zone they selected was in an open area near a village close to our laager.

Midnight came and went, and then we could hear the pleasant drone of the C-130s coming in low from the east in the direction of our winking fireflies. The drop was slightly off target, and so the large cargo parachutes deployed, floated down to earth and fell with a series of explosively loud thuds in the village itself; by the grace of God none of the heavy pallets flattened any of the huts or their occupants.

The troops appeared silently out of the night, grabbed their booty and disappeared equally silently into the darkness again. Sometimes when I lie awake at night I can't help smiling when I wonder what the hell those innocent civilians thought about the whole surreal happening. About the only downside to the whole thing was that in a moment of mental aberration the SAAFs air supply unit had packed the boxes of Windhoek Lager underneath a batch of spare Buffel wheels, so that some of our beers got flattened – war is hell, after all.

On 16 November Operation Daisy began to wither on the vine, to coin a phrase. The paratroopers were flown back to Ondangwa in several Dakota shuttles and the Tac HQ and MAOT at Ionde began closing down. Meanwhile we loitered quietly at Mupa. The troops were resting and at the same time languidly cleaning, repairing and maintaining their vehicles and equipment. There was a comfortable atmosphere in the laager.

Two of us, however – Giel Reinecke and Jakkals Jaeckel – were not resting on their laurels. Instead they were planning a pre-emptive attack of their own. For the first time we could make a proper assessment of the damage the bundu-bashing and general operational exposure had inflicted, and it was clear that all our equipment, especially the soft-skinned vehicles, had taken a severe hammering. They anticipated, with some reason, that those in logistical authority would demand an icy "explain, please" about why we were returning with such a sorry collection of wrecks even though we had not seen hard fighting.

Giel launched his attack by asking me to convene a board of inquiry and initiated the immediate taking of statements; another investigation on the side was set up to generate recommendations on the hardening of logistics vehicles and the improvement of our bush-breaking capabilities in general. The administration of the inquiry was to be completed before we left Ondjiva on 19 November, as planned, and the record of the inquiry as well as the recommendations would be sent up the chain of command as soon as we got back to SWA/Namibia (it worked, incidentally – there were no repercussions).

At first, though, it appeared that Daisy still had some life left. Oshakati radioed that according to fresh intelligence it had received, SWAPO's Northeastern Front and Northern Front headquarters were thought to be in the vicinity of Mupa – more specifically, at grid references WM 825 475 (Handa) and WM 819 900; Frans Botes and I were to plan a combined attack on their alleged position.

Frans and I made our arrangements by radio and stood by, ready to move immediately, while we waited for the information to be confirmed. I couldn't help thinking to myself: Has Military Intelligence concocted yet another fable? Or can we believe them this time? Only one thing was certain: The mission always came first!

So while everyone except Reinecke and Jaeckel relaxed, my command group was poring over maps again, assessing the situation and planning contingencies for an attack on 17 November, while Frans sent out reconnaissance teams to search for our elusive enemy and establish the exact locations of the headquarters, if they were there at all. We also requested that the SAAF keep some assets on standby at Dova in the event of an attack – one Alouette transport helicopter, three gunships and two Pumas – and likewise the Impalas and one Bosbok at Ondangwa.

But the attack came to nothing. The 201 Battalion recce teams reported that the enemy had withdrawn the previous day; once again we had missed the wily enemy by a hair's breadth. Apparently the insurgents had been tipped off by some local inhabitants, who had seen the recce elements scouting out the enemy's position. Reconnaissance sweeps by the Alouette helicopters over the alleged target areas were equally futile. It was yet another huge disappointment.

Our attempt at pre-emptive action was not necessarily the only reason why the insurgents had decamped – to us mere mortals on the scene it seemed that SWAPO was not truly keen on meeting up with us at the present time, and were legging it to any place except where we were. I might add that although such evasion was obviously their prerogative, it was damn infuriating to us. It was like looking for a needle in a haystack with a mailed fist, if you will permit me to mix my metaphors.

While at Mupa I visited the large and well-kept Roman Catholic Church, which looked almost like a small cathedral from the outside. There I met an elderly Portuguese gentleman named Quental who was married to a woman of the area's Kwanyama tribe and lived in a local village. He had devoted his life to looking after the church and showed me around it with glowing pride.

Mupa was not a rich area and the church's interior was bare by the standards of the big cities. Its only source of music at services was a small, ancient pedal organ which I recognised immediately, because in times past there had been many a "traporrel" like this one in isolated South African farmhouses. Sure enough, this one had come to Angola with the South African "Dorsland Trekkers" of the late 19th Century.

I didn't know it, but Mr. Quental and his precious traporrel were to pop up in my life again. More of that later.

By 17 November Operation Daisy was nearing its natural conclusion. For us this meant that the bludgeon would be going home to reflect about the way it had – literally – beaten about the Angolan bush. Sector 10's counterinsurgency tactics, and the tactics used in Operation Daisy, clearly required some serious reconsideration and reinvention. That we would be back at some stage was a certainty. All we didn't know was how, why, where and when. In the meantime our maxim, as always, remained "always search for forward ground".

On 18 November 61 Mech marched out of Mupa, bound for Ondjiva and then Omuthiya. Our mission now was simply to withdraw the ground forces to safety. On the way, however, Sector 10 informed me that yet another suspected enemy base was located close by – about three kilometres to the west of the Mupa-Evale road.

I took this with a pinch of salt, but we went quickly into an allround mutually supporting open laager alongside the road. This done, I sent out a small reconnaissance party under the leadership of a mischievous young paratrooper, Lieutenant Jan Viljoen (one of General Constand Viljoen's sons), to investigate. He soon returned with the news that there was a base, but its occupants were long gone. On the other hand, Viljoen's excursion had not been totally fruitless, since he came back at the wheel of a large, brand new red Scania truck the insurgents had left behind.

The Scania went southwards with us. We did not envisage any problems at the border, since one advantage of a war is that customs officials and other troublesome people of that ilk are usually conspicuous by their absence. The only potential fly in the ointment was Brigadier Badenhorst, who had a penchant for laying hands on liberated items of this kind and enlisting them in Sector 10's service. So we told nobody about the Scania, and subsequently it was put to good use at Omuthiya.

As we headed southwards I received an urgent radio call from Frans Botes of 201 Battalion: "Roland, please, we ran out of oil filters for our Buffels – do you have some spare for me?" I saw a gap worth taking. We had enough oil filters but were suffering from a drastic shortage of toilet paper. I had earlier made a pointed remark about this to Giel Reinecke, who had silenced me by replying that the reason for the shortage was that the advance party had used up most of his supplies while marking our approach route on the night of D-1/D-Day (moral: Never fight a loggie on ground of his choice. He will bludgeon you to death with indents and inventories every time).

In any case, we rendezvoused with 201 Battalion close to Evale and I swopped some of my spare oil filters for a number of rolls of white gold. The lesson to be learned from this is that you must never get caught in the bush without enough toilet paper or oil filters – you might find yourself involved in some dirty business.

Hugging the bushline, we made our way via Evale and Anhanca to Ondjiva, where we laagered near the airfield for the night. It was a comfortable feeling. We were still 245 km away from Omuthiya, but there would be a stopover at Ondangwa, and we would be able to patronise Portuguese café owner Tony Banana's establishment and buy russians and chips. For those who don't know, "russians" were a specific type of spicy beef sausage with which generations of Border troopies liked to stuff themselves. Why "russians?" That is yet another great military mystery. Incidentally, they are not to be confused with "Ovambos", a species of tinned pork sausage issued by the SADF.

Phase 7: Withdrawal of the Combat Force to SWA on 19 November (D+15)

On 19 November 61 Mech found its way south from Ondjiva via Santa Clara and Ondangwa to Omuthiya. Homeward bound, it was plain sailing all the way because this time we were travelling by road. By the 20th we were back at Omuthiya. I did not know then that 61 Mech would soon find its way back to southern Angola – somewhat hastily, I might add – when Sector 10 launched Operation Makro on 29 December 1981.[15]

In a sense, Operation Daisy did not end for me until a day after our return, when I happened to be walking past Padre Koos Rossouw's tent while he was conducting a service. There was nothing unusual about this, except that the melodious commotion included an element that I had not heard at Omuthiya before. I went to investigate and, much to my surprise, found Koos and some of his congregants banging happily away on an old pedal organ which bore an uncanny resemblance to the one Mr. Quental had shown me in Mupa's church.

I carried out an interrogation for information of primary tactical importance, as we say in the Army, and found that in fact this was Mr. Quental's "traporrel". I pressed on, and the pious congregation and its shepherd then admitted that the tiffies had laid reverent but unauthorised hands on the venerable instrument before we left Mupa and brought it back in one of the trucks, totally unbeknown either to me or to my military police. I was solemnly informed that the tiffies had considered this the righteous thing to do.

I was furious, but maintained my composure, as all good commanders sometimes do, and closed my gaping mouth so that I would not use the words I was tempted to use in the presence of my preacher, of whom I was very fond.

Next day, while I was considering what to do, I received a call from Brigadier Badenhorst, whose near-real-time intelligence of what was going on at our units and in Angola verged on the uncanny (how he didn't find out about Jan Viljoen's looted Scania I don't know). I assured him that the matter was being rectified, and the organ was promptly flown back to Mupa in a Puma, together with a set of gilded chalices which had also surfaced at Omuthiya.

There is an ending to this odd tale. In October 2011 I found myself back at Mupa while on a battlefield tour with some veterans of 61 Mech and 32 Battalion, and I met a nun called Sister Eria with whom I had a wonderful discussion about bygone days. She told our little group that Mr. Quental had since passed on, but she knew about the pedal organ. It had been used until it had finally become unserviceable, and had then been replaced by another old "traporrel". Question: How many of the things have they got squirreled away in Angola?

Closure – Sharing Thoughts on Camaraderie

Daisy could have been the perfect operation. For all practical purposes the plan was nearly without flaws, except that (as we realised early on) our tactical intelligence was not up to scratch.

From an SADF perspective Daisy had all the required ingredients needed to strike at the enemy. We understood that the finding and fixing of our wily foe were the weak parts. We fully realised that the quest for accurate tactical intelligence was a major challenge

15 See Chapter 14.

which would remain so for the foreseeable future. Real-time and near-real-time tactical intelligence were not readily available to us most of the time, partly because of the difficult terrain in which we were fighting. All these elements we understood and did our best to deal with tactics wise.

But when we added to this mix the elusiveness factor so typical of counter-revolutionary warfare, the unpredictability of people, inconsistent politics and wavering grand strategies, it became clear that we were dealing with more than just a marginal neglect of tactical intelligence. We were also faced with a lack of strategic intelligence, which would bite the SADF in the backside in 1987–88 during the high-intensity conventional operations we fought at the end of the war.

The signs were there, particularly the hostile air environment. The war was escalating rapidly, with the enemy's Russian-built MiG-21s roaming and probing the skies ever further southwards. The enemy's radar screens and anti-aircraft systems were gradually encircling and stifling the Area-In-Dispute. The SAAFs Mirages were growing older by the minute, while the enemy's ring of fire swelled with reinforcements. And clearly it would not remain at that level.

The Operation Daisy debrief was held on 25 November at HQ Sector 10 at Oshakati.[16] Army HQ submitted a supplementary report, of which the final paragraph apologised that it had been submitted so late. The report contained one important lesson for 61 Mech and the Army, dealing with deliberate planning and the ability to move a large mechanised force stealthily into and out of Angola:

"From enemy radio messages intercepted," it said, "it was clear that the initial approach by 61 Mech from the border to their forming-up place was never observed by the enemy. This could be attributed to their choice of a far easterly approach. The main attack by 61 Mech was realistic and went according to plan."

The following four important lessons were officially recorded:

- Intelligence was noted as the root cause of the Daisy dilemma, euphemistically stated. It was proposed by the Army's Chief of Staff Operations that better use should be made in future of local inhabitants as sources of intelligence. It was also suggested that the patrolling effort in southern Angola and the domination of no-man's land should be increased. Better use should also be made in future of UNITA as a source for information. The glaring predicament concerning intelligence was left at that.
- Clearly, in future, the employment of 61 Mech as a main strike force against an insurgent target should be reconsidered. The problem was rooted in the final noisy minute-by-minute approach. No sensible insurgent was going to wait for a menacing 61 Mech and circling gunships to appear on the scene. Those days were past.
- The future role of 61 Mech for employment in area type operations also required reconsideration. The status quo represented a true wastage of a mechanised unit's combat potential and its vitality. More suitable employment opportunities needed

16 The meeting was chaired by Commandant Anton van Graan and the minutes signed by Brigadier Witkop Badenhorst, the officer commanding Sector 10; under reference Sector 10/309/1/ Operation Daisy, dated 1 December 1981. Evaluation of the tactics for cross border operations were furthermore recorded in an official document submitted by Chief of the Army: C Army/D Ops/309/1/Ops Daisy, dated 30 January 1982; signed by Brigadier B.A. Ferreira, Director of Army Operations.

to be found.

- Logistical vehicles were currently not suited for this type of mobile operation and impeded the mobility of mechanised forces in the dense bush (something good came from this observation – logistical vehicles were soon to be appropriately hardened and equipped for bush-breaking capabilities. Full marks to Major Giel Reinecke and Captain Jakkals Jaeckel, who proposed some of these recommendations).

Looking at the strategic level of war for a moment: How far north of the northern border of SWA did the SADF want to drive FAPLA and SWAPO? What was Pretoria thinking and concocting ... likewise Moscow ... and Havana ... and Luanda? Was Operation Daisy another match that lit a bushfire?

Operation Protea had pushed FAPLA and the key operational bases of SWAPO to the outward fringes of the Area-In-Dispute.[17] Before the enemy could consolidate, the next deep operation was upon them, with umpteen mechanised and airborne forces and fighter jets. The physical battle line had now shifted much further northwards; right up to the Namibe-Menongue railway line. Once again the enemy insurgents had scattered all over into the sanctuary of the surrounding bush.

FAPLA still refrained from fighting back, even preventing their air force from intervening with the ongoing ground and air actions of the SADF in the contested area. But I had learned early in life that if you push people and organisations, even armies, they are going to push back at some stage; the observable fact of cause and effect. For that matter, Sun Tzu had said as long ago as 500 B.C.: "Never press a desperate foe too hard; always leave an outlet free!" How far was far enough? How long would FAPLA, the Russians and Cubans remain content with the SADF's occupation of the Area-In-Dispute? How long would we remain content if we had been in their shoes? How was the enemy going to counter us?

The military strategy of keeping FAPLA at bay and making life miserable for SWAPO in the Area-In-Dispute through counterinsurgency operations was a fine one while it lasted. The simultaneous actions on the diplomatic and political fronts, however, left much to be desired. Were the signs not clear that the war was escalating rapidly as more and more modern Russian military hardware and Cuban forces steadily made their way to the war zone? What was going to give, where, when and how? The enemy's ring of steel to the north of SWA was strengthening. The situation was about to become a pressure cooker!

The SADF was to enjoy a short period of potent domination in southern Angola for a little while longer. Gallivanting security forces were shrouded in false security as the political hoo-ha continued. What was needed was to "unbundle" the threatening political-military situation and then reassemble it – to find out what the hell was truly going on.

With the exception of Operation Askari and, to a lesser extent, Operation Meebos, large-scale external operations became a phenomenon of the past for the time being. The glory days were replaced by a myriad of smaller scale counterinsurgency and covert operations.

The latter remained mere exercises with bloodshed and a treading of water until the war was driven to its cusp by May–August 1988.[18] This would suddenly find a few politicians painted into a corner on both sides of the wall. What remained as the war gradually

17 See Map 5.
18 See Chapter 16.

escalated were shades of political mediocrity and military patchiness. Let us wait and see.

Back to basics: Collectively our young commanders and troops had learned a great deal and had done well at the tactical level. The learning applied especially to the skill needed for planning and executing a large-scale operation deep inside Angola at battle group level, and included the art of manoeuvring in dense bush during both day and night, and the organising of the logistical support and maintenance such a large force required far away from its home base.

I was extremely satisfied with the commitment of our men to the mission, many of them young national servicemen. All of their operational experience and exposure contributed to the overall tactical prowess of the South African combat forces and support services. In this regard Daisy was a sound investment for future warfare in the demanding milieu of the African battle space. Together, as a fighting team, we had learned and we had shared responsibility and some danger.

61 Mech was developing into a fighting force second to none. To this day I can see the young smiling faces in my mind's eye. They were my men. Our young sons were warriors – it was in their make-up.

And thus ended a long and arduous military journey.

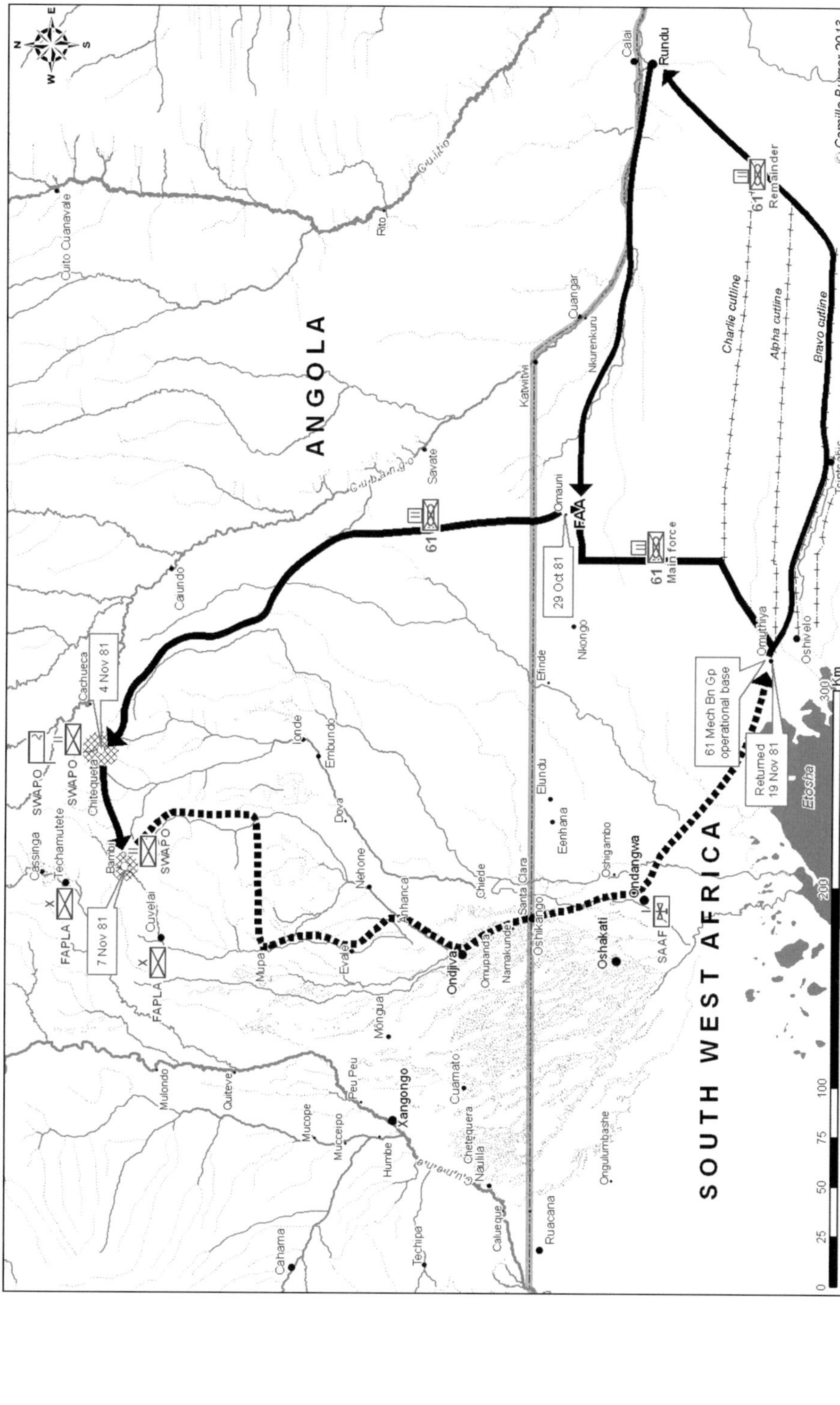

Map 11: Operation Daisy, October to November 1981 – Overview

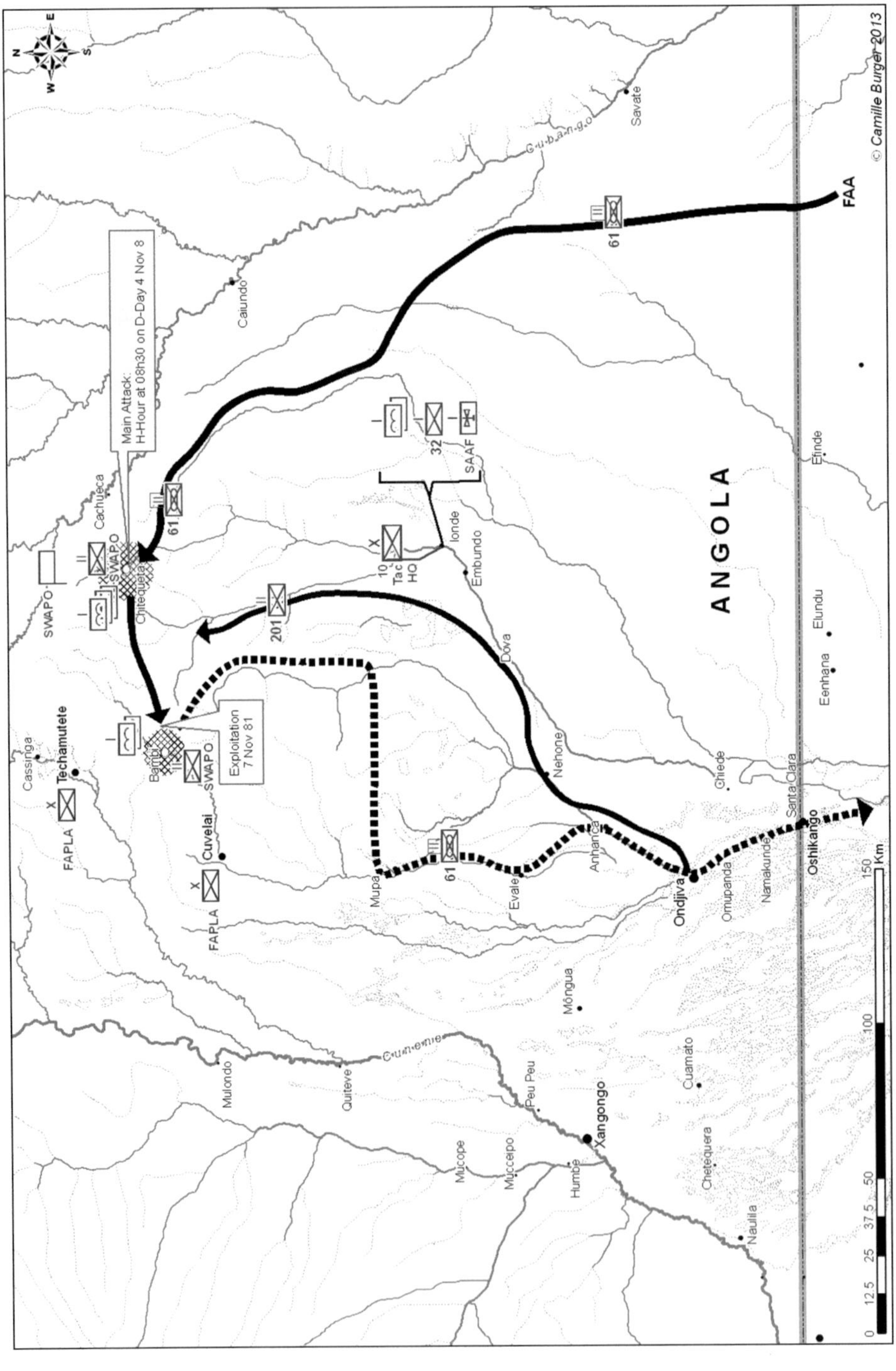

Map 12: Operation Daisy, October to November 1981 – Target Zone

14

High Readiness

Operations Makro and Meebos

Rapidity is the essence of war; take advantage of the enemy's lack of readiness, make your way by unexpected routes, and attack unguarded spots.
Sun Tzu - The Art of War (500 B.C.)

Prelude to Action – State of Play by the End of 1981

Politics Come from the Barrel of a Gun – Fight-Fight, Talk-Talk

Had the Border War become a way of life – a comfort zone for the South African Defence Force (SADF) by 1982? Was military operations more of the same and the border just another place to be transferred to – "we are going to the border" ("ons gaan grens toe")? Had we become an extremely smart counterinsurgency army; nothing more, nothing less? Still, it was exciting times for a soldier, no complaints.

The SADF had successfully completed Operation Protea in August 1981, gathering up the Area-In-Dispute as a spoil. However the question remained: Was South Africa making any headway with the war in Southwest Africa? Not only progress with the counterinsurgency battle but the political one as well. What were the military and political grandmasters doing with the territorial gains and the time that was bought with blood and guts by the men on the ground, to bring the war to an end? Or was I making an unnecessary fuss about this? Anyhow, it was interesting to think about all of this as a unit commander while the lingering Border War passed into yet another year. This was going to be a captivating period for me as I could clearly understand why Mao Tse-tung had stated that "politics come out of the barrel of a gun ... that guerrilla warfare knocks at the door of strategy."

Time as far as protracted war was concerned was on our enemy's side, was it not? African space, African lethargy, African fighting numbers, African time ... I was thinking that they could only beat us with their lethargy because of our speediness. It was a helluva thing to say, time would tell. The enemy could, however, not beat us at the fluid, fast moving tactical game – never. So what, if the faltering politicking came into play ... ? The enemy counted their political successes day-by-day, whilst the then SADF powers seemed more concerned with the demise of individual enemy soldiers ("Koppe tel!"). The macro versus the micro!

How did I as a soldier see the unfolding military and political trials and tribulations developing all around me in those fighting heydays of 1981–82? The mode of conventional-cum-semi-conventional type operations against FAPLA during the two-year Border War period discussed so far was influenced by a series of high-level ongoing international peace negotiations at political and military level. This happened at alternating overseas venues and usually involved the South Africans, Angolans, Americans, Soviets and Cubans. Who wanted what according to the gospel of Roland de Vries: The international community, including the United Nations (UN) wanted South Africa out of SWA/Namibia and Angola – the driving force was to have the UN Security Council Resolution 435 implemented as soon as possible so that peace and democracy could hopefully find its foothold in SWA/Namibia; the Americans went all out for peacemaking in Southern Africa and yes, it would be nice to get rid of the Soviets and Cubans in that part of the conflict world and for the bothersome Cold War (still huffing and puffing at gale force) to just, please, go away; Fidel Castro of Cuba wanted to be the hero of the revolution and to liberate Africa from its racist oppressors, the infamous Apartheid Regime; South Africa wanted to win the bush war and for this FAPLA and the Cubans needed to stop supporting SWAPO in southern Angola. "Yes, the Cubans must leave before the implementation of UN Resolution 435 is even considered, or for that matter, the withdrawal of the SADF from southern Angola – up yours, take that world, put that in your pipes and smoke it!"

Sorry, I nearly forgot: What the hell did the Angolans want, did they really know or was that decision neatly taken out of their hands by the Soviets and the Cubans? One fact was for damn sure – the MPLA government dearly wanted the SADF out of their country. Strangely enough, SWAPO and UNITA seemed to me as if they had been left out of this warring loop more or less for the moment; as if they did not matter at all. Where again did the notion stem from that "we do not negotiate with terrorists"; sorry somebody else's freedom fighters?

All the while, what was happening at the time with the internal politics in South Africa? With the all-powerful National Party government and their super Afrikaners? With the African National Council (ANC) and its sizzling Soweto and rolling mass action? (When was the Church Street Bomb?) All this while the casualties on the Border were mounting in concert with rising international pressures against Apartheid and its escalating political and economical embargoes.

A passing thought: What did "South Africa" truly want for "South Africa" and who were calling the shots? Were "they" looking for something "they" would only recognize once "they" found it? The tipping point would come on the banks of the Cuito Cuanavale River by August 1987. The warring situation in SWA and southern Angola would be drawn to its final conclusion on the banks of the Cunene by August 1988. For all the contestants of the elongated Bush War that is – the Cubans would soon leave the shores of Africa with a sigh of relief: the SADF ousted from a free Namibia! Let us soldier on in the meantime and rather concern ourselves with the simpler things in life – fighting to keep the Area-In-Dispute intact from FAPLA and to slaughter SWAPO relentlessly within its confines. Somebody was probably flying to the Cape Verde Islands at that very moment in high luxury to sort out things for us.

As we knew, bouts of peace negotiations had commenced in all seriousness shortly after the successful completion of Operation Protea in August 1981. Among others, Foreign Affairs Minister Pik Botha was involved on the political side and General Jannie Geldenhuys, the Chief of the SADF, on the military side of these high-level affairs. This series of negotiations dramatically influenced the South African political and military strategic guidelines generated for operational conduct in SWA and Angola. For example: In 1981 we had a full go at FAPLA during Operation Protea. Later in 1981–1982, owing to the peace talks this changed to a more cautious approach limiting full operational confrontation with the conventional army of Angola. Later still, during Operation Askari, this changed back to fuller confrontation when 61 Mech threatened a FAPLA Brigade at Cahama in December 1983; even more so when 61 Mech annihilated FAPLA's 11th Brigade at Cuvelai in January 1984. Much later still, during Operation Modular in 1987 in southeastern Angola, it was open sights and more or less all systems go again – at least with the few SADF units thrown piecemeal into battle within the "realistic," but somewhat restrictive rule of: "Keep casualties to the minimum and do not overly contribute to the escalation of the war."

Fight-fight, talk-talk, one step forward and two steps backwards, three steps forward. Now you shoot FAPLA; now you don't ... It happened in such a way that it bent some rules and influenced the tactics and its aesthetics on the ground. More and more we found that the politics and diplomacy up high started interfering with the mission and the tactics down below. It became a serious case of micro managing the battlefield. The cusp was reached during the major conventional battles fought in southern Angola from 1987 until 1988. As the war escalated beyond proportion the politicians and senior militarists on all sides became more than jittery, while the soldiers doggedly continued to fight it out on the ground.

Getting Down to Fighting Business – Turning the Tables on the Enemy

FAPLA was effectively neutralised in the Area-In-Dispute from mid-1981 until mid-1984 – the tables were neatly turned on the enemy for a while. Maintaining this favourable status quo was the operational responsibility of two military stalwarts, namely Brigadiers Witkop Badenhorst and Joep Joubert. Both Badenhorst (1981–82) and Joubert (1983–84) had commanded Sector 10 from Oshakati and maintained a forward operational base at Ondjiva. This favourable situation soon changed after the 11th Brigade of FAPLA was destroyed by 61 Mech at Cuvelai during Operation Askari in January 1984 under the command of Commandant Epp van Lill. After Askari the peace talks between South Africa and Angola once again flared up in all seriousness. This allowed FAPLA to finally filter back into their natural habitat from where they were ousted in August 1981 – cause and effect. For the SADF this meant losing its hard earned initiative vested in that piece of prime fighting space.

In between Protea and Askari the SADF and SWATF had to contend with operations such as Makro and Meebos. These external operations were a merry mix of counterinsurgency and semi-conventional modes of warfare. Meanwhile the conventional army of Angola stared longingly over their earthy ramparts from the fringes of the Area-In-Dispute and continued to remain a latent threat to these ongoing counterinsurgency operations. It was logical that the enemy would reorganise themselves and even make an all-out effort to recapture Xangongo, Môngua and Ondjiva from the SADF. For elusive SWAPO it remained insurgency business as usual.

From September 1981 onwards a tactical headquarters (Tac HQ) and forward operational base was established at Ondjiva as an extension of Oshakati. Adequate counterinsurgency forces were allocated for operations on a rotational basis by the SADF as well as SWATF respectively. This included units on a more permanent footing such as 32 Battalion; 201 Battalion (Bushmen); 1 Parachute Battalion; 2 Parachute Battalion (citizen force). From Ondjiva Alouette gunships and Puma helicopter troop carriers could be employed at leisure wherever the SADF chose to strike. Operation Makro-Meebos was all about keeping FAPLA from reclaiming their birth right after they had shamefully offered Xangongo and Ondjiva to the SADF during Operation Protea. In the meantime the hunt for the scatterings of SWAPO in the enormity of this quarter of contested earth in the central part of southern Angola was continuing. The quest of the South African Defence Force and the Southwest Africa Territorial Force by then was to keep it that way for as long as possible. This was to buy time for politicians to either make more war, or amends, or peace or whatever the hell it was they were after.

SWATF at the time was commanded by Major General Charles Lloyd from Bastion in Windhoek as was Sector 10 by Brigadier Witkop Badenhorst from Oshakati. Their instructions were clear-cut: FAPLA for the time being was a no-no; SWAPO was a go-go; unless otherwise ordered by the reigning power!

61 Mechanised Battalion Group was destined to strike three times into the cauldron of the Area-In-Dispute, looming 110 km to the north of Omuthiya as the crow flew. These were Operation Makro in December–January; Meebos One in March; and Meebos II in July–August. In between 61 Mech had to crush SWAPO's Special Unit in the Death Triangle in April–May during Operation Yahoo. Within our all-powerful conventional warfare structure I had 1,000 national service soldiers and a handful of permanent force members to care for; and the families of the latter living "peacefully" in Tsumeb. Did the families and girlfriends of our conscript soldiers know where they were and what they were up to?

Battle Design for Operation Meebos

Colonel Jan Pieterse, an accomplished anti-aircraft gunner from army HQ in Pretoria, was appointed as the operational commander at Ondjiva. The SAAF established a forward air force command post, which at this level was referred to as a mobile air operations team (MAOT). Special Forces as well as UNITA provided liaison staffs for these operations. Reconnaissance teams from Special Forces as well as 32 Battalion and 201 Battalion supported these external operations on a continued footing. The famous scout from 32 Battalion, Captain Willem Ratte, was deployed in theatre virtually throughout. The local mobile reserve for operations by Sector 10 was 10 Armoured Car Squadron (Eland-90s) commanded by Major Eddie van Jaarsveld from Oshakati. The overarching operation was nicknamed Meebos and consisted of two subsidiary operations, namely Handsak (Handbag) to the east and Makro to the west. The boundary between these two operations was an imaginary north-south line drawn through Môngua on a map.

- Operation Handsak to the east included Môngua, Xangongo and Ondjiva. 32 Battalion, under command of Commandant Deon Ferreira, was responsible for Handsak. Three companies of 32 Battalion and two companies from 101 Battalion resorted under his command. The operation included search-and-destroy missions against SWAPO and to prevent FAPLA from capturing Xangongo from Cahama. To this end, 32 Battalion had launched quite a few successful ambushes against elements of FAPLA's 21 Brigade which were probing along the tarred road from Cahama towards Xangongo over the period September 1981 until March 1982.
- Operation Makro to the west included the areas of Ondjiva-Anhanca-Evale-Mupa-Cuvelai-Techamutete. Initially 2 Parachute Battalion, a citizen force unit under command of Commandant Monty Brett, was responsible for Makro until January 1982. Afterwards 61 Mech ran the show for a short while until the responsibility was handed over to Commandant James Hills on 21 January, the officer commanding 1 Parachute Battalion. His task force comprised three

paratrooper companies and three reconnaissance groups of 201 Battalion. Makro entailed hunting for SWAPO and spoiling all interests expressed by FAPLA to reconnoitre or probe towards Ondjiva.

On 29 December 1981 several of the foot patrols of 2 Parachute Battalion under command of Commandant Monty Brett was in the dense entangled bush near Evale feverishly probing for the illusive insurgents of PLAN. It was a relentless day and night affair. At that very moment 61 Mech was standing by as the conventional mobile reserve of SWATF at Omuthiya.

61 Mech at High Readiness – Race to the Swift

For 61 Mech it was living at high readiness in the northern border region every minute of the day. The enemies could either be SWAPO or FAPLA or both simultaneously. This was what 61 Mech was all about, what it had been designed for as the conventional mobile reserve of SWATF.

I visited the HQ of Sector 10 at Oshakati regularly from Omuthiya with my key staff members to remain abreast of the operational developments to our north. I was usually accompanied by my second-in-command Major Thys Rall; logistics officer Major Giel Reinecke; intelligence officer Captain Gerrie Hugo. Our main concern was the conventional forces of FAPLA and the Cubans that could threaten the Area-In-Dispute at any time. Our mission was simply "To deny the Area-In-Dispute to FAPLA in the advent of the enemy attempting re-entry or re-capture. A secondary mission was to support the forces deployed for Operation Meebos in event of crisis." As the designated mobile reserve our fighting unit operated customarily in rapid deployment mode, which underscored the concept of speedy employment of an immediately available 61 Mech to particular trouble spots. Critical performance criteria centred on time (rapid) and distance (deployment.) Force deployment and redeployment was therefore viewed by 61 Mech as the ability to mount, move and stage our unit between its home location and a designated area of operations and between areas of operations. It also implied returning 61 Mech safely back to its home location at Omuthiya. In many instances 61 Mech operated under operational command of Sector 10 as was done for operations Protea, Daisy, Makro and Meebos in the Area-In-Dispute. At other times our fighting unit was placed under command of Sector 30 for operations such as Carrot and Yahoo in the Death Triangle. Our status of command could therefore switch at moment's notice from one mode of warfare to the other; from one sector to the other. We were ready to move at three hours' notice. (Task organisation of 61 Mech for Makro – refer to Figure 16 and Appendix A.) The mere fact that 61 Mech was deployed at Omuthiya or wherever we operated at high readiness as a potential threat to any foe, indicated that we were doing our work! My neverending quest was to keep 61 Mech mission and combat ready at all times As such, the high readiness of 61 Mech was one of the proud achievements of my military career.

At times of troop exchanges 61 Mech was at its most vulnerable as this unavoidable predicament could not be offered as an excuse not to be ready. As such, at the beginning of December 1981 Alpha and Bravo companies under command of Major Leon Marais and Captain Koos Liebenberg respectively, were exchanged with two new ones from 1 South African Infantry Battalion in Bloemfontein. The two incoming companies were commanded by Major Fred Burger and Captain Thomas Dreyer. In the same way the armoured car squadron of Captain Frik Schade was replaced with a new one from 1 Special

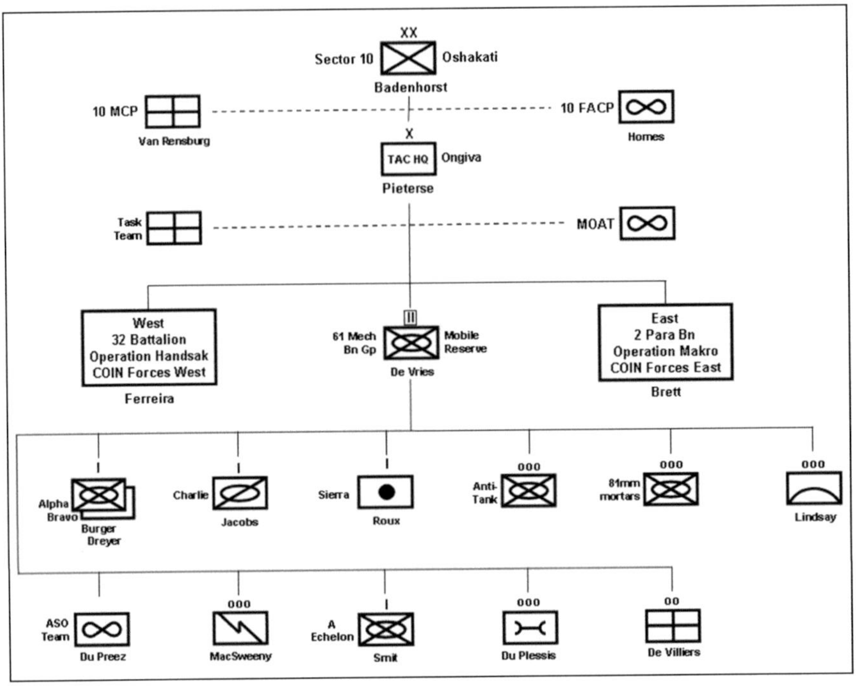

Figure 16: Task Organisation for Operation Makro

Service Battalion in Bloemfontein. Charlie Squadron was now commanded by Major Jakes Jacobs. 61 Mech said farewell to our outgoing subunits. The national servicemen had to return to their respective home units in South Africa to clear out and return to "Civvy Street." Our soldiers proudly wore their 61 Mech operational badges on their right chests as they departed Omuthiya; the emblem they fondly referred to as the "61 Meg Balkie" – the fighting dagger with the lightning flashes angled diagonally across the blade. They were veterans now! My leader group and I never slackened pace before we achieved combat-readiness to our satisfaction by the end of December. A pent-up sigh of relief escaped me!

Christmas Day arrived at Omuthiya. Our soldiers had their Christmas lunch. Our national servicemen were served by the permanent force members. That was the habit of 61 Mech. The hot festive season transpired peacefully into a languid 29 December closing in on New Year. It was to be an exhilarating year for us, even though the loss of a few good men would wrench our souls!

Operation Makro December 1981 – January 1982; 61 Mech to the Rescue

A Fluttering in the Coop – Hello, an Enemy Brigade Suddenly Appeared at Evale

In the meantime an enemy brigade, later to be confirmed as being 19 Brigade, had secretively advanced in stops and starts from Techamutette via Cuvelai to Evale early in December. They had bundu-bashed along the western bank of the Cuvelai River; the latter move in itself being surprising as our conventional foe rarely left the roads. Consequently the enemy's covered advance was not sensed by radio intercepts, neither own aerial nor ground reconnaissance. On reaching Evale the enemy stopped and dug in resolutely, camouflaging their fresh trench rows with stacks of withering Mopani, setting out their interlocking arcs of defensive fire and carefully positioning their artillery and air defences. This was the firm base from where FAPLA wanted to recapture Ondjiva and then Xangongo.

The enemy had guts, for sure, but was their move under existing operational circumstances not folly? Was their thoughtless offensive manoeuvre not the result of command imprudence? We shall see ... At Evale they were out on a limb. However, came 29 December our own security forces at Ondjiva did not know they were there – it came as slightly more than a surprise. The minor drama which unfolded caused tremors to be felt at Sector 10's tactical HQ deployed at Ondjiva, and to the logistics and the helicopters and so forth kept there. It was far more than just a fluttering in the coop at Ondjiva. The counterinsurgency force deployed there was without the weapon systems reasonably required to stop a conventional enemy. A feeling of strong insecurity rapidly found its way from Ondjiva to Oshakati and then Windhoek and Pretoria, much further to the south.

The particulars of the unfolding crisis at Evale reached the ears of 61 Mech early on 29 December at Omuthiya when Brigadier Witkop Badenhorst called me to the radio urgently. He explained to me that the paratroopers of 2 Parachute Battalion had unexpectedly made contact with a brigade of FAPLA near Evale. During a fiery mêlée an Alouette III gunship of the SAAF had been downed by hostile air defence fire. My instructions were for 61 Mech to hastily make its way to Ondjiva where I would be briefed on our impending mission by Colonel Jan Pieterse.

By twelve noon, less than three hours later, 61 Mech was on the move, hell bent for Ondjiva – standing operating procedure. On the way northwards one of our 18-ton Ratels overturned on a steep incline near Okatope during a brief 10-minute halt. Miraculously no one was hurt, neither was the protruding barrel of its 20 mm quick-firing gun damaged. The light workshop troop (LWT) of 61 Mech summarily plucked the monster back onto its six wheels with a recovery vehicle.

The Trigger Event – A Vicious Contact with FAPLA at Evale

On 29 December one of the small patrols of 2 Parachute Battalion had walked smack bang into the FAPLA brigade at Evale. Suddenly 15 paratroopers were fighting for their lives against more than 3,000 conventionally trained and equipped enemy soldiers of 19 Brigade. Alouette gunships from Ondjiva were immediately scrambled to support the firefight on the ground. Captain A.W. Walker and Sergeant C. W. Botes carried out the aforementioned close air support mission, with Walker acting as the flight leader. Air defence fire erupted in continuous streams from the defensive position of 19 Brigade as the helicopters entered the battle zone. The gunships continued to fire downward as they turned and twisted to evade the scathing fire streaming upwards from the ground. During the fiery fray the Alouette III gunship of Lieutenant Serge Bovy and Sergeant Dolf van Rensburg was shot down. The aircraft crash-landed in the midst of the heavily defended locality of FAPLA. It was a miracle that the two crew members were still alive.

Their situation was dire, as they were completely surrounded by the enemy. Without hesitation and with total disregard for their personal safety Captain Walker and his crewman landed their Alouette near the wrecked helicopter and immediately searched for the crew. Eventually the situation became suicidal, compelling Walker and his crewman to withdraw. When airborne they spotted the missing crew and yet again, without hesitation and despite the fact that virtually all enemy fire was now directed in their direction, they landed and scooped the crew to safety. They returned to the contact area once again to provide top cover for a Puma assigned for casualty evacuation, the gunship repeatedly subjected to heavy enemy anti-aircraft fire. Captain A.W. Walker and his flight engineer, Sergeant C.W. Botes, were later on awarded Honoris Crux decorations for bravery under life-threatening circumstances. Their actions at Evale were outstanding displays of military professionalism, devotion to duty and courage. During the firefight the paratroopers extricated themselves from the battle in leapfrogging bounds of fire and movement and returned to the illusive safety of Ondjiva. That was where 61 Mech found them the afternoon of the fateful 29th.

Arriving at the Tac HQ at Ondjiva and about Meeting the Paratroopers

Slightly beyond midday 61 Mech arrived at Ondjiva and subsequently deployed in an open laager on its southern outskirt. I immediately moved forward to the Tac HQ of Colonel Jan Pieterse at the airfield. In the meantime 61 Mech would refuel and do the necessary repairs to our battle array. I was swiftly briefed about the precarious situation surrounding the unexpected engagement with the 19th Brigade. Of course, the imminent threat to Ondjiva and the integrity of the operation was mentioned. Yes, we were to recover the wreck of the gunship as well. It was not to be left for the enemy to use for propaganda purposes. There was not much tactical intelligence to go on. In the meantime an airstrike had been called in from Ondangwa and Evale had been bombed by the Mirages.

What to do, 61 Mech? Attack the position at Evale and destroy the enemy or drive them back from whence they came. I was thinking what the enemy commander of 19 Brigade at Evale would do according to their traits and doctrine as I knew them. The MAOT confirmed that the Alouette gunships at Ondjiva and the Mirages and Impalas from Ondangwa would be on standby for close air support the next morning. I requested a reconnaissance team from 32 Battalion to be put under my operational command immediately. I met the team leader and told him to muster his men and join me at my HQ on the southern outskirts of Ondjiva. Let's go, no time left with which to play. I then moved off to find the paratroopers to gather some more firsthand information about the Evale situation and to learn about my enemy's intentions, their strengths, capabilities, equipment and deployments.

When I stopped in my Ratel-Command near the position of the paratroopers I could see that they were exasperated, tired, dirty, battle-weary, their faces still smeared with black-is-beautiful. I dismounted and walked towards Commandant Monty Brett, their commander. He was still wound up but relieved when he saw me and my Ratel. We knew each other well from our training heydays at Infantry School, Oudtshoorn; from the time I was his course leader on a company commander's course. We made ourselves comfortable in army camp chairs, having a talk, having coffee, battle maps lying at our feet in front of us in the sand. This fleeting interlude was relaxed, the discussions serious.

Let's talk about Evale now. His paratroopers were lying down behind us along a hedgerow, utterly exhausted, but composed. Lots of fight still left in them. I then motored back to my HQ. A quick battle appreciation followed: Time and map appreciation; terrain; possible enemy courses of action; own forces; time and distance; surprise; approaches; pre-deployments. Quick orders soon followed. 61 Mech was ready to move again, eastwards towards Anhanca. We needed to reach Anhanca, 39 kilometres away, before night set in, and prepare for the actions of the following day. The reconnaissance team of 32 Battalion were tasked to reconnoitre the enemy position at Evale the same night and report the situation to me by first light. They were to be deployed by helicopter to get closer to their target area. I could see that the approach planned by the team leader edged along the Cuvelai River through the dense bushes from the western side. Quick extraction plans for our fearless scouts were finalised – cool, calm and collected. The Alouette and the Puma were on standby for them as well.

61 Mech moved due northeast and deployed in allround defence near Anhanca before nightfall, the diesel tanks were filled to the brim and final repairs completed once again. We completed our planning for the following day as we waited patiently for the intelligence on Evale from our reconnaissance team to be confirmed. 61 Mech was "march and combat ready" to strike towards Evale at first light.

What was our enemy doing in the meantime? Where would they deploy their reconnaissance? Where was the enemy's indirect fire missions registered on the ground? How will the enemy react when we attacked from the northeast? Where was their mobile reserve located? Our operational plan called for a full-blown mechanised attack on Evale from the northeast with indirect artillery and mortar fire support. The paratroopers at Ondjiva had informed me that the defensives at Evale were facing south – our enemy's usual way. We did not call for an aerial pre-bombardment. The aircraft were on standby for close air support anyway.

Offensive Move by 61 Mech on Evale

Through the night our reconnaissance team from 32 Battalion successfully completed their scouting mission. They reported that an eerie silence enclosed Evale. There were no of the usual sighs of cooling metal, the quiet nervous chatter of soldiers, erratic snoring or the clatter of AK-47 magazines. Had the enemy suddenly withdrawn, as quietly as they had come? Were the previous day's fiery encounters from the ground and the air and the aerial bombardment too much for them to stomach? Nonetheless, 61 Mech would go in that day, guns blazing, if so required – the planning assumption was that the enemy would still be there at Evale. Therefore, take no chances. Secure the start line, work from one firm base to the next.

By first light 61 Mech was well on the way to our forming-up place (FUP) 7 km to the northeast of Evale. I reported to Ondjiva that we were moving offensively towards Evale to attack if the enemy was still there. The go-ahead was given. 61 Mech advanced towards Evale in assault formation ready to engage the enemy at moment's notice and proceed with fire and movement. The immediate front remained quiet. As our forward line approached the hamlet I could see some buildings appearing just across the Anhanca-Evale-Mupa road. No incoming fire. We could now clearly discern wide-ranging phalanxes of abandoned trenches in front of us. The trenches were fresh-fresh. The red gum of the Mopani used for camouflage was still oozing from the breaks and cuts of the branches. The assault formation of 61 Mech entered Evale directly from where the enemy's flank was deployed as they defended southwards. Abandoned equipment was left strewn everywhere.

The enemy must have left in a hurry, probably during early darkness the previous day. We had missed our valiant enemy by a whisker. This was a disappointment to us. We had looked forward to a scrap with FAPLA. 61 Mech swept through the position in battle formation. There was no sign of the enemy. We found fresh tracks where they had retreated across the Cuvelai River. Their escape route led northwards.

I eventually gave the command to adopt allround defence so that we could assess the situation. All at once, there was a sudden welcoming torrential downpour by the buckets, as one could only experience in Angola. On the spur of the moment I gave the command: Stop, switch off, have a bath. At a moment's notice the soldiers of 61 Mech were naked alongside our battle array, having a well-deserved wash in the pouring rain – utterly refreshing, laughter everywhere – a catharsis.

I walked around the erstwhile enemy position with some of the members of my command group. We were very wary of personnel mines and booby traps, watching out for the telltales. Empty shell casings lay strewn everywhere. It must have been a helluva fight by the paratroopers and the gunships. We found the wreck of the Alouette 111 of Bovy and Janse van Rensburg. It lay in a cluster of bushes in the centre of the defensive position. It was extremely close to the anti-aircraft position which had shot it down. Countless shells lay strewn. How the hell could they have been rescued by Walker under such conditions and still make it out alive? Totally amazing; divine intervention and utmost bravery all rolled into one.

The Alouette wreck of Bovy and Janse van Rensburg was loaded on to a SAMIL-100 cargo truck by the Tiffies. The wreck was later returned to the air force base at Ondangwa. Further to the rear we found the abandoned position of the enemy's erstwhile administrative and logistics position. A few broken down Russian Urals were left abandoned, as well. The area was a total mess – spare parts lay scattered and floods of old oil inundated the sandy soil. It was approaching late afternoon and we laagered 61 Mech in allround defence at Evale for the night. A comprehensive situation report (Sitrep) was submitted to Ondjiva about the situation at Evale. There was instant relief that the conventional enemy threat had dissipated to the north from whence it had come. I informed Ondjiva that we were going to pursue the enemy northwards the following day.

61 Mech spent a peaceful night at Evale. Through the hours of darkness the 120 mm mortar battery of Major Chris Roux did sporadic harassing fire all around. We could hear the lethal bombs through our weary sleep ever so often exploding in the distance – most comforting.

Pursuit into Nothingness – Beyond Mupa and Back to Evale

Evale at first light on 31 December was pleasant to experience with the fresh smell of rain and foliage and earth, the noises of 61 Mech comforting to my ear as our fighting unit prepared to move out in pursuit of 19 Brigade. The rapid pursuit followed through dense bushes on the tracks and the oil spills of our fleeing enemy northwards towards Cuvelai. The enemy retreated along the way they had come – through the bushes to the west of the Cuvelai River. FAPLA had dissipated like morning mist in the hot Angolan sun. The enemy had retreated much faster than they had advanced – gifted in that area, more likely. A few kilometres north of Mupa I received instructions from Ondjiva that we should halt and not engage FAPLA – politics and perhaps some slight apprehension of harming the ongoing peace talks – most infuriating.

We used the time well for some firing practices with the Ratels and harassing fire missions with the 120 mm mortars northwards in the direction of the receding foe – just to indicate that we were serious and that we knew what force projection was all about. After two more days of manoeuvrings in the area we returned empty handed to Evale. Brigadier Witkop Badenhorst visited 61 Mech soon afterwards. It was decided that 61 Mech would remain in the area a little longer from where the enemy's northern approaches could be influenced.

We kept ourselves busy and productive at Evale by means of occasional patrolling for SWAPO and by war-gaming. In between moments of high activity the leader group indulged in terrain analysis and contingency planning. Occasionally we threw 120 mm mortar rounds to whomever. This all increased the combat readiness of 61 Mech and added insult to FAPLA's injury. This was all in a day's work of projecting force as 61 Mech thought best. Careful calculations ensured that we did not blow innocent civilians residing in the kraals around us to smithereens.

I enjoyed sitting on top of my Ratel playing enemy and force commander at the same time during the two-sided field exercises we held. The combat teams took turns in fighting through 19 Brigade's erstwhile defensive positions. It was a joy to watch them manoeuvring aggressively on receiving snippets of information and responding rapidly to quick commands – fire and movement forwards and backwards and sideways. It was emotionally satisfying to experience the confidence and self-esteem of our men as they exercised and trained. The local inhabitants could report what they saw to the north, for all we cared.

After a few days we deployed southwards to Ondjiva where we had the chance to do some necessary maintenance on our equipment. A massive stable parade was held on the airfield at Ondjiva, flaunting our stuff to SWAPO and FAPLA in the process. By 21 January our fighting unit returned to Omuthiya and continued to fulfil its mission as the mobile reserve of SWATF, a force to be reckoned with by the enemy. FAPLA was back where they belonged on the fringes of contested ground. An uneasy stalemate remained as politics, diplomacy and peace talks continued, seemingly indifferent.

Meebos I in March 1981 – Sabre Rattling

By March 1982 there were devious moves afoot by FAPLA's 21 Brigade to recapture Xangongo from Cahama. Up to now 32 Battalion had clashed a few times with their reconnaissance elements probing towards Xangongo. For this reason Sector 10 had requested 61 Mech to conduct a hasty force projection exercise to Xangongo, Môngua and Ondjiva and to physically dominate the Cunene Province with our military might. These were all well-known haunts of 61 Mech from the heydays of Operation Protea. Meebos One was therefore intended as a show of force to be executed from 1 to 7 March. No fighting with FAPLA was anticipated. This swift intervention was to serve as a fair warning to the conventional enemy to remain at bay: At Cahama, west of the Cunene River and at Techamutete and Cassinga to the north – stay there, enemy, or else!

61 Mech considered: What was the best way to project military force towards the enemy at Cahama? We drove boldly to Xangongo by road via Ondjiva and Môngua for all to see and to report. Then we parked our Ratels in a firing line on the eastern bank of the Cunene River and shot at harmless targets on the western bank to improve our gunnery and fire-control techniques. Through the evenings and days Major Chris Roux and his gunners had fun directing indirect harassing fire missions with their 140 mm guns at our lamenting foe residing to the west.

61 Mech used the time in Angola well for extremely realistic joint training exercises with live ammunition as we mock-battled through all the derelict enemy positions gracelessly left for us by FAPLA at Xangongo and Ondjiva. The exercises also included sharpening our house clearing and street fighting skills. We had fun "fighting" through the streets of Xangongo and later on at Ondjiva. Our fighting unit gradually made its way back to Omuthiya, training on the hoof as we moved southwards.

By 7 March 61 Mech was back at Omuthiya on three hour's standby ... once again. In the meantime Alpha Company was replaced by a new incoming one under command of the astute Captain Jan Malan from 1 South African Infantry Battalion, Bloemfontein.

We had 61 Mech up and ready just in time to conduct Operation Yahoo from 14 April until 25 May 1982. Yahoo, although extremely successful, had been arduous. Many lives had been lost and many of our soldiers had been wounded in the fighting sequel. By 25 May 61 Mech was back at Omuthiya on three hours' standby ... once again. By 11 July 61 Mech was called upon to participate in the next offensive phase in southern Angola, which was known as Operation Meebos II.

Meebos II In July–August 1982 With a Mechanised Flavour

Overview of the Situation – Prelude to Meebos II

Meebos II was a fair operation considering the difficulty of hunting an elusive enemy in dense bush with meagre intelligence. It was conducted in the typical aggressive South African pre-emptive fighting manner. To our military way of thinking the deep attack, which threatened the enemy's strategic base areas, command systems and logistic lines gave the best leverage. Who could argue with that sound military theory, bar the enemy?

In July Sector 10 was building up seriously towards the next deliberate offensive phase ... It was time to light the next prairie fire underneath the backsides of SWAPO. A total of 345 insurgents were killed during Meebos II, whilst the security forces lost only 29 soldiers. There was great enjoyment as our fighting Mirages and Alouette gunships calmly reigned supreme over the hostile skies to cover our offensive ground manoeuvres. This happened in spite of the gradual intensification of the flagging bush war. The focus of the main effort was SWAPO's command and fighting structures located in the central area of southern Angola.

There was enough enemy to go around as intelligence reports were received of numerous SWAPO HQ deployments and operational bases in the area of Anhanca-Mupa-Cuvelai-Techamutette. In addition SWAPO's Special Unit was reported in the vicinity of Chifufua near the Mulola River; at the time it acted as the transit unit for SWAPO insurgents operating more to the east towards the Okavango. The battle indications were furthermore clear that FAPLA was not at all happy with the current state of play. It did not do their self-esteem any good by merrily twiddling thumbs on the fringes of the contested area, starring longingly inwards. We did not care a hoot about their ego states. To the west, across the Cunene River, the 21 Brigade of FAPLA guarded the portals of Lubango from Cahama. The 19th Brigade was reportedly dug in at Quiteve alongside the Cunene River, about 65 km map distance to the west of Mupa. The SADF's military intelligence had previously considered the possibility of 19 Brigade making a move on Mupa. The domicile of the 11th Brigade was the small Angolan hamlet of Cuvelai nestling on the shores of the river with the same name. Here our dear conventional enemy sat in defence with their heavy armaments, waiting patiently and wide-eyed behind their earthy ramparts for something exciting to happen. Some of the other fighting and support elements of 11 Brigade was located at Techamutete. Within the area of influence of Meebos II there were Cuban forces deployed at Techamutete-Cassinga and at Donga. One FAPLA brigade plus defended Menongue to the northwest and one FAPLA brigade Caiundo to the east. We reckoned that it was only the combined FAPLA-Cuban conventional warfaring deployments at Quiteve, Cuvelai and Techamutete-Cassinga which could really interfere with Meebos II – that is to say time and space-wise if the conventional enemy had the will to fight.

Interestingly enough, at times like these South Africa's Minister of Foreign Affairs Mr. Pik Botha and General Jannie Geldenhuys, the Chief of the SADF spent countless hours flying to and from Pretoria dialoguing for peace in Washington and other venues, such as the Cape Verde Islands. In actual fact, in July–August 1982, whilst Operation Meebos was rolling out in southern Angola, Botha and Geldenhuys were in and out of Washington doing just that.

Design for Battle – Find, Fix and Strike

Meebos II was commanded by Colonel Jan Pieterse from a roving forward Tac HQ supported by the air force and medical and logistic services from way up front. For this purpose a number of helicopter administrative areas (HAA) were established in succession, hidden away in the bush to the north of Cuvelai. The South African Air Force (SAAF) provided the required air support for counter air operations as well as for ground attacks. The Mirages and Impalas were based at Ondangwa. The fury unleashed was directed at SWAPO's command structures and operational bases in the vicinity of Mupa, Cuvelai and Techamutete. The operation was performed by a joint brigade-sized SADF/SWATF task force over the period 13 July 1982–30 August 1982. (Refer to Figure 17 and Appendix A.) It was found that such operations usually petered out after six weeks. Then time was needed for things to settle down again until the next repeat of flurry and fight; of finding, fixing and striking at the enemy again and again!

Meebos II consisted of a number of deceptive moves followed by sequential ground and air attacks in the form of Puma heli-borne assaults supported by Alouette gunships. The Puma and Alouette flew back to Ondangwa every evening and returned the following day – talk about maintaining momentum. The distance from prospective HAA positions in the northern sector of operations was approximately 280 km from the airfield at Ondangwa. This was a laborious process as flying time just from Ondangwa to Ondjiva was 55 minutes. Attacks were preceded by the gathering of near real-time intelligence through high altitude aerial reconnaissance, enemy radio intercepts and information gathered from the local population. The final work of fixing the enemy and gathering real-time intelligence was left in the capable hands of the reconnaissance teams of Captain Willem Ratte of 32 Battalion. To facilitate guaranteed communications between the scouts and the Tac HQ an Impala jet fighter roved the skies high above to act as a relay station at critical moments. Two companies from 32 Battalion and one from 1 Parachute Battalion operated as the main striking capability – our own guerrilla force. The companies from 32 Battalion were respectively commanded by Captains Eric Rabie and Tinus van Rensburg and the one from 1 Parachute Battalion by Major Jab Swart. These three seasoned veterans of the Bush War were tactically gifted; rather have them with you than against you.

The operation had a mechanised flavour, one in which the extrapolative deterrent value of 61 Mech increased the success rate of this particular operation significantly as the mobile reserve of the force. At least the initiative and freedom of action so desperately required could be maintained by curbing FAPLA. 61 Mech was sanctioned to strike hard at FAPLA if they dared to intervene with the operation on the ground. It was, however, emphasised over and over from our military high command that actions against FAPLA were only, but only allowed, when they interfered.

When appreciating the fighting guise of our task force I invariably thought about the wise words of Mao Tse-tung: "We should strive to make mobile warfare the principle

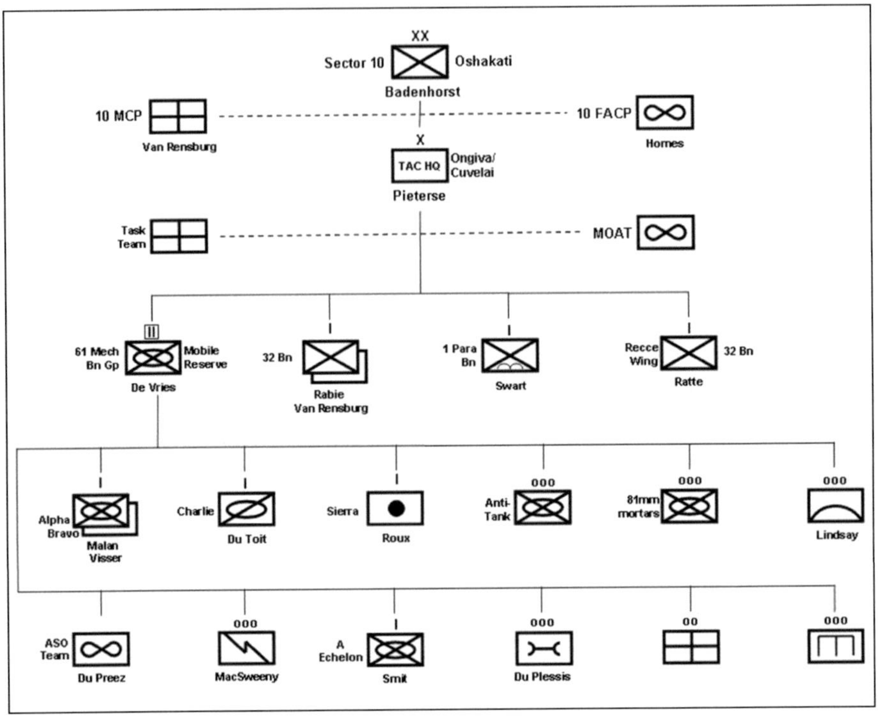

Figure 17: Task Organisation for Operation Meebos II

means of fighting ... Concentration of force does not imply the abandonment of the operations of the guerrillas. The operations of the guerrillas and the conventional force are complimentary to each other ... like the right and the left arm of a man. It would be like a warrior with one arm if there were only the conventional force without the guerrillas."

Meebos II could not have been achieved successfully if it had not been for the substantial and enthusiastic participation of the SAAF. Their fighting gunships were commanded by tactical astute and daring young SAAF Captain Neall Ellis. Their task force mustered for the operation comprised the following air assets: One Alouette helicopter for command and trooping purposes armed with a Browning 7,62 mm machine gun; seven Alouette gunships armed with 20 mm cannons; nine Puma transport helicopters for trooping and helicopter-landed operations; a number of C-130, C-160 and Dakota transport aircraft on standby for air transportation and air drop missions; two squadrons of Mirage and Impala fighter aircraft on standby for air support missions from Ondangwa.

The first attack on a SWAPO base in the northwestern sector of the Area-In-Dispute near the Calonga River was planned for the last week in July. Captain Willem Ratte and his reconnaissance teams were already deep inside Angola searching for the enemy.

The Mission of 61 Mech for Operation Meebos and the Plan – Vague but Factual

I received my orders for Operation Meebos II from Brigadier Witkop Badenhorst on 9 July 1982 and issued my orders at Omuthiya the next day. Everything happened very quickly. Our mission received was reasonably vague and stated that: 61 Mech should execute a deception operation in the lower quarter of central southern Angola from 13 July 1982 until further notice. The end date for the operation was specified as possibly being at the close of July or the middle of August 1982.

The first phase of our operation was shaped as a series of mobile actions in the areas of Ondjiva, Môngua and Xangongo. The aim was to disrupt and overwhelm the enemy's intelligence collection capabilities. Therefore, the more movements, radio chatter, ruses and feints by separate mechanised entities in that quarter east of the Cunene River the better. The second phase was to take place at Xangongo and also formed part of the deception tactics. The intention was that the enemy should observe the overtly aggressive action of 61 Mech. The opportunity was also to be used productively to exercise our unit for the coming operation. Force preparation and integration with freshly attached force elements needed to be completed by 27 July. On completion of the deception operation at Xangongo 61 Mech needed to disappear off FAPLA's radar screen. This phase entailed moving 61 Mech stealthily to a deployment area in the vicinity of Evale-Mupa and to await further instructions from Sector 10. Our unit's commitment entailed high readiness for offensive actions and to be ready to launch a counter-offensive operation against FAPLA and/or SWAPO when so ordered.[1] D-Day was 13 July – the day Charlie Squadron under command of Captain Chris du Toit deployed to Xangongo via Ondjiva as the mobile reserve of Task Force Meebos. The latter status of command remained until the remainder of 61 Mech joined up with the squadron at Xangongo on 18 July.

The combat Group HQ of 61 Mech and the two mechanised infantry companies of Captains Jan Malan and Vissie Visser moved to Xangongo on 18 July. Our support group followed suit under command of Major Giel Reinecke, with Alpha Echelon commanded by RSM WO1 H.G. Smit. Sierra Battery under command of Major Chris Roux moved to Ondjiva on 19 July to complete their training on the eight 120 mm mortars. This was to make them more versatile for future employment. The battery was already fully trained on their eight trusted 140 mm guns. The battery joined up with the remainder of 61 Mech at Xangongo on 24 July. While at Xangongo we heard that the Mirages had attacked the air defences at Cahama on 21 July, again ... This was second nature to the SAAF, who by now reckoned they had shares in Cahama.

Our unit completed its conventional warfare training by means of a few combat team and combat group attacks in the erstwhile trenches of FAPLA surrounding Xangongo. By 27 July I regarded 61 Mech as combat ready for mobile conventional operations and was extremely satisfied with the high level of combat discipline, tactical prowess and esprit de corps demonstrated by the respective subunits and their commanders. We were ready to be employed for whatever, whenever, wherever. 61 Mech now needed to disappear off the enemy's radar screen as we ventured stealthily towards the area of Mupa from where the unfolding operation would be supported.

Tactical Manoeuvres – Deploying for Operation Meebos Proper

On 27 July 61 Mech left Xangongo and deliberately followed the tarred road for 45 km towards Môngua for anyone to see and report. At Môngua our fighting 55 km unit left-wheeled sharply and disappeared from sight into the bushes. From there it was bundu-bashing for approximately 65 km, where 61 Mech occupied a hide until 29 July.

That day I flew by Puma to Oshivello to receive my follow-up orders from Sector 10 for

1 See Map 15.

Meebos II as the mobile reserve of the task force. I had the opportunity to meet both Mr. Pik Botha and General Jannie Geldenhuys during a pleasant interlude in the African bush with a Windhoek beer in hand. Mr. Botha, dressed in military fatigues as the honouree colonel of the SAAF walked up to me and said tongue in cheek: "Ah ... Roland, nice to meet the commander of 61 Mech ... It is a great privilege ... Your troops are doing a splendid job ... As you well know, your fighting unit is not in Angola at the moment". I was thinking of my troops who were at that exact moment calmly laagered north of Môngua, deep inside Angola, 120 km north of the SWA-Angola border. General Jannie Geldenhuys said to me, "Remember, no shooting at FAPLA". As I flew back in the Puma to join up with 61 Mech I found myself pondering the way in which politics in war so severely influenced everything happening on the ground in the real world. I did not know it then, but by 5 August I would receive a subtle reprimand from General Jannie Geldenhuys in Washington. This was for shooting at FAPLA on the road between Techamutete and Cuvelai. The reprimand, however, came with a smile. I thought that I could understand what Mao Tse-tung had meant when he said: "Developments of things in life are full of twists and turns and do not run in a straight line. It is the same in war and only a formalist cannot understand this truth." The next day at daybreak, still in the laager north of Môngua, some of my troops mischievously said to me, "Hey commandant, we picked up over our short wave radios that we are not in Angola. Where are we?" Funny, very funny! I adored the young men of 61 Mech and their young at heart spirit. With them you could fight a hole through any enemy, no matter the numerical odds. In 61 Mech every man – every one of the gallant one thousand souls – counted.

On the 30 July 61 Mech left its comfortable hide and bundu-bashed due east to join up with the two companies of 32 Battalion in a forward assembly area (FAA) 25 km east of Mupa. After crossing the Mupa-Evale gravel road and grinding through the dense foliage for about 15 km our vanguard was presented with one of those rare juicy operational optional extras in the African bush – the dear Lord has a fine sense of humour. An unsuspecting two-vehicle FAPLA reconnaissance patrol blundered into the front end of the awesome 61 Mech – the sharp end that is. The enemy scouts suddenly saw the impressive array of combat vehicles steadily approaching them from the south with 20 mm guns pointing aggressively at the high ready. From my Ratel-Command I could see the whites of the enemy's eyes and read total astonishment on their faces, soon to be replaced by stark terror. As if by signal the enemy soldiers suddenly jumped from their moving Land Rovers and fled in all the wind directions never to be seen or heard from again. They were probably marked down for desertion by FAPLA for life.

Meanwhile the two vehicles came to a shuddering, grinding halt against the sloping armour of the Ratel right in front of our 55 km extended armoured column. The enemy had disappeared so quickly from the scene of the crime that we did not get a chance to shoot at them. So be it. Good luck, FAPLA! Operations in Angola had its moments of levity. We took account of the booty and destroyed the two dilapidated vehicles. It was once again quite an experience to view how disorderly the equipment of FAPLA was stowed on their ramshackle vehicles. Field maintenance and orderliness was not their forte. 61 Mech could teach them something about combat discipline and maintenance. Our revered enemy never ceased to amaze us.

Whilst we moved towards the FAA tragedy struck at the heart of 61 Mech. My logistics officer, Major Giel Reinecke had requested me for an armoured escort for a logistics convoy to join up with us from Ondjiva. Energetic 19 year-old national service Second Lieutenant Stephanus Steyn, of Captain Chris du Toit's Charlie Squadron was selected for the job. Steyn commanded a troop of Ratel-90s. With him in his vehicle during the escort mission was an old school friend from Kroonstad, Lance Corporal J.H. Schultz. The rest of the crew consisted of Corporal I. Kriel, Rifleman C.H. Fouché, Rifleman A.R. Coony and Rifleman D. P. Crouser. With the ensemble of a few Ratel-90s and Ratel-20s travelled an 81 mm mortar fire group and a few logistics vehicles. Steyn travelled second from the front in the marching order of the convoy.

Suddenly there was an immense explosion and flames and black smoke erupted from beneath the Ratel Steyn was commanding. One of the middle wheels had detonated a double tank mine, throwing the eighteen ton six-wheeler a few meters to one side. For a moment the crew did not know what had happened to them – they were totally stunned and overwhelmed by the sudden turn of the event. Steyn and his mates then jumped out of the stricken Ratel, totally disoriented, thinking that they were in the midst of an enemy ambush.

Crew members Kriel, Coony and Fouché were already clear of the vehicle taking cover in the bushes without their rifles. Steyn shouted at his fellow soldiers to come back. In the meantime Steyn had evacuated his turret and was grabbing their rifles from a gaping hole on the right side of the Ratel and throwing it to those soldiers already outside. This was the side where Rifleman Crouser had been lying asleep on the interior crew seats. The bomb rack of forty three 90 mm projectiles was clearly visible through the large hole ripped into the side of the Ratel. By this time the vehicle was ablaze. Steyn then saw his friend Schultz lying inside as if dead. He immediately tried to evacuate him from the flames but the fatigues of Schultz hooked onto metal protrusions. Steyn then shouted at Corporal Kriel to come and help. With the support of the others they recovered Schultz to safety, about 50 m away from the burning vehicle.

Without hesitation and without thinking about his own safety, Steyn then rushed back to the Ratel to evacuate Rifleman Crouser from the flames. The first pieces of ammunition inside the wreck now started exploding. Steyn grabbed Crouser and dragged him to safety as the Ratel exploded behind them and was ripped to pieces. Rifleman Crouser was dead. The Pumas arrived a few minutes later to evacuate the wounded colleagues of Steyn and the body of their friend Crouser to Ondangwa. The level-headed Second Lieutenant Stephanus Steyn climbed into the next available Ratel and continued with his escort mission. For selfless conduct and utmost bravery in the direst situation imaginable Second Lieutenant Stephanus Steyn was awarded the Honoris Crux Decoration. Later Steyn related with deep-felt sorrow about Crouser to us, "He was my gunner and my orderly, he was a good soldier".[2]

By late afternoon 61 Mech reached the FAA and married up with the two companies of 32 Battalion. Somewhere, 91 km to the northwest of us, in the dense bush near the Calonga River, Captain Willem Ratte had established the first viable target for Meebos II near the Calonga River. One of the first tasks of 61 Mech was to set up a Helicopter Administrative Area (HAA) at first light on 31 July. The position selected by the task force for its first HAA was approximately 18 km due east of the small town of Cuvelai on the northern bank of the Cuvelai River.

2 Also refer to Chapter 9 about the fallen of 61 Mech.

Meebos Unfurled in All its Fury – the Neverending Quest for Tactical Intelligence

Operation Meebos II was ready to uncoil in all its fury ... To be fair, for most counterinsurgency type operations, such as Meebos, the lack of near real-time and real-time intelligence remained the two key deceiving elements. Those two disruptive factors always bedevilled the successful conduct of counterinsurgency operations; more so, to my mind, than typical conventional operations. However, the few scouts on the ground of 32 Battalion were our champions this time around. They worked overtime under the most hazardous of operational conditions anyone could have imagined. Captain Willem Ratte, originally a Selous Scout from the Rhodesian Armed Forces, was such a man. All I could say about Ratte was that There was none bolder with good broad shoulder. He fought many affray, and fought and won. He'd seen the glory, he'd told the story ... Of battles glorious and deeds victorious ... (By the way, at best Willem Ratte should never be requested to wear smart military "step-outs" – he looks very uncomfortable in those.)

The first objective was codenamed "Smelling Rat" and was located on 30 July by Willem Ratte on the southern bank of the fast flowing Calonga River, 31 km southwest of Techamutete. Ratte had infiltrated for more than 25–30 km on foot, wearing captured enemy boots with soles which had been reversed. He followed comprehensive countertracking procedures. He eventually lurked well-hidden and camouflaged inside the enemy base. From this extremely dangerous position he dispatched bits of information to the Tac HQ via an Impala aircraft relay which flew high above and to the side out of hearing range. Every so often Ratte needed to stop sending scraps of information as some of the enemy passed close to him. He truly lived on the edge for hours on end.

Following on Ratte's scouting missions a number of minor as well as more significant contacts were destined to be made with SWAPO. This occurred sporadically from the last week in July until the end of August. The elusive headquarters of the enemy were however never found. Many times the crafty reconnaissance teams of 32 Battalion would find the enemy, only to be rewarded with an empty lair once the ground assault went in. The enemy was extremely sensitive to strange moves in their immediate environs. They were observing carefully for the telltales of any unwelcome reconnaissance. Then it was up-sticks for the enemy within minutes, only to disappear over the next bushy horizon.

The first joint helicopter and airborne assault was planned for 31 July – the opening gambit. The plan called for the paratrooper company of Major Jab Swart to be inserted by parachute from C-130/160-s at 05:00 to the north of the enemy's position as a stopper line. The two companies of 32 Battalion would then be trooped in by Puma helicopter and attack from the west, east and south of the enemy objective. The Alouette gunships were to be used for close air support. All the Meebos forces were positioned through the night of 30–31 July ready to go for it by first light. The enemy just needed to stay were Ratte had located them ... This is how it went during the operation in ever-widening ripples: Scout, find, fix and then hopefully strike at the enemy.

Let the Games Begin – The Airborne Attack on Smelling Rat on 31 July 1982

As soon as it was dark 61 Mech started bundu-bashing 65 km northwards towards a selected crossing point across the Cuvelai River to establish the first HAA at first light. It was to be a touch-and-go thing. The position chosen from aerial photography by the task force HQ was approximately 18–22 km due east of Cuvelai on the northern bank of the river. Please bear in mind that the village of Cuvelai was ardently defended by FAPLA's 11th Brigade.

The Techamutete-Cuvelai gravel road served as their axis of command as well as for logistics supply. It was used by SWAPO for the same purpose.

The vanguard of 61 Mech arrived on the southern bank of the Cuvelai in the dark. As first light was upon us a suitable fording site needed to be found hastily, especially for the logistics vehicles and the SAMIL gun tractors to get through. The Pumas and Alouette would soon be arriving for the attack on "Smelling Rat." The ideal crossing site was eventually found approximately 18 km due east of the FAPLA's Brigade position at Cuvelai. We crossed the river in darkness and soon found what we thought to be an ideal open area, suitable for the HAA – think again.

It was time for a relaxing coffee break as we watched some of the helicopters arriving and settling down in the flat grassland around us. Captain Neall Ellis, who commanded the gunships, moved over to my Ratel and was invited to a welcome brew of coffee and some chit-chat. I had immense respect for this daring gunship pilot who had loads of hair-raising operational experiences.

As it became lighter I could see some high ground in the middle distance to the northwest. I still wondered by myself: "Hell, would the enemy have observation posts on the high rises?"

All of a sudden it seemed to us as if the sun was rising from the wrong side in the sky. Far to the west towards Cuvelai we could see ominous flashes reflected in the clouded sky. Massive explosions started ripping up the earth about 700 m to the west and northwest of us. It was far enough away, but still seemed uncomfortably close. My friend, Captain Neall Ellis did not seem to be impressed by the current position of the HAA. On my command we left an unending cacophony of exploding enemy artillery shells in our wake. The Alouette helicopters of the not-smiling Captain Neall Ellis followed suit – we had livened up the day for the SAAF. We hastily decided to move the HAA a few kilometres to the east and this was achieved in no time. I still wonder whether an outpost of 11 Brigade had observed the movement of 61 Mech to their east and had called for the fire of their long-range Russian D-70s by radio. Anyway, they were expending their entire brigade's artillery ammunition on nothing for quite a while – it was an impressive fire display. Mark you, the expenditure of all their artillery ammunition without restraint was going to cost them dearly on 4 August.

With the alternative HAA rapidly established, Task Force Meebos was ready for its first action. The Tac HQ under command of Colonel Jan Pieterse moved from Ondjiva to the HAA. I then forthwith detached the Anti-Aircraft Troop of Captain Carl Lindsay to provide added air and ground protection to the HAA until the end of Operation Meebos. The 20 mm anti-aircraft guns of Lindsay, mounted on the rear of the SAMIL-20s (Ystervark), were potent weapons in the ground role. Lindsay was super-efficient and the HAA would be able to employ his troop well.

The first attack on Smelling Rat was less than spectacularly successful. The airborne part of the operation was called off by Captain Willem Ratte when a suitable drop zone (DZ) for the parabats could not be found in time. The Hercules aircraft consequently returned to Ondangwa without completing the airborne part of the assault. The attack was now delayed for some hours and there were strong indications that the enemy had started withdrawing. In the meantime, the Puma helicopters had returned to Ondangwa to troop the paratroopers to their original target area. The attack force was eventually on the ground and started skirmishing through the enemy objective, only to find a small number of SWAPO strays. A few fleeing Gaz trucks were knocked out by some of the gunships.

The attack on Smelling Rat was ticked off as a lost opportunity. No versatile guerrilla-like foe would afford his enemy the luxury of deploying so languidly, where surprise and precision engagement was of the essence.

61 Mech used some of the spare time on hand to move the HAA to a more suitable position about 8 km northeastwards up river. We laagered close by, approximately 8 km upriver. Adjacent to this splendid river our troops had time for some hard-earned rest, bathing in the crystal clear water and washing their dirty fatigues. All of us were laughing and splashing in the water, Meebos forgotten for the moment.

The Tac HQ Plans and Executes its Attack on SWAPO's Alpha Battalion

1 August found the freshly deployed Tac HQ alongside the Cuvelai River excited by the prospect of striking at the Alpha Battalion of SWAPO soon. The enemy target had been located near a shona in densely covered terrain to the north of the HAA near the Bambi River. It was expected that there were about two hundred insurgents in the base. The initial plan formulated by the Tac HQ was to strike the enemy with Mirages on 2 August. An airborne assault by Puma helicopters were then to be carried out by the company of Captain Eric Rabie. The Alouette gunships would be deployed to cut off the fleeing foe and for close air support for the ground attack.

The attack went in as planned just before midday with Brigadier Witkop Badenhorst accompanying Captain Neall Ellis in the command Alouette. As the air attack went in the Mirages and the gunships started drawing fire from enemy 14,5 mm anti-aircraft guns and RPG-7 rockets. The gunships were now shooting profusely at the enemy on the ground. Eventually it seemed to Neall Ellis in his Alouette flying overhead that the enemy had started fleeing. The company of Captain Rabie was then deposited by the Pumas and the ground attack went in. A fierce firefight ensued on the ground. The Pumas flew back to the HAA area and returned with the first stick of paratroopers from the company of Major Jab Swart. As soon as they were on the ground Swart's paratroopers became heavily engaged with some of the fleeing SWAPO. By this time a raging bushfire resulting from the air attack and threatening the troops on the ground. The battle ended after some fierce fighting, leaving one soldier of 32 Battalion killed and two wounded. Of the enemy 144 lay dead in the immediate vicinity where the fighting had taken place. A large booty of weapons and ammunitions was captured. Monday 2 August had been one of the successful days for Meebos II.

61 Mech Goes into Action – Surprise Attack on FAPLA from a Hidden Position

On 31 July we heard on radio intercepts our revered FAPLA brigade at Cuvelai screaming for help against the background thunder of their useless and wasteful artillery barrage – it was actually funny. "We need more artillery ammunition … ! We have fired all our artillery ammunition at the enemy! Our situation is abnormal! We are surrounded by the South Africans! We are going to be attacked at any moment … !"

From the enemy's sporadic and frantic staccato cries two things became crystal clear. The commander of 11 Brigade was trapped for the moment at Techamutete during one of his liaison visits there and the brigade at Cuvelai was absolutely sure that they were on the priority list to be attacked next. Apparently General Jannie Geldenhuys had not informed them about the ongoing peace negotiations in Washington and we were definitely not going to set them right.

The consequence was absolute terror and prolonged agony for 11 Brigade, a phenomenon I had referred to as the "Catastrophe Theory" in Chapter 8. The humorous part was that the FAPLA brigade commander informed Cuvelai by radio that there was enough artillery ammunition left in one of the warehouses. "Yes," the reply came, "the man who has the key has fled, because of all the excitement". We listened in amazement to these "comics" as our intelligence community referred to them.

On the afternoon of 3 August we received extremely valuable intelligence about the enemy's predicament through another radio intercept. FAPLA was going to dispatch a large logistics convoy from Techamutette that same night to replenish 11 Brigade along the treacherous 60 km route. We knew that FAPLA, true to their dogmatic form, would follow the main bush track.

At about 16:00 I was briefed about the unfolding situation at the HAA by Colonel Jan Pieterse. From Oshakati the message by Colonel Joep Joubert, Chief of Staff of Sector 10, Oshakati, was clear and simple: 61 Mech was to take out the enemy convoy that same night. I did a quick map-and-time appreciation and discussed my plan with Colonel Jan Pieterse and SAAF Captain Neall Ellis. Time was too short and the distance too great to respond with the whole of 61 Mech in an ambush of the enemy relief column alongside the road. Our unit was still laagered approximately eight kilometres away from the HAA next to the Cuvelai River. The distance from the laager position to the road was close on 20 km through immensely dense bush. I was also apprehensive of losing the element of surprise by closing in on a prospective ambush position with a noisy mechanised force in the dark.

My plan was simple: 61 Mech would ambush the enemy column with a single platoon and then pounce on the disrupted enemy with the Alouette gunships at first light. I would accompany Neall Ellis in the command aircraft to coordinate the ground action. I arranged with Ellis to pick me up at 61 Mech at first light the following morning. Done deal, let's move now, but let's move fast.

Time was of the essence and 61 Mech had to respond rapidly as dusk was approaching. I therefore immediately requested the Alouette gunships of Captain Neall Ellis to remain in the HAA for the night. I also requested the Pumas to undertake one more sortie before they left for the safety of Ondangwa – to drop one of my platoons (35 men) near a possible ambush position close to the Techamutete-Cuvelai gravel road. I subsequently requested a sortie of Mirages to fly a combat air patrol over the Cuvelai-Techamutete road the next morning as soon as it was light. Captain Neall Ellis would act as the on-board forward air controller.

I was now on my way with my Ratel driving swiftly towards 61 Mech. My choice for the ambush commander was tactical astute enthusiastic young mechanised infantry Captain Jan Malan, the commander of Alpha Company. Travelling with me was Captain Willem Ratte, scout supreme. I had asked him to brief my troops on enemy convoy tactics and counter-ambush drills. He had brought one of the enemy's landmines, as his other chore was to teach one of our ambushers how to lay it as a little surprise gift for the unsuspecting foe. I gave quick radio orders to Captain Jan Malan on the move and requested him to hastily prepare a platoon for the ambush. He was to personally command the minute force and was to take some 60 mm mortars with the 35-man fighting contingent. When I arrived at 61 Mech's position, Malan and his platoon were ready – excited, armed to the teeth and suitably camouflaged. They were the best of men anxiously awaiting the command to fly westwards into the unknown. I experienced a moment of apprehension on their behalf –

what will the night hold for them? At the same time I felt exhilaration at an opportunity to strike at the enemy.

Malan had already completed his appreciation of the mission and had selected a suitable ambush position on the map. He was ready to brief the commander of the lead Puma. As we finished the final verbal briefings our Chaplain Koos Rossouw said his prayer and the Puma helicopters started coming in. The platoon duly emplaned and flew off to the west as the sun was setting. The scene was set for fireworks.

"An ambush is a surprise attack on a moving enemy from a hidden position"

As the ambush platoon flew away into the setting sun I briefed my command group about the impending events. We would occupy some high ground nearby to maintain first-class communications with the ambush party of Captain Jan Malan throughout the night. The communication part was left in the capable hands of our trusty signals officer, Captain Sean MacSweeny. He would also activate the relay station of Mrs. Pompie van der Westhuizen on a farm near Tsintsabis in northern SWA – just to make damn sure of our radio communications. Our second-in-command Major Thys Rall would take charge of 61 Mech at first light and advance as swiftly as possible the next day to a link-up position with the ambush party of Malan near the Cuvelai-Techamutete road. I thought with some apprehension about our lonely platoon of thirty five men lying in ominous silence next to the road in ambush. Had we catered for every possible risk? It was now a waiting game! Our thoughts and prayers were constantly with our few at the front. Was somebody out there praying for the enemy?

At stages during the night we encountered some problems with our radio communication and those bedevilling skip distances. However, close to bewitching first light Jan Malan reported, his voice crystal clear and calm: He could hear the far-off drone of the enemy's approaching vehicles – excitement stirred all around. I reported the news about the approaching enemy convoy to the Tac HQ and confirmed that the gunships and the Mirages must be ready to fly at first light. The platoon-sized force of 61 Mech stopped the FAPLA column of more than 22 enemy vehicles dead in their tracks on the winding gravel road, approximately 13 km north of Cuvelai. It was an remarkably successful ambush.

I am now going to pick up the enthralling ambush story as told by Captain Jan Malan. This is from a report he wrote at my request a few years later (July 1986) when we served together at the Army Battle School. The report included a sketch (see Figure 18) he made of the contact with the enemy that night. I kept his report and gave him a copy two years ago. Jan Malan, still my friend to date, was ecstatic when he received the report he had written 22 years ago. Here is his story:

> My ambush party comprised my command element; three infantry sections; two Sappers from the Field Engineer troop attached to 61 Mech; my company signaller; one medical orderly. I instructed the two sappers to take five tank mines with their booty. We were as ready as can be to deploy westwards where the sun was already hanging low in the fiery Angolan sky. We arrived at our ambushing position selected with a few precious minutes daylight to spare. This was time enough for a final reconnaissance and to determine our exact deployments for the night. This was followed by final orders for the impending action. I decided to keep the ambushing platoon reasonably closely grouped for the night.
>
> There were huge trees alongside the road and dense under cover. I therefore

deployed the killing group reasonably close to the road, approximately 20 to 25 metres from the killing area selected. The ambush was set up as follows: Two infantry sections with two RPG-7 rocket launchers and three light machine guns were deployed in an extended formation parallel to the road; my HQ position was selected in the centre of the formation with the platoon commander acting as my second-in-command; the 60 mm mortar was positioned close to my HQ position under control of the platoon sergeant; the third infantry section deployed in a half-moon formation behind us to ensure allround defence; alternative positions were selected for the depth section on the northern flank to thwart a possible enemy counter-attack on our position from that direction, if it came to that. There was no time to dig into the ground, so each member of the ambush party filled two sandbags each with loose sand and placed it in front of them for cover against possible enemy fire. The platoon sergeant and two sappers were now instructed to plant the tank mines as well as Claymore shrapnel mines in front of us on the road. In addition a few trip flares (illumination) were placed in the tree line on the other side of the road.

Within 30 minutes of returning the two sappers reported to me that with all the excitement they had forgotten to arm the mines. Somewhat disappointed I decided to leave the mines as they were. In retrospect this was a divine intervention as we would have been too close to its explosions if activated by the enemy. The sign to unleash hell on the enemy would be the activation of the trip flares and the illumination of the killing area with 300m illumination flares. By now the 60 mm patrol mortar had found a suitable position to fire northwards over the trees towards the rear of the expected enemy convoy. We now established communications with the combat group HQ with a B25 radio and a dipole antennae and the waiting began.

At times through the night the troops in the killing area dozed off. They were kept awake by means of jerks on a communications rope, which we had strung from the one to the other. At about 04:00 we lost communications for a while with the combat group HQ. We felt very lonely out there in front in the total darkness and vastness of Africa. At about 05:30 we heard the subtle engine drone of the enemy convoy approaching our position from the north. All in the ambushing party were wide awake by now, nerves on end, excitements were stirring amongst us, adrenaline surging.

We reported to the Combat Group HQ that contact was imminent. I told the signaller to dismantle the B25 radio. He said quietly to me that the oncoming vehicles sounded to him like Bedford's. I now deployed the depth section to our northern flank. The section knew that they had to protect our northern flank from a possible enemy counter-attack as soon as our party started withdrawing from the killing area. All the troops by now had packed their kit and were carrying it in rucksacks on their backs. At about 05:45 the first two enemy vehicles entered the killing area right in front of us. We could hear from the exchanging of gears further back that the enemy convoy was slowing down one-by-one, as they caught up with the next vehicle on the rise. The first two vehicles were extremely close to each other and were now in the centre of our killing area – they looked like Russian Ural cargo trucks. The enemy was driving with all their vehicle lights switched off.

At this moment I gave the command to open fire on the two enemy vehicles in front of us. The troops immediately adopted firing positions standing up and started firing short bursts into the killing area. The light machine guns and RPG-7 rocket launcher fire added to the mayhem right in front of us. The two Claymore mines were set off at the same moment. The remains of the exploding enemy vehicles were clearly silhouetted by the blazing trip flares in the trees on the other side of the road. It was not necessary to fire the illumination flares, as the whole area was lit up in front of us. Massive explosions rippled as the trucks had obviously been loaded with mortar and artillery ammunition. It was astonishing that none of us were killed or maimed by the shrapnel flying all around. The 60 mm patrol mortar started firing speculatively on the enemy convoy further to the north.

There was instant chaos amongst the enemy's ranks. We could hear vehicles turning around, people shouting frantically, gears gnashing in panic and metal tearing as some of the vehicles crashed into each other. The convoy to the rear was trying to escape northwards back towards Techamutete, away from the pandemonium. After a short while I gave the killing group the order to cease fire and to make ready to withdraw on my command. The section on our northern flank was now given the command to open fire to cover our withdrawal.

All our actions were unfolding calmly as if we were busy with a drill exercise on a parade ground. The killing group started to withdraw orderly along our southeastwardly withdrawal route to a prearranged checkpoint. I looked at my watch and observed the hour-hand closing in on 15 minutes before first light. Our ambushing party withdrew for a distance of approximately 3 km and then doubled back to lay in ambush on our tracks. The welcoming pleasantness of first light arrived and we could start discerning dirty smiling features all around. Our camaraderie was protected by the denseness of the African bush against any hostiles, which may lurk in our immediate environ.

We re-established communications with the combat group HQ and gave them the good news and a brief Sitrep (situation report). There was happiness for our safety and success and congratulations were duly expressed. Commandant Roland de Vries

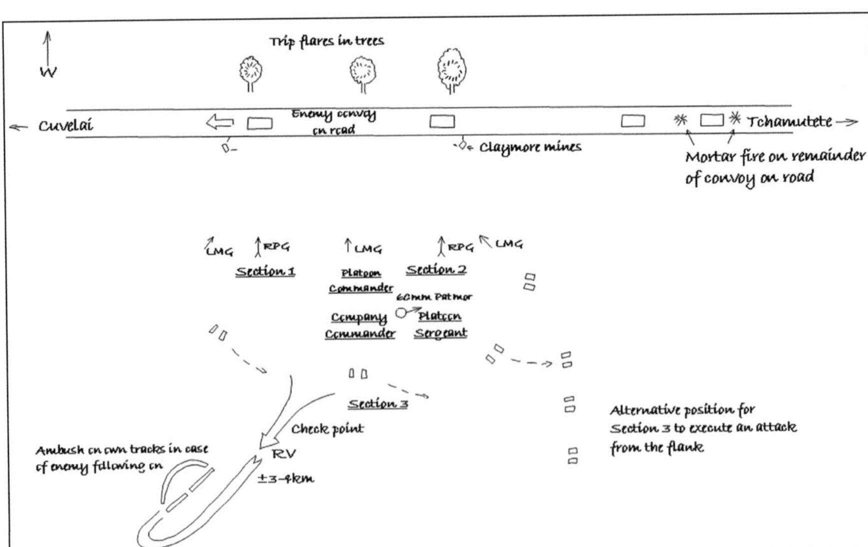

Figure 18: Ambush Sketch by Captain Jan Malan

informed me that two Mirages were on their way from Ondangwa to patrol the road between Cuvelai and Techamutete. He confirmed that he was on his way with the Alouette gunships. Our ambush party was furthermore tasked to sweep the ambush site as soon as the gunships arrived on the scene, which would provide close air support.

We prepared for our next mission. We were extremely tired, although we felt confident and highly satisfied by the extraordinary outcomes of the night. More so, we were fired up, ready to undertake the mopping-up operation with enthusiasm. As we formed into a sweep line to patrol back towards the killing area the gunships arrived. I established communications with the command Alouette of Captain Neall Ellis and with Commandant Roland de Vries. There were happy smiles allround. I thought that it was amazing what a small group of men could achieve through surprise – that was the magic about ambushing.

Captain Neall Ellis picked me up at first light with his command Alouette and the open formation of gunships flew aggressively westwards in the direction of the ambush site. I was sitting next to Ellis with his 7,62 mm Browning machine gunner poised and ready on the jump seat just behind us. The platoon of Captain Jan Malan was now about one kilometre from the ambush site. Two Mirages overhead reported that they could neither observe enemy activity on the road, nor see the vehicles that we say had been allegedly destroyed through the night. We responded, "Search for two black smudges on the road." The Mirage pilots soon observed the black smudges, but even so, there were no discernible signs of other Ural trucks. By now the platoon of Malan was sweeping steadily southwards in open formation using the road towards Techamutete as the axis of advance. The gunships started firing with 20 mm cannons at FAPLA soldiers on the ground. It was obvious from the air that the enemy remnants were wholly terrified and disoriented. Some of the enemy soldiers were staring up at the gunships with stark terror as they started fleeing in all directions. I momentarily felt a pang of sorrow for the hapless – it was a turkey shoot. Who was stupid enough to could have given the ill-fated the command to travel the road of death through the night?

Two wretched soldiers of FAPLA were running away from the sweeping platoon of Captain Jan Malan. I instructed Malan to capture one as we dearly required information from our enemy. As I uttered my command I saw the two luckless soldiers being felled by a hail of fire erupting from the platoon. Apparently one of the FAPLA soldiers killed was the convoy commander. He was already wounded and was about to throw a hand grenade at the platoon. Incidentally, one of the FAPLA soldiers had worn his badge of rank on his left breast pocket. One of our troops had neatly double-tapped the enemy soldier through his rank insignia. Jan Malan took the rank with the two bullet holes as a memento and still has it in his possession to this day.

The platoon came across two Urals that were left completely intact by FAPLA. Our soldiers took possession of their spoils of war. The vehicles were haphazardly loaded with piles of uniform and food, all jumbled together in the Ural. We later found loads of Norwegian tuna fish and spaghetti from Spain amongst the bits and pieces of FAPLA uniform. The two vehicles were now driven by two South African national servicemen (without official FAPLA driver's licences.) Seven other Russian Urals were found by the platoon in the surrounding bushes. Those that were not mobile any longer were destroyed with RPG-7 fire.

The gunships commenced with its sweep along the road in a northerly direction towards Techamutete. I was watching closely for dust clouds from the approximate positions of Cuvelai to the south and Techamutete to the north; that would have been an indication of possible enemy counter-actions after the early morning bedlam. All, however, was quiet on our northern and southern fronts. The avenging gunships kept on firing at clusters of enemy on the ground. It was altogether a strange feeling to have a bird's eye view of the fighting going on all around. It was captivating in a sense as one experienced a surreal feeling of complete safety, as if nobody could touch you up there. On the other hand there was a complete focus on particular segments of events unfolding down below. There was the calm chatter coming from microphone and headset, the drone of the aircraft's engine, now and then the stutter of the machine gun next to you ... We flew for approximately 20 km northwards and found another eleven vehicles that had been rushed away by the enemy during the night and early morning hours. Many were left abandoned, haphazardly driven into the bushes beside the road; a few had overturned.

It was almost macabre to see a gunship hovering, placing a few accurate 20 mm cannon shells into an Ural and, as flames erupted from the truck, drifting over to the next vehicle to repeat the treatment.

We flew back to the original position of our victorious platoon. There were eighteen spirals of black smoke gracing the cool Angolan sky. At about 08:00 the ambush operation and the mopping-up had been successfully completed. A complete convoy of 20 FAPLA vehicles had been annihilated and two captured. Well done, the gallant 35 young men of 61 Mech under command of Captain Jan Malan! Well done, Captain Neall Ellis and his gallant airborne fighters flying the fighting Alouette – those respected and courageous chopper boys doing their job, without regard to how completely vulnerable they were up there during operations such as Meebos. What a day it was for them!

The remainder of 61 Mech soon linked up with the exhausted platoon of Malan. The gallant 35 were extremely pleased to get back into their six-wheeled Ratels again. I was dropped off by Captain Neall Ellis close to 61 Mech and re-joined my combat group HQ. We moved about 8 km northeastwards where we occupied a laager position for the night. It was time to celebrate and congratulate our victorious young warriors. The spoils of the enemy's goodies were evenly distributed through the ranks of 61 Mech for a feast of Norwegian tuna and Spanish spaghetti. The two Urals – under new management – proudly took up position in the marching order of 61 Mech.

The successful ambush on the FAPLA convoy north of Cuvelai engendered a subtle reprimand from General Jannie Geldenhuys and Foreign Minister Pik Botha out of Washington one day later. Wow, rumours really spread fast! That kept the politicians busy for a while. The Angolan government had reacted heatedly – that will teach them to let fly with all their artillery ammunition at us near Cuvelai. The peace talks in Washington were obviously still in progress. Operation Meebos was evidently ongoing as well. It was utterly bizarre to me how things could be connected in different worlds. What was going on in the minds of my fighting youngsters, national servicemen, and 19 years-old? Those we had to keep alive? What were those terrified soldiers of FAPLA thinking in their trenches at Cuvelai? Did anybody inform them about the politics playing out in Washington? If you can think, but not make thoughts your aim – focus, Roland!

Well-known military author Al J. Venter in later years wrote a book with the title "Chopper Boys" in which he quotes Neall Ellis saying the following about the aforementioned contact with the convoy of FAPLA (incidentally Venter recorded the year as 1983 while it actually happened in 1982): "The following day we were told that the politicians in Pretoria were unhappy with the fact that the convoy had been knocked out. That FAPLA openly sided with our enemy, SWAPO, seemed to make no difference to the distant observers and we were aware that reports like this did tend to lower morale. We could never understand that if we were required to wage war against SWAPO, then everything and anyone opposed to us should be wiped out, particularly if they got in our way."

I could not discern anything amiss with the morale of 61 Mech that evening of 4 August 1982 ... laagering comfortably in the African bush somewhere between Cuvelai and Techamutete. On the contrary, I was not fired the following day, neither Colonel Joep Joubert who had given the instruction to slaughter the enemy convoy ... Wowee!

During a battle field tour in October 2010 I had the privilege to visit the ambush site with a few veterans of 61 Mech and 32 Battalion. It was 29 years later to be exact. My close friends, Camille Burger, Louis Bothma, Koos Moorcroft and Jaap Steyn were strolling along with me as I explained what had happened to our victorious platoon and the luckless FAPLA many years ago. We photographed the wrecks of all the FAPLA trucks which were destroyed in the ambush. All 20 of them are still lying there today alongside the road in the bushes. The local people seemed totally relaxed and unperturbed by the interest our few veterans showed in the broken relics of a bygone war. We casually walked about picking up exploded FAPLA mortar and artillery shells and the expended R4 rounds of Jan Malan's national servicemen ambush platoon. My thoughts wandered way back, as I thought of them. I kept a few of their R4 rounds as souvenirs. At that specific moment, on the gravel road surrounded by the thick Angola bush and in the sweltering African heat, I felt extremely proud to have commanded those young soldiers.

61 Mech Adopts a Mobile Ambushing Position along the Cuvelai-Techamutete Road

From 6 to 9 August I deployed 61 Mech in ambushing positions alongside the Techamutette-Cuvelai road in anticipation of unfolding enemy actions. We were given clear instructions by the Tac HQ that we were not to attack FAPLA unless we received authorisation from higher up. Yes sir! Noted ...

Our battle maps were put up against the sides of the Ratels of my command group underneath the camouflage nets. During the days I kept my leader group busy with map exercises, mini war-gaming and the preparation of contingency plans. I could see that they were enjoying the intellectual stimulation. The electronic warfare section was closely monitoring the enemy chatter. FAPLA was not at all happy with what had happened to their ill-fated convoy, we discovered.

The Tac HQ, 25 km to our east, was still in the same position next to the Cuvelai River. If they became too comfortable and did not move soon they would invite an unwelcome attack on their position by SWAPO for sure. They eventually moved their position about 15 km upstream on 8 August. No fresh intelligence on possible new positions of SWAPO to attack was available. We were waiting patiently for the next moves, either by own forces or the enemy. What will it be?

Disaster Strikes on 9 August 1982 – We Lose Fifteen Splendid Soldiers in One Foul Swoop

9 August – a crisp winter's morning found 61 Mech in an ambush position to the east

of the Cuvelai-Techamutete road close to where it intersected with the Mui River. The frustration of finding the next viable target for the Tac HQ was now the thing bedevilling the momentum and continuation of Meebos. Was the show petering out?

Captain Willem Ratte and his scouts were eagerly searching for the infamous Bravo Battalion of SWAPO – the main enemy 61 Mech had sought and with whom they had had a few skirmishes during Operation Daisy in November 1981. Roaming the wilderness somewhere as well were the Central and Eastern Area HQs and assorted loose elements of SWAPO.

Where the hell was the enemy, in six figure map grid reference's terms, please ... ? Show yourself damn it!

The target search by Ratte had now shifted to an area to the northwest of Cuvelai where fresh spoor of the enemy had been found. It was within two hour's striking distance from where 61 Mech was influencing the road between Techamutete and Cuvelai. The Tac HQ decided to launch an area operation into the suspect area: Fly in with Puma transport helicopters and Alouette gunships and hope for a lucky strike; fly out again, tally-ho! – was this a plan?

Eight Pumas were poised for the trooping mission of the splendid soldiers of 32 Battalion and 1 Parachute Battalion. Ready to go ... Right after midday the Pumas started flying the troops to their target zone just north of the Mui River, about 15 km to the west of the Cuvelai-Techamutete road. The flying pathway from the HAA almost took them over the deployment position of 61 Mech hidden in the bushes below and further along the dry river bed of the Mui. With their first flight the Pumas unwittingly flew over a deployed SWAPO anti-aircraft position lurking in a bushy patch of the Mui, approximately 15 km west of the Cuvelai-Techamutete road. The second time around, at about 15:00, four Pumas flew in a flurry with their precious cargo over the SWAPO position once again on the way to a landing zone. A curtain of enemy anti-aircraft fire suddenly erupted from below and slammed into the second Puma piloted by Captain John Twaddle. The Puma plummeted to the ground, exploded and burst into flames. Three SAAF crew members and twelve paratroopers were killed – for a brief moment one of the paratroopers was still alive ... This was a devastating tragedy; we had lost fifteen splendid soldiers in one foul swoop.

Soon afterwards the Alouette gunships went into action against more than thirty SWAPO soldiers running towards the crash site. A battle ensued and some of the Alouette took hits from below. One Alouette pilot reported seeing more than hundred SWAPO insurgents dancing around the stricken Puma. More gunships were scrambled and were on their way to the contact site. By this time the Tac HQ had informed 61 Mech about the unfolding tragedy in the Mui River. We immediately responded and started moving at best speed towards the position where we knew the fight with SWAPO and the gunships was raging, approximately 23 km to our west.

It took our vanguard close on one hour of bundu-bashing to get there. Move! Move! The battle was still raging at the site of the downed Puma as we moved in. The Alouettes were taking fire from SWAPO's formidable 14,5s and SAM-7s. The gunships needed to return to the HAA to re-arm and refuel. At this stage Captain Willem Ratte was still deployed further to the north, close to the Calonga River searching for enemy bases. 61 Mech reached the crash site in little more than an hour. As we deployed in an allround defensive open laager around the crash site we could hear a mini battle raging just to the north of our position.

My first instruction was for all of 61 Mech to remain extremely alert and to stay mounted on their Ratels until I had assessed the situation. I halted my Ratel next to the Puma helicopter, which was still smouldering. Looking down into the wreck we could see a number of charred remains of the paratroopers. It was obvious that nobody could be alive. However, our biggest fear was that the enemy could have captured someone. As this was as much an army as an air force show, SAAF Major Jaap du Preez[3] and I dismounted to inspect the blazing sight and analyse what had happened – our remaining fear centred on the possibility that some of the soldiers had been captured.

About fifty metres to the north we could see where the 14,5s had been positioned – the area was strewn with empty shell cases. The whole area was covered with the chevron boot print of SWAPO. Of the enemy themselves there was no sign at this stage. Realizing that SWAPO would have expected us, Jaap du Preez and I looked at each other and concurrently warned, "Watch out for booby traps and personnel mines." It was an eerie situation ... The three SAAF crew members had clearly been removed from the wreck by the SWAPO soldiers. The three bodies were propped up in their seats as if someone had posed them for a photograph in their scorched flying suits. Incidentally: In a contact with the enemy a day later a few Polaroid photographs were found on dead SWAPO insurgents, as well as some of the "dog tags" (two metal identification disks worn around the neck) of the paratroopers.

As I stood next to the wreck I momentarily felt an immense sadness, a heavy weight settling on my chest ... silent crying. I was thinking of those back home who did not yet know what had happened in the Mui on this fateful 9 August. My pondering did not last long as I was interrupted by a Ratel-90 approaching the crash site. Close to me lay one of the doors of the Puma which had been blown to one side. The approaching Ratel-90 belonged to Second Lieutenant Dewald Weideman, one of the troop commanders of Captain Chris du Toit of Charlie Squadron. Weideman dismounted and started walking in my direction ... Why? Chris du Toit shouted at him to get back on his Ratel. As I put up my hand and echoed the warning to halt him there was a tremendous explosion right in front of me. Weideman was flung into the air, one foot and the bottom part of his torso was blown to bits, but our man was alive ... Medics! Doctor! Medics! Quick! Call for a Puma casevac now! Again I shouted: "No one, but NO ONE get off your Ratels! Repeat my message down the chain of command now, AGAIN!" There was an eerie respectful silence that enshrouded the death site.

Jaap du Preez and I then found a drag mark from the Puma wreck to a lonely tree approximately thirty yards away. We could see the body of one of the paratroopers propped up against the stem of a Mopani tree. We walked very carefully towards the site, searching the earth for signs of booby traps or personnel mines. The paratrooper was dead yet he must have been alive for a while, probably thrown from the Puma by the explosion. His skin was blistered and hung in tatters from him. The pain must have been excruciating. He was shot through the centre of his forehead – was this a *coup de grace* by the enemy?

Du Preez and I returned to the wreck and started counting the bodies. We repeated the count six times to make very sure that all had been accounted for. We then confirmed our counts. I then instructed one of the Ratels to drive towards the Puma wreck and for our soldiers to carefully transfer the remains into body bags. The body bags were not enough and some of the charred remains had to share bags. A Puma was called in to fly the

3 Air support officer of the SAAF, who was deployed with 61 Mech for the duration of Meebos II.

remains to the HAA and then back to SWA. 61 Mech then left the Puma site to laager a few kilometres to the north of the Mui River for the night. We would return the next day to evacuate the helicopter wreck – we were definitely not going to leave it for SWAPO to use for propaganda purposes later on.

Sadness permeated the laager of 61 Mech as the sun set in the west over the Calonga River. Somewhere out there was Captain Willem Ratte and his scouts and the enemy in the darkness ... That night Major Alex Britz made our command group a potjie. He had made a deep hole in the ground for his fire so that the glow could not be discerned by any watchful enemy. We sat on our camp chairs in the bush in camaraderie, surrounded by darkness and the silence from within.

At midnight I was called to the radio by my signals officer Captain Sean MacSweeny. It was the Tac HQ. They had sifted through the remains of our slain soldiers and could only find signs of fourteen. One was missing. I replied: "No ways, check again." Captain Jaap du Preez and I checked our counting procedure of the day once again. We were very sure of the numbers; we had counted fifteen, over and over.

At 03:00 the next morning I was contacted again by radio. The Tac HQ informed me that the medical staff at the HAA had found fifteen unique bones, which affirmed the count was correct. Relief washed over me.

In Memoriam –The three crew members of the South African Air Force: Captain John Twaddle; Lieutenant Chris Pietersen and; Flight Engineer Sergeant Grobbies Grobbelaar. The twelve paratrooper national servicemen of 1 Parachute Battalion: Corporal Esuas Lombaard (20); Lance Corporal Stephen Hoare (20); Rifleman Andre Wolmerans (21); Rifleman Grant Krull (20); Rifleman Craig Moody (20); Rifleman Andries Hermias van Niekerk (20); Rifleman Anton Kruger (22); Rifleman Martin le Roux (22); Rifleman James Marshall (20); Rifleman Alan de Klerk (19); Rifleman Shane Patrick Mallon (21) and; Rifleman Ruffle Hilton-Barret (21).

In later years I came across the following message on an internet site: "3 April 2009. My brother died in Angola together with 12 parabats and 2 more pilots on 9 August 1982. Chris Pietersen I still miss you and love you to bits. Your sis ... "

As darkness settled over the laager, some of it also settled in the souls of the 1,000 soldiers of 61 Mech who became the lone victims of their own apprehensions and thoughts once again.

10 August 1982 – One Whopper of a Contact by the Strike Force on the Calonga

The next day 61 Mech returned to the Puma site. The field engineers carefully cleared the area of the wreck of booby traps and other explosive devices left by the foe. Our RSM, WO1 H.G. Smit, and the tiffies (technical personnel) then loaded the helicopter wreck onto one of our SAMIL cargo trucks. The Puma would be returning home with 61 Mech. Incidentally: This would be the third SAAF helicopter 61 Mech would be taking home in two years. The first was an Alouette gunship shot down by FAPLA during Operation Protea at Môngua on 25 August 1981. The second was an Alouette gunship shot down by FAPLA at Evale on 29 December 1981.

In the meantime the strike force at the HAA on the Cuvelai River was raring to go; they wanted to get back at the enemy. Colonel Jan Pieterse was on his way to 61 Mech at about 08:00 with the command Alouette of Captain Neall Ellis to join us for a few moments. However, on the way one of the reconnaissance teams of Captain Willem Ratte reported that they had sighted suspected enemy movement in the vicinity of the Calonga River to the north of us. Captain Neall Ellis with his command Alouette and two gunships veered away to go and investigate. Approximately 30 km north of Cuvelai along the Calonga River Neall Ellis and the two gunships came across a large enemy group who started firing SAM-7s, RPG-7 rockets, 14,5 mm anti-aircraft and small arms at them. Ellis immediately suspected that this was the mother lode. The target area was vast as the enemy was spread out over an area of more than two square kilometres. The other gunships were immediately scrambled. Unfortunately, it was still early in the morning and the Pumas were still on their way north to the HAA from Ondangwa.

The Mirages were called in and with the gunships started taking a heavy toll of the enemy on the ground. The enemy was fleeing in the direction of a fording site over the Calonga River Captain Willem Ratte had come across during one of his earlier scouting missions. Eventually the helicopters had to return to the HAA to re-arm and refuel. The fighting Alouette soon returned to the contact zone. Close to 11:00 the infantry companies of 32 Battalion and 1 Parachute Battalion were trooped into the contact zone guided by the gunships. At the end of the day 116 SWAPO insurgents had been killed and two captured. Many of the enemy's 14,5s were taken during the fighting. Own forces were intact; none were killed on this victorious day.

It was a great pity that on such a productive fighting day critical minutes had been lost by the Pumas, which had to return after spending the night at Ondangwa ... Precious hours were lost each day because of this particular SAAF safety practice.

As soon as 61 Mech had completed the job at the crash site on the Mui River we moved about 18 km northwest and leaguered close to the fast flowing Calonga River. The position was close to the old enemy base "Smelling Rat," which had been attacked on 31 July. We had driven through this abandoned position of SWAPO and could see their trenches. We were now in a position to either react towards the Techamutete road or to support the task force with the fight against SWAPO in the area, if called upon to do so.

The Calonga River was the same river into which paratrooper Human had disappeared with his parachute during Operation Reindeer on Cassinga on 4 May 1978, never to be found.

Following on 11 August 1982 – Operation Meebos Starts Petering Out

On 11 August 61 Mech moved east and then swung north to occupy a hide to the north of the HAA. We were now deployed slightly to the east of the high ground of Techamutete. It was rumoured that there was a possible SWAPO logistics base to be attacked at Techamutete and we wanted to be close to the action. Captain Willem Ratte later on reported that SWAPO had withdrawn from the suspected position.

Early the next morning my command group was assembled around me in the centre of the laager. It was time for our five-minute standing conference and quick orders by yours truly and a snap prayer by our chaplain, Koos Rossouw. Under the prayer I spotted one of our soldiers running at high speed towards us from due south. He shouted at me, "Commandant, terrorists, 6 o'clock, they are passing our laager." I immediately hissed at Koos Rossouw, "Koos, say Amen. Terrorists, 6 o'clock from our position, they are passing our laager!"

Needless to say, the few "terrs" had by now spotted the laagered array of Ratels and were hightailing it from the danger zone before we could react. I could not recollect whether Koos had prayed for them as well. Anyhow, the Dear Lord was good to a few hapless SWAPO that morning.

We could feel that things were quieting down. The next day we moved to the HAA a few kilometres due south of us. The news was that Colonel Johan Roos, an armour man, was taking over command of the task force from Colonel Jan Pieterse.

Area operations still continued for a while but did not produce any spectacular results. Here and there a few small contacts were still joined with the enemy. It seemed as if SWAPO had evaded to the north in the direction of Jamba (a small Angolan settlement near the railway line, approximately 50 km northwest of Techamutete not to be confused with UNITA's traditional base, Jamba, in the far southeast of Angola). Colonel Johan Roos subsequently gave instructions to end Operation Meebos and decided to move the Tac HQ and the task force back to Ondjiva.

61 Mech followed the Mui River via Môngua back to Ondjiva – it was like a dusty highway. One more spectacle would befall my eyes on the way to Môngua. It would make me adore and appreciate the troops of 61 Mech so much more. Early one morning a Ratel mounted infantry section of Captain Jan Malan's forever spirited Alpha Company rolled past, trailing dust. Tethered to the spare wheel on the roof of the said combat ready Ratel was a goat (for messing purposes only, it was later to be confirmed by me). I said to myself, de Vries let it be, a mobile mechanised goat, what the hell next?

However, the next day I encountered the same Ratel. This time there were a few mechanised chickens neatly tethered to the camouflage net, cackling happily on the move! I was curious and stopped the Ratel for a moment with a hand signal. I asked the troops what the hell was going on, were they farming or what and what had happened to the goat of yesterday? They said to me in a serious tone, "No commandant, we swopped our goat for a few chickens yesterday, it is a bargain, the goat had died – we gave them Ratpacks (24-hour ration packs) as well." I bade them to dash forth and to enjoy their dinner that evening in the dust, wherever.

Goodbye Ratel, goodbye chickens ...

We spent a few leisurely days at Ondjiva airfield where we did maintenance chores on all our vehicles and equipment and by 25 August returned to Omuthiya. On 10 January 1983 I would hand over command of 61 Mech to Commandant Gert van Zyl. Thus, one of the most exciting periods of my military career came to an end, after two years of service with awesome 61 Mech in the field; and those wonderful young soldiers with whom I had shared my life and from whom I had learned so much.

Epilogue – Simmering Fighting Power and Muttered Threats

So what, I thought when 61 Mech returned to Omuthiya by the end of August? Our fighting unit had done what it had been asked to do in a first-class, professional manner. Was every sixty seconds worth the distance ran? I thought so. Notwithstanding the politics and the military grand strategies ... I was proud of 61 Mech and each one of our young soldiers who had done their duty. I will never forget them! Soldiers like Rifleman D.P. Crouser, the only one 61 Mech had lost during Operation Meebos, had his place in our hearts!

The operation had definitely been a success as far as this type of counterinsurgency operation goes and the enemy had suffered dearly from its proceeds. Winning either a revolutionary or counter-revolutionary war takes massive organisation, dedication, sacrifice and time. Meebos was such an operation. Any government, such as ours, needed to decide whether it was willing to pay the price. Half-measures lead only to protracted, costly defeats. I was not only thinking of our slain fifteen soldiers of 9 August 1982. The war was not over yet and the conflict was escalating seemingly out of control. How far were the opposing governments, South Africa, Angola and Cuba, prepared to go with the Bush War?

What was the military situation in southern Angola by the end of August 1982 as the war for SWA/Namibia continued? The hunt for SWAPO in the Area-In-Dispute continued relentlessly. For some time this advantageous situation would be maintained without FAPLA's undue interference, until 1984 that is.

FAPLA and the Cubans, supported by the Soviets kept on fighting UNITA. They now started focussing seriously on ousting UNITA from southeast Angola, which had become the thorn in their flesh – the guerrilla strongholds of Dr. Jonas Savimbi at Mavinga and Jamba nestled slap-bang within his liberated zone and had become the sought-after targets of FAPLA and the Cubans – they were soon going to bleed out there repeatedly, they just did not know it yet.

In the meantime, the enemy bided their time with the SADF. The plot was thickening in terms of military man and machine. Angola and Cuba kept on reinforcing their menacing military screen hemming the Area-In-Dispute. Wide-ranging enemy air defences besieged the area of operations of the SADF, and impressively so. At the same time FAPLA forces were continually reimbursed with more and more Cuban combat units flowing in from Havana and military hardware from Moscow. By 1987–88 the Cubans had built their force to a cool 55,000 soldiers. The Cubans, as were countless FAPLA brigades, were being ardently equipped with the most modern Russian military hardware. The unnerving question was how much the South African military and national intelligence knew and understood about this?

Things were building up nicely towards a vicious conventional battle waiting for the SADF in southeast Angola in August 1987 – a piece of hallowed ground at the far end of the earth between the Lomba and Cuito rivers – somewhere between heaven and hell!

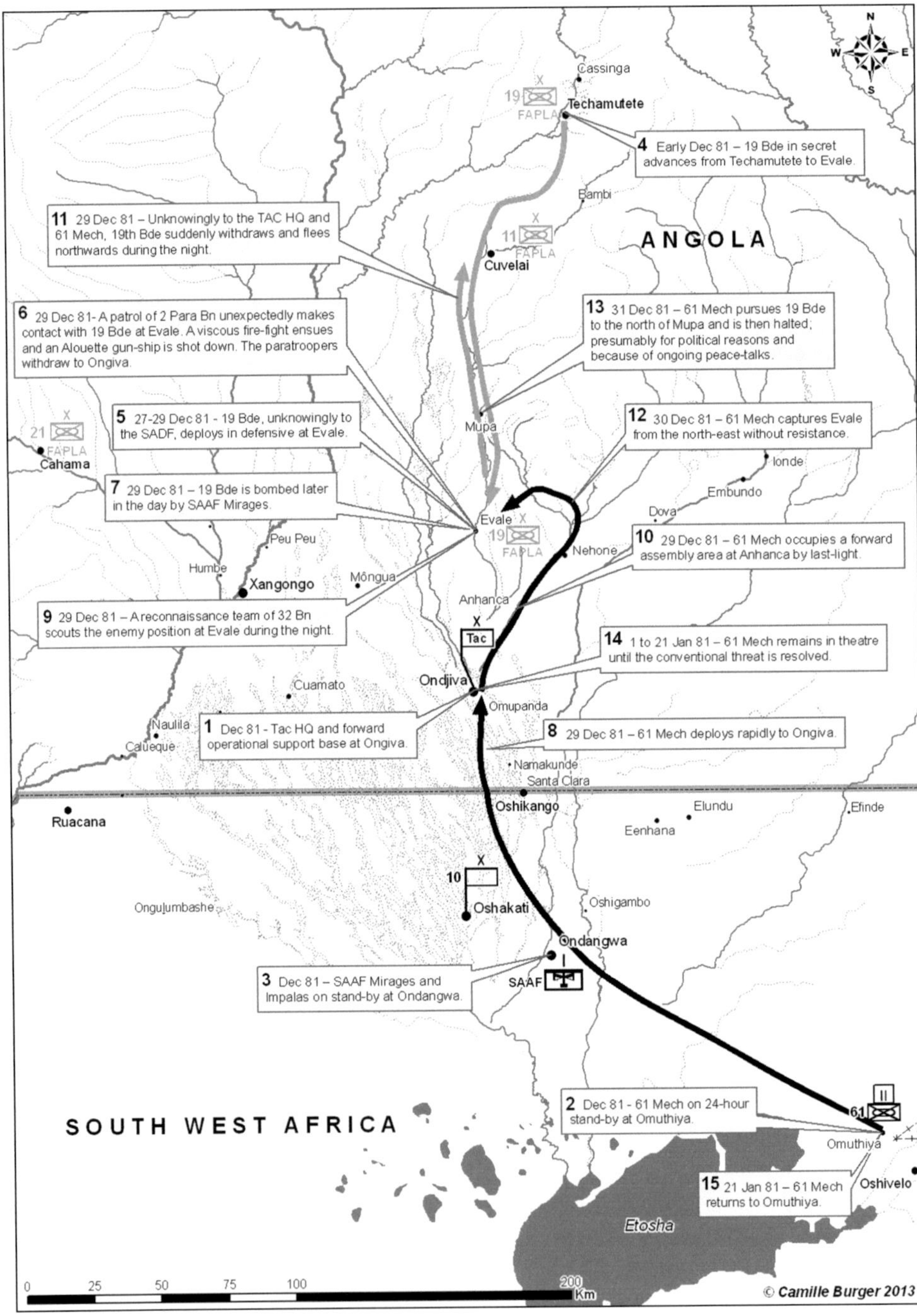

Map 14: Operation Makro, December 1981 to January 1982

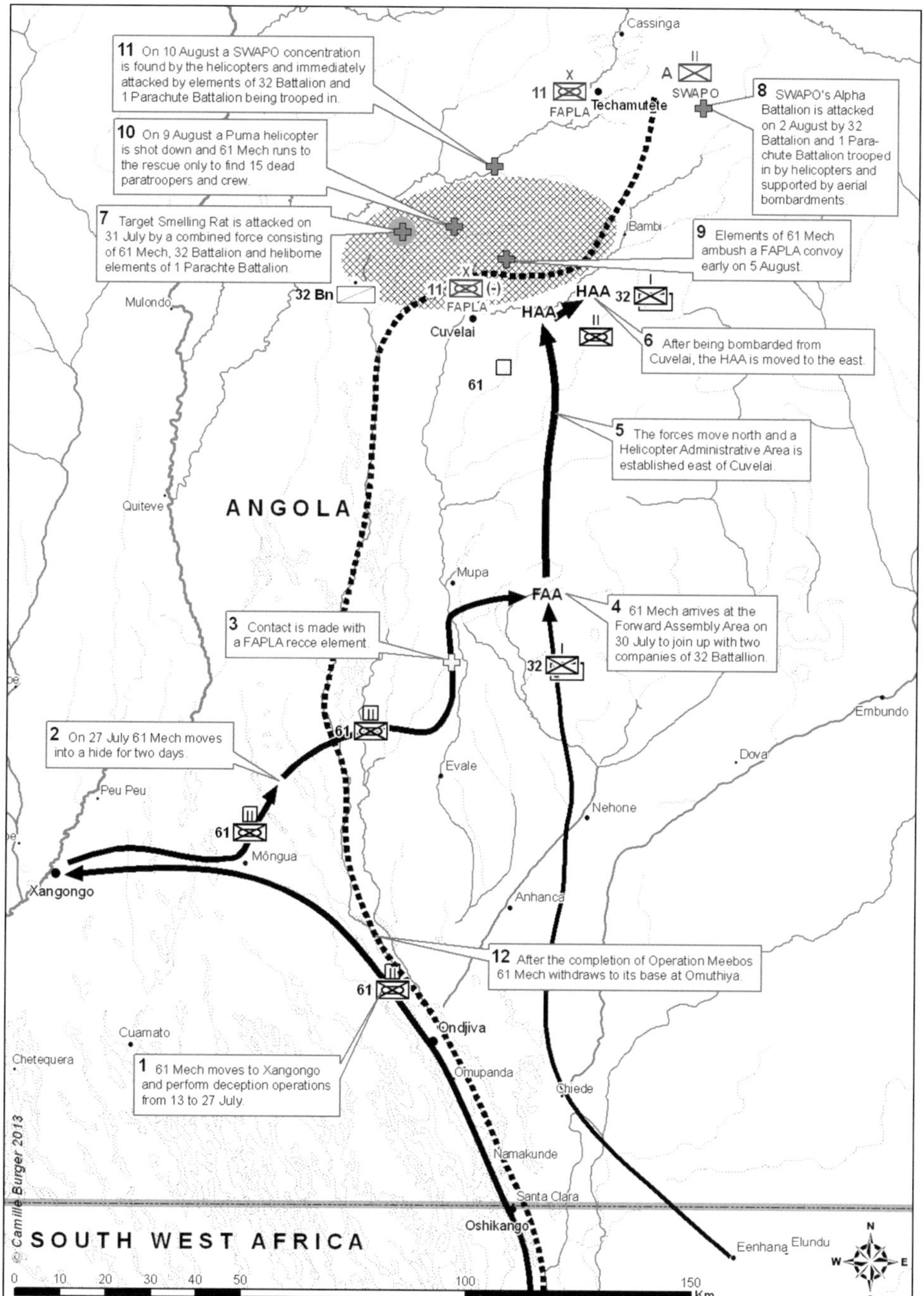

Map 15: Operation Meebos, July to August 1982

15

Manoeuvre Battles on the Chambinga

Somewhere between Heaven and Hell

Our strategy is to pit one against ten while our tactic is to pit ten against one ... Concentration of forces is the first and most essential condition.

Mao Tse-tung

(In southeast Angola the SADF broke this rule, and fought with one against twenty ... and won!)

Preamble – Where Angels Feared to Tread

My next story is about the final chapter of Operation Modular, a phase the enemy came to fear! This campaign played out in mystical southeast Angola in the magical months of October–December 1987. For the SADF storming in offensively against all odds where angels feared to tread in support of UNITA and winning all the way through manoeuvre was seemingly the logical thing to do. As such the small SADF brigade inserted into this firestorm needed to fight from the relative safety of the eye. The fighting units, unlikely as it seems, could find pockets of safety by means of controlled dispersion and concentration in the denseness and darkness of the African bush!

During the battle for southeast Angola a diminutive combined South African mechanised formation, nicknamed 20 Brigade and a few UNITA guerrilla battalions faced more than eight hostile mechanised brigades and two tactical groups in the field. At no stage during this war were more than 3,000 South African soldiers pitted against the more than 30,000 of the enemy – a Gideon's band of young national servicemen who fought like true heroes.

The success of this battle hinged on the crossing site over the Chambinga River. It was not a bridge, but a log and wreck-strewn fording place with considerable scatterings of human bones and decaying remains of past battles. From there one needed to fight approximately 27 kilometres further westwards through dense African bush and interlocking rows of heavily defended trenches and minefields to get to Cuito Cuanavale and its bridge of vital strategic and tactical importance. It was a place for any prudent manoeuvrist to avoid; obviously!

Little did South Africa know then that the aftermath of the epic mobile fights for the Lomba and Chambinga would lead to a mammoth grinding struggle to be fought east of Cuito Cuanavale later on in January-August 1988. Let nobody mislead you; a real battle was fought on its eastern shore. Three of our Olifant main battle tanks still lie in the minefields where our troops had fought courageously , where precious lives were sacrificed and the enemy had suffered dearly! I think of those sacrifices today with compassion instead of resentment for what had ultimately been achieved: These battles were the triggers for peacemaking come August–December 1988. However, let us for the moment focus on its prelude, the manoeuvre battle on the Chambinga that was fought successfully at the operational and tactical levels of war.

This significant episode of the South African Border War was intertwined with the Angolan Civil War and unfolded somewhere between heaven and hell at the far end of the earth. The ground became saturated with the blood of many enemy soldiers. The dense entangled African bushveld was literally strewn with the metal remnants of the enemy's military hardware and white-bleached bones; even from battles fought there in the past. Over this piece of disputed earth the Russian MiGs screamed uncontested from the skies and bombed the South African and UNITA forces.

31 SADF soldiers were killed in action by December; close on three thousand guerrilla fighters of UNITA had died in the field; on the Cuban-Angolan side four thousand and eighty five soldiers were sacrificed. More than 194 pieces of armour, 92 pieces of other military hardware, 9 MiG combat aircraft and 9 helicopters of Russian origin had been destroyed. In stark comparison 3 tanks, 5 Ratel infantry fighting vehicles, 5 other varieties, 1 Bosbok light reconnaissance aircraft and 2 Mirage combat aircraft of the SADF had been destroyed. These vast quantified differences were mind boggling and the reasons for this beg to be explained.

How far could an unending string of tactical successes by a few South African and UNITA warriors take them in southeast Angola? In the process of analysing the battle for Chambinga one should not become overly subjective or emotionally involved on any side.

Centre Stage for Battle – Forsaken Soil

The erstwhile hunting field of the Portuguese in southeast Angola had become the guerrilla-liberated area of UNITA led by Jonas Savimbi in their long drawn-out fight against the MPLA. This piece of contested ground was the thorn in the flesh of the MPLA government who were supported by the collective might of close on 55,000 Cuban troops and umpteen Russian military advisers.

Notwithstanding, Fidel Castro the dictator of Cuba had warned FAPLA countless times not to venture so far east, as they would burn more than their fingers and bleed out in the bush on forsaken soil, as he had reaffirmed in his memoirs: "I should say that we had always been opposed to those offensives against Jamba, because every time it happened South Africa intervened at the last moment with its modern air power, its powerful artillery and its armoured forces, able to inflict such heavy losses on the Angolan troops – and they couldn't be stopped ... We discussed this matter with the Soviets and the Angolans every year. 'Don't carry out X offensive, don't get into such wasting, costly and pointless offensives. And count us out if you do...' Once in a while we'd convinced them but it was an annual exercise".

These futile annual exercises about which Castro grumbled about started in 1981. In 1985 and 1986 such fruitless operations led to FAPLA's bloody demise every time through the subtle intervention by the SADF in support of UNITA. The 127 mm Valkiri rockets had a field day each time. This was when FAPLA started voicing their unbounded fear for the fiery metal balls of the Valkiri nicknamed the "Shindungu" – the red pepper that burns. During one of FAPLA's ambitious advances in 1985 towards Mavinga the Impalas of the SAAF ambushed six Russian Hind MI-14 combat helicopters by shooting them down one-by-one as they flew interspersed southwards along the Cuito River. However, by 1987 the enemy's air force had gained supremacy in the skies over Angola.

FAPLA and the Cubans did not learn from their mistakes nor heeded the warning of Castro. On 14 August 1987 they trundled southeastwards with their unwieldy mechanised force from their well-prepared bridgehead at Cuito Cuanavale with the purpose of capturing illusive Mavinga and mystical Jamba. They advanced right into the jaws of death waiting for them on the floodplains of the Lomba. Apparently, like so many before in the history of warfare, FAPLA did not realise that winning did not lie in numbers, but in artful manoeuvre and leadership. Notwithstanding, this time FAPLA had surprised the SADF with their large force they had quietly mustered and by the initial ferocity showed during the advance. Had the government of South Africa and the high command of the SADF misread the "subtle warning signs" and for that reason became the victim of subjective thinking?

Early in March South African Special Forces reconnaissance teams operating deep inside Angola had reported about a massive enemy build-up towards the southeast. There was other intelligence about huge Soviet Ilyushin transport aircraft flying military supplies and heavy equipment from Russia to Luanda for months. This was supported at a steady pace with large military convoys moving from Luanda to Menongue with close on 400 logistic vehicles at a time. The balance of military power in Angola was progressively shifting in favour of the MPLA government and its African army.

On Wednesday 13 May 1987 *The Manila Standard* (Manila being the capital city of the Philippines) published an article by David B. Ottaway of *The Washington Post* about the Soviet build-up in Angola from which I took the following extract:

> Washington – The Soviet Union has completed a major arms build-up in Angola for what the Reagan administration thinks will be a substantial summer offensive against US-armed rebels fighting the Marxist government there. A senior administration official said US intelligence sources estimate that Moscow had sent $1 billion worth of arms to Angola in the last year, bringing total Soviet military aid to $4 billion in the last decade. Hundreds of flights during the past four months have transported heavy arms and war material from the capital of Luanda to Huambo in South-Central Angola for an offensive that could begin late this month, the official said ... The shipments included a sizable number of ground-to-air missiles for use against the South Africans, which support the rebel forces. US analysts have been watching the build-up closely, not only to assess the military threat to the guerrillas, who are led by Jonas Savimbi, but also to determine Soviet leader Mikhail Gorbachev's intentions in Southern Africa. Both the United States and South Africa back Savimbi. Many authorities contend that the Soviet Union under Gorbachev is less interested in the Third World generally than it was under his predecessors and is reluctant to make major new commitments there ... But the arms build-up in Angola ... suggests that this judgement may be premature.

When reading such articles now one's blood runs ice cold to imagine what could have happened during that particular military scuffle in southeast Angola.

Steadily, but unobtrusively a large number of enemy brigades had made their way southeastwards. In March there were only two brigades and by August there were 8 mechanised brigades and two tactical groups with their MiGs comfortably nested at Cuito Cuanavale ready to march. Did South Africa lack in the department of strategic intelligence? Hello, weren't there a few surprises coming? Next would be the enemy's massive reinforcement of the southeastern front in November, followed by the uncomfortable appearance of Castro's elite 50th Cuban Division in May 1988 near Cahama in the west. The war situation had escalated dramatically and the fighting situation on the ground had become ... quite interesting and extremely dangerous for all belligerent parties. This time it was not going to be a walkover for the gallant SADF and their UNITA allies. By the same token, a few nasty surprises were waiting for FAPLA and the Cubans as well.

Once again the SADF would intervene to support UNITA and to check the enemy's advance on Mavinga and Jamba. Once again it would be done with negligible fighting numbers, but with much more ferocity than ever before. Yes, granted, this brave move by the SADF was advantageous for the counterinsurgency war in northern SWA: For as long as UNITA controlled southeast Angola, SWAPO was kept at bay and away from the doorstep of the Okavango Province and Caprivi on the far eastern border. The stage was set for the next vicious round of fighting with FAPLA and the Cubans. What political and high level outcomes would ensue from this exceptional fight in isolated southeast Angola?

Overview of the Situation – Those Compelled to Defend and Those about to Counter-Attack

When Operation Modular started in 1987 I was the second-in-command of the South African Army Battle School at Lohatlha. The commander was Brigadier Eddie Webb. As enthusiastic conventional soldiers we were both interested in and concerned about the precarious operational situation flaring up in the Western Sub-Theatre of War. Although the SADF kept Modular hush-hush we were kept abreast of unfolding events by a few of our officers returning from the front such as anti-aircraft officer Major Francois Cilliers.

The battle commenced in all seriousness when FAPLA started advancing deliberately southeastwards on 14 August to establish their next bridgehead over the Lomba River. Their offensive developed over a wide front on separate approaches with four frontline fighting brigades and two tactical groups leading the charge. These were: 47 Brigade reinforced by Tactical Group 1; 59 Brigade; 21 Brigade; and 16 Brigade supported by Tactical Group 2. The enemy was highly confident because of their overwhelming strength and did not contemplate defeat. Meanwhile the enemy's rear area at Cuito Cuanavale was defended by 13, 25 and 66 Brigades, while 8 Brigade ferried logistics between Menongue and Cuito Cuanavale (192 km). All in all, the enemy possessed more than 150 modern Russian T-54/55 main battle tanks in their arsenal.

The SADF had "almost" no other option but to launch Modular in support of UNITA. The war aim was limited and simply intended to halt FAPLA on the Lomba River and to drive them back from whence they came. Underlying the military mission of the South Africans was the political wish that the enemy should be harmed so severely that they would not contemplate returning at least within a year. Hope for South Africa not to become openly involved on a large scale faded as the SADF was about to be drawn deeper and deeper into an all-out conventional war.

First to be employed against FAPLA in mid-August were a few teams of Special Forces, soon to be followed up by elements of 32 Battalion and a few 155 mm G-5 guns, 127 mm Valkiri Multiple Rocket Launchers and 120 mm mortar batteries. Eventually the SAAF ground attack aircraft were given permission to join the fight. A number of vicious skirmishes ensued with the advancing brigades, but to no avail as the enemy came marching on. Then 32 Battalion became fully committed near the end of August to be followed by 61 Mechanised Battalion Group (61 Mech) during the first week of September. These few units were originally commanded by Colonel Jock Harris, the commander of 32 Battalion at the time.

It was rumoured that he did not see eye-to-eye with Major General Willie Meyer, the commander of the South West Africa Territorial Force (SWATF) on the way the campaign was being conducted and Colonel Deon Ferreira took over from him on 5 September and was now commanding the newly established 20 Brigade while Brigadier J.T. Louw manned the operations node of SWATF at the HQ of Sector 20 in Rundu. There followed a number of successive defensive blows against the enemy supported by devastating air and artillery strikes. From 9–16 September 32 Battalion under command of Commandant Robbie Hartslief softened up FAPLA's 47th Brigade in a series of significant skirmishes close to the source of the Lomba. In the same fighting sequel 21 Brigade was seriously mauled when the enemy's armoured formation tried to cross the river at the confluence of the Cunzumbia River on its way to Mavinga. On 3 October the enemy hordes were stopped decisively on the Lomba at the confluence of the Cuzuzi River in an epic engagement. This was the day 61 Mechanised Battalion Group under command of Commandant Kobus ("Bok") Smit destroyed the 47th Brigade of FAPLA and removed them from the Angolan troop list forever. In the process all four of the enemy's offensive frontline brigades, namely 47, 59, 21 and 16 Brigade and their two tactical groups had been progressively mauled up to then. A fair share of the mutilations accrued to the formidable 155 mm G-5 gun, the 127 mm Valkiri Multiple Rocket Launchers and Mirage and Buccaneer ground attack aircraft of the South Africans.

The enemy's overwhelming ground and air power had not visibly succeeded in dampening the ferocious combat edge of South African and UNITA's relatively small fighting force, or for that matter in marring their fighting spirit. The enemy's air force was Worrisome, make no mistake. The casualties of FAPLA mounted as the progressive battering of their brigades continued. There were a few shocking losses on the side of the SADF and UNITA as well, which started ebbing morale. It boggles the mind that the Angolan Air Force never attacked Rundu from where the SADF's fighting was supported.

Within the context of manoeuvre warfare the battle of the Lomba on 3 October was a decisive turning manoeuvre. The unnerving blow had caused the enemy to flee back north in disarray and panic in unplanned defeat to occupy intermediate defensive positions between the Lomba and Chambinga rivers. In the memoirs of Russian military adviser Lieutenant Igor Zhdarkin who served with 21 Brigade, he pronounced their disastrous retreat as "indeed being a harrowing experience, since FAPLA troops were under continuous bombardment by the SADF, along with the sniping, mining, and other harassment by the UNITA forces on the ground". The author furthermore related that even Russians who had served in Afghanistan had never experienced such "horrors" as the barrages of SADF artillery across the Lomba River. "Under fire from the G-5 guns and the Mirage and Buccaneer aircraft FAPLA brigades panicked and deserted the field in flight, leaving behind their Soviet equipment in a graveyard of tanks, trucks, ammunition, and other material." The enemy's flight was followed by a lull in battle during the latter part of October characterised by the relentless pounding of FAPLA's brigades by any physical and psychological means possible; from devastating direct and indirect fire means and loudspeaker-hailing (typically referred to as "ground shout" by the SADF), to a succession of well-coordinated and directed ground attacks by the resolute Mirages and Buccaneers of the SAAF.

It was probably due to political and military reasons for caution that South African forces were inserted piecemeal into battle. In this way the neglect of a fundamental principle of warfare, namely the concentration of forces, plagued the SADF throughout this campaign. The outcome was that a few South African soldiers fought desperately in the frontline for life and death with minimal equipment and operational reserves and logistics against this numerically superior power. Incidentally, 4 South African Infantry Battalion (4 SAI being similarly organised as 61 Mech) and a squadron of 13 Olifant main battle tanks only arrived on 20 October at Rundu from Middelburg, South Africa. At last, an additional mechanised unit and the few tanks were now available for the counteroffensive. That was it, concerning own forces mobilised for the war in southeast Angola. Astonishing!

In this sense I had a serious issue on how we fought conventionally in Angola as it had become a trait to fight with a combat group against a brigade instead of mustering the text book ratio of at least three to one in our favour. (Operation Protea in August 1981 was an exception where the SADF attacked the enemy's brigades more or less on a par.) Naturally this regretful practice hampered three important principles of the offensive, namely: The maintenance of momentum; to be organised in depth; and to maintain adequate operational reserves. There were never really enough forces available at the front to achieve this. This practise exerted extreme pressure on our fighting units in the field and gradually marred their morale as well. More so, when planning for the counter-attack commenced, an explicit instruction from on high was issued to spare the battle-weary 61 Mech in the coming fight. As one of our arms was now tied behind our back, the new kid on the block, namely Combat Group Charlie (4 SAI), was destined to bear the brunt of the impending battle.

I arrived at Rundu on Monday 12 October to participate in the final phase of Modular. By this time five of the enemy's leftover mechanised brigades, a battalion-sized tactical group and two infantry battalions lay in intermediate defence of Cuito Cuanavale and its bridge to the east of the river. Only 13 Brigade defended Cuito Cuanavale – the enemy's main defensive strongpoint and backstop – whilst 8 Brigade ferried logistics from Menongue. The intermediate defensive shield of FAPLA extended approximately 45 kilometres from the Chambinga River in the north to the Mianei River in the south. Until now the enemy still had some fight left in them and even seriously contemplated resuming their offensive to assail southeast Angola once again from the west. By mid-November – December this proved to be an unrealistic hope on their side.

FAPLA's lopsided defence was based on the smaller tributaries flowing into the Cuito River, especially at its sources and confluences. Their brigades were deployed in defended localities and lay observably so, isolated for lack of mutual support. It was obvious to me from the outset that the enemy's defensive layout made them extremely vulnerable against concerted attacks, although they had adequate depth and reserves. Their weaknesses in defence were in all probability due to a lack of strategic and tactical insight and guidance from higher up resulting in improper planning, if any at all.

By appreciating the overall situation it became clear to me that one could attack the enemy either from the east or the west of the Cuito River. The enemy's defences were deployed as follows by 9 November and would soon crumble in the face of a ferocious counter-attack by the SADF. (See Frame 1.)

In essence a typical FAPLA brigade was a well-balanced all-arms combat formation. It was able-bodied for the African battle space, barring dynamic leadership and doctrine

Frame 1: FAPLA Deployments

- The operational command post of FAPLA was located near the Viposto high ground.
- 8 Brigade ferried logistics between Menongue and Cuito Cuanavale.
- 13 Brigade defended Cuito Cuanavale from the western bank of the river.
- 25 Brigade (minus one battalion) defended in the area of Tumpo on the eastern bank.
- 16 Brigade defended at the source of the Chambinga River (our initial point of main effort).
- Tactical Group 2, with approximately fifteen T-54/55 tanks, were deployed close to the Viposto high ground, approximately 20 km to the west-southwest of 16 Brigade.
- 66 Brigade (to be replaced by the fleeing 59th Brigade from 14 November 1987) was deployed to protect the vital crossing over the Chambinga River.
- 59 Brigade defended at the source of the Vimpulo River.
- An infantry battalion of 66 Brigade defended further to the east at the confluence of the Cuito and Mianei rivers.
- An infantry battalion of 25 Brigade was deployed at the source of the Mianei River.
- 21 Brigade defended on the Mianei slightly to the west of the battalion of 25 Brigade.

and consisted of approximately 3,000 combatants, armed heavier than its South African opposite number. A typical FAPLA brigade usually fielded the following unit types and Russian military equipment and armaments within its fighting structures. (See Frame 2.)

The war by the SADF in southeast Angola was conducted at the tactical and high tactical levels of war. It formed part of the SADF's counterrevolutionary strategy and campaigns conducted in the Western Sub-Theatre of War by Major General Willie Meyer, the commanding general of SWATF. I found many a time that the decisions lower down the chain were overridden by either the headquarters of the Army or SADF. Another problem perceived was that the respective HQs were deployed one on top of the other: The brigade in the field, then the command node of SWATF deployed in Rundu, followed in series by the HQ of SWATF in Windhoek and the Army and SADF in Pretoria. To the commanders on the ground this situation occasioned grave frustration as command-and-control became contaminated by micro management and the perplexity about who made what decisions! It seemed as if SWATF and those at Rundu were playing a video game from their consoles outside Angola.

The South African units fighting in the frontline were commanded by highly experienced and dedicated combat officers and were designated: Combat Group Alpha (61 Mech) commanded by Commandant Mike Müller; Combat Group Bravo (32 Battalion) under Commandant Robbie Hartslief; Combat Group Charlie (4 SAI) under Commandant Leon Marais; and 20 Artillery Regiment under Colonel Jean Lausberg with Commandant Frans van Eeden as his second-in-command. A Guerrilla Battalion of UNITA was grouped with each combat group and air support officers were attached to each combat group. In combination these were powerful battle compositions with the support of 20 Artillery Regiment and the SAAF. They were also extremely flexible at grouping and regrouping in the field at the flick of a radio preset switch or verbal command.

Major Cubby van Rooyen commanded 20 Medical Task Force and Commandant Coen van den Berg the Mobile Air Operations Team in support of Modular. Both these

Frame 2: Organisation of a FAPLA Brigade

- Brigade headquarters.
- Three motorised infantry battalions transported in armoured personnel carriers, either BTR-60s or BTR-152s. In some instances the infantry were transported with Ural military trucks. Each battalion had three companies with three platoons each and in addition support weapons such as light machine guns, 60 mm mortars and shoulder launched RPG-7 anti-tank missile systems. There were sufficient hands holding entrenching tools to dig deep into the ground.
- One tank company usually equipped with ten Russian T-54/55 main battle tanks.
- One composite artillery battalion usually organised into six batteries. Of these two batteries were equipped with six 122 mm D-30 long range guns. Two batteries were armed with four older version 76 mm ZIS-3 type guns. An additional battery was armed with BM-21 multiple rocket launchers – those the South Africans preferred to call the "Rooi Oog" – the "Red Eye." The sixth battery had six 120 mm mortars. This was a handy assortment of indirect fire support systems; that is to say if the enemy gunners were up to effective fire planning and coordination.
- One reconnaissance company with PT-76 amphibious tanks and BRDM-2 armoured reconnaissance vehicles.
- One field engineering company or a platoon.
- One mortar platoon per battalion with six 82 mm mortars.
- One anti-tank platoon per battalion with either six B-10 recoilless guns or Sagger anti-tank missile systems.
- One grenade launcher platoon per battalion armed with six AGS-17 launchers.
- One air defence platoon with three teams equipped with shoulder launched SA-7s and four 14,5 mm ZPU-1 heavy machine guns.FAPLA formations had adequate air defence systems and mechanical bridge and mine laying systems available in the front-line.

officers and their command teams formed part of the Brigade HQ. A Liaison Team from UNITA under the leadership of Colonel Fred Oelschig and Colonel Shevukuvuku of UNITA moved with the HQ as well. The force compositions for the final phase of Operation Modular are set out in Appendix A.

There were approximately 5,000 UNITA guerrilla fighters deployed for the war against FAPLA in southeast Angola which were organised into five full battalions. Mavinga was the home to the Eastern Front Headquarters of Savimbi. Their force in the field was directed by General Demosthenes, the Chief of Staff of UNITA. They operated in a guerrilla and semi-conventional warfaring mode and for this reason was organised into regular, semi-regular and penetration type battalions. One of their guerrilla units was used to operate effectively in the rear area of the enemy between Menongue and Cuito Cuanavale. Guerrilla units were armed with Stinger shoulder-launched missile systems supplied by the United States of America, which gave some measure of comfort to us as the enemy's MiGs were cautious to fly below 12,000 feet.

When the preparation started for the counteroffensive by mid-October the HQ of 20 Brigade under Colonel Deon Ferreira was still controlling the ongoing battle from a position slightly south of the Lomba, approximately 28 km west of Mavinga; Combat Group Alpha (61 Mech) was deployed in a hide near Mavinga; Combat Group Bravo (32 Battalion) was still skirmishing in the vicinity of the source of the Chambinga; and Combat Group Charlie (4 SAI) with the tank squadron was approaching Mavinga from Rundu.

A well-concealed formation administrative area (FAA) was located close to Mavinga and its strategically important gravel airfield. The area was a hubbub of activity at night with SAAF Hercules C-130s and Transall C-160s transporters coming and going. From Rundu the earthbound logistical umbilical cord extended through Mavinga to the forward edge of the battle area. These tracks were forged through sheer human tenacity and by "bundu-bashing." From Rundu to Mavinga was a horrendous 280 km for the transportation of veritable mountains of ammunitions, fuels, lubricants, wheels, engines, axles, spare parts, batteries, rations ... and more. The fighting units were maintained by their A-Echelons (administrative) commanded by regimental sergeant-majors. A key challenge remained the G-5s and the Valkiri – they were consuming ammunition as if it were going out of fashion. For the men the menu was strict 24-hour ration packs. Casualties were treated in and just behind the fighting line by an outstanding South African medical support system. The high priority casualties were flown out at night from anywhere in the field by helicopter and then by fixed-wing aircraft from any of the forward airfields.

By mid-October the scene was set and the table laid for the counteroffensive against FAPLA.

The General's Instruction – Calling to Be Northward Bound

On 10 October 1987 the Chief of the Army, Lieutenant General Kat Liebenberg officiated at a parade in Kuruman. It was a splendid occasion where the freedom of Kuruman was granted to the South African Army Battle School and the Kuruman Commando. During the luncheon Lieutenant General Liebenberg called me and Brigadier Eddie Webb aside and said, "I want Roland to report to me on Monday. I am sending him to southeast Angola to participate in Operation Modular".

I packed my meagre firstline operational kit. Sunday came and I greeted my wife, Henriette and my children. Our youngest son, Pieter had just turned two. I left home and flew in a light aircraft from Sishen to Waterkloof Air Force base in Pretoria. I never saw my home in Kathu again or "cleared out" from the Battle School in true military fashion. In November my family would move on their own to Pretoria for my new posting as the officer commanding of the South African Army College where I met up with them again in mid-December to take up my new position.

At 10:30 on Monday 12 October I had tea with the Chief of the Army in his office at Army Headquarters in Potgieter Street. I liked him, he was sharp-witted, outgoing and easy to talk to. From the right top drawer of his imposing desk he took a folded battle map which demarcated the area of operations for Modular in southeast Angola. Circled in red were the vital crossing sites over the Cuito and Chambinga rivers.

General Liebenberg described to me the run of the battle as he saw it. He was extremely satisfied with the turn of events following on the destruction of the enemy's 47th Brigade at the Lomba on 3 October. He then told me that he was seriously contemplating attacking Cuito Cuanavale from the west of the river and that I was the designated force commander if that was decided. The enemy brigades deployed to the east of the river would then be fixed by a force under command of Colonel Deon Ferreira. However, the attack envisaged from the west was not fait accompli. All the available operational options for the counteroffensive still required careful consideration. This was part of my work. Liebenberg emphasised over and over his trepidation at unnecessarily losing South African lives and expressed his disquiet at the many lives already sacrificed. Another irksome fear he expressed was the possibility of the war in Angola escalating beyond proportion. The enemy's trump remained his overwhelming air force. If the enemy wanted to they could bomb the main towns and military installations in the northern border region at their heart's content. "By the way, we are there to support UNITA and not to take Angola," Liebenberg explained.

I knew that the headquarters of 20 Brigade lacked mobility. I thus grasped my opportunity and requested two favours. The first was to get six Ratel-Command vehicles despatched as soon as possible to the front from 7 Division Mobilisation Centre either in Bloemfontein or Wallmansthal (north of Pretoria). Next, I requested that Commandants Cassie Schoeman and C.P. du Toit be detached to the front as operational staff officers for the brigade headquarters forthwith. The general gave the nod to both requests without thinking twice. I was contented with these decisions taken so swiftly and immediately set things in motion. Schoeman was tasked to mobilise the pride of Ratel-Commands and to lead them right up to Mavinga as soon as possible.

That same day I flew to Rundu in a Learjet provided by Chief of Staff Intelligence, SADF. I was deep in thought about everything I had learned. With a feeling of exhilaration and high expectation came the pressing burden of responsibility. I knew that I was in for challenging and dangerous times. I had three books with me as I flew to Rundu. The one was my small leather-bound Bible of 61 Mech 1981–1982 vintage with Psalm 23 torn halfway out from overuse. The other book was my own work on "Mobile Warfare – A perspective for Southern Africa," published in August 1987. The other book was also about mobile warfare and by Richard Simpkin, appropriately entitled "Race for the Swift" which I was still busy reading.

Dusk was setting in as we landed and taxied into Rundu. The doors of the Learjet opened and the heavy, humid air of Africa enveloped me. The well-known smell of aircraft fuel floated sharply on the balmy evening air. To one side, a Puma helicopter gracefully poised, rotors speeding up as the air frame vibrated faster and faster with sliding doors open. A nutria-clad operations officer rushed up to me and shouted, "Get into the Puma; you are flying out to the brigade HQ at the Lomba". It was a starry moonlit night as we swept low over the dense canopy of the African foliage. Here and there I could spot lonely cooking fires and the lights of a number of South African mobile columns manoeuvring under cover of darkness below us. I kept to myself my anticipation and excitement in the overbearing hum of the chopper.

The night flight ended long past midnight at a cleared helicopter landing zone in the bush, close to the tactical headquarters (Tac HQ) of 20 Brigade. I found Colonel Deon Ferreira sitting on a camp chair in front of his battle map. The large 250,000 topographical map, marked in blue, red, green and brown, with "China Graph Pens," was suspended from a piece of Mopani branch. It hung in an Army tent, 16x16 drab veldt-coloured. A few lights flickered through Barracuda camouflage nets cladding the scattered operational vehicles; the creaking cooling metal hulls were scattered under the high trees. Some of the planning staffs were still working. The gaslights were mired by countless fluttering moths and mosquitoes. The monotonous hum of the military radios was comforting. I was shown to my mosquito net and foxhole and rolled open my sleeping bag.

To my delight when first light came I saw artillery officers Colonel Jean Lausberg and Commandant Frans van Eeden, close compatriots from Operation Protea. They were sitting on camp chairs next to a camouflaged SAMIL-100 "fire support coordination centre" poring over situation reports from their forward artillery observation officers and the gun lines. Daily fire missions were being planned for the 155 mm G-5s and the 127 mm Valkiri.

As I walked around and greeted the staff, two Mirage ground attack aircraft swept low over us. The SAAF was hell bent at vandalising some or other FAPLA brigade slightly to the north of us. Since it was my first day with 20 Brigade I was subjected to a thorough grounding on the battle. I was catapulted into the operational situation at the front – a sense of immense commitment, countless maps, busy staff officers and humming radios. We sweated profusely as we teemed over the battle maps, notwithstanding some canvas screening against the unfaltering African sun. We were uncomfortably swamped by hordes of flies, our sweat-darkened nutria-coloured fatigues covered by their unwholesome black spots; ever so often a fly was squashed with less than gracious ceremonial indifference. We deliberated about terrain, enemy, own forces, time and space and operational lessons learned thus far. Now and then there were spurts of excitement as the gunners and the Mirages blew another piece of FAPLA into oblivion. Real-time tactical intelligence was filtering through in dribs and drabs from the young artillery officers deployed the furthest forward, UNITA and the few Special Forces operatives on the ground out there in front. The common operating picture was becoming clearer and clearer to me by the minute; if we do this, what will the enemy do? We started contemplating a number of possible courses of action in outline for the counteroffensive, ardently war-gaming in the sand and on the maps. West-flanking was uppermost in our minds. We could do it.

As we worked I wondered ... Had a proper military and campaign strategy been formulated higher up for the war unfolding in southern Angola, or had it just happened in the course of things? To intervene or not to intervene were probably some of the questions originally posed, I could imagine. How many counteractions were considered, or was there only the obvious one, namely to halt the enemy at the Lomba? It was interesting to war-game, even by myself. What would have happened if the SADF had allowed FAPLA to gain confidence in their own might, as they did once? Imagine if FAPLA was allowed to take Mavinga and then in the course of their advance to Jamba to capture Cuito Cuanavale behind them, oh well ... It is well to reason that a military strategy depends for success on a sound calculation and coordination of the ends and the means towards the attainment of the political object of that war – the goal which should have been clearly defined by a fundamental policy of the South African government. Until today I still speculate about this and shake my head in amazement on how things had panned out in the end! Were the encouraging outcomes during the closing stage of the war by August–December 1988 due to Providence, more than anything else, or what?

It was decided that I would return to Rundu for a short while to muster our new planning team and to lead the joint operational planning for the counteroffensive. This was to occur under the oversight of Brigadier Fido Smit, the newly appointed designee who had taken over the operational responsibility from Brigadier J.T. Louw. Louw had been in Rundu for some time as the representative from the HQ of SWATF. With Smit was Colonel Hennie Blaauw, his Chief of Staff from 7 SA Division. So, one starry night it was back to Rundu for me by Puma, at least for a short while.

Ferreira stayed behind to direct operations in the field. Every day and night the astute and the brave sallied forth to be out there close to the enemy – Commandant Les Rudman and his merry men were pestering FAPLA 59th Brigade with loudspeaker hailing reverberating through the night from their four-wheeled Casspir – extreme sports – amplified sounds of tanks advancing mixed with other intimidating stuff. There was the more than occasional satisfying rumbling of the big guns, interspersed with smaller interesting tactical innovations, all debited to FAPLA's physical and psychological account. The enemy did not have the luxury of long distance artillery or guerrilla forces like we had, to hound and to hunt behind the lines. There were some pamphlet-carrying 155 mm shells evenly distributing creative propaganda to FAPLA – at times to their amusement. War at times was fun as well. You seek him here, you seek him there ... However, there was no rest for the weary.

Building up towards the Planning Bout – Time Spent on Reconnaissance was Never Wasted

As I walked into the office of Brigadier J.T. Louw, which was adjacent to the Sector 20 operation centre in Rundu, I saw him cutting a crossword puzzle from the "Rundu Daily". I was somewhat taken aback, thinking that a crossword puzzle was no substitute for a battle map; the cryptic clues from it not to be confused with the principles of warfare.

After a briefing I had some precious moments to discuss the unfolding operational situation in southeast Angola with Colonels Piet Muller, Jock Harris and Fred Oelschig. Piet Muller was an extremely able infantry officer who commanded Sector 20 in Rundu. He had the counterinsurgency warfaring responsibility of overseeing the Okavango Province in SWA. Jock Harris commanded 32 Battalion. He had borne the brunt of the external operations against FAPLA and the Cubans through the uncertain, careering heydays with very few forces from July until handing over command to Colonel Deon Ferreira on 5 September. Harris, to my mind an extremely conscientious and competent officer, reaffirmed that in some way he had not seen eye-to-eye with Major General Willie Meyer on the running of operational affairs nor the future planning of it.

In July Muller, Harris and Oelschig had presented to SWATF and Army HQ a comprehensive well-deliberated plan for an assault on Cuito Cuanavale from the west. The plan was not accepted. Presumably, it was believed to be too risky and politically unsavoury and too many forces were needed at the time. Thinking back to the recent briefing of myself by the Chief of the Army in his office, the geopolitical deck of cards must have been reshuffled; the plan for the west was now off the table again and needed to be re-appraised. I carefully tapped into the thinking of these three operationally experienced officers to learn more about their insights, of going west-flanking and the likes. My next move was to experience firsthand what the terrain in southeast Angola actually felt like to jarring marrow and bone compared to what I had experienced in 1981–82 in the west. Terrain was the neutral factor – the commander who could read and use it the best was favoured by the gods of war.[1]

One early morning bright and bushy-tailed Brigadier Fido Smit and I sauntered off into the rising sun with a SAMIL truck we had mobilised for reconnaissance – not the most luxurious for touring southern Angola. We stood uncomfortably in the back, hugging the shaking cab for dear life. We crossed the Okavango and eventually the Cuito River,

1 Refer to Chapter 5 regarding the appraisal of terrain.

dutifully following the logistics' "Luengue 1 and Luengue 2 Route" towards Mavinga. The bush was dense and the going extremely tough. We finally met up with a SAM-8 surface to air missile system that was captured during the Lomba battles on the way to its new home at Rundu and then to Kentron in South Africa – to the victors went the spoils of war. (Incidentally, the SAM-8 was a sophisticated system which was sought after by the Western World and this was the first to be taken by any Western nation.) Content with the fresh knowledge about the terrain Smit and I eventually turned around and returned to Rundu. We could clearly fathom why logistic support to the front line was a major challenge. Time spent on reconnaissance was never wasted.

Our next important undertaking was to recce possible crossings over the Cuito and the Longa rivers we had selected and marked on a map. We convinced the air force to undertake a recce flight in daytime northwards along the Cuito. The area as far as the Longa was still reasonably devoid of regular MiG interference. We were aiming at a specific spot where the Longa branched in a northwesterly direction out of the Cuito. Crossing here provided access to a vast manoeuvre area sweeping northwards, hemmed in between the Cuito and the Longa. The Longa crossed the road to Menongue approximately 90 kilometres to the west of the town of Cuito Cuanavale. Here it would be possible to cut off the enemy from interfering with our potential operations to the east towards Cuito Cuanavale, if it came to that, as well as their logistics. It would therefore be possible to compartmentalise the battlefield, if needs be; when the time came, we thought. Northward bound and airborne we spotted a number of wrecks of Russian helicopters lying abandoned in the field, either MI-8 transport helicopters or MI-24 combat helicopters. As we landed and deplaned at our selected landing spot my heart stopped beating for one crushing moment. As if by signal, silently out of nowhere, the African bush around us became alive with camouflaged clad AK-47 armed soldiers. Fortunately, they were UNITA already guarding this valued crossing site. I held my pose and casually started breathing again. The UNITA soldiers smiled spontaneously and greeted us in a hail of friendship and waving AKs. Did we have South African ration packs and cigarettes? We shared what we had. There was already an improvised fording point in place established with logs bound together in the most innovative manner by our soldierly friends for the Ural and SAMIL trucks used by UNITA. Our field engineers could easily convert it into something acceptable for the crossing of a mechanised attack force.

The Planning Framework for the Counteroffensive – Holistic Thinking

There was no time to waste in Rundu with our newly established joint planning team in the planning of the counteroffensive. The joint planning team comprised a range of staff compartments, namely: Operations, intelligence, operational security, artillery, air defence, combat engineers, military police, signals, electronic warfare, psychological warfare, communication operations, logistics, technical services, personnel and finances. Of course, with any joint operation the respective arms of the service, in this instance the Army, Air Force and Medical Services all formed an integral part of the planning affair. In terms of my designated responsibility as the elect west-flanking attacking commander I had the privilege to lead the process over three days. We used an extremely effective joint operational planning method of the Israeli Defence Force which we had customised over time. I experienced a remarkable openness in the sharing of knowledge and responsibility by all participants in an exercise that was intense and thought-provoking. An important first step was to assess what the overarching mission was and what exactly needed to be achieved at the end of the fighting process. This took some deep reflective thinking in warfaring terms and was principles-bound – the principles of warfare, that is.[2]

We started with the operational and intelligence staff teams doing their separate appreciations. Meanwhile, the other supporting staff compartments commenced with their own planning and relevant staff checks. Factors were carefully considered, assessed and developed into fundamental conclusions and main consideration as the plan gradually started unfolding. Judgement about the final plan was suspended as long as possible. This allowed for ample creative and objective processing. Factors such as terrain, enemy, own forces, time and distance, weather conditions, surprise and deception, and an assessment of tasks and the probable courses of action were carefully considered and woven into a thorough fabric of deliberate planning. During the first part of the process the main conclusions and probable courses of action, both from the viewpoint of our enemy and own forces, were presented. This result became the baseline for further planning by the support staffs. Finally all the interlocking plans were subjected to thorough testing in which advantages, disadvantages and risks were assessed and finally war-gamed. The principles of warfare served as the supreme planning guideline as the whole warfaring game was centred on preventing the enemy from acting on sound principles; on the other hand, a supreme planning effort was to enable own forces to exploit these principles in order to facilitate the achievement of our own objectives. What had we derived from our planning?

By glancing at the planning map the manoeuvre-oriented military mind invariably started thinking about what Rommel had surmised in the North African desert in 1942: "One should endeavour to concentrate one's own forces both in time and space, while at the same time seeking to split the opposing forces and destroying them at different times." As it were, our enemy's force was already split, were they not? Those deployed spread out in defence east of the Cuito Cuanavale and the two brigades operating vulnerably, exposed and isolated to its west, with only one vital and vulnerable bridge linking them across the river – excellent!

There was one frustrating aspect which needed constant consideration for the planning and execution of any operation from our side. We had to consider weather conditions and wind direction. This was due to the slight apprehension that the enemy could bombard us with chemical weapons. There were clear intelligence indications about this, although it had not been substantiated as truth yet. At one stage it was rumoured that the enemy had buried some of their chemical shells at the Lomba during a fracas in September. The enemy even spread rumours that we had used such weapons on them – untrue of course. At times vile-smelling battle smoke had drifted over them at the Lomba, which could have caused them to come to such a conclusion.

During the planning we were desperately seeking the chink in the enemy's armour – where the focus of main effort should be! The British military strategist and historian, Sir B.H. Liddell Hart provided some guidance when he wrote: "The object of obliquity is to find the chink in the armour, the mental armour at that. One's object is the psychological disruption of the opposing command and the yardstick of success is the degree of freedom of action one enjoys at the end of the process."[3] There were three areas where we surmised we should hit the enemy simultaneously, if it were feasible: "To cut the enemy's lines of

2 Refer to Chapter 7 regarding the planning of operations and the application of the principles of warfare.
3 Liddell Hart, B.H.: *Strategy*. Faber and Faber Ltd, London, 1967, p. 385.

communication, thus paralysing his physical build-up; to seal him from his lines of retreat, thus undermining the enemy's will and destroying his morale; to hit his centres of administration and disrupting his communications, thus severing the link between his brain and his limbs."[4] To my way of thinking the enemy in southeast Angola was more or less served to us on a tray.

From our countless deliberations the obvious points where the enemy was extremely vulnerable became clear. In the west it was the vital crossings over the Cuito and the Longa. The taking thereof from the west could lead to the leisurely destruction of its total force kicking its heels to the east of the river. If achieved properly such a manoeuvre could make the enemy's war for southeast Angola irrelevant and break their fighting spirit. Alternatively in the east, by destroying the enemy brigade at the source of the Chambinga River and threatening the crossing site 20 km to its west, the enemy's defensives south of Chambinga could be rendered irrelevant. It should furthermore cause collapse of their bridgehead on their eastern front and entice uncontrolled flight to the banks of the Cuito River, we reasoned. Any attack should be organised in depth and should develop progressively from one firm base to the next, while the start of the attack needed to be secured. More importantly any attack should enjoy maximum fire support and momentum had to be maintained at all cost. Sustained logistics remained a worrying factor.

Two main designs for attack were presented to our generals in the conference room at Sector 20 in Rundu on 20 October. The battle recipes described below differed in the sense that from the west it was more about destroying the enemy and from the east more about annoying them into submission.

The Plan to Attack from the West of the Cuito River – Destroy the Enemy

The focus of main effort for an attack from the west lay in successfully capturing the crossing over the Cuito River, not necessarily intact. The bridge was the pivotal point, being both vital to our esteemed enemy and vulnerable. One brigade stood in the way. The mission would be to encircle and annihilate FAPLA's Regional HQ and the 13th Brigade defending Cuito Cuanavale, the enemy's nerve centre. At a glance, contemplating the enemy's defence, it was clear that they never truly considered an attack from the west, which was astounding. The main conditions for such an élan adventure implied that the bridge should be taken swiftly and the enemy to the east of the river kept out of the fighting business. Furthermore, the achievement of surprise would be imperative so as not to draw unnecessary flies to the honey pot at Cuito Cuanavale, and any undue interference from Menongue needed to be halted on the Longa River, about ninety kilometres to the west. Finally, something substantial needed to be done about the enemy's overwhelming air threat for the duration of the attack.

All of the latter was possible – even with the limited South African force at our disposal. This time around it was contemplated that UNITA would really have to put in an immense effort for such a combined swooping manoeuvre of encirclement and annihilation. According to our military appreciation what we truly required was one full mechanised brigade for the western attack and one smaller mixed mechanised-motorised brigade as a fixing force to the east of the river. One additional Olifant tank squadron and 155 mm G-5 battery would be dearly appreciated. What we had were 61 Mech, 4 SAI, one

4 Ibid, p. 387.

tank squadron and about three UNITA battalions to attack along the western approach. To the east 32 Battalion and the remainder of UNITA would have to suffice as the fixing force. This was the plan in outline favoured by the tactical planners and was put forward as the preferred option to the generals.

The Plan to Attack from the East of the Cuito River – Annoy the Enemy

This battle design centred on an attack in depth to break FAPLA's bridgehead based on the Chambinga River and to twist them around for a second time after the Lomba battle. The central idea was to make the battlefield fluid and grab each killing opportunity presented to destroy as much of their men and machines possible. We knew that we did not have sufficient forces and operational reserves available to achieve complete annihilation of the enemy! The enemy, who was our immediate military threat, straddled the pathway to Cuito and had to be removed; not that the tacticians then immersed in the planning of the counteroffensive even remotely considered taking Cuito Cuanavale head-on from the east. That, for any simple rational thinking tactician, would have been downright crazy; especially those few who still had their whitish venerable and vulnerable hides intact. Success therefore hinged on manoeuvre and in avoiding from getting fixed by the enemy. To achieve this we needed to assail the rational mind of the enemy. Feints and strikes were to become the norm of the battle. In the words of Stonewall Jackson: "Mystify, mislead and surprise. To mystify and mislead constitutes distraction, while surprise is the essential cause of dislocation. It is through the distraction of the enemy commander's mind that the distraction of his forces follows. The loss of his freedom of action is sequel to the loss of his freedom of conception."[5]

FAPLA's reinforced 16th Brigade, that guarded the enemy's vulnerable eastern flank in depth and escape route to Cuito Cuanavale, was selected as our first main point of attack. Lurking close to the 16th's hideous rear was the worrisome Tactical Group 2 near Viposto. Not too far away to the west within eighteen kilometres or so striking distance skulked the 66th Brigade, confidently straddling the Chambinga crossing, which was described as follows by one of FAPLA's Russian advisors: "The crossing of the Chambinga River is quite uncomfortable. It is sufficient to say that it is completely open on both its banks and moreover swampy. The Angolans call such a surface area, 'Shana', the same as 'flood lands' in Russian. Only one single road, mined on each side, leads to the river through this 'Shana', so that nowhere can one turn around. If the enemy is able to successfully get this road within his gun sights, then it can become one of the seven circles of biblical hell."[6] From there the defensive line dotted the landscape 45 km further southwards to the source of the Mianei River.

I used the Battle of Gazala (May–June 1942) by Field Marshal Erwin Rommel as a benchmark for our planning. Rommel had successfully routed the British Eighth Army in the Western Desert by using probing attacks, feints and ruses to deceive and to fix the enemy over their 45 km front. Then he struck far and wide and hard going east, flanking behind his enemy's lines, causing a complete rout, which turned into the "Gazala Gallop."

5 Ibid, p. 328.

6 Recollections from the tape-recorded memories of the Russian officer, Lieutenant Colonel Igor Anatolevich Zhdarkin that were produced at the Africa Institute of the Russian Academy of Sciences on 28 October 2000: "We did not see it even in Afghanistan" – Memoirs of a participant of the Angolan war (1986-1988).

Although this was viewed as one of the greatest in German military annals, everything did not go according to Rommel's plan. This phenomenon is not unusual, due to fluid semi-unpredictable situations and restricted force levels. A large portion of the British Eighth Army succeeded in escaping the trap. The battle however was a major success and placed Rommel in an advantageous position for the next round of fighting. Similarly, as planners we predicted the flight of the entire enemy in unquestioned defeat by taking Chambinga in a similar manner and started expressing its possible outcome as the "Chambinga Gallop".

I also used the planning opportunity at Rundu to discuss the concept of psychological dislocation with our operational psychologist Dr. Coetzee Badenhorst. In essence we were looking at how we could use varying shock-inducing factors, such as creating anxiety and exploiting alienation, to paralyse the enemy's mind.[7] In the end this was achieved through the combination of various interrelated activities that was built into the plan. Everything of course relied on careful timing – even the selection of H-Hour and D-Day. A fraction of our plan suggested the insertion of a substantial raiding force behind enemy lines operating between Menongue and Cuito Cuanavale for the continued physical and psychological disruption of the opposing command and its forces. This was not approved and only later on became a reality when such a penetration force under Commandants Robbie Hartslief and Jan Hougaard, probably the best raiders in the business, was inserted behind enemy lines in December.

The crux of the plan for the counteroffensive was rooted in the initial shock to be induced on FAPLA by attacking 16 Brigade in the north on 9 November, whilst deceiving in the south. For the opening battle on 16 Brigade it was planned that Combat Group Charlie (4 SAI) would lead the surprise attack from the northeast with the Olifant tank squadron.[8] As the force of main effort they would enjoy the preponderance of combat power. On completion of the main attack Charlie would remain in readiness to follow up the attacks against FAPLA as the battle unfolded. Combat Group Alpha (61 Mech) would be in support, firstly to launch a deception attack from the southeast on 16 Brigade and then, secondly, to act as mobile reserve. Combat Group Bravo (32 Battalion) was tasked to launch a deception attack against FAPLA's 21st Brigade in the south at the Mianei River and thereafter to offensively support the continuation of the mobile battle as it unfolded. 20 Artillery Regiment and the SAAF were the deadly force multipliers organised to provide fire support throughout the operation.

An important component of the plan included the creation of a favourable air situation for 4 SAI on the day of the attack. The fighting was not only about the progressive annihilation of the foe, but also about survival of our valued few. Here we relied heavily on the planned indirect fire by UNITA to be brought to bear on the enemy airfield at Menongue at the time of the attack. This requirement was later to be coordinated very carefully by me and Colonels Jean Lausberg and Fred Oelschig at Mavinga with Savimbi and his generals prior to the attack on 16 Brigade. I will mention more about this activity later.

After 9 November it was predicted that things would loosen up quite swiftly. The endgame foreseen included endless nerve-taxing and energy-sapping manoeuvres and attacks from

7 Refer to Chapter 8 concerning the catastophe theory.

8 The few South African tanks saw battle for the first time in Africa since the Second World War at Chambinga. Another Olifant tank squadron was added to the frontline force for Operation Hooper and Packer in January 1988. Interestingly enough, a few World War Two vintage Sherman tanks had seen action with the South Africans during the Korean War in the early fifties.

the ground and the air. What was now required was to get the job done before the enemy changed their plan!

Presentation of the Plans to the Generals – West Flanking or East Flanking

The day arrived for the presentation of the plans of the counteroffensive to the generals in Rundu. What would the balance of consequences lead to in finally deciding whether to go west or east flanking? My expectations and hopes were high on attacking Cuito Cuanavale from the west. The atmosphere in the conference room in the headquarters of Sector 20 bristled and our spirits were high. Decision time! Large battle maps covered in layers of talc subjugated the scene.

General Jannie Geldenhuys as the Chief of the South African Defence Force (SADF) led the procession of high-ups with his usual flair – the high command was there: Lieutenant General Kat Liebenberg, Chief of the Army; Lieutenant General Dennis Earp, Chief of the Air Force; Lieutenant General Niel Knobel, Surgeon General; Lieutenant General Jan van Loggerenberg, Chief of Staff Operations; Vice Admiral Dries Putter, Chief of Staff Intelligence; Major General Willie Meyer, General Officer Commanding SWATF. In the wake of the generals followed a throng of senior staff officers either from Pretoria or Windhoek – an impressive array dressed in field regalia.

The proposed courses of action for the counter offensive were presented in utmost detail. This included the well-structured reasoned thinking behind it; all-embracing main conclusions and considerations – delivered with true military professionalism, poise and self-assurance – belief in self and the operational team. There was an amicable atmosphere. Discussions were open, frank, truthful and to the point. No burring stone was left untouched – possibility thinking to the uttermost.

At some stage during the heady deliberations Colonel Rinus van Rensburg from the office of the Surgeon General, a medical doctor of high standing with substantial operational experience, stood up to say his say with self-assurance, "We have to consider that if we run into trouble in a heavy fight for Cuito that we could incur more casualties than what we bargain for. It will be a major undertaking to evacuate large numbers of high priority casualties from the Cuito front; considering we can only do it at night." I knew from the talking in the army passageways that the casualty attrition rate of our young conscripts had become a major political issue. Fathers and mothers were already expressing their misgiving in more than serious open verbalisation about their young dying "for what?" in southeast Angola. Loads of pressure came from the international community and the media as well. Political moods in South Africa were already wavering with powerful gusts of change which could influence the future voting.[9] I was not perturbed by voting, never was, more about substantial operational planning and effectual execution, which should not be paid for in excessive blood. The soldiers needed to be given a fighting chance, especially considering the weighty odds against them.

At some stage during discussions I presented the option for the attack on Cuito Cuanavale from the west. General Jannie Geldenhuys interrupted and said, "Listen to what is being presented. I believe that the current politics could even favour such an option for going west-flanking." Being somewhat forward as I usually am, I immediately interrupted

9 The Minister of Defence, General Magnus Malan only announced publicly by 13 November that the SADF was fighting a serious conventional battle in southeast Angola. The operation could not be kept secret anymore.

and said, General, one moment please. What about going all out for Menongue, still further to the West? General Geldenhuys thought for a moment and said, untroubled and somewhat to my surprise, considering the loaded politics up to now, "Yes, even that is something plausible to look at." Whether these high-level deliberations were some form of clever change management induced for the more fiery I never established; anyway, it was intellectually stimulating. It was now decision time. General Geldenhuys then took the lead up front. He divided our operational planning group into syndicates, each team under one of his generals. The task was simple. "Make a final evaluation of the proposed courses of action and make a recommendation based on your judgements".

I drew the match to be in the syndicate of Lieutenant General Jan van Loggerenberg (Chief of Staff Operations of the SANDF and former Chief of the Air Force). So, off we went. Van Loggerenberg was a coolheaded professional with an open and friendly demeanour. I respected him and enjoyed working with him. For more than one hour the respective syndicates deliberated the advantages versus disadvantages and the risks of either going west or east-flanking. We returned to the conference centre and the generals presented their findings to the Chief of the Defence Force. The arguments for the counteroffensive along the eastern approach were heavily weighted and the more cautious line of counter-attack was therefore favoured by the generals. The decision was taken as such by General Jannie Geldenhuys and the die was cast for the counteroffensive. To my mind, the plan for the attack from the west was not approved for prudent political and military reasons. Some of these were most probably the caution of incurring undue casualties and of escalating the war. There was also a real threat of the enemy coming over the border to bomb Oshakati, Ondangwa, Grootfontein and Rundu to smithereens with their MiGs, when angered enough.

We finalised the plan for the counteroffensive and converted it into an operations order which was duly issued to all combat participants and supporting staffs and units.

Command Disposition for the Counteroffensive along the Eastern Approach[10]

The frontline fighting force for the counteroffensive along the eastern approach was divided in two components for command-and-control purposes. A new operational level headquarters (HQ) was established at Rundu under the command of Brigadier Fido Smit (officer commanding 7 South African Division). Smit now commanded Task Force 10, Combat Group Bravo and 20 Regiment with his HQ comprising key personnel from 7 Division's HQ.[11]

The command disposition of 20 Brigade was changed for the final phase of Modular as it now reverted to a smaller taskforce status designated Task Force 10, with Combat Groups Alpha and Charlie placed under its command. The mobile Tac HQ was to be kept small and was organised to command from the front, close to where the action would be.

To my mind the operational level command-and-control disposition was somewhat dysfunctional. As it was one coordinated affair all forces in the frontline should have remained under the command of Task Force 10 for the impending counteroffensive. Anyhow, this was how it materialised on the ground as practical expediency and force cohesion already established in the front line transcended the command-and-control

10 See Map 16.

11 Refer to Appendix A. Incidentally, 7 Division's HQ was located at Kensington in Johannesburg.

deviation decided upon. Rundu for that matter, as an extension of SWATF, did not have the necessary reserves to influence the outcome of the forward battle. Until today I still wonder where the respective responsibilities and accountabilities for the planning and conduct of the war in southeast Angola lay. Was it in Rundu, Windhoek or Pretoria?

Preparing for the Next Round – Continued Fighting and Anticipation

Without a brigade, I was now appointed as the second-in-command of Task Force 10 and the advisor for the employment of our mobile forces in the field – whatever advisor implied. I never waited to ask. I flew back to the Tac HQ of 20 Brigade near the Lomba by Puma during the night carrying a few beers for my friends. Brigadier Fido Smit and Colonel Hennie Blaauw accompanied me and were hosted at our HQ for a while. Welcomes extended, they duly enjoyed their chosen spot on the ground, shared our precious army camp chairs and diverted some of the flies and the mosquitoes.

With my kit I had a small knapsack, my sleeping roll, mosquito net, R-5 Rifle, trusted army prismatic compass and my favourite army camp chair. Inside the knapsack I had two spare beers for an emergency, my small leather Bible (also for emergencies), two other such books on mobile warfare, two sets of brown fatigues, my bush hat, my shaving kit, two water bottles, one small mirror, metal mug, plate, fork, spoon, penknife, three sets of jockey underpants, two white interlock vests (which my mother told me to wear at all times as it absorbs the sweat), three pairs of brown army socks, one pair of combat boots, one pair of "Vellies," spare toilet paper, insect repellent, Zam-Buk ointment, a flat tin of preserved oysters, and a few cakes of soap. No spade or gas mask, I am sorry to say – I later acquired a spade rapidly by means of affirmative shopping after a harrowing experience in the Catato Woods.

Smit and I discussed the Rundu planning and its results in detail with Colonel Deon Ferreira, as well as my future role with Task Force 10. It was now time to prepare for the next offensive battle and to issue orders down the chain of command. We were rearing to go. Apart from the ongoing operation we were poring over maps and marking them again for the next battle. By 23 October the name of 20 Brigade changed to Task Force 10. Ferreira remained in command with me now appointed as the second-in-command. Brigadier Fido Smit took over as overall force commander and established his mini divisional type HQ at Rundu.

The ongoing battle until 8 November was characterised by indecisive jostling. It was similar to dangerous fencing without any protective tips on the foils. The probing and reconnoitring of own forces were followed by the counter-probing and counter-reconnoitring by enemy forces. Push and shove was the name of the game. The G-5 was the backyard bully standing out amongst those shoving and shoeing. The enemy was desperately trying to sort themselves out after their bitter thrashing at the Lomba. However, we had a few restraining orders on them as they battled to get some of their depleted numbers safely back to Cuito Cuanavale. This happened in dribs and drabs across the extremely vulnerable Chambinga crossing point, the ideal target for the South Africans and UNITA – insistently hounding the enemy by guerrilla attack and artillery onslaught. The enemy numbers were progressively depleted over time and space. One of their greatest challenges was to get logistics through from Menongue across the derelict bridge at Cuito and then to the frontline.

Intelligence concerning the enemy were mainly gathered by means of radio intercepts and from our very few wary forward eyes on the battlefield – the forward observation officers of the artillery, UNITA and the scouts from either 32 Battalion or Special Forces. Unmanned Aerial Vehicles (UAV) and light aircraft were not considered; the enemy had already shot down a Bosbok light reconnaissance aircraft over the Lomba as well as a "Seeker" UAV from Kentron. Intelligence was followed up with visual aerial and photographic reconnaissance by the SAAF; mostly when the enemy was stationary. We did not have much to work on; close contact with the enemy was the thing; rather on our terms than theirs.

We were thinking circumspectly of requesting an H-2 laser guided bomb strike on the Cuito River bridge at the right moment. The "smart" Kentron bomb was extremely expensive and the launching of such a weapon needed to be considered thoroughly. The large laser-guided bomb, similar to a mini cruise missile, was carried comfortably under the belly of an Air Force Buccaneer. The bomb was launched approximately 60 kilometres from its target. The aircraft then turned around and flew back to base, whilst the co-pilot guided the bomb accurately onto the target by means of a television screen and a joystick. Two such bombs were employed during the operation with marginal success.

Our long distance artillery was pounding Cuito Cuanavale and its strategically important airfield and bridge day and night to the great distress of the enemy. A few enemy aircraft and helicopters had already been destroyed on the airfield by the undaunted G-5 – the deadly 155 mm projectile flying an uncontested 48 kilometres to its targets. The G-5 and the Valkiri became such a great problem for the enemy that they started searching for them on the ground and from the air.

For a period early in November I acted as the brigade commander as Ferreira flew away to the south for a short well-earned respite. It was now 1 November and time was fast closing in on FAPLA's chosen one, 16 Brigade. D-Day, 9 November and counting. We had already started with the preparatory movements, groupings and regroupings for the coming operation. Hubbubs of preparatory activities happened in shrouded security in the bush and in darkness. At times the enemy, for some strange uncalled-for reason, did not leave us in peace.

It was one of those days to do a dance with them in triple quick time. Night was closing in on our comfortable setting near the Lomba when I saw Colonel Jean Lausberg and Commandant Frans van Eeden mysteriously appearing from their artillery command post on the double ... The guns on the front had reported by radio that they were in dire straits. An enemy armoured column was out there aggressively seeking out one of our 155 mm G-5 gun emplacements near the Mianei River. A second armoured column was soon on its way to join the first. The guns were stranded in thick sand and it was difficult to extricate them as the clutches of the SAMIL gun-tractors were slipping and there were no firstline spares available.

A switch immediately flipped over in my mind: Observation, orientation, decision, action. The G-5 guns could not be taken by the enemy. What to do? Close to the stranded guns was Major Theo Wilken, one of our seasoned artillery observation officers with his eyes glued to the front. Comfortably close to the unfolding dilemma was Combat Group Bravo commanded by Commandant Robbie Hartslief. We needed additional resources to reinforce at the trouble spot. My choice fell on one of the combat teams of 61 Mech deployed in a hide near Mavinga, commanded by stout-hearted Major Dawid Lotter. We were going to take no chances as time was of the essence. As I explained the situation over the radio to Lotter I could hear that our chosen man was not too happy with yours truly. Him and his little manoeuvre group comprising one mechanised infantry company and an anti-tank platoon with eight Ratel-90s had just come out of some serious fighting on the Lomba and they were bone tired. Orders were given, received, acknowledged, maps marked and Lotter's combat team was soon traversing from east to west across our front into the unknown. I was praying along with them as this would become one of my longest nights

I now had to report our unfolding predicament by radio to Brigadier J.T. Louw in Rundu. Strangely enough he was unhappy about my decision about dispatching Lotter's combat team to the rescue of the guns. He was apparently worried that we would not get Major Lotter and his combat team back in time to join up with 61 Mech for the deception attack on the 9th. However, our Tac HQ had already conceived an alternative plan for that anyway. I was amazed – first things first, save the guns. I remember saying, Rundu, this is Task Force 10, the decision concerning the plight of the guns and the woes and the ways of Lotter has already been taken. They are already moving. Out. Ignore, I thought and focus on the job on hand.

In the meantime the situation on the front had worsened. Both the enemy tank columns were closing in on our stranded guns; two kilometres away or so, contact was imminent. Lotter soon joined up with the combat team of remarkable Major Hannes Nortmann of 32 Battalion: One motorised infantry company from 32 Battalion, two companies from 101 Battalion and the renowned Ratel-90 anti-tank platoon of Nortmann itself. At approximately 20:00 a violent battle ensued with the rogue FAPLA columns. Lotter's 81 mm mortars were literally firing on to the attacking line of Hannes Nortmann. Eventually the enemy broke contact and started to withdraw to their brigade defensive position of 59 Brigade. The retreating enemy had encountered heavy casualties. Fortunately no South African casualties were suffered, none whatsoever. Only two of Nortmann's vehicles were damaged. The 127 mm Valkiri started engaging the retreating enemy causing further havoc and destruction. At least two enemy vehicles were observed burning profusely. The G-5 guns were eventually hauled slightly further southwards for comfort. The next day 59 Brigade, who had sprouted the marauders, was pounded by the Mirages – vengeance was sweet. The combat team of Lotter was placed temporarily under the command of Commandant Robbie Hartslief of 32 Battalion. Close calls such as these were the spice of life. Adrenaline levels were settling again.

It was time for coffee and friendly chat on canvas camp chairs amongst close comrades. Phew![12] In the meantime, rumour had it that the enemy was contemplating moving 16 Brigade away from the source of the Chambinga. This was bad news as it did not suit our plans for them. A number of attacking Mirages and Buccaneers were duly dispatched to sort out this little problem, bombing 16 Brigade into submission, pegging them down to wait for the unexpected attack by 4 SAI and the tanks.

By now Ferreira had joined up with our Tac HQ. A few days before the scheduled attack on 16 Brigade I flew by Puma to Mavinga at night, accompanied by Colonels Jean Lausberg and Fred Oelschig. On landing at Mavinga airfield the three of us were whisked away in a brand new Casspir of Jonas Savimbi – compliments of P.W. Botha. Under my arm was the lengthy rolled-up battle map depicting the plan for the attack on 16 Brigade

12 Majors Dawid Lotter and Theo Wilken later on served with me at the South African Army College in friendlier years. With boundless practical experience and exposure they became extraordinary assets to the military and I was eternally indebted to such outstanding officers.

displayed on talc. The meeting happened in a dimly-lit underground command post at Mavinga. Savimbi was in the presence of his trusted generals Demosthenes, Ben-Ben and Bok. They were sitting around a beautiful wooden conference table on blue leathered office chairs stamped "Made in South Africa". We had the privilege of coordinating the plan of attack against FAPLA's 16 Brigade and what we predicted was to follow in its explosive aftermath. Savimbi and his generals were highly satisfied with the unfolding offensive state of affairs. We were ensured by them that the UNITA forces would be there on time at every point of impact as well as taking account of the enemy's unwelcome flying from Menongue. Content with the planning and the coordination thereof the three of us flew back to our Tac HQ at the Lomba – a full night's work satisfactorily completed – it was now time for a few minutes of well-deserved shuteye.

My friend, Commandant Cassie Schoeman by now had reached Mavinga with our small herd of trusted steeds; our six Ratel-Commands – a comforting thought as our Tac HQ was going to be mobile at last. We summarily moved our Buffel and Casspir-mounted Tac HQ from the Lomba to Mavinga. We left days of deeply trodden tracks at our former position and trailed many thoughts in the diesel wake of our lean procession moving towards Mavinga. Some of the thoughts were reminiscent of a few scary moments; mostly it was about fond memories and gratefulness shared amongst close comrades. Slightly to the north on the left of us lay the Lomba River's silvery watercourse in the moonlight as we progressively drove eastwards. Close on seventy kilometres to the north nestled the Chambinga in the night – the next offensive.

On arrival at Mavinga we rapidly reorganised the mobile command post of Task Force 10. We were now mobile and ready to move and to command and attack on the hoof. By the 7th our Tac HQ and all the respective combat groupings deployed towards forward assembly areas in readiness for the attack on 16 Brigade. Our Tac HQ left Mavinga in single file, crossed the Lomba and headed north. We were on our way to join 4 SAI and the tank squadron at their forward assembly area approximately 45 kilometres to the east of 16 Brigade. Their position was slightly north of the mine-infested "Old Portuguese Road."

I had one unsavoury chore to fulfil when we reached 4 SAI and I was not looking forward to it. I had to inform Major Vincent Harmse, who was one of the company commanders with 4 SAI, to withdraw from Modular. This was on the direct instruction of the Chief of the Army, Lieutenant General Kat Liebenberg who had contacted me in this regard the previous day. Harmse's father, Desmond was killed in an airplane crash during Operation Savannah (1975–1976) and his brother, Louis during Operation Protea on 25 August 1981. I knew that Harmse was making his first appearance in an external conventional operation. This was something every career officer dreamed of (I will not use the expression, "to die for"). It was not going to be easy for me to convey the message; much less so for him. Of course, the commander of 4 SAI would be party to the conveyance of this unpleasant instruction. I knew exactly what Commandant Leon Marais was going to think about this not so opportune disruption of his command the night before the assault on 16 Brigade. Any such leadership disturbance normally plays hell with organisational cohesion and force morale. However, orders were orders. Personally I thought the instruction for Vincent Harmse to withdraw at this late hour was grossly unfair, both to him and his unit – this was the soldier thinking. Whilst we had our talk with Harmse, Combat Group Alpha reached their deployment area somewhere to the southeast of 16 Brigade.

Our Tac HQ spent some precious moments with 4 SAI and the tank squadron as the fighting men did their finals before striking westward towards the enemy's 16 Brigade. Final orders were given on sand models, a church parade was held in the bush, the latest information on enemy dispositions affirmed – Combat Group Charlie was "march and combat ready." Our Tac HQ said their cheers. Soon after midnight our lean command procession moved slightly south, crossed the "Old Portuguese Road" and then struck westward. Before first light we reached our command position close to Combat Group Alpha's attacking position ready to command the battle. Commandants Cassie Schoeman and C.P. du Toit pushed extended high frequency radio antennas up into the tall trees to keep a listening watch on the combat net of Major André Retief's fighting tank squadron. Combat Group Bravo reported readiness further to the south near the Mianei River. The artillery and the SAAF were ready. Our UNITA fighting compatriots were ready – to the east and the west of the Cuito Cuanavale. H-Hour was approaching fast now. Soon after first light we could hear some Russian MiG fighters tearing through the skies high above us – ever prevalent and menacing. Dear Lord, please heed our prayers for our people on the ground – life on the edge.

Something about the Tac HQ of Task Force 10

Our Task Force HQ constituted a close-knit clan of seasoned and well-experienced fighters; a high-performance team, so to speak. We knew how to plan and conduct the fluid battle under these circumstances and also how to lead and inspire the stouthearted. As such, Colonel Deon Ferreira was a highly experienced commander and had a flair for tactics. We were both veterans from Operation Protea as were many of our staff officers who knew each other closely. There was no local protection element allotted to our Tac HQ. We depended on near real-time information about enemy movements, stealth and camouflage and concealment for survival. One important factor was not to be stationary at any one position for longer than three days at a time. Although the flatness and denseness of the terrain did not afford observation for command purposes, the close proximity to the frontline commanders and their fighting units were imperative. This allowed getting together rapidly once in a while for command and staff interaction when so required. This also afforded the command group an actual feel for the situation – the finger on the pulse so to speak.

The mobile headquarters constituted a small field staff representing the respective command functions of operations, intelligence, signals, electronic warfare, artillery, air support, logistics and medical support. These were officers the likes of Cassie Schoeman, C.P. du Toit, Lambert Smit, Coen van den Berg, Jean Lausberg, Francois van Eeden and Cubby van Rooyen; to mention some of the precious few. Many of these officers could at moment's notice take over the command of the operation. They were the best any commander could wish for. Sergeant-major Crocodile van Rensburg trailed in the rear with a single SAMIL truck carrying the bare necessities. Moving with us was the small liaison team from UNITA of Colonels Fred Oelschig and Shevukuvuku (UNITA). We were transported in six armoured Ratel-Commands and a few Casspir mine-protected vehicles. No more than about eleven in total. We normally adopted a dispersed well-camouflaged position. Barracuda nets, foliage and entrenching tools became our closest friends. The vehicles for operations and intelligence were more closely grouped. Within close proximity was the command post (fire support coordination centre) of the artillery of Lausberg and Van Eeden, who also kept a close vigil on the safety of own aircraft. This all formed part of the meticulous coordination of ground fire and manoeuvre with air defence, air attack and indirect fire support. SAAF Commandant Coen van den Berg formed part of the indirect and aerial fire support planning, coordination and control team.

The military staffs were ever vigilant maintaining situational awareness. Assessing and planning endlessly day and night, formulating options and presenting it for decision. At times this happened every hour on the hour, especially when the scene of battle changed consistently. Tactical decisions taken were borne with great responsibility and therefore considered the best interests of the soldiers at limb in the field. If decisions here and there went somewhat askew because of inadequate information at hand at a given moment, so be it. The next prudent decision then needed to be made by the undaunted and it had to be taken rapidly as, in the words of Sun Tzu, "rapidity is the essence of war".

When stationary we lived in shallow shell scrapes under the momentary comfort of mosquito nets. Our diet was mainly 24-hour ration packs. Deservedly so lukewarm beer, fresh meat and bread were enjoyed when the higher beings flew in occasionally in the dark of night by Puma helicopter. This was usually for a one-night stand to be briefed on the operation. In the same vein operational instructions and guidelines were conveyed from the higher layers of headquarters presiding over our fate at the front. Our masters and their few staff officers in attendance usually departed for Rundu, Windhoek and Pretoria before first light. Simply stated, command was about successfully achieving military missions and giving our soldiers a fair chance to make it out alive.[13]

9 November 1987 – The Attack on 16 Brigade and Diversionary Tactics in the South

In the writing of this chronicle of the battle for Chambinga I was offered the opportunity to reflect deeply about the past. I sometimes wondered how our forces did it, especially those young conscript warriors facing combat for the first time in their lives – through willing compulsion and utmost dedication. The minute South African combat force and the few UNITA soldiers were fighting in southeast Angola under the harshest operational conditions imaginable – few against many.[14] There were remarkable, endearing human exploits taking place during the battle for Chambinga and these stories need to be told. Space does not allow me to include all these tales. Here follows the essence of the chronicle relating to the bloody encounter for Chambinga.

Combat Group Bravo's diversionary attack struck at the battalion of 25 Brigade and 21 Brigade at the source of the Mianei River at 01:00 on the 9th. The battle for Chambinga was on. By 06:00 Combat Group Charlie under command of Commandant Leon Marais was approximately four kilometres northeast of their objective and started deploying in attacking formation.

It was an unforgettable morning in the war as the sun rose over a magnificent African landscape. Several attacking Mirages were already screaming through the air to attack 16 Brigade unknowingly competing with the 155 mm G-5 rounds slewing in on the same target. Combat Group Alpha delivered its diversionary attack from the southeast, which was preceded by the shattering roar of the lethal 155 mm artillery shells slamming into the

13 Refer to Chapter 8 on command and leadership.

14 Without knowing it then, by mid-November Fidel Castro was furiously rushing huge numbers of military reinforcements to Cuito Cuanavale from Cuba. This information was only confirmed to us by own intelligence at a much later date. The war for southern Angola was escalating beyond proportion.

16th at 06:30. The artillery onslaught was augmented by lethal pre-fragmentation bombs delivered by the low-level attacking Mirages. The diversionary force immediately started drawing artillery fire from the enemy guns. The enemy's T-54/55 tanks started forming up in readiness for a counter-attack. Commandant Mike Müller instructed Combat Group Alpha to withdraw to a safer distance to perform its work as mobile reserve. The artillery continued seeking out their targets amongst the enemy defences. The deliberate attack by Combat Group Charlie went in at 07:00.

One Russian military advisor, somewhat misinformed as he did not know that the attack at the Mianei in the south was part of our deception plan, wrote the following in his memoirs: "All night we heard the rumble of engines and nearby explosions ... Around eight o'clock we got information that 16 Brigade (20 km away) had been subjected since three o'clock in the morning to heavy fire and attacks from regular South African battalions. The advisors attached to 25 Brigade (battalion at the Mianei) informed us that at around one in the morning the enemy had tried to penetrate their defensive line. When they failed, the attackers began to throw everything they had at the brigade. Later on they again tried several times to break through and have continued with their racket up to now. The position of 25 Brigade is precarious."[15]

In the north the approach to contact through the dense bush by Combat Group Charlie was led by an infantry company from 32 Battalion and UNITA as a screening force. They soon became embroiled in a vicious battle with FAPLA. By now the enemy had heard the approaching roar of the attacking Ratels and the tanks. Their radios started buzzing and the South African electronic warfare operators mounted in their Ratels listened in and reported what they were saying. It was discerned that the enemy's Tactical Group 2 acting as mobile reserve with at least a company of T-54/55 tanks had been alerted for counter-attack from the Viposto area. One of the exposed flanks of the attacking formation of Combat Group Charlie was now under threat as well. Marais swiftly instructed Retief and his squadron of Olifant tanks to counter the enemy tank threat. It was an excellent decision.

A mechanised infantry company of Ratel-20s rapidly regrouped and integrated with the tank squadron for the counter action. Meanwhile, true to form the Cubans deployed with 16 Brigade, started withdrawing southwestward to safety. Similarly the Russian military advisors with the beleaguered enemy were shouting for helicopter extraction. A few minutes later the Olifant tanks started engaging the Russian T-54/55s. Lieutenant Hein Fourie's Olifant and his crew of three killed the first enemy tank. Our Tac HQ cheered when the first enemy tank was destroyed. The commanding voices over the radios were cool, calm and collected, as we listened in from our command post. We felt extremely proud of our commanders and their soldiers. This was true to their fighting form as we knew them. Minutes later the second enemy tank was destroyed by Lieutenant Abrie Strauss and his crew. The scathing well-directed fire of the 105 mm guns of the Olifant and its turret-mounted 7,62 mm Browning machine guns started exerting its toll from the enemy defenders. The tanks were supported by the quick-firing guns of the Ratel-20s, whilst supporting fire from the 155 mm G-6 guns and 81 mm mortars rained down relentlessly on the enemy. By 09:00 the damage to the enemy became apparent. Through swift calculation it was assessed that there were more than 22 enemies killed in the battle so far. Up to now, miraculously so, there were no own forces casualties encountered. A plan of the enemy's defensive layout was

15 Shubin, Gennady and Tokarev, Andrei: *Bush War – The Road to Cuito Cuanavale*. Chapter 2, p.24.

captured together with two FAPLA soldiers.

By 10:00 the resistance from those remaining in defence of 16 Brigade became fiercer still. Three South African soldiers were killed by now. The battle became a close affair and was extremely difficult to control. One of the Ratel-20s became entangled with a Russian T-54/55 and the staunch Ratel crew had to pour ripples of 20 mm armour piercing into the tank until it eventually exploded. The same Ratel was hit by another enemy tank, instantly killing both the gunner and the driver. An Olifant tank immediately took revenge and destroyed the T-54/55. Five enemy tanks were now destroyed and one was captured intact. The see-saw battle continued unabatedly. At approximately 11:00 Combat Group Charlie came under attack by enemy MiG-23s. By 12:00 the enemy's resistance suddenly collapsed and they started fleeing desperately westwards. It was now the ideal moment for Combat Group Charlie to exploit its success and to hunt down the fleeing foe. For some strange reason Commandant Leon Marais halted the attack and withdrew his combat force to safer ground. A moment for further decisive killing had passed by as a number of 16 Brigade soldiers and their hardware were afforded the opportunity to escape.

At about 18:00 approximately 45 km to the south, Combat group Bravo came under attack by two battalions of 21 Brigade and one of 59 Brigade supported by tanks. Combat Group Bravo withdrew to safety as they had been instructed to avoid contact with the enemy tanks. Night settled in. The diversionary work in the south had been performed well.

The completely exhausted Combat Group Charlie now withdrew to a laager position east of the enemy's defences to replenish and to reorganise. The dead and the wounded needed to be evacuated as well. As they withdrew they came under attack from enemy MiG-21s and MiG-23s.

Enemy losses accounted for were: Thirteen tanks; two BM-21s multiple rocket launchers; two 76 mm anti-aircraft guns; fourteen SA-7/SA-14s; one 14,5 mm heavy machine gun; four 23 mm anti-aircraft guns; one 82 mm mortar; 32 military trucks. It was a terrible loss to them. 75 FAPLA soldiers were killed in action and six captured.

Seven soldiers of Combat Group Charlie were killed and nine wounded. One Ratel-20 infantry combat vehicle was destroyed and one damaged. One Olifant tank was also damaged. This was a heavy price to pay for one battle according to our norm – truly, in the sense of incurring heavy casualties the South Africans were far below the median for conventional war fighting in accordance with international standards. We were fortunate in the war thus far – it was probably due to a magic mix of superior tactics and sheer providence, which had served us well. We had to guard against becoming complacent.

16 Brigade was beaten but not butchered. They were able to flee and fight again another day. This was not completely according to the original plan. It was however another nail in the coffin of FAPLA. There was anger expressed by Colonel Deon Ferreira at the discontinuation of the attack. Generally speaking the attack had gone so well, however, Commandant Leon Marais the commander on the ground stood by his decision to halt the attack. The members of our HQ were understandably disappointed that the attack had not been pushed home. I however need to point out that the terrible and sudden loss of the many South African soldiers came as a shock to the living – those who had experienced war and its bloody aftermath firsthand for the first time in their young, so far innocent, lives. The most harrowing experience was to attack under insistent air bombardments.

During the night of 10 November Combat Group Charlie lay enclosed in the dense foliage of their next hide about 15 km to the west of the source of the Cunzumbia. The combat force had already received orders to strike deeper at enemy objectives lying further southwest the next day. The young conscript soldiers had become veterans in one day, living on the sharp edge of combat.

The HQ of 16 Brigade and one of its battalions had withdrawn to halfway between the sources of the Chambinga and Hube rivers. Another battalion of 16 Brigade had moved towards the Chambinga crossing. Tactical Group 2 of the enemy was somewhere in the dense bush close to the source of the Hube River with 15 T-54/55 tanks. 59 Brigade had started moving steadily in the direction of the source of the Hube as they had been ordered to return to Tumpo to take over the old defensive line of 25 Brigade. The operational command post of the enemy remained at the Viposto High ground as did 21 Brigade and the battalion of 25 Brigade at the Mianei. All-in the entire enemy disposition during the night 10/11 November became somewhat vague to the Task Force HQ as the enemy started scurrying into new positions. The dislodgement of FAPLA's entire defence from Chambinga in the north right down to the Mianei in the south had begun. The fight was loosening up, but not in intensity and the expenditure of fuel and ammunition and lives.

By now we had started encountering substantial problems with logistics, which took its toll on our combat readiness and in maintaining mobility and momentum. Bear in mind that there was a considerable distance involved: By road from Pretoria to the logistic base at Grootfontein in SWA was 2 268 km; from Grootfontein to Rundu 258 km; from Rundu to Mavinga 280 km by jarring bush track. To the fighting line it was a further 120–150 km to be bundu-bashed mostly at night. Perpetual movement made it impossible to stockpile at the temporary deployment positions and hides of the frontline fighting units and artillery batteries. There were just not enough support capacity and wheels to go around as logistic support units had been deployed in bits and pieces. Just maintaining enough spare wheels and bread-and-butter spares at the front was a major problem. The observable fact was that a few drivers thrown into the fight did not make up a well-organised transport company; a few loose mechanics did not constitute a capable technical support group. The tracks of the Olifant tanks started stretching, which took extreme maintenance effort and time to repair; the mobile fuel pumps became unserviceable, which required digging holes so as to fill the fighting vehicles by gravitation. Some of these logistic challenges were downright irritating and some were daunting; all these consumed precious bits of time. In war you can make great demands of your men, but if circumstances bite into their well-earned, all too short, periods of rest, it destroys momentum. Without momentum the mobile battle dies a horrifying death. These minor hindrances were not going to get us down. There were always magical moments for a few miracles to be performed by the wily survivalist South Africans. The greater the pressure, the better they performed – remarkable people.

Another pressing challenge for the fighting force was the mere fact that the national service troops had to demobilise the latest by 15 December. This restriction put undue pressure on the fighting process and forced some unrealistic operational instructions from the higher HQs. SWATF wanted the enemy deploying east of the Cuito River to be destroyed before 15 December. This decision to my mind smacked of an ineffectual military appreciation of the true circumstances of the war. Notwithstanding this number of bothersome challenges the fury of the South Africans and UNITA up front towards the enemy never ceased as the progressive killing continued.

11 November 1987 – Resuming the Counter-Attack

The Task Force HQ wanted Combat Group Charlie to resume its attack on 10 November. There was however some discourse about the true enemy picture. This needed to be confirmed by means of intelligence as soon as possible. UNITA played an important role in this regard as well – could their intelligence be trusted? Combat Group Alpha, as the mobile reserve, remained in its hide, in close proximity to the enemy, quietly so, as not to be observed.

By 15:00 Combat Group Charlie was ready to resume its attack from the north on the remnants of 16 Brigade and the tactical group. As the combat force moved out, enemy MiGs flew over its position. The MiGs then flew over the concealed position of Combat Group Alpha and proceeded to bomb the old positions of 16 Brigade. All movement halted as Combat Group Charlie hastily sought concealment. Radio intercepts in the meantime confirmed that the enemy had observed that Combat Group Charlie was on its way to attack Tactical Group 2. Urgent support was requested by the enemy. Some more mishaps occurred with Combat Group Charlie as they had an unfortunate shooting incident. This expended more valuable time. The enemy mistakenly bombed their own forces with MiGs at the Chambinga crossing, while the South African Mirages attacked the position of 25 Brigade. Tactical Group 2 in the meantime was reinforced with combat elements from 16 Brigade, which included tanks. Came nightfall 59 Brigade further to the south was well on its way to escape over the Chambinga crossing. By now it was too late to continue the attack.

Planning through the night concluded that there were two viable targets to strike at the following day. Objective Alpha was a FAPLA force with some tanks deployed close to the source of the Hube River. Objective Bravo was another stronger enemy force located slightly south of the Chambinga River. Further to the south it was required from Combat Group Bravo once again to fix the attention of 21 Brigade and elements from 25 Brigade on 11 November through probing attack.

During the night of 10–11 November we moved the mobile tactical headquarters further to the southwest aiming for the cover of the Catato Woods in readiness for the next offensive which was scheduled for the 11th; once again to be executed by the newly blooded Combat Group Charlie and the more seasoned combatants of Combat Group Alpha. At midnight we drove through the laager of Combat Group Charlie with our meagre procession of command Ratels. The young troopers were asleep alongside their Ratels, arms and limbs outstretched, rifles in hand, utterly fatigued. Nobody challenged our whining low-revving diesel march-past as we drove through. The enemy could have taken our gallant warriors that night without a fight, they were so completely exhausted. I felt deep respect for the tenacity of our soldiers and their commanders. Respect on the one hand and remorse for their suffering were shaped into one emotion – seeing our young troopers, exhausted to the bone, exposed to their own vulnerability in every sense of the word. These were feelings, due to the limitations of the spoken and written word ... not easily explained. No wonder that their morale started waning under these terrible conditions. Just too much was expected from them. The next day, come first light, our soldiers were ready to do battle again. The perilous game thus played was emotionally wrenching and physically taxing to the extreme.

Our mobile headquarters was now in front of the fighting line. The next morning, soon after daybreak, slightly to the west of our command procession, we could see the Russian MiGs running just above the tree line. With some apprehension we watched our dust trailing and immediately slowed down. Our Tac HQ was approaching the Catato Woods from a northeasterly direction. The 81 mm Mortar Platoon of 4 SAI passed by our mobile headquarters at high speed; there was no more dust suspended in our dual wake and trailing tracks. The eyes of the young sparkled, they waved at us and smiled as they passed by – young enthusiastic dirt-streaked faces. The mortarists needed to take up position somewhere in front of us to support the next offensive move by Combat Group Charlie. The mortar platoon was now in front of our Tac HQ – a comfortable feeling.

We hightailed for the Catato Woods to get under cover from the marauding MiGs. On the way we had to stop to take cover rapidly and dig in feverishly as a few enemy aircraft started circling ominously above us, searching ardently for something lucrative to slam. At some stage we could hear a few Russian MiGs throwing cluster bombs slightly to our west – an extremely distasteful experience – first an explosive rupture and then the parachute opening, followed a few seconds later by the lethal ripple of the cluster bombs as its fiery mini munitions exploded. We were becoming quite used to these bothersome ruptures in the sky and on the ground around us.

At 09:00 on 11 November, Combat Groups Alpha and Charlie were ordered to launch consecutive attacks at enemy objectives Alpha and Bravo. Combat Group Charlie was to launch the main attack, while Combat Group Alpha diverted and acted as the mobile reserve. The attacking recipe allowed for softening blows by the artillery and attacking Mirages. During the approach to contact Combat group Charlie was attacked by enemy MiGs. Fortunately, only one member of the anti-aircraft troop was wounded. Some more MiG attacks were encountered later with the enemy's bombing becoming more accurate. The attacking units had immense control problems as they progressively penetrated the thickest bush imaginable on the way to Objective Alpha. They started drawing indirect fire as the enemy at Alpha summarily fled to the west.

Combat Group Charlie consolidated their position after Alpha was cleared. They were now ready to attack Objective Bravo further to the north. A tough target of approximately two enemy battalions and 22 tanks were awaiting them at Bravo. This was becoming a long, tiring day for the young attackers – sheer exhaustion was gradually eating into muscle and soul as enemy fire and African sun exerted its toll. Artillery onslaught and Mirage attack preceded the assault on Objective Bravo. The troops were becoming tired and extremely thirsty as they progressively moved forward. As the force rested for a while they drew indirect as well as accurate sniper fire. Major André Retief with the tanks in front immediately ordered a fire-belt action and resumed the attack on Bravo. There were several radio intercepts indicating that there were about three enemy tank groupings manoeuvring in close proximity to the attacking force. There was a real danger of the attackers being enveloped. Combat Group Charlie and the tank squadron subsequently became embroiled in a serious close-in battle. The mechanised companies started running short on ammunition and had to replenish in the fighting line. The attackers were drawing heavy artillery and multiple rocket launcher fire as they closed in on an enemy minefield. Commandant Leon Marais withdrew his force in apprehension of becoming fixed in the minefield, while drawing attack from the enemy's air force at the same time.

By 15:00 the attacking Combat Group Charlie was running low on ammunition and Marais withdrew them in bounds to safety. As they withdrew the BM-21 rockets rained down on the minefield. A damaged Olifant tank was safely recovered. The Mirages were called in to hit the enemy position once again. Müller's Combat Group Alpha was ordered to resume the attack after integrating with the Olifant tanks of André Retief. Combat Group Charlie now acted as the mobile reserve.

Dusk settled by 18:00. It became too dark to remain on the offensive. The enemy had withdrawn their position from Objective Bravo to safer high ground more to the west. The combat groups withdrew to safe laager positions. The troops were exhausted to the bone. It had been their longest day with some miraculous escapes. Through the many hours the artillery had kept on pounding targets in the vicinity of the Chambinga crossing and the SAAF had repeatedly bombed 25 Brigade into obedience. The artillery destroyed almost a battalion's worth of infantry who had formed up at the Chambinga crossing in the afternoon. Approximately 40 of their vehicles had been destroyed in the furious artillery encounter. All these actions had neatly kept the enemy surplus out of interfering with the attacks by Combat Groups Alpha and Charlie on Objectives Alpha and Bravo. It evenly contributed to the enemy's diminishing numbers.

Remnants of 16 Brigade and Tactical Group 2 were closing in on the Chambinga crossing. Their moves were closely watched by artillery observers, Majors Cassie van der Merwe and Koos Breytenbach, who duly responded with a G-5 onslaught and destroyed two enemy tanks at the crossing. The enemy's 59 Brigade which had already been ordered on 10 November to withdraw to Tumpo, now regrouped at the Chambinga crossing to cover the retreating FAPLA. Meanwhile, 21 Brigade and the battalion from 25 Brigade remained in defence at the Mianei River. They still desperately sought out the G-5s of the South Africans deployed in the south, notwithstanding having lost nine tanks since the battle had commenced on 9 November. The enemy's command, fearing an attack on Cuito Cuanavale, realised that they had to rapidly withdraw the force at the Mianei for defence of their main position straddling the river. Their escape route went via the source of the Hube and Viposto high ground. This contested area was now dominated by South Africa's mobile forces. As such all the remaining positions of the enemy south of the Chambinga had become untenable – even though they were the larger force by far.

By the end of the day 394 FAPLA soldiers were killed. The enemy had lost 15 T-54/55 tanks; three armoured fighting vehicles; three anti-aircraft guns; 12 trucks. The South African forces lost five soldiers killed; nineteen wounded. Two Ratel-20s were destroyed. Some of those precious souls were enthusiastic earlier on and had been smiling notwithstanding personal apprehensions. Once again there were some disappointments at the end of the day's offensive moves. The wily enemy was still eluding the clutches of the South Africans and UNITA. The enemy once again was severely wounded, but not slain. Did we truly have enough forces availably to properly corner the foe?

On this day the following was reported by one of the Russian advisers by telegram to Cuito (Telegram 91 on 11 November at 09:00): "The enemy hits each brigade separately one by one ... Thus all the brigades will be killed off one by one ... Commanding officers of all ranks are scared. They are scared to start counteractions against the enemy ... Something quite unimaginable is happening. The Angolan troops are almost completely demoralised; the brigades are on average at 45% strength. For every 10 to 15 shells launched by the enemy, the Angolans are able to send only one, if even that much. Our reconnaissance operates poorly and the enemy knows everything about us. The Angolans fear the South Africans like fire and if they hear that their "Buffalo" (32 Battalion) is part of an attack, they throw away all their equipment in panic and flee.[16]

13-17 November 1987 – The Chambinga Gallop

From 13 to 17 November the FAPLA brigades and units that were deployed east of the Cuito River started escaping across the Chambinga back to the safety of Cuito Cuanavale. There were just not sufficient own forces available to stop all the gaps. At this stage the logistic staying power and battle momentum of the South Africans were dwindling dimensionally in comparison with the immense fighting effort expended. During this crucial fighting period Task Force 10 endeavoured to trap 21 Brigade sandwiched between the Vimpulo and the Mianei. Subsequently as the enemy slipped the noose the fighting progressed to a battle arena lying near the source of the Hube River. The initial plan called for Combat Group Charlie to cut off the enemy's escape route across the Vimpulo, while continuously depleting the enemy's numbers by means of fire and attack. Combat Group Alpha was instructed to deploy halfway between the Mianei and the Vimpulo on the eastern flank to strike at the fleeing enemy. Ambushing was to be the prime method applied. In our book an ambush was a surprise attack on a moving enemy from a hidden position. The challenge remained the close control and effective coordination of own offensive operations in the dense bushes. Another was the problem of maintaining operational security. True navigation day and night in dense terrain posed its own unusual challenges. The other issue of high importance was the collection and interpretation of real-time and near real-time intelligence. The danger of the lurking and pouncing enemy air force during day time never ceased. All precautions had to be taken not to be cornered by the overwhelming numbers of the enemy. It took some effort to sort out the fluid battle situation. Building a true enemy picture minute-by-minute remained an immense challenge.

The mobile games were scheduled to commence by 13 November. The previous day was used to allow for some rest and logistic replenishment of the weary South African and UNITA soldiers. The artillery never ceased to strike at any viable target being presented either at the Mianei or the Chambinga crossing. A number of unsuccessful MiG attacks were launched close to our forces in hiding on the 12th. Further to the south near the Mianei Bravo was all set to support.

59 Brigade was halfway across the Chambinga by now. 66 Brigade was also in that vicinity with some of its remnants waiting to cross. Elements of 16 Brigade had now moved into a defensive line between the Chambinga and Hube rivers. Tactical Group 2 was east of the source of the Hube with their eight remaining T-54/55 tanks. 21 Battalion and the battalion of 25 Brigade were still at the Mianei. There was a clear possibility that the battalion of 66 Brigade from their deployment at the confluence of the Mianei and the Cuito had joined up with 21 Brigade. The operational command group of FAPLA was still deployed in the vicinity of Viposto.

Early on 13 November the tactical group near the Hube reported their position untenable due to logistic problems and the mere fact that some of their troops were hightailing it out of there. The enemy was not having it all their way. Waning soldiery discipline it seemed was eating its way into morale and was sapping their combat resilience. There were clear indications that the forces at the Mianei were readying to move out of their defences. The battle scene, so it seemed, was set.

16 Shubin, Gennady and Tokarev, Andrei: *Bush War – The Road to Cuito Cuanavale*. Chapter 2, p.27.

Our two most northerly combat groups reported intensified enemy air activity and bombing over their respective positions. The air threat remained an unnerving factor. Slowly but surely our own forces were showing strain as we gradually started running out of human resilience, mechanical spares and consumables. The G-5s were losing their ability for sustained fire support due to mechanical hitches – overutilization was gradually exerting its toll. There were no human spare parts available either. By the afternoon of 13th 21 Brigade was ready to escape northwards. We had not expected them to move so quickly. All of these untimely enemy actions caused continuous reassessment of the operational situation vis-à-vis the disposition of own forces, time and terrain. Every unnecessary move by own forces used up available killing time, human tether and logistics. At times I wondered what flashed through the minds of the soldiers of the 21st and how they felt being out here on a limb to the south. The remaining enemy brigades were now sprinting for home base during darkness knowing that they were going to run the gauntlet.

The three G-6s had in the meantime in their usual dashing style deployed onto the Chambinga high ground close to the Cuatir; all on their lonesome own some. The guns were leisurely bombarding Cuito Cuanavale. The deployment of a South African force north of the enemy's position at Chambinga came as a severe shock to them. The guns had to withdraw two days later because of technical hitches.[17]

By the close of 13 November the enemy's Chambinga Gallop had commenced in all seriousness – their whole defence collapsed like a house of cards just as we had predicted at Rundu. The suddenness and speed of their feverish escape still came as a surprise. We were not accustomed to the enemy making quick decisions and moving that swiftly. We had however become accustomed to their uncontrolled flight on numerous occasions, such as the 16th Brigade on the 9th. The enemy's swift retreat was taxing the restricted force levels and response capability of our own forces. Throughout the enemy intercepts indicated severe discontent with their own situation with continuous losses of men and material. The Soviet military advisors hastened to flee the closing trap leaving those advised to their own devices. 59 Brigade took over the defence of the Chambinga crossing, whilst 66 Brigade redeployed south of the Hube as the enemy was preparing to cover the escape of 21 Brigade.

At first light 21 Brigade was still floundering around at the Mianei after having been pinned down effectively by the G-5s. The battalion of 25 brigade moving westward at snail's pace was struggling to link up with the 21st under withering 155 mm fire. At about 16:00 on the 14th there was a brief skirmish when the 21st Brigade was caught between Combat Groups Alpha and Charlie. The enemy succeeded in evading. Catching the enemy crossing the Vimpulo was the next challenge – where would this be? Some tactical mishaps by Combat Group Charlie saved the bacon of 21 Brigade. Notwithstanding some bloody clashes and skirmishes, following night and day, 21 Brigade unfortunately succeeded in escaping towards the Viposto by first light on the morning of the 15th passing close by the ambush position of Charlie. Their next desperate move was to cross the Chambinga the same night. Due credit goes to FAPLA's 21st Brigade. They had executed an amazingly difficult manoeuvre through an extremely challenging night by successfully escaping the wrath of both Combat Groups Alpha and Charlie. Alpha forthwith reconnoitred the Mianei-Vimpulo basin in strength to ensure that it was clear of any enemy leftovers. Further plans were made on 15 November to pin down 21 Brigade on their last run towards the

17 The G-6 guns were being tried and tested for the first time in battle with very few spares available. Commandant Faan Bothma of the artillery was their project officer.

Chambinga River. Combat Group Charlie rushed towards the source of the Hube as fast as the difficult terrain would allow. The stops and starts of the enemy were continuously shelled by the artillery.

On the night of 14–15 November 16 Brigade reported that nearly all their troops had deserted their position and were fleeing towards the flesh pots of Cuito Cuanavale. A deserting enemy battalion commander was also ardently sought by his brigade commander to be figuratively or literally "shot at dawn". During the night Combat Group Alpha deployed towards the Hube continuously monitoring enemy movements ready to strike at a moment's notice. Combat Group Bravo deployed to the north to act as the Task Force mobile reserve. Combat Group Charlie was slightly too far eastward of their previous position at the Vimpulo and as such unexpectedly ran into an enemy minefield. Two mine-breaching "Plofadders" were fired by the combat group to forge a way through the minefield during darkness. This advent did not bode well for the ambushing of 21 Brigade when secrecy was required. Not one of the Plofadders functioned optimally. The combat group now used illumination rounds to navigate their movement through the minefield. This was another bad omen for ambushing and a dead giveaway of their position to any observant enemy. The same night 21 Brigade tried to cross the Hube but was unsuccessful. This was due to marshy crossing conditions and movement problems. At this stage 21 Brigade had a complement of twelve tanks and their four infantry battalions. By first light on 16 November 21 Brigade passed Viposto. The enemy's air force was on standby to strike at Combat Group Charlie near the source of the Hube and was in high readiness to support the final withdrawal of the 21st towards Chambinga. In the meantime Hartslief with Combat Group Bravo had closed up in support as mobile reserve. Under Hartslief's command Major Dawid Lotter with his combat team from 61 Mech and the combat team of Hannes Nortmann were ready to join in the fight.

Combat Group Charlie experienced another bout of faulty deployments and difficult manoeuvrings. Some of the enemy's advancing forces were met head-on instead of from a flank as was originally intended. A vicious close-in battle ensued in which the combat teams of Hannes Nortmann and Dawid Lotter also became involved. Fortunately during this fray the enemy MiGs went off-target and threw some of their wasted bombs in the vicinity of our Tac HQ. At 10:30 further fighting ensued between the enemy and Task Force Bravo which was operating on the flank of Charlie. Soon after, at approximately 11:00, the brigade commander of the 21st was wounded. His BTR-60 armoured command vehicle was shot out from under him. In the meantime 59 Brigade attempted to come to the rescue of the 21st from their position at the Hube. The withering fire of the G-5s successfully prevented this counter-attack from the north. Lotter's combat team now became involved in the fighting slightly east of the source of the Hube. Nearly all South Africa's combat groupings were entangled in the battle, which became a free for all making it extremely difficult to control. During this battle there were recorded and unrecorded acts of bravery and stories of human sacrifice and endeavour from both sides. Armoured fighting vehicles, soft skin trucks and flesh and blood became entangled. At some stage the enemy dropped their BM-21 Rocket packs to fire directly at their tormentors. One such BM-21 exploded amongst our own forces sending exploding rockets reeling in all directions. Surviving this endless ordeal became the watchword. By 13:00 on the 16th some of South Africa's combat forces needed replenishing and rest for a while. The fighting soon resumed as fire came in from all sides. A number of FAPLA infantry had infiltrated through the skirmish line and were fighting behind the South Africans. At 15:00 the MiG-23s were at it again strafing Combat Group Charlie up close with cannon fire and rockets. Fortunately, they were off target once again. Shortly thereafter the MiGs attacked in the vicinity of the Task Force HQ. UNITA fired two Stinger missiles at them without effect.

21 Brigade halted their advance and started digging in right in front of the fighting line of Combat Group Charlie who had manoeuvred through the night and up to that moment had been involved in an intense battle for more than six hours. Still there was no rest for the weary. Once again battlefield logistics were taking its toll as the fighting units ran short of ammunition and fuel. It became necessary to break contact with the enemy to replenish. Charlie moved five kilometres to the east to rendezvous with their administrative echelon. Nortmann was not pleased at all with the decision by Marais to break contact with the enemy. In the meantime Lotter had moved his combat team back to a position where he could cover the gap in the abandoned minefield of FAPLA. 21 Brigade similarly used the time to come to their senses, replenish, reorganise and prepare for the next fighting round. Combat Group Alpha by now was also busy with replenishment. The next plan was for Combat Groups Alpha and Charlie to integrate with Nortmann's force and to resume the attack on the 21st. The artillery maintained pressure on the foe in an all out effort to keep them pinned down. Night was approaching fast – still no rest for the weary.

Lady Luck and sheer providence smiled upon the depleted 21st. A heavy tropical downpour erupted from the African skies as they pulled a fast one. In this way we had underestimated our foe. As Combat Group Charlie and the combat team of Nortmann broke contact the enemy slipped the noose. They used the rain to mask their movement from the artillery observers and rapidly moved around the source of the Hube escaping to the safety of the high ground towards the Chambinga.

21 Brigade, breathing a sigh of relief now settled down in defence on the high ground south of the Chambinga River by nightfall on the 16th. Tactical Group 2 was still south of the Chambinga slightly to the east of the 21st. They were out on a limb and as usual crying for logistic replenishment. The enemy was logistics wise worse off than we were, it seemed.

The clash of arms near the source of the Hube River on the 16th was one of those extraordinary battles. It could be likened to a grinding mechanised contest of the Second World War. The South African soldiers and those of UNITA had experienced endless days and nights of manoeuvring and fighting, similar to the worst of times during the Second World War. The five days in November were crucial to the further decisive destruction of FAPLA east of the Cuito. Somehow our task force could not succeed in fixing our wily foe. The few combat groups in the field with the available time were just not completely up to the challenge. 21 Brigade eventually slipped away over the Chambinga River and came under the protection of 59 Brigade defending the crossing.

The situation which had so suddenly unfolded from 13 to 16 November in a sense came as a disappointment to our taskforce. We could have done with two more combat groups by the way – wishful thinking. The enemy had escaped the trap too quickly – accept it. In the crucial battle south of the Chambinga 21 Brigade had 131 soldiers killed in action. Seven T-54/55 tanks, one BTR-60, two BM-21s and four trucks were forfeited in the fighting process.

Miraculously only four soldiers of Combat group Charlie were killed in what can only be referred to as an epic mobile struggle. Nineteen South Africans were wounded. Combat Group Charlie only lost one recovery vehicle and an armoured ambulance. The combat team of Hannes Nortmann upped their score with three of the T-54/55 enemy tanks bagged to their credit. They suffered no casualties through the day's vicious fighting. I could clearly sense that the endless fighting and exposure to the enemy's relentless onslaughts from the skies were slowly eating away at the spirited morale of own forces. I did not want to know how the enemy felt. FAPLA had borne astonishing casualties due to continuous warfare.

By 16 and 17 November large concentrations of enemy forces in the vicinity of the Chambinga crossing were worn out and thus extremely vulnerable to any form of attack. The crossing had become hallowed ground for the South African artillery; neither to be spared by the attacking Mirages and Buccaneers of the SAAF. However the tactical ground surrounding the Chambinga crossing favoured defence by FAPLA. Our battle map at the Tac HQ now had one giant red circle drawn around the fording site at the Chambinga. We still had a few aces up the sleeve for the endgame. Everything now centred on the Chambinga crossing and the no-man's land towards the next portal at Cuito. If we did not watch out we could ourselves be caught in a trap between the Chambinga and the Cuito. We started feeling closely hemmed in – claustrophobic, more likely. Fortunately, to our west and south lay wide open spaces not easy to be influenced by the fleeing foe. The enemy was in a corner. First light on 17 November found the enemy desperately trying to cross the Chambinga at best speed. Indirect fire slewed relentlessly into the enemy concentrations, mowing down infantry and vehicles found in the open by scathing 155 mm shells and 127 mm rockets.

It was decided to launch another attack at the enemy defending the Chambinga crossing. The dice fell on Müller's Combat Group Alpha and the tank squadron of Retief. Alpha lay in a hide to the south of the Old Portuguese road and the source of the Chambinga. By this time they knew the terrain they were fighting over quite well. Any further pressure exerted on the disorganised foe south and east of Chambinga would force them into extreme vulnerability as they tried to escape through the choke point. By no means could the enemy effectively control their growing dilemma. Intelligence gained from FAPLA prisoners taken earlier further indicated that the enemy was planning to make a beeline for Tumpo on the night 17–18 November.

The line of attack on 17 November was to follow a westerly approach towards the crossing over the Chambinga. Combat Group Bravo remained as a mobile reserve to the south, deployed slightly to the east of the source of the Hube River ready to launch deceptive moves as planned. Combat Group Charlie was still busy with replenishment and would serve as an additional mobile reserve. A small combat team was dispatched to retrieve the recovery vehicle and armoured ambulance from the battlefield at the Hube where they had been left the previous day.

Combat Group Alpha attacked at approximately 08:30 striking towards the original Objective Bravo. UNITA foot soldiers covering the flanks reported that the area southwest of "Bravo" had been mined by FAPLA. Awareness of mines impeded momentum and drained away time. Meanwhile an enemy concentration, apparently 21 Brigade, was observed to the west of Alpha's attacking line and Müller decided to attack. The combat group found themselves battling through dense forest, which slowed them down tremendously. Momentarily as Alpha was pinned down by patrolling enemy MiGs the enemy made good their escape towards the west. Alpha started moving again as the forward elements of the 21st closed in on the Chambinga crossing. At 16:30 they made contact with the rear guard of the enemy and knocked out two of their tanks. UNITA warned about incoming MiG fighters and Alpha once again dispersed and took cover. Precious moments were lost as 21 Brigade escaped across the Chambinga. The day was drawing to a close as Alpha closed in on the crossing at Chambinga by 17:00. The fortunate 21 Brigade once again succeeded in escaping the fury of the pursuing South African and UNITA forces. The artillery had scored more than thirty enemy trucks killed as they tried to escape across the Chambinga. On 18 November UNITA forces became embroiled in a heavy fight with some FAPLA leftover in the vicinity of the Chambinga-Hube triangle.

Due credit goes to the enemy's 59 Brigade who had done an excellent job at controlling the escaping enemy across the Chambinga choke point. There were numerous acts of bravery reported on the side of the enemy. Many of their soldiers ran the 155 mm fiery gauntlet to recover broken down vehicles and those stranded in the marshes. The bridge crossing site over the river was reinforced with logs. Three fords adjacent to each other bore the brunt of countless artillery onslaughts. The fight of 18 November was over and the South African Combat groupings withdrew to laager positions. UNITA was out there scouting and hunting somewhere in the bush. The South African gunners kept on peppering the enemy.

The enemy had suffered tremendous equipment losses and from 9–18 November they had lost more than 600 of their soldiers killed. Many more were wounded. In comparison the South Africans had lost 17 soldiers killed in action and 41 wounded. The enemy force had been driven across the Chambinga. The original plan for the battle had envisaged more of the enemy slain. We had only been partially successful. What was next on the fighting agenda?

A Short Story about Our Tac HQ – A Few Interesting Moments Shared

What follows is a mini chronicle supplementary to the narrative above.

Our small headquarters had its own minor ordeals in the field, especially within the protective foliage of the Catato Woods. What we did not know was that due to its particular denseness it stood out to aerial observation. It had a derelict Portuguese concrete beacon in the centre ... of which we were also quite oblivious. FAPLA on the other hand knew this area well. From here the advance of 59 and 47 Brigade to Mavinga had commenced on 14 August. The Catato Woods was also an important way point for the MiG fighters. We therefore neglected the infantry lesson that one should not use distinctive cover. On the 13th at approximately 10:00 two MiG-23s bombed precariously close to us without undue effect. We were getting quite used to the enemy's speculative bombing in our vicinity. It remained uncomfortable when clouds of explosives' smoke drifted over. A platoon of UNITA soldiers came along that same day and casually camped alongside our command position. We appreciated the fact that they sported a few Stinger anti-aircraft launchers.

To cut a long story short: Early on 17 November two MiG-21s casually sauntered over in our direction and promptly strafed our well-camouflaged Tac HQ position. The next moment the cannon shots from the diving aircraft pattered lazily among us. We could see the red star on the helmet of one of the Cuban pilots. The cordite cloud from the aircraft's firing settled down indifferently over our position. From the radio intercept we discerned that the two Cuban pilots had a suspicion that something eerie was lurking in the shadows below. They talked about "strata, strata" over the radios – meaning "street" in Spanish. Later we found that close by the clear tracks of the Olifant tanks lay to one side of our Tac HQ position. Live and learn. Impulsively, our UNITA friends fired two Stinger missiles at the two MiGs. Vapours trailed endlessly ... and then exploded uselessly in the sky. The MiGs would be back. The Cuban pilots now knew where we were. We frowned in the direction of our UNITA compatriots.

I was suddenly very interested in inconspicuously making my shallow foxhole deeper using a metal Dixie; extremely embarrassing. This was to the utter enjoyment of Gunners Jean Lausberg and Frans van Eeden – these two had a yawning excavation next to their Ratel-Command. We dragged the somewhat hefty Deon Ferreira from beneath the axle of his own Ratel-Command. Coen van den Berg, our trusted air support officer in blue, casually sauntered out of the bush with a roll of toilet paper and tools entrenching, tying his belt. Apparently he was caught in a compromising position, white bits shining towards heaven like fluorescent "Dayglo" as he took cover in the deep sandy tracks left by a Ratel. These little things usually happened to air force officers when they were on mother earth with the "Brown Jobs". I immediately borrowed his small spade. The very deep foxhole of Lausberg and van Eeden was my benchmark

The same night a battery of 155 mm guns came rolling into position slightly to the east of our HQ position. They did not even know we were there. That night they treated us to a spectacular fireworks display firing 155 mm base-bleed shells relentlessly at Cuito for a fast and furious 30 minutes directly over our heads. Then it was up-sticks for them, and they were gone, like ghosts in the night. Soon after the departure of our staunch artillery friends we started drawing their counter bombardment from the enemy's BM-21s on to our position. Thank you very much, esteemed long gone G-5 battery, truly appreciated. The shrapnel of the BM-21 were screaming through the trees like banshees. This unexpected nerve-racking, ear-splitting din shortly after midnight found Cassie Schoeman suddenly positioned comfortably on top of C.P. du Toit, who was sitting on one of the jump seats of our Ratel-Command. I observed the spectacle from the flank seat. Not one drop of precious whisky was spilled from Schoeman's tin cup. Waste not, want not.

After our twin fiery ordeals at Catato Schoeman became extremely wary. He did not necessarily appreciate my remark, but smiled when I said, "Female intuition". By the 17th he seriously wanted us to depart the home comforts of Catato. Early the next day we folded the camouflage nets and drove away into the rising sun. We were travelling slowly avoiding a dust trail; bushes were packed onto the top of our vehicles. After 30 minutes moving due east, as we looked back, we could see Russian MiGs screaming in to attack the position we had just evacuated. A silent prayer went up, eyes to heaven; thank you, Dear Lord for intuitive Cassie Schoeman. Two UNITA soldiers were killed in the attack behind us. It was another ordinary, but interesting, day in the life of a mobile Tac HQ in the Angolan bush.

On the way towards the Cunzumbia we crossed the erstwhile enemy tracks of 59 and 47 Brigades and Tactical Group 1. A bit of nostalgia there, because 47 Brigade will never leave such tracks again. The tracks were five neat rows as they had moved in close proximity for ground protection and control purposes ... stupid. Where the enemy had halted the close-knit dug-ins could be clearly viewed. No wonder the G-5, Valkiri and Mirage had mauled them. Each temporary halt we came across were decorated with a number of burned metal relics. The trees were browned and blown clean of leaves. Our HQ settled for a few days next to the Cunzumbia for some hard earned respite during the lull in battle. The time was used by the fighting force for some desperate rest, recuperation, replenishment and maintenance. Logistics needed to catch up as well. Our Tac HQ remained there from 19–22 November. The relative safety of the dense bush and high trees was comforting.

Colonel Deon Ferreira returned to Rundu for two days to report on operational progress and to do forward planning with Brigadier Fido Smit regarding the demobilisation of the national service intake and handover to the incoming force to commence with Operation Hooper. Units such as 32 Battalion and elements of 101 Battalion and those of UNITA would be required to continue with the harassing and fixing the enemy during the changeover. At the Tac HQ we did a thorough assessment of the operational situation and indulged in contingency planning. One relaxing morning, as our HQ staff bathed and washed clothes in the crystal clear stream of the Cunzumbia two MiGs came screaming down the river line and we hastily jumped for cover in the reeds. During the night Ferreira returned by helicopter after his quick visit to Rundu. We now had some beer, fresh meat and bread. For one day we lived in extreme luxury.

Decision Time – Time was Fast Running Out for Operation Modular

With the demobilisation deadline of the conscript force approaching by mid-December there was no time left to pursue the enemy to the eastern bank of the Cuito. The situation was exacerbated by the dwindling morale of our national servicemen who were tired of the drawn-out fighting and clearly wanted to return home. Fuel was furthermore in short supply and some of the combat vehicles had to share fuel to make do for a short while as reserves were rushed to the frontline. This left us with an extremely uncomfortable feeling; it was not nice to be caught with your pants down. The consolation was that the enemy would not resume an offensive towards Mavinga and Jamba in the coming year. FAPLA had rather decided to defend Cuito Cuanavale and their logistics base at Tumpo in desperation. They were feverishly reinforcing their depleted numbers and strengthening their strongpoint defence straddling the river. The chance of attacking Cuito Cuanavale from the west had passed us by as it would take an immense effort to dislodge FAPLA from well-grounded defence; if that had ever been considered feasible: We had succeeded in painting ourselves and the enemy into a corner. It was decision time for the higher ups as fresh operational insights and new plans were urgently required. What would be the SADF's strategic decisions?

At the tactical level there was a small window of opportunity left for one final offensive fling at FAPLA on 25–26 November before Modular ended and the SADF forfeited momentum for a while, yet again! The dice to lead the next offensive charge invariably fell on UNITA. They knew the terrain well as they were fighting in their own backyard. Come to think of what was coming next! It was not really the ideal situation for a guerrilla force to get mauled and killed in frontal attack by overwhelming mechanised numbers firmly, I may humbly add. UNITA was going to be left no choice this time around; so we should have expected what came next. The enemy now defended terrain north of the Chambinga which was extremely difficult to attack frontally with mechanised forces in the face of concentrated artillery and air power. There was also no time left for smart manoeuvres to go around the enemy's frontline to, as "Blood and Guts Patton" had so aptly stated, " ... grab the enemy by the nose and kick him in the arse."

By mid-November the SADF generals were confronted with three broad strategic courses of action: One, end Modular and withdraw from southeast Angola; two, attempt to drive FAPLA across the Cuito River, hand over to UNITA and then withdraw the main force to SWA; three, go all out to attack FAPLA and capture Cuito Cuanavale. The last option would have entailed destroying the enemy in southeast Angola by any means. What were the South African generals going to choose? We knew what the tacticians would have chosen. What we did not know was that the enemy had a better ace up their sleeve as Castro had ordered his elite 50th Cuban Division to deploy to southwest Angola from Cuba in what was to be a surprise manoeuvre about which our strategic intelligence knew nothing. Whilst the Cuban generals planned their moves; the South African generals contemplated what do about Cuito Cuanavale.

By 22 November our Tac HQ was deployed in the dense bush halfway between the sources of the Cunzumbia and Cuzuzi rivers under high African hardwoods. It was almost not necessary to use Barracuda nets for camouflage. Through the foliage we could just see the blue Angolan sky where the MiGs of the enemy freely roamed. We were ready to command the final throes of Modular in another attempt to pressurise FAPLA into withdrawal from the Chambinga high grounds. If a few more enemies succumbed in the mauling, so be it. The war now started feeling to me like a creeping barrage, similar to what was probably experienced when the front on the Somme became bogged down during the First World War. What I quietly feared was that if we did not do something soon to wrest initiative and mobility from the tightening noose, we would inevitably be drawn into an attrition trap at Cuito.

It happened again. The senior generals and a few of their staff officers flew in at night to our Tac HQ with General Jannie Geldenhuys in the lead of the procession deplaning from the Puma. During our night-time deliberations the plan of attack for 25–26 November became a fait accompli – attack the Chambinga from east to west, tally-ho! I experienced some apprehension as I was not someone who favoured the frontal attack. It was now time to start discussing the courses of action in outline for the continuation of the campaign. It was clear to me that for the follow-up of the counteroffensive there were wavering consensus by the generals on the state of the enemy's resolve to defend Cuito Cuanavale. Some of them believed that the enemy was close on being smitten and ready to withdraw completely. This assumption probably drove the decision by Geldenhuys to attack Cuito Cuanavale from January until April 1988 along extremely limited eastern approaches. However, the enemy had been driven into a corner from which they could defend well towards the east. They were now on familiar ground of their own choosing and their morale had improved considerably. I mentioned my misgivings to the high-ups and candidly said that it would be unwise to play into the enemy's hands by forfeiting our hard-earned mobility and in fighting them where they were strong across their interlocking trenches and minefields. "Perhaps", it was suggested, "if we fired a few more shots at the enemy they would fold and flee Cuito Cuanavale ... We know how they are ... "

Then the high procession was off again to the far south flying into endless darkness with a twirl of rotor and dust. I said to Deon Ferreira, it does not matter how many plausible operational options we present, it always seems, excuse my language, that the "shittiest" option gets selected. One of the many options we presented was not to become involved in a grinding fight east of Cuito Cuanavale after Modular ended. We had inter alia proposed to withdraw the main force. The idea would then have been to keep the enemy under wraps with a complement of G-5s and Valkiri and a small holding force supporting UNITA.

The next day we received an operational instruction from Army HQ with commensurate guidelines on what had been decided the previous night – exquisite staff work – acknowledge receipt. I felt that we were being press-ganged into a situation which was not going to bear any fruit of substance. The final offensive throe of Modular was another major effort to pressurise the foe into submission. This however was wishful thinking. Our dear friend,

Fidel Castro, the esteemed President of Cuba, still wanted to revenge the slamming defeat at the Lomba. Ego and esteem was still heavily in play on both sides of the fence.

25-26 November 1987 – Charge of the Light Brigade

Our next mission stated that the enemy had to be bludgeoned into particles and driven back across the Cuito River. If this did not succeed, then at least the high ground of Chambinga should be denied our esteemed enemy, it was ordered. To my mind, the last part of the mission was the more feasible when appreciating own combat means available. In the meantime, as the fresh offensive moves commenced, the see-saw air and artillery war continued. It was not fun to be resident in Cuito Cuanavale as the 155 mm shells progressively ate away at the enemy's numbers.

25 Brigade was the most easterly defensive echelon and defended the Chambinga crossing. Slightly to the southwest lay the remnants of 16 Brigade and Tactical Group 2 deeply entrenched at the confluence of the Chambinga and Cuito Rivers. Further to the north 21 Brigade defended Tumpo and straddled the approach leading to the bridge at Cuito Cuanavale. 59 Brigade defended halfway between the Cuatir and Dala rivers across northern approaches leading to Tumpo and Cuito Cuanavale. The forward command post of FAPLA was back in Cuito Cuanavale while 13 Brigade and 24 Air Defence Brigade had the honour of guarding the town. The river constituted a formidable natural obstacle. Any casual observer could see sand flying everywhere as enemy soldiers enthusiastically dug deeper and sowed layers of minefields around their defences. Meanwhile, the SADF was struggling to get their replenishment sorted, while preparing for the next round of fighting.

The combined SADF/UNITA plan for 25 November basically entailed a frontal attack from the east over extremely difficult terrain led by the 3rd and 5th Regular Battalions of UNITA. The attacking South African artillery, Mirages and Buccaneers were to be in the thick of things, as usual. Combat Groups Bravo and Charlie were tasked to fight on the northern flank of UNITA in a supporting role. To the north of UNITA was Bravo and to their north was Charlie. On completion of the main attack the two South African combat groups would exploit the target area. Charlie would then move further northwestwards to block any counter-attack which could materialise from Tumpo. If opportunities were presented the two combat groups were to be ready to exploit success. On completion of the operation they would follow the command to safely withdraw into hides already selected towards the west. Combat Group Alpha was deployed on the Chambinga high ground slightly to the north of the main attacking formation, ready to protect its flank and to eventually cover its withdrawal.

The attack started shoddily when UNITA failed to join up in time and H-Hour, which had been selected for 06:30, was further postponed due to the slow mechanised movement caused by difficult terrain. Very soon the attacking force started running into its own creeping artillery barrage due to poor visibility on the ground. Contact with the enemy occurred sporadically and 25 Brigade continuously whimpered for air support. Bravo unexpectedly ran into an enemy minefield and was subsequently delayed in advancing further as planned. The enemy's MiGs furthermore confused the advance to contact by speculative bombings all over. As UNITA made contact with 25 Brigade the defenders simply withdrew to stronger alternative defensive positions further westward. At about 15:00 Bravo drew accurate 82 mm mortar fire as they struggled through the entangled foliage. Commandant Robbie Hartslief decided to withdraw his force to safety and discontinue the attack as dusk was settling. The G-5s continued shelling the enemy satisfactorily and a substantial number of their vehicles were set ablaze. By sunset the 5th Regular Battalion of UNITA had suffered dearly and their commander had been wounded. Compounding the problems on the ground in coordinating the battle was poor intelligence received throughout. The fighting's results at the end of the day came as a huge disappointment to us.

On 26 November the battle continued. It was up to Marais's Combat Group Charlie and UNITAs 4th Regular Battalion to bear the brunt of the next fight. Early morning found the enemy MiGs rampant in the skies searching and bombing targets of opportunity. Sporadic small arms fire was encountered all over. One recovery vehicle of Charlie trampled a mine and subsequently drew enemy mortar fire. At about 16:00 Charlie drove into yet another abandoned FAPLA defensive position, only finding some abandoned equipment. It was a game of hide-and-seek and the enemy was not doing so poorly. Own attacking forces were now running into the enemy's registered artillery fire tasks from its D-30 and M-46 guns as well as their BM-21s deployed within the safety of the Cuito Cuanavale defensive enclave. It was utterly frustrating as up to now no substantial defensive position of the enemy had been encountered. A close air support mission of the Mirages was closely followed by an attack by the MiGs onto the same enemy position. The heavy concentrated artillery onslaught of FAPLA was too much for the UNITA guerrillas to bear and the assault petered out – understandably so. The guerrillas were used to surviving, to live and fight again another day, under conditions that suited them better. The South African and UNITA combat groupings were withdrawn to safety to occupy hides further to the west. The South African artillery continued its shelling of the enemy. There was not much more left to do. 26 November for Task Force 10 was another huge disappointment.

To be fair about the attacks of 25 and 26 November – some additional pressure was exerted on the foe and some more of their mortal remains ended up in the soil. By 27 November the game was over. By 28 November one of the Russian advisors reported: "All night and the morning, there was an exhausting, protracted silence – not a shot to be heard, no sounds of engines – nothing. And we couldn't fall asleep because of it."[18] The enemy had decided to withdraw their defences further to the west, towards Tumpo. This left the Chambinga high ground free to be exploited by the SADF later in January for their attacks into the Tumpo cauldron.

In observing the spectacle of the final throes of Operation Modular at Chambinga I thought about something I had read somewhere ... Ah! The poem by Alfred Tennyson on the charge of the Light Brigade at Balaclava on 25 October 1854 during the Crimean War (Anglo-French Turkish campaign). The purpose was to capture the port and fortress of Cuito Cuanavale, excuse me, Sevastopol. In the instance of the Light Brigade their fateful charge was the result of a miscommunication in such a way that the brigade attempted a much more difficult objective than intended by the overall commander, Lord Raglan. Blame for the miscommunication has remained controversial, as the original order itself was vague. The charge produced no decisive gains and resulted in very high casualties and is best remembered as the subject of this poem. The lines of the poem emphasise the valour of the cavalry in carrying out their orders, even "though" the soldier knew that someone had blundered: "Half a league, half a league, half a league onward, all in the valley of death rode the six hundred. Forward the Light Brigade! Charge for the guns!" he said. "Into the valley

18 Shubin, Gennady and Tokarev Andrei: *Bush War – The Road to Cuito Cuanavale.* Jacana Media (Pty) Ltd, South Africa, Sunnyside, 2011, p. 80.

of Death rode the six hundred."

FAPLA was now well entrenched on the high ground straddling the restricted eastern approaches towards Cuito Cuanavale. What will follow next? Will it be a charge by the light brigade or something else? Decision pending by South Africa and UNITA – not that UNITA had much of a say, even if it was their war. Would maintenance of mobility and initiative be reconsidered; or will our precious forces, together with UNITA, be thrown into the cauldron – onto a slow-burning African cooking fire; from the cooking pot into the fire? Or was the fight done for now?

My close friend, Colonel Paul Fouché was already on his way to Rundu to take over command from Ferreira. Operation Hooper was firing up. Fouché and I had served together at the Army Battle School. He was a veteran from 61 Mech and had participated in Operation Sceptic in 1980. By then he was the commander of 82 Mechanised Brigade in Potchefstroom, a seasoned and fiery operational commander – the right man for the job. The problem lay with the job. Charismatic Commandant Cassie Schoeman was soon to replace Marais in the field as the commanding officer of 4 SAI. He was a deeply religious officer and cared for his people in a special way and was one of the SADF's gifted leaders. Ferreira would take up his position as the senior staff officer operations at the HQ of SWATF and I would become the officer commanding of the Army College in Pretoria.

Winding Up in December 1987 – Sorry to Say

From 30 November onwards the weary national service soldiers of the fighting Task Force 10 demobilised for Christmas. Their precarious retrograde operation towards Mavinga and then Rundu had to be completed by 15 December. The national service troops needed to clear out at their respective units in South Africa and rejoin civilian life.

This whole laborious demobilisation process allowed our beloved enemy valuable time for respite. They gathered their senses, cried over spilt diesel, petrol and gunpowder and licked their wounds. They were reorganising and reinforcing furiously, laying mines feverishly and digging in profusely. Come January 1988 the FAPLA soldiers were glaring over their earthy parapets in an easterly direction, their fields of fire carefully laid out by their Cuban henchmen, whips in hand. The enemy had decided to make a stand.

On 5 December we moved our Tac HQ back to Mavinga. We parked the vehicles at the formation administration area and performed the required maintenance. There the command vehicles remained under watchful eyes until it was received by Colonel Paul Fouché and the incoming command and staff team later in December.

On 8 December the South African Mirages mauled the 8th Brigade of the enemy on the road between the Longa River and Cuito Cuanavale while ferrying logistics. This was the hard-earned proceeds of South African Special Forces and part and parcel of an endeavour to continuously strike deep at the enemy. Our loud cheers could be heard in Rundu as we handed over to the command team of Colonel Paul Fouché.

The South African generals now decided to attack FAPLA's strongpoint defence located east of the strategic town of Cuito Cuanavale. The attrition battle had begun. The first attack of Operation Hooper was to be launched at 21 Brigade between the Dala and Cuatir rivers east of Cuito Cuanavale on 13 January 1988. Six more indecisive attacks would follow until the SADF withdrew from southeast Angola by the end of August.

During December 1987 until March 1988 a raiding force of 32 Battalion under Commandants Jan Hougaardt and Robbie Hartslief was inserted deep behind enemy lines. Their mission entailed harassing the enemy's logistic line between Menongue and Cuito Cuanavale. This was second best to the aborted attack from the west we had seriously contemplated in mid-October 1987. Some of the missions of the raiding force entailed moving right up to Menongue and harassing the enemy positions, especially the airfield, with indirect fire.

I hitched a lift home in the front cab of a Hercules C-130 from Rundu to Waterkloof with my friend Frans van Eeden. The airframe was filled with dirty, stinking, smiling national servicemen. I felt deep affection for them. What were the stories they were going to tell at home? There was no space in the back for the "permanent force". We flew without safety belts – no sweat. We had gotten used to it. Our families were waiting for us. What would a meal in a restaurant be like?

Modular was concluded by 15 December 1987. The enemy had put assailing Mavinga and Jamba out of their minds. In the meantime the 155 mm G-5 shells continued to rain down relentlessly on Cuito Cuanavale.

Reflective Thinking and ... Gratefulness ... Without Any Regrets

So many individuals, so many truths, with each story having more than three sides. Even the myths spread by Fidel Castro about FAPLA winning the battle of Cuito Cuanavale, bless his leathered hide. We knew well that everything did not always go our way in the successive battles fought for southeast Angola. However, the mere fact remains that we were never defeated tactically. As such I found the reflective thinking and the telling of this warfaring chronicle most enlightening, liberating, satisfying and rewarding in discharging my responsibility – without any regrets.

To my mind the South African commanders in the field had done their job extremely well in balancing two consistent pressing responsibilities – the one battling to outweigh the other and the scale was mostly tipped at a precarious angle under dire operational circumstances. At the one end of the gauge the responsibility to win tactically at all costs tipped the scales, because there was no alternative. On the other end hinged the responsibility not to incur undue casualties and to bring our troops safely home. This they had done.

My final strategic question is a critical one, albeit politically and military-strategically loaded. Why, oh, why did we ever allow ourselves to get bogged down in the enemy's killing ground and minefields east of Cuito Cuanavale in early 1988? This came at the price of forfeiting the mobility on which the success of our battles in southeast Angola depended. Let us not answer yet ... At Cuito Cuanavale FAPLA and the Cubans held the line ... The withdrawal by the SADF from that front in Angola by August 1988 afforded the opportunity to Fidel Castro to proclaim his so-called (mythical) victory through sheer propaganda – something at which the South African government was never any good. However "we" and "they" knew what actually happened on the ground. The enemy had never taken Mavinga or Jamba! Of course, some of the SADF's strategic and operation level thinking and planning could have been somewhat imperfect, who knows? And, of course, we were somewhat disillusioned by all the enemy reinforcements pouring into Cuito Cuanavale from November 1987 onwards; and by the 50th Cuban Division surprise appearance on our doorstep in southwest Angola in May 1988.[19] Could this be due to some

19 See Chapter 16.

apparent deficiencies in strategizing and strategic intelligence or what?

I hold fond memories of our troops and their courageous fight for ... whatever ... For time to pass and political and military circumstances to change for the better? They had achieved their mission every time and I was proud of them. In this sense I recall the words of Mao Tse-tung who believed that " ... the object of war is specifically to preserve oneself and destroy the enemy ... to destroy the enemy means to disarm him or deprive him of his power to resist, and does not mean to destroy every member of his forces physically". Never was so much done, by so few, in such little time, under such trying and dangerous circumstances. It was an honour for me to have been able to serve with our gallant commanders and their young troops in the field. By divine grace many live today to tell their story; also in poignant recognition and memory of the 31 men who did not make it out alive. I also salute FAPLA and the Cubans who had suffered so much more of the wrath of that particular war between the Lomba and the Cuito River. So be it if a few of them came out unscathed during the "Chambinga Gallop."

Yesterday, today and tomorrow I can only feel and express gratefulness. Our combined best proved good enough.

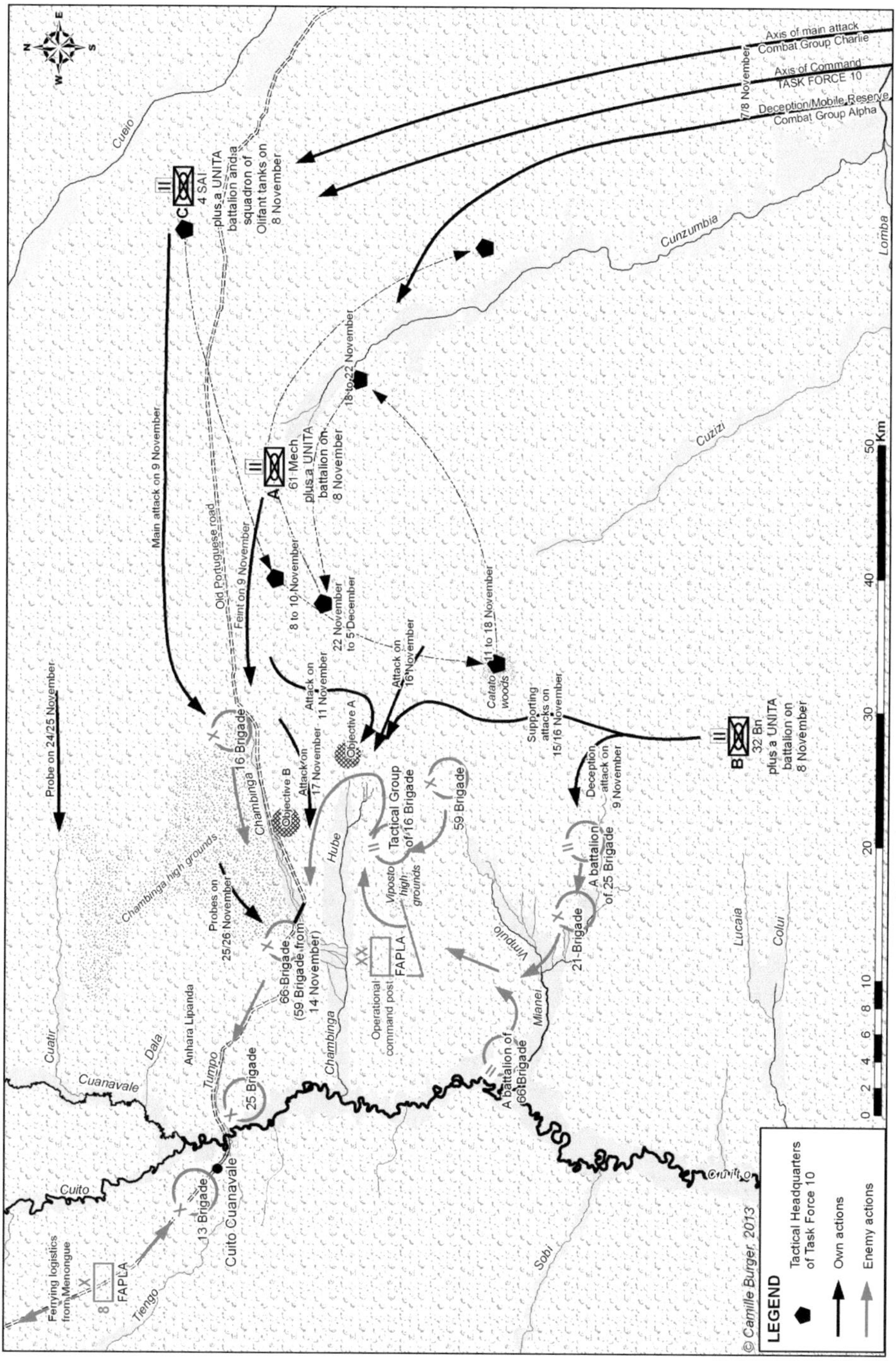

Map 16: Opration Modular – The Final Phase

16

The War that Never Was

Operation Prone

He restored matters by delay.
Quintus Fabius Maximus Verrucosus called Cunctator

An Attack without Warning – Surprise, Surprise

A surprise occurs unexpectedly and enshrouds one with a sudden feeling of astonishment. It often makes the blood run cold when it relates to war! In such an instance it leaves a coppery taste in the mouth. This was what happened to the South African government and the South African Defence Force (SADF) in May 1988. Hello, where did the elite 50th Cuban Division of Fidel Castro from Cuba so suddenly come from with their awe-inspiring mechanised force and modern air power? Surprise, surprise! This newest edition to FAPLA's overwhelming conventional army was already at Cahama with their tanks and their MiGs marching offensively towards Calueque just across the border when the SADF was shaken awake. Castro openly boasted that he was going to give the South Africans a 'bloody nose' and a military beating second to none.

Let us see what actually happened.

I gave Fidel Castro, the dictator of Cuba, credit for his military strategy. It was the ultimate turning manoeuvre, causing the SADF to rush its immediately available conventional fighting units such as 32 Battalion, 61 Mechanised Battalion Group (61 Mech) and 4 South African Infantry Battalion (4 SAI) helter-skelter to contain the newest conventional threat from southwest Angola. The men of all these South African units were bone tired and their equipment the worse for the wear as they had only recently returned from Operation Packer in southeast Angola by 30 April 1988. 32 Battalion and 61 Mech would soon cross swords with the vanguard of the 50th Cuban Division just across the border north of Ruacana near Techipa.

These fiery causes had the makings of an all-out conventional war in Southern Africa. Fortunately, the politicians from all sides involved in the conflict came to their senses and ended the war through peace negotiations by 22 December 1988. The precarious political-military conflict festering in southern Angola and northern Southwest Africa at the time was described as follows by the Maldon Institute, Washington, DC, on 1 July 1988: "The dramatic transformation of the military status quo in Southern Angola and Namibia during May and June has the potential of setting the stage for a regional war in Southern Africa."

The menacing military threat and ensuing military clashes on the northwestern border of SWA was veiled in smouldering politics from all sides and was teetering on a knife's edge. This issue came under the intense scrutiny of the United States of America and the Soviet Union, who collectively pushed hard for peace creation in southern Africa and for the independence of SWA (Namibia) through the implementation of United Nations Security Council Resolution 435. By then "Glasnost" and "Perestroika" had been introduced by Mikhail Gorbachev in the Soviet Union. His policies called for increased openness and transparency in government institutions and activities in the Soviet Union and its restructuring. As such Gorbachev's political reforms contributed to the government of South Africa's acceptance to end the war in SWA and at the same time to embark on major political change in our country and to end apartheid. Of course there were many other reasons for South Africa seeing the light in becoming a fully democratic state – reasons I do not wish to dwell on. Nonetheless, let us make no mistake that one of the triggers for peacemaking in southern Africa stemmed from the fierce conventional battles fought in southern Angola from August 1987 until August 1988.

In between the shooting and the peacemaking I have an interesting war story to tell about a military campaign that was referred to by the SADF as Operation Prone. In the event the SADF was prepared swiftly to go to war if push came to shove. However, in the end a final pitch battle was avoided by means of tactics of harassment, deception and delay. Prone was initially codenamed Hilti and lasted from 30 May until 22 December 1988. It was the final conventional warring phase of the South African Border War between the SADF vis-à-vis the combined might of the Angolan and Cuban army in southern Angola, supported by the South West Africa People's Organisation (SWAPO). In this context it formed an important part in the military history of southern Africa. Incidentally, UNITA did not participate in this last dramatic episode of the war in the west.

Prone was interesting in the sense that it included mobile defence as a key ingredient to its overall battle design. This was a form of warfare rarely undertaken by the SADF during the Border War, as they were more accustomed to counterinsurgency warfare and by taking the offensive to the enemy through pre-emptive border strikes such as Operation Protea in August 1981. As such Operation Prone was complex. It was characterised by large-scale military mobilisations and manoeuvres, enhanced force levels and elaborate command-and-control arrangements from all sides. Warfare schemes contained a fair mix of revolutionary and conventional war-fighting methods all rolled into one.

On the side of the SADF the campaign involved the army, air force, navy, medical services and Special Forces. It all came about in the Western Sub-theatre of War straddling southwestern Angola's 5th Military Region and Sector 10 in Ovamboland. What was further interesting to us as mere soldiers on the ground was how quickly the conflict turned from a serious shooting match on 26 and 27 June 1988 near Techipa to a negotiated ceasefire by 5 August in Geneva, to the signing of a ceasefire agreement at Calueque on 22 August, to a peace settlement in New York by 22 December. More so, how the highest political collusions and international mediation so rapidly and directly influenced what was happening with the tactics on the ground. Literally, in the blink of an eye, serious fighting was transformed into solemn peace-making. The rapid changing of opposing minds of the political "gifted" could therefore be viewed in wonderment.

What converted those strangely aloof so abruptly? It is amazing that the changing of minds through ages of war and politics never cost much; other things did. The already menacing situation was augmented by one command from Castro to move a massive mechanised division and air armada to Angola in complete secrecy and surprise. It took one signal from Chief of the Army on 30 May 1988 to swiftly release a vast number of forces for the war. With the rattling of sabres Calueque on the border between SWA and Angola became the focal point of politics and war. Ironically, this was where the war would also end. It emerged from a fiery cauldron – the final battle between South African and

Cuban mechanised forces took place on 26–27 June 1988 halfway between Techipa and Calueque in southwest Angola. From this final quarrel a strategically important military standoff transpired after the dust and the cordite had settled.

One small South African combat unit of less than brigade strength stopped the Cubans dead in their tank tracks north of the SWA-Angolan border near Techipa. This outstanding work was done by 61 Mech reinforced by combat elements from 32 Battalion and 101 Battalion under command of Commandant Mike Müller. It was heartrending to observe that it was these few first-line fighting units enduring the sharpest edge of combat imaginable once again. I felt extremely proud of them – a deep emotion not easily explained to others. I had seen these units in action during Operation Modular and had commanded 61 Mech during a number of operations in 1981–1982. During Protea I had also crossed with 61 Mech into Angola at Calueque in August 1981, where Müller had entered and exited on 26–27 June 1988 to fight off the advance guard of the 50th Cuban Division. What could have materialised from this final epic military clash was a grand war. What prevailed in the end was peace. This is my story about the war that fortunately never came to be!

Castro's Plan for Southern Africa – Grand Strategy

November 1987 heralded a turning point in the conventional war fought in southern Angola. A second war front was about to be opened by the Cubans in the 5th Military Region in the southwest they referred to as their Southern Front. By then Cuba was actively preparing for the major escalation of the conventional war in southern Angola under the direct leadership of President Fidel Castro. Both the USSR and Cuba at the time saw the struggle for the region as a major strategic concern that went beyond the defeat of UNITA. By 1987–88 Castro was fully committed to the demise of South Africa and the ending of apartheid in support of Angola, SWA/Namibia, the Frontline States and the other African revolutionary movements, such as the African National Congress (ANC), involved with their respective "liberation struggles." In this sense, the SADF's intervention in southern Angola was interpreted by the Soviets and the Cubans as South Africa's determination not to give up SWA willy-nilly, nor to allow the collapse of UNITA. It was furthermore viewed as a measure to prevent Cuban forces from deploying near the SWA-Angolan border.

Cuba therefore considered the fighting near Cuito Cuanavale as extremely important for the liberation of southern Africa. The USSR and Cuba decided to turn the military defeat they had suffered between the Lomba and Chambinga rivers into a political victory. *Bastion*, the official publication of the Cuban Ministry of Defence, emphasised in April 1988 that:

> The Cuito Cuanavale fighting was a turning point in the ongoing struggle for the liberation of Southern Africa. The new military situation means that the racist troops will not be able to act with impunity in Southern Angola as they had been doing in recent years with an absolute disregard for international law. At the same time, the situation confirms that the Cuban soldiers, together with their African brothers, will fulfil the internationalist mission entrusted to them by the party and the revolution to the end.

Their main enemy now was the SADF and not UNITA. The second strategic thrust of Castro therefore aimed at southwest Angola and was intended to recapture FAPLA and SWAPO infrastructure from the SADF and to revive the terrorist campaign against Namibia and South Africa. This ideal initiated the build-up of a Cuban-Angolan task force for a large-scale military campaign to be launched in May under the direct orders of Fidel Castro. Incidentally, the withdrawal of the South African forces from the southeastern front by 29 August was considered a major milestone for the liberation struggle as a whole. The mere fact that the SADF did not attempt to capture Cuito Cuanavale was considered by the Cubans as a victory.

Official sources would soon claim that Cuba had seized the initiative in southern Africa and that they were moving to consolidate their strategic ideals under protection of diplomatic dynamics and international negotiations. It was further proclaimed that Cuba operated in close coordination with the USSR and that they were collectively pursuing the objectives of the Soviet grand strategy for southern Africa. Castro was clearly in charge of the political and military moves in southern Angola and not the USSR. In this way Cuba and its African allies were ready to consolidate their gains on the "Namibian" border before the southern winter set in (mid-June–August) as this his could impede the major conventional fighting because of the rains. They were determined to escalate the fighting in the southern spring (September–October) should the need arise. Havana left no doubt that Fidel Castro had the initiative and that he was in full command of the acceleration of the war. Castro subsequently re-emphasised "Cuba's solidarity with the Namibian cause, Angolan territorial integrity and peace in the Atlantic strip of the African Southern Cone". He equally reiterated Cuba's commitment to the revolutionary causes of SWAPO and the ANC, namely the destruction of South Africa and the demise of apartheid.

In pursuit of Soviet-Cuban strategic objectives in southern Africa, Cuba continued to take unilateral steps without consultation or even notification thereof to Angola's president Jose Eduardo Dos Santos. In mid-May, MPLA sources in Lisbon complained that "the recent Cuban reinforcements in Angola were carried out without the knowledge of the ruling MPLA government in Luanda". They described Dos Santos as being 'upset' over the manner in which Cuba reinforced its troops in Angola and the degree of independence with which Cuba operated in his country. A situation had been reached where the Cubans were prepared to pursue the South African forces into SWA in support of SWAPO and in order to block South African support for UNITA; even to hinder any other form of SADF intervention in Angola. The SADF's heydays of gallivanting freely in the Area-In-Dispute since Operation Protea in August-September 1981 abruptly came to an end!

With its restrictive world view, inadequate resources and limited international support at the time did South Africa have a similar grand strategy to pursue its political and military objectives in southern Africa, to mobilise external support and to counter the wills and woes of Castro – or was what followed based on crises and luck management by the minute? Who had the initiative from the opposing sides and from where to when, to control the crises reaching its cusp in southern Africa?

The Build-Up towards All-Out War – Political and Military Methods or Madness and Chance

To counter the threat of the Cubans from southwest Angola the SADF was about to launch Operation Hilti/Prone by 30 May 1988. Before that they just did not know it yet. This campaign was the dramatic sequel to Operations Modular, Hooper and Packer which took place in southeast Angola from July 1987 until August 1988. During the latter three operations the SADF gave military support to the UNITA resistance movement in order to check the FAPLA advance on Mavinga and Jamba. By the end of November the combined Angolan-Cuban conventional army deployed east of the Cuito River had been defeated tactical blow after tactical blow by a diminutive South African and UNITA coalition force. The defeated enemy was driven back to Cuito Cuanavale where they decided to make a stand and were soon heavily reinforced, deeply entrenched and adequately protected by interlocking rows of minefields from both sides of the river. The strategic and political dominoes were set to tumble swiftly as politics continued to erupt from the barrels of many guns from opposing sides!

The build-up to what could become an all-out war in the region and the chronological account about Operation Prone follows below. The cross-impact of important political, diplomatic and military occurrences locally and in other parts of the world relevant to this conflict is indicated throughout the script as dated summarised inputs. It is interesting to see how swiftly these either started developing or unravelling with Calueque being the focal point. It therefore provided interesting perspectives to what was actually happening on the ground in the combat zone. What were some of these interesting views to be observed and important questions to be asked by any objective analyst about the war in southern Angola and its subsequent outcomes? One such query was whether South Africa had the required strategic intelligence to be forewarned about the evolving political and military threat – the one, that is, which came with a surprise? Or for that matter, to have prior knowledge and insight to foresee, predict and influence unfolding political and military strategic events by means of viable stratagem? To thy own self speak the truth! As ordinary soldiers on the ground we sometimes wondered about the nebulous world of higher politics and diplomacy, the elevated realm of the military and about their grand strategies. Did things happen more or less by chance, or was there method in political and military madness? I still speculate about this. Time and again it will become clear that the South African soldier on the ground saved the day for our politicians. Terrain in itself, as one of the neutral factors in war, exerted a major influence on how this final military campaign was conducted by the South Africans. I therefore advise a quick review on Chapter 5 relating to what I refer to as the "western and central manoeuvring sectors" and the "Western Front".

As could be expected, the defeat of the combined Angolan-Cuban force east of the Cuito River and the considerable loss of prestige came as a massive blow to Castro. This was not going to happen again, according to Castro's calculation and he decided to restore the military balance of power in southern Angola in no uncertain way. Interestingly enough, on 25 November the United Nations (UN) Security Council demanded the SADF's unconditional withdrawal from Angola by 10 December, a demand which was ignored of course. Through to December the situation for the besieged Angolans at Cuito Cuanavale became critical as the SADF prepared to tighten its noose. The 155 mm G-5 shells rained down on Cuito Cuanavale day and night. By 12 December Operation Modular ended followed by Hooper with a fresh contingent of national servicemen. Hooper focused on the continued destruction of the Angolan and Cuban forces still deployed east of the Cuito River.

Fidel Castro decided that the line against the South Africans and UNITA had to be held at all cost. For this reason Cuba feverishly rushed large contingents of military reinforcements and additional modern military hardware to the war front at Cuito

Cuanavale and southwest Angola. More than 15,000 fresh Cuban combatants and some of their best fighter pilots soon reached the shores of Angola. By now the Cuban troop strength in Angola had increased to about 55,000 men with 40,000 deployed in southern Angola alone. Castro furthermore decided to deploy his elite 50th Cuban Division to southwest Angola and in this way catch the South Africans unawares. The deadline for his surprise manoeuvre as far south as the SWA-Angolan border near Calueque was set for May 1988. He later on explained his massive reinforcement effort for southern Angola in his book entitled *My Life* as follows:

> In a titanic effort, despite the grave danger of military aggression that we ourselves faced here in Cuba with the proximity of the United States, the military and political leaders of the Revolution decided to solve the problem once and for all – which we had proposed more than once to the Soviets; pull together the troops and material needed for handling a definitive defeat to the South African forces. A flood of units and combat equipment was quickly sent across the Atlantic and disembarked on the southern coast of Angola, in order to attack the enemy from the southwestern part of Angola, towards Namibia. Meanwhile 800 kilometres to the east, a complete brigade of tanks, after sweeping the road for almost 100 kilometres for mines, was advancing towards Cuito Cuanavale, where the Angolan troops in retreat under the South African attack was reassembling ... Our combatants and their brilliant commanders prepared a mortal trap for the powerful South African forces advancing on the airport – a trap into which the racist army fell and was overpowered. So there was a great deal at stake, much more than some people could imagine. That time, 55,000 Cubans had been sent to Angola, and mobilized. That way, while the South African troops were being bled slowly dry in Cuito Cuanavale, down in the southwest 40,000 Cuban soldiers, 30,000 Angolan troops and some 3,000 Namibian guerrilla fighters from SWAPO, backed by 600 tanks, hundreds of artillery pieces, 1,000 anti-aircraft weapons and the daring MiG-23 air units that took over the skies, advanced towards the Namibian border, ready literally to sweep away the South African forces that were quartered in that main direction – sweep them away, but by means of many hard, unexpected hits, without any big battles; that was our principle.

There were a few blatant lies embedded in Castro's strong wording quoted above as could be expected from the master propagandist. No way had the South Africans been entrapped by the Cubans at Cuito Cuanavale. In reality Cuito Cuanavale had become FAPLA's slaughterhouse. At the end of April 1988 the South African main force leisurely left of their own accord. It was the Cubans and FAPLA soldiers who remained trapped in the ground that was to their undoing. The river, their minefields, a few South Africans, UNITA and the formidable G-5s were their downfall. No counter-attack in the southeast came forth from the languid foe. Mavinga and Jamba, as erstwhile important military objectives to be captured from UNITA, were conveniently set aside, even forgotten.

Meanwhile on the home front: Early in January, as the commanding officer of the Army College, I was approached by General Jannie Geldenhuys to support him with the design of a war game for his high command and some of the politicians so as to determine the future conduct and directions of the war in southern Angola. For this reason I was invited to attend one of his conferences held at the Military Intelligence School in Waterkloof as a silent observer to get a feel for the situation. During their deliberations it became clear to me that there were conflicting views about the way forward. Geldenhuys subsequently told me that his high-level assembly were not ready for such a strategic planning event yet and that we should postpone it for the time being. To my knowledge the war game that he had envisioned never happened.

I used my position as commander of the Army College to send some of my directing staff to participate in Operations Hooper and Packer as staff officers in the brigade HQ of Colonel Paul Fouché, and for the time that he served, Colonel Pat McLoughlin. These were officers of calibre such as Commandants Craig Harrison, Andrew Hudson and Mike Nel. The days were past that officers and non-commissioned officers would say that we only preached theory at the army college. In my many lectures at the college on mobile warfare I used Cuito Cuanavale as a case study on how easy one could become embroiled in a war of attrition. I subsequently received a subtle warning from a brigadier at army HQ to refrain from saying that ...

From 13 January until 23 March the South Africans launched seven major ground assaults on the entrenched FAPLA positions east of Cuito Cuanavale as the midpoint of the conventional war until then. Operation Hooper was followed by Packer in March which included the next changeover of fighting men. This time units from the citizen force were given a chance. None of these attacks delivered tangible results apart from the progressive destruction and demoralising of the enemy. Unknown to the South Africans a large Cuban-FAPLA relief column was on its way from Menongue to Cuito Cuanavale. Progress of the column and subsequent logistic provisioning in the rainy season was slow and cumbersome. This was due to the clearing of UNITA mines and fending against possible ambushes along the route. The enemy relief column did not reach Cuito Cuanavale in time to take part in the first engagement on 13 January. During the same period South African Special Forces and a raiding force of 32 Battalion supported by the SAAF struck relentlessly at targets of opportunity along the main supply route of FAPLA 192 km from Menongue to Cuito Cuanavale.

In the meantime the counterinsurgency war fought against SWAPO in northern SWA continued as intense as before. The focal point hinged on Ovamboland, the northwestern operational theatre of SWA. This was the designate area of operations of Sector 10 under command of Brigadier Chris Serfontein who commanded from Oshakati. Angola's 5th Military Region was situated across Sector 10 in southern Angola from where the fresh conventional threat was about to erupt.

By March South Africa's Foreign Minister Pik Botha and the Assistant US Secretary of State for African Affairs, Chester Crocker, reached an agreement on SWA/Namibian independence at a meeting held in Geneva. These high-level talks encapsulated the implementation of UN Resolution 435/78. Political dialogue and peace talks between South Africa, Angola and Cuba were ongoing at the time. The peacemaking process was initially loosely structured. Apparent misgiving and open animosity continued to exist amongst the respective negotiators. These peacemaking processes were continuously mediated and facilitated by key political representatives from the USA and USSR.

On 10 March Fidel Castro commanded his elite 50th Cuban Division to deploy from Cuba to southern Angola, a move to which the high command of the SADF was still oblivious. Because of these rapid developments and the crises Castro specifically faced at Cuito Cuanavale, the most influential Cuban generals now started taking command.

They were all veterans of the 1975–76 Cuban campaign in Angola, namely: Major General Arnaldo Ochoa Sanchez, Major General Leopoldo Cintra Frias, Brigadier General Patricio De Laguardia Font and Brigadier General Francisco Boraso. Sanchez was also a veteran of the 1977–78 tank battles in the Ogaden Desert of Ethiopia.

In order to facilitate the anticipated strategic escalation a new military high command was established by the Cubans under the command of Sanchez to accommodate the "Southern Front". He was now in overall command of the combined Angolan-Cuban army in southern Angola. His central strategic headquarters was located at Cuito Cuanavale. Two forward strategic headquarters (command posts) were established in Lubango and Xangongo. Brigadier General Patricio De Laguardia Font was appointed the commander of the new offensive formation (50th Cuban Division) and General Cintras Frias was made commander at Cuito Cuanavale. The Angolan commanders were summarily pushed to the rear of the command procession as the Cubans forcefully took over control. Castro commanded the military situation in southern Angola from his operation room in Havana.

All the Cuban generals were not overly content with Castro's commanding stance from his armchair position in Cuba. This caused some serious internal friction and even an attempt at desertion by one of his generals. Military matters therefore became awry within the inner circle of Cuba's high command, which came as a lucky break for South Africa as time and divine intervention were desperately required to grasp some initiative a propos the escalating war situation. Discord apparently reigned between Castro and Sanchez and with some of his other commanding generals deployed in southern Angola. On 27 March General Francisco Cruz Borsao was killed under suspicious circumstances in Angola. Approximately 26 Cuban officers formed part of a planned defection with General Borsao. The aircraft of the Cuban escapees were allegedly shot down by a MiG-23 as they flew southward to SWA from Huambo in Angola. The defectors, it was believed, wanted to follow in the footsteps of Cuban Brigadier General Rafael del Pino Diaz who had defected to the USA on 28 May 1987. Del Pino by now was safely in the hands of the CIA in America. He had notified South Africa through the American intelligence channels that he did not believe that Cuba could launch a deliberate attack on SWA/Namibia. His assertion was that Cuba lacked the required training, organisational ability, communication means and logistics.

Furthermore, by April there were clear indications all round that the USSR was experiencing political turmoil as "Perestroika" and "Glasnost" dawned as a reality. It became more and more apparent that the Russians no longer were able to sustain their current level of political and military support for Angola and other similar surrogate forces in Africa. These assumptions about the political changes in the USSR however still needed to be authenticated by the respective international intelligence communities who were monitoring the political developments. The final collapse of the USSR to follow in 1989–1991 was not yet foreseen by the international community. At the same time it became glaringly evident that both Cuba and South Africa were taking serious strain from the cost of war in Angola and its mounting casualties. By April Mr. P.W. Botha, the State President of South Africa, pronounced his intention to withdraw all South African forces from Angola.

During the same period it became clear to the SADF that something out of the ordinary was afoot in the 5th Military Region. To their surprise a light combat force of 101 Battalion involved in counterinsurgency operations against SWAPO in the vicinity of Xangongo came under attack by a Cuban combat force. It was therefore fortunate that by 29 April it became evident to South Africa that no further tactical advantage could be gained by continued engagement on the Cuito Cuanavale front. The main South African combat force withdrew to SWA and was therefore available for other unforeseen crisis situations which could develop. A diminutive South African holding force of approximately 1,000 combatants remained behind to support UNITA in keeping the besieged FAPLA-Cuban force firmly locked in their defensive position. This part of the campaign was referred to as Operation Displace.

By May the pressure was mounting on Fidel Castro to get his military job in southern Angola done as swiftly as possible to save his reputation. He knew well that he would soon have to end his "Internationalist Mission of Cuba's Revolutionary Armed Forces in Angola". This was evident from his earlier political announcement to his "National Council of State" on 9 July 1987 about his dilemma in southeast Angola as he had clearly stated that: "We ourselves understood that even though we were in no way responsible for the errors that had led to that situation, we could not sit still and allow a military and political catastrophe to occur". There was also extreme international pressure on Cuba to withdraw their armed forces from Angola. Over the same period the joint Ronald Reagan-Mikhail Gorbachev gathering of leaders from the USA and USSR met in Moscow. A resolution was jointly undertaken by the grouping that the Cuban forces would withdraw from Angola as soon as the SADF withdrew from SWA. In the advent of a South African and Cuban force withdrawal from Angola the USSR undertook to withdraw its military support and military advisers from Angola. This was understandable as the Soviet Union was suffering at its own hand from internal political strife and the pressing demands of "Glasnost" and "Perestroika." Russia therefore wanted the political and military burden of Angola to disappear and Cuba probably felt the same. The resolute SADF in their staunch support to UNITA did nothing to lessen the pressure on Cuba and due to their humiliating military defeat in southeast Angola Castro could not let go – self-esteem and ego became the governing factors. This became a Catch-22 situation as the war in southern Angola remained a millstone. As such the words of Sun Tzu come to mind: "Never press a desperate foe too hard; always let an outlet free". To save face Castro needed to deploy the 50th Cuban Division to southwest Angola by May to get the ball rolling.

From 3 to 4 May a first round of peace talks between South Africa, Cuba and the Angolan MPLA government commenced in all seriousness in London. The purpose was to reach a negotiated peace settlement plan for southern Africa and for the implementation of Resolution 435. The feasibility of a negotiated settlement plan for SWA was also considered as the super powers were positive that it could be reached. Chester A. Crocker (at the time the US Assistant Secretary of State for African Affairs) led the mediation process. His major effort to facilitate further peace talks was wholeheartedly supported by the USSR. Crocker's mediating counterpart was Russian diplomat Anatoly Adamishin. These two politicians subtly coerced the belligerents towards peacemaking. The South African delegation was led by Dr. Neil van Heerden, the Chief of South Africa's National Intelligence Services, and included General Jannie Geldenhuys, the Chief of the SADF, and Major General Neels van Tonder, who was seconded from South Africa's Military Intelligence Services. The Cubans and the Angolans fielded a joint team led by Cuba's Jorge Risquet. General Ulysses Rosales, Cuba's Military Chief of Staff, was the deputy leader of their delegation. Afonso van Dunemen, Angola's Minister for Foreign Affairs and Dr. Fernando José de França Dias

Van-Dúnem, Minister of Justice, were also members of their joint delegation.

Political dialogue was directed at the ending of hostilities in Angola as well as the implementation of UN Resolution 435. The first round in London ended on a positive note, although the gruelling process did not happen without strife and mishap. The US and USSR henceforth collectively and progressively exerted more and more pressure on South Africa, Angola and Cuba to remain positively involved in negotiations for peace. The meeting in London was to be followed by a next round of negotiations scheduled for 23–25 June 1988 in Congo-Brazzaville. Resolution 435 served as the baseline for the implementation of the peace settlement as well as the independence for Namibia. The process obviously entailed the eventual withdrawal of all Cuban forces from Angola and the SADF from Namibia. What was enshrouded in the peace offering? It seemed as if a win-win situation could just, but just, come forward for the embattled as such:

- Cuba could withdraw from Angola with honour, having earned significant prestige as Africa's redeemer. The further cost of war, loss of Cuban lives and prestige in Angola's futile war would be prevented in this way.
- Both the Soviet Union and South Africa could prevent further war in Angola – it was a war they could not afford anymore and neither did it seem winnable in the foreseeable future.
- Russia would gain some respect in the aftermath as one of the key mediators for peace-making in Africa, enshrined in the warmth of "Glasnost" and "Perestroika."
- The Americans themselves could step forward as champions. They would be viewed as one of the key international players in saving Southern Africa from themselves and in preventing further war in Angola and Namibia. A peace settlement reached would furthermore pave the way for achieving Resolution 435.
- The international community and the UN would be quite appreciative if this worrisome war in the South ended – especially if it was to be followed by the long-awaited realization of Resolution 435 for peace and democracy in Namibia; even for the same to happen in South Africa.
- The African frontline states would be equally happy. A peace settlement would move South Africa forward to full democracy; with inclusion of the ANC, who would most definitely win a free and fair election. The end of "apartheid" was in sight.
- Angola was teetering on the brink of bankruptcy and could not really afford further war with South Africa and UNITA. There were furtive hopes that in the advent of a peace settlement that UNITA would move towards open democracy for Angola.
- SWAPO would eventually achieve its revolutionary goal, namely to free the yoke of Namibia from its oppressor.
- All and sundry were excited about the fact that they would see the last of the Cuban forces in Angola, and even possibly in Africa. Of course, the South African military forces would be required to depart from Namibian soil as well, thus ending the Border War, which had lasted for more than twenty two years.
- South Africa would be able to end the war without further loss of life – especially those of their White conscripts. The Nationalist Government would now be able to focus on resolving its own internal dispute with the ANC. This would permit progress towards a long-awaited democracy.

Notwithstanding the peace initiative the war continued escalating. The Cubans clearly foresaw the possibility of crossing offensively into SWA. The main Cuban military build-up on the Southern Front was well-organised and became fully stabilised by May-June:

- The first round of fresh reinforcements, totalling 8 600 troops, arrived from Cuba between 17 April and 7 May 1988. The units included some 2,000 "special purpose troops" (Cuban SPETSNAZ) and 200 Cuban pilots organised into a "pilot brigade."
- The reinforcements arrived fully equipped by sea and air through Luanda and Namibe and from there they were deployed to the south.
- The second round of reinforcements arrived by 10–12 May. They were a few thousand and brought the new southern Cuban forces to over division strength. This included infantry as well as heavy artillery and anti-aircraft units.
- Simultaneously, a Cuban tank brigade, with some 100 new tanks, was transferred from northern Angola to the south. The tank brigade had received new upgraded T-62 tanks and combat equipment in January–February. They were deployed in a quiet area in northern Angola for advance training. Once declared operationally ready the tank brigade was assigned to the Southern Front.
- The best and most loyal FAPLA units were moved from northern and central Angola to augment the Cuban forces in the south.
- Large quantities of modern equipment were delivered directly from the USSR by air and sea.
- On 4 May a combat force comprising mainly Cuban soldiers attacked elements of 101 Battalion operating against SWAPO insurgents in an area slightly south of Humbe. Rifleman Johan Papenfus was taken prisoner of war during the skirmish. These offensive actions by the Cubans augmented the anger of the high command of the SADF and ignited the operational planning for Operation Hilti/Excite. On 9–12 May Commandant Jan Hougaard of 32 Battalion was summoned to the Headquarters of Sector 10 at Oshakati and given instructions by Brigadier Chris Serfontein to begin with the preparation to attack the enemy at Techipa.

Intelligence indications were that a large SWAPO force was based at Techipa and that they were preparing for their habitual "Winter Games" – a deliberate incursion by their "Special Unit" as far south as the White farming area into the so-called "Tsumeb-Otavi-Grootfontein Death Triangle." The intelligence regarding the enemy's disposition in southern Angola and especially at Techipa was sketchy. There were however numerous battle indications that something awesome was brewing and that the Cubans were in the thick of things. It was decided to gather more accurate intelligence on the enemy's disposition before mounting a deliberate attack. Intelligence now started pouring in which indicated a massive Cuban military build-up in southwest Angola.

On 15 May the Cuban-Angolan objectives in the London negotiations with South Africa were clarified in a media interview with Johnny Makatini of the ANC wherein he explained that the participation of Cuba and Angola in the negotiations with South Africa was an important move to ensure US disengagement from UNITA and the Republic of South Africa (RSA). In his words: "It is necessary for Angola to talk because if there is a Democratic administration in the US, we can expect the establishment of diplomatic relations with Angola. And that will mean no assistance to Savimbi and his UNITA bandits and no economic assistance to the South Africans and full sanctions against South Africa".

From 16 to 19 May in preparation for Operation Hilti/Excite 32 Battalion established a tactical HQ at Ruacana under command of their intelligence officer Captain Herman Mulder. Two three-man reconnaissance teams were dispatched to gather more substantial intelligence on enemy strengths and deployments for operational planning purposes. One team reconnoitred the area southeast of Techipa along the Devangulu Mountains. The other reconnaissance team operated stealthily in the Handa-Rotunda area. This area lay west of the Cunene River slightly south of Humbe. The respective reconnaissance missions were only partially successful and both teams were extracted by 19 May. Techipa was therefore never reached. Numerous tank tracks were however sighted by both teams on gravel roads crossing the said areas reconnoitred. The first reconnaissance team was subsequently redeployed to Techipa. They now reported the presence of a heavy Cuban mechanised ground force. The intelligence regarding the presence of large Cuban mechanised forces and heavy vehicle movement in the operational area was confirmed by other combat elements of 201 Battalion and 32 Battalion also operating in the area.

The new threat situation developing in the 5th Military Region across northern SWA was extremely unnerving to the SADF. Additional mechanised forces such as 61 Mech were urgently required for the evolving conventional threat on hand. As such the conventional force levels of the SADF in the northern operational area were stretched to its limit. 32 Battalion in the meantime was given the task to engage the enemy at Techipa. A heavy engagement ensued in which 32 Battalion was confronted by an aggressive tank force. The outcome of the battle was inconclusive and 32 Battalion withdrew southward across the SWA-Angolan border into a forward holding position close to Ruacana.

By 20 May the Cubans openly contradicted assurances by Angolan President José Eduardo dos Santos that Cuban forces would not cross the border into SWA. Cuban officials stated publically that MiG-23 and SU-22s (Russian Sukhoi fighter aircraft) had flown reconnaissance missions into SWA. Similarly, official Cuban sources in Washington said that "Cuba does not rule out the possibility of Cuban forces operating inside Namibia". They explained that the "Cuban soldiers are prepared psychologically to cross into Namibia in pursuit of the South Africans". The Cuban sources further pointed out that: "Such intervention can take place both in support of SWAPO and in order to block South African support for UNITA or any other form of intervention in Angola".

A most declaratory position of the USSR was provided by M. Ponomarev, writing in "Krasneya Zvezda" on 20 May 1988, wherein he highlighted the Soviet and Cuban internationalist support for Angola. Ponomarev justified why Cuba and Angola agreed to negotiate with South Africa at all. The Soviets explained that because of the extent of South Africa's intervention and support for UNITA, "the Peoples Armed Forces for the Liberation of Angola have not been able, even with the help of the Cubans, to decisively defeat the enemy and drive him out of the territory of the country. The result fairly speaking was an impasse. There can only be two ways out of such an impasse – a political solution or a military decision."

On 24 May a combat element of 201 Battalion deployed at Cuamato, east of the Cunene River, came under attack from a combined FAPLA-Cuban force operating from Xangongo. A fierce skirmish ensued in which 201 Battalion lost a vehicle. The enemy attack was however repelled. On the same day Oliver Tambo stated that the ANC would intensify the armed struggle in South Africa until apartheid was dismantled. He explained that the ANC had widened the scope of activities in South Africa to include sophisticated forms of sabotage and military confrontation.

By 26 May the 50th Cuban Division had advanced from Lubango to Ondjiva then progressively spearheaded towards the SWA-Angolan border via Techipa, approximately 50 km from Calueque. The Chief of the SADF General Jannie Geldenhuys announced that a heavily armed combined Cuban-FAPLA-SWAPO force had moved south to within 60 km of the SWA-Angolan border. The swift advance of the Cubans as far as Techipa came as another unpleasant surprise for the SADF. The battle front abruptly switched from Cuito Cuanavale in the east to Calueque in the west, close on 700 km, through this initiative taken by the Cubans.

Cuba Ready to Strike with a Combined Task Force Optimised for Conventional War

The 50th Division was considered Castro's personal division. It was proclaimed the best combined arms division of the Cuban Armed Forces and was manned by loyal army regulars and not conscripts. In the past units from the 50th (formerly known as Military Unit No. 1973) saw action in the Golan Heights in Syria in 1973–75 and in the main offensives in Angola.

The Cuban-Angolan task force was described by observers as the heaviest force used by the Cubans to date on the Southern Front. It was estimated that three of its brigade-sized task forces were equipped with more than 200 tanks each. Half of the tanks were T-54/55s, plus 100 newly upgraded T-62 tanks, which the Cubans had received in January–February. There were more than two divisions worth of enemy forces deployed on the Southern Front of 21,000 combatants, which included 16,000 Cubans. The Cubans emphasised the participation of "combative SWAPO fighters" in their new offensive. Three combined battalions of 200 Cuban and 250 SWAPO each, supported by armour and artillery units, were based respectively at Xangongo (Tiger Battalion), Cahama (Lion Battalion) and Mupa (Zebra Battalion). An additional combat grouping of 300 SWAPO guerrilla fighters were deployed with the Cubans at Techipa. (See Frame 1 for a more detailed account of the task force).

The combined Cuban-Angolan forces in southwest Angola by the end of May was firmly entrenched as far as Cahama, Techipa, Xangongo and Ondjiva. The air base at Cahama in the meantime was being feverishly upgraded and the landing strip at Xangongo extended by 524 metres to accommodate modern Russian MiG-23 combat aircraft. All of southern Angola was covered by a comprehensive radar network and modern Russian air defence systems such as the SA-8.

The enemy was in the position to attack across the border either from Cahama, Xangongo or Ondjiva, or simultaneously on two to three fronts. The main thrust of the 50th Cuban division was, however, directed at Ruacana. In the advent of South African counter-attacks the Cubans were prepared to destroy the Ruacana reservoirs and transformers and attack South African bases inside SWA. With their enhanced operational capability, preponderance in armour and air supremacy the enemy was now in position to attack any target of strategic value well inside SWA such as Rundu, Ruacana, Oshakati, Ondangwa and Grootfontein. The hydroelectric water scheme at Calueque was especially exposed to a combined enemy air and ground assault.

The Cubans openly declared that they had established bridgeheads for SWAPO to renew its cross border attacks, sporadic raids and over-the-border shelling by means of

Frame 1: Cuban Order of Battle and Operational Framework – Southern Front

- Three battalions of Cuban SPETSNAZ (Special Forces).
- One Cuban tank regiment/brigade with 105–110 tanks comprised of three tank battalions.
- One Cuban artillery regiment/brigade equipped with heavy artillery and rocket launchers.
- Six Cuban-Angolan combined-arms regiments/brigades of 1 500–2,000 troops each with tanks.
- Three Cuban-SWAPO raiding battalions (200 Cuban and 250 SWAPO elite soldiers each).
- Each of the abovementioned units included a detachment of Cuban intelligence services.
- Additional MI-17s (HIP) and MI-18s (HIND) combat helicopters were deployed from northern Angola. Some additional combat helicopters were delivered directly from the USSR.
- The Cubans paid special attention to the build-up of their formidable air combat and air defence capabilities. A squadron of the latest model MiG-23 (FLOGGER-K) fighter aircraft, with significantly improved performance, was deployed in southern Angola. Upgraded SU-22s were also deployed. Several airbases, including Cahama and Xangongo, were upgraded for modern air combat and ground attack aircraft. Cuban radar systems were upgraded so that they could control air operations well into SWA. This air defence system included the latest models of FLATFACE, SPOONREST and BARLOCK radars. Adequate SA-2c, SA-3, SA-6, SA-8b and SA-13 batteries were subsequently deployed with all mobile forces and at all garrisons.
- In May–June each of the six combined-arms regiments (brigades) in southern Angola was assigned an operational manoeuvre group – OGPZ in Cuban-Russian terms. The mission of an OGPZ was to serve as an advance guard for a combined-arms regiment (brigade size task force). This was most probably what 61 Mech clashed with on 26–27 June near Techipa.
- When necessary the combined Cuban-Angolan OGPZ could operate as a component of the combined-arms regiment or independently. The rest of the Cuban-Angolan regiment was normally comprised of:
  - One command echelon.
  - Two or three mechanised battalions with BTR-60 and truck mounted infantry.
  - One tank battalion of thirty three T-55/54 tanks.
  - One or more artillery regiments with twenty four pieces each.
  - One reconnaissance company.
  - Attached air defence components as required.
  - Logistic and other support units.

multiple rocket launchers (MRLs) and mortars. The tactics employed by the Cubans were variations of the doctrine applied by the Soviets for combined-arms warfare under "special conditions". Their operational manoeuvre groups could operate as independent "cluster forces" in any hostile environment, closely coordinated with combat helicopter strikes. They had high hopes that they could move over rapidly to the offensive and into the deep rear of South African combat groupings. Their aim was stated as disruption of the SADF so as to increase the effectiveness of the lower quality Angolan government forces.

The SADF Caught Off-Guard Hastily Prepares to Strike Back

Out of the blue the enemy was in the most aggressive combat position of the war for southern Angola since it had started in September 1987. In this way the SADF was caught off-guard by the 50th Cuban Division's unexpected appearance on the SWA-Angolan Border near Calueque and placed in a Catch-22 position; attack or defend was the question – prepare for and be ready for any contingency and play for time were the few options left open. What will the outcome of the evolving threatening situation be for South Africa and SWA and particularly for Sector 10?

The first-line fighting units with conventional warfare experience operationally deployed in Sector 10 initially had to bear the brunt of the immense threat posed by the combined Cuban-Angolan-SWAPO task force. These units were 61 Mech commanded by Commandant Mike Müller, 32 Battalion by Colonel Mucho Delport and 101 Battalion by Colonel Leon Marais. 61 Mech was still resting, reorganising and recovering at Omuthiya from their harrowing warfare ordeal on completion of Operation Packer, whilst 32 Battalion and 101 Battalion were already operating against SWAPO externally in southern Angola under command of Sector 10. 4 South African Infantry Battalion (4 SAI) had returned from southeast Angola to Middelburg in South Africa on completion of Packer. This unit, similarly organised as 61 Mech, was hastily recalled to Sector 10 and was set to arrive fully combat ready by 25 July under command of Commandant Cassie Schoeman.

The civilian population and families of military personnel in the northern urban areas of SWA were suddenly at risk. In the words of Padre Loutjie Bouwer, who was the Chaplain of Sector 10 at Oshakati during Operation Prone:

> On 30th of May 1988 the situation in Ovamboland became precarious, suddenly ... overnight ... with the surprising appearance of the 50th Cuban Division across the SWA-Angola border near Cahama, especially as I and my family lived in Oshakati. My wife Arista and my children had become used to the firing of rockets by SWAPO from a distance onto Oshakati, but now the situation had become much more life threatening. I was of the opinion that the Cubans could cross the border offensively at any moment and attack us or bomb our homes at Oshakati with their MiGs. They reminded us of that possibility, including our inability to do much about it, through some low level fly-over at both Oshakati and Ruacana. My Volkswagen Kombi was packed with the bare necessities, facing southwards and ready to go at a moment's notice. I had given meticulous instructions to Arista on which obscure route to follow to safety when I gave her the signal. Fortunately, it never came to that.

On 27 May the senior command-and-staff course of the South African Army College held its annual Wildebeest Golf Tournament at the Zwartkops Country Club in Pretoria. As the officer commanding I was obliged to attend this event with my Chief Instructor of the Senior Command-and-Staff Course, Colonel André Kruger. The event was also attended by Major General J.A. Klopper, the Chief of Army Staff Operations, who was an ardent golfer. As soon as Klopper arrived early in the morning he advised me that I had been appointed as Chief of Staff of 10 South African (SA) Division. "The formation was hastily being formed to counter the surprise offensive move of the 50th Cuban Division in the 5th Military Region", Klopper said. Brigadier Chris Serfontein, as the commanding officer of Sector 10 at Oshakati had been appointed as the divisional commander. Serfontein was a resolute infantry officer who understood warfare in the African context. During his career he had commanded 52 Battalion in Sector 10 as well as the Infantry School. He knew the sector as well as the operational circumstances pertaining to the northern operational area. He was a veteran of operations Sceptic in 1980 and Protea in 1981. He was a man who was dauntless when it became necessary to take the hard decision; he was not afraid of the Cubans, FAPLA or SWAPO. In Serfontein the enemy had a worthy adversary. It later on became a pleasure for me to work with him during Operations Hilti/Prone. I was informed forthwith by Klopper that I would leave for Sector 10 on 7 June. A contingent of army staff officers would accompany me that were designated for operational planning, which was scheduled to take place at Oshakati from 7 until 17 June. The code word for the operation was Hilti. The conventional side of the operation was to be named Operation Faction/Excite.

FAPLA and the Cuban conventional forces meanwhile continued to deliberately strengthen their defensive strongholds at Techipa, Cahama, Xangongo and Ondjiva. Fidel Castro provided a detailed briefing to the leaders of the Non-aligned Movement and some African diplomats on the situation in southern Angola late in May. He outlined the Cuban plans for the future. He used maps and charts to survey the developments since late 1987. Castro emphasised that the Cuban-FAPLA-SWAPO forces had had established positions 50 km from the Namibian border. He emphasised that "the enemy was defeated by the Angolan and Cuban forces" and compared the current situation in Angola to that of 1975, adding that a major and decisive confrontation with South Africa might be inevitable. In his briefing Castro boasted that in case of renewed fighting the South Africans would be confronted by "a military force like never before" and concluded that, "although Cuba would prefer a diplomatic solution, we are in a position to take more military risks, because if the enemy wants a confrontation he can suffer a serious defeat". An operations instruction for Operation Hilti was issued by Chief of the Army, Lieutenant General Kat Liebenberg, in Pretoria on 30 May 1988. It was signed by Major General J.A. Klopper, Chief of Army Staff Operations. This operational instruction of the South African Army preceded the top secret operational instruction issued by Chief of Staff Operations of the SADF dated 1 June, which was a clear indication of how hectic it went. The latter operational instructions were followed up by Operational Instruction Number 2/88 of the General Officer Commanding (GOC) SWATF. These series of operational instructions initiated the formal planning and conduct of enhanced integrated counterinsurgency and conventional operations in northwest SWA and southwest Angola. Therein it was foreseen by the SADF that the enemy would complete their force build-up by the end of June in readiness to attack southward into SWA. A more aggressive stance could be expected from the Cuban forces henceforth, the SADF predicted. At the time a counteroffensive by the enemy from Cuito Cuanavale to capture Mavinga and Jamba from UNITA in southeast Angola in 1988 was not envisaged by the South African intelligence services. Such an eventuality would enable the release of South African forces in the east for employment in the west it was surmised.

On 30 May I was summoned to Army HQ by Major General Klopper and given a copy of the operations instruction for Operation Hilti. I was then further briefed by the army intelligence and operation staff in Blenny (Blenny was the underground command bunker of the SA Army in Potgieter Street). I was informed that the anticipated conventional operation by the South Africans in southwest Angola and northwest SWA was to be executed with increased force levels as is described in Appendix A. The initial overall military mission of the South African conventional force was to: "Extend the influence of UNITA in southern Angola so as to include the 'Area-In-Dispute' by 31 December 1988". The SADF therefore initially, in essence, envisaged an external offensive operation – attack, attack! Conventional operations were to be supported by deliberate deception and strategic communication actions, as was instructed from up high. Inevitably, it was predetermined, UNITA needed to be part of this battle design.

- Phase 1 of Operation Hilti was code-named Operation Excite. The aim of this particular sub-phase was to gain more military freedom of action for the SADF, SWATF and UNITA forces operating in southern Angola. This goal needed to be achieved by the end of August 1988.
- The second sub-phase of Hilti was an offensive code-named Faction. An operational period of up to twenty one days was foreseen for the successful completion of an attack of which the ultimate aim was to restore the military control of the SADF over the so-called "Area-In-Dispute." This was the same area which was captured from FAPLA during Operation Protea in August 1981.
- Operation Florentine was to follow on the successful completion of Operation Faction and intended to establish UNITA firmly in the areas captured by Operation Faction. This would in the aftermath, it was envisaged, "require a strong SADF presence in southern Angola to support UNITA against any possible counter-attack by FAPLA and the Cuban forces."

The overarching operational design of the SA Army for Operation Hilti (renamed Prone on 19 July) made provision for the following operational guidelines:

- The South African Army was responsible for the ground war and was appointed lead executor for Operation Hilti/Prone.
- The SAAF was responsible for the air war and was designated to provide the required air capabilities and support to the ground forces deployed in SWA and southern Angola.
- The South African Navy was poised for naval operations along the western coastline and to support special seaborne operations and Special Forces operations to be conducted strategically deep behind enemy lines in Angola.
- The Surgeon General was tasked to provide the required medical support and health services for the impending operation.
- The General Officer Commanding (GOC) Special Forces was tasked to provide specialised support to the SA Army as required. This implied deep strategic reconnaissance inside Angola as well as close reconnaissance on the immediate battle front. Operational deployments were aimed at monitoring enemy deployments in the 5th Military Region and to provide early warning of possible offensive manoeuvres or attacks by the enemy.
- Chief of Staff Intelligence was to provide the required intelligence services. In addition defence intelligence was responsible to liaise with UNITA so as to coordinate their continued cooperation and military support for the SA Army

in southern Angola; support the army in developing and executing deliberate deception and strategic communication actions.

- Dedicated Task Teams of the respective Arms of Service and Special Forces formed an integral part of the operational and support staff components of the combat forces on the ground. Operation Hilti/ Prone was to be a joint affair and therefore constituted a joint high-performance fighting team.
- Additional forces, including the citizen force, was mobilised for Operation Hilti/ Prone as part of 10 SA Division. Mobilisation was authorised by means of Operations Instruction C Army/D Ops/ 309/4/Hilti Number 21 of 1988, dated 27 May 1988 and was set to be achieved by 22 July.

I viewed the unfurling situation as the makings for a grand war, an offensive one, no holds barred. Active motions were immediately initiated by the SADF for the rapid mobilisation of the mechanised task force now named 10 SA Division, a large portion of which comprised the conventional citizen force. I returned to the Army College and immediately prepared one of the lecture rooms (General De Wet Lecture Room) as a planning centre and commenced with preliminary planning of the operation. There was very little information to work on. The enemy picture was a maze, a void. Who must attack what, where, when, why and how? From the terrain appreciation it became evident that Lubango, Namibe, Cahama, Xangongo and Ondjiva would have to be captured. This was where the main infrastructure, force deployments, command centres, logistics and forward airfields of the enemy for their Southern Front were strategically located. The blue sweeping attacking arrows on the planning map pointed northward into Angola. Possible enemy positions and choke points were marked in red. The battle planning map started looking very similar to the planning map for Operation Protea, which had been drawn up in September 1981, even though the latter had been on a much smaller scale.

In the meantime a sizeable training team was mobilised to deploy from the South African Army Battle School, based at Lohatlha, to the operational area. This was to support 10 SA Division with force preparation and mission training of the forces to be called up and mobilised forthwith. Further arrangements were rapidly undertaken to mobilise a main HQ for 10 SA Division. The divisional HQ was to be established at Oshakati and a mobile tactical HQ was to be formed as well. The Tac HQ was to be brought into readiness soonest to deploy in the field in the advent of the battle becoming fluid. Operational plans and contingency plans were immediately instituted by Sector 10 for the forces in situ, such as 61 Mech, 32 Battalion and 101 Battalion to retaliate if need be. They were the first responders as usual – operation normal.

Ironically, at the same time things were brewing up north. The Director Training of the South African Army, Brigadier Andy (M.B.) Anderson, released an instruction for the debriefing of Operations Modular, Hooper and Packer, which was scheduled for 16 June at SA Army HQ – one which I was instructed to attend.

In this debriefing later on it would become apparent ad nauseum that throughout this untidy conventional war the SADF faced two insurmountable problems. Firstly, due to the international arms embargo since 1977 South Africa's aging air force was outclassed by sophisticated Soviet-supplied air defence systems and air-strike capabilities fielded by the Cubans and Angolans. The South African Air Force (SAAF) was unable to uphold the air supremacy it had enjoyed for many years in SWA and southern Angola; its diminished counter-air-defence capability proved to be critical to the outcome of any conventional battle to be fought on the ground in the so called "Western Sub-Theatre of War". Secondly, generally speaking, the South African conventional forces in theatre were outnumbered by approximately twelve combat groupings to one on the ground. The imbalance in combat power especially accounted to heavy armament such as tanks, artillery and air defence systems. The South Africans, however, clearly possessed the tactical prowess to outclass their conventional FAPLA-Cuban foe in the numerous mobile battles fought on the ground. Herein superior battle field command-and-control and the optimal tactical employment of the G-5 long distance artillery provided the combat edge. However, due credit was to be given to the 50th Cuban Division fielded in Angola for the first time; this force was another kettle of fish altogether. UNITA, as a formidable guerrilla army opposing FAPLA and the Cubans, in the end, played no significant role in the conventional conflict performed in the 5th Military Region. UNITA, however, remained overly active in southeastern Angola as well as the central and northern regions, where a large portion of FAPLA's brigades remained embroiled in their own vicious civil war.

Apart from the ongoing planning and preparation for the impending battle, feverishly so I may add, a brief spurt of hellfire was about to be released near Calueque came 26–27 June 1988.

The SADF Launches Operation Hilti/Prone

By the beginning of June Brigadier Chris Serfontein of Sector 10 was facing difficult choices. A dangerous situation was fast developing on the Techipa front which was covered by his command. This was not a low-key insurgency threat any more, but a conventional one, which was serious and imminent. As such tactical intelligence was notably lacking whilst adequate strategic intelligence from the higher realms of political and military powers in Pretoria was not truly forthcoming. Serfontein was probably thinking in similar vein as Stonewall Jackson of Chancellorsville had done. Jackson in facing similar odds during the American Civil War promptly uttered. "I was too weak to defend, so I attacked".

By now Colonel Mucho Delport and Commandant Jan Hougaardt of 32 Battalion had their Tac HQ firmly established at Ruacana. Hougaardt and his men knew the terrain on the other side in Angola well. In March 1982 he had commanded a fire-force of 32 Battalion and gave SWAPO a severe hiding in the same area during Operation Super. This time around 32 Battalion faced a conventional enemy on the same ground. It had become obvious to any prudent military tactician that a heavy conventional force was preparing to advance deliberately towards Calueque and the SWA-Angolan border.

What was next? It seemed that Calueque was their first objective, which included the strategically important water reservoir and hydroelectric water scheme as well as the two vital crossings over the Cunene River nearby. Since Operation Protea in August 1981 Calueque had been the sphere of influence of the SADF. To Serfontein, Delport and Hougaardt it was obvious that aggressive probing was required to gather more real-time intelligence. It was also vital that the persistent advances of the enemy be tempered. Time was furthermore required for the weightier 61 Mech and their squadron of Olifant main battle tanks and formidable G-5 battery to deploy from Omuthiya to Ruacana. A gaping unknown was the political and military will of the foe – will they cross the border, yes or no? The enemy picture, which was gradually becoming clear, was ominous.

Much further south in Pretoria an operations instruction marked exclusive and top secret was issued by Chief of the South African Army (Director Operations) to a restricted number of recipients, including me. This instruction authorised the mobilisation of the HQ of 81 Armour Brigade and a number of citizen force units for Operation Hilti. Call-up of the citizen force was to commence by 22 July, mobilisation completed by 25 July, movement to the operational area was scheduled from 26 to 31 July and force training and preparations for an offensive into Angola completed by 21 August. The fighting units were to be deployed in forward assembly areas ready for operational employment by 24 August. What was to be done on the ground in the period in-between while these additional force levels were mobilised to contain the imminent conventional threat?

On 6 June Brigadier Chris Serfontein issued his command appreciation for the planning and execution of Operation Hilti/Faction. The purpose of this was to initiate and guide the military planning for Operation Hilti and Faction as required respectively by the Chief of the SADF, Chief of the South African Army and the GOC SWATF. At the time General Jannie Geldenhuys presided as the Chief of the SADF, Lieutenant General Kat Liebenberg as the Chief of the South African Army, and Major General Willie Meyer was the GOC SWATF.

The mission originally stated by Serfontein was to recapture the Area-In-Dispute by the end of August. The operational framework for the impending offensive included target areas such as Cahama, Xangongo and Ondjiva. Both Serfontein and I knew these areas well from Operation Protea in August 1981. We clearly foresaw that offensive conventional operations by the SADF as planned would necessarily be conducted to the east as well as to the west of the Cunene River. This important natural obstacle posed a challenge to its crossing by both friend and foe and at the same time served as a vital feature for delaying and defensive tactics. It furthermore became apparent to us that one could not take Ondjiva, Xangongo, Humbe and Cahama if Lubango was not included in the offensive scheme. What about Namibe, the enemy's closest port on the Atlantic coast? It seemed that mission-creep was inevitable and that it could therefore lead to the escalation of the war if this was not realised by the South African government and high command of the SADF! On the same day a follow-up instruction was issued by Chief of the Army authorising a number of selected army personnel to report to the HQ of Sector 10 for operational planning from 7 June until 15 June 1988 (later extended to 17 June) to initiate Operation Hilti. The planning group was to depart by air from Waterkloof Air Force Base on 7 June at 06:30. Malaria tablets were to be taken beforehand it was habitually instructed. (See Appendix reflecting the names of the planning group).

On 7 June Fidel Castro, the President of Cuba, warned of a possible surprise attack by the SAAF against Cuban forces deployed in southwest Angola. He issued a direct command to General Ochoa Sanchez to launch an immediate counter-attack with his air force in such an advent. On 8 June the SADF commenced with the planning for the mobilisation of the citizen force to augment its conventional war-fighting capability in SWA. A strong message was therefore sent to the Cubans that the South African government was more than ready to respond strongly to any conventional war threat to the territorial integrity of SWA. On 9 June SWAPO haughtily announced that they had launched a number of military offensives from across the border into Namibia. They explained that some of these attacks were carried out in close corporation with joint Cuban-Angolan forces. As a preliminary action preceding Hilti, Colonel Mucho Delport was instructed by Sector 10 on 13 June to deploy a holding force with 32 Battalion immediately north of the SWA-Angolan border near Ruacana. Another part of the force under Commandant Jan Hougaardt was given the task to attack Techipa, where it was believed that the HQ of a large Cuban force was deployed. Hougaardt as a master tactician knew that he could not outmanoeuvre a large Cuban mechanised force in an all-out conventional battle and that his actions therefore required clever probing and delaying tactics. In the meantime 61 Mech under Commandant Mike Müller was making ready to move swiftly to Calueque to team up with 32 Battalion. Little did Hougaardt and approximately five hundred experienced fighters of 32 Battalion know that they were about to face more than eleven thousand Cubans and more than two hundred SWAPO combatants in the next fighting round.

There were two possible enemy approaches to be covered by the two combat groupings of 32 Battalion. The one enemy approach led from Cahama via Techipa southward directly towards Calueque to the west of the Cunene. The other axis of advance lay in the Cunene valley from Xangongo via Naulilato Ruacana to the east of the river. Mechanised patrols of the Cubans had already probed as far as twelve kilometres from Calueque. These preliminary actions were carefully undertaken and supported by rolling artillery barrages supported by a company of twelve T-55 tanks and Russian MiGs flying combat air patrols overhead. Their cautiousness was a clear indication that they were new to the game and still finding their feet in unforgiving Africa.

The primary mission of 32 Battalion was to fight for intelligence and hold the line until 61 Mech could join their ranks. As an exponent of guerrilla warfare Hougaard chose a modus operandi based on guerrilla tactics, African style. A number of enemy advance posts had been located between Techipa and Calueque and the next move entailed mobile offensive action to the flanks and rear of the conventional enemy. 32 Battalion was now set to launch a series of probing attacks and to harass the enemy through day and night by means of relentless mortar bombardments and fiery skirmishes. The fluid battle which materialised took place under dangerous conditions and in extremely difficult terrain. A number of murderous mechanised counter-attacks by the enemy followed, supported by scathing indirect fire and air attacks. Some of the reconnaissance elements of 32 Battalion were forced to flee by foot. Others had to escape and evade from danger over vast distances. The gallant bush warriors left some equipment behind that was shot to pieces. Miraculously so, all the soldiers of 32 Battalion returned safely home.

Brigadier Chris Serfontein now realised that his most recent enemy was not going to be an easy nut to crack. The numerical superiority of the conventional foe was immense. More forces were required than the mere combined fighting strengths of 32 Battalion and 61 Mech. It however remained imperative in the interim to do something significant about the threatening enemy situation. What was required was the systematic planning and executions of successive offensive engagements to annihilate the enemy – find, fix and strike once again. The main enemy force furthermore needed to be coerced into the open, where they would be more vulnerable to the South African's mobile tactics and the murderous effect of the 155 mm G-5 guns. The South Africans had learnt valuable lessons in the past: The enemy's inadequate command-and-control in fluid battle and the dense African bush prevented the effective utilisation of their air weapons and artillery.

In addition, own forces were still ardently fishing for more substantial tactical intelligence about the latest enemy they were facing. Recent intelligence gained indicated that the enemy's mobile columns were supported by excessive numbers of surface-to-air missile systems. The SAAF dearly required something to be done about this major problem. It was cramping their style to hit effectively at the enemy's ground forces. In a recent ground attack attempt the Impalas had to withdraw because of withering air defence fire. The fear was that the lethal SAM-6 of the Cubans was in theatre, bringing the employment of the SAAF in the ground attack role to a grinding halt.

Sector 10, however, went forth to hastily assemble a conventional task force in the area of Calueque for the next round of fighting. Colonel Mucho Delport of 32 Battalion was placed in command of a brigade-sized task force comprising 32 Battalion, 61 Mech and 101 Battalion. From this force a formidable combat grouping was formed under command of Commandant Mike Müller to execute an offensive mission towards Techipa. His force comprised 61 Mech and additional subunits from other sources – refer to the composition of the force as depicted in Appendix A. Crossing effortlessly in an out of Angola over the partially damaged low-water bridge at Calueque with heavy equipment, including tanks, was a substantial challenge. This required a major engineering effort by 25 Field Engineer Regiment who was up to the challenge.

In the interim, from 7 to 17 June, Brigadier Chris Serfontein and the newly established staff team of 10 SA Division completed the preliminary planning for Operation Hilti/Faction at the HQ of Sector 10 in Oshakati. I was responsible to lead the planning for mobile conventional operations, whilst Colonel Eddie Viljoen, the Chief of Staff of Sector 10, remained responsible for counterinsurgency. Our integrated planning process inter alia catered for the arrangements to mobilise 10 SA Division as swiftly as possible. As a guideline Chief of the Army had predetermined that the offensive operation itself should preferably be completed within 21 days and not 36 days. This was due to the demobilisation requirements of the citizen force. Thereafter Hilti/Faction was to be continued by first line combat units such as 61 Mech, 4 South African Infantry Battalion, 32 Battalion and 101 Battalion. This was a tall order. However, we were raring to go.

On 15 June I issued a supplementary warning order for Operation Faction as the Chief of Staff on behalf of 10 SA Division, which reiterated our main mission as: "The capturing of the Area in Dispute by 31 December 1988". This warning order unambiguously dealt with the actions for Faction summarised in Frame 2. Following suit, preliminary courses of action for the impending offensive were presented to Major General Willie Meyer and the senior staff of SWATF on 16 June. Resolutions that were taken served as the baseline to activate the preparations for Hilti/Faction.

It is important to realise at this point in time that South Africa was teetering on the brink of an all-out regional war with Angola. The political and military situation became extremely fluid and unpredictable within the next crucial nine weeks. This was best illustrated by the original intention of South Africa to launch a major offensive into southern Angola by 22 August. Miraculously, this was the day that a ceasefire agreement was signed between South Africa, Cuba and Angola at Calueque and the order given to 10 SA Division to plan for mobile defence in case of the derailment of the ensuing peace negotiations.

How did this all come about at our level of war at the front?

I returned to Pretoria on 17 June with the main portion of the staff team to set in motion the further planning and preparation for Hilti/Faction. For this purpose a secure planning room was set up at the Army College in Voortrekkerhoogte, where a core planning team under my guidance commenced with extended operational planning and preparations for Hilti/Faction. At this stage the military appreciation still focused on a deliberate offensive to recapture the Area-In-Dispute. Potential targets were situated to

Frame 2: Summarised Version of the Warning Order for Operation Faction – Capturing of the Area in Dispute

- Continuation of the preliminary joint operational planning cycle for Operation Hilti/Faction (which had started on 7 June) to be completed by 17 June.
- Presentation of possible operational courses of action to the GOC SWATF by 16 June.
- Establishment of the intelligence and logistics office of 10 SA Division by 16 June.
- Establishment of a skeleton divisional HQ by 15 July and the main HQ by 2 August.
- Mobilisation and movement of the designated forces for Faction to the operational area.
- Operational plans for Hilti/ Faction to be finalised over the period 27 July to 1 August.
- Deployment of the Senior Command and Staff Course of the South African Army College and the other personnel earmarked for the HQ of 10 SA Division by air on 27 July.
- Presentation of the final operational concepts and plans to the Chief of the SADF, Chief of the Army, Chief of the Air Force, Surgeon General, GOC Special Forces and GOC SWATF on 1 August at the HQ of 10 SA Division, Oshakati.
- Mission training and exercises of the combat force to be conducted by the Army Battle School under supervision of Director Training over the period 2 until 21 August.
- Final orders to be issued down the command chain from 2 until 7 August.
- A motivational talk by the commander of 10 SA Division to the troops on 17 August.
- A final joint rehearsal for Faction by the respective brigades from 18 until 19 August.
- Final maintenance, repairs and operational inspections completed by 20 August.
- Motivational speeches by the State President, Chief of the SADF and Chief of the Army on 21 August in the training area or forward assembly areas.
- Final preparation, rest and inspections of the combat force on 21 August.
- Movement by the respective combat groupings to forward assembly areas for the impending attack by 22–24 August.

the west and east of the Cunene River and extended as far as Lubango and Namibe in the west and Techamutete and Cassinga in the north. Namibe on the Atlantic Coast of southern Angola was earmarked as a potential target for an airborne assault, supported by the SAAF, SA Navy and Special Forces. At the same time I set in motion the arrangements we had made at Oshakati for the mobilisation and training of 10 SA Division. For this purpose Chief of the Army had appointed the HQ of 8 Armour Division under command of Brigadier J.C. Nel to oversee the mobilisation and movement of the citizen force to the operational area and the Army Battle School under command of Brigadier Eddie Web to conduct the force training in northern SWA.

From 23 to 25 June the second meeting between the peace negotiators from South Africa, Angola and Cuba took place in Congo-Brazzaville. The Russian diplomat Anatoly Adamishin once again supported Chester Crocker in the course of peacemaking. Together the two politicians worked desperately towards a win-win situation for all those who were intimately involved in this particular conflict. General Magnus Malan, South Africa's Minister of Defence led the South African delegation. Dr. Neil Barnard and General Jannie Geldenhuys were part of the team once again. The joint Cuban-Angolan negotiation team was headed by Jorge Risquet and Afonso Van-Dúnem. After some heated arguments the respective delegations eventually fielded their views and wish lists in writing. It was clear to all that the procession was steadily moving towards a peace settlement. It took until 5–8 August for a negotiated ceasefire to be reached between South Africa, Angola and Cuba in Geneva.

In the meantime the line was held at Cuito Cuanavale in the east by a combined SADF-UNITA holding force, whilst the 155 mm G-5 shells rained down on the little African village and its surrounding defences. By 26–27 June 1988 blood would flow at Techipa.

Close Encounters of the Most Vicious Kind – Teetering on the Brink of Regional War

By 26/27 June the SADF was ready to launch Operation Excite to test Cuban forces in the area north of Calueque, which centred on the enemy's mechanised force located at Techipa. For this purpose a number of Special Forces teams, active against the enemy across the Cunene River, provided vital real time tactical intelligence to Sector 10 as Brigadier Chris Serfontein was about to launch the reinforced combat group of Commandant Mike Müller at the Cubans. However, uncertainty still remained regarding the exact intention, strength and composition of the overall conventional enemy now being faced head-on. One thing was certain, the enemy now opposed was far more competent than those engaged by the SADF in the past and they were not shy in any way to cross swords. Their advance guard was steadily closing in on Calueque as their forward elements aggressively probed southeastwards under the continuous protection of artillery supporting fire and ever prevalent MiG-23s air combat patrolling. The Cubans were so self-assured that they had informed the local population to carry a simple, but striking message to the South Africans: "Boers, we are here to kick your backsides". It was now becoming a game of cat and mouse; sheer battle craft, tactics and superior command-and-control were going to exert its toll – may the best man win.

The terrain conditions were not favourable to the South African mobile forces due to more open rugged country in this western quarter. In this way, own forces were much more vulnerable to attack by the enemy's overwhelming air force. These were all relevant factors Commandant Mike Müller carefully considered when he made his military appreciation and planned for the impending offensive. Keeping the enemy away from Calueque and causing maximum casualties in a flowing mobile battle, was the underlying concept. The enemy's HQ was sought after for attack. It was however too well protected by their ground forces and therefore became a priority target for the long distance G-5s. There were just too many of the enemy.

By 26 June the South African task force was ready to take on an overwhelming 50th Cuban Division who was advancing steadily southeastwards towards Calueque. That same night Müller crossed into Angola at Calueque with three combat teams. Techipa was bombarded with 155 mm G-5 long-range artillery. This massive artillery onslaught to a large extent marginalised the effect of the Cubans' artillery. A heavy mobile battle ensued between 61 Mech and forward combat elements of the 50th Cuban Division in the area between Techipa and Calueque. Major Hannes Nortmann and his formidable Ratel ZT-3s formed part of the impressive combat array. In the fighting mêlée the South Africans were surprised at the suddenness and scale of the Cuban advance and their offensive spirit. A series of running fire fights and spoiling attacks followed between the Cuban armoured force and the South Africans. It was a grinding battle, hard relentless, exerting toll on man and machine.

Commandant Jan Hougaardt was controlling the battle from his Tac HQ position at Ruacana. From there he could support the close-in fighting with deception actions and the adjustment of artillery fire. In preparation for the battle the South Africans had used decoys to provoke SAM sites into revealing their positions. The sites located through these means became targets for the G-5. For more than six hours a murderous G-5 onslaught affected its toll on Techipa. There were countless casualties reported by the enemy as the battle smoke drifted over enemy concentrations and the village of Techipa.

The enemy continued to advance persistently southeastward. The mechanised odds were just too much for the South Africans to counter, who were now in grave danger of being enveloped. By 27 June Serfontein gave Müller permission to withdraw his fighting task force further southward to safety. The Cubans retaliated with a successful air attack by six Russian MiG-23 combat aircraft against a South African air defence position held at Calueque on the same day. During the first bombing run one South African soldier was killed. During the second attack another eleven soldiers of 8 South African Infantry Battalion were killed and damage caused to the bridge and some hydroelectric installations.

The South African combat force eventually broke contact with the enemy ground force and withdrew orderly and safely southwards towards the Cunene River. This manoeuvre by Müller was in apprehension of being encircled and overwhelmed by a numerical superior Cuban combat force, as they could be cut off at Calueque. The idea now was to fall back and occupy an intermediary defensive line on the high ground slightly north of Calueque.

The crossing sites over the Cunene River were restricted. The low-water bridge at Calueque had now been partially destroyed by the MiG-23 attack. This situation placed pressure on Müller pertaining to the safe withdrawal southwards of his combat force. Fortunately, an alternative crossing was available further southwestward, which was left intact by the enemy. The advancing enemy was constantly kept under fire by the South African artillery. At midnight Müller received the command to cross over into SWA under the cover of darkness – for him and his men this had been a long arduous day. At the same time Hougaardt received an instruction from Sector 10 to withdraw all the troops of 32 Battalion from Angola.

The engagement at Techipa and the enemy air attack at Calueque heralded the last fighting between the South Africans and the combined Angolan-Cuban force in the war for southern Angola. More than three hundred Cuban soldiers succumbed in the fighting, who were shocked by their losses. With the withdrawal of the SADF into SWA on 27 June the hostilities ceased. The Cubans now controlled Calueque and the crossing sites over the Cunene River.

After the attack by the Cuban MiG–23s at Calueque the South African community became seriously perturbed by the military situation in the northern operational area. Seven of the twelve South African soldiers killed were 19 years old; the eldest was 23. Questions directed at the politicians and generals were sharp, damning and less than flattering.[1]

1 Bridgland, Fred: *The War for Africa: Twelve Months That Transformed a Continent.* Ashanti Publishing Limited, Gibraltar, 1990, p. 363. Also refer to Chapter 9.

"In South Africa it caused waves of wrath, anguish and fear as international newspapers blazoned that "Pretoria's plans had gone awry!" The South African as well as Cuban forces remained on high alert after the battle smoke cleared up over the fields of Techipa and Calueque. Any side could now expect a strong response from its adversary at any moment. A kind of an impasse was reached. A weary calm settled over the battlefield.

The SADF immediately re-evaluated its military-strategic posture in northern SWA and southern Angola in light of rapidly changing military and political developments. High-level political and military considerations and decisions were influenced by some of the following factors:

- The recent operational developments relevant to the surprise encounter with the 50th Cuban Division in southern Angola. This situation changed the threat environment overnight and therefore influenced the overall balance of military power in the region.
- The fast changing political landscape in South Africa was a clear indication that the ending of "apartheid" had dawned. There were furthermore clear signs that the South African government wanted to withdraw their military forces from Angola and SWA. Parents in South Africa were staring hard at the government ruled by the National Party. Casualties were steadily mounting in the operational area and this factor would inevitably influence future voting. The mood by the South African community for fighting in the north was waning.
- The pressure by the UN and the international community on South Africa, Angola and Cuba to establish peace in Southern Africa was increasing steadily. This was intensified by increased coercion on South Africa and Cuba to withdraw their military forces from the conflict zone, which was collectively mediated by the US and the USSR through ongoing peace talks – Chester Crocker played a huge role in this regard. The day for the implementation of Resolution 435 for the independence of SWA had finally dawned.

From these high-level political and military considerations a decision was made by the SADF to switch the offensive nature of Operation Hilti/Faction to a defensive posture. Instructions were subsequently issued to the SADF to withdraw from Angola's 5th Military Region and for 10 SA Division to be readied forthwith for mobile defence, which included a deliberate counteroffensive. The overarching mission for Operation Faction therefore remained the destruction of the enemy's conventional force either in SWA or Angola in the advent of an attack across the border. Only at the command of the Chief of the SADF would forces in Sector 10 be authorised to cross the border into southern Angola. In this way a complete paradigm shift by the South African government and SADF came into affect literally overnight.

If You Want Peace, Prepare for War – Operation Prone in the Making

On 30 June South Africa's Minister of Defence, General Magnus Malan and Minister for Foreign Affairs, Mr. Pik Botha made an announcement to the media about the developing war situation in SWA. They proclaimed that the air attack by FAPLA on 27 June at Calueque was proof that the Cuban forces in Angola were not subservient to the Angolan military high command. The recent Cairo peace talks were mentioned, as well; it was declared that an agreement had been reached that the hydroelectric installation at Calueque would be protected against any attack. They pronounced that the peace talks between South Africa and Angola had reached a point where military engagement was no longer needed but that the Cubans were discontent with this development and were attempting to derail the process.

In response to the Cuban aggression a decision was made by the South African government to mobilise additional forces, comprising citizen forces as well, to contend with the heightened military threat in the northern operational area.

On 5 and 6 July I held a planning conference at the Army College in Pretoria for the finalisation of mobilisation and movement arrangements of South African forces to the operational area. The conference was attended by the commanders of 71 Motorised Brigade, 81 Armour Brigade, 44 Parachute Brigade; 10 Artillery Brigade and 4 South Infantry Battalion. Representatives from the following institutions attended as well: The HQ of SWATF; Sector 10; SAAF, South African Medical Services; Quarter Master General; Directorate Army Intelligence and Counter Intelligence; Chief of the Army, Directorate Training; directorates from all the combat participants namely infantry, amour, artillery, anti-aircraft and engineers; Director Logistic Services; Logistic Command; Directorate Signals; Directorate Technical Services; South African Defence Force Institute (SADFI). I used the conference to brief the respective attendees on the latest operational developments in theatre. I subsequently appointed Commandant Andrew Hudson as the coordinating officer for 10 SA Division to set our resolutions taken into action.

From 7–19 July Brigadier Chris Serfontein and the staff of Sector 10 and 10 SA Division commenced with the planning of Operation Hilti at Oshakati in accordance with the revised operational directives received from above. It was decided to fuse the HQ of Sector 10 into the one now being organised for 10 SA Division. The focus now was to finalise the operational plans and orders for the force being mobilised as quickly as possible. Serfontein was assisted by his two chiefs of staff, namely Colonel Eddie Viljoen who oversaw the planning for the counterinsurgency side, while I was responsible for the conventional warfaring part of Hilti/Prone.

By 19 July the name for Hilti changed to Prone, which was subdivided into Operations Linger and Pact. On this day 10 SA Division promulgated its written operations order for Operation Prone – Top Secret/OPSO 1/88/309 Op Prone/dated 19 July 1988. This allowed for an integrated operational framework for counterinsurgency as well as mobile conventional war as described in outline below:

- Operation Prone: Prone encapsulated the counterinsurgency as well as the conventional components of the war in northwest SWA and southwest Angola. The aim of which was to ensure military stability and to protect the territorial integrity of SWA.
- Operation Linger: Linger contained the counterinsurgency component of the war against SWAPO (PLAN) in Ovamboland and southern Angola, the aim of which was to neutralise the military capability of SWAPO. This included enhancement of closer relationships between second-tier local government structures and the security forces. It was equally set at protecting the infrastructure held by the security forces and state institutions against terrorism.
- Operation Faction, later renamed Pact: Faction/Pact was the operational framework established to contain the conventional threat posed by the 50th Cuban Division and their allies and intended to counter a conventional or semi-conventional attack by Cuban or any other force composition in Sector 10's area

of operations. The military mission was to protect the territorial integrity of SWA. In such an advent the SADF was prepared to destroy the conventional force of the enemy either inside SWA or externally in Angola. This operation had now turned to mobile defence. It was initially to be carried out within the borders of SWA. The battle design did not preclude later taking the offensive to the enemy within southern Angola.

The operational plan for Prone was based on a series of formal military appreciations and subsequent ongoing contingency planning by 10 SA Division. All the operational plans of the division were formally presented to and approved by the command structures of the SADF and SWATF. Military appreciations and assessments, contingency planning, directives, orders and instructions provided the principal means by which the intentions of 10 SA Division were conveyed to subordinate formations, staff bodies and units. This formed a critical link in the chain of command and thus became the indispensable tools of command-and-control. The process was supplemented by means of regular war-gaming.

The initial military appreciation about the enemy was based on deficient intelligence. A feasible operational plan however needed to be made as quickly as possible. Colonel Deon Steyn, with the intelligence teams from both the army and air force, were jointly responsible for the intelligence function of 10 SA Division. The original operational planning was founded on two possible enemy courses of action which the intelligence staffs produced, namely:[2]

Most probable course of action: The most probable enemy course of action foresaw the conventional enemy consolidating its tactical gains and reinforcing its defences right up to the border with SWA. The enemy's combined Cuban-Angolan-SWAPO conventional force would continue with strategic force projection in the region so as to establish viable deterrence. Such operational moves would support the high level political and military objectives of the Cuban and Angolan governments. The conventional force would deploy into positions from where a deliberate offensive could be launched into SWA if this became necessary. This option included high-density area operations in southern Angola by the enemy, intended to drive the counterinsurgency forces of the SADF and SWATF south across the border. These operations would be characterised by increased terror and political actions conducted purposefully inside SWA, simultaneously with deep penetrations by SWAPO's special Typhoon unit directed at the Tsumeb-Otavi-Grootfontein farming area. The overall operation would be supported by deliberate combined Cuban-SWAPO (PLAN) guerrilla raids launched at military bases at night. Possible targets identified were: Mahanene, Ombalantu, Okalongo, Etale, Onhangwena, Eenhana and a number of water towers. From the most probable operational mode the enemy could switch over to its most dangerous course of action at moment's notice.

Most dangerous course of action: The most dangerous enemy course of action considered pre-emptive enemy air assaults on Oshakati, Ondangwa and Grootfontein. The initiating phase, it was predicted, would follow the most probable enemy course of action. This would coincide with high level aerial reconnaissance over Ovamboland. Enemy forward assembly areas for a major offensive were assessed to be selected at Naulila, Cuamato and Ondjiva. Pre-aerial bombardments were expected on selected SADF military targets on D-Day at first light from the east out of the sun. The main enemy attack was expected to be launched

2 See Map 17.

along the tar road against Ondangwa from Namacunde via Santa Clara-Oshikango – an easterly flanking manoeuvre via Oshigambo was also considered. Two supporting attacks were anticipated. The one secondary attack leading from Cuamato to Oshakati; the other from Cuamato towards Ruacana. It was anticipated that the enemy's mobile reserve would employ in the vicinity of Cuamato. From there the mobile reserve could strike to the east or the west at the command of its forward command post. A reaction time of up to nine hours was allocated. A variety of envelopment and encirclement options, which could be taken by the enemy ground forces, were furthermore considered.

Priority targets selected for the counteroffensive: The following priority targets were identified and analysed by the intelligence staff: First priority: Xangongo, Ondjiva, Quiteve, Naulila, Cuamato, Nanquete, Capira, Calueque, Môngua, Lubango, Leba Pass and the train tunnel, Namibe, Chitado, Epupa falls, Oncocua and Mulemba. Second priority: Humbe, Catequero, Mucope, Evale, Anhanca, Techipa, Cahama and Tombua. Third priority: Mupa, Cuvelai and Mulondo. Fourth priority: Chibemba and Techamutete. Fifth priority: Matale and Jamba (near Indungo).

Battle indications: A list of battle indications (intelligence signatures) by the enemy was compiled. These intelligence telltales were carefully monitored on a daily basis so as to provide insight into the enemy's preparations of which anticipated course of action they were following; and for early warning. Situational awareness was maintained on a minute-to-minute basis.

The overarching mission for Prone was formulated as: "10 SA Division is to destroy any enemy force operating in the area of operations of Sector 10 from 2 August 1988 onwards." It was based on the strategic intent as set out by Chief of the SADF, SA Army and SWATF, namely: "The creation of a safe and secure environment in SWA with the underlying purpose of supporting political development and peaceful coexistence in the region."

The battle design of 10 SA Division for Operation Pact (conventional war-fighting component) relied on mobile defence in depth by buying time and causing casualties by yielding space. Rather than defeating the Cuban-FAPLA force with a single strong defensive line, defence in depth relied on the tendency of an attack to lose momentum over time as it covers a large area. Once the attacker had lost momentum and had overextended his logistics the intention was to counter-attack. As such Operation Pact was intended to be executed in three phases, namely:[3]

- Phase 1 – This phase made provision for the conduct of a deliberate well-planned deception operation against the enemy and to play for time. The aim as set was to deceive the enemy with regards to the disposition, strengths and intentions of own forces. This included the neutralisation of the enemy's intelligence-gathering capability. The preparation of the battlefield and the forces for future operations formed one of the foundations of the plan; another was to support counterinsurgency operations and to conduct counteroffensives against SWAPO raiders. Special Forces were deployed for early warning of possible enemy attacks and to monitor enemy movements and deployments on the front.
- Phase 2 – This phase of the operation was to be executed in the advent of a deliberate enemy offensive threatening the territorial integrity of SWA. 10 SA Division was to be employed aggressively so as to delay and channel the enemy

3 See Map 17.

into killing zones of own choosing. The underlying aim was to effect maximum casualties through the fighting process. The overall intention of Phase 2 depended on the scale of the enemy's offensive. The ultimate outcome envisaged was to halt and destroy the enemy with the available force levels in theatre if possible.

- Phase 3 – This part of the plan was to be executed in the advent of Phase 2 not being completely successful – as a last resort. It made provision for a retrograde operation and included rendering maximum destruction to the enemy by means of a delaying battle. The enemy was to be halted near Tsumeb-Otavi on defendable terrain if it came down to it and adequately fixed for a final destruction battle. The final contingency plan still needed to be devised for the deliberate counteroffensive. Additional force levels were to be mobilised for the final destruction of the enemy should this become necessary.

The Order of Battle of 10 SA Division and the Operational Plan in Outline (Refer to Appendix A)

The division comprised three brigade-sized task forces, which were supported by: 10 Artillery Brigade, the SAAF, South African Navy, South African Medical Services; Special Forces and the required army support formations, units and services.[4]

- For the initial phase of the operation: Colonel Leon Marais was appointed commander of Task Force X-Ray; Colonel Mucho Delport of Task Force Zulu; Colonel Jan Lusse of Task Force Yankee; Colonel Jean Lausberg commanded 10 Artillery Brigade.
- The standard counterinsurgency motorised infantry battalions of Sector 10 formed an integral part of the main combat force for the execution of Prone. These units included: 51 Battalion (Ruacana); 53 Battalion (Ondangwa); 54 Battalion (Eenhana). 101 Battalion based at Ondangwa formed part of the fighting gathering. 101 Battalion was well experienced in counterinsurgency and mobile conventional war-fighting; especially the aggressive offensive part thereof. Their fighting Casspirs were manned by seasoned combat leaders and Ovambo guerrilla fighters.
- The logistic and medical installations of Sector 10 were located at Oshakati and Ondangwa.
- Air assets were deployed at Ondangwa (OA) and Grootfontein (GFTN). This included some Mirage and Impala combat aircraft, Alouette Gun-ships and Puma transport helicopters. All of these military installations mentioned above obviously formed potential targets for the enemy's conventional means (refer to the air force plan discussed in more detail below).
- A mobile airborne reaction force of company strength from 1 Parachute Battalion was based at Ondangwa. Ondangwa was also home to a contingent of army intelligence and Special Forces operatives.

All the northern operational sectors such as Sector 10, 20, 30 and 70 were supported with logistics and medical services from Northern Logistics Command (NLC) and its second-line service support units based at Grootfontein.

For the initial counterinsurgency phase, as well as Phase 1 of Operation Pact, the area

4 See Maps 2, 3, 4 and 17.

of Sector 10 was demarcated into two operational zones. The road leading from Ondangwa to Oshikango-Santa Clara was the inter-taskforce boundary, inclusive for Task Force X-Ray. Task Force X-Ray was responsible for the eastern operational zone; Task Force Zulu for the western operational zone. The main immediate mechanised threat lurked across the western sector from the recent fighting at Techipa. Task Force Zulu was therefore suitably grouped with tanks to counter this initial threat. Task Force Yankee was the designated mobile reserve for 10 SA Division during Phase I of Operation Pact. At the same time Task Force Yankee, forces from 81 Armour Brigade, 71 Motorised Brigade and 10 Artillery Brigade were to be prepared for the conventional war fighting mission for Phase 1–3 of the operation as specified above.

One of the specific actions planned over this period as a contingency was an airborne operation called Operation Magersfontein against Namibe (known as Moçâmedes during the reign of the Portuguese). Namibe lay on the coast of Angola in the south.[5] It was a remote coastal town with a harbour and was therefore quite vulnerable to attack from the sea and the air; definitely not from the land. From Namibe major logistics flowed by road through the exceptionally difficult Leba pass on the way to Lubango-Cahama-Ondjiva. This included fuel and spares, which was the lifeblood of the large Cuban-FAPLA mechanised force deployed in southern Angola. The nature of the target and its supply route to the east was equally susceptible to attack by Special Forces and guerrilla marauders. The other main enemy supply route as far as Ondjiva in the south stretched from Luanda in the far north. The route was extended and arduous. The South Africans and UNITA knew that the logistic troops of FAPLA could never truly protect themselves adequately; far less than their regular combat forces who never really impressed.

Namibe was the ideal target to strike at the enemy in depth, so as to cause psychological paralysis and physical disruption of the enemy's logistics and command. There was however one problem. A restriction had been placed by the Chief of the SADF on the employment of large-scale airborne forces in the operational area. This was due to the enemy's formidable air defences covering southern Angola, which was adequately enclosed by Russian-manned air control and radar systems. South Africa could not run the risk of losing one transporter aircraft filled with young national service paratroopers at the time – it would have been a military as well as a political disaster. It was however assumed by the South African planners that the restriction would be lifted on the airborne forces in the advent of the war escalating.

The man responsible for the planning of the airborne operation against Namibe in all secrecy was Commandant McGill Alexander. He was a seasoned paratrooper with adequate operational experience, soon to be appointed the officer commanding of 44 Parachute Brigade and subsequently to be promoted to colonel. Alexander was an exquisite operational planner. He was positioned against the back wall in the Askari Hall with his maps and a small planning team, enthusiastically planning his airborne strike at Namibe. Alexander duly commenced with the planning of the airborne operation, which was later on developed into a full-blown exercise held at Walvis Bay. The SAAF, South African Navy and Special Forces formed part of the planning and exercising formalities. 2 Parachute Battalion (citizen force) as well as national service paratroopers from 1 Parachute Battalion in Bloemfontein were mobilised for the exercise. This included the necessary supporting

5 Refer to Chapter 5 on terrain.

elements required to form a composite combat grouping. The airborne combat force was designated 14 Parachute Battalion Group, under command of citizen force Commandant Jet van Zyl. The airborne combat grouping consisted of a parachute battalion; an artillery battery; an anti-aircraft troop; a field engineer troop; an anti-tank platoon equipped with Ferret reconnaissance cars and; the required medical, signal and logistic support. The paratroopers planned to capture Namibe in one day. On completion of the exercise at Walvis Bay the paratroopers returned to Sector 10 and deployed as part of Prone. They remained on standby for the execution of the airborne assault at a moment's notice.

The purpose of the SAAF plan for Operation Pact (conventional operation) was to support the land battle against the enemy's conventional forces. All allocated and deployed air assets for Operation Prone, including SAAF air defence and radar units were under control of 310 Air Force Command Post in Windhoek. In case of an all-out battle, the SAAF considered the pre-emptive bombing of the enemy's air assets on all their forward airfields, while most of the attack aircraft were still on the ground. Another idea catered the possibility of enticing some of the fighter aircraft into flight and then to bomb the airfields whilst the enemy aviators were airborne. They would then have the wide choice of Africa to land in. The SAAF had special bombs which could penetrate and crater the reinforced tar and concrete surfaces of airfields. These bombs had been used successfully in the past wars in Angola. Target acquisition, analysis and planning catered inter alia for the enemy's command-and-control systems; forward command posts; communication relay stations; convoys; enemy concentrations and reserves; communication lines. Fighter aircraft were kept safely in reserve, but remained on immediate standby to support forward operations. Adequate air-to-ground communications had already been established with all combat participants. Logistic preparations and forward dumping for an all-out air battle to support the land battle were already in progress.

The SAAF plan for Operation Linger continued to support counterinsurgency operations and to aid in neutralising the military capability of SWAPO (PLAN). The air assets were deployed at forward airfields and at Ondangwa.

I had requested the participation of the Senior Command and Staff Course of the Army and their directing staff (DS) in the operational planning from 26 July until 4 August. This gave them a golden opportunity to gather operational experience and to support our HQ with the development of a wide range of contingency plans. Their chief instructor was the operationally experienced Colonel André Kruger, a veteran of both Operations Reindeer and Protea. The members returned to the Army College in Voortrekkerhoogte, on 4 August, but were kept on standby to perform duties as key personnel of 10 SA Division if this became an operational necessity.

Force and mission training of the incoming force was held at Oshivello from 31 July to 12 August. The force then moved to a designated training area southeast of Ruacana in Ovamboland for more advanced joint combat training and exercises to prepare for Pact. The Training occurred under supervision of the training team of the Army Battle School led by Colonel Wouter Lombaard, who was the second-in-command of the school. Training was done as realistically as possible and was based on the contingency planning for Pact and was done with live ammunition. All of the training formed part and parcel of the deception plan. Such deception initiatives were augmented by means of communication operations and rumour offensives. In addition heavy vehicular and armament movements were regularly planned and executed on the road between Grootfontein-Oshivello-

Ondangwa-Oshakati-Ruacana. This included increased radio communications and the sporadic deployment and movement of the mobile tactical HQ of the division in the area of operations. Through these means the SADF bought time and space to restore the balance of power and to regain the initiative the enemy had momentarily enjoyed. In the meantime Taskforce X-Ray and Yankee continued with counterinsurgency operations as the remainder of the force was made combat ready for their main mission. Holding and deception operations thus formed an integral component of the battle design designated as key tasks for Phase 1 during Operation Prone. Over the same period I requested Colonel Deon Steyn and his intelligence and security staffs to undertake a study on the command and operational disposition of the 50th Cuban Division as previously described.

By 4 August Sector 10 issued its operations order for Operation Linger (counterinsurgency) as re-appreciated under the guidance of Colonel Eddie Viljoen. The intention of this plan was to exploit the higher force levels Sector 10 was now fortunate to have deployed in its area of operations.[6] The plan covered the period from 20 August to 1 November and the mission read as follows: "Sector 10 is to militarily counter the revolutionary war of SWAPO in the area of operations so as to effectively support the current peaceful political developments in SWA". The plan made provision for high-density counterinsurgency as well as deception operations and invariably supported the battle design for conventional war in the sector and vice versa.

The Enemy Tests the SADF's Defences on the Border – The Proof Lies in the Eating

A water tower named Alpha Tower on the border near Santa Clara/Oshikango was attacked by the enemy with rockets and mortars on 26 July. It was obvious from intelligence gathered that the enemy was probing the SADF's defences and resolve and that they were enticing them to cross the border. Similarly, on 1 August from 00:10 until 01:20 a combined Cuban-FAPLA-SWAPO raiding force attacked the temporary military base at Okalongo on the SWA-Angolan border with rockets and mortars. I had accounted for this ordeal experienced by a company of 1 South African Coloured Corps and on how I had exercised the Tac HQ of 10 SA Division from Oshakati via Okalongo to Etale and back again in Chapter 5 on leadership and command. A combination of more than 50 122 mm rockets and 82 mm mortar bombs had been fired into the base; fortunately none of the inhabitants were killed. From an intelligence report (handwritten – 10 Art Bde/302/Op Prone/9 Aug 88) compiled by Major Clive Wilsworth, intelligence staff officer 10 Artillery Brigade, it became apparent:

> The enemy raiding force had come from southern Angola and was escorted and protected by eighteen Russian BTR60 armoured troop carriers. The enemy used sophisticated measurement techniques for the locating of fire positions and adjustment of indirect fire; in their wake they left two harassing minefields in advent of pursuit. The local population were informed by the raiders that there was 'a big war coming.'

It was deduced that the enemy was from SWAPO's "Artillery Striking Unit", who were operating in close cahoots with FAPLA and the Cubans. This was not an insurgent party;

6 Operation Linger Counterinsurgency Plan, hand written, dated 1 August 1988 (in possession of the author).

it was a determined conventional force of more than company strength. There was now a thinking enemy on the other side. The war had become extremely interesting and perhaps much more serious than in the past.

By 4 August I was satisfied that our Tac HQ was combat-ready and duly reported such to Brigadier Chris Serfontein. All the key personnel required for the main HQ as well as the mobile Tac HQ of 10 SA Division had not yet arrived at Oshakati. Force planning and preparation however continued unabatedly. The HQ personnel of the division comprised permanent force, citizen force and national service members. The Mobile Tac HQ consisted of 13 Ratel-Command vehicles and other assortments of transport. (See Appendix A for the allocation of key personnel to vehicles.) A small administrative logistic tail was added to the HQ array. A HQ defence section of ten men was responsible for local protection and general duties. A paratrooper defence (protection) company was on stand-by to accompany the Tac HQ during field deployments for added protection. The defence company was equipped with seventeen mine-protected Buffel troop carriers.

The Main HQ of 10 SA Division as well as those of the brigade-sized task forces became fully operational by 4 August. The Main HQ of 10 SA Division and its Tac HQ operated from Oshakati, whilst an alternative HQ was located at the HQ of 53 Battalion at Ondangwa.

From 4 August until 1 September the following missions were performed by Task Forces X-Ray and Zulu for Phase 1 of Prone, while the remainder of the division was made combat and mission ready: Border protection; counterinsurgency; planning and preparation to counter-attack any enemy force threatening own operational bases and installations; protection of infrastructure; communication operations (psychological operations); intelligence gathering; deception operations; preparation for the control of the emergency evacuation of the civilian population and families of the military staff under threat if this became necessary; preparation for participation in the destruction battle against a conventional or semi-conventional enemy when so required and ordered.

A Ceasefire was Reached by 22 August 1988 – from War to Peace in the Blink of an Eye

It eventually became necessary for the SADF only to execute Phase 1 of Operation Pact. The reason for this being that events were overtaken by a ceasefire agreement which was signed by South Africa, Angola and Cuba in Geneva on 5 to 8 August. The final signing of the ceasefire agreement by the warring parties followed on 22 August at Calueque. In all honesty, the move by Castro's 50th Cuban Division and the fighting with South African forces at Calueque had driven the lagging negotiations for peace to a cusp. Something of value had materialised from these recent gigantic military clashes and manoeuvres. The provisions of the ceasefire in southern Angola inter alia related to the ending of hostilities and the subsequent withdrawal of the SADF from Angola. The Geneva Protocol furthermore applied arrangements for the progressive northwardly withdrawal of the Cuban forces from southern Angola and eventually from Angola and their return to Cuba.

A Joint Military Monitoring Commission (JMMC) was subsequently set up at Ruacana on 16 August to further negotiate the peace and the ceasefire terms of reference at the more practical operational level. Meetings of the JMMC took place on a daily basis on the southern bank of the Cunene River, close to Calueque and Ruacana. This particular arrangement was mutually agreed to by the South African, Angolan and Cuban delegations.[7] The SADF provided the infrastructure in the field for these gatherings. The process included comprehensive arrangements for the implementation of the higher-level ceasefire provisions and the final ending of hostilities. Arrangements determined by the JMMC extended to the ongoing monitoring of mutual agreements relating to the implementation of the ceasefire and peace settlement process which was to follow. These said additional JMMC monitoring activities alternated between Angola and SWA, as was mutually scheduled and agreed to.

The JMMC comprised members from the South African, Cuban and Angolan Armed forces. Colonel Archie Moore (deceased) was appointed by Chief of the Army and the GOC SWATF to lead the military delegation of the SADF. I used the opportunity to second Commandants Craig Harrison and Andrew Hudson to the JMMC as both these officers were members of the South African Army College and with me at Oshakati at the time.

Negotiations were initially plagued by misgiving and apprehension from both sides. The joint negotiation working party soon settled down and a strange form of camaraderie developed. Colonel Archie Moore and Commandants Craig Harrison and Andrew Hudson did magnificent work. The joint team progressively developed close cohesion and interdependence. Negotiations for peace subsequently became a joint affair within a friendly atmosphere.

Harrison and Hudson diligently kept the minutes of the negotiations with the Cubans and Angolans. It was then typed on an Olivetti XT computer running off a generator in a tent at Ruacana (not at the base of 51 Battalion, but literally in the bush close to the Cunene River). Finishing touches to the minutes included a Cuban lieutenant helping the South African delegation with Spanish translation. The English, Spanish and Portuguese were typed by Harrison with various members of the joint delegation spelling out the words one by one. The word processing software at the time was PFS Write (long before MS-Word!) and a 9-pin dot matrix printer. Language accents were carefully added by hand with a black pen in Spanish and Portuguese. At one point Brigadier Chris Serfontein insisted on an Afrikaans copy as well. He was quickly outvoted (even by the SADF members). The finished document was of historical importance and needed to be "dollied" up. Harrison and Hudson used three white cardboard pages and three clear transparencies for this purpose. Red ribbon of about one metre long was purchased from a nearby cuca shop at Ruacana for R1,00. The final documents were bound with red ribbons and bows. These were the originals signed on behalf of the three countries. Somewhere in the archives in Pretoria, Havana and Luanda lies a triple-signed document tied up with red ribbon from a cuca shop and with the accents neatly added to the typing by hand!

During the same period a few of the military families, living at Oshakati and Ruacana, enjoyed the opportunity of meeting some of the Cuban and FAPLA negotiating members; those who were representing our erstwhile enemy. These social interactions were relaxed and occurred on the bank of the Cunene River near Ruacana and Calueque. At times these events were accompanied with a pleasant "braai". During such interactions crabs from Moçâmedes, Cuban cigars and Havana rum were exchanged for biltong and South African red wine. Across the river lurked the military hardware of the 50th Cuban Division. Near Calueque a few sparsely camouflaged T-55 tanks and BMP Armoured Personnel Carriers, halfway dug into the ground, were clearly visible from across the border. We could see

7 Interestingly enough SWAPO and UNITA did not form part of these peace negotiations.

the enemy's hardware – the strong smell of diesel wafted across the border in the warm Angolan breeze.

During a short visit to Oshakati in late August my wife, Henriette and young son, Pieter (then three and a half years old) were given the opportunity to visit the JMMC. They flew by Puma helicopter along the road from Oshakati to Ruacana. Underneath they could fleetingly view a number of telephone poles which had been demolished by SWAPO insurgents the previous night. At the Cunene River they met some interesting people. One was a tall Angolan MiG-21 pilot who's friend had been shot down recently during Operation Modular – as he flew next to him – by South African air defences in southeast Angola. Another was a Cuban colonel with the strange family name of Richard Wilson – son to an English father and Cuban mother – Wilson was an ardent socialist with whom Henriette had the opportunity to exchange some interesting ideas regarding his views on capitalism, communism, socialism and the war for Angola.

I used the same opportunity to take Henriette and Pieter to the helicopter landing site of the Cubans across the border near Calueque, using the Datsun Stanza of the commander of 51 Battalion at Ruacana, Commandant Leon Lamprecht. A short journey was taken across the border with some minefields glaringly visible. Young Pieter was given the opportunity to play in the cockpit of a Russian MI-8 helicopter with a few of the Cuban pilots. From their spontaneity and positive reactions it was clear that they had been away from home for some time and were missing their own children. Henriette was quite apprehensive about her youngest offspring literally being in enemy hands. She was therefore not too happy with this playful encounter. The De Vries family trio soon returned safely to Ruacana. Two days later Henriette and Pieter returned to Pretoria in a Hercules C-130 after their unique experience in the northern operational area of SWA.

A formal Peace Treaty was signed on 22 August near Ruacana on the southern bank of the Cunene River which effectively ended the hostilities between the South African, Angolan and Cuban military forces in southern Angola. The SADF/SWATF was represented by Major General Willie Meyer at the Ruacana signing ceremony. The Cuban forces were represented by General Leopoldo Frias and the Angolans by Colonel Antonio José. This significant historical step not only ended the said hostilities, it also ended the severe effect of the Cold War in southern Africa. The way was now paved for full-scale disengagement of the Cuban forces from Angola and the SADF from SWA. Plans for the implementation of UN Resolution 435 were subsequently set in motion at the higher political realm.

The next round of peace negotiations began in Congo Brazzaville on 24 August. On the same day the State President Mr. PW Botha, referring to the crisis in SWA, warned a joint session of Parliament that: "Experience has taught us not to expect too much too soon". At the talks in Brazzaville the timetable for the Cuban withdrawal was discussed. No decision was made and the parties agreed to continue their discussions in Brazzaville at a later date. The latter discussions in no way deterred SWAPO from continuing with its terrorist campaign. On the evening of 1 September two people were killed and at least fifteen injured when two powerful explosive devices rocked the central part of Windhoek.

Remaining Combat and Mission Ready Just in Case – Being Prepared

The overlay order of 10 SA Division was issued for Operation Prone on 26 August as a supplementary to the main division order (OPSO 1/88/Op Prone), which had been issued on 19 July. A number of map overlays were provided to the respective commanders as a foundation for the further planning and conduct of the operation; just in case of all-out war, if the ongoing peace negotiations became disrupted. The military mission in the overlay order was confirmed as: "The destruction of any enemy force entering the area of operations of Sector 10." The plan was supported by a comprehensive operational forecast of events. All of these ensued from a deliberate military appreciation and continued war-gaming. The order included a well worked out list of code words and nicknames, which were used as control measures for command-and-control.

The main challenge regarding the mobile defensive scheme remained the short distance the enemy's conventional forces needed to traverse from the border to key objectives inside Sector 10 – from the border to Oshakati and Ondangwa was a mere sixty kilometres. The operation therefore still made provision for a manoeuvre battle with the aim of rendering the enemy maximum casualties. Through the manoeuvre battle time was to be gained for the SA Army to mobilise its war reserve if need be. As such additional forces in South Africa were brought into readiness as a war reserve and were placed on stand-by in the advent of all-out war.

The enemy's disposition was monitored on a continuous basis. This was underpinned by the original military appreciation and continuous update of the operational, intelligence and other supporting plans. Contingency planning continued unabated. The main operational plan of 10 SA Division was therefore viewed as a basis for change. The operational plan was designed to buy South Africa time and to restore the equilibrium on the war front. Initiative and freedom of action needed to be regained at the political and military spheres. In the meantime the combat force remained ready to strike at moment's notice. To my mind symmetry at the front had been established by 2 August.

Operation Displace came to an end in southeast Angola near Cuito Cuanavale on 30 August. The South African holding force withdrew safely and unhindered by FAPLA and the Cuban forces to SWA. UNITA was left to fend for themselves in Angola without the support of the SADF.

The final withdrawal of all South African forces from Angola had been completed.

Aftermath of the War That Never was – Winding Down as Peace Settles

10 SA Division was disbanded by the SADF and SWATF on 1 September and the citizen forces were demobilised and returned home. This formality followed on the successful implementation of the ceasefire and the peace settlement.

A core SADF planning team continued with the development and maintenance of a range of contingency plans for Operation Prone. This was upheld in the advent of the peace agreement breaking down and hostilities resuming. I remained involved in this process. Firstline combat units deployed in northern SWA, such as 61 Mechanised Battalion Group, 32 Battalion and 101 Battalion remained at high readiness as a back-stop.

I returned to Pretoria on 3 September to resume command of the SA Army College, but remained on standby as the Chief of Staff of 10 SA Division in the advent of conventional war resuming in SWA. I continued with the maintenance and upgrading of the respective operational contingency plans for Sector 10 as was applicable for Operation Pact. This included operational planning conducted for mobile operations in the rainy season within northern SWA and southern Angola. For the latter study I was supported by citizen force Lieutenant Jacob Helberg, a very able university graduate who specialised in this particular field. Optimal utilisation was made of the extensive studies undertaken by Potchefstroom University for the SADF in this regard. Helberg was provided with an office at the Army College for this purpose.

On 3 September I sent a telex message (Secret/309/Op Prone/Contingency Planning) from Sector 10 to Chief Army Operations. This was to initiate some of the selected contingency planning with the priority focusing on the destruction of the enemy's tanks in Sector 10 and the 5th Military Region, should this become necessary. The study relating to enemy tank destruction was to be based on the enemy's most dangerous course of action – it is a large scale deliberate armour and air offensive into SWA. Intelligence indicated that the enemy by now possessed close on three hundred and seventy nine (379) tanks in theatre. These were modern T-54/55 and T-62 main battle tanks. Some of these tanks were equipped with modern laser rangefinders and reactive armour. I requested Chief of the Army to appoint Colonel Anton Fourie (directorate armour) as the chief coordinator for the study. Brigadier Chris Serfontein was to act as the chairperson for the first meeting, which was scheduled to take place at Oshakati from 6 to 7 October 1988. Chief of the Army was also requested to provide specialists and some of the members requested to attend were Majors André Retief and Tim Rudman. These two seasoned officers had participated in tank battles during operations in southeast Angola before. Other members were Colonel Jan Breytenbach (called up from retirement) and Major Les Rudman. These two officers had extensive operational experience and they had also participated in a study relating to guerrilla war and fighting against tanks within a Southern Africa context.

On 6 September the peace-talks were resumed in Congo-Brazzaville. At this meeting it was noted that the SADF had in terms of the Geneva Protocol withdrawn from Angola before 1 September and that the JMMC was still functioning satisfactorily. The respective delegations reaffirmed their commitment to Resolution 435 and Cuba subsequently offered to withdraw its forces from Angola over the next three years.

During the joint session at Congo-Brazzaville the South African delegation raised the issue of the alleged shipment of additional Cuban troops and ordnance. The Cuban delegation strongly denied these allegations which were, inter alia, made in Washington by officials of the American Government. They stated that they were continuing with the normal supplying of their soldiers as well as the replacing of troops who had completed their term of duty in Angola. The discussions ended without adopting any important resolutions and the respective delegations returned home to report to their governments.

The discussions were again resumed in Congo-Brazzaville on 26–27 September. At the first combined session on 27 September the Cuban delegation accused South Africa of using delaying tactics. The biggest stumbling block, however, remained the withdrawal of the Cuban forces from Angola. Although a combined statement to the contrary was issued after the discussions, it became clear that the proposed date of implementation of Resolution 435 on 1 November was not possible.

More than a month elapsed before the parties met on 10 November in Geneva for the next round of peace talks. On this occasion the timetable for the Cuban withdrawal became a focal point of the negotiations and the respective parties made a concerted effort to reach an agreement. Certain proposals concerning the Cuban withdrawal were tentatively agreed upon and were submitted to the respective governments. These were later on accepted.

On 17 November the General Assembly of the UN once again appealed to South Africa to relinquish SWA. It also rejected the withdrawal of Cubans from Angola as a prerequisite for the implementation of Resolution 435 and confirmed its support for SWAPO. By this action the decisions taken a few days before at Geneva, were completely ignored. The discussions were continued in Brazzaville on 1–2 December. At this meeting the Director General of Foreign Affairs, Mr. Neil van Heerden, and his team negotiated with the Cuban and Angolan delegations for verification of the Cuban withdrawal.

The Minister of Defence, General Magnus Malan referred to the activities of the SADF in Angola at a passing out parade at Dunnottar on 1 December by saying that "the SADF had gained an impressive victory over the forces of Cuba and the MPLA government of a magnitude which has not yet been achieved in the modern history of semi-conventional warfare". General Malan added that this victory had forced Cuba and the MPLA regime to the conference table. "It is in a spirit of victory that our forces were withdrawn from Angola. There never were more than three thousand men and they had a prescribed and limited task".

The following day General Magnus Malan accompanied Mr. Pik Botha to Brazzaville to sign a formal agreement with Cuba and the MPLA Government. On their arrival at Mayo-Mayo, the two ministers were briefed on developments by the South African negotiating team. Thereafter further discussions were held with the US Assistant Secretary of State for African Affairs and Chairman of the Brazzaville meeting, Dr. Chester Crocker. There was every indication that an important breakthrough had been made and that the Brazzaville Protocol would soon be signed. This, however, did not materialise at this round of talks. The South African delegation returned to South Africa on 4 December. The obvious and sudden departure of the South Africans were severely criticised by the Cuba and Angolan delegates.

On 13 December the South African delegation was back in Brazzaville. This time no fundamental differences surfaced and the Brazzaville Protocol was signed, formally ending hostilities in Angola. The signing ceremony took place in the Palais de Peuple (the people's palace) in the presence of 200 representatives from many countries, the Congo and the international media. In terms of the provisions of the Brazzaville Protocol it was recommended to the Secretary General of the UN that 1 April 1989 be the date of implementation of Resolution 435. The parties would also meet in New York on 22 December to sign the final tripartite agreement and the bilateral peace treaty between South Africa, Cuba and the MPLA government. The Brazzaville Protocol also provided for the setting up of a combined commission to act as a forum for discussion and solving matters concerning the interpretation and application of the subsequent tripartite agreement. It was further agreed that prisoners of war would be exchanged after the tripartite agreement was signed on 22 December.

After signing the Brazzaville Protocol, President José Eduardo dos Santos of Angola made a plea for international financial assistance to finance the withdrawal of the Cubans. He estimated the cost at R1 840 million (800 million dollars). At the same time, in Lusaka the secretary for information and publicity of SWAPO, Mr. Hidipo Hamutenja, welcomed the signing of the Brazzaville Protocol.

The signing of the Brazzaville Protocol was not the only newsworthy happening on that day in the history of SWA. On that day two Angolan MiG-21 fighter aircraft crossed the border and flew in a southerly direction across the SWA-Angolan border. One of the aircraft later returned, but the second made a forced landing on a farm near Otjiwarongo. The pilot landed safely and was taken prisoner. After this incident the Minister of Defence

General Magnus Malan said that although the aircraft were observed on radar screen by the security forces they were not shot down because the SAAF acted in keeping with the spirit of the Brazzaville Protocol.

Incidentally, the State Security Council of South Africa approved the provisions of the proposed tripartite agreement at an extraordinary meeting held in Cape Town on 20 December. That evening the South African delegation, under the leadership of Mr. Pik Botha, was already on their way to the UN in New York to sign the agreement. The tripartite peace accord was reached between South Africa, Angola and Cuba in New York on 22 December, in accordance with the so-called "New York Three Powers Accord" and the "Brazzaville Protocol". The accord was signed by the three ministers of foreign affairs. The said agreement inter alia made provision for: The independence of Namibia in accordance with the United Nations (UN) Resolution 435; the withdrawal of the Cuban forces from Angola; the withdrawal of South African forces from Namibia. Further provisions of the peace treaty entailed the establishment of a "Joint Monitoring Commission (JMC)" to oversee the implementation of the peace accord in Angola and Namibia. Provision was made for representatives from the US and USSR, as official observers, to monitor the peace implementation process. This important agreement paved the way for the implementation of Resolution 435 and the negotiated settlement plan for SWA.

The Cuban withdrawal from Angola, as well as that of the SADF, was aligned with the mutually agreed to political process for the implementation of Resolution 435 in Namibia. The following provisions were mutually agreed to for the withdrawal of the said forces respectively from Angola and Namibia:

SADF withdrawal from SWA/Namibia: In terms of the agreement the negotiated settlement plan would be implemented on 1 April 1989. The RSA's military personnel would, in terms of the provisions of Resolution 435, be withdrawn from South West Africa from this date. It was undertaken that on 13 May 1989 there would be a maximum of 13,000 South African soldiers in SWA and on 24 June this figure would be no more than 1 500. This meant that only 1 500 would be in specific camps on polling day (1 November 1989). One week after certification by the UN of the result of the elections all remaining South African troops would be withdrawn from SWA. The SWATF had to be demobilised six weeks after the implementation of Resolution 435 (on 13 May 1989).

The Cuban withdrawal from Angola: The bilateral treaty between Cuba and the MPLA government concerning the Cuban withdrawal from Angola was also signed on 22 December 1988. This provided for the withdrawal of approximately 50,000 Cuban soldiers from Angola over a period of 27 months. The withdrawal and regrouping of Cuban forces were to start on 22 December and by 1 April 1989 the withdrawal of 3,000 soldiers needed to be finalised. The withdrawal would be monitored by a team of 90 men known as UNAVEM (United Nations Angola Verification Mission). UNAVEM consisted of a headquarters in Luanda and several observation teams to be deployed on 1 April 1989. According to the timetable for the Cuban withdrawal all Cuban troops should have withdrawn by 1 August 1989 to the north of an adjusted 15th parallel. On 1 November 1989 (the polling date for SWA) all Cuban soldiers should withdraw north of an adjusted 13th parallel. On the same date half of all Cuban forces in Angola needed to be withdrawn and on 1 April 1990 two thirds of their force. By October 1990 76% of the troops should have left Angola. By 1 January 1991 there should not be more than 1 200 troops in Angola and, six months later, all Cuban troops should have left the country.

The implementation of UN Resolution 435 for the independence of Namibia officially commenced on 1 April 1989. A ceasefire agreement between the SADF, SWATF and SWAPO came into effect. A combined UN civilian and peacekeeping force, under Finnish diplomat Martti Ahtisaari, was deployed to supervise the military withdrawals of Cuban and South African forces. His work included the return of SWAPO exiles and the holding of Namibia's coming first ever one-person one-vote election for a constituent assembly and its final independence.

On 1 April 1989 SWAPO (PLAN) launched a major surprise incursion over the Namibian-Angolan border from the 5th Military Region into neighbouring Ovamboland. The PLAN offensive occurred soon after the JMMC was dissolved. The purpose of SWAPO was to establish a position of strength, as basis for political manipulation for the oncoming democratic election. Their devious act was a gross violation of the peace accord. Some SADF/SWATF/Koevoet operational units, including 61 Mech and 101 Battalion were summarily released from base. A series of vicious battles ensued with a large number of PLAN insurgent combat units resulting in close on 300 PLAN fighters being killed and many more wounded during this disastrous foray of SWAPO. The Security Forces suffered 125 casualties during the same period. A total of 21 Casspir mine-protected vehicles of Koevoet as well as one Ratel infantry combat vehicle of the SADF were destroyed in contacts with the insurgents. This battle was referred to as "The Nine Day War" and by the SADF as "Operation Merlyn." This deliberate act of war by SWAPO became a political catastrophe for them as was seen through the eyes of the UN and the international community. South Africa was clearly committed to withdraw from Namibia and the incursion did not change their resolve in this regard. On 4 April British Prime Minister Margaret Thatcher clearly expressed her dissatisfaction regarding the devious incursion by PLAN and condemned it as a direct contravention of the agreed UN peace process. The so called "Mount Etjo Agreement" undertaken jointly between the SADF, SWATF and SWAPO on 9 April ended the tragedy.

On 22 June 1989 the Angolan MPLA government and UNITA agreed on a ceasefire. The MPLA was represented by President dos Santos and UNITA by Dr. Jonas Savimbi at the signing ceremony. The formality took place in Gbadolite, Zaire. The ceasefire was broken in July 1989 and hostilities between the MPLA and UNITA subsequently resumed.

By November 1989 the last remaining South African forces departed from Namibia. On the 7th Namibia held its first ever national election. The election was won by SWAPO although it did not gain the two-thirds majority it had hoped for; the South African-backed Democratic Turnhalle Alliance (DTA) became the official opposition party in Namibia.

Interestingly enough, on 9 November 1989 the Iron Curtain completely collapsed overnight. The historic event formed part of the "Autumn of Nations Revolution" in the Soviet Union. The abrupt fall of the "Iron Curtain" was symbolized by the opening of the Berlin Wall. All of these happenings in the Soviet Union came as a surprise to the West. The Soviet Union was dissolved by the end of 1991 and resulted in Russia and fourteen nations declaring their independence from the Soviet Union, which brought an end to the Cold War. The fall of the Soviet Union further stimulated the process for peacemaking and political reconciliation in Namibia as well South Africa.

Namibia celebrated its independence in Windhoek on 21 March 1990 and Sam Nujoma was sworn in as the first Black president of a democratic Namibia. South Africa's former protectorate finally obtained its independence after 106 years of foreign occupation by Germany, Britain and South Africa. Namibia has held free and fair elections every five years ever since. (On 4 April 2002 a ceasefire agreement was finally reached between the Angolan government and UNITA, effectively ending their civil war which had lasted for 27 years.[8])

South Africa achieved its independence as a fully democratic state on 27 April 1994 and Nelson Mandela was sworn in as South Africa's first Black State President in Pretoria on 10 May.[9]

Closure – Afterthoughts about the War That Never Was

The year of 1988 had been an interesting one for southern Africa and all its weary and somewhat anxious onlookers worldwide. Could the South African Border War, which had lasted for more than twenty-two years, truly be ended and long-lasting peace achieved in Southern Africa? In all fairness, the politics and international pressure raging internationally and regionally vis-à-vis the conflict in southern Africa at the time was most probably the balancing factors which prevented all-out war. However, it was the conventional war-fighting in southern Angola as such, which had ignited this amazing drive for peacemaking and the democratic changes experienced in Namibia and South Africa in its aftermath.

On the other hand, if it had happened Operation Prone would have been a grand-marshal affair and a colossal clash of arms which would have been a huge test of military men, their mettle and war machines. I truly believed at the time and still do that the South Africans at the operational and tactical levels of war were more than a match for FAPLA and their supporting Cuban armed forces. The two single factors I put forward were the tactical prowess and combat leadership of the South African soldier which caused FAPLA-Cuban weariness. South Africa's superior military capability at the tactical level of war was clearly demonstrated by the vastly outnumbered South African fighting brigade during Operations Modular, Hooper and Packer in southeast Angola in 1987–88.

This particular war had nothing to do with the numbers of men or the tonnage of machines and material; it was about human will, sheer endurances and tactical dexterity. In addition, the nature of the terrain and operational space were well-suited for integrated mobile conventional and guerrilla warfare as applied by the SADF. This was the forte of the South African fighting men and not of the FAPLA and Cuban soldier who were overly accustomed to positional warfare.

A few afterthoughts: Castro was probably somewhat wary of giving the American armed forces an excuse to intervene in Southern Africa, if he went too far. The US lurked within close striking distance. As such, the shipping lane from Havana to Moçâmedes (Namibe) and Luanda was extremely exposed. The enemy's supply and reinforcement route was susceptible to attack by any air or naval means. Furthermore, the USSR during this particular quarrel in southern Angola and the dwindling cold war was becoming progressively less and less of a political and military factor in the region.

The question then remains: Why did the Cubans not take the initiative in May–June 1988 to offensively cross the border into SWA, even with their added advantages of overwhelming mechanised combat forces and uncontested air power? With all due respect, the enemy required far more than two or even three conventional divisions to seriously take on the South Africans militarily in southern Angola and northern SWA. A staunch

8 Government troops killed Jonas Savimbi on February 22, 2002, in Moxico province.

9 See Chapter 17.

and unfaltering political and military will was another important missing ingredient. The Cubans knew well that if they crossed the battle line that the South Africans would be unforgiving. So be it at the operational and tactical levels of war.

At the strategic level they were cautious of not being drawn into their own "Vietnam" in Africa. The battlefield was notoriously well suited for protracted war. If it came to that it could be used extremely well to exchange time and space for the progressive attrition of enemy numbers and materiel. On the other hand, perhaps, just perhaps the Cubans were apprehensive of South Africa's nuclear arsenal?

We will never know what would have happened if a gigantic clash of arms had occurred across the SWA-Angolan border? In my heart and mind I knew that we could have beaten them – intuitively and practically speaking. However, it would have been worth nobody's while.

What I learned was that this particular conventional war in southern Angola and the real possibility of its escalation had caused a better form of peace in southern Africa! The question remains: Will history repeat itself and bring about war once again?

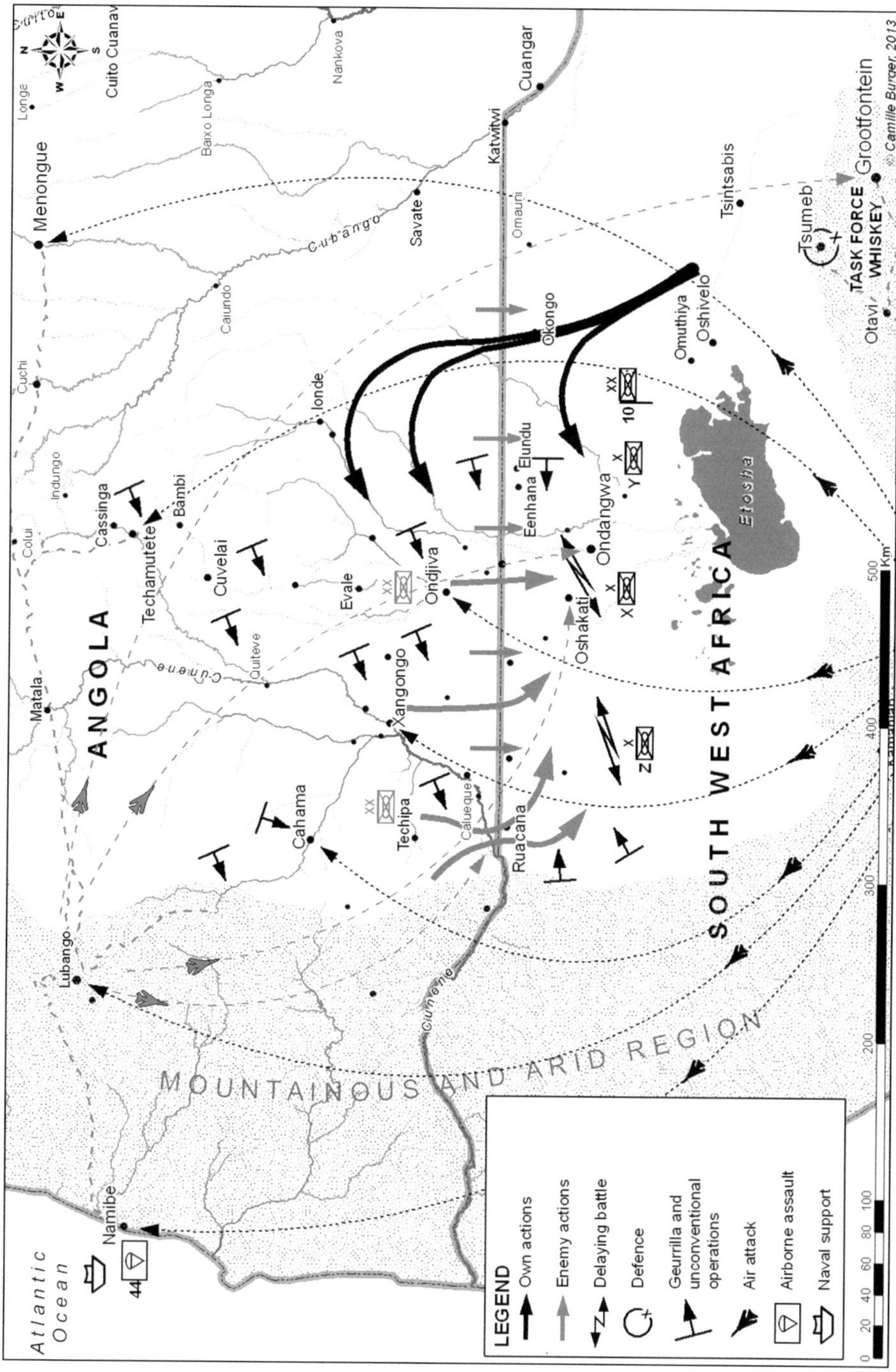

Map 17: Operation Prone – Contingency Plan for Mobile Defence

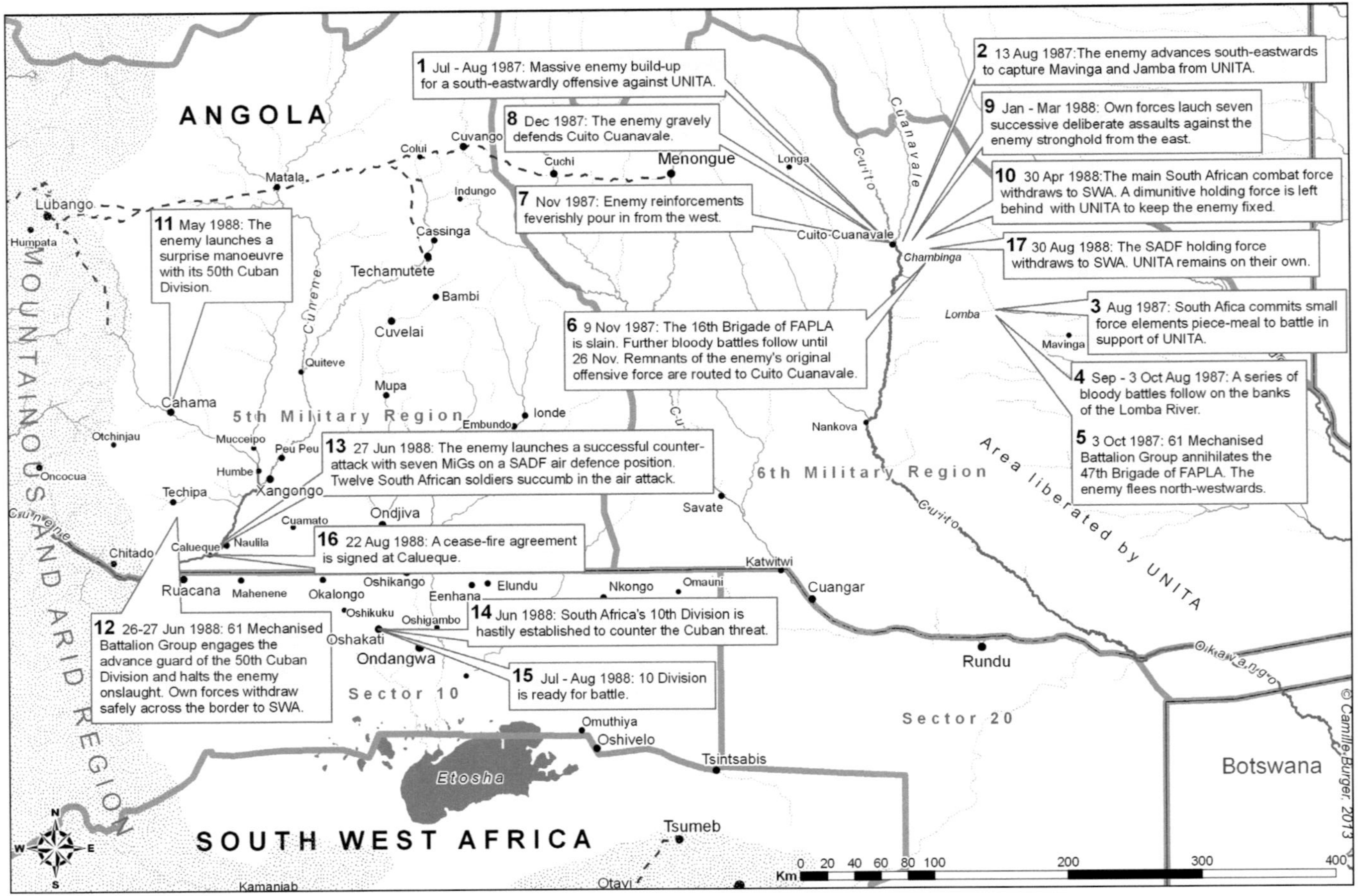

Map 18: From Operation Modular to Prone, 1987–88 – The Final Battle

PART 3

Recovering from Life – the Journey was Worth it

This was the point in time I realised that life for me had more facets and took more daring than just the military and warfare

Life is preparing for the middle adulthood stage and the last stage is recovering from it. Perhaps that is because as older adults we can often look back on our lives with happiness and are content, feeling fulfilled with a deep sense that life has meaning and we've made a contribution to life, a feeling Erikson calls integrity. Our strength comes from a wisdom that the world is very large and we now have a detached concern for the whole of life, accepting death as the completion of life. On the other hand, some adults may reach this stage in despair at their experiences and perceived failures. They may fear death as they struggle to find a purpose to their lives, wondering: "Was the trip worth it?"

So what was it to you Roland? Had you filled every unforgiving minute with sixty seconds' worth of distance run? Was the journey worth it?

17

A New Order of Things

Walking the Tightrope

There is nothing more difficult to carry out, nor more doubtful of success, nor more dangerous to handle than to initiate a new order of things.
Machiavelli

At Long Last: Political Change – A New Order of Things

Shock action! By 1994 long sought political change was upon South Africa. It was the sincere hope of millions in our country that the change would result in lasting peace and political stability and save our country from the imminent bloody revolution that had been in the offing!

On 27 April 1994 the African National Congress (ANC) won the first ever multiracial democratic election in South Africa and Nelson Mandela was inaugurated as our first Black President and the Supreme Commander of the newly formed South African National Defence Force (SANDF). This dramatic world event happened soon after the ANC and similar political organisations were unbanned and the ANC leader Nelson Mandela released from prison in February 1990 by President F.W. de Klerk. The apartheid system in South Africa was now ended through a series of negotiations between 1990 and 1993 and through unilateral steps taken by the government of De Klerk. These negotiations between the governing National Party, the ANC and a variety of other political organisations began in all seriousness on 20 December 1991 at the World Trade Centre in Kempton Park. It was known as the "Convention for a Democratic South Africa" (CODESA) and happened against a backdrop of political violence, including allegations of a "state sponsored third force" destabilising the country.

Through sheer determination from all sides the process was navigated through the stormy waters and eventually resulted in South Africa's first multiracial election on 27 April 1994. Today De Klerk is best known for engineering the end of apartheid and South Africa's racial segregation policy. Along with Mr. Nelson Mandela he supported the transformation of South Africa into a multiracial democracy for which they were jointly awarded the Nobel Peace Prize in 1993.

In January 1994 the advent of these dramatic political changes hit the South African Defence Force (SADF) like the surge of an Olifant main battle tank. Try to appreciate the situation from the perspective of soldiers swollen with pride within the ranks of a defence force that was reckoned to be the best on the continent of Africa: It had emerged from the Union Defence Force established by General Jan Smuts in 1912 and had fought with distinction in German South West Africa in 1915 and through two world wars.[1] The SADF

1 General J.C Smuts was the person who gave lead to the establishment of the Union Defence Force as defence minister by signing "The South African Defence Act" in 1912. By 1957 the New Defence Act (Act No.44 of 1957) was passed, which merged the former Union Defence Force into the South African

as an extremely effective military force had contained the threat on our northern border in Southwest Africa (SWA) from 1966 until 1989.

The transformation course the SANDF now embarked upon required clear heads and a well-structured programme. It played out as a three-act drama from 1994 until 1999 on a new global playing field and would necessitate the (1) awakening of the organisation to fundamental change, (2) the envisioning of its future and (3) re-architecting of its force design and structure as well as its organisational dynamics. It therefore entailed a sober perspective of both endings and new beginnings. This would include the integration of seven armed forces, some of them former adversaries, into one national defence force. These were the SADF, the former "Homeland Armies" of Transkei, Venda, Bophuthatswana and Ciskei as well as the former guerrilla forces of the ANC – Umkhonto we Sizwe, colloquially known as MK – and the Pan Africanist Congress's Azanian People's Liberation Army (APLA). Later on the Self-Protection Units of the Inkatha Freedom Party (IFP) were incorporated in the integration process. As such the transformation of the SANDF was considered by many informed global change management specialists as one of the most comprehensive and successful ever undertaken.

I would soon learn that to be effective, transformation implied taking ownership of the process and strong leadership and that it meant a change of heart, mind and spirit of all those who participated in this great patriotic challenge. The greatest challenge was to get people involved and excited about the endeavour, helping each other and generating high levels of positive emotional energy. I understood very well from the word go that it was going to be a dangerous and difficult path to follow requiring the proponents of change to walk a tightrope. I had no illusion that trust would be a major key to success. The latter was more fragile than a soft whisper.

As such I was privileged to fully participate in this process from 1994 until 1999: Initially from 17 January until 21 April 1994 as the co-leader of an army work group; later on from 1 October 1995 until 1 April 1997 as Director Transformation Management of the SANDF; from 1 April 1997 until 1 July 1979 as Chief of Joint Training, SANDF; and from 1 July 1998 until 30 April 1999 as Deputy Chief of the South African Army.

This was the point at which I, at the age of 55, decided to retire from the military in order to try my hand at things completely out of the ordinary for me – I only realised much later that it had remained "suspiciously military" in nature.

Participating intimately in the transformation of the SANDF for the next five years required all the battlefield and leadership skills I had accumulated throughout my military career. I would become to understand the wise words uttered by Machiavelli many years ago:

> There is nothing more difficult to carry out, nor more doubtful of success, nor more dangerous to handle than to initiate a new order of things. For the reformer has enemies in all who profit by the old order and only lukewarm defenders in all those who would profit by the new order!

In this chapter I chart difficult terrain. In difficult terrain you can expect unexpected attacks or hostile fire from the flanks or the rear. Let us now enter a few firestorms and occasionally return to the safety of its eye. What needed to be achieved in the SANDF,

Defence Force (SADF) as we knew it until 1994.

and the ways in which to accomplish it within the next five years, would defy traditional thinking and resonate for eternity! The time had passed for those in our defence force cleaving to non-dynamic mechanistic thinking. Let us leave the ordinary and enjoy the rhythms of manoeuvre.

Imperatives for and Resistance to Transformation – Death and Rebirth Processes

What did transformation mean to the "old" SADF and other integrating armies being redesigned as a new national defence force; one that was required to fit into a newly crafted democracy and rapidly changing strategic environment? Remember that the Berlin Wall had fallen and South Africa's war in South West Africa (Namibia) and with Angola and the Cubans had ended quite abruptly in 1988–89. Transformation therefore implied the unleashing of a dynamism which would have an impact on the whole organisation. It involved radical change, not a mere series of incremental remedies – it was like changing the course of the Titanic instead of just rearranging a few folding chairs on deck. For this reason transformation was not a few change programmes to improve productivity and standards, reduce personnel and cut costs. It required fundamental change: To organisational structures, to leadership, managerial and command structures, to the culture and behaviour of its members.

Why was transformation necessary? All of a sudden nobody was angry at South Africa anymore – probably more astounded than anything else – and the doors of the international community opened up in recognition and acceptance. The imperatives for change were clear-cut as our defence force needed to meet new requirements in its strategic environment and altered defence needs, such as, for example, to participate in peace operations in Africa instead of fighting against the "frontline states" as in the recent past.[2]

Furthermore fundamental political change and a shift in national priorities to socio-economic issues resulted in altered government's spending priorities and a reduced defence budget.

These changes suggested that a smaller defence force was needed for South Africa. However, as a result of the integration process required by the constitutional settlement, there was suddenly a larger SANDF. Democratic political imperatives furthermore resulted in the necessity for a transformed public service that was more representative of the whole South African population with new requirements for civil control, transparency and representation. Therefore, there was a need to design a defence force with an eye on its future tasks. These needs were eventually reflected in the newly approved White Paper on Defence (1996), which described the national defence policy, and were further expanded in the Defence Review (1998) and Defence Act (2002). The SANDF had to undergo fundamental transformation to meet these changing defence needs.

Nobody said that transformation was going to be easy. These were harrowing times for

2 The Frontline States (FLS) was established to achieve democratic majority rule in South Africa. It no longer exists. Former members included Angola, Botswana, Lesotho, Mozambique, Tanzania, Zambia and Zimbabwe. United States relations with the Front Line States were at its peak during the human rights push of the Carter administration. During the Reagan administration Assistant Secretary of State for Africa Chester A. Crocker, and the Front Line States were engaged diplomatically to achieve landmark peace accords between South Africa, Mozambique, Angola (Lusaka Protocol) and Namibia (New York Accords) – From Wikipedia, the free encyclopaedia.

South Africa as many incidents and individuals threatened to derail the negotiations. The transition that followed was a miracle and proceeded relatively peaceful, notwithstanding many innocent people who would still die violently, even "necklaced" with burning tyres to install fear. It was as if there were a conscious as well as unconscious conspiracy to make evolving peace and political changes fail! Dangerous and unfortunate things happened at the cusp of transformation, which caused a few firestorms to erupt from unexpected avenues. To mention only a few of these:

- Soon after the second plenary session of CODESA in June 1992 a massacre took place at Boipatong killing 46 residents by mainly-Zulu hostel dwellers. Mandela accused De Klerk's government of complicity in the attack and withdrew the ANC from the negotiations. This led to the abrupt end of CODESA for a while. The ANC took to the streets with "rolling mass action," which resulted in the Bisho massacre in September 1992. It was a tragedy when the ostensibly independent Homeland Army of Ciskei opened fire on protest marchers killing 28. Ronnie Kasrils himself had to duck for cover.
- This Bisho incident opened old wounds and conversely triggered the urgency to search for a fresh political settlement. Incidentally, Brigadier Mo Oelschig commanded the Ciskei Defence force at the time. In 1995 he was appointed as the Chief Director Transformation of the SANDF as a Major General by General George Meiring – later on this warranted the question of how insightful this particular appointment was. Notwithstanding of being a smart individual, Mo Oelschig had to bear the brunt of serious resistance from the two newly appointed ANC ministers of defence (Messrs. Joe Modise and Ronnie Kasrils) as well as the Joint Standing Committee on Defence, in particular its Chairman, Mr. Tony Yengeni.
- On 10 April 1993 Chris Hani, the leader of the South African Communist Party (SACP) and a prominent leader of the ANC, was assassinate. This act of defiance by white right-wingers brought the country to the brink of disaster. The situation was however superbly managed by Nelson Mandela and afterwards all the influential parties resolutely pushed ahead for a political settlement.
- The resumption of CODESA was dramatically interrupted in June 1993 when the right-wing Afrikaner Weerstandsbeweging (AWB), stupidly to my mind, barged into the World Trade Centre in Kempton Park with an armoured car, briefly disrupting the proceedings.
- Finally ... Remember the abortive coup in the tribal homeland of Bophuthatswana by heavily armed para-militarist white supremacist members of the AWB in March 1994 which included the mutiny of the Bophuthatswana Defence Force. President Lucas Mangope had requested the right-wing Afrikaner Volksfront (AVF) to assist with peacekeeping, which involved retired Chief of the SADF, General Constand Viljoen himself. Heavily armed, paramilitary members of the AWB invaded the territory claiming to have done so at the behest of Mangope. Three White South African militiamen were subsequently shot dead in front of filming cameras, while more than a hundred Bophuthatswana soldiers were killed – this blatant act of foolishness shook the South African community and the world.
- It is prudent to remember that this was the dark side to the obscure world of transformation we were living in. There were even a few minor things on the side

which I found interesting and relevant to mention; then I will draw a line regarding undue interruptions of the transformation process. In 1996 riotous ex-combatants of MK, those that were undergoing integration at Wahlmanstahl a few kilometres north of Pretoria, enthusiastically set the new subsidy car of Lieutenant General Siphiwe Nyanda ablaze while he was visiting and overseeing the process. This brought a few childish sniggers from certain quarters, but nonetheless indicated how precarious the transformation endeavour in the SANDF truly was!

- There were major doubts about defence transformation in the offing as well.[3] There was an apparent unawareness of the implications of transformation and this resulted in the projection of non-committal attitudes by many officers in top leadership positions. The Department of Defence (DOD) was riddled with pockets of resistance where passive as well as active defiance could be camouflaged through the guise of ongoing command and management. In many ways this was simply rooted in high degrees of anxiety and uncertainty about the future without being malicious in any way and was especially prevalent among the lower ranks. Entrenched cultures of the integrating forces had an impact in many ways on new forms of shared values, leadership, command and management to such an extent that it was difficult to unravel. The almost entrenched counterinsurgency culture, ways and means of the former SADF consistently made it difficult to clarify the new vision, mission, roles and tasks of the transforming defence force.
- The few transformers leading the process were filled with apprehension that political interference could result in misunderstandings, rash decisions and unrealistic demands. They were acutely aware of the magnitude of the task and the timeframe in which transformation had to be achieved, and filled with trepidation that it might fail because of the wild expectations of some of the transforming armies.
- In 1995 it was stated by the Council on Defence that transformation needed to be irrevocably on track and almost completed within a three-year time frame, a tall order.

Where did I Stand?

I have always been an optimist and to my mind there was hope for the future. I decided that in my small way I would participate enthusiastically in the process of creating the future plans of our defence force for posterity. It was a decision of will and with my family I felt extremely comfortable about this. To provide insight into where I stood from the outset regarding impending political change in South Africa I wish to express that I was pleased with what was happening in our country.

The career of arms required from those who seek it or were called upon to pursue certain military virtues: Courage, fidelity, patriotism ... Until now I had experienced in the military a common bond of interdependence, mutual interests, open communication and enthusiasm to build the best army in Africa. I would endeavour full-heartedly to do that once again as a member of the newly created SANDF. My enthusiasm and outspokenness, however, began to take its toll as certain cliques started targeting me maliciously as I moved into a more prominent position within the realms of transformation. I imagined that my

3 As formally expressed by the core defence transformation team of the SANDF on 11 April 1996 and presented to the Defence Staff Council (document in the authors possession).

zest to see transformation through was not appreciated by many of those I thought of as the "Pretoria guard." I was not going to forfeit my principles for their whims or the sake of promotion.

I had attended the Joint Staff Course at the Defence College, commanded by Brigadier George Kruys, in 1985. Kruys was a gifted strategist and one of our senior officers I truly respected and considered to be enlightened – that was probably why he eventually retired as a lowly brigadier and not as a general as he should have. He held exercises with us in which we had to state our future aspirations as the "other nationalities" living in South Africa as Blacks, Indians or Coloureds, and to compare the constitution of South Africa with the Freedom Charter of the ANC. I found these exercises most revealing. As this particular course was used as the gateway to future senior appointments and general's rank in the SADF for the selected few we could strategize to our heart's content and speak freely – this I truly enjoyed. I can remember well that three of the ideas our course recommended was for the governing National Party to sort out their restrictive politics soonest, to unban the ANC and to free Nelson Mandela. Wow, did that come from one of those authoritarian, hard-core militarists?

On the contrary, in 1989 certain extremely senior defence officials still declared vehemently that we would not negotiate with terrorists. This unwieldy outlook soon changed dramatically by 1990 when the ANC was disbanded by President F.W. de Klerk, and Nelson Mandela was freed.

Furthermore, I can recollect while I was the Chief of Staff of Northern Transvaal Command under command of Brigadier Gert Opperman, attending a workshop at the Hartebeespoort Dam early in 1991, when he was suddenly recalled to Defence Headquarters. This was to attend an urgent tête-à-tête with other members of the military command. He soon returned and told his brethren of colonels and other senior staff officers that he needed to assess our mood about the impending political changes. Was this beginning change management or something to that effect, or what?

As the most senior amongst equals I duly put up my hand to answer. Opperman said: "No, Roland, you speak last." So he took the answers of his colonels and other senior staff members first from left to right. Their replies, more or less true to form, questioned the wisdom of negotiating with the so-called terrorists. Last in line was yours truly, of course answering that it would be damn stupid not to do so and that it was about time. Little did I know what I was letting myself in for! I believed that many serving members in the defence force at the time thought that the phenomenon of apartheid would last forever. Nothing lasts forever. The governing ANC should take note of this as well – history tends to repeat itself.

I sincerely respected those difficult times in the history of South Africa when severe internal and external pressures over long duration had moved the Nationalist Government to finally accept the advent of full democracy. It was crystal clear that apartheid could neither be maintained by force forever nor overthrown by the opposition without considerable suffering.

I can remember well travelling to Plettenberg Bay on holiday in late December 1991 with my family, as we all listened to the CODESA proceedings over the radio, that we were highly excited about these new developments.

The aftermath of CODESA saw the establishment of a "Transitional Executive Council" created to manage the run-up to the democratic election. A "Joint Military Coordinating

Council" (JMCC) was formed to oversee the first wave of defence transformation and to kick-start the integration and demobilisation processes of the respective armies.

General George Meiring was appointed as the Chief of the SANDF with Lieutenant General Siphiwe Nyanda, a former MK commander, as his deputy. Lieutenant General Pierre Steyn was civilianised and became the Secretary for Defence and Head of the Department with Mr. Aboobaker Ismail serving as his new Chief of Policy and Planning.[4] To me, looking in from the outside, it was clear that there existed some friction between Meiring and Steyn, probably due to the position of Steyn as the new head of the department, although the two appointments had the same seniority level. Mr. Joe Modise was appointed as the Minister for Defence and Mr. Ronnie Kasrils as the Deputy Minister. At the time Mr. Ron Hayward was retained in the post of Chairman of Armscor. Together the two ministers, the chief of the defence force and the chairman of Armscor formed the new Council on Defence that was responsible to lead the transformation process.

Now I shall tell my story on how I perceived defence transformation to unfurl. It was an exciting (and somewhat dodgy) world we lived in, Master Jack!

The First Wave of Defence Transformation – Meeting Former Foes

Came 16 January 1994 I was peacefully commanding 7 South African Division, having an enjoyable time and minding my own business, when I received a telephone call from Chief of the Army, Lieutenant General Hattingh Pretorius who said, "Roland, please come and see me immediately".

Imagine my thoughts as I hastily steamed due north 56 km in my army Camry from the headquarters of 7 Division, which was located at Kensington in Johannesburg, to Army HQ in Potgieter Street.

"Sit down please, would you like some coffee?"

Yes, thanks General.

Hattingh Pretorius was an extremely experienced infantry officer and highly intelligent, having served as a military attaché in France and as a senior staff officer at Chief of Staff Intelligence before commanding Natal Command and eventually the army. I liked and respected him and had a good relationship with him. We had served together at the Infantry School in 1970–76 and in 1985 attended the Joint Staff Course together at the Defence Staff College in Pretoria.

General Pretorius duly informed me that he was appointing me as the leader of the army work group for transformation. My mission was to develop the vision, mission, mission success factors and force design and structure and implementation plan for the new army by 21 April 1994, as the change in government was scheduled for 27 April following national elections. He enlightened me that my team would be working for a Joint Military Coordinating Council (JMCC), which formed part of the planning mechanisms of the new transitional government. My liaison at Army HQ was Major General A.K. de Jager, Chief of Army Staff Planning. Pretorius told me to report at Kasteelpark the next morning, at Denel Head Office, where the JMMC would be working. The army workgroup would

4 Both Siphiwe Nyanda and Aboobaker Ismail had become well-known for the role they had played in the Church Street bombing in Pretoria on 20 May 1983 by Umkhonto we Sizwe (MK), the military wing of the African National Congress (ANC). The bombing killed 19 and wounded 217 and was one of the largest attacks by the ANC during its armed struggle against apartheid. The attack had been executed by a special operations unit of MK commanded by Ismail.

consist of selected members from the SADF, MK, APLA and the Homeland defence forces (Ciskei, Transkei, Bophuthatswana and Venda). The process also concerned the integration of the seven different defence forces into one new national defence system, he said. I was told to take cognisance of the fact that I could expect distrust and animosity from especially the members of MK and APLA, our former enemies. We would furthermore work side-by side with the teams from the air force, navy, medical services and the likes I was informed. All the work would be coordinated by the JMMC on a weekly basis; in actual fact, I now reported to them and not to the Army; however I needed to keep Pretorius and de Jager abreast of developments.

I stood up, deep in thought, saluted and said, "Yes sir, thank you sir."

I made a few requests, one of which was for the assistance of Colonel André Kruger, which was appropriate as he was serving on the staff of Directorate Army Management Services. Kruger was my friend and colleague of long standing, soon to be promoted to brigadier. He was a smart officer, extremely articulate, forward looking, enlightened and above all a loyal compatriot. I also requested the use of the Army War Game Centre at the Army College in Voortrekkerhoogte to work at. Major General A.K. de Jager subsequently promised us his full support. His guidance to me and Andre Kruger throughout the next gruelling three months proved invaluable. He was a charismatic leader, who had commanded the Western Province Command before taking up the senior planning position at army HQ.

I offered a silent prayer: Dear Lord, why me? I subsequently temporarily handed over command of 7 SA Division to my extremely capable Chief of Staff, Colonel Hans Heinze. The next day at 07:00 on the 17th I reported at Kasteelpark to tackle the transformation of the Army.

I met the army workgroup at Kasteelpark and we were briefed by the JMMC. Our new team looked at me wide-eyed with expectation. I said, "Let's meet at the War Game Centre of the Army College and start with the work tomorrow". I explained to all the outsiders how to get there.

On the 18th we set up office at the Army College. I jokingly told the guys from MK and APLA that they had fired rockets at this place a few years earlier and had missed, even so that the swimming pool had been cracked. This allowed me in 1988 as the commander of the College to request funds to have it repaired and the whole recreation area revived. I jestingly thanked MK and APLA for that!

MK member Solly Mollo and I were duly selected as the co-leaders of the workgroup. Mollo asked me whether MK member, Dr. Rocky Williams could join us in addition to the MK team. I said, "Fine, especially if he is good with a computer". We decided that we would visit our respective HQs to receive more specific guidelines for planning, so that we could start working furiously the next day. We did not have much time left until 21 April to produce the final plans. As it were we rarely slept over the next few weeks and never enjoyed a weekend off during the Easter holidays. André Kruger and I duly visited General Pretorius to receive our guidelines. He said to us, jokingly, "The two of you know what must be done: Keep what we have." When we left I said to Kruger, we are in deep shit!

The next day the MK team was late. The excuse was that they did not have official transport as we had. Their grumbles, to my mind, were fully justified. I requested my logistics officer, Colonel Chris Beukes of 7 Division to somewhat "informally" arrange an Avis rental car for our former foes, now our new-found colleagues – remember they were not on the strength of the SANDF as yet. I said don't make an accident, or I will be in serious trouble. We then started with our first proceedings.

We opened with scripture reading and prayer. Mollo did the praying for us. Wow, I suddenly realised that some MKs were also Christians – later that evening Solly Mollo and the others of MK would sing Sarie Marais for us. They told us that they had sung it in the bushes in Africa due north during exile when they longed for South Africa. Hell, that made us Whities bear up.

Mollo was a smart operator. When I asked him to commence with the session he said, "No, Brigadier, you first, you are more senior". I decided to be straightforward and said, We are the future senior commanders and staff officers of a new national army; we need to be honest with each other and develop trust amongst ourselves if we want to generate a viable army plan by 21 April. I am going to tell you what the Chief of my Army told me and André Kruger yesterday when we asked for guidelines. He told us to keep what we have.

Everyone then burst out laughing and replied that they had received similar instructions. How the hell were we going to design a new army based on those norms?

The ice was broken and we started working seriously. In the evenings we shared around the campfire some interesting and emotional stories from our collective pasts. We developed a close-knit friendship from working focused and closely together over long hours. Our work included many visits to military installations. This was part of the induction of the members from the outside of the "old" army.

During a visit to the Woman's College at George in the Southern Cape in early April we stayed over at the Army Foundation Holiday Resort at Plettenberg Bay. I told the MKs that I would take them sailing in the bay with my Hobie Cat. They were somewhat apprehensive at first, but said that they were game nonetheless. I prayed for wind. The next day I took them sailing one by one and it was a fun day. When Solly Mollo and I went out the wind was howling. Quite far from shore we capsized and Mollo grabbed hold of me. We were bobbing up and down in the rough sea, but eventually succeeded in righting the catamaran together and tacked for shore. While sailing back Mollo suddenly said to me, smiling, "Roland, this thing of you Whities that Unity is Strength (motto on the former National Coat of Arms of South Africa) is a lot of nonsense; diversity is strength, we had just proven it". His words out there on the bay cemented our friendship for life.

In later years Solly Mollo, Rocky Williams and I would tell many transformation teams in Africa that Red Wine and campfires are crucial for successful transformation the African way!

Our workgroup delivered a comprehensive army plan and implementation framework for the new SA Army by 21 April 1994 and it was approved by Transitional Military Council. The organisation of the old army was more or less retained to as structure for the integration of the other forces into the new army. The many issues to be managed during the next transitional phase was neatly identified and described. The most sensitive for MK and APLA was the future of the commando system.

Before we finished our work in April we were introduced to the incoming members of the British Military Advisory Training Team (BMATT), who had been requested by the transitional government to support the SANDF with the integration and demobilisation processes. On 22 April I resumed command of 7 South African Division.

Internal Politics in between – Machiavellian Times and Other Forms of Manoeuvre

I wish to share a few interesting things that came to pass at 7 South African Division in 1994–95, after I had successfully completed my assignment regarding the initial phase of the Army's transformation. Some of that which followed was exhilarating and others were downright infuriating.

Shortly after I returned to 7 Division I was appointed by Chief of the Army as the deputy chairman of a workgroup under Major General du Preez Coetzee, Chief of Army Staff Personnel, to investigate the prospects of a future voluntarily military system (VMS) and the impending changes and expectations regarding the future of our part-time force system. Colonel Ian Deetlefs, a bright young part-time officer and business entrepreneur served with me and Coetzee on the workgroup. Colonel Solly Mollo, then serving with Army Management Services, was co-opted to serve on this workgroup as well. Our studies took Du Preez, Deetlefs and myself to Belgium and Britain to benchmark possible future part-time force concepts. I later had an opportunity to investigate the system applied by the Swiss Army. We eventually submitted a comprehensive report expressing recommendations for the future of part-time force system. Retired Lieutenant General Ian Gleeson was subsequently called up by Defence HQ to work on the practical modalities for such future implementation. In April 1997 Ian Deetlefs was promoted by the Minister of Defence as a Major General in the part-time forces to establish an office for the Part-Time Force Division and to direct and guide its function. The new voluntary military service was instituted in South Africa in 1995.

Early in May 1994 I was called to Army HQ and informed by Lieutenant General Hattingh Pretorius and Major General Du Preez Coetzee that I had done well with my transformation assignment and that my knowledge gained was indispensable and that I was being considered for promotion to major general in a strategic planning capacity. Take note Roland, but do not put your hopes on this, you know the system. Incidentally, each of the members of the Army transformation work group had received a "Chief of the Army Commendation" signed by Pretorius – this was a first for members of the former MK and Homeland Armies. I returned to 7 Division's HQ with my army Camry to continue the work I enjoyed. Shortly afterwards General Hattingh Pretorius fell tragically ill with Parkinson's Disease and was medically boarded and Major General Du Preez Coetzee retired from the army. There followed almost a complete changeover of the army's general staff and Lieutenant General Reg Otto was appointed Chief of the Army. Forthwith, for reasons of propriety, I will refrain from referring to the names of certain newly appointed army generals.

In May I requested that Colonel Solly Mollo be transferred to 7 Division and I appointed him as my senior staff officer personnel. He was extremely intelligent, had a legal degree and was gifted in working with and relating to people. I gave him one instruction, I said, Colonel Solly Mollo, don't read that cumbersome personnel code of the Army, follow your gut. Each morning Mollo had his military and civilian staffs in his office and they conversed intimately about the division and personnel management issues – it was high communication par excellence and everyone was having fun.

Within weeks I started receiving feedback from my part-time force units spread out all over South Africa, "What the hell is happening at the division, the personnel management services has improved dramatically!" Everybody enjoyed our new MK foundling and Mollo was excelling at his work. I soon received a message from a certain general at army HQ, who said, "Who the hell are you, Brigadier, to appoint a former MK member as a senior personnel officer?" I somewhat laconically replied that I am the commander of 7 Division, that is who I am. It was left at that. In 1995 7 Division came out tops with the inspection by Inspector General, Major General Shylock Mulder, in comparison with the territorial commands and other Army formations. We especially excelled in the measurement of the management climate throughout the army – I have kept the latter result just in case until today.

Something else quite interesting happened at 7 Division: Mollo brought many of the former MK cadres to our HQ after hours for me to start tutoring them on the subject of conventional warfare to prepare them for their promotion courses. In addition I gave them books to read on the subject. Similarly, Brigadier Godfrey Ngwenya, acting in a double-up capacity as Chief of Staff of Witwatersrand Command phoned me, "Roland, I am going on the next command and staff course. Would you help me getting acquainted with mobile warfare?"[5] So at least three times per week for a while he ventured over to 7 Division in his red Camry and spent fruitful hours in my office where we conversed about the concepts of mobile warfare and mission command on my whiteboard.

By mid-1995 it was rumoured that the nine territorial commands were being upgraded to major general posts. This was strange to me as this was not in accordance with the future plans of the army. Transformation implied making the army smaller and not larger; as such a move would imply gross rank inflation. I said to myself, Ah, Roland, this is a scheme by the Pretoria guard to out-general MK and APLA with the integration that will follow soon! I viewed the cumbersome static commands as power structures of the former military order eating up large chunks of the defence budget. Many a time in jest I compared the commands to Mercedes-Benz. If they should stop making cars, they would continue to thrive on administration and boards of inquiry. I should know. I had been the Chief of Staff of Northern Transvaal command for two years in 1991–92. Soon I was called to Army HQ in Pretoria and told that there were going to be a few promotions to major general's rank, but that I would only later be considered for promotion. "You are being transferred to the staff of CSANDF as Director Transformation Management," I was told, "because you have acquired this particular competency and are needed to first perform important work in the capacity of defence transformation."

For the first time in my life I was transferred out of the Army and I was fuming. It was clear to me that I was being marginalised. One of my close colleagues in Army HQ – no names, no pack drill – said to me. "My friend you have an enemy up there, watch out, I think you are a threat to him. It is rumoured that you are too enthusiastic in pursuing these coming changes."

In October 1995 I handed over command of 7 Division to Colonel Hans Heinze and went forth to the "Glass Palace" which housed Defence HQ in Erasmuskloof, Pretoria, to assume my new position as Director Transformation Management of the SANDF.

Soon after I became intimately embroiled in defence transformation, Solly Mollo and I were approached by Mark Gevisser of the Mail and Guardian to do a profile on us. We did

5 In 1999 Major General Godfrey Ngwenya served with me on the army general staff and in 2000 he was appointed CSANDF. He currently serves as South Africa's ambassador in Angola. He was highly regarded by MK, was wounded in a military operation somewhere in Africa and his combat name was "Brattie".

the interview at Voortrekkerhoogte. An article titled "SANDFs new brothers in arms", was consequently published in the 8–14 September 1995 issue of Mail and Guardian. I thought it was an interesting article illustrating the coming together of the integrating armies, elucidating the captivating elements of transformation and on how Solly Mollo and I had become friends. Mark Gevisser ended his article by writing: " ... Despite the scathamiya songs that drift over from the training fields, despite the way Mollo greets an old comrade with an eita da as well as a salute, this is still Voortrekkerhoogte, a fortress of conformity and hierarchy and control. If I had to do the pro patria mori routine and was given a choice of commander to follow into battle, it would be de Vries. But if I was 18 again, and there were still conscription, I'd be outta there."

Was this article appreciated by certain circles in the military? I don't think so. There were murmurings from the Blue and the Red Carpet areas, but nothing more. In 1996 a book was published by Mark Gevisser, Portraits of Power by Creda Press, South Africa, Epping, which contained the same article. I was starting to really enjoy this game. However, I was confronted with a reality check. I was called to the office of Minister Joe Modise and he said to me in a serious, but animated manner, "Listen, you must be careful; I have ascertained from certain sources that your life may be in danger from rightist groupings". I thanked him and left.

A month later I had a situation where the tyres of my small diesel Mercedes C250 were damaged on several occasions by what seemed to be metal pop rivets. Henriette had to come and fetch me at Defence HQ ever so often to have my tyres repaired. Then after a month these malicious acts stopped. I kept a close watch to my front and rear, as if I were on the "Border" again. I was reasonably fit in those days from regularly playing squash. Notwithstanding, I started tearing muscles in my legs. A military doctor said to me, what's going on, are you stressed out? I replied that I didn't think so. Henriette, my "personal psychologist'"said to me, "Hey, I know that you are enjoying your work, but you better watch out. You are living on surges of adrenaline energy." Oh, is that what it was?

In addition I need to share the following titbit before I reveal the interesting story of the next phase of defence transformation: In 1996 I was nominated by the SANDF to attend the "Programme in Strategic Transformation" of the University of Stellenbosch Business School (USB in Bellville, Western Cape, South Africa. The "experiential" phase to the Far East from 26 May until 15 June was led by Professor Hein Oosthuizen and Mr. Hennie Olivier. This included visits to Bangkok, Singapore, Seoul (South Korea), Beijing and Hong Kong. Incidentally, Brigadier Jack Grundling from the Secretary for Defence, Mr. Anton Botes from Deloitte and Touche, Mr. Johan Ackerman from Denel and Mr. Pierre Hoffmann of Armscor were with me on the same programme.

I thought deeply about my situation in the SANDF and decided that I "had it up to you know where." The first morning I arrived in Beijing I phoned Henriette and said, Find out everything there is about severance packages, I am leaving the defence force!

When I returned in June I submitted my papers for retirement. When my resignation reached the office of the ministers, I was called in. They said no way was I leaving now. According to Modise and Kasrils many members of former MK, from the former SADF and reserve forces had requested them to halt my request to leave. I said, Ministers with all due respect I am not too well liked by you know who. If I decide that I am going to stay on, how are we going to manage the procedure to withdraw my previous request?

Deputy Minister Ronnie Kasrils merely said, "Just write a short letter to Army HQ and say that you are withdrawing your request, and do not give any reasons why." To me this sounded like fun.

A few days later my secretary, Mrs. Elaine Roos, informed me that she had received a telephone call and that I had to report urgently to a certain general (that one) at Army HQ. I said to her, Phone him and tell him that I am not under his command. If he wants to see me he can make an appointment through you and come to my office. At this stage of my career I did not care a hoot about my own position anymore. I just wanted to see the job through. This sort of gave me a good sense of feeling untouchable – the wheel had turned. I heard nothing from the man. Next I was invited for an interview with Chief of the Army. It was a good conversation where General Reg Otto told me that he admitted that I had been treated unfairly (the words used in Afrikaans was "te na gekom.") I sincerely appreciated his gesture.

At one stage after I became Director of Transformation in October 1995, Henriette and I were invited to the home of Ronnie Kasrils in Parkhurst, Johannesburg. I saw an unpretentious man who was fond of his family and easy to talk to. As we shared a few beers I asked him why he had joined the ANC and MK. He told me that when he was young he saw the suffering of people. The ANC wanted to talk to the National Party Government in the early days when the struggle began, but they were not prepared to listen. His deep caring for people and our new defence force left a lasting impression.

The Second Wave of Transformation – Walking the Tightrope

Early in 1995 CSANDF General George Meiring decided to subject the SANDF to a second wave of transformation due to further serious budget cuts. This decision was soon taken out of his hands by Minister Joe Modise and Deputy Minister Ronnie Kasrils, who decided that the whole of the DOD should be subjected to this process. This would include the Secretary for Defence, led by Lieutenant General Pierre Steyn, now serving in civilian capacity, soon to be appointed as the Head of the Department. The transformation endeavour was subsequently managed at the level of the newly established Council on Defence (COD – Two ministers, Secretary for Defence, CSANDF and Chairman of Armscor).

A Chief Directorate Transformation was formed to support the Office of the Minister, CSANDF as well as the Secretary for Defence with the programme. For administrative purposes our transformation team operated within the Division of Chief of Staff Operations headed by Lieutenant General Wessel Kritzinger. Our team comprised Major General Mo Oelschig as Chief Director, myself as the Director Transformation, Naval Captain Fanie Uys and SAAF Colonel Hennie Prinsloo. Both Uys and Prinsloo were gifted in the area of business process re-engineering and could teach Mike Hammer a few lessons. I would learn much from these two over the next few months. As there was no representative of one of the former liberation movements I requested that Colonel Solly Mollo be transferred to our team; after a "who-hah", this was subsequently granted.

We worked closely with a small transformation team appointed by the Secretary for Defence, the team being the Chief of Policy and Planning Aboobaker Ismail, Army Brigadier André Kruger, SAAF Brigadier Len Le Roux and former MK Dr. (Colonel) Rocky Williams. Both Williams and Le Roux were intimately involved with the Defence White Paper and Defence Review process. This was probably one of the best-managed and most consultative processes I observed happening in the Public Sector. It took months to complete and incorporated a wide range of stakeholders within the public as well as private sector. Through the coming months I established a close relationship with the two ministers, General Pierre Steyn, and his team from the Secretary for Defence – together we formed a kinship. All the members participating in the transformation venture were extremely dedicated. A project team from Deloitte and Touche was subsequently contracted to support defence transformation and was led by Mr. Pierre Tredoux. He had a few smart consultants working with him whom I wish to mention: Dr. Gys Wessels, Mr. Anton Botes, and Mr. Deon Crafford.

I knew instinctively that when I embarked on transformation that I was venturing into my next firestorm and that I would have to find its eye once again to manoeuvre in. When you walk a tightrope, don't look down. Furthermore the leadership proclaiming change needed to accept that they were going to become vulnerable – in for a cent, in for a rand; I decided that nothing and nobody was going to get me down, come hell or high water – especially from being side-tracked by the open animosity coming from a few influential members of the Pretoria old guard. So be it, no love lost! In a way I was looking forward to the next challenge, a skirmish more likely, that would require nimble manoeuvring.

Soon after I was appointed Director Transformation in October 1995 I was instructed to support the high command of the Malawi Army with a three-week strategic planning exercise. This was for the design of their new vision, force design and structure, including an implementation plan. I called up – sort of illegally – one of my erstwhile part-time force chaplains, Kobus Myburgh of 7 South African Division to assist me with the workshop. We travelled by car via Harare, Kariba, Lusaka and Lilongwe to Salima, where the workshop was held. The Command and Staff College of the Malawi Army was located at Salima, close to the Livingstonian Beach Hotel, adjacent to the Malawi Lake, where we were accommodated. I was soon joined by Colonel (SAAF) "PegLeg" van Rensburg to support me with the threat analysis for Malawi. He is a helicopter pilot who had lost both his legs whilst flying in the Rhodesian Bush War in 1979. Colonel Giel Reinecke, our military attaché in Malawi gave our team outstanding support throughout.

I started referring to the general staff of the Malawi Army as the "Seventeen Wise Men" and I could see that they enjoyed the nickname I had coined. I took packets of Jelly Beans with me as well as a few bottles of "mampoer" (South African moonshine), which part time force officer Commandant Boet Schoeman of Regiment De La Rey had given me. During sessions I dished out sweets to any contributor of a bright idea. Those who made negative remarks received a shooter of mampoer.

Lieutenant General Kelvin Shimwaka soon performed a coup and took over this part of my work as he said to me, "Roland, I am now in control of the sweets and the Mampoer. From now on we will turn the process around; those with bright remarks will receive a tot of schnapps".

Came the evenings my new-found army high command was slightly intoxicated. Oh well, the Greeks during the middle ages did their creative planning in a similar fashion. General Shimwaka later on requested Kobus Myburgh to open our sessions with scripture reading and prayer. Each time Myburgh received a standing ovation from the "Seventeen Wise Men." We had a ball of a time! I still maintain close friendship ties with the current Chief of the Malawi Army, General Mark Shisuku, who was a brigadier in those days. Many a time afterwards he phoned me or contacted me through his military attaché based in Pretoria – at the time I could help him with critical issues. In 2007 I could link him and his Ministry for Defence with ISS when the Malawi Army embarked on a process to once again rejuvenate their military system.

Soon after I returned from Malawi our core transformation team was requested to fly to Cape Town to brief the Parliamentary Joint Standing Committee on Defence on the progress we were making with the process. At the time Mr. Tony Yengeni was its Chairman. An explicit instruction was given to Major General Mo Oelschig, Chief Director Transformation, not to attend due to the Bisho legacy. Deputy Minister Ronnie Kasrils, Mr. Pierre Tredoux and Dr. Gys Wessels of Deloitte and Touche, the press and yours truly duly found us in one of the conference halls near Parliament. Mr. Tony Yengeni was raving on and on about Bisho and the legacy of apartheid from up high on his podium preventing the proceedings from getting started. The deputy minister on my left jabbed me in the side with his elbow and said, "Roland, do something!"

I stood up and walked out in front of the gathering, looked up at Mr. Yengeni and said, Sir with all due respect, we are not here for Bisho, but to report back about defence transformation, which is serious business and we dearly need your input!

He was taken aback for a moment, looked down at the white guy in front of him and said, "The Brigadier is right, let us continue".

Smartly dressed Winnie Madikizela-Mandela was sitting in the front row. Afterwards Pierre Tredoux said to me that Deloitte and Touche owed me a coffee. I said, phew!

Our work continued in all seriousness with the redesign of the Defence Force and its internal processes. Simultaneously other high level workgroups were busy with the formulation of the new military strategy and high level defence policies such as the White Paper and Defence Act. The work included the ongoing management of the integration and demobilisation processes which were directed by Lieutenant Generals Siphiwe Nyanda and Andrew Masondo in particular and were supported by BMATT. Nyanda was backed by Colonel Craig Harrison who was his personal staff officer. During the process six closely interlinked goals of transformation embraced the dimensions that were selected as focal areas:

- To take full advantage of the operational capability of the SANDF and to establish the most advantageous force design: This process focused on the development of a professional, balanced and modern defence force aligned with its foreseen future mission, roles and tasks with the guidelines set out in the emerging White Paper on Defence.
- To optimise the effectiveness, economy and efficiency of the defence function through the improvement of its processes and support structures: This process inter alia focused on rationalising and streamlining internal processes and structures with the purpose of efficiency and effectiveness and minimising of defence cost – the tooth-to-tail ratio as we referred to it.
- To ensure durability and continuity of optimal performance through the institutionalisation of appropriate leadership, command and management principles, processes and practices (LCAMPS): It was accepted that leadership would provide the decisive edge and for this purpose was viewed as the most essential dynamic to ensure astounding success in daily work and operations. This was further supported by the need to conduct civic education programmes to teach young and even older military leaders the important role they needed to play in our emerging democracy and to be nonpartisan. It was therefore found necessary

to design an appropriate integrated leadership, command and management (as well as culture) concept for the future defence force.

- To affect management of the transformation programme: It was accepted that vigorous programme management would be required to achieve synergy and coordination of all transformation-related projects and its subsequent results. It was therefore necessary to establish a high-performance transformation management team with the necessary power and credibility to ensure outstanding project management.
- To provide ongoing communication and change management assistance: This was essential owing to the critical importance and specialised nature of internal and external communication and change management actions required during transformation.
- To design and establish new management information systems for the department while the transformation process was in progress: The management of the transformation process required extensive management information support so as to provide appropriate, timely and accurate management information. A mass of new knowledge, concepts and data was generated during the process, which needed to be captured and archived for future use. This system evolved to become the eventual management information system of the transformed SANDF.

Although the members of our small transformation team were involved in all of the above processes, I was appointed as the project leader to develop the integrated leadership, command, management and culture concepts and policies for the SANDF. This was fundamental to the establishment of a new code of conduct and to affect the required cultural change of the new national defence force. These programmes were carefully tied into the communication and change management enabling goal and civic education programme mentioned above. Leadership throughout all levels played an all-important part in facilitating durable change and it was therefore important to have top leadership fully committed in this regard. This was one project in the military I found immensely challenging and enjoyable, however it was accompanied by severe resistance from certain embedded pockets as could be imagined in the top leadership.

The overall project was defined in three phases over a three-year period: In 1996–7 a process was initiated to unfreeze the Department of Defence for change, to set up the guiding coalition and to create a frame of reference. During this part the core defence processes as mentioned above were designed in utmost detail. In 1997-98 the transformation management team and a first wave of project teams commenced with the planning of the new design and implementation and supporting activities. In 1998–99 implementation of the new force design and structure commenced.

A new integrated Department of Defence consisting of the Defence Secretariat and Defence Headquarters was created in April 1997, while macro level decisions were implemented and planning and implementations started moving to the lower levels of the newly created SANDF. This process led to a design workshop that was held towards the end of 1997 where all newly appointed Department of Defence top level incumbents and role players were tasked to develop their respective divisions in more detail. At this stage I was appointed as the Chief of the newly created Joint Training Division of the SANDF and member of the new Defence Staff Council with the post level of major general with effect from 1 April 1997.

It was rumoured in the passages that one of the senior generals entrapped in the fold of the "Old Guard" had said that he would hold my promotion back as long as possible – ignore and carry on, Roland, regardless. I was only promoted on 1 October when the Minister for Defence said to "him": "Do it, or else ... " I heard about my promotion while I was away on comprehensive bilateral staff talks with the German Defence Ministry in Bonn, Germany. It must have made that someone seriously frantic, somehow, somewhere. So be it, that's life, especially during transformation. Sleep well through the nights, my erstwhile colleague, for I have no regrets about what had happened. Notwithstanding, I had the privilege to serve on the Defence Staff Council and was now in a position where I could do something refreshing about what I had expressed above concerning "jointness," training and doctrine – this would require some careful footwork as there were a few "enemies" out there in the halls of power.

Establishing the Joint Training Division from April 1997 to July 1998

I have always nurtured an obsession about "jointness" whilst serving in the former SADF. This probably stemmed from my days with 61 Mechanised Battalion Group in the field in 1981–2 and from being caught up in Operations Modular and Prone in 1987–8.[6] Briefly: "Joint operations" involved more than one service, such as the Army and Air Force, operating together whereas a joint campaign implied a series of successively or simultaneously conducted major operations, designed to achieve the operational objective within a given time and space. This required the synchronisation of land, air forces and naval forces in one operation – add medical and health services and mutual support for good measure. Combined operations, on the other hand, referred to operations by the armed forces in an international setting working closely with the forces of other nations. It was clear that the SANDF as such, would become more and more involved in future in combined peace operations in Africa –something appropriate had to be devised for this.

During my operational and training heydays in the former SADF I had always alleged that there were deficiencies in the domains of jointness, especially at the operational level of war pertaining to joint campaign planning.[7] To my mind operational plans and guidelines which made it to the front were mostly too tactically oriented. They usually came down the command lines separately from the top to ground level via the respective single service HQs. I believed that this was due to overemphasis on the ethos of the respective services and in the way we trained our commanders and staff officers separately.

Incidentally, in those days it was still the practise to appoint the Army as the "main executor" for landward operations, skirting the need for a joint operational level HQ. Usually joint task forces were assembled for specific operations and were then disbanded on its completion – in this way we were more disjointed than jointed in battle. Providentially at ground level things usually worked out fine as the operators from the respective services knew each other well and had, in a sense, became a veritable "A-Team." There were only single service colleges in those days, which to my mind emphasised the need for a joint services command and staff institution to train officers at the different operational levels of war – there was a huge vacuum, in fact. I was equally exasperated by the fact that an appropriate doctrine at the operational level of war for mobile conventional operations and

6 Refer to Part 1, Chapter 4 and Part 2 from Chapters 9 to 16.

7 Refer to Chapter 7.

command and control never saw the light.[8]

I can say it now more openly than in the past. I had wondered many a time about the quality of our military strategies formulated in those earlier days; much more so the war stratagem connived at the political level! For military strategy is not merely concerned with the employment of forces, but with its medium to long-term outcomes as well. This was strikingly illustrated by the surprises sprung on the SADF in August 1987 during Operation Modular and during Prone in May 1988 and the way in which our forces were deployed piecemeal. As such the horizon of military strategy was bounded by the war itself, while higher strategy at the political level truly needed to look beyond the war to the subsequent peace – hello surprise!

Was this the disconnect which caused the SADF to be caught on the back foot – to the extent it was – in the Cuito Cuanavale situation of 1987? This question seems even more pertinent when dissecting the advance of the 50th Cuban Division which had the surprised SADF scrambling to contain the threat (refer to Chapters 15 and 16.) I hesitantly have to conclude that in our HQs many of our senior army officers focused on counterinsurgency rather than total warfare and the particular war making strategies and plans required by it. Fortunately there were also many talented officers scattered throughout our military system that did outstanding work and rescued the peace.

In those days a book written by Major General Charles A. Willoughby, Maneuver in Warfare (Harrisburg, P.A.: The Military Service Publishing Co., 1939) had a significant influence on my thinking. He explained that on 10 September 1935 an officer in the infantry, Colonel Wilson B. Burt, had drawn the following incisive conclusion in an official document at the Command and General Staff School, Fort Leavenworth, Kansas: "In the academic sequence of instruction at the command and general staff school, there is a period of transition from the reinforced brigade and division to the corps and the army. It is in the nature of things that this transition is abrupt ... Considering that the average student has rarely commanded more than a battalion, the intelligent manipulation, even on paper, of the masses represented by the corps and the army, called for a strategic imagination of a higher order; in the absence of practical experience, such an operative skill can only be acquired through a careful study of great campaigns ... It is significant that great military thinkers like Napoleon, Clausewitz, Moltke and Foch did not consider the tactical schooling of leaders as the most important thing – they esteemed above all an intellectual training derived from a comparative study of the past ... as an orientation course, this series at the command and general staff school aim particularly at enlarging the professional horizon from the inevitable limitation of small peace strength garrisons to the greater responsibilities of high command ... "

I dare say that during operations I have very often observed that plans dished out from up high were very similar to those originally conceptualised at tactical level. In support of my argument, let me point you to the strategic impact and outcome that was eventually achieved by our final military operations conducted in southern Angola in 1987–88 – management of good fortune – luck, if you prefer – in other words. I rest my case.

Perhaps, just perhaps, we could find some balm in the wise words expressed by Harry G. Summers in "On Strategy": "What went wrong in Vietnam? Among the points are the difference between the civilian planning done by the government bureaucracy and the

8 Refer to Chapters 6, 7 and 8 as well as Chapter 12 on Operation Protea, when this particular deficiency was noted.

actual strategy of military operations; our failure to learn from the Korean experience – how we took counsel of our fears and surrendered the initiative to the enemy; how we failed to distinguish the internal Vietnamese problem and the threat of North Vietnamese aggression or to discern how the North used insurgency to hide their real objective." The SADF's failing was a common one.

As Chief of Joint Training I had the Defence Staff College, Military Academy and School for Educational Technology as well as the Directorate Professional Development and Training (SANDF) under my command, I had substantial capacity to work with. This entailed establishing the Joint Training Division and crafting the high level policy for future professional development in the SANDF. It included joint command and staff training for officers as well as the development of other ranks in this regard.

I had the privilege to set up a joint workgroup to initiate the turf-breaking work and was supported by outstanding officers such as Major General (retired) Duncan Ralston; Major General (retired) Ben Vorster; Brigadier Ashwin Hurribunce; Brigadier Martin Rutsch; Colonel Johan Jooste; Colonel Solly Mollo; Captain (SA Navy) Herman de Vries; and many other stalwarts I cannot mention because of space constraints; an amazing team. I succeeded in having Brigadier Ashwin Hurribunce (a former MK member and medical doctor-cum-radiologist by profession) appointed as my deputy and Ms. Elaine Roos as my secretary – we were ready to roll. Hurribunce was an exceptional and highly intelligent individual who could talk circles around a few senior individuals embedded in those sombre unsmiling pockets of resistance found in the Defence Staff Council. He used to accompany me to these sessions. At times I would draw the fire to allow him to breach the lines of resistance and to push our proposals through one by bloody one – outflanking tactics.

During this period one of the project teams I personally kept on managing was the one concerned with the "Integrated Leadership Command and Management Concept" for the SANDF. This embraced transformational leadership, mission command, total quality management, public administration and civic education as an integrated entity. Mr. Deon Crafford (Deloitte and Touche), Mr. Danie Maritz (Productivity Development (Pty.) Ltd., Brigadier André Kruger (from the Secretary of Defence) and Colonel Solly Mollo formed part of my team. This concept was officially approved by the Defence Staff Council in April 1997. The new transformational leadership methods that were now accepted in the SANDF were used for change management interventions as well.

Transformational leadership as such enhances the motivation, morale, and performance of followers through a variety of mechanisms. These included connecting the follower's sense of identity and self to the work and the collective identity of the organization; being a role model for followers that inspired them and to keep them interested through intellectual stimulation and inspirational motivation; challenging followers to take greater ownership of their work, and understanding the strengths and weaknesses of followers so the leader could align tasks that enhanced their performance. Much of this I had described in Chapter 8 on leadership and command. Solly Mollo and I presented many of these programmes over the next two years. In this way we came to meet many of the young integrates in the SANDF.

I now put in a concentrated effort on the finalisation of joint doctrine regarding manoeuvre warfare and mission command. These were the concepts I had started working on while I commanded 61 Mechanised Battalion Group in 1981–82, served at the Army Battle School from 1983 until 1987 and the Army college from 1988 until 1990. In the process I befriended Major General Duncan Ralston (retired SAAF) who worked at Defence HQ in an office close to me and I intended to keep him close. Ralston took part as navigator of Maritime Reconnaissance during World War II and the amazing "Berlin Airlift" afterwards. He had spent his entire career in the SAAF and had flown DC3s, Oxfords, Wellingtons, Warwicks (a modified Wellington used for search and destroy missions on U-boats), Vampires and Harvards. I found General Ralston heading the Joint Warfare and Strategy Directorate after he had retired from the SADF as the Director General Planning and Strategy of the SAAF – what a remarkable man. We subsequently subtly generated the provisional doctrine for manoeuvre warfare as well as for mission command through his directorate, while I flew under the radar. These doctrines were soon approved by the Defence Staff Council. Some of the die-hards in the passageways were still frowning; however, a new world had passed them by. I was suffused by a surge of satisfaction when I started reading about manoeuvre warfare in the new strategy of the SANDF as it evolved day by day. One question remained in my mind afterwards: What was the new SANDF going to make of these new-fangled methods which had now been adopted; something I had worked on all my life? I knew that the military would need strong leadership, passion and understanding to see its institutionalisation through! In my heart of hearts I realised that it would take more than twenty years to build the next good defence force. So be it. They now had solid concepts to work on.

I had a passion to get a joint services command and Staff College established for the SANDF. In September–October 1997 I was afforded the opportunity to finalise the vision and plans for such an institution. Brigadier Martin Rutsch and I undertook an extensive study tour to Britain and Europe to benchmark joint services command and staff training. Our tour included visits to the Command and Staff College of the German Defence Force (Bundeswehr) in Hamburg as well as several similar training establishments of the British Defence Force such as Sandhurst, the Royal Military College of Science at Swindon and the Joint Services Command and Staff College (JSCSC) at its temporary location in Brecken.

The JSCSC was the one I was truly interested in. There Rutsch and I had an opportunity to meet Colonel Deon Holtzhausen of the South African Army, who was on a multinational course in which he later came first. We met the commandant of the college, remarkable Major General Sir Timothy Granville-Chapman GBE KCB ADC Gen – in later years he served as Vice Chief of the Defence Staff at the United Kingdom's Ministry for Defence, where he deputised for the Chief of the British Defence Force. He became Assistant Chief of the General Staff in 1994 and in 1997 was appointed to create the new Joint Services Command and Staff College, closing the former single Service Staff Colleges and negotiating the permanent location for the new Staff College at Shrivenham. Rutsch and I had an informative discussion with Granville-Chapman on the pros and cons of command and staff training and the establishment of such a joint institution. In the process he gave me a copy of the first directive he issued to establish the Joint Services Command and Staff College (JSCSC) at Shrivenham. The JSCSC is a British military academic establishment providing training and education to experienced officers of the Royal Navy, Army, Royal Air Force, Ministry of Defence, Civil Service, and serving officers of other states such as South Africa.

Our last visit was followed by a tour to Salisbury Plains and the Centre for Military Doctrine at Uphaven. Incidentally it was at Salisbury Plain where Sir B.H. Liddell Hart and Major General J.F.C. Fuller had demonstrated in 1936 to the world their concept of mobile warfare – those the German commanders such as Güderian, Von Manstein and Rommel later perfected as Blitzkrieg with which they beat the Allied Forces in May 1940 through their surprise offensive through the Ardennes Forest. At Uphaven Rutsch and I were treated with the newest British military doctrine on manoeuvre warfare and mission command. It interested me to compare it with my own concept already formulated in August 1987. I could take back manuals and CDs to hand over to Major General Duncan Ralston once we returned to Defence HQ.

With my staff from Joint Training we now started developing the planning framework for the establishment of a joint services command and training institution. When I was appointed Deputy Chief of the Army in July 1998 Brigadier (later Major General) Ashwin Hurribunce continued with the work, ardently supported by Lieutenant General Themba Matanzima. The South African National War College (SANWC) was subsequently established in Pretoria in 2000 to undertake joint command and staff training and to plan and conduct combined joint African peace keeping exercises as part of the SANDFs commitment to greater integration within AU and SADC military structures. In 2007 I was invited by the War College to participate in a panel discussion with the senior command and staff course on Operation Modular, Hooper and Packer that had played out in southeast Angola in 1987-88. The discussion was attended by members from Cuba, former MK members and well-known author Helmoed-Römer Heitman. Enjoying the company of the students that evening made me think back. I wondered whether they knew how it had all come about!

Later in October–November 1997 I was tasked to participate in a multi-nation fact-finding mission and planning exercise to establish the concept for a future African Standby Force for the Southern African Development Community (SADC). SADC is an inter-governmental organization headquartered in Gaborone, Botswana. Its goal was to further socio-economic collaboration and integration as well as political and security cooperation amongst fifteen Southern African states, Angola, Botswana, Democratic Republic of the Congo, Lesotho, Madagascar, Malawi, Mauritius, Mozambique, Namibia, Swaziland, Tanzania, Zambia, Zimbabwe, Seychelles, and South Africa. SADC complements the role of the African Union. Our mission was sponsored by the Danish Government and was facilitated by Colonel Kurt Mosgard who was the Head of the Danish-supported Peacekeeping Centre for SADC in Zimbabwe. We commenced with an all-encompassing workshop in Harare, Zimbabwe, after which we flew to Copenhagen in Denmark. There we studied the concept of peace operations at national level, which involved a number of workshops and interviews with senior Danish government and military officials. Then we flew to Bosnia by Danish Air Force Hercules and were hosted by the Nordic Brigade (Denmark, Norway and Sweden) to study peace operations at a multinational level. We completed our joint report and recommendations for the establishment of the SADC Standby Force once we returned to Harare, which were subsequently submitted to our respective governments and militaries. In the process I had the privilege to meet Foreign Minister Alfred Baphethuxolo Nzo, who was one of the instigators of this initiative – I gave him a framed front cover of a magazine I had found in Bosnia, with a colour photograph of him dressed in camouflage, wearing a "flak jacket." Nzo had served as the longest standing secretary-general of the ANC between 1969 and 1991. He was the South African minister for foreign affairs from 1994 to 1999.

In February 1998 something both interesting and surprising happened. The Chief of the SANDF General George Meiring personally handed President Nelson Mandela a report alleging that there was a left-wing plot to topple the government.[9] The report generated by Military Intelligence was based on questionable sources and implicated senior politicians, including Winnie Madikizela-Mandela, Bantu Holomisa and current SANDF Deputy Chief Lieutenant General Siphiwe Nyanda, amongst others. It claimed that they had conspired against the government and were linked to a range of criminal activities, including gun-running. The "Meiring Report" was subsequently rejected by the government as being an attempt by them to misinform and to destabilise. For this Meiring was effectively forced into early retirement. This misfortune also impelled the formation of a commission of inquiry to examine the functioning of the intelligence community in South Africa.

At the time I was serving as the Chief of Joint Training on the Defence Staff Council and we were all "invited" to the Union Buildings for a talking-to about the incident by President Nelson Mandela. I was impressed by the role this charismatic leader performed as the Supreme Commander of the SANDF; he greeted each of us by hand before he shared his views about this delicate dilemma, handling it superbly. Had there been a plan within a plan and by whom – a double threat?

In June 1998 I was informed by the Minister for Defence and Chief of the SANDF that I was going to be appointed as the Deputy Chief of the Army with effect from 1 July. I requested an interview with Defence Minister Joe Modise and Deputy Minister Ronnie Kasrils regarding the appointments of two future generals as soon as I learned of my new appointment. The first was about Ashwin Hurribunce, a former MK member, to be appointed in my place as Chief of Joint Training – he was a gifted individual and I knew that he would complete the work we had started together the past year; which he subsequently did. The next was to get André Kruger appointed as the Chief of Army Structures – I knew Kruger to be enlightened and highly energetic and by now he understood the politics through his ardent work done with the Secretary of Defence General Pierre Steyn and Mr. Aboobaker Ismail the past few months – this was said and done and the two officers were subsequently promoted and appointed.

On Becoming the Deputy Chief of the Army in July 1998

Our new Army general staff team appointed on 1 July 1998 was: Lieutenant General Gilbert Remano as the Chief of the Army; Major General Roland de Vries as the Deputy Chief of the Army; Major General André Kruger as Chief of Army Structures, with Brigadier General Barney Hlatswayo as his deputy; Major General Godfrey Ngwenya as the Chief of Army Force Preparation with Brigadier General Leon Wessels as his deputy; and Major General Themba Matanzima as the Chief Army Corporate Services, with Brigadier General Thinus Ackerman as his deputy. The legendary Sergeant-major Koos Moorcroft from Special Forces was reappointed as the sergeant-major of the Army. All I could say was: What a team! For the next few months I enjoyed it tremendously to work within this particular kinship. Our general staff team maintained an exceptional relationship with the Chief, who would refer to me as the "moving spirit," words I dearly appreciated.

On 24 August 1998 I held an intensive workshop for the Department of Defence at Lisedi, a cultural village near Broederstroom, thus completing some of the work I had

9 Stott, Noel: *Safeguarding South Africa for a better life for all*. Violence and Transition Series, Vol. 7, 2002.

started as Chief of Joint Training. This was to fuse the vision of the future leadership, command, management and culture concept of the Department Of Defence within the top leadership. This prestigious gathering included the two defence ministers and the members of the Council on Defence and Defence Staff Council. Throughout this process we received tremendous support from Defence Minister Joe Modise, Deputy Minister Ronnie Kasrils, Chief SANDF General Siphiwe Nyanda and Lieutenant General Andrew Masondo (former MK). To me, getting these leadership and command principles accepted engendered huge satisfaction.

The new Army Command Cadre set about swiftly building our new team and transforming the army within weeks, in many ways setting the pace within defence circles. This was done with the enthusiastic support of highly professional officers of the British Military Advisory Training Team (BMATT), working within our structures from the top down to unit level. Their role was to advise and help us oversee the fairness of the integration process down to grassroots. As such their work was indispensable to the success we achieved during those highly exciting, but extremely challenging times. BMATT had been intimately involved since April 1994 in the integration process which happened at Wallmansthal, a huge temporary military base where the former liberation army members were processed in phalanxes. This included adjudicating the former academic qualifications, training achievements and military experience to determine ranks and postings as well as the requirements for professional development, bridging and other training. Then the incumbents were put on the nominal roll of the SANDF and posted to their respective new units. It was a massive process and extremely complex, placing great pressure not only on the management staff, but on those individuals who were being integrated as well. The process made provision for appeal boards and BMATT ensured that everything was done above board. Of course there were major frictions ... and sheer resistance to change. In the first three months we re-staffed the army from top to bottom with new incumbents; made the decision to close down the nine cumbersome territorial commands, which caused a ripple through the system; created a new Army HQ staffed with 220 people as opposed to original 1 800 staff members. The message was clear; we were serious about impending change and what we were doing.

Our work entailed crafting a new strategy and implementation plan to install the new force design and structure of the Army as well as its re-engineered internal processes. We held umpteen workshops and mounted numerous project teams to get the work done. At times in addressing members in large gatherings and in briefing work groups I spoke in a whisper as I had become hoarse from all the talking. I was almost never in my office and my family rarely saw me at home. General Gilbert Remano and I would visit the units in the field on many occasions, sitting on camp chairs amongst our people, talking comfortably with them about our current realities and the future. From them materialised the vision that we fashioned and started voicing for our new army: "The SA Army, our people one in spirit, has the commanding presence and power of a pride of lions. We are an excellent military force, forever professional and ready, making a difference wherever serving South Africa." Incidentally, it was quite easy to arrive at the latter vision statement. When we asked our troops jokingly in the field, would you like our new defence force to be like a donkey, they vehemently and passionately replied: "No, like a lion!" – that was Africa for you. Officers such as Colonel Kobus (Bok) Smit played an indispensible role as Senior Staff

Officer Transformation (Army) to design the new structures and processes.[10]

The vision of our new army was unmistakably linked to the major change of the Army's future role, which was now to provide combat ready landward forces to the Chief of the SANDF (CSANDF), in so much to be employed by the newly established Chief of Joint Operations on behalf of CSANDF. The Army however continued to play a leading role in sustaining a credible and cohesive joint landward defence capability. This needed to be done in concert with the other major role players be it the air, naval, medical support components or in combination.

I had befriended Major General Michael Willcocks, the Assistant Chief of the British Army General Staff in England during a visit in 1997. His responsibilities as such had set out the conditions for the British Army to contribute to success on operations and ensured coherence across the "Defence Lines of Development for the Army of the Future" – we could learn from him. He was a fine strategist and extremely knowledgeable about manoeuvre warfare. Early in 1989 I invited him for an official visit to South Africa. I said no uniforms and no speeches – he replied in a letter to me that this would be a first for him and should prove to be invigorating. He requested to bring his Aide de Camp, a Special Forces captain, with him.

Major General André Kruger, Colonel Swannie Swanepoel and I hosted our two friends from Britain. We toured the picturesque Mpumalanga Province and numerous military bases with a small luxury bus. Along the way we visited a few British cemeteries from the Anglo-Boer War (1899–1902). We arranged a parachute jump for his captain when we visited and stayed over at 5 Reconnaissance Regiment, Special Forces, at Phalaborwa. Brigadier General Borries Bornman, the officer commanding Special Forces was in attendance when we arrived. We toured the Kruger National Park in the company of knowledgeable range wardens afterwards. At one of the "hippo pools" along the Sabie River we presented the Army strategy on a graphic roll-out we had prepared and discussed future developments and how the British Military Training and Advisory Team (BMATT) could support us in future. Every evening we discussed military doctrine. Mike Wilcox left our shores highly revitalized, having not once worn his uniform. This was one of me and André Kruger's memorable times together.

Within this aforementioned changing environment there was one unhappy incident which occurred in September 1998, while I was the acting Chief of the Army. In September the SANDF launched Operation Boleas under the auspices of the Southern African Development Community (SADC) to subdue an army rebellion in the small mountain kingdom of Lesotho. The operation lasted from 16 September to 3 December. Colonel Robbie Hartslief was in command of a combined brigade-sized SADNF-Botswana Defence Force (to give it a SADC flavour) taskforce – it should be mentioned that it was reported that the contingent from Botswana arrived somewhat late at the scene. However it is relevant to mention that their force was well-trained, spirited and well-disciplined. Nine South African soldiers and over 50 soldiers of the Lesotho Defence Force (LDF) and 40 civilians were killed during the ensuing action. The operation was widely criticised in national as well as international circles and was presented as a "debacle and a failure." The large number of deaths in what should have been a relatively small operation was interpreted as the new SANDF's lack of fighting capacity and lack of military discipline.

10 Former officer commanding 61 Mechanised Battalion Group during Operation Modular in 1987 – refer to Chapter 15.

The South African government and the military later conceded that the level of resistance encountered by the diminutive Lesotho defence force had surprised them and that tactical shortcomings and inadequate intelligence had resulted in poor performance. In the *Star* of 4 November 1998 it was reported that General Siphiwe Nyanda CSANDF and Lieutenant General Deon Ferreira, Chief of Joint Operations, had truthfully said to parliament and the Joint Standing Committee on Defence that: " … our troops had not been combat ready and that planning and preparation had been poor."

The *Star* furthermore stated: "The high cost of the intervention in Lesotho – R24 million to date – had strained the SANDF's budget to breaking point."

Perhaps the most startling admission was that the Government lacked a clear national security policy which would determine conditions for participation in foreign military operations. The generals are to be commended for their brutal honesty. They have not spared themselves, or the politicians. I was hopping mad when I heard about the Lesotho invasion. Of course the Army knew that our forces were training for such a contingency as we had allowed its provision to Chief of Joint Operations for just that. However, neither General Gilbert Remano as the Chief of the Army or I as his deputy had given our consent for operational employment – the force had not been declared combat ready as such by us yet! Apparently CNN had waited for our force to cross the Maseru Bridge on D-Day as intelligence had been a mess.

To my mind Lesotho was the next wake-up call. In the media around 3 October it was reported that the most damning critique came from me as the Deputy Chief of the Army. This followed a discussion I had at the Infantry Symposium at 4 South African Battalion in Middelburg. Major General André Kruger and Brigadier General Bornman of Special Forces had accompanied me and in our usual open manner we discussed the pros and cons of the operation with the members of the symposium. Unknown by me there were a few military correspondents of the media in the large gathering … or known by me … So the next day there was fire and brimstone in the circles of the military top brass and I was called to Defence HQ and asked why I had said what I had said. I explained my viewpoint and the next day issued my own media statement. I also had a discussion with the defence ministers to whom I openly asked a straightforward question about which I was extremely serious: Ministers, who gave permission for our troops to be employed in operations before being declared combat ready? Was there a proper campaign strategy formulated that was irrevocably linked to a clear political-military goal? Finally, was the coming operation thoroughly war-gamed? The reply was that I had made my point.

Straightaway I held a comprehensive debriefing session and map exercise in the Army concerning Operation Boleas. Next Sergeant-major Koos Moorcroft and I visited my friend and colleague Colonel Robbie Hartslief in Lesotho, for whom I had the utmost respect and affection. I spoke to senior officers in Lesotho about the debacle. Many of them said to me straight out, "If your defence force told us beforehand that your military wanted to invade, we would have yielded … "

When people stop talking, war starts! I then approached Lieutenant General Deon Ferreira: "Let us hold a proper planning conference and sort out once and for all how we are going to manage the process of providing combat ready forces to Joint Operations for optimal employment". Said and done. I could now settle down. In November 1998 I held an all-encompassing media briefing and conference at Army HQ which included all the members of our top brass about transformation (Salut, January 1999.) Salut stated: "The

Army sets the pace ... as it discloses major changes." This was to clearly indicate the path that the Army was taking. I told the media in no uncertain terms that we were progressively integrating seven armies into one united army and that this had resulted in the fusion of various leadership and command and control processes. I also stated that the integration process had provided us with the opportunity to combine the guerrilla warfare competencies of the former liberation movements with those of mobile conventional tactics applied by the former SADF. I emphasised that transformation did not only entail the hard issues of structures and processes, but that it also impacted on the hearts and minds of individuals and the spirit of our organisation.

Colonel Kobus Smit expressed to the media that the DOD would be staffed to represent the population of South Africa at large and that civilians must also be utilised. Major General Themba Matanzima explained the staffing imperatives and that the Army was looking for well-trained professionals, but at the same time that we were looking for representivity.

In the new structures at management level by December 1999 there had to be 50% black representivity and 30% women at this level – the challenges were enormous. Those suitable candidates who were not trained according to professional standards would be afforded the opportunity. According to Colonel Johann Preller at the media briefing the staffing of the new structures was proving to be very emotional as it would result in identifying huge numbers of personnel to be rationalised.

The changes earmarked for the new SA Army, although it seemed harsh to many, needed to meet the imperatives of a smaller, representative, affordable and effective public service combined with the other Arms of Service so as to protect our country and the new Constitution. So we steered our path through a fiery cauldron and ran the gauntlet from day to day.

In February 1999 one of our senior officers, Colonel Japie Dreyer, on the personal staff of General Gilbert Remano and one of my personal friends approached me and said: "General, do you realise that you are becoming 55 in May? If you do not opt for a severance package now you will have to remain in the service until you are 60." The revelation hit me like a ton of bricks and I needed to sit down momentarily and think about this. I said to Japie Dreyer: I will speak to Henriette this evening and give you an answer by tomorrow, thank you for telling me. That day I made the hardest decision of my life by deciding to leave my beloved army.

Henriette's advice was: "Roland, one swallow does not make a summer. It is time for you to spend more time with your family; there is life beyond the Army!" So that was it. For the second time I submitted my papers for retirement; this time I was serious about it. General Gilbert Remano was extremely troubled and he arranged for me to discuss the situation with our two defence ministers. They both said to me that I had a promising career ahead of me and that in due course I would be promoted to the next rank. I replied:

> Ministers, I dearly appreciate your gesture and it was an extreme privilege and honour to work with you. However, please let me go, as I owe this to my family and I dearly need to think about a second career. What you need now is a person that can create stability in the organisation, as up to now I had thrived on change and sincerely believe that I had done what I had been called for. I shall make myself available to join the reserve force and will be ready to be called upon at moment's notice.

My papers were signed. A few years later when I met Ronnie Kasrils at a function, he jokingly referred to me as "the General that got away."

I made sure that the concept of mission command for mobile warfare was written into the Army's doctrine before I retired. As such the South African Army's leadership, command and management manual was published in May 2000 (ICN: 7610-18-035-1555). Some of my articles relating to mission command, as well as command and staff work in general, were published in the manual. I felt pleased that the concepts of mobile warfare and mission command had finally taken root in the Army. It was ironic, after so many years in trying to get it through that it was the newly transformed Army which accepted these concepts.

I held my last massive strategic workshop for the Army at Buffelspoort, west of Hartebeespoort Dam, in February 1999. It was in the form of a war game for the majority of all the newly appointed incumbents; close on 450 people attended. Each new incumbent had the opportunity to introduce himself to his colleagues and to say what his role and tasks were all about. We started with Lieutenant Gilbert Remano, the Chief of the Army. I was next. For me this was an emotional moment. Deloitte and Touche fielded a feedback report to the CSANDF soon afterwards stating that they were disturbed by the fact that I was leaving at this critical juncture of defence transformation, due to the leadership role I had performed thus far.

Beeld, one of the well-known newspapers in South Africa stated on 27 April that "Major General Roland de Vries, Deputy Chief of the Army has played a huge role in the transformation of the Army. According to informed sources it was not going to be easy to find a replacement for him as he was an outstanding leader and good strategist. Furthermore it can be said that de Vries had gained huge support in the ranks of the Army."

These positive announcements did not alleviate my sombre mood in any way ... although I already felt the stirring of excitement for other things waiting on the other side of the hill. In April I held an intimate meeting with the general staff to plan the way forward and then handed the "sword" over to them. On 30 April I gave my last speech and I was out of uniform. How can I ever explain to anyone what I felt!

Aftermath of Defence Transformation

Despite real or perceived shortcomings of the SANDF there was substantial progress made during the transformation process, which was now truly in motion and carried forward. Civilian control over the military was well established. Even the operational conduct was fair as the SANDFs emergency relief operations with the floods in Mozambique in 1999–2000 were widely acclaimed. The overall staff reduction targets were being realised as the full-time component of the SANDF had been reduced from more than 113,000 to 78,000 members with still further downsizing foreseen in the near future. In addition, a proper voluntary military system (VMS) had been established. As such affirmative action policies were satisfactorily implemented: Blacks made up 60.6%, Asians 1.2%, Coloureds 12.1% and Whites 26.1% as of 1 April 2001 of the SANDF's full-time complement.

As of 2004 the transformation and its integration process was considered complete, with the integrated personnel having been incorporated into a modified structure with many of the substructures and equipment of the former SADF being retained. Four armed services made up the new SANDF, namely the: South African Army, South African Air Force, South African Navy, and South African Military Health Service. The SANDF had since participated in a number of peacekeeping operations in places such as the Democratic Republic of the Congo and Burundi. A peacekeeping mission to Sudan had recently begun and is scheduled to be increased to brigade strength. It is clear from the information I received from a number of United Nations officials working in countries like Sudan that our military of today was generally plagued by criminality and ill-discipline. To me it was sad to hear this.

One serious issue confronting the SANDF was our rapidly aging soldier community being plagued by high HIV percentages – the fact was that our infantry soldiers were some of the oldest in the world. In addition there are severe shortages of pilots and naval combat officers due to the replacement and emigratingon of white officers from the former SADF. This was exacerbated by a serious loss of trained personnel the last decade and the gradual diminishing and decommissioning of much needed equipment due to funding issues. All of the latter negative admissions raised questions regarding the fighting efficiency of the SANDF. Some of these issues were being addressed with the introduction of military skills development (MDC) programmes as well as aggressive recruitment and training by the reserve force regiments. Nonetheless, there is some good news as a few reports have also been received that our troops are doing extremely well in peace operations in Africa. This was usually due to the presence of outstanding leadership; it was heartening to hear this. There were pockets of outstanding leadership in the SANDF who were truly trying their darnedest to restore the combat potential and discipline of the SANDF. There are general officers such as Lieutenant General Derek Ngwebe and Major General Les Rudman who truly cared about the future of our military. Order and progression are usually only restored when there is a serious shake-up of the military and many lives are lost, similarly to what the former SADF experienced during Operation Savannah in 1975–76.

The creation of the SANDF since the advent of South Africa's non-racial democracy in 1994 had been one of the most successful episodes in the transformation of the Republic's civil service. However, on the cusp of the new millennium, critical questions about the Defence Force's budget allocations, its personnel levels, and equipment still raised many concerns about its effectiveness. By itself there were many complaints uttered that the new defence structures were dysfunctional in comparison with those of the former SADF. The sheer truth according to me was that no structure could perform optimally if the appropriately developed leadership was not in place. By the way, it takes years to build a smart defence force. I have yet to see a smart all-African standing army. Perhaps with the genetic memory of the old SADF, just perhaps, the new SANDF stood a chance; if this reality was appreciated and respected by the reigning political power and senior military leadership – let us wait and see. I would dearly wish to be proud of our defence force before I retire permanently – those in command of the military and who have the political say in our country do need to get their act together swiftly; please!

An Ending – a Farewell to Arms

I have fought through a firestorm not dissimilar to war. I felt strangely comfortable and satisfied; I had achieved what I had set out to do and was at peace with myself and the world.

I have enjoyed a thrilling and fulfilling career of 37 years in the military. I belonged to an Army I was extremely proud of from 1963 until 1999 – its trials and tribulations and all. At times I was subtly reprimanded by my dear wife Henriette about what she referred to as "your blind loyalty to the military... Roland!" ... Yes my dear Henriette, I know...! I was part of a defence force which had started out as a small, inappropriately equipped military organisation before growing into one of the most powerful on the continent by the 1980s. I was now swayed by my responsibility to my family to take up the next challenge in civilian life – a family that had supported me loyally over a long service career. Fight through the objective Roland – not up to it! There is life beyond the Army!

18

Life Beyond the Army

To Live is to Experience

If you can dream – and not make dreams your master ... !
"If" - Rudyard Kipling

The Story of My Later Life – Bouts of Anticipation and Thrills

Sure enough, it turned out that there is life after the Army. Ever since leaving the military I continued having a full and interesting life. Although it probably deserves a detailed book I will attempt to briefly highlight in this chapter some of the main episodes.

I enjoyed my life in the military tremendously for all those years; it was all I knew. I loved my Army and my soldiers. Many a time after I had retired from the military I asked myself the question (I need to share this openly with you): "Roland, would you really have been able to make a difference in this 'new' army of ours? Or, would you eventually have become bogged down in stagnation; failing to make progress and to effect the necessary change that was so dearly required? Could this 'new' army be turned into something of value that would generate respect from the people it served, its country, and the outside world? Or would it be turned into an ugly construction site filled with the self-righteously ignorant, a force-field of resentment guarding every interaction?"

The mere thought was too ghastly to contemplate and I put such thinking forcefully behind me. My time had come to leave the military. It was now time to do something else. Would I be able to add value on the outside?

On leaving the South African Defence Force on 30 April 1999 I was pleasantly surprised to discover that I could apply umpteen things from the military in the business sector which I knew best: Planning, strategising, tactics, deception, command, leadership and going all-out, fighting on your feet. I would soon realise that transformational leadership in the public and private sectors were akin to mission command (as I reviewed these concepts in Chapter 8 of this book.) Where I found flourishing systems this all-powerful ingredient was present. If not, I found corruption, open resentment, divergence, quarrel, tension and inconsistency, which from my vantage point invariably led to failed families, failed businesses and failed states.

I was soon thinking that MBAs could use the proven "joint operational planning cycle" of the Israeli defence force as part of their management toolkit, as well as the honest to goodness "operations instruction" to put their many plans into action. I would put this forward to them very carefully – don't become pushy, Roland, you must still get used to wearing a suit.

Wow, at the same time this was rather scary and otherwise electrifying – manoeuvre warfare all over again, requiring the knack to operate from the eye of firestorm! I was about to enter a world of good things and bad things, a boutique of conflict not dissimilar to the military where great strides of progress could be marred by surges of corruption (the latter is extremely worrying.) The flames thrown at you by battalions of civilians dressed in suits, smelling more of aftershave and less of cordite could be just as lethal – the time-proven principle of Sun Tzu applied: "Know your enemy, know yourself or succumb in every battle".

I was ready to indulge in high adventure as an outsider in a world that was still foreign to me. As such I shall set forth the last thirteen years of my life in surges of excitement. This chapter is about my final career in civilian life until I started writing Eye of the Firestorm in 2010. This became possible when Henriette and I decided to spend a few exciting years in the Middle East. (Okay, let me be honest, she decided and I obeyed!)

"Civvy Street" – a Daunting Prospect!

Interestingly enough, many of my civilian friends as well as those in the military plus a few senior members of my family had their reservations. They cautioned that I had no reason to think that military successes would inevitably lead to a thriving career as a civilian. Although I never saw myself as a "businessman" I decided to prove them wrong and was set to venture out and have some fun in "Civvy Street". My core belief was that if I were open to it, life could still fling up many exhilarating new experiences and I would have plenty opportunities to openly, with no strings attached, share the knowledge I had acquired over so many years in uniform.

If I had a fear, it was that I would be bored. No thank you! I wasn't signing up for that, even if I had to leopard-crawl to the next piece of tactical ground just to glance over it with a pair of eyes progressively growing dimmer. I soon found out that living was about experiences and that networking was the mega-trend of the future – manoeuvring by other means.

Thirteen Years in Civvy Street – Filled with Fun and Excitement

The first of May 1999 was D-Day for me in a battle of another kind in "Civvy Street" – break in, break through, break out by manoeuvring and applying the principles of warfare was the only way I knew.

I found marketing similar to the functions of battle: Find the customer, fix the customer and strike the customer. I quickly had to master the principles of management the "civvy way" – the most important being that to maintain close contact with your customer did not lead to one of you dying!

In the few paragraphs below I shall now briefly explain the different ventures in which I was involved. Many of these happened simultaneously as I did not want to get bogged down in one activity only and could now freely share my hours amongst a variety of endeavours. I was following the manoeuvrist approach where campaign planning and pace was important – maintain the momentum, run a few risks and accept open flanks. One way or the other, I was employed more or less full time for almost four years as an independent contractor by Denel from 2001 until 2004; and again by Grintek Integrated Defence Solutions (GRIDS, a subsidiary of SAAB-GRINTEK) in 2005.

I developed a certain consultancy expertise on my feet and essentially enjoyed and presented it in two main areas to a variety of clients, both locally and abroad, namely: (1) Leadership and management development; and (2) the provision of integrated defence, security and disaster management solutions. In all these areas I found that I could apply the expertise I had acquired in the military. This followed the simple dictum that for many solutions one must to be able "to see, decide and act" and that strategy was simply finding the answers to the "ends, ways and means" – of course, sound leadership always remained the force multiplier in getting things done. Voila, Roland! Charge forth, do it and – most important of all – enjoy it! In the process I could also have the joy of working with Henriette and supporting Pieter to get his degree – including honours – since he was studying from home. Through this I could sharpen my wits on some of his management subjects for free, play squash and enjoy sailing with him (reconnoitre in force and not dig in!)

Initially, Danie Maritz, Managing Director of Productivity Development, (Pty.) Ltd., in Johannesburg requested me to join his company for a few months so that I could find my feet. This was more or less to establish a solid base from which I could "fight." In this way, he was extremely kind to me and I am eternally thankful for his kind gesture. Danie Maritz, André Kruger, Solly Mollo and I had cemented a solid friendship during our collective involvement in the defence transformation programme from 1994–99. By the same token we had established a good relationship with Deputy Defence Minister Ronnie Kasrils when we started implementing transformational leadership as a basis to manage change in the SANDF.

I ventured out as a civilian with Maritz in May 1999 visiting obscure corners in South Africa and elsewhere to consult on leadership and management development, forays that brought tremendous enrichment. During this time I had opportunity to visit the "Luftkrigsskolen" (Air Fighter School) in Trondheim, Norway to lecture on defence transformation and transformational leadership precepts.

Productivity Development was associated with the Leadership Institute of Dr. Bernard Bass and Dr. Bruce Avolio in San Francisco in the United States. We subsequently received an invitation to address leadership seminars in the USA on how we had institutionalised transformational leadership within the SANDFs formula for integrated leadership, command and management. This was quite applicable as the US military was experimenting with similar theories after finding that transformational leadership significantly improved the performance of military organisations. Incidentally, I had written an article published in *Salut*[1] just before I retired from the army in April 1999 on "Developing the Perfect Platoon," based on similar principles. In fact, the Sergeant-Major of the Army, Koos Moorcroft, and I had started a pilot project to initiate such a venture.

Providing Integrated Solutions within the Domain of Civil Security – See, Decide and Act

Early in 2000 I was approached by Nedbank to assist them with the design of an integrated security strategy against violent crime. Serious crimes, such as bank robberies and cash-in-transit heists, had an enormously negative and traumatic effect on their personnel. Crime is not dissimilar to war and therefore fighting crime required practices not dissimilar to that of making war. They had heard from someone somewhere that I had the knack to strategize.

The driving force to find a creative solution was Mr. Pete Backwell, the head of Nedbank, supported by Mr. Johan van Schalkwyk and Mr. Loutjie Bouwer. So I dug in and did just that, finding the work highly satisfying. This gave me the opportunity to establish Oak Solutions, (Pty.) Ltd., in partnership with my wife, Henriette and Craig Harrison. Craig Harrison was a military intelligence specialist who had become a family friend ever

1 The official monthly issued military journal of the SANDF.

since the days we served together at the Army College in 1988–90.

Apart from designing the security strategy for Nedbank, Oak Solutions was also contracted by Nedcor's Safety and Security Division to undertake a survey amongst their technology and operations (T&O) personnel in several branches of Nedbank, Permanent Bank and Peoples Bank and to make recommendations to improve overall security. For practical and financial reasons this survey was limited to twenty branches in mainly the Gauteng West Region.

Information available to Oak Solutions soon indicated that the corporation and especially its security division, was very aware of the increasing crime situation in the country. They also discovered that the T&O personnel in branches operated on the frontline where an increasing number of fraud and robberies actually took place. It is believed that it was this knowledge that urged the Safety and Security Division to formally seek the opinions of T&O personnel in the branches regarding possible improvements that could be made. We deemed this an excellent idea (participative leadership works.) Their opinions were put to good value in the process of improving security and thereby decreasing asset loss, as well as personnel trauma caused by issues such as robberies and fraud. Once again, I realised that in life one could learn much from the people on the ground and that dynamic organisations were ecologies of ideas – the study of the relationships between the living and their interactions with their natural or developed environments and the risks they were involved in from day to day.

Nedbank had been an exciting project, from which I learned together with Henriette and Craig how to operate successfully in the shady world of commerce. Now we needed to venture forward and find other exciting endeavours.

Our newly established small company soon operated in close alliance with another small company named Disaster Management Solutions (DMS) (Pty.) Ltd. The owner was Ferdie Mocke whom we had befriended after Nedbank whilst working together on several disaster management projects. To me this was similar to "joint operations" requiring finely tuned marrying-up drills and integration of effort. I thoroughly enjoyed this challenge.

For some time our two companies were productively involved in management consulting and training and in providing integrated security and disaster management solutions to not only government institutions but also to different companies in the private sector. Craig Harrison and I had worked closely together with the Department of Provincial and Local Government (DPLG) in developing a comprehensive strategy to implement the Disaster Management Act and Policy Framework and conducting national workshops throughout South Africa. In this way we befriended Mr. Louis Buys who was the undisputed head of the National Disaster Management Centre. Subsequent projects with DMS included the development of disaster management strategies and policy frameworks for six provinces, two metropoles and two district municipalities as well as for the South African Police Services and Johannesburg City Power.

The work that Harrison and I did as independent consultants included the development and implementation of integrated safety and security solutions for key financial institutions and a number of security businesses locally and in Africa. At times we worked closely with Ulwazi Management Solutions (Pty.) Ltd. owned by Dr. Frans Volschenk, a very competent and amiable executive. Similarly Craig and I did an extremely interesting and successful project for South Africa's main electricity supplier Eskom from April 2002 until October 2005.

Let us digress for a moment and venture into the shadow of serious economic crime, namely conductor theft, a plague in the whole of South Africa.

The Eskom Project and its Aftermath – Unexpectedly Different (2002–2005)

Because of its unique nature the Eskom project demands the spotlight for a moment. Due to corruption ingrained and rife within Eskom and as such all of their esteemed customers were being subjugated to perpetual power surges and outages, oh well: Africa my beginning, Africa my end!

The focus of the project was to terminate conductor theft in the central region of Gauteng Province. It was an experiment initiated by a handful of innovative Eskom engineers to find a creative solution for this bothersome issue. Klaas Gouws was the man behind the idea. For a while the few engineers ran the gauntlet and took it out of the hands of their own security division, which involved seizing the initiative internally that triggered much animosity in the process; also towards us, as the new kids of light complexion on the block who, ironically so, became instrumental in solving the problem.

The engineers had approached me and Craig Harrison to tender for the project due to our Nedbank experience and said that the criterion for contract award was not "Black Economic Empowerment" (BEE) this time around but securing a creative solution. This included running a six-month pilot project before a three-year contract would be awarded to the successful company. There was good money in this venture.

Know your enemy: The criminals we encountered in this nebulous world of crime talked about the money bills (money suspended from the pylons) hanging from the beautiful star-lit South African sky. Rains were good for us budding crime fighters as the criminals feared electrifications. This dramatically reduced the number of thefts, which lowered the incidence, which improved our performances bonuses (wow, suddenly ex-military guys were working for real money!). It seems that in Africa crime pays in several ways since it is one of our fastest growing industries (an estimated 17% per year). Okay, so this was going to be predominantly a night operation, a game we knew well. Typically African-style this was to be a "low-tech war."

The thieves of these conductors used wooden brandering with hacksaws affixed to the end with wire to cut at the overhead conductor; or they simply pulled the cable out of the ground with a stolen bakkie (a small truck.) Quite often we apprehended the perpetrators with metal filings embedded in their wiry curls (Mozambican, Zimbabwean, Somalian or Nigerian.) I soon discovered that the battle was not dissimilar to what we had experienced during Operation Carrot and Yahoo in the Death Triangle (Chapter 11), but without the killing.

To do the job Craig and I established a company, "Global Strategic Solutions" (GSI – similar to a combat group such as 61 Mech) in partnership with Mr. Hentie Botha, a former operative of the security Branch of the South African Police. In turn, we sub-contracted a Black-owned guarding company and a Black-owned intelligence company for this purpose – our forces were marshalled for the next exciting "fighting" mission. GSI was awarded the contract against the bidding of twelve other contenders. Also, without exception the twelve had offered guarding solutions – an attritionist approach – while we had adopted a manoeuvrist approach.[2] We had declared quite boldly that we wanted to prove a concept

2 Refer to Chapter 6.

and therefore we would close down the crime and our own company (GSI) within three years, with the sole purpose to prove a point! It was our express purpose to use our military expertise.

I was convinced that in various ways many security companies often unwittingly perpetuated crime instead of ending it (as the Americans are perpetuating counterinsurgency in Iraq and Afghanistan.) I say this tongue in cheek since I came to exactly this conclusion after working in this field for nine years. In addition, I believed that many security companies, knowingly or unknowingly provided a home for the intelligence sources of organised as well as petty crime gangs – this nebulous world where many of the perpetrators originally came from Nigeria, Mozambique, Zimbabwe and Somalia. Don't forget our local boys! As ordinary business people did their networking openly, so the main criminals did theirs in places like Turffontein Race Track all hush-hush and illegally.

Our "surprisingly different" paramilitary solution offered to Eskom included command-and-control, providing intelligence and a rapid response capability. We ran a 24/7 operations centre out of Centurion. Pretoria. Our outlook was not to focus on hitting the criminal at the place of the crime since this opportunity lasted only for a few minutes. Instead, our primary objective was the criminal's underground world where intelligence was gathered and the plans were made. We needed "agents" and the local community as sources of intelligence to infiltrate the shadowy world of the criminal. An additional part of the solution was to close down their market, countless illegal scrap metal dealers. Once apprehended, criminals had to appear in court without delay, had to be tried swiftly and then convicted. It was also imperative to spread the word that the matter of conductor theft was a serious economic crime of national proportion. GSI appointed a fulltime advocate to run that part of our business, Advocate Johan le Roux.

Giel Reinecke was the project leader; no, the commander of the operation. You might recall that Reinecke had served with me at 61 Mech in 1981–82 and at the Army College in 1988–90 and we had remained close friends ever since. The remarkable Johan Potgieter became our intelligence officer, a covert intelligence expert. Moreover, we trained our "forces" as we had done at 61 Mech in 1981–82, transforming ordinary guards into extraordinary operators and blending them into a high-performance crime-fighting team – we successfully applied the principle of see, decide and act.

We trained our teams during the week and over weekends until they experienced a paradigm shift. It resembled preparing 61 Mech for battle all over again. We decided that bonuses accrued for performance would find its way to our people on the ground and not to management. We were justifiably proud of our all-African ground force. Many of them came from the disbanded 32 Battalion. In the process we developed a comprehensive doctrine and standing operating procedure (SOP) for the demise of conductor theft. I consistently thought of the battle doctrine and SOP we had developed for 61 Mech in 1981–82. Live and learn.

Giel Reinecke is presently employed as a senior security consultant for the government of Saudi-Arabia. He has fond memories of his role in the Eskom project:

It was exhilarating to apply my military mind and to solve a problem of crime in a civilian context. More so, to participate in a project where I could literally experience how a well-devised strategy could be implemented to the letter, practically and enthusiastically, at grassroots over a three-year period. This included the successful implementation of a number of operational plans and the development of a standing operating procedure for

Eskom to eradicate conductor theft.

It was extremely satisfying to transform ordinary security guards into a formidable crime fighting team. This included the cross-cultural friendships forged amongst our more than one hundred operatives in the field and to participate in their teamwork, commitment and resourcefulness. It proved what could be done through good leadership and caring. Then there were our impromptu "field barbecues" in the field with our off-duty "observers" after a night of hard work and how these times of friendship were so positively enjoyed by our down-to-earth crews.

My greatest "wow!" was when we arrested Wally Meadon, a prominent scrap metal dealer in Springs for illegal trade in stolen conductors. This particular operation was meticulously planned and executed by us in close cooperation with the highly effective "Scorpions" crime investigation unit. It is interesting to note that the Scorpions were later on disbanded (2009) by the South African President, Mr. Jacob Zuma. "Were they getting too close to exposing major corruption in government circles?" I wondered ...

I now want to summarise the entire Eskom project, heralded as one of their most successful security projects, particularly in reducing the crime rate within 36 months from an average of 140 cable theft incidents per month to zero. On completion of our project our company was summarily ousted by Eskom and the work awarded to a Black-owned Security Company offering a clumsy guarding solution. Within three months the crime rate was higher than ever. The enterprising engineers of Eskom who had worked so intimately with GSI just shook their heads in astonishment. Don't pursue this issue about the proven competency of GSI, their bosses said, or your own jobs would be in jeopardy. Was Eskom truly interested in delivery, or was there something else to it? But, this is Africa... and the broader business world... who knows?

In March 2007 City Power Johannesburg requested a submission on stamping out conductor theft. I wrote a detailed proposal that included providing strategic crime intelligence, rapid response capability and the means to investigate cable theft effectively. I did the work on behalf of a three-company consortium, namely: Ulwazi Management (Pty.) Ltd., AMAHLO Consulting CC and Quemic (Pty.) Ltd., who in the end was awarded the contract. City Power had benchmarked at Eskom and was advised that we could provide an innovative solution. I was proud of this achievement – an integrated concept to defeat crime had proved itself. Hello South African Police Service! Put that in your pipe and smoke it.

Two of my favourite local projects were to support Quemic (Pty.) Ltd., an extremely inventive medium-sized security company, with the development of an integrated security solution for Metrorail Western Cape and Transnet (National Rail and Freight Transport and Logistics Business.) The work included a comprehensive threat and vulnerability assessment as well as the design of an operational plan for Transnet Pipelines. The integrated national security strategy for Transnet was signed off by their group chief executive, Maria Ramos, at the end of February 2009, just before embarking on her tenure as CEO of ABSA. Ms. Ramos is considered one of the architects of South Africa's new and improved economy. It was a privilege to meet this dynamic businesswoman who had been rightfully described in the South African business and financial circles as a "gem." Not surprisingly she featured on Fortune magazine's list of most powerful women in international business for four consecutive years from 2004 to 2007.

Next in line as one of my favourite security projects with Ferdie Mocke of DMS was to support Mr. Roelf Kruger, CEO of G4S in Nigeria, with the development of a concept for a guard force for the capital, Abuja. This was typical military work: "Provide strategic direction, leadership and management; provide forces, support forces, and employ forces." It proved to be the perfect challenge.

I truly believe that the civvies can learn from the military, especially about integrated planning, operational orders and precision engagement – this should become MBA material!

My Sporadic Interactions with the SANDF after May 1999

Now to venture back in time for a wee bit ... I somehow just could not succeed in shunning the military – and history has a tendency to repeat itself.

A final event which I shared with 61 Mech after my retirement was the memorial service held at Lohatlha on 17 November 2005 to close the unit. It was an extreme honour to participate in this historical event and to lay a wreath to honour the 61 Mech soldiers who had fallen in battle. 61 Mech was disbanded at Lohatlha on 18 November 2005, to be merged with 8 South African Infantry Battalion at Upington. The last serving commanding officer was Lieutenant Colonel Etienne Visagie. The final chapter followed when the colours of 61 Mech were laid up in Bloemfontein at 1 SAI on 2 December 2005. The closing-down work was handled with utmost dignity!

Soon after I retired from the SANDF I was requested by part-time force officers Ray van Zandten and Gerhardt Kamfer to assist them with the advancement of the Reserve Force association and I was selected national chairman. We worked closely with Dr. John Job, Major general (retired) Reginald Modise and Mr. Keith Mokoape of the Reserve Force Council. The council before long became a statutory body with Job appointed as its national chairman and Mokoape as his deputy.[3] We succeeded in fusing the association and council into one body and subsequently developed its strategic framework and positioning for the future. For some years to come I had the pleasure of working closely with the Reserve Force Council and with two outstanding part-time officers who were promoted to major general, Ian Deetlefs and Roy Anderson. This was to establish the future reserve force of South Africa.[4] The work entailed a number of workshops held with part-time force members across our country as well as with members of parliament. In many instances this included work done with Dr. (Colonel) Rocky Williams and Solly Mollo, whom I had befriended during our army's transformation in 1994. I resigned as chairman of the Reserve Force Association and member of the Reserve Force Council once I started to work extensively in Africa from 2009 onwards.

I had the opportunity to work three more times for the SANDF after my retirement in April 1999 in an official capacity as a member of its reserve force. In 1999 I was recalled by General Siphiwe Nyanda to conduct a sensitive board of enquiry on the coup d'état in the Transkei. Major General Solly Shoke was a member of my board and soon afterwards he was promoted to Lieutenant-General and appointed as Chief of the Army. He currently serves as the Chief of the SANDF.

Furthermore, in 2005 I was asked by Brigadier Solly Mollo, then commanding the Military Academy in Saldanha, to support him with the design of his strategy and five-

3 Former head of intelligence of MK. He later became a major general in the Reserve Force. I was instrumental in supporting his later promotion.

4 At the time Roy Anderson was the Chairman of Liberty Life. He was a good friend as we were connected through his service as a senior part-time force officer and myself as the commander of 7 South African Division and later on as the deputy chief of the army.

year business plan for his institution. In 2006 Mollo was promoted to major general and appointed as the Chief of Human Resource Management for Defence. He requested Lieutenant General Derek Ngwebe for my assistance in supporting his division with the development of their human resource management strategy, which we subsequently did through a number of fruitful workshops.

Post-Military Career Highlights within the Defence Sector

It was providential for me to be drawn in to some extremely interesting defence projects after my military career. With such ventures came a variety of juicy optional extras. My first major undertaking was to become involved with the elaborate Ground-Based Air Defence Programme of the SANDF, Armscor and Denel. Denel was founded in 1991 and established as a state-owned aerospace and defence technology business under the Ministry of Public Enterprises in April 1992. It was created when the manufacturing subsidiaries of Armscor were split up in order for Armscor to become the sole procurement agency for the SADF and later on for the SANDF.

In January 2001 I was approached by Mr. Willie van Biljon, CEO of Kentron, a subsidiary of Denel, to lead the GBADS bidding process as the campaign leader. What followed was a complex bidding process with BAE Systems (United Kingdom), Reutech Radar Systems, Reutech Defence Solutions, GRINTEK Communication Systems and LOG-TEK Engineering Solutions (Pty.) Ltd. all siding with Denel. I had the opportunity to soon make the acquaintance of formidable engineers and technologists within these defence industry circles, many of them being legendary such as Paul Bester, Schalk Verwey, James Verster, Piet Smit, James Kerr, Lex Jackson, Donald Marwick and Pieter van der Bijl, to name but a few. Through the complex work undertaken I had the opportunity to work closely with the CEO of Denel, Mr. Flip Botha and with Messrs. Nick Francs and Andrew Humphreys of BAE. I quickly learnt much more about the intricacies of business politics, systems engineering, complex bidding processes, the quirks of engineers, competitor analysis and industrial participation than I'd previously thought possible. It was truly like fighting a huge military campaign. Fortunately we had the super-efficient executive secretary Elmarie Bierman to support us – more like our chief of staff. Our main competitor was THALES Defence (France), who was in cahoots with African Defence Systems (ADS).[5] During the initial bid building process I requested Kentron to employ Craig Harrison to manage Industrial Participation.[6] He soon became an expert and for his outstanding work in this field was commended by Armscor, Denel and BAE.

Armscor requested a re-submission of the GBADS tender after the first bid was entered due to certain technical controversies. A decision by Denel-BAE and THALES-ADS to submit a joint bid with Denel acting as the bid leader and joint systems integrator followed. Mr. Schalk Verwey of Denel was appointed lead systems engineer. It was decided to base the bid on the short-range shoulder-launched man-portable air defence missile of THALES, known as Starstreak, developed and manufactured by THALES Air Defence Systems in Belfast, Ireland (previously known as Shorts Air Defence Company.) Finally, on Thursday,

5 ADS became well known in later years due to the corruption trial of Shabir Shaik and his alleged deceitful relationship with Jacob Zuma.

6 Whilst Craig Harrison and I were involved with the Denel GBADS programme we directed the Eskom Defeat Conductor Theft programme after-hours and over weekends while it was superbly managed by Hentie Botha and Giel Reinecke on a full-time base.

28 November 2002, Armscor announced that it had contracted Denel for delivery of the Local Warning Segment of the GBADS programme with a total value of ZAR 796 700 389, 00. It was said that Denel, as the prime contractor, would utilize various South African and foreign sub-contractors and suppliers to do the work. Mr. Paul Bester was appointed by Denel as the Programme Manager. I worked two more fruitful years for Denel, providing services as marketing consultant and for new business development. During this time I supported Armscor with studies pertaining to the new generation anti-tank and mortar systems for mechanised infantry. I was also involved in writing a paper on the future employment of mechanised infantry when Denel (Lyttleton Engineering Works) entered the bidding process for the provision of a new generation infantry combat vehicle system for the Army. One of my exciting ventures for Denel over the same period was to work closely with Mr. George Tate, based in the United Arab Emirates (UAE). I subsequently consulted for the Chief of the UAE Land Forces Brigadier General Saeed Mohamed Al Rumaithy (soon to be promoted to Major General) in April–May 2003 regarding the enhancement of the manoeuvre capability and combat readiness of their mechanised forces. This included providing insights into the establishment of an army combat centre for the UAE.

Kentron was subsequently renamed Denel Integrated System Solutions (DISS). The GBADS programme was successfully completed by 2010 and delivered into service with the Air Defence Formation based in Kimberley. I felt satisfied when I received the good news. I could not help thinking that it was a misfortune that we did not have Starstreak available when the Russian MiGs harassed us in southern Angola in 1987–88 during operations such as Modular and Prone.

Following on our work for Denel, Harrison and I were requested by CEO Riaz Saloojee to work with Grintek Integrated Defence Solutions, a subsidiary of SAAB-GRINTEK, for another year. This was to develop business within the domains of defence and civil security. The work took us to SAAB in Stockholm (Sweden) and entailed the design of a marketing strategy for Africa and technology system enhancements in the fields of civil security and disaster management. Through this involvement we succeeded in linking up Mr. Louis Buys of the National Disaster Management Centre (NDMC) of the Department of Provincial and Local Government (DPLG) with the Swedish Rescue Services. These ventures included a number of enthralling visits to Sweden. Incidentally, Mr. Riaz Saloojee was recently appointed CEO of Denel.

Manoeuvrings in Africa and Sharing Thoughts on Defence Transformation with Others

Over the last decade fortune smiled on me as I was afforded ample opportunities to consult in Africa on defence transformation, leadership and command subjects – this was what I truly enjoyed doing. These ventures at times involved working closely with Dr. Jakkie Cilliers, Major General (retired) Len le Roux and Colonel (retired) Henri Boshoff from the Institute of Security Studies for Africa (ISS); at other times it took me to Nigeria to work with Danie Maritz of Productivity Development in support of the Nigerian Army. For many of these enthralling moments I was accompanied by my friend, Solly Mollo (former MK) as well as business partner, Craig Harrison.

In 2007 I was approached by South African filmmaker, Katinka Heyns and Tobie Cronje of Sonneblom Films to do an interview about my defence transformation exploits, which included my family and a few close friends.[7] This one-hour programme subsequently became part of a television series aired by kykNET.

On Various Transformation Initiatives

I wish to summarise only a few of my African experiences that were highlights regarding defence transformation bouts on our continent. This I do apart from those specifically mentioned below. I shared such experiences with a number of military as well as civilian leaders all over the African continent. This included monitoring and tutoring senior level government and military officials in formal groups and informal individual sessions from countries such as Malawi, Zambia, Sri Lanka, Nepal and Southern Sudan – this I did many times as a freelance and for which I did not expect payment. I furthermore facilitated the Burundi transformation process by tutoring various political and military groupings in transformation and modalities for their peace processes. This was done in co-operation with Lieutenant General Andrew Masondo of the SANDF, Mr. Gary Dixon of Scribe Communications and my business partner, Craig Harrison. I also conducted a number of workshops locally in cooperation with the Institute for Security Studies for the Defence teams of Sierra Leone and Southern Sudan. Other juicy adventures were sharing experiences and conducting workshops on transformation in Ghana and the Democratic Republic of Congo. I produced a paper on the latter experience which was published by the Institute for Security Studies (African Security Review, Volume 15, No. 4, dated 2006, www.issafrica.org). The article gives a picture of Defence Transformation in South Africa and shares the experience with the military forces of the Democratic Republic of Congo. Listening to what happened during the rebellion at Gomo in November 2012 near the Rwanda border showed that my article was not widely read by Congolese military. That is Africa!

On to Antananarivo, Madagascar in 2004

Madagascar is an exotic island that is home to 300 species of frogs, 75 species of chameleons, 3 dozen species of lemurs and strange species of politicians claiming to run the country. One of my transformation ventures took me, Craig Harrison and Gary Dixon (our newly found friend and CEO of Scribe Communications) without passports and visas to Madagascar in 2004 at the request of President Marc Ravalomanana. This was to share thoughts on defence transformation with his defence ministry and army general staff.

The first step was to visit President Ravalomanana at his palace at his request, yes sir, Mister President. We waited for a while before we were summoned into his office. Apparently he was more of a business mogul than a President since he owned several of the enterprises flourishing outside the palace grounds. Shoprite was there as well with shelves as bare as those in Mother Hubbard's cupboard.

Whilst we waited Craig Harrison enviously eyed the president's heavily armoured Mercedes Geländewagen. Craig was already contracting major dysentery from working with "dirty" Madagascan money and eating peanuts in a bar we had just visited. This was okay as he still had his full SADF medical benefit as a retired officer.

Then we went into the presidential office. It was a pleasant interlude with the charismatic

---

7 Katinka Heyns' role in Jans Rautenbach's "Katrina" (1969) gained her national recognition. She subsequently went on to star in several feature films. In conjunction with her husband, Afrikaans novelist and critic, Chris Barnard, they then established Sonneblom Films. Tobie Cronjé is a South African comedian and actor, especially known for appearing in annual pantomimes.

Ravalomanana and interesting to hear him explaining to the three of us in detail how he had planned his coup d'état that brought him to power. He carefully showed us his planning maps and overlays. Then we discussed his requirements for defence transformation. He told us that we would next have a meeting with the Minister of Defence before giving a comprehensive briefing to his general staff and a large gathering of senior officers covering the SANDFs recent successful transformation. No, he was not going to attend since it was a Saturday. Before we left he told us that he wanted to change the operating language in his country to English as he was pissed off with the French and that he had instituted an English television programmes to achieve just that. This is extremely interesting Sir, thank you for this valuable titbit of information.

We would soon find out that the minister, our French interpreter and French-speaking audience were upset and quite unhappy about the President's order to meet on a Saturday. I am still uncertain whether they were genuinely interested in transformation. So much for stifling authoritarian governance. Our French interpreter facilitated the proceeding which followed and in between we used their toilets with great care since we were not issued with gumboots. It was an interesting morning ... captivating is probably more apt. There were rows of old generals – no, they did not retire, but were kept on in the system with pay. What is this that you are talking about, they asked us, about making a defence force smaller and more effective, about rationalisation and demobilisation? Afterwards the younger officers cornered me and Craig and Gary and asked whether it was truly possible to transform a defence force in a democracy. Did this really happen in your army ... ? There was excitement amongst the young. However, the three of us realised that it would soon wane and be smothered through the brutal authority of their old guard (I thought about the cliché of teaching old dogs new tricks.) Craig, Gary and I looked at each other, feeling sorry for the young officers, realising that the time for fundamental change for them had not dawned yet. Will it ever, this was Africa. Let us get out of here.

Just to clarify our fascinating experience: Marc Ravalomanana became the new President of Madagascar on 6 July 2001 after he had ousted President Didier Ratsiraka through a successful military coup. More so, Ravalomanana had gained diplomatic recognition of his government since the Malagasy High Constitutional Court in April 2002 had declared him the legitimate President after a recount of the December 2001 poll, which indicated that he had won outright. This proved to be the turning point as Western governments one by one started to recognise his government.

Notwithstanding Ravalomanana's initial successes, it was announced on 17 March 2009 that he was stepping down to hand over power to the military following a successful coup. In the process soldiers and armoured vehicles had seized the central bank and had occupied the offices of the embattled president, including seizing his Geländewagen. The army chief of staff, Colonel Andre Ndriarijaona proclaimed that his forces were 99 percent behind opposition leader and former mayor, Andry Rajoelina, who led early protests against the president and who in the meantime had installed a rival government. Rajoelina and his supporters had accused President Marc Ravalomanana of being a dictator who cared nothing about the people in one of the world's poorest countries, where more than half of its 20 million people live on less than $1 a day. This was interesting to me, Gary and Craig; our efforts to share information on defence in a democracy had obviously not borne fruit. Chuckled at the irony. The story of Africa.

In case you wondered: Neither Gary, Craig nor I were involved in any way.

Defining the Role of the Nigerian Army in a Democratic Setting in 2004

In May 2004 Danie Maritz and I advised Major General OA Azazi and the transformation team of the Nigerian Army at Port Harcourt with the design of the future role of their military within a democracy. Their primary objective was to develop a master plan which described the processes, procedures and guidelines for implemented change including the milestones to be achieved over the next ten years. The work entailed their future force posture and structure as well as training and professional development programmes. As one of the key imperatives for transformation General Azazi stated that: "The overall picture of what I saw was that 18 years of regression had made us less than contemporary even amongst African countries." The officers with whom we worked were extremely professional and the workshop was a thrill and most enlightening.

As there was too much sand in the air from the Sahara Desert storms we could not fly to Lagos to catch our flight back to South Africa. We had to traverse the Niger River Delta and Benin Province through the night as well as sixty eight illegal roadblocks, travelling in a rusty, dilapidated beige Mercedes-Benz taxi with holes all over the floor panels. I said to myself, wow, this is the place to fight a delaying battle. General Azazi phoned me the next day when he heard we had travelled by car, he said: "My G... , you Whiteys, I don't even travel on that road myself. You could get killed!" By the way, watch out South Africa. In due course the economy as well as the army of Nigeria will surpass ours.

Workshop for the African Union in Addis Ababa, Ethiopia, on the African Standby Force in 2007

In July 2007 I acted as the key facilitator and map exercise leader to enhance the concepts of the Rapid Deployment Capability of the African Standby Force. 58 officers and other officials from all over Africa including the Seychelles and Madagascar attended. The workshop took place under the auspices of the Peace Support Operations Division of the United Nations (UN) in Addis Ababa, Ethiopia. I acted as an independent consultant on behalf of the Institute for Security Studies, South Africa (ISS). This exercise was very enjoyable and most illuminating.

I could fall back on what I had learned and achieved at 61 Mech in 1981–82 during Operations Makro and Meebos concerning high readiness and rapid deployment. I delivered a draft paper on rapid deployment for this occasion and worked closely with Mr. Bereng Mtimkulu, Head Peace Support Operations Division AU Commission; South African Naval Captain Johan Potgieter seconded to the Peace Support Operations Division; Mr. Nicholas Seymour, Senior Political Officer UN; Brigadier General (Retired) Dick Baly (UK).

The Addis Ababa experience was followed up by a visit to the Peacekeeping School at Karen in Kenya with Dr. Jakkie Cilliers in August 2007. The latter initiative was in support of the Eastern Brigade of the Standby Force with the development of their role and functions and mechanisms to prepare for and manage multidimensional peace missions.
I truly appreciated participating in these latter ventures as I could follow up on the creation of the concept for the standby force for the Southern African Development Community (SADC) created in 1979 while I was serving as Chief of Joint Training. [8]

8 Refer to Chapter 2. I had then participated as the Chief of Joint Training of the SANDF in a multilateral international process sponsored by the Danish government.

Historic Turning Point at Cuito Cuanavale

On 28 May 2008 I was invited to Rhodes University, Grahamstown, together with Minister Ronnie Kasrils of Intelligence Services to talk about our epic battle that was fought in southeast Angola in 1987.[9] Ronnie Kasrils expressed his point about how he viewed Cuito Cuanavale as one of the historic turning points in the history of South Africa. I detailed our view about how our gallant brigade was never defeated on the battlefield. During his address Kasrils said the following: "I am pleased to participate in this event as part of our country's commemoration of the 20th anniversary of the historic outcome of the Battle at Cuito Cuanavale. I take this opportunity to state that we need our universities and other institutions. I am therefore encouraged by the presence of retired General Roland de Vries, who served both our democratic defence force and the former apartheid military, as I know him to be an emancipated and sober-minded person who was directly connected with the period under discussion and I look forward to his input. In fact, interaction such as this should take place between all the belligerents of the time, to relate their account of what took place. I am therefore encouraged by his presence ... " If he had said this to me in 1994–1999 I would probably have been fired by "them" – and at times it came close ... For me this was a compliment from a man I had learned to respect during the time we worked together on defence transformation from 1994–1999. During a pleasant social interlude that evening Ronnie Kasrils said to me: "Roland, how the hell did you guys do it on the ground, against those overwhelming numbers and the air threat; one day you must tell me?" Coming from an informed former adversary I considered this quite a compliment!

Supporting the Sudan People's Liberation Army with Transformation in 2009

In 2009 I supported the Southern Sudan Security Sector Development and Defence Transformation Programme as a senior defence advisor with a British consultancy company. They had secured a contract sponsored by the UK Department for International Development. Out of courtesy I am not going to mention the name of the company because I wish to say a few negative things about them, although I had a great time working with their respective ex-military and other civilian consultants, and, for that matter, with the Sudan People's Liberation Army (SPLA).

The history of Sudan has been plagued by internal conflict and civil wars since its independence in 1956. The First Sudanese Civil War took place in 1955–1972 and the second in 1983–2005. After 23 years of vicious fighting it all ended with the signing of a "Comprehensive Peace Agreement" (CPA) between the North and South. This peace accord established the foundation for a comprehensive disarmament, demobilisation and reintegration (DDR) in Sudan.

A comprehensive "Security Sector Development and Defence Transformation Project" (SSDDT) was subsequently launched in Southern Sudan in 2009 with the overall goal of achieving sustainable peace and security in the country. The underlying purpose was to transform the Southern People's Liberation Army (SPLA) from a guerrilla force into an affordable, professional, disciplined army operating under democratic civil control.

Beforehand, early in 2004, Craig Harrison and I had the opportunity of interacting with a number of officers from the SPLA who were in South Africa as guests of the

9 Refer to Chapters 15 and 16.

government to learn more about democracy and defence transformation. At the behest of Major General Solly Mollo, Craig Harrison and I were introduced to the well-known and respected Dr. John Garang de Mabior in Pretoria. He was a charismatic Sudanese politician and military leader who had led the SPLA during the Second Sudanese Civil War. Following the peace agreement he briefly served as First Vice President of Sudan until his unfortunate death in a helicopter crash in the southern part of Sudan close to the Ugandan border in July 2005. Garang was the man who had shaped the "New Sudan" model.

A few weeks after I had met Garang I was requested by ISS to address a fact-finding team of the SPLA on defence transformation at their head office at Brooklyn in Pretoria. During this session Lieutenant General Oyay Deng Ajak, SPLA Chief of General Staff, asked what one of my key recommendations about the future of their military would be? I immediately replied: "Sir, never lose your superb guerrilla fighting capability, no matter what!" He said: "Perhaps you must come to Juba once we embark on our transformation programme."

In October I was approached by said British company to join them as an independent consultant supporting the transformation process of the SPLA, which I was happy to do. The project was kick-started with a fact-finding mission to Juba, South Sudan, in November 2008. We moved lock, stock and barrel to Juba in February 2009, and commenced with the work. This entailed working with the SPLA high command at its interim headquarters on the outskirts of Juba near the airport. It was not a place easily reached with a 4X4-vehicle when it rained or a good place to use a toilet. I soon realised that our young British Project Leader was a micro-manager expert who knew nothing about defence matters and did not allow any initiative to flourish. He knew even less about working with and motivating experienced military consultants. This led to utmost frustration and the gnashing of teeth amongst our team members. I soon realised that for him his career and the continuation of future business was more important than the future effectiveness and livelihood of the SPLA. I could only smile knowingly one day when General Oyay Deng Ajak coolly said to him in a talk-to at the SPLA HQ: "You receive money for consultancy from the British Government; I would rather have the money to buy modern air defence weapons for my army." So the project leader went on to manage the objectives set for him, without realising how important it was to first establish a rapport with his client in the African way. I ignored my project leader and happily went on doing what needed to be done, which included establishing a great relationship with the officers of the SPLA and growing thinner by the day. Among other things my work entailed supporting the development of the SPLA military strategy, the design of a proposed training and education plan and policy and the crafting of a proposed logistic system. I became a close friend of a great man, the up-and-coming Lieutenant-Colonel Africano Mande. He was soon posted to the USA for a while to complete his military academic studies with the emphasis on defence transformation. I supported him throughout, even while he was away in America. In 2010 he wrote me a personal letter thanking me for the support I had given him during the transformation of the SPLA and his studies which he had completed by then. I enjoyed working with the SPLA for the year I had spent in Southern Sudan.

In January 2011 a referendum was held on independence for Southern Sudan and the South voted overwhelmingly to secede later that year as the Republic of South Sudan. Its capital was officially established at Juba and General Salva Kiir Mayardit was elected as its first president. President Al-Bashir of the North announced that he accepted the result but violence soon erupted in the disputed region of Abyei, claimed by both the North and the South. Strife in the two Sudans and the war in Darfur continue to this day. In addition the issue regarding claims to oil resources in central Sudan and the international borders between the North and the South have not been satisfactorily resolved. I wait anxiously for the two Sudans to prove that Africa is changing for the better; or is that hope in vain?

Leaving South Africa for a While and on Deciding to Write *Eye of the Firestorm*

In November 2009 when I returned from Southern Sudan I said to Henriette I have had it fighting the Anglo Boer War all over again with the British company mentioned above. So I went for a minor operation which made it difficult for me to sit down for a while and then I left on a sabbatical for two months to visit my sister and her family in England and to do some more battlefield excursions in Europe. I was joined after a month in the snow by Henriette and Pieter.

Henriette subsequently informed me that she had been transferred to the Middle East Bureau of the World Food Programme (WFP) for the United Nations (UN) – once again as the staff counsellor for UN personnel. She had done the same work from 2002 until 2010 in Africa. She said: "Stop working for a while as a consultant; come to Amman, Jordan, with me and write your book". So I replied "yes dear, thank you dear," because this was her chance in life and she's a tough one! She obtained her black belt in Judo at the age of nineteen; in service of WFP she had ventured all over Africa, slept in a hammock in central Lesotho, meandered into Liberia with a jeep and a UN driver through rebel country to remote areas and attended a Swedish army survival course for the UN at the age of 54 in Malmö, Sweden. Her new venture took her to Afghanistan, Iraq, Yemen, Palestine, East Timor, Cambodia, Thailand, Pakistan and Nepal. I often accompanied her. In February 2013 we visited the battlefield at Dien Bien Phu.

How could I refuse accompanying her to the Middle East and later also Asia and from writing *Eye of the Firestorm*!

Optional Add-Ons – Battlefields Afar – Living and Experiencing

I had always believed that it was necessary to study military campaigns so as to master the art of war and to excel at campaign planning and its successful execution. Many members who served in the military just never got enough opportunity to participate in a variety of military operations and even more so to do their thing at the different organisational levels. I believe that this was one of the main reasons that often we were subjugated on the ground due to inappropriate military stratagems and operational plans. See the many leadership lessons coming to the fore by studying the disastrous attack by the British on Spioenkop during the Anglo-Boer War. Take heed civilians: read and study business campaigns of corporates of note, otherwise you will become victims of that structuring evil and the doing before the right strategy has been formulated, followed by the laborious measuring of the wrong objectives so meticulously planned – management by objectives, is it?

I therefore wish to add the following few paragraphs as an optional extra to this chapter as it was something that meant so much to me and many of my family members and friends. It was something exhilarating we could share and learn through our lives together.

During snap prayers now and then I had expressed to the Dear Lord quite assertively that I wished to travel to battlefields afar – I saw these excursions as intellectual studies and to improve my own grasp of military strategy and campaign planning as mentioned above. He had granted me my desire and I could fulfil it at times with my family, or only with Henriette, at other times with a few of my erstwhile military comrades, or even on my own. As concentrated moments of enlivening and enrichment from the past these were forever and a day experienced as revitalizing ... those moments on the battlefields of yore were for eternity filled with endearing for those whose glory shall never fade.

To live, I realised, was to experience. Throughout my married life with Henriette I used every opportunity possible to take my family to the battlefields in South Africa or elsewhere. At times I had to carry infant Pieter across rugged territory, his pram hooked under my left arm or even bundu-bash with his four-wheeler across some uneven terrain. Occasionally, I had to use a kinetic rope on Henriette to get her up a mountain. This involved heavy lifting as her traction was quite severe but exciting and it kept me fit. In the boot of the car we had a book of the Anglo-Boer War with short descriptions of all the battles illustrated with hand-drawn maps. We went from Stormberg to Magersfontein; the war sites surrounding Colenso, Ladysmith and Dundee; to Isandlwana and Rorke's Drift and Blood River and many others; even the skirmishes trail of Breaker Morant where he had terrorised the local Boer communities near Louis Trichardt. I could tell my children what Sir Arthur Conan Doyle had written about an astonishing people who had made their mark in military history because of their staunch religion and ability to fight skilfully with weapons and horsemanship against all odds when very few others would have prevailed. I told my children how the offspring of those same Boers had fought with courage and tactical prowess facing unbearable odds during the final epic conventional war in southern Angola in 1987-88. That they had survived, never to be defeated on the battlefield. That this small community of White People will continue to make their mark positively on the history of South Africa and elsewhere in the world, no matter the odds. To quote the words of Sir Arthur Conan Doyle: "No one can know or appreciate the Boer who does not know his past, for he is what his past has made him!"

One of my most memorable visits was to Kinmen (Quemoy) Island on the shores of Mainland China in 1973, where one of the final battles was fought between the Nationalist Kuomintang Government of Chiang Kai-shek and the communists of Mao Tse-tung in 1949. Kinmen Island is 150 km west of Taiwan and only 2 km from the mainland where the Taiwan-China split took place. Another such memorable experience was to drive up "Snipers Alley", through Sarajevo in Bosnia to the Latin bridge in 1997. This was the site where Archduke Franz Ferdinand of Austria and his wife Sophie, Duchess of Hohenberg, were shot dead by six Bosnian Serb assassins on 28 June 1914. Austria-Hungary and Germany used the Sarajevo assassination as a pretext for the armed attack on Serbia that marked the beginning of World War I one month later (1914–18.)

For the last few years Henriette and I had lived in Jordan while she was stationed in Amman for the UN WFP. From 2010 onwards we had wonderful opportunities to visit the different historical sites in the area. One of our battlefield tours included Yarmuk on the Israel-Syria-Jordan border southeast of the Sea of Galilee. This battle consisted of a series of engagements that lasted for six days in August 636 A.D. near the Yarmuk River. The result of the battle was a complete Muslim victory which ended Byzantine rule in Syria. Yarmuk is regarded as one of the most decisive battles in military history and it marked the first great wave of Islamic conquests after the death of prophet Muhammad, heralding the rapid advance of Islam into the then Christian Levant.

We also travelled down the magnificent north-south mountain range where the Crusader battles had taken place near Ajlun and Karak, way down alongside the Hejaz Railway line, which had been attacked by Lawrence of Arabia and his marauding Arabs from the desert, and then travelled southwards to the well-known Wadi Rum and Fort Aqaba. The Battle of Aqaba took place on 6 July 1917 when the attacking forces of the Arab Revolt led by Auda ibu Tayi and T.E. Lawrence ("Lawrence of Arabia") overcame the Turkish defenders. A really terrific read from those times is T.E. Lawrence's "The Seven Pillars of Wisdom," about the Arab revolt in the desert against the Turks during the First World War in 1918.

I always found it incredible what you could learn from studying these past military campaigns, especially if you visited a particular battlefield and experienced the atmosphere and the terrain firsthand.[10] I encountered this phenomenon across the many battlefields I visited in Europe, North Africa, across the Bar-Lev Defence line aligning the Suez Canal from the 1973 Yom Kippur War era, and through the Sinai Desert. Even to the coast-line of Spain-Portugal at Gibraltar and Cadiz, which guarded the entrance to the Mediterranean through the ages, and up the spine of Italy from Monte Casino across the Po Valley, where 6 South African Armoured Division under the legendary Major General W.H.E. Poole had made their mark during the Second World War. The many historical sites in the Middle-East and in Asia were particularly captivating. As I walked across these battlefields it was as if the spirits of the past where still there. From many such erstwhile conflicts one could learn so much from the influence of terrain, the effects of leadership, about command decisions taken and the human side of war, if you wanted to. For example, it was remarkable that the outcome of the battle of Waterloo, where Wellington defeated Bonaparte near Leuven in Belgium on 18 June 1815, hinged on thirteen critical command decisions taken – amazingly exciting facts!

On the human side I can remember well how Henriette just suddenly burst out crying when we arrived on the beach at Gallipoli in Turkey one crisp early morning in August 2011. Here the fateful landing of the Australia and New Zealand Army Corps (ANZAC) took place on 18 March 1915. The atmosphere was overwhelming. What gripped me and Henriette most were the words that were uttered by the Turkish victor, Mustafa Kemal Atatürk in 1934: "Those heroes that shed their blood and lost their lives ... You are now lying in the soil of a friendly country. Therefore rest in peace. There is no difference between the Johnnies and the Mehmets to us where they lie side by side here in this country of ours ... You, the mothers, who sent your sons from faraway countries, wipe away your tears; your sons are now lying in our bosom and are in peace. After having lost their lives on this land they have become our sons as well."

The ANZAC veterans and the Turks still commemorate this battle together until today – there is a lesson for Southern Africa in this, especially for a few dyed-in-the-wool soldiers and politicians who still gripe about the past.

This experience made the moment when Henriette and I could visit Albany in Southern Australia, from where the Australian forces had embarked for Gallipoli, especially poignant. Just as the battle of Gallipoli was a turning point in the creation of a proud new Turkey,

10 The most costly action by the South African forces during WW 1 on the Western Front was the Battle of Delville Wood in 1916. Of the 3,000 men from the brigade who entered the wood only 768 emerged unscathed. Henriette, Pieter and I also had the opportunity to visit Cambria nearby, where tanks were used in war for the first time to break the stalemate of linear trench warfare.

the battle of Cuito Cuanavale in 1987 was a trigger in a series of turning events paving the way for the creation of a peaceful Southern Africa. Of course there were other pivotal events such as the demise of communism from 1989 onwards, the fact that Namibia could eventually transform peacefully into democracy after the Cubans and the SADF had left and when the Black Nationalist parties were disbanded and Nelson Mandela was freed from imprisonment in 1990 – these were magical things of those times we should well appreciate today. The words of Atatürk expressed in 1934 to commemorate the battle of Gallipoli should serve as a sobering lesson and reminder to those who are short-sighted and self-centred, still arguing fruitlessly about whom had won or lost at Cuito Cuanavale in August 1988.

On finalising this chapter in November 2012 Henriette and I had the opportunity to visit the Thai-Burma "Death Railway" near Kanchanaburi, which was popularised by the 1957 film "Bridge on the River Kwai". For the archaeologically minded, Kanchanaburi is most interesting, as the incidents which occurred in World War II have recently and quite by chance led to the discovery of Neolithic burial sites in the region. It was from here that the Japanese put the Allied prisoners of war to work to construct 415 km of rail leading to the Three Pagoda Pass at the Burmese Border. It is estimated that 100,000 ordinary labourers as well as 16,000 Allied prisoners died due to the beatings, starvation, overwork and malaria when constructing the railway. At Kanchanaburi endless rows of war graves mark the resting place of 6 982 Allied soldiers.

Henriette and I also had the opportunity to visit the site of the Great Wall of China to the north of Beijing as well as the Terracotta Warriors unearthed at Xian. The latter visit included a quick excursion to Sri Lanka which included a visit to Jaffna in the north. This was true guerrilla-fighting terrain and I could imagine its influence on this particular civil war which ended only three years ago. This visit was particularly interesting to me as I had the opportunity to work with a few of the Tamils and government officials from Sri Lanka in Cape Town in 2008 to share our experiences with them on defence transformation. The Liberation Tigers of Tamil Eelam; commonly known as the LTTE or the Tamil Tigers, was a separatist militant organisation that was based in northeast Sri Lanka with Jaffna serving as one of their main bases of operation. Founded in May 1976 by Velupillai Prabhakaran, it waged a violent secessionist and nationalist campaign to create an independent state in the northeast of Sri Lanka for Tamil people. This campaign evolved into the Sri Lankan Civil War, which ran from 1983 until 2009 when the LTTE was defeated by the Sri Lankan Military. It was interesting to see that Sri Lanka had been bludgeoned by ethnic strife as many countries and Africa still experience. Do not leave South Africa out of this loop where things still simmer and at times finds its outlet in ongoing xenophobic reprisals. What goes around, comes around.

In October 2010 I had the opportunity to visit the battlefields in Namibia and southern Angola with a few of my veteran friends from 61 Mechanised Battalion Group and 32 Battalion. In a sense it was a soldier's crusade and a most memorable one at that. This visit gave us the opportunity to link-up with a few former foes of the past who had now become our friends. What was most valuable to me was to re-assess the terrain and its influences on the past battles and to discuss it with my colleagues. We could trek along our old routes and haunts from the Death Triangle, to Omuthiya and Xangongo, way up north past Mupa and Cuvelai to Cassinga, Indungo, Menongue and Cuito Cuanavale.[11] We could visit Savate on the western bank of the Cubango River on the return trip, where 32 Battalion had fought a momentous battle on 21 May 1980 and lost fifteen of their soldiers. We could laugh and shed a few tears in close camaraderie. At the going down of the sun and in the mornings during this amazing tour we could remember our fallen. Newspaper journalist, Deon Lamprecht of Rapport wrote a few great articles on our visit and how we connected and reconciled with former foes from SWAPO[12]. Well-known author, Louis Bothma also wrote a memorable book in Afrikaans about this tour entitled "Anderkant Cuito" ("Beyond Cuito.") Surprisingly enough a few former military die-hards responded vehemently in public and the media by saying, "What was this all about, former SADF soldiers crying in front of the enemy?" I did not even respond to this and only thought, "What silly people," and felt deeply sorry for them! It was, however, heartening to see that the public response was overwhelmingly positive.

On the bucket list of more planned battlefield travels Henriette and I have the Volga River and Operation Barbarossa jotted down for August 2013. Barbarossa was the largest military operation in human history, in both manpower and casualties, lasting from June until December 1941, during which more than 4 million troops of the Axis powers invaded the Soviet Union along a 2 900 km front. In addition to troops, Barbarossa involved 600,000 motor vehicles and 750,000 horses. The German invasion of the Soviet Union ultimately resulted in 95% of all German Army casualties from 1941 to 1944 and 65% of all Allied military casualties accumulated throughout the war. Its failure was a turning point in the Third Reich's failed destiny to conquer Europe which ultimately led to the demise of Adolf Hitler. As such the well-known Battle of Stalingrad changed the tide of World War Two. We had our own mini Stalingrad at Cuito Cuanavale in 1988, which caused the battle to ebb when FAPLA and the Cubans stood their ground. One difference was that the SADF as the attackers was never defeated in southern Angola.

Now for a final wish: to visit Libya where Rommel's Afrika Korps defeated the Allied Eighth Army in May–June 1942 at Gazala. This was the battle I used as a case study for the planning of the attack and subsequent defeat of FAPLA's 16th Brigade at the source of the Chambinga River in southeast Angola on 9 November 1987. After this my wanderlust would be expended somewhat... I think ... almost! I do not want to utter these words too loudly for the Dear Lord to pay attention to.

To Whom it May Concern – Common Bonds of Friendships and Interests

Now, only for a moment, I will come back again to real life and precious friendships for the finalisation of the eighteenth chapter of my living being.

What happened to some of my friends? Gert Minnaar, Ariel Hugo and Camille Burger, as one of their main hobbies and zests for life, fervently serve the interests of the military veterans of 61 Mechanised Battalion Group. Where I can I help them, share a few beers with my many close compatriots and tell a few stories about our collective pasts. Craig Harrison is currently working for the United Nations in New York as one of their outstanding security analysts, after having spent a number of years in the rough neighbourhoods of Afghanistan – much safer than Jo'burg. Giel Reinecke had become a super security consultant working all over the Middle East. He is currently eating sand in Saudi Arabia, whilst consulting on

11 See Maps 3 and 4.
12 South West Africa People's Organisation.

security. Is this better than gorging flies in southern Angola?

Something about amazing Lekoa Solly Mollo, who has many a time referred to himself as Van Vuuren, because Mollo means fire. After the first democratic elections in South Africa in 1994 Solly Mollo joined the SANDF as an integrated Umkhonto we Sizwe (MK) member. He became known for his work on the integration and transformation of military forces, both locally and internationally and also developed extensive experience in the field of strategic planning. He has facilitated the security sector transformation for several African defence forces and was member of a team that developed a strategy for Regional Defence Cooperation. While serving as the officer commanding at the Military Academy in 2004–06 he was appointed professor at Stellenbosch University – the latter was affiliated to the Military Academy. Mollo retired from the SANDF as a major general in 2008. I gave a speech at his farewell function – his remarkable mother was there as well. I had the opportunity to tell the ANC high brass about some of our exploits shared during defence transformation and how we manoeuvred deftly through certain difficult areas and how enjoyable our collaboration had been. Many of them gawked, others smiled knowingly. Mollo was then appointed Professor at the University of Witwatersrand on his retirement from the SANDF. As Professor he participated in the establishment of the Defence Management Programme at the University of Witwatersrand. Lekoa Solly Mollo is currently the Director General at the National Academy of Public Administration for the government in Johannesburg. He also serves as the President of the South African Military History Commission (under UNESCO). It was great to observe what happened to him after we had met at the Army War Game Centre for the first time on 17 January 1994 and developed the "Integrated Leadership Command and Management Concept of the SANDF" together, which was officially approved in 1998. To pull the thread of transformation through I need to add something: In 1999, after I had retired from the army, I was approached by Dan Cohen who was writing a book in partnership with John Kotter of the Harvard Business School on real-life stories of how people had changed their organisations[13]. In this book, entitled, *The Heart of Change*, Kotter and Cohen emphasised the importance of transformation by proclaiming that change was not merely about structures and operations of an organisation – "you need to change people's behaviour and that is never easy." In the book the authors shared the experience of Solly Mollo and me on how we had developed a trust relationship to perform complex transformation. To quote the authors: "In Chapter 2 (guiding team), the army officer (Roland de Vries) doesn't pull together his new change team with a rational argument. Instead, he shocks them by taking a risk for the greater good with his comments in a meeting. He then helps them to begin to tell emotion-packed stories around a campfire. More positive feelings and trust grow, making them act as an effective team." Stories like these reveal a core pattern associated with successful change... "Successful see-feel-change tactics tend to be clever, not clumsy, and never cynically manipulative."[14] I am justly proud of my friend, Solly Mollo who was once my enemy!

I have truly started enjoying this writing thing, especially where my good friends Willem Steenkamp, Friedel Hansen, Gustav Venter and Camille Burger are happy to help me with the editing part –English tenses are like trenches and minefields.

13 John P. Kotter is the author of international bestseller 'Leading Change'.

14 Kotter, John, P. and Cohen, Dan S.: *The Heart of Change*. Harvard Business School Press, Boston, Massachusetts, pp. 8 and 9 and 50–53.

Camille Burger and I have already started writing "The African Way of Warfare" – manoeuvring through the bushes at its best. It is a sequel to my book, Mobile Warfare – a Perspective for Southern Africa, which was published in 1987. Camille and I are also writing a book entitled, "Our Sons Were Warriors", because they were. Camille will include plenty of maps and we have collected a number of juicy real-life stories about the Border War. On the side I still do the odd consulting venture here and there, provided it promises to be exciting.

In Closure – Fruits of Life

Wow, did I enjoy operating on that fluid battlefield, adrenaline surging. I now understood what high productivity, simultaneous action, job satisfaction and individual growth truly meant. In the process I sincerely hoped that my efforts had meant something to others. I am still alive and well, I need to report to friend and foe. To my adversaries who might have been seared in the firestorm, no hard feelings. I wish to end with the words by Rudyard Kipling: "If you can make one heap of all your winnings and risk it on one turn of pitch-and-toss..." Then life should be a ball!

19

Trust Yourself

If You Can Make One Heap of All Your Winnings

And risk it on one turn of pitch-and-toss ...
"If" – Rudyard Kipling

Afterthoughts – Mind, Body and Soul

First light at 05:00, Amman Jordan. It was time for stand to in military terms, as the sun rose to the east over this foreign country. Countless loudspeakers were blaring praises to Allah as I stood on the high ground of the Citadel overlooking the old city; it was the same place where Uriah had died in the times of King David of the Bible. I was doing my daily twelve kilometre walk and celebrating the writing of this chapter I had completed the previous evening. At sixty eight I stopped jogging and reverted to walking. This was due to a landmine explosion endured at the hands of SWAPO[1] many years ago, which had started taking its toll on the body, especially my back and crooked left elbow. The landmine had been planted by some damned illusive insurgent from the People's Liberation Army of Namibia, bless his soul. Take note, I am not upset with SWAPO today; just perhaps, afford me the luxury to be mad at a few politicians and a few other enemies, I could specify if you wanted me to or write about the Broederbond in general. I shall however reserve my judgement and keep those thoughts to myself.

I had left Henriette (with her I exercise in shopping malls) and my small leather clad Bible behind in our apartment where we lived together in Al Webdeh. It was the same Bible I had diligently carried with me during all military operations in southern Africa ... the one with Psalm 23 partially torn out, hanging precariously on its thin papery fringes. The damage was causal from overusage; I still needed to file a damage report, Dear Lord. I had a few pieces torn out of self from overuse as well. I realised that I had done my fair share to tax Him and a few others I may add; so be it – fortunately, He did not need excessive paperwork to be done or damage reports filed. He knew everything, what I was thinking and doing and about the day, not too far off, that I would receive my final merit report; the one which really counts. I am quite content with that idea in mind, peace of mind, body and soul.

As it were, Henriette and I had just received a telephone message that the Syrian border to the north of us had been closed due to civil unrest. The Syrian Army was deploying quickly to subdue and kill a few sorrowful souls, their own people. There were many poor, unhappy people in the Middle East as is the case in Africa. All around us the Arabian world was wakening up for what they coined "The Arab Spring". It is however clear the majority were not sure of the details or of the turmoil and unwarranted killings ... perhaps similar to what we have experienced for many years in Africa ourselves. Far to the south I thought my own South Africa was reasonably peaceful after many years of undue strife.

---

1 South West Africa People's Organisation.

However, its stupid, boring politics were blared forth unabatedly as in the past; as were the blaring loudspeakers in Amman. I thought: when would stupid politics and the dogmas of intolerant religions become obsolete, if ever? Anyhow, that was just a fleeting thought I wished to share with you.

The writing of this book therefore meant much to me in finding simple answers to life, much more than just searching my soul and ordering my thoughts. I could through the writing connect with many of you in meaningful ways. At least I had found a pattern which made sense to me. It was the pattern of connecting with others, the pattern of learning and teaching through worthy dialogue, the pattern of enjoying life and in nurturing trust relationships. I thought by myself that if one should break this pattern, one would necessarily destroy the quality of life. To my mind this kind of intimacy lay at the heart of competence. It made me free somehow. However, I was still far from completing my learning and establishing enough meaningful relationships. My efforts to further explore life in other exciting ways, as I had done during military operations, and the many different nuances of life itself was certainly not over yet. So in my own way, I have searched for the truth in the writing of this account, at times being openly frank about own expressed views. Amen.

War and Peace, Fear and Hope – Meaning Questioned

I have learned that fear can spread rapidly and widely even through rumour or lie. The counter to fear is truth and hope. Hopefully, after the current wars in southern Africa are over, fear will be removed and to be replaced by confidence for the future. Otherwise, the fighting which had been done by me, my former friends and foes would have been for nothing. However, we must forever remain realistic and aware of our surroundings.

What has been heartrending until now, considering a notably stretched period of peace and so-called freedom in southern Africa, is that the destitute, the poor, the crime and corruption still remain. For the state of the poor, crime and corruption all over Africa, even apartheid cannot be blamed anymore. From Cape to Cairo perpetual political instability still afflicts the African continent. The unrest in Africa has highlighted ethnic, sectarian and tribal differences for many years and it still exists. This has happened through the ages in the Middle East as well and it is currently being ruthlessly rekindled. Don't throw Europe or other parts of the western and eastern worlds away. Countries such as obtuse America is clearly supercharging this negative downward spiral at the whim of a will in many places all over the world, for the sake of politics and riches and oil. At times it feels as if there is nothing anyone can do to stop it. Amidst global turmoil the African world especially struggles to produce a few innovations and signs of hope.

Hope however prevails, especially for countries such as South Africa as a benchmark, where the hope is that the political map will not unravel. In a world where leaders are encouraged to embrace democratic change, the question still remains whether democratic governances can hold under pressure. What might emerge from the African and other developing environs two or three generations from now is therefore beyond anyone's capacity to predict. As individuals Africans are as talented and productive as anyone else in the world. I have witnessed peoples all over, so there is hope. For the time being however I fear that Africa like many other countries in the world are entwined in a failing culture. This alone can be substantiated beyond doubt by the many countries in Africa and elsewhere still ruled by corruption and fear. Hopefully in the years to come this will not be an incidental fact of life. Otherwise the examples set by South Africa and Namibia's democratic triumphs through contemporary military operations such as Protea and Modular and the sacrifice of many precious lives in achieving peace would have been in vain.

To my mind the war in southern Africa was not for nothing. Struggle over time brought peoples and politicians to their senses. I trust that those in power today will remember this. Not to forget the old adage by Liddell Hart that the only thing we learn from history is that we don't learn from history.

Posterity – Meaning Revealed

Many of my former military compatriots and civilian friends and their families, either living in South Africa or other parts of the world, such as Africa, the Middle East and Australia today, occupy key leadership positions and render meaningful work. I find that those do not complain of undeserved practices such as affirmative action. They carry on with their lives positively and successfully so, even under challenging circumstances. Many of them serve in international organisations such as the United Nations, such as Henriette, my wife. My youngest daughter, Melanie is in Australia with her family; my youngest son, Pieter works in Saudi Arabia and sails in Bahrain; Roland junior and Elmarie and their families are still in Southern Africa; nothing gets them down.

I witness all over that our children are of warrior stock; the calibre who knows how to triumph against all odds, also in Africa. They will triumph and create their own destinies, whatever may come their way! Peace combined with personal freedom is the greatest gift of all. It is something to fight for if it becomes necessary!

Our children are of the old South Africa, as my soldiers were. They are strong children, a beautiful product, cognitively and genetically speaking. We find our children everywhere in the world today ... all over Africa, in the Middle East, Europe, in Australia, in New Zealand ... everywhere in leadership positions, because they can work hard, are honest, creative and have the leadership ability. They are open, not racially biased and hardworking. They are sought-after employees in the world and we can be proud of them.

My One Conclusive Answer to What We Faced in Warring Southern Africa in the Past

Was the South African Border War worth it? My one conclusive answer is: yes, it was worth it! It was so much more than just win or lose. It took us far beyond a satisfactory conclusion. It taught us about life and death, about peoples and their ways, about vulnerabilities and strengths. It taught me about life in the military, life with my family, my colleagues, my friends, even that former enemies could become new friends. I meet young friendly Russian tourists in Dubai. I invite them to come and visit magnificent Cape Town. Firstly, I tell them, fly via Angola and visit Cuito Cuanavale where your older generation had fought against us in the war for southern Angola. Read about their exploits and hardships in a book they had written about that war: "Bush War – The Road to Cuito Cuanavale" by Gennady Shubin and Andrei Tokarev Andrei. At times I sit around a campfire during battlefield tours to Namibia and Angola and talk to those people who had endured that war, as we share memories and tears and laughter about the fighting years of yore. During one such visit in October 2010 we visited the Heroes Acre of SWAPO in Windhoek. A few of the veterans from erstwhile 61 Mechanised Battalion Group and 32 Battalion shared a memorable occasion in reaching out to our former enemies from SWAPO; one of them spontaneously voiced to our small group: "There are no winners here today; peace is the only victor ... Come again, this is your home from home." Our former enemies touched our souls through such simple utterances.

I sincerely believe that through such simple gestures we in southern Africa today have a better form of peace and optimism than in the past. If we could but just make one heap of all our winnings and fill every unforgiving minute with hope, every sixty seconds distance we had ran thus far would have been worthwhile.

Endings and New Beginnings

I had a career in the military and another in civilian life which I both cherished and thoroughly enjoyed in good health. For the latter I am humbly thankful. I have a family I adore, my few soldiery and civilian friends I treasure and a number of enemies I still appreciate. All of them taught me the importance of keeping the combat edge sharpened. I had the pleasure of writing this book, which was truly indicative of what it meant for me to fight through an objective and not onto it.

Every year, come hell or high water as my dad used to say, for as long as it is possible, as before Henriette and I will put up a Christmas tree with fluttering tinsel and flickering Chinese lighting for our children and our grandchildren,; and ride on trains or boats just for fun somewhere and laugh just because we are alive and well. Life is full of potential and patiently awaits our attitudes and choices as we manoeuvre along.

To my readers, thank for your kind attention. It was nice meeting you in this way. Dear Lord, thank you for all of this, as you know, if I had a choice I would choose to do the same again! Now for the next exciting thing You are going to send over my path? Life is a continuum of endings and new beginnings? Life can be a heap of winnings! It all depends on our attitude. And now, Dear Lord, I am ready to move on, I have no heavy luggage, only a small duffel bag.

20

Epilogue

Understanding Motion

What is impossible with man is possible with God.
Luke 18:27

I am the conductor of the music of the rhythm of my life; the commander directs and instructs the troops he commands. I walk, I run, I jump. The commander coordinates the movement and the rhythm of the battle. The conductor defines harmony with a slight gesture of the baton. Life moves with a certain rhythm. War resonates with its own movement and tempo. Music has its own certain rhythm and movement. Like music, movement incorporates an assortment of rhythms. Sometimes very slow (adagissimo!), sometimes very fast (prestissimo!)

The same is true for the soldier. Movement on the battlefield or in daily life is like composing music: it has its own tempo and rhythm. The numbers of your adversary determines the pace of your march. Many triumphs take place because of positive actions: a propensity for warfare and life is a talent to define movement.

In any movement the men and women in your care should come first because every man and woman counts. I believe that this presents the most solemn and grave of all responsibilities, not promotion or positional power! I believe that success comes to those who are in motion, those who experience the proceeds and joys of either deliberate or spontaneous manoeuvre, the ever-changing adaptation to the benefits of shifting positions – even if just for the mere fun of it! This is the ability of the prudent strategist and tactician to make the most of "terrain" as a neutral factor in either warfare or ordinary life. It requires talent, confidence, understanding and nearness, a type of intimacy.

The most exciting and challenging times of my life was spent in the intimacy of the African bush in southern Angola with my soldiers. Knowing well that serenity was elusive, I found calmness in its closeness. I learned that in any hostile situation, or amiable venture for that matter, there is room for a clever person to manoeuvre; especially when using methods surprisingly different to what the adversary, or even ally, is used. To my mind this principle applies to life in the military, family, business and ordinary society. The instinctive analysis of "terrain" and skilful utilisation thereof allows you to strike at whomever, wherever, whenever, from unexpected directions; at the same time to evade any fury from the ground, air and even an opponent's mind with relative ease through manoeuvre. Clever utilisation of "terrain" and manoeuvrability allows the small to outdo the big by means of a clever strategy or tactic; in other words to turn disadvantageous inflections into advantageous dispositions by taking the high ground – to operate effectively within the eye of any firestorm.

During years of operational experience in the Army I realised that there was no substitute for the military appreciation with regards to analysis of the physical environment; I found that I could use this same method in a business context during a second career:

Own forces, the enemy, terrain, time and distance, time and space – the battle of wills, and risks and contingency plans to counter those. For example: Significant questions inevitably asked by us on the ground in the Operational Area were: Where is the enemy the most vulnerable? Where are we the strongest? Where is key terrain? What does the terrain compel the enemy and own forces to do? What does the terrain allow the enemy and own forces to do? Where should the point of main effort be?

All of the aforementioned factors have a psychological dimension to it. It is very easy to "lose it" in the closeness of the African bush; so guard against it. The troops used to refer to this phenomenon as "bossies raak." One could exploit this singular marvel vis-à-vis the adversary to one's own advantage by adding a few disquieting optional extras, such as: A surprising, "deadly" onslaught at the right moment and place; attacking far to the adversary's rear when least expected; by striking at unguarded spots; by overloading the opponent's intelligence-gathering means at critical moments – through dislocation, disruption and surprise yet again and again within the physical, psychological and sensory milieus. We found that stress in the ranks of our African enemy, for example, could be caused trough alienation; chaos brought about by exploiting the denseness of the bush and darkness of the nights; fear and exasperation of the unknown and primal belief systems used to instigate uncontrolled anxiety. Business opponents have these weaknesses to.

To take complete advantage of terrain in warfare or otherwise requires mobility to the fullest, and creative thinking; mobility in the physical as well as the psychological realms. Thus, mobility in totality and not only movement by means of track, wheel, rotor, wing or foot, but mobility of the mind, as well.

Watch out, "terrain," especially in Africa, can become a daunting adversary, even more so than any human adversary – so read and use it well. Undoubtedly the instruments of true mobility are men and machines who are hardened to move swiftly and to survive in the environment of the natural medium without loss of "combat" effectiveness.

The race goes to the swift, to those of substance with a firm belief in their methods and in self. In the field under dire straits this has a direct bearing on the development of individual character and self-esteem, in truly caring for your people and in developing them continuously; on the ground where you are all the time. In the words of Napoleon: "The psychological is to the physical as three is to one!" Therefore: Know yourself, know your adversary, and know the terrain and manoeuvre. Then be successful under either adverse or favourable circumstances, or for that matter, through any firestorm which may blow your way! Strength lies in mobility! There is always a way!

If you can dream... And not make dreams your master; if you can think... and not make thoughts your aim...
"If" – Rudyard Kipling

About Mobility

Give me a place to stand and I will move the earth ...
– Archimedes

The comprehension and exploitation of the spatial characteristics of the battlefield can give the commander leverage on the enemy. So it is with life as well... location in space, a static concept, can become dynamic. Mobile warfare is an ever-changing adaptation to the benefits of shifting positions.

Listen to your inner voice!

Seek forward ground!

Be surprisingly different!

At any spur of the moment render random acts of kindness!

Try out the benefits of movement, by being hospitable to the unusual person!

The Life Stages of Erik Erikson

1. Infancy: Birth to 18 Months
Ego Development Outcome: Trust vs. Mistrust
Basic Strengths: Drive and Hope

2. Early Childhood: 18 Months to 3 Years
Ego Development Outcome: Autonomy vs. Shame
Basic Strengths: Self-Control, Courage and Will

3. Play Age: 3 to 5 Years
Ego Development Outcome: Initiative vs. Guilt
Basic Strength: Purpose

4. School Age: 6 to 12 Years
Ego Development Outcome: Industry vs. Inferiority
Basic Strengths: Method and Competence

5. Adolescence: 12 to 18 Years
Ego Development Outcome: Identity vs. Role Confusion
Basic Strengths: Devotion and Fidelity

6. Young Adulthood: 18 to 35
Ego Development Outcome: Intimacy and Solidarity vs. Isolation
Basic Strengths: Affiliation and Love

7. Middle Adulthood: 35 to 55 or 65
Ego Development Outcome: Generatively vs. Self Absorption or Stagnation
Basic Strengths: Production and Care

8. Late Adulthood: 55 or 65 to Death
Ego Development Outcome: Integrity vs. Despair
Basic Strength: Wisdom

Appendix A

Composition of Forces for Operations

Operation Carrot April 1981 – Chapter 11

Composition of 61 Mechanised Battalion Group

Commander: Commandant Roland de Vries.
Second-in-Command: Major Thys Rall.
Regimental Sergeant-Major (RSM): Warrant Officer Class 1 M.C. Barnard.
Intelligence Officers: Captains Rolf van Zyl and Gerrie Hugo (seconded from Sector 30).
Signals Officer and Commander of the Signals Troop: Captain Paul Roos.
Unit Chaplain: Padre Koos Rossouw.
Logistics Officer: Captain Giel Reinecke.
Personnel Officer: Lieutenant Willem van der Vyfer.
Alpha Company Commander (Ratel-20): Captain Cassie Schoeman.
Bravo Company Commander (Ratel-20): Captain Koos Liebenberg.
Charlie Squadron Commander (Ratel-90): Major Joe Weyers.
Sierra Battery Commander (140 mm Gun/120 mm Mortar): Captain Bernie Pols.
Anti-Tank Platoon Commander: Second Lieutenant Chris Walls.
Mortar Platoon Commander: Second Lieutenant: Ettienne Gertzen.
Light Workshop Troop (LWT) Commander: WO1 Duppie du Plessis.

Forces Under Command of 61 Mechanised Battalion Group for Carrot

61 Mechanised Battalion Group – organised as laid out above.
The Area Force Units (AFU) of Etosha (Tsumeb), Grootfontein, Otavi and Outjo.
One Parachute Company Provided by 1 Parachute Battalion.
The Northern Border Company – newly established at Tsintsabis.
The SAAF Provided Air Assets – consisting of a number of Alouette and Puma helicopters and Bosbok light reconnaissance aircraft. In addition one/two commando (part-time force) aircraft deployed from SWATF.
The South African Medical Services (SAMS) Provided – one Regimental Medical Post at Tsumeb.
The South African Police Provided One Specialist Counterinsurgency Platoon – which was used only for follow-ups.
Elements of the South African Police (SAP), SWA Police and SAP (Security Branch) – were deployed for maintenance of law and order; intelligence operations and clandestine operations.

Operation Yahoo April-May 1982 – Chapter 11

Forces Deployed For Yahoo

The Headquarters of Sector 30 Based at Otjiwarongo (In Overall Command – Colonel J.T. Louw).

Sector 30 had the following forces available for employment in its immediate locale:

- The Area Force Unit (AFU) of Otjiwarongo.
- The restricted services of the Damaraland AFU. The latter AFU was still being formed and its recruits were undergoing training.
- Task Force Nutcracker. The force comprised two motorised infantry companies, which could be employed for area operations, follow-ups, road blocks and observation posts.

Task Force East Comprised the Following Force Structure Elements under Command of Tac HQ EAST Commanded by Commandant Roland de Vries (HQ 61 Mech):

61 Mechanised Battalion Group: Organised and employed as discussed above.

- 1 SWA Special Unit: The HQ of the unit also provided the Tac HQ for Otavi. The specialist elements of this unit were used for their specialists functions as and when required, namely: Tracking; mounted horse and motorcycle patrols; tracker and patrol dogs.
- The Area Force Units (AFU) Etosha (Tsumeb), Grootfontein and Otavi: Used for traditional infantry tasks. Valuable supports were rendered as guides, who could be integrated with and move with the respective forces in the field, as well as liaison with the community. Their most valuable asset was the numerous tracker teams, which assisted the many follow-up groups. Important tasks of the AFUs were home-and-hearth protection and the protection of vulnerable points.
- Two Parachute Companies were Provided by 1 Parachute Battalion. The paratroopers were employed for follow-ups; ambushes; rapid reaction forces; cross-tracking and; observation posts.
- The capability of the Northern Border Company was reinforced with an additional two companies from 203 Battalion and 201 Battalion respectively. A Tac HQ was established at Tsintsabis. The sub-unit was almost at battalion strength. The Tsintsabis force component was responsible for the patrolling of the Alpha, Bravo and Charlie cut-lines. This included area operations and restricted follow-ups in the Mangeti Block.
- A Motorised Company was Provided by 6 South African Infantry Battalion (Grahamstown). The company was used to supplement farm protection operations as well as for area ambushing ahead of enemy surges.
- An Additional Motorised Company was Provided by 911 Battalion, Windhoek. This company was utilised for observation posts and stopper groups.
- One Part-Time Force Company from Witwatersrand Rifles (WR): Provided farm protection duties.
- The Transvaal State Artillery (TSA – citizen force): Provided additional personnel for farm protection duties.
- 911 Battalion Provided an Additional Platoon: Used for the protection of National Key Points (NKP) in the region.
- One Field Engineer Troop: Provided to fulfil traditional engineering tasks and the lifting of mines. Their work included the provisioning of purified drinking water for

forces deployed in the field.

- Two Infantry Platoons: From Sectors 50 and 60 provided to undertake farm protection duties.
- The SAAF Provided Air Assets for: Helicopter gunship support; medical evacuation; trooping; liaison flights; aerial reconnaissance; aerial radio relay; fixing of the enemy. The following air assets were deployed at the Tsumeb Air Field: Three Alouette gunships; one Alouette helicopter for command and trooping purposes; two Bosbok light reconnaissance aircraft; two commando (part-time force) aircraft from SWATF; three Puma transport helicopters.
- The South African Medical Services (SAMS) Provided the Following Deployments: One Regimental Medical Post at Tsumeb; one medical officer at Otavi; one medical officer at Tsintsabis; one medical team at Grootfontein.
- The South African Police Provided One Specialist Counterinsurgency Platoon: Used only for follow-up operations.
- The Koevoet ("Crowbar") Force of the South African Police Provided Nine Follow-Up Groups: Each group comprised 340 men. Koevoet was employed for hot-pursuits, cross tracking and for clandestine work. This force did outstanding work and received the accolades of their friends from the taskforce. The name Koevoet (crow bar) indicated "covert operations." This was a term which covered many functions, such as tracking terrorists internally in SWA as well as across the international border into southern Angola. Koevoet was also used for interrogation, negotiating with local people, and other mainly policing duties, for which regular military forces were not normally suited.
- Elements of the South African Police (SAP), SWA Police and SAP (Security Branch): Deployed for maintenance of law and order; intelligence operations, clandestine operations.
- Task Force West Comprised the Following Force Structure Elements under Command of Tac HQ West Commanded by Commandant Stoffel Rothman (HQ Outjo AFU): The Outjo AFU; an infantry company deployed at Onaiso; an infantry platoon deployed at Uis.

Composition of 61 Mechanised Battalion Group

Commander: Commandant Roland de Vries.
Second-in-Command: Major Thys Rall.
Regimental Sergeant-Major (RSM): Warrant Officer Class 1 (WO1) H.G. Smit.
Intelligence Officer: Captain Gerrie Hugo.
Signals Officer and Commander of the Signals Troop: Captain Sean McSweeney.
Unit Chaplain: Padre Koos Rossouw.
Logistics Officer: Major Giel Reinecke.
Personnel Officer: WO1 Jack Sindon.
Alpha Company Commander (Ratel-20): Captain Jan Malan.
Bravo Company Commander (Ratel-20): Captain Vissie Visser.
Charlie Squadron Commander (Ratel-90): Major Jakes Jacobs.
Sierra Battery Commander (140 mm Gun/120 mm Mortar): Major Chris Roux.
Light Workshop Troop (LWT) Commander: WO1 Duppie du Plessis.

In addition to the above-mentioned force composition for Yahoo 61 Mech boasted a Ratel-90 anti-tank platoon, an 81 mm Mortar platoon, a medical section and a signals platoon. At the time of Operation Yahoo the 81 mm mortar platoon had been detached to Sector 10 to participate in Operation Meebos in Southern Angola. Included in the 61 Mech arsenal was a Headquarters Company (support company), which was commanded by Major Giel Reinecke, my logistics officer. He was assisted by our RSM, WO1 H.G. Smit, who commanded Alpha Echelon (administrative echelon). The latter extremely important establishments provided first-line combat service support wherever 61 Mech moved: Administrative; financial; logistical; technical; catering.

Employment of 61 Mechanised Battalion Group For Yahoo

- The HQ of 61 Mech served as the Task Force HQ East (Tsumeb).
- The HQ of Sierra Battery provided the HQ and the detachments for farm protection operations.
- Mechanised infantry companies were used for follow-ups; cross-tracking; observation posts; stopper groups; listening posts; ambushes; mobile and foot patrols; visiting and patrolling of farms.
- The armoured squadron and anti-tank platoon were employed for the monitoring and patrolling of routes; road blocks; stopper lines; channelling of the enemy through movement and noise; escort tasks and convoy protection.
- The artillery battery provided farm protection duties and harassing fire missions into mountainous areas.
- HQ Company and Alpha Echelon for establishing and maintaining the operational base and for supply support and technical maintenance of the task force as a whole.

Operation Protea August 1981 – Chapter 12

Composition of 61 Mechanised Battalion Group (Battle Group 10)

HQ of Battle Group 10:

Officer Commanding: Commandant Roland de Vries.
Second-in-Command: Major Thys Rall.
Regimental Sergeant-Major (Alpha Echelon): Warrant Officer Class 1 MC Barnard.
Operations Officer: Commandant Epp van Lill.
Intelligence Officer: Commandant Joe Aveling.
Logistics Officer and Commander of the Administrative Support Company: Major Giel Reinecke.
Senior Engineer Officer: Major Leon Terblanche.
Technical Services Officer: Captain Philip "Jakkals" Jaeckel.
Adjutant: Lieutenant Henri "Bossie" Boshoff.
Signals Officer: Captain Thinus van Wyk.
Personnel Officer: Lieutenant Willem van der Vyfer.
Medical Officer: Dr. Reitz Malherbe.
Chaplain: Padre Koos Rossouw.

Sub-Units:

Alpha Company: Captain Pale van der Walt (1 Parachute Battalion).
Bravo Company: Captain Koos Liebenberg.
Charlie Squadron: Major Joe Weyers.
Protection Company (701 Battalion) and Garrison Force Commander: Major Dawid Mentz.
Sierra Battery Commander: Captain Bernie Pols and Captain Francois van Eeden.
81 mm Mortar Platoon: Second Lieutenant Etienne Gertzen.
Alpha Troop – Field Engineer Troop from 25 Field Engineer Squadron: Lieutenant Martin Olivier.
Protection Platoon (Phantom Squad): Second Lieutenant Marshall Michau.
Light Workshop Troop Commander: Warrant Officer Class 1 Duppie du Plessis.
Mobile Reserve of Task Force Alpha – Detached from 61 Mechanised Battalion Group to HQ Task Force Alpha until Completion of the Attack on Ondjiva.
Alpha Company: Captain Hannes van der Merwe. Anti-Tank Platoon (Ratel-90): Lieutenant Chris Walls.

Composition of Battle Groups of Task Force Alpha

- Battle Group 10: 1 x mechanised infantry company; 1 x motorised paratrooper company; 1 x motorised protection company; 1 x armoured car squadron with two Ratel-90 armoured car troops, two Eland-90 armoured car troops and four support sections; 1 x medium artillery troop; 1 x field engineer troop; 1 x 81 mm mortar platoon; 1 x protection platoon (nicknamed Phantom).
- Battle Group 20: 1 x mechanised infantry company; 2 x motorised infantry companies; 1 x armoured car squadron with two Ratel-90 armoured car troops and two Eland-90 armoured car troops; 1 x medium artillery troop; 1 x 81 mm mortar platoon; 1 x field engineer troop; 1 x assault pioneer platoon; 2 x protection platoons.

- Battle Group 30: 3 x motorised infantry companies; 1 x Eland-90 armoured car squadron; 1 x 120 mm mortar battery; 1 x 81 mm mortar platoon; 1 x field engineer troop; 2 x protection platoons.
- Battle Group 40: 3 x motorised infantry companies; 3 x Eland-90 armoured car troops; 1 x 120 mm mortar battery; 1 x field engineer troop; 4 x anti-tank teams; 2 x protection platoons.
- Mobile Reserve: 1 x mechanised infantry company; 1 x Ratel-90 anti-tank platoon; 2 x Ratel-60 support sections; 1 x medium artillery troop; 2 x protection platoons.

Composition of Battle Groups of Task Force Bravo

- Battle Group 30: As for above; on completion of attack on Xangongo.
- Battle Group 40: As for above; on completion of attack on Ondjiva.
- Battle Group 50: 4 x motorised infantry companies; 1 x 81 mm mortar platoon.
- Battle Group 60: 4 x motorised infantry companies; 1 x 81 mm mortar platoon.
- Task Force Reserve: 2x paratrooper companies; 1x pathfinder platoon from 1 Parachute Battalion; Special Forces teams from 52 Reconnaissance Regiment.

Operation Daisy November 1981 – Chapter 13

Composition of The Ground Force

The ground force was provided by the South African Army and South West Africa Territorial Force (SWATF) and comprised a sizeable contingent of mechanised, motorised and airborne forces, which included:

- A Tactical HQ provided for the operation by Sector 10.
- 61 Mechanised Battalion Group.
- 201 Battalion (Bushmen).
- One motorised company from 32 Battalion.
- One company from 1 Parachute Battalion as mobile reserve.
- One company from 1 Parachute Battalion under command of 61 Mechanised Battalion Group.
- Three parachute companies from 3 Parachute Battalion (Citizen Force).
- A number of reconnaissance teams from Special Forces.
- A liaison team of UNITA, which accompanied 61 Mech for the duration of the operation.
- A mobile tactical command team of Special Forces, which accompanied 61 Mech for a major portion of Operation Daisy.

Composition of 61 Mechanised Battalion Group

Officer Commanding: Commandant Roland de Vries.
Second-in-Command: Major Thys Rall.
Air Support Officer: Major Rod Penhall (SAAF).
Regimental Sergeant-Major: Warrant Officer Class 1 MC Barnard.
Logistics Officer and Support Company Commander: Major Giel Reinecke.
Intelligence Officers: Commandant Louwtjie de Beer (attached for Operation Daisy from Army HQ) and Captain Gerrie Hugo.
Technical Services Officer: Captain Philip "Jakkals" Jaeckel (originally 1 Parachute

Battalion).
Personnel Officer: Lieutenant Willem van der Vyfer.
Chaplain: Padre Koos Rossouw.
Adjutant and Operations Officer: Captain Cassie Schoeman (originally 1 South African Infantry Battalion).
Commander Alpha Company Mechanised: Major Leon Marais (originally 1 South African Infantry Battalion).
Commander Bravo Company Mechanised: Captain Koos Liebenberg (originally 1 South African Infantry Battalion).
Commander Charlie Squadron: Captain Frik Schade (originally 2 Special Service Battalion).
Commander Delta Company Motorised: Captain Pale van der Walt (originally I Parachute Battalion).
Commander Sierra Battery 120 mm Mortars (from 4 Medium Field Artillery Regiment Permanently Attached to 61 Mech): Captain Bernie Pols.
Platoon Leader 81 mm Mortar Platoon: Major Kobus (Bok) Smit (originally 1 South African Infantry Battalion).
Platoon Leader Anti-Tank Platoon: Second Lieutenant Chris Walls (originally 1 South African Infantry Battalion).
Troop Leader Alpha Troop, Field Engineers (Detached from 25 Field Engineer Squadron): Major Tallies Taljaard.
Troop Leader Anti-Aircraft Troop (20 mm Ystervark and SAM-7): Captain Carl Lindsey.
Commander Protection Group: Major Andy Anderson.
Light Workshop Troop Commander: Warrant Officer Class 1 Duppie du Plessis.
A Liaison Team of UNITA.
A Mobile Command Team of Special Forces.

Air Force Participation

The South African Air Force (SAAF) support for Operation Daisy was awe inspiring. The air force operated mainly from its forward airfields located at Grootfontein and Ondangwa. The gravel airfield at Ionde was to be used for the holding and deployment of Dakota transport aircraft, Bosbok light fixed wing aircraft, Alouette gunships and Puma transport helicopters. The following forces were deployed in theatre as an all-out air effort to support the ground forces and the air war:

- 12 x Mirage F1AZ
- 8 x Mirage F1CZ
- 2 x Mirage R2Z
- 10 x Impala Mark IIs equipped for daylight operations
- 4 x Impala Mark IIs equipped for night operations
- 1 x Impala reconnaissance aircraft
- 3 x Buccaneer
- 9 x Puma transport helicopters
- 10 x Alouette III helicopters
- 2 x Super Frelon helicopters
- 9 x Bosbok light aircraft
- 4 x Dakota transport aircraft

- 6 x C130 Hercules and C160 Transall transport aircraft
- 1 x Douglas DC4 Skymaster electronic surveillance aircraft
- Operation Makro – Meebos 1982 – Chapter 14

Composition of 61 Mechanised Battalion Group

At the time of Operation Makro-Meebos in December 61 Mech was about 1 000 men strong. Our fighting unit was readily trained for mobile conventional as well as counterinsurgency operations. 61 Mech comprised the following key personnel and organisational sub-groupings at the time:

For Operation Makro:
Commander: Commandant Roland de Vries.
Second-in-Command: Major Thys Rall.
RSM: WO1 H.G. Smit and commander of Alpha Echelon.
Intelligence Officer: Captain Gerrie Hugo.
Signals Officer and Commander of the Signals Troop: Captain Sean McSweeney.
Unit Chaplain: Padre Koos Rossouw.
Medical Officer and Commander of the Medical Section: Major Neels de Villiers.
Logistics Officer: Major Robbie Robertze.
Alpha Company Commander (Ratel-20): Major Fred Burger.
Bravo Company Commander (Ratel-20): Captain Thomas Dreyer.
Charlie Squadron Commander (Ratel-90): Major Jakes Jacobs.
Artillery Battery Commander (120 mm Medium Range Mortar): Major Chris Roux.
LWT Commander: WO1 Duppie du Plessis.

For Operation Meebos II:
Commander: Commandant Roland de Vries.
Second-in-Command: Major Thys Rall.
Regimental Sergeant-Major (RSM): Warrant Officer Class 1 (WO1) H.G. Smit.
Air Support Officer (ASO) SAAF: Major Jaap du Preez.
Operations Officer: Major Jakes Jacobs.
Intelligence Officer: Captain Gerrie Hugo.
Signals Officer and Commander of the Signals Troop: Captain Sean McSweeney.
Unit Chaplain: Padre Koos Rossouw.
Logistics Officer: Major Giel Reinecke.
Personnel Officer: WO1 Jack Sindon.
Alpha Company Commander (Ratel-20): Captain Jan Malan.
Bravo Company Commander (Ratel-20): Captain Vissie Visser.
Charlie Squadron Commander (Ratel-90): Captain Chris (CP) Du Toit.
Sierra Battery Commander (140 mm medium guns and 120 mm Medium Range Mortar): Major Chris Roux.
Anti-Aircraft Troop: Captain Carl Lindsay.
Light Workshop Troop (LWT) Commander: WO1 Duppie du Plessis.

In addition to the above-mentioned force composition 61 Mech boasted a Ratel-90 anti-tank platoon, an 81 mm Mortar platoon, a medical section and a signals platoon. Included in the

61 Mech arsenal was a Headquarters Company (support company,) which was commanded by Major Giel Reinecke, my logistics officer. He was assisted by our RSM, WO1 H.G. Smit, who commanded Alpha Echelon (administrative echelon). The latter extremely important establishments provided first-line combat service support, wherever 61 Mech moved: administrative; financial; logistical; technical. A field engineer troop, an air support officer (ASO) and team and an electronic warfare (EW) section were attached to 61 Mech for the duration of Operation Makro-Meebos. The EW section was suitably equipped with Ratels and appropriate telecommunications equipment to support electronic warfare practices and to intercept and interpret enemy radio communications.

Operation Modular 1987 – Final Phase – Chapter 15

Composition of the Task Force for Southeast Angola

Operational Level HQ at Rundu

Commanded by Brigadier Fido Smit with the following forces under command:

- Task Force 10.
- Combat Group Bravo (32 Battalion).
- 10 Artillery Regiment.

The Composition of Task Force 10

- Combat Group Alpha (61 Mech).
- Combat Group Charlie (4 SAI).
- One tank squadron.
- UNITA Liaison Team.
- Mobile Air Operations Team.
- Medical Task Team.

Composition of Combat Group Alpha (61 Mech)

Combat Group Alpha was based on 61 Mech. The unit was commanded by Commandant Mike Müller who had taken over in the field from Commandant Kobus (Bok) Smit. The unit organisation entailed: One UNITA guerrilla battalion, two mechanised infantry companies, one armoured car squadron, an 81 mm mortar platoon, an ant-aircraft platoon, a field engineer troop and an assault pioneer platoon.

Composition of Combat Group Bravo (32 Battalion)

Combat Group Bravo was based on 32 Battalion under command of Commandant Robbie Hartslief with under command: One UNITA guerrilla battalion, four motorised infantry companies, two from 32 Battalion and two from 101 Battalion. In addition there were the unit's organic anti-tank squadron and its support company.

Composition of Combat Group Charlie (4 SAI)

Combat Group Charlie as the main assault force enjoyed the preponderance of combat power. The unit was based on 4 South African Infantry Battalion (4 SAI) and was commanded by Commandant Leon Marais with under command: One UNITA guerrilla battalion; two mechanised infantry companies; two motorised infantry companies from 32 Battalion; one squadron of thirteen Olifant main battle tanks from the School of Armour,

Bloemfontein; one Ratel-90 armoured car squadron; one Ratel-90 anti-tank platoon; one 81 mm mortar platoon; one 120 mm mortar battery with an infantry company attached for local protection; an administrative echelon.

Composition of 20 Artillery Regiment

20 Artillery Regiment was commanded by Colonel Jean Lausberg and his second-in-command was Commandant Frans van Eeden. Under command were Quebec and Sierra Battery each with eight 155 mm G-5 guns; Juliet Troop with three 155 mm G-6 self-propelled guns; Papa Battery boasted eight and India Troop four of the deadly 127 mm Valkiri Multiple Rocket Launchers; and an additional battery had eight 120 mm mortars.

Additional Information Concerning the Organisation of Mechanised Battalions

The headquarters of a mechanised battalion was usually equipped with four Ratel-Command vehicles. In addition a mechanised battalion usually consisted of two mechanised infantry companies with fourteen Ratel-20 infantry combat vehicles each; one armoured car squadron hosting twelve Ratel-90s; an anti-tank platoon either equipped with eight Ratel-90s or with a mix of six Ratel-90s and two ZT-3 anti-tank missile systems; the mortar platoon fielded eight 81 mm or alternatively eight 120 mm mortars; the anti-aircraft platoon was armed with twelve 20 mm guns mounted on an Ystervark mine protected vehicle. Combat service support elements brought up the rear of these fighting units. This support grouping consisted of logistics, technical services, signals, field engineers and medical services. The assortment of support elements grouped together was called A Echelon and was led by trustworthy and competent regimental sergeant-majors. A Echelon moved very close to the fighting force. At the Lomba and Chambinga they virtually supported the front line fighting under fire. A number of medical doctors manning sophisticated and well equipped forward medical and resuscitation posts were found in A Echelon. The forward fighting elements were referred to as F Echelon.

Operation Prone 1988 – Chapter 16

Composition of South African Forces Mobilised for Hilti/Prone

- HQ 10 SA Division (Newly Established):
  Main HQ – Oshakati.
  Mobile tactical HQ – Ratel-Command.
  Administrative echelon.
- 61 Mechanised Battalion Group (61 Mech, including one Olifant tank squadron).
- 4 South African Infantry Battalion – similarly organised as 61 Mech (minus a tank squadron).
- 32 Battalion.
- 101 Battalion.
- 81 Armour Brigade:
  Brigade tactical HQ.
  One tank regiment (three tank squadrons – Pretoria Regiment).
  One mechanised battalion (1 Regiment Northern Transvaal).
  One armoured car regiment (2 Light Horse Regiment).
  One field engineer regiment (15 Field Regiment).

One anti-aircraft battery (Regiment East Transvaal).
One engineer support squadron.
One signal unit (81 Signal Regiment).
One maintenance unit (20 Maintenance Unit).
One field workshop (32 Field Regiment).
One medical battalion group (6 Medical Battalion Group).
One provost platoon (military police – from 8 Provost Unit).

- 71 Motorised Brigade:
Battalion Group HQ (Cape Town Highlanders – CTH).
Two mechanised infantry companies (CTH).
Support weapon's company (81 mm mortar platoon and an anti-tank platoon – CTH).
One armoured car regiment (Regiment Orange River).
One field engineer troop (6 Field Engineer Regiment).
One anti-aircraft troop (7 Light Anti-Aircraft Regiment).
One signal troop (7 Signal Group).
One composite maintenance platoon (from 4 Maintenance Unit).
One medical battalion (3 Medical Battalion).
One light workshop troop (71 Field Regiment).
One provost platoon (military police – from 7 Provost Unit).
- Parachute Battalion Group (from 44 Parachute Brigade):
Battalion Group HQ.
Three parachute companies.
One parachute support company.
One light anti-aircraft troop – 12,7 mm.
One field engineer troop.
One signal troop.
One composite maintenance platoon.
One reconnaissance section – Ferret Armoured Reconnaissance Car.
One light workshop troop.
One provost platoon.
One medical task team.
Two mobile air operations teams (MAOT).
- 10 Artillery Brigade:
HQ 10 Artillery Brigade.
HQ 14 Artillery Regiment (minus – as regimental HQ).
G-5 155 mm battery (4 SAI).
G-5 155 mm battery (61 Mech).
G-2 140 mm battery (17 Field Regiment).
G-2 140 mm battery (TSA – Transvaal State Artillery).
G-2 140 mm battery (51 Battalion – Ruacana).
One multiple rocket launcher battery (127 mm Valkiri – 32 Battalion).
One multiple rocket launcher battery (127 mm Valkiri – 4 Artillery Regiment).
One M-5 battery (120 mm mortar – 4 Artillery Regiment).
One M-5 battery (120 mm mortar – 18 Light Artillery Regiment Parachute Brigade).
Two meteorological sections (from 1 Locating Battery and 32 Battalion respectively).

- Additional Force Elements Allocated to 10 SA Division or Earmarked as Reserves:
  HQ elements from the HQ of 71 Motorised Brigade.
  HQ elements from the HQ of 8 Armour Division.
  HQ elements from the HQ of 44 Parachute Brigade.
  Reserve drivers under training from the pool of Chief of the Army.
  The current G-5 Battery deployed in South East Angola in reserve.
  One G-2 battery of 71 Motorised Brigade in reserve.
  8 Maintenance Unit.
  30 Corps Maintenance Unit.
  Two 35 mm anti –aircraft batteries with effect from 14 August 1988.
  One provost platoon earmarked for the logistics area.

Names of the Planning Group for Operation Hilti/Prone – June 1988

Col M.J.D. Bernardo, directorate training; Colonel D.M. Bossenger, army intelligence; Colonel R. de Vries, officer commanding SA Army College as designate Chief of Staff of 10 SA Division; Colonel P.J.J.S. du Plessis, directorate engineers; Colonel L. du Toit, army personnel; Commandant C.J. Harrison, SA Army College; Colonel H.A. Kotze, army intelligence; Colonel J.A. Laubscher, directorate artillery; Colonel J.L. Lausberg, officer commanding 10 Artillery Brigade; Colonel J. Lusse, officer commanding 81 Armour Brigade; Colonel J. McLoughlin, officer commanding 71 Motorised Brigade; Colonel D.J. Moore, officer commanding 44 Parachute Brigade; Colonel W.G. Mouton, directorate anti-aircraft; Colonel C.F.W. Müller directorate permanent force personnel; Col D. Steyn, North West Command and designate Senior Staff Officer Intelligence for 10 SA Division; Colonel C.J.Tosen, directorate logistic support; Colonel A.E. Tucker, directorate engineers; Colonel C.J. Venter, directorate technical services; Commandant E.G.M. Alexander, 44 Parachute Regiment; Commandant D. Boshoff, army intelligence; Commandant C.P. du Toit, 81 Armour Brigade; Commandant I. Fordred, directorate signals; Commandant G.A. Taylor, 2 Signal Regiment; Commandant S.J. van Vuuren, Free State Command; Commandant M.J.H. van Wyk, 5 Signal Regiment; Major J.J. van der Merwe, 2 Field Engineer Regiment; Captain S.C. Fourie, directorate engineers.

Colonel Roland de Vries (as Chief of Staff 10 Division and commander of the SA Army College) requested Chief of the Army to detach the following two officers from the SA Army College to the divisional HQ, namely: Commandant A. Hudson as staff officer class 1 operational planning and Commandant C.S. Harrison as staff officer class 1intelligence.

The following army personnel were provisionally earmarked to fill some of the staff posts in the HQ of 10 SA Division, which was to be co-located with the HQ of Sector 10 at Oshakati and established as soon as possible. They were: Colonel B. van Heerden as senior staff officer operational control; Colonel P.S. Fouché as senior staff officer force training; Commandant J. Britz as staff officer class 1 logistic control; Commandant G. Erlank as staff officer class 1 operations; Commandant C.H. Kruger as staff officer class 1 signal planning; Commandant E. Muller as staff officer class 1 force training; Commandant S.P.J. van Vuuren as force security officer; Commandant D. Wessels as staff officer class 1 engineers; Major S. Barnard as assistant force security officer; Major J. Groenewald as staff officer class 2 signal logistics; Major C.S. Wilsworth as staff officer class 2 artillery.

Order of Battle 61 Mech for the Attack on Techipa 26-27 June 1988

- Fighting Sub-Units from 61 Mech:
  Two mechanised infantry companies – Ratel-20.
  One Olifant tank squadron.
  One anti-tank platoon – Ratel-90.
  One 81 mm mortar platoon – Ratel-81.
  One troop of 120 mm mortars.
- Reinforced with the Following Combat Elements:
  Three motorised infantry companies (1 Para Bn, 202 and 701 Bn).
  Four motorised infantry companies in Casspirs (32 Battalion).
  One anti tank group – Ratel ZT-3 (anti tank missile system).
  One anti tank group – Ratel-90.
  One artillery battery 155 mm G-5.
  One artillery troop 140 mm G-2 (from 51 Battalion at Ruacana).
  One artillery troop 127 mm – Valkiri Multiple Rocket Launcher.

Allocation of Key Personnel to Vehicles – Tac HQ 10 Division

- Command (Ratel-Command) – Call sign 0: Brigadier C.J. Serfontein; Colonel A. Bestbier (Special Forces); Commandant A. Hudson; crew
- Alternative Command (Ratel-Command) – Call sign OA: Colonel R. de Vries; Commandant B. van Heerden; Commandant N.S. Ackerman; crew
- Intelligence Centre (Ratel-Command) – Call sign OB1: Colonel D. Steyn; Commandant H. Coetzee; Major D. Drew; Corporal M. Aldrich; crew.
- Fire Support Coordination Centre (Ratel-Command) – Call sign OG: Colonel J. Lausberg; Commandant M. Schalekamp; Major C.S. Wilsworth; Second-Lieutenant K. Hollenbach; Second- Lieutenant D. Bothma; Bombardier K. Pretorius; crew.
- Battle Support Control Centre (Ratel-Command) – Call sign OE: Colonel M. Nel; Commandant S.P.J. van Vuuren; Commandant J.H. Potgieter; Major T. Botha; crew (engineers, security, deception, telecommunication support and medical).
- Logistic Support centre (Ratel-Command) – Call sign OF: Colonel M.F. Reinecke; Commandant T. Petzer; crew.
- Mobile Air Operation Centre (Ratel-Command) – Call sign LM1: Commandant N. Muller; SAAF personnel; crew.
- Air force Intelligence Centre (Ratel-Variant) – Call sign LMR: SAAF personnel; crew.
- Signal Communication Centre One (Ratel-Variant) – Call sign OC1: Commandant I. Fordred; crew.
- Signal Communication Centre Two (Ratel-Variant) – Call sign OC2: Signal personnel; crew.
- Electronic Warfare Control Centre (Ratel-Variant) – Call sign OB2: Signal personnel; crew.
- Electronic Warfare Technical Support Centre (Ratel-Variant) – Call sign OB3: Signal personnel; crew.
- Administrative Echelon Command (Ratel-Command) – Call sign 9F: Warrant Officer Class One M. van Baalen; Warrant Officer Class One F. Venter; Commandant J.A.L. van der Merwe; crew.
- Signal Logistics Support (Samil-20) – Call sign 9F1: Crew.

- Technical Services Support (Samil-100) – Call sign 9F2: Crew.
- Technical Recovery (Samil-100 Withings) – Call sign 9F3: Crew.
- Logistic Support (Samil-100) – Call sign9F4: Crew.
- Logistic Support (Samil-100) – Call sign 9F5: Crew.
- Logistic Support (Samil-100) – Call sign 9F6: Crew.
- Diesel Bowser – Call sign 9F7: Crew.
- Diesel Bowser – Call sign 9F8: Crew.
- Mobile Fuel Pump (Samil-20 Lappiespomp) – Call sign 9F10: Crew.
- Water Bunker – Call sign 9F11: Crew.
- Water Bunker – Call sign 9F12: Crew.
- Field Kitchen and Pantry (Samil-50) – Call sign 9F13: Crew.

Order of Battle – 10 SA Division for Operation Prone

- Task Force X-Ray under Command of Colonel Leon Marais – Eastern Zone, designated deployment area Ondangwa: 53 Battalion; 54 Battalion; 4 SAI; one sub-unit from 101 Battalion (modular combat wing); one tank squadron from 81 Armour Brigade; Regimental HQ of 17 Field Regiment; Oscar Battery 155 mm G-5 (4 SAI); one battery 140 mm G-2 of 17 Field Regiment; one 127 mm Multiple Rocket Launcher battery from 44 Battery; one meteorological section from 1 Locating Regiment; one anti-aircraft battery from Regiment Vaal River.
- Task Force Zulu under Command of Colonel Mucho Delport – Western Zone, designated deployment area Ruacana: 51 Battalion; 52 Battalion; 102 Battalion; 32 Battalion; 61 Mech (including one tank squadron); one sub-unit from 101 Battalion (modular combat wing); 10 Armoured Car Squadron; Regimental HQ of 14 artillery Regiment; one battery 140 mm G-2 of Transvaal State Artillery Regiment; one 35 mm anti-aircraft troop from regiment Orange Free State; two 20 mm anti-aircraft troop of Regiment Eastern Transvaal.
- Task Force Yankee under Command of Colonel Jan Lusse – division mobile reserve, designated deployment area Ondangwa: Tactical HQ of 81 Armour Brigade; 10 Artillery Brigade HQ; one tank regiment (minus one tank squadron) from 81 Armour Brigade; one mechanised infantry company from 81 Armour Brigade; one armoured car squadron from 2 Light Horse Regiment; two armoured car squadrons (national service) from 1 and 2 Special Service Battalion; one 120 mm M-5 mortar battery from 4 Artillery Regiment.
- Task Force Whiskey – comprised all the counterinsurgency units organised for area defence in the Tsumeb – Grootfontein-Otavi area on completion of Operation Linger.
- 10 Artillery Regiment – under command of Colonel Jean Lausberg.
- In Addition:
  - Medical, provost and engineer assets were to be allocated to the respective task forces on completion of force training.
  - Deployed in the operational area of Task Force Zulu near Ruacana were one radar detachment and a 23 mm anti-aircraft troop of the SAAF.
  - From 11 August 1988 one tank squadron was to be detached to Task Force X-Ray as well.

Composition of First Line Conventional Fighting Units for Operation Pact

- 4 South African Infantry Battalion (4 SAI) – under command of Commandant Cassie Schoeman: Combat Group HQ; two mechanised infantry companies; one armoured car squadron; one anti-tank platoon; one 81 mm mortar platoon (minus one fire group); one 20 mm anti-aircraft troop (Etale).
- 32 Battalion – under command of Commandant Jan Hougaardt: Battalion HQ; three motorised infantry companies; one anti-tank group; one 81 mm mortar fire group; one machine gun group; one 127 mm Multiple Rocket Launcher battery; one 20 mm anti-aircraft troop (Ruacana); one metrological section.
- 61 Mechanised Battalion Group – under command of Commandant Mike Müller: Combat Group HQ; two mechanised infantry companies; one tank squadron; one armoured car squadron; one anti-tank platoon; one 81 mm mortar platoon (minus one fire group); one battery 155 mm G-5; one battery 140 mm G-2; one 20 mm anti-aircraft troop (Ondangwa).

Deployment of Sector 10 Forces for Operation Linger – Counterinsurgency

- HQ Sector 10 – Oshakati
- 102 Battalion: Opuwa – HQ 102 Battalion; one 81 mm mortar section; three intelligence teams.
  Okongwati – one infantry company; one 81 mm mortar section; two assault pioneer sections;
  Ehomba – One infantry company; one 81 mm mortar section; one assault pioneer section; Ondururundu – one infantry company; one 81 mm mortar section.
- 51 Battalion: Ruacana – HQ 51 Battalion; one mounted infantry company; one infantry company from 701 Battalion; one infantry company from 301 Battalion; one infantry company from 201 Battalion; one reaction force company from 101 Battalion; one armoured car troop from 10 armoured Car Squadron; three assault pioneer sections; three 81 mm mortar sections; one 20 mm anti-aircraft troop from 32 Battalion; three intelligence teams. Ombalantu – one infantry company from 911 Battalion; one 81 mm mortar section. Hurricane Base – protection personnel; one 140 mm G-2 battery.
- 53 Battalion: Ondangwa – HQ 53 Battalion; one infantry company from 1 South African Coloured Corps (SACC); one infantry company from 5 South African Infantry Battalion (5 SAI); one infantry company from 1 Parachute Battalion; one reaction force company from 101 Battalion; one armoured car troop from 10 Armoured Car Squadron; five intelligence teams; two 81 mm mortar sections; one 20 mm anti-aircraft troop (61 Mech); one assault pioneer section; Okalongo – one infantry company (SACC); one 81 mm mortar section; one assault pioneer section; Ogongo – one infantry company (SACC); one 81 mm mortar section; one assault pioneer section; Oshigambo – two infantry platoons from 2 South African Infantry Battalion; one 81 mm mortar section; one assault pioneer section; Etale – three infantry platoons from 2 South African Infantry Battalion; one 81 mm mortar section; one assault pioneer section; one 20 mm anti-aircraft troop from 4 SAI; Alpha, Charlie, Delta and Echo Water towers – one infantry company from 121 Battalion; one 81 mm mortar section (Alpha tower).
- 54 Battalion: Eenhana – HQ 54 Battalion; one infantry company (SACC); two

support companies (SACC); one reaction force company from 101 Battalion; three intelligence teams.

- Nkongo – one infantry company (5 SAI); one 81 mm mortar section; one assault pioneer section; Okankolo – one infantry platoon from 8 SAI; one 81 mm mortar section; one assault pioneer section; Miershoop – one infantry company from 1 Special Training Unit; one 81 mm mortar section; five assault pioneer sections; Okatope – one infantry company from 8 SAI; one 81 mm mortar section; five assault pioneer sections.
- 101 Battalion: Ondangwa – HQ 101 Battalion and a Mobile Wing with four reaction force companies; one 81 mm mortar platoon; one reconnaissance company; one assault pioneer section; fourteen intelligence teams; detached – one reaction force company deployed at 51 Battalion; One reaction force company deployed at 53 Battalion; One reaction force company deployed at 54 Battalion.
- 10 Training Unit: Oshivello – HQ 10 Training Unit; two infantry platoons from Cape Regiment (SACC); a number of infantry companies as scheduled for training.
- 10 Armoured Car Squadron: Oshakati – HQ 10 Armoured Car Squadron; seven armoured car troops; one infantry company from 8 SAI; one support company from 8 SAI; one 35 mm anti-aircraft battery; one 25 pounder G-1 troop (only equipment); one 120 mm mortar battery.
- 25 Field Squadron (Engineers): Oshakati – seven field engineer troops.
- SWA Police Services (SWAPOL) – SWAPOL elements respectively deployed at Mahanene and Onhangwena.

SAAF Assets for Operation Pact – Conventional Operation

- 310 Air Force Command Post: Windhoek.
- 1 SAAF Squadron: Was destined to operate either from Ondangwa or Grootfontein in a ground attack role with six Mirage F1AZs.
- 2 SAAF Squadron: Were to be employed in air defence and air reconnaissance configurations from Ondangwa with six Mirage III RZs.
- 3 SAAF Squadron: Were earmarked for offensive counter air operations with six Mirage CZs from Ondangwa. These fighter aircraft could also be used for air defence purposes and escort duties.
- Eight Impalas: were tasked to perform close air support missions for the ground forces. The Impalas were not to operate within a sophisticated enemy air defence environments.
- 10 SAAF Squadron: was to operate with the Kentron Seeker UAV's in the role of reconnaissance and artillery weapons delivery guidance support from any air field available.
- 12 SAAF Squadron: maintained four Canberra bombers on standby at Waterkloof Air Force Base in Pretoria for bombing and air reconnaissance missions.
- 24 SAAF Squadron: was to operate from Grootfontein with three Buccaneers for special missions as well as for toss bombing.
- Six Puma Helicopters: were deployed at Ondangwa for trooping and search and rescue missions.
- One Hercules C-130: was held at Grootfontein for traditional transport missions. An additional four Hercules air transport aircraft were kept on standby at Waterkloof.
- One Boeing 707 Electronic Warfare (EW) Aircraft: operated either from Pretoria or

Grootfontein, depending on the operational requirements.

- One EW Skymaster DC4: was kept on standby at Windhoek, ready to be deployed to the operational area if so required.
- 122 and 129 Air Defence Squadrons: were to be deployed to Ovamboland for the static air defence of air force assets.
- 140 SAAF Squadron: maintained its services as a Sector Control Centre (SCC) and for the control of radar assets at Ondangwa. An additional SCC was deployed at Umbulantu.
- GARRA, the Unmanned Aerial Vehicle (UAV): was available in theatre to support the artillery with fire control.

SAAF Assets for Operation Linger – Counterinsurgency Operation

- Eight Impala Jet Aircraft – were employed in the close air support role and for air reconnaissance purposes.
- Four Bosbok Light Aircraft – were used for aerial reconnaissance, the dropping of illumination flares at night, Telstar duties (aerial communication relay) and convoy escorts. An additional two Bosbok aircraft were kept on standby in South Africa. This was in the advent of Kaokoland being activated by SWAPO (PLAN) and if the distance bombing of military bases should increase.
- Two Kudu Light Aircraft – were in theatre for communication and liaison duties and the evacuation of casualties.
- One Cessna Light Aircraft – was maintained at the ready for communication flights and for 'air shout' purposes – it was equipped with loudspeakers.
- Light Commando Aircraft (from the Local SWA Part-Time Force Squadron) – were used in a similar role as the light aircraft of the SAAF.
- Three Dakota DC3 Aircraft – were on standby at Ondangwa for communication flights, Lunar Operations (parachute delivered operations and reaction force) and Bantam Operations (20 mm close air support, air shout and pamphlet distribution operations).
- Seven Alouette III Gunships – were used for close air support, Lunar Operations, communication flights, trooping, evacuation of casualties and reaction force operations. Four Alouette IIIs were kept in readiness in South Africa.
- Four Puma Transport Helicopters – were used for trooping, air resupply, communication flights, evacuation of casualties and reaction force operations.
- Two Mobile Air Operation Teams (MAOT) – were deployed in the operational area. A third MAOT was on standby in South Africa or Kaokoland.
- The Following Air Assets were Kept on Standby in South Africa – in case of a deep penetration by SWAPO (PLAN) to the white farming area in the Tsumeb district: One MAOT, four Alouette IIIs, two Pumas, one Bosbok and one light commando aircraft.

Appendix B

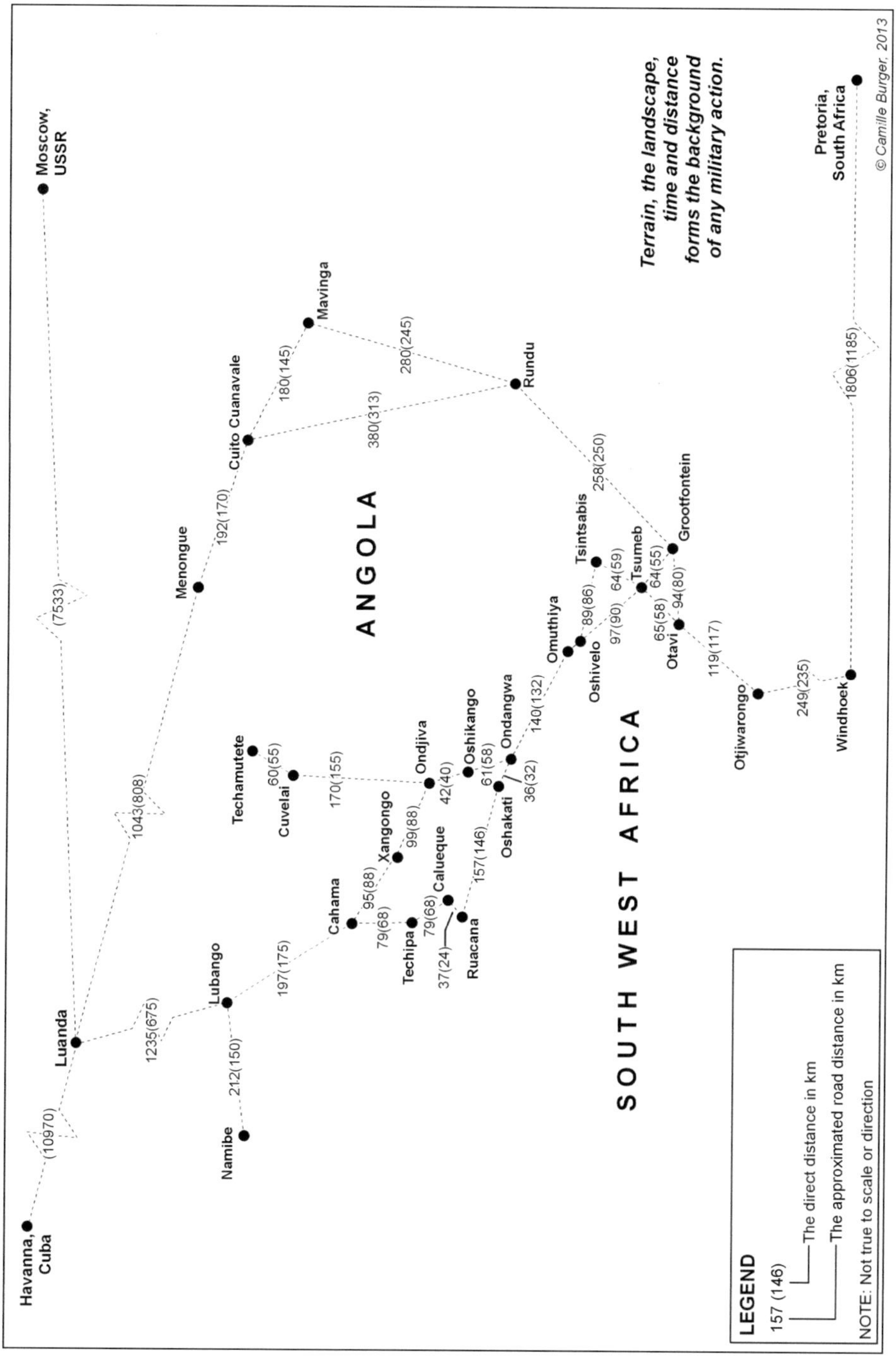

Chart with Distances Relevant to the Border War

Bibliography

Askin, Mustafa: *Gallipoli – A Turning Point.* Keskin Color Kartpostalcilik, Turkey, 2010.

Avolio, Bruce and Bass, Bernard M.: *Full Range Leadership Development.* Copyright Bruce, J. Avolio and Bernard, M. Bass, 1990.

Bass, B.M.: *From Transactional to Transformational Leadership.* Organisational Dynamics, USA, 1990.

Bridgland, Fred: *The War for Africa – Twelve Months That Transformed a Continent.* Ashanti Publishing Limited, Gibraltar, 1990.

Boon, Mike: *The African Way – The Power of Interactive Leadership.* Zebra Publishers, 1997.

Castro, Fidel with Ramonet, Ignacio: *My Life.* Penguin Group Ltd, 80 Strand, London WC2R, England, 2007.

Coroalles, Anthony M., Captain: *Maneuver to Win.* Military Review, September 1981.

De Vries, Roland, Brigadier: *Lei Met Grasie (Lead with Grace).* Saluut, Pretoria, November 1995, Vol 1, No.11.

De Vries, Roland: *Defence Transformation in South Africa: Sharing the Experience with the Forces Armées de la République Démocratique du Congo.* Institute for Security Studies (ISS), African Security Review, Vol 15, No 4, 1 December 2006.

De Vries, Roland, Kolonel: *Die Militêre Waardering – Kreatiewe Denke of Geykte Dogma (The Military Appreciation – Creative Thinking or Rigid Dogma).* Infanterie Forum, Oudtshoorn, 1985.

De Vries, Roland, Kolonel: *Die Verbetering van die SA Leër se Mobiliteit en Vuurkrag tydens Konvensionele Oorlogvoering (The Improvement of the SA Army's Mobility and Fire Power during Conventional Operations).* Infanterie Forum, Oudtshoorn, 1984.

De Vries, Roland, Kolonel: *Mobiele Oorlogvoering – 'n Perspektief vir Suider-Afrika (Mobile Warfare – A Perspective for Southern Africa).* FJM Harman Publishers, Pretoria, 1987.

De Vries, Roland, Major General: *Dynamic Leadership and Command Concepts for Africa – The Future.* Armed Forces, a monthly journal related to defence matters in South Africa, December –January 1999.

De Vries, Roland, Major General: *The Commander.* Armed Forces, a monthly journal related to defence matters in South Africa, November 1998.

De Vries, Roland, Major General: *The Military Staff and its Work.* Armed Forces, a monthly journal related to defence matters in South Africa, March 1999.

De Vries, Roland, Major General (Ret): *Warfare the African Way – Fundamentals of Warfare within the Future African Battle Space.* Paper presented on behalf of Denel SOC Ltd (South African state owned aerospace and defence technology conglomerate established in 1991) at a Technology Seminar in Stockholm, Sweden, 2003.

De Vries, Roland, Colonel and McCaig, G.I., Lieutenant: *Mobile Warfare in Southern Africa.* Institute for Strategic Studies, University of Pretoria Bulletin (ISSUP), August 1987.

De Wet, Christiaan Rudolf: *Three Years War.* Scripta Africana. Hans Strydom Publishers, Johannesburg, May 1985. (Copy no 66 of only 1,000).

Doyle, P. and Bennett, M.R.: *Fields of Battle: Terrain in Military History.* Wikipedia.

Dupuy, T.N., Colonel: *A Genius for War.* Congress Catalogue in Publication Data,

USA, 1989.

Dupuy, T.N., Colonel: *A Genius for War – The German Army and General Staff 1807–1945.* A.T.N. Dupuy Associates Books, MacDonald and Janes, London, 1977.

Elliot-Bateman, Michael: *Defeat in the East.* London Oxford University Press, 1967.

Fuller, J.F.C.: *The Conduct of War.* Whitstable Litho Ltd, Kent, 1957.

Gevisser, Mark: *Portraits of Power.* Creda Press, South Africa, Epping, 1996.

Gouillart, Francis J. and Kelly, James N: *Transforming the Organisation.* McGraw-Hill, Inc, New York, 1995.

Güderian, Heinz: *Panzer Leader.* Zenger Publishing Co. Inc., Washington, 1979.

Heitman, Helmoed-Römer: *War in Angola – The Final South African Phase.* Ashanti, Gibraltar, 1990.

Human, P.: *A Blueprint for Transformation*, Yenza, 1998.

International Freedom Foundation: *Special Report June 1988 – Castro's Plans for Southern Africa.* The Maldon Institute, Washington DC, June 1988.

International Freedom Foundation: *Strategic Implications of Cuba's Angolan Military Build-up.* The Maldon Institute, Washington DC, 1 July 1988.

Institute for Strategic Studies, University of Pretoria Bulletin (ISSUP): *National Security in the RSA. The Strategic Importance of South and Southern Africa: The Pretoria View.* June 1981.

Institute for Strategic Studies, University of Pretoria Bulletin (ISSUP): *South Africa – Conventional Deterrence,* May 1980.

Institute for Strategic Studies, University of Pretoria Bulletin (ISSUP): Bulletin. *The RSA and Conventional Threat Perception.* No 2/85, 1985.

Institute for Strategic Studies, University of Pretoria Bulletin (ISSUP): *The White Paper on Defence and Armaments Supply of 1982.* August 1982.

Jaster, Robert S.: *South Africa's Narrowing Security Options.* Adelphi Papers: The International Institute for Strategic Studies, London, No 159, 1980.

Kasrils, Ronnie: *Cuito Cuanavale – A paradox of History.* Address by Ronnie Kasrils (MP) Minister for Intelligence Services, South African Government, Havana, Cuba, 24 April 2008.

Kasrils, Ronnie: *Historic Turning Point at Cuito Cuanavale.* Address by Ronnie Kasrils (MP), Minister for Intelligence Services, South African Government, Rhodes University, Grahamstown, 28 May 2008 (the author participated as a speaker on the subject of war in Angola during the same address).

Kotter, John P. and Cohen, Dan S.: *The Heart of Change.* Harvard Business School Press, Boston, Massachusetts, 2002.

Lawrence, T.E.: *Seven Pillars of Wisdom.* Penguin Books, 1971.

Lehmann, Joseph H.: *The First Boer War.* Tonathan Cape, Thirty Bedford Square, 1972, London, 1972.

Liddell Hart, B.H.: *History of the First World War.* Pan Books, London, 1972.

Liddell Hart, B.H.: *History of the Second World War.* G.P. Putnam, New York, 1971.

Liddell Hart, B.H.: *Strategy.* Faber and Faber Ltd, London, 1967.

Liddell Hart, B.H.: *The Rommel Papers.* Library of Congress Catalog Card No 53 –5656, 1953.

Liddell Hart, B.H.: *Why Don't We Learn From History.* George Allen and Unwin Ltd, Ruskin House, Museum Street, London, 1972.

McCuen, John J.: *The Art of Counter Revolutionary War.* Faber and Faber Ltd, London, 1969.

Marshall, S.L.A.: *Men against Fire.* William Morrow, New York, 1966.

Messenger, Charles: *The Art of Blitzkrieg.* Ian Allen Ltd, Shepperton, Surrey, UK, 1976.

Mao Tse-tung: *Quotations from Chairman Mao Tse-Tung.* Foreign Language Press, Peking, 1972.

Mao Tse-tung: *Selected Military Writings.* Foreign Language Press, Peking, 1968.

Mao Tse-tung: *Six Essays on Military Affairs.* Foreign Language Press, Peking, 1972.

Mao Tse-tung: *The Selected Works of Mao Tse-tung.* Lawrence and Wishart Ltd, London, 1954.

Morris, Michael F., Major, USMC: *Flying Columns in Small Wars – An OMFTS Model.* A Thesis on the Angolan War of 1987 to 1988, United States Marine Corps, 2000.

Myburgh, Kobus and Nkhata, Nelson, Major: *African Armed Forces Journal: The Scotoma Busters: The Malawi Army Strategic Planning – a Double-sided Perspective.* Article, March 1996.

Orpen, Neil: *Total Defence.* Nasionale Boekhandel Ltd, Cape Town, 1967.

Pakenham, Thomas: *Die Boere-oorlog (The Boer War).* Jonathan Ball Publishers, Johannesburg, 1981.

Perret, Bryan: *Lightning War: A History of Blitzkrieg.* Panther Books Granada Publishing Ltd, 1985.

Rawlinson, Geoffrey J.: *Creative Thinking and Brainstorming.* Gower, 1984.

Ritter, E.A.: *Shaka Zulu.* Penguin Books, Harmondsworth, England, 1985.

Shubin, Gennady and Tokarev, Andrei: *Bush War – The Road to Cuito Cuanavale.* Jacana Media (Pty) Ltd, South Africa, Sunnyside, 2011.

Simpkin, Richard: *Race to the Swift.* Brassey's, London, 1984.

Slim, Viscount, Field-Marshal: *Defeat into Victory.* British Library Cataloguing in Publication Data, London, 1986.

South African White Paper on Defence: Chapter 1, The Challenge of Transformation, 1996.

Stott, Noel: *Safeguarding South Africa for a better life for all,* Violence and Transition Series, Vol. 7, 2002.

Summers, Harry G. Jr.: *On Strategy.* Presido Press, Novato USA, 1982.

Sun Tzu: *The Art of War.* Literature House, Taiwan, Taipei, 1964.

The McAlvany Intelligence Advisor: *The Accelerating Revolution in South Africa.* P.O. Box 39810, Phoenix, Arizona, April, 1986.

Tichy, N.M.: *The Transformational Leader.* John Wiley & Sons, New York, 1990.

Tichy, Noel M. and Sherman, Stratford: *Control your Own Destiny or Someone Else Will.* Doubleday Publishing Group, New York, January 1993.

Turton, Anthony, Dr.: *A South African Diary: Contested Identity, My Family – Our Story* Part F: 1975 – 2007, tony@anthonyturton.com, updated April 2010.

US Army War College: *Air land Battle Doctrine.* June 1983.

Vessey, General (Ret.): *Preface* of *Military Geography for Professionals and the Public* by John M. Collins. Repressed Publishing, US, 2012.

Von Mellenthin, F.W., Major General: *Panzer Battles.* University of Oklahoma Press, Norman, Oklahoma, 1956.

Wallace, P. Franz, Colonel: *Maneuver – The Dynamic Element of Combat.* Military Review, May 1983.

Wallace, P. Franz, Colonel: *Operational Concepts.* Military Review, July 1984.

White Paper on Defence (Witskrif): *Verdediging en Krygstuigvoorsiening.* RSA Departement van Verdediging, 1984.
Williamson, John M.: *The Leader Manager.* John Wiley and Sons, New York, 1986.
Woodmansee Jr., John W., Major General: *Blitzkrieg and the Air land Battle.* Military Review, August 1984.
Wesley, Yale W., White Isaac D., Von Manteuffel, H.: *Alternative to Armageddon: The Peace Potential of Lightning War.* Rutgers University, New Jersey, 1970.
Zeeman, E.C.: *Catastrophe Theory.* Addison-Wesley Publishing Company, Massachusetts, 1976.
Zhdarkin, Igor: *We Did Not See It Even in Afghanistan – Memoirs of a Participant of the Angolan War (1986–1988), from A Russian View of the Angolan War.* Moscow: Memories Mockba, 2008. Translated by Tamara Reilly, ISBN 978-5-903116-57-7, reviewed by Elaine Windrich, published on H-SAfrica (November, 2008), commissioned by Peter C. Limb.

Documents of the SADF in Possession of the Author (Chronological)

Operations Order Number 1/81 (Top Secret): Operation Protea, 61 Mechanised Battalion Group, Omuthiya, dated *14 August 1981.*
Minutes Debriefing Conference Operation Protea (Secret), dated *9 and 10 September 1981,* Grootfontein: Chief Army/Inspector General/ 305/3/1, dated *23 September 1981.*
Operations Order Number 2/81 (Top Secret): Operation Daisy, 61 Mechanised Battalion Group, Omuthiya, dated *28 October 1981.*
Letter from Lieutenant General Jannie Geldenhuys Chief of the Army to Commandant Roland de Vries, Officer Commanding 61 Mechanised Battalion Group: Letter Chief Army 511/4/5, dated *19 November 1981* concerning the soccer game at Xangongo during Operation Protea.
Minutes Debriefing Conference Operation Daisy (Secret), dated *25 November 1981,* Sector 10, Oshakati: Sector 10/ 309/1, Ops Daisy, dated *1 December 1981.*
Minutes Debriefing Conference Operation Yahoo (Secret): Sector 30/305/3/1, dated *11 June 1982,* Headquarters Sector 30, Otjiwarongo.
De Vries, Roland: *Personal Notes on Conventional Operations in Southern Angola and Northern Namibia, 1987 to 1988.* SA Army College, *1988.*
Scans Relating to Operation Modular – Digital Electronic Text Messages (Transmissions) (DETs) by the Second in Command of 10 Task Force *(November 1987)* Colonel Roland de Vries.
Official briefing to senior officers of the SADF on Operations Modular and Hooper (Suid-Afrikaanse Leër: *Voorligting aan senior offisiere van die Suid Afrikaanse Weermag oor Opreasies Modular en Hooper).* Official Document of the SADF – Copy No. 11 of 11 Copies, H Leer/D OPS/309/4 Operations Moduler and Hooper, *1987.*
Instruction from Chief of the Army, Director Training, regarding the debriefing of Operations Modular, Hooper and Packer (C Army/Drg/309/1/Modular/Hooper/Packer) dated *30 May 1988.*
Operations instruction for Operation Hilti issued by Chief of the Army Lieutenant General Kat Liebenberg in Pretoria on *30 May 1988* – C Army/D Ops/ 309/4/Hilti Number 21 of 1988, dated *30 May 1988.* It was signed by Major General J.A. Klopper, Chief of Army Staff Operations. This operations instruction of the South African Army preceded the

top secret operational instruction issued by Chief of Staff Operations of the SADF dated 1 June – CS/Top Secret/309/4/Hilti No 6/88 dated 1 June 1988. The latter operational instructions were followed up by Operations Instruction Number 2/88 of the General Officer Commanding (GOC) SWATF. These series of operations instructions initiated the formal planning and conduct of Operation Hilti/Prone.

Operations Instruction regarding Operation Hilti (supplementary) from Chief of the Army on *1 June 1988*: Top Secret/Director Operations/679/01 June 1988 – C Army/D Ops/309/4/Hilti.

Signal from Chief of the Army relating to the mobilisation of the citizen force for Operation Hilti – *1 June* 1988 (C Army/D Ops/309/4 Op Hilti, dated *1 June 1988*).

Signal from Chief of the Army on *6 June 1988* (Director Army Staff Manpower – Top Secret/ DSM/271/6 Jun 88 – C Army/DSMP/309/1/Op Hilti) relating to the assembly of the planning group for Operation Hilti.

Instruction regarding Operation Hilti from Sector 10: Sector 10/301/Op Hilti dated *6 June 1988*.

Command Appreciation for Operation Hilti by Brigadier Chris Serfontein, 10 SA Division Operation Hilti dated *6 June 1988* (Top Secret – Copy Number 4 of 18 Copies: Sek 10/301/Op Hilti, dated *6 June 1988*).

Memorandum by Colonel Jean Lausberg to the Chief of Staff of 10 SA Division relating to the infiltration observation posts (OP) of 10 Artillery Brigade, dated *9 June 1988*.

Warning Order No 1/88 by Colonel Roland de Vries, Chief of Staff, 10 SA Division for Operation Faction, dated *15 June 1988*.

Programme and Schedule for the SA Army Senior Command and Staff Course attendance of the operational planning Cycle for Operation Hilti/Faction over the period 26 Jul to 4 August 1988: Signal by Sector 10 (Colonel Roland de Vries) to Army 31, dated *3 July 1988*.

Document 10 SA Division Tactical Headquarter (Tac HQ) – Allocation of Personnel to Vehicles.

The Operations Plan of 10 SA Division, dated *19 July 1988*, including the following documents:

Landward planning document relating to Operation Prone (Appendix G).

Document about the enemy's deployments – Operation Hilti.

Document relating to the enemy's intelligence and reconnaissance capability in southern Angola.

Operations Order for Operation Prone (OPSO 1/88 OP PRONE) dated *19 July 1988* comprising the following documents: Main Document with plans reflected in the following appendices:

A: Intelligence.
B: Artillery.
C: Anti-aircraft.
D: Engineers.
E: Signals.
F: Personnel: Logistics.
G: Logistics.
H: Technical Services.
I: Counter Intelligence.

J: Communication Operation.
K: Air Force.
L: Medical.
M: Guidelines for Planning.
N: Risks.
O: Overlays and Deployment areas.
P: Attachments and Detachments 10 Div.

Document on the appreciation on terrain sectors and planning for the rainy season *(August 1988)*.

Operation Linger counterinsurgency plan, handwritten, dated *1 August 1988*.

Artillery intelligence document by Major Clive Wilsworth (10 Art Bde/302/Op Prone/9 Aug 88) dated *9 August 1988*.

Document on Major General Arnaldo Ochoa Sanchez (*Departamento de Intelligencia Para: Buro Politico* Regarding Arnaldo T. Ochoa – Divisional General) dated *16 August 1988*.

A case study on the Ogaden Campaign of the Cubans compiled by Commandant R. Gibson (army intelligence) – C Army/GS2/205/1 dated *23 August 1988*.

Overlay plan of 10 SA Division for Operation Prone, dated *26 August 1988*.

Signal by Colonel Roland de Vries to Chief of Army Staff Operations Ops (From Sector 10 to Army 31), Sep 88 regarding the destruction of enemy's tanks.

Range of planning documents on:
Enemy Courses of Action.
Own Forces Deployments.
10 Artillery Brigade Planning.
SAAF Plan for Operation Prone.

South African Defence Force: Lessons Learned during Conventional Operations in the Western Sub-Theatre Concerning Operations Modular, Hooper, Packet and Hilti/Prone – Confidential (the author participated in the compilation of this document), Official SADF Publication, *December 1988*.

Department of Defence, South Africa. *Proposed Integrated Philosophy on Leadership, Command, Management and Culture: Guidelines for New Concepts*. Pretoria, 1997 (the author was instrumental in the design of this thesis, as well as being one of the co-authors).

Command Doctrine, Department of Defence (DOD) 5 Part 1: Joint Secretary for Defence/ Chief of the Defence Force Publication, *30 July 1997* (the author was instrumental in the design of this thesis, as well as being one of the co-authors).

South African Army's leadership, command and management manual published in *May 2000* (ICN: 7610-18-035-1555) (the author was instrumental in the design of this thesis, as well as being one of the co-authors).

In Acknowledgement – the Thoughts Reflected in this Book Emerged through Countless Discussions and Work Done with the Following People and/or Institutions:

- Major General (Deceased) F.W. von Mellenthin, German Defence Force – Second World War: Discussion with regard to *Blitzkrieg*, *Auftragstaktik* and other German operational concepts.
- Many African officers not listed herein, concerning war-faring traits of Africa and on Defence Transformation from Ghana, Ethiopia, Kenya, the Democratic Republic of Congo, Nigeria, Southern Sudan and Malawi.

- The transformation teams of the SADF and Delloitte and Touche, since the integration of the respective armed forces that commenced in 1994. Acknowledgement is given to Major General (Ret.) Len le Roux, Major General Solly Mollo, Colonel Craig Harrison, Dr. Rocky Williams and Mr. Roger Kibasomba, with whom I consulted in Africa on transformation. Special acknowledgement is given to the team of SADC who I accompanied to the Democratic Republic of Congo (DRC) in May 2004 to discuss transformation with our colleagues from the DRC. Our team was effectively led and guided by Lieutenant General L.M. Fischer, Commander of the Botswana Defence Force. A special word of appreciation is extended to President Olivier Kamitatu Etsu of the DRC National Assembly, who gave us clear insight into the challenges faced by the DRC and a clear vision of what the Congolese wished to achieve.
- Some of the thoughts shared in this paper were gained from Mr. Dan Cohen who wrote the *Heart of Change* with Prof. John Kotter from the Harvard Business School in Boston.
- Dr. Jakkie Cilliers and Colonel (Ret.) Henri Boshoff (Deceased) of the Institute for Security Studies (ISS) for valuable exchanges of thoughts and ideas on transformation initiatives in Africa.
- Professor Eboe Hutchful from Ghana on security issues relating to Africa.
- Lieutenant Colonel Africano Mande, Southern Sudan People's Liberation Army (SPLA).
- Lieutenant General Mark Shisuku, the current Chief of the Malawi Defence Force.
- Mr. Bereng Mtimkulu (Head Peace Support Operations Division AU Commission), Mr. Nicholas Seymour (Senior Political Officer UN) and Brigadier General (Ret.) Dick Baly, (UK). In July 2007 the author acted as the key facilitator and exercise leader to enhance the concepts of the Rapid Deployment Capability of the African Standby Force. The workshop occurred under the auspices of the Peace Support Operations Division of the UN in Addis Ababa, Ethiopia and in support of the Institute for Security Studies, South Africa. The author (Roland de Vries) delivered a draft paper for this occasion and worked in close liaison with the aforementioned officials. This was followed up by a visit to the Peacekeeping School at Karen in Kenya in August 2007 with Dr. Jakkie Cilliers (ISS), in support of the Eastern Brigade of the Standby Force with the development of their role and functions and mechanisms to prepare for and manage multidimensional peace missions.